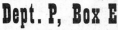

The
Paperback
PRICE GUIDE™

First Edition

By
Kevin B. Hancer

DEDICATION: To Aileen and Colin, this one's for you.

SPECIAL RESEARCH ADVISOR TO THIS EDITION

Rahn Kollander

SPECIAL CONTRIBUTORS TO THIS EDITION

- Lance Casebeer
- Mardi Kirklin
- Steve Sayles
- Robert Selvig
- Jon Warren

COVER: The cover of this edition is the work of two exciting Minnesota artists, Steve Fastner and Rich Larson. It is a tribute to the classic bug-eyed monster (BEM) cover often used for early science-fiction paperbacks and pulp magazines, especially as popularized by Earle Bergey.

THE PAPERBACK PRICE GUIDE No. 1 is copyrighted 1980 by Kevin B. Hancer, Editor, 5813 York Ave. S., Edina, MN 55410. All rights are reserved. Send all pricing and corrective data to above address. Printed in U.S.A. Distributed to the collectors market by Overstreet Publications, Inc., 780 Hunt Cliff Dr. NW, Cleveland, TN 37311. Distributed to the book trade by Harmony Books, a division of Crown Publishers, Inc., One Park Ave., New York, N. Y. 10016. ISBN: 0-517-542250.

INTRODUCTION

In the mid-eleventh century, a Chinaman named Pi Sheng introduced moveable type to the world and four hundred years later, Johann Gutenburg introduced it to Europe. This development made books available to people who previously could not afford to buy laboriously handwritten copies.

Books became even more accessible to the general public when cheap paperback editions were introduced, but paperback publication was generally not a commercial success until the mid-20th century. Much as mechanically printed books were not initially accepted, neither was the paperbound book. It was not until the growth of leisure time for the modern working classes, coupled with the development of proper sales and marketing techniques, that publishing became a widespread, profitable venture.

The modern era of the paperback book, which is the subject of this volume, began with issuance of ten titles by Pocket Books, each in a limited printing of 10,000 copies and distributed within New York City. Once opened, the floodgates were never closed.

The paperback book has become a multi-million dollar business today. As inflation drives the price of hardcover books higher and higher, experts predict that the future of the book industry will largely belong to that once scorned and unsuccessful item, the paperback book.

FORMAT OF THIS BOOK

The Paperback Price Guide is an attempt to list all mass market paperback books, both regular and digest sized, published in the United States between 1939 and 1959. Selected post-1959 and Canadian books are included and more will be added to updated editions.

Book listings are arranged according to the imprint name, which is the identifiable series title, and then listed in numerical order. Where there is no identifiable series title, the listings are arranged alphabetically by publisher. Rather than organizing books alphabetically by title and author, this method was chosen to assist those who collect individual series rather than special authors or genres.

Where available, data has been included to identify books that are either original or first editions. A first edition is the first appearance of a novel or collection of short stories in book form. An original edition is the first appearance of a novel or collection of short stories in any form. An original edition is always a first edition.

Collector interest in certain artists warrants identification of book covers done by them. These artists include:

Rudolph Belarski	Robert Maguire
Earle Bergey	Richard Powers
L. B. Cole	Mac Raboy
Heade	Alex Schomburg
Everett Raymond Kinstler	Wally Wood

As post-1959 data is added to future editions, cover identification of artists like Frank Frazetta and Roy Krenkel, among others, will be added.

Pricing is provided in three grades: good, fine, and mint. For explanations of what these terms mean, check the section Grading of Paperbacks. Prices given are for first printings only.

Many entries also include a letter code at the far right margin. This is a genre classification, used to identify books that belong to a particular area of the book field. The genre codes used are:

A =	Adventure	C =	Combat
B =	Biography	E =	Esoteric

H =	Humor		R =	Romance
HO =	Horror		S =	Sports
M =	Mystery		SF =	Science-fiction
NF =	Non-fiction		W =	Western

The following abbreviations are used with the cover reproductions throughout the book for copyright credit purposes. The companies they represent are listed here:

(Abra) Abrams, Harry N., Inc.
(Ace) Ace Books, Inc.
(Anson) Anson Bond Publ., Inc.
(Archer) The Archer Press, Ltd.
(Argyle) Argyle Press
(Arrow) Arrow Publ.
(Astro) Astro Dist. Corp.
(Atomic) Atomic Books, Inc.
(Avon) Avon Publ., Inc.
(Banner) Banner Mystery
(Bantam) Bantam Books
(Bard) Bard Publ. Corp.
(Bart) Bartholomew House, Inc.
(BB) Ballantine Books
(Belmt) Belmont Books
(Berk) Berkley Publ. Corp.
(Bowker) R. R. Bowker Co.
(CBS) Columbia Broadcasting System
(Cen) Century Publications
(Check) Checkerbooks, Inc.
(Close) Close-up, Inc.
(Col) Columbia Publ. Inc.
(Cor) Corinth Publ., Inc.
(CP) Colonial Press, Inc.
(Crest) Crestwood Publ., Inc.
(Cross) Crossword Pleasure, Inc.
(Croy) Croyden Publ. Co.
(Daggar) Daggar House, Inc.
(DD) Doubleday & Co., Inc.
(Death) Death Library, Inc.
(Dell) Dell Publ. Co., Inc.
(Delta) Delta Library, Inc.
(Design) Design Publ. Corp.
(Det) Detective House, Inc.
(Div) Diversey Publ. Corp.
(Duch) Duchess Printing & Publ. Co., Ltd.
(Edell) Edell Co.
(Eerie) Eerie Publ. Co.
(ERB) Edgar Rice Burroughs
(Eton) Eton Books, Inc.
(Export) Export Publ. Ent., Ltd.
(Falcon) Falcon Books, Inc.
(Faw) Fawcett Publ., Inc.
(Fed) Federal Publ. Co.
(Fem) Femack Co., The
(Glxy) Galaxy Publ. Corp.
(Great) Great American Publ., Inc.
(Green) Green Publ. Co.
(GW) Golden Willow Press, Inc.
(Handi) Handi-book Publ.
(Hanro) Hanro Corp.
(Hart) Horace Hart, Inc.
(HB) Harlequin Books
(Hill) Hillman Periodicals, Inc.
(Holl) Holloway House Publ. Co.
(How) Howard Publ.
(Ideal) Ideal Dist. Co.
(Infan) Infantry Journal, Inc.

(Jon) Jonathan Press, Inc.
(Knic) Knickerbocker Publ., Inc.
(KW) Keep-Worthy Books, Inc.
(Larch) Larch Publ.
(Leisure) Leisure Library, Inc.
(Lion) Lion Books, Inc.
(Mag) Magazine Village, Inc.
(MCG) Marvel Comics Group (Atlas)
(Merc) Mercury Publs.
(Metro) Metro Publ.
(MH) Mohawk Publ. Corp.
(Mid) Midwood Ent., Inc.
(Oceana) Oceana Publ.
(Orig) Original Novels, Inc.
(Padell) Padell Book & Magazine Co.
(Par) Parsee Publ.
(Pen) Penquin Books
(Perma) Perma Books
(Phan) Phantom Mystery Publ.
(Phoen) Phoenix Books
(PI) Parents' Institute
(Pitman) Pitman Publ. Corp.
(Pkb) Pocket Books
(Poplib) Popular Library, Inc.
(Pub) Publishers Productions, Inc.
(Put) Putnam's Sons G. P.
(Pyb) Pyramid Books
(Quinn) Quinn Publ. Co.
(RC) Readers Choice Library
(Red) Red Arrow Books
(Retail) Retail Distributors, Inc.
(Rio) Rio Publ. Corp.
(RL) Reader's League of America
(RN) Romantic Novels
(Royce) Royce Publ.
(S&S) Street & Smith
(SB) Scholastic Book Services
(SG) Star Guidance, Inc.
(SH) Stamford House
(Sigb) Signet Books
(Simon) Simon & Schuster
(Sol) Solomon & Gelman, Inc.
(Spot) Spotlight Publ.
(Star) Star Publ., Inc.
(Stj) St. John Publ. Co.
(Tech) Tech Books, Inc.
(Toby) Toby Press, Inc.
(Univ) Universal Publ. Co., Inc.
(Value) Value Books, Inc.
(Vulcan) Vulcan Publ., Inc.
(Mil) Military Service Publ. Co.
(MP) Magazine Productions, Inc.
(NA) New American Library
(New) New International Library, Inc.
(NH) National Home Library Foundation
(Novel) Novel Library
(NS) Novel Selections, Inc.

WHY PEOPLE COLLECT PAPERBACKS

Anything that exists or was produced on this planet is undoubtedly collected by someone, somewhere. Collecting is a peculiar passion that affects many people in varying degrees and is often hard to explain.

Book collecting has been a popular hobby for many years. Where paperbacks are concerned, there are several easily recognizable reasons for the collecting impulse. Since books are meant to be read, of course, many people collect books that they like to read. Depending on how voracious the reader is, this could mean all books by a certain author or all books of a certain type, such as mystery or science-fiction.

Some collect paperbacks as examples of popular culture because they are reflective of the time periods in which they were published. While a book might have been written centuries or just years earlier, the design packaging and cover art will be distinctive of the times. For example, the first Home Library Edition of Rostand's **Cryano de Bergerac** was initially packaged as a classic novel with a simple, stylish look in 1932. When reprinted years later, the book was retitled "**The Art of Love** by a Parisian Casanova" and the cover depicts a young couple in a heated embrace! The reason is simple. Publishers discovered that suggestive covers helped to sell books and many quality books published in the forties and fifties were designed to look as though they were a little spicy and risque...esoteric if you will.

A lot of people collect paperbacks for the cover art, as many paperback book covers are bright and colorful. A Dutch architect is reported to have collected over 3,000 of them for this reason.

HOW TO START COLLECTING

A good place to begin collecting is at your neighborhood bookstore, buying the kind of new books you are interested in.

There are thousands of used bookstores throughout the United States, and thousands more if you count swap shops, trading centers, and second-hand shops. Many bargains are available in places like these.

A lot of mail-order dealers sell collectible paperbacks. Through ads in this book and elsewhere, you will be able to receive sales catalogues and lists that you can buy from.

STORAGE OF A COLLECTION

Rare and collectible books should be protected from damage that would reduce their value.

Valuable books should be stored in a cool, dry, and dark place. The paper on which most paperbacks were printed will get brown and brittle with age. Heat, humidity, and light will hasten the deterioration of books.

Many collectors use specially designed plastic bags to protect their paperbacks. Because of non-inert elements in plastic bags that might damage them over the years, some collectors prefer not to use them.

HOW TO SELL PAPERBACKS

If you have a collection of paperbacks that you wish to sell, there are several ways to do this.

The easiest method is to take your books to a bookdealer who sells collectible paperbacks and request an offer. Many bookdealers, if they want the material, will pay between 10 and 70 percent of retail value. Because dealers buy with the idea of selling for profit, they will pay only what they can afford based on what they think they can sell for, the amount of overhead (those expenses involved with the cost of operating a business), and the amount of demand they may have for particular books. Mail-order dealers may buy books too, if a listing is provided.

It is possible for the novice to sell his paperbacks by himself and realize more money from them. This involves the compiling of a detailed list of the books, giving book numbers, title, author, condition, and price. There are many instant printing businesses where copies of a price list can be inexpensively printed. These can then be sent to people who might wish to buy them. Names of interested people can be obtained from ads placed in collectors publications such as this one.

There are drawbacks to either method. With the first, although relatively easy, the full value will not be realized. With the second, a lot of work is involved and many books could be left over, if they sell at all. The decision as to which method to choose may depend on the individual's experience or lack of it.

GRADING OF PAPERBACK BOOKS

The condition of a book is the most important factor affecting its value as a collectible item. The following guidelines are suggested, and to be effective, they should be closely followed.

MINT (M): As issued. The book is absolutely brand-new and perfect in every way. The cover will be bright, crisp, and unfaded, with no imperfections of any kind. The original plastic lamination (if any) is intact. The spine is tight, square, and clean. The pages are white. Color staining of the margins (if any) is not faded.

NEAR MINT (NM): Almost perfect. The cover will still be bright, crisp, and unfaded, with perhaps a few minor wear marks along the extremities. Plastic lamination (if any) may be starting to slightly peel or chip along the edges. The spine will be tight, square, and clean, with a few minor wear spots. Pages will still remain virtually white. Color edge staining (if any) might be slightly faded. Any defects will be minor in nature.

VERY FINE (VF): Slight wear beginning to show. There may be some slight fading of the cover or spine, and slight creasing along the spine edge to indicate that the book was carefully read once. Still, all aspects of the book will be clean and fresh with no major flaws.

FINE (FN): This copy may have been carefully read several times, but the spine will still be relatively tight although perhaps a little bent. Stress lines along the spine will be more pronounced. No creases or bends in the cover themselves. Pages will still be largely white or slightly browning. Cover lamination (if any) may be peeling at corners and other spots. Possible light fading of the cover. Edge staining faded. Light wear, rubbing, or color flaking noticeable along the extremities. An assortment of minor defects are acceptable, but this is still a well preserved copy.

VERY GOOD (VG): An obviously read copy. Cover lustre and gloss virtually gone. Plastic lamination (if any) may be totally missing or peeling in a number of spots. Slight creases or bends in the cover. Pages fresh but slightly browned. Spine may be bent due to several readings. Wear spots, rubbing, and flaking or chipping more pronounced. No tears in the cover and no tape used anywhere. Spine is loose but repairable, and may be slightly splitting at the top and bottom.

GOOD (G): The average used copy but still complete with no pages missing. Cover has bends, creases, and is faded. Spine may be splitting and possibly is rolled. Possible tears. Although obviously well-read, this is still an acceptable worn copy missing no pieces of the cover.

FAIR (f): Very heavily read and soiled but still complete and readable. Torn cover or pages. Slightly rolled spine. Possible stains or damaged by the elements.

POOR (p): Damaged, heavily worn and soiled. Pages or parts of the cover are missing. Unreadable and unsuitable for collecting.

IMPORTANT: Books that are miscut, misbound, or have covers misprinted are not worth as much as they would be without these defects. The use of tape or the utilizing of color dyes to hide rubbing spots is not recommended and also detracts from book condition.

A WORD ABOUT REPRINTS

Reprint editions of most paperback books will not be worth the same as first printings. Fortunately, in these cases the reprints are usually easy to detect.

Some publishers, like Pocket Books, made this quite easy. If collectors check the indicia or copyright page of the book (almost always on the reverse side of the title page), reprintings will generally be noted. On the subject of Pocket Books, it is useful to mention that the accuracy of their reprint information on some books has been questioned, but I have yet to hear the validity of the first printing identification made suspect.

For many publishers, it was easier to re-issue a book under a new number rather than reprint it under the old number. Still others, like Dell and Popular Library, would sometimes add 1000 to the original number. For example, the reprint of Popular Library No. 392 became No. 1392.

Reprints are often worth 25 to 50 percent less than the original printings with a number of exceptions. Perhaps the most striking example of this exists with the first ten Pocket Book titles. Because the first printings were limited to 50,000 copies and distributed within the New York City area only, reprints will be worth significantly less...at least 90 percent less.

A SPECIAL PLEA

Inasmuch as future editions of **The Paperback Price Guide** are planned, the editor urgently requests that notification of omissions or corrections be sent to me at the following address for inclusion in future editions: Kevin Hancer, 5813 York Avenue S., Edina, Minnesota 55410.

I welcome any comments from dealers and collectors regarding this book and future editions, because it is a fact that thoughtful feedback can help to increase the usefulness of this publication to everyone in the hobby.

The editor is especially interested in obtaining materials, whether in the nature of books, magazines, catalogues, or films, that relate to the paperback industry, past and present.

A WORD OF CAUTION

The prices contained in this book reflect prices that have been realized for paperback books in recent years. Before anyone buys books at these prices, or prices books to sell at these prices, a few things must be considered.

First, these prices reflect prices from a collectors market. Obviously, many secondhand stores and the like cannot expect to obtain these prices if they don't have a collectors clientele.

Secondly, the paperback collectors market is only now being known to the general public. As happened in the comics field, warehouses of material may surface that would force prices down dramatically. The market may fluctuate a great deal before it stabilizes.

The paperback book field is growing every day, and the exercise of a little caution and common sense is heartily recommended.

GOOD LUCK AND HAPPY READING!

Kevin B. Hancer

HANCER'S BOOKHOUSE

Hancer's Bookhouse is not a mass merchandising book 'supermarket', and I don't 'just' sell books. I sell knowledge. I sell thrills and adventure. I sell voyages to exotic isles where the palm trees sway and cannibals lurk in the undergrowth. I sell free-fall flights in fantasy and hair-raising rides in the American West. I love books, for they are the key to all the knowledge and entertainment of mankind's lush imagination. I intend that this love is reflected in Hancer's Bookhouse.

CATALOGUES NOW AVAILABLE:

Vintage Paperbacks	Comic Character Collectibles
Edgar Rice Burroughs items	Popular Fiction
Motion Picture/Television	Each list $1.00

FOR SALE:

These collectible books are all in near mint condition, add $1.50 shipping per order.

Avon 277 - Perelandra - $40.00
Avon 327 - One Man Show - $15.00
Avon 354 - Werewolf of Paris - $35.00
Avon 370 - The Moon Pool - $35.00
Avon 389 - Saturday Evening Post Fantasy Stories - $15.00
Avon 396 - His First Million Women - $15.00
Dell 536 - Tarzan and the Lost Empire - $15.00
Dell 600 - Rogue Queen - $20.00
Dell F115 - The Misfits (Monroe-Gable movie ed.) - $7.50
Pocket Book 452 - Dracula - $20.00
Popular Library 273 - The Big Eye - $10.00
         326 - Behind the Flying Saucers - $10.00
Belmont L504 - The Brigitte Bardot Story - $10.00

A full-color poster of the cover of the Paperback Price Guide is available for $3.00 plus $1.00 shipping. A limited, signed print is available for $10.00 plus shipping.

WANTED TO BUY:

1 - Paperback books of all kinds, from all publishers, both in digest and standard size. Will buy one or 1,000+ in all fields. Top prices paid. Will buy original paperback cover art as well.
SPECIAL NEEDS: Ace (all early doubles, singles-all types, 1960's science fiction esp. Tolkien-Vance-The Prisoner series), All Picture Mystery, Archer, Armed Services (mystery, horror, science fiction-especially Tarzan and Superman titles), Atomic, Avon (all early titles, all digests, all pulps and magazines), Ballantine, Bantam of Los Angeles, Bart House, Beacon, Bonded, Broadway, Bronze Books, Chartered Checkerbooks, Dell, Dell digests, Dell 10-cent, Dell Told in Pictures, Dell un-numbered, Diversey, Eton, Gold Medal, Handi-Books, Harlequin, Leisure Library, Lion, Novel Library, Phantom, Popular Library, Prize, Pyramid, Quick Reader, Red Arrow,

HANCER'S BOOKHOUSE

Royal Stallion, Stork, Trophy, Universal, Yogi Mystery.
SPECIAL BOOKS WANTED: Frederic Brown-All, Edgar Rice
Burroughs-All Bantam, Dell, Armed Services, Carpozi-The Elvis
Presley Story (Hillman 130), Raymond Chandler-All, Dashiell
Hammett-All, Holmes-Rocket to the Morgue, Irish-All, Jackson-
The Lottery (Lion 14), Kerouac-Maggie Cassidy, Tristessa,
William Lee-Junkie (Ace D-15), Leske-I was a Nazi Flyer (Dell
21), Lieber-Conjure Wife (Lion 179), Millard-Mansion of Evil
(Gold Medal 129), Slesar-20 Million Miles to Earth, Swados-
Reform School Girl, Tolkien-All Ace editions, Vance-Most,
esp. Dying Earth and Bad Ronald, movie/TV titles, all books in
dust jackets, most puzzle-cooking-cartoon books, and novels
concerned with juvenile delinquency or drugs.
ALWAYS READY TO BUY LARGE ASSORTMENTS IN
BETTER CONDITION.

2 - Edgar Rice Burroughs/Tarzan items of any kind, esp. books
in dust wrappers, scrapbooks, magazines, pulps, comics, toys,
fanzines, paper items of any kind.

3 - Any books, etc. with imitation Tarzan/ERB characters.
Example: Azan, Shuna, Sheena, Jacare, Kaspa, Morgo, etc.

4 - Hardcover photoplay editions, especially in dust wrappers.
KING KONG is especially wanted.

5 - Zorro, Lone Ranger, Hopalong Cassidy, Tom Corbett, Steve
Canyon, boys and girls series, etc. hardcover books, especially
in dust wrappers.

6 - All books by Charles Thurley Stoneham (African and
Canadian fact and fiction), Jimm Hatlo (cartoons), Robert
Ripley (cartoons), Bill Mauldin (WWII and cartoons), Carl
Claudy (Adventures in the Unknown series).

7 - Books (paperback or hardcover) by Louis L'amour and any
pulp magazines with stories by L'amour under his own name
or his pen names of Jim Mayo or Tex Burns (Hopalong
Cassidy items).

8 - Quality detective fiction, children's books, illustrated books,
movie magazines, TV GUIDE issues, old comics, pulp magazines,
movie posters and paper ephmera, big little books, Little
Golden Books, fact/fiction pertaining to pirates/foreign legion/
exotic adventure, wrestling magazines, pinups, art posters,
Beatle items.

9 - Original art by J. Allen St. John, Gustaf Tenggren, and
Mahlon Blaine. Also any books or magazines illustrated by
them.

HANCER'S BOOKHOUSE

5813 York Avenue South
Edina, Minnesota 55410
612-922-9144

PAPERBACKS
1939-1969

SEND $1.00 FOR
 HUGE LIST TO:

STEWART GIPP
371 DIAMOND ST.
SAN FRANCISCO, CA.
        94114

AVON
POCKET BOOKS
SIGNET
POPULAR
DELL MAP BACKS
PERMA BOOKS
SCIENCE FICTION
MOVIE EDITIONS
T.V. EDITIONS
BEATLES
GRAPHIC MYSTERY
LION BOOKS
AND MANY, MANY MORE....

ALSO,
DRUG BOOKS
SABER
MONARCH
BEACON
ETC....

BOOKS
S. W. Gipp
371 DIAMOND ST.
SAN FRANCISCO, CA. 94114

Ace D-1, c. Ace

Ace D-10, c. Ace

Ace D-15, c. Ace

ACE

(Ace Books, Inc./A. A. Wynn, Inc.)

D 1	The Grinning Gismo - Samuel W. Taylor				M
	c-Saunders				
	Too Hot for Hell - Keith Vining	25.00	60.00	100.00	M
	c-Saunders				
	1952				
D 2	Bad Man's Return - W. Colt MacDonald				W
	Bloody Hoofs - J. Edward Leithead	4.00	8.00	15.00	W
	c-Saunders				
D 3	Twist the Knife Slowly- Kate Clugston				M
	aka A Murderer in the House				
	The Big Fix - Mel Colton	4.00	8.00	15.00	M
	Orig., 1952				
D 4	Rimrock Rider - Walter A. Tompkins				W
	c-Saunders				
	Massacre at White River - L. B. Patten	4.00	8.00	15.00	W
	Orig., 1952				
D 5	Drawn to Evil - Harry Whittington				M
	Orig., 1952, c-Saunders				
	The Scarlet Spade - Eaton K. Goldthwaite	5.00	10.00	20.00	M
	aka Cut for Partners, c-Saunders				
D 6	The Branded Lawman - William E. Vance				W
	Plundor Valley - Nelson Nye	4.00	8.00	15.00	W
D 7	So Dead My Love - Harry Whittington				M
	I, the Executioner - Stephen Ransome	4.00	8.00	15.00	M
	1953				
D 8	Terror Rides the Range - Alan K. Echols				W
	Orig., 1953				
	Gunsmoke Gold - Tom West	4.00	8.00	15.00	W
D 9	Decoy - Michael Morgan				M
	Orig., 1953				
	If I Die Before I Wake - Sherwood King	4.00	8.00	15.00	M
D10	The Brazos Firebrand - Leslie Scott				W
	Orig., 1953				
	Hell on Hoofs - Gordon Young	4.00	8.00	15.00	W
	aka Quarter Horse, c-Ralph Smith				
D11	Mrs. Homicide - Day Keene				M
	Orig., 1953				
	Dead Ahead - William L. Stuart	4.00	8.00	15.00	M
	aka The Dead Lie Still				
D12	The Man From Boot Hill - Dean Owen				W
	Orig., 1953				
	Wild Horse Range - Dan J. Stevens	4.00	8.00	15.00	W
D13	The Judas Goat - Leslie Edgley				M
	Cry Plague! - Theodore S. Drachman	15.00	35.00	60.00	SF
D14	Maverick with a Star - George Kilrain				W
	Vultures on Horseback - Paul Evan Lehman	4.00	8.00	15.00	W
D15	Junkie - William Lee (William Burroughs)				E
	Orig., 1953				
	Narcotic Agent - Maurice Helbrant	30.00	65.00	100.00	E
D16	Germinie - Jules de Goncourt & Edmond				
	de Goncourt				
	c-Saunders				
	Crime d'amour - Paul Bourget	5.00	10.00	20.00	

D17	Shakedown - Roney Scott c-Saunders				M
	The Darkness Within - Walter Erickson	4.00	8.00	15.00	M
D18	The Lead Slingers - J. Edward Leithead c-Saunders				W
	The Hanging Hills - Brad Ward	4.00	8.00	15.00	W
D19	Fear No More - Leslie Edgley				M
	Never Kill a Cop - Mel Colton	4.00	8.00	15.00	M
D20	The Desperate Code - Roy Manning aka Six-Gun Sheriff				W
	Double-Cross Brand - Alan K. Echols Orig., 1953	4.00	8.00	15.00	W
D21	Nightshade - John N. Makris Orig., 1953, c-Saunders				M
	High Stakes - Lester Dent aka Dead at the Take-off	5.00	10.00	20.00	M
D22	Badlands Masquerader - Leslie Scott				W
	Mavericks of the Plains - Bliss Lomax	4.00	8.00	15.00	W
D23	Bring Back Her Body - Stuart Brock Orig., 1953				M
	Passing Strange - Richard Sale	4.00	8.00	15.00	M
D24	Vulture Valley - Tom West				W
	The Sidewinders - John Callahan	4.00	8.00	15.00	W
D25	The Code of the Wooster - P. G. Wodehouse c-Saunders				H
	Quick Service - P. G. Wodehouse	7.50	15.00	30.00	H
D26	The Impotent General - Charles Pettit c-Saunders				E
	Love in a Junk & Other Exotic Tales - Harold Acton & Lee Yi-Hsieh aka Four Cautionary Tales	10.00	25.00	40.00	E
D27	The Fingered Man - Bruno Fischer c-Saunders				M
	Double Take - Mel Colton	4.00	8.00	15.00	M
D28	Gunsmoke Kingdom - Paul Evan				W
	Avenger from Nowhere - William E. Vance Orig., 1953	4.00	8.00	15.00	W
D29	Dead Man Friday - J. F. Hutton aka Too Good to be True				M
	The Fast Buck - Ross Laurence Orig., 1953	5.00	10.00	20.00	M
D30	Johnny Sundance - Brad Ward c-Saunders				W
	South to Santa Fe - George Kilrain Orig., 1953	4.00	8.00	15.00	W
D31	Universe Maker - A. E. Van Vogt Orig., 1953				SF
	The World of Null-A - A. E. Van Vogt	4.00	8.00	15.00	SF
D32	Cookbook for Beginners - Dorothy Malone aka Cookbook for Brides	4.00	8.00	15.00	NF
D33	Murder by the Pack - Carl G. Hodges Orig., 1953				M
	About Face - Frank Kane	5.00	10.00	20.00	M
D34	Hellion's Hole - Ken Murray Orig., 1953				W
	Feud in Piney Flats - Ken Murray Orig., 1953, c-Saunders	4.00	8.00	15.00	W
D35	Open All Night - Jack Houston				E

Ace D-16, c. Ace

Ace D-25, c. Ace

Ace D-26, c. Ace

Ace D-36, c. Ace

Ace D-43, c. Ace

Ace D-52, c. Ace

(ACE, continued)

Orig., 1953				
The Marina Street Girls - Rae Loomis	4.00	8.00	15.00	E
D36 Conan the Conqueror - Robert E. Howard				SF
The Sword of Rhiannon - Leigh Brackett	10.00	25.00	40.00	SF
Orig., 1953				
D37 The Drowning Wire - Marvin Claire				M
Departure Delayed - Will Oursler	4.00	8.00	15.00	M
D38 Showdown at Yellow Butte - Jim Mayo				W
Orig., 1953				
Outlaw River - Bliss Lomax	4.00	8.00	15.00	W
c-Saunders				
D39 Quantrill's Raiders - Frank Gruber				W
Orig., 1954, c-Saunders				
Rebel Road - Frank Gruber	4.00	8.00	15.00	W
aka Outlaw				
1954				
D40 Waltz into Darkness - William Irish				M
Scylla - Malden Grange Bishop	5.00	10.00	20.00	M
Orig., 1954				
D41 Mourning After - Thomas B. Dewey				M
Death House Doll - Day Keene	4.00	8.00	15.00	M
Orig., 1954				
D42 One Against a Bullet Horde - Walker A.				
Tompkins				W
Law for Tombstone - Charles M. (Chuck)				
Martin	4.00	8.00	15.00	W
D43 Salome, My First 2,000 Years of Love -				
George Sylvester Viereck & Paul Eldridge	5.00	10.00	20.00	SF
D44 Sentinels of Space - Eric Frank Russell				SF
The Ultimate Invader - Don Wollheim	4.00	8.00	15.00	SF
Orig., 1954				
D45 Death Hitches a Ride - Martin L. Weiss				M
Tracked Down - Leslie Edgley	4.00	8.00	15.00	M
aka The Angry Heat				
D46 Vengeance Valley - Roy Manning				W
Law from Back Beyond - Chuck Martin	4.00	8.00	15.00	W
Orig., 1954, c-Saunders				
D47 Kiss and Kill - Joe Barry				M
Orig., 1954				
On the Hook - Richard Powell	4.00	8.00	15.00	M
aka Shark River				
D48 Utah Blaine - Jim Mayo				W
Orig., 1954				
Desert Showdown - Brad Ward	4.00	8.00	15.00	W
aka The Spell of the Desert, c-Saunders				
D49 The Golden Temptress - Charles Grayson				E
Tongking! - Dan Cushman	4.00	8.00	15.00	M
Orig., 1954				
D50 The Mating Call - Wilene Shaw				E
Ban 'un - Ozro Grant	4.00	8.00	15.00	E
D51 Over the Edge - Lawrence Treat				M
Switcheroo - Emmett McDowell	4.00	8.00	15.00	M
Orig., 1954				
D52 Crossfire Trail - Louis L'amour				W
Orig., 1954				
Boomtown Buccaneers - William Colt	4.00	8.00	15.00	W
MacDonald				
D53 Gateway to Elsewhere - Murray Leinster				SF
Orig., 1954				

(ACE, continued)

The Weapon Shops of Isher - A. E. Van Vogt	4.00	8.00	15.00	SF
S 54 The Naked Fear - Carl Offord	3.00	6.00	12.00	E
Orig., 1954				
D55 Kill-box - Michael Stark				M
aka Run for Your Life				
The Tobacco Auction Murders - Robert Turner	4.00	8.00	15.00	M
Orig., 1954				
D56 Ambush at Coffin Canyon - Bliss Lomax				W
Hellbent for a Hangrope - Clement Hardin	4.00	8.00	15.00	W
D57 Treachery in Trieste - Charles L. Leonard				A
Counterspy Express - A. S. Fleischman	5.00	10.00	20.00	A
Orig., 1954				
S 58 Vice, Inc. - Joachim Joesten	4.00	8.00	15.00	E
D59 Spiderweb - Robert Bloch				M
Orig., 1954				
The Corpse in my Bed - David Alexander	4.00	8.00	15.00	M
aka Most Men Don't Kill				
S 60 The Marshall of Medicine Bend - Brad Ward	2.00	4.00	7.50	W
D61 Cosmic Manhunt - L. Sprague de Camp				SF
Orig., 1954				
Ring Around the Sun - Clifford D. Simak	4.00	8.00	15.00	SF
D62 Ken Murray's Giant Joke Book - Ken Murray	3.00	6.00	12.00	H
D63 You'll Die Next - Harry Whittington				M
Orig., 1954				
Drag the Dark - Frederick C. Davis	4.00	8.00	15.00	M
D64 Bullets Don't Bluff - Paul Evan Lehman				W
Orig., 1954				
Under the Mesa Rim - Chandler Whipple	3.00	6.00	12.00	W
D65 Tornado - Juanita Osborne				E
Orig., 1954				
Night Fire - Edward Kimbrough	4.00	8.00	15.00	E
S 66 Return to Tomorrow - L. Ron Hubbard	4.00	8.00	15.00	SF
S 67 The Will to Kill - Robert Bloch	4.00	8.00	15.00	M
D68 Deadwood - Walker A. Tompkins				W
Bullet Brand Empire - William Hopson	3.00	6.00	12.00	W
D69 Daybreak-2250 A. D. - Andre Norton				SF
aka Star Man's Son				
Beyond Earth's Gates - C. W. Moore & Lewis Padgett	3.00	5.00	12.00	
S 70 Luisita - Rae Loomis	4.00	8.00	15.00	E
D71 Drop Dead - Gordon Ashe				M
The Case of the Hated Senator - Margaret Scherf	4.00	8.00	15.00	M
aka Dead: Senate Office Building				
D72 Nightrider Deputy - Ralph R. Perry				W
The Devil's Saddle - Norman A. Fox	3.00	6.00	12.00	W
D73 Adventures in the Far Future - D. A. Wollheim				SF
Tales of Outer Space - Donald A. Wollheim	3.00	6.00	12.00	SF
S 74 Heat Lightning - Wilene Shaw	2.00	4.00	7.50	E
S 75 Cartoon Annual - Ralph Shikes	4.00	8.00	15.00	H
S 76 Shame - Emile Zola	2.00	4.00	7.50	E
D77 Catch the Brass Ring - Stephen Marlowe				M
Stranger at Home - George Sanders	3.00	6.00	12.00	M
D78 Lobo Legacy - Tom West				W
The One-Shot Kid - Nelson Nye	3.00	6.00	12.00	W
D79 The Brain Stealers - Murray Leinster				SF
Atta - Francis Rufus Bellamy	3.00	6.00	12.00	SF

Ace D-53, c. Ace

Ace D-59, c. Ace

Ace D-61, c. Ace

Ace D-65, c. Ace	Ace S-66, c. Ace		Ace D-88, c. Ace	

(ACE, continued)

S 80	The Fear and the Guilt - Wilene Shaw	2.00	4.00	7.50	E
D 81	Too Many Sinners - Sheldon Stark				M
	Liability Limited - John A. Saxon	3.00	6.00	12.00	M
S 82	Kilkenny - Louis L'Amour	4.00	8.00	15.00	W
S 83	The Steel Noose - Arnold Drake	2.00	4.00	7.50	E
D 84	An Earth Gone Mad - Roger Dec				SF
	The Rebellious Stars - Isaac Asimov	2.00	4.00	7.50	SF
	aka The Stars, Like Dust				
S 85	The Bachelor's Widow - Maurice Dekobra	3.00	6.00	12.00	E
D 86	Tangled Trail - Roy Manning				W
	Sentinel Peak - Richard Brister	3.00	6.00	12.00	W
S 87	Why Am I so Beat - Nolan Miller	2.00	4.00	7.50	E
	1955				
D 88	The 7-day System for Gaining Self-Confidence, Popularity and Financial Success - Dexter Davis	4.00	8.00	15.00	NF
D 89	Death Watch - Ruth Wilson & Alexander Wilson				M
	aka The Town is Full of Rumors				
	Turn Left for Murder - Stephen Marlowe	4.00	8.00	15.00	W
S 90	The Chaos Fighters - Rbt. Moore Williams	3.00	6.00	12.00	SF
S 91	End of the Line - Stanley Baron	2.00	4.00	7.50	E
D 92	The Drifter - Burt Arthur				W
	The Longhorn Trail - Richard Wormser & Dan Gordon	2.00	4.00	7.50	W
S 93	Modern Casanovas Handbook - Horace T. Elmo	3.00	6.00	12.00	H
D 94	One Against Eternity - A. E. Van Vogt				SF
	aka The Weapon Makers				
	The Other Side of Here - Murray Leinster	3.00	6.00	12.00	SF
S 95	The Naked Jungle - Harry Whittington	2.00	4.00	7.50	M
D 96	The Last Planet - Andre Norton				SF
	aka Star Rangers				
	A Man Obsessed - Alan E. Nourse	3.00	6.00	12.00	SF
D 96	The Last Planet - Andre Norton Special edition	4.00	8.00	15.00	SF
S 97	Death has 2 Faces - Norman Herries	2.00	4.00	7.50	M
D 98	The Lobo Horseman - Sam Peoples				W
	The Texas Tornado - Nelson Nye	3.00	6.00	12.00	W
	aka Rustler's Roost				
D 99	The Galactic Breed - Leigh Brackett				SF
	aka The Starmen				
	Conquest of the Space Sea - Rbt. Moore Williams	3.00	6.00	12.00	SF
S 100	The Caves - Henry Lewis Nixon	2.00	4.00	7.50	E
D 101	Knock 'em Dead - Jack Karney				M
	Point of No Escape - Mel Colton	3.00	6.00	12.00	
S 102	Oath of Seven - George Albert Glay	4.00	8.00	15.00	A
D 103	Solar Lottery - Philip K. Dick				SF
	The Big Jump - Leigh Brackett	3.00	6.00	12.00	SF
S 104	Left Bank of Desire - R. V. Cassill & Eric Protler	2.00	4.00	7.50	E
S 105	The Fires of Youth - Edward DeRoo Orig., 1955	3.00	6.00	12.00	JD
D 106	Lawman without a Badge - Dorothy L. Bonar				W
	Four Texans North - Lee Floren	2.00	4.00	7.50	W
S 107	The Gilded Hideaway - Peter Twist	2.00	4.00	7.50	E
S 108	Lie Like a Lady - C. S. Cody	2.00	4.00	7.50	E
D 109	I See Red - Sterling Noel				M

(ACE, continued)

	Mambo to Murder - Dale Clark	3.00	6.00	12.00	M
D110	The 1000 Year Plan - Isaac Asimov	4.00	8.00	15.00	SF
D110	No World of Their Own - Poul Anderson				SF
	Special Edition				
	The 1000 Year Plan - Isaac Asimov	3.00	6.00	12.00	SF
	aka Foundation				
S111	The Smoldering Fire - Harry Harrison				
	Kroll	2.00	4.00	7.50	E
D112	Trigger Gospel - Henry Sinclair Drago				W
	Border Buccaneers - Frank Castle	3.00	6.00	12.00	W
D113	The Transposed Man - Dwight V. Swain				SF
	First ed., 1955				
	One in 300 - J. T. McIntosh	3.00	6.00	12.00	
S114	Living it Up - Edward Adler	4.00	8.00	15.00	E
D115	Shady Lady - Cleve F. Adams				M
	One Got Away - Harry Whittington	3.00	6.00	12.00	M
S116	Words Fail Me! - Brant House	2.00	4.00	7.50	H
S117	Dark Rapture - Kim Darien	2.00	4.00	7.50	E
D118	Dome Around America - Jack Williamson				SF
	The Paradox Men - Charles L. Harness	2.00	4.00	7.50	SF
S119	The Driven Flesh - Lawrence Easton	2.00	4.00	7.50	E
D120	Bounty Man - John McGreevey				W
	Call of the Gun - Samuel A. Peeples	2.00	4.00	7.50	W
D121	The Stars are Ours! - Andre Norton	3.00	6.00	12.00	SF
	Special Edition				
D121	3 Faces of Time - Sam Merwin, Jr.				SF
	The Stars are Ours! - Andre Norton	2.00	4.00	7.50	SF
S122	The Preying Streets - Ledru Baker, Jr.	2.00	4.00	7.50	E
D123	Love Me to Death - Frank Diamond				M
	The Squeeze - Gil Brewer	2.00	4.00	7.50	M
S124	House of Deceit - Rae Loomis	2.00	4.00	7.50	E
D125	The Man Who Upset the Universe - Isaac				
	Asimov	2.00	4.00	7.50	SF
	aka Foundation and Empire				
S126	Washington Bachelor - A. H. Berzen	2.00	4.00	7.50	E
D127	Alexander and the Camp Follower - Robert				
	Payne	4.00	8.00	15.00	A
	aka Alexander the God				
D128	Way Station West - William E. Vance				W
	High Saddle - William Hopson	2.00	4.00	7.50	W
D129	Silenced Witnesses - Norman C. Rosenthal				M
	The Dangling Carrot - Day Keene	2.00	4.00	7.50	M
S130	Backlash - Sidney Weissman	2.00	4.00	7.50	
D131	The Ripening - Eugene Wyble	2.00	4.00	7.50	E
S132	Cartoon Annual no. 2 - Brant House	2.00	4.00	7.50	H
S133	Adventures on Other Planets - Donald A.				
	Wollheim	2.00	4.00	7.50	SF
D134	Tornado on Horseback - Nelson Nye				W
	aka Fiddle-Back Ranch				
	The Outsiders - Gene Olson	2.00	4.00	7.50	W
D135	Dead Ringer - James Hadley Chase				M
	Maid for Murder - Milton K. Ozaki	3.00	6.00	12.00	M
S136	A Taste of Sin - R. V. Cassill	2.00	4.00	7.50	E
S137	Violent Night - Ralph Jackson	2.00	4.00	7.50	E
D138	Haven of the Hunted - T. V. Olsen				W
	Gunsmoke over Sabado - Paul Evan	2.00	4.00	7.50	W
	1956				
D139	The Atom Curtain - Nick Bodie Williams				SF
	Alien from Arcturus - Gordon R. Dickson	3.00	6.00	12.00	SF
S140	Honeymoon Humor - Horace T. Elmo	2.00	4.00	7.50	H

Ace S-90, c. Ace

Ace D-127, c. Ace

Ace D-181, c. Ace

S141 Blood on the Branches - Oliver Crawford	2.00	4.00	7.50	
S142 Masquerade in Blue - Glenn M. Barns	2.00	4.00	7.50	E
S143 A Woman on the Place - Harry Whittington	2.00	4.00	7.50	E
D144 The Man From Stony Lonesome - Jay Albert				W
A Killer Comes Riding - Rod Patterson	2.00	4.00	7.50	W
S145 The Little Monsters - Brant House	2.00	4.00	7.50	H
D146 The Forgotten Planet - Murray Leinster				SF
Contraband Rocket - Lee Correy	2.00	4.00	7.50	SF
D146 The Forgotten Planet - Murray Leinster	3.00	6.00	12.00	SF
D147 Prowl Cop - Gregory Jones				M
My Private Hangman - Norman Herries	3.00	6.00	12.00	M
S148 The Man from Andersonville - Brad Ward	2.00	4.00	7.50	W
D149 A Run for the Money - Dale Clark				M
The Thin Edge of Mania - Mack Macklin	2.00	4.00	7.50	M
D150 Agent of the Unknown - Margaret St. Clair				SF
The World Jones Made - Philip K. Dick	2.00	4.00	7.50	SF
S151 Climb a Broken Ladder - Robert Novak	1.50	3.50	5.00	E
S152 Medic Mirth - Henry G. Felsen	2.00	4.00	7.50	H
S153 The Wild Seed - Hallam Whitney	1.50	3.50	5.00	E
D154 Voyage to Somewhere - Sloan Wilson	1.50	3.50	5.00	C
D155 Journey to the Center of the Earth - Jules Verne	1.50	3.50	5.00	SF
D156 Thruway West - Lee Floren				W
c-Leone				
The Naked Range - Stephen C. Lawrence	2.00	4.00	7.50	W
D157 Stab in the Dark - Louis Trimble				M
Never Say no to a Killer - Jonathan Gant	2.00	4.00	7.50	M
S158 Golden Girl - Kim Darien	2.00	4.00	7.50	E
S159 She Shark - John Farr	2.00	4.00	7.50	
D160 Decision at Sundown - Michael Carder				W
Action Along the Humboldt - Karl Kramer	2.00	4.00	7.50	W
S161 Gag Writer's Private Joke Book - Eddie Davis	2.00	4.00	7.50	H
D162 The Mars Monopoly - Jerry Sohl				SF
The Man Who Lived Forever - R. DeWitt Miller & Anna Hunger	2.00	4.00	7.50	SF
D163 Woman's Doctor - Russell Boltar	2.00	4.00	7.50	E
D164 Mankind on the Run - Gordon R. Dickson				SF
The Crossroads of Time - Andre Norton	2.00	4.00	7.50	SF
S165 Love and Hisses - Brant House	2.00	4.00	7.50	H
D166 Whispering Canyon - Stuart Breck				W
Terror of Tres Alamos - Samuel A. Peeples	1.50	3.50	5.00	W
D167 Destroying Angel - John Creighton				M
Never Say Die - Milton K. Ozaki	1.50	3.50	5.00	M
S168 Riverboat Girl - P. A. Hoover	2.00	4.00	7.50	E
D169 Star Bridge - Jack Williamson & James E. Gunn	1.50	3.50	5.00	SF
D170 Black Fire - Lawrence Goldman				
Flight by Night - Day Keene	1.50	3.50	5.00	
S171 Campus Joke Book - Eddie Davis	2.00	4.00	7.50	H
D172 Johnny No-Name - Ben Smith				W
Stages South - Robert Steelman	1.50	3.50	5.00	W
D173 Overlords from Space - Joseph E. Kelleam				SF
The Man Who Mastered Time - Ray Cummings	2.00	4.00	7.50	SF
S174 B-Girl - Robert Novak	2.00	4.00	7.50	E
D175 Best TV Humor of the Year - Irving Settel	2.00	4.00	7.50	H
D176 3 Thousand Years - Thomas Calvert McClary				SF
The Green Queen - Margaret St. Clair	2.00	4.00	7.50	SF
D177 The Girl in the Cop's Pocket - Robert Turner				M
Violence is Golden - C. H. Thames	2.00	4.00	7.50	M
D178 The Savage City - Jean Paradise	2.00	4.00	7.50	A
S179 Squelches - Brant House	2.00	4.00	7.50	H
D180 The No-Gun Fighter - Nelson Nye				W
One Step Ahead of the Posse - Walt Coburn	1.50	3.50	5.00	W
D181 The Exploits of Sherlock Holmes - John Dickson Carr & Adrian Conan Doyle	2.00	4.00	7.50	M
D182 Shame - Emile Zola				E
Therese Raquin - Emile Zola	2.00	4.00	7.50	
S183 The End of the World - Don Wollheim Orig., 1956	2.00	4.00	7.50	SF
D184 The Big Ivy - James McCague	1.50	3.50	5.00	
D185 The Humming Box - Harry Whittington				M
Build my Gallows High - Geoffrey Homes	2.00	4.00	7.50	M
D186 Ex-Marshall - Ray Hogan				W

(ACE, continued)

	Steel Horizon - Edward Churchill	1.50	3.50	5.00	W
D187	The Pawns of Null-A - A. E. Van Vogt	4.00	8.00	15.00	SF
	First ed., 1956				
S188	They Goofed - Brant House	1.50	3.50	5.00	H
D189	Dead on Arrival - Stephen Marlowe				M
	Weep for a Wanton - Lawrence Treat	1.50	3.50	5.00	M
S190	The Golden Couch - Henry Lewis Nixon	1.50	3.50	5.00	
D191	Apalachee Gold - Frank G. Slaughter	1.50	3.50	5.00	
D192	Beware of this Tenderfoot - Roy Manning				W
	Bad Blood at Black Range - John Callahan	1.50	3.50	5.00	W
D193	The Man Who Japed - Philip K. Dick				SF
	The Space Born - E. C. Tubb	3.00	6.00	12.00	SF
D194	Moscow - Theodor Plievier	1.50	3.50	5.00	C
D195	The Deep End - Owen Dudley				M
	The Quaking Widow - Robert Colby	1.50	3.50	5.00	M
196	The Night Branders - Walt Coburn				W
	The Highwayman - Frank Gruber	1.50	3.50	5.00	W
D197	Counterfeit Corpse - Ferguson Findley				M
	TNT for Two - James Byron	1.50	3.50	5.00	M
S198	Tokyo Intrigue - William Bender, Jr.	1.50	3.50	5.00	
D199	Planet of No Return - Poul Anderson				SF
	Star Guard - Andre Norton	2.00	4.00	7.50	SF
	1957				
D200	Report on Unidentified Flying Objects -				
	Edward J. Ruppelt	1.50	3.50	5.00	UFO
D201	Saturday Mountain - Nathaniel Jones				E
	Across that River - Harry Whittington	2.00	4.00	7.50	E
D202	The Color of Green - Leonard Kaufman	1.50	3.50	5.00	
D203	Uneasy Lies the Head - William L. Rohde				M
	Cain's Girl Friend - William Grote	2.00	4.00	7.50	M
D204	The Desperate Donigans - Gordon Donalds				
	John Law, Keep Out! - Paul Durst	1.50	3.50	5.00	
D205	Who Speaks of Conquest? - Lan Wright				SF
	The Earth in Peril - Don A. Wollheim	2.00	4.00	7.50	SF
D206	Great Day in the Morning - Robert Hardy				
	Andrews	1.50	3.50	5.00	W
D207	Hollywood Doctor - Charles Grayson	2.00	4.00	7.50	E
D208	Blind Man's Bullets - Glenn Balch				W
	The Prodigal Gun - Barry Cord	1.50	3.50	5.00	W
D209	Three Times a Victim - F. L. Wallace				M
	A Night for Treason - John Jakes	2.00	4.00	7.50	
D210	The Lion at Morning - Stephen Longstreet	1.50	3.50	5.00	E
D211	Eye in the Sky - Philip K. Dick	2.00	4.00	7.50	SF
S212	Hollywood Humor - Horace T. Elmo	1.50	3.50	5.00	H
D213	How to Stop Killing Yourself - Peter J.				
	Steincrohn	2.00	4.00	7.50	NF
D214	Hate Alley - Martin Weiss	2.00	4.00	7.50	
D215	Three to Conquer - Eric Frank Russell				SF
	Doomsday Eve - Robert Moore Williams	3.00	6.00	12.00	SF
D216	Ridin' Through - William Colt MacDonald				W
	Savage Valley - Barry Cord	1.50	3.50	5.00	W
	aka Dry Range				
D217	Downwind - Bob McKnight				M
	A Rage to Kill - B. E. Lovell	1.50	3.50	5.00	M
D218	Tigrero! - Sasha Siemel	1.50	3.50	5.00	A
S219	Backwater Woman - P. A. Hoover	1.50	3.50	5.00	E
D220	Wear a Fast Gun - John Jakes				W
	The Friendless One - Ray Hogan	2.00	4.00	7.50	W
D221	The Terror Package - Robert Chavis				M
	You've Bet Your Life - Gordon Ashe	1.50	3.50	5.00	M
D222	First on the Rope - R. Frison-Roche	1.50	3.50	5.00	A
D223	This Fortress World - James E. Gunn				SF
	The 13th Immortal - Robert Silverberg	2.00	4.00	7.50	SF
D224	Desire in the Ozarks - Shelby Steger	1.50	3.50	5.00	E
D225	A Lonely Walk - M. E. Chaber				M
	Loser by a Head - Harry Giddings	1.50	3.50	5.00	M
D226	Doc Colt - Sam A. Peeples				W
	Showdown at Warbird - Edwin Booth	1.50	3.50	5.00	W
D227	Crisis in 2140 - H. Beam Piper & John J.				
	McGuire				SF
	Gunner Cade - Cyril Judd	3.00	6.00	12.00	SF
D228	We Die Alone - David Howarth	1.50	3.50	5.00	NF
D229	Take it Out in Trade - Walter Whitney	1.50	3.50	5.00	E
D230	Boss of Barbed Wire - Barry Cord				W
	Burn 'Em Out - Lee Floren	1.50	3.50	5.00	W

8

Ace D-187, c. Ace   Ace D-238, c. Ace   Ace D-270, c. Ace

(ACE, continued)

D231	Point of Peril - Edward Ronns				M
	Murder for Charity - Owen Dudley	1.50	3.50	5.00	M
D232	The Fixers - Willard Manus	1.50	3.50	5.00	E
D233	First on Mars - Rex Gordon	1.50	3.50	5.00	SF
D234	Look of the Eagle - Robert L. Scott, Jr.	1.50	3.50	5.00	
D235	The Lady and the Snake - John Farr				M
	Nothing to Lose but My Life - Louis Trimble	1.50	3.50	5.00	M
D236	Jinx Rider - Edwin Booth				W
	Walk a Lonely Trail - Ray Hogan	1.50	3.50	5.00	W
D237	The Secret Vistors - James White				SF
	Master of Life and Death - Robert Silverberg	2.00	4.00	7.50	SF
D238	Go - Clellon Holmes	5.00	10.00	20.00	JD
D239	Earth Satellites and the Race for Space Superiority - G. Harry Stine	1.50	3.50	5.00	NF
D240	Broken Wheel Ranch - Wayne C. Lee				W
	Torture Trail - Tom West	1.50	3.50	5.00	W
D241	The Hired Target - Wilson Tucker				M
	One Deadly Dawn - Harry Whittington	2.00	4.00	7.50	M
D242	Empire of the Atom - A. E. Van Vogt				SF
	Space Station No. 1 - Frank B. Long	2.00	4.00	7.50	SF
D243	The Roving Eye - Michael Wells	1.50	3.50	5.00	E
D244	Night Raider of the Atlantic - Terrence Robertson	1.50	3.50	5.00	C
D245	Off on a Comet - Jules Verne	1.50	3.50	5.00	SF
D246	The Magnate - John Harriman	1.50	3.50	5.00	
D247	Look Out Behind You - Ken Lewis				M
	Not so Evil as Eve - John Creighton	1.50	3.50	5.00	M
D248	Longhorn Law - Ray Hogan				W
	Cross Me in Gunsmoke - Clement Hardin	1.50	3.50	5.00	W
D249	The Cosmic Puppets - Philip K. Dick				SF
	Sargasso of Space - Andrew North	2.00	4.00	7.50	SF
D250	The Terrible Swift Sword - Arthur Steuer	2.00	4.00	7.50	M
D251	Windward Passage - Hamilton Cochran	2.00	4.00	7.50	A
D252	The Rawhide Breed - John Callahan				W
	Prairie Terror - Rod Patterson	1.50	3.50	5.00	W
D253	The Buried Motive - Bruce Cassiday				M
	Marked Down for Murder - Spencer Dean	1.50	3.50	5.00	M
D254	The Lash of Desire - Marcos Spinelli	2.00	4.00	7.50	E
D255	Star Ways - Poul Anderson c-Emsh				SF
	City Under the Sea - Kenneth Bulmer	2.00	4.00	7.50	
S 256	The General - Karlludwig Opitz	1.50	3.50	5.00	C
D257	Tiger in the Streets - Louis Malley	3.00	6.00	12.00	JD
D258	The Long Walk - Slavomir Rawicz	1.50	3.50	5.00	NF
D259	The Case of the Violent Virgin - Michael Avallone				M
	The Case of the Bouncing Betty - Michael Avallone	2.00	4.00	7.50	M
D260	Land of the Stranger - Ray Hogan				W
	The Saddle Wolves - Lee Floren	1.50	3.50	5.00	W
D261	The Variable Man and Other Stories - Philip K. Dick c-Emsh	2.00	4.00	7.50	SF
S 262	Attack! - Leland Jamieson c-Emsh	1.50	3.50	5.00	C
S 263	See How They Run - Wilene Shaw	1.50	3.50	5.00	E
D264	Cain Basin - Barry Cord				W

Brother Outlaw - Lee E. Wells	1.50	3.50	5.00	W
D265 Terror in the Night and Other Stories - Robert Bloch				M
Shooting Star - Robert Bloch	2.00	4.00	7.50	M
D266 Twice Upon a Time - Charles L. Fontenay c-Emsh				SF
The Mechanical Monarch - E. C. Tubb	2.00	4.00	7.50	SF
D267 Speed Demon - Jim Bosworth	2.00	4.00	7.50	E
D268 Lincoln's Wit - Brant House	2.00	4.00	7.50	H
D269 Death in the South Atlantic - Michael Powell	1.50	3.50	5.00	NF
D270 D for Delinquent - Bud Clifton	3.00	6.00	12.00	JD
D271 Lovers and Libertines - Cliff Howe	1.50	3.50	5.00	NF
D272 Riders in the Night - Lee Floren				W
Backlash at Cajon Pass - William Hopson	1.50	3.50	5.00	W
D273 The Midnight Eye - Mike Roscoe				M
Shakedown Hotel - Ernest Jason Fredericks	1.50	3.50	5.00	M
D274 World Without Men - Charles Eric Maine c-Emsh	7.50	15.00	30.00	SF
S 275 Cartoon Annual No. 3 - Brant House	1.50	3.50	5.00	H
D276 The Gunsmoke Trail - Boney Cord				W
Lead in His Fists - Tom West	1.50	3.50	5.00	W
D277 City on the Moon - Murray Leinster c-Emsh				SF
Men on the Moon - Donald A. Wollheim	2.00	4.00	7.50	SF
D278 This Bright Sword - Donald Barr Chidsey	2.00	4.00	7.50	
D279 Bye-Bye, Baby! - J. Harvey Bond				M
Murder Mutual - Bob McKnight	1.50	3.50	5.00	M
D280 The Story of Wake Island - James P. S. Devereux	1.50	3.50	5.00	NF
D281 Guideposts - Norman Vincent Peale	1.50	3.50	5.00	NF
D282 Scoundrels, Fiends & Human Monsters - Cliff Howe	2.00	4.00	7.50	NF
D283 City - Clifford D. Simak	2.00	4.00	7.50	SF
D284 The Man Who Killed Tex - Edwin Booth				W
The Guns of Hammer - Barry Cord	1.50	3.50	5.00	W
D285 The Brass Shroud - Bruce Cassiday				M
Odd Woman Out - Joseph Linklater	2.00	4.00	7.50	M
D286 Invaders from Earth - Robert Silvergerg c-Emsh				SF
Across Time - David Grinnell	2.00	4.00	7.50	SF
D287 Coral and Brass - Gen. Holland M. Smith & Percy Finch	1.50	3.50	5.00	NF
D288 The Trail to Tomahawk - Edwin Booth				W
Law Beyond the Law - John Callahan	1.50	3.50	5.00	W
D289 This'll Slay You - Alan Payne				M
Violent City - John & Ward Hawkins 1958	1.50	3.50	5.00	M
D290 A Woman Called Trouble - P. A. Hoover	1.50	3.50	5.00	E
D291 Lest We Forget Thee, Earth - Calvin M. Knox				SF
People Minus X - Raymond Z. Gallun c-Emsh	3.00	6.00	12.00	SF
D292 The Insiders - Booth Mooney	1.50	3.50	5.00	E
D293 The Unknown Soldier - Vaino Linna	1.50	3.50	5.00	C
D294 Beyond the Wild Missouri - Walt Coburn				W
Bad Bunch of the Brasada - John H. Latham	1.50	3.50	5.00	W
D295 Big Planet - Jack Vance				SF
Slaves of the Klau - Jack Vance	4.00	8.00	15.00	SF
D296 Run the River Gauntlet - John Clagett	2.00	4.00	7.50	A
D297 The Cut of the Whip - Peter Rabe				M
Kill One, Kill Two - Rbt. H. Kelston	1.50	3.50	5.00	M
D298 Thunder Creek Range - Paul Evan				W
Outlaw's Welcome - William E. Vance	1.50	3.50	5.00	W
D299 A Planet for Texans - John J. McGuire				SF
Star Born - Andre Norton	2.00	4.00	7.50	SF
D300 The Dance Merchants - J. Walter Small	1.50	3.50	5.00	E
D301 The Deadly Combo - John Farr				M
Murder Isn't Funny - J. Harvey Bond	2.00	4.00	7.50	M
D302 The Iron King - Maurice Druon	2.00	4.00	7.50	A
D303 War of the Wing-Men - Poul Anderson				SF
The Snows of Ganymede - Poul Anderson	1.50	3.50	5.00	SF
D304 River to the Sunset - Archie Joscelyn				W
Trouble at Breakdam - Ben Smith	1.50	3.50	5.00	W
D305 Free-Lance Murder - Vic Rodell				M
Cornered - Louis King	1.50	3.50	5.00	M

Ace D-274, c. Ace   Ace D-331, c. Ace   Ace D-343, c. Ace

(ACE, continued)

D306	All Shook Up - Peyson Antholz	2.00	4.00	7.50	JD
D307	From Eve On - Brant House	1.50	3.50	5.00	H
D308	Gunman's Gamble - Jack M. Bickham				W
	Draw and Die! - Roy Manning	1.50	3.50	5.00	W
D309	The Island of Dr. Moreau - H. G. Wells	2.00	4.00	7.50	SF
D310	Mocambu - Marcos Spinell	3.00	6.00	12.00	E
D311	Stepsons of Terra - Robert Silberberg				SF
	A Man Called Destiny - Lan Wright	2.00	4.00	7.50	SF
D312	The Deadly Streets - Harlan Ellison	7.50	15.00	30.00	JD
	First ed., 1958				
D313	The Deadly Boodle - J. M. Flynn				M
	Design for Dying - Samuel A. Krasney	2.00	4.00	7.50	M
D314	Deeds of Darkness - Blair Ashton	2.00	4.00	7.50	
D315	Six Worlds Yonder - Eric Frank Russell				SF
	The Space Willies - Eric Frank Russell	3.00	6.00	12.00	SF
D316	Mesquite Johnny - Barry Cord				W
	A Time for Guns - Rod Patterson	1.50	3.50	5.00	W
D317	The Wayward Blonde - John Creighton				M
	The Big Bite - Gerry Travis	1.50	3.50	5.00	M
D318	Captain Crossbones - Donald Barr Chidsey	2.00	4.00	7.50	A
D319	The Man with Three Faces - Hans-Otto				
	Meissner	1.50	3.50	5.00	NF
D320	The Last Shoot Out - William Hopson				W
	The Rangemaster - Robert McCaig	1.50	3.50	5.00	W
D321	The Smell of Trouble - Louis Trimble				M
	Trial by Perjury - John Creighton	1.50	3.50	5.00	M
D322	The Void Beyond and Other Stories -				
	Robert Moore Williams				SF
	The Blue Atom - Williams	2.00	4.00	7.50	SF
D323	The Violent Ones - Brant House	3.00	6.00	12.00	JD
D324	Brigands of the Moon - Ray Cummings	1.50	3.50	5.00	SF
	c-Emsh				
D325	July, 1863 - Irving Werstein	1.50	3.50	5.00	NF
D326	Battling the Bombers - Wilhelm Johnen	1.50	3.50	5.00	C
D327	First on the Moon - Jeff Satton	1.50	3.50	5.00	SF
	c-Emsh				
D328	The Fourth Gunman - Merle Constiner				W
	Slick on the Draw - Tom West	1.50	3.50	5.00	W
D329	Stamped for Death - Emmett McDowell				M
	Three for the Gallows - Emmett McDowell	1.50	3.50	5.00	M
D330	Muscle Boy - Bud Clifton	2.00	4.00	7.50	E
D331	The Secret of Zi - Kenneth Bultner				SF
	c-Emsh				
	Beyond the Vanishing Point - Ray Cummings	2.00	4.00	7.50	SF
D332	Stranger in Sundown - Ben Smith				W
	Blood on Boot Hill - Kermit Welles	1.50	3.50	5.00	W
	1959				
D333	Scream Street - Mike Brett				M
	Stranglehold - John Creighton	1.50	3.50	5.00	M
D334	Queen of the flat-tops - Stanley Johnston	1.50	3.50	5.00	NF
D335	War of Two Worlds - Poul Anderson				SF
	Threshold of Eternity - John Brunner	2.00	4.00	7.50	SF
D336	Morals Squad - Samuel A. Krasney	1.50	3.50	5.00	E
D337	Play it Cool - Jack Gerstine	3.00	6.00	12.00	JD
D338	The Fires of Youth - Edward DeRoo	3.00	5.00	12.00	JD
D339	Ring Around the Sun - Clifford D. Simak	4.00	8.00	15.00	SF
D340	Solar Lottery - Philip K. Dick	1.50	3.50	5.00	SF

(ACE, continued)

D341	The Marina Street Girls - Rae Loomis	1.50	3.50	5.00	E
D342	Queen's Blade - Nicholas Gorham	2.00	4.00	7.50	A
D343	The Young Wolves - Edward De Roo	3.00	6.00	12.00	JD
D344	Desert Fury - Gordon Landsborough	1.50	3.50	5.00	C
	aka Battery from Hellfire				
D345	Plague Ship - Andrew North				SF
	Voodoo Planet - Andrew North	2.00	4.00	7.50	SF
D346	Sheriff of Big Hat - Barry Cord	1.50	3.50	5.00	W
	Wanted! Alive! - Ray Hogan				
D347	The Corpse without a Country - Louis Trimble				M
	Play for Keeps - Harry Whittington	2.00	4.00	7.50	M
D348	The Man from Nowhere - T. V. Olsen				W
	The Avenging Gun - John L. Shelley	1.50	3.50	5.00	W
D349	The Guilty Bystander - Mike Brett				M
	Kill Me with Kindness - J. Harvey Bond	1.50	3.50	5.00	M
D350	Red Alert - Peter Bryant	2.00	4.00	7.50	SF
D351	The Sun Smasher - Edmond Hamilton				SF
	Star Haven - Ivar Jorgenson	1.50	3.50	5.00	SF
G352	Fire and Morning - Francis Leary	1.50	3.50	5.00	A
D353	The Macabre Reader - Donald A. Wollheim	1.50	3.50	5.00	HO
D354	The Hidden Planet - Donald A. Wollheim	1.50	3.50	5.00	SF
D355	The Beachhead Spies - Bill Strutton & Michael Pearson	1.50	3.50	5.00	C
	aka The Secret Invaders				
D356	Kansan Guns - Paul Durst				W
	The Cactus Kid - Tom West	1.50	3.50	5.00	W
D357	Lady in Peril - Lester Dent				M
	Wired for Scandal - F. L. Wallace	1.50	3.50	5.00	M
D358	The Plot Against Earth - Calvin M. Knox				SF
	Recruit for Andromeda - Milton Lesser	1.50	3.50	5.00	SF
D359	The Haunted Strangler - John C. Cooper	3.00	6.00	12.00	HO
D360	War in Peaceful Valley - Barry Cord				W
	Johnny Sixgun - John H. Latham	1.50	3.50	5.00	W
D361	Murder Mistress - Robert Colby				M
	Dangerous to Know - James P. Duff	1.50	3.50	5.00	M
D362	The 100th Millenium - John Brunner				SF
	Edge of Time - David Grinnell	1.50	3.50	5.00	SF
D363	The Rapist - Samuel A. Krasney	2.00	4.00	7.50	E
D364	The Pipes Are Calling - Donald Barr Chidsey	2.00	4.00	7.50	A
	First ed., 1959				
D365	Mig Alley - Robert Eunson	1.50	3.50	5.00	C
	First ed., 1959				
D366	The Invaders are Coming - Alan E. Nourse & J. A. Meyer	1.50	3.50	5.00	SF
	c-Emsh				
D367	Negative of a Nude - Charles E. Fritch				M
	First ed., 1959				
	Till Death Do Us Part - Louis Trimble	1.50	3.50	5.00	M
D368	A Score to Settle - Joseph Gage				W
	Hangman's Valley - Ray Hogan	1.50	3.50	5.00	W
	First ed., 1959				
D369	Vanguard from Alpha - Brian Aldiss				SF
	The Changeling Worlds - Kenneth Bulmer	1.50	3.50	5.00	SF
D370	Cry Flood! - Ernest Jason Fredericks	1.50	3.50	5.00	E
G371	Berlin - Theodor Plievier	1.50	3.50	5.00	C
D372	Grass Greed - Glenn Balch	1.50	3.50	5.00	W
	Cimarron Territory - Dan Kirby				

Ace D-347, c. Ace

Ace D-359, c. Ace

Ace D-417, c. Ace

12

D373	Scarlet Starlet - Doug Warren				M
	The Knave of Diamonds - Jack Karney	1.50	3.50	5.00	M
	First ed., 1959				
D374	The Thoroughbred and the Tramp -				
	Burgess Leonard	1.50	3.50	5.00	E
	First ed., 1959				
D375	Masters of Evolution - Damon Knight				SF
	c-Emsh				
	Fire in the Heavens - George O. Smith	1.50	3.50	5.00	SF
G376	The Big Company Look - J. Harvey Howells	1.50	3.50	5.00	
D377	Bombs in Orbit - Jeff Sutton	1.50	3.50	5.00	SF
	First ed., 1959				
D378	Out for Kicks - Wilene Shaw	1.50	3.50	5.00	
D379	Drink with the Dead - J. M. Flynn				M
	Mistress of Horror House - William Woody	1.50	3.50	5.00	M
D380	Concho Valley - Barry Cord				W
	My Brother the Gunman - William Heuman	1.50	3.50	5.00	W
D381	Secret of the Lost Race - Andre Norton				SF
	First ed., 1959				
	One Against Herculum - Jerry Sohl	1.50	3.50	5.00	SF
G382	The Willing Maid - C. T. Ritchie	1.50	3.50	5.00	A
D383	The Murder Specialist - Bud Clifton	1.50	3.50	5.00	M
	First ed., 1959				
D384	Feud Fury - Jack M. Bickham				W
	First ed., 1959				
	Mountain Ambush - Louis Trimble	1.50	3.50	5.00	W
D385	Echo in the Skull - John Brunner				SF
	First ed., 1959				
	Rocket to Limbo - Alan E. Nourse	1.50	3.50	5.00	SF
	c-Emsh				
G386	The Sulu Sword - Richard O'Connor	2.00	4.00	7.50	A
D387	Fare Prey - Laine Fisher				M
	The Bikini Bombshell - Bob McKnight	1.50	3.50	5.00	M
D388	When the Sleeper Wakes - H. G. Wells	2.00	4.00	7.50	SF
	c-Emsh				
D389	No Entry - Manning Coles	1.50	3.50	5.00	
G390	Long Pig - Russell Foreman	1.50	3.50	5.00	
D391	The World Swappers - John Brunner				SF
	First ed., 1959				
	Seige of the Unseen - A. E. Van Vogt	1.50	3.50	5.00	SF
D392	Twisted Trail - Tom West				W
	The Man From Salt Creek - Archie Joscelyn	1.50	3.50	5.00	W
D393	Dictators Die Hard - Robert A. Levey				M
	Evil is the Night - John Creighton	1.50	3.50	5.00	M
	First ed., 1959				
D394	The Flaming Island - Donald Barr Chidsey	2.00	4.00	7.50	A
D395	Thunder at Harper's Ferry - Allan Keller	1.50	3.50	5.00	NF
D396	Luisita - Rae Loomis	1.50	3.50	5.00	E
D397	Journey to the Center of the Earth -				
	Jules Verne	1.50	3.50	5.00	SF
D398	Why I Am So Beat - Nolan Miller	1.50	3.50	5.00	E
D399	Living it Up - Edward Adler	1.50	3.50	5.00	
D400	Last Chance at Devil's Canyon - Barry Cord				W
	Shadow of a Gunman - Gordon D. Shirreffs	1.50	3.50	5.00	W
D401	Obit Deferred - Louis Trimble				M
	First ed., 1959				
	I Want Out - Tedd Thomey	1.50	3.50	5.00	M
G402	Kiboko - Daniel P. Mannix	3.00	6.00	12.00	A
D403	The Pirates of Zan - Murray Leinster				SF
	First ed., 1959, c-Emsh				
	The Mutant Weapon - Murray Leinster	2.00	4.00	7.50	SF
D404	The Hollow Hero - Clifford Anderson	1.50	3.50	5.00	
	First ed., 1959				
D405	First to the Stars - Rex Gordon	1.50	3.50	5.00	SF
	First ed., 1959				
D406	Go, Man, Go! - Edward De Roo	3.00	6.00	12.00	JD
	First ed., 1959				
D407	The Planet Killers - Robert Silverberg	2.00	4.00	7.50	SF
	We Claim These Stars! - Poul Anderson				
D408	Wyoming Welcome - Edwin Booth	2.00	4.00	7.50	W
	Law of the Trigger - Giles A. Lutz				
D409	Terror Tournament - J. M. Flynn				M
	Cargo for the Styx - Louis Trimble	2.00	4.00	7.50	M
	First ed., 1959				
D410	Buccaneer's Blade - Donald Barr Chidsey	2.00	4.00	7.50	A
	First ed., 1959				

(ACE, continued)

D411	Swamp Sanctuary - Bob McKnight	2.00	4.00	7.50	E
	First ed., 1959				
D412	Apache Butte - Gordon R. Shirreffs				W
	Ride the Long Night - E. A. Alman	1.50	3.50	5.00	W
	First ed., 1960				
D413	A Touch of Infinity - Harlan Ellison				SF
	The Man with Nine Lives - Harlan Ellison	5.00	9.00	17.50	SF
G414	The Companions of Jehu - Alexandre Dumas	2.00	4.00	7.50	A
D415	Dead Certain - Stewart Sterling				M
	First ed., 1960				
	Fire on Fear Street - Stewart Sterling	1.50	3.50	5.00	M
D416	The Big Question - John Kenneth	1.50	3.50	5.00	E
	First ed., 1960				
D417	Rumble at the Housing Project - Edward DeRoo	3.00	6.00	12.00	
418					
D419	A Slice of Death - Bob McKnight				M
	First ed., 1960				
	Open Season - Bernard Thielen	1.50	3.50	5.00	M
D420	The Angry Ones - John A. Williams	1.50	3.50	5.00	E
	First ed., 1960				
D421	Dr. Futurity - Philip K. Dick				SF
	First ed., 1960				
	Slavers of Space - John Brunner	1.50	3.50	5.00	SF
D422	The Best from Fantasy and Science Fiction, 3rd Series - Anthony Boucher & J. Francis McComas	1.50	3.50	5.00	SF
D423	Tidal Wave - Browning Norton	1.50	3.50	5.00	
	First ed., 1960				
D424	Wild Justice - Robert McCaig				W
	Shoot-out at the Way Station - Lee Richards	1.50	3.50	5.00	W
D425	Dig Her a Grave - Paul Kruger				M
	A Half Interest in Murder - John Creighton	1.50	3.50	5.00	M
	First ed., 1960				
D426	Penal Colony - Robert S. Close	3.00	6.00	12.00	E
	aka Eliza Callaghan				
D427	World of the Masterminds - Robert Moore Williams				SF
	To the End of Time and Other Stories - R. M. Williams	2.00	4.00	7.50	SF
	First ed., 1960				
D428	Scowtown Woman - P. A. Hoover	2.00	4.00	7.50	E
D429	The Anatomy of Violence - Charles Runyon	2.00	4.00	7.50	E
	First ed., 1960				
430					
D431	Lost in Space - George O. Smith				SF
	Earth's Last Fortress - A. E. Van Vogt	1.50	3.50	5.00	SF
	First ed., 1960				
D432	Convention Queen - Donn Broward	1.50	3.50	5.00	E
	First ed., 1960				
D433	If Hate Could Kill - Jack Bradley				M
	First ed., 1960				
	The Smasher - Talmadge Powell	1.50	3.50	5.00	M
D434	The Purchase of the North Pole - Jules Verne	1.50	3.50	5.00	SF
D435	Lady in Bondage - C. T. Ritchie	2.00	4.00	7.50	A
D436	The Challenger - Giles A. Lutz				W
	The Phantom Pistoleer - Tom West	1.50	3.50	5.00	W
D437	And Then the Town Took Off - Richard				

Ace D-426, c. Ace

Ace D-432, c. Ace

Ace D-452, c. Ace

	Wilson				SF
	The Sioux Spaceman - Andre Norton	1.50	3.50	5.00	SF
D438	The Panic Button - Charles Fogg First ed., 1960	1.50	3.50	5.00	C
D439	Run If You Can - Owen Dudley First ed., 1960				M
	The Devil's Punchbowl - Duane Decker	1.50	3.50	5.00	M
G440	Letter of Marque - Andrew Hepburn	2.00	4.00	7.50	A
D441	Skip Bomber - Lloyd E. Olson	1.50	3.50	5.00	C
D442	Rider of the Rincon - Rod Patterson				W
	Killer's Paradise - Jack M. Bickham	1.50	3.50	5.00	W
D443	Bow Down to Nul - Brian W. Aldiss First ed., 1960				SF
	The Dark Destroyers - Manly Wade Wellman	1.50	3.50	5.00	SF
D444	Desire Island - Shepard Rifkin First ed., 1960	2.00	4.00	7.50	E
D445	Bloodline to Murder - Emmett McDowell First ed., 1960				M
	In at the Kill - Emmett McDowell	1.50	3.50	5.00	M
D446	Flight 685 is Overdue - Edward Moore First ed., 1960	1.50	3.50	5.00	M
D447	The Hot Chariot - J. M. Flynn				M
	Kiss the Babe Goodbye - Bob McKnight First ed., 1960	2.00	4.00	7.50	M
D448	Pistol - Whipper - Lee Floren				W
	Winter Range - Al Cody	1.50	3.50	5.00	W
D449	The Genetic General - Gordon R. Dickson First ed., 1960				SF
	Time to Teleport - Gordon R. Dickson	2.00	4.00	7.50	SF
D450	Side Me with Sixes - Tom West				W
	The Ridgerunner - Roy Hogan	1.50	3.50	5.00	W
D451	Odds Against Linda - Steve Ward First ed., 1960				M
	A Key to the Morgue - Robert Martin	1.50	3.50	5.00	M
D452	The Color of Hate - Joe L. Hensley	2.00	4.00	7.50	M
D453	The Games of Neith - Margaret St. Clair First ed., 1960				SF
454	The Earth Gods Are Coming - Kenneth Bulmer	2.00	3.75	6.50	SF
D455	The Best From Fantasy and Science Fiction - Fourth Series - Anthony Boucher	1.50	3.50	5.00	SF
D456	The Desperate Dude - Edwin Booth				W
	Danger Trail - Edwin Booth	1.50	3.50	5.00	W
D457	Vulcan's Hammer - Philip K. Dick First ed., 1960				SF
	The Skynappers - John Brunner	1.50	3.50	5.00	SF
D458	Womanhunt - Mark Derby	1.50	3.50	5.00	A
D459	The Hot Diary - Howard J. Olmsted First ed., 1960				M
	Ring Around a Rogue - J. M. Flynn	1.50	3.50	5.00	M
460					
D461	The Time Traders - Andre Norton	1.50	3.50	5.00	SF
462					
D463	Dying Room Only - Stewart Sterling				M
	The Body in the Bed - Stewart Sterling	1.50	3.50	5.00	M
464					
D465	The Martian Missile - David Grinnell				SF
	The Atlantic Abomination - John Brunner First ed., 1960	2.00	3.75	6.50	SF
466					
D467	Five, Four, Three, Two, One - Pfftt - William C. Anderson First ed., 1960	4.00	8.00	15.00	SF/H
D468	Sentinels of Space - Eric Frank Russell c-Schulz	1.50	3.50	5.00	SF
D469	Running Scared - Bob McKnight First ed., 1960				M
	Man-Killer - Talmage Powell	1.50	3.50	5.00	M
470					
D471	Sanctuary in the Sky - John Brunner				SF
	The Secret Martians - Jack Sharkey First ed., 1960	1.50	3.50	5.00	SF
D472	A Night for Screaming - Harry Whittington	1.50	3.50	5.00	M
D473	The Greatest Adventure - John Taine	3.00	6.00	12.00	SF

(ACE, continued)

G474	Lost Mines and Hidden Treasure - Leland Lovelace	2.00	4.00	7.50	NF
475					
D476	Double-Cross Dinero - Tom West				W
	Lost Valley - Edwin Booth	1.50	3.50	5.00	W
D477	The Duchess of Skid Row - Louis Trimble				M
	Love Me and Die - Louis Trimble	1.50	3.50	5.00	M
D478	Spacehive - Jeff Sutton	1.50	3.50	5.00	SF
	First ed., 1960				
D479	To the Tombaugh Station - Wilson Tucker				SF
	First ed., 1960				
	Earthman Go Home! - Poul Anderson	2.00	4.00	7.50	SF
480					
D481	The Biggest Holdup - Joseph F. Dinneen	1.50	3.50	5.00	NF
	aka The Alternate Case				
D482	The Weapon Shops of Isher - A. E. Van Vogt	1.50	3.50	5.00	SF
D483	The Corpse in the Picture Window - Bruce Cassidy				M
	If Wishes Were Hearses - J. Harvey Bond	1.50	3.50	5.00	M
	First ed., 1961				
D484	Dead Man's Spurs - Al Cody				W
	First ed., 1961				
	Ambush at Riflestock - Ray Hogan	1.50	3.50	5.00	W
D485	The Puzzle Planet - Robert A. W. Lowndes				SF
	First ed., 1961				
	The Angry Espers - Lloyd Biggle, Jr.	1.50	3.50	5.00	SF
D486	The Little Caesars - Edward DeRoo	3.00	6.00	12.00	JD
D487	Four-Year Hitch - Leonard Sanders	1.50	3.50	5.00	C
	First ed., 1961				
D488	Third Time Down - Dan Brennan	1.50	3.50	5.00	C
	First ed., 1961				
D489	Somebody's Walking Over My Grave - Robert Arthur				M
	First ed., 1961				
	Dally with A Deadly Doll - John Miles	1.50	3.50	5.00	M
D490	Adventures on Other Planets - Donald A. Wollheim	1.50	3.50	5.00	SF
D491	The Big Time - Fritz Leiber				SF
	First ed., 1961				
	The Mind Spider and Other Stories - Fritz Leiber	3.00	6.00	12.00	SF
492					
D493	The Queen's Awards/Fifth Series - E. Queen	2.00	4.00	7.50	M
D494	Log Jam - Leslie Turner White	1.50	3.50	5.00	A
D495	A Mania for Blondes - Samuel A. Krasney	1.50	3.50	5.00	M
	First ed., 1961				
D496	With Blood in Their Eyes - Steven Lawrence				W
	Killer's Canyon - Tom West	1.50	3.50	5.00	W
D497	Wandl the Invader - Ray Cummings				SF
	First ed., 1961				
	I Speak for Earth - Keith Woodcott	2.00	4.00	7.50	SF
D498	Galactic Derelict - Andre Norton	1.50	3.50	5.00	SF
D499	Night Drop - Frederick C. Davis				M
	High Heel Homicide - Frederick C. Davis	1.50	3.50	5.00	M
G500	The Bad Man of the West - George D. Hendricks	2.00	4.00	7.50	NF
D501	Let Him Go Hang - Bud Clifton	1.50	3.50	5.00	M
D502	Long Night at Lodgepole - Al Cody				W
	First ed., 1961				
	Troubled Range - Paul Evan Lehman	1.50	3.50	5.00	W
D503	The Girl in the Death Seat - Fan Nichols	1.50	3.50	5.00	M
D504	Master of the World - Jules Verne	2.00	4.00	7.50	SF
	Movie tie-in				
D505	The Surfside Caper - Louis Trimble				M
	In a Vanishing Room - Robert Colby	2.00	4.00	7.50	M
	First ed., 1961				
D506	The Brazen Dream - Harry Harrison Kroll	1.50	3.50	5.00	E
	First ed., 1961				
D507	Meeting at Infinity - John Brunner				SF
	First ed., 1961				
	Beyond the Silver Sky - Kenneth Bulmer	1.50	3.50	5.00	SF
D508	More Macabre - Donald A. Wollheim	2.00	4.00	7.50	HO
D509	Star Hunter - Andre Norton				SF
	First ed., 1961				
	The Beast Master - Andre Norton	1.50	3.50	5.00	SF
D510	The Searching Rider - Harry Whittington				W

Ace D-513, c. Ace   Ace D-530, c. Ace   Ace D-531, c. Ace

(ACE, continued)

	Hangman's Territory - Jack M. Bickham	1.50	3.50	5.00	W
D511	Drop Dead, Please - Bob McKnight				M
	First ed., 1961				
	One for the Death House - J. M. Flynn	1.50	3.50	5.00	M
D512	Marooned - Donald Barr Chidsey	2.00	4.00	7.50	A
	First ed., 1961				
D513	The Juvies - Harlan Ellison	7.50	15.00	30.00	JD
D514	Ride a Lone Trail - Gordon D. Shirreffs				W
	Hangin' Pards - Gordon D. Shirreffs	1.50	3.50	5.00	W
D515	Kill Me a Fortune - Robert Colby				M
	First ed., 1961				
	Five Alarm Funeral - Stewart Sterling	1.50	3.50	5.00	M
D516	The Swordsman of Mars - Otis Adelbert Kline	2.00	4.00	7.50	SF
D517	The Trouble with Tycho - Clifford D. Simak				SF
	Bring Back Yesterday - A. Bertram Chandler	1.50	3.50	5.00	SF
	First ed., 1961				
D518	Nightmare Cruise - Wade Miller	1.50	3.50	5.00	M
D519	Air Rescue - Carroll V. Glines, Jr. & Wendell F. Moseley	1.50	3.50	5.00	NF
D520	One Foot in Hell - Wilene Shaw	1.50	3.50	5.00	E
	First ed., 1961				
D521	The Girl in the White Cap - Margaret Howe	.75	1.75	3.00	R
D522	A Nest of Fear - Hal Ellson	2.00	4.00	7.50	JD
D523	Strike the Black Flag - Jay Scotland	2.00	4.00	7.50	A
	First ed., 1961				
D524	Overseas Nurse - Jennifer Ames	.75	1.75	3.00	R
D525	This World is Taboo - Murray Leimster	2.00	4.00	7.50	SF
	First ed., 1961				
526					
D527	Star Guard - Andre Norton	1.50	3.50	5.00	SF
D528	Forgotten Planet - Murray Leinster	1.50	3.50	5.00	SF
D529	The Pirate and the Lady - Leslie Turner White	2.00	4.00	7.50	A
	First ed., 1961				
D530	The Day they H-Bombed Los Angeles - Robert Moore Williams	3.00	6.00	12.00	SF
	First ed., 1961				
D531	The Outlaws of Mars - Otis Adelbert Kline	2.00	4.00	7.50	SF
D532	Nurse Craig - Isabel Cabot	.75	1.75	3.00	R
D533	Mad Ave - H. T. Elmo	1.50	3.50	5.00	H
D534	Daybreak - 2250 A. D. - Andre Norton	1.50	3.50	5.00	SF
	1962, aka Star Man's Son				
D535	The Shadow Girl - Ray Cummings	2.00	5.00	10.00	SF
D536	The Nurse and the Pirate - Peggy Gaddis	.75	1.75	3.00	R
D537	The Island of Dr. Moreau - H. G. Wells	1.50	3.50	5.00	SF
D538	The 1,000 Year Plan - Isaac Asimov	2.00	4.00	7.50	SF
	aka Foundation				
D539	Psychiatric Nurse - Mary Mann Fletcher	.75	1.75	3.00	R
	First ed., 1962				
D540	School Nurse - Arlene Hale	.75	1.75	3.00	R
D541	Scavengers in Space - Alan E. Nourse	1.50	3.50	5.00	SF
D542	The Last Planet - Andre Norton	1.50	3.50	5.00	SF
	aka Star Rangers				
D543	Small Town Nurse - Harriet Kathryn Myers	.75	1.75	3.00	R
	First ed., 1962				

(ACE, continued)

D544 Space Station No. 1 - Frank Belknap Long	2.00	3.50	5.00	SF
D545 Emergency Nurse - Suzanne Roberts	.75	1.75	3.00	R
First ed., 1962				
D546 The Crossroads of Time - Andre Norton	1.50	3.50	5.00	SF
D547 The Super Barbarians - John Brunner	2.00	4.00	7.50	SF
D548 End of the World - Dean Owen	2.00	4.00	7.50	SF
Movie tie-in				
D549 Spotlight on Nurse Thorne - Tracy Adams	.75	1.75	3.00	R
First ed., 1962				
D550 No World of Their Own - Poul Anderson	2.00	4.00	7.50	SF
D551 Red Alert - Peter Bryant	1.50	3.50	5.00	SF
D552 Hollywood Nurse - Patricia Libby	.75	1.75	3.00	R
D553 The House on the Borderland - William				
Hope Hodgson	3.00	6.00	12.00	SF
D554 Runaway Nurse - Ethel Hamill	.75	1.75	3.00	R
D555 The Trial of Terra - Jack Williamson	2.00	4.00	7.50	SF
First ed., 1962				
D556 A Nurse for Dr. Sterling - Ruth MacLeod	.75	1.75	3.00	R
D557 Hope Wears White - Florence Stuart	.75	1.75	3.00	R
D558 Campus Nurse - Suzanne Roberts	.75	1.75	3.00	R
D559 Ski Resort Nurse - Jane L. Sears	.75	1.75	3.00	R
D560 Medic in Love - Rowena Boylan	.75	1.75	3.00	R
D561 Nell Shannon, R. N. - Ann Rush	.75	1.75	3.00	R
1963				
D562 Cover Girl Nurse - Patricia Libby	.75	1.75	3.00	R
D563 Leave it to Nurse Kathy - Arlene Hale	.75	1.75	3.00	R
D564 Prodigal Nurse - Harriet Kathryn Myers	.75	1.75	3.00	R
D565 The Heart of Dr. Hilary - Ray Dorien	.75	1.75	3.00	R
D566 Julie Jones, Cape Canaveral Nurse -				
Suzanne Roberts	.75	1.75	3.00	R
First ed., 1963				
D567 A Challenge for Nurse Melanie - Isabel Moore	.75	1.75	3.00	R
First ed., 1963				
D568 Star Ways - Poul Anderson	1.50	3.50	5.00	SF
D569 Dude Ranch Nurse - Arlene Hale	.75	1.75	3.00	R
First ed., 1963				
D570 Spanish Grant - L. L. Foreman	1.50	3.50	5.00	W
D571 Princess of White Starck - Katherine				
McComb	.75	1.75	3.00	R
First ed., 1963				
D572 Arizona Rider - Frank Wynne	1.50	3.50	5.00	W
D573 Whispering Canyon - Stuart Brock	1.50	3.50	5.00	W
D574 Kilkenny - Louis L'Amour	2.00	4.00	7.50	W
D575 A Nurse Called Hope - Peggy Dern	.75	1.75	3.00	R
D576 Border Nurse - Dorothy Dowdell	.75	1.75	3.00	R
D577 Legacy of Love - Frances Sarah Moore	.75	1.75	3.00	R
c-Schinella				
D578 The Lawbringers - Brian Wynne Garfield	1.50	3.50	5.00	W
D579 Hootenanny Nurse - Suzanne Roberts	.75	1.75	3.00	R
First ed., 1964				
D580 Symptoms of Love - Arlene Hale	.75	1.75	3.00	R
D581 Co-ed in White - Suzanne Roberts	.75	1.75	3.00	R
First ed., 1964				
D582 My Love an Altar - Joan Sargent	.75	1.75	3.00	R
c-Schinella				
D583 Hotel Nurse - Tracy Adams	.75	1.75	3.00	R
First ed., 1964				
D584 Airport Nurse - Monica Edwards	.75	1.75	3.00	R
D585 Nurse Marcie's Island - Arlene Hale	.75	1.75	3.00	R
First ed., 1964				
D586 San Francisco Nurse - Barbara Grabendike	.75	1.75	3.00	R
First ed., 1964				
D587 Nurse Connor Comes Home - Arlene Hale	.75	1.75	3.00	R
First ed., 1964				
D588 Short-trigger Man - Merle Constiner	1.50	3.50	5.00	W
First ed., 1964				
D589 The Nurse with the Silver Skates - Virginia				
B. McDonnell	.75	1.75	3.00	R
590				
D591 Northwest Nurse - Arlene Fitzgerald	.75	1.75	3.00	R
First ed., 1964				
D592 Gunslick Mountain - Nelson Nye	1.50	3.50	5.00	W
D593 Sisters in White - Suzanne Roberts	.75	1.75	3.00	R
First ed., 1965				
D594 The Desperate Deputy of Cougar Hill -				
Louis Trimble	1.50	3.50	5.00	W

18

Adv. Novel Classic 2, c. Hill   Adv. Novel Classic 31, c. Hill   All-Picture Mystery nn, c. Stj

(ACE, continued)

First ed., 1965				
D595 Nurse Ann in Surgery - Ruth MacLeod	.75	1.75	3.00	R
First ed., 1965				
D596 Nurse on the Run - Arlene Hale	.75	1.75	3.00	R
First ed., 1965				
597				
D598 Disaster Area Nurse - Arlene Hale	.75	1.75	3.00	R
First ed., 1965				
D599 Winged Victory for Nurse Kerry - Patricia Libby	.75	1.75	3.00	R

ADVENTURE NOVEL CLASSIC

(Hillman Periodicals, Inc./Novel Selections, Inc.)

Digest size

2 Bardelys the Magnificent - Rafael Sabatini	1.50	3.50	5.00	A
5 The Queen's Messenger - Rafael Sabatini	1.50	3.50	5.00	A
7 Hands Up! - A. Treynor	1.50	3.00	5.00	A
10 Connie Morgan Hits the Trail - James Hendryx	1.50	3.00	5.00	A
11 The Vengeance of Hurricane Williams - Gordon Young	.75	1.75	3.00	A
13 Gone North - Charles Alden Seltzer	1.50	3.00	5.00	W
14 Rivermen Die Broke	.75	1.75	3.00	A
15 The Courage of Marge O'Doone - James Oliver Curwood	1.50	3.00	5.00	A
16 Out from Shanghai - Sydney Parkman	.75	1.75	3.00	A
17 Death Heads North - James Hendryx	1.50	3.00	5.00	A
18 River of Fear	.75	1.75	3.00	A
21 Hawk of the Desert - A. Treynor	1.50	3.00	5.00	A
22 Secret Command - John & Ward Hawkins	.75	1.75	3.00	A
23 Hard Money - Luke Short	.75	1.75	3.00	A
24 Jungle Murder - Alan Amos aka Pray for a Miracle	.75	1.75	3.00	A
26 Montana Rides - Evan Evans	.75	1.75	3.00	W
28 Riot at Red Water - Frederick R. Bechdolt	.75	1.75	3.00	W
29 Broken River - John & Ward Hawkins	.75	1.75	3.00	A
30 Arizona - Clarence Budington Kelland	.75	1.75	3.00	W
31 Death Charter - Eustace L. Adams	1.50	3.50	5.00	A
33 Stagecoach Kingdom - Harry Sinclair Drago	.75	1.75	3.00	W
34 Journey to Murder - Robert Portner Koehler	.75	1.75	3.00	M
41 Hard Rock Man - James Hendryx	1.50	3.00	5.00	A

ALL-PICTURE MYSTERY

(St. John Publishing Company)

Digest size

nn The Case of the Winking Buddha - Manning Lee Stokes	2.50	6.00	10.00	M

(ALL-PICTURE MYSTERY, continued)
    Orig., 1950, comic book style
nn It Rhymes with Lust   5.00   10.00   20.00   M
    Orig., 1951, comic book style with Matt
    Baker art

AMAZING STORIES SCIENCE FICTION NOVEL

(Ziff-Davis Publishing Company)

Digest size

nn 20 Million Miles to Earth - Henry Slesar   2.00   4.00   7.50   SF
    1957, Movie tie-in

AMERICAN FOLK-LORE AND HUMOR

(Atomic Books, Inc.)

Digest size

nn(1) The True Story of Billy the Kid: The Outlaw	4.00	8.00	15.00	B
nn(2) The True Story of "Wild Bill" Hickok: Gun Fighter - J. W. Buel 1946	4.00	8.00	15.00	B
nn(3) The True Story of Jesse James: King of Robbers	4.00	8.00	15.00	B

ARCHER BOOKS

(Kaywin Publishers, Inc./ Archer Press Ltd.)

2 Dames are No Dice	2.00	4.00	7.50	E
3 Take It, and Like It - Spike Morelli 1951, c-Heade	3.00	6.00	12.00	E
4 This Thing Called "Sin"	2.00	4.00	7.50	E
5 Dame in my Bed - Michael Storme 1951, c-Heade	3.00	6.00	12.00	E
6 Satan's Sister - Tony Angelo c-Heade	3.00	6.00	12.00	
8 You'll Never Get Me - Spike Morelli 1952, c-Heade	3.00	6.00	12.00	E
10 The Body Ran Home	2.00	4.00	7.50	M
11 Coffin for a Cutie	2.00	4.00	7.50	M
12 Sinner's Shroud - Tony Angelo	2.00	4.00	7.50	E
13 The Worms Have Eaten Them	2.00	4.00	7.50	E
14 Shipwreck Passion	2.00	4.00	7.50	E
15 Lost Souls of Bohemia	2.00	4.00	7.50	E
28 Girl from Tiger Bay	2.00	4.00	7.50	E
31 Two Smart Dames	2.00	4.00	7.50	E

Amaz. Stories SF Novel, c. Z-D   Archer Books 3, c. Archer

Archer Books 5, c. Archer

Archer Books 8, c. Archer

Archer Books 35, c. Archer

Archer Books 52, c. Archer

(ARCHER BOOKS, continued)

33 Come Into My Parlor	2.00	4.00	7.50	E
35 Vice Rackets of Soho - Roland Vane	5.00	10.00	20.00	E
36 Flame - Paul Renin	3.00	6.00	12.00	E
37 Willing Sinner - Roland Vane	2.50	6.00	10.00	
38 Where They Breed	2.00	4.00	7.50	E
39 Black Mistress	2.00	4.00	7.50	E
40 Sin Stained	2.00	4.00	7.50	E
42 Eternal Conflict	2.00	4.00	7.50	E
44 Pleasure's Price - Paul Renin	2.00	4.00	7.50	E
45 When Passion Rules	2.00	4.00	7.50	E
47 Double Life	2.00	4.00	7.50	E
48 Passionate Puritan	2.00	4.00	7.50	E
49 Sultry Love	2.00	4.00	7.50	E
50 Sex - Paul Renin	2.50	6.00	10.00	E
1951				
51 Night Haunts of Paris - Roland Vane	2.50	6.00	10.00	E
1951				
52 Sinful Sisters - Roland Vane	3.00	6.00	12.00	E
1951, c-Heade				
53 Love - Paul Renin	2.50	6.00	10.00	E
54 Fortnight's Folly - Paul Renin	2.00	4.00	7.50	E
57 Plaything of Passion - Jeanette Revere	3.00	6.00	12.00	E
1951, c-Heade				
68 White Slaves of New Orleans - Roland Vane	4.00	8.00	15.00	E
c-Heade				
69 Ladies of the Red Lamp - Roland Vane	3.00	6.00	12.00	E
c-Heade				
70 The Silken Lure - Pierre Flammeche	3.00	6.00	12.00	E
c-Heade				
71 Unlucky Virgin - Michael Storme	2.50	6.00	10.00	E
72 Ladies Sleep Alone - Lew Della	2.00	4.00	7.50	E
1951				
81 Outrage	2.00	4.00	7.50	E
82 Virtue	2.00	4.00	7.50	E
83 Men Women Love	2.00	4.00	7.50	E
84 Make Mine a Harlot - Michael Storme	2.50	6.00	10.00	E
96 Spoiled Lives - Pierre Flammeche	3.00	6.00	12.00	E
1952, c-Heade				

ARGYLE

(Argyle Press)

Digest size

nn Germany Must Perish! - Theodore N. Kaufman	4.00	8.00	15.00
Anti-Nazi war propaganda			

ARMED SERVICES EDITIONS

(Editions for the Armed Services, Inc.)

(ARMED SERVICES EDITIONS, continued)

A- 1 The Education of Hyman Kaplan - L. Q. Ross 1943	2.00	4.00	7.50	
A- 2 Report from Tokyo - J. C. Grew	1.50	3.50	5.00	
A- 3 Good Intentions - Ogden Nash	1.50	3.50	5.00	
A- 4 Mama's Bank Account - K. Forbes	1.50	3.50	5.00	
A- 5 There Go the Ships - Robert Carse	1.50	3.50	5.00	
A- 6 Sophie Halenczik, American - R. C. Field	1.50	3.50	5.00	
A- 7 Mr. Winkle Goes to War - Theodore Pratt	1.50	3.50	5.00	
A- 8 Oliver Twist - Charles Dickens	2.00	4.00	7.50	
A- 9 Tortilla Flat - John Steinbeck	1.50	3.50	5.00	
A-10 World Series - John R. Tunis	1.50	3.50	5.00	B
A-11 My World and Welcome to It - James Thurber	2.00	4.00	7.50	H
A-12 Peace Marshall - Frank Gruber	1.50	3.50	5.00	W
A-13 Heathen Days - H. L. Mencken	1.50	3.50	5.00	
A-14 The Ship - C. S. Forester	1.50	3.50	5.00	A
A-15 The Human Comedy - William Saroyan	1.50	3.50	5.00	
A-16 Wind, Sand and Stars - Antoine De Saint - Exupery	1.50	3.50	5.00	
A-17 The Making of Modern Britain - J. B. Brebner	1.50	3.50	5.00	NF
A-18 The Arabs - P. K. Hitti	1.50	3.50	5.00	
A-19 The Unvanquished - Howard Fast	1.50	3.50	5.00	
A-20 Miracles of Military Medicine	1.50	3.50	5.00	NF
A-21 A Time for Greatness - H. Agar	1.50	3.50	5.00	
A-22 The Ministry of Fear - Graham Greene	1.50	3.50	5.00	M
A-23 Happy Landings - M. J. Herzberg	1.50	3.50	5.00	
A-24 Typee - Herman Melville	2.00	4.00	7.50	A
A-25 George Washington Carver - R. Holt	1.50	3.50	5.00	B
A-26 Lord Jim - Joseph Conrad	2.00	4.00	7.50	A
A-27 Storm Over the Land - Cart Sandburg	2.00	4.00	7.50	
A-28 Action at Aquila - Hervey Allen	1.50	3.50	5.00	
A-29 Reprisal - Grace Zaring Stone	1.50	3.50	5.00	
A-30 The Fireside Book of Dog Stories - J. Goodman	1.50	3.50	5.00	A
B-31 Let the Hurricane Roar - R. W. Lane 1943	1.50	3.50	5.00	
B-32 Dynamite Cargo - F. Herman	1.50	3.50	5.00	A
B-33 Come In - Robert Frost	2.00	4.00	7.50	
B-34 Ethan Frome - Edith Wharton	1.50	3.50	5.00	
B-35 Suds in Your Eye - M. Lasswell	1.50	3.50	5.00	
B-36 Fight for Powder Valley! - Peter Field	1.50	3.50	5.00	W
B-37 Our Hearts were Young and Gay - C. O. Skinner	1.50	3.50	5.00	
B-38 Gentle Annie - MacKinlay Kantor	1.50	3.50	5.00	
B-39 Benchley Beside Himself - Robert Benchley	2.00	4.00	7.50	H
B-40 To Walk the Night - William Sloane	1.50	3.50	5.00	
B-41 The Gaunt Woman - E. Gilligan	1.50	3.50	5.00	
B-42 Winter Range - Alan LeMay	1.50	3.50	5.00	W
B-43 Painted Buttes - A. H. Gooden	1.50	3.50	5.00	W
B-44 Chicken Every Sunday - R. Taylor	1.50	3.50	5.00	
B-45 Father and Glorious Descendant - P. Lowe	1.50	3.50	5.00	
B-46 Life in a Putty Knife Factory - H. Allen Smith	1.50	3.50	5.00	H
B-47 Lightship - A. Binns	1.50	3.50	5.00	
B-48 Get Thee Behind Me - H. Spence	1.50	3.50	5.00	

Archer Books 68, c. Archer   Archer Books 96, c. Archer   Armed Services Editions F-180

22

B-49	My Friend Flicka - M. O'Hara	1.50	3.50	5.00	A
B-50	Moscow Dateline - H. C. Cassidy	1.50	3.50	5.00	
B-51	The Uninvited - D. Macardle	1.50	3.50	5.00	
B-52	Rome Haul - Walter D. Edmonds	1.50	3.50	5.00	
B-53	Powder River - S. Burt	1.50	3.50	5.00	W
B-54	The Natives Return - L. Adamic	1.50	3.50	5.00	
B-55	The Yearling - M. K. Rawlings	1.50	3.50	5.00	
B-56	Hostages - S. Heym	1.50	3.50	5.00	
B-57	Good Neighbors - H. Herring	1.50	3.50	5.00	
B-58	Klondike Mike - M. Denison	1.50	3.50	5.00	
B-59	Delilah - M. Goodrich	1.50	3.50	5.00	
B-60	Arctic Adventure - Peter Freuchen	2.00	4.00	7.50	A
C-61	North Africa - A. H. Brodrick 1944	1.50	3.50	5.00	
C-62	The Sea of Grass - Conrad Richter	1.50	3.50	5.00	A
C-63	The Mind in the Making - J. H. Robinson	1.50	3.50	5.00	
C-64	Candide - Voltaire	2.00	4.00	7.50	
C-65	The Forest - S. E. White	1.50	3.50	5.00	
C-66	Pistols for Hire - Nelson E. Nye	1.50	3.50	5.00	W
C-67	Seven Men - M. Beerbohm	1.50	3.50	5.00	
C-68	Swamp Water - V. Bell	1.50	3.50	5.00	
C-69	Unlocking Adventure - C. Courtney	1.50	3.50	5.00	A
C-70	Penrod - Booth Tarkington	1.50	3.50	5.00	
C-71	Green Mansions - W. H. Hudson	2.00	4.00	7.50	F
C-72	Hopalong Cassidy Serves a Writ - Clarence E. Mulford	2.00	4.00	7.50	W
C-73	U. S. Foreign Policy - Walter Lippman	1.50	3.50	5.00	NF
C-74	Star Spangled Virgin - D. B. Heyward	1.50	3.50	5.00	
C-75	Black-out in Gretley - J. B. Priestley	1.50	3.50	5.00	
C-76	The Adventures of Tom Sawyer - Mark Twain	2.00	4.00	7.50	A
C-77	The Short Stories of Stephen Vincent Benet - Stephen Vincent Benet	1.50	3.50	5.00	F
C-78	Miracle in Hellas - B. Wason	1.50	3.50	5.00	
C-79	Fathoms Below - F. Meier	1.50	3.50	5.00	A
C-80	Australian Frontier - E. Hill	1.50	3.50	5.00	
C-81	Storm - G. R. Stewart	1.50	3.50	5.00	A
C-82	Kabloona - G. DePoncins	1.50	3.50	5.00	
C-83	The Forest and the Fort - Hervey Allen	1.50	3.50	5.00	A
C-84	The Hawkeye - H. Quick	1.50	3.50	5.00	
C-85	...and a Few Marines - J. W. Thomason	1.50	3.50	5.00	
C-86	Starbuck - J. Selby	1.50	3.50	5.00	
C-87	Great Smith - Edison Marshall	1.50	3.50	5.00	A
C-88	Paul Revere - Edith Forbes	1.50	3.50	5.00	A
C-89	Coronet - M. Komroff	1.50	3.50	5.00	
C-90	The Grapes of Wrath - J. Steinbeck	2.00	4.00	7.50	
D-91	The Story of Dr. Wassell - James Hilton 1944	1.50	3.50	5.00	
D-92	Love at First Flight - C. Spalding	1.50	3.50	5.00	
D-93	Blazed Trail Stories - S. E. White	1.50	3.50	5.00	A
D-94	Tumbling River Range - W. C. Tuttle	1.50	3.50	5.00	W
D-95	Colonel Effingham's Raid - B. Fleming	1.50	3.50	5.00	A
D-96	Without Orders - M. Albrand	1.50	3.50	5.00	
D-97	Death Comes for the Archbishop - Willa Cather	1.50	3.50	5.00	M
D-98	The Trees - Conrad Richter	1.50	3.50	5.00	A
D-99	The Night of the Summer Solstice - M. Van Doren	1.50	3.50	5.00	
D-100	Valley of the Sun - Clarence Buddington Kelland	1.50	3.50	5.00	W
D-101	Evidence of Things Seen - Edith Daly	1.50	3.50	5.00	M
D-102	Java Head - J. Hergesheimer	1.50	3.50	5.00	
D-103	Mystery Ship - G. S. Bryan	1.50	3.50	5.00	
D-104	Burma Surgeon - G. S. Seagrave	1.50	3.50	5.00	
D-105	On Being a Real Person - H. E. Fosdick	1.50	3.50	5.00	
D-106	Rats, Lice and History - H. Zinsser	1.50	3.50	5.00	NF
D-107	R. F. D. - C. A. Smart	1.50	3.50	5.00	
D-108	McSorley's Wonderful Saloon - J. Mitchell	1.50	3.50	5.00	
D-109	Country Lawyer - B. Partridge	1.50	3.50	5.00	
D-110	The Adventures of Huckleberry Finn - Mark Twain	1.50	3.50	5.00	A
D-111	Blanche Fury - J. Shearing	1.50	3.50	5.00	
D-112	Cross Creek - M. K. Rawlings	1.50	3.50	5.00	
D-113	The Keys of the Kingdom - A. J. Cronin	1.50	3.50	5.00	
D-114	We Cannot Escape History - J. T. Whitaker	1.50	3.50	5.00	NF
D-115	Slim - W. W. Haines	1.50	3.50	5.00	

D-116	The Best American Short Stories of 1942 - M. Foley	1.50	3.50	5.00	
D-117	A Tree Grows in Brooklyn - B. Smith	1.50	3.50	5.00	
D-118	The Robe - Lloyd C. Douglas	1.50	3.50	5.00	
D-119	Rivers of Glory - F. VanWyck Mason	1.50	3.50	5.00	
D-120	So Little Time - J. P. Marquand	1.50	3.50	5.00	
E-121	State Fair - P. Stong	1.50	3.50	5.00	
	1944				
E-122	Seven Essays - R. W. Emerson	1.50	3.50	5.00	
E-123	Ghost Trails - W. C. Tuttle	1.50	3.50	5.00	W
E-124	The Range Hawk - A. H. Gooden	1.50	3.50	5.00	W
E-125	The Mountain Divide - F. H. Spearman	1.50	3.50	5.00	
E-126	A Sense of Humus - B. Damon	1.50	3.50	5.00	
E-127	Bushido - Alexandre Pernikoff	2.00	4.00	7.50	E
E-128	The Moon and Sixpence - W. Somerset Maugham	1.50	3.50	5.00	
E-129	Saddle and Ride - Ernest Haycox	1.50	3.50	5.00	W
E-130	Seven Keys to Baldpate - Earl Derr Biggers	2.00	4.00	7.50	M
E-131	Science Year Book of 1943 - J. D. Ratcliff	1.50	3.50	5.00	NF
E-132	Green Hell - J. Duguid	1.50	3.50	5.00	
E-133	Ship of the Line - C. S. Forester	1.50	3.50	5.00	A
E-134	Ordeal by Hunger - G. R. Stewart, Jr.	1.50	3.50	5.00	
E-135	The Gambler Takes a Wife - M. Brinig	1.50	3.50	5.00	
E-136	Stories for Men - C. Grayson	1.50	3.50	5.00	
E-137	Jamaica Inn - Daphne DuMaurier	1.50	3.50	5.00	
E-138	Random Harvest - James Hilton	1.50	3.50	5.00	
E-139	A Connecticut Yankee in King Arthur's Court - Mark Twain	2.00	4.00	7.50	F
E-140	Cimarron - Edna Ferber	1.50	3.50	5.00	W
E-141	I Married Adventure - Ona Johnson	1.50	3.50	5.00	
E-142	Windswept - M. E. Chase	1.50	3.50	5.00	
E-143	Roughly Speaking - L. R. Pierson	1.50	3.50	5.00	
E-144	Hell on Ice - C. E. Ellsberg	1.50	3.50	5.00	
E-145	Doctors on Horseback - J. T. Flexner	1.50	3.50	5.00	
E-146	The Late George Apley - J. P. Marquand	1.50	3.50	5.00	
E-147	Selected Short Stories - Stephen Crane	2.00	4.00	7.50	
E-148	One Man's West - D. Lavender	1.50	3.50	5.00	
E-149	Drums Along the Mohawk - Walter D. Edmonds	1.50	3.50	5.00	A
E-150	King's Row - H. Bellamann	1.50	3.50	5.00	
F-151	Messer Marco Polo - D. Byrne	1.50	3.50	5.00	
	1944				
F-152	Night Flight - Antoine DeSaint-Exupery	1.50	3.50	5.00	
F-153	The Selected Writings - Abraham Lincoln	2.00	4.00	7.50	
F-154	Black Majesty - John W. Vandercook	1.50	3.50	5.00	A
F-155	Going Fishing - N. Farson	1.50	3.50	5.00	
F-156	Lassie Come Home - E. Knight	1.50	3.50	5.00	
F-157	Flying Colours - C. S. Forester	1.50	3.50	5.00	A
F-158	Clear the Tracks - J. Bromley	1.50	3.50	5.00	
F-159	Happy Days - H. L. Mencken	1.50	3.50	5.00	
F-160	Border Breed - William MacLeod Raine	1.50	3.50	5.00	W
F-161	Jungle Peace - W. Beebe	1.50	3.50	5.00	
F-162	Selected Short Stories - Bret Harte	1.50	3.50	5.00	
F-163	The Bar 20 Rides Again - Clarence E. Mulford	2.00	4.00	7.50	W
F-164	The Border Trumpet - Ernest Haycox	1.50	3.50	5.00	W
F-165	So Big - Edna Ferber	1.50	3.50	5.00	
F-166	West with the Night - B. Markham	1.50	3.50	5.00	
F-167	Land Below the Wind - A. N. Keith	1.50	3.50	5.00	
F-168	Under a Lucky Star - R. C. Andrews	1.50	3.50	5.00	
F-169	The Horse and Buggy Doctor - A. E. Hertzler	1.50	3.50	5.00	
F-170	Here is Your War - Ernie Pyle	1.50	3.50	5.00	NF
F-171	The Blazed Trail - S. E. White	1.50	3.50	5.00	W
F-172	Round Up - Ring Lardner	1.50	3.50	5.00	
F-173	Old Jules - Mari Sandoz	1.50	3.50	5.00	W
F-174	Life on the Mississippi - Mark Twain	1.50	3.50	5.00	
F-175	The Essays of Charles Lamb - Charles Lamb	1.50	3.50	5.00	
F-176	A Subtreasury of American Humor - E. B. White	1.50	3.50	5.00	
F-177	Wellington - P. Guedalla	1.50	3.50	5.00	
F-178	Casuals of the Sea - W. McFee	1.50	3.50	5.00	
F-179	Dr. Dogbody's Leg - J. N. Hall	1.50	3.50	5.00	
F-180	The Sea-wolf - Jack London	2.00	4.00	7.50	A
G-181	The Glorious Pool - Thorne Smith	2.00	4.00	7.50	H
	1944				

G-182	White Fang - Jack London	2.00	4.00	7.50	A
G-183	Low Man on a Totem Pole - H. Allen Smith	1.50	3.50	5.00	A
G-184	Trail's End - William MacLeod Raine	1.50	3.50	5.00	W
G-185	My Antonia - Willa Cather	1.50	3.50	5.00	
G-186	Long, Long Ago - Alexander Woolcott	1.50	3.50	5.00	
G-187	Sam Small Flies Again - E. Knight	1.50	3.50	5.00	
G-188	Taps for Private Tussie - J. Stuart	1.50	3.50	5.00	
G-189	Kamongo - H. W. Smith	1.50	3.50	5.00	
G-190	The Trusty Knaves - E. M. Rhodes	1.50	3.50	5.00	W
G-191	Little Caesar - W. R. Burnett	2.00	4.00	7.50	M
G-192	Inside Benchley - Robert Benchley	2.00	4.00	7.50	H
G-193	How to Think Straight - R. H. Thouless	1.50	3.50	5.00	
G-194	The Mirror of the Sea - Joseph Conrad	2.00	4.00	7.50	
G-195	Raiders of the Rimrock - Luke Short	1.50	3.50	5.00	W
G-196	A Crystal Age - W. H. Hudson	1.50	3.50	5.00	
G-197	Laught with Leacock - S. Leacock	1.50	3.50	5.00	H
G-198	Kim - Rudyard Kipling	1.50	3.50	5.00	A
G-199	Journey into America - D. C. Peattie	1.50	3.50	5.00	
G-200	As the Earth Turns - G. H. Carroll	1.50	3.50	5.00	
G-201	Young Man of Caracas - T. R. Ybarra	1.50	3.50	5.00	
G-202	Arouse and Beware - MacKinlay Kantor	1.50	3.50	5.00	A
G-203	This Chemical Age - W. Haynes	1.50	3.50	5.00	NF
G-204	Thunderhead - M. O'Hara	1.50	3.50	5.00	A
G-205	The Fleet in the Forest - C. D. Lane	1.50	3.50	5.00	
G-206	The Best American Short Stories of 1943 - ed. M. Foley	1.50	3.50	5.00	
G-207	Rogues' Company - H. H. Kroll	1.50	3.50	5.00	
G-208	H. M. Pulham, Esq. - J. P. Marquand	1.50	3.50	5.00	
G-209	Moby Dick - Herman Melville	2.00	4.00	7.50	
G-210	East of the Giants - G. R. Stewart	1.50	3.50	5.00	
H-211	C/O Postmaster - Corp. T. R. St. George 1944	1.50	3.50	5.00	
H-212	Beyond the Desert - Eugene Manlove Rhodes	1.50	3.50	5.00	W
H-213	Payment Deferred - C. S. Forester	1.50	3.50	5.00	A
H-214	Buried Alive - A. Bennett	1.50	3.50	5.00	
H-215	Western Star - Stephen Vincent Benet	1.50	3.50	5.00	
H-216	Laughing Boy - O. LaFarge	1.50	3.50	5.00	
H-217	The Republic of Plato - I. A. Richards	1.50	3.50	5.00	
H-218	Forward the Nation - D. C. Peattie	1.50	3.50	5.00	
H-219	Three Times I Bow - C. Glick	1.50	3.50	5.00	
H-220	Night Over Fitch's Pond - C. Jarrett	1.50	3.50	5.00	
H-221	The Cruise of the Snark - Jack London	2.00	4.00	7.50	
H-222	Riders of the Night - Eugene Cunningham	1.50	3.50	5.00	W
H-223	Danger in the Cards - M. MacDougall	1.50	3.50	5.00	
H-224	Burning an Empire - Stewart H. Holbrook	1.50	3.50	5.00	
H-225	Animal Reveille - R. Dempewolff	1.50	3.50	5.00	
H-226	Red Raskall - C. McMeekin	1.50	3.50	5.00	
H-227	Corson of the J C - Clarence E. Mulford	2.00	4.00	7.50	W
H-228	Captain Caution - K. Roberts	1.50	3.50	5.00	
H-229	The Cold Journey - G. Z. Stone	1.50	3.50	5.00	
H-230	The Bishop's Jaegers - Thorne Smith	1.50	3.50	5.00	H
H-231	Innocent Merriment - F. P. Adams	1.50	3.50	5.00	
H-232	Carmen of the Rancho - F. H. Spearman	1.50	3.50	5.00	
H-233	Cardigan - R. W. Chambers	1.50	3.50	5.00	
H-234	Box Office - M. Barrows	1.50	3.50	5.00	
H-235	The Pacific Ocean - F. Riesenberg	1.50	3.50	5.00	
H-236	The Travels of Marco Polo - Manuel Komroff	1.50	3.50	5.00	A
H-237	The Ringed Horizon - E. Gilligan	1.50	3.50	5.00	
H-238	Botany Bay - Charles Nordhoff	1.50	3.50	5.00	A
H-239	How Green Was My Valley - R. Llewellyn	1.50	3.50	5.00	
H-240	Chad Hanna - Walter D. Edmonds	1.50	3.50	5.00	
I-241	Avalanche - K. Boyle 1944	1.50	3.50	5.00	
I-242	Semper Fidelis - K. Ayling	1.50	3.50	5.00	
I-243	Mr. and Mrs. Cugat - I. S. Rorick	1.50	3.50	5.00	
I-244	Ol' Man Adam an' His Chillun - R. Bradford	1.50	3.50	5.00	
I-245	The Mystery of the Red Triangle - W. C. Tuttle	1.50	3.50	5.00	
I-246	We Followed Our Hearts to Hollywood - E. Kimbrough	1.50	3.50	5.00	
I-247	Deserts on the March - P. B. Sears	1.50	3.50	5.00	
I-248	Rogue Male - Geoffrey Household	1.50	3.50	5.00	M

I-249	High Tension - W. W. Haines	1.50	3.50	5.00	
I-250	The Book Nobody Knows - Bruce Barton	1.50	3.50	5.00	
I-251	Stage Coach Kingdom - Harry Sinclair Drago	1.50	3.50	5.00	W
I-252	Selected Short Stories - K. Mansfield	1.50	3.50	5.00	
I-253	The Middle-aged Man on the Flying Trapeze James Thurber	2.00	4.00	7.50	
I-254	Deep West - Ernest Havcox	1.50	3.50	5.00	W
I-255	Arizona - Clarence Buddington Kelland	1.50	3.50	5.00	W
I-256	Cow by the Tail - J. J. Benton	1.50	3.50	5.00	
I-257	Hopalong Cassidy's Protege - Clarence E. Mulford	2.00	4.00	7.50	W
I-258	Coast Guard to the Rescue - K. Baarslag	1.50	3.50	5.00	
I-259	On the Bottom - E. Ellsberg	1.50	3.50	5.00	
I-260	Ashenden - Somerset Maugham	1.50	3.50	5.00	M
I-261	Queen Victoria - L. Strachey	1.50	3.50	5.00	
I-262	The Tides of Malvern - F. Griswold	1.50	3.50	5.00	
I-263	Ten...and Out - A. Johnston	1.50	3.50	5.00	
I-264	Victory - Joseph Conrad	1.50	3.50	5.00	
I-265	Mrs. Parkington - L. Bromfield	1.50	3.50	5.00	
I-266	The Sea-Hawk - Rafael Sabatini	2.00	4.00	7.50	A
I-267	Honey in the Horn - H. L. Davis	1.50	3.50	5.00	
I-268	Jane Eyre - Charlotte Bronte	1.50	3.50	5.00	
I-269	Paradise - Edith Forbes	1.50	3.50	5.00	
I-270	My son, My son! - H. Spring	1.50	3.50	5.00	
J-271	The Proud Sheriff - Eugene Manlove Rhodes 1944	1.50	2.50	5.00	W
J-272	My Name is Aram - William Saroyan	1.50	3.50	5.00	
J-273	The Shadow Line - Joseph Conrad	2.00	4.00	7.50	
J-274	Tree Toad - B. Davis	1.50	3.50	5.00	
J-275	Riot at Red Water - F. R. Bechdolt	1.50	3.50	5.00	W
J-276	Past the End of the Pavement - C. J. Finney	1.50	3.50	5.00	
J-277	Lou Gehrig - F. Graham	1.50	3.50	5.00	B
J-278	You Know Me, Al - Ring Lardner	1.50	3.50	5.00	
J-279	The Phantom Filly - G. A. Chamberlain	1.50	3.50	5.00	
J-280	Sheriff of Yavisa - C. H. Snow	1.50	3.50	5.00	
J-281	Davy Crockett - C. Rourke	1.50	3.50	5.00	B
J-282	A High Wind in Jamaica - R. Hughes	1.50	3.50	5.00	A
J-283	The Gangs All Here - H. Smith	1.50	3.50	5.00	
J-284	Skin and Bones - Thorne Smith	1.50	3.50	5.00	H
J-285	The Last Adam - J. G. Cozzens	1.50	3.50	5.00	
J-286	South of Rio Grande - Max Brand	1.50	3.50	5.00	W
J-287	George M. Cohan - W. Morehouse	1.50	3.50	5.00	B
J-288	The Golden Fleece - N. Lofts	1.50	3.50	5.00	
J-289	End of Track - W. Weaver	1.50	3.50	5.00	
J-290	Selected Stories - Paul Gallico	1.50	3.50	5.00	
J-291	February Hill - V. Lincoln	1.50	3.50	5.00	
J-292	The Sea and the Jungle - H. M. Tomlinson	1.50	3.50	5.00	A
J-293	No Life for a Lady - A. M. Cleaveland	1.50	3.50	5.00	
J-294	The Bayous of Louisiana - H. T. Kane	1.50	3.50	5.00	
J-295	The Wake of the Prairie Schooner - I. D. Paden	1.50	3.50	5.00	
J-296	Vanity Fair - W. M. Thackery	1.50	3.50	5.00	
J-297	Selected Stories - Edgar Allen Poe	1.50	3.50	5.00	
J-298	Young Ames - Walter D. Edmonds	1.50	3.50	5.00	A
J-299	The Apostle - Sholem Asch	1.50	3.50	5.00	
J-300	Good Night, Sweet Prince - G. Fowler	1.50	3.50	5.00	
J-301	Forty-niners - A. B. Hulbert	1.50	3.50	5.00	
J-302	Indians Abroad - C. T. Foreman	1.50	3.50	5.00	
K- 1	This Simian World - Clarence Day 1944	1.50	3.50	5.00	
K- 2	The Old Soak - D. Marquis	1.50	3.50	5.00	
K- 3	The Call of the Wild - Jack London	2.00	4.00	7.50	A
K- 4	The Dark Gentleman - G. B. Stern	1.50	3.50	5.00	
K- 5	The Secret of Dr. Kildare - Max Brand	1.50	3.50	5.00	
K- 6	The Noise of Their Wings - MacKinlay Kantor	1.50	3.50	5.00	
K- 7	Bounty of the Wayside - W. B. Wilder	1.50	3.50	5.00	
K- 8	Stepsons of Light - Eugene Manlove Rhodes	1.50	3.50	5.00	W
K- 9	Selected Short Stories - Ernest Hemingway	1.50	3.50	5.00	
K-10	The Life and Death of Little Jo - R. Bright	1.50	3.50	5.00	
K-11	Rebel of Ronde Valley - C. H. Snow	1.50	3.50	5.00	
K-12	The St. Lawrence - H. Beston	1.50	3.50	5.00	
K-13	Ethan Allen - Stewart H. Holbrook	1.50	3.50	5.00	A
K-14	The Wild Bunch - Ernest Haycox	1.50	3.50	5.00	W

K-15	The Stray Lamb - Thorne Smith	1.50	3.50	5.00	H
K-16	Selected Short Stories - O. Henry	1.50	3.50	5.00	
K-17	The Eight Million - M. Berger	1.50	3.50	5.00	
K-18	Moon Tide - W. Robertson	1.50	3.50	5.00	
K-19	The Journey of the Flame - A. D. F. Blanco	1.50	3.50	5.00	
K-20	Young Man of the World - T. R. Ybarra	1.50	3.50	5.00	
K-21	Winter Wheat - M. Walker	1.50	3.50	5.00	
K-22	Walt Whitman - H. S. Canby	1.50	3.50	5.00	B
K-23	Andrew Jackson: The Border Captain - M. James	1.50	3.50	5.00	B
K-24	Babbitt - Sinclair Lewis	1.50	3.50	5.00	
K-25	Yankee Lawyer, The Autobiography of - E. Tutt	1.50	3.50	5.00	
K-26	Suckers Progress - H. Asbury	1.50	3.50	5.00	
K-27	The Robe - L. C. Douglas	1.50	3.50	5.00	
K-28	A Tree Grows in Brooklyn - B. Smith	1.50	3.50	5.00	
K-29	AP: The Story of News - O. Gramling	1.50	3.50	5.00	NF
K-30	Benjamin Franklin - Carl Van Doren	1.50	3.50	5.00	B
K-31	Tristram Shandy - Laurence Sterne	1.50	3.50	5.00	
K-32	Rise to Follow - A. Spalding	1.50	3.50	5.00	
L- 1	A Book of Americans - R & S. V. Benet	1.50	3.50	5.00	B
	1944				
L- 2	My Life and Hart Times - James Thurber	2.00	4.00	7.50	H
L- 3	Kilgour's Mare - H. G. Lamond	1.50	3.50	5.00	
L- 4	Etched in Moonlight - J. Stephens	1.50	3.50	5.00	
L- 5	Porgy - D. B. Heyward	1.50	3.50	5.00	
L- 6	Great Poems from Chaucer to Whitman - L. Untermeyer	1.50	3.50	5.00	
L- 7	What Became of Anna Bolton - Louis Bromfield	1.50	3.50	5.00	
L- 8	Montana Rides Again - Evan Evans (Max Brand)	1.50	3.50	5.00	W
L- 9	The Sherriff's Son - William MacLeod Raine	1.50	3.50	5.00	W
L-10	Happy Stories Just to Laugh At - Stephen Leacock	1.50	3.50	5.00	H
L-11	Roaring River Range - A. H. Gooden	1.50	3.50	5.00	W
L-12	There's One in Every Family - F. Eisenberg	1.50	3.50	5.00	
L-13	The King Bird Rides - Max Brand	1.50	3.50	5.00	W
L-14	The Sea is so Wide - E. Eaton	1.50	3.50	5.00	
L-15	Omoo - Hermen Melville	2.00	4.00	7.50	A
L-16	Hackberry Cavalier - G. S. Perry	1.50	3.50	5.00	
L-17	Turnabout - Thorne Smith	1.50	3.50	5.00	
L-18	400 Million Customers - C. Crow	1.50	3.50	5.00	
L-19	Fish and Tin Fish - Philip Wylie	1.50	3.50	5.00	
L-20	Eminent Victorians - L. Strachey	1.50	3.50	5.00	
L-21	Country Cured - Homer Croy	1.50	3.50	5.00	
L-22	Science at War - G. W. Gray	1.50	3.50	5.00	NF
L-23	Bedford Village - Hervey Allen	1.50	3.50	5.00	
L-24	The Lady and the Arsenic - J. Shearing	1.50	3.50	5.00	
L-25	Dracula - Bram Stoker	7.50	15.00	30.00	HO
L-26	Wickford Point - J. P. Marquand	1.50	3.50	5.00	
L-27	I, Claudius - Robert Graves	1.50	3.50	5.00	B
L-28	Selected Short Stories - Thomas Mann	1.50	3.50	5.00	
L-29	Lust for Life - Irving Stone	1.50	3.50	5.00	B
L-30	Of Human Bondage - W. Somerset Maugham	1.50	3.50	5.00	
L-31	The Land is Bright - A. Binns	1.50	3.50	5.00	
L-32	Four Years in Paradise - Ona Johnson	1.50	3.50	5.00	
M- 1	Selected Poems - A. E. Houseman	1.50	3.50	5.00	
	1944				
M- 2	Is Sex Necessary - James Thurber	2.00	4.00	7.50	H
M- 3	Selected Short Stories of "Saki" - H. H. Munro	1.50	3.50	5.00	
M- 4	20,000 Leagues Under the Sea or David Copperfield - Robert Benchley	2.00	4.00	7.50	
M- 5	Pere Marquette - A. Repplier	1.50	3.50	5.00	
M- 6	Copper Streak Trail - Eugene Manlove Rhodes	1.50	3.50	5.00	W
M- 7	Dune Boy - E. W. Teale	1.50	3.50	5.00	
M- 8	Paul Bunyon - J. Stevens	1.50	3.50	5.00	
M- 9	Science Yearbook of 1944 - J. D. Ratcliff	1.50	3.50	5.00	NF
M-10	The Chicken-wagon Family - B. Benefield	1.50	3.50	5.00	
M-11	The Big Ones Get Away - Philip Wylie	1.50	3.50	5.00	
M-12	Old McDonald Had a Farm - A. McDonald	1.50	3.50	5.00	
M-13	Action by Night - Ernest Haycox	1.50	3.50	5.00	W
M-14	The Border Kid - Max Brand	1.50	3.50	5.00	W

M-15	Fighting Men of the West - Dane Coolidge	1.50	3.50	5.00	W
M-16	Tarzan of the Apes - Edgar Rice Burroughs	10.00	25.00	40.00	A
M-17	The Boomer - H. Bedwell	1.50	3.50	5.00	
M-18	Such Interesting People - R. J. Casey	1.50	3.50	5.00	
M-19	Call her Rosie - E. Bruce	1.50	3.50	5.00	
M-20	Larrish Hundred - A. R. B. Giddings	1.50	3.50	5.00	
M-21	Country Editor - H. B. Hough	1.50	3.50	5.00	
M-22	With a Dutch Accent - D. C. DeJong	1.50	3.50	5.00	
M-23	Four Modern American Plays - Hellman, Thurber, Nugent, Chodorov, Fields, & Kingsley	2.00	4.00	7.50	
M-24	A Treasury of the Worlds Great Letters - M. L. Schuster	1.50	3.50	5.00	
M-25	Indigo - C. Weston	1.50	3.50	5.00	
M-26	Barnum - M. R. Werner	1.50	3.50	5.00	
M-27	Show Me a Land - M. R. McMeekin	1.50	3.50	5.00	
M-28	New Stories for Men - Capt. C. Grayson	1.50	3.50	5.00	
M-29	The Moonstone - Wilkie Collins	1.50	3.50	5.00	M
M-30	Der Fuehrer - K. Heiden	1.50	3.50	5.00	
M-31	Stars on the Sea - F. Van Wyck Mason	1.50	3.50	5.00	
M-32	While Still we Live - Helen MacInnes	1.50	3.50	5.00	
N- 1	The Mysterious Stranger - Mark Twain	1.50	3.50	5.00	
	1944				
N- 2	The Dream Department - S. J. Perelman	1.50	3.50	5.00	H
N- 3	America - Stephen Vincent Benet	1.50	3.50	5.00	
N- 4	The Man Nobody Knows - Bruce Barton	1.50	3.50	5.00	
N- 5	The Crock of Gold - J. Stevens	1.50	3.50	5.00	
N- 6	Selected Poems - Carl Sandburg	2.00	4.00	7.50	
N- 7	Let Your Mind Alone - James Thurber	2.00	4.00	7.50	
N- 8	We Pointed them North - E. C. Abbot	1.50	3.50	5.00	
N- 9	Rim of the Desert - Ernest Haycox	1.50	3.50	5.00	W
N-10	Useless Cowboy - Alan Lemay	1.50	3.50	5.00	W
N-11	The Fallen Sparrow - Dorothy B. Hughes	1.50	3.50	5.00	M
N-12	Snow Above Town - D. Hough	1.50	3.50	5.00	
N-13	Kidnapped - Robert Louis Stevenson	2.00	4.00	7.50	A
N-14	The Summing Up - W. Somerset Maugham	1.50	3.50	5.00	
N-15	The Iron Trail - Max Brand	1.50	3.50	5.00	W
N-16	Riata and Spurs - Charles A. Siringo	1.50	3.50	5.00	W
N-17	Duel in the Sun - Niven Busch	1.50	3.50	5.00	W
N-18	Thunder Mountain - Thedore Pratt	1.50	3.50	5.00	
N-19	I Dive for Treasure - H. E. Riesenberg	1.50	3.50	5.00	
N-20	Prophet by Experience - Jack Iams	1.50	3.50	5.00	
N-21	Hangman's House - D. Byrne	1.50	3.50	5.00	
N-22	The Great American Novel - C. B. Davis	1.50	3.50	5.00	
N-23	Fire Bell in the Night - C. Robertson	1.50	3.50	5.00	
N-24	Bonin - R. Standish	1.50	3.50	5.00	
N-25	Mathematics and the Imagination - J. Newman	1.50	3.50	5.00	
N-26	Magnus Merriman - E. Linklater	1.50	3.50	5.00	
N-27	Look Away, Look Away - L. T. White	1.50	3.50	5.00	
N-28	Martin Eden - Jack London	2.00	4.00	7.50	A
N-29	The Turning Wheels - Stuart Cloete	1.50	3.50	5.00	
N-30	Perilous Journey - C. M. Sublette	1.50	3.50	5.00	
N-31	David Copperfield - Charles Dickens	2.00	4.00	7.50	
N-32	The Big Rock Candy Mountain - Wallace Stegner	1.50	3.50	5.00	
O- 1	Selected Poems - Percy Bysshe Shelley				
	1945	2.00	4.00	7.50	
O- 2	The Prophet - Kahlil Gibran	1.50	3.50	5.00	
O- 3	The Art of Illusion - J. Mulholland	1.50	3.50	5.00	
O- 4	They Played the Game - H. Grayson	1.50	3.50	5.00	
O- 5	Tales of the Pampas - W. H. Hudson	2.00	4.00	7.50	A
O- 6	Plowmans Folly - E. H. Faulkner	1.50	3.50	5.00	
O- 7	Mr. Glencannon Ignores the War - Guy Gilpatric	1.50	3.50	5.00	
O- 8	My Dear Bella - A. Kober	1.50	3.50	5.00	
O- 9	Donovan's Brain - Curt Siodmak	4.00	8.00	15.00	SF
O-10	Wild Horse Shorty - C. Nelson Nye	1.50	3.50	5.00	
O-11	Journey Into the Fog - C. Goodhue	1.50	3.50	5.00	
O-12	The African Queen - C. S. Forester	1.50	3.50	5.00	A
O-13	Lost Worlds - A. T. White	1.50	3.50	5.00	
O-14	I Never Left Home - B. Hope	1.50	3.50	5.00	
O-15	Island in the Sky - Ernest K. Gann	1.50	3.50	5.00	A
O-16	Crazy Weather - C. L. McNichols	1.50	3.50	5.00	
O-17	Nobody Lives Forever - W. R. Burnett	2.00	4.00	7.50	M

O-18 Runyon A La Carte - Damon Runyon	1.50	3.50	5.00	
O-19 The Lost Weekend - Charles Jackson	2.00	4.00	7.50	
O-20 Selected Short Stories - John Russell	1.50	3.50	5.00	
O-21 On the Danger Line - Georges Simenon	2.00	4.00	7.50	M
O-22 The Return of Tarzan - Edgar Rice Burroughs	10.00	25.00	40.00	A
O-23 Men Like Gods - R. Sturgis	1.50	3.50	5.00	
O-24 The Three Black Pennies - J. Hergesheimer	1.50	3.50	5.00	
O-25 Selwood of Sleepy Cat - Frank Spearman	1.50	3.50	5.00	W
O-26 We Live In Alaska - C. Helmericks	1.50	3.50	5.00	
O-27 The Red Cock Crows - F. Gaither	1.50	3.50	5.00	
O-28 Selected Short Stories - M. R. James	1.50	3.50	5.00	
O-29 Leave Her to Heaven - B. A. Williams	1.50	3.50	5.00	
O-30 Blessed are the Meek - Z. Kozzak	1.50	3.50	5.00	
O-31 Look Homeward Angel - Thomas Wolfe	1.50	3.50	5.00	
O-32 Look to the Mountain - L. Cannon, Jr.	1.50	3.50	5.00	
P- 1 Lady Into Fox - D. Garnett	1.50	3.50	5.00	
1945				
P- 2 Boomerang - W. Chambliss	1.50	3.50	5.00	C
P- 3 Rookie of the Year - John R. Tunis	1.50	3.50	5.00	S
P- 4 Hotel Splendide - L. Bemelmans	1.50	3.50	5.00	
P- 5 Lost Island - James Norman Hall	1.50	3.50	5.00	A
P- 6 Not Quite Dead Enough - Rex Stout	2.00	4.00	7.50	M
P- 7 The Great Bustard and Other People - Will Cuppy	1.50	3.50	5.00	
P- 8 The Fighting Four - Max Brand	1.50	3.50	5.00	W
P- 9 Valley of the Sky - H. D. Skidmore	1.50	3.50	5.00	
P-10 The Kingdom of Swing - Goodman & Kolodin	1.50	3.50	5.00	NF
P-11 Lie down in Darkness - H. R. Hays	1.50	3.50	5.00	
P-12 The Valley of Silent Men - James Oliver Curwood	1.50	3.50	5.00	A
P-13 Mother Wore Tights - M. Young	1.50	3.50	5.00	
P-14 Pilotin' Come Natural - F. Way, Jr.	1.50	3.50	5.00	
P-15 Starlight Pass - Tom Gill	1.50	3.50	5.00	W
P-16 Trail Town - Ernest Haycox	1.50	3.50	5.00	W
P-17 Blood Upon the Snow - Hilda Lawrence	1.50	3.50	5.00	M
P-18 Many Happy Days I've Squandered - A. Loveridge	1.50	3.50	5.00	
P-19 Stories by Erskine Caldwell - Erskine Caldwell	1.50	3.50	5.00	
P-20 Danger is My Business - Capt. J. D. Craig	1.50	3.50	5.00	
P-21 Botts in War, Botts in Peace - W. H. Upson	1.50	3.50	5.00	
P-22 World's Great Humorous Stories - I. S. Cobb	1.50	3.50	5.00	
P-23 Aunt Beardie - J. Shearing	1.50	3.50	5.00	
P-24 Rebellion of Leo McGuire - C. B. Davis	1.50	3.50	5.00	
P-25 O. Henry Prize Stories - H. Brickell	1.50	3.50	5.00	
P-26 One Mans Meat - E. B. White	1.50	3.50	5.00	
P-27 Dragonwyck - Anna Seton	1.50	3.50	5.00	
P-28 Slogum House - Mari Sandoz	1.50	3.50	5.00	
P-29 The Republic - C. A. Beard	1.50	3.50	5.00	
P-30 Brave Men - Ernie Pyle	1.50	3.50	5.00	NF
P-31 A Treasury of Science - H. Shapley	1.50	3.50	5.00	NF
P-32 Yankee from Olympus - C. D. Bowen	1.50	3.50	5.00	
Q- 1 Excuse It, Please! -	1.50	3.50	5.00	
1945				
Q- 2 The Postman Always Rings Twice - James M. Cain	2.00	4.00	7.50	M
Q- 3 The Story of George Gershwin - D. Ewen	1.50	3.50	5.00	B
Q- 4 The Education of T. C. Mits - L. R. Lieber & H. Gray	1.50	3.50	5.00	
Q- 5 The Feather Merchants - Max Shulman	1.50	3.50	5.00	
Q- 6 The World Ends at Hoboken - M. Heimer	1.50	3.50	5.00	
Q- 7 High Time - M. Lasswell	1.50	3.50	5.00	
Q- 8 Keystone Kids - John R. Tunis	1.50	3.50	5.00	S
Q- 9 Selected Short Stories - S. Anderson	1.50	3.50	5.00	
Q-10 Give 'em the Ax - A. A. Fair	2.00	4.00	7.50	M
Q-11 Prairie Guns - E. E. Halleran	1.50	3.50	5.00	W
Q-12 Watch Out for Willie Carter - T. Naidish	1.50	3.50	5.00	
Q-13 The Passionate Witch - Thorne Smith	2.00	4.00	7.50	H
Q-14 Guerrilla - Lord Dunsany	3.00	6.00	12.00	
Q-15 The Corpse without a Clue - R. A. J. Walling	2.00	4.00	7.50	M
Q-16 Man in the Saddle - Ernest Haycox	1.50	3.50	5.00	W
Q-17 The Amethyst Spectacles - Frances Crane	2.00	4.00	7.50	M
Q-18 Beat to Quarters - C. S. Forester	1.50	3.50	5.00	A
Q-19 The Heritage of the Desert - Zane Grey	2.00	4.00	7.50	W
Q-20 Devil on his Trail - John & Ward Hawkins	1.50	3.50	5.00	W

Q-21 Salt Water Daffy - Philip Wylie	1.50	3.50	5.00	
Q-22 The House of Cobwebs - M. Reisner	1.50	3.50	5.00	
Q-23 Luck in all Weather - D. H. Haines	1.50	3.50	5.00	
Q-24 Happy Jack - Max Brand	1.50	3.50	5.00	W
Q-25 Mom Counted Six - M. Gardner	1.50	3.50	5.00	
Q-26 Take Them Up Tenderly - M. C. Harriman	1.50	3.50	5.00	
Q-27 The Green Years - A. J. Cronin	1.50	3.50	5.00	
Q-28 The Saddle and the Plow - R. M. Taylor	1.50	3.50	5.00	
Q-29 The Lively Lady - K. Roberts	1.50	3.50	5.00	
Q-30 Reckon with the River - C. McMeekin	1.50	3.50	5.00	
Q-31 The Razor's Edge - W. Somerset Maugham	1.50	3.50	5.00	
Q-32 Strange Fruit - L. Smith	1.50	3.50	5.00	
Q-33 The Seventh Cross - A. Seghers	1.50	3.50	5.00	
Q-34 Wild is the River - Louis Bromfield	1.50	3.50	5.00	
Q-35 Selected Plays - Eugene O'Neill	1.50	3.50	5.00	
Q-36 The Shadow and the Glory - John Jennings	1.50	3.50	5.00	
Q-37 Time Out of Mind - R. Field	1.50	3.50	5.00	
Q-38 The Sea Witch - A. Laing	1.50	3.50	5.00	
Q-39 The Strange Woman - B. A. Williams	1.50	3.50	5.00	
Q-40 The Education of Henry Adams - Henry Adams	1.50	3.50	5.00	
R- 1 The Ugly Dachshund - G. B. Stern	1.50	3.50	5.00	
1945				
R- 2 Selected Poems - John Keats	1.50	3.50	5.00	
R- 3 One More Spring - Robert Nathan	1.50	3.50	5.00	
R- 4 Selected Short Stories - Dorothy Parker	1.50	3.50	5.00	
R- 5 After 1903 - What? - Robert Benchley	1.50	3.50	5.00	
R- 6 Psychology You Can Use - W. H. Roberts	1.50	3.50	5.00	NF
R- 7 Selected Radio Plays - N. Corwin	1.50	3.50	5.00	
R- 8 You Wouldn't Know Me from Adam - Col. Stoopnagle	1.50	3.50	5.00	
R- 9 Sea Duty - J. Marmur	1.50	3.50	5.00	
R-10 The Dark Page - S. M. Fuller	1.50	3.50	5.00	
R-11 War on the Cimarron - Luke Short	1.50	3.50	5.00	W
R-12 Geography in Human Destiny - R. Peattie	1.50	3.50	5.00	NF
R-13 Bermuda Calling - David Garth	1.50	3.50	5.00	
R-14 A Shorter History of Science - Sir W. C. Dampier	1.50	3.50	5.00	NF
R-15 Crime on my Hands - G. Sanders	1.50	3.50	5.00	
R-16 The American Character - D. W. Brogan	1.50	3.50	5.00	
R-17 Our Hearts Were Young and Gay - Kimbrough & Skinner	1.50	3.50	5.00	
R-18 Winter Range - Alan LeMay	1.50	3.50	5.00	W
R-19 The Gaunt Woman - E. Gilligan	1.50	3.50	5.00	
R-20 Painted Buttes - A. H. Gooden	1.50	3.50	5.00	W
R-21 Selected Short Stories - K. A. Porter	1.50	3.50	5.00	
R-22 Cluny Brown - M. Sharp	1.50	3.50	5.00	
R-23 Of Men and Music - Deems Taylor	1.50	3.50	5.00	NF
R-24 The Long Chance - Max Brand	1.50	3.50	5.00	W
R-25 Kitty Foyle - Christopher Morley	1.50	3.50	5.00	
R-26 Combustion on Wheels - D. L. Cohn	1.50	3.50	5.00	
R-27 Earth and High Heaven - G. Graham	1.50	3.50	5.00	
R-28 Young 'Un - H. Best	1.50	3.50	5.00	
R-29 Gamble's Hundred - C. Dowdey	1.50	3.50	5.00	
R-30 The Bridal Wreath - S. Undset	1.50	3.50	5.00	
R-31 Try and Stop Me - Bennett Cerf	1.50	3.50	5.00	
R-32 Captain Blood - Rafael Sabatini	2.00	4.00	7.50	A
R-33 Sleep No More - August Derleth	3.00	6.00	12.00	
R-34 Of Smiling Peace - S. Heym	1.50	3.50	5.00	
R-35 The Time for Decision - S. Welles	1.50	3.50	5.00	
R-36 For My Great Folly - Thomas B. Costain	1.50	3.50	5.00	
R-37 Disputed Passage - Lloyd C. Douglas	1.50	3.50	5.00	
R-38 The Way Our People Lived - W. E. Woodward	1.50	3.50	5.00	
R-39 Deep River - H. Buckmaster	1.50	3.50	5.00	
R-40 Canal Town - S. H. Adams	1.50	3.50	5.00	
S- 1 A Wartime Whitman - Maj. W. A. Aiken	1.50	3.50	5.00	
1945				
S- 2 Dear Baby - William Saroyan	1.50	3.50	5.00	
S- 3 I Love You, I Love You, I Love You - L. Bemelmans	1.50	3.50	5.00	
S- 4 Castaway - J. G. Cozzens	1.50	3.50	5.00	
S- 5 My World and Welcome To it - James Thurber	2.00	4.00	7.50	H
S- 6 Peace Marshall - Frank Gruber	1.50	3.50	5.00	W
S- 7 Not Too Narrow, Not Too Deep - Richard Sale	2.00	4.00	7.50	M

S- 8 Selected Short Stories - Philip Wylie	1.50	3.50	5.00	
S- 9 Selected Short Stories - Mark Twain	1.50	3.50	5.00	
S-10 Young Man with a Horn - D. Baker	1.50	3.50	5.00	
S-11 A Pearl in Every Oyster - F. Sullivan	1.50	3.50	5.00	
S-12 Unexpected Uncle - Eric Hatch	1.50	3.50	5.00	
S-13 The Mauve Decade - T. Beer	1.50	3.50	5.00	
S-14 In What Torn Ship - E. Eaton	1.50	3.50	5.00	
S-15 Clipper Ship Men - A. Laing	1.50	3.50	5.00	
S-16 Alarum and Excursion - V. Perdue	1.50	3.50	5.00	
S-17 Captain Retread - D. Hough	1.50	3.50	5.00	
S-18 Guns of the Frontier - William MacLeod Raine	1.50	3.50	5.00	W
S-19 Your Kids and Mine - J. E. Brown	1.50	3.50	5.00	
S-20 After-dinner Story - William Irish	2.00	4.00	7.50	M
S-21 The Case of the Black-eyed Blonde - Erle Stanley Gardner	1.50	3.50	5.00	M
S-22 Lost in the Horse Latitudes - H. Allen Smith	1.50	3.50	5.00	H
S-23 Hunted Riders - Max Brand	1.50	3.50	5.00	W
S-24 The Ox-bow Incident - W. Van Tillburg Clark	1.50	3.50	5.00	
S-25 The St. Louis Cardinals - F. G. Lieb	1.50	3.50	5.00	S
S-26 Selected Short Stories - Algernon Blackwood	2.00	4.00	7.50	
S-27 An Almanac for Moderns - D. C. Peattie	1.50	3.50	5.00	
S-28 The Night Life of the Gods - Thorne Smith	2.00	4.00	7.50	H
S-29 People On Our Side - E. Snow	1.50	3.50	5.00	
S-30 The Great Lakes - H. Hatcher	1.50	3.50	5.00	
S-31 The Farm - Louis Bromfield	1.50	3.50	5.00	
S-32 The Bolinvars - M. F. Bayliss	1.50	3.50	5.00	
S-33 The Yearling - M. K. Rawlings	1.50	3.50	5.00	
S-34 Klondike Mike - M. Denison	1.50	3.50	5.00	
S-35 Henry Esmond - W. M. Thackery	1.50	3.50	5.00	
S-36 The Hustory of Rome Hanks - J. S. Pennell	1.50	3.50	5.00	
S-37 Henry the Eighth - F. Hackett	1.50	3.50	5.00	
S-38 Arundel - Kenneth Roberts	1.50	3.50	5.00	
S-39 Green Dolphin Street - E. Goudge	1.50	3.50	5.00	
S-40 Boston Adventure - J. Stafford	1.50	3.50	5.00	
T- 1 Dithers and Jitters - C. O. Skinner	1.50	3.50	5.00	
1945				
T- 2 The Time Machine - H. G. Wells	5.00	10.00	20.00	SF
T- 3 Anything Can Happen - G. & H. Papashvily	1.50	3.50	5.00	
T- 4 Men of Popular Music - D. Ewen	1.50	3.50	5.00	NF
T- 5 Cannery Row - John Steinbeck	2.00	4.00	7.50	
T- 6 This is Murder - T. Fuller	1.50	3.50	5.00	
T- 7 A Smattering of Ignorance - Oscar Levant	1.50	3.50	5.00	H
T- 8 The Fireside Book of Verse - Louis Untermeyer	1.50	3.50	5.00	
T- 9 Coming, Major! - W. & Stone E. Melick	1.50	3.50	5.00	
T-10 Men Against the Sea - Charles Nordhoff & James Norman Hall	1.50	3.50	5.00	A
T-11 We Farm for a Hobby and Make it Pay - H. Tetlow	1.50	3.50	5.00	
T-12 The Stone of Chastity - M. Sharp	1.50	3.50	5.00	
T-13 Benchley Beside Himself - Robert Benchley	1.50	3.50	5.00	H
T-14 Gentle Annie - MacKinlay Kantor	1.50	3.50	5.00	
T-15 The Outlaw Years - R. M. Coates	1.50	3.50	5.00	
T-16 The Range Boss - Charles Alden Seltzer	1.50	3.50	5.00	W
T-17 Puzzle for Puppets - Patrick Quentin	2.00	4.00	7.50	M
T-18 Daisy Miller and Other Stories - Henry James	1.50	3.50	5.00	
T-19 Ridin' the Rainbow - R. Taylor	1.50	3.50	5.00	
T-20 Pistol Passport - Eugene Cunningham	1.50	3.50	5.00	W
T-21 Riders of the Plains - Max Brand	1.50	3.50	5.00	W
T-22 Tunnel from Calais - D. Rame	1.50	3.50	5.00	
T-23 The Edge of Running Water - William Sloane	1.50	3.50	5.00	
T-24 The New York Yankees - F. Graham	1.50	3.50	5.00	S
T-25 The Best Plays of 1943-44 - B. Mantle	1.50	3.50	5.00	
T-26 Freedom Road - Howard Fast	1.50	3.50	5.00	
T-27 Blow for a Landing - B. L. Burman	1.50	3.50	5.00	
T-28 Wolf Law and Three Other Stories - Nafziger Foster	1.50	3.50	5.00	
T-29 The General's Lady - E. Forbes	1.50	3.50	5.00	
T-30 Genesee Fever - C. Carmer	1.50	3.50	5.00	
T-31 Battle Report - Karig & Kelley	1.50	3.50	5.00	C
T-32 The World We Live In - Louis Bromfield	1.50	3.50	5.00	
T-33 The Citadel - A. J. Cronin	1.50	3.50	5.00	
T-34 Whistle Stop - M. M. Wolff	1.50	3.50	5.00	

T-35	The Loon Feather - I. Fuller	1.50	3.50	5.00	
T-36	Rebecca - Daphne DuMaurier	1.50	3.50	5.00	
T-37	Delilah - M. Goodrich	1.50	3.50	5.00	
T-38	Arctic Adventure - Peter Freuchen	1.50	3.50	5.00	A
T-39	Forever Amber - K. Winsor	1.50	3.50	5.00	
T-40	Anna and the King of Siam - Margaret Landon	1.50	3.50	5.00	
655	Portrait of Jenny - R. Nathan	1.50	3.50	5.00	
	1945				
656	Adventures of Superman - George Lowther	10.00	25.00	40.00	A
657	Barefoot boy with Cheek - Max Shulman	1.50	3.50	5.00	H
658	The Charge of the Light Brigade - Alfred				
	Lord Tennyson	1.50	3.50	5.00	
659	What's On Your Mind? - J. Dunninger	1.50	3.50	5.00	
660	The Outermost House - H. Beston	1.50	3.50	5.00	
661	Look to the Frontiers - R. Peattie	1.50	3.50	5.00	
662	My Family, Right or Wrong - J. P. Sousa, III	1.50	3.50	5.00	
663	Murder and the Married Virgin - Brett				
	Halliday	2.00	4.00	7.50	M
664	Where Away - Perry & Leighton	1.50	3.50	5.00	
665	The Old Dark House - J. B. Priestley	1.50	3.50	5.00	
666	Laura - Vera Caspary	1.50	3.50	5.00	
667	To Have and Have Not - Ernest Hemingway	2.00	4.00	7.50	
668	Mrs. Egg and Other Barbarians - T. Beer	1.50	3.50	5.00	
669	Mademoiselle Fifi and Other Stories - Guy De				
	Maupassant	1.50	3.50	5.00	
670	Gunman's Chance - Luke Short	1.50	3.50	5.00	
671	The Glorious Pool - Thorne Smith	1.50	3.50	5.00	
672	White Fang - Jack London	2.00	4.00	7.50	
673	Low Man on a Totem Pole - H. Allen Smith	1.50	3.50	5.00	
674	Trail's End - William MacLeod Raine	1.50	3.50	5.00	
675	The 17th Letter - D. C. Disney	1.50	3.50	5.00	
676	Esquire's Jazz Book 1944 - P. E. Miller	1.50	3.50	5.00	
677	Selected Short Stories - Walter D. Edmonds	1.50	3.50	5.00	
678	Western Union - Zane Grey	1.50	3.50		
679	The Captain from Connecticut - C. S.				
	Forester	1.50	3.50	5.00	
680	Calamity Town - Ellery Queen	2.00	4.00	7.50	
681	Tomorrow Will Sing - E. Arnold	1.50	3.50	5.00	
682	Science Remakes the World - J. Stokley	1.50	3.50	5.00	
683	Bugles in the Afternoon - Ernest Haycox	1.50	3.50	5.00	
684	Prodigal Genius - J. J. O'Neill	1.50	3.50	5.00	
685	The Cadavar of Gideon Wyck - A. Laing	1.50	3.50	5.00	
686	Western Story Omnibus - W. Targ	1.50	3.50	5.00	
687	Seven Gothic Tales - I. Dinesen	1.50	3.50	5.00	
688	Barren Ground - E. Glasgow	1.50	3.50	5.00	
689	Great Smith - Edison Marshall	1.50	3.50	5.00	A
690	The Grapes of Wrath - John Steinbeck	2.00	4.00	7.50	
691	Pickwick Papers - Charles Dickens	2.00	4.00	7.50	
692	Lock, Stock and Barrel - D. & E. Rigby	1.50	3.50	5.00	
693	Immortal Wife - Irving Stone	1.50	3.50	5.00	
694	Journey in the Dark - M. Flavin	1.50	3.50	5.00	
695	The McKenneys Carry On - R. McKenney	1.50	3.50	5.00	
	1945				
696	Quo Vadimus? - E. B. White	1.50	3.50	5.00	
697	Thunder Over the Bronx - A. Kober	1.50	3.50	5.00	
698	The Island of Dr. Moreau - H. G. Wells	5.00	10.00	20.00	HO
699	Meet Me in St. Louis - S. Benson	1.50	3.50	5.00	
700	A Home in the Century - F. F. Vam de Water	1.50	3.50	5.00	
701	Another Claudia - R. Franken	1.50	3.50	5.00	
702	I Am Gazing Into My 8-Ball - Earl Wilson	1.50	3.50	5.00	
703	The Pastures of Heaven - John Steinbeck	2.00	4.00	7.50	
704	Paul Revere's Ride and Other Poems - H. W.				
	Longfellow	1.50	3.50	5.00	
705	The Middle-Aged Man on the Flying Trapeze -				
	James Thurber	2.00	4.00	7.50	
706	Deep West - Ernest Haycox	1.50	3.50	5.00	W
707	Arizona - Clarence Buddington Kelland	1.50	3.50	5.00	W
708	Cow by the Tail - J. J. Benton	1.50	3.50	5.00	
709	To the Indies - C. S. Forester	1.50	3.50	5.00	A
710	Eddie and the Archangel Mike - B. Benefield	1.50	3.50	5.00	
711	Wings of Fear - Mignon G. Eberhart	2.00	4.00	7.50	M
712	The Three Mesquiteers - William Colt				
	MacDonald	1.50	3.50	5.00	W
713	The Golden Rooms - V. Fisher	1.50	3.50	5.00	
714	Lad: A Dog - A. P. Terhune	1.50	3.50	5.00	

Armed Services Editions 719   Armed Services Editions 730   Armed Services Editions 822

(ARMED SERVICES EDITIONS, continued)

715 Gunman's Gold - Max Brand	1.50	3.50	5.00	
716 Tall Tale America - W. Blair	1.50	3.50	5.00	
717 Webster's New Handy Dictionary - A. Merriam Webster	1.50	3.50	5.00	NF
718 Webster's New Handy Dictionary - A. Merriam Webster	1.50	3.50	5.00	NF
719 The Sad Sack - Sgt. George Baker	5.00	10.00	20.00	H
720 Voyage of the Golden Hind - E. Gilligan	1.50	3.50	5.00	
721 The Purple Land - W. H. Hudson	1.50	3.50	5.00	
722 Sunset Pass - Zane Grey	1.50	3.50	5.00	W
723 The Woman in the Window - J. H. Wallis aka Once Off Guard	2.00	4.00	7.50	
724 South Moon Under - M.K. Rawlings	1.50	3.50	5.00	
725 Pitcairn's Island - Charles Nordhoff & James Norman Hall	1.50	3.50	5.00	A
726 Jazzmen - Ramsey & Smith	2.00	4.00	7.50	NF
727 Death and the Dancing Footman - Ngaio Marsh	2.00	4.00	7.50	M
728 Farewell to Sport - Paul Gallico	1.50	3.50	5.00	
729 Mankind So Far - W. Howells	1.50	3.50	5.00	
730 The Dunwich Horror and Other Weird Tales - H. P. Lovecraft	10.00	25.00	40.00	SF
731 ....And a Few Marines - Col. J. W. Thomason	1.50	3.50	5.00	
732 Starbuck - J. Selby	1.50	3.50	5.00	
733 The Cross and the Arrow - A. Maltz	1.50	3.50	5.00	
734 Lower than the Angels - Walter Karig	1.50	3.50	5.00	
735 A Little Night Music - G. W. Johnson 1945	1.50	3.50	5.00	
736 My Heart Leaps Up and Other Poems - William Wordsworth	1.50	3.50	5.00	
737 The Enchanted Voyage - Robert Nathan	2.00	4.00	7.50	F
738 Lives - G. Eckstein	1.50	3.50	5.00	
739 Prize Winners in Special Services Art Contest	2.00	4.00	7.50	
740 Cartoons for Fighters - Sgt. F. Brandt	2.00	4.00	7.50	H
741 Pipe Night - John O'Hara	1.50	3.50	5.00	
742 Joe, the Wounded Tennis Player - M. Thompson	1.50	3.50	5.00	
743 Brag Dog and Other Stories - V. Bell	1.50	3.50	5.00	
744 Harvard Has a Homicide - T. Fuller	1.50	3.50	5.00	M
745 The War of the Worlds - H. G. Wells	5.00	10.00	20.00	SF
746 Kid Galahad - F. Wallace	1.50	3.50	5.00	
747 Death on the Aisle - Frances & Richard Lockridge	2.00	4.00	7.50	M
748 Starlight Rider - Ernest Haycox	1.50	3.50	5.00	W
749 Looking for a Bluebird - J. Wechsberg	1.50	3.50	5.00	
750 Cup of Gold - John Steinbeck	2.00	4.00	7.50	A
751 The Big Sleep - Raymond Chandler	5.00	10.00	20.00	M
752 The Valley of Dry Bones - A. H. Gooden	1.50	3.50	5.00	W
753 Diamond River Man - Eugene Cunningham	1.50	3.50	5.00	W
754 Adventures of Hiram Holliday - Paul Gallico	1.50	3.50	5.00	
755 Let Your Mind Alone - James Thurber	2.00	4.00	7.50	H
756 We Pointed Them North - Smith & Abbott	1.50	3.50	5.00	
757 The Eight Million - M. Berger	1.50	3.50	5.00	
758 Moon Tide - W. Robertson	1.50	3.50	5.00	
759 Buck Peters, Ranchman - Clarence E. Mulford	2.00	4.00	7.50	W
760 Died in the Wool - Ngaio Marsh	2.00	4.00	7.50	M
761 Keep 'em Crawling - W. H. Upson	1.50	3.50	5.00	
762 Joseph Lister - R. Truax	1.50	3.50	5.00	

763	Listen for a Lonesome Drum - C. Carmer	1.50	3.50	5.00	
764	The Asiatics - F. Prokosch	1.50	3.50	5.00	
765	Worlds Great Tales of the Sea - W. McFee	1.50	3.50	5.00	A
766	Double Indemnity and Two Other Stories - James M. Cain	2.00	4.00	7.50	M
767	Selected Stories - Edgar Allan Poe	1.50	3.50	5.00	
768	Young Ames - Walter D. Edmonds	1.50	3.50	5.00	A
769	Life with Father and Mother - Clarence Day	1.50	3.50	5.00	
770	Quietly my Captain Waits - E. Eaton	1.50	3.50	5.00	
771	Myths After Lincoln - L. Lewis	1.50	3.50	5.00	
772	The Years - V. Woolf	1.50	3.50	5.00	
773	Timber Line - G. Fowler	1.50	3.50	5.00	
774	Night Unto Night - Philip Wylie	1.50	3.50	5.00	
775	Some Like Them Short - W. March	1.50	3.50	5.00	
	1945				
776	The Collected Poems - R. Brooke	1.50	3.50	5.00	
777	Canary - G. Eckstein	1.50	3.50	5.00	
778	A Genius in the Family - H. P. Maxim	1.50	3.50	5.00	
779	On Borrowed Time - L. E. Watkin	1.50	3.50	5.00	
780	Horsethief Creek - Bliss Lomax (H. S. Drago)	1.50	3.50	5.00	W
781	Lou Gehrig - F. Graham	1.50	3.50	5.00	B
782	You Know Me AL - Ring Lardner	1.50	3.50	5.00	
783	The Phantom Filly - G. Chamberlain	1.50	3.50	5.00	
784	Sheriff of Yavisa - C. H. Snow	1.50	3.50	5.00	W
785	The So Blue Marble - Dorothy B. Hughes	2.00	4.00	7.50	M
786	Blind Man's Bluff - Baynard Kendrick	2.00	4.00	7.50	M
787	Patrick Henry and the Frigate's Keel - Howard Fast	1.50	3.50	5.00	
788	The Bruiser - E. L. McKenna	1.50	3.50	5.00	
789	Payoff for the Banker - Frances & Richard Lockridge	2.00	4.00	7.50	M
790	This is Our World - P. B. Sears	1.50	3.50	5.00	
791	Trail Smoke - Ernest Haycox	1.50	3.50	5.00	W
792	Apartment in Athens - G. Wescott	1.50	3.50	5.00	
793	The Barefoot Mailman - Theodore Pratt	1.50	3.50	5.00	
794	The Long Valley - John Steinbeck	2.00	4.00	7.50	
795	King Solomon's Mines - H. Rider Haggard	5.00	10.00	20.00	A
796	Mr. Tutt Finds a Way - Arthur Train	1.50	3.50	5.00	
797	Forlorn River - Zane Grey	1.50	3.50	5.00	W
798	Pattern for Murder - I. S. Shriber	2.00	4.00	7.50	M
799	Butterfield 8 - John O'Hara	1.50	3.50	7.50	
800	The Bishop's Wife and Two Other Novels - Robert Nathan	1.50	3.50	5.00	
801	When Worlds Collide - Edwin Balmer & Philip Wylie	4.00	8.00	15.00	SF
802	Winter's Tales - I. Dinesen	1.50	3.50	5.00	
803	Five Western Stories - Coburn, Foster, Ranger, McCulley & Wilson	1.50	3.50	5.00	W
804	Commodore Hornblower - C. S. Forester	1.50	3.50	5.00	A
805	Yankee Woman - E. Baume	1.50	3.50	5.00	
806	The Hudson - C. Carmer	1.50	3.50	5.00	
807	Sun in Their Eyes - M. Barrett	1.50	3.50	5.00	
808	Men Against Death - P. de Kruif	1.50	3.50	5.00	
809	Men of Science in America - B. Jaffe	1.50	3.50	5.00	
810	Great Stories From Great Lives - H. V. Prochnow	1.50	3.50	5.00	
811	Mrs. Parkington - Louis Bromfield	1.50	3.50	5.00	
812	The Sea Hawk - Rafael Sabatini	2.00	4.00	7.50	A
813	Author's Choice - MacKinlay Kantor	1.50	3.50	5.00	
814	Ride With Me - Thomas B. Costain	1.50	3.50	5.00	
815	The Voice of the Turtle - J. Van Druten	1.50	3.50	5.00	
	1945				
816	In the Fog - R. H. Davis	1.50	3.50	5.00	
817	Pal Joey - John O'Hara	1.50	3.50	5.00	
818	Rackety Rax - J. Sayre	1.50	3.50	5.00	
819	The New Yorker's Baedeker	1.50	3.50	5.00	
820	Selected Poems - John Masefield	1.50	3.50	5.00	
821	The Half-Haunted Saloon - R. Shattuck	1.50	3.50	5.00	
822	Up Front - Bill Mauldin	2.00	4.00	7.50	H
823	O Pioneers! - Willa Cather	1.50	3.50	5.00	
824	Electronics Today and Tomorrow - J. Mills	1.50	3.50	5.00	NF
825	A Rose for Emily and Other Stories - William Faulkner	2.00	4.00	7.50	
826	Coming of Age in Samoa - Margaret Mead	1.50	3.50	5.00	NF
827	The Indigo Necklace - Frances Crane	1.50	3.50	5.00	M

828	The Delicate Ape - Dorothy B. Hughes	2.00	4.00	7.50	M
829	Payment Deferred - C. S. Forester	1.50	3.50	5.00	A
830	Buried Alive - A. Bennett	1.50	3.50	5.00	
831	Virgin with Butterflies - T. Powers	1.50	3.50	5.00	
832	The Sporting Gesture - T. L. Stix	1.50	3.50	5.00	
833	Square Deal Sanderson - Charles Alden Seltzer	1.50	3.50	5.00	W
834	Bar 20 Days - Clarence E. Mulford	2.00	4.00	7.50	W
835	American Guerilla in the Phillipines - Ira Wolfert	1.50	3.50	5.00	C
836	Claudia and David - Rose Franken	1.50	3.50	5.00	
837	Sundown Jim - Ernest Haycox	1.50	3.50	5.00	W
838	The Lady in the Lake - Raymond Chandler	5.00	10.00	20.00	M
839	River Song - H. Hamilton	1.50	3.50	5.00	
840	The Biscuit Eater and Other Stories - J. Street	1.50	3.50	5.00	
841	The Upstart - Edison Marshall	1.50	3.50	5.00	A
842	Twin Sombreros - Zane Grey	1.50	3.50	5.00	
843	Young Bess - M. Irwin	1.50	3.50	5.00	
844	Little Orvie - Booth Tarkington	1.50	3.50	5.00	
845	Pleasant Valley - Louis Bromfield	1.50	3.50	5.00	
846	McGraw of the Giants - F. Graham	1.50	3.50	5.00	S
847	Cuckoo Time - R. Temple	1.50	3.50	5.00	
848	Time to be Young - W. Burnett	1.50	3.50	5.00	
849	Bedford Village - Hervey Allen	1.50	3.50	5.00	
850	The Lady and the Arsenic - J. Shearing	1.50	3.50	5.00	
851	Dracula - J. Shearing	5.00	10.00	20.00	HO
852	Wickford Point - John P. Marquand	1.50	3.50	5.00	
853	A Lion Is in the Streets - A. L. Langley	1.50	3.50	5.00	
854	Captain from Castile - Samuel Shellabarger	1.50	3.50	5.00	A
855	A Book of Americans - Stephen Vincent Benet	1.50	3.50	5.00	
856	My Life and Hard Times - James Thurber	2.00	4.00	6.00	
857	Lyrics and Sonnets - Edna St. Vincent Millay	1.50	3.50	5.00	
858	The Rumelhearts of Rampler Ave. - M. S. Delavan	1.50	3.50	5.00	
859	Tacey Cromwell - Conrad Richter	1.50	3.50	5.00	
860	The Royal Game - S. Zweig	1.50	3.50	5.00	
861	The Pearl Lagoon - Charles Nordhoff	1.50	3.50	5.00	A
862	The Great Gatsby - F. Scott Fitzgerald	2.00	4.00	7.50	
863	The Gray Champion and Other Tales - Nathaniel Hawthorne	2.00	4.00	7.50	
864	Ariel: The Life of Shelley - A. Maurois	1.50	3.50	5.00	
865	My Ten Years in a Quandry - Robert Benchley	2.00	4.00	7.50	H
866	Tragic Ground - Erskine Caldwell	1.50	3.50	5.00	
867	Rim of the Desert - Ernest Haycox	1.50	3.50	5.00	W
868	Useless Cowboy - Alan LeMay	1.50	3.50	5.00	W
869	The Fallen Sparrow - Dorothy B. Hughes	2.00	4.00	6.00	M
870	Snow Above Town - D. Hough	1.50	3.50	5.00	
871	Green Thoughts and Other Strange Tales - John Collier	2.00	4.00	7.50	F
872	Crazy Like a Fox - S. J. Perelman	2.00	4.00	7.50	H
873	The Confidential Agent - Grahan Greene	2.00	4.00	7.50	M
874	Ramrod - Luke Short	1.50	3.50	5.00	W
875	Mostly Canallers - Walter D. Edmonds	1.50	3.50	5.00	
876	The Countess to Boot - Jack Iams	1.50	3.50	5.00	M
877	Danger Trail - Max Brand	1.50	3.50	5.00	W
878	Deadline at Dawn - William Irish	2.00	4.00	7.50	M
879	Wind Before Rain - J. D. Weaver	1.50	3.50	5.00	
880	Walden - H. David Thoreau	2.00	4.00	7.50	
881	She - H. Rider Haggard	5.00	10.00	20.00	A
882	Colour Scheme - Ngaio Marsh	2.00	4.00	7.50	M
883	Desert Gold - Zane Grey	1.50	3.50	5.00	
884	Ruggles of Red Gap - H. L. Wilson	1.50	3.50	5.00	
885	The Strange Case of Dr. Jekyll and Mr. Hyde - Robert Louis Stevenson	7.50	15.00	30.00	SF
886	White Sales Crowding - E. Gilligan	1.50	3.50	5.00	
887	The Virginian - Owen Wister	1.50	3.50	5.00	W
888	Head O'W-Hollow - J. Stuart	1.50	3.50	5.00	
889	Five Acres and Independence - M. G. Kains	1.50	3.50	5.00	
890	Busman's Honeymoon - Dorothy L. Sayers	2.00	4.00	7.50	M
891	Hatter's Castle - A. J. Cronin	1.50	3.50	5.00	
892	The Sky's the Limit - B. A. Botkin	1.50	3.50	5.00	
893	The Loom of Language - F. Bodmer	1.50	3.50	5.00	
894	Reveille in Washington - M. Leach	1.50	3.50	5.00	

895	Dear Sir and Dumb-belles Letters - Juliet Lowell 1946	1.50	3.50	5.00	H
896	How to do Practically Anything - Goodman & Green	1.50	3.50	5.00	
897	Bowleg Bill - J. Digges	1.50	3.50	5.00	
898	Walls Rise Up - G. S. Perry	1.50	3.50	5.00	
899	Mr. Wilmer - R. Lawson	1.50	3.50	5.00	
900	The Full Life and Other Stories - D. D. Beauchamp	1.50	3.50	5.00	
901	The Daniel Jazz and Other Poems - V. Lindsay	1.50	3.50	5.00	
902	My Bitter Half and Other Stories - J. Weaver	1.50	3.50	5.00	
903	Keep Your Head Down - W. Bernstein	1.50	3.50	5.00	
904	The Story of Penicillin - B. Sokoloff, M.D.	1.50	3.50	5.00	
905	Lost Island - James Norman Hall	1.50	3.50	5.00	A
906	Not Quite Dead Enough - Rex Stout	1.50	3.50	5.00	
907	The Great Bustard and Other People - Will Cuppy	2.00	4.00	7.50	
908	The Fighting Four - Max Brand	1.50	3.50	5.00	
909	Frankenstein - Mary Wollstonecraft Shelley	7.50	15.00	30.00	SF
910	The Happy Time - R. Fontaine	1.50	3.50	5.00	
911	Mantrap - Sinclair Lewis	2.00	4.00	7.50	
912	Ironies - R. Connell	1.50	3.50	5.00	
913	Best Sport Stories of 1944 - Marsh & Ehre	1.50	3.50	5.00	S
914	The Lucky Stiff - Craig Rice	2.00	4.00	7.50	M
915	The Case of the Golddiggers Purse - Erle Stanley Gardner	1.50	3.50	5.00	M
916	Canyon Passage - Ernest Haycox	1.50	3.50	5.00	W
917	The Trail Horde - Charles Alden Seltzer	1.50	3.50	5.00	W
918	"Tex" - Clarence E. Mulford	2.00	4.00	7.50	
919	The Folded Leaf - W. Maxwell	1.50	3.50	5.00	
920	Jazz - R. Goffin	1.50	3.50	5.00	NF
921	Concerning a Woman of Sin and Other Stories - Ben Hecht	1.50	3.50	5.00	H
922	Rain in the Doorway - Thorne Smith	1.50	3.50	5.00	H
923	Aunt Beardie - J. Shearing	1.50	3.50	5.00	
924	Rebellion of Leo McGuire - C. B. Davis	1.50	3.50	5.00	
925	The Odyssey of Homer - T. E. Shaw	1.50	3.50	5.00	
926	The Giaconda Smile and Other Stories - Aldous Huxley	1.50	3.50	5.00	
927	The Last Time I Saw Paris - E. Paul	1.50	3.50	5.00	
928	Fortitude - Hugh Walpole	1.50	3.50	5.00	
929	Names on the Land - G. R. Stewart	1.50	3.50	5.00	
930	God's Angry Man - L. Ehrlich	1.50	3.50	5.00	
931	A. Woollcott - S. H. Adams	1.50	3.50	5.00	B
932	Two Solitudes - H. MacLennan	1.50	3.50	5.00	
933	The Bedside Tables - Peter Arno	1.50	3.50	5.00	H
934	The Best from Yank - Editors of Yank	1.50	3.50	5.00	
935	Dear Ruth - N. Krasdan 1946	1.50	3.50	5.00	
936	Set 'Em Up - J. Madden	1.50	3.50	5.00	
937	The Deadly Dove - Rufus King	2.00	4.00	7.50	M
938	Admirals of the Caribbean - F. R. Hart	1.50	3.50	5.00	
939	Love Poems - Robert & Elizabeth Barrett Browning	2.00	4.00	7.50	
940	The Great God Pan and Other Weird Stories - Arthur Machen	4.00	8.00	15.00	HO

Armed Services Editions 878

Armed Services Editions 885

Armed Services Editions 954

941	Artie Greengroin, Pfc. - H. Brown	1.50	3.50	5.00	
942	The World, the Flesh and Father Smith - B. Marshall	1.50	3.50	5.00	
943	Bedelia - Vera Caspary	1.50	3.50	5.00	
944	The Ransom of Red Chief and Other Stories - O. Henry	1.50	3.50	5.00	
945	God's Little Acres - E. Caldwell	1.50	3.50	5.00	
946	Deadlier than the Male - J. Gunn	1.50	3.50	5.00	
947	Comanche Kid - E. B. Mann	1.50	3.50	5.00	
948	Laugh It Off - M. E. Derrickson	1.50	3.50	5.00	
949	The Boss of the Lazy Y - Charles Alden Seltzer	1.50	3.50	5.00	W
950	Killing the Goose - Frances & Richard Lockridge	2.00	4.00	7.50	M
951	Prairie Guns - E. E. Halleran	1.50	3.50	5.00	W
952	Watch Out for Willie Carter - T. Naidish	1.50	3.50	5.00	
953	The Passionate Witch - Thorne Smith	1.50	3.50	5.00	H
954	Guerrila - Lord Dunsany	4.00	8.00	15.00	
955	The New Yorker Profiles	1.50	3.50	5.00	
956	Cartridge Carnival - William Colt MacDonald	1.50	3.50	5.00	W
957	Winds, Blow Gently - R. Kirkbride	1.50	3.50	5.00	
958	The Food of the Gods - H. G. Wells	4.00	8.00	15.00	SF
959	Great Son - Edna Ferber	1.50	3.50	5.00	
960	Rockets and Jets - H. S. Zim	1.50	3.50	5.00	
961	Marta of Moscovy - P. Stong	1.50	3.50	5.00	
962	Science Yearbook of 1945 - J. D. Ratcliff	1.50	3.50	5.00	NF
963	The Brooklyn Dodgers - F. Graham	1.50	3.50	5.00	B
964	Trail of the Money Bird - D. Ripley	1.50	3.50	5.00	S
965	Esquire's First Sports Reader - H. Graffis	1.50	3.50	5.00	S
966	So Well Remembered - J. Hilton	1.50	3.50	5.00	
967	There's Laughter in the Air! - Gaver & Stanley	1.50	3.50	5.00	
968	Rickshaw Boy - L. Shaw	1.50	3.50	5.00	
969	Cass Timberlane - Sinclair Lewis	2.00	4.00	7.50	
970	The Thurber Carnival - James Thurber	2.00	4.00	7.50	H
971	The Razor's Edge - W. Somerset Maugham	1.50	3.50	5.00	
972	Strange Fruit - Lillian Smith	1.50	3.50	5.00	
973	Against These Three - Stuart Cloete	1.50	3.50	5.00	
974	The City of Trembling Leaves - W. Van Tillburg Clark	1.50	3.50	5.00	
975	Gentleman Overboard - H. C. Lewis	1.50	3.50	5.00	
	1946				
976	My Remarkable Uncle and Other Sketches - Stewart Leacock	1.50	3.50	5.00	
977	Buy and Acre - P. Corey	1.50	3.50	5.00	
978	The Helicopters Are Coming - C. B. Macauley	1.50	3.50	5.00	
979	The Doctor's Son and Other Stories - John O'Hara	1.50	3.50	5.00	
980	Silversides - R. Trumbull	1.50	3.50	5.00	
981	I'm A Stranger Here Myself - Ogden Nash	1.50	3.50	5.00	
982	Silvertip's Search - Max Brand	1.50	3.50	5.00	W
983	An Eye for an Eye - W. Bayer	1.50	3.50	5.00	
984	The Man Who Was Thursday - G. K. Chesterton	3.00	6.00	12.00	F
985	Slow Train to Yesterday - A. Robertson	1.50	3.50	5.00	
986	Our United States Secret Service - Irving Crump	1.50	3.50	5.00	
987	"Beau" Rand - Charles Alden Seltzer	1.50	3.50	5.00	W
988	Lay that Pistol Down - R. Powell	1.50	3.50	5.00	
989	Who Wants to Live Forever? - William MacLeod Raine	1.50	3.50	5.00	W
990	Louis Beretti - Donald Henderson Clarke	2.00	4.00	7.50	M
991	The Curse of the Bronze Lamp - Carter Dickson	2.50	6.00	10.00	M
992	Chicago Murders - S. P. Wright	1.50	3.50	5.00	
993	Sports Extra - S. Frank	1.50	3.50	5.00	
994	The Private Life of Helen of Troy - John Erskine	2.00	4.00	7.50	A
995	The Amethyst Spectacles - Frances Crane	1.50	3.50	5.00	M
996	Beat to Quarters - C. S. Forester	1.50	3.50	5.00	A
997	The Heritage of the Desert - Zane Grey	1.50	3.50	5.00	W
998	Devil on his Trail - John & Ward Hawkins	1.50	3.50	5.00	
999	Rooster Crows for a Day - P. E. Burman	1.50	3.50	5.00	
1000	Esquire's 1945 Jazz Book - P. E. Miller	2.00	4.00	7.50	NF

1001 Black Moon - C. McMeekin	1.50	3.50	5.00	
1002 Twenty Careers of Tomorrow - D. & F. Huff	1.50	3.50	5.00	
1003 Dan Sickles - E. Pinchon	1.50	3.50	5.00	
1004 January Thaw - B. Partridge	1.50	3.50	5.00	
1005 Arms and the Man and Two Other Plays - G. B. Shaw	1.50	3.50	5.00	
1006 The Birth of Mischief - Rafael Sabatini	1.50	3.50	5.00	
1007 All Brides are Beautiful - T. Bell	1.50	3.50	5.00	
1008 Atoms in Action - G. R. Harrison	1.50	3.50	5.00	
1009 The Green Years - A. J. Cronin	1.50	3.50	5.00	
1010 The Saddle and the Plow - R. M. Taylor	1.50	3.50	5.00	
1011 Best Short Stories - Jack London	2.00	4.00	7.50	
1012 Some of these Days - S. Tucker	1.50	3.50	5.00	
1013 Of Time and the River - T. Wolfe	1.50	3.50	5.00	
1014 Northwest Passage - Kenneth Roberts	1.50	3.50	5.00	
1015 Selected Poems - A. E. Housman	1.50	3.50	5.00	
1946				
1016 Is Sex Necessary - Thurber & White	2.00	4.00	6.00	H
1017 I'll Try Anything Twice - F. Russell	1.50	3.50	5.00	
1018 Your Personal Plane - J. P. Andrews	1.50	3.50	5.00	
1019 Parlor, Bedlam and Bath - Perelman & Reynolds	2.00	4.00	7.50	H
1020 Till I Come Back to You - T. Bell	1.50	3.50	5.00	
1021 The Wolf Pack of Lobo Butte - W.C. Tuttle	1.50	3.50	5.00	W
1022 Rusty Guns - Bliss Lomax	1.50	3.50	5.00	W
1023 The State of Music - V. Thomson	1.50	3.50	5.00	NF
1024 Liberal Education - M. Van Doren	1.50	3.50	5.00	NF
1025 Dreamland - Clarence Buddington Kelland	1.50	3.50	5.00	
1026 The King is Dead on Queen Street - F. Bonnamy	1.50	3.50	5.00	
1027 Big Ben - E. S. Miers	1.50	3.50	5.00	
1028 Red Sand - T. S. Stribling	1.50	3.50	5.00	
1029 Is It Anyone We Know? - G. Price	1.50	3.50	5.00	
1030 "Drag" Harlan - Charles Alden Seltzer	1.50	3.50	5.00	W
1031 The Corpse in the Snowman - N. Blake	1.50	3.50	5.00	
1032 Make the Most of Your Life - D. E. Lurton	1.50	3.50	5.00	
1033 O Genteel Lady! - E. Forbes	1.50	3.50	5.00	
1034 Panic - H. McCloy	1.50	3.50	5.00	
1035 Mahogany - A. Segre	1.50	3.50	5.00	
1036 Buckaroo - Eugene Cunningham	1.50	3.50	5.00	W
1037 Frank Leahy and the Fighting Irish - A. Ward	1.50	3.50	5.00	S
1038 They Tell No Tales - Manning Coles	1.50	3.50	5.00	
1039 The Case of the Half-Wakened Wife - Erle Stanley Gardner	1.50	3.50	5.00	M
1040 The Japanese Nation - J. F. Embree	1.50	3.50	5.00	NF
1041 The Lost Weekend - C. Jackson	1.50	3.50	5.00	
1042 Selected Short Stories - J. Russell	1.50	3.50	5.00	
1043 The Diamond as Big as the Ritz and Others - F. Scott Fitzgerald	2.00	4.00	7.50	
1044 New World of Machines - H. Manchester	1.50	3.50	5.00	
1045 Storm - G. Stewart	1.50	3.50	5.00	
1046 Kabloona - G. de Poncins	1.50	3.50	5.00	
1047 Three O'clock Dinner - J. Pinckney	1.50	3.50	5.00	
1048 Trelawny - M. Armstrong	1.50	3.50	5.00	
1049 Oil for the Lamps of China - A. T. Hobart	1.50	3.50	5.00	
1050 Modern American Short Stories - Bennett Cerf	1.50	3.50	5.00	
1051 The Builders of the Bridge - D. B. Steinman	1.50	3.50	5.00	
1052 Saints and Strangers - G. F. Willison	1.50	3.50	5.00	
1053 The White Tower - J. R. Ullman	1.50	3.50	5.00	
1054 The Stars Look Down - A. J. Cronin	1.50	3.50	5.00	
1055 Hunter's Moon and Other Stories - E. Gilligan	1.50	3.50	5.00	
1946				
1056 The Love Poems of Robert Herrick - Louis Untermeyer	1.50	3.50	5.00	
1057 Excuse It, Please! - C. O. Skinner	1.50	3.50	5.00	
1058 The Postman Always Rings Twice - James M. Cain	2.00	4.00	6.00	M
1059 The Story of George Gershwin - D. Ewen	1.50	3.50	5.00	
1060 The Education of T. C. Mits - Gray & Lieber	1.50	3.50	5.00	
1061 One Day on Beetle Rock - S. Carrighar	1.50	3.50	5.00	
1062 Jumper - N. Kalashnikoff	1.50	3.50	5.00	

1063	Atomic Energy in the Coming Era - David Dietz	1.50	3.50	5.00	NF
1064	Block that Bride and Other Stories - C. S. Brooks	1.50	3.50	5.00	
1065	Kazan - James Oliver Curwood	1.50	3.50	5.00	A
1066	The New Yorker Reporter At Large	1.50	3.50	5.00	
1067	Hold Autumn in Your Hand - G. S. Perry	1.50	3.50	5.00	
1068	Inside the F. B. I. - J. J. Floherty	1.50	3.50	5.00	NF
1069	The Department of Queer Complaints - Carter Dickson	3.00	6.00	12.00	M
1070	Enrico Caruso - D. Caruson	1.50	3.50	5.00	B
1071	The Vengeance of Jefferson Gawne - Charles Alden Seltzer	1.50	3.50	5.00	W
1072	The Man from Bar-20 - Clarence E. Mulford	1.50	3.50	5.00	W
1073	Gold and Guns on Halfaday Creek - James B. Hendryx	1.50	3.50	5.00	W
1074	The Sunday Pigeon Murders - Craig Rice	2.00	4.00	7.50	M
1075	The Murder that had Everything - Hulbert Bootner	1.50	3.50	5.00	M
1076	Comic Relief - R. N. Linscott	1.50	3.50	5.00	H
1077	We Took to the Woods - L. D. Rich	1.50	3.50	5.00	
1078	My True Love - D. L. Teilhet	1.50	3.50	5.00	
1079	The Story of the Great Geologists - Fenton & Fenton	1.50	3.50	5.00	NF
1080	Tales by Tolstoy - Leo Tolstoy	1.50	3.50	5.00	
1081	You and Your Future Job - Campbell & Bedford	1.50	3.50	5.00	NF
1082	The Black Rose - Thomas B. Costain	1.50	3.50	5.00	A
1083	Baseball Recorder - W. Tulley	1.50	3.50	5.00	
	1946				
1084	Repent in Haste - J. P. Marquand	1.50	3.50	5.00	
1085	Best Cartoons of the Year 1945 - Lawrence Lariar	2.00	4.00	7.50	H
1086	The Lunatic at Large - J. S. Clouston	1.50	3.50	5.00	
1087	Biography of the Earth - G. Gamow	1.50	3.50	5.00	
1088	The Double Take - Roy Huggins	2.00	4.00	7.50	M
1089	If the Prospect Pleases - L. Haystead	1.50	3.50	5.00	
1090	Straight, Place and Show - R. S. Dowst	1.50	3.50	5.00	
1091	The War of the Worlds - H. G. Wells	4.00	8.00	15.00	SF
1092	Kid Galahad - F. Wallace	1.50	3.50	5.00	
1093	Death on the Aisle - Frances & Richard Lockridge	2.00	4.00	7.50	M
1094	Starlight Rider - Ernest Haycox	1.50	3.50	5.00	W
1095	A Small Store and Independence - Greenberg & Schindall	1.50	3.50	5.00	
1096	Steamboat Round the Bend - B. L. Burman	1.50	3.50	5.00	
1097	Out of Control - Baynard Kendrick	2.00	4.00	7.50	
1098	V as in Victim - Lawrence Treat	2.00	4.00	7.50	M
1099	Typhoon and the End of the Tether - Joseph Conrad	2.00	4.00	7.50	
1100	The Egg and I - Betty MacDonald	1.50	3.50	5.00	H
1101	The Ranchman - Charles Alden Seltzer	1.50	3.50	5.00	W
1102	My Three Years with Eisenhower - Capt. H. C. Butcher	1.50	3.50	5.00	
1103	The Well-tempered Listener - Deems Taylor	1.50	3.50	5.00	NF
1104	The Manatee - N. Bruff	1.50	3.50	5.00	
1105	The Theory and Practice of Earning a Living - J. F. Wharton	1.50	3.50	5.00	
1106	The Big Midget Murders - Craig Rice	2.00	4.00	7.50	M
1107	The Border Legion - Zane Grey	1.50	3.50	5.00	W
1108	The Saga of Billy the Kid - Walter Noble Burns	2.00	4.00	7.50	B
1109	Mr. Digby - D. Welch	1.50	3.50	5.00	
1110	White Water and Black Magic - R. C. Gill	1.50	3.50	5.00	
1111	Saratoga Trunk - Edna Ferber	1.50	3.50	5.00	
1112	Radio's 100 men of Science - O. E. Dunlap, Jr.	1.50	3.50	5.00	
1113	Days and Nights - K. Simonov	1.50	3.50	5.00	
1114	John Brown's Body - Stephen Vincent Benet	1.50	3.50	5.00	
1115	Prater Violet - Christopher Isherwood	1.50	3.50	5.00	
	1946				
1116	The Wolf - Sgt. L. Sansone	1.50	3.50	5.00	
1117	Come in Like a Yankee and Other Stories - H. V. Dixon	1.50	3.50	5.00	
1118	Joe Louis: American - M. Miller	1.50	3.50	5.00	B

1119 The Zebra Derby - Max Shulman	1.50	3.50	5.00	
1120 Dingo - H. G. Lamond	1.50	3.50	5.00	
1121 The Crock of Gold - J. Stephens	1.50	3.50	5.00	
1122 Selected Poems - Carl Sandburg	2.00	4.00	7.50	
1123 Port of Seven Strangers - K. M. Knight	1.50	3.50	5.00	
1124 Safari - M. Johnson	1.50	3.50		
1125 The Bitter Tea of General Yen - Grace Zaring Stone	2.00	4.00	7.50	
1126 The Great American Customer - C. Crow	1.50	3.50	5.00	
1127 Valiant is the Word for Carrie	1.50	3.50	5.00	
1128 My Greatest Day in Baseball - J. P. Carmichael	1.50	3.50	5.00	
1129 Courage Stout - William MacLeod Raine	1.50	3.50	5.00	W
1130 The Noose is Drawn - Barber & Schabelitz	1.50	3.50	5.00	
1131 The Case of the Black-eyed Blonde - Erle Stanley Gardner	1.50	3.50	5.00	M
1132 Lost in the Horse Latitudes - H. Allen Smith	1.50	3.50	5.00	H
1133 Hunted Riders - Max Brand	1.50	3.50	5.00	W
1134 The Ox-bow Incident - Van Tillburg Clark	1.50	3.50	5.00	W
1135 Troopers West - F. Parkhill	1.50	3.50	5.00	W
1136 Woman at Bay - George Harmon Coxe	2.00	4.00	7.50	M
1137 Tales for Males - E. Fitzgerald	1.50	3.50	5.00	
1138 The Small General - R. Standish	1.50	3.50	5.00	
1139 Caribbean Treasure - I. T. Sanderson	1.50	3.50	5.00	
1140 Miracles Ahead - Carlisle & Latham	1.50	3.50	5.00	
1141 The Bar-20 Three - Clarence E. Mulford	2.00	4.00	7.50	W
1142 Shakespeare - M. Van Doren	1.50	3.50	5.00	
1143 Where Do People Take Their Troubles? - L. R. Steiner	1.50	3.50	5.00	
1144 The Cherokee Strip - M. James	1.50	3.50	5.00	
1145 Modern Woman in Love - Stead & Blake	1.50	3.50	5.00	
1146 That Girl from Memphis - W. D. Steele	1.50	3.50	5.00	
1147 Pal Joey - John O'Hara	1.50	3.50	5.00	
1946				
1148 Rackety Rax - J. Sayre	1.50	3.50	5.00	
1149 Anything Can Happen - G. & H. Papashvily	1.50	3.50	5.00	
1150 Men of Popular Music - D. Ewen	1.50	3.50	5.00	NF
1151 Many Long Years Ago - Ogden Nash	1.50	3.50	5.00	
1152 Winter Meeting - Grace Zaring Stone	1.50	3.50	5.00	
1153 Wheels in His Head - M. M. Musselman	1.50	3.50	5.00	
1154 The End of the Trail - Peter Field	1.50	3.50	5.00	
1155 The Owl in the Cellar - M. Scherf	1.50	3.50	5.00	
1156 The Dark Ship and Other Selections from the New Yorker	1.50	3.50	5.00	
1157 The Story of the Moon - C. Fisher	1.50	3.50	5.00	
1158 The Tenderfoot - W. H. B. Kent	1.50	3.50	5.00	W
1159 It's Still Maloney - R. Maloney	1.50	3.50	5.00	
1160 Meet Your Ancestors - R. C. Andrews	1.50	3.50	5.00	
1161 Tomorrow's Another Day - W. R. Burnett	2.00	4.00	7.50	
1162 Murder Within Murder - Frances & Richard Lockridge	2.00	4.00	7.50	M
1163 Starlight Pass - Tom Gill	1.50	3.50	5.00	W
1164 Trail Town - Ernest Haycox	1.50	3.50	5.00	W
1165 The Salvation of Pisco Gabar and Other Stories - Geoffrey Household	2.00	4.00	7.50	
1166 She Came Back - P. Wentworth	1.50	3.50	5.00	
1167 Your Servant the Molecule - W. S. Landis	1.50	3.50	5.00	NF
1168 Treasure Below - E. Comm. Ellsberg	1.50	3.50	5.00	
1169 The Edge of Running Water - W. Sloane	1.50	3.50	5.00	
1170 The New York Yankees - F. Graham	1.50	3.50	5.00	S
1171 Top Stuff - H. Hart	1.50	3.50	5.00	
1172 The Gashouse Gang - J. R. Stockton	1.50	3.50	5.00	S
1173 I Wouldn't be in Your Shoes - William Irish	2.00	4.00	7.50	M
1174 Green Fire - P. W. Ranier	1.50	3.50	5.00	
1175 Cobb's Cavalcade - B. D. Zevin	1.50	3.50	5.00	
1176 The King's General - Daphne du Maurier	1.50	3.50	5.00	
1177 Arch of Triumph - Erich Marie Remarque	1.50	3.50	5.00	C
1178 While You Were Gone - J. Goodman	1.50	3.50	5.00	
1179 Last Chapter - Ernie Pyle	1.50	3.50	5.00	C
1946				
1180 Third Avenue, New York - J. McNulty	1.50	3.50	5.00	
1181 Ravaged Range - Peter Field	1.50	3.50	5.00	W
1182 Williwaw - Gore Vidal	1.50	3.50	5.00	
1183 Outlaw on Horseback - Will Ermine	1.50	3.50	5.00	W
1184 Coroner Creek - Luke Short	1.50	3.50	5.00	W

1185	The Unforeseen - D. Macardle	2.50	6.00	10.00	F
1186	Let's Kill George - L. Cores	1.50	3.50	5.00	
1187	Lord Hornblower - C. S. Forester	1.50	3.50	5.00	A
1188	With Bated Breath - A. Campbell	1.50	3.50	5.00	
1189	A Solo in Tom-Toms - G. Fowler	1.50	3.50	5.00	
1190	The Saturday Evening Post Stories 1942-1945	1.50	3.50	5.00	
1191	Denver Murders - L. Casey	1.50	3.50	5.00	M
	1946				
1192	By Way of Wyoming - C. Bishop	1.50	3.50	5.00	
1193	A Rock in Every Snowball - F. Sullivan	1.50	3.50	5.00	
1194	Death's Old Sweet Song - Jonathan Stagge	2.00	4.00	7.50	
1195	The World in His Arms - Rex Beach	1.50	3.50	5.00	A
1196	Clattering Hoofs - William MacLeod Raine	1.50	3.50	5.00	W
1197	The Chicago Cubs - W. Brown	1.50	3.50	5.00	S
1198	Man-eaters of Kumaon - James Corbett	1.50	3.50	5.00	A
1199	Jim Bridger, Mountain Man - Stanley Vestal	2.00	4.00	7.50	B
1200	Blaze of Noon - Ernest K. Gann	1.50	3.50	5.00	
1201	All the King's Men - R. P. Warren	1.50	3.50	5.00	
1202	Tell Your Sons - W. Gibbs	1.50	3.50	5.00	
1203	Mister Roberts - T. Heggen	1.50	3.50	5.00	
	1946				
1204	Football Coach - A. Sampson	1.50	3.50	5.00	
1205	Benefit Performance - Richard Sale	2.00	4.00	7.50	M
1206	Double Cross Trail - E. E. Halleran	1.50	3.50	5.00	W
1207	Pikes Peek or Bust - Earl Wilson	1.50	3.50	5.00	
1208	Thunderbird Trail - William Colt MacDonald	1.50	3.50	5.00	W
1209	Stranger Than Truth - Vera Caspary	1.50	3.50	5.00	
1210	Companions of the Left Hand - G. Tabori	1.50	3.50	5.00	
1211	Green Grass of Wyoming - Mary O'Hara	1.50	3.50	5.00	
1212	Driftwood Valley - T. C. S. Fletcher	1.50	3.50	5.00	
1213	The Best Stories of W. D. Steele - W. D. Steele	1.50	3.50	5.00	
1214	Under the Red Sea Sun - Com. E. Ellsworth	1.50	3.50	5.00	
1215	The Big Clock - K. Fearing	1.50	3.50	5.00	
	1947				
1216	Mountain Riders - Max Brand	1.50	3.50	5.00	W
1217	Mr. Adam - Pat Frank	2.00	4.00	7.50	SF
1218	The Case of the Borrowed Brunette - Erle Stanley Gardner	1.50	3.50	5.00	
1219	The Sudden Guest - C. LaFarge	1.50	3.50	5.00	
1220	White Man - Peter Freuchen	1.50	3.50	5.00	
1221	Frontier on the Potomac - J. Daniels	1.50	3.50	5.00	
1222	The Silent Speaker - Rex Stout	2.00	4.00	7.50	M
1223	Strange and Fantastic Stories - J. A. Margolies	1.50	3.50	5.00	
1224	Holdfast Gaines - Shepard & Shepard	1.50	3.50	5.00	
1225	B. F's Daughter - J. P. Marquand	1.50	3.50	5.00	
1226	The Salem Frigate - John Jennings	1.50	3.50	5.00	A
1227	Boy from Nebraska - R. G. Martin	1.50	3.50		
	1947				
1228	Francis - D. Stern	1.50	3.50	5.00	H
1229	Surreptitious Entry - W. George	1.50	3.50	5.00	
1230	Courage of the North - James B. Hendryx	1.50	3.50	5.00	W
1231	Death of a Tall Man - Frances & Richard Lockridge	2.00	4.00	7.50	M
1232	The Wayward Bus - John Steinbeck	2.00	4.00	7.50	
1233	But Look, the Morn - MacKinlay Kantor	1.50	3.50	5.00	
1234	Saigon Singer - Van Wyck Mason	1.50	3.50	5.00	
1235	Fabulous Empire - F. Gibson	1.50	3.50	5.00	
1236	The Colorado - F. Waters	1.50	3.50	5.00	
1237	Eagles Fly West - E. Ainsworth	1.50	3.50	5.00	
1238	Toil of the Brave - I. Fletcher	1.50	3.50	5.00	
1239	Treasure of the Brasada - Les Savage, Jr.	1.50	3.50	5.00	W
	1947				
1240	Six Gun Showdown - T. West	1.50	3.50	5.00	W
1241	The Silver Leopard - Helen Reilly	2.00	4.00	7.50	M
1242	The Face of the Clam - L. Whiteman	1.50	3.50	5.00	
1243	Command Decision - W. W. Haines	1.50	3.50	5.00	
1244	The Shadowed Trail - A. H. Gooden	1.50	3.50	5.00	W
1245	The Natural History of Nonsense - B. Evans	1.50	3.50	5.00	H
1246	My Late Wives - Carter Dickson	2.50	6.00	10.00	M
1247	The Quarry - M. Walker	1.50	3.50	5.00	
1248	Tales of the South Pacific - J. A. Michener	1.50	3.50	5.00	
1249	Look South to the Polar Star - H. Cahill	1.50	3.50	5.00	
1250	Not So Wild a Dream - Eric Sevareid	1.50	3.50	5.00	

1251	The Barber of Tubac - Nelson C. Nye 1947	1.50	3.50	5.00	W
1252	The Magnificent Barb - D. Faralla	1.50	3.50	5.00	
1253	Mixture for Men - F. Feldkamp	1.50	3.50	5.00	
1254	Buckaroo's Code - Wayne D. Overholser	1.50	3.50	5.00	W
1255	Pick Your Victim - P. McGerr	2.00	4.00	7.50	M
1256	The Widow-Makers - M. Blankfort	1.50	3.50	5.00	
1257	The Border Bandit - Evan Evans (Max Brand)	1.50	3.50	5.00	W
1258	The Middle of Midnight - W. G. Beymer	1.50	3.50	5.00	
1259	Jeremy Bell - C. B. Davis	1.50	3.50	5.00	
1260	The Detroit Tigers - F. G. Lieb	1.50	3.50	5.00	B
1261	Wake of the Red Witch - Garland Roark	1.50	3.50	5.00	A
1262	The Walls of Jericho - Paul I. Wellman	1.50	3.50	5.00	
1263	Valley of Vanishing Men - Max Brand 1947	1.50	3.50	5.00	W
1264	Gambler's Gold - Peter Field	1.50	3.50	5.00	W
1265	Aurora Dawn - Herman Wouk	1.50	3.50	5.00	
1266	The Strumpet Wind - G. Merrick	1.50	3.50	5.00	
1267	Long Storm - Ernest Haycox	1.50	3.50	5.00	W
1268	Gentleman's Agreement - L. Z. Hobson	1.50	3.50	5.00	
1269	Final Curtain - Ngaio Marsh	2.00	4.00	7.50	M
1270	Death of a Doll - Hilda Lawrence	2.00	4.00	7.50	M
1271	The Boston Red Sox - F. G. Lieb	1.50	3.50	5.00	S
1272	9 Lives Before Thirty - M. Manus	1.50	3.50	5.00	
1273	Blood Brother - E. Arnold	1.50	3.50	5.00	
1274	This is the Story - D. L. Cohn	1.50	3.50	5.00	
1275	Shadow Range - C. Bishop 1947	1.50	3.50	5.00	
1276	So Long at the Fair - A. Thorne	1.50	3.50	5.00	
1277	Silver Spurs - M. Layton	1.50	3.50	5.00	
1278	Alaska: Land of Tomorrow - E. A. Herron	1.50	3.50	5.00	
1279	With Intent to Deceive - Manning Coles	1.50	3.50	5.00	
1280	The Sleeping Sphinx - John Dickson Carr	2.50	6.00	10.00	
1281	Mr. On Loong - Robert Standish	1.50	3.50	5.00	
1282	Go-devil - M. Eyssen	1.50	3.50	5.00	
1283	There Was Once a Slave - S. Graham	1.50	3.50	5.00	
1284	My Name is Christopher Nagel - C. W. Grafton	1.50	3.50	5.00	
1285	The Wild Yazoo - J. M. Myers	1.50	3.50	5.00	
1286	Jed Blaine's Woman - E. Wells	1.50	3.50	5.00	
1287	Within the Ropes - H. Rice 1947	1.50	3.50	5.00	
1288	Trail Dust - Bliss Lomax	1.50	3.50	5.00	W
1289	How Green was My Father - David Dodge	1.50	3.50	5.00	
1290	The Drifting Kid - Will Ermine	1.50	3.50	5.00	W
1291	Puzzle for Pilgrims - Patrick Quentin	2.00	4.00	7.50	M
1292	Ghost of a Chance - Roos Kelley	2.00	4.00	7.50	
1293	Think of Death - Richard & Frances Lockridge	2.00	4.00	7.50	M
1294	Valley of Wild Horses - Zane Grey	1.50	3.50	5.00	W
1295	Mrs. Mike - B. & N Freedman	1.50	3.50	5.00	
1296	Little Gate - A. Ewing	1.50	3.50	5.00	
1297	The Big Sky - A. B. Guthrie, Jr.	1.50	3.50	5.00	W
1298	Famous Stories of Code and Cipher - R. T. Bond	2.00	4.00	7.50	
1299	Hang and Rattle - A. R. Bosworth	1.50	3.50	5.00	
1300	Trail from Needle Rock - Peter Field	1.50	3.50	5.00	W
1301	Flannigan's Folly - G. Milburn	1.50	3.50		
1302	The Case of the Fan-Dancers Horse - Erle Stanley Gardner	2.00	4.00	7.50	M
1303	Blood Money - R. Bellamy	1.50	3.50	5.00	
1304	Master of the Mesa - William Colt MacDonald	1.50	3.50	5.00	W
1305	Tomorrow's a Holiday - A. Loveridge	1.50	3.50	5.00	
1306	Boston: Cradle of Liberty - John Jennings	1.50	3.50	5.00	
1307	Comrade Forest - M. Leigh	1.50	3.50	5.00	
1308	The Side of the Angels - R. McLaughlin	1.50	3.50	5.00	
1309	The Thresher - H. Krause	1.50	3.50	5.00	
1310	Vermilion - I. Jones	1.50	3.50	5.00	
1311	The False Rider - Max Brand 1947	1.50	3.50	5.00	W
1312	The Blue Horse of Taxco - Kathleen Moore Knight	1.50	3.50	5.00	
1313	Los Angeles Murders - Craig Rice	2.00	4.00	7.50	M
1314	Passing By - E. Merrick	1.50	3.50	5.00	
1315	On My Way Home - R. Phenix	1.50	3.50	5.00	
1316	Strikeout Story - B. Feller	1.50	3.50	5.00	S

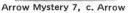

Arrow Mystery 7, c. Arrow   Astro 12, c. Astro   Atlas Mystery nn, c. MCG

(ARMED SERVICES EDITIONS, continued)

1317 The Harder They Fall - Budd Schulberg	1.50	3.50	5.00	
1318 Raw North - C. E. Gillham	1.50	3.50	5.00	
1319 The Story of Mrs. Murphy - N. A. Scott	1.50	3.50	5.00	
1320 The Moneyman - Thomas B. Costain	1.50	3.50	5.00	
1321 Prince of Foxes - Samuel Shellabarger	1.50	3.50	5.00	A
1322 Home Country - Ernie Pyle	1.50	3.50	5.00	

ARROW MYSTERY

(Arrow Publishers)

Digest size

5 Murder on High Heels - Richard Burke	2.00	4.00	6.00	M
6 Murder on Friday - Harriette Ashbrook aka The Purple Onion Mystery	2.00	4.00	6.00	M
7 Death Takes a Redhead - Anthony Gilbert 1944, aka Dear Dead Woman	2.00	4.00	6.00	M
8 The Kissed Corpse - Asa Baker (Brett Halliday)	2.00	4.00	6.00	M
9 Invitation to Murder - Manning Long aka False Alarm	2.00	4.00	6.00	M
10 Death Hides a Mask - M. E. Corne	2.00	4.00	6.00	M
11 Design for Murder - Frederic Arnold Kummer	2.00	4.00	6.00	M

ASTRO

(Astro Distributing Corporation)

Digest size

1 Part-Time Virgin - James Clayford	1.50	3.50	5.00	E
2 Week-end Girl - James Clayford	.75	1.75	3.00	E
10 Confessions of a Good-Time Girl - Ethel Owen	.75	1.75	3.00	E
12 Shakedown Dame - Dorothy Herzog 1948, aka Undercover Woman	1.50	3.50	5.00	E
14 Shameless Virgin - Peggy Gaddis 1948, aka One More Woman	.75	1.75	3.00	E

ATLAS MYSTERY

(Bard Publishing Corporation)

Digest size

nn The Singing Widow - Veronica Parker Johns 1945	1.50	3.50	5.00	M

ATLAS MYSTERY

(Cornell Publishing Corporation)

Digest size

nn Murder Goes to College - Kurt Steel   1.50   3.50   5.00   M
    1944

ATLAS MYSTERY

(Hercules Publishing Corporation)

Digest size

nn The Lisping Man - Frank Rawlings   1.50   3.50   5.00   M
    1944

ATLAS MYSTERY

(London Publishing Corporation)

Digest size

nn Rattle his Bones - Julian Shore   1.50   3.50   5.00   M
    1944

ATLAS MYSTERY

(Mohawk Publishing Corporation)

Digest size

nn Kill One, Kill Two - W. W. Anderson   1.50   3.50   5.00   M
    1944

ATLAS MYSTERY

(Select Publications, Inc.)

Digest size

nn The Golden Dress - Ione Montgomery   1.50   3.50   5.00   M
    1944

Atlas Mystery nn, c. MCG

Atlas Mystery nn, c. MCG

Atlas Mystery nn, c. MCG

Atlas Mystery nn, c. MCG   Atlas Mystery nn, c. MCG   Atlas Mystery nn, c. MCG

ATLAS MYSTERY

(Vital Publications, Inc./Current Detective Stories, Inc.)

Digest size

1 Looks that Kill! - Walter B. Gibson Orig., 1948	3.00	6.00	12.00	M
2 A Blonde for Murder - Walter B. Gibson Orig., 1948	3.00	6.00	12.00	M

ATLAS MYSTERY

(Zenith Publishing Corporation)

Digest size

nn Murder with Long Hair - H. Donald Spatz 1944	1.50	3.50	5.00	M

ATOMIC BOOKS

(Atomic Books, Inc.)

Digest size

nn The Case of the Golden Blonde - Maurice LeBlanc 1946, Sherlock Holmes pastiche	7.50	15.00	30.00	M

AVON

(Avon Book Company/New Avon Library/Avon Publishing Co., Inc./Avon Publications, Inc./Avon Book Division - Hearst Corporation)

nn(1) Elmer Gentry - Sinclair Lewis 1941	15.00	35.00	60.00	
nn(2) The Rubiyat of Omar Khayam - Edward Fitzgerald	7.50	15.00	30.00	
nn(3) The Big Four - Agatha Christie	10.00	25.00	40.00	M
nn(4) Ill Wind - James Hilton	5.00	10.00	20.00	
nn(5) Dr. Priestly Investigates - John Rhode	7.50	15.00	30.00	M
nn(6) The Haunted Hotel and 25 other Ghost				

Atlas Mystery nn, c. MCG   Atomic Books nn, c. Atomic   Avon 1, c. Avon

(AVON, continued)

	Stories - Wilkie Collins (ed. W. Bob Holland)	7.50	15.00	30.00	M/HO
nn(7)	The Plague Court Murders - Carter Dickson	7.50	15.00	30.00	M
nn(8)	The Corpse in the Green Pajamas - R. A. J. Walling	7.50	15.00	30.00	M
nn(9)	Willful and Premeditated - Freeman Wills Crofts	4.00	8.00	15.00	M
nn(10)	Dr. Thorndyke's Discovery - R. Austin Freeman	7.50	15.00	30.00	M
nn(11)	Count Bruga - Ben Hecht	4.00	8.00	15.00	M
nn(12)	Mosquitoes - William Faulkner	7.50	15.00	30.00	
nn(13)	Mystery at Spanish Hacienda - Jackson Gregory	5.00	10.00	20.00	M
	1942				
nn(14)	Call Her Savage - Tiffany Thayer	7.50	15.00	30.00	E
nn(15)	The Avon Book of Modern Short Stories - aka My Best Story	5.00	10.00	20.00	
nn(16)	Murder at Midnight - R. A. J. Walling	7.50	15.00	30.00	M
nn(17)	The Agony Column - Earl Derr Biggers	7.50	15.00	30.00	M
nn(18)	The Man Who Murdered Himself - Geoffrey Holmes	7.50	15.00	30.00	M
nn(19)	48 Saroyan Stories - William Saroyan	5.00	10.00	20.00	
nn(20)	The League of Frightened Men - Rex Stout	7.50	15.00	30.00	M
nn(21)	The Avon Book of Detective and Crime Stories - John Rhode aka Line Up	7.50	15.00	30.00	M
nn(22)	The Red Headed Woman - Katharine Brush	7.50	15.00	30.00	
nn(23)	Suspicious Characters - Dorothy L. Sayers	7.50	15.00	30.00	M
	1943				
nn(24)	Ashenden, or the British Agent - W. Somerset Maugham	7.50	15.00	30.00	M
nn(25)	Trumpet in the Dust - Gene Fowler	5.00	10.00	20.00	
nn(26)	Seven Footprints to Satan - A. A. Merritt	10.00	25.00	40.00	SF
nn(27)	The Avon Book of Puzzles	10.00	25.00	40.00	NF
nn(28)	Tonight at 8:30 - Noel Coward	5.00	10.00	20.00	
nn(29)	The Sabotage Murder Mystery - Margery Allingham	5.00	10.00	20.00	M
nn(30)	Gorgeous Ghoul Murder Case - Dwight V. Babcock	5.00	10.00	20.00	M

Avon 3, c. Avon   Avon 14, c. Avon   Avon 26, c. Avon

Avon 29, c. Avon   Avon 38, c. Avon   Avon 43, c. Avon

(AVON, continued)

nn(31)	Doctor's Son - John O'Hara	5.00	10.00	20.00	
nn(32)	Stage Door Canteen - Delmer Daves Movie tie-in	7.50	15.00	30.00	C
nn(33)	Corpse in the Waxworks - John Dickson Carr	7.50	15.00	30.00	M
nn(34)	The Saint Goes On - Leslie Charteris	7.50	15.00	30.00	M
nn(35)	Poison for One - John Rhode	7.50	15.00	30.00	M
nn(36)	The Avon Book of Great Mystery Stories				M
	Note: This book apparently does not exist. It was later released as no. 86 in the series.				
nn(37)	Coffin for One - Francis Beeding	5.00	10.00	20.00	M
nn(38)	The Big Sleep - Raymond Chandler	10.00	25.00	40.00	M
nn(39)	Rage in Heaven - James Hilton	4.00	8.00	15.00	
nn(40)	In the Teeth of the Evidence - Dorothy L. Sayers	5.00	10.00	20.00	M
41	The Narrow Corner - W. Somerset Maugham 1944	4.00	8.00	15.00	
42	The Passionate Year - James Hilton	4.00	8.00	15.00	
43	Burn Witch Burn - A. A. Merritt	10.00	25.00	40.00	SF
44	The Saint in New York - Leslie Charteris	5.00	10.00	20.00	M
45	Germany - Past, Present and Future - Lord Vansittart	5.00	10.00	20.00	NF
46	Death on the Nile - Agatha Christie	5.00	10.00	20.00	M
47	Shoe the Wild Mare - Gene Fowler	3.00	6.00	12.00	
48	The Road to Victory - Cardinal Francis J. Spellman	3.00	6.00	12.00	
49	The London Spy Murders - Peter Cheyney aka The Stars are Dark	4.00	8.00	15.00	M
50	Cakes and Ale - W. Somerset Maugham	3.00	6.00	12.00	
51	Nobody's in Town - Edna Ferber	3.00	6.00	12.00	
52	The Man Who Had Everything - Louis Bromfield	3.00	6.00	12.00	
53	Mystery of the Red Triangle - W. C. Tuttle	4.00	8.00	15.00	W
54	See What I Mean? - Lewis Browne	4.00	8.00	15.00	C
55	Presenting Lily Mars - Booth Tarkington	3.00	6.00	12.00	
56	Theatre - W. Somerset Maugham	3.00	6.00	12.00	
57	The Hills Beyond - Thomas Wolfe	3.00	6.00	12.00	
58	Winged Victory - Moss Hart	3.00	6.00	12.00	C
59	Heaven's My Destination - Thornton Wilder 1945	3.00	6.00	12.00	
60	Double Indemnity - James M. Cain	4.00	8.00	15.00	M

Avon 49, c. Avon   Avon 53, c. Avon   Avon 54, c. Avon

Avon 68, c. Avon

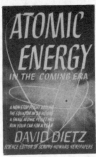

Avon 76, c. Avon

Avon 82, c. Avon

(AVON, continued)

61	Murder in Three Acts - Agatha Christie	4.00	8.00	15.00	M
62	Over My Dead Body - Rex Stout	4.00	8.00	15.00	M
63	Five Murderers - Raymond Chandler	7.50	15.00	30.00	M
64	Back Stage - Vicki Baum	4.00	8.00	15.00	
65	Now I'll Tell One - Harry Hershfield	4.00	8.00	15.00	H
66	Little Caesar - W. R. Burnett	7.50	15.00	30.00	M
	Note: Same cover as the comic Famous Gangsters no. 3				
67	Action This Day - Bishop Francis J. Spellman	3.00	6.00	12.00	
68	A Homicide for Hannah - Dwight V. Babcock	4.00	8.00	15.00	M
69	The Stray Lamb - Thorne Smith	4.00	8.00	15.00	H
70	Poirot Loses a Client - Agatha Christie	4.00	8.00	15.00	M
71	The Saint Intervenes - Leslie Charteris	4.00	8.00	15.00	M
72	The Avon Story Teller	4.00	8.00	15.00	
	Orig., 1945				
	Note: Includes Merritt, Chandler, Others				
73	A Goodly Heritage - Mary Ellen Chase	3.00	6.00	12.00	
74	The Ghost Patrol and Other Stories - Sinclair Lewis	3.00	6.00	12.00	
75	The Mysterious Affair at Styles - Agatha Christie	4.00	8.00	15.00	M
76	Atomic Energy in the Coming Era - David Dietz	4.00	8.00	15.00	NF
77	The Long Valley - John Steinbeck	4.00	8.00	15.00	
78	To Step Aside - Noel Coward	3.00	6.00	12.00	
	1946				
79	Catherine Herself - James Hilton	3.00	6.00	12.00	
80	You Can't Keep the Change - Peter Cheyney	4.00	8.00	15.00	M
81	Bad Girl - Vina Delmar	3.00	6.00	12.00	E
82	The Red Box - Rex Stout	3.00	6.00	12.00	M
83	Sight Unseen and the Confession - Mary Roberts	3.00	6.00	12.00	
84	Mistress Wilding - Rafael Sabatini	4.00	8.00	15.00	A
	Note: Same cover as Modern Short Story Monthly no 36.				
85	The Regatta Mystery - Agatha Christie	4.00	8.00	15.00	M
86	Avon Mystery Story Teller - anthology	3.00	6.00	12.00	M
	Note: Includes Irish, Wallace, Carr. Christie				
87	The Private Affairs of Bel Ami - Guy de				

Avon 89, c. Avon

Avon 90, c. Avon

Avon 98, c. Avon

Avon 106, c. Avon	Avon 108, c. Avon	Avon 110, c. Avon

(AVON, continued)

		3.00	6.00	12.00	
	Maupassant Movie tie-in				
88	Five Sinister Characters - Raymond Chandler	7.50	15.00	30.00	M
89	Death in the Air - Agatha Christie	4.00	8.00	15.00	M
90	Avon Ghost Reader - ed. Herbert Williams	7.50	15.00	30.00	SF
	Note: Includes Merritt, Lovecraft, Derleth, Stoker.				
91	The French Key Mystery - Frank Gruber	3.00	6.00	12.00	M
92	Loose Ladies - Vina Delmar	3.00	6.00	12.00	E
93	The Dark Street Murders - Peter Cheyney	3.00	6.00	12.00	M
94	Butterfield 8 - John O'Hara	3.00	6.00	12.00	
95	Black Orchids - Rex Stout	4.00	8.00	15.00	M
96	Black Angel - Cornell Wodrich	4.00	8.00	15.00	M
97	Wedding Ring - Beth Brown	3.00	6.00	12.00	R
98	The Virgin and the Gypsy - D. H. Lawrence	4.00	8.00	15.00	E
99	The Embezzler - James M. Cain	3.00	6.00	12.00	
100	The Secret Adversary - Agatha Christie	4.00	8.00	15.00	M
101	Avon Improved Cook Book - Pearl V. Metzelthin	5.00	10.00	20.00	
102	The Three Wise Guys and Other Stories - Damon Runyon	4.00	8.00	15.00	
103	Where There's a Will - Rex Stout	4.00	8.00	15.00	M
104	If I Should Die Before I Wake - William Irish	4.00	8.00	15.00	M
	Note: Same cover as Murder Mystery Monthly No. 13 and Avon Detective Mystery no. 2.				
105	Lady Ann - Donald Henderson Clarke	3.00	6.00	12.00	E
	Note: Same cover as Avon no. 78.				
106	The Black Path of Fear - Cornell Woolrich	4.00	8.00	15.00	M
107	The Marriage Racket - Vina Delmar	3.00	6.00	12.00	
108	A Taste for Honey - H. F. Heard	4.00	8.00	15.00	M
109	Avon Bedside Companion	3.00	6.00	12.00	
	1947				
110	Terror at Night	7.50	15.00	30.00	SF
111	The Imperial Orgy - Edgar Saltus	4.00	8.00	15.00	E
112	The Squealer - Edgar Wallace	4.00	8.00	15.00	M
	Note: Same cover as Avon no. 17.				

Avon 112, c. Avon	Avon 114, c. Avon	Avon 117, c. Avon

Avon 118, c. Avon

Avon 119, c. Avon

Avon 123, c. Avon

(AVON, continued)

113	Aphrodite - Pierre Louys	4.00	8.00	15.00	E
114	Sinister Errand - Peter Cheyney	4.00	8.00	15.00	M
	Note: Same cover as the comic Parole Breakers no. 2.				
115	The Avon Book of W. Somerset Maugham	3.00	6.00	12.00	
116	Kelly - Donald Henderson	3.00	6.00	12.00	E
117	Creep Shadow Creep - A. A. Merritt	10.00	25.00	40.00	SF
118	The Saint in Action - Leslie Charteris	4.00	8.00	15.00	M
	aka The Ace of Knaves				
	Note: Same cover as the comic Saint no. 7.				
119	The Better Taylors - Richard Taylor	4.00	8.00	15.00	
120	Alabam - Donald Henderson Clarke	3.00	6.00	12.00	E
121	Kept Woman - Vina Delmar	3.00	6.00	12.00	E R
122	Unconscious Witness - R. Austin Freeman	4.00	8.00	15.00	M
	Note: Same cover as the pulp magazine Private Detective Stories October, 1944, and Avon Detective Mysteries no. 3.				
123	The Case of the Dark Hero - Peter Cheyney	4.00	9.00	15.00	A
	Note: Same cover as the comic Saint no. 12.				
124	Holiday for Murder - Agatha Christie	4.00	8.00	15.00	M
125	The Door with Seven Locks - Edgar Wallace	4.00	8.00	15.00	M
126	Cold Blooded Murder - Freeman Wills Crofts	4.00	8.00	15.00	M
127	Eastern Shame Girl	10.00	25.00	40.00	E
128	Ten Nights of Love	4.00	8.00	15.00	E
129	The Gentleman in the Parlour - W. Somerset Maugham	3.00	6.00	12.00	
130	The Saint Goes West - Leslie Charteris 1948	4.00	8.00	15.00	M
131	Death Takes a Bow - Frances & Richard Lockridge	4.00	8.00	15.00	M
132	14 Great Short Stories from the Long Valley - John Steinbeck	3.00	6.00	12.00	
133	Naughty 90's Joke Book - Harold Meyers	4.00	8.00	15.00	H
134	Georgia Boy - Erskine Caldwell	3.00	6.00	12.00	E
135	The Woman and the Puppet - Pierre Louys	3.00	6.00	12.00	E
136	The Lurking Fear - H. P. Lovecraft	10.00	25.00	40.00	SF
137	Double Indemnity - James M. Cain	3.00	6.00	12.00	M
138	The Hard-Boiled Virgin - Jack Woodford	3.00	6.00	12.00	E
	aka Lady Killer				

Avon 126, c. Avon

Avon 127, c. Avon

Avon 136, c. Avon

Avon 144, c. Avon

Avon 159, c. Avon

Avon 160, c. Avon

(AVON, continued)

139 Liza of Lambeth - W. Somerset Maugham	3.00	6.00	12.00	E
140 In Bed We Cry - Ilka Chase	3.00	6.00	12.00	
141 Career in C Major - James M. Cain	3.00	6.00	12.00	
142 Killing the Goose - Frances & Richard Lockridge 1948	4.00	8.00	15.00	M
143 Casey - Hard Boiled Detective - George Harmon Coxe	4.00	8.00	15.00	M
144 Hope of Heaven - John O'Hara	3.00	6.00	12.00	E
145 The Restless Passion - Vina Delmar aka Women Live too Long	3.00	6.00	12.00	E
146 The Abortive Hussy - Jack Woodford	3.00	6.00	12.00	E
147 The Avenging Saint - Leslie Charteris	4.00	8.00	15.00	M
148 Love, Health, and Marriage - John Cowan & Arthur Rose Guerard	4.00	8.00	15.00	NF
149 John Bartel Jr. - Donald Henderson Clarke	3.00	6.00	12.00	E
150 A Love Episode - Emile Zola	4.00	8.00	12.00	E
151 Where the Girls Were Different - Erskine Caldwell	4.00	8.00	12.00	E
Note: Same cover as the comic Campus Romances no. 2.				
152 Georgie May - Maxwell Bodenheim	3.00	6.00	12.00	E
153 Valley Vixen - Ben Ames Williams aka Hostile Valley	3.00	6.00	12.00	E
154 When She Was Bad... - Katherine Brush aka You Go Your Way	3.00	6.00	12.00	E
155 The Unfaithful Lady - Charles Pettit	4.00	8.00	15.00	E
156 Pardners of the Badlands - Bliss Lomax	3.00	6.00	12.00	W
157 Yesterday's Love - James T. Farrell	3.00	6.00	12.00	
158 Now I'll Tell One - Harry Hershfield	4.00	8.00	15.00	H
159 This is Murder, Mr. Herbert - Day Keene First ed., 1948	4.00	8.00	15.00	M
160 Casanova's Homecoming - Arthur Schnitzler	3.00	6.00	12.00	E
161 Love's Lovely Counterfeit - James M. Cain	3.00	6.00	12.00	
162 The Avon Book of Complete Crosswords and Cryptograms - Clark Kinnaird	5.00	10.00	20.00	NF
163 Love in the Latin Quarter - Henri Murger	3.00	6.00	12.00	E
164 The Moving Finger - Agatha Christie	4.00	8.00	15.00	M
165 The Stone of Chastity - Margery Sharp	4.00	8.00	15.00	F
Note: Same cover as the comic Women to Love				

Avon 175, c. Avon

Avon 179, c. Avon

Avon 183, c. Avon

Avon 184, c. Avon

Avon 186, c. Avon

Avon 189, c. Avon

(AVON, continued)

166	Psyche - Pierre Louys	3.00	6.00	12.00	E
167	Piping Hot - Emile Zola	4.00	8.00	15.00	E
168	A Virtuous Girl - Maxwell Bodenheim	3.00	6.00	12.00	E
169	The Amboy Dukes - Irving Shulman	4.00	8.00	15.00	E
	Note: Three cover variations exist on this number.				
170	Bronc Buckaroo - J. Edward Leithead	3.00	6.00	12.00	W
171	Amorous Philandre - Jean-Gall: De Bibiena	4.00	8.00	15.00	F
172	Bubu of Montparnasse - Charles-Louis Philippe	4.00	8.00	15.00	E
173	On the Spot - Edgar Wallace	4.00	8.00	15.00	
174	Sinful Woman - James M. Cain	3.00	6.00	12.00	
175	A Woman's Heart - Guy De Maupassant	3.00	6.00	12.00	E
176	Whose Body? - Dorothy L. Sayers	4.00	8.00	15.00	M
177	Midsummer Passion - Erskine Caldwell	3.00	6.00	12.00	E
178	Fast One - Paul Cain	4.00	8.00	15.00	M
179	Blondie Iscariot - Edgar Lustgarten	4.00	8.00	15.00	E
	Note: Same cover as the comic Prison Break no. 3.				
180	French Summer - Guy Gilpatric	3.00	6.00	12.00	E
181	Her Private Passions - Marty Holland	3.00	6.00	12.00	E
	aka The Glass Heart				
182	New Avon Bedside Companion 1949	3.00	6.00	12.00	
183	Burial of the Fruit - David Dortort	4.00	8.00	15.00	E
184	The Girl with the Hungry Eyes - ed. Don Wollheim	10.00	25.00	40.00	SF
	First ed., 1949				
185	Never Come Morning - Nelson Algren	4.00	8.00	15.00	E
186	Night Cry - William L. Stuart	4.00	8.00	15.00	M
187	Love Trap - Vina Delmar	4.00	8.00	15.00	E
188	Fools and their Folly - W. Somerset Maugham	3.00	6.00	12.00	
	aka Then and Now				
189	The Daughter of Fu Manchu - Sax Rohmer	15.00	35.00	60.00	M
190	The Life and Loves of a Modern Mr. Bluebeard - Ward Greene	4.00	8.00	15.00	E
	aka Ride the Nightmare				
191	Replenishing Jessica - Maxwell Bodenheim	3.00	6.00	12.00	E
192	Young Man of Manhattan - Katharine Brush	3.00	6.00	12.00	

Avon 190, c. Avon

Avon 195, c. Avon

Avon 207, c. Avon

Avon 208, c. Avon

Avon 211, c. Avon

Avon 212, c. Avon

(AVON, continued)

193 The Impatient Virgin - Donald Henderson Clarke	4.00	8.00	15.00	E
194 Avon Book of New Stories of the Great Wild West - Don Wollheim	4.00	8.00	15.00	W
195 Out of the Silent Planet - C. S. Lewis	10.00	25.00	40.00	SF
196 Memory of Love - Bessie Breuer	3.00	6.00	12.00	
197 The Son of the Grand Eunuch - Charles Pettit	4.00	8.00	15.00	E
198 Yvette and Other Stories - Guy de Maupassant	3.00	6.00	12.00	
199 The Miller and the Mayor's Wife - Pedro DeAlarcon	3.00	6.00	12.00	E
200 Your Most Intimate Problems - Lawrence Gould	3.00	6.00	12.00	NF
201 Strange Desires - Len Zinberg	4.00	8.00	15.00	E
aka What D'ya Know for Sure				
Note: Same cover as the comic Campus Romances no. 3.				
202 From Gags to Riches - Joey Adams	4.00	8.00	15.00	H
203 Quartet - W. Somerset Maugham	4.00	8.00	15.00	
204 Portrait of a Man with Red Hair - Hugh Walpole	4.00	8.00	15.00	HO
205 The Last Frontier - Howard Fast	3.00	6.00	12.00	W
206 The Palace of Pleasure - Jacques-Rochette de la Morliere	3.00	6.00	12.00	E
207 Virgie, Goodbye - Nathan Rothman	4.00	8.00	15.00	E
Note: Same cover as the comic Romantic Love no. 6.				
208 The Devil Thumbs a Ride - Robert C. Du Soe	4.00	8.00	15.00	E
209 New Orleans Lady - Vina Delmar	3.00	6.00	12.00	
210 Wicked Sister - Helen Topping Miller	3.00	6.00	12.00	E
211 Scarf of Passion - Robert Bloch	6.00	15.00	25.00	HO
Note: Same cover as Avon Monthly Novel no. 9.				
212 Iron Man - W. R. Burnett	6.00	15.00	25.00	
Note: Same cover as the comic Romantic Love no. 10.				
213 Nina - Donald Henderson Clarke	3.00	6.00	12.00	E
214 The Fox Woman and Other Stories - A. A. Merritt	10.00	25.00	40.00	SF
First ed., 1949				

Avon 214, c. Avon

Avon 216, c. Avon

Avon 219, c. Avon

Avon 220, c. Avon	Avon 222, c. Avon	Avon 230, c. Avon

(AVON, continued)

215	All the Brothers were Valiant - Ben Ames Williams	3.00	6.00	12.00	
216	Gladiator - Philip Wylie	10.00	25.00	40.00	SF
217	Miss Jill from Shanghai - Emily Hahn	3.00	6.00	12.00	E
218	Anyone Can Win at Gin Rummy and Canasta - Alfred Drake	3.00	6.00	12.00	NF
219	Finger Man - Raymond Chandler	5.00	10.00	20.00	M
220	I Married a Dead Man - William Irish	4.00	8.00	15.00	M
221	Don Juan - Ludwig Lewisohn	3.00	6.00	12.00	E
222	Neon Wilderness - Nelson Algren	7.50	15.00	30.00	
	Note: Same cover as the comic Intimate Confessions no. 1.				
223	Three Loves Had Margaret - James Hilton	3.00	6.00	12.00	
224	Port Afrique - Bernard Victor Dryer	3.00	6.00	12.00	E
225	Anyone Can Have a Great Vocabulary - J. L. Stephenson	3.00	6.00	12.00	NF
226	I Can Get it for You Wholesale! - Jerome Weidman	3.00	6.00	12.00	
227	Just What the Doctor Ordered - Dr. Anthony Bassler	3.00	6.00	12.00	NF
228	Gilbert and Sullivan Operas - William Schwenck Gilbert & Arthur Sullivan 1950	3.00	6.00	12.00	
229	All About Girls	4.00	8.00	15.00	H
230	The Big Fights - Harold Meyers Orig., 1950	4.00	8.00	15.00	S
231	Butterfield 8 - John O'Hara	3.00	6.00	12.00	
232	Alabam - Donald Henderson Clarke	2.00	4.00	7.50	E
233	The Servant - Robin Maugham	3.00	6.00	12.00	E
234	The Old Goat - Tiffany Thayer	2.00	4.00	7.50	E
235	Seven Footprints to Satan - A. A. Merritt	10.00	25.00	40.00	SF
236	Venus of the Counting House - Emile Zola	4.00	8.00	15.00	E
237	Tawny - Donald Henderson Clarke	3.00	6.00	12.00	E
238	The First Lady Chatterley - D. H. Lawrence	3.00	6.00	12.00	E
239	Bad Girl from Maine - Katharine Brush	3.00	6.00	12.00	
240	End as a Man - Calder Willingham	3.00	6.00	12.00	
241	What's in if for Me? - Jerome Weidman	3.00	6.00	12.00	E
242	The Case of the Untidy Murder - Frances & Richard Lockridge	4.00	8.00	15.00	M

Avon 235, c. Avon	Avon 242, c. Avon	Avon 245, c. Avon

Avon 250, c. Avon   Avon 255, c. Avon   Avon 256, c. Avon

(AVON, continued)

243	Mysterious Mickey Finn - Elliot Paul	4.00	8.00	15.00	M
244	Cry Tough! - Irving Shulman	3.00	6.00	12.00	E
245	The Big Four - Agatha Christie	7.50	15.00	30.00	M
246	A Shropshire Lad - Housman	3.00	6.00	12.00	
247	The Midsummer Fires - James Aswell	3.00	6.00	12.00	E
248	Love Among the Haystacks - D. H. Lawrence	3.00	6.00	12.00	E
249	It Happens Every Spring - Valentine Davies	3.00	6.00	12.00	F
250	Carlotta - Robert Briffault aka Fandango Note: Same cover as the comic Intimate Confessions no. 3.	4.00	8.00	15.00	E
251	Sonnets from the Portuguese - Elizabeth Barrett Browning	3.00	6.00	12.00	
252	A Hell of a Good Time - James T. Farrell Note: Same cover as the comic Romantic Love no. 1.	3.00	6.00	12.00	
253	Confidential - Donald Henderson Clarke	3.00	6.00	12.00	E
254	Flame Vine - Helen Topping Miller	3.00	6.00	12.00	E
255	Tropical Passions - anthology	4.00	8.00	15.00	E
256	The Case of the Black Orchids - Rex Stout	5.00	10.00	20.00	M
257	Aphrodite - Pierre Louys	4.00	8.00	15.00	E
258	Hope of Heaven - John O'Hara	3.00	6.00	12.00	E
259	For a Night of Love - Emile Zola	3.00	6.00	12.00	E
260	Yesterday's Love - James T. Farrell	3.00	6.00	12.00	E
261	Avon Improved Cook Book - P. V. Metzelthin	5.00	10.00	20.00	NF
262	The Rubiyat of Omar Khayam - Edward Fitzgerald	4.00	8.00	15.00	
263	The Gangs of New York - Herbert Asbury	4.00	8.00	15.00	NF
264	Six Deadly Dames - Frederick Nebel First ed., 1950	5.00	10.00	20.00	M
265	Mortgage on Life - Vicki Baum	3.00	6.00	12.00	E
266	Death in the Deep South - Ward Greene	5.00	10.00	20.00	E
267	A Bullet for Billy the Kid - Nelson Nye	3.00	6.00	12.00	W
268	Seven Slayers - Paul Cain	3.00	6.00	12.00	M
269	Jadie Greenway - I.S. Young	3.00	6.00	12.00	E
270	The Chastity of Gloria Boyd - Donald Henderson Clarke	3.00	6.00	12.00	E
271	Nana's Mother - Emile Zola	2.50	6.00	10.00	E

Avon 264, c. Avon   Avon 265, c. Avon   Avon 266, c. Avon

Avon 268, c. Avon   Avon 272, c. Avon   Avon 272, c. Avon

(AVON, continued)

272	Europa - Robert Briffault			
	Girl by map	4.00	8.00	15.00	
	Girl in bondage	7.50	15.00	30.00	
	Note: Two cover variants noted.				
273	Imperial City - Elmer Rice	3.00	6.00	12.00	E
274	T as in Trapped - Lawrence Treat	3.00	6.00	12.00	M
275	My Bride in the Storm - Theodore Pratt	3.00	6.00	12.00	E
276	Madwoman? - Emily Harvin	5.00	10.00	20.00	
277	Perelandra - C. S. Lewis	7.50	15.00	30.00	SF
278	A Killer is Loose Among Us - Robert Terrall	4.00	8.00	15.00	M
279	The Price is Right - Jerome Weidman	3.00	6.00	12.00	E
280	Dangerous Love - Jack Woodford	5.00	10.00	20.00	E
	aka Temptress				
281	Into Plutonian Depths - Stanton A. Coblentz	10.00	25.00	40.00	SF
282	Lovely Lady, Pity Me - Roy Huggins	4.00	8.00	15.00	M
283	She Posed for Death - Russell Gordon	4.00	8.00	15.00	M
	aka Dead Level				
	Note: Same cover as the comic Parole				
	Breakers no. 1.				
284	Madam is Dead - Robert Terrell	4.00	8.00	15.00	M
	1951				
285	An Earthman on Venus - Ralph Milne Farley	15.00	35.00	60.00	SF
	aka The Radio Man				
286	Kept Woman - Vina Delmar	3.00	6.00	12.00	E
287	How to Play Samba Canasta - Richard L. Frey	3.00	6.00	12.00	NF
	1951				
288	Front for Murder - Guy Emery	3.00	6.00	12.00	M
289	Friday for Death - Lawrence Lariar	3.00	6.00	12.00	M
	Note: Same cover as the comic The Saint				
	no. 10.				
290	Gas-House McGinty - James T. Farrell	3.00	6.00	12.00	
291	Call Her Savage - Tiffany Thayer	4.00	8.00	15.00	E
292	Four Boys, a Girl and a Gun - Willard Wiener	4.00	8.00	15.00	JD
	aka Four Boys and a Gun				
	Note: Same cover as the comic Gangsters and				
	Gun Molls no. 1.				
293	Hellbox - John O'Hara	3.00	6.00	12.00	
294	Sappho - Alphonse Daudet	4.00	8.00	15.00	

Avon 277, c. Avon   Avon 281, c. Avon   Avon 285, c. Avon

Avon 300, c. Avon

Avon 308, c. Avon

Avon 314, c. Avon

(AVON, continued)

295	Avon Book of Puzzles for Everybody - John Paul Adams	5.00	10.00	20.00	NF
296	A Modern Lover - D. H. Lawrence	3.00	6.00	12.00	E
297	Untamed Darling - Jack Woodford aka Iris	4.00	8.00	15.00	IE
298	House of Fury - Felice Swados	15.00	35.00	60.00	E
	Note: Later titled Reform School Girl and adapted into a very rare and popular comic book of the same name.				
299	The Round-up - Oscar J. Friend	3.00	6.00	12.00	W
300	The Amboy Dukes - Irving Shulman	4.00	8.00	15.00	E
	Note: Two cover variants exist of this number.				
301	We Are Not Alone - James Hilton	3.00	6.00	12.00	
302	Perversity - Francis Carco	4.00	8.00	15.00	E
303	Dream Street - Robert Sylvester	3.00	6.00	12.00	E
304	Song Without Sermon - James Woolf	4.00	8.00	15.00	
	Note: Same cover as the comic Intimate Confessions no. 4.				
305	God Wears a Bow Tie - Lyle Stuart	5.00	10.00	20.00	E
306	Gone to Texas - John W. Thomason, Jr.	3.00	6.00	12.00	W
307	Big League Baseball	5.00	10.00	20.00	S
308	Musk, Hashish, and Blood - Hector France	7.50	15.00	30.00	E
309	Midsummer Passion - Erskine Caldwell	4.00	8.00	15.00	E
310	Bubu of Montparnasse - Charles-Louis Phillippe	4.00	8.00	15.00	E
311	The Saturday Evening Post Western Stories - ed. Barthold Fles	4.00	8.00	15.00	W
312	The Mysterious Affair at Styles - Agatha Christie	4.00	8.00	15.00	M
313	The Ugly Duchess - Lion Feuchtwanger	4.00	8.00	15.00	E
314	Nigger Heaven - Carl Van Vechten	10.00	25.00	40.00	E
315	The Metal Monster - A. A. Merritt	10.00	25.00	40.00	SF
316	Murder in Three Acts - Agatha Christie	4.00	8.00	15.00	M
317	Death on the Nile - Agatha Christie	5.00	10.00	20.00	M
318	Dear Sir - Juliet Lowell	4.00	8.00	15.00	H
319	Along the Broadway Beat - Louis Sobol	4.00	8.00	15.00	E
320	Gorgeous Ghoul Murder Case - Dwight V. Babcock	5.00	10.00	20.00	M

Avon 315, c. Avon

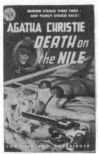

Avon 317, c. Avon

Avon 320, c. Avon

Avon 324, c. Avon   Avon 329, c. Avon   Avon 339, c. Avon

(AVON, continued)

321	The Saint in New York - Leslie Charteris	4.00	8.00	15.00	M
322	Slipping Beauty - Jerome Weidman aka The Horse that could Whistle 'Dixie'	4.00	8.00	15.00	E
323	The Furies in her Body - Guy Endore aka Methinks the Lady	4.00	8.00	15.00	F
324	The Ship of Ishtar - A. A. Merritt	10.00	27.50	45.00	SF
325	Ill Wind - James Hilton	3.00	6.00	12.00	
326	Burial of the Fruit - David Dortort	4.00	8.00	15.00	E
327	One Man Show - Tiffany Thayer	5.00	10.00	20.00	F
328	Strong Poison - Dorothy L. Sayers	4.00	8.00	15.00	M
329	Little Caesar - W. R. Burnett	5.00	10.00	20.00	M
	Note: Same cover as the comic Police Line- Up no. 2.				
330	Desperate Men - James D. Horan	4.00	8.00	15.00	NF
331	Trio - W. Somerset Maugham	3.00	6.00	12.00	
332	A Homicide for Hannah - Dwight V. Babcock	4.00	8.00	15.00	M
333	Line on Ginger - Robin Maugham	5.00	10.00	20.00	E
334	Red Bone Woman - Carlyle Tillery	4.00	8.00	15.00	E
335	In the Teeth of the Evidence - Dorothy L. Sayers	4.00	8.00	15.00	M
336	The Housekeeper's Daughter - Donald Henderson Clarke	3.00	6.00	12.00	E
337	The Agony Column - Earl Derr Biggers	4.00	8.00	15.00	M
338	Hollywood Bedside Reader	4.00	8.00	15.00	
339	The Terror of the Leopard Men - Juba Kennerley	10.00	25.00	40.00	NF
	First American ed., 1951				
340	Midsumer Passion - Erskine Caldwell	4.00	8.00	15.00	E
341	The Saint Sees it Through - Leslie Charteris	4.00	8.00	15.00	M
342	The Woman Aroused - Ed Lacy	5.00	10.00	20.00	E
343	Six-Gun Melody - William Colt MacDonald	3.00	6.00	12.00	W
344	The Chinese Parrot - Earl Derr Biggers	7.50	15.00	30.00	M
345	I Lost My Girlish Laughter - Jane Allen	3.00	6.00	12.00	E
346	Possess Me Not - Fan Nichols	7.50	15.00	30.00	E
347	The Saint at the Thieves' Picnic - Leslie Charteris	4.00	8.00	15.00	M
348	Jealous Woman - James M. Cain	4.00	8.00	15.00	M
	Note: Same cover as the comic Campus Romance no. 1.				

Avon 342, c. Avon   Avon 344, c. Avon   Avon 346, c. Avon

Avon 354, c. Avon   Avon 355, c. Avon   Avon 362, c. Avon

(AVON, continued)

349	Mistress Murder - Peter Cheyney	4.00	8.00	15.00	M
350	Charlie Chan Carries On - Earl Derr Biggers	7.50	15.00	30.00	M
351	Millie's Daughter - Donald Henderson Clarke	3.00	6.00	12.00	E
352	Ninth Avenue - Maxwell Bodenheim	4.00	8.00	15.00	E
353	Poirot Loses a Client - Agatha Christie	4.00	8.00	15.00	M
354	The Werewolf of Paris - Guy Endore	6.00	12.00	25.00	HO
355	No Orchids for Miss Blandish - James Hadley Chase	4.00	8.00	15.00	M
356	I Can Get If for You Wholesale! - Jerome Weidman Movie tie-in	4.00	8.00	15.00	E
357	All About Girls	4.00	8.00	15.00	H
358	Woman and the Puppett - Pierre Louys	3.00	6.00	12.00	E
359	Can Can Americana - Harold Meyers First ed., 1951	5.00	10.00	20.00	NF
360	As They Reveled - Philip Wylie Note: Same cover as the comic Realistic Romance no. 7.	4.00	8.00	15.00	E
361	Does not exist				
362	Calamity Jane of Deadwood Gulch - Ethel Hueston	4.00	8.00	15.00	W
363	Murder is Served - Frances & Richard Lockridge	4.00	8.00	15.00	M
364	The Point of Honour - W. Somerset Maugham	3.00	6.00	12.00	
365	The Impatient Virgin - Donald Henderson Clarke	5.00	10.00	20.00	E
366	They'll Do It Every Time - Jimmy Hatlo	4.00	8.00	15.00	H
367	Outlaw Guns - E. E. Halleran	3.00	6.00	12.00	W
368	All the Girls he Wanted - John O'Hara	3.00	6.00	12.00	
369	The Dishonest Murderer - Francis & Richard Lockridge	4.00	8.00	15.00	M
370	The Moon Pool - A. A. Merritt	10.00	25.00	40.00	SF
371	The Regatta Mystery - Agatha Christie	4.00	8.00	15.00	M
372	Cry Tough! - Irving Shulman	4.00	8.00	15.00	E
373	The Blue Negro - Robert Payne	7.50	15.00	30.00	E
374	Gun Fight at Horsethief Range - B. M. Bower	3.00	6.00	12.00	W
375	Babes and Sucklings - Philip Wylie Note: Same cover as the comic Intimate Confessions no. 8.	3.00	6.00	12.00	E

Avon 370, c. Avon   Avon 371, c. Avon   Avon 373, c. Avon

Avon 376, c. Avon   Avon 377, c. Avon   Avon 384, c. Avon

(AVON, continued)

#	Title				
376	Home to Harlem - Claude McKay	10.00	25.00	40.00	E
377	Taffy - Philip B. Kaye	7.50	15.00	30.00	E
378	Marshal of Deer Creek - Al Cody	3.00	6.00	12.00	W
379	Death in the Air - Agatha Christie	4.00	8.00	15.00	M
380	If This Be Sin - Loren Wahl	3.00	6.00	12.00	E
381	Nothing So Strange - James Hilton	3.00	6.00	12.00	M
382	Tough Kid from Brooklyn - Robert Mende	4.00	8.00	15.00	
383	The Untamed Wife of Louis Scott - W. Carroll Munro	3.00	6.00	12.00	E
	aka The Gift of Glory				
384	Louis Beretti - Donald Henderson Clarke	4.00	8.00	15.00	M
385	Cat and Mouse - Christianna Brand 1952	4.00	8.00	15.00	M
386	Does not exist.				
	Note: Announced as The Face in the Abyss by A. Merritt but instead was released as Murder Mystery Monthly no. 29.				
387	Maniac Rendezvous - Marc Brandel	5.00	10.00	20.00	M
	aka Rain Before Seven				
388	Does not exist.				
	Note: Announced as After Many a Summer Dies the Swan - Aldous Huxley and later released as Avon AT435.				
389	The Saturday Evening Post Fantasy Stories	4.00	8.00	15.00	SF
390	The Savage Gentleman - Philip Wylie	7.50	15.00	30.00	F
391	Maidens in the Midden - Oliver Anderson	3.00	6.00	12.00	E
	aka In for a Penny				
392	Burn, Witch, Burn - A. A. Merritt	10.00	25.00	40.00	SF
393	The Moron - Marc Brandel	4.00	8.00	15.00	M
	aka The Choice				
394	Murderer's Holiday - Donald Henderson Clarke	4.00	8.00	15.00	M
395	The Drunk the Damned, and the Bedeviled - Terence Ford	4.00	8.00	15.00	E
	aka He Feeds the Birds				
396	His First Million Women - George Weston	5.00	10.00	20.00	SF
397	Nina - Donald Henderson Clarke	3.00	6.00	12.00	
398	Element of Shame - Cicely Schiller	4.00	8.00	15.00	E
399	... Plus Blood in Their Veins - Robert Paul Smith	5.00	10.00	20.00	E

Avon 389, c. Avon   Avon 393, c. Avon   Avon 396, c. Avon

Avon 411, c. Avon   Avon 413, c. Avon   Avon 434, c. Avon

(AVON, continued)

1952, aka So it Doesn't Whistle

400	Jule: Alabama Boy in Harlem - George Wylie Henderson	4.00	8.00	15.00	E
401	Perversity - Francis Carco	3.00	6.00	12.00	E
402	Dangerous Love - Jack Woodford	3.00	6.00	12.00	E
403	Untamed Darling - Jack Woodford aka Iris	3.00	6.00	12.00	E
404	The Blackmailer - Ernst Klein Orig., 1952	2.50	6.00	10.00	
405	How Brave We Live - Paul Monash	3.00	6.00	12.00	E
406	Two Beds for Roxane - Stephen Longstreet aka The Sound of an American	2.50	6.00	10.00	E
407	Strange Brother - Blair Niles	3.50	6.00	10.00	
408	Tawny - Donald Henderson	2.50	6.00	10.00	E
409	Does not exist. Note: Announced as The Rites of Love by Jack Woodford.				
410	The Secret Adversary - Agatha Christie	2.50	6.00	10.00	M
411	Hospital Happy - Bob Dunn	4.00	8.00	15.00	H
412	Waiting for Willy - Jack Houston	2.50	6.00	10.00	
413	Dwellers in the Mirage - A. A. Merritt	7.50	15.00	30.00	SF
414	The Gringo Bandit - William Hopson	3.00	6.00	12.00	W
415	Musk, Hashish, and Blood - Hector France	5.00	10.00	20.00	E
416	The Frenchman in Mohammed's Harem - Mario Uchard	5.00	10.00	20.00	E
417	Star Lust - Jach Hanley	4.00	8.00	15.00	E
418	Call Her Savage - Tiffany Thayer	3.00	6.00	12.00	E
419	Never Come Morning - Nelson Algren	2.50	6.00	10.00	E
420	The Saint Goes West - Leslie Charteris	2.50	6.00	10.00	M
421	Love's Lovely Counterfeit - James M. Cain	2.50	6.00	10.00	
422	Butterfield 8 - John O'Hara	2.50	6.00	10.00	
423	Love Among the Haystacks - D. H. Lawrence	2.50	6.00	10.00	E
424	The Neon Wilderness - Nelson Algren Note: Same cover as the comic Intimate Confessions no. 1.	5.00	10.00	20.00	E
425	The Tragedy of X - Ellery Queen	3.00	6.00	12.00	M
426	Guns Blaze at Sundown - Al Cody	2.50	6.00	10.00	W
427	Georgie May - Maxwell Bodenheim	3.00	6.00	12.00	E
428	The Servant - Robin Maugham	2.50	6.00	10.00	E
429	The Price is Right - Jerome Weidman	2.50	6.00	10.00	E
430	House of Fury - Felice Swados	10.00	25.00	40.00	E
431	That Mrs. Renney - Donald Henderson Clarke	2.50	6.00	10.00	E
432	Saint Overboard - Leslie Charteris	3.00	6.00	12.00	M
433	Juvenile Delinquents - Leonard Kaufman aka The Lower Part of the Sky	3.00	6.00	12.00	E
434	Murder Comes First - Frances & Richard Lockridge	3.00	6.00	12.00	M
AT435	After Many a Summer Dies the Swan - Aldous Huxley	4.00	8.00	15.00	SF
A436	Too Dangerous to Be Free - James Hadley Chase	3.00	6.00	12.00	M
437	The Battle at Apache Pass - Harold Conrad Orig., 1952, Movie tie-in	3.00	6.00	12.00	W
438	Confidential - Donald Henderson Clarke	2.50	6.00	10.00	E
439	Diplomatic Corpse - Phoebe Atwood Taylor	2.50	6.00	10.00	M
440	The Saint at the Thieves' Picnic - Leslie Charteris	2.50	6.00	10.00	M

(AVON, continued)

441	A Mouse is Born - Anita Loos	3.00	6.00	12.00	H
442	Slipping Beauty - Jerome Weidman aka The Horse that Could Whistle 'Dixie'	2.50	6.00	10.00	E
443	A Holiday for Murder - Agatha Christie	2.50	6.00	10.00	M
444	Four Boys, a Girl and a Gun - Willard Wiener aka Four Boys and a Gun Note: Same cover as the comic Gangsters and Gun Molls no. 1.	3.00	6.00	12.00	E
AT445	End as a Man - Calder Willingham	2.50	6.00	10.00	E
446	The Outcasts of Poker Flat - Bret Harte Movie tie-in	2.50	6.00	10.00	W
AT447	Red Canvas - Marcel Wallenstein	2.50	6.00	10.00	E
448	The Last of Mr. Norris - Christopher Isherwood	2.50	6.00	10.00	E
449	The Virgin and the Gypsy - D. H. Lawrence	2.50	6.00	10.00	E
450	The Tragedy of Y - Ellery Queen	3.00	6.00	12.00	M
451	Gone to Texas - John W. Thomason, Jr.	2.50	6.00	10.00	W
452	Red Bone Woman - Carlyle Tillery	2.50	6.00	10.00	E
453	Glamor Girls - Don Flowers	3.00	6.00	12.00	H
454	The Challenge of Smoke Wade - Robert J. Hogan	2.50	6.00	10.00	W
455	The Root of his Evil - James M. Cain	2.50	6.00	10.00	
456	The Chastity of Gloria Boyd - Donald Henderson Clarke	2.50	6.00	10.00	E
457	Bimini Run - Howard Hunt	2.50	6.00	10.00	
458	Because of My Love - Robert Paul Smith	2.50	6.00	10.00	E
459	Mademoiselle Fifi and Other Stories - Guy de Maupassant	2.50	6.00	10.00	
460	Outlaw Justice at Hangman's Coulee - Al Cody	2.50	6.00	10.00	W
461	Lady, Don't Die on my Doorstep - Joseph Shallit	3.00	6.00	12.00	M
462	Pardners of the Badlands - Bliss Lomax (H. S. Drago)	2.00	4.00	7.50	W
463	The Saint in Action - Leslie Charteris aka The Ace of Knaves	2.50	6.00	10.00	M
464	The Rough and the Smooth - Robin Maugham	2.50	6.00	10.00	E
465	The Tragedy of Z - Ellery Queen	3.00	6.00	12.00	M
466	Gas-House McGinty - James T. Farrell	2.50	6.00	10.00	
467	Hell-Bent with Jake - Russell LaDue aka No More with Me	2.50	6.00	10.00	E
468	A Hell of a Good Time - James T. Farrell	2.50	6.00	10.00	
469	Roaring Guns at Apache Landing - Robert J. Hogan	2.50	6.00	10.00	W
470	Low Company - Mark Benney	2.50	6.00	10.00	
471	Mr. and Mrs. North Meet Murder - Frances & Richard Lockridge	2.50	6.00	10.00	M
472	The Headstrong Young Man - Donald Henderson Clarke aka Regards to Broadway	2.50	6.00	10.00	E
473	The Saint's Getaway - Leslie Charteris	2.50	6.00	10.00	M
474	Outlaw Ambush on the Drumfire Trail - Tom J. Hopkins	2.50	6.00	10.00	W
475	Yesterday's Love - James T. Farrell	2.50	6.00	10.00	E
476	The Bride of Newgate - John Dickson Carr	3.00	6.00	12.00	M
477	The Saint Meets the Tiger - Leslie Charteris	2.50	6.00	10.00	M
478	A Bullet for Billy the Kid - Nelson C. Nye aka Pistols for Hire	2.50	6.00	10.00	W

Avon 437, c. Avon

Avon 451, c. Avon

Avon 476, c. Avon

(AVON, continued)

479	Jealous Woman - James M. Cain	2.50	6.00	10.00	
480	Millie - Donald Henderson Clarke	2.00	4.00	7.50	
481	The Hucksters - Frederic Wakeman	2.00	4.00	7.50	E
482	Avon Bedside Companion	2.50	6.00	10.00	
483	A Lady Named Lou - Donald Henderson Clarke	2.50	6.00	10.00	E
484	Murder in a Hurry - Frances & Richard Lockridge	2.50	6.00	10.00	M
485	12 Chinks and a Woman - James Hadley Chase	3.00	6.00	12.00	E
486	Bronc Buckaroo - J. Edward Leithead	2.00	4.00	7.50	W
487	Feud at Sundown - Robert Jasper 1953	2.50	6.00	10.00	W
488	Drury Lone's Last Case - Ellery Queen	2.50	6.00	10.00	M
489	The Saint Meets his Match - Leslie Charteris	2.50	6.00	10.00	M
490	Yell Bloody Murder - Joseph Shallit	2.50	6.00	10.00	M
491	Mesquiteer Mavericks - William Colt MacDonald	2.50	6.00	10.00	W
492	Waiting for Willy - Jack Houston	2.00	4.00	7.50	
493	Strange Brother - Blair Niles	2.00	4.00	7.50	
494	The Scarf - Robert Bloch	2.00	4.00	7.50	
495	Rebel's Roundup - W. Edmunds Claussen	2.50	6.00	10.00	W
496	Fast One - Paul Cain	2.00	4.00	7.50	M
497	A Night with Mr. Primrose - Whitfield Cook	2.50	6.00	10.00	
498	Six-Gun Melody - William Colt MacDonald	2.00	4.00	7.50	W
499	Chorus of Cuties - E. Simms Campbell	3.00	6.00	12.00	H
500	Colorado - William MacLeod Raine	2.50	6.00	10.00	W
501	The Untamed Wife of Louis Scott - W. Carroll Munro aka The Gift of Glory	2.50	6.00	10.00	E
502	Mr. and Mrs. North and a Pinch of Poison - Frances & Richard Lockridge	2.50	6.00	10.00	M
503	The Housekeeper's Daughter - Donald Henderson Clarke	2.00	4.00	7.50	E
504	The Chase - Richard G. Huber	2.00	4.00	7.50	E
505	Gun Fight at Horsethief Range - B. M. Bower aka Five Furies of Leaning Ladder	2.00	4.00	7.50	W
506	Nonce - Michael Brandon	2.50	6.00	10.00	E
507	Straw Boss - E. E. Halleran	2.00	4.00	7.50	W
508	He Swung and He Missed - Eugene O'Brien	2.00	4.00	7.50	
509	The Four of Hearts - Ellery Queen	2.00	4.00	7.50	M
510	The Thin Line - Edward Atiyah	2.00	4.00	7.50	
511	Marshal of Deer Creek - Al Cody	2.00	4.00	7.50	W
512	The Gifted - Roswell G. Ham, Jr.	2.00	4.00	7.50	
513	Bachelor's Joke Book - Leo Guild	3.00	6.00	12.00	H
514	The Vanishing Gun Slinger - William Colt MacDonald	2.00	4.00	7.50	W
515	Murder Out of Turn - Frances & Richard Lockridge	2.50	6.00	10.00	M
516	The Gringo Bandit - William Hopson	2.00	4.00	7.50	W
517	The Fat Boy's Book - Elmer Wheeler	3.00	6.00	12.00	NF
518	The Avenging Saint - Leslie Charteris	2.00	4.00	7.50	M
519	Dennis the Menace - Hank Ketcham	3.00	6.00	12.00	H
520	Scratch the Surface - Edmund Schiddel	2.00	4.00	7.50	E
521	The Prisoner Ate a Heary Breakfast - Jerome Ellison	2.00	4.00	7.50	E
522	Outlaw Guns - E. E. Halleran	2.00	4.00	7.50	W
523	The American Gun Mystery - Ellery Queen	2.50	6.00	10.00	M
524	The New Jimmy Hatlo Book - Jimmy Hatlo First ed., 1953	3.00	6.00	12.00	H
525	Guns Blaze at Sundown - Al Cody	2.00	4.00	7.50	W
526	Call for the Saint - Leslie Charteris	2.00	4.00	7.50	M
527	All About Girls	2.50	6.00	10.00	
528	Kiss the Killer - Joseph Shallit	2.50	6.00	10.00	M
529	Gunshot Empire - Lee E. Wells	2.00	4.00	7.50	W
530	Impatient Virgin - Donald Henderson Clarke	3.00	6.00	12.00	E
531	The Wages of Fear - Georges Arnaud	2.00	4.00	7.50	
532	Trouble in the Saddle - Arthur Henry Gooden	2.00	4.00	7.50	W
533	Follow the Saint - Leslie Charteris	2.00	4.00	7.50	M
534	The Time and the Place - Robert Paul Smith	2.00	4.00	7.50	E
535	Dead as a Dinosaur - Frances & Richard Lockridge	2.50	6.00	10.00	M
536	Three - Notch Cameron - William Colt MacDonald	2.00	4.00	7.50	W
537	The Innocent Villa - Barnaby Conrad	2.00	4.00	7.50	
538	Dope, Inc. - Joachim Joesten Orig., 1953	4.00	8.00	15.00	

539	Hardcase - Matt Kinkaid	2.00	4.00	7.50	
540	Pistols on the Pecos - Paul Evan Lehman	2.00	4.00	7.50	W
541	Burial of the Fruit - David Dortort	2.00	4.00	7.50	E
542	Call Me Killer - Max Carter	2.50	6.00	10.00	
543	Millie's Daughter - Donald Henderson Clarke	2.00	4.00	7.50	
544	The Saint and the Last Hero - Leslie Charteris	2.00	4.00	7.50	M
545	Circle of Desire - Robert Paul Smith aka The Journey	2.00	4.00	7.50	E
546	The Hoodlums - John Eagle Orig., 1953	2.00	4.00	7.50	E
547	Southern Daughter - Daniel White	2.00	4.00	7.50	
548	Away & Beyond - A. E. Van Vogt	2.50	6.00	10.00	
A549	Tales of Love and Fury - anthology First ed., 1953	2.00	4.00	7.50	E
550	Renegade Guns - Robert J. Hogan	2.00	4.00	7.50	W
551	Stool Pigeon - Louis Malley	2.00	4.00	7.50	M
552	Man on the Tightrope - Neil Paterson	2.00	4.00	7.50	E
553	Rusty Desmond - Steve January 1954	2.00	4.00	7.50	E
554	I'll Call Every Monday - Orrie Hitt	2.00	4.00	7.50	
555	Rue Pigalle - Francis Carco	2.00	4.00	7.50	E
556	Guns of Circle 8 - Jeff Cochran	2.00	4.00	7.50	W
557	Glamor Girls - Don Flowers	2.50	6.00	10.00	H
558	Case of the Billion Dollar Body - Joseph Shallit	2.00	4.00	7.50	M
559	A Cartoon Guide to the Kinsey Report - Charles Preston	3.00	6.00	12.00	H
560	Gang Girl - Wenzell Brown	2.50	6.00	10.00	JD
561	Enter Without Desire - Ed Lacy	2.00	4.00	7.50	
562	Call of the Range - Arthur Henry Gooden	2.00	4.00	7.50	W
563	The Creepers - John Creasey	2.00	4.00	7.50	M
564	Every Bet's A Sure Thing - Thomas B. Dewey	2.00	4.00	7.50	M
565	Thunder Below - Thomas Rourke	2.00	4.00	7.50	E
566	Go For the Body - Ed Lacy	2.00	4.00	7.50	
567	Ship Ahoy	3.00	6.00	12.00	H
568	I Worked for Lucky Luciano - anonymous	3.00	6.00	12.00	NF
569	Gunhead from Texas - William Heuman	2.00	4.00	7.50	W
570	Devil's Daughter - Floyd Shaw	2.00	4.00	7.50	
571	As they Reveled - Philip Wylie	2.00	4.00	6.00	E
572	Laughter Came Screaming - Henry Kane	2.00	4.00	7.50	M
573	The Long Noose - Lee E. Wells	2.00	4.00	7.50	W
574	Make My Bed in Hell - John B. Sanford aka Seventy Times Seven	2.00	4.00	6.00	E
575	Louis Beretti - New York Hoodlum - Donald Henderson Clarke	2.00	4.00	6.00	M
576	Forbidden - Leo Brattes	2.00	4.00	7.50	
577	Jule: Alabama Boy in Harlem - George Wylie Henderson	2.00	4.00	7.50	
578	The Girl on the Left Bank - Joan Shepherd	2.00	4.00	7.50	
579	Rebel Ranger - William Colt MacDonald	2.00	4.00	7.50	W
580	The Guy from Coney Island - Jack Hanley	2.00	4.00	7.50	E
581	Love's Lovely Counterfeit - James M. Cain	2.00	4.00	6.00	
582	How Rough Can It Get? - Joe Weiss	2.00	4.00	7.50	
583	Death Has a Small Voice - Frances & Richard Lockridge	2.00	4.00	7.50	M
584	Few Die Well - Sterling Noel	2.00	4.00	6.00	
585	Keeping Women in Line - Mischa Richter	2.00	4.00	7.50	
586	The Riddle of Ramrod Ridge - William Colt MacDonald	2.00	4.00	7.50	W
587	The Virgin and the Gypsy - D. H. Lawrence	2.00	4.00	6.00	E
588	Saint Errant - Leslie Charteris	2.00	4.00	7.50	
589	The Other Side of the Night - Edmund Schiddel	2.00	4.00	7.50	
590	The Figure in the Dusk - John Creasey	2.00	4.00	6.00	M
591	The Wrong Turn - Daniel Harper	2.00	4.00	6.00	
592	The Phantom Pass - William Colt MacDonald	2.00	4.00	6.00	W
593	Nina - Donald Henderson Clarke	2.00	4.00	6.00	
594	The Pennycross Murders - Maurice Proctor	2.00	4.00	7.50	M
595	How Brave We Live - Paul Monash	2.00	4.00	6.00	
596	Gun Feud at Stampede Valley - Samuel A. Peeples	2.00	4.00	7.50	W
597	Night Cry - William L. Stuart	2.00	4.00	7.50	M
598	More all About Girls	2.50	6.00	10.00	H
599	Sinful Woman - James M. Cain	2.00	4.00	7.50	

600 More Dennis the Menace - Hank Ketcham	3.00	6.00	12.00	H
601 Love for a Stranger - John Pleasant McCoy	2.00	4.00	6.00	
602 My Business is Murder - Henry Kane	2.00	4.00	7.50	M
603 Avon Bedside Companion - ed. Wollheim	2.00	4.00	6.00	
604 The Case of the Burning Bride - Alan Hynd aka Alan Hynd's Murder	2.00	4.00	7.50	M
605 Death Hits the Jackpot - John Tiger	2.00	4.00	6.00	
606 The Kansan - Richard Brister	2.00	4.00	6.00	W
607 Bubu of Montparnasse - Charles-Louis Philippe	2.00	4.00	7.50	E
608 Curtain for a Jester - Frances & Richard Lockridge	2.00	4.00	7.50	M
609 French Postcards	3.00	6.00	12.00	H
610 The Saint Steps in - Leslie Charteris	2.00	4.00	6.00	M
611 The Saint in Europe - Leslie Charteris	2.00	4.00	6.00	M
612 The New Jimmy Hatlo Book - Jimmy Hatlo	2.50	6.00	10.00	H
613 Break-Up - Edmund Schiddel	2.00	4.00	7.50	E
614 And Dream of Evil - Tedd Thomey	2.00	4.00	7.50	
615 Tawny - Donald Henderson Clarke	2.00	4.00	6.00	
616 A Holiday for Murder - Agatha Christie	2.00	4.00	6.00	M
617 Battle of the Sexes - Charles Preston	3.00	6.00	12.00	H
618 Trinity in Violence - Henry Kane	2.00	4.00	6.00	M
619 The Saint Sees it Through - Leslie Charteris	2.00	4.00	6.00	M
620 Death in the Desert - Lee E. Wells	2.00	4.00	6.00	W
621 It Walks by Night - John Dickson Carr	2.00	4.00	7.50	M
622 Hellbound - Paul Monash	2.00	4.00	7.50	E
623 Beat Not the Bones - Charlotte Jay	2.00	4.00	6.00	
624 The Stone of Chastity - Margery Sharp	2.00	4.00	7.50	F
625 A Taste for Murder - H. F. Heard	2.00	4.00	6.00	M
626 The Case of the Murdered Model - Thomas B. Dewey	2.00	4.00	6.00	M
627 Caveman Cartoons - Harold Meyers	3.00	6.00	12.00	H
628 The Monk and the Hangman's Daughter - Ambrose Bierce	2.00	4.00	6.00	
629 The Saint and Mr. Teal - Leslie Charteris	2.00	4.00	6.00	M
630 20 Great Ghost Stories	2.50	6.00	10.00	HO
631 Murderer's Holliday - Donald Henderson Clarke	1.50	3.50	5.00	M
632 Jet Pilot - Tedd Thomey	1.50	3.50	5.00	
633 Klever Kid Kartoons - Harold Meyers	2.50	6.00	10.00	H
634 Miss Lonelyhearts - Nathanel West	2.00	4.00	6.00	
635 The Saint Goes West - Leslie Charteris	2.00	4.00	6.00	M
636 The Moving Finger - Agatha Christie	2.00	4.00	6.00	M
637 Animals are Funnier than People - Harold Meyers	2.50	6.00	10.00	H
638 Tropical Passions - anthology	2.00	4.00	6.00	E
639 Cartoons by Jimmy Hatlo First ed., 1955	3.00	6.00	12.00	H
640 The Man Who Never Was - Ewen Montague	2.00	4.00	6.00	
641 The Case of the Acid Throwers - John Creasey	2.00	4.00	7.50	M
642 The Fighting Texan - Paul Evan Lehman	2.00	4.00	6.00	W
643 South Sea Cartoons - Harold Meyers c-Ward	5.00	10.00	20.00	H
644 Stories for Tonight - anthology First ed., 1955	2.00	4.00	7.50	
645 Puzzles for Everybody - John Paul Adams	3.00	6.00	12.00	NF
646 The Case of the Murdered Madam - Henry Kane	2.50	6.00	10.00	M
647 Unfaithful - John Baxter	2.00	4.00	6.00	
648 Murder in three Acts - Agatha Christie	1.50	3.50	5.00	M
649 Nudist Cartoons - Harold Meyers	2.50	6.00	10.00	H
650 Confidential - Donald Henderson Clarke	1.50	3.50	5.00	
651 Murder in Las Vegas - Jack Waer	2.00	4.00	6.00	M
652 Hatlo's Inferno - Jimmy Hatlo First ed., 1955	4.00	8.00	15.00	H
653 The Saint Goes on - Leslie Charteris	1.50	3.50	5.00	M
654 Bloody Kansas - Chuck Martin First ed., 1955	1.50	3.50	5.00	W
655 Seven Who Were Hanged - Leonid Andreyev	1.50	3.50	5.00	
656 Impatient Virgin - Donald Henderson Clarke	1.50	3.50	5.00	
657 The Doctor's Woman - H. P. Koenig	1.50	3.50	5.00	
658 Death in the Air - Agatha Christie	1.50	3.50	5.00	M
659 Hell-town in Texas - Leslie Ernenwein	1.50	3.50	5.00	W
660 Wake Up to Murder - Day Keene	1.50	3.50	5.00	M
661 Stories of Venial Sin - John O'Hara	1.50	3.50	5.00	

(AVON, continued)

662 Teen-age Cartoons and Jokes - Harold Meyers	2.50	6.00	10.00	H
663 The Ace of Knaves - Leslie Charteris	1.50	3.50	5.00	M
664 Desire in the Deep South - Ward Greene	2.00	4.00	7.50	E
665 Dennis the Menace - Hank Ketcham	2.00	4.00	7.50	H
666 A Key to Death - Frances & Richard Lockridge	2.00	4.00	6.00	M
667 The Range Bum - Kenneth Fowler	1.50	3.50	5.00	W
668 Woman and the Puppet - Pierre Louys	1.50	3.50	5.00	E
669 Sensualite - Georges de La Fouchardiere	1.50	3.50	5.00	E
670 The Fugitive Eye - Charlotte Jay	1.50	3.50	5.00	
671 A Lady Named Lou - Donald Henderson Clarke	1.50	3.50	5.00	E
672 Too French and Too Deadly - Henry Kane	2.00	4.00	6.00	
673 Henry Morgan's Joke Book - Henry Morgan	2.00	4.00	7.50	H
674 The Challenge of Smoke Wade - Robert J. Hogan	1.50	3.50	5.00	W
675 A Room in Berlin - Gunther Birkenfeld	1.50	3.50	5.00	
676 White Barrier - Noel Clad	2.00	4.00	6.00	
677 Case of the Black, Black Hearse - Frederic Freyer	1.50	3.50	5.00	M
678 The Fighting Kid from Eldorado - William Colt MacDonald	1.50	3.50	5.00	W
679 Hellbox - John O'Hara	1.50	3.50	5.00	
680 The Saint--The Happy Highwayman - Leslie Charteris	1.50	3.50	5.00	M
681 Showgirl Cartoons, Photographs, Stories - Harold Meyers	2.50	6.00	10.00	H
682 Chinese Love Tales - Edward Powys Mathers	2.00	4.00	7.50	
683 Coming, Aphrodite!	2.00	4.00	6.00	
684 The Passion Murders - Day Keene	1.50	3.50	5.00	M
685 Alibi Baby - Stewart Sterling	1.50	3.50	5.00	M
686 The Hungering Shame - R. V. Cassill Orig., 1956	.75	1.75	3.00	E
687 Vegas, Gunman Marshal - William Hopson	1.50	3.50	5.00	W
688 The Art Studio Murders - Edward Ronns	1.50	3.50	5.00	M
689 Riders of the Whistling Skull - William Colt MacDonald	1.50	3.50	5.00	W
690 The Big Four - Agatha Christie c-Kinstler	2.00	4.00	7.50	M
691 Sappho - Alphonse Daudet	1.50	3.50	5.00	E
692 The Counterfeit General Montgomery - M. E. Clifton James	1.50	3.50	5.00	
693 The Hotshot - Fletcher Flora	1.50	3.50	5.00	
694 The Saint - Wanted for Murder - Leslie Charteris aka Wanted for Murder	1.50	3.50	5.00	M
695 The Jungle of Love - Robin Maugham aka Behind the Mirror	1.50	3.50	5.00	
696 Murder Somewhere in this City - Maurice Procter aka Hell in a City	1.50	3.50	5.00	M
697 The Girl with the Golden Eyes - Honore De Balzac	1.50	3.50	5.00	E
698 Smoking-room Jokebook - Harold Meyers	2.50	6.00	10.00	H
699 Counterspy Murders - Peter Cheyney	1.50	3.50	5.00	M
700 Mirror of Your Mind - Joseph Whitney Orig., 1956	2.00	4.00	7.50	NF

Avon 652, c. Avon

Avon 682, c. Avon

Avon 704, c. Avon

(AVON, continued)

701	The Anatomy of a Crime - Joseph F. Dinneen	1.50	3.50	5.00	
702	The Room in the Dragon Inn - Joseph Sheridan LeFann	1.50	3.50	5.00	A
	aka The Room and the Dragon Volant				
703	Armchair in Hell - Henry Kane	1.50	3.50	5.00	
704	Whiplash War - Al Cody	1.50	3.50	5.00	W
705	Hunt the Killer - Day Keene	1.50	3.50	5.00	
706	Operation Intrigue - Walter Hermann	1.50	3.50	5.00	
707	Hatlo Cartoons of 1956 - Jimmy Hatlo	3.00	6.00	12.00	H
	First ed., 1956				
708	Arrest the Saint! - Leslie Charteris	1.50	3.50	5.00	M
709	Montana Gunslinger - William Hopson	1.50	3.50	5.00	W
710	The Wound of Love - R. V. Cassill	1.50	3.50	5.00	
711	Experiment in Crime - Philip Wylie	2.00	4.00	6.00	
712	The Man Nobody Saw - Peter Cheyney	2.00	4.00	6.00	M
	c-Kinstler				
713	The Outraged Sect - Jada M. Davis	2.00	4.00	6.00	E
	Orig., 1956				
714	The Case of the Black Orchids - Rex Stout	1.50	3.50	5.00	M
715	The Vengeance Trail - Paul Evan Lehman	1.50	3.50	5.00	W
716	Poirot Investigates - Agatha Christie	2.00	4.00	6.00	M
717	How Rough Can it Get? - Joe Weiss	1.50	3.50	5.00	
718	Enter the Saint - Leslie Charteris	1.50	3.50	5.00	M
719	Few Die Well - Sterling Noel	1.50	3.50	5.00	
720	Give a Man a Gun - John Creasey	1.50	3.50	5.00	M
	aka A Gun for Inspector West				
721	Lilly's Story - Ethel Wilson	1.50	3.50	5.00	
722	Gang Girl - Wenzell Brown	2.00	4.00	7.50	JD
723	Yucca City Outlaw - William Hopson	1.50	3.50	5.00	W
724	Empty Saddles - Al Cody	1.50	3.50	5.00	W
725	The Case of the Bludgeoned Teacher - Jim Hollis	1.50	3.50	5.00	M
726	The Tragedy of Z - Ellery Queen	1.50	3.50	5.00	M
727	The Smuggled Atom Bomb - Philip Wylie	2.00	4.00	7.50	
728	Safari to Dishonor - Edmund Schiddel	1.50	3.50	5.00	
729	The Battle at Apache Pass - Harold Conrad	1.50	3.50	5.00	W
730	The Case of the Hypnotized Virgin - John Roeburt	1.50	3.50	5.00	M
731	Operation Tokyo - Ted Middleton	1.50	3.50	5.00	
732	The Kansan - Richard Brister	1.50	3.50	5.00	W
733	Who Killed Sweet Sue? - Henry Kane	1.50	3.50	5.00	M
734	The Case of the Dark Hero - Peter Cheyney	1.50	3.50	5.00	M
735	Dennis the Menace - Hank Ketcham	2.00	4.00	7.50	H
736	The Yellow Turban - Charlotte Jay	1.50	3.50	5.00	
737	And Dream of Evil - Tedd Thomey	1.50	3.50	5.00	
738	Invitation to Murder - Rex Stout	1.50	3.50	5.00	M
739	Hired Gun - Archie Joscelyn	1.50	3.50	5.00	W
740	Park Avenue Girl - Floyd Shaw	1.50	3.50	5.00	
741	Outlaw Loot - Paul Evan Lehman	1.50	3.50	5.00	W
742	KKK - Paul E. Walsh	2.00	4.00	7.50	
	Orig., 1956				
743	Love Affair - William Russell	1.50	3.50	5.00	
744	The Saint and the Sizzling Saboteur - Leslie Charteris	1.50	3.50	5.00	M
745	Martinis and Murder - Henry Kane	1.50	3.50	5.00	M
746	The Girl with the Frightened Eyes - Lawrence Lariar	1.50	3.50	5.00	
747	Tawny - Donald Henderson Clarke	1.50	3.50	5.00	E
748	Gunsight Showdown - Johnston McCulley	2.00	4.00	6.00	
749	Violent Maverick - Walt Coburn	1.50	3.50	5.00	W
750	Southern Daughter - Daniel White	2.00	4.00	6.00	
751	Murder of the Park Avenue Playgirl - Henry Kane	1.50	3.50	5.00	
	1957				
752	Death by Moonlight - Michael Innes	1.50	3.50	5.00	M
	aka The Man from the Sea				
753	The Passionate Seekers - Peter Matthiessen	1.50	3.50	5.00	
754	The Long Noose - Lee E. Wells	1.50	3.50	5.00	W
755	A Spy in the House of Love - Anais Nin	1.50	3.50	5.00	
756	The Saint - The Brighter Buccaneer - Leslie Charteris	1.50	3.50	5.00	M
757	Inspector Maigret & The Dead Girl - Georges Simenon	2.00	4.00	7.50	M
	c-Kinstler				
758	Arizona Dead-shot - Nelson Nye	1.50	3.50	5.00	W
759	Fighting Buckaroo - Paul Evan Lehman	1.50	3.50	5.00	W

(AVON, continued)

No.	Title				
760	Love of Seven Dolls - Paul Gallico	1.50	3.50	5.00	
761	Death on the Double - Henry Kane	1.50	3.50	5.00	M
762	The Hotel Murders - Stewart Sterling	1.50	3.50	5.00	M
763	Vice Squad Cop - Michael Carey	1.50	3.50	5.00	
764	The Dark Street Murders - Peter Cheyney	1.50	3.50	5.00	M
765	California Gunman - William Colt MacDonald	1.50	3.50	5.00	W
766	Mr. & Mrs. North and the Poisoned Playboy - Frances & Richard Lockridge	1.50	3.50	5.00	M
	aka Death of an Angel				
767	The Murder Room - Paul Walsh	1.50	3.50	5.00	M
768	Sinful Woman - James M. Cain	1.50	3.50	5.00	
769	The Phantom Pass - William Colt MacDonald	1.50	3.50	5.00	W
770	Outlaw Fury - Burt Arthur	1.50	3.50	5.00	W
771	The Saint on the Spanish Main - Leslie Charteris	1.50	3.50	5.00	
772	Murder in Manhattan - John Roeburt	1.50	3.50	5.00	
773	The Woman and the Prowler - Stuart Friedman	1.50	3.50	5.00	
774	Gunfight at the O. K. Corral Movie tie-in	2.00	4.00	7.50	W
775	The Tall T - Elmore Leonard Movie tie-in	2.00	4.00	7.50	W
776	Sinister Murders - Peter Cheyney	1.50	3.50	5.00	M
777	Kiss and Kill - Reed McCary aka Sleep with the Devil	2.00	4.00	7.50	
778	Tales of Midsummer Passion - anthology	2.00	4.00	6.00	
779	Gunsmoke Vengeance - Johnston McCulley aka South of the Pass, c-Kinstler	2.00	4.00	7.50	W
780	The Lonely Man - Robert Turner Movie tie-in	2.00	4.00	7.50	W
781	The Calypso Murders - P. J. Mulholland Note: Same cover as Avon no. 506.	1.50	3.50	5.00	M
782	Gun Feud at Stampede Valley - Samuel A. Peeples	1.50	3.50	5.00	W
783	Hot Rod Gang Rumble - Meyer Dolinsky	2.00	4.00	6.00	JD
784	Murder in Las Vegas - Jack Waer	1.50	3.50	5.00	M
785	Gun Play at the X-Bar-X - Burt Arthur	1.50	3.50	5.00	W
786	Murder, My Love - Edward Atiyah	1.50	3.50	5.00	M
787	The Case of the Murdered Model - Thomas B. Dewey	1.50	3.50	5.00	M
788	Six-gun Sawbones - Archie Joscelyn	1.50	3.50	5.00	W
789	More They'll Do It Every Time - Jimmy Hatlo First ed., 1957	3.00	6.00	12.00	H
790	My Business is Murder - Henry Kane	1.50	3.50	5.00	M
791	Texas Revenge - Archie Joscelyn	1.50	3.50	5.00	W
792	Murder in Lima - Robert A. Leuey	1.50	3.50	5.00	M
793	The Moving Finger - Agatha Christie	1.50	3.50	5.00	M
794	The Ripper Murders - Maurice Proctor	1.50	3.50	5.00	M
795	Blood on the Saddle - Johnston McCulley	1.50	3.50	5.00	W
796	A Mask for Murder - Henry Kane	1.50	3.50	5.00	M
797	Cocktails and the Killer - Peter Cheyney	1.50	3.50	5.00	M
798	Outlaw - Archie Joscelyn 1958	1.50	3.50	5.00	W
799	Powdersmoke Range - William Colt MacDonald	1.50	3.50	5.00	W
800	Case of the Murdered Redhead - Frances & Richard Lockridge	1.50	3.50	5.00	M

Avon 742, c. Avon

Avon 774, c. Avon

Avon 780, c. Avon

(AVON, continued)

801 Night Cry - William L. Stuart	1.50	3.50	5.00	M
802 Murder in Baracoa - Paul Walsh	1.50	3.50	5.00	M
803 Featuring the Saint - Leslie Charteris	1.50	3.50	5.00	M
804 Flesh and Fire - Georges Arnaud	.75	1.75	3.00	
805 The Tough Texan - Paul Evan Lehman	.75	1.75	3.00	W
806 Bandit in Black - Paul Evan Lehman	1.50	3.50	5.00	W
807 Wine, Women and Murder - John Roeburt	.75	1.75	3.00	M
808 A Taste for Murder - H. F. Heard	.75	1.75	3.00	M
809 The Vice Net - Michael Carey	.75	1.75	3.00	
810 Montana Helltown - Al Cody	.75	1.75	3.00	W
811 Let Me Kill You, Sweetheart - Fletcher Flora	.75	1.75	3.00	M
812 Bloody Wyoming - Al Cody	.75	1.75	3.00	W
813 Fighting Kid from Texas - Archie Joscelyn	.75	1.75	3.00	W
814 It's a Sin to Kill - Day Keene	.75	1.75	3.00	M
815 Bachelor's Guide to the Opposite Sex - Max Lieg & Georges Pichard	2.00	4.00	7.50	H
816 Thunderbolt Range - Paul Evan Lehman aka The Sheep Killers	.75	1.75	3.00	W
817 The Doctor's Woman - H. P. Koenig	.75	1.75	3.00	
818 Alias the Saint - Leslie Charteris	1.50	3.50	5.00	M
819 Cheyenne Kid - Archie Joscelyn	.75	1.75	3.00	W
820 Stampede Canyon - Robert J. Hogan	.75	1.75	3.00	W
821 Guns Blaze on Spiderweb Range - Walt Coburn	.75	1.75	3.00	W
822 Montana Dead-Shot - Chuck Martin	.75	1.75	3.00	W
823 Cry Killer! - Kenneth Fearing	.75	1.75	3.00	W
824 Notched Guns - William Hopson	.75	1.75	3.00	W
825 Gun-Whipped! - Paul Evan Lehman Orig., 1958	.75	1.75	3.00	W
826 Another New Jimmy Hatlo Book - Jimmy Hatlo First ed., 1958	3.00	6.00	12.00	H
827 The Saint on Guard - Leslie Charteris	1.50	3.50	5.00	M
828 Tall in the Saddle - Chuck Martin	.75	1.75	3.00	W
829 Hell Range in Texas - J. E. Grinstead	.75	1.75	3.00	W
830 The Bitch - Gil Brewer	1.50	3.50	5.00	
831 Renegade Marshal - Paul Evan Lehman aka Devil's Doorstep, c-Abbett	1.50	3.50	5.00	W
832 Disaster Trail - Al Cody	.75	1.75	3.00	W
833 The Wolf Streak - Richard Brister	.75	1.75	3.00	W
834 Concerning the Saint - Leslie Charteris	1.50	3.50	5.00	M
835 Too Hot to Kill - Stewart Sterling	.75	1.75	3.00	M
836 Unfaithful - John Baster	.75	1.75	3.00	
837 Long Ride to Abilene - William Hopson	.75	1.75	3.00	W
838 The Dead Ride Hard - Lynn Westland	.75	1.75	3.00	W
839 Leave Her to Hell! - Fletcher Flora	.75	1.75	3.00	
840 Cartoon Guide to the Battle of the Sexes - Charles Preston 1959	2.00	4.00	7.50	H
841 Day of Vengeance - Chuck Martin	.75	1.75	3.00	W
842 Wyoming Ambush - Al Cody	.75	1.75	3.00	W
843 Gunsmoke at Buffalo Basin - Paul Evan Lehman	.75	1.75	3.00	W
844 Deadly Draw - Lee Floren	.75	1.75	3.00	W
845 The Man from the Badlands - Paul Evan Lehman	.75	1.75	3.00	W
846 Born Reckless - Milton Rogers	.75	1.75	3.00	
847 My Name is Violence - John D. Matthews & Jeffrey Roche	.75	1.75	3.00	
848 The Saint Cleans Up - Leslie Charteris	.75	1.75	3.00	M
849 It Happened at Thunder River - Bliss Lomax (H. S. Drago)	.75	1.75	3.00	W
850 The Manhunter - Paul Evan Lehman aka Law of the Forty-five	.75	1.75	3.00	W
851 Ship Ahoy	2.00	4.00	7.50	H
852 Fast Gun - Walt Coburn	.75	1.75	3.00	W
853 French Postcards -	2.00	4.00	7.50	H
854 Make Mine Vengeance - Robert Colby	.75	1.75	3.00	
855 Then Came Mulvane - William Heuman	.75	1.75	3.00	W
856 Bullet Law - Johnston McCulley	.75	1.75	3.00	W
857 The Newest Jimmy Hatlo Cartoon Book - Jimmy Hatlo First ed., 1959	2.50	6.00	10.00	H
858 Branded - Walt Coburn	.75	1.75	3.00	W
859 More all About Girls	2.00	4.00	7.50	H
860 Caveman Cartoons - Harold Meyers	2.00	4.00	7.50	H

(AVON, continued)

861	Six Bullets Left - Barry Cord	.75	1.75	3.00	W
862	Renegade Lawman - Gordon D. Shirreffs	.75	1.75	3.00	W
863	Bloody Kansas - Chuck Martin	.75	1.75	3.00	W
864	The Deadly Game - Norman Daniels	.75	1.75	3.00	M
	c-Abbett				
1001	Jew Suss - Lion Feuchtwanger	4.00	8.00	15.00	E
	1951, interior illos - Kinstler				
1002	The Avon All-American Fiction Reader	3.00	6.00	12.00	
	1951				

AVON G-SERIES

(Avon Publishing Company, Inc.)

G1003	The Collected Works of Pierre Louys	3.00	6.00	12.00	E
	1951				
G1004	Giant Mystery Reader	4.00	8.00	15.00	M
G1005	Geraldine Bradshaw - Calder Willingham	2.50	6.00	10.00	E
G1006	Men at War - Ernest Hemingway	3.00	6.00	12.00	A
	1952				
G1007	Avon Webster English Dictionary	2.50	6.00	10.00	NF
G1008	Temptation - John Pen	4.00	8.00	15.00	E
G1009	The Big Brokers - Irving Shulman	2.00	4.00	6.00	
	1953				
G1010	Out of this World to Forbidden Tibet -				
	Lowell Thomas	2.00	4.00	7.50	NF
	1954				
G1011	Master of the World - Cothburn O'Neal	2.00	4.00	7.50	A
G1012	Send Me Down - Henry Steig	2.00	4.00	6.00	
G1013	The Human Beast - Emile Zola	2.00	4.00	6.00	
G1014	Journey to the End of the Night - Louis-				
	Ferdinand Celine	2.00	4.00	6.00	
G1015	Queen's Caprice - George Preedy	2.00	4.00	7.50	A
G1016	Avon Book of Modern Writing No. 2 -				
	William Phillips & Philip Rahr	1.50	3.50	5.00	
G1017	The Third Angel - Jerome Weldman	1.50	3.50	5.00	E
	1955				
G1018	The Collected Works of Pierre Louys	2.00	4.00	7.50	E
	1955				
G1019	Temptation - John Pen	2.00	4.00	7.50	E
G1020	Point Counter Point - Aldous Huxley	1.50	3.50	5.00	
G1021	Women in Love - D. H. Lawrence	1.50	3.50	5.00	E
G1022	Death on the Installment Plan - Louis-				
	Ferdinand Celine	1.50	3.50	5.00	
G1023	The Big Brokers - Irving Shulman	1.50	3.50	5.00	
G1024	Crime and Punishment - Fyodor				
	Dostoyevsky	2.00	4.00	6.00	
	1956				
G1025	Aaron's Rod - D. H. Lawrence	1.50	3.50	5.00	E
G1026	Your Daughter Iris - Jerome Weidman	1.50	3.50	5.00	
G1027	Those Barren Leaves - Aldous Huxley	1.50	3.50	5.00	
G1028	The Rainbow - D. H. Lawrence	1.50	3.50	5.00	E
G1029	Dishonored Flesh - Joseph Pennell	1.50	3.50	5.00	IE
G1030	Conquests of Tamerlane - Cothburn O'Neal	2.00	4.00	7.50	A
	1957				

Avon 1001, c. Avon

Avon G-1008, c. Avon

Avon G-1018, c. Avon

Avon AT-54, c. Avon   Avon T-94, c. Avon   Avon T-98, c. Avon

(AVON G-SERIES, continued)

G1031	Point Counter Point - Aldous Huxley	1.50	3.50	5.00	
G1032	The Third Angel - Jerome Weidman 1958	1.50	3.50	5.00	
G1033	Temptation - John Penn 1959	2.00	4.00	6.00	E
G1034	A Death in the Family - James Agee	1.50	3.50	5.00	
G1035	Maggie Cassidy - Jack Kerouac First ed., 1959	3.00	6.00	12.00	
G1036	Last Summer - Boris Pasternak	1.50	3.50	5.00	
G1037	They Hanged My Saintly Billy - Robert Graves	1.50	3.50	5.00	
G1038	The Rainbow - D. H. Lawrence	1.50	3.50	5.00	E
G1039	Aaron's Rod - D. H. Lawrence	1.50	3.50	5.00	E
G1040	Great Short Stories by Soviet Authors	1.50	3.50	5.00	
G2001	After Many a Summer Dies the Swan - Aldous Huxley	1.50	3.50	5.00	SF
G2002	Butterfield 8 - John O'Hara	.75	1.75	3.00	

AVON T/AT-SERIES

(Avon Book Company/Avon Publishing Co., Inc.)

T- 1	Return Postage Guaranteed - Holborn G. Croydon 1954	1.50	3.50	5.00	
T- 2	Aaron's Rod - D. H. Lawrence	1.50	3.50	5.00	E
AT-51	Bad Girl - Vina Delmar 1953	1.50	3.50	5.00	E
AT-52	The Night Air - Harrison Dowd	1.50	3.50	5.00	E
AT-53	The Second Oldest Profession - Robert Sylvester	1.50	3.50	5.00	E
AT-54	Madame Serpent - Jean Plaidy	2.00	4.00	7.50	A
AT-55	The Rake's Progress - Philip Lindsay	2.00	4.00	7.50	A
AT-56					
AT-57	Jessamy John - Phil Stong	1.50	3.50	5.00	
AT-58	The Scorpion - Anna Elisabet Weirauch	1.50	3.50	5.00	E
AT-59	The Rose and the Flame - Jonreed Lauritzen	1.50	3.50	5.00	
AT-60	Kings Mountain - Florette Henri	1.50	3.50	5.00	
AT-61	Stories in the Modern Manner	1.50	3.50	5.00	
AT-62	Powder Mission - Herbert E. Stover	1.50	3.50	5.00	
AT-63	The Hand of the Hunter - Jerome Weidman	1.50	3.50	5.00	E
AT-64	Son of Egypt - James Busbee, Jr.	1.50	3.50	5.00	A
AT-65	Sex Habits of American Women - Dr. Fritz Wittels	2.00	4.00	7.50	NF
AT-66	The Avon Book of Modern Writing - ed. William Phillips & Philip Rahr	1.50	3.50	5.00	
AT-67	Dark Passions Subdue - Douglas Sanderson	1.50	3.50	5.00	
AT-68	I, Claudius - Robert Graves	2.00	4.00	6.00	A
AT-69	Intimacy - Jean-Paul Sartre	1.50	3.50	5.00	
AT-70	Turn Back the River - W. G. Hardy	1.50	3.50	5.00	
T-71	Painted Veils - James Huneker	1.50	3.50	5.00	E
T-72	Tide of Empire - Bates Baldwin	2.00	4.00	7.50	A
T-73	Yankee Mariner - James Busbee, Jr. 1954	1.50	3.50	5.00	

T-74 Never Leave Me - Harold Robbins	1.50	3.50	5.00	E
T-75 After Many a Summer Dies the Swan - Aldous Huxley	1.50	3.50	5.00	SF
T-76 Blade of Conquest - Jonreed Lauritzen	1.50	3.50	5.00	A
T-77 More Stories in the Modern Manner	.75	1.75	3.00	F
T-78 A Foreign Affair - John Baxter	.75	1.75	3.00	
T-79 The Scarlet Petticoat - Nard Jones	1.50	3.50	5.00	A
T-80 No Time Like the Future - Nelson Bond	2.00	4.00	6.00	SF
T-81 Captain Adam - Donald Barr Chidsey	2.00	4.00	6.00	A
T-82 I'll Never Go There Any More - Jerome Weidman	.75	1.75	3.00	
T-83 The Bitterweed Path - Thomas Hal Phillips	.75	1.75	3.00	
T-84 Naked Acre - Francis Mitchell aka The Wing and the Yoke	1.50	3.50	5.00	E
T-85 Gone to Texas - John W. Thomason, Jr.	1.50	3.50	5.00	W
T-86 Savage Holiday - Richard Wright	.75	1.75	3.00	
T-87 Dawn on Our Darkness - Emmanuel Robles	.75	1.75	3.00	
T-88 Send them Summer - Hansford Martin	.75	1.75	3.00	
T-89 The Merry Mistress - Philip Lindsay	1.50	3.50	5.00	
T-90 Nine Days to Mukalla - Frederic Prokosch	1.50	3.50	5.00	A
T-91 The Dark Journey - Julian Green	.75	1.75	3.00	
T-92 Belly Laughs Annual - Harold Meyers	2.00	4.00	6.00	H
T-93 What D'ya Know for Sure? - Len Zinberg	.75	1.75	3.00	
T-94 Diary of a Chambermaid - Octave Mirbeau	2.00	4.00	6.00	E
T-95 Honeymoon Guide - Harold Meyers	2.00	4.00	6.00	H
T-96 Lord of the Isles - Donald Barr Chidsey	1.50	3.50	5.00	A
T-97 I Can Get it for you Wholesale! - Jerome Weidman	.75	1.75	3.00	
T-98 Chattels of Eldorado - Edgar Jean Bracco c-Kinstler	2.00	4.00	7.50	A
T-99 Tough Kid from Brooklyn - Robert Mende	.75	1.75	3.00	
T-100 The Flesh and the Sea - John Dobbin	.75	1.75	3.00	
T-101 Life and Death of a Tough Guy - Benjamin Appel First ed., 1955	.75	1.75	3.00	M
T-102 Droll Stories - Honore de Balzac	1.50	3.50	5.00	
T-103 What's in it for Me? - Jerome Weidman	.75	1.75	3.00	E
T-104 Love in the Shadows - John Evans	.75	1.75	3.00	E
T-105 Juvenile Delinquents - Lenard Kaufman	1.50	3.50	5.00	JD
T-106 Confessions of a Princess - H. R. H.	2.00	4.00	6.00	A
T-107 Butterfield 8 - John O'Hara	.75	1.75	3.00	
T-108 Never Come Morning - Nelson Algren	.75	1.75	3.00	E
T-109 Various Temptations - anthology	2.00	4.00	6.00	
T-110 Royal Scandal - Philip Lindsay c-Kinstler	2.00	4.00	7.50	A
T-111 Dishonor - Gerald Kersh aka Night and the City	.75	1.75	3.00	
T-112 An Artist in Love - Philip Lindsay	.75	1.75	3.00	
T-113 Stories of Scarlet Women	1.50	3.50	5.00	E
T-114 The First Lady Chatterley - D. H. Lawrence	.75	1.75	3.00	E
T-115 Seven Footprints to Satan - A. A. Merritt 1956	2.00	4.00	7.50	SF
T-116 Suzanne, Savage Vixen - Jonreed Lauritzen	.75	1.75	3.00	
T-117 Typee: A Peep at Polynesian Life - Herman Melville c-Gauguin	2.00	4.00	7.50	E
T-118 The Loves of Liberace - Leo Guild	2.00	4.00	7.50	NF
T-119 Ashenden, or the British Agent - W. Somerset Maugham c-Kinstler	2.00	4.00	7.50	M
T-120 The Kiss and the Duel - Anton Chekhov	1.50	3.50	5.00	
T-121 Down and Out in Paris and London - George Orwell	1.50	3.50	5.00	
T-122 To Love by Candlelight - Philip Lindsay aka A Piece for Candlelight	1.50	3.50	5.00	E
T-123 Girls--for Men Only - John Paul Adams	1.50	3.50	5.00	H
T-124 Cry Tough! - Irving Shulman	.75	1.75	3.00	
T-125 The Neon Wilderness - Nelson Algren	1.50	3.50	5.00	E
T-126 Gold for the Gay Masters - Harriet Gray	.75	1.75	3.00	
T-127 Out of the Silent Planet - C. S. Lewis c-Kinstler	2.50	6.00	10.00	SF
T-128 Emma: My Lord Admiral's Mistress - F. W. Kenyon	.75	1.75	3.00	
T-129 The Gin Palace - Emile Zola	.75	1.75	3.00	
T-130 The Savage Soldiers - Harold Waters & Aubrey Wisberg	.75	1.75	3.00	

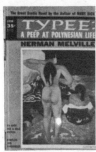

Avon T-117, c. Avon   Avon T-127, c. Avon   Avon T-165, c. Avon

(AVON T/AT-SERIES, continued)

T-131	Slipping Beauty - Jerome Weidman	.75	1.75	3.00	E
T-132	Naked Acre - Francis Mitchell	.75	1.75	3.00	E
T-133	Polikushka and Two Hussars - Leo Tolstoy	1.50	3.50	5.00	
T-134	Captain Adam - Donald Barr Chidsey	1.50	3.50	5.00	A
T-135	The Moon Pool - A. A. Merritt	1.50	3.50	5.00	SF
T-136	Sir Naked Blade - Philip Lindsay	1.50	3.50	5.00	A
T-137	The Bride Comes to Yellow Sky - Stephen Crane	1.50	3.50	5.00	W
T-138	The Amboy Dukes - Irving Shulman	1.50	3.50	5.00	
T-139	The Gifted Sinners - Roswell G. Ham, Jr.	.75	1.75	3.00	E
T-140	Temptation in Paris - Honore De Balzac aka Illusions Perdues	1.50	3.50	5.00	E
T-141	The Tragedy of X - Ellery Queen	1.50	3.50	5.00	
T-142	Murder in Port Afrique - Bernard Dryer	.75	1.75	3.00	
T-143	Burial of the Fruit - David Dortort	1.50	3.50	5.00	E
T-144	Coming Up for Air - George Orwell	1.50	3.50	5.00	
T-145	Diary of a Chambermaid - Octave Mirbeau	1.50	3.50	5.00	E
T-146	21st Century Sub - Frank Herbert aka The Dragon in the Sea	.75	1.75	3.00	SF
T-147	Money, Money, Money - David Wagoner	.75	1.75	3.00	
T-148	Around the World in 80 Days - Jules Verne Movie tie-in	1.50	3.50	5.00	SF
T-149	Death on the Nile - Agatha Christie	1.50	3.50	5.00	M
T-150	Zarak - A. J. Beran Movie tie-in	1.50	3.50	5.00	A
T-151	Hannibal: Scourge of Imperial Rome - Mary Dolan 1957, aka Hannibal of Carthage	1.50	3.50	5.00	A
T-152	The Ship of Ishtar - A. A. Merritt	1.50	3.50	5.00	SF
T-153	I'll Never Go There Any More - Jerome Weidman	.75	1.75	3.00	
T-154	26 Men and a Girl - Maxim Gorky	1.50	3.50	5.00	
T-155	Gladiator - Philip Wylie	1.50	3.50	5.00	SF
T-156	Bride of Violence - Harriet Gray	.75	1.75	3.00	E
T-157	Perelandra - C. S. Lewis	1.50	3.50	5.00	SF
T-158	A Man Can Love Twice - Robert Paul Smith	.75	1.75	3.00	
T-159	Intrigue in Paris - Sterling Noel	.75	1.75	3.00	
T-160	After the Fireworks and other Stories - Aldous Huxley aka Brief Candles	.75	1.75	3.00	E
T-161	Face in the Abyss - A. A. Merritt	1.50	3.50	5.00	SF
T-162	Teen-age Mobster - Benjamin Appel aka Life and Death of a Tough Guy	1.50	3.50	5.00	JD
T-163	Love Among the Haystacks - D. H. Lawrence	.75	1.75	3.00	E
T-164	The Scarlet Petticoat - Nard Jones	.75	1.75	3.00	
T-165	Boy on a Dolphin - David Divine Movie tie-in	2.00	4.00	7.50	A
T-166	Josephine, The Great Lover - N. P. Nezelof	.75	1.75	3.00	E
T-167	7 Dials Mystery - Agatha Christie	.75	1.75	3.00	M
T-168	Tomorrow Plus X - Wilson Tucker	.75	1.75	3.00	SF
T-169	The Unholy Wife - John Roeburt Movie tie-in	2.00	4.00	7.50	E
T-170	Juvenile Hoods - Joseph Shallit	2.00	4.00	6.00	JD
T-171	The Duke's Temptation - Paula Batchelor	.75	1.75	3.00	
T-172	The Metal Monster - A. A. Merritt	.75	1.75	3.00	SF
T-173	Naked Morning - R. V. Cassill	.75	1.75	3.00	
T-174	The Young Killers - Willard Wiener	.75	1.75	3.00	JD

T-175	From Outer Space - Hal Clement	.75	1.75	3.00	SF
T-176	A Holiday for Murder - Agatha Christie	.75	1.75	3.00	M
T-177	Man on Fire - Owen Aherne Movie tie-in	1.50	3.50	5.00	
T-178	Beyond Mombasa - Joseph Hilton Movie tie-in	1.50	3.50	5.00	A
T-179	Cry Slaughter! - E. K. Tiempo	.75	1.75	3.00	
T-180	The Space Plague - George O. Smith	.75	1.75	3.00	SF
T-181	Pickup Alley - Edward Ronns Movie tie-in	1.50	3.50	5.00	E
T-182	An Affair to Remember - Owen Aherne Movie tie-in	1.50	3.50	5.00	
T-183	Butterfield 8 - John O'Hara	.75	1.75	3.00	
T-184	Drury Lane's Last Case - Ellery Queen	.75	1.75	3.00	M
T-185	The Jungle - Nelson Algren	.75	1.75	3.00	
T-186	The Time Dissolver - Jerry Sohl	.75	1.75	3.00	SF
T-187	Temptations of Valerie - Harry Whittington Movie tie-in	1.50	3.50	5.00	E
T-188	Action of the Tiger - James Wellard Movie tie-in	1.50	3.50	5.00	A
T-189	Make My Bed in Hell - John B. Sanford	.75	1.75	3.00	
T-190	The Hunchback of Notre Dame - Victor Hugo Movie tie-in	2.50	6.00	10.00	HO
T-191	Bomber Crew - Joseph Landon	.75	1.75	3.00	C
T-192	Poirot Loses a Client - Agatha Christie	.75	1.75	3.00	M
T-193	Year 2018! - James Blish	.75	1.75	3.00	SF
T-194	The Wild One - Bonnie Golightly	.75	1.75	3.00	
T-195	The Flesh Agents - Jean Bosquet	.75	1.75	3.00	
T-196	Man in the Shadow - Harry Whittington Movie tie-in	1.50	3.50	5.00	
T-197	Panzer Ghost Division - Thomas Goethals	.75	1.75	3.00	C
T-198	Ride out for Revenge - Burt Arthur	.75	1.75	3.00	W
T-199	The Saint vs. Scotland Yard - Leslie Charteris	.75	1.75	3.00	M
T-200	Diary of a 16-year Old French Girl - Sidonie Colette	.75	1.75	3.00	
T-201	The Long Haul - Mervyn Mills Movie tie-in	1.50	3.50	5.00	
T-202	The Planet Explorer - Murray Leinster	1.50	3.50	5.00	SF
T-203	Les Girls - Constance Tomkinson Movie tie-in	1.50	3.50	5.00	
T-204	The Mysterious Affair at Styles - Agatha Christie	.75	1.75	3.00	M
T-205	U-Boat Killer - Donald MacIntyre	.75	1.75	3.00	E
T-206	Soldier's Weekend - Hansford Martin	.75	1.75	3.00	
T-207	The Price is Right - Jerome Weidman	.75	1.75	3.00	E
T-208	Seven Footprints to Satan - A. A. Merritt	2.00	4.00	7.50	SF
T-209	Don Gastone and the Women - Geoffredo Parise aka Don Gastone and the Ladies	.75	1.75	3.00	E
T-210	The Secret Adversary - Agatha Christie 1958	.75	1.75	3.00	M
T-211	The Tortured Planet - C. S. Lewis	1.50	3.50	5.00	SF
T-212	Case of the Dark Wanton - Peter Cheyney	.75	1.75	3.00	M
T-213	I Survived Hitler's Ovens - Olga Lengyel	1.50	3.50	5.00	NF
T-214	Hot Spell - Lonnie Coleman Movie tie-in	1.50	3.50	5.00	E
T-215	Tobruk Commando - Gordon Landsborough	.75	1.75	3.00	C
T-216	Case of the Red Box - Rex Stout	.75	1.75	3.00	M
T-217	Juvenile Delinquents - Lenard Kaufman aka The Lower Part of the Sky	2.00	4.00	6.00	JD
T-218	A Modern Lover - D. H. Lawrence	.75	1.75	3.00	E
T-219	Juvenile Jungle - Firth Counsel	1.50	3.50	5.00	JD
T-220	The Regatta Mystery - Agatha Christie	.75	1.75	3.00	M
T-221	Children of the Atom - Wilmar H. Shiras	1.50	3.50	5.00	SF
T-222	Officers' Plot to Kill Hitler - Constantine Fitzgibbon	1.50	3.50	5.00	NF
T-223	Never Come Morning - Nelson Algren	.75	1.75	3.00	
T-224	Passiontide - Wirt Williams	.75	1.75	3.00	
T-225	Earthman, Come Home - James Blish	1.50	3.50	5.00	SF
T-226	Raid at Dieppe - Quentin Reynolds	.75	1.75	3.00	C
T-227	Belly Laughs Annual - Harold Meyers	1.50	3.50	5.00	H
T-228	The Lady Takes a Flyer - Edward Ronns Movie tie-in	1.50	3.50	5.00	M
T-229	Young and Wild - Morton Cooper	.75	1.75	3.00	

T-230	Cry Baby Killer - Joseph Hilton	1.50	3.50	5.00	
	Movie tie-in				
T-231	Rogue's March - Maristau Chapman	1.50	3.50	5.00	A
T-232	2nd Foundation: Galactic Empire - Isaac Asimov	1.50	3.50	5.00	SF
T-233	Impatient Virgin - Donald Henderson Clarke	.75	1.75	3.00	
T-234	The Saint in Miami - Leslie Charteris	.75	1.75	3.00	M
T-235	Gang Girl - Wenzell Brown	2.00	4.00	7.50	JD
T-236	The Secret Raiders - David Woodward	.75	1.75	3.00	
T-237	High Cost of Loving - Bonnie Golightly	1.50	3.50	5.00	
	Movie tie-in				
T-238	VOR - James Blish	.75	1.75	3.00	SF
T-239	D-Day - John Gunther	.75	1.75	3.00	C
T-240	I Can Get It For You Wholesale! - Jerome Weidman	.75	1.75	3.00	
T-241	Teen-age Jungle - Harry Whittington	2.00	4.00	6.00	JD
T-242	The Four of Hearts - Ellery Queen	.75	1.75	3.00	M
T-243	Murder in Three Acts - Agatha Christie	.75	1.75	3.00	M
T-244	Naked Sin - Gordon Clark	.75	1.75	3.00	E
	Orig., 1958				
T-245	The Tuesday Club Murders - Agatha Christie	.75	1.75	3.00	M
T-246	Sunk! - Mochitsura Hashimoto	.75	1.75	3.00	C
T-247	Delinquent! - Morton Cooper	2.00	4.00	6.00	JD
	Orig., 1958				
T-248	Chattels of Eldorado - Edgar Jean Bracco	.75	1.75	3.00	A
T-249	Worlds Apart - J. T. McIntosh	.75	1.75	3.00	SF
T-250	The Saint in England - Leslie Charteris	.75	1.75	3.00	M
T-251	The Young Who Sin - John Haase	.75	1.75	3.00	
T-252	The Mind Cage - A. E. Van Vogt	1.50	3.50	5.00	SF
T-253	Breathe No More, My Lady - Ed Lacy	.75	1.75	3.00	
T-254	Death of a Fool - Ngaio Marsh	.75	1.75	3.00	M
T-255	Of All My Sins - Thomas Rourke	.75	1.75	3.00	
T-256	Jet Ace - Tedd Thomey	.75	1.75	3.00	C
T-257	High School Confidential - Morton Cooper	1.50	3.50	5.00	
	Movie tie-in				
T-258	The G-String Murders - Gypsy Rose Lee	.75	1.75	3.00	M
	Note: Actually written by Craig Rice				
T-259	Hiroshima Diary - Michihiko Hachiya	1.50	3.50	5.00	C
T-260	Painted Veils - James Huneker	.75	1.75	3.00	
T-261	Waldo: Genius in Orbit - Robert A. Heinlein	1.50	3.50	5.00	SF
T-262	Gang Rumble - Edward Ronns	1.50	3.50	5.00	JD
T-263	Love in the Shadows - John Evans	.75	1.75	3.00	E
	aka Shadows Flying				
T-264	Trinity in Violence - Henry Kane	.75	1.75	3.00	M
T-265	Cry Attack! - John Burgan	.75	1.75	3.00	C
T-266	The Vice Trap - Elliott Gilbert	.75	1.75	3.00	
T-267	Naked Tide - Roderic Hastings	.75	1.75	3.00	
T-268	ESPer - James Blish	1.50	3.50	5.00	SF
T-269	Mitsou - Sidonie Colette	.75	1.75	3.00	
T-270	Run for Your Life! - Sterling Noel	.75	1.75	3.00	M
	Orig., 1958				
T-271	Raw Wind in Eden - Ed Robinson	1.50	3.50	5.00	
	Movie tie-in				
T-272	I am a Marked Woman - anonymous	.75	1.75	3.00	E
T-273	The Bitterweed Path - Thomas Hal Phillips	.75	1.75	3.00	
T-274	West of the Law - Al Cody	.75	1.75	3.00	W
T-275	Destination: Infinity - Henry Kuttner	1.50	3.50	5.00	SF
T-276	Fistful of Death - Henry Kane	.75	1.75	3.00	M
T-277	Sinful - Bart Frame	.75	1.75	3.00	
T-278	Out for a Killing - John W. Vandercook	.75	1.75	3.00	
T-279	The Triumph of Time - James Blish	1.50	3.50	5.00	SF
T-280	Death Hits the Jackpot - Walter Wager	.75	1.75	3.00	M
T-281	Lustful Summer - R. V. Cassill	.75	1.75	3.00	E
	Orig., 1958				
T-282	Honeymoon Guide - Harold Meyers	1.50	3.50	5.00	H
T-283	A Hell of a Murder - Warren Carrier	.75	1.75	3.00	M
T-284	Horror! - H. P. Lovecraft	1.50	3.50	5.00	HO
T-285	Shameless - James M. Cain	.75	1.75	3.00	
T-286	The Merry Mistress - Philip Lindsay	.75	1.75	3.00	
T-287	The Death Dealers - Isaac Asimov	1.50	3.50	5.00	M
T-288	Shakedown for Murder - Ed Lacy	.75	1.75	3.00	
T-289	BR-R-R! - Groff Conklin	.75	1.75	3.00	SF
	1959				
T-290	Prelude to Murder - Sterling Noel	.75	1.75	3.00	

T-291	Death is the Last Lover - Henry Kane	.75	1.75	3.00	M
T-292	The American Gun Mystery - Ellery Queen	.75	1.75	3.00	M
T-293	The Buccaneer - R. V. Cassill	1.50	3.50	5.00	A
	Movie tie-in				
T-294	Waiting for Willy - Jack Houston	.75	1.75	3.00	
T-295	The Hot Half Hour - Robert L. Foreman	.75	1.75	3.00	
T-296	Over My Dead Body - Rex Stout	.75	1.75	3.00	M
T-297	Doomsday Morning - C. L. Moore	1.50	3.50	5.00	SF
T-298	Break-up - Edmund Schiddel	.75	1.75	3.00	
T-299	Halfway to Hell - Harry Whittington	.75	1.75	3.00	
T-300	Confidential - Donald Henderson Clarke	.75	1.75	3.00	
T-301	Claudine - Sidonie Colette	.75	1.75	3.00	
T-302	The Subterraneans - Jack Kerouac	1.50	3.50	5.00	
	Note: Origional preface by Henry Miller				
T-303	Cry Tough! - Irving Shulman	1.50	3.50	5.00	
	Movie tie-in				
T-304	Aliens 4 - Theodore Sturgeon	1.50	3.50	5.00	SF
T-305	The Naked Sword - Donald Barr Chidsey	1.50	3.50	5.00	A
T-306	The Night Was Made for Murder - Will				
	Cotton	.75	1.75	3.00	M
T-307	Doorway to Death - Dan Marlowe	.75	1.75	3.00	M
T-308	And Sin No More - H. P. Koenig	.75	1.75	3.00	
T-309	Mark It for Murder - Douglas Sanderson	.75	1.75	3.00	M
T-310	Beat Girl - Bonnie Golightly	1.50	3.50	5.00	
T-311	Anything for Kicks - Morton Cooper	.75	1.75	3.00	
T-312	The Lonely Gun - Gordon D. Shirreffs	.75	1.75	3.00	W
T-313	Diary of a Geisha Girl - Kimiko Omura &				
	William Vaneer	.75	1.75	3.00	E
T-314	Undressed to Kill - Peter Cheyney	.75	1.75	3.00	M
T-315	Death in the Desert - Lee E. Wells	.75	1.75	3.00	W
T-316	Ginny - Morton Cooper	.75	1.75	3.00	
T-317	The Saint in New York - Leslie Charteris	.75	1.75	3.00	M
T-318	Lord of the Isles - Donald Barr Chidsey	.75	1.75	3.00	A
T-319	Too Innocent to Kill - Doris Miles Disney	.75	1.75	3.00	M
T-320	The Blonde in Suite 14 - Stewart Sterling	.75	1.75	3.00	M
T-321	They Who Sin - John Roeburt	.75	1.75	3.00	E
T-322	The Hard Man - Philip Ketchum	.75	1.75	3.00	W
T-323	Pnin - Vladimir Nabokov	.75	1.75	3.00	
T-324	The Jungle - Nelson Algren	.75	1.75	3.00	
T-325	The Savage Warriors - Henry Treece	1.50	3.50	5.00	A
	aka The Dark Island				
T-326	Never Leave Me - Harold Robbins	.75	1.75	3.00	E
T-327	Gun for Sale - Lee E. Wells	.75	1.75	3.00	W
T-328	The Real Cool Killers - Chester Himes	.75	1.75	3.00	
T-329	The Shame - Richard Himmel	.75	1.75	3.00	
T-330	Blonde Bait - Stephen Marlowe	.75	1.75	3.00	M
T-331	Savage Star - Lewis B. Patten	.75	1.75	3.00	W
T-332	How Rough Can it Get? - Joe Weiss	.75	1.75	3.00	
T-333	The Devil's Bride - Carter A. Vaughan	1.50	3.50	5.00	A
T-334	The Amboy Dukes - Irving Shulman	.75	1.75	3.00	
T-335	Sugar - Gil Brewer	.75	1.75	3.00	E
	Orig., 1959				
T-336	The Strange Co-ed - Bart Frame	.75	1.75	3.00	
T-337	The Tragedy of Y - Ellery Queen	.75	1.75	3.00	M
T-338	Nadia - Assia Djebar	.75	1.75	3.00	
T-339	The Man Who Rode Alone - Lewis B. Patten	.75	1.75	3.00	W
T-340	The Subterraneans - Jack Kerouac	.75	1.75	3.00	
T-341	Iron Lover - Gardner F. Fox	1.50	3.50	5.00	A
T-342	The Unholy Lovers - Paul Monash	.75	1.75	3.00	E
T-343	Find Eileen Hardin - Alive! - Andrew Frazer	.75	1.75	3.00	
T-344	Three Loves Had She - Mark Schorer	.75	1.75	3.00	
T-345	Monsters and Such - Murray Leinster	1.50	3.50	5.00	SF
T-346	Bachelor's Joke Book - Leo Guild	1.50	3.50	5.00	H
T-347	Strange Bargain - Harry Whittington	.75	1.75	3.00	
T-348	This Range is Mine - Dean Owen	.75	1.75	3.00	W
T-349	Killer with a Key - Dan Marlowe	.75	1.75	3.00	M
T-350	Love for a Stranger - John Pleasant McCoy	.75	1.75	3.00	
T-351	Murder is an Art - Michael Innes	.75	1.75	3.00	M
	aka One Man Show				
T-352	Fort Suicide - Gordon D. Shirreffs	.75	1.75	3.00	W
T-353	The Town that God Forgot - William Colt				
	MacDonald	.75	1.75	3.00	W
T-354	Beyond the Night - Cornell Woolrich	1.50	3.50	5.00	M
	Orig., 1959				
T-355	Bachelor Summer - Herbert D. Kastle	.75	1.75	3.00	

Avon Bard 5, c. Avon   Avon Bedside Novel 2, c. Avon   Avon Book Dividend 2, c. Avon

(AVON T/AT-SERIES, continued)

T-356	Girl in a Jam - James Savage	.75	1.75	3.00	
T-357	The Crazy Kill - Chester Himes	.75	1.75	3.00	
T-358	The Mistress - Theodora Keogh	.75	1.75	3.00	
T-359	Rusty Desmond - Steve January	.75	1.75	3.00	JD
T-360	We Who Survived...the Fifth Ice Age - Sterling Noel	1.50	3.50	5.00	SF
T-361	Run, Killer, Run! - Lionel White	.75	1.75	3.00	
T-362	The Man Who Could Cheat Death - Barre Lyndon & Jimmy Sangster Movie tie-in	2.00	4.00	7.50	SF
T-363	The Pagan Queen - Henry Treece aka Red Queen, White Queen	1.50	3.50	5.00	A
T-364	Young Awakening - Robert Fontaine	.75	1.75	3.00	
T-365	The Terrible Night - Peter Cheyney	.75	1.75	3.00	M
T-366	The Figure in the Dusk - John Creasey	.75	1.75	3.00	M
T-367	Avon Bedside Companion	.75	1.75	3.00	
T-368	Cheyenne War Cry - Noel M. Loomis	.75	1.75	3.00	W
T-369	Ambush at Scorpion Valley - William Colt MacDonald	.75	1.75	3.00	W
T-370	The Captive - Norman Daniels Orig., 1959	.75	1.75	3.00	E
T-371	Planet in Peril - John Christopher	.75	1.75	3.00	SF
T-372	The Long Night - Orid Demaris	.75	1.75	3.00	
T-373	Law Killer - Richard Brister	.75	1.75	3.00	W
T-374	Where There's a Will - Rex Stout	.75	1.75	3.00	M
T-375	I, Barbarian - Jay Scotland (John Jakes) Orig., 1959	2.00	4.00	6.00	A
T-376	Beat Not the Bones - Charlotte Jay	.75	1.75	3.00	
T-377	McHugh - Jay Flynn	.75	1.75	3.00	M
T-378	The Naked Land - Lee E. Wells	.75	1.75	3.00	W
T-379	The Blockhouse - Jean-Paul Clebert 1960	.75	1.75	3.00	NF

AVON ANNUAL

(Avon Book Company)

Digest size

nn(1)	Avon Annual 1944	4.00	8.00	15.00
nn(2)	Avon Annual 1945	3.00	6.00	12.00
nn(3)	Avon Annual 1946	3.00	6.00	12.00
nn(4)	Avon Annual 1947	3.00	6.00	12.00

AVON BARD

(Avon Publications, Inc./Avon Book Division - Hearst Corporation)

(AVON BARD, continued)

Bard	1	The Rubaiyat of Omar Khayyam 1955	1.50	3.50	5.00	
Bard	2	The Meaning and Psychology of Dreams - Wilheim Stekel	1.50	3.50	5.00	NF
Bard	3	Anyone Can Have a Great Vocabulary - S. L. Stephenson	1.50	3.50	5.00	NF
Bard	4	Favorite Stories - W. Somerset Maugham	1.50	3.50	5.00	
Bard T 05	5	My Lord What a Morning - Marian Anderson 1958	1.50	3.50	5.00	
Bard T 06	6	You and the Atom - Gerald Wendt	1.50	3.50	5.00	NF
Bard T 11	11	Sonnets from the Portugese - Elizabeth Barrett Browning	1.50	3.50	5.00	

AVON BEDSIDE NOVELS

(Avon Publishing Company, Inc.)

Digest size

1	The Rites of Love - Jack Woodford	4.00	8.00	15.00	E
2	The Hard-boiled Virgin - Jack Woodford 1950	4.00	8.00	15.00	E
3	Queer Patterns - Lilyan Brock	4.00	8.00	15.00	E
4	Bedroom Eyes - Maurice Dekobra	4.00	8.00	15.00	E
5	Male and Female - Jack Woodford	4.00	8.00	15.00	E
6	The Passionate Princess - Jack Woodford aka Proxy Princess	4.00	8.00	15.00	E

AVON BOOK DIVIDEND

(Avon Publishing Company, Inc.)

Digest size

1	The Abortive Hussy - Jack Woodford	4.00	8.00	15.00	E
2	Star Lust - Jack Hanley	4.00	8.00	15.00	E
3	New York Madness - Maxwell Bodenheim	4.00	8.00	15.00	E
4	Grounds for Divorce - Jack Woodford	4.00	8.00	15.00	E
5	Her Private Passions - Marty Holland	4.00	8.00	15.00	E
6	Teach Me to Love - Jack Woodford	4.00	8.00	15.00	E
7	Tropical Passions - anthology	4.00	8.00	15.00	E

AVON FANTASY NOVELS

(Avon Publishing Company)

 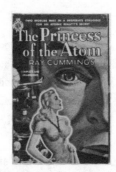 

Avon Book Dividend 3, c. Avon   Avon Fant. Novels 1, c. Avon   Avon Fant. Novels 2, c. Avon

Avon Fant. Reader 1, c. Avon   Avon Fant. Reader 3, c. Avon   Avon Fant. Reader 14, c. Avon

(AVON FANTASY NOVELS, continued)

1 Princess of the Atom - Ray Cummings 1950	10.00	20.00	35.00	SF
2 The Green Girl - Jack Williamson 1950	12.50	25.00	40.00	SF

Note: Coblentz' Into Plutonian Depths and Farley's Earthman on Venus were planned as no. 3 and 4 of the series but instead became no. 281 and 285 of the regular Avon series.

AVON FANTASY READER

(Avon Book Company/Avon Novels, Inc.)

Digest size

1 Includes Leinster, Derleth, Merritt, Smith, Others 1947	5.00	10.00	20.00	SF
2 Includes Pratt, Howard, Endore, Keller, 1947	3.00	6.00	12.00	SF
3 Includes Merritt, Lovecraft, Moore, Bradbury, Others 1947	4.00	8.00	15.00	SF
4 Includes Miller, Bradbury, Smith, Van Vogt, Others 1947	3.00	6.00	12.00	SF
5 Includes Moore, Bloch, Jacobi, Kornbluth 1947	3.00	6.00	12.00	SF
6 Includes Lovecraft, Merritt, Hamilton, McClusky, Others 1948	4.00	8.00	15.00	SF
7 Includes Moore, Rohmer, Howard, Merritt, Others 1948	4.00	8.00	15.00	SF
8 Includes Howard, Bradbury, Lovecraft, Bierce, Others 1948	4.00	8.00	15.00	SF
9 Includes Smith, Leiber, Kline, Bloch, Others 1949	3.00	6.00	12.00	SF
10 Includes Howard, Lovecraft, Breuer, Wollheim, Others 1949	3.00	6.00	12.00	SF
11 Includes Quinn, Bond, Stribling, Bradbury, Others 1949	3.00	6.00	12.00	SF
12 Includes Howard, Smith, Rohmer, Wellman, Others	3.00	6.00	12.00	SF
13 Includes Long, Cummings, Derleth, Wandrel, Others 1950	3.00	6.00	12.00	SF
14 Includes Howard, Bradbury, Cummings, Keller, Others 1950	4.00	8.00	15.00	SF

15	Includes Weinbaum, Smith, Kornbluth, Miller, Others 1951	3.00	6.00	12.00	SF
16	Includes Bloch, Shiel, Wandrei, Long, Others 1951	3.00	6.00	12.00	SF
17	Includes Bradbury, Lovecraft, Price, Chesterton, Others 1951	4.00	8.00	15.00	SF
18	Includes Howard, Hodgson, Blackwood, Clark, Others 1952	4.00	8.00	15.00	SF

AVON LOVE BOOK MONTHLY

(Avon Publishing Company, Inc.)

Digest size

1	Blonde Baggage - Marty Holland	4.00	8.00	15.00	E
2	Chorus Girl - Thyra Samter Winslow	4.00	8.00	15.00	E

AVON MONTHLY NOVEL

(Avon Publishing Co., Inc.)

Digest size

1	Sinful Woman - James M. Cain Orig., 1947	4.00	8.00	15.00	E
2	Her Private Passions - Marty Holland	4.00	8.00	15.00	E
3	The Regenerate Lover - D. H. Clarke	4.00	8.00	15.00	E
4	The Villain and the Virgin - J. H. Chase	4.00	8.00	15.00	E
5	Uneasy Virtue - Dana Wilson 1948, aka Make with the Brains, Pierre	4.00	8.00	15.00	E
6	Strange Desires - Len Zinberg aka What D'ya Know for Sure	4.00	8.00	15.00	E
7	12 Chinks and a Woman - J. H. Chase	8.00	16.00	30.00	E
8	Virgie, Goodbye - Nathan Rothman Note: Same cover as the comic Romantic Love no. 7	4.00	8.00	15.00	E
9	The Scarf of Passion - Robert Bloch aka The Scarf Note: Same cover as Avon 211 and an unnumbered Avon Special of the same name.	4.00	8.00	15.00	E
10	The Lady Said Yes - G. V. Martin	4.00	8.00	15.00	E
11	The Devil is Loneliness - Elma K. Lobaugh	4.00	8.00	15.00	E
12	Little Sins - Katharine Brush	4.00	8.00	15.00	E
13	Carlotta - Robert Briffault	4.00	8.00	15.00	E
14	The Man Who Drove Girls Wild - M. H. Hanline	3.00	6.00	12.00	E
15	The Darling of Paris - Marty Holland Orig., 1949	3.00	6.00	12.00	E

Avon Monthly Nov. 1, c. Avon   Avon Monthly Nov. 9, c. Avon   Avon SF & Fant. 1, c. Avon

Avon SF Reader 1, c. Avon   Avon Specials nn, c. Avon   Avon West. Novel 1, c. Avon

(AVON MONTHLY NOVEL, continued)

16 Millie's Daughter - D. H. Clarke	3.00	6.00	12.00	E
17 Jealous Woman - J. M. Cain	3.00	6.00	12.00	E
18 I'll Get You for This - J. H. Chase	3.00	6.00	12.00	E
19				
20 Ecstasy Girl - Jack Woodford	3.00	6.00	12.00	E
21 Tomcat in Tights - Jack Hanley	3.00	6.00	12.00	E

AVON SCIENCE FICTION AND FANTASY READER

(Avon Novels, Inc./Stratford Novels, Inc.)

Digest size

1 Includes Clarke, Christopher, Jakes, Others 1953	2.50	6.00	10.00	SF
2 Includes Vance, Clarke, Jakes, Others 1953	2.00	4.00	7.50	SF

AVON SCIENCE FICTION READER

(Avon Novels, Inc.)

Digest size

1 Includes Hamilton, Merritt, Williamson, Smith, Others 1951	4.00	8.00	15.00	SF
2 Includes Wandrei, Smith, Cummings, Dunsany, Others 1951	3.00	6.00	12.00	SF
3 Includes Long, Wright, Lovecraft Bok, Others 1952	3.00	6.00	12.00	SF

AVON SPECIALS

(Avon Publishing Company, Inc.)

Digest size

nn Seduction - Leo Guild	4.00	8.00	15.00	E
nn A Lady Named Lou - D. H. Clarke	4.00	8.00	15.00	E
nn Peeping Tom - Woodford	4.00	8.00	15.00	E
nn Night Club Girl - John Wilstach 1951, aka Fiddler's Fee	4.00	8.00	15.00	E
nn Three Gorgeous Hussies - Woodford	4.00	8.00	15.00	E
nn Free Lovers - Woodford	4.00	8.00	15.00	E
nn Scarf of Passion - Robert Bloch Note: Same cover as Avon 211 and Avon Monthly Novel 9.	4.00	8.00	15.00	E

AVON WESTERN NOVEL MONTHLY

(Avon Publishing Co., Inc.)

Digest size

1 The Gun-Wolf of Tubac - Nelson C. Nye 1949, aka The Barber of Tubac	3.00	6.00	12.00	W
2 Cattle War Buckaroo - William Hopson 1950, aka The Laughing Vaquero	3.00	6.00	12.00	W
3 Arizona Roundup - William Hopson	3.00	6.00	12.00	W

AVON WESTERN READER

(Avon Book Company)

Digest size

1	3.00	6.00	12.00	W
2 Includes White, Drago, Haycox, Others 1947	3.00	6.00	12.00	W

BALLANTINE BOOKS

(Ballantine Books, Inc.)

1 Executive Suite - Cameron Hawley 1952	2.00	4.00	7.50	
2 The Golden Spike - Hal Ellson Orig., 1952	3.00	6.00	12.00	E
3 All My Enemies - Stanley Baron	2.00	4.00	7.50	
4 Saddle by Starlight - Luke Short	2.00	4.00	7.50	W
5 The Witch's Thorn - Ruth Park	2.00	4.00	7.50	
6 Tides of Time - Emile Danoen First ed., 1952, aka Dust in the Wind	2.00	4.00	7.50	E
7 Blood on the Land - Frank Bonham	2.00	4.00	7.50	W
8 The World of Li'l Abner - Al Capp	4.00	8.00	15.00	H
9 The Red Gate - LaSelle Gilman	2.00	4.00	7.50	
10 Concannon - Frank O'Rourke	2.50	6.00	10.00	W
With dust jacket c-Saunders	5.00	10.00	20.00	
11 War Bonnet - Clay Fisher	2.00	4.00	7.50	W
12 Heyday - W. M. Spackman Orig., 1953	1.50	3.50	5.00	
13 First Blood - Jack Schaefer Orig., 1953	2.00	4.00	7.50	W
14 Why Did They Kill? - John Bartlow Martin	2.00	4.00	7.50	NF
15 The Wheel and the Hearth - Lucia B. Moore	2.00	4.00	7.50	
16 Star Science Fiction Stories - Frederik Pohl	3.00	6.00	12.00	SF
17 The Racer - Hans Ruesch	2.00	4.00	7.50	

Avon West. Reader 2, c. Avon   Ballantine Books 1, c. BB   Ballantine Books 2, c. BB

Ballantine Books 10, c. BB   Ballantine Books 28, c. BB   Ballantine Books 41, c. BB

(BALLANTINE BOOKS, continued)

18	Kingdom of the Spur - Gene Markey	2.00	4.00	7.50	W
19	Stories of Sudden Truth - Elizabeth Abell & Joseph I. Green	2.00	4.00	7.50	
20	I Thought of Daisy - Edmund Wilson	2.00	4.00	7.50	
21	The Space Merchants - F. Pohl & C. M. Kornbluth	4.00	8.00	15.00	SF
	Orig., 1953, c-Powers				
22	The Big Range - Jack Schaefer	2.00	4.00	7.50	W
23	Patrol - Fred Majdalany	2.00	4.00	7.50	
24	Desert Passage - Richard Poole	2.00	4.00	7.50	W
25	The Undying Fire - Fletcher Pratt	3.00	6.00	12.00	SF
	Orig., 1953, c-Powers				
26	The City of Anger - William Manchester	2.00	4.00	7.50	
	Orig., 1953				
27	Summer Street - Hal Ellson	2.00	4.00	7.50	
	Orig., 1953, c-Maguire				
28	The Secret Masters - Gerald Kersh	3.00	6.00	12.00	SF
	Orig., 1953, aka The Great Wash, c-Powers				
29	Indian Country - Dorothy M. Johnson	2.00	4.00	7.50	
30	Ahead of Time - Henry Kuttner	2.50	6.00	10.00	SF
31	A Gradual Joy - Alma Routsong	1.50	3.50	5.00	
32	The Far Command - Elinor Chamberlain	2.00	4.00	7.50	
33	Childhood's End - Arthur C. Clarke	2.50	6.00	10.00	SF
34	The Best Short Stories of 1953	1.50	3.50	5.00	
35	Gun Hand - Frank O'Rourke	2.00	4.00	7.50	
36	Earthly Creatures - Charles Jackson	2.00	4.00	7.50	
37	Silent Army - Chin Kee Onn	2.00	4.00	7.50	C
38	Bring the Jubilee - Ward Moore	1.50	3.50	5.00	SF
39	New Poems by American Poets - Rolfe Humphries	2.00	4.00	7.50	
40	Yellow Hair - Clay Fisher	2.00	4.00	7.50	W
41	Fahrenheit 451 - Ray Bradbury	4.00	8.00	15.00	SF
42	Ratoons - Daphne Rooke	2.00	4.00	7.50	A
43	Silver Rock - Luke Short	2.00	4.00	7.50	W
44	The Valiant Virginians - James Warner Bellah	2.00	4.00	7.50	W
45	The Canyon - Jack Schaefer	2.00	4.00	7.50	W
46	More than Human - Theodore Sturgeon	2.50	6.00	10.00	SF
47	King of Abilene - Thomas Thompson	2.00	4.00	7.50	W
48	The Burl Ives Song Book - Burl Ives	2.00	4.00	7.50	NF
49	Ride West - Frank O'Rourke	2.00	4.00	7.50	W
50	Out of the Deeps - John Wyndham	2.00	4.00	7.50	SF
	Orig., 1953, aka The Kraken Wakes				
51	Law Man - Lee Leighton	2.00	4.00	7.50	W
52	Expedition to Earth - Arthur C. Clarke	2.50	6.00	10.00	SF
53	Edge of the World - Vincent McHugh	2.00	4.00	7.50	
54	The Bounty Hunters - Elmore Leonard	2.00	4.00	7.50	W
55	Star Science Fiction Stories No. 2 - Frederik Pohl	2.00	4.00	7.50	SF
56	Dark Dominion - David Duncan	2.00	4.00	7.50	SF
	Orig., 1954				
57	Brandon's Empire - Dave Hardin	2.00	4.00	7.50	W
58	Riders to the Stars - Curt Siodmak	2.00	4.00	7.50	SF
59	The Tall Men - Clay Fisher	2.00	4.00	7.50	W
60	The Peacemaker - Richard Poole	2.00	4.00	7.50	W
	Orig., 1954				
61	Search the Sky - Frederik Pohl & C. M. Kornbluth	2.50	6.00	10.00	SF
	Orig., 1954, c-Powers				

(BALLANTINE BOOKS, continued)

62	The Night Winds - Brian Talbot Cleeve	2.00	4.00	7.50	
63	New Short Novels - Mary Louise Aswell	1.50	3.50	5.00	
	Orig., 1954				
64	Night Raid - Frank Bonhaur	2.00	4.00	7.50	W
65	West of Justice - John Hunter	2.00	4.00	7.50	W
	Orig., 1954				
66	The Coasts of the Earth - Harold E. Livingston	1.50	3.50	5.00	
	Orig., 1954				
67	Aircraft Carrier - Joseph Bryan III	2.00	4.00	7.50	NF
68	Prelude to Space - Arthur C. Clarke	2.00	4.00	7.50	SF
69	Thunder in the Sun - Frank O'Rourke	2.00	4.00	7.50	W
70	Broken Wagon - Norman A. Fox	2.00	4.00	7.50	W
71	Hero's Walk - Robert Crane	2.50	6.00	10.00	SF
	Orig., 1954				
72	Prize Articles 1954 - Llewellyn Miller	2.50	6.00	10.00	
	Orig., 1954				
	Note: Contains first book appearance of a Ray Bradbury story.				
73	Untouched by Human Hands - Robert Sheckley	2.50	6.00	10.00	SF
	Orig., 1954				
74	Trouble Rider - Thomas Thompson	2.00	4.00	7.50	W
	Orig., 1954				
75	American Accent - Elizabeth Abell	1.50	3.50	5.00	
76	Trumpets of Company K - William Chamberlain	2.00	4.00	6.00	W
	Orig., 1954				
F77	Break Down the Walls - John Bartlow Martin	2.00	4.00	6.00	NF
78	The Real Story of Lucille Ball - Eleanor Harris	3.00	6.00	12.00	B
79	An Indian's Tale - Jefferson McCall	2.00	4.00	7.50	W
80	Brain Wave - Poul Anderson	2.00	4.00	7.50	SF
81	The One I Love - E. A. Fishman	1.50	3.50	5.00	
82	High Vengeance - Frank O'Rourke	2.00	4.00	7.50	W
83	The Deadly Derringer - Sam Meriwether	2.00	4.00	7.50	W
84	They Brought Their Guns - Thomas Thompson	2.00	4.00	7.50	W
85	The Feud at Spanish Ford - Frank Bonham	2.00	4.00	7.50	W
86	The Explorers - C. M. Kornbluth	2.00	4.00	7.50	SF
	Orig., 1954				
87	Fire in the Desert - Ford Logan	2.00	4.00	6.00	
88	Strange Conquest - Alfred Neumann	2.00	4.00	6.00	
89	Star Short Novels - Frederik Pohl	2.00	4.00	7.50	SF
90	Security and the Middle East	1.50	3.50	5.00	NF
91	Shadows in the Sun - Chad Oliver	2.00	4.00	7.50	SF
	Orig., 1954				
92	A Life for a Life - Horst Fanyer	2.00	4.00	6.00	
93	The Mad Reader - Harvey Kurtzman	3.00	6.00	12.00	H
94	Messiah - Gore Vidal	4.00	8.00	15.00	SF
	1954, c-Powers				
95	Brave Harvest - Richard Cargoe	1.50	3.50	5.00	W
	Orig., 1954				
96	Star Science Fiction Stories No. 3 - Frederik Pohl	2.00	4.00	7.50	SF
97	Earthlight - Arthur C. Clarke	2.00	4.00	7.50	SF
98	Violence at Sundown - Frank O'Rourke	2.00	4.00	6.00	W
99	Of all Possible Worlds - William Tenn	2.50	6.00	10.00	SF
	Orig., 1955, c-Powers				
100	Young - Miriam Colwell	1.50	3.50	5.00	
101	The Dam Busters - Paul Brickhill	2.00	4.00	7.50	NF
102	Beyond Eden - David Duncan	2.00	4.00	7.50	SF
	Orig., 1955, c-Powers				

Ballantine Books 45, c. BB

Ballantine Books 50, c. BB

Ballantine Books 63, c. BB

Ballantine Books 78, c. BB   Ballantine Books 99, c. BB   Ballantine Books 108, c. BB

(BALLANTINE BOOKS, continued)

103 Rock - Hal Ellson	2.00	4.00	7.50	
104 Re-Birth - John Wyndham	2.00	4.00	7.50	SF
Orig., 1955, c-Powers				
105 How to Play with Your Child - A. F. Arnold	1.50	3.50	5.00	NF
106 Mad Strikes Back - Harvey Kurtzman	3.00	6.00	12.00	H
107 Gladiator-at-Law - Frederick Pohl & C. M. Kornbluth	2.00	4.00	7.50	SF
c-Powers				
108 Marilyn Monroe as the Girl - Sam Shaw	5.00	10.00	20.00	
109 Far and Away - Anthony Boucher	2.00	4.00	7.50	SF
Orig., 1955				
110 The Mackenzie Raid - Red Reeder	2.00	4.00	7.50	W
111 Car Deal! - Frank O'Rourke	2.00	4.00	7.50	
Orig., 1955				
112 My Lady Greensleaves - Constance Beresford-Howe	2.00	4.00	6.00	A
113 Another Kind - Chad Oliver	2.00	4.00	7.50	SF
Orig., 1955, c-Powers				
114 The Guests of Faine - Daniel Stern	1.50	3.50	5.00	
115 The Power of Negative Thinking - Charles Preston	1.50	3.50	5.00	H
116 Jet - Frank Harvey	2.00	4.00	6.00	C
117 The Girls from Planet 5 - Richard Wilson	3.00	6.00	12.00	SF
Orig., 1955, c-Powers				
118 Great Dog Stories - Stanley Kaufmann	2.00	4.00	7.50	
119 Caviar - Theodore Sturgeon	2.50	6.00	10.00	
Orig., 1955				
120 U-Boats at War - Harald Busch	2.00	4.00	7.50	NF
121 Lone Gun - Clark Brooker	2.00	4.00	6.00	W
122 No Boundaries - Henry Kuttner & C. L. Moore	2.00	4.00	7.50	
Orig., 1955				
123 A Town is Drowning - C. M. Kornbluth & Frederik Pohl	4.00	8.00	15.00	
124 Inside Mad - Harvey Kurtzman	3.00	6.00	12.00	H
125 North to Texas - Noel M. Loomis	2.00	4.00	6.00	W
126 Citizen in Space - Robert Sheckley	2.00	4.00	7.50	SF
Orig., 1955				
127 How to Succeed in Business Without Really Trying - Shepherd Mead 1956	2.00	4.00	7.50	H
128 Hot Iron - Elmer Kelton	2.00	4.00	6.00	W
129 Tell them Nothing - Hal Ellson	2.00	4.00	6.00	
130 Alternating Currents - Frederick Pohl	2.00	4.00	7.50	SF
c-Powers				
F131 A Woman of Bangkok - Jack Reynolds	2.00	4.00	6.00	
132 In One Head and Out the Other - Roger Price	1.50	3.50	5.00	H
F133 The Best Short Stories of 1955 - Martha Foley	1.50	3.50	5.00	
134 Beyond Courage - Clay Blair, Jr.	2.00	4.00	6.00	NF
135 Reach for Tomorrow - Arthur C. Clarke	2.00	4.00	6.00	SF
136 The Pioneers - Jack Schaefer	2.00	4.00	7.50	W
137 The God of Channel 1 - Donald Stacy	2.00	4.00	7.50	
138 My First 10,000,000 Sponsors - Frank Edwards	2.00	4.00	6.00	
F139 The October Country - Ray Bradbury	5.00	10.00	20.00	SF
140 New Short Novels II	2.00	4.00	7.50	
Orig., 1956, c-Powers, Note: Contains Norman Mailer				

(BALLANTINE BOOKS, continued)

141	Never Plead Guilty - Bernard Averbuch & John Wesley Noble	2.00	4.00	6.00	NF
142	Devil's Canyon - E. E. Halleran	2.00	4.00	6.00	W
143	Flood - David Dempsey	2.00	4.00	6.00	
144	Presidential Year - C. M. Kornbluth & Frederik Pohl	4.00	8.00	15.00	
145	God is My Co-Pilot - Robert L. Scott, Jr.	2.00	4.00	6.00	C
146	Sea Songs of Sailing, Whaling and Fishing - Burl Ives	2.00	4.00	7.50	
147	Bright Phoenix - Harold Mead	2.50	6.00	10.00	SF
148	Beyond the Pass - Lee Leighton	2.00	4.00	7.50	W
149	Hard Men - Frank O'Rourke	2.00	4.00	6.00	W
F150	The Power and the Prize - Howard Swiggett	1.50	3.50	5.00	
151	Nerves - Lester del Ray	2.00	4.00	6.00	SF
152	I'm for Me First - Roger Price Orig., 1956	1.50	3.50	5.00	H
153	Blazing Border - E. E. Halleran	1.50	3.50	5.00	W
154	Hoops of Steel - Evans Rolfe	1.50	3.50	5.00	
155	The Wright Brothers - Fred C. Kelly	1.50	3.50	5.00	
156	Brother Buffalo - Jefferson McCall	2.00	4.00	7.50	
157	Eight for Control - David Karr	1.50	3.50	5.00	
158	The Night of the Coyotes - Philip Ketchum	2.00	4.00	6.00	W
159	The Human Angle - William Tenn	2.50	6.00	10.00	SF
160	Best Television Plays - Gore Vidal	1.50	3.50	5.00	
161	Olympic Cavalcade of Sports - John V. Grombach Orig., 1956	1.50	3.50	5.00	NF
F162	The Cruiser - Warren Tute	1.50	3.50	5.00	
163	Grab Your Socks - Shel Silverstein	1.50	3.50	5.00	
164	Frontier - Marvin De Vries	2.00	4.00	6.00	W
165	I, Libertine - Frederick R. Ewing (Theodore Sturgeon & Jean Shepherd) Orig., 1956, c-Freas	5.00	10.00	20.00	H
166	Scout - R. M. Roberts Orig., 1956	2.00	4.00	6.00	W
167	To Live Forever - Jack Vance	3.00	6.00	10.00	SF
168	The Road to Stalingrad - Bruno Zeiser	1.50	3.50	5.00	NF
F169	The Scourge of the Swastika - Lord Russell of Liverpool	3.00	6.00	12.00	NF
170	Wagon Captain - F. E. Halleran	2.00	4.00	6.00	W
171	The Wild Reader - Bernard W. Shir-Cliff	2.00	4.00	6.00	
172	The World of Li'l Abner - Al Capp	2.00	4.00	6.00	H
173	Turn the Tigers Loose - Col. Walt Lasly	1.50	3.50	5.00	W
174	The Big Ball of Wax - Shepherd Mead	2.00	4.00	7.50	H
175	Fish the Strong Waters - N. C. McDonald Orig., 1956	2.00	4.00	6.00	A
176	Kansas Trail - Hascal Giles	2.00	4.00	6.00	W
177	I Drive the Turnpikes—And Survive - Paul Kearney	2.00	4.00	7.50	NF
178	Utterly Mad - William M. Gaines	3.00	6.00	12.00	H
179	E Pluribus Unicorn - Theodore Sturgeon	2.50	6.00	10.00	SF
180	James Dean: A Biography - William Bast	2.50	6.00	10.00	B
181	Hangtown - Les Savage, Jr.	2.00	4.00	6.00	W
182	Tales of Gooseflesh & Laughter - John Wyndham Orig., 1956, c-Powers	2.50	6.00	10.00	SF
183	Defeat at Sea - C. D. Bekker	1.50	3.50	5.00	NF

Ballantine Books 118, c. BB   Ballantine Books 141, c. BB   Ballantine Books 165, c. BB

Ballantine Books 168, c. BB   Ballantine Books 177, c. BB   Ballantine Books 220, c. BB

(BALLANTINE BOOKS, continued)

184 The German Raider Atlantis - Wolfgang Frank & Bernhard Rogge 1957	1.50	3.50	5.00	NF
185 Shadow on the Border - George C. Appell	1.50	3.50	5.00	W
186 Tales from the White Hart - Arthur C. Clarke	2.50	6.00	10.00	SF
187 Buffalo Wagons - Elmer Kelton	1.50	3.50	5.00	W
188 Cavalry Raid - S. E. Whitman	1.50	3.50	5.00	W
189 Fire Mission - William P. Mulvihill	1.50	3.50	5.00	
190 The Battle of the Bulge - Robert E. Merriam	1.50	3.50	5.00	NF
191 Halfway to Heaven - Terrance Flair	1.50	3.50	5.00	
192 Slave Ship - Frederik Pohl	1.50	3.50	5.00	SF
F193 The First and the Last - Adolf Galland	1.50	3.50	5.00	
194 The Spotted Horse - John Dillon	1.50	3.50	5.00	
F195 Wing Leader - J. E. Johnson	.75	1.75	3.00	NF
196 The Lonely Women - Gerda Rhoads	.75	1.75	3.00	
197 The Frozen Year - James Blish	1.50	3.50	5.00	SF
198 Fight at Sun Mountain - Clark Brooker	1.50	3.50	5.00	W
199 Edge of the City - Frederik Pohl	4.00	8.00	15.00	
200 Cycle of Fire - Hal Clement	1.50	3.50	5.00	SF
F201 Zero - Martin Caidin	1.50	3.50	5.00	NF
202 Yellowhorse - Dee Brown	1.50	3.50	5.00	W
203 Paris Blues - Harold Flender	.75	1.75	3.00	
F204 The Best American Short Stories of 1956 - Martha Foley	.75	1.75	3.00	
205 The Hostile Hills - E. E. Halleran	1.50	3.50	5.00	W
206 The Case Against Tomorrow - Frederik Pohl	1.50	3.50	5.00	SF
207 U-boat 977 - Heinz Schaeffer	1.50	3.50	5.00	NF
208 Lawman's Pay - Frank C. Robertson	.75	1.75	3.00	W
209 Commando Extraordinary - Charles Foley	.50	1.25	2.50	
210 The Green Odyssey - Philip Jose Farmer Orig., 1957	2.50	6.00	10.00	SF
211 Legend in the Dust - Frank O'Rourke	1.50	3.50	5.00	W
212 Gun Hand - Frank O'Rourke	1.50	3.50	5.00	W
213 Violence at Sundown - Frank O'Rourke	1.50	3.50	5.00	W
214 High Vengeance - Frank O'Rourke	1.50	3.50	5.00	W
215 Sometime, Never - John Wyndham, William Golding & Mervyn Peake	1.50	3.50	5.00	SF
216 Serenade to the Big Bird - Bert Stiles	.75	1.75	3.00	
217 Between the Elephant's Ears - Robert L. Scott, Jr.	.75	1.75	3.00	A
218 High Vacum - Charles Eric Maine	.75	1.75	3.00	SF
219 Spanish Ridge - E. E. Halleran	.75	1.75	3.00	W
220 The Deep South Says Never - John Barttow Martin	1.50	3.50	5.00	NF
221 The Password Is Courage - John Castle	.75	1.75	3.00	NF
222 One Minute to Ditch - Cornelius Ryan	.75	1.75	3.00	
223 A Woman in Berlin	.75	1.75	3.00	
F224 Midway - Mitsuo Fuchida & Masatake Okumiya	1.50	3.50	5.00	NF
F225 Panzer Leader - Heinz Guderian	.75	1.75	3.00	NF
226 New Poems by American Poets No. 2 - Rolfe Humphries	.50	1.25	2.00	
227 The Battle for Leyte Gulf - C. Vann Woodward	.50	1.25	2.00	NF
228 Aircraft Carrier - Joseph Bryan	.50	1.25	2.00	NF
229 Sergeant Bilko - Nat Hiken	2.00	4.00	7.50	H
230 Occam's Razor - David Duncan	2.00	4.00	6.00	SF
F231 The 85 Days - R. W. Thompson	.75	1.75	3.00	NF
232 Disaster Valley - Frank C. Robertson	.75	1.75	3.00	W

233	The Crack in the Picture Window - John Keats	.75	1.75	3.00	
F234	The Bridge at Remagen - Ken Hechler	.75	1.75	3.00	
235	Best TV Humor of 1957 - Irving Settel	1.50	3.50	5.00	H
236	Gunsmoke - Don Ward Orig., 1957, TV tie-in	2.00	4.00	7.50	W
237	Those Idiots from Earth - Richard Wilson	1.50	3.50	5.00	SF
238	Best TV Plays: 1957 - Florence Britton	1.50	3.50	5.00	
239	The Wild Sweet Wine - Don Congdon Orig., 1958	1.50	3.50	5.00	
240	Chain Link - Owen Evens	.75	1.75	3.00	
241	Indian Country - Dorothy M. Johnson	.75	1.75	3.00	W
242	The Humbug Digest - Harvey Kurtzman	2.00	4.00	6.00	H
243	Man of Earth - Algis Budrys	1.50	3.50	5.00	SF
244	Kamikaze - Gordon T. Allred & Yasuo Kuwahara	.75	1.75	3.00	NF
245	The Dam Busters - Paul Brickhill	.50	1.25	2.00	NF
246	Robots and Changelings - Lester del Rey	1.50	3.50	5.00	SF
247	Barbed Wire - Elmer Kelton	1.50	3.50	5.00	W
F248	Samurai! - Martin Caidin & Others	.75	1.75	3.00	
249	Earthlight - Arthur C. Clarke	.75	1.75	3.00	SF
250	The Big Boxcar - Alfred Maund	.75	1.75	3.00	
251	Sun Dance - Fred Grove	.75	1.75	3.00	W
F252	The Battle of Cassino - Fred Majdalany	.75	1.75	3.00	NF
253	Patrol - Fred Majdalany	.75	1.75	3.00	
254	Blood on the Land - Frank Bonham	.75	1.75	3.00	W
255	Tomahawk - Lee Leighton	.75	1.75	3.00	W
256	A Case of Conscience - James Blish	.75	1.75	3.00	SF
257	The Graveyard Reader - Groff Conklin	2.00	4.00	7.50	HO
F258	The Sea Wolves - Wolfgang Frank	1.00	2.00	3.50	
259	The Return of the Texan - L. L. Foreman Orig., 1958	.75	1.75	3.00	W
260	Deadly Image - Edmund Cooper	.75	1.75	3.00	SF
F261	The Big Show - Pierre Clostermann	.75	1.75	3.00	
F262	The One that Got Away - Kendal Burt & James Leasor	.75	1.75	3.00	
263	The Mad Reader - Harvey Kurtzman	.75	1.75	3.00	H
264	Mad Strikes Back - Harvey Kurtzman	.75	1.75	3.00	H
265K	Inside Mad - Harvey Kurtzman	.75	1.75	3.00	H
266K	Utterly Mad - William M. Gaines	.75	1.75	3.00	H
267K	The Brothers Mad-- William M. Gaines	.75	1.75	3.00	H
268	On an Odd Note - Gerald Kersh	.75	1.75	3.00	SF
269K	Hardrock - Frank Bonham	.75	1.75	3.00	W
270K	More Equal than Others - Roy Michaels	.75	1.75	3.00	
271K	The Monster of the Butte - Sam Meriwether	.75	1.75	3.00	W
272K	Star Science Fiction Stories No. 4 - Frederik Pohl	.75	1.75	3.00	SF
F273K	V-2: The Nazi Rocket - Walter Dornberger	1.50	3.50	5.00	NF
274K	The Hanging Tree - Dorothy M. Johnson	.75	1.75	3.00	W
275K	Those About to Die - Daniel P. Mannix	1.50	3.50	5.00	NF
F276K	Stuka Pilot - Hans Ulrich Rudel	.75	1.75	3.00	NF
F277K	This Woman - Pietro di Donato	.50	1.25	2.00	
278K	Count Five and Die - Barry Wynne	.50	1.25	2.00	
279K	Tomorrow's Gift - Edmund Cooper	.75	1.75	3.00	SF
F280K	The Call Girl - Harold Greenwald	.75	1.75	3.00	NF
281K	The Old Copper Collar - Dan Cushman	.75	1.75	3.00	
282K	Colorado Gold - Lee Leighton & Chad Merriman	.75	1.75	3.00	W

Ballantine Books 229, c. BB

Ballantine Books 259, c. BB

Ballantine Books 298, c. BB

(BALLANTINE BOOKS, continued)

283K The Sledge Patrol - David Howarth	.50	1.25	2.00	
284K After the Rain - John Bowen	.75	1.75	3.00	SF
285K Rebel Ranger - S. E. Whitman	.75	1.75	3.00	W
286K Ingenue - Millicent Brower	.50	1.25	2.00	
287K How to Succeed with Women Without Really Trying - Shepherd Mead	.75	1.75	3.00	H
288K The Bright Road to Fear - Richard Martin Stern	.75	1.75	3.00	M
289K The Avengers - Chad Merriman	.75	1.75	3.00	W
290K The Tide Went Out - Charles Eric Maine	.75	1.75	3.00	SF
F291K Battle for the Rhine - R. W. Thompson	.75	1.75	3.00	NF
292K Brain Surgeon - William Sharpe	.50	1.25	2.00	
293K Heat Wave - Caesar Smith	.50	1.25	2.00	
294K Apache Wells - Robert Steelman	.75	1.75	3.00	
F295K The Burl Ives Song Book - Burl Ives	.75	1.75	3.00	NF
296K The Mad Reader - Harvey Kurtzman	.75	1.75	3.00	H
297K Mad Strikes Back - Harvey Kurtzman	.75	1.75	3.00	H
298K Sergeant Bilko Joke Book	2.00	4.00	7.50	H
299K The Midwich Cuckoos - John Wyndham	2.00	4.00	6.00	SF
300K End of a War - Edward Loomis	.75	1.75	3.00	
301K Ride the Nightmare - Richard Matheson	2.00	4.00	6.00	M
302K The Beast - Daniel P. Mannix	2.00	4.00	7.50	NF
303K The Marching Morons - C. M. Kornbluth	.75	1.75	3.00	SF
304K Shadow of a Star - Elmer Kelton	.75	1.75	3.00	W
305K Sensual Love - Don Congdon	.75	1.75	3.00	
306K Tiger in the Sky - Robert L. Scott, Jr.	.50	1.25	2.00	
F307K Air Spy - Constance Babington-Smith	1.50	3.50	5.00	NF
308K Star Science Fiction Stories No. 5 - Frederik Pohl	.75	1.75	3.00	SF
309K Fort Starke - Wade Everett	.75	1.75	3.00	
310K False Witness - Helen Nielsen	.50	1.25	2.00	
311K Sex, Vice and Business - Monroe Fry	.75	1.75	3.00	NF
312K Witch Doctor - N. C. McDonald	.75	1.75	3.00	
F313K Who Dares, Wins - Virginia Cowles	.50	1.25	2.00	
314K God is My Co-Pilot - Robert L. Scott, Jr.	.50	1.25	2.00	
315K Bunch Quitter - Chad Merriman	.50	1.25	2.00	W
316K The Fourth "R" - George O. Smith	.50	1.25	2.00	SF
317K Kamikaze - Gordon T. Allred & Yasuo Kuwahara	.75	1.75	3.00	NF
F318K The Coast Watchers - Eric D. Feldt	.75	1.75	3.00	
319K Stairway to Nowhere - Hal Ellson	.75	1.75	3.00	
320K The Chemical Elements - Helen Miles Davis	.50	1.25	2.00	NF
321K Outlaw Woman - Sam Meriwether	.50	1.25	2.00	W
F322K Boeing 707 - Martin Caidin	.50	1.25	2.00	NF
F323K Thunderbolt! - Martin Caidin & Robert S. Johnson	.50	1.25	2.00	NF
324K No Bugles, No Glory - Fred Grove	.50	1.25	2.00	W
325K Tomorrow Times Seven - Frederik Pohl	.50	1.25	2.00	SF
326K Deals with the Devil - Basil Davenport	2.00	4.00	7.50	HO
327K Seed of Light - Edmund Cooper	.50	1.25	2.00	SF
328K Black Rock Valley - S. E. Whitman	.50	1.25	2.00	W
329K Air Force! - Frank Harvey	.75	1.75	3.00	C
330K The Whirligig - of Love - E. A. Fishman	.50	1.25	2.00	
331K Suspense - Richard Martin Stern	.50	1.25	2.00	
F332K Zeebrugge - Barrie Pitt	.75	1.75	3.00	NF
F333K Great Cases in Psychoanalysis - Harold Greenwald	.75	1.75	3.00	
334K Winter of the Sioux - Robert Steelman	.50	1.25	2.00	W
335K Wolfbane - Frederik Pohl & C. M. Kornbluth	.75	1.75	3.00	SF
Orig., 1959, c-Powers				
F336K Defeat in the East - Jurgen Thorwald	.75	1.75	3.00	NF
337K Life Among the Savages - Shirley Jackson	.50	1.25	2.00	H
338K Harvey Kurtzman's Jungle Book - Harvey Kurtzman	2.00	4.00	7.50	H
F339K To Live and Kill - Stefan Gazel	.75	1.75	3.00	
340K Cartoon Countdown - Bernard Wiseman	.75	1.75	3.00	H
341K The Outward Urge - John Wyndham & Lucas Parkes	.50	1.25	2.00	SF
342K Raising Demons - Shirley Jackson	.50	1.25	2.00	H
343K Stampede - Chad Merriman	.50	1.25	2.00	W
344K First Command - Wade Everett	.50	1.25	2.00	
345K The Funhouse - Benjamin Appel	2.00	4.00	6.00	SF
S346K Poronography and the Law - Drs. Eberhard & Phyllis Kronhausen	.50	1.25	2.00	NF

347K	Rumor, Fear and the Madness of Crowds	2.00	4.00	6.00	NF
348K	Eagle in the Bathtub - Jule Mannix	.50	1.25	2.00	NF
F349K	American Aces - Edward H. Sims	.50	1.25	2.00	NF
350K	The World of Li'l Abner - Al Capp Movie tie-in	2.00	4.00	6.00	H
351					
352K	Ordeal at Blood River - James Warner Bellah Orig., 1959	.50	1.25	2.00	W
353K	Star Science Fiction Stories No. 6 - Frederik Pohl	.50	1.25	2.00	SF
354K	The Hell Fire Club - Daniel P. Mannix	2.00	4.00	7.50	NF
355K	Those About to Die - Daniel P. Mannix	.75	1.75	3.00	
F356K	The Plague and I - Betty MacDonald	.50	1.25	2.00	H

BANNER MYSTERIES

(Fact and Fiction Publications)

Digest size

1	The Sunday Pigeon Murders - Craig Rice c-Raboy 1945	5.00	10.00	20.00	M
2	Death Goes to School - Q. Patrick c-Raboy 1945	4.00	8.00	15.00	M

BANTAM A-SERIES

(Bantam Books, Inc.)

See Bantam Books for other A volumes

A1	Men and Volts at War - John A. Miller 1948	.75	1.75	3.00	NF
A2	Model Railroading 1950	.75	1.75	3.00	NF
A3	Main Street Merchant - Norman Beasley 1950	.75	1.75	3.00	B
A4	How to Use Premiums in Your Business to Increase Your Sales and Profits 1950	.75	1.75	3.00	NF
A5	The Power of People - Charles P. McCormick 1952	.75	1.75	3.00	NF

BANTAM BIOGRAPHIES

(Bantam Books, Inc.)

Ballantine Books 354K, c. BB   Banner Mysteries 2, c. Banner   Bantam A-Series A-2, c. Bantam

Bantam Biog. FB415, c. Bantam   Bantam Books 1, c. Bantam   Bantam Books 37, c. Bantam

(BANTAM BIOGRAPHIES, continued)

FB400	Cleopatra - Emil Ludwig ,1956	.75	1.75	3.00	B
FB401	Henry the Eighth - Francis Hackett	.75	1.75	3.00	B
FB402	The Great Pierpont Morgan - Frederick Lewis Allen	.75	1.75	3.00	B
FB403	Venetian Adventurer: Marco Polo - Henry Hart	1.50	3.50	5.00	B
FB404	Autobiography of Benvenuto Cellini	1.50	3.50	5.00	B
FB405	The Last Billionaire, Henry Ford - William C. Richards	.75	1.75	3.00	B
FB406	Up from Slavery - Booker T. Washington	.75	1.75	3.00	B
FB407	The Borgias - J. Lucas-Dubreton	1.50	3.50	5.00	B
FB408	Andrew Jackson - Gerald Johnson	.75	1.75	3.00	B
FB409	Madame de Pompadour - Nancy Mitford 1957	.75	1.75	3.00	B
FB410	The Memoirs of Catherine the Great ,1957	.75	1.75	3.00	B
FB411	Yankee from Olympus - Catherine Drinker Bowen	.75	1.75	3.00	B
FB412	Genghis Khan - Harold Lamb	1.50	3.50	5.00	B
FB413	The Life and Time of Rembrandt - Hendrik Willem Van Loon	1.50	3.50	5.00	B
FB414	Five and Ten - John K. Winkler	.75	1.75	3.00	B
FB415	The Memoirs of Casanova - Giacomo Casanova 1958	1.50	3.50	5.00	B
FB416	Charlemagne - Harold Lamb ,1958	1.50	3.50	5.00	B
FB417	Ashurbanipal - Washington Young	1.50	3.50	5.00	B
FB418	Clarence Darrow for the Defense - Irving Stone	.75	1.75	3.00	B

BANTAM BOOKS

(Bantam Books, Inc.)

1	Life on the Mississippi - Mark Twain 1945	5.00	10.00	20.00	
2	The Gift Horse - Frank Gruber	2.00	4.00	7.50	M
3	Nevada - Zane Grey	2.00	4.00	6.00	W
4	Evidence of Things Seen - Elizabeth Daly	2.00	4.00	6.00	M
5	Scaramouche • Rafael Sabatini	2.00	4.00	6.00	A
6	A Murder by Marriage - Robert George Dean	2.00	4.00	6.00	M
7	The Grapes of Wrath - John Steinbeck	3.00	6.00	12.00	
8	The Great Gatsby - F. Scott Fitzgerald	2.00	4.00	7.50	
	With dust jacket	7.50	15.00	30.00	
9	Rogue Male - Geoffrey Household	2.00	4.00	6.00	A
10	South Moon Under - Marjorie Kinnan Rawlings	2.00	4.00	6.00	E
11	Mr. and Mrs. Cugat - Isabel Scott Rorick	2.00	4.00	6.00	B
12	Then There Were Three - Geoffrey Homes	2.00	4.00	6.00	
13	The Last Time I Saw Paris - Elliot Paul	2.00	4.00	6.00	
14	Wind, Sand, and Stars - Antoine de Saint-Exupery	2.00	4.00	6.00	A
15	Meet Me in St. Louis - Sally Benson	2.00	4.00	6.00	H
16	The Town Cried Murder - Leslie Ford	2.00	4.00	6.00	M
17	Seventeen - Booth Tarkington	2.00	4.00	6.00	H
18	What Makes Sammy Run? - Budd Schulberg	2.00	4.00	6.00	

19 One More Spring - Robert Nathan	2.00	4.00	6.00	
20 Oil for the Lamps of China - Alice Tisdale Hobart	2.00	4.00	6.00	
21 Men, Women, and Dogs - James Thurber 1946	2.00	4.00	6.00	H
22 Babbitt - Sinclair Lewis	2.00	4.00	7.50	
With dust jacket	7.50	15.00	30.00	
23 The Fog Comes - Mary Collins	2.00	4.00	6.00	M
24 Valiant is the Word for Carrie - Barry Benefield	2.00	4.00	6.00	
25 Bugles in the Afternoon - Ernest Haycox 1946	2.00	4.00	6.00	W
26 Net of Cobwebs - Elisabeth Sanxay Holding	2.00	4.00	6.00	M
With dust jacket	7.50	15.00	30.00	
27 Only Yesterday - Frederick Lewis Allen	2.00	4.00	6.00	
28 Night in Bombay - Louis Bromfield	2.00	4.00	6.00	
29 Was it Murder? - James Hilton	2.00	4.00	6.00	M
30 Citizen Tom Paine - Howard Fast	2.00	4.00	6.00	B
31 The Three Hostages - John Buchan	2.00	4.00	6.00	A
32 The Great Mouthpiece - Gene Fowler	2.00	4.00	6.00	B
33 The Prisoner of Zenda - Anthony Hope	2.00	4.00	6.00	A
34 First Come, First Kill - Francis Allan	2.00	4.00	6.00	M
35 My Dear Bella - Arthur Kober	2.00	4.00	6.00	H
36 Trail Boss - Peter Dawson	2.00	4.00	6.00	W
37 Drawn and Quartered - Chas. Addams	4.00	8.00	15.00	H
38 Anything for a Quiet Life - A. A. Avery	2.00	4.00	6.00	M
39 Long, Long Ago - Alexander Woollcott	2.00	4.00	6.00	
40 Captain from Connecticut - C. S. Forester	2.00	4.00	6.00	A
41 David Harum - Edward Noyes Westcott	2.00	4.00	6.00	
42 Road to Folly - Leslie Ford	2.00	4.00	6.00	M
43 The Lives of a Bengal Lancer - Francis Yeats-Brown	1.50	3.50	5.00	A
44 The Cold Journey - Grace Zaring Stone	2.00	4.00	6.00	
45 A Bell for Adano - John Hersey	2.00	4.00	6.00	
46 Escape the Night - Mignon G. Eberhart	2.00	4.00	6.00	M
47 Home Ranch - Will James	2.00	4.00	7.50	NF
48 The Laughter of My Father - Carlos Bulosan	2.00	4.00	6.00	H
49 The Amethyst Spectacles - Frances Crane	1.50	3.50	5.00	M
50 The Buffalo Box - Frank Gruber	2.00	4.00	6.00	M
51 Death in the Blackout - Anthony Gilbert	2.00	4.00	6.00	M
52 No Hands on the Clock - Geoffray Homes	2.00	4.00	6.00	M
53 Nothing Can Rescue Me - Elizabeth Daly	2.00	4.00	6.00	M
54 The Love Letters - Chris Massie	2.00	4.00	6.00	R
55 Tutt and Mr. Tutt - Arthur Train	2.00	4.00	6.00	H
56 The Tonto Kid - Henry Herbert Knibbs	2.00	4.00	7.50	W
57 Anything for a Laugh - Bennett Cerf	2.00	4.00	6.00	H
58 "Captains Courageous" - Rudyard Kipling	2.00	4.00	7.50	A
59 Wild Animals I Have Known - E. Thompson Seton	2.00	4.00	7.50	NF
60 The Kennel Murder Case - S. S. Van Dine	4.00	8.00	15.00	M
61 The Bantam Concise Dictionary	2.00	4.00	7.50	
62 Dead Center - Mary Collins	2.00	4.00	6.00	M
63 Green Mansions - W. H. Hudson	3.00	6.00	12.00	F
64 Harriet - Elizabeth Jenkins	2.00	4.00	6.00	
65 South Wind - Norman Douglas	2.00	4.00	6.00	A
66 She Loves Me Not - Edward Hope	2.00	4.00	6.00	H
67 The Bruiser - Jim Tully	2.00	4.00	6.00	S
68 Guns from Powder Valley - Peter Field	2.00	4.00	6.00	W
69 The Grandmothers - Glenway Wescott	2.00	4.00	6.00	
70 Lay That Pistol Down - Richard Powell	2.00	4.00	6.00	M
71 Mountain Meadow - John Buchan	2.00	4.00	7.50	A
72 No Bones About It - Ruth Sawtell Wallis	2.00	4.00	6.00	
73 The Law of Plainsmen - Zane Grey	2.00	4.00	6.00	W
74 Halo in Blood - John Evans	2.00	4.00	6.00	M
75 Cannery Row - John Steinbeck 1947	2.00	4.00	6.00	
76 Drink to Yesterday - Manning Coles	2.00	4.00	6.00	
77 Pistol Passport - Eugene Cunningham	2.00	4.00	6.00	W
78 Deadly Nightshade - Elizabeth Daly	2.00	4.00	6.00	M
79 A Tree Grows in Brooklyn - Betty Smith	2.00	4.00	6.00	
80 False to Any Man - Leslie Ford	2.00	4.00	6.00	M
81 Puzzles, Quizzes, and Games - Phyllis Fraser & Edith Young	4.00	8.00	15.00	NF
82 Ride the Man Down - Luke Short	2.00	4.00	7.50	W
83 Up Front - Bill Mauldin	2.00	4.00	7.50	H
84 The World, the Flesh and Father Smith - Bruce Marshall	1.50	3.50	5.00	

Bantam Books 81, c. Bantam Bantam Books 83, c. Bantam Bantam Books 101, c. Bantam

(BANTAM BOOKS, continued)

85	Death at the Door - Anthony Gilbert aka He Came by Night	1.50	3.50	5.00	M
86	Border Roundup - Allan R. Bosworth	2.00	4.00	7.50	W
87	Apartment in Athens - Glenway Wescott	3.00	6.00	12.00	
88	Trigger Kid - Bennett Foster aka The Maverick	2.00	4.00	7.50	W
89	Finders Keepers - Geoffrey Homes	2.00	4.00	7.50	M
90	The Uninvited - Dorothy Macardle	3.00	6.00	12.00	F
91	The 17th Letter - Dorothy Cameron Disney	2.00	4.00	7.50	M
92	My Life and Hard Times - James Thurber	3.00	6.00	12.00	H
93	Dagger of the Mind - Kenneth Fearing	2.00	4.00	7.50	M
94	The Crimson Horseshoe - Peter Dawson	2.00	4.00	7.50	W
95	Assignment Without Glory - Marcos Spinelli	1.50	3.50	5.00	M
96	The Scarab Murder Case - S. S. Van Dine	4.00	8.00	15.00	M
97	Swamp Water - Vereen Bell	2.00	4.00	7.50	
98	Cry Wolf - Marjorie Carleton	2.00	4.00	7.50	
99	Comanche Chaser - Dane Coolidge	2.00	4.00	7.50	W
100	The Cautious Amorist - Norman Lindsay 1947	2.00	4.00	7.50	
101	The Problem of the Green Capsule - J. D. Carr	3.00	6.00	12.00	M
102	Range Rider - W. H. B. Kent	2.00	4.00	7.50	W
103	The Bells of St. Mary's - George Victor Martin	1.50	3.50	5.00	
104	Powder Valley Pay-Off - Peter Field	2.00	4.00	7.50	W
105	Our Hearts Were Young and Gay - Cornelia Otis Skinner & Emily Kimbrough	1.50	3.50	5.00	
106	Asylum - William Seabrook	2.00	4.00	7.50	
107	Murder in Brass - Lewis Padjett	4.00	8.00	15.00	M
108	Quick Draw - Curtis Bishop	2.00	4.00	7.50	
109	Blood from a Stone - Ruth Sawtell Wallis	2.00	4.00	7.50	M
110	Romance for Sale - Maysie Greig	1.50	3.50	5.00	R
111	Trouble Shooter - Robert Travor	2.00	4.00	7.50	
112	Hardcase - Luke Short	2.00	4.00	7.50	W
113	Riders of the Night - Eugene Cunningham	2.00	4.00	7.50	W
114	Old Lover's Ghost - Leslie Ford	2.00	4.00	7.50	M
115	Women Will be Doctors - Hannah Lees	2.00	4.00	7.50	R
116	Great Stories from the Saturday Evening Post	2.00	4.00	7.50	
117	Stiffs Don't Vote - Geoffrey Homes aka Forty Whacks	2.00	4.00	7.50	M
118	A Toast to Tomorrow - Manning Coles	2.00	4.00	7.50	
119	Double Deal - Allan R. Bosworth aka Hang and Rattle	2.00	4.00	7.50	W
120	Secret Beyond the Door - Rufus King Movie tie-in	2.00	4.00	7.50	
121	My Man Godfrey - Eric Hatch aka Irene, the Stubborn Girl	1.50	3.50	5.00	E
122	A Certain French Doctor - Elizabeth Seifert	1.50	3.50	5.00	R
123	A Treasury of Folk Songs - Sylvia & John Kolb	3.00	6.00	12.00	NF
124	To Mary with Love - Richard Sherman	1.50	3.50	5.00	
125	February Hill - Victoria Lincoln 1947	1.50	3.50	5.00	E
126	Quality - Cid Ricketts Sumner	2.00	4.00	7.50	E
127	Chicago Murders - Sewell Peaslee Wright	2.00	4.00	7.50	NF
128	Six-Gun Outcast - Charles N. Heckelmann	2.00	4.00	7.50	W
129	"Whip" Ryder's Way - Grant Taylor	2.00	4.00	7.50	W
130	The Cinnamon Murder - Frances Crane	2.00	4.00	7.50	M
131	The Pearl - John Steinbeck	2.00	4.00	7.50	

(BANTAM BOOKS, continued)

132	Date With Death - Eaton K. Goldthwaite	2.00	4.00	7.50	M
133	Kid Galahad - Francis Wallace	1.50	3.50	5.00	
134	Hell for Breakfast - Alan LeMay	2.00	4.00	7.50	W
135	Mama's Bank Account - Kathryn Forbes Movie tie-in	2.00	4.00	7.50	
136	Up at the Villa - W. Somerset Maugham	1.50	3.50	5.00	
137	Wings of Fear - Mignon G. Eberhart 1948	2.00	4.00	7.50	M
138	Murder Cheats the Bride - Anthony Gilbert	1.50	3.50	5.00	M
139	Station West - Luke Short	2.00	4.00	7.50	W
140	Coroner Creek - Luke Short	2.00	4.00	7.50	W
141	Scandals of Clochemerle - Gabriel Chevallier	2.00	4.00	7.50	
142	Treasure Island - Robert Louis Stevenson	2.00	4.00	7.50	A
143	The She-Wolf - H. H. Munro aka A Saki Sampler Note: Exists only as a Bantam dust jacket on Superior M656.	10.00	25.00	40.00	F
144	The Mighty Blockhead - Frank Gruber Note: Exists only as a Bantam dust jacket on Superior M655.	7.50	15.00	30.00	
145	The Love Nest - Ring Lardner Note: Exists only as a Bantam dust jacket on Superior M646.	7.50	15.00	30.00	H
146	The Rynox Murder Mystery - Philip MacDonald Note: Exists only as a Bantam dust jacket on Superior M642.	7.50	15.00	30.00	M
147	Only the Good - Mary Collins	2.00	4.00	7.50	
148	On Ice - Robert George Dean Note: Exists only as a Bantam dust jacket on Superior M654.	7.50	15.00	30.00	M
149	Good Night, Sheriff - Harrison R. Steeves Note: Exists only as a Bantam dust jacket on Superior M657.	7.50	15.00	30.00	
150	The Informer - Liam O'Flaherty Note: Exists only as a Bantam dust jacket on Superior M650. 1948	7.50	15.00	30.00	
151	The Navy Colt - Frank Gruber Note: Exists only as a Bantam dust jacket on Superior M649.	7.50	15.00	30.00	
152	Mrs. Mike - Benedict & Nancy Freedman	2.00	4.00	7.50	
153					
154	Twenty Grand Short Stories - Ernest Taggard	2.00	4.00	7.50	
155	Storm - George R. Stewart Note: Exists only as a Bantam dust jacket on Penguin Special s238.	7.50	15.00	30.00	
156	Boomerang! - William C. Chambliss Note: Exists only as a Bantam dust jacket on Infantry Journal J101.	7.50	15.00	30.00	
157	The Curse of the Fen - Brad Levin	2.00	4.00	7.50	
158	The Sign of the Ram - Margaret Ferguson Movie tie-in	2.00	4.00	7.50	E
200	Western Triggers - Arnold Hano 1948	2.00	4.00	7.50	W
201	Trail South from Powder Valley - Peter Field	2.00	4.00	7.50	W
202	The Tenderfoot - W. H. B. Kent	2.00	4.00	7.50	W
203	Sugarfoot! - Clarence Budington Kelland	2.00	4.00	7.50	W

Bantam Books 107, c. Bantam Bantam Books 123, c. Bantam   Bantam 143 w/dj, c. Bantam

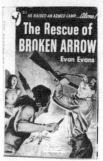

Bantam 150 w/dj, c. Bantam   Bantam Books 203, c. Bantam   Bantam Books 211, c. Bantam

(BANTAM BOOKS, continued)

204	Blood on the Moon - Luke Short aka Gunman's Chance	2.00	4.00	7.50	W
205	Red River - Borden Chase aka Blazing Guns on the Chisholm Trail	2.00	4.00	7.50	W
206	Deputy Marshall - Charles N. Heckelmann c-Saunders	2.50	6.00	10.00	W
207	Short Grass - Thomas W. Blackburn c-Saunders	2.50	6.00	10.00	W
208	Dead Man's Range - Tom J. Hopkins aka Bullets Over Broken Leg	2.00	4.00	7.50	W
209	Hard Money - Luke Short 1949, c-Saunders	2.50	6.00	10.00	W
210	Land Grabber - Peter Field aka Fight for Powder Valley	2.00	4.00	7.50	W
211	The Rescue of Broken Arrow - Evan Evans	2.00	4.00	7.50	W
212	Fighting Man - Frank Gruber	1.50	3.50	5.00	W
213	Hell or High Water - Dick Pearce aka Desert Steel	2.00	4.00	7.50	W
214	Rio Grande Kid - R. M. Hankins aka Lonesome River Justice, c-Saunders	2.50	6.00	10.00	W
227	American Sexual Behaviour & the Kinsey Report - Morris L. Ernst & David Loth	2.00	4.00	7.50	NF
250	The Stagline Feud - Peter Dawson 1948	2.00	4.00	7.50	W
251	Relentless - Kenneth Perkins aka Three Were Thoroughbreds	2.00	4.00	7.50	W
252	Barbed Wire - Bennett Foster aka Powdersmoke Fence	2.00	4.00	7.50	W
253	Wild Justice - Alan LeMay aka The Smoky Years	2.00	4.00	7.50	W
254	Border Bandit - Evan Evans c-Saunders	2.50	6.00	10.00	W
255	Badlands - Bennett Foster c-Saunders	2.50	6.00	10.00	W
256	Western Roundup - Arnold Hane	2.00	4.00	7.50	W
257	Arizona - Clarence Budington Kelland	2.00	4.00	7.50	W
258	Raiders of the Rimrock - Luke Short 1949	2.00	4.00	7.50	W
259	The Man from Wyoming - R. M. Hankins	2.00	4.00	7.50	W

Bantam Books 214, c. Bantam   Bantam Books 254, c. Bantam   Bantam Books 255, c. Bantam

260 Pay-off at Ladron - Bennett Foster	2.00	4.00	7.50	
261 The Wild Bunch - Ernest Haycox	2.50	6.00	10.00	W
c-Saunders				
262 A Ghost Town on the Yellowstone - Elliot Paul	2.00	4.00	7.50	W
300 The Kidnap Murder Case - S. S. Van Dine	4.00	8.00	15.00	M
301 Headlined for Murder - Edwin Lanham	2.00	4.00	7.50	M
302 The Fabulous Clipjoint - Fredric Brown	4.00	8.00	15.00	M
303 Siren in the Night - Leslie Ford	2.00	4.00	7.50	M
304 The Problem of the Wire Cage - John Dickson Carr	2.00	4.00	7.50	
305 Hanged for a Sheep - Richard & Francis Lockridge	2.00	4.00	7.50	M
306 The Day He Died - Lewis Padjett	1.50	3.50	5.00	M
307 The Bride Saw Red - Robert Carson	1.50	3.50	5.00	
308 The Silent Speaker - Rex Stout	2.00	4.00	7.50	M
309 The Case of the Mexican Knife aka Street of the Crying Woman	2.00	4.00	7.50	M
310 Murder in the Glass Room - Edwin Rolfe & Lester Fuller	1.50	3.50	5.00	M
311 Saigon Singer - F. Van Wyck Mason	1.50	3.50	5.00	
312 The Indigo Necklace Murders - Frances Crane	1.50	3.50	5.00	M
313 The Chasm - Victor Canning	1.50	3.50	5.00	
314 The Yellow Room - Mary Roberts Rinehart	1.50	3.50	5.00	M
315 Brighten Rock - Graham Greene	1.50	3.50	5.00	M
316 Gentlemen Prefer Corpses - Max Arthur	1.50	3.50	5.00	M
317 Murder is Cheap - Anthony Gilbert	1.50	3.50	5.00	M
350 Your Red Wagon - Edward Anderson Movie tie-in	1.50	3.50	5.00	
351 The Lying Ladies - Robert Finnegan	1.50	3.50	5.00	
352 Miss Agatha Doubles for Death - H. L. V. Fletcher	1.50	3.50	5.00	M
353 The Book of the Dead - Elizabeth Daly	1.50	3.50	5.00	M
354 San Francisco Murders - Joseph Henry Jackson	1.50	3.50	5.00	NF
355 The Man Within - Graham Greene	1.50	3.50	5.00	M
356 Sorry, Wrong Number - Lucille Fletcher & Allan Ullman	1.50	3.50	5.00	
357 The Sealed Verdict - Lionel Shapiro	1.50	3.50	5.00	
358 The Voice of the Corpse - Max Murray	2.00	4.00	7.50	M
359 All for the Love of a Lady - Leslie Ford 1949	1.50	3.50	5.00	M
360 One More Unfortunate - Edgar Lustgarten	1.50	3.50	5.00	M
361 The Dead Ringer - Fredric Brown	5.00	10.00	20.00	M
362 The Dragon Murder Case - S. S. Van Dine	4.00	8.00	15.00	M
363 Many a Monster - Robert Finnegan	1.50	3.50	5.00	
364 Fire in the Snow - Hammond Innes	1.50	3.50	5.00	
365 The Man Who Could Not Shudder - John Dickson Carr	2.00	4.00	7.50	M
366 The Hound of the Baskervilles - Sir Arthur Conan Doyle	5.00	10.00	20.00	M
400 Winter Meeting - Ethel Vance	1.50	3.50	5.00	
401 Yesterday's Madness - Marian Cockrell	1.50	3.50	5.00	
402 The Red Pony - John Steinbeck	1.50	3.50	5.00	
403 Beggar's Choice - George Axelrod	1.50	3.50	5.00	
404 Hiroshima - John Hersey	1.50	3.50	5.00	
405 The Hucksters - Frederic Wakeman	1.50	3.50	5.00	

Bantam Books 302, c. Bantam Bantam Books 361, c. Bantam Bantam Books 366, c. Bantam

96

406 Mickey - Peggy Goodin aka Clementine, Movie tie-in	1.50	3.50	5.00	
407 Behold this Woman - David Goodis	1.50	3.50	5.00	
408 Doctor Kim - Lucy Agnes Hancock	1.50	3.50	5.00	E
409 Low Man on a Totem Pole - H. Allen Smith	.75	1.75	3.00	
410 The Grass is Always Greener - George Malcolm-Smith	1.50	3.50	5.00	F
411 Hotel Hostess - Faith Baldwin	1.50	3.50	5.00	R
412 Encore for Love - Katharine Dunlop	1.50	3.50	5.00	R
413 Family Honeymoon - Homer Croy Movie tie-in	1.50	3.50	5.00	
414 Spendthrift - Eric Hatch	1.50	3.50	5.00	E
415 Something Wonderful to Happen - Darwin L. Teilhet	1.50	3.50	5.00	
416 Miss Dilly Says No - Theodore Pratt	1.50	3.50	5.00	
417 Confession - Dorothy Les Tina	1.50	3.50	5.00	
418 Someone Called Maggie Lane - Frances Shelley Wees	1.50	3.50	5.00	
419 My Flag is Down - James Maresca	1.50	3.50	5.00	
420 Illusion - Allane Corliss aka Marry for Love	1.50	3.50	5.00	E
421 No Place to Hide - David Bradley	2.00	4.00	7.50	SF
422 Office Nurse - Adelaide Humphries	1.50	3.50	5.00	R
423 Stranger in Paris - W. Somerset Maugham	1.50	3.50	5.00	
424 Now You See Me, Now You Don't - Roy Michaels	1.50	3.50	5.00	
425 My Sister, My Bride - Merriam Modell	1.50	3.50	5.00	
426 The Stranger - Lillian Bos Ross	1.50	3.50	5.00	W
427 Prison Nurse - Louis Berg	3.00	6.00	12.00	
450 Moonlit Voyage - Elizabeth Dunn 1948	1.50	3.50	5.00	
451 Love is the Winner - Natalie Shipman aka Who Wins His Love	1.50	3.50	5.00	
452 Cabbage Holiday - Anthony Thorne	1.50	3.50	5.00	E
453 Five Nights - Eric Hatch aka Five Days	1.50	3.50	5.00	
454 The Chinese Room - Vivian Connell	.75	1.75	3.00	
455 Love is a Surprise! - Faith Baldwin	1.50	3.50	5.00	R
456 Yankee Storekeeper - R. E. Gould	1.50	3.50	5.00	
457 The Weird Sisters - Douglas M. Alver	1.50	3.50	5.00	
458 Dr. Woodward's Ambition - Elizabeth Seifert	1.50	3.50	5.00	E
459 Joan of Arc - Frances Winwar Movie tie-in	2.00	4.00	7.50	A
460 Earth and High Heaven - Gwethalyn Graham	1.50	3.50	5.00	E
461 Back Home - Bill Mauldin	1.50	3.50	5.00	
462 What Became of Anna Bolton? - Louis Bromfield	1.50	3.50	5.00	
463 The Other Room - Worth Tuttle Hedden	2.00	4.00	7.50	E
464 Nurse into Woman - Marguerite Mooers Marshall	1.50	3.50	5.00	R
465 Bitter Forfeit - Mabel Louise Robinson	1.50	3.50	5.00	E
466 The Big Town - Ring Lardner	1.50	3.50	5.00	H
467 A Farewell to Arms - Ernest Hemingway	1.50	3.50	5.00	
468 Monarch of the Vine - Thomas Skinner Willings	1.50	3.50	5.00	
469 Lady Godiva and Master Tom - Raoul C. Faure	3.00	6.00	12.00	E
470 The Men in Her Life - Edith Roberts	1.50	3.50	5.00	
471 Marry for Money - Faith Baldwin	1.50	3.50	5.00	R
472 The Secret Memoirs of a Chicken - Andrew B. Stephens	1.50	3.50	5.00	
473 Danger Trail - Theodore Pratt	1.50	3.50	5.00	
474 Hazard - Roy Chanslor	1.50	3.50	5.00	E
475 The Little Green Men - Douglas M. Alver	1.50	3.50	5.00	
476 Road Show - Eric Hatch	1.50	3.50	5.00	E
477 The Fascination - Jean Pedrick	1.50	3.50	5.00	E
500 My Greatest Day in Baseball - J. P. Carmichael	2.00	4.00	7.50	S
501 Strikeout Story - Bob Feller	2.00	4.00	7.50	S
502 The Unexpected - Bennett Cerf	2.00	4.00	7.50	SF
503 First Love - Elizabeth Abell & Joseph I. Green	1.50	3.50	5.00	R
504 Kick-Off - Ed Fitzgerald	1.50	3.50	5.00	S
505 Babe Ruth - Tom Meany	3.00	6.00	12.00	B
506 Lucky to be a Yankee - Joe DiMaggio 1949	3.00	6.00	12.00	S

(BANTAM BOOKS, continued)

No.	Title			
507	Clowning through Baseball - Al Schacht	2.00	4.00	7.50	S
550	Out of my Trunk - Milton Berle	1.50	3.50	5.00	H
551	The ABC of Horseracing - Dan Parker	2.00	4.00	7.50	NF
552	The Gashouse Gang - J. Roy Stockton	3.00	6.00	12.00	S
553	The Big Bet - Edward Harris Heth	1.50	3.50	5.00	E
554	Hot Leather - Beulah Marie Dix & Bertram Millhauser	1.50	3.50	5.00	
555	Great Stories from the Saturday Evening Post, 1947 - ed. Ben Hibbs	1.50	3.50	5.00	
556	The Story of the Brooklyn Dodgers - Ed Fitzgerald	2.00	4.00	7.50	S
557	Jack Dempsey - Nat Fleischer	2.00	4.00	7.50	B
700	Blackjack - Joseph E. Kelleam 1949	1.50	3.50	5.00	W
701	Dead as a Dummy - Geoffrey Homes	1.50	3.50	5.00	M
702	The Rustlers - Luke Short	1.50	3.50	5.00	W
703	Hands Off! - Luke Short	1.50	3.50	5.00	W
704	The Memoirs of Sherlock Holmes - Sir Arthur Conan Doyle	2.00	4.00	7.50	M
705	Kingsblood Royal - Sinclair Lewis	1.50	3.50	5.00	
706	The Other Woman - Isabel Moore	1.50	3.50	5.00	
707	The Harder they Fall - Budd Schulberg	.75	1.75	3.00	
708	The Captive Women - Walter D. Edmonds aka In the Hands of the Senecas	2.00	4.00	7.50	A
709	The Web of Days - Edna Lee	.75	1.75	3.00	E
710	The Pitfall - Jay J. Dratler	1.50	3.50	5.00	E
711	Summer Lightning - Allene Corliss	1.50	3.50	5.00	E
712	The African Queen - C. S. Forester	2.00	4.00	7.50	
713	Murder Listens In - Elizabeth Daly aka Arrow Pointing Nowhere	1.50	3.50	5.00	M
714	The Gilded Rooster - Richard Emery Roberts	1.50	3.50	5.00	
715	My Greatest Day in Football - Murray Goodman & Leonard Lewin c-Saunders	2.50	6.00	10.00	S
716	High Pressure - Ahmad Kamal aka Full Fathom Five	1.50	3.50	5.00	E
717	The Sun Also Rises - Ernest Hemingway	1.50	3.50	5.00	
718	Death Warmed Over - Mary Collins	1.50	3.50	5.00	M
719					
720	Action at Three Peaks - Frank O'Rourke	1.50	3.50	5.00	W
721	Hollywood Without Makeup - Pete Martin	2.00	4.00	7.50	NF
722	Too Many Women - Rex Stout	1.50	3.50	5.00	M
723	The Dark Wood - Christine Weston	1.50	3.50	5.00	E
724	The Heller - William E. Henning	1.50	3.50	5.00	E
725	Blackleg Range - Bennett Foster	1.50	3.50	5.00	W
726	Desert Law - Clarence Budington Kelland c-Saunders	2.50	6.00	10.00	W
727	City Limits - Hollis Summers	2.00	4.00	7.50	JD
728	I Escaped from Devil's Island - Rene Belbenoit aka Dry Guillotine	2.00	4.00	7.50	NF
729	Belvedere - Gwen Davenport	1.50	3.50	5.00	H
730	Dark Interlude - Peter Cheyney	1.50	3.50	5.00	M
731	Sheriff's Revenge - Peter Field c-Saunders	2.50	6.00	10.00	W
732	Valley of the Shadow - Charles M. Warren	1.50	3.50	5.00	W
733	The Valley of Fear - Sir Arthur Conan Doyle	3.00	6.00	12.00	M

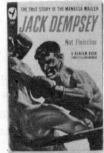

Bantam Books 469, c. Bantam   Bantam Books 557, c. Bantam   Bantam Books 704, c. Bantam

Bantam Books 731, c. Bantam   Bantam Books 733, c. Bantam   Bantam Books 751, c. Bantam

(BANTAM BOOKS, continued)

734	Panther's Moon - Victor Canning Movie tie-in	1.50	3.50	5.00	M
735	A Plot for Murder - Fredric Brown	4.00	8.00	15.00	M
736	The Wine of Astonishment - Martha Gellhorn	2.00	4.00	7.50	
737	The Darker Brother - Bucklin Moon	2.00	4.00	7.50	
738	The Big Clock - Kenneth Fearing	1.50	3.50	5.00	M
739	The White Dress - Mignon G. Eberhart	1.50	3.50	5.00	M
740	Bullet Breed - Leslie Ernenwein c-Saunders	2.50	6.00	10.00	W
741	Gale Warning - Hammond Innes	1.50	3.50	5.00	
742	Husbands and Lovers - Jos. Greene & Elizabeth Abell	.75	1.75	3.00	E
743	Twelve O'Clock High - Sy Bartlett & Beirne Lay, Jr.	1.50	3.50	5.00	C
744	The Spring Begins - Helen Rich	1.50	3.50	5.00	E
745	Camille - Alexandre Dumas	1.50	3.50	5.00	E
746	Politics is Murder - Edwin Lanham 1950	1.50	3.50	5.00	M
747	Bull-Whip - Luke Short	1.50	3.50	5.00	W
748	And the Wind Blows Free - Luke Short	1.50	3.50	5.00	W
749	The Angry Woman - James Ronald	1.50	3.50	5.00	
750	Thieves' Market - A. I. Bezzerides	1.50	3.50	5.00	
751	Shot in the Dark - Judith Merril	4.00	8.00	15.00	SF
752	The Wayward Bus - John Steinbeck	1.50	3.50	5.00	
753	Midnight Lace - MacKinlay Kantor	1.50	3.50	5.00	E
754	The Hour of Truth - David Davidson	1.50	3.50	5.00	
755	Wayward Angel - Verne Chute	1.50	3.50	5.00	M
756	The Smell of Murder - S. S. Van Dine	3.00	6.00	12.00	M
757	Ace-in-the-Hole Haygarty - R. M. Hankins	1.50	3.50	5.00	W
758	Desperate Choice - Dorothy Speare	1.50	3.50	5.00	
759	Tacey Cromwell - Conrad Richter	1.50	3.50	5.00	W
A760	This Side of Innocence - Taylor Caldwell	1.50	3.50	5.00	
761	Explosion - Dorothy Cameron Disney	1.50	3.50	5.00	M
762	Seven Slash Range - Bennett Foster	1.50	3.50	5.00	W
763	Baseball's Greatest Teams - Tom Meany	2.00	4.00	7.50	S
764	Range Drifter - Thomas Thompson	1.50	3.50	5.00	W
765	Border City - Hart Stilwell	4.00	8.00	15.00	
766	Jassy - Norah Lofts	.75	1.75	3.00	E
767	No Marriage in Paradise - Myron Brinig	1.50	3.50	5.00	E
768	Death Lifts the Latch - Anthony Gilbert	1.50	3.50	5.00	M
769	Valley of Violence - Louis Trimble	1.50	3.50	5.00	
770	The Whip - Sara Elizabeth Mason	1.50	3.50	5.00	
A771	Leave Her to Heaven - Ben Ames Williams	1.50	3.50	5.00	
772	Flying Colors - C. S. Forester	2.00	4.00	7.50	A
773	Come Clean, My Love - Rosemary Taylor	1.50	3.50	5.00	
774	Heritage of the River - Muriel Elwood	1.50	3.50	5.00	
775	Hell's Corner - Peter Field	1.50	3.50	5.00	W
776	Only the Valient - Charles M. Warren	1.50	3.50	5.00	
777	The Furies - Niven Busch	1.50	3.50	5.00	
778	Irene - Ronald Marsh	1.50	3.50	5.00	
779	The Case of the Unhappy Angels - Geoffrey Homes	1.50	3.50	5.00	M
780	Walk the Dark Streets - William Krasner	1.50	3.50	5.00	
781	The Enchanted Heart - Marjorie Worthington	1.50	3.50	5.00	
782	The Keys of the Kingdom - A. J. Cronin	2.00	4.00	7.50	
783	The Bloody Moonlight - Fredric Brown	4.00	8.00	15.00	M
784	Gunman's Legacy - Evan Evans	1.50	3.50	5.00	W

(BANTAM BOOKS, continued)

785 Pleasure Island - William Maier	1.50	3.50	5.00	E
786 Sins of New York - Milton Crane	1.50	3.50	5.00	
787 The Sister of Cain - Mary Collins	1.50	3.50	5.00	M
788 Long Storm - Ernest Haycox	1.50	3.50	5.00	W
789 Mary Hallam - Susan Ertz	1.50	3.50	5.00	
790 The Blazing Land - Norman Collins aka Flames Coming Out of the Top	1.50	3.50	5.00	
791 The Feud at Single Shot - Luke Short	1.50	3.50	5.00	W
792 War on the Cimarron - Luke Short	1.50	3.50	5.00	W
793 Till Death Do Us Part - John Dickson Carr	2.00	4.00	7.50	M
794 Angels Camp - Kay Morrison	2.00	4.00	7.50	JD
795 My Sister, Goodnight - Gordon McDonell	1.50	3.50	5.00	
796 Lord and Master - Robert Standish aka Elephant Walk	1.50	3.50	5.00	
797 The Third Man - Graham Greene	1.50	3.50	5.00	
A798 The Underworld - Ira Wolfert aka Tucker's People	1.50	3.50	5.00	E
799 Thunder on the Buckhorn - Frank O'Rourke c-Saunders	2.50	6.00	10.00	
800 Halo for Satan - John Evans	1.50	3.50	5.00	M
801 The Steeper Cliff - David Davidson	1.50	3.50	5.00	
802 Fire - George R. Stewart	1.50	3.50	5.00	
803 Killer by Proxy - Selwyn Jepson	1.50	3.50	5.00	
A804 Drums Along the Mohawk - Walter D. Edmonds	1.50	3.50	5.00	A
A805 H. M. Pulham Esquire - John P. Marquand	1.50	3.50	5.00	
A806 Woman of Property - Mabel Seeley	1.50	3.50	5.00	E
A807 The Gallery - John Horne Burns	1.50	3.50	5.00	
808 The Owl Hoot Trail - Bennett Foster	.75	1.75	3.00	W
809 Wicked Water - MacKinlay Kantor	.75	1.75	3.00	
810 The Moon and Sixpence - W. Somerset Maugham	1.50	3.50	5.00	E
811 Any Shape or Form - Elizabeth Daly	1.50	3.50	5.00	M
812 Cotton Country - Hubert Creekmore aka The Fingers of Night	1.50	3.50	5.00	E
813 Sailor Town - Paul Fox	1.50	3.50	5.00	
A814 Never Love a Stranger - Harold Robbins	1.50	3.50	5.00	
A815 A Lion is in the Street - Adria Locke Langley	1.50	3.50	5.00	
816 Payment Deferred - C. S. Forester	2.00	4.00	7.50	M
817 The Whipping - Roy Flannagan	4.00	8.00	15.00	E
A818 The Black Rose - Thomas B. Costain Movie tie-in	4.00	8.00	15.00	A
819 Donovan's Brain - Curt Siodmak	3.00	6.00	12.00	SF
820 The Purple Plain - H. E. Bates	2.00	4.00	7.50	
821 Reflections in a Golden Eye - Carson McCullers	2.00	4.00	7.50	
822 The Member of the Wedding - Carson McCullers	2.00	4.00	7.50	
823 Range Pirate - L. P. Holmes	2.00	4.00	7.50	W
824 And Be a Villain - Rex Stout	2.00	4.00	7.50	M
825 A Private Killing - James Benet	2.00	4.00	7.50	M
826 High Sierra - W. R. Burnett	2.00	4.00	7.50	
827 Thunder on the River - Charlton Laird	2.00	4.00	7.50	
828 American Guerrilla in the Philippines - Ira Wolfert	2.00	4.00	7.50	
829 An Affair of State - Pat Frank	1.50	3.50	5.00	
830 Anna Becker - Max White	1.50	3.50	5.00	E

Bantam Books A760, c. Bantam   Bantam Books 769, c. Bantam   Bantam Books 817, c. Bantam

Bantam Books A818, c. Bantam   Bantam Books 855, c. Bantam   Bantam Books 945, c. Bantam

(BANTAM BOOKS, continued)

831	The Screaming Mimi - Fredric Brown	3.00	6.00	12.00	M
832	Six-gun Doctor - Paul S. Powers	2.00	4.00	7.50	W
833	Shane - Jack Schaefer	2.00	4.00	7.50	W
834	The Golden Salamander - Victor Canning	1.50	3.50	5.00	
835	What Mad Universe - Fredric Brown	2.00	4.00	7.50	SF
836	Long Hunt - James Boyd	2.00	4.00	7.50	
837	The Green Flames - Marcos Spinelli	2.00	4.00	7.50	
	aka From Jungle Roots				
838	The Rebellion of Leo McGuire -				
	Clyde Brion Davis	1.50	3.50	5.00	
839	Mission: Danger - Dod Orsborne	1.50	3.50	5.00	
	aka Master of the Girl Pat				
840	Bold New Program - Willard R. Espy	1.50	3.50	5.00	
841	Rider of the Rifle Rock - Bennett Foster	2.00	4.00	7.50	W
842	The Wooden Horse - Eric Williams	2.00	4.00	7.50	
843	Ordeal by Slander - Owen Lattimore	1.50	3.50	5.00	
844	Brazes - Ross McLaury Taylor	2.00	4.00	7.50	
845	How to Survive an Atomic Bomb - Richard				
	Gerstell	3.00	6.00	12.00	NF
846	This is My Story - Eleanor Roosevelt	1.50	3.50	5.00	B
A847	The Strange Woman - Ben Ames Williams	2.00	4.00	7.50	
848	The Queen Bee - Edna Lee	1.50	3.50	5.00	E
849	Another Woman's House - Mignon Eberhart	2.00	4.00	7.50	
850	Mayhem in B-flat - Elliot Paul	2.00	4.00	7.50	
851	The Innocent Bottle - Anthony Gilbert	2.00	4.00	7.50	M
852	Catalina - W. Somerset Maugham	1.50	3.50	5.00	
853	Ambush - Luke Short	2.00	4.00	7.50	W
854	Fiddlefoot - Luke Short	2.00	4.00	7.50	W
855	A Sort of a Saga - Bill Mauldin	2.00	4.00	7.50	
856	The Rim of Terror - Hildegarde Tolman				
	Teilhet	1.50	3.50	5.00	
857	The Haters - Theodore Strauss	1.50	3.50	5.00	
858	With Naked Foot - Emily Hahn	1.50	3.50	5.00	
859	Cyrano de Bergerac - Edmond Rostand	2.00	4.00	7.50	
A860	Captain from Castile - Samuel Shellabarger	2.00	4.00	7.50	
861	Verdict in Dispute - Edgar Lustgarten	2.00	4.00	7.50	M
862	The Mesh - Lucie Marchal	1.50	3.50	5.00	E
863	The Hangman's Tree - Dorothy Cameron				
	Disney	2.00	4.00	7.50	M
864	Broken Valley - Thomas Thompson	1.50	3.50	5.00	W
865	The Hunter - Hugh Fosburgh	1.50	3.50	5.00	
A866	Bright Feather - Robert Wilder	1.50	3.50	5.00	A
	1950				
A867	Tender is the Night - F. Scott Fitzgerald	1.50	3.50	5.00	
	1951				
A868	The Grapes of Wrath - John Steinbeck	1.50	3.50	5.00	
A869	Night in Bombay - Louis Bromfield	1.50	3.50	5.00	
870	Evered - Ben Ames Williams	1.50	3.50	5.00	
A871	Bridal Journey - Dale Van Every	1.50	3.50	5.00	
872	The Passionate Pilgrim - Charles Terrot	1.50	3.50	5.00	
873	The Cow Thief Trail - Bennett Foster	1.50	3.50	5.00	W
874	Murder on the Purple Water - Frances Crane	1.50	3.50	5.00	M
875	Something for Nothing - H. Vernor Dixon	1.50	3.50	5.00	E
876	Compliments of a Fiend - Fredric Brown	3.00	6.00	12.00	M
877	Dog Eat Dog - Mary Collins	1.50	3.50	5.00	M
878	Ticket to Oblivion - Robert Parker	1.50	3.50	5.00	
879	Low Down - Reynolds Packard	1.50	3.50	5.00	E
	aka The Kansas City Milkman				

880 Tasker Martin - Diana Gaines	2.00	4.00	7.50	
881 Repent in Haste - John P. Marquand	1.50	3.50	5.00	E
882 Lone Hand - Evan Evans	1.50	3.50	5.00	W
A883 For Whom the Bell Tolls - Ernest Hemingway	1.50	3.50	5.00	
A884 The Fires of Spring - James A. Michener	1.50	3.50	5.00	
885 House of Storm - Mignon G. Eberhart	1.50	3.50	5.00	M
886 The Martian Chronicles - Ray Bradbury	3.00	6.00	12.00	SF
887 The Husband Who Ran Away - Hildegarde Dolson	1.50	3.50	5.00	
888 Nobody Lives Forever - W. R. Burnett	2.00	4.00	7.50	
889 Dark Hunger - Theodore Strauss	1.50	3.50	5.00	
890 Run by Night - Hammond Innes	1.50	3.50	5.00	
891 Wolf Song - Harvey Fergusson	1.50	3.50	5.00	
892 Gunsmoke Justice - Louis Trimble	1.50	3.50	5.00	W
A893 Cass Timberlain - Sinclair Lewis	1.50	3.50	5.00	
A894 The Cours of the Lion - Robert W. Krepps	2.00	4.00	7.50	A
895 Nightmare in Manhattan - Thomas Walsh	1.50	3.50	5.00	
896 He Who Whispers - John Dickson Carr	2.00	4.00	7.50	M
897 Death Has a Past - Anita Boutell	1.50	3.50	5.00	M
898 Black Sage - L. P. Holmes	1.50	3.50	5.00	W
899 The Pastures of Heaven - John Steinbeck	1.50	3.50	5.00	
900 Arouse and Beware - MacKinlay Kantor	1.50	3.50	5.00	C
901 Shake Well Before Using - Bennett Cerf	.75	1.75	3.00	H
A902 The Flames of Time - Baynard Kendrick	4.00	8.00	15.00	E
A903 The Burnished Blade - Lawrence Schoonover	2.00	4.00	7.50	A
A904 The Great Mouthpiece - Gene Fowler	1.50	3.50	5.00	B
905 Strangers in a Train - Patricia Highsmith	2.00	4.00	7.50	M
906 Bend of the Snake - Bill Gulick	1.50	3.50	5.00	W
907 The Case Against Myself - Gregory Tree	2.00	4.00	7.50	M
908 So Many Doors - Oakley Hall	1.50	3.50	5.00	E
909 The Narrow Corner - W. Somerset Maugham	1.50	3.50	5.00	
A910 Wild is the River - Louis Bromfield	1.50	3.50	5.00	C
911 Vengeance Valley - Luke Short	1.50	3.50	5.00	W
A912 Captain Horatio Hornblower - C. S. Forester Movie tie-in	4.00	8.00	15.00	A
913 The Saturday Review Reader	1.50	3.50	5.00	
A914 Stories for Here and Now - Elizabeth Abell & Joseph I. Green	1.50	3.50	5.00	
915 The Unforseen - Dorothy Macardle	2.00	4.00	7.50	F
916 Blackwater - Frank O'Rourke	1.50	3.50	5.00	W
917 To the Indies - C. S. Forester	2.00	4.00	7.50	A
A918 Blood Brother - Elliott Arnold	2.00	4.00	7.50	
A919 B. F.'s Daughter - John P. Marquand	1.50	3.50	5.00	
920 Scottsboro Boy - Earl Conrad & Haywood Patterson	3.00	6.00	12.00	NF
921 12 Against Crime - Edward D. Raoin	2.00	4.00	7.50	
922 Apache - Will Levington Comfort	2.00	4.00	7.50	W
923 Hot Rod - Henry Gregor Felsen	1.50	3.50	5.00	
924 Saddle-man - Matt Stuart	1.50	3.50	5.00	W
925 Trouble in Triplicate - Rex Stout	1.50	3.50	5.00	M
926 Night Without Sleep - Elick Moll	1.50	3.50	5.00	
927 The Judas Cat - Dorothy Salisbury Davis	1.50	3.50	5.00	M
A928 Flamingo Road - Robert Wilder	1.50	3.50	5.00	
929 Steel to the Sunset - Allan R. Bosworth	1.50	3.50	5.00	W
A930 The Citadel - A. J. Cronin	1.50	3.50	5.00	
931 Louisville Saturday - Margaret Long	1.50	3.50	5.00	E
932 Torch for a Long Journey - Lionel Shapiro	1.50	3.50	5.00	
A933 Look to the Mountain - Le Grand Cannon, Jr.	1.50	3.50	5.00	
934 Blues for the Prince - Bart Spicer	1.50	3.50	5.00	
F935 A Rage to Live - John O'Hara	1.50	3.50	5.00	
936 Previews of Entertainment - Gilbert Seldes	1.50	3.50	5.00	NF
937 Bright Victory - Baynard Kendrick	1.50	3.50	5.00	
A938 W. C. Fields: His Follies and His Fortunes	3.00	6.00	12.00	B
A939 All the King's Men - Robert Penn Warren	2.00	4.00	7.50	
940 Apache Gold and Yagui Silver - J. Frank Doble	2.00	4.00	7.50	NF
941 Sundown Riders - Thomas Thompson	1.50	3.50	5.00	W
942 Romelle - W. R. Burnett	2.00	4.00	7.50	
943 Here Comes a Candle - Fredric Brown	3.00	6.00	12.00	M
A944 Timeless Stories for Today and Tomorrow - Intro Ray Bradbury	2.00	4.00	7.50	SF
945 Tomboy - Hal Ellson , Intro by F. Wertham	4.00	8.00	15.00	E
946 No Survivors - Will Henry	1.50	3.50	5.00	W
947 A Room on the Route - Godfrey Blunder	1.50	3.50	5.00	

948	A Forest of Eyes - Victor Canning	1.50	3.50	5.00	
949	Woman of the World - W. Somerset Maugham	1.50	3.50	5.00	
A950	Fifty Great Short Stories - Milton Crane	1.50	3.50	5.00	
A951	For My Great Folly - Thomas B. Costain	2.00	4.00	7.50	A
952	Death of a Salesman - Arthur Miller	1.50	3.50	5.00	
953	Burning Bright - John Steinbeck	1.50	3.50	5.00	
A954	Grant of Land - Lucile Finlay	1.50	3.50	5.00	
A955	The Dream Merchants - Harold Robbins	1.50	3.50	5.00	
A956	The Earth Is the Lords - Taylor Caldwell 1952	2.00	4.00	7.50	A
957	Colorado - Louis Bromfield	1.50	3.50	5.00	
958	Raton Pass - Thomas W. Blackburn	1.50	3.50	5.00	W
959	The Best Go First - Frank O'Malley	1.50	3.50	5.00	M
960	Cheaper by the Dozen - Ernestine Carey & Frank B. Gilbreth, Jr.	1.50	3.50	5.00	
961	What a Man Wants - Harvey Fergusson aka The Life of Riley	.75	1.75	3.00	E
962	The Trees - Conrad Richter	1.50	3.50	5.00	
963	The God that Failed - Richard Crossman	1.50	3.50	5.00	
A964	Terror in the Streets - Howard Whitman c-Maguire	4.00	8.00	15.00	
A965	Signal Thirty-two - Mackinlay Kantor	1.50	3.50	5.00	
966	Sawdust and Sixguns - Evan Evans	1.50	3.50	5.00	W
967	A Man Without Friends - Margaret Echard	1.50	3.50	5.00	
968	Dig Me a Grave - John Spain	2.00	4.00	7.50	M
969	The Little Princesses - Marion Crawford	1.50	3.50	5.00	B
970	Jackson Mahaffey - Fred Ross	1.50	3.50	5.00	
971	The Confidential Agent - Graham Greene	1.50	3.50	5.00	
972	Dollar Cotton - John Faulkner	2.00	4.00	7.50	
A973	The Prince of Foxes - Samuel Shellabarger	2.00	4.00	7.50	A
974	The Outlaw of Longbow - Peter Dawson	1.50	3.50	5.00	W
975	The Golden Door - Bart Spicer	1.50	3.50	5.00	
976	The Gambler - William Krasner	1.50	3.50	5.00	
977	The Silver Hook - John Mortimer	1.50	3.50	5.00	E
978	Mima - Tom Hanlin aka Yesterday Will Return	1.50	3.50	5.00	E
A979	Model Railroading	2.00	4.00	7.50	NF
A980	Bugles in the Afternoon - Ernesy Haycox	1.50	3.50	5.00	W
A981	The Shining Mountains - Dale Van Every	1.50	3.50	5.00	
982	Operation Cicero - L. C. Moyzisch	2.00	4.00	7.50	C
A983	God Has a Long Face - Robert Wilder	1.50	3.50	5.00	
A984	Ride with Me - Thomas B. Costain	2.00	4.00	7.50	A
A985	His Eye Is on the Sparrow - Ethel Waters with Charles Samuels	1.50	3.50	5.00	B
A986	Wyatt Earp, Frontier Marshal - Stuart N. Lake	2.00	4.00	7.50	NF
A987	Point of No Return - John P. Marquand	1.50	3.50	5.00	
988	Dead Man's Saddle - L. P. Holmes	1.50	3.50	5.00	W
989	Johnny Christmas - Forrester Blake	1.50	3.50	5.00	
990	Night of the Jabberwock - Fredric Brown	3.00	6.00	12.00	M
991	The Illustrated Man - Ray Bradbury	3.00	6.00	12.00	SF
992	Circus Doctor - J. Y. Henderson & Richard Taplinger	2.00	4.00	7.50	NF
993	The Gun - C. S. Forester	2.00	4.00	7.50	A
A994	The Gentle Infidel - Lawrence Schoonover	2.00	4.00	7.50	A
A995	The Witch Diggers - Jessamyn West	2.00	4.00	7.50	
996	The Sleeping Sphinx - John Dickson Carr	2.00	4.00	7.50	M
997	12 Against the Law - Edward D. Radin	2.00	4.00	7.50	
998	Tomorrow's Another Day - W. R. Burnett	2.00	4.00	7.50	
A999	Return to Paradise - James A. Michener	2.00	4.00	7.50	
A1000	The Voice of Asia - James A. Michener	1.50	3.50	5.00	NF
1001	Stormy Range - Dwight Bennett	1.50	3.50	5.00	W
A1002	Web of Destiny - Muriel Edwood	1.50	3.50	5.00	
A1003	Far from Home - Raymond Mason	1.50	3.50	5.00	
1004	High Prairie - E. E. Halleran	1.50	3.50	5.00	W
1005	Warbonnet Law - Frank O'Rourke	1.50	3.50	5.00	W
1006	Step Right Up!- Daniel P. Mannix	2.00	4.00	7.50	NF
1007	Castaway - James Gould Cozzens	1.50	3.50	5.00	
A1008	Long Remember - MacKinlay Kantor	1.50	3.50	5.00	
A1009	The Devil in Velvet - John Dickson Carr	3.00	6.00	12.00	M
1010	Laughter, Incorporated - Bennett Cerf	.75	1.75	3.00	H
1011	Rifleman Dodd - C. S. Forester	2.00	4.00	7.50	A
1012	Murder on the West Bank - Elliot Paul	1.50	3.50	5.00	M
1013	The Clay Hand - Dorothy Salisbury Davis	1.50	3.50	5.00	M
1014	Alibi at Dusk - Ben Benson	1.50	3.50	5.00	M

1015				
A1016	The Judas Tree - Neil H. Swanson	1.50	3.50	5.00	
A1017	Ann Carmeny - Hoffman Birney	1.50	3.50	5.00	
1018	Gun Law at Vermillion - Matt Stuart	1.50	3.50	5.00	W
1019	A Rough Shoot - Geoffrey Household	2.00	4.00	7.50	
1020	Theresa - Emile Zola	1.50	3.50	5.00	
F1021	Soldier of Democracy - Kenneth S. Davis	1.50	3.50	5.00	
A1022	Scaramouche - Rafael Sabatini	2.00	4.00	7.50	A
1023	Men Working - John Faulkner	1.50	3.50	5.00	
1024	The Survivors - Hammond Innes	1.50	3.50	5.00	
1025	Dark Madonna - Richard Summers	1.50	3.50	5.00	E
1026	Big Shot - Lawrence Trent	1.50	3.50	5.00	M
A1027	High Towers - Thomas B. Costain	2.00	4.00	7.50	A
A1028	Written on the Wind - Robert Wilder	1.50	3.50	5.00	
1029	Angel of Gaiety - Joseph Hitrec	1.50	3.50	5.00	
1030	The Frightened Dove - Peter Hardin	1.50	3.50	5.00	M
1031	West of Abilene - Vingie Roe	1.50	3.50	5.00	W
1032	The Second Confession - Rex Stout	2.00	4.00	7.50	M
A1033	Inside U. S. A., Volume 1 - John Gunther	.75	1.75	3.00	NF
A1034	Inside U. S. A., Volume 2 - John Gunther	.75	1.75	3.00	NF
1035	Live with Lightning - Mitchell Wilson	1.50	3.50	5.00	
1036	The Grand Portage - Walter O'Meara	1.50	3.50	5.00	
A1037	Harper's Magazine Reader	1.50	3.50	5.00	
1038	Don't Touch Me - MacKinlay Kantor	2.00	4.00	7.50	E
1039	The Desert of Love - Francois Muriac	1.50	3.50	5.00	
1040	Death Has Many Doors - Fredric Brown	3.00	6.00	12.00	M
F1041	The Silent Drum - Neil H. Swanson	1.50	3.50	5.00	
F1042	The Stars Look Down - A. J. Cronin	1.50	3.50	5.00	
A1043	Fighting Men of the West - Dane Coolidge	2.00	4.00	7.50	NF
A1044	The Affairs of Flavie - Gabriel Chevallier	1.50	3.50	5.00	E
1045	The Grass is Singing - Doris Lessing	2.00	4.00	7.50	
1046	The Farmers Hotel - John O'Hara	1.50	3.50	5.00	
1047	The End of My Life - Vance Bourjaily	1.50	3.50	5.00	E
1048	Summer Range - L. P. Holmes	1.50	3.50	5.00	W
1049	Black Sheep, Run - Bart Spicer	1.50	3.50	5.00	
A1050	Grand Canary - A. J. Cronin	1.50	3.50	5.00	
A1051	The Disenchanted - Budd Schulberg	1.50	3.50	5.00	
A1052	The Last Englishman - Hebe Weenolsen	2.00	4.00	7.50	A
A1053	No People Like Show People - Maurice Zolotow	1.50	3.50	5.00	NF
1054	Cage of Darkness - Rene Masson	1.50	3.50	5.00	
1055	Pagoda - James Atlee Phillips	1.50	3.50	5.00	
1056	The Lonesome Quarter - Richard Wormser	1.50	3.50	5.00	W
1057	Cimarron Crossing - Michael Carder	1.50	3.50	5.00	W
1058	The Angry Mountain - Hammond Innes	1.50	3.50	5.00	
1059	The 31st of February - Julian Symons	1.50	3.50	5.00	M
A1060	The Keys of the Kingdom - A. J. Cronin	1.50	3.50	5.00	
1061	Arizona - Clarence Budington Kelland	1.50	3.50	5.00	W
1062	The Tonto Kid - Henry Herbert Knibbs	1.50	3.50	5.00	W
1063	Ride the Man Down - Luke Short	1.50	3.50	5.00	W
1064	Trail Boss - Peter Dawson	1.50	3.50	5.00	W
1065	Cannery Row - John Steinbeck	1.50	3.50	5.00	
1066	The Pastures of Heaven - John Steinbeck	1.50	3.50	5.00	
1067	Nevada - Zane Grey	1.50	3.50	5.00	W
1068	Valley of the Shadow - Charles M. Warren	1.50	3.50	5.00	
A1069	Only Yesterday - Frederick Lewis Allen	1.50	3.50	5.00	
	1953				
1070	Beware the Pale Horse - Ben Benson	1.50	3.50	5.00	M
A1071	Brave New World - Aldous Huxley	3.00	6.00	12.00	SF
A1072	Nightrunners of Bengal - John Masters	2.00	4.00	7.50	
A1073	An Unfound Door - Al Hine	1.50	3.50	5.00	
1074	Berenstain's Baby Book - Janice & Stanley Berenstein	1.50	3.50	5.00	
1075	Play a Lone Hand - Luke Short	1.50	3.50	5.00	W
1076	Final Copy - Jay Barbette	1.50	3.50	5.00	M
1077	Space on My Hands - Fredric Brown	2.00	4.00	7.50	SF
1078	Hold Back the Night - Pat Frank	1.50	3.50	5.00	
1079	Is Another World Watching? - H. F. Heard	2.00	4.00	7.50	UFO
1080	Single-handed - C. S. Forester	2.00	4.00	7.50	A
1081	Harbin's Ridge - Henry Giles	1.50	3.50	5.00	E
1082	Gunman Brand - Thomas Thompson	1.50	3.50	5.00	W
1083	A Gentle Murderer - Dorothy Salisbury Davis	1.50	3.50	5.00	M
A1084	The Looking Glass - William March	1.50	3.50	5.00	E
A1085	Storm Centre - Robert Standish	1.50	3.50	5.00	E

A1086	Green Fire - Peter Rainier	1.50	3.50	5.00
F1087	So Little Time - John P. Marquand	1.50	3.50	5.00
A1088	Delilah - Marcus Goodrich	1.50	3.50	5.00
A1089	Coronado's Children - J. Frank Dobie	2.00	4.00	7.50	NF
A1090	The Captive Witch - Dale Van Every	1.50	3.50	5.00
A1091	The Heart is a Lonely Hunter - Carson McCullers	1.50	3.50	5.00
1092	Parole Chief - David Dressler	1.50	3.50	5.00
1093	The Day of the Locust - Nathanael West	1.50	3.50	5.00
1094	A Drum Calls West - Bill Gulick	1.50	3.50	5.00	W
1095	The Smoky Trail - Matt Stuart	1.50	3.50	5.00	W
1096	Spin the Glass Web - Max Ehrlich	1.50	3.50	5.00
A1097	Come Fill the Cup - Harlan Ware	1.50	3.50	5.00
A1098	The Story of Ernie Pyle - Lee Miller	1.50	3.50	5.00	B
A1099	Rome Haul - Walter D. Edmonds	1.50	3.50	5.00
A1100	Roger Sudden - Thomas H. Raddall	1.50	3.50	5.00
1101	The Mountains Have No Shadow - Owen Cameron	1.50	3.50	5.00
1102	Strange Courage - Evan Evans	1.50	3.50	5.00	W
1103	Black Sage - L. P. Holmes	1.50	3.50	5.00	W
1104	Ambush - Luke Short	1.50	3.50	5.00	W
1105	Fiddlefoot - Luke Short	1.50	3.50	5.00	W
A1106	Fancies and Goodnights - John Collier	3.00	6.00	12.00	SF
A1107	Sunrise to Sunset - Samuel Hopkins Adams	1.50	3.50	5.00	A
1108	Full of Life - John Fante	1.50	3.50	5.00
1109	Clara - Lonnie Coleman	1.50	3.50	5.00
1110	Road Kid - Howard Pease	1.50	3.50	5.00
1111	Brazos - Ross McLaury Taylor	1.50	3.50	5.00	W
1112	Badlands - Bennett Foster	1.50	3.50	5.00	W
1113	The Crimson Horseshoe - Peter Dawson	1.50	3.50	5.00	W
1114				
1115	The Wild Bunch - Ernest Haycox	1.50	3.50	5.00	W
1116	Trigger Kid - Bennett Foster	1.50	3.50	5.00	W
1117	The Last Apaches - William Hopson	1.50	3.50	5.00	W
1118	Saturday Review Reader No. 2	.75	1.75	3.00
1119	Below Suspicion - John Dickson Carr	2.00	4.00	7.50	M
1120	Gaptown Law - Louis Trimble	1.50	3.50	5.00	W
A1121	The Golden Exile - Lawrence Schoonover	2.00	4.00	7.50	A
1122	Nigger John - Sam Meriwether	2.00	4.00	7.50
A1123	Of Former Love - Emma Laird	1.50	3.50	5.00	E
1124	Little Men, Big World - W. R. Burnett	2.00	4.00	7.50
1125	Air Bridge - Hammond Innes	1.50	3.50	5.00
1126	The Long Green - Bart Spicer	1.50	3.50	5.00
1127	Genghis Khan - Harold Lamb	2.00	4.00	7.50	B
1128	Thin Edge of Violence - William O'Farrell	1.50	3.50	5.00
A1129	Now You See Me, Now You Don't - Roy Michaels	1.50	3.50	5.00
D1130	Green Centuries - Caroline Gordon	1.50	3.50	5.00
A1131	The King's Cavalier - Samuel Shellabarger	2.00	4.00	7.50	A
1132	Rim of the Caprock - Noel M. Loomis	1.50	3.50	5.00	W
1133	The Far Cry - Fredric Brown	3.00	6.00	12.00	M
1134	The Fabulous Clipjoint - Fredric Brown	2.00	4.00	7.50	M
1135	Rock Bottom - Earl Conrad	1.50	3.50	5.00
A1136	Lament for Four Virgins - Lael Tucker	1.50	3.50	5.00
A1137	The Lute Player - Norah Lofts	1.50	3.50	5.00
A1138	Hill of the Hawk - Scott O'Dell	1.50	3.50	5.00
A1139	Melissa - Taylor Caldwell	1.50	3.50	5.00
1140	Night Man - Lucille Fletcher & Allan Ullman	1.50	3.50	5.00
1141	Lost Wolf River - Dwight Bennett	1.50	3.50	5.00	W
1142	Antic Hay - Aldous Huxley	2.00	4.00	7.50
1143	Mountain Meadow - John Buchan	1.50	3.50	5.00	A
A1144	Westward the River - Dale Van Every	1.50	3.50	5.00
A1145	The Great Rascal - Jay Monaghan	1.50	3.50	5.00
A1146	The Gallery - John Horne Burns	1.50	3.50	5.00
1147	A Cry of Children - John Horne Burns	1.50	3.50	5.00
1148	The Price of Salt - Claire Morgan	1.50	3.50	5.00
1149	Gold Under Skull Peak - Frank O'Rourke	1.50	3.50	5.00
1150	The Night Watch - Thomas Walsh	1.50	3.50	5.00
A1151	Paradise - Esther Forbes	1.50	3.50	5.00
F1152	Model Railroading	1.50	3.50	5.00	NF
1153	A Worthy Man - Robert Standish	1.50	3.50	5.00
1154	Man Drowning - Henry Kuttner	2.00	4.00	7.50
A1155				
A1156	Reflections in a Golden Eye - Carson McCullers	1.50	3.50	5.00

A1157	Empress of Byzantium - Helen A. Mahler	2.00	4.00	7.50	A
A1158	Argosy Book of Adventure Stories - Rogers Terrill	1.50	3.50	5.00	A
A1159	The Forbidden Ground - Neil H. Swanson	1.50	3.50	5.00	
A1160	Juan Belmonte: Killer of Bulls - Juan Belmonte Y Garcia & Manuel Chaves Nogales	2.00	4.00	7.50	B
1161	Missing - Egon Hostovsky	1.50	3.50	5.00	
A1162	And Ride a Tiger - Robert Wilder	1.50	3.50	5.00	
F1163	What to Wear Where	1.50	3.50	5.00	NF
1164	Short Grass - Thomas W. Blackburn	1.50	3.50	5.00	W
F1165	Flee the Angry Strangers - George Mandel	1.50	3.50	5.00	
1166	Laughter, Incorporated - Bennett Cerf	.75	1.75	3.00	H
1167	Southwest - John Houghton Allen	1.50	3.50	5.00	
1168	No Survivors - Will Henry	1.50	3.50	5.00	W
1169	The Paradise Below the Stairs - Andre Brincourt	1.50	3.50	5.00	
1170	The General - C. S. Forester	2.00	4.00	7.50	A
F1171	50 Great Artists - Bernard Myers	2.00	4.00	7.50	NF
A1172	Bright Feather - Robert Wilder	1.50	3.50	5.00	
1173	In the Best Families - Rex Stout	2.00	4.00	7.50	M
A1174	My Brother, My Enemy - Mitchell Wilson	1.50	3.50	5.00	
1175	Warwhoop - MacKinlay Kantor	1.50	3.50	5.00	
1176	We All Killed Grandma - Fredric Brown	3.00	6.00	12.00	M
1177	Bird of Prey - Victor Canning	1.50	3.50	5.00	
1178	The Quick Brown Fox - Lawrence Schoonover	1.50	3.50	5.00	
1179	Four Steps to the Wall - Jon Edgar Webb	1.50	3.50	5.00	
1180	Gunfighters Pay - William Hopson	1.50	3.50	5.00	W
A1181	Wait for Tomorrow - Robert Wilder	1.50	3.50	5.00	E
A1182	The Bizarre Sisters - Jay & Audrey Walz	1.50	3.50	5.00	
A1183	The Weight of the Cross - Robert O. Bowen	1.50	3.50	5.00	
1184	Cup of Gold - John Steinbeck	.75	1.75	3.00	
A1185	Dance to the Piper - Agnes deMille	.75	1.75	3.00	
	1954				
F1186	The Moneyman - Thomas B. Costain	.75	1.75	3.00	
1187	The Deceivers - John Masters	1.50	3.50	5.00	
1188	Dead Pigeon - Robert P. Hanson	1.50	3.50	5.00	M
1189	Gunflame - John S. Daniels	1.50	3.50	5.00	W
A1190	The Wonderful Country - Tom Lea	1.50	3.50	5.00	
1191	Son of Haman - Louis Cochran	.75	1.75	3.00	
A1192	The Other Room - Worth Tuttle Hedden	.75	1.75	3.00	E
A1193	Here Comes Joe Mungin - Chalmers S. Murray	.75	1.75	3.00	
1194	Ask the Dust - John Fante	.75	1.75	3.00	
1195	Catch a Tiger - Owen Cameron	1.50	3.50	5.00	
A1196	The Ship - C. S. Forester	1.50	3.50	5.00	A
1197	Dead on Arrival - George Bagby	.75	1.75	3.00	M
1198	Broken Lance - Frank Gruber	.75	1.75	3.00	W
A1199	Monarch of the Vine - Thomas Skinner Willings	.75	1.75	3.00	
F1200	Melville Goodwin, USA - John P. Marquand	.75	1.75	3.00	
A1201	Manhattan - Seymour Krim	.75	1.75	3.00	
1202	Rhapsody in Death - S. Jerod Chouinard	.75	1.75	3.00	M
F1203	The Kings of the Road - Ken W. Purdy	1.50	3.50	5.00	NF
A1204	The Hate Merchant - Niven Busch	.75	1.75	3.00	
A1205	The Man from Brazil - E. B. Garside	.75	1.75	3.00	
1206	Royal Gorge - Peter Dawson	.75	1.75	3.00	W
1207	The Burning Court - John Dickson Carr	2.00	4.00	7.50	M
1208	The Sea of Grass - Conrad Richter	1.50	3.50	5.00	A
A1209	Gal Young 'Un - Marjorie Kinnan Rawlings	.75	1.75	3.00	
A1210	Our American Government - Wright Patman	.75	1.75	3.00	NF
A1211	The Wild Ohio - Bart Spicer	.75	1.75	3.00	
A1212	The Mustangs - J. Frank Dobie	1.50	3.50	5.00	NF
A1213	Some Faces in the Crowd - Budd Schulberg	.75	1.75	3.00	
A1214	Someday, Boy - Sam Ross	.75	1.75	3.00	
1215	The Deep End - Fredric Brown	2.00	4.00	7.50	M
1216	The Dead Ringer - Fredric Brown	1.50	3.50	5.00	M
A1217	The Power and the Glory - Graham Greene	.75	1.75	3.00	
1218					
1219	Hiroshima - John Hersey	.75	1.75	3.00	
A1220	Picaroon - Ernest Dudley	.75	1.75	3.00	
A1221	Troubling of a Star - Walt Sheldon	.75	1.75	3.00	
1222					
1223					
1224					

Bantam 1207, c. Bantam

Bantam A1234, c. Bantam

Bantam A1262, c. Bantam

(BANTAM BOOKS, continued)

1225	Swamp Water - Verenn Bell	.75	1.75	3.00	
1226	Blood will Tell - George Bagby	.75	1.75	3.00	M
A1227	A Treasury of Folk Songs - Sylvia & John Kolb	1.50	3.50	5.00	NF
A1228	The Great Gatsby - F. Scott Fitzgerald	.75	1.75	3.00	
A1229	The God that Failed - Richard Crossman	.75	1.75	3.00	
A1230	Cyrano de Bergerac - Edmond Rostand	.75	1.75	3.00	A
A1231	Good for A Laugh - Bennett Cerf	.50	1.25	2.00	H
1232	A Man Gets Around - John McNulty	.75	1.75	3.00	
F1233	Eyeless in Gaza - Aldous Huxley	.75	1.75	3.00	
A1234	Suleiman the Magnificent - Harold Lamb	.75	1.75	3.00	A
A1235	Seven - Carson McCullers	.75	1.75	3.00	
A1236	Walt, Son, October is Near - John Bell Clayton	.75	1.75	3.00	
1237	The Daughter of Bugle Ann - MacKinlay Kantor	.75	1.75	3.00	
1238	Wicked Water - MacKinlay Kantor	.75	1.75	3.00	
A1239	The Restless Border - Dick Pearce	.75	1.75	3.00	W
A1240	A Farewell to Arms - Ernest Hemingway	.75	1.75	3.00	
A1241	The Golden Apples of the Sun - Ray Bradbury	1.50	3.50	5.00	SF
A1242	The Saturday Review Reader No. 3	.50	1.25	2.00	
1243	Sword and Candle - Sidney Herschel Small	1.50	3.50	5.00	A
A1244	Restless House - Emile Zola	.75	1.75	3.00	
A1245	A Good Man - Jefferson Young	.75	1.75	3.00	
A1246	Billy the Kid - Edwin Corle	1.50	3.50	5.00	
1247	Man Alone - William Doyle & Scott O'Dell	.75	1.75	3.00	
1248					
A1249	The Sun Also Rises - Ernest Hemingway	.75	1.75	3.00	
A1250	The Trembling Earth - Dale Van Every	.50	1.25	2.00	
1251	Line to Tomorrow - Lewis Padgett	1.50	3.50	5.00	SF
1252	Murder by the Book - Rex Stout	.75	1.75	3.00	M
1253	What Mad Universe - Fredric Brown	1.50	3.50	5.00	SF
A1254	The Boyds of Black River - Walter D. Edmonds	.75	1.75	3.00	
A1255	The Woods Colt - Thames Williamson	.50	1.25	2.00	
1256					
A1257	Sea Struck - Bennett Stanley	.50	1.25	2.00	
A1258	Autumn Thunder - Robert Wilder	.50	1.25	2.00	
1259					
A1260	Crome Yellow - Aldous Huxley	.75	1.75	3.00	
1261	The Martian Chronicles - Ray Bradbury	.75	1.75	3.00	SF
A1262	Utopia 14 - Kurt Vonnegut, Jr.	2.00	4.00	7.50	SF
1263					
1264	The Light in the Forest - Conrad Richter	.50	1.25	2.00	
1265					
1266	Cannery Row - John Steinbeck	.50	1.25	2.00	
F1267	East of Eden - John Steinbeck	.50	1.25	2.00	
A1268	The Chinese Room - Vivian Connell	.50	1.25	2.00	E
1269	The Bridges at Toko-ri - James A. Michener	.50	1.25	2.00	C
1270					
1271	The Venus Death - Ben Benson	.50	1.25	2.00	M
1272	Crazy Weather - Charles L. McNichols	.50	1.25	2.00	
1273	Case File: FBI - the Gordons	.50	1.25	2.00	M
F1274	Best of the Bedside Esquire - Arnold Gingrich	.50	1.25	2.00	
A1275	In the Years of Our Lord - Manuel Komroff	.75	1.75	3.00	
A1276	The Streak - Paul Darcy Boles	.50	1.25	2.00	
1277	The Stagline Feud - Peter Dawson	.50	1.25	2.00	W

Num	Title				
1278	Costigan's Needle - Jerry Sohl	.75	1.75	3.00	SF
F1279	Battle Cry - Leon Uris	.50	1.25	2.00	C
1280					
A1281	White Hunter, Black Heart - Peter Viertel	.50	1.25	2.00	
1282	The Illustrated Man - Ray Bradbury	.75	1.75	3.00	SF
1283	Sailor Town - Paul Fox	.50	1.25	2.00	
F1284	Lord Vanity - Samuel Shellabarger 1955	.75	1.75	3.00	A
1285	The Lights in the Sky are Stars - Fredric Brown	1.50	3.50	5.00	SF
1286	Shakedown - Richard Ellington	.50	1.25	2.00	M
1287	Bitter Sage - Frank Gruber	.50	1.25	2.00	W
1288	The Cautious Amorist - Norman Lindsay	.50	1.25	2.00	
A1289	The Undaunted - John Harris	.50	1.25	2.00	
A1290	The Kill - Emile Zola	.50	1.25	2.00	
A1291	Tamerlane - Harold Lamb	.75	1.75	3.00	A
A1292	War with the Newts - Karel Capek	1.50	3.50	5.00	SF
1293	And the Wind Blows Free - Luke Short	.50	1.25	2.00	W
1294	Third from the Sun - Richard Matheson	1.50	3.50	5.00	SF
1295	The Name is Archer - John Ross MacDonald	1.50	3.50	5.00	M
A1296	How to Buy Stocks - Louis Engel	.50	1.25	2.00	NF
1297	Shane - Jack Schaefer	1.50	3.50	5.00	W
1298	Nevada - Zane Grey	.50	1.25	2.00	W
F1299	The Thorndike - Barnhart Handy Pocket Dictionary - Clarence Barnhart	.50	1.25	2.00	NF
A1300	Never Love a Stranger - Harold Robbins	.50	1.25	2.00	
F1301	The Grapes of Wrath - John Steinbeck	.50	1.25	2.00	
F1302	Fifty Great Short Stories - Milton Crane	.50	1.25	2.00	
A1303	Twenty Grand Short Stories - Ernestine Taggard	.50	1.25	2.00	
A1304	Far from Customary Skies - Warren Eyster	.50	1.25	2.00	
A1305	Mr. Midshipman Hornblower - C. S. Forester	.75	1.75	3.00	A
A1306	The End of the Affair - Graham Greene	.50	1.25	2.00	
A1307	Man Without a Star - Dee Linford	.50	1.25	2.00	
1308	Drop Dead - George Bagby	.50	1.25	2.00	M
1309	1001 Valuable Things You Can Get Free - Mort Weisinger	.50	1.25	2.00	NF
1310	More Adventures in Time and Space - Raymond J. Healy & J. Francis McComas	.75	1.75	3.00	SF
1311	The Natural Way to Better Golf - Jack Burke	.50	1.25	2.00	NF
1312	The Screaming Mimi - Fredric Brown	1.50	3.50	5.00	M
1313	High Gear - Evan Jones	.50	1.25	2.00	
A1314	To the Indies - C. S. Forester	.50	1.25	2.00	A
1315	Murder Points a Finger - David Alexander	.50	1.25	2.00	M
1316	This Gun for Hire - Graham Greene	.50	1.25	2.00	
1317	The Syndic - C. M. Kornbluth	1.50	3.50	5.00	SF
A1318	Sayonara - James A. Michener	.50	1.25	2.00	
A1319	The Enchanted Cup - Dorothy James Roberts	.50	1.25	2.00	
A1320	Peace of Mind - Joshua Loth Liebman	.50	1.25	2.00	
F1321	Beyond this Place - A. J. Cronin	.50	1.25	2.00	
A1322	Death of a Salesman - Arthur Miller	.50	1.25	2.00	
1323	Target in Taffeta - Ben Benson	.50	1.25	2.00	M
A1324	To a God Unknown - John Steinbeck	.50	1.25	2.00	
1325	The Nine Wrong Answers - John Dickson Carr	1.50	3.50	5.00	
1326	Prisoner's Base - Rex Stout	.75	1.75	3.00	
1327	The Schirmer Inheritance - Eric Ambler Mentioned in Parade Of Pleasure, pg. 174	.50	1.25	2.00	M
1328	Frontiers in Space - Everett F. Bleiler & T. E. Dikty	.75	1.75	3.00	SF
A1329	Of Mice and Men - John Steinbeck	.50	1.25	2.00	
1330	But That's Unprintable - Dave Breger	.50	1.25	2.00	
A1331	Captain Lightfoot - W. R. Burnett	.75	1.75	3.00	A
A1332	The Time of the Fire - Marc Brandel	.50	1.25	2.00	
1333	Orient Express - Graham Greene	.75	1.75	3.00	M
1334	Strange as it Seems - Elsie Hix	.50	1.25	2.00	
A1335	The Lotus and the Wind - John Masters	.50	1.25	2.00	
A1336	The Kentuckians - Janice Holt Giles	.50	1.25	2.00	
F1337	The Cobweb - William Gibson	.50	1.25	2.00	
F1338	All the King's Men - Robert Penn Warren	.50	1.25	2.00	
A1339	The Moon and Sixpence - W. Somerset Maugham	.50	1.25	2.00	
A1340	Don't Tread on Me - Horace V. Bird & Walter Karig	.50	1.25	2.00	

1341					
A1342	Laughter, Incorporated - Bennett Cerf	.50	1.25	2.00	H
1343	The Man from Tomorrow - Wilson Tucker	1.50	3.50	5.00	SF
1344	High Dive - Frank O'Rourke	.50	1.25	2.00	
1345	The Far Shore - Gordon Webber	.50	1.25	2.00	
1346	Cattle, Guns and Men - Luke Short	.50	1.25	2.00	W
1347	Johnny Vengeance - Frank Gruber	.50	1.25	2.00	W
1348	F. B. I. Story - The Gordons	.50	1.25	2.00	M
1349	Death's Long Shadow - Jay Barbette	.50	1.25	2.00	M
F1350	The Fires of Spring - James A. Michener	.50	1.25	2.00	
1351	God and My Country - MacKinlay Kantor	.50	1.25	2.00	
1352	Science Fiction Thinking Machines - Groff Conklin	.75	1.75	3.00	SF
A1353	Alexander of Macedon - Harold Lamb	.75	1.75	3.00	A
A1354					
A1355	View from the Air - Hugh Fosburgh	.50	1.25	2.00	
1356	Station West - Luke Short	.50	1.25	2.00	W
A1357	The Informer - Liam O'Flaherty	.50	1.25	2.00	
A1358	Women and Children First - Paul Steiner	.50	1.25	2.00	H
1359	The Girl in the Cage - Ben Benson	.50	1.25	2.00	M
1360	Find a Victim - John Ross MacDonald	.75	1.75	3.00	
1361	The Big Outfit - Peter Dawson	.50	1.25	2.00	W
1362	Deep Space - Eric Frank Russell	.75	1.75	3.00	SF
1363	The Killers - Peter Dawson	.50	1.25	2.00	W
1364	Honey, I'm Home - Marione R. Nickles	.50	1.25	2.00	
F1365	The Complete Book of First Aid - John Henderson	.50	1.25	2.00	NF
F1366	The Spider King - Lawrence Schoonover	.75	1.75	3.00	A
1367	New Campus Writing - Nolan Miller	.50	1.25	2.00	
A1368	The Second Happiest Day - John Philips	.50	1.25	2.00	
A1369	Brave New World - Aldous Huxley	.75	1.75	3.00	SF
A1370	Port Royal - Noel B. Gerson	.75	1.75	3.00	A
1371	The Seven Year Itch - George Axelrod	.50	1.25	2.00	
1372	Tears for the Bride - Robert Martin	.50	1.25	2.00	
1373	Hardcase - Luke Short	.50	1.25	2.00	W
A1374	The Case for the UFO - M. K. Jessup	.50	1.25	2.00	UFO
A1375	They Went Wrong - Croswell Bowen	.50	1.25	2.00	
1376	Giveaway - Steve Fisher	.50	1.25	2.00	
1377	Scandals of Clochemerle - Gabriel Chevallier	.50	1.25	2.00	
A1378	The Art of Italian Cooking - Maria Lo Pinto & Milo Miloradovich	.50	1.25	2.00	NF
F1379	The Time of the Gringo - Elliott Arnold	.50	1.25	2.00	
1380					
F1381	Bhowani Junction - John Masters	.50	1.25	2.00	
A1382	Genghis Khan - Harold Lamb	.75	1.75	3.00	A
1383	The Sands of Karakorum - James Ramsey Ullman	.50	1.25	2.00	
1384	Delta Deputy - L. P. Holmes	.50	1.25	2.00	W
1385	Winter Ambush - E. E. Halleran	.50	1.25	2.00	W
1386	The Black Mountain - Rex Stout	.75	1.75	3.00	M
1387	The Golden Spiders - Rex Stout	.75	1.75	3.00	M
1388	Three Men Out - Rex Stout	.75	1.75	3.00	M
1389	The Howls of Ivy - Henry Boltinoff	.50	1.25	2.00	H
1390	Guns of the Timberlands - Louis L'Amour	.75	1.75	3.00	W
A1391	Hunter - J. A. Hunter	.50	1.25	2.00	A
A1392	The Do-it-Yourself Gadget Hunter's Guide - William Manners	.75	1.75	3.00	NF
F1393	The Alaskan - Robert Lund	.50	1.25	2.00	
1394	Trouble in Triplicate - Rex Stout	.75	1.75	3.00	M
1395	Too Many Women - Rex Stout	.75	1.75	3.00	M
1396	Dead Man Pass - Peter Dawson	.50	1.25	2.00	W
1397	The Widow and the Web - Robert Martin	.50	1.25	2.00	
1398	Pagan is Paradise - Susanne McConnaughey	.75	1.75	3.00	
A1399	Stranger in Paris - W. Womerset Maugham	.50	1.25	2.00	
1400	Time: X - Wilson Tucker	1.50	3.50	5.00	SF
A1401	Frontier: 150 Years of the West - Luke Short	.75	1.75	3.00	NF
A1402	King's Rebel - James D. Horan	.75	1.75	3.00	
A1403	Best Loved Books of the Twentieth Century - Vincent Starrett	1.50	3.50	5.00	NF
1404	Hazel - Ted Key	.75	1.75	3.00	H
A1405	Hotel Tallegrand - Paul Hyde Donner	.50	1.25	2.00	
1406	The Red Pony - John Steinbeck	.50	1.25	2.00	
1407	The Steel Web - Thomas Thompson	.50	1.25	2.00	W
	1956				

1408	Terror on Broadway - David Alexander	.50	1.25	2.00	M
1409	The Taming of Carney Wilde - Bart Spicer	.50	1.25	2.00	
A1410	The Courts of the Lion - Robert W. Krepps	.75	1.75	3.00	A
A1411	Who Rides with Wyatt - Will Henry	.75	1.75	3.00	W
A1412	Sweet Thursday - John Steinbeck	.50	1.25	2.00	
A1413	The Fifty-Minute Hour - Robert Lindner	.50	1.25	2.00	
A1414	3 Weeks to a Better Memory - Brendan Byrne	.50	1.25	2.00	NF
F1415	Away All Boats - Kenneth Dodson	.50	1.25	2.00	C
F1416	Coromandel! - John Masters	.50	1.25	2.00	
F1417	Three Complete Western Novels - Luke Short	.75	1.75	3.00	W
A1418	The Complete Book of Roses - Dorothy H. Jenkins	.75	1.75	3.00	NF
1419	Deep Hills - Matt Stuart	.50	1.25	2.00	W
1420	Dead Fall - Dale Wilmer	.50	1.25	2.00	
1421	The Burning Fuse - Ben Benson	.50	1.25	2.00	M
1422	Hope of Heaven - John O'Hara	.50	1.25	2.00	
1423	Star Shine - Fredric Brown	1.50	3.50	5.00	SF
A1424	The Heart of the Matter - Graham Greene	.50	1.25	2.00	
A1425	The Long Swords - Edward Franklin	.75	1.75	3.00	A
A1426	Last Frontier - Richard Emery Roberts	.50	1.25	2.00	
A1427	The Round-the-World Cookbook - Myra Waldo	.50	1.25	2.00	NF
F1428	The Day Lincoln was Shot - Jim Bishop	.75	1.75	3.00	
F1429	The Citadel - A. J. Cronin	.50	1.25	2.00	
F1430	Model Railroading	.50	1.25	2.00	NF
F1431	The Dream Merchants - Harold Robbins	.50	1.25	2.00	
1432	Woman Doctor - Hannah Lees	.50	1.25	2.00	R
1433	Graduate Nurse - Lucy Agnes Hancock	.50	1.25	2.00	R
1434	Ward Nurse - Marguerite Mooers Marshall	.50	1.25	2.00	R
1435	Haywire Town - Robert McCaig	.50	1.25	2.00	W
1436	His Name was Death - Fredric Brown	2.00	4.00	7.50	M
1437	Street Rod - Henry Gregor Felsen	.50	1.25	2.00	
1438	Violent Saturday - William L. Heath	.50	1.25	2.00	
A1439	The Four Lives of Mundy Tolliver - Ben Lucien Burman	.50	1.25	2.00	
A1440	Rap Sheet - My Forty Years Outside the Law - Blackie Audett	.75	1.75	3.00	
F1441	The Golden Argosy - Van H. Cartmell & Charles Grayson	.50	1.25	2.00	
F1442	The Inspirational Reader - William Oliver Stevens	.50	1.25	2.00	
A1443	Forbidden Planet - W. J. Stuart	1.50	3.50	5.00	SF
F1444	For My Great Folly - Thomas B. Costain	.50	1.25	2.00	A
F1445	Life on the Mississippi - Mark Twain	.75	1.75	3.00	
1446	High Vermilion - Luke Short	.50	1.25	2.00	W
1447	The Third Bullet - John Dickson Carr	.75	1.75	3.00	M
1448	Million Dollar Murder - Thomas Black	.50	1.25	2.00	
1449					
A1450	Ben-Hur - Lew Wallace	.50	1.25	2.00	
1451	Crossfire - Louis Trimble	.50	1.25	2.00	W
A1452	Man Against Nature - Charles Neider	.50	1.25	2.00	
F1453	Sincerely, Willis Wayde - John P. Marquand	.50	1.25	2.00	
F1454	Point of No Return - John P. Marquand	.50	1.25	2.00	
1455	The Case of the Talking Bug - The Gordons	.50	1.25	2.00	M
F1456	The Burnished Blade - Lawrence Schoonover	.75	1.75	3.00	A
1457	Picnic - William Inge	.50	1.25	2.00	
A1458	Cyrano de Bergarac - Edmund Rostand	.75	1.75	3.00	A
F1459	The Sixth of June - Lionel Shapiro	.50	1.25	2.00	

Bantam 1390, c. Bantam

Bantam A1411, c. Bantam

Bantam 1518, c. Bantam

1460 Why the Long Puss? - Reamer Keller	.50	1.25	2.00	
1461 Cry Viva! - William Hopson	.50	1.25	2.00	W
A1462 So Help Me God - Felix Jackson	.50	1.25	2.00	
A1463 The Harder They Fall - Budd Schulberg	.50	1.25	2.00	
A1464 A Wonderful World for Children - Peter Cardozo	.50	1.25	2.00	NF
A1465 Tiger of the Snows - Tenzing Norgay & James Ramsey Ullman	.50	1.25	2.00	
1466 Rimrock - Luke Short	.50	1.25	2.00	W
1467 The Renegade - John Prescott	.50	1.25	2.00	W
1468 The Silver Cobweb - Ben Benson	.50	1.25	2.00	M
1469 Trouble Comes Double - Robert P. Hansen	.50	1.25	2.00	M
A1470 Timeliner - Charles Eric Maine	1.50	3.50	5.00	SF
1471 My Flag is Down - James Maresca	.50	1.25	2.00	
A1472 Captain Cut-Throat - John Dickson Carr	.75	1.75	3.00	M
F1473 The Wine of Youth - Robert Wilder	.50	1.25	2.00	
F1474 The Keys of the Kingdom - A. J. Cronin	.50	1.25	2.00	
1475 Campaign Train - The Gordons	.50	1.25	2.00	M
1476 Some Die Slow - William E. Heber	.50	1.25	2.00	
1477 Here's Hazel - Ted Key	.75	1.75	3.00	H
A1478 The Pastures of Heaven - John Steinbeck	.50	1.25	2.00	
1479 With Naked Foot - Emily Hahn	.50	1.25	2.00	
A1480 The Shipwrecked - Graham Greene	.50	1.25	2.00	
A1481 The Raiders - Will Henry	.50	1.25	2.00	W
A1482 The Fourth Horseman - Will Henry	.50	1.25	2.00	
A1483 Pillars of the Sky - Will Henry	.50	1.25	2.00	
A1484 The Great Short Stories of John O'Hara	.50	1.25	2.00	
1485 Vengeance Valley - Luke Short	.50	1.25	2.00	W
1486 The Burning Hills - Louis L'Amour	.75	1.75	3.00	W
1487 A Cry in the Night - Whit Masterson	.50	1.25	2.00	M
1488 The Limping Goose - Frank Gruber	.50	1.25	2.00	
1489 Up at the Villa - W. Somerset Maugham	.50	1.25	2.00	
A1490 The Genius and the Godders - Aldous Husley	.75	1.75	3.00	
A1491 Guns of Chickamauga - Richard O'Connor	.50	1.25	2.00	C
A1492 Not this August - C. M. Kornbluth	1.50	3.50	5.00	SF
A1493 Analyze Yourself - William Gerhardi & Leopold Loewenstein	2.50	6.00	10.00	NF
F1494 Lost Pony Tracks - Ross Santee	.50	1.25	2.00	W
F1495 Apache Land - Ross Santee	.50	1.25	2.00	W
1496 Nurse Landon's Challenge - Adelaide Humphries	.50	1.25	2.00	R
S1497 War and Peace - Leo Tolstoy	.75	1.75	3.00	C
1498 Doctor Jane - Adeline McElfresh	.50	1.25	2.00	R
A1499 Dining Out in any Language - Myra Waldo	.50	1.25	2.00	NF
F1500 Blood Brother - Elliott Arnold	.50	1.25	2.00	
1501 A Very Silent Symphony - J. Jerod Chouinard	.50	1.25	2.00	M
1502 Follow the New Grass - Cliff Farrell	.50	1.25	2.00	M
1503 The Problem of the Wire Cage - John Dickson Carr	.75	1.75	3.00	M
1504 The Man Who Could Not Shudder - John Dickson Carr	.75	1.75	3.00	M
1505 The Problem of the Green Capsule - John Dickson Carr	.75	1.75	3.00	M
1506 Hammer Me Home - Richard R. Werry	.50	1.25	2.00	
1507 Reincarnation—the Whole Startling Story - R. DeWitt Miller	.50	1.25	2.00	NF
A1508 The Green Cockade - Frederic F. Van de Water	.50	1.25	2.00	A
A1509 "Captains Courageous" - Rudyard Kipling	.75	1.75	3.00	A
F1510 Waterfront - Budd Schulberg	.50	1.25	2.00	
1511 Hold Back the Night - Pat Frank	.50	1.25	2.00	
1512				
1513 Mama's Bank Account - Kathryn Forbes	.50	1.25	2.00	
1514 Somewhere they Die - L. P. Holmes	.50	1.25	2.00	W
1515 The Buscadero - Noel M. Loomis	.50	1.25	2.00	W
1516 Campbell's Kingdom - Hammond Innes	.50	1.25	2.00	
1517 Satan's Rock - Carl D. Burton	.50	1.25	2.00	
1518 Bus Stop - William Inge Movie tie-in	1.50	3.50	5.00	
A1519 The Circus of Dr. Lao and Other Improbable Stories - Ray Bradbury	1.50	3.50	5.00	SF
F1520 The Count of Monte Cristo - Alexandre Dumas	.50	1.25	2.00	A
A1521 Cleaning House - Wolfgang von Drech	.50	1.25	2.00	
1522				

1523 Sex Rears its Lovely Head - Jerome Beatty, Jr.	.50	1.25	2.00	
1524				
A1525 Royalist - Edward Grierson	.50	1.25	2.00	
F1526 The Hunchback of Notre Dame - Victor Hugo	.50	1.25	2.00	A
1527 Bitter Sage - Frank Gruber	.50	1.25	2.00	
A1528 Common Sense Book of Puppy and Dog Care - Harry Miller	.50	1.25	2.00	NF
1529 Hiroshima - John Hersey	.50	1.25	2.00	
1530				
1531 Sunset Graze - Luke Short	.50	1.25	2.00	W
1532 Gunman's Chance - Luke Short	.50	1.25	2.00	W
1533 Coroner Creek - Luke Short	.50	1.25	2.00	W
1534 Paint the Town Black - David Alexander	.50	1.25	2.00	M
1535 The Pale Door - Lee Roberts	.50	1.25	2.00	
F1536 The Green Years - A. J. Cronin	.50	1.25	2.00	
F1537 Shannon's Way - A. J. Cronin	.50	1.25	2.00	
1538 Rag Top - Henry Gregor Felsen	.50	1.25	2.00	
1539 A Night to Remember - Walter Lord	.50	1.25	2.00	NF
A1540 Written on the Wind - Robert Wilder	.50	1.25	2.00	
1541 The Age of the Tail - H. Allen Smith	.50	1.25	2.00	H
1542 Beast in View - Margaret Millar	.50	1.25	2.00	M
1543 Dead, She was Beautiful - Whit Masterson	.50	1.25	2.00	M
1544 The Pearl - John Steinbeck	.50	1.25	2.00	
A1545 Omar Khayyam - Harold Lamb	.75	1.75	3.00	A
A1546 Martians, Go Home - Fredric Brown	1.50	3.50	5.00	SF
1547 Adobe Walls - W. R. Burnett	.75	1.75	3.00	W
1548				
1549 Latigo - Frank O'Rourke	.75	1.75	3.00	W
A1550 19 Tales of Terror - Whit & Hallie Burnett	.50	1.25	2.00	HO
1551 The Boss of Broken Spur - Nick Sumner	.50	1.25	2.00	W
1552 Broken Shield - Ben Benson	.50	1.25	2.00	M
A1553 Forbidden Area - Pat Frank	.75	1.75	3.00	SF
F1554 Ten North Frederick - John O'Hara	.50	1.25	2.00	
A1555 The Wayward Bus - John Steinbeck	.50	1.25	2.00	
F1556 A New Southern Harvest - Albert Erskine & Robert Penn Warren	.50	1.25	2.00	
A1557 The Siege - Jay Williams	.50	1.25	2.00	
F1558 Cartoon Treasury - Lucy Black & Pyke Johnson, Jr.	.50	1.25	2.00	H
1559 The Rainmaker - N. Richard Nash	.75	1.75	3.00	
A1560 Antic Hay - Aldous Huxley	.75	1.75	3.00	
1561 Tomboy - Hal Ellson	.75	1.75	3.00	JD
1562 Nurse Fairchild's Decision - Zillah K. MacDonald	.50	1.25	2.00	R
F1563 Monarch of the Vine - Thomas Skinner Willings	.50	1.25	2.00	
1564 Dead Freight for Piute - Luke Short	.50	1.25	2.00	W
1565 The Wench is Dead - Fredric Brown	2.00	4.00	7.50	M
1566 The Fabulous Clipjoint, Fredric Brown	1.50	3.50	5.00	M
1567 Death Has Many Doors - Fredric Brown	2.00	4.00	7.50	M
F1568 Island in the Sun - Alec Waugh	.50	1.25	2.00	
A1569 Dragoon - Nelson & Shirley Wolford	.50	1.25	2.00	
A1570 Your Own Beloved Sons - Thomas Anderson	.50	1.25	2.00	
A1571 The Shores of Space - Richard Matheson	1.50	3.50	5.00	
F1572 Cass Timberlane - Sinclair Lewis	.50	1.25	2.00	
1573				
1574 Full of Life - John Fante	.50	1.25	2.00	
1575 Nurse with Wings - Marguerite Mooers Marshall	.50	1.25	2.00	R
1576 Tejas Country - Frank Miller	.50	1.25	2.00	
1577 The Tough Die Hard - Robert Martin	.50	1.25	2.00	
A1578 The Year of the Tempest - Peter Matthiessen	.50	1.25	2.00	
F1579 Bitter Creek - James Boyd	.50	1.25	2.00	
F1580 Native Stone - Edwin Gilbert	.50	1.25	2.00	
S1581 The Boston Cooking-School Cook Book - Rannie Farmer	.50	1.25	2.00	NF
A1582 Fear Strikes Out - Al Hirshberg & Jim Piersall	.75	1.75	3.00	B
F1583 A Rage to Live - John O'Hara	.50	1.25	2.00	
1584 Captain McRae - William Herman	.50	1.25	2.00	
1585 Dr. Woodward's Ambition - Elizabeth Seifert	.50	1.25	2.00	E
A1586 Seventeen - Booth Tarkington	.50	1.25	2.00	H

A1587	The Good Shepherd - C. S. Forester	.50	1.25	2.00	
1588	The Feud at Single Shot - Luke Short	.50	1.25	2.00	W
1589	Live Bait for Murder - William E. Herber	.50	1.25	2.00	
1590	The Sound of White Water - Hugh Fosburgh	.50	1.25	2.00	
F1591	A Crossbowman's Story - George Millar	.75	1.75	3.00	A
1592	Stop Dieting! Start Losing! - Ruth West	.50	1.25	2.00	NF
A1593	The Power - Frank M. Robinson	1.50	3.50	5.00	SF
1594	The Farmers Hotel - John O'Hara	.50	1.25	2.00	
1595	The Bells of St. Mary's - George Victor Martin	.50	1.25	2.00	
1596	The Baron of Boot Hill - Brad Ward	.50	1.25	2.00	W
F1597	Lord Jim - Joseph Conrad	.50	1.25	2.00	A
A1598	The Big Land - Frank Gruber	.50	1.25	2.00	W
F1599	The Cross of Iran - Willi Heinrich	.50	1.25	2.00	C
A1600	The Package Deal - W. T. Ballard	.50	1.25	2.00	
1601	Shoot a Sitting Duck - David Alexander	.50	1.25	2.00	M
1602	Square in the Middle - William Campbell Gault	.50	1.25	2.00	M
A1603	West of the River - Charlton Laird	.50	1.25	2.00	
F1604	Harry of Monmouth - A. M. Maughan	.75	1.75	3.00	A
1605					
1606	1001 Valuable Things You Can Get Free, No. 2 - Mort Weisinger	.50	1.25	2.00	NF
1607	Nora Meade, M. D. - Elizabeth Weslery	.50	1.25	2.00	
A1608	The Pass - Thomas Savage	.50	1.25	2.00	
S1609	A Treasury of Short Stories - Rudyard Kipling	.50	1.25	2.00	
1610	The Gun - C. S. Forester	.50	1.25	2.00	A
A1611	Randall and the River of Time - C. S. Forester	.50	1.25	2.00	A
1612	Starlight Basin - Giff Cheshire	.50	1.25	2.00	W
1613	The Barbarous Coast - John Ross MacDonald	.50	1.25	2.00	
1614	Visiting Nurse - Jeanne Judson	.50	1.25	2.00	R
A1615	Science Fiction Carnival - Fredric Brown & Mack Reynolds	2.00	4.00	7.50	SF
F1616	Amy Vanderbilt's Everyday Etiquette - Amy Vanderbilt	.50	1.25	2.00	NF
A1617	What Makes Sammy Run? - Budd Schulberg	.50	1.25	2.00	
1618	For All Your Life - Emilie Loring	.50	1.25	2.00	
A1619	The Ship - C. S. Forester	.50	1.25	2.00	A
F1620	Only Yesterday - Frederick Lewis Allen	.50	1.25	2.00	
A1621	The Chinese Room - Vivian Connell	.50	1.25	2.00	E
F1622	Eyeless in Gaza - Aldous Huxley	.50	1.25	2.00	
1623	Mating Manual - Reamer Keller	.50	1.25	2.00	
F1624	A Thing of Beauty - A. J. Cronin	.50	1.25	2.00	
A1625	Arouse and Beware - MacKinlay Kantor	.50	1.25	2.00	C
A1626	Beau James - Gene Fowler	.50	1.25	2.00	
A1627	Long Storm - Ernest Haycox	.50	1.25	2.00	W
1628	The Wild Bunch - Ernest Haycox	.50	1.25	2.00	
1629					
A1630	Chocolates for Breakfast - Pamela Moore	.50	1.25	2.00	
A1631	Triple Jeopardy - Rex Stout	.75	1.75	3.00	M
A1632	Before Midnight - Rex Stout	.75	1.75	3.00	M
A1633	Three Witnesses - Rex Stout	.75	1.75	3.00	M
A1634	The Golden Princess - Alexander Baron	.50	1.25	2.00	
A1635	A Face in the Crowd - Bud Schulberg	.50	1.25	2.00	
A1636	Goodbye, Mr. Chips - James Hilton	.50	1.25	2.00	
F1637	God Has a Long Face - Robert Wilder	.50	1.25	2.00	
1638	Day of the Ram - William Campbell Gault	.50	1.25	2.00	M
1639	Return of the Outlaw - Michael Carder	.50	1.25	2.00	W
1640	A Family Party - John O'Hara	.50	1.25	2.00	
A1641	Sayonara - James A. Michener	.50	1.25	2.00	
1642	Man on the Buckskin - Peter Dawson	.50	1.25	2.00	W
F1643	Jonathan Eagle - Alexander Laing	.50	1.25	2.00	
1644					
1645	Her Soul to Keep - Marguerite Mooers Marshall	.50	1.25	2.00	R
A1646	Pebble in the Sky - Isaac Asimov	1.50	3.50	5.00	SF
F1647	The Joker is Wild - Art Cohn	.50	1.25	2.00	
F1648	Drums Along the Mohawk - Walter D. Edmonds	1.50	3.50	5.00	A
F1649	New Campus Writing, No. 2 - Nolan Miller	.50	1.25	2.00	
A1650	The Bridge at Andau - James A. Michener	.50	1.25	2.00	C
A1651	How to Buy Stocks - Louis Engel	.50	1.25	2.00	NF
1652	Raiders of the Rimrock - Luke Short	.50	1.25	2.00	W

A1653	Will Success Spoil Rock Hunter? - George Axelrod	.50	1.25	2.00	
1654	Wagon Train - John Prescott	.50	1.25	2.00	W
1655	Die, Little Goose - David Alexander	.50	1.25	2.00	M
A1656	The Man Who Paid His Way - Walt Sheldon	.50	1.25	2.00	
A1657	The Scimitar - Samuel Edwards	.75	1.75	3.00	A
A1658	100 Stories of Business Success	.50	1.25	2.00	
F1659	The Last Hurrah - Edwin O'Connor	.50	1.25	2.00	
F1660	The Strange Woman - Ben Ames Williams	.50	1.25	2.00	
F1661	Indian-Fighting Army - Fairfax Downey	.75	1.75	3.00	
F1662	The Old Santa Fe Trail - Stanley Vestal	.75	1.75	3.00	
S1663	Model Railroading	.50	1.25	2.00	NF
A1664	Flamingo Road - Robert Wilder	.50	1.25	2.00	
F1665	A Parent's Guide to Children's Illnesses - John Henderson	.50	1.25	2.00	NF
1666	Bugles West - Frank Gruber	.50	1.25	2.00	W
1667	Carol Trent, Air Stewardess - Jeanne Judson	.50	1.25	2.00	R
1668	The Whip - Luke Short	.50	1.25	2.00	W
A1669	The Quiet American - Graham Greene	.50	1.25	2.00	
A1670	The Frozen Jungle - Lawrence Earl	.50	1.25	2.00	
A1671	State of Siege - Eric Ambler	.50	1.25	2.00	
A1672	Pilgrimage to Earth - Robert Sheckley	1.50	3.50	5.00	SF
F1673	The Queen's Cross - Lawrence Schoonover	.75	1.75	3.00	A
F1674	Return to Paradise - James A. Michener	.50	1.25	2.00	
F1675	H. M. Pulham, Esq. - John P. Marquand	.50	1.25	2.00	
A1676	Wild Animals I Have Known - Ernest Thompson Seton	.50	1.25	2.00	NF
A1677	The Bridge over the River Kwai - Pierre Boulle	.50	1.25	2.00	C
F1678	The Hunchback of Notre Dame - Victor Hugo	.50	1.25	2.00	A
1679	Pal Joey - John O'Hara	.50	1.25	2.00	
1680	Colt's Law - Luke Short	.50	1.25	2.00	W
1681	Silver Canyon - Louis L'Amour	.75	1.75	3.00	W
1682	Patrick Butler for the Defense - John Dickson Carr	.75	1.75	3.00	M
1683	Till Death Do Us Part - John Dickson Carr	.75	1.75	3.00	M
1684	He Who Whispers - John Dickson Carr	.75	1.75	3.00	M
A1685	Wagons to Tucson - Ed Newsom	.50	1.25	2.00	W
1686					
F1687	Dodge City: Queen of Cowtowns - Stanley Vestal	.75	1.75	3.00	NF
F1688	The Art of Mixing Drinks - Frederic A. Birmingham	.50	1.25	2.00	
A1689	Porgy - Du Bose Heyward	.50	1.25	2.00	
A1690	Stopover: Tokyo - John P. Marquand	.50	1.25	2.00	
A1691	Thank You, Mr. Moto - John P. Marquand	.75	1.75	3.00	M
S1692	50 Great Artists - Bernard Myers	.50	1.25	2.00	NF
A1693	Death of a Man - Lael Tucker Wertenbaker	.50	1.25	2.00	
1694	My Man Godfrey - Eric Hatch	.50	1.25	2.00	E
1695	Trail Boss - Peter Dawson	.50	1.25	2.00	W
1696	Gun Smoke Showdown - Matt Stuart	.50	1.25	2.00	W
1697	The Secret World of Roy Williams - Roy Williams	1.50	3.50	5.00	
A1698	The Ninth Hour - Ben Benson	.50	1.25	2.00	M
A1699	Touch of Evil - Whit Masterson	.50	1.25	2.00	M
A1700	The Hunters - James Salter	.50	1.25	2.00	
A1701	Rogue in Space - Fredric Brown	1.50	3.50	5.00	SF
F1702	The Earth is the Lord's - Taylor Caldwell	.50	1.25	2.00	A
F1703	Fancies and Goodnights - John Collier	2.00	4.00	7.50	SF
A1704	The Day of the Locust - Nathanael West	.50	1.25	2.00	
F1705	The Fires of Spring - James A. Michener	.50	1.25	2.00	
A1706	Knock and Wait Awhile - William Rawle Weeks	.50	1.25	2.00	
	1958				
F1707	The Big War - Anton Myrer	.50	1.25	2.00	C
A1708	The Heller - William E. Henning	.50	1.25	2.00	
1709	Outlaw's Code - Evan Evans	.50	1.25	2.00	W
1710	Ambush - Luke Short	.50	1.25	2.00	W
1711	Special Nurse - Margaret Howe	.50	1.25	2.00	R
1712	The Lenient Beast - Fredric Brown	2.00	4.00	7.50	M
A1713	Sitka - Louis L'Amour	.75	1.75	3.00	W
F1714	Bugles and a Tiger - John Masters	.50	1.25	2.00	
F1715	Day of Infamy - Walter Lord	.50	1.25	2.00	NF
1716					
A1717	Nevada - Zane Grey	.50	1.25	2.00	W

A1718	The Last of the Plainsmen - Zane Grey	.50	1.25	2.00	W
A1719	The Spanish Gardener - A. J. Cronin	.50	1.25	2.00	
F1720	Tolbecken - Samuel Shellabarger	.50	1.25	2.00	
A1721	The Big Nickelodeon - Maritta Wolff	.50	1.25	2.00	
F1722	The Great World and Timothy Colt - Louis Auchincloss	.50	1.25	2.00	
F1723	Rachel Cade - Charles Mercer	.50	1.25	2.00	
A1724	Captain Ironhand - Rosamond Marshall	.75	1.75	3.00	A
1725	Red River - Borden Chase	.50	1.25	2.00	W
1726	Tales of Wells Fargo - Frank Gruber TV tie-in	.75	1.75	3.00	W
1727	Halo in Brass - John Evans	.50	1.25	2.00	M
1728	Halo in Blood - John Evans	.50	1.25	2.00	M
1729	Halo for Satan - John Evans	.50	1.25	2.00	M
A1730	Reprieve - John Resko	.50	1.25	2.00	
A1731	The Naked Sun - Isaac Asimov	1.50	3.50	5.00	SF
A1732	The Life of the Party - Bennett Cerf	.50	1.25	2.00	H
1733					
S1734	The Red and the Black - Stendahl	.50	1.25	2.00	
F1735	Crime and Punishment - Fyodor Dostoyevsky	.75	1.75	3.00	
1736	The Murder of Whistler's Brother - David Alexander	.50	1.25	2.00	M
1737	The Light in the Forest - Conrad Richter	.50	1.25	2.00	A
F1738	Lancet - Garet Rogers	.50	1.25	2.00	
A1739	An End to Dying - Sam Astrachan	.50	1.25	2.00	
F1740	Say, Darling - Richard Bissell	.50	1.25	2.00	
1741	Peace Marshal - Frank Gruber	.50	1.25	2.00	W
1742	Lonesome River - Frank Gruber	.50	1.25	2.00	W
1743	Fighting Man - Frank Gruber	.50	1.25	2.00	W
F1744	Our Valiant Few - F. Van Wyck Mason	.50	1.25	2.00	
A1745	The Memoirs of a Chicken - Andrew B. Stephens	.50	1.25	2.00	
A1746	Miracle Gardening - Samm Sinclair Baker	.50	1.25	2.00	NF
F1747	The Bantam Book of Correct Letter Writing - Lilian E. Watson	.50	1.25	2.00	NF
A1748	The Lives of a Bengal Lancer - Francis Yeats-Brown	.50	1.25	2.00	A
F1749	Cowhand: The Story of a Working Cowboy - Fred Gipson	.75	1.75	3.00	NF
1750					
1751	Nancy Ross, Private Secretary - Jeanne Judson	.50	1.25	2.00	R
A1752	Never Love a Stranger - Harold Robbins	.50	1.25	2.00	
A1753	The Short Reign of Pippin IV - John Steinbeck	.50	1.25	2.00	
A1754	Cimarron - Edna Ferber	.50	1.25	2.00	W
1755	Fiddlefoot - Luke Short	.50	1.25	2.00	W
1756	Mr. Taxicab - James Maresca	.50	1.25	2.00	
1757	The Screaming Mimi - Fredric Brown Movie tie-in	1.50	3.50	5.00	M
1758	Riddle of a Lady - Anthony Gilbert	.50	1.25	2.00	M
A1759	Yonder - Charles Beaumont	1.50	3.50	5.00	SF
A1760	The Invisible Curtain - Joseph Anthony	.50	1.25	2.00	
F1761	The Member of the Wedding - Carson McCullers	.50	1.25	2.00	
F1762	The Heart is a Lonely Hunter - Carson McCullers	.50	1.25	2.00	
F1763	Reflections in a Golden Eye - Carson McCullers	.50	1.25	2.00	
F1764	Ballad of the Sad Cafe - Carson McCullers	.50	1.25	2.00	
A1765	Satellite! - William Beller & Erik Bergaust	.50	1.25	2.00	NF
A1766	Satellite E One - Jeffrey Lloyd Castle	1.50	3.50	5.00	SF
F1767	Silver Spoon - Edwin Gilbert	.50	1.25	2.00	
A1768	Thieves' Market - A. I. Bezzerides	.50	1.25	2.00	
1769	The Land Grabbers - John S. Daniels	.50	1.25	2.00	W
A1770	Rescue! - Elliott Arnold	.50	1.25	2.00	
1771	Sorry, Wrong Number - Lucille Fletcher & Allan Ullman	.50	1.25	2.00	
A1772	Epitaph for a Spy - Eric Ambler	.50	1.25	2.00	
A1773	The Confidential Agent - Graham Greene	.50	1.25	2.00	
A1774	The Tyrant of Bagdad - Glenn Pierce	.75	1.75	3.00	A
F1775	The Art of Barbecue and Outdoor Cooking	.50	1.25	2.00	NF
1776	Calling Doctor Jane - Adeline McElfresh	.50	1.25	2.00	R
F1777	South Wind - Norman Douglas	.50	1.25	2.00	A
F1778	The Mustangs - J. Frank Dobie	.75	1.75	3.00	NF
A1779	The Wind Cannot Read - Raymond Mason	.50	1.25	2.00	

1780	Teacher's Pet - Michael & Fay Kanin	.50	1.25	2.00	
A1781	Life at Happy Knoll - John P. Marquand	.50	1.25	2.00	
1782	The Big Frame - The Gordons	.50	1.25	2.00	M
F1783	Alabama Empire - Welbaurn Kelley	.50	1.25	2.00	
A1784	The Teen-age Diet Book - Ruth West	.50	1.25	2.00	NF
A1785	They Fought for the Sky - Quentin Reynolds	.50	1.25	2.00	C
A1786	Time in Advance - William Tenn	.75	1.75	3.00	SF
1787	What, then, is Love - Emilie Loring	.50	1.25	2.00	R
F1788	Folk Songs of the Caribbean - James Morse	.75	1.75	3.00	NF
F1789	Three Plays - Thornton Wilder	.50	1.25	2.00	
A1790	A Wonderful World for Children, No. 2 - Peter Cardoze & Lilli Taylor	.50	1.25	2.00	NF A
F1791	Rally Round the Flag, Boys! - Max Shulman	.50	1.25	2.00	H
A1792	The Lady - Conrad Richter	.50	1.25	2.00	
A1793	Age and Essence - Aldous Huxley	.50	1.25	2.00	
1794	The Lawbringers - William Porter	.50	1.25	2.00	
A1795	Might as Well be Dead - Rex Stout	.75	1.75	3.00	M
A1796	Three for the Chair - Rex Stout	.75	1.75	3.00	M
A1797	The Silent Speaker - Rex Stout	.75	1.75	3.00	M
A1798	Sierra Baron - Thomas W. Blackburn	.50	1.25	2.00	W
1799	Eve Cameron, M. D. - Ann Rush	.50	1.25	2.00	R
A1800	The Inn of the Sixth Happiness - Alan Burgess Movie tie-in	.75	1.75	3.00	
A1801	Getting Along in French - John Fisher & Marlo Pei	.50	1.25	2.00	NF
A1802	Getting Along in Italian - Marlo Pei	.50	1.25	2.00	NF
F1803	Typee - Herman Melville	.75	1.75	3.00	A
F1804	Tales of Fair and Gallant Ladies - Abbe de Brantome	.75	1.75	3.00	
F1805	Far, Far the Mountain Peak - John Masters	.50	1.25	2.00	
1806	Gidget - Frederick Kohner	.50	1.25	2.00	R
F1807	Home Before Dark - Eileen Bassing	.50	1.25	2.00	
A1808	Wilderness Passage - Forrester Blake	.50	1.25	2.00	
A1809	Johnny Christmas - Forrester Blake	.50	1.25	2.00	
1810	Think Fast, Mr. Moto - John P. Marquand	.75	1.75	3.00	M
A1811	Lieutenant Hornblower - C. S. Forester	.50	1.25	2.00	A
A1812	Honeymoon in Hell - Fredric Brown	2.00	4.00	7.50	SF
1813	If You Like Hazel - Ted Key	.75	1.75	3.00	H
F1814	The New Art of Selling - Elmer G. Leterman	.50	1.25	2.00	NF
A1815	Mr. Midshipman Hornblower - C. S. Forester	.50	1.25	2.00	A
A1816	Beat to Quarters - C. S. Forester	.50	1.25	2.00	A
F1817	The Philadelphian - Richard Powell	.50	1.25	2.00	
F1818	The Drummond Tradition - Charles Mercer	.50	1.25	2.00	
A1819	Underdog - W. R. Burnett	.75	1.75	3.00	
A1820	Great Circle - Robert Carse	.50	1.25	2.00	
1821	Play a Lone Hand - Luke Short	.50	1.25	2.00	W
1822	The Plunders - L. P. Holmes	.50	1.25	2.00	W
1823	The Stag Party - William Krasner	.50	1.25	2.00	
A1824	Echo of a Bomb - Mark Derby	.50	1.25	2.00	
A1825	Station in Space - James E. Gunn	.50	1.25	2.00	SF
A1826	Helmet for My Pillow - Robert Leckie	.50	1.25	2.00	
A1827	The Art of French Cooking - Fernande Silve Garvin	.50	1.25	2.00	NF
A1828	Harry Black - David Walker	.50	1.25	2.00	
1829	Sonata with Bullets - J. Jerod Chouinard	.50	1.25	2.00	M
1830					
A1831	The Price of Salt - Claire Morgan	.50	1.25	2.00	
F1832	Patterns - Rod Serling	.75	1.75	3.00	
F1833	The Wapshot Chronicle - John Cheever	.50	1.25	2.00	
A1834	The Temple of Gold - William Goldman	.50	1.25	2.00	
A1835	The Killing Ground - Elleston Trevor	.50	1.25	2.00	
A1836	Tubie's Monument - Peter Keveson	.50	1.25	2.00	
1837	Outlaw Valley - Evan Evans	.50	1.25	2.00	W
1838	The Trail from Texas - Dale Homer	.50	1.25	2.00	W
1839	Blue City - John Ross MacDonald	.50	1.25	2.00	
1840	The Dark Window - Thomas Walsh	.50	1.25	2.00	
1841	A Nurse for Galleon Key - Ethel Hamill	.50	1.25	2.00	R
A1842	Bell, Book and Candle - John van Druten	.50	1.25	2.00	
S1843	One Basket - Edna Ferber	.50	1.25		
F1844	Rascals in Paradise - James A. Michener & A. Grove Day	.50	1.25	2.00	
A1845	The Blue Chips - Jay Deiss	.50	1.25	2.00	
F1846	The Spiral Road - Jan de Hartog	.50	1.25	2.00	
A1847	Fire, Burn! - John Dickson Carr	1.50	3.50	5.00	M
A1848	Louisville Saturday - Margaret Long	.50	1.25	2.00	E

A1849	The Sleeping Sphinx - John Dickson Carr	.75	1.75	3.00	M
A1850	The Fields - Conrad Richter	.50	1.25	2.00	
F1851	The Town - Conrad Richter	.50	1.25	2.00	
A1852	The Trees - Conrad Richter	.50	1.25	2.00	
1853	Radigan - Louis L'Amour	.75	1.75	3.00	W
F1854	1000 Ways to Make $1,000 - Helen Hoke	.50	1.25	2.00	NF
1855	The North Star - Will Henry	.50	1.25	2.00	
1856	The Outlaw of Longbow - Peter Dawson	.50	1.25	2.00	W
A1857	Proud Land - Logan Forster	.50	1.25	2.00	
1858	The Canvas Dagger - Helen Reilly	.50	1.25	2.00	M
A1859	First Train to Batylon - Max Ehrlich	.50	1.25	2.00	
A1860	The Big Eye - Max Ehrlich	.50	1.25	2.00	SF
1861	Write me a Poem, Baby - H. Allen Smith	.50	1.25	2.00	
F1862	Pigboats - Theodore Roscoe	.50	1.25	2.00	
1863					
A1864	Jalna - Mazo de la Roche	.50	1.25	2.00	
1865	Rawhide and Bob-wire - Luke Short	.50	1.25	2.00	W
1866	Summer of the Smoke - Luke Short	.50	1.25	2.00	W
A1867	A Stranger in my Arms - Robert Wilder	.50	1.25	2.00	
A1868	The Journey - George Tabori	.50	1.25	2.00	
F1869	Soomar - Ernie Kovacs	.75	1.75	3.00	
F1870	The Prisoners of Combine D - Len Giovanitti	.50	1.25	2.00	
A1871	Little Caesar - W. R. Burnett	.75	1.75	3.00	
F1872	The Earthbreakers - Ernest Haycox	.50	1.25	2.00	W
1873	Modoc, the Last Sundown - C. P. Holmes	.75	1.75	3.00	W
1874					
1875	No Vacation for Maigret - Georges Simenon	1.50	3.50	5.00	M
1876	Rival to my Heart - Ann Pinchot	.50	1.25	2.00	
F1877	TV Movie Almanac and Ratings, 1958-1959 - Steven H. Schever	.75	1.75	3.00	NF
F1878	Green Mansions - W. H. Hudson	.75	1.75	3.00	F
S1879	The Sound of Thunder - Taylor Caldwell	.50	1.25	2.00	
A1880	My Face for the World to See - Alfred Hayes	.50	1.25	2.00	
1881					
F1882	A Single Step - Lin Yung	.50	1.25	2.00	
1883	Death of a Postman - John Creasey	.50	1.25	2.00	M
1884	The Gelignite Gang - John Creasey	.50	1.25	2.00	M
A1885	The Martian Chronicles - Ray Bradbury	.50	1.25	2.00	SF
A1886	The Tall Captains - Bart Spicer	.50	1.25	2.00	
1887					
A1888	Bat Masterson - Richard O'Connor TV tie-in	1.50	3.50	5.00	W
F1889	Having a Gay Old Time - Shirley James Fagerty	.50	1.25	2.00	
A1890	Across the Everglades - Budd Schulberg	.50	1.25	2.00	
A1891	Meet Me in St. Louis - Sally Benson	.50	1.25	2.00	H
A1892	Hot Rod - Henry Gregor Felsen	.50	1.25	2.00	
1893	Rio Bravo - Leigh Brackett	.75	1.75	3.00	W
A1894	Our Hearts Were Young and Gay - Cornelia Otis Skinner & Emily Kimbrough	.50	1.25	2.00	
F1895	East of Eden - John Steinbeck	.50	1.25	2.00	
F1896	Hitler, a Study in Tyranny - Alan Bullock	.75	1.75	3.00	B
A1897	The Betty Bissell Book of Home Cleaning - Betty Bissell	.50	1.25	2.00	NF
1959					
A1898	So Many Doors - Oakley Hall	.50	1.25	2.00	E
A1899	Cry for Happy - George Campbell	.50	1.25	2.00	
F1900	Maggie Now - Betty Smith	.50	1.25	2.00	
A1901	The Hon. Rocky Slade - William Wister Haines	.50	1.25	2.00	
F1902	Slim - William Wister Haines	.50	1.25	2.00	
F1903	Ben-Hur - Lew Wallace	.50	1.25	2.00	
A1904	Mrs. Mike - Benedict & Nancy Freedman	.50	1.25	2.00	
1905	The First Fast Draw - Louis L'Amour	.75	1.75	3.00	W
1906					
1907	Nurse Howard's Assignment - Virginia Roberts	.50	1.25	2.00	R
A1908	The Price of Courage - Curt Anders	.50	1.25	2.00	
1909	The Black Mirror - Ben Benson	.50	1.25	2.00	M
1910	The Running Man - Ben Benson	.50	1.25	2.00	M
1911	I Take this Man - Emilie Loring	.50	1.25	2.00	
F1912	Ice Palace - Edna Ferber	.50	1.25	2.00	
F1913	Crack of Doom - Willis Heinrich	.50	1.25	2.00	
A1914	Love Me Little - Amanda Vail	.50	1.25	2.00	
F1915	Ride the Red Earth - Paul I. Wellman	.50	1.25	2.00	

1916	And the Wind Blows Free - Luke Short	.50	1.25	2.00	W
A1917	The Hunger and Other Stories - Charles Beaumont	1.50	3.50	5.00	SF
1918					
A1919	The Red Knight of Germany - Floyd Gibbons	.75	1.75	3.00	B
G1920	And Save them for Pallbearers - James Garrett	.50	1.25	2.00	
A1921	The Hard Sell - David Delman	.50	1.25	2.00	
A1922	Dandelion Wine - Ray Bradbury	1.50	3.50	5.00	
1923	The Mesh - Lucie Marchal	.50	1.25	2.00	E
A1924	The Teen-age Diet Book - Ruth West	.50	1.25	2.00	NF
1925	Silent River - Wayne Roberts	.50	1.25	2.00	
1926	Barbed Wire Kingdom - C. William Harrison	.50	1.25	2.00	W
1927	The Convertible Hearse - William Campbell Gault	.50	1.25	2.00	M
A1928	Conducted to a Grave - J. Jerod Chovinard	.50	1.25	2.00	M
1929	Young Doctor Randall - Adeline McElfresh	.50	1.25	2.00	R
A1930	Theatre - W. Somerset Maugham	.50	1.25	2.00	
A1931	The Narrow Corner - W. Somerset Maugham	.50	1.25	2.00	
F1932	The Disenchanted - Bud Schulberg	.50	1.25	2.00	
1933					
1934	Outlaw - Frank Gruber	.50	1.25	2.00	W
A1935	Reckoning at Yankee Flat - Will Henry	.50	1.25	2.00	W
1936	The Doctor is a Lady - Beth Myers	.50	1.25	2.00	
A1937	The Witches - Jay Williams	.75	1.75	3.00	
1938	My Dearest Love - Emilie Loring	.50	1.25	2.00	
A1939	Barefoot Boy with Cheek - Max Shulman	.50	1.25	2.00	H
A1940	The Feather Merchants - Max Shulman	.50	1.25	2.00	H
A1941	The Naked Maja - Samuel Edwards	.50	1.25	2.00	
A1942	Night of the Quarter Moon - Franklin Coen	.50	1.25	2.00	
A1943	Getting Along in Spanish - Mario Pei & Eloy Vaquero	.50	1.25	2.00	NF
A1944	Getting Along in German - Mario Pei, & Robert Politzer	.50	1.25	2.00	NF
1945	A Night to Remember - Walter Lord	.50	1.25	2.00	NF
F1946	The Image Makers - Bernard Dryer	.50	1.25	2.00	
F1947	The Northern Light - A. J. Cronin	.50	1.25	2.00	
1948	The Hours After Midnight - Joseph Hayes	.50	1.25	2.00	
1949	Gunfighter's Return - Ben Smith	.50	1.25	2.00	W
1950					
1951	Hill Country Nurse - Adeline McElfresh	.50	1.25	2.00	R
A1952	Point Ultimate - Jerry Sohl	1.50	3.50	5.00	SF
A1953	Goren Presents the Italian Bridge System - Charles H. Goren	.50	1.25	2.00	NF
A1954	The Summer Lovers - Hollis Alpert	.50	1.25	2.00	
F1955	The Violated - Vance Bourjaily	.50	1.25	2.00	
F1956	The Wonderful Country - Tom Lea	.50	1.25	2.00	A
A1957	Blue Denim - James Leo Herlihy & William Noble	.50	1.25	2.00	
A1958	Solomon and Sheba - Jay Williams	.75	1.75	3.00	A
A1959	Hard Money - Luke Short	.50	1.25	2.00	W
1960					
A1961	If Death Ever Slept - Rex Stout	.75	1.75	3.00	M
1962					
1963					
A1964	Command Decision - William Wister Haines	.50	1.25	2.00	
1965					
A1966	Middle of the Night - Paddy Chayefsky	.75	1.75	3.00	
1967					
F1968	The Bramble Bush - Charles Mergendahl	.50	1.25	2.00	
1969					
A1970	Nothing But the Night - James Yaffe	.50	1.25	2.00	
A1971	The Transcendent Man - Jerry Sohl	1.50	3.50	5.00	SF
F1972	Hoof Trails and Wagon Tracks	.75	1.75	3.00	
1973	Bitter Ground - W. R. Burnett	.75	1.75	3.00	
1974	The Blonde in Black - Ben Benson	.50	1.25	2.00	M
1975	Nurse on Location - Virginia Roberts	.50	1.25	2.00	R
F1976	His Eye is on the Sparrow - Ethel Waters & Charles Samuels	.50	1.25	2.00	B
1977	Taggart - Louis L'Amour	.75	1.75	3.00	W
A1978	Earth is Room Enough - Isaac Asimov	.75	1.75	3.00	SF
1979					
F1980	Warlock - Oakley Hall	.50	1.25	2.00	W
A1981	Sports Shorts - Mac Davis	.50	1.25	2.00	S

A1982	The Mouse that Roared - Leonard Wibberley	.50	1.25	2.00	H
A1983	Ask Any Girl - Winifred Wolfe	.50	1.25	2.00	
1984	The Savages - Peter Dawson	.50	1.25	2.00	W
1985					
A1986	The Fume of Poppies - Jonathan Kozol	.50	1.25	2.00	
F1987	The Detroiters - Harold Livingston	.50	1.25	2.00	
F1988	The Voyagers - Dale Van Every	.50	1.25	2.00	
A1989	War on the Cimarron - Luke Short	.50	1.25	2.00	W
1990	One for the Road - Fredric Brown	2.00	4.00	7.50	M
A1991	Immortality, Inc. - Robert Sheckley	1.50	3.50	5.00	SF
A1992	Dr. John's Decision - Dorothy Worley	.50	1.25	2.00	
1993					
1994					
S1995	Exodus - Leon Uris	.50	1.25	2.00	C
F1996	Battle Cry - Leon Uris	.50	1.25	2.00	C
1997					
A1998	Town Tamer - Frank Gruber	.50	1.25	2.00	W
A1999	The Crimson Horseshow - Peter Dawson	.50	1.25	2.00	W
A2000	Fear is the Same - Carter Dickson	4.00	8.00	15.00	M
2001	The Affair of the Exotic Dancer - Ben Benson	.50	1.25	2.00	M
2002	Debutante Nurse - Margaret Howe	.50	1.25	2.00	R
2003					
F2004	The End of the Affair - Graham Greene	.50	1.25	2.00	
2005					
A2006	Silver Rock - Luke Short	.50	1.25	2.00	W
F2007	The Shining Mountains - Dale Van Every	.50	1.25	2.00	
A2008	Prision Nurse - Louis Berg	.50	1.25	2.00	
A2009	Irene - Ronald Marsh	.50	1.25	2.00	
A2010	The Forest Lord - Noel B. Gerson	.50	1.25	2.00	
F2011	The God that Failed - Richard Crossman	.50	1.25	2.00	
A2012	Sleep till Noon - Max Shulman	.50	1.25	2.00	H
S2013	Women and Thomas Harrow - John P. Marquand	.50	1.25	2.00	
2014					
F2015	Wyatt Earp, Frontier Marshal - Stuart N. Lake	.75	1.75	3.00	NF
A2016	And Four to Go - Rex Stout	.75	1.75	3.00	M
A2017	1001 Valuable Things You Can Get Free, No. 3 - Mort Weisinger	.50	1.25	2.00	NF
A2020	Rock - David Wagoner	.50	1.25	2.00	
A2021	The Marshal - Frank Gruber	.50	1.25	2.00	W
A2024	The Doomsters - John Ross MacDonald	.50	1.25	2.00	
2031	Hill Smoke - L. P. Holmes	.50	1.25	2.00	W
F2033	Beloved Infidel - Gerold Frank & Sheilah Graham	.50	1.25	2.00	
A2034	Look Back in Anger - John Osborne	.50	1.25	2.00	
F2035	The Day Lincoln Was Shot - Jim Bishop	.75	1.75	3.00	NF
A2036	Saddle by Starlight - Luke Short	.50	1.25	2.00	W
A2060	Sink the Bismarck! - C. S. Forester	.75	1.75	3.00	C
A2063	The Methods of Maigret - Georges Simenon	1.50	3.50	5.00	M
F2070	The Russian Revolution - Alan Moorehead	.50	1.25	2.00	
A2073	Cheaper by the Dozen - Ernestine Carey & Frank B. Gilbreth, Jr.	.50	1.25	2.00	H

BANTAM BOOKS (LOS ANGELES)

(Bantam Publications)

Note: Later printings of 21, 22, 23, 26, 27 (and probably others) have pictorial covers whereas first printings do not. Later variants are equal in value and desirability with first printings.

A 1	The Red Threads - Rex Stout	10.00	25.00	40.00	M
1	The Spanish Cape Mystery - Ellery Queen	10.00	25.00	40.00	M
2	Little Known Facts About Famous People - Dale Carnegie	7.50	15.00	30.00	NF
3	Your Health Questions - M. M. D. Fishbein	7.50	15.00	30.00	NF
4	Everybody's Dream Book, Your Dreams Explained	7.50	15.00	30.00	NF
5	How to Make Friends Easily - S. Currie	7.50	15.00	30.00	NF
6	Everybody's Book of Jokes and Wisecracks - J. Gregory	7.50	15.00	30.00	H
7	The Voice of Experience	7.50	15.00	30.00	
8	Favorite Poems: Popular Selections from the World's Literature	7.50	15.00	30.00	

(BANTAM BOOKS, continued)

9 Enter the G-Men - William Engle	10.00	25.00	40.00	M
10 1000 Facts Worth Knowing	7.50	15.00	30.00	NF
11 How to Win and Hold a Husband - L. Martin	7.50	15.00	30.00	NF
12 The World's Great Love Affairs - Hendrik Willem Van Loon	7.50	15.00	30.00	
13 Poems of Passion - Ella Wheeler Wilcox	7.50	15.00	30.00	
14 The Lone Ranger and the Secret of Thunder Mountain - Fran Striker aka Heigh-Yo Silver: A Story of The Lone Ranger	15.00	35.00	60.00	W
15 Children's Favorite Stories	10.00	25.00	40.00	
16 Grimms' Fairy Tales	10.00	25.00	40.00	
17 Private Lives of the Movie Stars - Eleanor Packer	10.00	25.00	40.00	NF
18 Love on the Run - Fred MacIsaac	10.00	25.00	40.00	
19 The Tower of Flame/Jaragu of the Lost Islands - Rex Beach	10.00	25.00	40.00	A
20 The Story of Rabelais and Voltaire - Hendrik Willem Van Loon	7.50	15.00	30.00	
21 The Shadow and the Voice of Murder - Maxwell Grant	15.00	35.00	60.00	M
22 The Green Death - Brett Hutton	10.00	25.00	40.00	M
23 Tarzan in the Forbidden City - Edgar Rice Burroughs 1940	15.00	35.00	60.00	A
24 Humorous Anecdotes and Funny Stories	7.50	15.00	30.00	H
25 Nobody Heard the Shot - Donald Barr Chidsey	10.00	25.00	40.00	M
26 Mystery of the Blue Geranium and Other Tuesday Club Murders - Agatha Christie	10.00	25.00	40.00	M
27 Danger Mansion - Philip Wylie	10.00	25.00	40.00	M
28 Stranger in Flight - Mignon G. Eberhart	10.00	25.00	40.00	M

BANTAM CLASSICS

(Bantam Books, Inc.)

AC 1 Brave New World - Aldous Huxley	1.50	3.50	5.00	SF
FC 2 Four Great Comedies of the Restoration and Eighteenth Century	.75	1.75	3.00	
SC 3 The Complete Short Stories of Mark Twain	.75	1.75	3.00	
SC 4 The Idiot - Fyodor Dostoyersky	.75	1.75	3.00	
FC 5 Four Great Plays - Anton Chekhov	.75	1.75	3.00	
FC 6 Sister Carrie - Theodore Dreiser	.75	1.75	3.00	
FC 7 Lord Jim - Joseph Conrad	.75	1.75	3.00	
FC 8 The Octopus - Frank Norris	.75	1.75	3.00	
FC 9 Henry the Eighth - Francis Hackett	.75	1.75	3.00	B
FC10 Emma - Jane Austen	.50	1.25	2.00	
FC11 The Voyage of the Beagle - Charles Darwin	.75	1.75	3.00	NF
AC12 Of Mice and Men - John Steinbeck	.75	1.75	3.00	
FC13 Penguin Island - Anatole France	.75	1.75	3.00	
AC14 The Day of the Locust - Nathanael West	.75	1.75	3.00	
FC15 Only Yesterday - Frederick Lewis Allen	.50	1.25	2.00	
FC16 Four Short Novels - Herman Melville	.75	1.75	3.00	
AC17 Eugenie Grandet - Honore de Balzac	.75	1.75	3.00	
AC18 Cannery Raw - John Steinbeck	.75	1.75	3.00	

Bantam 1977, c. Bantam   Bantam (L. A.) 14, c. Bantam   Bantam (L. A.) 23, c. Bantam

(BANTAM CLASSICS, continued)

AC19	Cyrano de Bergerac - Edmond Rostand	.75	1.75	3.00	
FC20	Two Years Before the Mast - Richard Henry Dana	.75	1.75	3.00	A
FC21	Barchester Towers - Anthony Trollope	.75	1.75	3.00	
AC22	Crome Yellow - Aldous Huxley	.75	1.75	3.00	
FC23	Four Great Plays by Ibsen - Henrik Ibsen	.75	1.75	3.00	
FC24	Canterbury Tales - Geoffrey Chaucer	.75	1.75	3.00	
AC25	The Moon and Sixpence - W. Somerset Maugham 1959	.75	1.75	3.00	
AC26	Hiroshima - John Hersey	.50	1.25	2.00	
FC27	Cleopatra - Emil Ludwig	.75	1.75	3.00	B
FC28	Manhattan Transfer - John Dos Passos	.75	1.75	3.00	
FC29	Fifty Great Short Stories - Milton Crane	.50	1.25	2.00	
FC30	Crime and Punishment - Fyodor Dostoyevsky	.75	1.75	3.00	
AC31	The Crucible - Arthur Miller	.75	1.75	3.00	
FC32	Marriage and Morals - Bertrand Russell	.75	1.75	3.00	
NC33	50 Great Artists - Bernard Myers	.50	1.25	2.00	
FC34	All the King's Men - Robert Penn Warren	.50	1.25	2.00	
AC35	Madame Bovary - Gustave Flaubert 36	.50	1.25	2.00	
FC37	Up from Slavery - Booker T. Washington	.75	1.75	3.00	B
AC38	Washington Square - Henry James	.50	1.25	2.00	
FC39	Life on the Mississippi - Mark Twain	.75	1.75	3.00	
SC40	The Red and the Black - Stendhal	.75	1.75	3.00	
FC41	Fathers and Sons - Ivan Turgenev	.75	1.75	3.00	
AC42	Rashomon and Other Stories - Ryunosuke Akutagawa	1.50	3.50	5.00	
SC43	The Age of Reason - Jean-Paul Sartre	.75	1.75	3.00	
FC44	Citizen Tom Paine - Howard Fast 45	.75	1.75	3.00	B
FC46	War With the Newts - Karel Capek	1.50	3.50	5.00	SF
FC47	The Finest Stories of Sean O'Faolain - Sean O'Faolain	.75	1.75	3.00	
AC48	Seventeen - Booth Tarkington	.50	1.25	2.00	H
FC49	Beyond the Pleasure Principle - Sigmund Freud	.75	1.75	3.00	
AC50	Pudd'nhead Wilson - Mark Twain 1959	.75	1.75	3.00	
AC51	Candide - Voltaire	.75	1.75	3.00	
FC52	Man and Superman - George Bernard Shaw	.50	1.25	2.00	

BANTAM UN-NUMBERED

(Bantam Books, Inc.)

nn	Roosevelt and Hopkins, Volume I - Robert E. Sherwood 1950	1.50	3.50	5.00	NF
nn	Roosevelt and Hopkins, Volume 2 - Robert E. Sherwood 1950	1.50	3.50	5.00	NF

BARD

(Bard Publishing Corporation)

Digest size

nn	Dead Giveaway - Dorothy Wheelock 1944	1.50	3.50	5.00	M

BART HOUSE

(Barthomew House, Inc.)

nn(1)	The Hand in the Cobbler's Safe - Seth Bailey 1944	4.00	8.00	15.00	M

(BART HOUSE, continued)

nn(2)	The Delinquent Ghost - Eric Hatch	3.00	6.00	12.00	M
3	The Spy Trap - William Gilman	2.50	6.00	10.00	
4	Weird Shadow over Innsmouth - H. P. Lovecraft	15.00	30.00	55.00	SF
5	John Smith Hears Death Walking - Wyatt Blassingame	7.50	15.00	30.00	
6	Rebirth - Thomas Calvert McClary	10.00	25.00	40.00	SF
7	The Shivering Bough - Noel Burke	2.50	6.00	10.00	M
8	The Blue Geranium - Dolan Birkley	2.50	6.00	10.00	M
9	The Waltz of Death - P. B. Maxon	3.00	6.00	12.00	M
10	The Devil Drives - Virgil Markham	2.50	6.00	10.00	M
11	Murder Meets Mephisto - Queena Mario 1945	2.00	4.00	7.50	M
12	The Dunwich Horror - H. P. Lovecraft	15.00	35.00	60.00	SF
13	4 Feet in the Grave - Amelia Reynolds Long	2.50	6.00	10.00	M
14	The Wheelchair Corpse - Will Levinrew aka Murder on the Palisades	2.50	6.00	10.00	M
15	Three Short Biers - Jimmy Starr	2.00	4.00	6.00	M
16	Murder Is Out - Lee Thayer	2.50	6.00	10.00	M
17	The Deaths of Lora Karen - Roman McDougald	2.50	6.00	10.00	M
18	Terry - Harriet T. Comstock	2.00	4.00	7.50	E
19	Said with Flowers - Anne Nash	2.50	6.00	10.00	M
20	Motionless Shadows - Kathleen Norris aka Come Back to Me, Beloved	2.00	4.00	7.50	R
21	The Promise - Pearl S. Buck 1946	2.00	4.00	7.50	
22	Checkmate to Murder - E. C. R. Lorac	2.50	6.00	10.00	M
23	Roughly Speaking - Louise Randall Pierson	2.00	4.00	6.00	H
24	Murder Secretary - William Beyer aka Eenie, Meenie, Minie - Murder!	2.50	6.00	10.00	M
25	Hollywood Mystery - Ben Hecht aka I Hate Actors	2.00	4.00	7.50	M
26	Bury the Hatchet - Manning Long	2.50	6.00	10.00	M
27	Design for Dying - Louis Trimble	2.50	6.00	10.00	M
28	Grand Hotel - Vicki Baum	2.50	6.00	10.00	
29	Puzzle in Porcelain - Robin Grey	2.50	6.00	10.00	M
30	The Lion's Skin - Rafael Sabatini	3.00	6.00	12.00	A
31	The Blue Cloak - Temple Bailey	2.50	6.00	10.00	R
32	Hangman's Tie - Christopher Hale	2.50	6.00	10.00	M
33	A Smattering of Ignorance - Oscar Levant	2.00	4.00	6.00	H
34	Death in the Cards - Ann T. Smith	2.50	6.00	10.00	M
35	The Clue in the Clay - D. B. Olsen	2.50	6.00	10.00	M
36	Murder Among Friends - Lange Lewis	2.50	6.00	10.00	M
39	Can You Top This? - Ed Ford, Harry Hershfield & Joe Laurie, Jr.	2.00	4.00	6.00	H
101	Mr. Ace - Helen Christy 1946, movie tie-in	2.00	4.00	6.00	M
102	The Sin of Harold Diddlebock - Harry Hershfield 1947, movie tie-in	3.00	6.00	12.00	H
103	Honeymoon - Elisabeth Ogilvie Movie tie-in	3.00	6.00	12.00	R

BEACON

Bard nn, c. Bard

Bart House 4, c. Bart

Bart House 6, c. Bart

122

Bart House 12, c. Bart   Beacon B105, c. Univ   Beacon B108, c. Univ

(BEACON, continued)

(Universal Publishing and Distributing Corporation)

B101 She Got What She Wanted - Orrie Hitt	2.00	4.00	7.50	E
Orig., 1954				
B102 Pawn - Fan Nichols	1.50	3.50	5.00	E
B103 Rooming House - Fred Malloy	1.50	3.50	5.00	E
Orig., 1954				
B104 Shabby Street - Orrie Hitt	1.50	3.50	5.00	E
Orig., 1954				
B105 King of the Khyber Rifles - Talbot Mundy	4.00	8.00	15.00	A
B106 Walk in Darkness - Hans Habe	1.50	3.50	5.00	E
B107 Stable Boy - Adam Rebel	1.50	3.50	5.00	E
B108 Gutter Gang - Jay de Bekker	2.50	6.00	10.00	JD
B109 Pick-up - Charles Willeford	2.00	4.00	6.00	E
Note: Same cover as Royal Giant no. 21.				
B110 Keyhole Peeper - Jay de Bekker	1.50	3.50	5.00	E
B111 Liz - Frank Kane	1.50	3.50	5.00	E
B112 Lady Cop - J. T. Pritchard	1.50	3.50	5.00	E
B113 Highlights from Yank - the Army Weekly	2.50	6.00	10.00	C
B114 Scandalous Lady - Fan Nichols	1.50	3.50	5.00	E
B115 Gonzaga's Woman - John Jakes	3.00	6.00	12.00	E
B116 Hired Girl - Valerie Taylor	1.50	3.50	5.00	E
B117 The Hussy - Idabel Williams	1.50	3.50	5.00	E
B118 The Woman He Wanted - Daoma Winston	1.50	3.50	5.00	E
B119 Forbidden Fruit - Curtis Lucas	1.50	3.50	5.00	E
B120 Confessions of a Psychiatrist - Henry Lewis				
Nixon	2.00	4.00	6.00	E
B121 Warped Women - Janet Pritchard	1.50	3.50	5.00	E
B122 Dolly - Fan Nichols	1.50	3.50	5.00	E
B123 Passion in the Pines - Jack Woodford & John				
B. Thompson	1.50	3.50	5.00	E
B124 Honey - Jack Woodford & John B.				
Thompson	1.50	3.50	5.00	E
B125 Swamp Hoyden - Jack Woodford & John B.				
Thompson	2.00	4.00	6.00	E
B126 Unfaithful Wives - Orrie Hitt	1.50	3.50	5.00	E
B127 Savage Eve - Jack Woodford & John B.				
Thompson	1.50	3.50	5.00	E
B128 Witch on Wheels - William Boltin	1.50	3.50	5.00	E
B129 Bayou Girl - John Thompson	1.50	3.50	5.00	E
B130 High Priest of California - Charles Willeford	2.00	4.00	6.00	E
B131 Rock'N Roll Gal - Ernie Weatherall	2.00	4.00	6.00	E
B132 The Sucker - Orrie Hitt	1.50	3.50	5.00	E
B133 French Model - Cecil Barr	1.50	3.50	5.00	E
B134 Twisted - George Jones	2.00	4.00	6.00	E
c-Gross				
Note: Same cover as Intimate no. 19.				
B135 Queer Affair - Carol Emery	1.50	3.50	5.00	E
B136 Shack Baby - Lon Williams	1.50	3.50	5.00	E
B137 Nudist Camp - Orrie Hitt	1.50	3.50	5.00	E
B138 Hitch-hike Hussy - John B. Thompson &				
Jack Woodford	1.50	3.50	5.00	E
B139 Pushover - Orrie Hitt	1.50	3.50	5.00	E
B140 Sugar Doll - Jack Woodford & John B.				
Thompson	1.50	3.50	5.00	E

(BEACON, continued)

B144	Girls of the French Quarter - John B. Thompson	1.50	3.50	5.00	E
B146	Ladies Man - Orrie Hitt	.75	1.75	3.00	E
B147	Footloose Fraulein - Hans Habe	1.50	3.50	5.00	E
B148	Lovel Fraud - Joe Weiss	.75	1.75	3.00	E
B149	Call Her Wanton - Lon Williams	.75	1.75	3.00	E
B150	Blonde Trap - Ernie Weatherall	.75	1.75	3.00	E
B151	Dolls and Dues - Orrie Hitt	.75	1.75	3.00	E
B152	Adam and Two Eves - anonymous	1.50	3.50	5.00	E
B153	Trailer Tramp - Orrie Hitt	.75	1.75	3.00	E
B154	Sinful Virgin - John B. Thompson	.75	1.75	3.00	E
B155	Gang Girl - Joe Weiss	1.50	3.50	5.00	E
B156	Twilight Women - Les Scott	1.50	3.50	5.00	E
	Note: Same cover as Universal Giant no. 9.				
B157	Paprika - Eric Von Stroheim	1.50	3.50	5.00	E
	Note: Same cover as Universal Giant no. 2.				
B158	Teaser - Orrie Hitt	.75	1.75	3.00	E
B159	Ellie's Shack - Orrie Hitt	.75	1.75	3.00	E
B160	Honey Gal - Charles Willeford	.75	1.75	3.00	E
B161	Back of Town - Herbert Pruett	.75	1.75	3.00	E
B162	Hill Hoyden - Lon Williams	.75	1.75	3.00	E
B163	Hell Bent - H. P. Ames	.75	1.75	3.00	E
B164	Suburban Wife - Orrie Hitt	.75	1.75	3.00	E
B165	Gutter Gang - Jay de Bekker	1.50	3.50	5.00	E
B166	The Private Pleasures of Mary Linton - William Arthur	.75	1.75	3.00	E
B167	Play for Pay - Wright Williams	.75	1.75	3.00	E
B169	Wild Oats - Orrie Hitt	.75	1.75	3.00	E
B170	Side Street - Wright Williams	.75	1.75	3.00	E
B171	Wild Hunger - Fred Malloy	.75	1.75	3.00	E
B172	Woman He Wanted - Daoma Winston	.75	1.75	3.00	E
B173	Forbidden Fruit - Curtis Lucas	.75	1.75	3.00	E
B175	Lust is a Woman - Charles Willeford	.75	1.75	3.00	E
B176	Call South 3300: Ask for Molly! - Orrie Hitt	.75	1.75	3.00	E
B177	Hill Hellion! - Lon Williams	.75	1.75	3.00	E
B178	Fair Game - Clement Wood	.75	1.75	3.00	E
B179	The Girl in the Black Chemise - Les Scott	1.50	3.50	5.00	E
B182	Fast Girl - Token West	.75	1.75	3.00	E
B183	The Naked and the Fair - Hal Moore	.75	1.75	3.00	E
B184	Confessions of a Psychiatrist - Henry Lewis Nixon	.75	1.75	3.00	E
B185	Rooming House - Fred Malloy	.75	1.75	3.00	E
B186	Trapped - Orrie Hitt	.75	1.75	3.00	E
B187	The Lusting Breed - Mary S. Gooch	.75	1.75	3.00	E
B188	I Made My Bed - Celia Hye	.75	1.75	3.00	E
B189	Studio Affair - Clement Wood	.75	1.75	3.00	E
B190	Three Women - March Hastings	.75	1.75	3.00	E
B193	The Other Stranger - Daoma Winston	.75	1.75	3.00	E
B194	Shabby Street - Orrie Hitt	.75	1.75	3.00	E
B195	She Got What She Wanted - Orrie Hitt	.75	1.75	3.00	E
B200	Pick-up - Charles Willeford	1.50	3.50	5.00	E
	Note: Same cover as Royal Giant no. 21.				
B203	Hot Cargo - Orrie Hitt	1.50	3.50	5.00	E
	1958				
B204	Surabaya - James Fox	1.50	3.50	5.00	A
B205	Red Curtain - Duncan Taylor	1.50	3.50	5.00	E
	1959				

Beacon B156, c. Univ   Beacon B179, c. Univ   Beacon B203, c. Univ

Beacon B217, c. Univ   Beacon 236, c. Univ   Beacon B260, c. Univ

(BEACON, continued)

B208	Spawn of the Bayou - John B. Thompson	.75	1.75	3.00	E
B209	Rotten to the Core - Orrie Hitt	.75	1.75	3.00	E
B210	The Dispossessed - Geoffrey Wagner	.75	1.75	3.00	E
B211	Sheba - Orrie Hitt	.75	1.75	3.00	E
B212	Nudist Camp - Orrie Hitt	.75	1.75	3.00	E
B213	Hitch-Hike Hussy - John B. Thompson & Jack Woodford	.75	1.75	3.00	E
B214	Adulteress - Lon Williams	.75	1.75	3.00	E
B216	Steffi - Eunice Gray	.75	1.75	3.00	E
B217	Slave Ship - H. B. Drake	.75	1.75	3.00	E
B218	Strumpet's Seed - Fred Malloy	.75	1.75	3.00	E
B219	Tabasco - John B. Thompson	.75	1.75	3.00	E
B220	Scandalous Lady - Fan Nichols	.75	1.75	3.00	E
B221	The Hussy - Idabel Williams	.75	1.75	3.00	E
B222	The Widow - Orrie Hitt	.75	1.75	3.00	E
B223	Chris - Randy Salem	.75	1.75	3.00	E
B224	Half-caste - John B. Thompson	.75	1.75	3.00	E
B226	The Strange Ones - Ben Travis	.75	1.75	3.00	E
B227	Add Flesh to the Fire - Orrie Hitt	.75	1.75	3.00	E
B228	Nude in the Mirror - George Viereck	.75	1.75	3.00	E
B229	Alcoholic Woman - Ruth M. Walsh	.75	1.75	3.00	E
B230	Odd Girl - Artemis Smith	.75	1.75	3.00	E
B231	Tap Softly on My Bedroom Door - Roswell Lewis	.75	1.75	3.00	E
B232	Private Club - Orrie Hitt	.75	1.75	3.00	E
B233	Turncoat - Richard Fox	.75	1.75	3.00	E
B234	Night of Shame - Lewis Lester	.75	1.75	3.00	E
B235	Lita - Fred Malloy	.75	1.75	3.00	E
236	Odd John - Olaf Stapledon 1959	4.00	8.00	15.00	SF
B237	The Needle - Sloane M. Britain	.75	1.75	3.00	E
B238	Carnival Girl - Orrie Hitt	.75	1.75	3.00	E
B239	The Peeper - Orrie Hitt	.75	1.75	3.00	E
B240	Temple of Lust - John Burton Thompson	.75	1.75	3.00	E
B241	Street Walker - E. S. Seeley	.75	1.75	3.00	E
242	The Deviates - Raymond F. Jones	3.00	6.00	12.00	SF
B243	Hellcat - Dorine Clark	.75	1.75	3.00	E
B244	The Virgin - Don Morro	.75	1.75	3.00	E
B245	The Young Hoods - Joe Castro	1.50	3.50	5.00	JD
B246	The Divorcees - Scott Stone	.75	1.75	3.00	E
B247	Too Many Women - Barry Devlin	.75	1.75	3.00	E
B248	Margo - Scott Stone	.75	1.75	3.00	E
B250	Too Hot to Handle - Orrie Hitt	.75	1.75	3.00	E
B251	One-Kind of Woman - Ralph Dean	.75	1.75	3.00	E
B252	Cheating Wives - Barry Devlin	.75	1.75	3.00	E
B253	Nude in the Sand - John Burton Thompson	.75	1.75	3.00	E
B254	Sin Doll - Orrie Hitt	.75	1.75	3.00	E
B255	Make Sure I Win - Barry Devlin	.75	1.75	3.00	E
256	Troubled Star - George O. Smith 1959	2.50	6.00	10.00	SF
B257	Shack Woman - Kathie Reed	.75	1.75	3.00	E
B258	Wild Blonde - Jack Kelly	.75	1.75	3.00	E
B260	Basement Gang - David Williams 1959	2.00	4.00	7.50	JD
	Note: Virtually the same cover as Intimate no. 32 and Stallion no. 213.				
B261	Tawny - Orrie Hill	.75	1.75	3.00	E

(BEACON, continued)

B262	Danielle - Joseph Foster	.75	1.75	3.00	E
263	Pagan Passions - Randall Garrett & Larry M. Harris	3.00	6.00	12.00	SF
	First ed., 1959				
B264	Strange Thirsts - Michael Norday	.75	1.75	3.00	E
B265	Hot Blood - John B. Thompson	.75	1.75	3.00	E
B266	Strip-Tease Girl - Cal Anton	.75	1.75	3.00	E
B267	Ex-Virgin - Orrie Hitt	.75	1.75	3.00	E
B268	The Third Sex - Artemis Smith	.75	1.75	3.00	E
B269	Private School - J. C. Priest	.75	1.75	3.00	E
270	Virgin Planet - Poul Anderson	2.50	6.00	10.00	SF
	1960				
B271	Naked Desire - Henry Louis Nixon	.75	1.75	3.00	E
B272	Golden Tramp - Daoma Winston	.75	1.75	3.00	E
B273	Of G-Strings and Strippers - Mark Tryon	.75	1.75	3.00	E
B274	Suburban Sin - Orrie Hitt	.75	1.75	3.00	E
B275	Mimi - Lee Morell	.75	1.75	3.00	E
B276	Triangle of Sin - Manning	.75	1.75	3.00	E
277	Flesh - Philip Jose Farmer	7.50	15.00	25.00	SF
	First ed., 1960				
B278	Sorority Sin - E. S. Seeley	.75	1.75	3.00	E
B279	Convention Girl - Rick Lucas	.75	1.75	3.00	E
B280	Warped - Michael Norday	.75	1.75	3.00	E
B281	Strange Circle - Gale Sydney	.75	1.75	3.00	E
B282	Mavis - Justin Kent	.75	1.75	3.00	E
B283	Night of the Lash - Barry Devlin	.75	1.75	3.00	E
284	The Sex War - Sam Merwin	2.50	6.00	10.00	SF
	1960, aka The White Widows				
B285	Ex-Mistress - Thomas Stone	.75	1.75	3.00	E
B286	Helena's House - Kim Savage	.75	1.75	3.00	E
B287	Pound of Flesh - Simms Albert	.75	1.75	3.00	E
B288	Wayward Girl - Orrie Hitt	.75	1.75	3.00	E
B289	Warped Desire - Kay Addams	.75	1.75	3.00	E
B290	Scarlet City - Winchell Barry	.75	1.75	3.00	E
291	A Woman a Day - Philip Jose Farmer	7.50	15.00	30.00	SF
	First ed., 1960				
B292	Male Virgin - Jack Woodford & John Burton Thompson	.75	1.75	3.00	E
B293	Station Wagon Wives - Janet Pritchard	.75	1.75	3.00	E
B294	The Torrid Teens - Orrie Hitt	.75	1.75	3.00	E
B295	Song of the Whip - Barry Devlin	.75	1.75	3.00	E
B296	Very Private Secretary - Jack Hanley	.75	1.75	3.00	E
B297	Summer Resort Women - Gordon Semple	.75	1.75	3.00	E
298	The Mating Cry - A. E. Van Vogt	4.00	8.00	15.00	SF
	1960, aka The House that Stood Still				
B299	Ask for Therese - Evans Wall	.75	1.75	3.00	E
B300	Lingerie Limited - Ralph Dean	.75	1.75	3.00	E
B301	One More for the Road - John Burton Thompson	.75	1.75	3.00	E
B302	Doctor Prescott's Secret - Pegy Gaddis	.75	1.75	3.00	E
B303	Restless Women - Rick Lucas	.75	1.75	3.00	E
B304	From Door to Door - Orrie Hitt	.75	1.75	3.00	E
	1960				
305	The Male Response - Brian Aldiss	2.50	6.00	10.00	SF
	First ed., 1961				
B306	Gutter Girl - Leo Rifkin & Tony Norman	1.50	3.50	5.00	JD
B307	Pleasure Alley - Ralph Carter	.75	1.75	3.00	E
	Note: Same cover as Intimate no. 20.				

Beacon 270, c. Univ   Beacon 291, c. Univ   Beacon 298, c. Univ

Beacon Envoy E102, c. Univ   Belmont Books 204, c. Belmt   Belmont Books 230, c. Belmt

(BEACON, continued)

B308	Lucy - Kay Addams	.75	1.75	3.00	E
B309	Hucksters' Women - Rick Lucas	.75	1.75	3.00	E
B310	Infidelity - Fred Malloy	.75	1.75	3.00	E
B311	Different - Dorene Clark	.75	1.75	3.00	E
312	Sin in Space - Cyril Judd (Judith Merril & C. M. Kornbluth	2.50	6.00	10.00	SF
	1961, aka Outpost Mars				
B313	Private Chauffeur - N. R. DeMexico	.75	1.75	3.00	E
B315	She Learned the Hard Way - Scott Stone	.75	1.75	3.00	E
B317	Trailer Camp Woman - Doug Duperrault	.75	1.75	3.00	E
B318	Philanderer's Women - Lewis Lester	.75	1.75	3.00	E
B321	Lust for Love - Florence Stonebreaker	.75	1.75	3.00	E
B322	Intimate Physician - Florenz Branch	.75	1.75	3.00	E
B323	Wanton - Ben Smith	.75	1.75	3.00	E
B324	She Made Her Bed - Evans McKnight	.75	1.75	3.00	E
B325	Tell Them Anything - Orrie Hitt	.75	1.75	3.00	E
B327	Play Girl - Barney DeForest	.75	1.75	3.00	E
B328	Marijuana Girl - N. R. DeMexico	2.00	4.00	6.00	E
B329	The Eager Ones - John Burton Thompson	.75	1.75	3.00	E
B330	Alcoholic Wife - G. G. Revelle	.75	1.75	3.00	E

BEACON ENVOY

(Universal Publishing and Distributing Corporation)

E102	Horns of Ecstasy - David Williams	.75	1.75	3.00	E
	1961				

BELMONT BOOKS

(Belmont Productions, Inc.)

201	Temptress - Andre Maurois	1.50	3.50	5.00	E
	1960, aka September Roses				
202	The Question - Henri Alleg	1.50	3.50	5.00	NF
203	Payola Woman - Carson Bingham	.75	1.75	3.00	E
204	Johnny Havoc - John Jakes	2.00	4.00	7.50	M
205	Who Live in Shadow - Judge John Murtagh & Sara Harris	1.50	3.50	5.00	NF
206	Bloody Precinct - Bill Douglas	.75	1.75	3.00	M
207	The Cruel City - Joe Mackey	.75	1.75	3.00	E
208	The Slave - Micheline Maurel aka An Ordinary Camp	1.50	3.50	5.00	NF
209	Hong Kong Kill - Bryan Peters	.75	1.75	3.00	E
210	The Oldest Profession - Jean Campbell	.75	1.75	3.00	E
211	Cage of Passion - Isa Mari Movie tie-in	1.50	3.50	5.00	E
212	Something Wild - Alex Karmel Movie tie-in, aka Mary Ann	1.50	3.50	5.00	E
213	The Blanket - A. A. Murray	.75	1.75	3.00	
214	Come-on Girl - Stuart Friedman	.75	1.75	3.00	E
215	Lights, Camera, Murder - John Shepherd	.75	1.75	3.00	M

216	Concha - Philippe Sollers aka A Strange Solitude	.75	1.75	3.00	E
217	Sugar Shannon - Adam Knight	.75	1.75	3.00	M
218	Sex-Clusive - Jack Heller	1.50	3.50	5.00	H
219	Hitler's Woman - Antoni Gronowicz aka Hitler's Wife	1.50	3.50	5.00	B
220	South Pacific Affair - Ed Lacy 1961	.75	1.75	3.00	E
221	Vice Cop - Richard Deming	.75	1.75	3.00	M
222	A Wind Is Rising - William Russell	.75	1.75	3.00	E
223	Skid Row U. S. A. - Sara Harris	1.50	3.50	5.00	NF
224	Lonely Boy Blues - Alan Kapelner	.75	1.75	3.00	
225	Foxhole in Cairo - Leonard Mosley	.75	1.75	3.00	
226	Niether Sin nor Shame - Ann Marie & Michael Burgess	.75	1.75	3.00	
227	The Borgia Blade - Gardner F. Fox	2.00	4.00	7.50	A
228	The Ladies Man - Carl Winston Movie tie-in	1.50	3.50	5.00	
229	Ten Against the Third Reich - Stan Smith	1.50	3.50	5.00	NF
230	Creeps by Night - Dashiell Hammett	2.00	4.00	7.50	HO
231	My Life and Loves in Greenwich Village - Maxwell Bodenheim	2.00	4.00	6.00	B
232	The Day the War Ends - Irwin Shaw	1.50	3.50	5.00	NF
233	Nightmares - Robert Bloch	2.00	4.00	7.50	HO
234	Love Doctor - Florence Stonebraker	.75	1.75	3.00	E
235	A Gun for Cantrell - Harry Sinclair Drago	.75	1.75	3.00	W
236	Markham - Lawrence Block TV tie-in	1.50	3.50	5.00	M
237	Stronger than Fear - Richard Tregaskis	.75	1.75	3.00	C
238	13 Against the Rising Sun - Stanley E. Smith	1.50	3.50	5.00	NF
239	The Red Brain - Dashiell Hammett	2.00	4.00	7.50	HO
240	Lover Boy - John B. Flint	.75	1.75	3.00	E
241	The Trial of Johnny Dice - Harry Sinclair Drago	.75	1.75	3.00	W
242	The Back of the Tiger - Richard Cargoe	.75	1.75	3.00	E
243	The Love Mill - Louis Malley	.75	1.75	3.00	E
244	Nurse Durand's Affair - Peggy Gaddis	.75	1.75	3.00	R
245					
246	The Horror Expert - Frank B. Long	2.00	4.00	7.50	HO

BELMONT BOOKS L-SERIES

(Belmont Productions, Inc.)

L501	Varieties of Love - Herbert Kubly	.75	1.75	3.00	
L502	The Incorrigibles - William Wiegand aka The Treatment Man	.75	1.75	3.00	
L503	Sex Life of the Modern Adult - Dr. Leland E. Glover	.75	1.75	3.00	NF
L504	The Brigitte Bardot Story - George Carpozi, Jr.	2.50	6.00	10.00	B
L505	The Cheat - Charles Jackson aka Earthly Creatures	1.50	3.50	5.00	
L506	The Secret Agent's Badge of Courage - ed. Ernest Hemingway	.75	1.75	3.00	

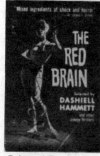

Belmont Books 239,
c. Belmt

Belmont Books 246,
c. Belmt

Belmont L-Series L504,
c. Belmt

L507	Meet the Mob - Detective Mullady & Bill Kofoed	2.00	4.00	7.50	NF
L508	Marilyn Monroe: "Her Own Story" - George Carpori, Jr.	3.00	6.00	12.00	B
L509	The Battle of Leyte Gulf - Stan Smith	.75	1.75	3.00	NF
L510	Most Likely to Succeed - John Dos Passos	.75	1.75	3.00	
L511	The Traitor - W. Somerset Maugham	.75	1.75	3.00	
L512	The Shadow in the Rose Garden - D. H. Lawrence	.75	1.75	3.00	E
L513	How to Get Rich Buying Stocks - Ira U. Cobleigh	.50	1.25	2.00	NF
L514	Sinatra and His Rat Pack - Richard Gehman	2.50	6.00	10.00	B
L515	Memoirs - Admiral Karl Doenitz	1.50	3.50	5.00	NF
L516	The Ambassador - Aldous Huxley	.75	1.75	3.00	
L517	Eat Your Troubles Away - Dr. Lelord Kordel	.50	1.25	2.00	NF
L518	Come into My Parlor - Charles Washburn	.50	1.25	2.00	E
L519	Khrushchev's "Mein Kampf" - Harrison E. Salisbury	.75	1.75	3.00	NF
L520	Black-Shirt - Graham Fisher & Michael McNair-Wilson	1.50	3.50	5.00	NF
L521	The Integration of Maybelle Brown - Bonnie Golightly	.75	1.75	3.00	E
L522	Behind Every Door - Julius Horwitz	.50	1.25	2.00	
L523	Sex Life of the Modern Teen-ager - Dr. Leland E. Glover	.75	1.75	3.00	NF
L524	Berlin Betrayal - Willi Frischaver	.75	1.75	3.00	NF

BELMONT BOOKS X-SERIES

(Belmont Productions, Inc.)

X201	The Family Survival Handbook - Martin A. Smith & William E. Eliason	.50	1.25	2.00	NF

BERKLEY

(Berkley Publishing Corporation)

101	The Pleasures of the Jazz Age - William Hodapp 1955	2.00	4.00	7.50	NF
102	Loveliest of Friends - G. Sheila Donisthorpe	1.50	3.50	5.00	
103	S. S. San Pedro - James Gould Cozzens	1.50	3.50	5.00	
104	Fever Pitch - Frank Waters	2.00	4.00	7.50	
105	Death of an Ad Man - Alfred Eichler	1.50	3.50	5.00	
106	Three Day Pass--to Kill - James Wakefield Burke & Edward Grace	1.50	3.50	5.00	
107	Border Raider - William Hopson	1.50	3.50	5.00	W
108	They Shoot Horses, Don't They? - Horace McCoy	2.00	4.00	7.50	
109	So It Doesn't Whistle - Robert Paul Smith	1.50	3.50	5.00	
110	All The Girls We Loved - Prudencio DePereda	1.50	3.50	5.00	
111	Torture Garden - Octave Mirbeav	3.00	6.00	12.00	
112	Mask of Glass - Holly Roth	2.00	4.00	7.50	
313	Saddle Hawks - Bliss Lomax (H.S. Drago)	2.00	4.00	7.50	W
314	Andrew's Harvest - John Evans	1.50	3.50	5.00	
315	Eleven Blue Men - Berton Roueche	.75	1.75	3.00	
316	Pattern for Panic - Richard S. Prather	1.50	3.50	5.00	M
317	Roadside Motel - Arthur Herbert Bryant	1.50	3.50	5.00	
318	White Hell - Don Tracy	1.50	3.50	5.00	
319	Portrait of a Woman - John Hyde Preston	1.50	3.50	5.00	
320	Sweetie Pie - Nadine Seltzer	2.00	4.00	7.50	H
321	Gunfighter Breed - Nelson Nye	1.50	3.50	5.00	W
322	Danger at Sea - Georges Simenon	2.00	4.00	7.50	M
323	The Temptation of Roger Heriott - Edward Newhouse	1.50	3.50	5.00	
324	Cowpoke Justice - William Hopson	1.50	3.50	5.00	W
325	Oh, Doctor! - Charles Preston 1955	1.50	3.50	5.00	H
326	The Velvet Whip - Leonard Snyder	2.00	4.00	7.50	
327	We Too Are Drifting - Gale Wilhelm	2.00	4.00	7.50	

328	I Should Have Stayed Home - Horace McCoy	2.00	4.00	7.50	
329	Who's in Charge Here? - George Price	1.50	3.50	5.00	H
330	Cartridge - Case Law - Nelson Nye	1.50	3.50	5.00	W
331	Joe and Jennie - Donald Henderson Clarke	1.50	3.50	5.00	
332	The Twisted Trail - Paul Evan Lehman	1.50	3.50	5.00	W
333	Cue for Murder - Matt Bryant	1.50	3.50	5.00	M
334	Manhunt - Philip Van Doren Stern	2.00	4.00	7.50	
335	Powder Burns - Al Cody	1.50	3.50	5.00	
336	Mopsy - Gladys Parker	1.50	3.50	5.00	H
337	Only a Woman - Francis Carco	1.50	3.50	5.00	
338	The Man With My Face - Samuel W. Taylor	1.50	3.50	5.00	M
339	The Girl With the Golden Yo-Yo - Edmund Schiddel	1.50	3.50	5.00	
340	Danger Ashore - Georges Simenon	2.00	4.00	7.50	M
341	Outlaw of Hidden Valley - William Hopson	1.50	3.50	5.00	W
342	The Postman - Roger Martin du Gard	1.50	3.50	5.00	
343	Gunshot Trail - Nelson Nye	1.50	3.50	5.00	W
344	Mission to the Stars - A. E. Van Vogt	2.00	4.00	7.50	SF
345	Cruel is the Night - Howard Hunt	1.50	3.50	5.00	
346	The $64,000,000 Answer - Charles Preston	1.50	3.50	5.00	H
347	Tombstone Stage - William Hopson 1956	1.50	3.50	5.00	W
348	Dupree Blues - Dale Curran	1.50	3.50	5.00	
349	Strictly Business - Dale McFeatters	1.50	3.50	5.00	
350	Saddle Bow Slim - Nelson Nye 1956	1.50	3.50	5.00	W
351	The Magician - Georges Simenon	2.00	4.00	7.50	M
352					
353	Forbidden River - Al Cody	1.50	3.50	5.00	W
354	The Narrowing Circle - Julian Symons	1.50	3.50	5.00	M
355	Back Issves - Evans Rolfe	1.50	3.50	5.00	
356	Outlaws of Lost River - Paul Evan Lehman	1.50	3.50	5.00	W
357	When in Doubt, Kill - Merlyn Estin	1.50	3.50	5.00	
358	Bailey's Daughters - John De Meyer	1.50	3.50	5.00	
359	Loveliest of Friends - G. Sheila Donisthorpe	1.50	3.50	5.00	
360	Sweetie Pie - Nadine Seltzer	2.00	4.00	7.50	H
361	Seven Men from Now - Burt Kennedy movie tie-in	2.00	4.00	7.50	W
362	Pattern for Panic - Richard S. Prather	1.50	3.50	5.00	M
363	Ranger's Revenge - Nelson Nye	1.50	3.50	5.00	W
364	Pistol Law - Paul Evan Lehman	1.50	3.50	5.00	W
365	No Money Down--36 Months to Pay! - Charles Preston 1957	1.50	3.50	5.00	H
366	Ramrod Vengeance - William Hopson	1.50	3.50	5.00	W
357	We Too Are Drifting - Gale Wilhelm	2.00	4.00	7.50	
368	Kinkaid of Red Butte - Leslie Ernenwein	1.50	3.50	5.00	W
369	Only a Woman - Francis Carco	1.50	3.50	5.00	
370	Texas Vengeance - Paul Evan Lehman	1.50	3.50	5.00	W
371	Bubu of Montparnasse - Charles-Louis Philippe	1.50	3.50	5.00	E
372	Rustlers of the Rio Grande - Paul Evan Lehman	1.50	3.50	5.00	W
373	The Devil His Due - William O'Farrell	1.50	3.50	5.00	
374	Red Man's Range - Al Cody	1.50	3.50	5.00	W
375	The Lost and the Damned - Warren Carrier 1957	1.50	3.50	5.00	

Belmont L-Series L508, c. Belmt

Berkley 112, c. Berk

Berkley Diamond D2012, c. Berk

(BERKLEY, continued)

376	We Dare You to Solve This! - John Paul Adams	2.00	4.00	7.50	P
377	Twist of the Knife - Victor Canning	1.50	3.50	5.00	M
378	Brand of Iron - Al Cody	1.50	3.50	5.00	W
379	The Burial of Monsieur - Bouvet-Georges Simenon	1.50	3.50	5.00	M
380	The Time Machine - H. G. Wells	2.00	4.00	7.50	SF
381	More Sweetie Pie - Nadine Seltzer	2.00	4.00	7.50	H
382	Tizzy - Kate Osann 1958	1.50	3.50	5.00	
383	Will-Yum - Fred Neher	1.50	3.50	5.00	H
384	Baby Sitter's Guide - Mary Furlong Moore 1959	.75	1.75	3.00	NF
385	Hi-teens - Fred Neher	.75	1.75	3.00	H
386	Phyllis - Ted Key	.75	1.75	3.00	H

BERKLEY DIAMOND

(Berkley Publishing Corporation)

D2001	Cruel is the Night - Howard Hunt 1959	1.50	3.50	5.00	
D2002	Guns Along the Arrowhead - Lee Floren	.75	1.75	3.00	W
D2003	The Big Kiss-off - Day Keene	.75	1.75	3.00	M
D2004	Shack Road Girl - Harry Whittington	.75	1.75	3.00	E
D2005	Descent to Darkness - Fritz Peters	.75	1.75	3.00	
D2006	Wildcats of Tonto Basin - Nelson Nye	.75	1.75	3.00	W
D2007	Dressed to Kill - Milton K. Ozaki	.75	1.75	3.00	M
D2008	Hideaway - Fan Nichols	.75	1.75	3.00	
D2009	Rifle Law - Lee Floren	.75	1.75	3.00	W
D2010	Kill Me In Shimbashi - Earl Norman c-Maguire	2.00	4.00	7.50	M
D2011	Vengeance Trail - Charles M. Martin	.75	1.75	3.00	W
D2012	Messalina - Vivian Crockett c-Maguire	2.00	4.00	7.50	E
D2013	Drift Fence - Walt Coburn	.75	1.75	3.00	W
D2014	Twin Mavericks - William Hopson	.75	1.75	3.00	W
D2015	Renegade Cop - Jonathan Craig	.75	1.75	3.00	
D2016	Murder Doll - Milton K. Ozaki	.75	1.75	3.00	M
D2017	Guns Along the Pecos - Lee Floren	.75	1.75	3.00	W
D2018	Desert Desperados - Nelson Nye	.75	1.75	3.00	W
D2019	Married to Murder - Harry Whittington	.75	1.75	3.00	M
D2020	Naked Fury - Day Keene	.75	1.75	3.00	E

BERKLEY G/BG-SERIES

(Berkley Publishing Corporation)

G	1	The Lost Weekend - Charles Jackson 1955	1.50	3.50	5.00	
G	2	Sexual Conduct of the Teen-ager - Jules Archer & S. V. Lawton	1.50	3.50	5.00	NF
G	3	Possible Worlds of Science Fiction - Groff Conklin	.75	1.75	3.00	SF
G	4	South Street - William Gardner Smith	.75	1.75	3.00	
G	5	Salambo - Gustave Flaubert	2.00	4.00	7.50	
G	6	If He Hollers Let Him Go - Chester Himes	.75	1.75	3.00	
G	7	A Seed Upon the Wind - William Michelfelder	.50	1.25	2.00	
G	8	The Devil's Brigadier - Don Ryan	.75	1.75	3.00	
G	9	Naked Hollywood - Mel Harris, Weegee	.75	1.75	3.00	H
G	10	Lone Star Preacher - J. W. Thomason, Jr.	.75	1.75	3.00	W
G	11	Diana - Diana Fredericks	.50	1.25	2.00	
G	12	Crazy Mixed-Up Kids - William Hodapp	.75	1.75	3.00	
G	13	The Sign of Eros - Paul Bodin	.50	1.25	2.00	
G	14	Messalina - Vivian Crockett	1.50	3.50	5.00	
G	15	A Lust to Live - E. B. Garside 1956, aka Whirligig	.50	1.25	2.00	
G	16	Jungle Fury - Robb White	2.00	4.00	7.50	E
G	17	The Thorn in the Flesh - D. H. Lawrence	.75	1.75	3.00	

B G 18	Modern Writing No. 3 - William Phillips & Philip Rahv	.50	1.25	2.00	
G 19	The Rat Race - Alfred Bester	.75	1.75	3.00	
G 20	Paris, My Love - Henry Calet	.50	1.25	2.00	
G 21	Bessie Cotter - Wallace Smith	.50	1.25	2.00	
G 22	Renee - H. R. Lenormand	.50	1.25	2.00	
G 23	The Place of Jackals - Ronald Hardy	.50	1.25	2.00	
G 24	Adios, O'Shaughnessy - Robert Tallman	.50	1.25	2.00	
G 25	A Girl in Every Port - Donald R. Morris 1956	.50	1.25	2.00	
G 26	Love on the Rocks - Elliott Chaze	.50	1.25	2.00	
G 27	The Blaze of Noon - Rayner Heppenstall	.50	1.25	2.00	
G 28	Young Man of Paris - Henri Calet	.50	1.25	2.00	
G 29	Hypnotism Comes of Age - Raymond Rosenthal & Bernard Wolfe	.75	1.75	3.00	
G 30	Intimacy - Jean-Paul Sartre	.50	1.25	2.00	
G 31	Science Fiction Omnibus - Groff Conklin	.75	1.75	3.00	SF
G 32	Six Days in Marapore - Paul Scott	.75	1.75	3.00	
G 33	Perversity - Francis Carco	.75	1.75	3.00	
G 34	Alabam - Donald Henderson Clarke	.75	1.75	3.00	
B G 35	Night Rider - Robert Penn Warren	.75	1.75	3.00	
G 36	The Strange Case of Miss Annie Spragg - Louis Bromfield	.75	1.75	3.00	SF
G 37	Virgie, Goodbye - Nathan Rothman	.75	1.75	3.00	
G 38	Escape from Colditz - P. R. Reid	.50	1.25	2.00	NF
G 39	Torture Garden - Octave Mirbeau	2.00	4.00	7.50	E
G 40	Daughters of Eve	.75	1.75	3.00	
G 41	Astounding Science Fiction Anthology - John W. Campbell, Jr.	.75	1.75	3.00	SF
G 42	To Wake the Dead - John Dickson Carr	1.50	3.50	5.00	M
G 43	The Captain's Doll - D. H. Lawrence	.75	1.75	3.00	
G 44	My Sister, My Beloved - Edwina Mark 1957	.50	1.25	2.00	
G 45	Scratch the Surface - Edmund Schiddel	.50	1.25	2.00	
G 46	Aphrodite - Pierre Louys	.75	1.75	3.00	
G 47	Astounding Tales of Space and Time - John W. Campbell, Jr.	.75	1.75	3.00	SF
G 48	The Eight of Swords - John Dickson Carr	1.50	3.50	5.00	M
G 49	A Dime a Throw - Jerome Weidman	.50	1.25	2.00	
G 50	Diana - Diana Fredericks 1957	.50	1.25	2.00	
G 51	The Body of Love - Charles Keats	.50	1.25	2.00	
G 52	The Virgin and the Gypsy - D. H. Lawrence	.75	1.75	3.00	
G 53	The Big Book of Science Fiction - .ed Groff Conklin	.75	1.75	3.00	SF
G 54	The Sign of Eros - Paul Bodin	.50	1.25	2.00	
G 55	Love in a Hot Climate - Edmund Schiddel	.50	1.25	2.00	
G 56	Jungle Fury - Robb White	1.50	3.50	5.00	
G 57	Take Me as I Am - Loren Wahl	.50	1.25	2.00	
G 58	How Cheap Can You Get? - Martin Abzug aka Seventh Avenue Story	.75	1.75	3.00	E
G 59	The Woman Who Rode Away - D. H. Lawrence	.75	1.75	3.00	
G 60	The Case of the Constant Suicides - John Dickson Carr c-Maguire	4.00	8.00	15.00	M
G 61	Andrew's Harvest - John Evans	.50	1.25	2.00	
G 62	The Most Dangerous Game	.75	1.75	3.00	

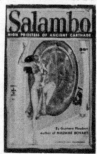

Berkley G/BG-Series G-5,
c. Berk

Berkley G/BG-Series G12,
c. Berk

Berkley G/BG-Series G40,
c. Berk

Berkley BG66, c. Berk Berkley BG73, c. Berk Berkley G92, c. Berk

(BERKLEY G/BG-SERIES, continued)

G 63	A Treasury of Science Fiction - .ed Groff Conklin	.75	1.75	3.00	SF
G 64	The Tripitz - David Woodward	.75	1.75	3.00	NF
G 65	A Seed Upon the Wind - William Michelfelder	.50	1.25	2.00	
B G 66	Time Must Have a Stop - Aldous Huxley c-Maguire	4.00	8.00	15.00	
G 67	Spy Catcher - Oreste Pinto	.50	1.25	2.00	
G 68	This is My Body	.50	1.25	2.00	
G 69	Affair in Capri - Mario Soldati	.50	1.25	2.00	
B G 70	The Last Days of Hitler - H. R. Trevor-Roper	1.50	3.50	5.00	NF
G 71	Strangers in the Universe - Clfford D. Simak	.75	1.75	3.00	SF
G 72	Poison in Jest - John Dickson Carr c-Maguire	4.00	8.00	15.00	
B G 73	Salambo - Gustave Flaubert c-Maguire	5.00	10.00	20.00	E
G 74	Olivia - Olivia	.50	1.25	2.00	
G 75	The Case of the Lady Who Took a Bath - Alan Hynd 1957	.50	1.25	2.00	
G 76	The Chastity of Gloria Boyd - Donald Henderson Clarke	.75	1.75	3.00	
G 77	Beachheads in Space - August Derleth	.75	1.75	3.00	SF
G 78	Harlem is My Heaven - Ian Gordon	.75	1.75	3.00	
G 79	Gun-quick - Nelson Nye	.75	1.75	3.00	W
G 80	The Blind Barber - John Dickson Carr	1.50	3.50	5.00	M
G 81	Depravity - Francis Carco	.75	1.75	3.00	
B G 82	Graf Spee - Dudley Pope	.75	1.75	3.00	NF
G 83	Martha Crane - Charles Gorham	.50	1.25	2.00	
G 84	The Corpse with Sticky Fingers - George Bayby	.75	1.75	3.00	M
G 85	Three of a Kind - P. J. Wolfson	.50	1.25	2.00	
G 86	Juvenile Jungle	1.50	3.50	5.00	
G 87	Gunthrower - William Hopson	.75	1.75	3.00	W
G 88	Trish - Margaret Maze Craig	.50	1.25	2.00	
G 89	Great Sports Stories - Herman L. Masin	.75	1.75	3.00	S
B G 90	Drive to Victory - Robert S. Allen	.50	1.25	2.00	
G 91	The Four False Weapons - John Dickson Carr c-Maguire	4.00	8.00	15.00	M
G 92	Legend of the Lost - Bonnie Golightly Movie tie-in	2.00	4.00	7.50	
G 93	All Woman's Flesh - Paul Bodin	.50	1.25	2.00	
G 94	The Tunnel Escape - Eric Williams 1958	.50	1.25	2.00	
G 95	Such is My Beloved - Carol Hales	.50	1.25	2.00	
B G 96	Rommel, the Desert Fox - Desmond Young	.75	1.75	3.00	NF
G 97	Nude Croquet	.50	1.25	2.00	
G 98	Pattern for Panic - Richard S. Prather	.75	1.75	3.00	M
G 99	G Stands for Gun - Nelson Nye	.75	1.75	3.00	W
B G100	Finnley Wren - Philip Wylie 1958	.50	1.25	2.00	
G101	Death Watch - John Dickson Carr	1.50	3.50	5.00	M
B G102	Stalingrad - Theodor Plievier	.75	1.75	3.00	NF
G103	Forbid Me Not - Blair Fuller	.50	1.25	2.00	

G104	Beyond Time and Space - August Derleth	.75	1.75	3.00	SF
G105	Intimacy - Jean-Paul Sartre	.75	1.75	3.00	
G106	S. S. San Pedro - James Gould Cozzens	.50	1.25	2.00	
G107	Escape from Colditz - P. R. Reid	.50	1.25	2.00	NF
B G108	The Exurbanites - A. C. Spectorsky	.50	1.25	2.00	H
G109	Marsha - Margaret Maze Craig	.50	1.25	2.00	
B G110	The Theory and Practice of Hell - Eugen Kogon	1.50	3.50	5.00	NF
G111	The Strange Path - Gale Wilhelm	.75	1.75	3.00	
G112	Bessie Cotter - Wallace Smith	.50	1.25	2.00	
G113	The Girl of the Roman Night - Dante Arfelli aka The Unwanted	.50	1.25	2.00	
G114	The End of the Track - Andrew Garve	.50	1.25	2.00	
G115	Holocaust at Sea; the Drama of the Scharnhorst - Fritz-Otto Busch	.75	1.75	3.00	NF
G116	The Outer Reaches - August Derleth	.75	1.75	3.00	SF
G117	The Mad Hatter Mystery - John Dickson Carr	1.50	3.50	5.00	M
G118	Guns of Arizona - Nelson Nye	.75	1.75	3.00	W
G119	The Enormous Radio and Other Stories - John Cheever	5.00	10.00	20.00	SF
G120	Black Opium - Claude Farrere c-Maguire	7.50	15.00	30.00	E
B G121	The Fatal Decisions - Seymour Freidin & William Richardson	.50	1.25	2.00	
G122	Gideon of Scotland Yard - J. J. Marric Movie tie-in	.75	1.75	3.00	M
G123	To Whom it May Concern - Juliet Lowell	.50	1.25	2.00	
G124	Joe and Jennie - Donald Henderson Clarke	.50	1.25	2.00	
G125	So It Doesn't Whistle - Robert Paul Smith c-Maguire	3.00	6.00	12.00	
	1958				
G126	Naomi Martin - Clarkson Crane	.50	1.25	2.00	
S127	Men at War - Ernest Hemingway	.75	1.75	3.00	
B G128	Sex in Our Changing World - John McPartland	.50	1.25	2.00	NF
G129	Hag's Nook - John Dickson Carr -c-Maguire	1.50	3.50	5.00	
G130	Thieves Like Us - Edward Anderson	.50	1.25	2.00	
G131	Strange Ports of Call - August Derleth	.75	1.75	3.00	SF
G132	Tormented - Carolyn Weston	.50	1.25	2.00	
G133	Tropic Moon - Georges Simenon	2.00	4.00	7.50	M
G134	I Should Have Stayed Home - Horace McCoy	.75	1.75	3.00	
B G135	The German Generals Talk - B. H. Liddell Hart	.75	1.75	3.00	NF
G136	China Doll - Edgar Jean Bracco	.50	1.25	2.00	
G137	The 31st of February - Julian Symons c-Maguire	.50	1.25	2.00	M
G138	Gunfighter Brand - Nelson Nye	.75	1.75	3.00	W
G139	If He Hollers Let Him Go - Chester Himes	.75	1.75	3.00	
G140	Infamy - Frances Carco	.75	1.75	3.00	
G141	My Sister, My Beloved - Edwina Mark	.50	1.25	2.00	
G142	Low Level Mission - Leon Wolff	.50	1.25	2.00	
G143	The Corpse in the Waxworks - John Dickson Carr	1.50	3.50	5.00	M
G144	Proud Youth - Alexander Eliot	.50	1.25	2.00	

Berkley G119, c. Berk

Berkley G120, c. Berk

Berkley G169, c. Berk

G145	The Man Who Watched the Train Go By - Georges Simenon	2.00	4.00	7.50	M
G146	The Man Within - Graham Greene	.75	1.75	3.00	
G147	Bailey's Daughters - John DeMeyer	.50	1.25	2.00	
G148	Men, Martians and Machines - Eric Frank Russell	.75	1.75	3.00	SF
B G149	Ah King - W. Somerset Maugham	.50	1.25	2.00	
B G150	The First Lady Chatterley - D. H. Lawrence 1958	.75	1.75	3.00	
G151	The Golden Jungle - William Howard Harris	.75	1.75	3.00	
G152	Hell's Kitchen - Benjamin Appel	.75	1.75	3.00	
G153	The Last of Mr. Norris - Christopher Isherwood c-Maguire	4.00	8.00	15.00	
G154	Gunshot Trail - Nelson Nye	.75	1.75	3.00	W
G155	Perversity - Francis Carco	.75	1.75	3.00	
G156	Laughter in the Dark - Vladimir Nabokov	.50	1.25	2.00	
G157	The Crooked Hinge - John Dickson Carr	1.50	3.50	5.00	M
G158	Mystery Walks the Campus - Annette Turngren	.50	1.25	2.00	M
G159	Marcia, Private Secretary - Zillah K. MacDonald	.50	1.25	2.00	R
G160	Desire and Other Stories - Clement Wood	.50	1.25	2.00	
G161	The Wicked and the Warped - Max Alth	.75	1.75	3.00	
G162	The Evil That Men Do - George Victor Martin	.50	1.25	2.00	
G163	Worlds of Tomorrow - August Derleth	.75	1.75	3.00	SF
G164	Three Day Pass - to Kill - James Wakefield Burke & Edward Grace	.50	1.25	2.00	
G165	The Pub Crawler - Maurice Procter	.50	1.25	2.00	M
G166	Morning, Winter and Night - John Nairne Michaelson	.50	1.25	2.00	
G167	Adam and Evil - John Carlova	.50	1.25	2.00	
G168	Renee - H. R. Lenormand	.50	1.25	2.00	
G169	The Terrible Game - Dan Tyler Moore	.75	1.75	3.00	A
G170	Devil's Holiday - Fred Malloy	.50	1.25	2.00	
G171	Stag Stripper - Jack Hanley	.50	1.25	2.00	
G172	Loveliest of Friends - G. Sheila Donisthorpe	.50	1.25	2.00	
G173	We Too Are Drifting - Gale Wilhelm	1.50	3.50	5.00	
G174	Only a Woman - Francis Carco	.75	1.75	3.00	
G175	Olivia - Olivia 1958	.50	1.25	2.00	
G176	Mystery on Graveyard Head - Edith Dorian	.50	1.25	2.00	M
B G177	Pocket Battleship - H. J. Brennecke & Theodor Krancke	.75	1.75	3.00	
B G178	The Hucksters - Frederic Wakeman	.50	1.25	2.00	
G179	No Bed of Her Own - Cicely Schiller	.50	1.25	2.00	
G180	Boots and Saddles - Edgar Jean Braco TV tie-in	1.50	3.50	5.00	W
G181	Is My Flesh of Brass? - P. J. Wolfson	.50	1.25	2.00	
G182	Too Many Girls - Don Tracy	.50	1.25	2.00	
G183	Virgie, Goodbye - Nathan Rothman	.75	1.75	3.00	
G184	The Shameless Ones - Uberto Quintavalle	.50	1.25	2.00	
G185	Wicked Woman - Fred Malloy	.50	1.25	2.00	
G186	Scarlet Angel - Dorene Clark	.50	1.25	2.00	
G187	The Big Wheel - John Brooks	.50	1.25	2.00	
G188	The Incurable Wound - Berton Roueche	.50	1.25	2.00	
G189	Time to Come - August Derleth	.75	1.75	3.00	SF
G190	The Judge and His Hangman - Friedrich Durrenmatt	.50	1.25	2.00	
G191	Awakening - Jean-Baptiste Rossi	.50	1.25	2.00	
G192	Kill Me in Tokyo - Earl Norman	.50	1.25	2.00	
G193	South Street - William Gardner Smith	.50	1.25	2.00	
G194	The Postman - Roger Martin duGard	.50	1.25	2.00	
G195	Hot Money Girl - Arlo Wayne	.75	1.75	3.00	
G196	Passion in Panama - Richard Marshe	.50	1.25	2.00	
B G197	The Professional - W. C. Heinz	.50	1.25	2.00	
G198	Early to Rise - Arnold E. Grisman	.50	1.25	2.00	
G199	Make Me an Offer - Charles Gorham	.50	1.25	2.00	
G200	Sexual Conduct of the Teen-ager - Jules Archer & S. V. Lawton 1954	.75	1.75	3.00	NF
G201	Smoke Wagon Kid - Clem Colt	.75	1.75	3.00	W
B G202	Last in Convoy - James Pattinson	.50	1.25	2.00	
G203	Love Around the World	.50	1.25	2.00	

G204	The Blaze of Noon - Rayner Heppenstall	.50	1.25	2.00	
G205	Forbidden Pleasures - B. Devlin	.50	1.25	2.00	
G206	The Sinning Lens - Mark Tryon	.50	1.25	2.00	
G207	The Home Encyclopedia of Moving Your Family - Margaret Randall	.50	1.25	2.00	NF
G208	Mystery in Blue - Gertrude E. Mallette	.50	1.25	2.00	M
G209	The Singing Heart - Elizabeth Cadell 1959	.50	1.25	2.00	
G210	How to Make Your Emotions Work for You - Dorothy C. Finkelhor	.50	1.25	2.00	NF
B G211	73 North - Dudley Pope	.50	1.25	2.00	
B G212	Prettiest Girl in Town - Thomas Fall	.50	1.25	2.00	
B G213	First Person Singular - W. Somerset Maugham	.50	1.25	2.00	
G214	The Bowstring Murders - Carter Dickson	1.50	3.50	5.00	
G215	Away and Beyond - A. E. Van Vogt	.75	1.75	3.00	SF
G216	The Sign of Eros - Paul Bodin	.50	1.25	3.00	
G217	Love on the Rocks - Elliott Chaze aka The Golden Tag	.75	1.75	3.00	E
G218	Jule - George Wylie Henderson	1.50	3.50	5.00	E
G219	Sandy - John B. Thompson	.50	1.25	2.00	
G220	The Fire that Burns - Mark Tryon	.50	1.25	2.00	
G221	I'll Find My Love - Joan Dirksen	.50	1.25	2.00	
G222	The Big Book of Horse Stories - Page Cooper	.75	1.75	3.00	
G223	Beany Malone - Lenora Mattingly Weber	.50	1.25	2.00	
G224	I Flew for the Fuhrer - Heinz Knoke	.75	1.75	3.00	NF
G225	What D'ya Know for Sure? - Len Zinberg 1959	.50	1.25	2.00	
G226	All Woman's Flesh - Paul Bodin	.50	1.25	2.00	
G227	Blaze - Scott Stone	.50	1.25	2.00	
G228	Dreamboat - Rick Lucas	.50	1.25	2.00	
G229	Easy Living - Terence Ford	.50	1.25	2.00	
G230	Rambling Top Hand - William Hopson	.75	1.75	3.00	W
B G231	Dateline: Paris - Reynolds Packard	.50	1.25	2.00	
G232	Deadlier than the Male - James E. Gunn	.75	1.75	3.00	M
G233	Imagination Unlimited - T. E. Dikty & Everett F. Bleiler	.75	1.75	3.00	SF
G234	Guns of Horse Prairie - Nelson Nye	.75	1.75	3.00	W
G235	Channel Dash - Terence Robertson	.50	1.25	2.00	
G236	A Woman Called Desire - Richard Marshe	.50	1.25	2.00	
G237	Showroom Girls - Token West	.50	1.25	2.00	
B G238	The Lessons of Love - W. Carroll Munro	.50	1.25	2.00	
B G239	The Wooden Horse - Eric Williams	.50	1.25	2.00	
G240	House of Fury - Felice Swados	5.00	10.00	20.00	E
G241	Pattern for Panic - Richard S. Prather	.75	1.75	3.00	M
G242	Duel on the Range - Burt Arthur	.75	1.75	3.00	W
G243	Count Me In - Fan Nichols	.50	1.25	2.00	
G244	Vice Girl - Sim Albert	.75	1.75	3.00	
G245	The Odd Ones - Edwina Mark	1.50	3.50	5.00	E
G246	The Frogmen - James Gleeson & T. J. Waldron	.50	1.25	2.00	
G247	Box Star Buckaroo - Charles M. Martin	.75	1.75	3.00	W
G248	Three of a Kind - P. J. Wolfson	.50	1.25	2.00	
G249	The Other Side of the Moon - August Derleth	.75	1.75	3.00	SF
G250	Native Girl - Harry Whittington 1959	.75	1.75	3.00	
G251	Affairs of Marie-Odette - Cecil Saint-Laurent	.50	1.25	2.00	
G252	Immoral Woman - Jack Hanley	.50	1.25	2.00	
G253	Devil Take Her - Fan Nichols	.50	1.25	2.00	
B G254	A Man Escaped - Andre Devigny	.50	1.25	2.00	
G255	Hangman's Range - Lee Floren	.75	1.75	3.00	W
G256	The Incredible Truth - Chris Massie	.50	1.25	2.00	
G257	Woman of the Night - Robert Carse	.50	1.25	2.00	
G258	Wake Up to Murder - Day Keene	.75	1.75	3.00	M
G259	Harlem is My Heaven - Ian Gordon	.75	1.75	3.00	
G260	Shanty Boat Girl - Kirk Westley	.50	1.25	2.00	
G261	Strip Street - Jack Hanley	.50	1.25	2.00	
G262	Down and Out in Paris and London - George Orwell	.50	1.25	2.00	
B G263	The Knights of Bushide - Lord Russell	1.50	3.50	5.00	NF
B G264	The Ginger Man - J. P. Donleavy	.50	1.25	2.00	
G265	The Daughter of Time - Josephine Tey	.50	1.25	2.00	M

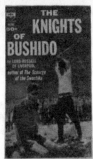
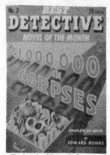

Berkley BG263, c. Berk   Best Detect. Novel 2, c. MCG   Best Detect. Selection 3, c. MCG

(BERKLEY G/BG-SERIES, continued)

G266	The Girl Beneath the Lion - Andre Pieyre de Mandiargues	.50	1.25	2.00
G267	The Plague Court Murders - Carter Dickson	1.50	3.50	5.00 M
G268	Cosmopolitans - W. Somerset Maugham	.50	1.25	2.00
G269	Money, Marbles and Chalk - Douglas Fairbairn	.50	1.25	2.00
G270	Thomas Alva Edison - G. Glenwood Clark	.75	1.75	3.00 B
G271	Deliver Us from Evil - Thomas A. Dooley	.50	1.25	2.00
G272	The Edge of Tomorrow - Thomas A. Dooley	.50	1.25	2.00
G273	Something Foolish, Something Gay - Jane & Glen Sire	.50	1.25	2.00
G274	Francie Comes Home - Emily Hahn	.50	1.25	2.00
G275	Comanche of the 7th - Margaret Leighton 1959	.75	1.75	3.00 W
G276	Sharon - Harriett H. Carr	.50	1.25	2.00
G277	Desert Love - Henry de Montherlant	.50	1.25	2.00
G278	Gideon's Month - J. J. Marric	.75	1.75	3.00 M
G279	Altars of the Heart - Richard Lebherz	.50	1.25	2.00
G280	A Touch of Strange - Theodore Sturgeon	.75	1.75	3.00 SF
G281	Death Turns the Tables - John Dickson Carr	1.50	3.50	5.00 M
G282	The Other Side of the Night - Edmund Schiddel	.50	1.25	2.00
G283	Aphrodite - Pierre Louys	.75	1.75	3.00 E
G284	My Sister Eileen - Ruth McKenney	.50	1.25	2.00
G285	Blue Ribbon Romance - Jane S. McIlvaine	.50	1.25	2.00 R
G286	Mystery of Hidden Village - Annette Turngren	.75	1.75	3.00 M
G287	The Emperor's Snuff Box - John Dickson Carr	1.50	3.50	5.00 M
G288	Flight Nurse - Adelaide Humphries	.50	1.25	2.00 R
G289	The Enemy Stars - Poul Anderson	1.50	3.50	5.00 SF
G290	The Thorn in the Flesh - D. H. Lawrence	.75	1.75	3.00
G291	Flight - Edgar Jean Bracco	.50	1.25	2.00
G292	Laughs Around the World	.50	1.25	2.00 H
G293	Meet the Malones - Lenora Mattingly Weber	.50	1.25	2.00
G294	Step to the Music - Phyllis A. Whitney	.50	1.25	2.00

BEST DETECTIVE NOVEL OF THE MONTH

(Select Publications, Inc.)

Digest size

Also see Best Detective Selection of the Month

2	$1,000,000 in Corpses - Edward Ronns 1942	2.00	4.00	7.50 M

BEST DETECTIVE SELECTION OF THE MONTH

(Select Publications, Inc.)

Digest size

Also see Best Detective Novel of the Month

3	Death Goes to a Party - Michael Jaffe	2.00	4.00	7.50	M
8	Modeled in Murder - Manning Long 1943	2.00	4.00	6.00	M
nn	The Corpse Hangs High - Edward Ronns 1943	2.00	4.00	6.00	M

BESTSELLER LIBRARY/MYSTERY

(The American Mercury, Inc./Mercury Publications)

Digest size

nn(1)	The Adventures of Ellery Queen - Ellery Queen	1.50	3.50	5.00	M
2	One More Spring - Robert Nathan	.50	1.25	2.00	
3	More Adventures of Ellery Queen - Ellery Queen	.75	1.75	3.00	
4	Life Begins at Forty - Walter B. Pitkin	.50	1.25	2.00	
5	Tobacco Road - Jack Kirkland (Erskine Caldwell)	.50	1.25	2.00	E
6	Twenty-Four Hours - Louis Bromfield	.50	1.25	2.00	
7	The Bellamy Trial - Frances Noyes Hart	.75	1.75	3.00	M
8	The Devil to Pay - Ellery Queen	.50	1.25	2.00	M
9	The Mysterious Mr. Quin - Agatha Christie	.75	1.75	3.00	M
10	The Case of the Curious Bride - Erle Stanley Gardner	.50	1.25	2.00	M
11	The Spanish Cape Mystery - Ellery Queen	.75	1.75	3.00	M
12	Thank You, Mr. Moto - John P. Marquand	.50	1.25	2.00	M
13	Lord Peter Views the Body - Dorothy L. Sayers	.75	1.75	3.00	M
14	The Greek Coffin Mystery - Ellery Queen	.75	1.75	3.00	M
15	Inquest - Percival Wilde	.50	1.25	2.00	M
16	Murder in Stained Glass - Margaret Armstrong	.50	1.25	2.00	M
17	The Egyptian Cross Mystery - Ellery Queen	.75	1.75	3.00	M
18	Dead Man's Mirror - Agatha Christie	.75	1.75	3.00	M
19	The Case of the Sleepwalker's Niece - Erle Stanley Gardner	.50	1.25	2.00	M
20	In the Teeth of the Evidence - Dorothy L. Sayers	.75	1.75	3.00	M
21	Murder in Three Acts - Agatha Christie	.50	1.25	2.00	M
22	The D. A. Holds a Candle - Erle Stanley Gardner	.50	1.25	2.00	M
23	Death in Ecstacy - Ngaio Marsh	.75	1.75	3.00	M
24	A Face for a Clue - Georges Simenon	.75	1.75	3.00	M
25	Partners in Crime - Agatha Christie	.75	1.75	3.00	M
26	Does not exist				
27	The Cairo Garter Murders - Van Wyck Mason	.50	1.25	2.00	M
28	The Tragedy of Y - Ellery Queen	.50	1.25	2.00	M

Bestseller nn (1), c. Merc

Bestseller B59, c. Merc

Bestseller B101, c. Merc

29	Murder Up My Sleeve - Erle Stanley Gardner	.50	1.25	2.00	M
30	The Man With No Face - Margaret Armstrong	.50	1.25	2.00	M
31	Some Buried Caesar - Rex Stout	.50	1.25	2.00	M
32	The Seven Dials Mystery - Agatha Christie	.50	1.25	2.00	M
33	Black Plumes - Margery Allingham	.50	1.25	2.00	M
34	The Department of Queer Complaints - Carter Dickson	2.00	4.00	7.50	M
35	This is Murder - Erle Stanley Gardner	.50	1.25	2.00	M
36	The Regatta Mystery - Agatha Christie	.75	1.75	3.00	M
37	The Whispering Cup - Mabel Seeley	.50	1.25	2.00	M
38	Hangman's Holiday - Dorothy L. Sayers	.50	1.25	2.00	M
39	The Boomerang Clue - Agatha Christie	.50	1.25	2.00	M
40	$106,000 Blood Money - Dashiell Hammett First ed., 1943	7.50	15.00	30.00	M
41	The Flemish Shop - Georges Simenon	.75	1.75	3.00	M
42	The G-String Murders - Gypsy Rose Lee	.50	1.25	2.00	M
43	Poirot Investigates - Agatha Christie	.75	1.75	3.00	M
44	Where There's a Will - Rex Stout	.75	1.75	3.00	M
45	Death in Five Boxes - Carter Dickson	.75	1.75	3.00	M
46	Death in the Doll's House - Hannah Lees & Lawrence Bachmann	.75	1.75	3.00	M
47	The Three Coffins - John Dickson Carr	.75	1.75	3.00	M
48	The Secret Adversary - Agatha Christie	.50	1.25	2.00	M
49	Dark Garden - Mignon G. Eberhart	.50	1.25	2.00	M
50	The Adventures of Sam Spade - Dashiell Hammett First ed., 1944	7.50	15.00	30.00	M
51	Police at the Funeral - Margery Allingham	.50	1.25	2.00	M
52	The Man in the Brown Suit - Agatha Christie	.50	1.25	2.00	M
53	Thirty Days Hath September - Dorothy Cameron Disney & George Sessions Perry	.50	1.25	2.00	M
54	Sad Cypress - Agatha Christie	.50	1.25	2.00	M
55	The Pattern - Mignon G. Eberhart	.50	1.25	2.00	M
56	Kingdom of Death - Margery Allingham	.50	1.25	2.00	M
57	The Washington Legation Murders - Van Wyck Mason	.50	1.25	2.00	M
58	Appointment with Death - Agatha Christie	.75	1.75	3.00	M
59	The Case Book of Ellery Queen - Ellery Queen	.75	1.75	3.00	M
60	Hangman's Whip - Mignon G. Eberhart	.50	1.25	2.00	M
61	Murder at Hazelmoor - Agatha Christie	.50	1.25	2.00	M
62	The Continental Op - Dashiell Hammett First ed., 1945	7.50	15.00	30.00	M
63	The Budapest Parade Murders - Van Wyck Mason	.50	1.25	2.00	M
64	Artists in Crime - Ngaio Marsh	.50	1.25	2.00	M
65	Compound for Death - Doris Miles Disney	.50	1.25	2.00	M
66	Alarm of the Black Cat - D. B. Olsen	.50	1.25	2.00	M
67	Dagger of the Mind - Kenneth Fearing	.50	1.25	2.00	M
68	Vintage Murder - Ngaio Marsh	.50	1.25	2.00	M
69	The Patience of Maigret - Georges Simenon aka Battle of Nerves	.75	1.75		M
70	Deadly Nightshade - Elizabeth Daly	.50	1.25	2.00	M
71	The Crimson Circle - Edgar Wallace	.75	1.75	3.00	M
72	The Parchment Key - Stanley Hopkins	.50	1.25	2.00	M
73	The Affair of the Crimson Gull - Clifford Knight	.50	1.25	2.00	M
74	Laura - Vera Caspary	.50	1.25	2.00	M
75	Miss Silver Deals with Death - Patricia Wentworth	.50	1.25	2.00	M
76	The Pricking Thumb - H. C. Branson	.50	1.25	2.00	M
77	While She Sleeps - Ethel Lina White	.50	1.25	2.00	M
78	Death Watch - John Dickson Carr	.50	1.25	2.00	M
79	Mr. Parker Pyne, Detective - Agatha Christie	.75	1.75	3.00	M
80	The Chuckling Fingers - Mabel Seeley	.50	1.25	2.00	M
81	Hammett Homicides - Dashiell Hammett First ed., 1946	7.50	15.00	30.00	M
82	Quoth the Raven - Bruno Fischer	.50	1.25	2.00	M
83	She Fell Among Actors - James Warren	.50	1.25	2.00	M
84	Sinners Never Die - A. E. Martin	.50	1.25	2.00	M
85	The Black Honeymoon - Constance & Gwenyth Little	.50	1.25	2.00	M
86	Murder in the Calais Coach - Agatha Christie	.50	1.25	2.00	M
87	The Corpse with Purple Thighs - George Bagby	.50	1.25	2.00	M
88	Whisper Murder - Vera Kelsey	.50	1.25	2.00	M
89	The Blonde Died First - Dana Chambers	.50	1.25	2.00	M

90	Deadline at Dawn - William Irish	.50	1.25	2.00	M
91	The Department of Dead Ends - Roy Vickers	.75	1.75	3.00	M
92	The Book of the Dead - Elizabeth Daly	.50	1.25	2.00	M
93	One Alone - Van Siller	.50	1.25	2.00	M
94	Cops and Robbers - O. Henry	.50	1.25	2.00	M
95	The Yellow Room - Mary Roberts Rinehart	.50	1.25	2.00	M
96	Dead at the Take-Off- Lester Dent	.50	1.25	2.00	M
97	The Man Who Slept All Day - Michael Venning	.50	1.25	2.00	M
98	Stranger at Home - George Sanders	.50	1.25	2.00	M
99	Cats Don't Need Coffins - D. B. Olsen	.50	1.25	2.00	M
100	The Hawk - Roy Vickers	.50	1.25	2.00	M
101	Lady to Kill - Lester Dent	.75	1.75	3.00	M
102	Kiss the Blonde Goodbye - Finlay McDermid aka Ghost Wanted	.50	1.25	2.00	M
103	Rope for an Ape - Dana Chambers	.50	1.25	2.00	M
104	Fear No More - Leslie Edgley	.50	1.25	2.00	M
105	So Deadly Fair - Gertrude Walker	.50	1.25	2.00	M
106	The Bleeding Scissors - Bruno Fischer	.50	1.25	2.00	M
107	Make My Bed Soon - John Stephen Strange	.50	1.25	2.00	M
108	Murder Picks the Jury - Harrison Hunt	.50	1.25	2.00	M
109	The Angry Heart - Leslie Edgley	.50	1.25	2.00	M
110	Bullets for a Blonde - Will Oursler aka Departure Delayed	.50	1.25	2.00	M
111	Death for My Beloved - Doris Miles Disney aka Enduring Old Charms	.50	1.25	2.00	M
112	The Book of the Lion - Elizabeth Daly	.50	1.25	2.00	M
113	In Cold Blood - George Bagby	.50	1.25	2.00	M
114	The Blue Horse of Taxco - Kathleen Moore Knight	.50	1.25	2.00	M
115	Lady Afraid - Lester Dent	.50	1.25	2.00	M
116	Fountain of Death - Hugh Lawrence Nelson	.50	1.25	2.00	M
117	Death Has Four Hands - Hilda Lawrence aka Composition for Four Hands	.50	1.25	2.00	M
118	Short Shrift - Manning Long	.50	1.25	2.00	M
119	The Dark River - Philip Clark	.50	1.25	2.00	M
120	Devious Design - D. B. Olsen	.50	1.25	2.00	M
121	Nightfall - David Goodis	.50	1.25	2.00	M
122	The Bleeding House - Hilda Lawrence aka The House	.50	1.25	2.00	M
123	Bait for Murder - Kathleen Moore Knight	.50	1.25	2.00	M
124	Think Fast, Mr. Moto - John P. Marquand	.75	1.75	3.00	M
125	Shark River - Richard Powell	.50	1.25	2.00	M
126	For the Love of Murder - Margaret Scherf aka Gilbert's Last Toothache	.50	1.25	2.00	M
127	The Dark Light - Bart Spicer	.50	1.25	2.00	M
128	The Monkey Murder - Stuart Palmer	.50	1.25	2.00	M
129	Place for a Poisoner - E. C. R. Lorac	.50	1.25	2.00	M
130	Kill to Fit - Bruno Fischer	.50	1.25	2.00	M
131	Kill 'Em With Kindness - Fred Dickenson	.50	1.25	2.00	M
132	Days of Misfortune - Aaron Marc Stein	.50	1.25	2.00	M
133	Too Like the Dead - Dana Chambers aka Too Like the Lightning	.50	1.25	2.00	M
134	A Lonely Way to Die - Hal Debrett	.50	1.25	2.00	M
135	Murder for Millions - Nancy Rutledge aka Emily Will Know	.50	1.25	2.00	M
136	Blood on My Shoes - Jean Leslie aka Shoes for My Love	.50	1.25	2.00	M
137	He Didn't Mind Danger - Michael Gilbert	.50	1.25	2.00	M
138	The Whitebird Murders - Thomas B. Black	.50	1.25	2.00	M
139	Death of a Big Shot - Clifford Knight	.50	1.25	2.00	M
140	Rather Cool for Mayhem - Lawrence G. Blochman	.50	1.25	2.00	M
141	Sinister Shelter - Charles L. Leonard	.50	1.25	2.00	M
142	Hot Tip - Jack Dolph	.50	1.25	2.00	M
143	Murder Makes a Deadline - Samuel M. Fuller aka The Dark Page	.50	1.25	2.00	M
144	Mr. Blessington's Imperialist Plot - John Sherwood	.50	1.25	2.00	M
145	Half-Past Mortem - John Saxon	.50	1.25	2.00	M
146	The Knife Behind You - James Benet	.50	1.25	2.00	M
147	The Man in the Mist - Francis Bonnamy	.50	1.25	2.00	M
148	Smallbone Deceased - Michael Gilbert	.50	1.25	2.00	M
149	These Arrows Point to Death - William O'Farrell	.50	1.25	2.00	M
150	The Kahuna Killer - Juanita Sheridan	.50	1.25	2.00	M

151 The 3-13 Murders - Thomas B. Black	.50	1.25	2.00	M
152 Alias Basil Willing - Helen McCloy	.50	1.25	2.00	M
153 FBI Story - The Gordons	.50	1.25	2.00	M
154 Fatal Lover - Van Siller	.50	1.25	2.00	M
aka The Last Resort				
155 The Mamo Murders - Juanita Sheridan	.50	1.25	2.00	M
156 Don't Kill, My Love - Rae Foley	.50	1.25	2.00	M
aka Wake the Sleeping Wolf				
157 F as in Flight - Lawrence Treat	.50	1.25	2.00	M
158 Mask for Murder - Aaron Marc Stein	.50	1.25	2.00	M
159 Divine and Deadly - Margaret Scherf	.50	1.25	2.00	M
aka The Curious Custard Pie				
160 Dead Ringer - Ferguson Findley	.50	1.25	2.00	M
aka The Man in the Middle				
161 The Fair and the Dead - John Stephen Strange	.50	1.25	2.00	M
aka Reasonable Doubt				
162 Murder is a Gamble - Glenn Barns	.50	1.25	2.00	M
163 Lust for Vengeance - Robert Bloomfield	.50	1.25	2.00	M
aka Vengeance Streets				
164 Death My Darling Daughters - Jonathan Stagge	.50	1.25	2.00	M
165 Vice Squad - Leslie T. White	.75	1.75	3.00	M
aka Harness Bull, Movie tie-in				
166 Dance of Death - Veronica Parker	.50	1.25	2.00	M
167 The Virgin Huntress - Elizabeth Sanxay Holding	.50	1.25	2.00	M
168 Dead Yesterday - Ruth Fenisong	.50	1.25	2.00	M
169 One Murder Too Many - Edwin Lanham	.50	1.25	2.00	M
170 Make Haste to Live - The Gordons	.50	1.25	2.00	M
171 One Blonde Died - Leslie Edgley	.50	1.25	2.00	M
aka The Runaway Pigeon				
172 Killer Loose! - Genevieve Holden	.50	1.25	2.00	M
173 The Corpse Who Had Too Many Firneds - Hampton Stone	.50	1.25	2.00	M
174 This Year's Death - John Godey	.50	1.25	2.00	M
175 Lawyers Don't Hang - Glenn Barns	.50	1.25	2.00	M
176 The Passionate Victims - Lange Lewis	.50	1.25	2.00	M
177 Terror Lurks in Darkness - Dolores Hitchens	.50	1.25	2.00	M
178 V as in Victim - Lawrence Treat	.50	1.25	2.00	M
179 Lovely in Death - William O'Farrell	.50	1.25	2.00	M
aka The Snakes of St. Cyr				
180 Killer at His Back - John Godey	.50	1.25	2.00	M
aka The Blue Hour				
181 You'll Fry Tomorrow - M. V. Heberden	.50	1.25	2.00	M
aka Exit This Way				
182 The Case of the Missing Corpse - Edwin Lanham Lanham	.50	1.25	2.00	M
aka Death of a Corinthian				
183 Embrace of Death - Carroll Cox Estes	.50	1.25	2.00	M
aka The Moon Gate				
184 The Fatal Flirt - Dolores Hitchens	.50	1.25	2.00	M
aka Beat Back the Tide				
185 Too Lovely Too Live - Ruth Fenisong	.50	1.25	2.00	M
aka Miscast for Murder				
186 They all Bleed Red - Richard Sted	.50	1.25	2.00	M
187 Buried for Pleasure - Edmund Crispin	.50	1.25	2.00	M
188 The Blonde Betrayer - John Godey	.50	1.25	2.00	M
aka The Man in Question				
189 Trap for a Redhead - Stuart Palmer	.50	1.25	2.00	M
aka Nipped in the Bud				
190 Trial and Terror - Lawrence Treat	.50	1.25	2.00	M
191 Shroud for a Lady - Elizabeth Daly	.50	1.25	2.00	M
aka The Wrong Way Down				
192 Another Morgue Heard From - Frederick C. Davis	.50	1.25	2.00	M
193 Catch and Kill - Nicholas Blake	.50	1.25	2.00	M
aka The Whisper in the Gloom				
194 Network of Fear - Alvin Yudkoff	.50	1.25	2.00	M
aka Circumstances Beyond Control				
195 No Time for Terror - Philip MacDonald	.50	1.25	2.00	M
aka Guest in the House				
196 Murder Muscles In - Max Franklin	.50	1.25	2.00	M
aka Justice Has no Sword				
197 Murder Makes an Entrance - Clarence Budington Kelland	.50	1.25	2.00	M
198 Black Alibi - Cornell Woolrich	.50	1.25	2.00	M
199 The Book of the Crime - Elizabeth Daly	.50	1.25	2.00	M

200	A Dirty Way to Die - George Bagby	.50	1.25	2.00	M
201	Tell Her It's Murder - Helen Reilly	.50	1.25	2.00	M
202	Take One for Murder - M. E. Chaber	.50	1.25	2.00	M
	aka As Old as Cain				
203	The Long Body - Helen McCloy	.50	1.25	2.00	M
204	I Wake up Screaming - Steve Fisher	.50	1.25	2.00	M
205	Don't Look Back - Miriam Borgenicht	.50	1.25	2.00	M
206	The Black Angel - Cornell Woolrich	.50	1.25	2.00	M
207	Hang the Man High - Geoffrey Household	.50	1.25	2.00	M
	aka Fellow Passenger				
208	The Deadly Truth - Helen McCloy	.50	1.25	2.00	M
209	Bridge to Vengeance - Winston Graham	.50	1.25	2.00	M
	aka The Little Walls				
	Note: After no. 209, the series became Bestseller Mystery Magazine.				

BIG GREEN DETECTIVE NOVEL

(Green Publishing Company)

Digest size

2	Hot Bullets for Love - Gentry Nyland	2.00	4.00	7.50	M
	aka Mr. South Burned his Mouth				
	Note: Same cover as Double Action Detective no. 2.				
3	Run Corpse Run - Guy Pember-Hiller	2.00	4.00	6.00	M
4	Murder with Love - Garland Lord	2.00	4.00	6.00	M
5	Target for Murder - Guy Elwyn Giles	2.00	4.00	6.00	M

BIG GREEN PUBLICATION

(Green Publishing Company)

Digest size

5	The Little Dog Barked - Anne Rowe	1.50	3.50	5.00	M

BLACK CAT DETECTIVE

(Crestwood Publishing Co., Inc.)

Digest size

1	3 Died Variously - Guy Elwyn Giles	2.00	4.00	7.50	M
2	Bait for a Tiger - Bayard Veiller	1.50	3.50	5.00	M
3	Dig Me a Grave - John Spain	1.50	3.50	5.00	M
5	The Case of the Cheating Bride - Milton				

Bestseller B165, c. Merc

Big Green Det. 2, c. Green

Big Green Publ. 5, c. Green

Black Cat Detective 15,
c. Crest

Black Cat Detective 19,
c. Crest

Black Cat Western 40,
c. Crest

(BLACK CAT DETECTIVE, continued)

	Propper	1.50	3.50	5.00	M
	1943				
6	Death Thumbs a Ride - Jean Lilly	1.50	3.50	5.00	M
7	The Beast Must Die - Nicholas Blake	2.00	4.00	6.00	M
8	The Body in the Road - Moray Dalton	1.50	3.50	5.00	M
	1944				
9	It Takes a Thief - Dan Billany	1.50	3.50	5.00	M
10	Crazy to Kill - Ann Cardwell	1.50	3.50	5.00	M
11	John Doe - Murderer - William Dale	1.50	3.50	5.00	M
12	6 Were to Die - Kirk Wales	1.50	3.50	5.00	M
13	Murder as Usual - Owen Fox Jerome	1.50	3.50	5.00	M
15	Head long for Murder - Merlda Mace	1.50	3.50	5.00	M
	1945				
16	The Crooked Circle - Gerald Verner	1.50	3.50	5.00	M
17	Motto for Murder - Merlda Mace	1.50	3.50	5.00	M
18	Murder Trouble - Louis Trimble	1.50	3.50	5.00	M
19	Murder in Miniatures - Sam Merwin, Jr.	1.50	3.50	5.00	M
20	Murder in Plain Sight - Gerlad Brown	1.50	3.50	5.00	M
	1946				
25	Dear Dead Professor - K. Alison LaRoche	1.50	3.50	5.00	M
27	The Bright Face of Danger - Julius Fast	1.50	3.50	5.00	M
	1947				

BLACK CAT WESTERN

(Crestwood Publishing Co., Inc.)

Digest size

30	Prairie Pioneers - Lynn Westland	1.50	3.00	5.00	W
38	Saddle River Spread - Lynn Westland	1.50	3.50	5.00	W
39	Nighthawk's Gold - Kim Knight	1.50	3.00	5.00	W
40	The Faceless Riders - Archie Joscelyn	1.50	3.50	5.00	W
41	Smoke in the West - Archie Joscelyn	1.50	3.50	5.00	W
42	Gunslammer - Lee Floren	1.50	3.50	5.00	W
43	Renegade Guns - James L. Rubel	1.50	3.50	5.00	W
44	Mad River Guns - Lee Floren	1.50	3.50	5.00	W
45	Outcast Law - Archie Joscelyn	1.50	3.50	5.00	W

BLACK KNIGHT

(Ideal Distributing Company)

Some digest size

15	Corpse in the Wind - Robert Portner Koehler	1.50	3.50	5.00	M
	Digest size				
16	Last Year's Snow - Don Tracey	1.50	3.50	5.00	M
	Digest size				
17	Death to Drumbeat - Jeremy Lane	1.50	3.50	5.00	M
	Digest size				

Black Knight 26, c. Ideal

Black Knight 27, c. Ideal

Black Knight 28, c. Ideal

(BLACK KNIGHT, continued)

18	Murder Behind the Mike - R. L. Goldman Digest size	1.50	3.50	5.00	M
25	Come Dwell with Death - M. W. Glidden	2.00	4.00	6.00	M
26	Death Is No Lady - M. E. Corne aka Death is a Masquerade	2.00	4.00	6.00	M
27	The Psychiatric Murders - M. Scott Michel	2.00	4.00	6.00	M
28	The Kidnappers - Albert E. Ullman	2.00	4.00	6.00	M
29	Green for a Grave - Manning Lee Stokes	2.00	4.00	6.00	M
30	Make Mine Murder - R. Sidney Bowen	2.00	4.00	6.00	M
32	Kill Him Tonight - Jeremy Lane If I Die-It's Murder! - Mari Ervin	2.00	4.00	6.00	M

BLEAK HOUSE

(Parsee Publications)

Some digest size

12	Design for Dying - Albert Jeffers aka Screen for Murder, Digest size	1.50	3.50	5.00	M
13	Murder Wore Green - Robert Portner Koehler Digest size	1.50	3.50	5.00	M
14	The Case of the Blood-stained Dime - Minna Barton aka Murder Does Light Housekeeping	2.00	4.00	6.00	M
15	The Case of the Missing Corpse - Joan Langar	2.00	4.00	6.00	M
16	The Corpse in the Guest Room - Clement Wood	2.00	4.00	6.00	M
17	The Skyscraper Murder - Samuel Spewack	2.00	4.00	6.00	M
18	Murder Menagerie - Jeremy Lane	2.00	4.00	6.00	M
19	If I Should Murder - Patrick Laing	2.00	4.00	6.00	M
20	The Terror of the Headless Corpse - William Dale	2.00	4.00	6.00	M
21	Here Come the Dead - Robert Portner Koehler	2.00	4.00	6.00	M

BOBLIN BOOK

Bleak House 12, c. Par

Bleak House 18, c. Par

Bleak House 20, c. Par

Boblin Book nn, c. Boblin   Bonded 2, c. Bond-Charteris   Bonded 5, c. Bond-Charteris

(BOBLIN BOOK, continued)

(Boblin Sales Company)

Digest size

nn	The Adventures of Buffalo Bill - William F. Cody movie tie-in	5.00	10.00	20.00	W
nn	The Jumping Frog and Sixteen Other Stories - Mark Twain	3.00	6.00	12.00	H
nn	Was it Murder? - James Hilton	3.00	6.00	12.00	W
nn	Judge Priest Turns Detective - Irvin S. Cobb	3.00	6.00	12.00	M

BONDED

(Bond-Charteris/Black/Jacobs/Shaw)

Digest size

1	The Saint Meets the Tiger - Leslie Charteris	2.00	4.00	7.50	M
2	Featuring the Saint - Leslie Charteris 1945	2.00	4.00	7.50	M
3	The Saint's Getaway - Leslie Charteris	2.00	4.00	7.50	M
4	The Saint's Choice of English Crime - ed. Leslie Charteris	2.00	4.00	7.50	M
5	Alias the Saint - Leslie Charteris	2.00	4.00	7.50	M
6	The Saint's Choice of American Crime - ed. Leslie Charteris	2.00	4.00	7.50	M
7	Paging the Saint - Leslie Charteris aka Wanted for Murder	2.00	4.00	7.50	M
8	The Saint's Choice of True Crimes - ed. Leslie Charteris	2.00	4.00	7.50	M
9	The Saint's Choice of Humorous Crime Stories ed. Leslie Charteris	2.00	4.00	7.50	M
10	Fast One - Paul Cain	2.00	4.00	7.50	M
10A	Atomic Bomb - Malcolm Jameson	4.00	8.00	15.00	SF
11	The Saint's Choice of Impossible Crime - ed. Leslie Charteris First ed., 1945	7.50	15.00	30.00	SF
12	The Craig Rice Mystery Digest - ed. Craig Rice	2.50	6.00	10.00	M
13	8 Faces at 3 - Craig Rice	2.00	4.00	7.50	M
14	The Saint Meets his Match - Leslie Charteris	2.00	4.00	7.50	M
15	Crime on my Hands - George Sanders	2.00	4.00	7.50	M
nn	Lady on a Train - Leslie Charteris Movie tie-in	3.00	6.00	12.00	M
nn	Guns of Powder River - Oscar J. Friend	2.00	4.00	7.50	W

BONDED MYSTERY

(Anson Bond Publications, Inc.)

Bonded 10A, c. Bond-Charteris   Bonded 11, c. Bond-Charteris   Bonded nn, c. Bond-Charteris

(BONDED MYSTERY, continued)

Some digest size

1	The Goose is Cooked - Emnett Hogarth Digest size	2.50	6.00	10.00	M
2	Murder of a Novelist - Sally Wood Digest size	2.00	4.00	7.50	M
3	The Hungry House - Lilian Lauferty Digest size	2.00	4.00	6.00	M
4	Murder Strikes Thrice - Charles G. Booth Digest size	2.00	4.00	6.00	M
5	I'll Eat You Last - H. C. Branson	2.00	4.00	7.50	M
6	The Thing in the Brook - Peter Storme	2.00	4.00	7.50	M
7	Death Blew Out the Match - Kathleen Moore Knight	2.00	4.00	7.50	M
8	Twittering Bird Mystery - H. C. Bailey	2.00	4.00	7.50	M
9	Murder Needs a Name - Ruth Fenisong	2.00	4.00	6.00	M
10	"B" as in Banshee - Lawrence Treat	2.00	4.00	7.50	M
11	Johnnie - Dorothy B. Hughes	2.00	4.00	6.00	M
12	Kingdom of Death - Margery Allingham	2.00	4.00	7.50	M
13	Harbour - Philip MacDonald	2.00	4.00	7.50	M
14	Who's Afraid? - Elisabeth Sanxay Holding	2.00	4.00	6.00	M
15	Footsteps in the Air - Susan Wells	2.00	4.00	6.00	M
16	This is Mr. Fortune - H. C. Bailey	2.00	4.00	7.50	M

BOWKER

(R. R. Bowker Company)

nn	Banned Books - Anne Lyon Haight 1955	2.00	4.00	7.50	NF

Note: Contains interesting information on the banning of some paperback books
either as pornography or because of lurid covers.

Bonded Mystery 5, c. Anson   Bonded Mystery 12, c. Anson   Bowker nn, c. Bowker

Broadway Novel Monthly 3,
c. Div

Bronze Books 2, c. Designs

Brussel nn, c. Brussel

BROADWAY NOVEL MONTHLY

(Diversey Periodicals, Inc.)

Digest size

1	Infidelity - Arthur Weigal	5.00	10.00	20.00	E
2	Venus on Wheels - Maurice Dekobra	5.00	10.00	20.00	E
3	Ladies of the Evening - Milton Herbert Gropper 1949	5.00	10.00	20.00	E
4	Tom's Temptations - Don Prince	5.00	10.00	20.00	E
5	Night Boat - Timothy Trent	5.00	10.00	20.00	E
6	Three Loose Ladies - M. H. Gropper	5.00	10.00	20.00	E
7	Fleshpots of Malibu - C. & G. Graham	5.00	10.00	20.00	E
8	Blonde Baby - Wilson Collison	5.00	10.00	20.00	E
9	Dangerous Love - Jack Woodford	5.00	10.00	20.00	E
10	Untamed Darling - Jack Woodford	5.00	10.00	20.00	E

BRONZE BOOKS

(Designs Publishing Co.)

Digest size

2	Hot Chocolate - Jesse Lee Carter Orig., 1952	2.50	6.25	10.00	E

BRUSSEL

(J. Brussel)

Digest Size

nn	Murder in the Bedroom - Gaston Leroux 1945	3.00	6.00	12.00	M

BULL'S-EYE DETECTIVE NOVELS

(Duchess Printing and Publishing Co., Ltd.)

Digest size

Canadian

1	Silent Terror · T. C. H. Jacobs 1944	1.50	3.50	5.00	M

CAMEO

(Detective House, Inc.)

Digest size

300	No Man of Her Own - Florence Stonebraker	1.50	3.50	5.00	E
301	The Loves of Alice Brandt - Gene Harvey	1.50	3.50	5.00	E
	Orig., 1951				
302	Night of Ecstasy - William Arnold	1.50	3.50	5.00	E
303	Conquest of Margie - Norman Bligh	1.50	3.50	5.00	E
304	Naughty Blonde - Florence Stonebraker	1.50	3.50	5.00	E
305	Pick-Up at Midnight - Gene Harvey	1.50	3.50	5.00	E
306	Passion C. O. D. - Albert L. Quandt	1.50	3.50	5.00	E
307	Sin Preferred - Kermit Welles	1.50	3.50	5.00	E
308	Secret Affair - Amos Hatter	1.50	3.50	5.00	E
	Orig., 1951				
309	A Girl Called Joy - Gene Harvey	1.50	3.50	5.00	E
310	Pleasure Bound - Kermit Welles	1.50	3.50	5.00	E
311	The Affairs of a Country Girl - Gail Jordan	1.50	3.50	5.00	E
312	Crossroads of Desire - Amos Hatler	1.50	3.50	5.00	E
313	Three-time Sinner - Norman Bligh	1.50	3.50	5.00	E
314	The Big Tease - William Arnold	1.50	3.50	5.00	E
	Orig., 1952				
315	Passion's Harvest - Florence Stonebraker	1.50	3.50	5.00	E
316	Soft Shoulders - Norman Bligh	1.50	3.50	5.00	E
317	Woman of Fire - Peggy Gaddis	1.50	3.50	5.00	E
318	Island Ecstasy - Amos Hatter	1.50	3.50	5.00	E
319	Beach Party - Ralph Douglas	1.50	3.50	5.00	E
320	Girl of the Midway - Amos Hatter	1.50	3.50	5.00	E
321	Tight Skirt - Frederic Spencer	1.50	3.50	5.00	E
322	Loose Women - Robert E. Reynolds	1.50	3.50	5.00	E
	Orig., 1952				
323	Wild Girl - L. Dixon c-Belarski	1.50	3.00	5.00	E
325	Mountain Girl - Peggy Gaddis	1.50	3.00	5.00	E
326	At Ruby's Place - Tucker	1.50	3.50	5.00	E
327	Cleo - Frederic Spencer	1.50	3.50	5.00	E
328	Country Girl - Gail Jordan	1.50	3.50	5.00	E
334	Office Sinner - Gene Harvey	1.50	3.50	5.00	E
	aka The Loves of Alice Brandt				
336	Doctor's Nurse - Gene Harvey	1.50	3.50	5.00	E
	aka A Girl Called Joy				
339	French Maid - M. Cooper	1.50	3.00	5.00	E
341	Country Girl - Gail Jordan	1.50	3.00	5.00	E
342	Shanty Girl - Jean Tucker	2.00	4.00	6.00	E
	c-Belarski				
344	Woman of Passion - Norman Bligh	1.50	3.00	5.00	E
346	Backwoods Bride - Robert E. Reynolds	1.50	3.50	5.00	E
357	Woman of Passion - Norman Bligh	1.50	3.50	5.00	E
	aka 3-Time Sinner				
359	Boy-Chaser - Nickerson	1.50	3.50	5.00	E
362	Mountain Bride - Peggy Gaddis	1.50	3.50	5.00	E
365	Boarding House - Frank Haskell	1.50	3.50	5.00	E
	aka House of Lost Women, c-Gross				
367	Lost Women - R. Reynolds	1.50	3.50	5.00	E

Bull's-Eye Det. Novels 1, c. Duch

Cameo 308, c. Det

Candid Love Novels 21, c. Crest

CANDID LOVE NOVELS

(Crestwood Publishing Co., Inc.)

Digest size

21 Wild Weekend - Gene Harvey 1949, aka Pack Up Your Sins, c-Wenzel	2.00	4.00	7.50	E

CARDINAL EDITIONS

(Pocket Books, Inc.)

C	1	Four Great Historical Plays - William Shakespeare	.75	1.50	3.00	
C	2	Kings Row - Henry Bellamann	.50	1.25	2.00	
C	3	In Tragic Life - Vardis Fisher	.50	1.25	2.00	
C	4	Cutlass Empire - F. Van Wyck Mason	.75	1.50	3.00	A
C	5	The Merriam - Webster Pocket Dictionary	.50	1.25	2.00	NF
C	6	Hungry Hill - Daphne du Maurier	.50	1.25	2.00	
C	7	A Short History of the Civil War Fletcher Pratt	.75	1.50	3.00	NF
C	8	Prince of Egypt - Dorothy Clarke Wilson	.75	1.50	3.00	A
C	9	The Pocket Bible	.50	1.25	2.00	NF
C	10	Lust for Life - Irving Stone	.50	1.25	2.00	
C	11	The Pocket Book of Verse - M. E. Speare	.50	1.25	2.00	
C	12	The Pocket Book of Short Stories - M. E. Speare	.50	1.25	2.00	
C	13	Roget's Pocket Thesaurus - Christopher Mawson, Katharine Whiting	.50	1.25	2.00	NF
C	14	Four Great Tragedies - William Shakespeare	.50	1.25	2.00	
C	15	Four Great Comedies - William Shakespeare	.50	1.25	2.00	
C	16	The Pocket Book of Quotations - Henry Davidoff	.50	1.25	2.00	
C	17	Tales from the Arabian Nights	1.25	2.50	5.00	
C	18	Honey in the Horn - H. L. Davis	50	1.25	2.00	
C	19	Cakes and Ale and Other Favorites - W. Somerset Maughan	.50	1.25	2.00	
C	20	Rand McNally - Pocket World Atlas 1952	.50	1.25	2.00	NF
C	21	Pride's Castle - Frank Yerby	.75	1.50	3.00	A
C	22	The Pepper Tree - John Jennings	.50	1.25	2.00	
C	23	Rivers of Glory - F. Van Wyck Mason	.50	1.25	2.00	
C	24	The 100 Most Important People in the World Today - Donald Robinson	.50	1.25	2.00	NF
C	25	A Short History of the American Revolution - John Hyde Preston 1952	.50	1.25	2.00	NF
C	26	Tap Roots - James Street	.50	1.25	2.00	
C	27	The Confessions of St. Augustine - Aurelius Augustinus	.50	1.25	2.00	
C	28	Lives of Famous French Painters - Herman J. Wechsler	.75	1.50	3.00	NF
C	29	The Pocket Book of Baby and Child Care - Benjamin Spock	.50	1.25	2.00	NF
C	30	The Way West - A. B. Guthrie, Jr.	.50	1.25	2.00	W
C	31	The Man with the Golden Arm - Nelson Algren With dust jacket	.50 10.00	1.25 20.00	2.00 35.00	
C	32	The Loyalty of Free Men - Alan Barth	.50	1.25	2.00	
C	33	Wuthering Heights - Emily Bronte	.50	1.25	2.00	
C	34	Mutiny on the Bounty - James Norman Hall, Charles Nordhoff	.75	1.50	3.00	A
C	35	A Tale of Two Cities - Charles Dickens	.75	1.50	3.00	
C	36	Famous Chinese Short Stories - Lin Yutang	.75	1.50	3.00	
C	37	Pride and Prejudice - Jane Austen	.50	1.25	2.00	
C	38	The Witching Pool - Robert Presnell, Jr.	.50	1.25	2.00	
C	39	Hour of Glory - Robert Lund	.50	1.25	2.00	
C	40	The Disappearance - Philip Wylie	.50	1.25	2.00	

(CARDINAL EDITIONS, continued)

C 41	The Conqueror - John Tebbel	.75	1.50	3.00	A
C 42	The Return of the Native - Thomas Hardy	.50	1.25	2.00	
C 43	Dawn's Early Light - Elswyth Thane	.50	1.25	2.00	
C 44	Moll Flanders - Daniel Defoe	.75	1.50	3.00	
C 45	Great Tales and Poems - Edgar Allen Poe	.50	1.25	2.00	
C 46	Kinfolk - Pearl S. Buck	.50	1.25	2.00	
C 47	Tess of the D'Urbervilles - Thomas Hardy	.50	1.25	2.00	
C 48	The Great Short Stories of Robert Louis Stevenson	.50	1.25	2.00	
C 49	Jubilee Trail - Gwen Bristow	.50	1.25	2.00	
C 50	Immortal Poems of the English Language - Oscar Williams	.50	1.25	2.00	
	1952				
C 51	Abraham Lincoln - Lord Charnwood	.75	1.50	3.00	NF
C 52	The Big Sky - A. B. Guthrie, Jr.	.50	1.25	2.00	W
C 53	Rebecca - Daphne du Maurier	.50	1.25	2.00	
C 54	The Golden Hawk - Frank Yerby	.75	1.50	3.00	A
C 55	The Complete Sonnets, Songs and Poems of Shakespeare - William Shakespeare	.50	1.25	2.00	
C 56	Caroline Hicks - Walter Karig	.50	1.25	2.00	
C 57	Three Harbours - F. Van Wyck Mason	.50	1.25	2.00	
C 58	River of the Sun - James Ramsey Ullman	.50	1.25	2.00	
C 59	Madame Bovary - Gustave Flaubert	.50	1.25	2.00	
C 60	Buddenbrooks - Thomas Mann	.50	1.25	2.00	
C 61	Questions and Answers from the Book of Knowledge - E. U. McLoughlin	.50	1.25	2.00	NF
C 62	The Golden Ass of Apuleius - Madaurensis Apuleius	.50	1.25	2.00	
C 63	Of Human Bondage - W. Somerset Maugham	.50	1.25	2.00	
C 64	The Turquoise - Anya Seton	.50	1.25	2.00	
C 65	The Scarlet Letter - Nathaniel Hawthorne	.50	1.25	2.00	
C 66	Dialogues of Plato	.50	1.25	2.00	
C 67	The Song of Bernadette - Franz Werfel	.50	1.25	2.00	
C 68	The Parasites - Daphne du Maurier	.50	1.25	2.00	
C 69	The Foundling - Francis J. Spellman	.50	1.25	2.00	
C 70	Morning Journey - James Hilton	.50	1.25	2.00	
C 71	The Cardinal - Henry Morton Robinson	.50	1.25	2.00	
C 72	The 42nd Parallel - John Dos Passos	.50	1.25	2.00	
C 73	Passions Spin the Plot - Vardis Fisher	.50	1.25	2.00	
	1953				
C 74	Tomorrow We Reap - James Childers, James Street	.50	1.25	2.00	
C 75	English through Pictures - Book 1 - Christine Gibson, I. A. Richards	.50	1.25	2.00	NF
	1953				
C 76	The White Tower - James Ramsey Ullman	.50	1.25	2.00	
C 77	My Six Convicts - Donald Powell Wilson	.75	1.50	3.00	
C 78	French through Pictures - I. A. Richards, Others	.50	1.25	2.00	NF
C 79	Ivanhoe - Walter Scott	.50	1.25	2.00	A
C 80	Discovery No. 1 - John W. Aldridge, Vance Bourjaily	.50	1.25	2.00	
C 81	Dinner at Belmont - Alfred Leland Crabb	.50	1.25	2.00	
C 82	Fight Against Fears - Lucy Freeman	.50	1.25	2.00	
C 83	Spanish through Pictures - I. A. Richards, Others	.50	1.25	2.00	NF

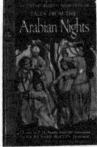

Cardinal Editions C17, c. PKB

Cardinal Editions C80, c. PKB

Cardinal Editions C226, c. PKB

C 84 The Producer - Richard Brooks	.50	1.25	2.00	
C 85 The Southern Cook Book - Marion Brown	.50	1.25	2.00	(NF)
C 86 The 100 Most Important People of 1953 - Donald Robinson	.50	1.25	2.00	(NF)
C 87 Floodtide - Frank Yerby	.50	1.25	2.00	(A)
C 88 Jane Eyre - Charlotte Bronte	.50	1.25	2.00	
C 89 The Ragged Ones - Burke Davis	.50	1.25	2.00	
C 90 The Pocket Household Encyclopedia - N. H. Mager, S. K. Mager	.50	1.25	2.00	(NF)
C 91 A Stone for Danny Fisher - Harold Robbins	.50	1.25	2.00	
C 92 Look Away, Look Away - Leslie Turner White	.50	1.25	2.00	
C 93 A Pocket Guide to the Trees - Rutherford Platt	.75	1.50	3.00	(NF)
C 94 The Pocket Book of Robert Frost's Poems	.50	1.25	2.00	
C 95 German through Pictures - I. A. Richards, Others	.50	1.25	2.00	(NF)
C 96 The Iron Mistress - Paul I. Wellman	.75	1.50	3.00	(A)
C 97 The Earthbreakers - Ernest Haycox	.50	1.25	2.00	(W)
C 98 The Pedlocks - Stephen Longstreet	.50	1.25	2.00	
C 99 The King's General - Daphne du Maurier	.50	1.25	2.00	
C100 Flesh and the Dream - George Williams	.50	1.25	2.00	
1953				
C101 Devils, Drugs and Doctors - Howard H. Haggard	.50	1.25	2.00	(NF)
C102 A Woman Called Fancy - Frank Yerby	.50	1.25	2.00	
C103 Yankee Stranger - Elswyth Thane	.50	1.25	2.00	
C104 The Imitation of Christ - Thomas A. Kempis	.50	1.25	2.00	
C105 Pavilion of Women - Pearl S. Buck	.50	1.25	2.00	
C106 Tales from the Decameron - Giovanni Boccaccio	.75	1.50	3.00	
C107 A Connecticut Yankee in King Arthur's Court - Mark Twain	.50	1.25	2.00	
1954				
C108 Come, My Beloved - Pearl S. Buck	.50	1.25	2.00	
C109 The Pocket Book of American Poems - Louis Untermeyer	.50	1.25	2.00	
C110 Lincoln McKeever - Eleazar Lipsky	.50	1.25	2.00	
C111 The Good Earth - Pearl S. Buck	.50	1.25	2.00	
C112 How to Stop Worrying and Start Living - Dale Carnegie	.50	1.25	2.00	(NF)
C113 Great Essays - Houston Peterson	.50	1.25	2.00	
C114 God's Men - Pearl S. Buck	.50	1.25	2.00	
C115 Discovery No. 2 - Vance Bourjaily	.50	1.25	2.00	
C116 Matthew Steel - Mildred Masterson McNeilly	.50	1.25	2.00	
C117 Captain Marooner - Louis B. Davidson, Eddie Doherty	.75	1.50	3.00	(A)
C118 Great Escapes - Basil Davenport	.80	1.25	2.00	
C119 We are Betrayed - Vardis Fisher	.50	1.25	2.00	
C120 Giant - Edna Ferber	.50	1.25	2.00	
C121 Young Ames - Walter D. Edmonds	.50	1.25	2.00	
C122 The University of Chicago Spanish-English, English-Spanish Dictionary - Carlos Castillo	.50	1.25	2.00	(NF)
C123 Yorktown - Burke Davis	.50	1.25	2.00	
C124 The Saracen Blade - Frank Yerby	.75	1.50	3.00	(A)
C125 Carol Curtis' Complete Book of Knitting and Crocheting - Carol Curtis	.50	1.25	2.00	(NF)
1954				
C126 The Court of Last Resort - Erle Stanley Gardner	.50	1.25	2.00	(M)
C127 Crimson is the Eastern Shore - Don Tracy	.50	1.25	2.00	
C128 God's Angry Man - Leonard Ehrlich	.50	1.25	2.00	
C129 Marye Dahnke's Salad Book - Marye Dahnke	.50	1.25	2.00	(NF)
C130 Discovery No. 3 - Vance Bourjaily	.50	1.25	2.00	
C131 1919 - John Dos Passos	.50	1.25	2.00	
C132 The Science Book of Wonder Drugs - Donald G. Cooley	.50	1.25	2.00	(NF)
C133 Winston Churchill - Robert Lewis Taylor	.50	1.25	2.00	(NF)
C134 Nana - Emile Zola	.50	1.25	2.00	
C135 The Exploration of Space - Arthur C. Clarke	.50	1.25	2.00	(NF)
C136 The Border Lord - Jan Westcott	.50	1.25	2.00	
C137 The Strange Brigade - John Jennings	.75	1.50	3.00	(A)
C138 Pleasant Valley - Louis Bromfield	.50	1.25	2.00	
C139 The Adventures of Huckleberry Finn - Mark Twain	.50	1.25	2.00	

C140 The Smoldering Sea - U. S. Anderson	.50	1.25	2.00	
C141 Jubal Troop - Paul I. Wellman	.50	1.25	2.00	(W)
C142 The Devil's Laughter - Frank Yerby	.75	1.50	3.00	(A)
C143 Discovery No. 4 - Vance Bourjaily	.50	1.25	2.00	
C144 Night Light - Douglass Wallop	.50	1.25	2.00	
C145 Six Minutes a Day to Perfect Spelling - Harry Shefter	.50	1.25	2.00	(NF)
C146 Call Me Lucky - Bing Crosby	1.25	2.50	5.00	(NF)
C147 Hope for the Troubled - Lucy Freeman	.50	1.25	2.00	
C148 Drawing Self-Taught - Arthur Zaidenberg	.50	1.25	2.00	(NF)
C149 The Bandit and the Priest - Audrey Erskine Lindop	.50	1.25	2.00	
C150 Freud: His Dream and Sex Theories	.50	1.25	2.00	(NF)
1954				
C151 The Chieftain - Robert Payne	.75	1.50	3.00	(A)
C152 The Pocket Book Magazine - Franklin Watts	.50	1.25	2.00	
C153 My Cousin Rachel - Daphne du Maurier	.50	1.25	2.00	
C154 The Story of the World - John van Duyn Southworth	.50	1.25	2.00	(NF)
C155 A Minute of Prayer - Christopher Cross	.50	1.25	2.00	
C156 Great Tales of Fantasy and Imagination - Philip Van Doren Stern	1.50	3.00	6.00	(SF)
C157 The Walsingham Woman - Jan Westcott	.50	1.25	2.00	
1955				
C158 The Pocket Book of Ogden Nash - Ogden Nash	.50	1.25	2.00	
C159 Discovery No. 5 - Vance Bourjaily	.50	1.25	2.00	
C160 The Pocket Book Magazine No. 2 - Franklin Watts	.50	1.25	2.00	
C161 The Razor's Edge - W. Somerset Maugham	.50	1.25	2.00	
C162 The Kingpin - Tom Wickes	.50	1.25	2.00	
C163 The Silent World - Jacques-Yves Cousteau, Frederic Dumas	.75	1.50	3.00	(NF)
C164 Ever After - Elswyth Thane	.50	1.25	2.00	
C165 Golden Admiral - F. Van Wyck Mason	.75	1.50	3.00	(A)
C166 Six Weeks to Words of Power - Wilfred Funk	.50	1.25	2.00	(NF)
C167 The 1955 Baseball Almanac - Hy Turkin	.75	1.50	3.00	(S)
C168 Kiss Me Again, Stranger - Daphne du Maurier	.50	1.25	2.00	
C169 Sex and the Nature of Things - N.J. Berrill	.50	1.25	2.00	(NF)
C170 Hebrew through Pictures - I. A. Richards	.50	1.25	2.00	(NF)
C171 Hebrew Reader - I. A. Richards, Others	.50	1.25	2.00	(NF)
C172 Silver Street Woman - Les Savage, Jr.	.50	1.25	2.00	
C173 N. Y., N. Y. - Will Oursler	.50	1.25	2.00	
C174 The Science Book of the Human Body - Edith E. Sproul	.50	1.25	2.00	(NF)
C175 The Vixens - Frank Yerby	.50	1.25	2.00	
1955				
C176 Disputed Passage - Lloyd C. Douglas	.50	1.25	2.00	
C177 No Villain Need Be - Vardis Fisher	.50	1.25	2.00	
C178 Sir Rogue - Leslie Turner White	.75	1.50	3.00	(A)
C179 A Marriage Manual - Hannah Stone, Abraham Stone	.50	1.25	2.00	(NF)
C180 Your Own Book of Camp Craft - Catherine T. Hammett	.50	1.25	2.00	(NF)
C181 The Pocket Cook Book - Elizabeth Woody	.50	1.25	2.00	(NF)
C182 Sign of the Pagan - Roger Fuller	.75	1.50	3.00	(A)
C183 A Subtreasury of American Humor - E. B. White, Katherine S. White	.50	1.25	2.00	
C184 Diane - Herbert Best	.50	1.25	2.00	
C185 Discovery No. 6 - Vance Bourjaily	.50	1.25	2.00	
C186 How to Make More Money - Marvin Small	.50	1.25	2.00	(NF)
C187 The Blackboard Jungle - Evan Hunter	1.00	2.00	4.00	
C188 The Duncan Hines Dessert Book - Duncan Hines	.50	1.25	2.00	(NF)
C189 Roanoke Renegade - Don Tracy	.50	1.25	2.00	
C190 Short Cuts to Effective English - Harry Shefter	.50	1.25	2.00	(NF)
C191 Aboard the Flying Swan - Stanley Wolpert	.50	1.25	2.00	
C192 Lord Grizzly - Frederick Manfred	1.00	2.00	4.00	(W)
C193 Best-Seller Digest No. 1	.50	1.25	2.00	
C194 American Captain - Edison Marshall	.75	1.50	3.00	(A)
C195 The French Quarter - Herbert Asbury	1.25	2.50	5.00	
C196 The Compact Treasury of Inspiration - Kenneth S. Giniger	.50	1.25	2.00	
C197 Buccaneer Surgeon - C. V. Terry	.75	1.50	3.00	(A)
C198 The Gown of Glory - Agnes Sligh Turnball	.50	1.25	2.00	

C199 The Toastmaster's and Speaker's Handbook - Herbert V. Prochnow	.50	1.25	2.00	(NF)
C200 The Pocket Book Magazine No. 3 - Franklin Watts	.50	1.25	2.00	
1955				
C201 Italian Through Pictures - I. A. Richards	.50	1.25	2.00	(NF)
1956				
C202 Never Victorious, Never Defeated - Taylor Caldwell	.50	1.25	2.00	
C203 The Last Hunt - Milton Lott	.75	1.50	3.00	(W)
C204 The Adventurers - Ernest Haycox	.50	1.25	2.00	(W)
C205 Have Tux, Will Travel - Bob Hope	.50	1.25	2.00	(H)
C206 Ann Pillsbury's Baking Book - Ann Pillsbury	.50	1.25	2.00	(NF)
C207 The Science Book of Space Travel - Harold Leland Goodwin	.50	1.25	2.00	(NF)
C208 Benton's Row - Frank Yerby	.50	1.25	2.00	(A)
C209 The Virginian - Owen Wister	.50	1.25	2.00	(W)
C210 Somebody up There Likes Me - Rowland Barber, Rocky Graziano	.50	1.25	2.00	
C211 Blue Hurricane - F. Van Wyck Mason	.50	1.25	2.00	
C212 The 1956 Baseball Almanac - Don Schiffer	.75	1.50	3.00	(S)
C213 The Long Goodbye - Raymond Chandler	1.25	2.50	5.00	(M)
C214 Bless This House - Norah Lofts	.50	1.25	2.00	
C215 The Gadget Maker - Maxwell Griffith	.50	1.25	2.00	
C216 Mary Anne - Daphne du Maurier	.50	1.25	2.00	
C217 Big Business: A New Era - David E. Lilienthal	.50	1.25	2.00	(NF)
C218 The Man from Mesabi - Sarah Lockwood	.50	1.25	2.00	
C219 79 Park Avenue - Harold Robbins	.50	1.25	2.00	
C220 Katrina - Jeramie Price	.50	1.25	2.00	
C221 "Before I Kill More..." - Lucy Freeman	.50	1.25	2.00	
C222 Anna and the King of Siam - Margaret Landon	1.00	2.00	4.00	
C223 The Great Man - Al Morgan	.50	1.25	2.00	
C224 My Brother's Keeper - Marcia Davenport	.50	1.25	2.00	
C225 The Lost Eagles - Ralph Graves	.50	1.25	2.00	
1956				
C226 Tales of the South Pacific - James A. Michener	1.00	2.00	4.00	
C227 Roxana - Marian Castle	.50	1.25	2.00	
C228 Carolina Corsair - Don Tracy	.75	1.50	3.00	(A)
C229 The View from Pompey's Head - Hamilton Basso	.50	1.25	2.00	
C230 The Man in the Gray Flannel Suit - Sloan Wilson	.50	1.25	2.00	
C231 The U. P. Trail - Zane Grey	.75	1.50	3.00	(W)
C232 The Complete Guide to Home Sewing - S. K. Mager	.50	1.25	2.00	(NF)
1957				
C233 The Gentleman - Edison Marshall	.50	1.25	2.00	(A)
C234 The Last Temptation - Joseph Viertel	.50	1.25	2.00	
C235 Heritage - Anthony West	.50	1.25	2.00	
C236 Quartet in "H" - Evan Hunter	.50	1.25	2.00	
C237 How to Develop Self-Confidence - Dale Carnegie	.50	1.25	2.00	(NF)
C238 Profiles in Courage - John F. Kennedy	1.00	2.00	4.00	(NF)
C239 The Border Legion - Zane Grey	.75	1.50	3.00	(W)
C240 Forgive Us Our Trespasses - Lloyd C. Douglas	.50	1.25	2.00	
C241 The Golden Journey - Agnes Sligh Turnbull	.50	1.25	2.00	
C242 Silver Leopard - F. Van Wyck Mason	.50	1.25	2.00	
C243 The Quick Cook Book - Lois S. Kellogg	.50	1.25	2.00	(NF)
C244 The Wanderer - Mika Waltari	.50	1.25	2.00	
C245 Tender Victory - Taylor Caldwell	.50	1.25	2.00	
C246 The Winged Sword - Leslie Turner White	.50	1.25	2.00	
C247 The Sudden Strangers - William E. Barrett	.50	1.25	2.00	
C248 Will Acting Spoil Marilyn Monroe? - Pete Martin	5.00	12.50	25.00	(NF)
C249 Captain Rebel - Frank Yerby	.75	1.50	3.00	(A)
C250 Hilda Manning - Allan Seager	.50	1.25	2.00	
1957				
C251 The Barbary Coast - Herbert Asbury	1.00	2.00	4.00	
C252 Dynasty of Death - Taylor Caldwell	.50	1.25	2.00	
C253 Pemmican - Vardis Fisher	.75	1.50	3.00	(A)
C254 Deluxe Tour - Frederic Wakeman	.50	1.25	2.00	
C255 Mary - Sholem Asch	.50	1.25	2.00	

C256	First Steps In Reading English - Christine Gibson, I. A. Richards	.50	1.25	2.00	(NF)
C257	Magnificent Obsession - Lloyd C. Douglas	.50	1.25	2.00	
C258	English through Pictures-Book 2 - Christine Gibson, I. A. Richards	.50	1.25	2.00	(NF)
C259	A First Workbook of French - I.A. Richards	.50	1.25	2.00	(NF)
C260	How to Work with Tools & Wood - Fred Gross	.50	1.25	2.00	(NF)
C261	The Painted Veil - W. Somerset Maugham	.50	1.25	2.00	
C262	The Swordsman - Jefferson Cooper	.75	1.50	3.00	(A)
C263	The Dark Angel - Mika Waltari	.50	1.25	2.00	
C264	The Drift Fence - Zane Grey	.75	1.50	3.00	(W)
C265	The World's Best Recipes - Marvin Small	.50	1.25	2.00	(NF)
C266	Jenny - Ada Cook Lewis	.50	1.25	2.00	
C267	These Thousand Hills - A. B. Guthrie, Jr.	.50	1.25	2.00	
C268	The Case of the Sun-Bather's Diary - Erle Stanley Gardner	.75	1.50	3.00	(M)
C269	Green Light - Lloyd C. Douglas	.50	1.25	2.00	
C270	The Pocket Book of Erskine Caldwell Stories - E. Caldwell	.50	1.25	2.00	
C271	Canton Barrier - Andrew Geer 1958	.50	1.25	2.00	
C272	The Voice at the Back Door - Elizabeth Spencer	.50	1.25	2.00	
C273	The Magician - W. Somerset Maugham	.50	1.25	2.00	
C274	The Strong City - Taylor Caldwell	.50	1.25	2.00	
C275	The Case of the Terrified Typist - Erle Stanley Gardner 1958	.75	1.50	3.00	(M)
C276	The Scapegoat - Daphne du Maurier	.50	1.25	2.00	
C277	Chance Elson - W. T. Ballard	.50	1.25	2.00	
C278	Jericho's Daughters - Paul I. Wellman	.50	1.25	2.00	
C279	The Prosecuter - Bernard Botein	.50	1.25	2.00	
C280	The Innocent Ambassadors - Philip Wylie	.50	1.25	2.00	
C281	The Case of the Runaway Corpse - Erle Stanley Gardner	.75	1.50	3.00	(M)
C282	The Case of the Glamorous Ghost - Erle Stanley Gardner	.75	1.50	3.00	(M)
C283	The Case of the Half-Wakened Wife - Erle Stanley Gardner	.75	1.50	3.00	(M)
C284	The Case of the Empty Tin - Erle Stanley Gardner	.75	1.50	3.00	(M)
C285	The Case of the Lazy Lover - Erle Stanley Gardner	.75	1.50	3.00	(M)
C286	Cast the First Stone - Sara Harris, John M. Murtagh	.50	1.25	2.00	
C287	The Etruscan - Mika Waltari	.75	1.50	3.00	(A)
C288	The Hidden Persuaders - Vance Packard	.50	1.25	2.00	
C289	Basketball - Arnold "Red" Auerbach	.75	1.50	3.00	(S)
C290	The Promoters - Stephen Longstreet	.50	1.25	2.00	
C291	The D.A. Calls a Turn - Erle Stanley Gardner	.75	1.50	3.00	(M)
C292	The D.A. Breaks a Seal - Erle Stanley Gardner	.75	1.50	3.00	(M)
C293	The D.A. Takes a Chance - Erle Stanley Gardner	.75	1.50	3.00	(M)
C294	The D.A. Breaks an Egg - Erle Stanley Gardner	.75	1.50	3.00	(M)
C295	The D. A. Calls It Murder - Erle Stanley Gardner	.75	1.50	3.00	(M)
C296	Halfway Down the Stairs - Charles Thompson	.50	1.25	2.00	
C297	The Case of the Nervous Accomplice - Erle Stanley Gardner	.75	1.50	3.00	(M)
C298	No Down Payment - John McPartland	.50	1.25	2.00	
C299	The Case of the Careless Kitten - Erle Stanley Gardner	.75	1.50	3.00	(M)
C300	Cherokee - Don Tracy 1958	1.00	2.00	4.00	
C301	Riders of Judgement - Frederick Manfred	.50	1.25	2.00	
C302	The Case of the Crooked Candle - Erle Stanley Gardner	.75	1.50	3.00	(M)
C303	How to Win Friends and Influence People - Dale Carnegie	.50	1.25	2.00	(NF)
C304	Care and Training of Dogs - Arthur Frederick Jones	.50	1.25	2.00	(NF)
C305	Monsieur Yankee - Leslie Turner White	.50	1.25	2.00	(A)

C306	Cast of Characters - Al Morgan	.50	1.25	2.00	
C307	The Case of the Forgotten Murder - Erle Stanley Gardner	.75	1.50	3.00	(M)
C308	Letter from Peking - Pearl S. Buck	.50	1.25	2.00	
C309	The Case of the Sulky Girl - Erle Stanley Gardner	.75	1.50	3.00	(M)
C310	Fairoaks - Frank Yerby	.50	1.25	2.00	
C311	The Final Hour - Taylor Caldwell	.50	1.25	2.00	
C312	Remembered Death - Agatha Christie	.75	1.50	3.00	(M)
C313	Cash McCall - Cameron Hawley	.50	1.25	2.00	
C314	A Parent's Guide to Children's Reading - Nancy Larrick	.50	1.25	2.00	(NF)
C315	Kings Go Forth - Joe David Brown	.50	1.25	2.00	
C316	Odds Against Tomorrow - William P. McGivern	.50	1.25	2.00	
C317	The Diary of a Young Girl - Anne Frank	.50	1.25	2.00	
C318	What Mrs. McGillicuddy Saw! - Agatha Christie	.75	1.50	3.00	(M)
C319	New Tales of Space and Time - Raymond J. Healy	.50	1.25	2.00	(NF)
	1959				
C320	The Case of the One-Eyed Witness - Erle Stanley Gardner	.75	1.50	3.00	(M)
C321	On the Midnight Tide - Don Tracy	.50	1.25	2.00	
C322	To Have and to Hold - Mary Johnston	.50	1.25	2.00	
C323	The Case of the Demure Defendant - Erle Stanley Gardner	.75	1.50	3.00	(M)
C324	The Case of the Curious Bride - Erle Stanley Gardner	.75	1.50	3.00	(M)
C325	The Case of the Haunted Husband - Erle Stanley Gardner	.75	1.50	3.00	(M)
	1959				
C326	Jamaica Inn - Daphne du Maurier	.50	1.25	2.00	
C327	"Where Did You Go?" "Out" "What Did You Do?" "Nothing" - Robert Paul Smith	.50	1.25	2.00	
C328	The Year the Yankees Lost the Pennant - Douglass Wallop	.50	1.25	2.00	
C329	The Case of the Lucky Legs - Erle Stanley Gardner	.75	1.50	3.00	(M)
C330	Kids Say the Darndest Things! - Art Linkletter	.50	1.25	2.00	(H)
C331	The Pocket Book of Esquire Cartoons	.50	1.25	2.00	(H)
C332	The Case of the Cautious Coquette - Erle Stanley Gardner	.75	1.50	3.00	(M)
C333	The Trail Driver - Zane Grey	.50	1.25	2.00	(W)
C334	The Angry Wife - Pearl S. Buck	.50	1.25	2.00	
C335	Death Comes as the End - Agatha Christie	.75	1.50	3.00	(M)
C336	White Banners - Lloyd C. Douglas	.50	1.25	2.00	
C337	The Case of the Gilded Lily - Erle Stanley Gardner	.75	1.50	3.00	(M)
C338	The Immortal - Walter Ross	.50	1.25	2.00	
C339	Dragonwyck - Anya Seton	.50	1.25	2.00	
C340	The Man who Broke Things - John Brooks	.50	1.25	2.00	
C341	The Case of the Lucy Loser - Erle Stanley Gardner	.75	1.50	3.00	(M)
C342	Young Mr. Keefe - Stephen Birmingham	.50	1.25	2.00	
C343	The Finishing Stroke - Ellery Queen	.75	1.50	3.00	(M)
C344	The Lady in the Lake - Raymond Chandler	1.00	2.00	4.00	(M)
C345	The D.A. Cooks a Goose - Erle Stanley Gardner	.75	1.50	3.00	(M)
C346	The D.A. Draws a Circle - Erle Stanley Gardner	.75	1.50	3.00	(M)
C347	The D.A. Goes to Trial - Erle Stanley Gardner	.75	1.50	3.00	(M)
C348	The D.A. Holds a Candle - Erle Stanley Gardner	.75	1.50	3.00	(M)
C349	Peril at End House - Agatha Christie	.75	1.50	3.00	(M)
C350	A Gift from the Boys - Art Buchwald	.50	1.25	2.00	
	1959				
C351	Valley of Wild Horses - Zane Grey	.50	1.25	2.00	(W)
C352	The Serpent and the Staff - Frank Yerby	.75	1.50	3.00	(A)
C353	The Nine Lives of Michael Todd - Art Cohn	.75	1.50	3.00	(NF)
C354					
C355	The Case of the Vagabond Virgin - Erle Stanley Gardner	.75	1.50	3.00	(M)

155

C356	Dear Abby - Abigail Van Buren	.50	1.25	2.00	(NF)
C357	Cat of Many Tails - Ellery Queen	.75	1.50	3.00	(M)
C358	Power Golf - Ben Hogan	.50	1.25	2.00	(S)
C359	The Low Calorie Diet - Marvin Small	.50	1.25	2.00	(NF)
C360	And Then There were None - Agatha Christie	.75	1.50	3.00	(M)
C361	Towards Zero - Agatha Christie	.75	1.50	3.00	(M)
C362	A Murder Is Announced - Agatha Christie	.75	1.50	3.00	(M)
C363	Lady Chatterley's Lover - D. H. Lawrence	.50	1.25	2.00	
C364	The 1959 Pro Football Handbook - Don Schiffer	.75	1.50	3.00	(S)
C365	Return of the Eagles - F. Van Wyck Mason	.50	1.25	2.00	
C366					
C367	The Foxes of Harrow - Frank Yerby	.50	1.25	2.00	
C368	Lucky Larribee - Max Brand	.50	1.25	2.00	
C369					(W)
C370	Action by Night - Ernest Haycox	.50	1.25	2.00	(W)
C371					
C372	The Long Love - Pearl S. Buck	.50	1.25	2.00	
C373	The Crossing - Clay Fisher	.50	1.25	2.00	(W)
C374					
C375					
	1959				
C376	The Case of the Dubious Bridegroom - Erle Stanley Gardner	.75	1.50	3.00	(M)

CARDINAL EDITIONS

GC Series

(Pocket Books, Inc.)

GC 1	The Cardinal - Henry Morton Robinson 1953	.50	1.25	2.00	
GC 2	Three Harbours - F. Van Wyck Mason	.50	1.25	2.00	
GC 3	Buddenbrooks - Thomas Mann	.50	1.25	2.00	
GC 4	The Story of Philosophy - Will Durant	.50	1.25	2.00	(NF)
GC 5	The Story of Mankind - Hendrik Willem Van Loon	.50	1.25	2.00	(NF)
GC 6	Stars on the Sea - F. Van Wyck Mason	.50	1.25	2.00	
GC 7	Langenscheidt's German-English, English-German Dictionary	.50	1.25	2.00	(NF)
GC 8	Oh, Promised Land - James Street	.50	1.25	2.00	
GC 9	Eagle in the Sky - F. Van Wyck Mason	.50	1.25	2.00	
GC 10	The Cruel Sea - Nicholas Monsarrat	.50	1.25	2.00	
GC 11	Napoleon - Emil Ludwig 1954	.50	1.25	2.00	(NF)
GC 12	The Wall - John Hersey	.50	1.25	2.00	
GC 13	The Office Encyclopedia - N. H. Mager, S. K. Mager	.50	1.25	2.00	(NF)
GC 14	The Devil Rides Outside - John Howard Griffin	.50	1.25	2.00	
GC 15	Immortal Poems of the English Language - Oscar Williams	.50	1.25	2.00	
GC 16	The Pocket Book of Modern Verse - Oscar Williams	.50	1.25	2.00	
GC 17	Proud New Flags - F. Van Wyck Mason	.50	1.25	2.00	
GC 18	The Pocket Guide to Birds - Allen D. Cruickshank	.50	1.25	2.00	(NF)
GC 19	The Pocket Household Encyclopedia - N. H. Mager, S. K. Mager	.50	1.25	2.00	(NF)
GC 20	The Female - Paul I. Wellman	.50	1.25	2.00	
GC 21	Marie Antoinette - Stefan Zweig	.50	1.25	2.00	
GC 22	Desiree - Annemarie Selinko	.50	1.25	2.00	
GC 23	The Lincoln Reader - Abraham Lincoln 1955	1.00	2.00	4.00	
GC 24	Larousse's French-English, English-French Dictionary	.50	1.25	2.00	(NF)
GC 25	The Whitman Reader - Walt Whitman 1955	.50	1.25	2.00	
GC 26	The Big Money - John Dos Passos	.50	1.25	2.00	
GC 27	Understanding Surgery - Robert E. Rothenberg	.50	1.25	2.00	(NF)
GC 28	Youngblood - John O. Killens	.50	1.25	2.00	
GC 29	An Act of Love - Ira Wolfert	.50	1.25	2.00	
GC 30	The Doctors Mayo - Helen Clapesattle 1956	.50	1.25	2.00	(NF)

GC 31	The Egyptian - Mika Waltari	.50	1.25	2.00	(A)
GC 32	Love is Eternal - Irving Stone	.50	1.25	2.00	
GC 33	A Baby's First Year - Benjamin Spock	.50	1.25	2.00	(NF)
GC 34	The Adventurer - Mika Waltari	.50	1.25	2.00	
GC 35	My Several Worlds - Pearl S. Buck	.50	1.25	2.00	
GC 36	The Nazarene - Sholem Asch	.50	1.25	2.00	
GC 37	The Search for Bridey Murphy - Morey Bernstein	.50	1.25	2.00	
GC 38	The Apostle - Sholem Asch	.50	1.25	2.00	
GC 39	Masters of Deceit - J. Edgar Hoover	.50	1.25	2.00	
GC 40	Baby and Child Care - Benjamin Spock	.50	1.25	2.00	(NF)
GC 41	Imperial Woman - Pearl S. Buck 1958	.50	1.25	2.00	
GC 42	King of Paris - Guy Endore	.50	1.25	2.00	(A)
GC 43	Moses - Sholem Asch	.50	1.25	2.00	
GC 44	Language for Everybody - Mario Pei	.50	1.25	2.00	(NF)
GC 45	The FBI Story - Don Whitehead	.50	1.25	2.00	
GC 46	The Townsman - Pearl S. Buck	.50	1.25	2.00	
GC 47	Mondadori's Pocket Italian-English, English-Italian Dictionary - Alberto Tedeschi	.50	1.25	2.00	(NF)
GC 48	A Stillness at Appomattox - Bruce Catton	.75	1.50	3.00	(NF)
GC 49	The Prophet - Sholem Asch	.50	1.25	2.00	
GC 50	Faster Reading Self-Taught - Harry Shefter 1958	.50	1.25	2.00	(NF)
GC 51	The Family of Man - Edward Steichen	.50	1.25	2.00	
GC 52	Baruch: My Own Story - Bernard Baruch	.50	1.25	2.00	(NF)
GC 53	The Robe - Lloyd C. Douglas	.50	1.25	2.00	
GC 54	The Nun's Story - Kathryn Hulme	.50	1.25	2.00	
GC 55	Kings Row - Henry Bellamann	.50	1.25	2.00	
GC 56	Strangers When we Meet - Evan Hunter 1959	.50	1.25	2.00	
GC 57	Madame Curie - Eve Curie	.50	1.25	2.00	(NF)
GC 58	The Kodak Camera Guide	.50	1.25	2.00	(NF)
GC 59	The Big Fisherman - Lloyd C. Douglas	.50	1.25	2.00	
GC 60	Diccionario del Idioma Espanol - Edwin B. Williams	.50	1.25	2.00	(NF)
GC 61	The Roots of Heaven - Romain Gary	.50	1.25	2.00	
GC 62	Generation of Vipers - Philip Wylie	.50	1.25	2.00	
GC 63					
GC 64					
GC 65	A Summer Place - Sloan Wilson	.50	1.25	2.00	
GC 66	Madison Avenue, U.S.A. - Martin Mayer	.50	1.25	2.00	
GC 67	High-Speed Math Self-Taught - Lester Meyers	.50	1.25	2.00	(NF)
GC 68	The Best of Everything - Rona Jaffe	.50	1.25	2.00	
GC 69	The Stars in the Making - Cecilia Payne-Gaposchkin	.50	1.25	2.00	
GC 70	Devils, Drugs and Doctors - Howard W. Haggard	.50	1.25	2.00	(NF)
GC 71					
GC 72	Parrish - Mildred Savage	.50	1.25	2.00	
GC 73	The Day Christ Died - Jim Bishop	.50	1.25	2.00	
GC 74					
GC 75	Ben-Hur - Lew Wallace 1959	.50	1.25	2.00	(A)
GC 76	Microbe Hunters - Paul Oekrulf	.50	1.25	2.00	NF
GC 77	The Winthrop Woman - Anya Seton 1953	.50	1.25	2.00	NF
nn	The 1954 Pocket Almanac 1954	.50	1.25	2.00	NF
GC1955	The 1955 Pocket Almanac 1955	.50	1.25	2.00	NF
GC1956	The 1956 Pocket Almanac 1956	.50	1.25	2.00	NF
GC750	The English-Portuguese Pocket Dictionary - Hygino Allandro	.50	1.25	2.00	NF
GC751	Cash McCall - Cameron Hawley 1957	.50	1.25	2.00	
GC752	Katherine - Anya Seton	.50	1.25	2.00	
GC753	Something of Value - Robert Ruark	.50	1.25	2.00	
GC754	1958				
GC755	The Tribe that Lost Its Head - Nicholas Monsarrat	.50	1.25	2.00	

GC756 Compulsion - Meyer Levin 1959	.50	1.25	2.00
GC757 The Last Angry Man - Gerald Green	.50	1.25	2.00

CARNIVAL

(Hanro Corporation)

Digest size

901 A Body to Own - Robert W. Harmon 1952, aka Pickup, aka Sacrifice	1.50	3.50	5.00	E
902 Midnight Sinners - John Caldwall	1.50	3.50	5.00	E
903 Lovers Bewitched - William E. Gordon	1.50	3.50	5.00	E
904 Borrowed Ecstasy - Watkins E. Wright aka Wild Passion	1.50	3.50	5.00	E
905 Strangers in the Dark - Peggy Gaddis aka Pushover, c-Gross	1.50	3.50	5.00	E
907 Tempting Tigress - John Underwood aka Bedtime Blonde	1.50	3.50	5.00	E
908 Girl-Hungry - William E. Gordon aka The Transgressor	1.50	3.50	5.00	E
910 Pick-Up - Albert L. Quandt aka Ticket to Passion	1.50	3.50	5.00	E
911 Affairs of a Ward Nurse - Mitchell Coleman aka Born to Be Bad	1.50	3.50	5.00	E
912 Wild Party - Frederic Spencer	1.50	3.50	5.00	E
913 Affairs of a Career Girl - Mitchell Coleman 1953, aka Fast, Loose, and Lovely, c-Gross	1.50	3.50	5.00	E
914 Girl of the Slums - Raymond Blair	1.50	3.50	5.00	E
916 Passion's Harvest - Peggy Gaddis aka Woman of Fire, c-Gross	1.50	3.50	5.00	E
918 Rapture Alley - Whit Harrison 1953	2.00	4.00	7.50	E
920 Hotel Waitress - Gene Harvey	1.50	3.50	5.00	E
924 Pick-Up - Albert L. Quandt 1954, aka Ticket to Passion	1.50	3.50	5.00	E
925 Reckless! - Kermit Welles aka Pleasure Bound	1.50	3.50	5.00	E
928 Frenchie - David Charlson	1.50	3.50	5.00	E
931 Backwoods Shack - Hallam Whitney	1.50	3.50	5.00	E
956 Big-Town Hellcat - Amos Hatler aka On Borrowed Love	1.50	3.50	5.00	E

CAVALCADE

(Delta Library, Inc.)

Digest size

nn Madman on a Drum	2.00	4.00	7.50	M
1 Men are Molehills - Ruth S. Livingston 1946	2.00	4.00	7.50	R

Carnival 904, c. Hanro

Carnival 914, c. Hanro

Carnival 918, c. Hanro

Cavalcade 2, c. Delta

Century 12, c. Cen

Century 18, c. Cen

(CAVALCADE, continued)
2 Magic for Murder - Armstrong Livingston   2.00   4.00   7.50   M

CENTURY

(Century Publications)

Some digest size

10 The Man Who Murdered Himself - Geoffrey Holmes Digest size	3.00	6.00	12.00	M
12 Murder without Makeup - Elda Benjamin Digest size	2.50	6.00	10.00	M
13 Here Comes the Corpse - George Bagby Digest size	3.00	6.00	12.00	M
14 Disagnosis: Murder - Rufus King Digest size	3.00	6.00	12.00	M
15 Ghost Trails - W. C. Tuttle Digest size	2.50	6.00	10.00	W
16 Renegade Roundup - William Colt MacDonald Digest size	2.50	6.00	10.00	W
17 As Good as Murdered - James O'Hanlon	2.50	6.00	10.00	M
18 Stab in the Back - Philip Wylie Digest size				M
Bottom Deal - Judson Philips	3.00	6.00	12.00	M
19 Fair Warning - Mignon E. Eberhart	3.00	6.00	12.00	M
20 Gun Bulldogger - Eugene Cunningham Digest size	2.50	6.00	10.00	M
21 The Sulu Sea Murders - Van Wyck Mason Digest size	3.00	6.00	12.00	M
23 Death Came Dancing - Kathleen Moore Knight Digest size	3.00	6.00	12.00	M
25 Time Off for Murder - Zelda Popkin	2.50	6.00	10.00	M
26 Fallen Angel - Marty Holland	3.00	6.00	12.00	E
27 Picture of the Victim - John S. Strange Digest size	3.00	6.00	12.00	M

Century 23, c. Cen

Century 32, c. Cen

Century 58, c. Cen

28	Bad for Business - Rex Stout	3.00	6.00	12.00	M
29	All Concerned Notified - Helen Reilly	2.50	6.00	10.00	M
30	Weekend to Kill - Frederick Nebel				M
	Secret Corridors - Hugh Pentecost	3.00	6.00	12.00	M
	Digest size				
31	The Dark Corner - Leonard Q. Ross	3.00	6.00	12.00	M
	Movie tie-in				
32	The Shanghai Bund Murders - Van Wyck				
	Mason	3.00	6.00	12.00	M
	Digest size				
33	Corpses at Indian Stone - Philip Wylie	2.50	6.00	10.00	M
	Digest size				
34	Red Gardenias - Jonathan Latimer	2.50	6.00	10.00	M
	Digest size				
35	The Glass Slipper - Mignon Eberhardt	2.50	6.00	10.00	M
	Digest size				
37	Singapore - Wm Bogert	3.00	6.00	10.00	M
	Movie tie-in, Digest size				
52	No Nice Girl - Perry Lindsay	2.00	4.00	7.50	E
53	Death Rides the Mesa - Tom Gill	2.00	4.00	7.50	W
54	Scarlet Sin - John Saxon	2.00	4.00	7.50	E
55	Love Business - William Arthur	2.00	4.00	7.50	E
55	Don Desperado - L. L. Foreman	2.00	4.00	7.50	W
56	The Phantom Pass - William Colt MacDonald	2.00	4.00	7.50	W
56	Cue for Passion - Gordon Semple	2.00	4.00	7.50	E
57	Buckskin Empire - H. S. Drago	2.00	4.00	7.50	W
58	Gringo Gunfire - Bliss Lomar (H. S. Drago)	2.00	4.00	7.50	W
	Digest size				
59	Secret of the Wasteland - Bliss Lomax	2.00	4.00	7.50	W
60	Peace Marshall - Frank Gruber	2.00	4.00	7.50	W
61	One More Lover - Thomas Stone	2.00	4.00	7.50	E
61	Roaring Lead - William Colt MacDonald	2.00	4.00	7.50	W
62	Colt Comrades - Bliss Lomax (H. S. Drago)	2.00	4.00	7.50	W
63	Body and Soul - Sam Merwin, Jr.	2.50	6.00	10.00	
	Movie tie-in, Digest size				
64	Outlaw - Frank Gruber	2.00	4.00	7.50	W
66	Sleep My Love - Leonard Q. Ross	2.00	4.00	7.50	E
67	No Nice Girl - Perry Lindsay	2.00	4.00	7.50	E
68	A Double Life - Manly Wade Wellman	2.50	6.00	10.00	
	Movie tie-in				
69	California Caballero - William Colt				
	MacDonald	2.00	4.00	7.50	W
70	Cairo Garter Murders - Van Wyck Mason	2.00	4.00	7.50	M
71	Sign of the Gun - Archie Joscelyn	2.00	4.00	7.50	W
72	Gunsight - Frank Gruber	2.00	4.00	7.50	W
73	Saddles West - H. B. Hickey	2.00	4.00	7.50	W
74	Notched Guns - William Hopson	2.00	4.00	7.50	W
75	Scarlet Sin - John Saxon	2.00	4.00	6.00	E
76	Powdersmoke Range - W. C. MacDonald	2.00	4.00	7.50	W
77	Blonde Trouble - Perry Lindsay	2.00	4.00	6.00	E
78	Gunsmoke - Lee Floren	2.00	4.00	7.50	W
79	Love Business - William Arthur	2.00	4.00	6.00	E
80	Cue for Passion - Gordon Semple	2.00	4.00	6.00	E
81	Dryguich Canyon - F. M. Bechdolt	2.00	4.00	7.50	W
	Digest size				
82	Ranger Justice - J. E. Grinstead	2.00	4.00	7.50	W
83	Ripe for Love - Carmen Snow	2.00	4.00	6.00	E
84	Marriage is for Two - Phyllis Arthur	2.00	4.00	6.00	E
85	Unashamed - Perry Lindsay	2.00	4.00	6.00	E
86	Bad Company - Gordon Semple	2.00	4.00	6.00	E
87	One More Lover - Thomas Stone	2.00	4.00	6.00	E
89	Common Passion - John Saxon	2.00	4.00	6.00	E
90	Too Loose - Carlotta Baker	2.00	4.00	6.00	E
91	Scandalous - Ralph Carter	2.00	4.00	6.00	E
92	Outlaw Justice - Leigh Carder	2.00	4.00	7.50	W
93	Fleshpots - Florenz Branch	2.00	4.00	7.50	E
94	Passion's Way - Gordon Semple	2.00	4.00	6.00	E
95	Teaser - Craig Shepard	2.00	4.00	6.00	E
96	Body for Sale - Eliot Brewster	2.00	4.00	6.00	E
97	Call it Love - Hall Bennett	2.00	4.00	6.00	E
98	Quick Passion - Ralph Carter	2.00	4.00	6.00	E
99	Nice and Naughty - Gordon Semple	2.00	4.00	6.00	E
100	Dark Memory - Jonathan Latimer	2.00	4.00	7.50	E
101	Bright Star of Danger - W. C. Chambers	2.00	4.00	7.50	
102	Hot Gold - Frederick R. Bechdolt	2.00	4.00	7.50	W
	Digest size				

Century 106, c. Cen

Century 116, c. Cen

Century 120, c. Cen

(CENTURY, continued)

103	Without Reservations - Jane Allen	2.00	4.00	6.00	E
104	The Green Man - Harold Sherman Digest size	2.50	6.00	10.00	SF
105	Man-Handled - Eliot Brewster	2.00	4.00	6.00	E
106	Marriage Later - William Arthur	2.00	4.00	6.00	E
107	Inherited Husband - Cecile Gilmore	2.00	4.00	6.00	E
108	Kept Woman - John Saxon	2.00	4.00	6.00	E
109	Passion's Lesson - Gordon Semple	2.00	4.00	6.00	E
110	Three Time Sin - Thomas Stone	2.00	4.00	6.00	E
111	Sinner Take All - William Arthur	2.00	4.00	6.00	E
112	Profane - Ralph Carter	2.00	4.00	6.00	E
113	Sinful Lady - Gordon Semple	2.00	4.00	6.00	E
114	Passion's Program - Florenz Branch	2.00	4.00	6.00	E
115	Two Time Lover - Gordon Semple	2.00	4.00	6.00	E
116	Time Trap - Rog Phillips 1949	3.00	6.00	12.00	SF
117	Red for Passion - Thomas Stone	2.00	4.00	6.00	E
118	Desperato - William Hopson	2.00	4.00	7.50	W
119	Love Slave - Gail Jordan	2.00	4.00	6.00	E
120	Forbidden Sin - William Arthur aka Burlesque Girl	2.00	4.00	6.00	E
121	Voluptueous - Charles Thornton	2.00	4.00	6.00	E
122	Passion's Sin - Ralph Carter aka The Quiet Passion	2.00	4.00	6.00	E
123	Past Folly - Florenz Branch	2.00	4.00	6.00	E
124	Worlds Within - Rog Phillips	2.50	6.00	10.00	SF
125	Trigger Trails - Hamilton Craigie	2.00	4.00	7.50	W
126	Street Girl - Eliot Brewster	2.00	4.00	6.00	E
127	Charming Sinner - Barry DeForest aka Partners in Sin	2.00	4.00	6.00	E
128	Bullet Trail - Burt Arthur	2.00	4.00	7.50	W
129	Tombstone Stage - William Hopson	2.00	4.00	7.50	W
130	Sinful Love - William Arthur aka Redhead	2.00	4.00	6.00	E
131	Reckless Range - Johnston McCulley	2.00	4.00	7.50	W
132	Six Gun Stampede - Jackson Cole	2.00	4.00	7.50	W
133	California Trail - H. Bedford Jones	2.00	4.00	7.50	W
135	Saddle Wolves - Allan K. Echols	2.00	4.00	7.50	W
136	Headed for a Hearse - Jonathan Latimer	2.00	4.00	7.50	M

Century 128, c. Cen

Century 135, c. Cen

Chartered 26, c. Bond-Charteris

CHARTERED
(Bond-Charteris Pub./Saint Enterprises, Inc.)
Digest size

16	I'll Hate Myself in the Morning - Elliott Paul	2.00	4.00	7.50	M
17	The Saint's Choice of Hollywood Crime Stories - ed. Leslie Charteris	2.00	4.00	7.50	M
18	Deadlier than the Male - James Gunn	2.00	4.00	7.50	M
19					
20					
21	Seven Slayers - Paul Cain	2.00	4.00	7.50	M
22	The Man Who Limped - Otis Adelbert Kline First ed., 1946	7.50	15.00	30.00	SF
23					
24					
25	The Last Door bell - Frank Gruber	2.00	4.00	7.50	M
26	The Brighter Buccaneer - Leslie Charteris	2.00	4.00	7.50	M
27	The Saint's Choice of Radio Thrillers - ed. Leslie Charteris	2.00	4.00	7.50	M
28	A Pocketful of Clues - James R. Langham	2.00	4.00	7.50	M

CHECKER BOOKS
(Checker Books, Inc.)

1	Terry and the Pirates: The Jewels of Jade - Edward J. Boylan, Jr. 1949, c-Wenzel	15.00	35.00	60.00	A
2	The Broadway Butterfly Murders - Tip Bliss	9.00	20.00	35.00	M
3	Make Mine Murder - Robert Bowen	9.00	20.00	35.00	M
4	Lost River Buckaroos - Charles M. Martin	7.50	15.00	30.00	W
5	Horror and Homicide - anthology 1949	10.00	25.00	40.00	M
6	Duke Herring - Maxwell Bodenheim 1949, c-Wenzell	9.00	20.00	35.00	M
7	Master-at-Arms - Rafael Sabatini 1949	7.50	15.00	30.00	A
8	Taxi - Abraham Bernstein	7.50	15.00	30.00	
9	The Florentine Dagger - Ben Hecht 1949	7.50	15.00	30.00	M
10	Lady, Mind that Corpse - Hank Janson 1949, c-Heade	10.00	25.00	40.00	M
11	The Practical Party Guide and Cook Book - Dorothy & Fifi Bannett	5.00	10.00	20.00	NF
12	Over 100 Best Cartoons - Patricia Fulford 1949	5.00	10.00	20.00	NF

COLUMBIA BROADCASTING SYSTEM

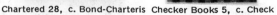

Chartered 28, c. Bond-Charteris   Checker Books 5, c. Check   Checker Books 6, c. Check

Checker Books 10, c. Check   Columbia Broadcasting nn, c. CBS   Comet Books 1, c. PKB

(Columbia Broadcasting System)

nn	From Pearl Harbor Into Tokyo - Orig., 1945	2.00	4.00	7.50	NF
nn	From D-Day through Victory in Europe - ed. Paul Hollister and Robert Strunsky Orig., 1945	2.00	4.00	7.50	NF

COMET BOOKS

(Pocket Books, Inc.)

Digest size, see Pocket Book Jr.

1	Wagons Westward - Armstrong Sperry 1948	2.00	4.00	7.50	W
2	Batter Up - Jackson Scholz	1.50	3.50	5.00	S
3	Star Spangled Summer - Janet Lambert	1.50	3.50	5.00	R
4	Tawny - Thomas C. Hinkle	1.50	3.50	5.00	A
5	300 Tricks You Can Do - Howard Thurston	1.50	3.50	5.00	NF
6	Peggy Covers the News - Emma Bugbee	1.50	3.50	5.00	
7	Winged Mystery - Alan Gregg	1.50	3.50	5.00	M
8	Your Own Joke Book - Gertrude Crampton	1.50	3.50	5.00	H
9	Sue Barton, Student Nurse - Helen Boylston	1.50	3.50	5.00	
10	The Tatooed Man - Howard Pease	1.50	3.50	5.00	A
11	Skycruiser - Howard M. Brier	1.50	3.50	5.00	
12	The Spanish Cave - Geoffrey Household	1.50	3.50	5.00	M
13	The Green Turtle Mystery - Ellery Queen Jr. 1949	2.00	4.00	7.50	M
14	Silver - Thomas C. Hinkle c-Powers	1.50	3.50	5.00	W
15	Strangers in the Desert - Alice Russell	1.50	3.50	5.00	
16	The Southpaw - Donal Hamilton Haines	1.50	3.50	5.00	S
17	Bat Boy of the Giants - Garth Garreau	1.50	3.50	5.00	S
18	Big Red - Jim Kjelgaard	1.50	3.50	5.00	
19	The Mystery of the Empty Room - Augusta Seaman	1.50	3.50	5.00	M
20	Husky: Co-Pilot of the Pilgrim - Rutherford Montgomery	1.50	3.50	5.00	
21	Starbuck Valley Winter - Roderick Haig-Brown	1.50	3.50	5.00	
22	Hobby Horse Hill - Lavinia R. Davis	1.50	3.50	5.00	
23	Your Own Party Book - Gertrude Crampton	1.50	3.50	5.00	NF
24	Gray Wolf - Rutherford Montgomery	1.50	3.50	5.00	
25	Fighting Coach - Jackson Scholz 1949, c-Powers	1.50	3.50	5.00	
26	Midnight - Rutherford Montgomery	1.50	3.50	5.00	
27	Forest Patrol - Jim Kjelgaard	1.50	3.50	5.00	
28	Scarface - Andre Norton	2.00	4.00	7.50	A
29	Lightning on Ice - Philip Harkins	1.50	3.50	5.00	S
30	No Other White Men - Julia Davis Interior Illustrations - Powers	2.00	4.00	7.50	
31	Indian Paint - Glen Balch	1.50	3.50	5.00	
32	Puppy Stakes - Betty Cavanna	1.50	3.50	5.00	
33	Long Wharf - Howard Pease	1.50	3.50	5.00	A
34	Fun With Puzzles - Joseph Leeming	1.50	3.50	5.00	NF

CREST BOOKS

(Fawcett Publications, Inc.)

114 Best Cartoons from True 1955	2.00	4.00	7.50	H
115 Run, Thief, Run - Frank Gruber	.75	1.75	3.00	M
116 Top Hand With a Gun - Harry Sinclair Drago	.75	1.75	3.00	W
117 Stranger at the Door - Gil Meynier	.75	1.75	3.00	
118 The Best from Captain Billy's Whizbang - Lester Grady	1.50	3.50	5.00	H
119 Love in Dishevelment - David Greenhood	.75	1.75	3.00	
120 Avenger from Texas - Will Ermine	.75	1.75	3.00	W
121 Affair - Emily Hahn	.75	1.75	3.00	
122 A Journey with Love - Denys Val Baker 1956	.75	1.75	3.00	
123 Riders by Night - Nelson Nye	.75	1.75	3.00	W
s124 The Golden Hussy - Octavus Roy Cohen	.75	1.75	3.00	
125 So Sweet, So Cruel - Julian Farren	.75	1.75	3.00	
126 Captive in the Night - Donald Stokes	.75	1.75	3.00	
127 The Education of a French Model - Kiki	.75	1.75	3.00	E
128 The Thundering Trail - Norman A. Fox	.75	1.75	3.00	W
s129 Son of the Giant - Stuart Engstrand	.75	1.75	3.00	
130 Jadie - I. S. Young	1.50	3.50	5.00	E
131 Gunsmoke on the Mesa - Davis Dresser	.75	1.75	3.00	W
132 Lie Down, Killer - Richard S. Prather	.75	1.75	3.00	M
s133 All My Sins - Norbert Estey	.75	1.75	3.00	E
134 Destination, Danger - William Colt MacDonald	.75	1.75	3.00	W
135 A Man's Affair - Dawn Powell	.50	1.25	2.00	
136 Down Through the Night - Julius Fast	.75	1.75	3.00	
137 War on the Range - Norman A. Fox	.75	1.75	3.00	W
138 The Memoirs of Maisie - Maude Hutchins 1956	.75	1.75	3.00	
139 So Nude, So Dead - Richard Marsten	.75	1.75	3.00	M
s140 Of Sin and the Flesh - Robert De Vries	.50	1.25	2.00	
141 Sex Withour Tears - Norman Lockridge & Virgil Partch	.75	1.75	3.00	H
142 Dagger of Flesh - Richard S. Prather	.75	1.75	3.00	M
s143 Hypnotism and the Power Within - S. J. VanPelt	.50	1.25	2.00	NF
s144 Come Desire Me - Anton Fereva	.75	1.75	3.00	
s145 You Can Live After Death - Harold Sherman	.50	1.25	2.00	
146 Code of the Gun - Gordon D. Shirreffs	.75	1.75	3.00	W
147 And the Girl Screamed - Gil Brewer	.75	1.75	3.00	E
s148 My First Two Thousand Years - Paul Eldridge & George Sylvester Viereck	1.50	3.50	5.00	F
149 The Comanche Scalp - William Colt MacDonald	.75	1.75	3.00	W
150 The Rule of the Pagbeasts - J. T. McIntosh aka The Fittest	2.00	4.00	7.50	SF
151 Saturday Night Town - Harry Whittington	.75	1.75	3.00	
152 Ambush at Buffalo Wallow - T. D. Allen	.75	1.75	3.00	W
153 The Golden Lure - Michael Barrett	.75	1.75	3.00	
154 Six-gun Vengeance - Dudley Dean	.75	1.75	3.00	W
155 Crazy Cartoons by VIP - Virgil Partch	.75	1.75	3.00	H
s156 The Trumpet Unblown - William Hoffman 1957	.75	1.75	3.00	W
d157 A Walk on the Wild Side - Nelson Algren	.75	1.75	3.00	
158 Badge for a Gunfighter - Clair Huffaker	.75	1.75	3.00	W
159 Office Laffs - Charles Preston	.75	1.75	3.00	H
d160 A Dream of Kings - Davis Grubb	.50	1.25	2.00	
161 Last Stand at Anvil Pass - Merle Constiner	.75	1.75	3.00	W
162 Seawife - J. M. Scott	.75	1.75	3.00	
s163 The Empire -- and Martin Brill - George deMare 1957	.50	1.25	2.00	
164 Gunswift - Stewart Gordon	.75	1.75	3.00	
165 The Right to Love - Markoosha Fischer	.75	1.75	3.00	
166 The Conquering Prince - Gardner F. Fox	1.50	3.50	5.00	A
167 Badman - Clair Huffaker Movie tie-in	1.50	3.50	5.00	W
s168 Way to Happiness - Fulton J. Sheen	.50	1.25	2.00	
169 Evil in the Night - Erico Verissimo	.75	1.75	3.00	
170 Fury Trail - Giles A. Lutz	.75	1.75	3.00	W
s171 Strangers in Paradise - Howard Otway	.75	1.75	3.00	
172 Case of the Brunette Bombshell - Hillary Waugh	.75	1.75	3.00	M

Crest Books 193, c. Faw   Crest Books 210, c. Faw   Crest Books 308, c. Faw

(CREST BOOKS, continued)

173	Little Tramp - Gil Brewer	1.50	3.50	5.00	E
174	Valley of Violent Men - Lewis B. Patten	.75	1.75	3.00	W
s175	The Loving and the Lost - James Lord	.50	1.25	2.00	
d176	Tom Jones - Henry Fielding	.75	1.75	3.00	
177	Border Renegade - Dudley Dean	.75	1.75	3.00	W
s178	The Spiked Heel - Richard Marsten	.75	1.75	3.00	
179	Walk With Evil - Robert Wilder	.75	1.75	3.00	
d180	According to Hoyle - Richard Frey	.50	1.25	2.00	NF
181	Gun the Man Down - Giles A. Lutz	.75	1.75	3.00	W
s182	Seed of Violence - Williams Forrest	.75	1.75	3.00	
s183	The Home Book of Italian Cooking - Angela Catanzaro	.50	1.25	2.00	NF
s184	City at World's End - Edmond Hamilton	1.50	3.50	5.00	SF
185	Top Gun - Gordon Donalds	.75	1.75	3.00	W
t186	The Heart Has Its Reasons - Duchess of Windsor	.50	1.25	2.00	
187	Whisper Their Love - Valerie Taylor	.75	1.75	3.00	E
s188	Beyond Defeat - Hans Werner Richter 1957	.75	1.75	3.00	
189	The Hell-Fire Kid - Steve Shannon	.75	1.75	3.00	W
s190	Sweepings - Lester Cohen	.50	1.25	2.00	
191	A Dram of Poison - Charlotte Armstrong	.75	1.75	3.00	M
192	Mantrap - Duane Yarnell	.75	1.75	3.00	E
193	Rider from Thunder Mountain - Clair Huffaker	.75	1.75	3.00	W
s194	And Come Back a Man - John Bell Clayton	.50	1.25	2.00	
195	Meet Morocco Jones - Jack Baynes	.75	1.75	3.00	M
196	The New Crest Crossword Puzzle Book - James Freeman	.75	1.75	3.00	NF
s197	Five Tales from Tomorrow - T. E. Dikty	.75	1.75	3.00	SF
198	West of Devil's Canyon - Richard Poole 1958	.75	1.75	3.00	
d199	Eastern Love - Edward Powys Mathers	1.50	3.50	5.00	
s200	Gas-House McGinty - James T. Farrell	.75	1.75	3.00	
s201	The Hungry Years - Annabel Johnson	.50	1.25	2.00	
t202	Mandingo - Kyle Onstott	.75	1.75	3.00	E
s203	House in Shanghai - Emily Hahn	.75	1.75	3.00	
s204	The Home Book of French Cooking - Anita Abbott & Lisa Andors	.50	1.25	2.00	NF
205	Texas Fury - John Callahan	.75	1.75	3.00	W
206	Baby Moll - Steve Brackeen	.75	1.75	3.00	
s207	Off Limits - Hans Habe	.75	1.75	3.00	
s208	The Magnificent Rascal - Thomas Sancton	.75	1.75	3.00	
s209	The 27th Day - John Mantley	1.50	3.50	5.00	SF
210	Swamp Babe - Robert Faherty	.75	1.75	3.00	E
211	High Hell - Steve Frazee	.75	1.75	3.00	W
s212	Night of Fire and Snow - Alfred Coppel 1958	.50	1.25	2.00	
213					
s214	Of Love Forbidden - Anna Elisabet Weirauch	.75	1.75	3.00	
s215	All Quiet on the Western Front - Erich Maria Remarque	.75	1.75	3.00	
s216	From the Earth to the Moon and Round the Moon - Jules Verne	.75	1.75	3.00	SF
s217	The Legion of the Damned - Sven Hassel	.75	1.75	3.00	
s218	A Fool There Was - John Manson	.50	1.25	2.00	
219	Dr. Anders' Dilemma - Henry & Sylvia Lieferaut	.50	1.25	2.00	
s220	The Best of Balzac - Honore de Balzac	.75	1.75	3.00	

s221 Yanqui's Woman - George McKenna	.75	1.75	3.00	
222 Posse from Hell - Clair Huffaker	.75	1.75	3.00	W
s223 How You Can Take Better Photos - Simon Nathan	.50	1.25	2.00	NF
224 Hand of the Mafia - Jack Baynes	.75	1.75	3.00	M
225 Root of Evil - James Cross	.75	1.75	3.00	
s226 Ralph 124C41+ - Hugo Gernsback	1.50	3.50	5.00	SF
s227 The Pink Hotel - Patrick Dennis & Dorothy Erskine	.75	1.75	3.00	
d228 The Durable Fire - Howard Swiggett	.50	1.25	2.00	
229 Wild - Gil Brewer	.75	1.75	3.00	E
230 The Widoe Wore Red - Richard Wormser	.75	1.75	3.00	M
s231 Awake Monique - Astrid Van Royen	.75	1.75	3.00	
d232 Blue Camellia - Frances Parkinson Keyes	.50	1.25	2.00	
s233 Small Town D. A. - Robert Traver	.50	1.25	2.00	
234 The Peeping Tom Murders - Jack Baynes	.75	1.75	3.00	M
235 The Red Sombrero - Nelson Nye	.75	1.75	3.00	W
s236 Stigma for Valor - Williams Forrest	.50	1.25	2.00	
s237 Ten Seconds to Hell - Lawrence Bachmann	.75	1.75	3.00	
238 The Vengeful Virgin - Gil Brewer	.75	1.75	3.00	E
1958				
239 Cartoon Laffs from True - Bill McIntyre	.75	1.75	3.00	H
s240 The Best of Crunch and Des - Philip Wylie	.75	1.75	3.00	
s241 The Power of Positive Living - Douglas Lurton	.50	1.25	2.00	NF
242 The Wind River Kid - Will Cook	.75	1.75	3.00	W
s243 The Dangerous Games - Tereska Torres	.75	1.75	3.00	
s244 The Unforgiven - J. Edward Leithead Movie tie-in	2.00	4.00	7.50	W
s245 Race to the Stars - Oscar J. Friend & Leo Margulies	.75	1.75	3.00	SF
246 The Long Nightmare - John Roeburt	.75	1.75	3.00	
247 Mask of Evil - Charlotte Armstrong	.75	1.75	3.00	M
248 End of a Call Girl - William Campbell Gault	.75	1.75	3.00	M
d249 The Black Obelisk - Erich Maria Remarque	.75	1.75	3.00	
s250 The Grand Seduction - Marcel Ayme	.75	1.75	3.00	
s251 The Doctor's Husband - Elizabeth Seifert	.50	1.25	2.00	R
s252 The House on the Beach - E. L. Withers	.50	1.25	2.00	
253 Murder Bait - Duane Yarnell	.75	1.75	3.00	M
s254 Bad Girls - Leo Margulies	.75	1.75	3.00	
255 Lie Down, Killer - Richard S. Prather	.75	1.75	3.00	M
d256 A Treasury of True - Charles N. Barnard	.50	1.25	2.00	
s257 Pappy's Women - Jack Gotshall	.75	1.75	3.00	E
s258 Six from Worlds Beyond - T. E. Dikty	.75	1.75	3.00	SF
s259 Devil's Prize - Samuel Edwards	.75	1.75	3.00	
260 Night Lady - William Campbell Gault	.75	1.75	3.00	
261 Gold at Kansas Gulch - Steve Frazee	.75	1.75	3.00	W
d262 Fun With Mathematics - Jerome S. Meyer	.50	1.25	2.00	NF
s263 Please Don't Eat the Daisies - Jean Kerr	.50	1.25	2.00	
1959				
d264 The Silver Mountain - Dan Cushman	.75	1.75	3.00	
s265 The Great Captains - Henry Treece	1.50	3.50	5.00	A
266 Clementine Cherie - Jean Bellus	.50	1.25	2.00	
s267 Edge of Twilight - Paula Christian	.75	1.75	3.00	
268 The Vanishing Vixen - Roy B. Sparkia	.75	1.75	3.00	
s269 The Great Religions by Which Men Live - Tynette Hills & Floyd H. Ross	.50	1.25	2.00	
s270 The Devil's Agent - Hans Habe	.75	1.75	3.00	
d271 Seven Keys to Koptic Court - Herbert D. Kastle	.75	1.75	3.00	
s272 Young and Deadly - Leo Margulies	.75	1.75	3.00	
s273 The Caves of Night - John Christoper	.75	1.75	3.00	
274 Fighting Rawhide - Lewis B. Patten	.75	1.75	3.00	W
s275 How to Retire and Enjoy It - Ray Giles	.50	1.25	2.00	NF
d276 The World's Ten Greatest Novels - W. Somerset Maugham	.50	1.25	2.00	
277 Dagger of Flesh - Richard S. Prather	.75	1.75	3.00	M
d278 Days in the Yellow Leaf - William Hoffman	.75	1.75	3.00	
s279 Enter Laughing - Carl Reiner	1.50	3.50	5.00	B
s280 The Damned Wear Wings - David Camerer	.75	1.75	3.00	
281 The Wayward Widow - William Campbell Gault	.75	1.75	3.00	E
s282 Three From Out There - Leo Margulies	.75	1.75	3.00	SF
s283 The Way to Inner Peace - Fulton J. Sheen	.50	1.25	2.00	
s284 How to Write and Speak Effective English - Edward Frank Allen	.50	1.25	2.00	NF
d285 Wine of Life - Charles Gorham	.50	1.25	2.00	

286	Dead Dolls Don't Talk - Day Keene	.75	1.75	3.00	M
287	The Cautious Bachelor - Sarel Eimerl	.50	1.25	2.00	
s288	Legacy of a Spy - Henry S. Maxfield	.75	1.75	3.00	
s289	Handsome's Seven Women - Theodore Pratt	.75	1.75	3.00	
s290	The Girls in 3-B - Valerie Taylor	.75	1.75	3.00	
s291	The Sergeant - Dennis Murphy	.75	1.75	3.00	
292	The Eighth Mrs. Bluebeard - Hillary Waugh	.75	1.75	3.00	M
d293	Steamboat Gothic - Frances Parkinson Keyes	.75	1.75	3.00	
294	Pardon My Blooper - Kermit Schafer	.75	1.75	3.00	H
s295	The Executioners - John D. MacDonald	1.50	3.50	5.00	M
296	Passport to Peril - Stephen Marlowe	.75	1.75	3.00	M
297	Doctor's Temptation - Henry & Sylvia Lieferant	.75	1.75	3.00	
298	In this Corner---Dennis the Menace - Hank Ketcham	.75	1.75	3.00	H
s299	The Way We Live Now - Warren Miller	.50	1.25	2.00	
d300	North from Rome - Helen MacInnes	.50	1.25	2.00	
s301	Shake Hands With the Devil - Rearden Conner	.75	1.75	3.00	
s302	The Girl Cage - Charles Mergendahl	.75	1.75	3.00	
303	Night of Violence - Louis Charbonneau	.75	1.75	3.00	
304	Creole Woman - Gardner F. Fox	1.50	3.50	5.00	E
d305	The Old Blood - Edgar Mittelholzer	.50	1.25	2.00	
s306	Sun in the Hunter's Eyes - Mark Derby	.50	1.25	2.00	
s307	The Horn - Clellon Holmes	.75	1.75	3.00	
s308	A Stir of Echoes - Richard Matheson	1.50	3.50	5.00	SF
309	Sweet Wild Wench - William Campbell Gault	.75	1.75	3.00	E
310	The Red Scarf - Gil Brewer	.75	1.75	3.00	
311	Crazy Cartoons by VIP - Virgil Partch	.75	1.75	3.00	H
d312	Showcase - Martin Dibner	.75	1.75	3.00	
313					
d314	Joy Street - Frances Parkinson Keyes	.75	1.75	3.00	
315	Rendezvous - Steve Frazee	.75	1.75	3.00	W
316	Danger in my Blood - Steve Brackeen	.75	1.75	3.00	
s317	The Insolent Chariots - John Keats	.50	1.25	2.00	H
s318	The Enjoyment of Love in Marriage - LeMon Clark	.50	1.25	2.00	NF
d319	Lost Summer - Christopher Davis	.50	1.25	2.00	
s320	Venus in Sparta - Louis Auchircloss	.75	1.75	3.00	
s321	The Shook-up Generation - Harrison S. Salisbury	.50	1.25	2.00	
s322	The Passionate City - Ian Stuart Black	.75	1.75	3.00	
323	You've Got Him Cold - Thomas B. Dewey	.75	1.75	3.00	
s324	Treasure Book of Fairy Tales - Ann McGovern	.75	1.75	3.00	
325	Morocco Jones in the Case of the Golden Angel - Jack Baynes	.75	1.75	3.00	M
t326	By Love Possessed - James Gould Cozzens	.75	1.75	3.00	
s327	Murder on the Mistral - Vincent Gaspard Malo	.75	1.75	3.00	M
s328	The Bystander - Albert Guerard	.75	1.75	3.00	
s329	The Star of Life - Edmond Hamilton	1.50	3.50	5.00	SF
d330	Tom Jones - Henry Fielding	.75	1.75	3.00	
s331	Drink and Be Merry - Lester Grady	.50	1.25	2.00	H
s332	Someone from the Past - Margot Bennett	.75	1.75	3.00	
d333	Victorine - Frances Parkinson Keyes	.75	1.75	3.00	
334	Kill My Love - Kyle Hunt	.75	1.75	3.00	M
s335	A Little Revolution - Paul Edmondson	.75	1.75	3.00	
s336	Strange Are the Ways of Love - Lesley Evans	.75	1.75	3.00	
s337	All Quiet on the Western Front - Erich Maria Remarque	.75	1.75	3.00	
d338	Lolita - Vladimir Nabokov 1959	1.50	3.50	5.00	
339	Lyn Darling, M. D. - Ray Dorien	.75	1.75	3.00	
340	Jimmy Hoffa's Hot - John Bartlow Martin	.75	1.75	3.00	
s341	The Badge - Jack Webb	1.50	3.50	5.00	M
s342	No Place on Earth - Louis Charbonneau	1.50	3.50	5.00	SF
s343	The Ruling Passion - George deMare	.75	1.75	3.00	
344	Meet Morocco Jones - Jack Baynes	.75	1.75	3.00	M

CRIME NOVEL SELECTION

(Red Circle Magazines, Inc.)

Digest size

(CRIME NOVEL SELECTION, continued)

1	Strangler's Holiday - Kurt Steel 1942, aka Murder in G-Sharp	2.00	4.00	7.50	M
4	Murder for What? - Kurt Steel	1.50	3.50	5.00	M
5	3 Girls and a Killer - H. Donald Spatz	1.50	3.50	5.00	M
nn	Death Is the Host - Lawrence Lariar 1943, aka Death Paints the Picture	1.50	3.50	5.00	M

CROSSWORD PLEASURE

(Crossword Pleasure, Inc.)

nn	Collector's Crosswords - with a Medical Twist - Jesse Jacobs First ed., 1961	1.50	3.50	5.00	NF
nn	Today's New, Enlarged Crossword Dictionary - David Shulman	1.50	3.50	5.00	NF

CROYDON

(Croydon Publishing Co./Star Publications, Inc.)

Digest size unless noted

nn	Vicious Circle - Manning Long 1945, c-Cole	2.50	6.00	10.00	M
nn	Many a Murder - Delia Van Deusen 1945, aka Murder Bicarb, c-Cole	2.50	6.00	10.00	M
nn	Murder's I've seen - Philip Mechem 1945, aka And Not for Love	2.00	4.00	7.50	M
nn	Slave of Desire - Gordon Semple Orig., 1951	2.00	4.00	7.50	E
nn	Here Lies Blood - M. M. Mannon	2.00	4.00	7.50	M
11	Cheaters at Love - Wright Williams c-Cole	2.50	6.00	10.00	E
13	Reckless Virgin - Glen Watkins c-Cole, Small size	2.50	6.00	10.00	E
14	Shadows of Lust - Ralph Carter c-Cole, Small size	2.50	6.00	10.00	E
15	Fool for Love - Wright Williams c-Cole, Small size	2.50	6.00	10.00	E
16	Sinner - Gordon Semple 1950, aka Life of Passion, c-Cole, Small size	2.50	6.00	10.00	E
17	Street of Sin - Wright Williams	2.00	4.00	7.50	E
20	The Shame at Vanna Gilbert - Glenn Watkins aka Sinful Life	1.50	3.50	5.00	E
24	Love-Hungry Doctor - Florence Stonebraker 1953	1.50	3.50	5.00	E
25	Spotlight on Sin - Duperrault	1.50	3.50	5.00	E
31	Army Mistress - William David Orig., 1953	1.50	3.50	5.00	E
36	Blonde Temptress - Gordon Semple Orig., 1953	1.50	3.50	5.00	E

Crossword Pleasure nn, c. Cross   Croydon nn, c. Croy   Croydon nn, c. Croy

Croydon 16, c. Croy   Croydon 17, c. Croy   Croydon 52, c. Croy

(CROYDON, continued)

39 Indiscretions of a French Model	1.50	3.50	5.00	E
40 Cellar Club Girl - Alan Bennett	2.00	4.00	7.50	E
44 Confessions of a B-Girl - Sim Albert	1.50	3.50	5.00	E
Orig., 1953				
45 Man-Hungry Widow - Peggy Gaddis	.75	1.75	3.00	E
49 Sinful Island Vacation - William Vaneer	1.50	3.50	5.00	E
52 Love Cult - William Vaneer	1.50	3.50	5.00	E
54 Scandalous French Doctor - Jean Calvert	1.50	3.50	5.00	E
Orig., 1954				
59 Scandals at a Country Club - Bart Frame	1.50	3.50	5.00	E
Orig., 1954				
60 Forbidden Passions - Wright Williams	1.50	3.50	5.00	E
aka Lust for Love				
63 Man-Crazy Hussy - Gordon Semple	.75	1.75	3.00	E
65 Indiscretions of a TV Sinner - Gordon Semple	.75	1.75	3.00	E
Orig., 1954				
69 Scandalous Nurse - Peggy Gaddis	.75	1.75	3.00	E
Orig., 1954				
70 Confessions of a Ladies Chauffeur - Florence				
Stonebraker	.75	1.75	3.00	E
72 Hoyden of the Mountains - D. Kingsland	.75	1.75	3.00	E
73 Woman-Crazy Doctor - S. Albert	.75	1.75	3.00	E
80 Lonely Soldiers - William David	.75	1.75	3.00	E
aka Army Mistress				
83 Affairs of a Party Girl - Bart Frame	.75	1.75	3.00	E
88 Maybelle - Georgia Girl in Harlem - Bart Frame	2.00	4.00	7.50	E
89 Shanty-Town Tease - Florence Stonebraker	.75	1.75	3.00	E
90 Man-Crazy Nurse - Peggy Gaddis	.75	1.75	3.00	E
92 Warped Desires - Gordon Semple	.75	1.75	3.00	E
93 Confessions of a B-Girl - S. Albert	.75	1.75	3.00	E
94 Tenement Girl - Alan Bennett	2.00	4.00	6.00	E
1955, aka Cellar Club Girl				
102 Shameful Love - Thomas Stone	.75	1.75	3.00	E
103 Sinner - Gordon Semple	.75	1.75	3.00	E
aka Life of Passion				
107 Intimate Affairs of a Sinful Model - J. Sherman	.75	1.75	3.00	E
110 Scandalous Career Girl - Gordon Semple	.75	1.75	3.00	E

CROYDON HOW-TO BOOKS

Croydon 73, c. Croy   Croydon 94, c. Croy   Croydon 107, c. Croy

(Croydon Publishing Company)

Digest size

11 The Giant Hobby Handbook 1953, c-Cole	2.00	4.00	6.00	NF

DAGGER HOUSE MYSTERY

(Dagger House, Inc.)

Digest size

24 If A Body Kill A Body - Peter Mortimer	2.00	4.00	7.50	M
26 You Can't Kill a Corpse - Louis Trimble 1947	2.00	4.00	7.50	M
28 Murder Makes a Marriage - Schuyler Broocks 1947	2.00	4.00	7.50	M

DEATH HOUSE

(William H. Wise & Co., Inc.)

Digest size

nn Vengeance Pulls the Trigger - Sturges Mason Schley aka Who'd Shoot a Genius?	2.00	4.00	7.50	M
nn Full Crash Dive - Allan R. Bosworth aka Murder Goes to Sea	2.00	4.00	7.50	M
nn Death Springs the Trap - Eaton K. Braithwaite aka You Did it	2.00	4.00	7.50	M
3 Murder on the Downbeat - Robert Avery	2.00	4.00	7.50	M
4 The Case of the Nameless Corpse - Eaton K. Braithwaite	2.00	4.00	7.50	M
5 Dead Reckoning - F. Bonnamy 5.00 10.00	2.00	4.00	7.50	M
6 Full Crash Dive - Allan R. Bosworth	2.00	4.00	7.50	M

DELL

(Dell Publishing Company, Inc.)

1 Death in the Library - Philip Ketchum 1943	15.00	35.00	60.00	M
2 Dead or Alive - Patricia Wentworth	7.50	15.00	30.00	M

Dagger House Myst. 26,
c. Dagger

Death House nn, c. WHW

Death House nn, c. WHW

Dell 1, c. Dell

Dell 13, c. Dell

Dell 19, c. Dell

(DELL, continued)

3 Murder-on-Hudson - Jennifer Jones	7.50	15.00	30.00	M
4 The American Gun Mystery - Ellery Queen aka Death at the Rodeo	5.00	10.00	20.00	M
5 Four Frightened Women - George Harmon Coxe	5.00	10.00	20.00	M
6 Ill Met by Moonlight - Leslie Ford	5.00	10.00	20.00	M
7 See You at the Morgue - Lawrence G. Blochman	5.00	10.00	20.00	M
8 The Tuesday Club Murders - Agatha Christie	5.00	10.00	20.00	M
9 Double for Death - Rex Stout	5.00	10.00	20.00	M
10 The Lone Wolf - Louis Joseph Vance	5.00	10.00	20.00	M
11 Hearses Don't Hurry - Stephen Ransome	5.00	10.00	20.00	M
12 Wife vs. Secretary - Faith Baldwin	4.00	8.00	15.00	R
13 Death Wears a White Gardenia - Zelda Popkin	5.00	10.00	20.00	M
14 The Doctor Died at Dusk - Geoffrey Homes	5.00	10.00	20.00	M
15 The Golden Swan Murder - Dorothy Cameron Disney	5.00	10.00	20.00	M
16 The Unicorn Murders - Carter Dickson	6.00	12.50	25.00	M
17 The Dead Can Tell - Helen Reilly	5.00	10.00	20.00	M
18 The Puzzle of the Silver Persian - Stuart Palmer	5.00	10.00	20.00	M
19 Death Over Sunday - James Francis Bonnell	5.00	10.00	20.00	M
20 Tambay Gold - Samuel Hopkins Adams	5.00	10.00	20.00	R
21 I Was a Nazi Flyer - Gottfried Leske	5.00	10.00	20.00	C
22 Homicide Holiday - Rufus King	5.00	10.00	20.00	M
23 The Private Practice of Michael Shayne - Bret Halliday	5.00	10.00	20.00	M
24 The Phantom of the Opera - Gaston Leroux	10.00	25.00	40.00	M
25 Speak No Evil - Mignon G. Eberhart	4.00	8.00	15.00	M
26 The Raft - Robert Trumbull	4.00	8.00	15.00	A
27 The Camera Clue - George Harmon Coxe	5.00	10.00	20.00	M
28 The Mountain Cat Murders - Rex Stout	5.00	10.00	20.00	M
29 Curtains for the Copper - Thomas Polsky	4.00	8.00	15.00	M
30 Memo to a Firing Squad - Frederick Hazlitt Brennan	4.00	8.00	15.00	C
31 The Fallen Sparrow - Dorothy B. Hughes	4.00	8.00	15.00	M
32 This Time for Keeps - John MacCormac	4.00	8.00	15.00	NF
33 Dance of Death - Helen McCloy 1944	4.00	8.00	15.00	M
34 Crime Hound - Mary Semple Scott	4.00	8.00	15.00	M

Dell 23, c. Dell

Dell 24, c. Dell

Dell 28 (back cover), c. Dell

35	The Cat Saw Murder - D. B. Olsen	4.00	8.00	15.00	M
36	The Hammersmith Murders - David Frome	4.00	8.00	15.00	M
37	Queen of the Flat-tops - Stanley Johnston	4.00	8.00	15.00	C
38	Liberty Laughs - Frances Cavanah & Ruth Weir	4.00	8.00	15.00	H
39	Murder Challenges Valcour - Rufus King	4.00	8.00	15.00	M
40	The Case of Jennie Brice - Mary Roberts Rinehart	4.00	8.00	15.00	M
41	The Man Who Didn't Exist - Geoffrey Homes	4.00	8.00	15.00	M
42	Murder at Scandal House - Peter Hunt	4.00	8.00	15.00	M
43	Midnight Sailing - Lawrence G. Blochman	4.00	8.00	15.00	M
44	Reply Paid - H. F. Heard	4.00	8.00	15.00	M
45	Too Many Cooks - Rex Stout	4.00	8.00	15.00	M
46	The Boomerang Clue - Agatha Christie	4.00	8.00	15.00	M
47	Keeper of the Keys - Earl Derr Biggers	5.00	10.00	20.00	M
48	The Cross-Eyed Bear Murders - Dorothy B. Hughes	4.00	8.00	15.00	M
49	The Feathered Serpent - Edgar Wallace	4.00	8.00	15.00	M
50	The Iron Spiders - Baynard Kendrick 1944	4.00	8.00	15.00	M
51	While the Wind Howled - Audrey Gaines	4.00	8.00	15.00	M
52	The Body that Wasn't Uncle - George Worthing Yates	4.00	8.00	15.00	M
53	Blood Money - Dashiell Hammett	7.50	15.00	30.00	M
54	Harvard Has a Homicide - Timothy Fuller	4.00	8.00	15.00	M
55	The D. A.'s Daughter - Herman Petersen	4.00	8.00	15.00	M
56	The Frightened Stiff - Kelley Roos	4.00	8.00	15.00	M
57	Murder at the White Cat - Mary Roberts Rinehart	4.00	8.00	15.00	M
58	Murder for the Asking - George Harmon Coxe	4.00	8.00	15.00	M
59	Turn on the Heat - A. A. Fair	4.00	8.00	15.00	M
60	Thirteen at Dinner - Agatha Christie	4.00	8.00	15.00	M
61	The Clue of the Judas Tree - Leslie Ford	4.00	8.00	15.00	M
62	The Strawstack Murder - Dorothy Cameron Disney	4.00	8.00	15.00	M
63	Mourned on Sunday - Helen Reilly	4.00	8.00	15.00	M
64	Blood on the Black Market - Brett Halliday	4.00	8.00	15.00	M
65	Scotland Yard Department of Queer Complaints - Carter Dickson	7.50	15.00	30.00	M
66	A Talent for Murder - Anna Mary Wells	4.00	8.00	15.00	
67	Hidden Ways - Frederic F. Van de Water	3.00	6.00	12.00	M
68	Juliet Dies Twice - Lange Lewis	3.00	6.00	12.00	M
69	Death from a Top Hat - Clayton Rawson 1945	4.00	8.00	15.00	M
70	The Red Bull - Rex Stout aka Some Buried Caesar	4.00	8.00	15.00	M
71	Murder in the Mist - Zelda Popkin	3.00	6.00	12.00	M
72	The Man in the Moonlight - Helen McCloy	3.00	6.00	12.00	M
73	Week-end Marriage - Faith Baldwin	3.00	6.00	12.00	R
74	The Murder that Had Everything - Hulbert Footner	3.00	6.00	12.00	M
75	The Affair of the Scarlet Crab - Clifford Knight 1945	3.00	6.00	12.00	M
76	Death in the Back Seat - Dorothy Cameron Disney	3.00	6.00	12.00	M
77	G. I. Jokes - Lou Nielsen	4.00	8.00	15.00	H
78	Murder Wears a Mummer's Mask - Brett Halliday	4.00	8.00	15.00	M

Dell 47, c. Dell

Dell 53, c. Dell

Dell 65, c. Dell

Dell 92, c. Dell   Dell 109, c. Dell   Dell 129, c. Dell

(DELL, continued)

79 The Hornet's Nest - Bruno Fischer	4.00	8.00	15.00	M
80 Prescription for Murder - Hannah Lees	3.00	6.00	12.00	M
81 The Glass Triangle - George Harmon Coxe	4.00	8.00	15.00	M
82 Curtains for the Editor - Thomas Polsky	3.00	6.00	12.00	M
83 With this Ring - Mignon G. Eberhart	3.00	6.00	12.00	M
84 Gold Comes in Bricks - A. A. Fair	3.00	6.00	12.00	M
85 The Savage Gentleman - Philip Wylie	4.00	8.00	15.00	A
86 The Man Who Murdered Goliath - Geoffrey Homes	4.00	8.00	15.00	M
87 Painted for the Kill - Lucy Cores	3.00	6.00	12.00	M
88 The Creeps - Anthony Abbot	5.00	10.00	20.00	M
89 Dell Book of Jokes - Frances Cavanah & Ruth Weir	4.00	8.00	15.00	H
90 A Man Called Spade - Dashiell Hammett	5.00	10.00	20.00	M
91 The Case of the Constant Suicides - John Dickson Carr	5.00	10.00	20.00	M
92 Suspense Stories - Alfred Hitchcock	7.50	15.00	30.00	M
93 Beyond the Dark - Kieran Abbey	3.00	6.00	12.00	
94 No Crime for a Lady - Zelda Popkin	3.00	6.00	12.00	
95 The Last Express - Baynard Kendrick	4.00	8.00	15.00	M
96 Skeleton Key - Lenore Glen Offord	3.00	6.00	12.00	
97 Trail Boss of Indian Beef - Harold Channing Wire	4.00	8.00	15.00	W
1946, aka Indian Beef				
98 Spring Harrowing - Phoebe Atwood Taylor	2.50	6.00	10.00	R
99 Now, Voyager - Olive Higgins Prouty	2.50	6.00	10.00	
100 The So Blue Marble - Dorothy B. Hughes	2.00	4.00	7.50	M
1946				
101 Murder with Pictures - George Harmon Coxe	4.00	8.00	15.00	
102 You Only Hang Once - H. W. Roden	4.00	8.00	15.00	M
103 Murder is a Kill-joy - Elisabeth Sanxay Holding	3.00	6.00	12.00	M
104 The Crooking Finger - Cleve F. Adams	3.00	6.00	12.00	M
105 Appointment with Death - Agatha Christie	4.00	8.00	15.00	M
106 Made Up to Kill - Kelley Roos	3.00	6.00	12.00	M
107 The Deadly Truth - Helen McCloy	3.00	6.00	12.00	M
108 Death in Five Boxes - Carter Dickson	5.00	10.00	20.00	M
109 Spill the Jackpot - A. A. Fair	3.00	6.00	12.00	M
110 Wall of Eyes - Margaret Millar	3.00	6.00	12.00	M
111 Greenmask - Jefferson Farjeon	3.00	6.00	12.00	M
112 Michael Shayne's Long Chance - Brett Halliday	3.00	6.00	12.00	M
113 The Whistling Hangman - Baynard Kendrick	3.00	6.00	12.00	M
114 Three Women in Black - Helen Reilly	2.50	6.00	10.00	M
115 The Broken Vase - Rex Stout	3.00	6.00	12.00	M
116 Honor Bound - Faith Baldwin	2.50	6.00	10.00	R
117 Women are Like That - Alice Elinor Lambert	2.50	6.00	10.00	R
118 Half Angel - Fanny Heaslip Lea	2.50	6.00	10.00	R
119 Robin Hill - Lida Larrimore	2.50	6.00	10.00	R
120 Man in the Saddle - Ernest Haycox	2.50	6.00	10.00	W
121 Footprints on the Ceiling - Clayton Rawson	3.00	6.00	12.00	M
122 Death in the Doll's House - Lawrence Bachmann & Hannah Lees	2.50	6.00	10.00	M
123 Too Many Bones - Ruth Sawtell Wallace	3.00	6.00	12.00	M
124 The Man in Lower Ten - Mary Roberts Rinehart	2.50	6.00	10.00	M
125 Dreadful Hollow - Irina Karlova	2.50	6.00	10.00	M
1946				

Dell 133, c. Dell

Dell 135, c. Dell

Dell 143, c. Dell

(DELL, continued)

126	Murderer's Choice - Anna Mary Wells	2.50	6.00	10.00	M
127	Old Bones - Herman Petersen	3.00	6.00	12.00	M
128	Murder and the Married Virgin - Brett Halliday	3.00	6.00	12.00	M
129	The Continental Op - Dashiell Hammett	7.50	15.00	30.00	M
130	The Harvey Girls - Samuel Hopkins Adams	2.50	6.00	10.00	
131	The Red Lamp - Mary Roberts Rinehart	2.50	6.00	10.00	
132	The Visitor - Carl Randau & Leane Zugsmith	2.50	6.00	10.00	
133	Cobweb House - Elizabeth Holloway	2.50	6.00	10.00	M
134	Wives to Burn - Lawrence G. Blochman	3.00	6.00	12.00	M
135	Meat for Murder - Lange Lewis	3.00	6.00	12.00	M
136	Wolf in Man's Clothing - Mignon G. Eberhart	3.00	6.00	12.00	M
137	Crimson Friday - Dorothy Cameron Disney	3.00	6.00	12.00	M
138	Men Are Such Fools - Faith Baldwin	3.00	6.00	12.00	R
139	Love—and the Countess to Boot - Jack Iams	2.50	6.00	10.00	R
140	Footprint of Cinderella - Philip Wylie	2.50	6.00	10.00	
141	The Swift Hour - Harriett Thurman	2.50	6.00	10.00	
142	Cold Steal - Alice Tilton	4.00	8.00	15.00	M
143	Bar the Doors! - Alfred Hitchcock	7.50	15.00	30.00	M
144	The White Brigand - Edison Marshall 1947	2.50	6.00	10.00	A
145	Murder in Mesopotamia - Agatha Christie	3.00	6.00	12.00	M
146	Alphabet Hicks - Rex Stout	3.00	6.00	12.00	M
147	The Lady is Afraid - George Harmon Coxe	3.00	6.00	12.00	M
148	Name Your Poison - Helen Reilly	3.00	6.00	12.00	M
149	The Blackbirder - Dorothy B. Hughes	2.50	6.00	10.00	M
150	Midsummer Nightmare - Christopher Hale 1947	2.50	6.00	10.00	M
151	Who's Calling? - Helen McCloy	2.50	6.00	10.00	M
152	Jokes, Gags and Wisecracks - Ted Shane	4.00	8.00	15.00	H
153	Western Stories - Gene Autry	4.00	8.00	15.00	W
154	Return of the Continental Op - Dashiell Hammett	7.50	15.00	30.00	M
155	Sailor, Take Warning! - Kelley Roos	3.00	6.00	12.00	M
156	Blow-down - Lawrence G. Blochman	3.00	6.00	12.00	M
157	Fire Will Freeze - Margaret Millar	3.00	6.00	12.00	M
158	The Devil in the Bush - Matthew Head	3.00	6.00	12.00	M
159	If a Body - George Worthing Yates	3.00	6.00	12.00	M
160	Double or Quits - A. A. Fair	2.50	6.00	10.00	M

Dell 144, c. Dell

Dell 158, c. Dell

Dell 172, c. Dell

Dell 175, c. Dell   Dell 185, c. Dell   Dell 207, c. Dell

(DELL, continued)

161 The Man Next Door - Mignon G. Eberhart	2.50	6.00	10.00	M
162 Odor of Violets - Baynard Kendrick	2.50	6.00	10.00	M
163 Self-made Woman - Faith Baldwin	2.50	6.00	10.00	R
164 The Left Leg - Alice Tilton	2.50	6.00	10.00	M
165 Wiped Out - John D. Newsom	3.00	6.00	12.00	A
166 The Wall - Mary Roberts Rinehart	2.50	6.00	10.00	M
167 White Fawn - Olive Higgins Prouty	2.50	6.00	10.00	
168 The Corpse Came Calling - Brett Halliday	2.50	6.00	10.00	M
169 Murdock's Acid Test - George Harmon Coxe aka The Barotique Mystery	2.50	6.00	10.00	M
170 Reluctant Millionaire - Maysie Greig	2.50	6.00	10.00	
171 Octagon House - Phoebe Atwood Taylor	2.50	6.00	10.00	M
172 Sad Cypress - Agatha Christie	4.00	8.00	15.00	M
173 Rim of the Pit - Hake Talbot	2.50	6.00	10.00	M
174 The Sheik - E. M. Hull	4.00	8.00	15.00	A
175 And So to Murder - Carter Dickson 1947	5.00	10.00	20.00	M
176 The Headless Lady - Clayton Rawson	4.00	8.00	15.00	M
177 The Hand in the Glove - Rex Stout	2.50	6.00	10.00	M
178 The Pink Camellia - Temple Bailey	2.50	6.00	10.00	R
179 Trail's End - William MacLeod Raine	2.50	6.00	10.00	W
180 The Rat Began to Gnaw the Rope - C. W. Grafton	2.50	6.00	10.00	M
181 Great Black Kanba - Gwenyth & Constance Little	3.00	6.00	12.00	M
182 No Time to Kill - George Harmon Coxe	3.00	6.00	12.00	M
183 American Acres - Louise Redfield Peattie	2.50	6.00	10.00	R
184 Murder is My Business - Brett Halliday	2.50	6.00	10.00	M
185 Too Busy to Die - H. W. Roden	4.00	8.00	12.00	M
186 She Ate Her Cake - Blair Treynor	2.00	4.00	7.50	M
187 N or M? - Agatha Christie	2.50	6.00	10.00	M
188 Splendid Quest - Edison Marshall	2.50	6.00	10.00	
189 Kind Are Her Answers - Mary Renault	2.50	6.00	10.00	R
190 Dead Man's Gift - Zelda Popkin	2.50	6.00	10.00	M
191 The Lady in the Tower - Katherine Newlin Burt	2.50	6.00	10.00	
192 Tugboat Annie - Norman Reilly Raine	2.50	6.00	10.00	
193 Scarecrow - Eaton K. Goldthwaite	2.50	6.00	10.00	M
194 The Innocent Mrs. Doff - Elisabeth Sanxay Holding	2.50	6.00	10.00	M
195 Beam Ends - Errol Flynn	2.50	6.00	10.00	A
196 Rich Girl, Poor Girl - Faith Baldwin	2.50	6.00	10.00	R
197 Kiss the Blood Off My Hands - Gerald Butler	2.50	6.00	10.00	M
198 The Glass Mask - Lenore Glen Offord	2.50	6.00	10.00	
199 The Secret of Chimneys - Agatha Christie	2.50	6.00	10.00	M
200 The Opening Door - Helen Reilly 1947	2.50	6.00	10.00	M
201 The First Men in the Moon - H. G. Wells	5.00	10.00	20.00	SF
202 Mrs. Murdock Takes a Case - George Harmon Coxe	2.00	4.00	7.50	M
203 The State vs. Elinor Norton - Mary Roberts Rinehart	2.00	4.00	7.50	
204 The Frightened Pigeon - Richard Burke	2.00	4.00	7.50	M
205 Dell Book of Crossword Puzzles - Kathleen Rafferty	5.00	10.00	20.00	NF
206 Hold Your Breath - Alfred Hitchcock	7.50	15.00	30.00	M

(DELL, continued)

207	The Crimson Feather - Sara Elizabeth Mason	4.00	8.00	15.00	M
208	The Black Curtain - Cornell Woolrich	3.00	6.00	12.00	M
209	The Iron Gates - Margaret Millar	2.50	6.00	10.00	M
210	Ride the Pink Horse - Dorothy B. Hughes 1948	2.50	6.00	10.00	M
211	Owls Don't Blink - A. A. Fair	2.50	6.00	10.00	M
212	Cue for Murder - Helen McCloy	2.50	6.00	10.00	M
213	Unidentified Woman - Mignon G. Eberhart	2.50	6.00	10.00	M
214	The Birthday Murder - Lange Lewis	2.50	6.00	10.00	M
215	Dr. Parrish, Resident - Sydney Thompson	2.50	6:00	10.00	R
216	Golden Earrings - Yolanda Foldes	2.50	6.00	10 00	
217	Gun Smoke Yarns - Gene Autry	3.00	6.00	12.00	W
218	H as in Hunted - Lawrence Treat	2.50	6.00	10.00	M
219	The Smell of Money - Matthew Head	2.50	6.00	10.00	
220	Hospital Nocturne - Alice Elinor Lambert	2.50	6.00	10.00	R
221	Dark Passage - David Goodis	2.50	6.00	10.00	
222	Marked for Murder - Brett Halliday	2.50	6.00	10.00	M
223	Hammett Homicides - Dashiell Hammett	5.00	10.00	20.00	M
224	How to Pick a Mate - Clifford Adams & Vance Packard	2.50	6.00	10.00	NF
225	Silent are the Dead - George Harmon Coxe 1948	2.50	6.00	10.00	M
226	Murder at the Vicarage - Agatha Christie	2.50	6.00	10.00	M
227	Trail Town - Ernest Haycox	2.50	6.00	10.00	W
228	Murder on Angler's Island - Helen Reilly	2.50	6.00	10.00	M
229	Murder within Murder - Richard & Frances Lockridge	4.00	8.00	15.00	M
230	Blind Man's Bluff - Baynard Kendrick	2.50	6.00	10.00	M
231	A Halo for Nobody - Henry Kane	2.50	6.00	10.00	M
232	The Rope Began to Hang the Butcher - C. W. Grafton	2.50	6.00	10.00	M
233	The Upstart - Edison Marshall	2.50	6.00	10.00	A
234	Student Nurse - Renee Shann	2.00	4.00	7.50	R
235	Red Threads - Rex Stout	3.00	6.00	12.00	M
236	Skyscraper - Faith Baldwin	2.50	6.00	10.00	R
237	House of Darkness - Allan MacKinnon	2.50	6.00	10.00	
238	Gunsight Pass - William MacLeod Raine	2.50	6.00	10.00	W
239	Candidate for Love - Maysie Greig	2.50	6.00	10.00	R
240	The Charred Witness - George Harmon Coxe	3.00	6.00	12.00	M
241	The Bat - Mary Roberts Rinehart	3.00	6.00	12.00	M
242	The Unafraid - Gerald Butler Movie tie-in	2.50	6.00	10.00	M
243	Owl's Don't Blink - A. A. Fair	2.50	6.00	10.00	M
244	Judas, Incorporated - Jaclen Steele	2.50	6.00	10.00	M
245	Wallflowers - Temple Bailey	2.50	6.00	10.00	R
246	Bar-20 Days - Clarence E. Mulford	2.50	6.00	10.00	W
247	One Angel Less - H. W. Roden	2.50	6.00	10.00	M
248	Dangerous Ground - Francis Wickware	2.50	6.00	10.00	M
249	Stars Still Shine - Lida Larrimore	2.50	6.00	10.00	R
250	Skyline Riders - Francis W. Hilton 1948	2.50	6.00	10.00	W
251	Banbury Bog - Phoebe Atwood Taylor	2.50	6.00	10.00	M
252	Benefit Performance - Richard Sale	2.50	6.00	10.00	
253	Treasure of the Brasada - Les Savage, Jr.	2.50	6.00	10.00	W
254	Bats Fly at Dusk - A. A. Fair	2.50	6.00	10.00	M
255	Enchanted Oasis - Faith Baldwin	2.50	6.00	10.00	R
256	Madonna of the Sleeping Cars - Maurice Dekobra	2.50	6.00	10.00	

Dell 217, c. Dell

Dell 223, c. Dell

Dell 235, c. Dell

Dell 262, c. Dell

Dell 264, c. Dell

Dell 265, c. Dell

(DELL, continued)

257	Murder in Retrospect - Agatha Christie	2.50	6.00	10.00	M
258	No Coffin for the Corpse - Clayton Rawson	4.00	8.00	15.00	M
259	Murder Wears Muklucks - Eunice Mays Boyd	2.50	6.00	10.00	M
260	Chinese Red - Richard Burke	2.50	6.00	10.00	M
261	Do Not Disturb - Helen McCloy	2.50	6.00	10.00	M
262	Rope - Alfred Hitchcock	7.50	15.00	30.00	M
	Movie tie-in				
	Note: Actually written by Don Ward				
263	The Panic-Stricken - Mitchell Wilson	2.50	6.00	10.00	M
264	Fear and Trembling - Alfred Hitchcock	7.50	15.00	30.00	M
265	Men Under the Sea - Frank Meier	2.50	6.00	10.00	A
266	Ghost of a Chance - Kelley Roos	2.50	6.00	10.00	M
267	Not Quite Dead Enough - Rex Stout	2.50	6.00	10.00	M
268	Blood on Biscayne Bay - Brett Halliday	2.50	6.00	10.00	M
269	The Invisible Man - H. G. Wells	7.50	15.00	30.00	SF
270	It Ain't Hay - David Dodge	4.00	8.00	15.00	M
	1949				
271	Gunsmoke and Trail Dust - Bliss Lomax	2.50	6.00	10.00	W
	aka Trail Dust				
272	The Velvet Fleece - Lois Eby & John C.	2.50	6.00	10.00	M
	Fleming				
273	Death Knell - Baynard Kendrick	2.50	6.00	10.00	M
274	The Body Missed the Boat - Jack Iams	2.50	6.00	10.00	M
275	Where There's Smoke - Stewart Sterling	2.50	6.00	10.00	M
	1949				
276	Murder for Two - George Harmon Coxe	2.50	6.00	10.00	M
277	Ex-Wife - Ursula Parott	2.50	6.00	10.00	R
278	Second Dell Book of Crossword Puzzles -	5.00	10.00	20.00	NF
	Kathleen Rafferty				
279	Sons of the Sheik - E. M. Hull	3.00	6.00	12.00	A
280	Counterfeit Wife - Brett Halliday	2.50	6.00	10.00	M
281	Anthony Adverse in Italy - Hervey Allen	2.50	6.00	10.00	A
282	Western Stories - William MacLeod Raine	3.00	6.00	12.00	W
283	Anthony Adverse in Africa - Hervey Allen	2.50	6.00	10.00	A
284	Outlaw on Horseback - Will Ermine	2.50	6.00	10.00	W
285	Anthony Adverse in America - Hervey Allen	2.50	6.00	10.00	A
286	Eisenhower Was My Boss - Kay Summersby	3.00	6.00	12.00	NF
287	The Silver Leopard - Helen Reilly	2.50	6.00	10.00	M
288	The Heart Remembers - Faith Baldwin	2.50	6.00	10.00	R

Dell 269, c. Dell

Dell 270, c. Dell

Dell 279, c. Dell

Dell 282, c. Dell

Dell 305, c. Dell

Dell 307, c. Dell

(DELL, continued)

289	Bitter Ending - Alexander Irving	2.50	6.00	10.00	
290	The Pioneers - Courtney Ryley Cooper	2.50	6.00	10.00	
291	So Dear to My Heart - Sterling North Movie tie-in	3.00	6.00	12.00	
292	Hits, Runs. & Errors - Robert Smith	2.50	6.00	10.00	S
293	Cards on the Table - Agatha Christie	2.50	6.00	10.00	M
294	Jim the Conqueror - Peter B. Kyne	2.50	6.00	10.00	W
295	The Goblin Market - Helen McCloy	2.50	6.00	10.00	M
296	Little Women - Louisa May Alcott & Jean Francis Webb Movie tie-in	3.00	6.00	12.00	
297	The Great Mistake - Mary Roberts Rinehart	2.50	6.00	10.00	M
298	Promise of Love - Mary Renault	2.50	6.00	10.00	R
299	Bad for Business - Rex Stout	3.00	6.00	12.00	M
300	The Paintin' Pistoleer - Walker A. Tompkins 1949	3.00	6.00	12.00	W
301	'Q' as in Quicksand - Lawrence Treat	2.50	6.00	10.00	M
302	The Dark Device - Hannah Lees	2.50	6.00	10.00	
303	The Mirabilis Diamond - Jerome Odlum	2.50	6.00	10.00	M
304	Doctor Hudson's Secret Journal - Lloyd C. Douglas	2.50	6.00	10.00	
305	Invasion from Mars - Orson Welles	5.00	10.00	20.00	SF
306	Brandy for a Hero - William O'Farrell	2.50	6.00	10.00	
307	Pick Your Victim - Pat McGerr	2.50	6.00	10.00	M
308	Dead Yellow Women - Dashiell Hammett	8.50	20.00	32.50	M
309	Satin Straps - Maysie Greig	2.50	6.00	10.00	R
310	West of Texas Law - Walker A. Tompkins	2.50	6.00	10.00	W
311	Bengal Fire - Lawrence G. Blochman	2.50	6.00	10.00	A
312	The Gaunt Woman - Edmund Gilligan	2.50	6.00	10.00	
313	Death of a Bullonaire - A. B. Cunningham	2.50	6.00	10.00	M
314	Dead Wrong - Stewart Sterling	2.50	6.00	10.00	M
315	Cats Prowl at Night - A. A. Fair	2.50	6.00	10.00	M
316	Armchair in Hell - Henry Kane	2.50	6.00	10.00	M
317	Alder Gulch - Ernest Haycox	2.50	6.00	10.00	W
318	Alimony - Faith Baldwin	2.50	6.00	10.00	R
319	The Man in the Brown Suit - Agatha Christie	2.50	6.00	10.00	M
320	The Cave Girl - Edgar Rice Burroughs	7.50	15.00	30.00	A
321	Assignment in Guiana - George Harmon Coxe	2.50	6.00	10.00	M
322	Death of a Tall Man - Richard & Frances Lockridge	2.50	6.00	10.00	M

Dell 308, c. Dell

Dell 320, c. Dell

Dell 339, c. Dell

Dell 371, c. Dell

Dell 382, c. Dell

Dell 383, c. Dell

(DELL, continued)

323 Murder and the Married Virgin - Brett Halliday	2.50	6.00	10.00	M
324 The Corpse Came Calling - Brett Halliday	2.50	6.00	10.00	M
325 Michael Shayne's Long Chance - Brett Halliday	2.50	6.00	10.00	M
1949				
326 Murder is My Business - Brett Halliday	2.50	6.00	10.00	M
327 Leave Cancelled - Nicholas Monsarrat	2.50	6.00	10.00	R
328 Cream of the Crop - Ed Fort	2.50	6.00	10.00	
329 Young Doctor Kildare - Max Brand	2.50	6.00	10.00	
330 Report for a Corpse - Henry Kane	2.50	6.00	10.00	M
331 Anna Lucasta - Jean Francis Webb	2.50	6.00	10.00	
332 Fact Detective Mysteries - W. A. Swanberg	2.50	6.00	10.00	
First ed., 1949				
333 Stampede - E. B. Mann	2.50	6.00	10.00	
334 The Case of the Seven Sneezes - Anthony				
Boucher	2.50	6.00	10.00	M
335 Double Treasure - Clarence Budington				
Kelland	2.50	6.00	10.00	W
336 Afterglow - Ruby M. Ayers	2.50	6.00	10.00	
337 Just Around the Corner - Stuart Brock	2.50	6.00	10.00	M
338 The Lady Regrets - James M. Fox	2.50	6.00	10.00	M
339 She - H. Rider Haggard	7.50	15.00	30.00	F
Note: Retold by Don Ward				
340 The Care of Your Child from Infancy to				
Six - William Rosenson & Bela Schick	5.00	10.00	20.00	NF
341 The Upstart - Edison Marshall	2.50	6.00	10.00	
342 Sons of the Sheik - E. M. Hull	2.50	6.00	10.00	
343 The Chinese Doll - Wilson Tucker	3.00	6.00	12.00	M
344 Bedeviled - Libbie Block	2.50	6.00	10.00	
345 Wake for a Lady - H. W. Roden	2.50	6.00	10.00	M
346 The Accomplice - Matthew Head	2.50	6.00	10.00	
347 Trail Town - Ernest Haycox	2.50	6.00	10.00	W
348 A Halo for Nobody - Henry Kane	2.50	6.00	10.00	M
349 Too Busy to Die - H. W. Roden	2.50	6.00	10.00	M
350 It Ain't Hay - David Dodge	4.00	8.00	15.00	
1949				
351 Showdown - Errol Flynn	3.00	6.00	12.00	A
352 Gunsmoke Graze - Peter Dawson	2.50	6.00	10.00	W
353 Yankee Pasha - Edison Marshall	4.00	8.00	15.00	A
354 The Philadelphia Murder Story - Leslie Ford	2.50	6.00	10.00	M
355 The One that Got Away - Helen McCloy	2.50	6.00	10.00	M
356 Death in the Doll's House - Lawrence				
Bachmann & Hannah Lees	2.50	6.00	10.00	M
357 Leave it to Psmith - P. G. Wodehouse	4.00	8.00	15.00	H
358 To a God Unknown - John Steinbeck	2.50	6.00	10.00	
359 Trail's End - William MacLeod Raine	2.50	6.00	10.00	W
360 Don Lorenzo's Bride - Juanita Savage	3.00	6.00	12.00	
361 Haunted Lady - Mary Roberts Rinehart	2.50	6.00	10.00	M
362 Silent in the Saddle - Norman A. Fox	2.50	6.00	10.00	W
363 Blue City - Kenneth Millar	2.00	4.00	7.50	
364 Forlorn Island - Edison Marshall	3.00	6.00	12.00	A
365 The Death of a Worldly Woman - A. B.				
Cunningham	2.50	6.00	10.00	M
366 Unfinished Business - Cary Lucas	2.50	6.00	10.00	M
367 Suspense Stories - Alfred Hitchcock	4.00	8.00	15.00	M
368 The Moon's Our Home - Faith Baldwin	2.50	6.00	10.00	R
1950				
369 Panic - Helen McCloy	2.50	6.00	10.00	M

370	He Wouldn't Kill Patience - Carter Dickson	4.00	8.00	15.00	M
371	Wisteria Cottage - Robert M. Coates	3.00	6.00	12.00	
372	Buckaroo's Code - Wayne D. Overholser	2.50	6.00	10.00	W
373	The Heart Has April Too - Gladys Taber	2.50	6.00	10.00	R
374	Night and the City - Gerald Kersh	2.50	6.00	10.00	M
375	Date with Darkness - Donald Hamilton 1950	2.50	6.00	10.00	
376	Out of Control - Baynard Kendrick	2.50	6.00	10.00	M
377	Alias the Dead - George Harmon Coxe	3.00	6.00	12.00	M
378	Last of the Longhorns - Will Ermine	2.50	6.00	10.00	W
379	Nightmare Town - Dashiell Hammett	5.00	10.00	20.00	M
380	Invitation to Live - Lloyd C. Douglas	2.50	6.00	10.00	
381	The Clever Sister - Margaret Culkin Banning	2.50	6.00	10.00	R
382	Celeste...the Gold Coast Virgin - Rosamond Marshall	5.00	10.00	20.00	E
383	Rutledge Trails the Ace of Spades - William McLeod Raine	2.50	6.00	10.00	W
384	Girl Meets Body - Jack Iams	2.50	6.00	10.00	M
385	Blood on the Stars - Brett Halliday	2.50	6.00	10.00	M
386	The Uncomplaining Corpses - Brett Halliday	2.50	6.00	10.00	M
387	Tickets for Death - Brett Halliday	2.50	6.00	10.00	M
388	Murders Wears a Mummer's Mask - Brett Halliday	2.50	6.00	10.00	M
389	Give 'Em the Ax - A. A. Fair	2.50	6.00	10.00	M
390	The Cabinda Affair - Matthew Head	2.50	6.00	10.00	M
391	Murder at Hazelmoor - Agatha Christie	2.50	6.00	10.00	M
392	Virgin with Butterflies - Tom Powers	2.50	6.00	10.00	
393	The Code of the Woosters - P. G. Wodehouse	4.00	8.00	15.00	H
394	Return to Night - Mary Renault	2.50	6.00	10.00	
395	Devil's Stronghold - Leslie Ford	2.50	6.00	10.00	M
396	After Midnight - Martha Albrand	2.50	6.00	10.00	
397	The Farmhouse - Helen Reilly	2.50	6.00	10.00	M
398	Murder in Any Language - Kelley Roos	2.50	6.00	10.00	M
399	The Ridin' Kid from Powder River - Henry Herbert Knibbs	2.50	6.00	10.00	W
400	Big City after Dark - Jack Lait & Lee Mortimer 1950	2.50	6.00	10.00	
401	They Can't All Be Guilty - M. V. Heberden	2.50	6.00	10.00	M
402	The Captive of the Sahara - E. M. Hull	2.50	6.00	10.00	A
403	The Man in Lower Ten - Mary Roberts Rinehart	2.50	6.00	10.00	M
404	The Case of Jennie Brice - Mary Roberts Rinehart	2.50	6.00	10.00	M
405	The Long Escape - David Dodge	2.50	6.00	10.00	
406	Cactus Cavalier - Norman A. Fox	2.50	6.00	10.00	W
407	To a God Unknown - John Steinbeck	2.50	6.00	10.00	
408	Blue City - Kenneth Millar	2.00	4.00	6.00	
409	Strangers May Kiss - Ursula Parrott	2.50	6.00	10.00	R
410	The Affair at the Boat Landing - A. G. Cunningham	2.50	6.00	10.00	M
411	A Man Called Spade - Dashiell Hammett	4.00	8.00	15.00	M
412	Seven Deadly Sisters - Pat McGerr	2.50	6.00	10.00	M
413	Arizona Feud - Frank R. Adams	2.50	6.00	10.00	W
414	Cleopatra's Nights - Allan Barnard	4.00	8.00	15.00	A
415	Ladies in Hades - Frederic Arnold Kummer	4.00	8.00	15.00	F
416	They Drive by Night - A. I. Bezzendes	2.50	6.00	10.00	

Dell 414, c. Dell

Dell 415, c. Dell

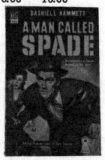

Dell 452, c. Dell

No.	Title			
417	Tell Me About Women - Harry Reasoner	2.00	4.00	6.00	
418	Gunsmoke and Trail Dust - Bliss Lomax	2.00	4.00	6.00	W
419	Murder is Mutual - Jack Dolph	2.00	4.00	7.50	M
420	Dead Sure - Stewart Sterling	2.00	4.00	7.50	M
421	Dead Yellow Women - Dashiell Hammett	7.50	15.00	30.00	M
422	Yankee Pasha - Edison Marshall	3.00	6.00	12.00	A
423	Murder in Havana - George Harmon Coxe	2.50	6.00	10.00	M
424	The Bandit Trail - William MacLeod Raine	2.00	4.00	7.50	W
425	Breakdown - Louis Paul	2.00	4.00	7.50	
	1950				
426	A Taste for Violence - Brett Halliday	2.50	6.00	10.00	M
427	Dead Man's Diary and Dinner at Dupre's - Brett Halliday	2.50	6.00	10.00	M
428	Call for Michael Shayne - Brett Halliday	2.50	6.00	10.00	M
429	The Private Practice of Michale Shayne - Brett Halliday	2.50	6.00	10.00	M
430	She Walks Alone - Helen McCloy	2.00	4.00	7.50	M
431	Benjamin Blake, Son of Fury - Edison Marshall	2.00	4.00	7.50	A
432	Stag Night - Phillips Rogers	2.50	6.00	10.00	A
433	King Solomon's Mines - H. Rider Haggard Movie tie-in Note: Actually written by Jean Francis Webb	2.50	6.00	10.00	A
434	Dell Crossword Puzzle Dictionary - Kathleen Rafferty	3.00	6.00	12.00	NF
435	Their Ancient Grudge - Harry Harrison Kroll	2.00	4.00	7.50	
436	Gone to Earth - Mary Webb	2.00	4.00	6.00	
437	Gunpowder Lightning - Bertrand W. Sinclair	2.00	4.00	6.00	W
438	All Men are Liars - John Stephen Strange	2.00	4.00	6.00	
439	The Border Lord - Jan Westcott	2.00	4.00	6.00	
440	New York Confidential - Jack Lait & Lee Mortimer	2.00	4.00	6.00	NF
441	Murder with Pictures - George Harmon Coxe	2.00	4.00	7.50	M
442	Root of Evil - Eaton K. Goldthwaite	2.00	4.00	7.50	M
443	Dinner at Antoine's - Frances Parkinson Keyes	2.00	4.00	6.00	
444	Tender Mercy - Lenard Kaufman	2.00	4.00	6.00	E
445	The High Road - Faith Baldwin	2.00	4.00	6.00	R
446	Yours Ever - Maysie Greig	2.00	4.00	6.00	R
447	The Woman in Black - Leslie Ford	2.00	4.00	7.50	M
448	Flaming Canyon - Walker A. Tompkins	2.00	4.00	6.00	W
449	West of Texas Law - Walker A. Tompkins aka Hang-Rope Harvest	2.00	4.00	6.00	W
450	Alder Gulch - Ernest Haycox	2.00	4.00	6.00	W
	1950				
451	The Long Rope - Francis W. Hilton	2.00	4.00	6.00	W
452	A Man Called Spade - Dashiell Hammett	4.00	8.00	15.00	M
453	The Camera Clue - George Harmon Coxe	2.00	4.00	7.50	M
454	Murder on the Links - Agatha Christie	2.00	4.00	7.50	M
455	Hang by Your Neck - Henry Kane	2.00	4.00	7.50	M
456	Gentlemen of the Jungle - Tom Gill	2.00	4.00	7.50	E
457	Death Draws the Line - Jack Iams	2.00	4.00	7.50	M
458	A Taste for Violence - Brett Halliday	2.00	4.00	7.50	M
459	Blood on Biscayne Bay - Brett Halliday	2.00	4.00	7.50	M
460	Give 'Em the Ax - A. A. Fair	2.00	4.00	7.50	M
461	Innocent Bystander - Craig Rice	2.00	4.00	6.00	M
462	Desperate Angel - Helen Topping Miller	2.00	4.00	6.00	
463	The Inconvenient Bride - James M. Fox	2.00	4.00	6.00	M
464	The Corpse in the Corner Saloon - Hampton Stone	2.00	4.00	7.50	M
465	Death Haunts the Dark Lane - A. B. Cunningham	2.00	4.00	7.50	M
466	Pirates of the Range - B. M. Bower	2.00	4.00	6.00	W
467	Money to Burn - Peter B. Kyne	2.00	4.00	6.00	
468	Jungle Hunting Thrills - Edison Marshall	2.00	4.00	7.50	A
469	Uncle Dynamite - P. G. Wodehouse	2.50	6.00	10.00	H
470	Flight of an Angel - Verne Chute	2.00	4.00	6.00	
	1951				
471	Vigilante - Richard Summers	2.00	4.00	6.00	
472	Crows Can't Count - A. A. Fair	2.00	4.00	6.00	M
473	The Steel Mirror - Donald Hamilton	2.00	4.00	6.00	
474	The Miracle of the Bells - Russell Janney	2.00	4.00	6.00	
475	Manhattan Nights - Faith Baldwin	2.00	4.00	6.00	R
	1951				

(DELL, continued)

476 My True Love Lies - Lenore Glen Offord	2.00	4.00	6.00	
477 Crosstown - John Held, Jr.	2.00	4.00	6.00	
478 Plunder of the Sun - David Dodge	2.00	4.00	6.00	A
479 The Web of Evil - Lucille Emerick	2.00	4.00	6.00	
480 The Thirsty Land - Norman A. Fox	2.00	4.00	6.00	W
481 The Skeleton in the Clock - Carter Dickson	3.00	6.00	12.00	M
482 Women Must Weep - Ruth Adams Knight	2.00	4.00	6.00	
483 What a Body! - Alan Green	2.00	4.00	7.50	
484 Untamed - Helga Moray	2.00	4.00	7.50	
485 The Queen and the Corpse - Max Murray	2.00	4.00	7.50	M
486 Blood Money - Dashiell Hammett	4.00	8.00	15.00	M
487 Castle in the Swamp - Edison Marshall	2.00	4.00	7.50	
488 Bombay Mail - Lawrence C. Blochman	2.00	4.00	7.50	
489 My Chinese Wife - Karl Eskelund	2.00	4.00	6.00	
490 The Stirrup Boss - Peter Dawson	2.00	4.00	6.00	W
491 The Labors of Hercules - Agatha Christie	2.00	4.00	7.50	M
492 Blood of the Lamb - Charles Baker, Jr.	2.00	4.00	6.00	
493 She Shall Have Murder - Delano Ames	2.00	4.00	6.00	M
494 Miss Pinkerton - Mary Roberts Rinehart	2.00	4.00	6.00	M
495 Double for Death - Rex Stout	2.00	4.00	7.50	M
496 Whispers in the Sun - Maysie Greig	2.00	4.00	6.00	R
497 The Three Roads - Kenneth Millar	2.00	4.00	6.00	
498 Staircase 4 - Helen Reilly	2.00	4.00	6.00	M
499 West of the Rimrock - Wayne D. Overholser	2.00	4.00	6.00	W
500 Blood and Sand - Vincente Blasco Ibanez	2.00	4.00	6.00	
1951				
501 The Demon Caravan - Georges Surdez	2.00	4.00	6.00	
502 The Groom Lay Dead - George Harmon Coxe	2.00	4.00	7.50	M
503 Marked for Murder - Brett Halliday	2.00	4.00	6.00	M
504 The Sunnier Side - Charles Jackson	2.00	4.00	6.00	
505 Murder with Southern Hospitality -				
Leslie Ford	2.00	4.00	6.00	M
506 The Window at the White Cat - Mary				
Roberts Rinehart	2.00	4.00	6.00	M
507 Francis - David Stern	2.50	6.00	10.00	H
508 The Baited Blonde - Robinson MacLean	2.00	4.00	6.00	
509 Blazing Trails - Francis W. Hilton	2.00	4.00	6.00	W
510 You Play the Black and the Red Comes Up -				
Richard Hallas	2.00	4.00	7.50	
511 Slippery Hitch - Gerald Butler	2.00	4.00	6.00	M
512 The Robbed Heart - Clifton Cuthbert	2.00	4.00	6.00	
513 Alarm in the Night - Stewart Sterling	2.00	4.00	6.00	M
514 Do Not Murder Before Christmas - Jack Iams	2.00	4.00	6.00	M
515 Message from a Stranger - Marya Mannes	2.00	4.00	6.00	
516 No Highway - Nevil Shute	2.00	4.00	6.00	
517 The Sagebrush Bandit - Bliss Lomax				
(H. S. Drago)	2.00	4.00	6.00	W
518 Shell Game - Richard Powell	2.00	4.00	6.00	M
519 Through a Glass, Darkly - Helen McCloy	2.00	4.00	6.00	M
520 Dead Giveaway - Hugh Lawrence Nelson	2.00	4.00	6.00	
521 Hell Cat - Idabel Williams	2.00	4.00	6.00	
522 The Glass Triangle - George Harmon Coxe	2.00	4.00	6.00	M
523 Zane Grey Western Award Stories	2.00	4.00	7.50	W
524 Once in Vienna - Vicki Baum	2.00	4.00	6.00	
525 Diamond Lil - Mae West	3.00	6.00	12.00	E
1951				
526 The Gentle Hangman - James M. Fox	2.00	4.00	6.00	M
527 Trouble Valley - Ward West	2.00	4.00	6.00	W

Dell 501, c. Dell

Dell 536, c. Dell

Dell 538, c. Dell

(DELL, continued)

528 Young Claudia - Rose Franken	2.00	4.00	6.00	
529 Sad Cypress - Agatha Christie	2.00	4.00	6.00	M
530 Love Stories of India - Edison Marshall	2.00	4.00	6.00	A
531 Death in Four Colors - Brandon Bird	2.00	4.00	6.00	M
532 The Incredible Year - Faith Baldwin	1.50	3.50	5.00	R
533 This is It, Michael Shayne - Brett Halliday	2.00	4.00	6.00	M
534 New York Confidential - Jack Lait & Lee Mortimer	1.50	3.50	5.00	NF
535 Edge of Panic - Henry Kane	2.00	4.00	6.00	M
536 Tarzan and the Lost Empire - Edgar Rice Burroughs	3.00	6.00	12.00	A
537 Hag's Nook - John Dickson Carr	2.00	4.00	7.50	M
538 The Creeping Siamese - Dashiell Hammett	3.00	6.00	12.00	M
539 Shadow on the Range - Norman A. Fox	2.00	4.00	6.00	W
540 Too Many Cooks - Rex Stout	2.00	4.00	6.00	M
541 Episode of the Wandering Knife - Mary Roberts Rinehart	2.00	4.00	6.00	M
542 Fools Die on Friday - A. A. Fair	2.00	4.00	6.00	M
543 A Graveyard to Let - Carter Dickson	2.00	4.00	7.50	M
544 Wait for the Dawn - Martha Albrand	1.50	3.50	5.00	
545 The Sheriff of San Miguel - Allan Vaughan Elston	2.00	4.00	6.00	W
546 Hunt with the Hounds - Mignon G. Eberhart	2.00	4.00	6.00	M
547 Date with Death - Leslie Ford	2.00	4.00	6.00	M
548 That Girl from Memphis - Wilbur Daniel Steele	2.00	4.00	6.00	
549 The Jade Venus - George Harmon Coxe	2.00	4.00	6.00	M
550 Mr. Parker Pyne, Detective - Agatha Christie	2.00	4.00	6.00	M
1951				
551 Manhunt West - Walker A. Tomkins	2.00	4.00	6.00	W
552 Murder Begins at Home - Delano Ames	2.00	4.00	6.00	M
553 The Mark of Zorro - Johnston McCulley	2.00	4.00	7.50	W
554 Letter to Five Wives - John Klempner	1.50	3.50	5.00	
555 Causeway to the Past - William O'Farrell	1.50	3.50	5.00	
556 Draw or Drag - Wayne D. Overholser	2.00	4.00	6.00	W
557 Backwoods Woman - Jack Boone	2.00	4.00	6.00	E
558 Do Evil in Return - Margaret Millar	2.00	4.00	6.00	M
559 Renegade Canyon - Peter Dawson	2.00	4.00	6.00	W
560 The Neat Little Corpse - Max Murray	2.00	4.00	6.00	M
561 Crescent Carnival - Frances Parkinson Keyes	2.00	4.00	6.00	
1952				
562 Raw Land - Luke Short	2.00	4.00	6.00	W
563 The King's Choice - Margaret Campbell Barnes	2.00	4.00	6.00	A
564 Death-watch - John Dickson Carr	2.00	4.00	7.50	M
565 The Red Tassel - David Dodge	2.00	4.00	6.00	
566 The Happy Time - Robert Fontaine	1.50	3.50	5.00	
567 The Harem - Louis-Charles Royer	2.00	4.00	7.50	E
568 Passport to Peril - Robert Parker	2.00	4.00	6.00	
569 Stormy in the West - Norman A. Fox	2.00	4.00	6.00	W
570 The Mysterious Mr. Quin - Agatha Christie	2.00	4.00	6.00	M
571 No Mask for Murder - Andrew Grave	2.00	4.00	6.00	M
572 Dark Moon of March - Emmett Gowen	2.00	4.00	6.00	
573 The Wheel is Fixed - James M. Fox	2.00	4.00	6.00	M
574 For Richer, for Poorer... - Faith Baldwin	1.50	3.50	5.00	R
575 Montana, Here I Be! - Dan Cushman	2.00	4.00	6.00	W
1952				
576 Murder at Arroways - Helen Reilly	2.00	4.00	6.00	M
577 Murder Twice Told - Donald Hamilton	2.00	4.00	6.00	M
578 Framed in Blood - Brett Halliday	2.00	4.00	6.00	M
579 Nobody Wore Black - Delano Ames	2.00	4.00	6.00	
580 Until You Are Dead - Henry Kane	2.00	4.00	6.00	M
581 The Lost Buckaroo - Bliss Lomax (H. S. Drago)	2.00	4.00	6.00	W
582 Trial by Marriage - Vereen Bell	1.50	3.50	5.00	
583 Dead of Night - Stewart Sterling	2.00	4.00	6.00	M
584 Proceed at Will - Burke Wilkinson	2.00	4.00	6.00	
585 The Circular Staircase - Mary Roberts Rinehart	2.00	4.00	6.00	M
586 Dangerous Legacy - George Harmon Coxe	2.00	4.00	6.00	M
587 The Stampeders - James B. Hendryx	2.00	4.00	6.00	W
588 The Unknown Path - Anne Meredith	1.50	3.50	5.00	
589 The Cabin in the Cotton - Harry Harrison Kroll	2.00	4.00	6.00	

(DELL, continued)

590	Counterfeit Wife - Brett Halliday	2.00	4.00	6.00	M
591	Rocket to the Morgue - Anthony Boucher	3.00	6.00	12.00	M
592	Rustlers' Bend - Will Ermine	2.00	4.00	6.00	W
593	Too Hot to Handle - Frank G. Presnell	2.00	4.00	6.00	M
594	Keep Cool, Mr. Jones - Timothy Fuller	2.00	4.00	6.00	M
595	My Enemy, My Wife - Allen Haden	1.50	3.50	5.00	
596	A Taste of Murder - Joanna Cannan	1.50	3.50	5.00	M
597	Georgia Girl - Margaret Rebecca Lay	2.00	4.00	6.00	
598	Return of a Fighter - Ernest Haycox	2.00	4.00	6.00	W
599	Heaven Ran Last - William P. McGivern	1.50	3.50	5.00	
600	Rogue Queen - L. Sprague de Camp	4.00	8.00	15.00	SF
	1952				
601	Before It.s Too Late - Stuart Palmer	2.00	4.00	6.00	M
602	Tequila - Margaret Page Hood	2.00	4.00	6.00	
603	Bedrooms Have Windows - A. A. Fair	2.00	4.00	6.00	M
604	Sudden Fear - Edna Sherry	2.00	4.00	6.00	M
605	The Congo Venus - Matthew Head	2.00	4.00	6.00	
606	Savage Range - Luke Short	2.00	4.00	6.00	W
607	Funny Side Up - James E. Gunn	2.00	4.00	7.50	H
608	The Human Beast - George Milburn & Emile Zola	2.00	4.00	6.00	
609	Brother Death - John Lodwick	1.50	3.50	5.00	
610	Dr. Norton's Wife - Mildred Walker	1.50	3.50	5.00	
611	How to Get Rich in Washington - Blair Bolles	1.50	3.50	5.00	
612	Follow, as the Night - Pat McGerr	1.50	3.50	5.00	M
613	Saddlebum - William MacLeod Raine	1.50	3.50	5.00	W
614	Jewels for a Shroud - Walter de Steiguer	1.50	3.50	5.00	M
615	The Sea is a Woman - Lonnie Coleman	1.50	3.50	5.00	
616	No Range is Free - E. E. Halleran	1.50	3.50	5.00	W
617	Dividend on Death - Brett Halliday	1.50	3.50	5.00	M
618	Man in the Saddle - Ernest Haycox	1.50	3.50	5.00	W
619	Spill the Jackpot - A. A. Fair	1.50	3.50	5.00	M
620	Turn on the Heat - A. A. Fair	1.50	3.50	5.00	M
621	Lament for the Bride - Helen Reilly	1.50	3.50	5.00	M
622	Age of Consent - Clem Yore	1.50	3.50	5.00	
623	Fatal in Furs - James M. Fox	1.50	3.50	5.00	M
624	Steel to the South - Wayne D. Overholser	1.50	3.50	5.00	W
625	Border Town - Carroll Graham	1.50	3.50	5.00	
	1952				
626	Three Doors to Death - Rex Stout	2.00	4.00	6.00	M
627	When Worlds Collide - Philip Wylie & Edwin Balmer	2.50	6.00	10.00	SF
628	Speak No Evil - Mignon G. Eberhart	1.50	3.50	5.00	M
629	Gunsight Pass - William MacLeod Raine	1.50	3.50	5.00	W
630	Untamed - Helga Moray	1.50	3.50	5.00	
631	What Rhymes with Murder? - Jack Iams	1.50	3.50	5.00	M
632	Border Ambush - Walker A. Tompkins	1.50	3.50	5.00	W
633	Three Blind Mice - Agatha Christie	1.50	3.50	5.00	M
634	Two if by Sea - Roger Bax	1.50	3.50	5.00	
635	To Wake the Dea - John Dickson Carr	2.00	4.00	7.50	M
636	Triggerman - Frank Austin	1.50	3.50	5.00	
637	Indian Beef - Harold Channing Wire	1.50	3.50	5.00	W
638	See You at the Morgue - Lawrence G. Blochman	1.50	3.50	5.00	M
639	Good Luck to the Corpse - Max Murray	1.50	3.50	5.00	M
640	The Life and Death of the Wicked Lady Skelton - Magdalen King-Hall	1.50	3.50	5.00	
641	Carry My Coffin Slowly - Lee Herrington	1.50	3.50	5.00	M

Dell 591, c. Dell

Dell 600, c. Dell

Dell 679, c. Dell

184

642	Tall Man Riding - Norman A. Fox	1.50	3.50	5.00	W
643	Deadline at Durango - Allan Vaughan Elston	1.50	3.50	5.00	W
644	The Fifth Key - George Harmon Coxe	1.50	3.50	5.00	M
645	The Body that Wasn't Uncle - George Worthing Yates	1.50	3.50	5.00	M
646	No Mourners Present - Frank G. Presnell	1.50	3.50	5.00	M
647	King Colt - Luke Short	1.50	3.50	5.00	W
648	Fabia - Olive Higgins Prouty	1.50	3.50	5.00	
649	The Kind Man - Helen Nielsen	1.50	3.50	5.00	
650	Night at the Mocking Widow - Carter Dickson	2.00	4.00	7.50	M
	1953				
651	Desperate Moment - Martha Albrand	.75	1.75	3.00	
652	The Bat - Mary Roberts Rinehart	1.50	3.50	5.00	M
653	Outlaw in Horseback - Will Ermine	1.50	3.50	5.00	W
654	Dell Crossword Puzzles - Kathleen Rafferty	2.50	6.00	10.00	NF
655	No Tears for Hilda - Andrew Garve	1.50	3.50	5.00	M
656	Badlands Justice - Dan Cushman	1.50	3.50	5.00	W
657	The Hunter - James Aldridge	1.50	3.50	5.00	
658	To Catch a Thief - David Dodge	1.50	3.50	5.00	
659	Stairway to an Empty Room - Dolores Hitchens	1.50	3.50	5.00	M
660	Buckskin Empire - Harry Sinclair Drago	1.50	3.50	5.00	W
661	Stormy Present - Hope Field	1.50	3.50	5.00	
662	Murder Leaves a Ring - Fay Grissom Stanley	1.50	3.50	5.00	M
663	The Arms of Venus - John Appleby	1.50	3.50	5.00	
664	The Boomerang Clue - Agatha Christie	1.50	3.50	5.00	M
665	Dead Weight - Frank Kane	2.50	6.00	10.00	M
666	The Law Busters - Bliss Lomax (H. S. Drago)	1.50	3.50	5.00	W
667	Four Fallen Women - anthology	2.00	4.00	6.00	E
668	Bodies Are Where You Find Them - Brett Halliday	1.50	3.50	5.00	M
669	Never Look Back - Mignon G. Eberhart	1.50	3.50	5.00	M
670	The Witching Night - C. S. Cody	2.00	4.00	7.50	
671	1953 Racing Almanac - Rowland Barber & John I. Day	2.00	4.00	7.50	NF
672	Don't Cry for Me - William Campbell Gault	1.50	3.50	5.00	M
673	Treasure of the Brasada - Les Savage, Jr.	1.50	3.50	5.00	W
674	The Broken Vase - Rex Stout	1.50	3.50	5.00	M
675	Hardly a Man is Now Alive - Herbert Brean	1.50	3.50	5.00	
	1953				
676	All Over Town - George Milburn	1.50	3.50	5.00	
677	Texas Fury - John Callahan	1.50	3.50	5.00	W
678	Fashioned for Murder - George Harmon Coxe	1.50	3.50	5.00	M
679	Night Has a Thousand Eyes - William Irish	2.00	4.00	7.50	M
680	First He Died - Clifford D. Simak	2.00	4.00	6.00	SF
681	The Picture of Dorian Grey - Oscar Wilde	2.50	6.00	10.00	H
682	The Gallows in My Garden - Richard Deming	1.50	3.50	5.00	M
683	An Overdose of Death - Agatha Christie	1.50	3.50	5.00	M
684	The Silver Star - Will Ermine	1.50	3.50	5.00	W
685	The Scarlet Slippers - James M. Fox	1.50	3.50	5.00	M
686	The Juggler - Michael Blankfort	1.50	3.50	5.00	
687	The Frightened Stiff - Kelley Roos	1.50	3.50	5.00	M
688	The Proud Sheriff - Eugene Manlove Rhodes	1.50	3.50	5.00	W
689	The Bahamas Murder Case - Leslie Ford	1.50	3.50	5.00	M
690	Behind the Crimson Blind - Carter Dickson	2.00	4.00	7.50	M
691	Bats Fly at Dusk - A. A. Fair	1.50	3.50	5.00	M
692	The River Road - Frances Parkinson Keyes	1.50	3.50	5.00	
693	Nightmare at Noon - Stewart Sterling	1.50	3.50	5.00	M
694	Roughshod - Norman A. Fox	1.50	3.50	5.00	W
695	The Other One - Catherine Turney	1.50	3.50	5.00	M
696	Slan - A. E. Van Vogt	2.50	6.00	10.00	SF
697	At Last, Mr. Tolliver - William Wiegand	1.50	3.50	5.00	
698	The Big Fist - Clyde Ragsdale	1.50	3.50	5.00	
699	Buckaroo's Code - Wayne D. Overholser	1.50	3.50	5.00	W
700	Curtains for the Copper - Thomas Polsky	1.50	3.50	5.00	M
	1953				
701	They Died Laughing - Alan Green	1.50	3.50	5.00	
702	Bounty Guns - Luke Short	1.50	3.50	5.00	W
703	The Stockade - Kenneth Lamott	1.50	3.50	5.00	E
704	The Chill - E. C. Bentley	1.50	3.50	5.00	M
705	Brutally with Love - Edith Pope	1.50	3.50	5.00	
706	The Mad Hatter Mystery - John Dickson Carr	2.00	4.00	7.50	M
707	Gold Brick Range - Allan Vaughan Elston	1.50	3.50	5.00	W
708	Mosquitoes - William Faulkner	1.50	3.50	5.00	
709	Three Women in Black - Helen Reilly	1.50	3.50	5.00	M
710	The Follower - Patrick Quentin	2.00	4.00	6.00	M

711 Challenge to Danger - William MacLeod Raine	1.50	3.50	5.00	W
712 The Natural - Bernard Malamud	1.50	3.50	5.00	
713 Strangle Hold - Mary McMullen	1.50	3.50	5.00	
714 Matador - Barnaby Conrad	2.00	4.00	6.00	A
715 Four Lost Ladies - Stuart Palmer	1.50	3.50	5.00	
716 Gunsmoke Graze - Peter Dawson	1.50	3.50	5.00	
717 Trial by Terror - Paul Gallico	1.50	3.50	5.00	
718 Double or Quits - A. A. Fair	1.50	3.50	5.00	M
719 The Iron Virgin - James M. Fox	1.50	3.50	5.00	M
720 The Ripper from Rawhide - Dan Cushman	1.50	3.50	5.00	W
721 Mercy Island - Theodore Pratt	1.50	3.50	5.00	
722 A Shot of Murder - Jack Iams	1.50	3.50	5.00	M
723 When Dorinda Dances - Brett Halliday	1.50	3.50	5.00	M
724 Guns Along the Yellowstone - Bliss Lomax (H. S. Drago)	1.50	3.50	5.00	W
725 Seeds of Contemplation - Thomas Merton 1953	1.50	3.50	5.00	
726 Blow Hot, Blow Cold - Gerald Butler	1.50	3.50	5.00	M
727 The Burden of Guilt - Ian Gordon	1.50	3.50	5.00	
728 The Dell Bowling Handbook - Joe Falcaro & Murray Goodman	2.00	4.00	6.00	NF
729 Fabulous Gunman - Wayne D. Overholser	1.50	3.50	5.00	W
730 Vanish in an Instant - Margaret Millar	1.50	3.50	5.00	M
731 Fetish - Christine Garnier	1.50	3.50	5.00	
732 The Double Man - Helen Reilly	1.50	3.50	5.00	M
733 The Fatal Caress - Richard Barker	1.50	3.50	5.00	M
734 The Lady is Afraid - George Harmon Coxe	1.50	3.50	5.00	M
735 A Corpse for Christmas - Henry Kane	1.50	3.50	5.00	M
736 The Cumberland Rifles - Noel B. Gerson	1.50	3.50	5.00	A
737 Ghostly Hoofbeats - Norman A. Fox	1.50	3.50	5.00	W
738 Nothing More than Murder - Jim Thompson	2.00	4.00	6.00	M
739 Hurry the Darkness - Maurice Procter	1.50	3.50	5.00	M
740 Blow-down - Lawrence G. Blochman	1.50	3.50	5.00	
741 Dr. Gatskill's Blue Shoes - Paul Conant	1.50	3.50	5.00	
742 Colorado Showdown - Allan Vaughan Elston	1.50	3.50	5.00	W
743 Mum's the Word for Murder - Brett Halliday	1.50	3.50	5.00	M
744 Death Has Deep Roots - Michael Gilbert	1.50	3.50	5.00	M
745 Venturous Lady - George Harmon Coxe	1.50	3.50	5.00	M
746 The Bloody Bokhara - William Campbell Gault	1.50	3.50	5.00	M
747 Dead on the Level - Helen Nielsen 1954	1.50	3.50	5.00	M
748 Trail Town - Ernest Haycox	1.50	3.50	5.00	W
749 Bare Trap - Frank Kane	1.50	3.50	5.00	M
750 The Gabriel Horn - Felix Holt 1954	1.50	3.50	5.00	
751 Barbary Hoard - John Appleby	1.50	3.50	5.00	
752 The Spider Lily - Bruno Fischer	1.50	3.50	5.00	M
753 Murder after Hours - Agatha Christie	1.50	3.50	5.00	M
754 Laughing on the Inside - Bill Yates	2.00	4.00	6.00	H
755 Smoky Range - E. E. Halleran	1.50	3.50	5.00	W
756 Whomsoever I Shall Kiss - Curt Siodmak	2.00	4.00	6.00	
757 The Hollow Needle - George Harmon Coxe	1.50	3.50	5.00	M
758 The Clock Strikes 13 - Herbert Brean	1.50	3.50	5.00	
759 Black Widow - Patrick Quentin	2.00	4.00	6.00	M
760 Outpost Mars - Cyril Judd	2.00	4.00	6.00	SF
761 Sex After Forty - John Gilmore & S. A. Lewin	2.00	4.00	6.00	NF
762 Silver Doll - Blair Treynor	1.50	3.50	5.00	M
763 The Key to Nicholas Street - Stanley Ellin	1.50	3.50	5.00	
764 Prairie Marshal - Walker A. Tompkins	1.50	3.50	5.00	W
765 By-line for Murder - Andrew Garve	1.50	3.50	5.00	M
766 Nell Gwyn: Royal Mistress - John H. Wilson	1.50	3.50	5.00	A
767 Dead Man's Plains - Mignon G. Eberhart	1.50	3.50	5.00	M
768 What Really Happened - Brett Halliday	1.50	3.50	5.00	M
769 Brand of Empire - Luke Short	1.50	3.50	5.00	W
770 Thirteen at Dinner - Agatha Christie	1.50	3.50	5.00	M
771 The Loved One - Evelyn Waugh	.75	1.75	3.00	
772 Top of the Heap - A. A. Fair	1.50	3.50	5.00	M
773 Evil Became Them - Pat Root	1.50	3.50	5.00	
774 Sam Snead's Natural Golf - Sam Snead	2.00	4.00	6.00	S
775 The Corpse in the Waxworks - John Dickson Carr 1954	2.00	4.00	7.50	M
776 Gun Bulldogger - Eugene Cunningham	1.50	3.50	5.00	W

777	The Tiger in the Smoke - Margery Allingham	1.50	3.50	5.00	M
778	Crows Can't Count - A. A. Fair	1.50	3.50	5.00	M
779	Widow's Won't Wait - Dolores Hitchens	1.50	3.50	5.00	M
780	Tall in the Saddle - Gordon Young	1.50	3.50	5.00	W
781	Beyond Infinity - Robert Spencer Carr	2.00	4.00	6.00	SF
782	The Red Lamp - Mary Roberts Rinehart	1.50	3.50	5.00	M
783	Long Lightning - Norman A. Fox	1.50	3.50	5.00	W
784	Dead Babes in the Woods - D. B. Olsen	1.50	3.50	5.00	M
785	Bullet Proof - Frank Kane	1.50	3.50	5.00	M
786	Hold it, Florence - Whitney Darrow, Jr.	.75	1.75	3.00	
787	The Long Memory - Howard Clewes	.75	1.75	3.00	
788	Murder is the Pay-off - Leslie Ford	1.50	3.50	5.00	M
789	Stagecoach Kingdom - Harry Sinclair Drago	1.50	3.50	5.00	W
790	The Corpse that Refused to Stay Dead - Hampton Stone	1.50	3.50	5.00	M
791	The Long Loud Silence - Wilson Tucker	2.00	4.00	7.50	SF
792	The Evil Men Do - Benedict Kiely aka Honey Seems Bitter	1.50	3.50	5.00	
793	The Bandit Trail - William MacLeod Raine	1.50	3.50	5.00	W
794	Sleep, my Love - Robert Martin	1.50	3.50	5.00	
795	The Canvas Coffin - William Campbell Gault	1.50	3.50	5.00	M
796	West of the Rimrock - Wayne D. Overholser	1.50	3.50	5.00	W
797	The Harlot Killer - Allan Barnard	1.50	3.50	5.00	
798	Cooking for Two - Janet McKenzie Hill	2.00	4.00	6.00	NF
799	Inland Passage - George Harmon Coxe	1.50	3.50	5.00	M
800	Daisy Miller and the Turn of the Screw - Henry James	.75	1.75	3.00	
	1954				
801	Riders of the Buffalo Grass - Bliss Lomax (H. S. Drago)	1.50	3.50	5.00	W
802	Asylum - William Seabrook	1.50	3.50	5.00	
803	One Night with Nora - Brett Halliday	1.50	3.50	5.00	M
804	Wide Loop - Nelson Nye	1.50	3.50	5.00	W
805	Murder in Mesopotamia - Agatha Christie	1.50	3.50	5.00	M
806	Obit Delayed - Helen Nielsen	1.50	3.50	5.00	M
807	Vile Bodies - Evelyn Waugh	1.50	3.50	5.00	
808	Deadlock - Ruth Fenisong	1.50	3.50	5.00	M
809	Some Women Won't Wait - A. A. Fair	1.50	3.50	5.00	M
810	Roundup on the Picketwire - Allan Vaughan Elston	1.50	3.50	5.00	W
811	The Unknown Quantity - Mignon G. Eberhart	1.50	3.50	5.00	M
812	Deep is the Night - James Wellard	1.50	3.50	5.00	
813	My Name is Michael Sibley - John Bingham	.75	1.75	3.00	M
814	Haunted Lady - Mary Roberts Rinehart	.75	1.75	3.00	M
815	Valley of Guns - Wayne D. Overholser	1.50	3.50	5.00	W
816	Five Alarm Funeral - Stewart Sterling	1.50	3.50	5.00	M
817	The Pigskin Bag - Bruno Fischer	1.50	3.50	5.00	
	1955				
818	The Golden Violet - Joseph Shearing	.75	1.75	3.00	
819	The Amazing Adventures of Father Brown - G. K. Chesterton	1.50	3.50	5.00	M
820	Is Sex Necessary? - James Thurber & E. B. White	2.00	4.00	7.50	H
821	Riders of Buck River - William MacLeod Raine	1.50	3.50	5.00	W
822	Poisons Unknown - Frank Kane	1.50	3.50	5.00	M
823	A Town of Masks - Dorothy Salisbury Davis	1.50	3.50	5.00	M
824	The Company She Keeps - Mary McCarthy	1.50	3.50	5.00	
825	Gunfire Men - L. L. Foreman	1.50	3.50	5.00	W
	1955				
826	Savage Range - Luke Short	1.50	3.50	5.00	W
827	Murder through the Looking Glass - Andrew Garve	1.50	3.50	5.00	M
828	Strawberry Roan - Clem Colt	1.50	3.50	5.00	W
829	Before I Wake - Brett Halliday	1.50	3.50	5.00	M
830	There is a Tide - Agatha Christie	1.50	3.50	5.00	M
831	The Rawhide Years - Norman A. Fox	1.50	3.50	5.00	W
832	The Stirrup Boss - Peter Dawson	1.50	3.50	5.00	W
833	Recipe for Homicide - Lawrence G. Blochman	1.50	3.50	5.00	M
834	The Strangers - William E. Wilson	1.50	3.50	5.00	
835	Blood on the Boards - William Campbell Gault	1.50	3.50	5.00	M
836	Gold Comes in Bricks - A. A. Fair	1.50	3.50	5.00	M
837	Detour to Death - Helen Nielsen	1.50	3.50	5.00	M
838	The Frightened Fiancee - George Harmon Coxe	1.50	3.50	5.00	M

839 Baseball's Greatest Players - Tom Meany	2.00	4.00	6.00	S
840 The Bridal Bed Murders - A. E. Martin	1.50	3.50	5.00	M
841 The Evil of Time - Evelyn Berckman	1.50	3.50	5.00	
842 The Corpse Came Calling - Brett Halliday	1.50	3.50	5.00	M
843 Man the Beast and the Wild, Wild Women - Virgil Partch	2.00	4.00	7.50	H
844 The Proud Diggers - William O. Turner	1.50	3.50	5.00	W
845 Death Commits Bigamy - James M. Fox	1.50	3.50	5.00	M
846 Tough Hand - Wayne D. Overholser	1.50	3.50	5.00	W
847 The Bad Seed - William March	1.50	3.50	5.00	
848 Give the Little Corpse a Great Big Hand - George Bagby	1.50	3.50	5.00	M
849 Wyoming Gun - Tom Roan	1.50	3.50	5.00	W
850 The Shocking Secret - Holly Roth 1955	.75	1.75	3.00	M
851 Run to Death - Patrick Quentin	2.00	4.00	6.00	M
852 The Affairs of Caroline Cherie - Cecil Saint-Laurent	1.50	3.50	5.00	
853 The Body on the Bench - Dorothy B. Hughes	1.50	3.50	5.00	M
854 Heather Mary - J. M. Scott	1.50	3.50	5.00	
855 The Witness for the Prosecution - Agatha Christie	1.50	3.50	5.00	M
856 To Walk the Night - William Sloane	1.50	3.50	5.00	M
857 Dead and Gone - Brandon Bird	1.50	3.50	5.00	M
858 Bury Me Not - Allan R. Bosworth	1.50	3.50	5.00	W
859 The Crooked Hinge - John Dickson Carr	2.00	4.00	7.50	M
860 Seeing Red - Theodora DuBois	1.50	3.50	5.00	
861 Saddle Up for Sunlight - Allan Vaughan Elston	1.50	3.50	5.00	W
862 My Favorite Football Stories - Red Grange	2.00	4.00	6.00	S
863 The Law at Randado - Elmore Leonard	1.50	3.50	5.00	W
864 The Thirsty Land - Norman A. Fox	1.50	3.50	5.00	W
865 Death Has Three Lives - Brett Halliday	1.50	3.50	5.00	M
866 Michael Shayne's Long Chance - Brett Halliday	.75	1.75	3.00	M
867 She Woke to Darkness - Brett Halliday	1.50	3.50	5.00	M
868 Run, Killer, Run - William Campbell Gault	1.50	3.50	5.00	M
869 Bounty Guns - Luke Short	1.50	3.50	5.00	W
870 The Danger Within - Michael Gilbert	1.50	3.50	5.00	
871 Murder in Retrospect - Agatha Christie	1.50	3.50	5.00	M
872 Grin and Bear It - George Lichty	2.00	4.00	6.00	H
873 The Tender Poisoner - John Bingham	1.50	3.50	5.00	M
874 The Big Money - Harold Q. Masur	1.50	3.50	5.00	M
875 The Violent Land - Wayne D. Overholser 1955	1.50	3.50	5.00	W
876 The Long Chase - James B. Hendryx	1.50	3.50	5.00	W
877 Man Missing - Mignon G. Eberhart	1.50	3.50	5.00	M
878 The Border Jumpers - Will C. Brown	1.50	3.50	5.00	W
879 Gold on the Hoof - Walker A. Tompkins	1.50	3.50	5.00	W
880 The Silent Women - Margaret Page Hood	1.50	3.50	5.00	
881 Fog of Doubt - Christianna Brand 1956	1.50	3.50	5.00	
882 The High Passes - John Reese	1.50	3.50	5.00	
883 The Murder that Wouldn't Stay Solved - Hampton Stone	1.50	3.50	5.00	M
884 Danger West! - Robert McCaig	1.50	3.50	5.00	W
885 Straw Man - Doris Miles Disney	1.50	3.50	5.00	M
886 Grave Danger - Frank Kane	1.50	3.50	5.00	
887 The Ponder Heart - Eudora Welty	.75	1.75	3.00	
888 Murder at the Vicarage - Agatha Christie	1.50	3.50	5.00	M
889 Trail's End - William MacLeod Raine	.75	1.75	3.00	W
890 My Son, the Murderer - Patrick Quentin	2.00	4.00	6.00	M
891 Blood on the Stars - Brett Halliday	1.50	3.50	5.00	M
892 Quick on the Shoot - George C. Appell	1.50	3.50	5.00	
893 The Frightened Fingers - Spencer Dean	.75	1.75	3.00	M
894 Thin Air - Howard Browne	.75	1.75	3.00	M
895 Raw Land - Luke Short	1.50	3.50	5.00	W
896 The Butcher's Wife - Owen Cameron	1.50	3.50	5.00	
897 The Twilighters - Noel M. Loomis	1.50	3.50	5.00	W
898 Gulf Coast Girl - Charles Williams c-Maguire	2.00	4.00	7.50	
899 Cats Prowl at Night - A. A. Fair	.75	1.75	3.00	M
900 The Woman on the Roof - Helen Nielsen 1956	1.50	3.50	5.00	M
901 Red Hot Ice - Frank Kane	.75	1.75	3.00	M
902 Eye Witness - George Harmon Cose	1.50	3.50	5.00	M
903 Draw or Drag - Wayne D. Overholser	.75	1.75	3.00	W
904 The Body in the Basket - George Bagby	.75	1.75	3.00	M

(DELL, continued)

905 In a Deadly Vein - Brett Halliday	.75	1.75	3.00	M
906 Day of the Outlaw - Lee E. Wells	.75	1.75	3.00	W
907 Shadow on the Range - Norman A. Fox	.75	1.75	3.00	W
908 Washington Whispers Murder - Leslie Ford	.75	1.75	3.00	M
909 Day of the Dead - Bart Spicer	.75	1.75	3.00	
910 The Restless Hands - Bruno Fischer	.75	1.75	3.00	
911 Lazy H Feud - Ed LaVanway	.75	1.75	3.00	W
912 Cards on the Table - Agatha Christie	.75	1.75	3.00	M
913 Goodbye to Gunsmoke - Ralph Catlin	.75	1.75	3.00	W
914 Stranger in Town - Brett Halliday	.75	1.75	3.00	M
915 Masterpiece in Murder - Richard Powell	.75	1.75	3.00	M
916 Last of the Longhorns - Will Ermine	.75	1.75	3.00	W
917 The Opening Door - Helen Reilly	.75	1.75	3.00	M
918 Green Light for Death - Frank Kane	.75	1.75	3.00	M
919 Their Guns were Fast - Harry Sinclair Drago	.75	1.75	3.00	W
920 The Lively Corpse - Margaret Millar	.75	1.75	3.00	M
921 The Cautious Maiden - Cecil Saint-Laurent	.75	1.75	3.00	
922 The Hidden Grave - Peter Hardin	.75	1.75	3.00	
923 Scout Commander - S. E. Whitman	.75	1.75	3.00	
924 Cast a Long Shadow - Wayne D. Overholser	.75	1.75	3.00	W
925 The Tall Dark Man - Anne Chamberlain 1956	.75	1.75	3.00	
926 Murder in the Raw - William Campbell Gault	.75	1.75	3.00	M
927 Stormy in the West - Norman A. Fox	.75	1.75	3.00	W
928 The Unquiet Corpse - William Sloane	.75	1.75	3.00	M
929 Dead Stop - Doris Miles Disney	.75	1.75	3.00	M
930 The Texas Pistol - James Keene 1957	.75	1.75	3.00	
931 Never Bet Your Life - George Harmon Coxe	.75	1.75	3.00	M
932 Rustlers' Bend - Will Ermine	.75	1.75	3.00	M
933 Murder at Nightfall - Edna Sherry	.75	1.75	3.00	M
934 A Taste for Violence - Brett Halliday	.75	1.75	3.00	M
935 Border Guns - Eugene Cunningham	.75	1.75	3.00	W
936 Worse than Murder - Evelyn Berckman	.75	1.75	3.00	
937 Murder at Hazelmoor - Agatha Christie	.75	1.75	3.00	M
938 Renegade Canyon - Peter Dawson	.75	1.75	3.00	W
939 Fools Die on Friday - A. A. Fair	.75	1.75	3.00	M
940 Escape from Five Shadows - Elmore Leonard	.75	1.75	3.00	
941 Murder is a Witch - John Bingham	.75	1.75	3.00	M
942 The Sagebrush Bandit - Bliss Lomax (H. S. Drago)	.75	1.75	3.00	W
943 The Man Who Had Too Much to Lose - Hampton Stone	.75	1.75	3.00	M
944 Bury Me Deep - Harold Q. Masur	.75	1.75	3.00	M
945 Alder Gulch - Ernest Haycox	.75	1.75	3.00	W
946 The Blonde Cried Murder - Brett Halliday	.75	1.75	3.00	M
947 The Settler - William O. Turner	.75	1.75	3.00	W
948 Steel to the South - Wayne D. Overholser	.75	1.75	3.00	M
949 Dead Storage - George Bagby	.75	1.75	3.00	M
950 Night Passage - Norman A. Fox 1957	.75	1.75	3.00	W
951 Murder in a Nunnery - Eric Shepherd	.75	1.75	3.00	M
952 Man in the Saddle - Ernest Haycox	.75	1.75	3.00	W
953 Dead of Summer - Dana Mosely	.75	1.75	3.00	
954 To Ride the River With - William MacLeod Raine	.75	1.75	3.00	
955 Postmark Murder - Mignon G. Eberhart	.75	1.75	3.00	M
956 Riding Gun - Eugene Cunningham	.75	1.75	3.00	W
957 This Is It, Michael Shayne - Brett Halliday	.75	1.75	3.00	M
958 Framed in Blood - Brett Halliday	.75	1.75	3.00	M
959 The Brass and the Blue - James Keene	.75	1.75	3.00	
960 Murder and the Married Virgin - Brett Halliday	.75	1.75	3.00	M
961 Mr. Parker Pyne, Detective - Agatha Christie	.75	1.75	3.00	M
962 King Colt - Luke Short	.75	1.75	3.00	W
963 Savage Range - Luke Short	.75	1.75	3.00	W
964 Inspector Maigret and the Burglar's Wife - Georges Simenon	2.00	4.00	7.50	M
965 Murder is My Business - Brett Halliday 1958	.75	1.75	3.00	M
966 The Diamond Hitch - Frank O'Rourke	.75	1.75	3.00	
967 Secret of the Wastelands - Bliss Lomax	.75	1.75	3.00	W
968 The Blonde Died Dancing - Kelley Roos	.75	1.75	3.00	M
969 Stranger from Arizona - Norman A. Fox	.75	1.75	3.00	W
970 Focus on Murder - George Harmon Coxe	.75	1.75	3.00	M
971 Seven Days Before Dying - Helen Nielsen	.75	1.75	3.00	M

(DELL, continued)

972	Gunlock - Wayne D. Overholser	.75	1.75	3.00	W
973	The Fatal Foursome - Frank Kane	.75	1.75	3.00	
974	Stampede at Blue Springs - Gene Olson	.75	1.75	3.00	
975	Return of a Fighter - Ernest Haycox	.75	1.75	3.00	W
	1958				
976	Dear Doctor - Juliet Lowell	1.50	3.50	5.00	H
977	Vertigo - Pierre Boileau & Thomas Narcejac	2.00	4.00	7.50	
	Movie tie-in				
978	Weep for a Blonde - Brett Halliday	.75	1.75	3.00	M
979	Bullet Brand - Nick Sumner	.75	1.75	3.00	W
980	Tall Man Riding - Norman A. Fox	.75	1.75	3.00	W
981	The Uncomplaining Corpses - Brett Halliday	.75	1.75	3.00	M
982	The Diehard - Jean Potts	.75	1.75	3.00	
983	The Demon Stirs - Owen Cameron	.75	1.75	3.00	
984	Man on a Rope - George Harmon Coxe	.75	1.75	3.00	M
985	So Young, So Cold, So Fair - John Creasey	.75	1.75	3.00	M
986	Man of the West - Will C. Brown	.75	1.75	3.00	W
987	Heads You Lose - Brett Halliday	.75	1.75	3.00	M
988	Shoot the Works - Brett Halliday	.75	1.75	3.00	M
989	Tickets for Death - Brett Halliday	.75	1.75	3.00	M
990	Here We Go Again and Bottle Fatigue - Virgil Partch	2.00	4.00	7.50	H
991	Deadly Beloved - William Ard	.75	1.75	3.00	
992	Don't Count the Corpses - Christopher Monig	.75	1.75	3.00	M
993	Desperate Man - Wayne D. Overholser	.75	1.75	3.00	W
994	Grounds for Murder - John Appleby	.75	1.75	3.00	M
995	Lady Killer - William M. Hardy	.75	1.75	3.00	
996	Now, Will You Try for Murder? - Harry Olesker	.75	1.75	3.00	M
	1959				
997	Cop Killer - George Bagby	.75	1.75	3.00	M
998	Lover Boy - Janice Berenstain & Stanley Berenstain	.75	1.75	3.00	H
999	The Trouble with Fidelity - George Malcolm-Smith	.75	1.75	3.00	
1000	Justice, My Brother! - James Keene	.75	1.75	3.00	
	1959				
1001	Dear Hollywood - Juliet Lowell	.75	1.75	3.00	
1002	The Badlands Beyond - Norman A. Fox	.75	1.75	3.00	W
1003	Once a Widow - Lee Roberts	.75	1.75	3.00	
1004	She Asked for Murder - Edna Sherry	.75	1.75	3.00	M
1005	Stranger with a Gun - Bliss Lomax (H. S. Drago)	.75	1.75	3.00	W
1006	Trapped! - Jean Hougron	.75	1.75	3.00	
1007	A Gem of a Murder - Carleton Keith	.75	1.75	3.00	
1008	The Lone Deputy - Wayne D. Overholser	.75	1.75	3.00	W

DELL D-SERIES

(Dell Publishing Company)

D101	Chicago Confidential - Jack Lait & Lee Mortimer	.75	1.75	3.00	NF
	1952				
D102	The Great Smith - Edison Marshall	1.50	3.50	5.00	A

Dell D-Series D102, c. Dell   Dell D-Series D204, c. Dell   Dell D-Series D266, c. Dell

D103 Gypsy Sixpence - Edison Marshall	.75	1.75	3.00	
D104 Tomorrow Will be Better - Betty Smith	.50	1.25	2.00	
D105 The Natchez Woman - Alice Walworth Graham	.50	1.25	2.00	
D106 Mrs. Craddock - W. Somerset Maugham	.50	1.25	2.00	
D107 Rivers Parting - Shirley Barker	.50	1.25	2.00	
D108 Washington Confidential - Jack Lait & Lee Mortimer	.50	1.25	2.00	NF
D109 The Chequer Board - Nevil Shute	.75	1.75	3.00	
D110 The Forest and the Fort - Hervey Allen	.50	1.25	2.00	
D111 Gold for My Fair Lady - Sidney H. Courtier	.50	1.25	2.00	
D112 Three Hundred Pillsbury Prize Recipes	.50	1.25	2.00	NF
D113 The Phantom Emperor - Neil H. Swanson	.75	1.75	3.00	
D114 Go Down to Glory - Richard Warren Hatch	.50	1.25	2.00	
D115 The Circle of the Day - Helen Howe	.50	1.25	2.00	
D116 Slogum House - Mari Sandoz	.50	1.25	2.00	
D117 Across the River and Into the Trees	.75	1.75	3.00	
1953				
D118 Really the Blues - Mezz Mezzrow & Bernard Wolfe	1.50	3.50	5.00	
D119 Castle in the Swamp - Edison Marshall	.50	1.25	2.00	
D120 Snowslide - Carl Jonas	.50	1.25	2.00	
D121 Caroline Cherie - Cecil Saint-Laurent	.50	1.25	2.00	
D122 The Infinite Woman - Edison Marshall	.50	1.25	2.00	
D123 The Legacy - Nevil Shute	.50	1.25	2.00	
D124 Jefferson Selleck - Carl Jonas	.50	1.25	2.00	
D125 Captain Ebony - Hamilton Cochran	.75	1.75	3.00	
1953				
D126 The Swimming Pool - Mary Roberts Rinehart	.50	1.25	2.00	M
D127 Diamond Head - Houston Branch & Frank Waters	.50	1.25	2.00	
D128 Bedford Village - Hervey Allen	.50	1.25	2.00	
D129 Boom Town - Jack O'Connor	.50	1.25	2.00	
D130 Round the Bend - Nevil Shute	.50	1.25	2.00	
D131 Gina - George Albert Glay	.50	1.25	2.00	
D132 Tallulah - Tallulah Bankhead	1.50	3.50	5.00	B
1954				
D133 Caroline Coquette - Cecil Saint-Laurent	.50	1.25	2.00	
D134 Fresh Water Fishing - Arthur Carhart	.75	1.75	3.00	NF
D135 Reap the Whirlwind - Jean Hougron	.50	1.25	2.00	
D136 The Rogue from Padua - Jay Williams	.75	1.75	3.00	
D137 The Bold Sabouteurs - Chandler Brossard	.50	1.25	2.00	
D138 Daughter of Strangers - Elizabeth Boatwright Coker	.50	1.25	2.00	
D139 The Viking - Edison Marshall	.75	1.75	3.00	A
D140 This Side of Paradise - F. Scott Fitzgerald	.75	1.75	3.00	
D141 Three to Get Married - Fulton J. Sheen	.50	1.25	2.00	
D142 The Story of America - Hendrik Willem Van Loon	.75	1.75	3.00	NF
D143 The Doctor on Bean Street - Simon Kent	.50	1.25	2.00	
D144 Rogue's Holiday - Hamilton Cochran	1.50	3.50	5.00	
D145 The Magnificent Bastards - Lucy Herndon Crockett	.50	1.25	2.00	
1955				
D146 How to Help Your Doctor Help You - Walter C. Alvarez	.50	1.25	2.00	NF
D147 The Long Rifle - Stewart Edward White	1.50	3.50	5.00	A
D148 Fresh and Salt Water Spinning - Eugene Burns	.75	1.75	3.00	NF
D149 The Night of the Hunter - Davis Grubb	.50	1.25	2.00	
D150 Who Goes There? - John W. Campbell, Jr.	.75	1.75	3.00	SF
1955				
D151 Sylvia - Edgar Mittelholzer	.50	1.25	2.00	
D152 Sunset Land - Eugene Manlove Rhodes	.50	1.25	2.00	W
D153 Herself Surprised - Joyce Cary	.50	1.25	2.00	
D154 The Frightened Wife - Mary Roberts Rinehart	.50	1.25	2.00	M
D155 Guns and Hunting - Pete Brown	.75	1.75	3.00	NF
D156 Tell it on the Drums - Robert Krepps	1.50	3.50	5.00	A
D157 Caravan to Xanadu - Edison Marshall	.75	1.75	3.00	A
D158 Indigo - Christine Weston	.50	1.25	2.00	
D159 The Man Who Killed Lincoln - Philip Van Doren Stern	.75	1.75	3.00	
D160 Trial - Don M. Mankiewicz	.50	1.25	2.00	
1956				

D161	The Tumult and the Shouting - Grantland Rice	.50	1.25	2.00	
D162	The Drinker - Hans Fallada	.50	1.25	2.00	
D163	Brideshead Revisited - Evelyn Waugh	.50	1.25	2.00	
D164	The Dark Arena - Mario Puza	.50	1.25	2.00	
D165	The Wall - Mary Roberts Rinehart	.50	1.25	2.00	M
D166	Bonjour Tristesse - Francoise Sagan	.50	1.25	2.00	
D167	The Picture of Dorian Grey - Oscar Wilde	2.00	4.00	7.50	
D168	Mosquitoes - William Faulkner	.50	1.25	2.00	
D169	Roads from the Fort - Arvid Shulenberger	.50	1.25	2.00	
D170	The Young Lovers - Julian Halevy	.50	1.25	2.00	
D171	The Steep Ascent - Anne Morrow Lindbergh	.50	1.25	2.00	
D172	Fourteen for Tonight - Steve Allen	.75	1.75	3.00	
D173	Benjamin Blake - Edison Marshall	.50	1.25	2.00	A
D174	An Affair of Dishonor - Louis A. Brennan	.50	1.25	2.00	
D175	The Far Country - Nevil Shute	.50	1.25	2.00	
	1956				
D176	Mrs. Craddock - W. Somerset Maugham	.50	1.25	2.00	
D177	Warhorse - John Cunningham	.50	1.25	2.00	
D178	The Golden Kazoo - John G. Schneider	.75	1.75	3.00	F
D179	The Yellow Room - Mary Roberts Rinehart	.50	1.25	2.00	M
D180	Child Behavior: Gesell Institute - Louise Bates Ames & Frances L. Ilg	.50	1.25	2.00	NF
D181	Daisy Miller and the Turn of the Screw - Henry James	.50	1.25	2.00	
D182	Listen! The Wind - Anne Morrow Lindbergh	.50	1.25	2.00	
D183	Nightmare - Guy Endore	.50	1.25	2.00	
D184	The Company She Keeps - Mary McCarthy	.50	1.25	2.00	
D185	Ship's Company - Lonnie Coleman	.50	1.25	2.00	
	1957				
D186	The Bride Wore Black - Cornell Woolrich	.75	1.75	3.00	M
D187	Trial by Fury - Craig Rice	.50	1.25	2.00	M
D188	Laura - Vera Caspary	.50	1.25	2.00	M
D189	No Man is an Island - Thomas Merton	.50	1.25	2.00	
D190	Blaze of the Sun - Jean Hougren	.50	1.25	2.00	
D191	Winter's Tales - Isak Dinesen	.75	1.75	3.00	F
D192	A Puzzle for Fools - Patrick Quentin	.50	1.25	2.00	M
D193	Aspects of Love - David Garnett	.50	1.25	2.00	
D194	Warrant for X - Philip MacDonald	.50	1.25	2.00	M
D195	The Wicked Village - Gabriel Chevallier	.50	1.25	2.00	
D196	Headed for a Hearse - Jonathan Latimer	.50	1.25	2.00	M
D197	The Circular Staircase - Mary Roberts Rinehart	.50	1.25	2.00	M
D198	The Loved and the Unloved - Thomas Hal Phillips	.50	1.25	2.00	
D199	Love in the South Seas - Bengt Danielsson	.50	1.25	2.00	
D200	Dell Crossword Puzzle Dictionary - Kathleen Rafferty	.50	1.25	2.00	NF
	1957				
D201	A Coffin for Dimitrios - Eric Ambler	.50	1.25	2.00	M
D202	Mountain Boy - Felix Holt	.50	1.25	2.00	
D203	The Red Right Hand - Joel Townsley Rogers	.50	1.25	2.00	M
D204	The Mark of Zorro - Johnston McCulley TV tie-in	1.50	3.50	5.00	A
D205	The Lonely Passion of Judith Hearne - Brian Moore	.50	1.25	2.00	
D206	A Certain Smile - Francoise Sagan	.50	1.25	2.00	
D207	Phantom Lady - William Irish	.75	1.75	3.00	M
D208	Seeds of Contemplation - Thomas Merton	.50	1.25	2.00	
	1958				
D209	Paths of Glory - Humphrey Cobb	.50	1.25	2.00	
D210	Owls Don't Blink - A. A. Fair	.50	1.25	2.00	M
D211	Spill the Jackpot - A. A. Fair	.50	1.25	2.00	M
D212	Bedrooms Have Windows - A. A. Fair	.50	1.25	2.00	M
D213	Give 'Em the Ax - A. A. Fair	.50	1.25	2.00	M
D214	A Charmed Life - Mary McCarthy	.50	1.25	2.00	
D215	Before the Fact - Frances Iles	.50	1.25	2.00	M
D216	The Long Rifle - Stewart Edward White	.75	1.75	3.00	A
D217	Sad Cypress - Agatha Christie	.50	1.25	2.00	M
D218	The Witness for the Prosecution - Agatha Christie	.50	1.25	2.00	M
D219	House Party - Virginia Rowans	.50	1.25	2.00	
D220	The Door - Mary Roberts Rinehart	.50	1.25	2.00	M
D221	Dead Sure - Herbert Brean	.50	1.25	2.00	M
D222	The Loved One - Evelyn Waugh	.50	1.25	2.00	

D223 Fer-de-lance - Rex Stout	.50	1.25	2.00	M
D224 No Time at All - Charles Einstein	.50	1.25	2.00	
D225 Ride the Pink Horse - Dorothy B. Hughes	.50	1.25	2.00	M
1958				
D226 A Real Gone Guy - Frank Kane	.50	1.25	2.00	M
D227 The Beast Must Die - Nicholas Blake	.75	1.75	3.00	M
D228 Two-thirds of a Ghost - Helen McCloy	.50	1.25	2.00	M
D229 A Houseful of Love - Marjorie Housepian	.50	1.25	2.00	
D230 The Amazing Adventures of Father Brown -				
G. K. Chesterton	.75	1.75	3.00	M
D231 12 Stories They Wouldn't Let Me Do on				
TV - Alfred Hitchcock	.75	1.75	3.00	M
D232 Tall, Dark and Deadly - Harold Q. Masur	.50	1.25	2.00	M
D233 The Bellamy Trial - Frances Noyes Hart	.50	1.25	2.00	M
D234 Death of a Ghost - Margery Allingham	.50	1.25	2.00	M
D235 Dead Man's Mirror - Agatha Christie	.50	1.25	2.00	M
D236 Appointment with Death - Agatha Christie	.50	1.25	2.00	M
D237 The Brain Pickers - Hallie Burnett	.50	1.25	2.00	
D238 Background to Danger - Eric Ambler	.50	1.25	2.00	M
D239 Grand Hotel— Vicki Baum	.50	1.25	2.00	
D240 Rage of Desire - Charles Mergendahl	.50	1.25	2.00	
D241 The Flower Drum Song - C. Y. Lee	.75	1.75	3.00	
Movie tie-in				
D242 Miss Pinkerton - Mary Roberts Rinehart	.50	1.25	2.00	M
D243 Secrets of Successful Selling -				
John D. Murphy	.50	1.25	2.00	NF
D244 Falling Through Space - Richard Hillary	.50	1.25	2.00	
D245 Corner Boy - Herbert Simmons	.50	1.25	2.00	
D246 A Mirror for Observers - Edgar Pangborn	.75	1.75	3.00	
D247 The Mystery of the Dead Police -				
Philip MacDonald	.50	1.25	2.00	M
D248 The Private Practice of Michael Shayne -				
Brett Halliday	.50	1.25	2.00	M
D249 The Man in the Brown Suit - Agatha Christie	.50	1.25	2.00	M
D250 Suddenly a Corpse - Harold Q. Masur	.50	1.25	2.00	M
1958				
D251 The Great Mistake - Mary Roberts				
Rinehart	.50	1.25	2.00	M
D252 The Mountain Cat Murders - Rex Stout	.50	1.25	2.00	M
D253 Turn on the Heat - A. A. Fair	.50	1.25	2.00	M
D254 The Secrets of Caroline Cherie -				
Cecil Saint-Laurent	.50	1.25	2.00	
1959				
D255 The Main in the Queue - Josephine Tey	.50	1.25	2.00	M
D256 The Living Bread - Thomas Merton	.50	1.25	2.00	
D257 The Decline and Fall of Practically Everybody -				
Will Cuppy	.50	1.25	2.00	H
D258 The Camp Followers - Ugo Pirro	.75	1.75	3.00	
D259 Another Man's Murder - Mignon G.				
Eberhart	.50	1.25	2.00	M
D260 Student Nurse - Renee Shann	.50	1.25	2.00	
D261 The Man in the Net - Patrick Quentin	.75	1.75	3.00	M
D262 The Secret of Chimneys - Agatha Christie	.50	1.25	2.00	M
D263 Into the Valley - John Hersey	.50	1.25	2.00	
D264 Slay Ride - Frank Kane	.50	1.25	2.00	M
D265 The Doctor's Secret - Hans Kades	.50	1.25		
D266 The Story of Walt Disney - Pete Martin &				
Diane Disney Miller	1.50	3.50	5.00	B
D267 The Golden Eagle - John Jennings	.75	1.75	3.00	A
D268 The Strange Bedfellow - Evelyn Berckman	.50	1.25	2.00	
D269 Call for Michael Shayne - Brett Halliday	.50	1.25	2.00	M
D270 Murder in Venice - Thomas Sterling	.50	1.25	2.00	M
D271 Murder on Their Minds - George Harmon				
Coxe	.50	1.25	2.00	M
D272 Shadow of a Killer - William Mole	.50	1.25	2.00	
D273 Focus - Arthur Miller	.50	1.25	2.00	
D274 The Third Level - Jack Finney	.50	1.25	2.00	
D275 A Hole in the Ground - Andrew Garve	.50	1.25	2.00	M
1959				
D276 The Man in Lower Ten - Mary Roberts				
Rinehart	.50	1.25	2.00	M
D277 Those Without Shadows - Francoise Sagan	.50	1.25	2.00	
D278 The Girl Who Kept Knocking them Dead -				
Hampton Stone	.50	1.25	2.00	M
D279 In Case of Emergency - Georges Simenon	1.50	3.50	5.00	M
D280 Trigger Mortis - Frank Kane	.50	1.25	2.00	M

D281	13 More Stories they Wouldn't Let Me Do on TV - Alfred Hitchcock	.75	1.75	3.00	M
D282	The Talented Mr. Ripley - Patricia Highsmith	.75	1.75	3.00	
D283	Murder on the Wanton Bride - Brett Halliday	.50	1.25	2.00	M
D284	Earthshaker - Robert W. Krepps	.75	1.75	3.00	A
D285	Lover's Point - C. Y. Lee	.50	1.25	2.00	
D286	The Gentle Murderer - Dorothy Salisbury Davis	.50	1.25	2.00	M
D287	The Meaning of Dreams - Calvin S. Hall	.50	1.25	2.00	NF
D288	Murder on the Links - Agatha Christie	.50	1.25	2.00	M
D289	Brand of Empire - Luke Short	.50	1.25	2.00	W
D290	Trail Town - Ernest Haycox	.50	1.25	2.00	W
D291	Marked for Murder - Brett Halliday	.50	1.25	2.00	M
D292	Dead Man's Diary and a Taste of Cognac - Brett Halliday	.50	1.25	2.00	M
D293	Dividend on Death - Brett Halliday	.50	1.25	2.00	M
D294	The Sensualists - Ben Hecht	.50	1.25	2.00	
D295					
D296	The Color of Murder - Julian Symons	.50	1.25	2.00	M
D297	Sophie - Geoffrey Wagner	.50	1.25	2.00	
D298	Murder on Broadway - Harold Q. Masur	.50	1.25	2.00	M
D299	One More Unfortunate - Edgar Lustgarten	.50	1.25	2.00	
D300	Long Shot - David Mark 1959	.50	1.25	2.00	
D301	The Woman in the Woods - Lee Blackstock	.50	1.25	2.00	
D302	The Hound of the Baskervilles - Arthur Conan Doyle	.75	1.75	3.00	M
D303	Only Akiko - Duncan Thorp	.50	1.25	2.00	
D304	Angel's Ransom - David Dodge	.50	1.25	2.00	
D305	The Labors of Hercules - Agatha Christie	.50	1.25	2.00	M
D306	The April Robin Murders - Ed McBain & Craig Rice	.50	1.25	2.00	M
D307	Gypsy - Gypsy Rose Lee	.75	1.75	3.00	B
D308	Kind Are Her Answers - Mary Renault	.50	1.25	2.00	R
D309	Top of the Heap - A. A. Fair	.50	1.25	2.00	M
D310	Boulevard - Robert Sabatier	.50	1.25	2.00	
D311	The Eighth Circle - Stanley Ellin	.50	1.25	2.00	
D312					
D313	The Silent Life - Thomas Merton	.50	1.25	2.00	
D314	Fit to Kill - Brett Halliday	.50	1.25	2.00	M
D315	The Search - Myrick Land	.50	1.25	2.00	
D316	The Confession and Sight Unseen - Mary Roberts Rinehart	.50	1.25	2.00	M
D317	The Heart Remembers - Faith Baldwin	.50	1.25	2.00	R
D318	The Shrew is Dead - Shelley Smith	.50	1.25	2.00	
D319	Child of Our Time - Michael del Castillo	.50	1.25	2.00	
D320	The Sunlit Ambush - Mark Derby	.50	1.25	2.00	
D321	The Red House Mystery - A. A. Milne	.75	1.75	3.00	M
D322	The Man with Two Wives - Patrick Quentin	.75	1.75	3.00	M
D323	The Three Coffins - John Dickson Carr	.75	1.75	3.00	M
D324					
D325	Quiet Horror - Stanley Ellin	.75	1.75	3.00	
D326	The Mysterious Mr. Quin - Agatha Christie	.50	1.25	2.00	M
D327	Bodies Are Where You Find Them - Brett Halliday	.50	1.25	2.00	M
D328	Moment of Danger - Donald MacKenzie				
D329	You Can't Live Forever - Harold Q. Masur	.50	1.25	2.00	M
D330	The Bat - Mary Roberts Rinehart	.50	1.25	2.00	M
D331	Murder in Miami - Brett Halliday 1959	.50	1.25	2.00	M

DELL F-SERIES

(Dell Publishing Company)

F50	Gus the Great - Thomas W. Duncan 1953	.50	1.25	2.00	
F51	Canal Town - Samuel Hopkins Adams	.75	1.75	3.00	
F52	Wake of the Red Witch - Garland Roark	.75	1.75	3.00	A
F53	War and Peace - Leo Tolstoy 1955	.50	1.25	2.00	

F54 Persephone - Thomas Skinner Willings	.50	1.25	2.00	
1956				
F55 The Brothers Karamazov - Fyodor Dostoyevsky	.50	1.25	2.00	
F56 The Story of Edgar Cayce - Thomas Sugrue	.50	1.25	2.00	B
F57 Bedside Book of Famous French Stories - Belle Becker & Robert N. Linscott	.50	1.25	2.00	
F58 Raintree County - Ross Lockridge, Jr.	.50	1.25	2.00	A
1957				
F59 Life of Christ - Giovanni Papini	.75	1.75	3.00	B
F60 The Ninth Wave - Eugene Burdick	.50	1.25	2.00	
F61 Peyton Place - Grace Metalious	.50	1.25	2.00	
F62 How to Take Better Pictures - Joseph C. Keeley	.50	1.25	2.00	NF
F63 Dodsworth - Sinclair Lewis	.50	1.25	2.00	
F64 The Savage Place - Leon Arden	.50	1.25	2.00	
1958				
F65 Make Each Day Count - James Keller	.50	1.25	2.00	NF
F66 Maybe I'm Dead - Joe Klaas	.50	1.25	2.00	
F67 The Viking - Edison Marshall	.75	1.75	3.00	A
F68 Brideshead Revisited - Evelyn Waugh	.50	1.25	2.00	
F69 Beloved - Vina Delmar	.50	1.25	2.00	
F70 David Copperfield - Charles Dickens	.75	1.75	3.00	
F71 The Bounty Lands - William Ellis	.50	1.25	2.00	
F72 The Upstart - Edison Marshall	.50	1.25	2.00	A
1959				
F73 Sharks and Little Fish - Wolfgang Ott	.50	1.25	2.00	NF
F74 A Handful of Dust and Decline and Fall - Evelyn Waugh	.50	1.25	2.00	
F75 Anatomy of a Murder - Robert Traver	.50	1.25	2.00	M
1959				
F76 The Horse Soldiers - Harold Sinclair Movie tie-in	1.50	3.50	5.00	A
F77 The Fiery Trial - Carl Sandburg	.75	1.75	3.00	
F78 Embezzled Heaven - Franz Werfel	.50	1.25	2.00	
F79 Ben-Hur - Lew Wallace	.50	1.25	2.00	A
F80 This Earth is Mine - Alice Tisdale Hobart	.50	1.25	2.00	
F81 The Raw Edge - Benjamin Appel	.50	1.25	2.00	
F82 The Circus in the Attic - Robert Penn Warren	.50	1.25	2.00	
F83 Theme for Ballet - Vicki Baum	.50	1.25	2.00	
F84 The Beat Generation and the Angry Young Men - Gene Feldman & Max Gartenberg	1.50	3.50	5.00	
F85 Ranchero - Stewart Edward White	.75	1.75	3.00	W
F86 On My Own - Eleanor Roosevelt	.50	1.25	2.00	
F87 Yankee Pasha - Edison Marshall	.50	1.25	2.00	A
F88 Baa Baa Black Sheep - Pappy Boyington	.75	1.75	3.00	NF
F89 Great True Adventures - Lowell Thomas	.50	1.25	2.00	NF
F90 Harrison High - John Farris	.50	1.25	2.00	
F91				
F92				
F93				
F94 The Intruder - Charles Beaumont	.50	1.25	2.00	
F95 The Magnificent Bastards - Lucy Herndon Crockett	.50	1.25	2.00	

DELL FIRST EDITIONS

(Dell Publishing Co.)

1E Down - Walt Grove	.75	1.75	3.00	
1953				
2E Madball - Frederic Brown, First ed., 1953	3.00	6.00	12.00	
D3 Women - A. M. Krich	.50	1.25	2.00	
4 Girl on the Beach - George Sumner Albee	.50	1.25	2.00	
5 The Bloody Spur - Charles Einstein	.50	1.25	2.00	M
6 Next Time is for Live - Paul Warren	.50	1.25	2.00	
7 Bold Rider - Luke Short	.75	1.75	3.00	W
8 Back Country - William Fuller	.50	1.25	2.00	
1954				
D9 6 Great Short Novels of Science Fiction - ed. Groff Conklin	.75	1.75	3.00	SF
F10 The Ribald Reader - ed. A. M. Krich	.50	1.25	2.00	
11 Arrow in the Dust - L. L. Foreman	.50	1.25	2.00	W

12	Area of Suspicion - Jonn D. MacDonald	1.50	3.50	5.00	M
13	Fever Heat - Angus Vicker	.50	1.25	2.00	
14	The Man from Laramie - T. T. Flynn	.50	1.25	2.00	W
D15	Men - A. M. Krich	.50	1.25	2.00	
F16	Short Story Masterpieces - ed. Albert Erskine, Robert Penn Warren	.50	1.25	2.00	
17	The Crooked City - Robert Kyle	.50	1.25	2.00	
18	Smoky Valley - Donald Hamilton	.50	1.25	2.00	W
19	Conduct Unbecoming - Charles Fenton	.50	1.25	2.00	
D20	I Detest All My Sins - Jack Weeks	.50	1.25	2.00	
21	French Cartoons - William Cole & Douglas McKee	.50	1.25	2.00	H
22	The Nothing Man - Jim Thompson	.75	1.75	3.00	
23	Teresa - Les Savage, Jr.	.50	1.25	2.00	W
24	The Joys She Chose - Matthew Peters	.50	1.25	2.00	
25	Trouble on Big Cat - Glenn Corbin	.50	1.25	2.00	
	1954				
26	The Deadly Mermaid - James Atlee Phillips	.50	1.25	2.00	
27	Night Walker - Donald Hamilton	.50	1.25	2.00	
28	Goat Island - William Fuller	.50	1.25	2.00	
29	Sole Survivor - Louis Falstein	.50	1.25	2.00	
30	Plain Murder - C. S. Forester	.50	1.25	2.00	
31	The Man on the Blue - Luke Short	.75	1.75	3.00	
32	Year of Consent - Kendell Foster Crossen	.75	1.75	3.00	SF
33	Two Faces West - T. T. Flynn	.50	1.25	2.00	W
34	The Calm Man - David Cort	.50	1.25	2.00	
F35	Six Great Modern Short Novels	.50	1.25	2.00	
36	The Golden Urge - Robert Kyle	.50	1.25	2.00	
37	Last of the Breed - Les Savage, Jr.	.50	1.25	2.00	W
38	The Book of Prayers - Elfrieda & Leon McCauley	.50	1.25	2.00	
39	Too Funny for Words - Bill Yates	.50	1.25	2.00	H
D40	The Handbook of Beauty - Constance Hart	.50	1.25	2.00	NF
41	Dakota Rifle - Frank O'Rourke	.50	1.25	2.00	W
42	The Body Snatchers - Jack Finney	.50	1.25	2.00	NF
43	New Ways to Greater Word Power - Roger B. Goodman & David Lewin	.50	1.25	2.00	NF
44	Now is the Time - Lillian Smith	.50	1.25	2.00	
45	City of Love - Daniel Talbot	.50	1.25	2.00	
46	Line of Fire - Donald Hamilton	.50	1.25	2.00	
47	The Only Game in Town - Charles Einstein	.50	1.25	2.00	
F48	The Complete Book of Gardening - W. W. Goodpasture	.50	1.25	2.00	NF
49	A Gun for Billy Reo - C. Hall Thompson	.50	1.25	2.00	W
	1955				
50	Marital Blitz - Janice & Stanley Berenstain	.50	1.25	2.00	H
51	Nice Guys Finish Last - Robert Kyle	.50	1.25	2.00	
52	Fort Sun Dance - Manly Wade Wellman	.75	1.75	3.00	
D53	Everybody's Book of Modern Diet and Nutrition - Henrietta Fleck & Elizabeth Munves	.50	1.25	2.00	NF
FE54	How to Draw and Paint - Henry Gasser	.50	1.25	2.00	NF
55	What, When, Where and How to Drink - David Meyers & Richard L. Williams	.50	1.25	2.00	NF
D56	Too Near the Sun - Gordon Forbes	.50	1.25	2.00	
57	Women of the Avalon - L. L. Foreman	.50	1.25	2.00	W
58	After Innocense - Ian Gordon	.50	1.25	2.00	
59	The Big Fifty - Frank O'Rourke	.50	1.25	2.00	W
60	Dell Crossword Puzzles - Rosalind Moore & Kathleen Rafferty	.50	1.25	2.00	NF
61	The Dirty Shame - John R. Humphries	.50	1.25	2.00	
62	A Bullet for Cinderella - John D. MacDonald	.75	1.75	3.00	M
63	Hunger Mountain - William R. Scott	.50	1.25	2.00	
64	More French Cartoons - William Cole & Douglas McKee	.50	1.25	2.00	H
65	Return to Warbow - Les Savage, Jr.	.50	1.25	2.00	W
66	A Tiger in the Night - Robert Kyle	.50	1.25	2.00	
67	The Fastest Gun - Dan Cushman	.50	1.25	2.00	W
68	Bought With a Gun - Luke Short	.50	1.25	2.00	W
FE69	Six Centuries of Great Poetry - ed. Albert Erskine, Robert Penn Warren	.50	1.25	2.00	
70	Marauders' Moon - Luke Shot	.50	1.25	2.00	W
71	Local Color - John Andrew Rice	.50	1.25	2.00	
D72	How to Build and Operate a Model Railroad - Marshall McClintock	.75	1.75	3.00	NF

Dell 1st Editions 78, c. Dell

Dell 1st Editions A125, c. Dell

Dell 1st Editions B138, c. Dell

(DELL FIRST EDITIONS, continued)

73	In His Blood - Harold R. Daniels	.50	1.25	2.00	
74	Queen's Own - George C. Appell	.75	1.75	3.00	A
FE75	The Long Playing Record Guide - Warren de Motte 1955	.75	1.75	3.00	NF
76	Wiretap! - Charles Einstein	.50	1.25	2.00	
77	Dangerous Dames - Mike Shayne	.50	1.25	2.00	M
78	Little Iodine - Jimmy Hatlo	2.00	4.00	7.50	H
79	The $64,000 Question Quiz Book	.50	1.25	2.00	NF
D80	Short Stories, Short Plays and Songs by Noel Coward	.75	1.75	3.00	
D81	Down - Walt Grove	.50	1.25	2.00	
82	Texas, Blood Red - Shepard Rifkin 1956	.50	1.25	2.00	W
83	Night Fell on Georgia - Louise & Charles Samuels	.50	1.25	2.00	
FE84	The New Hammond - Dell World Atlas	.50	1.25	2.00	NF
85	April Evil - John D. MacDonald	.75	1.75	3.00	M
D86	While the City Sleeps - Charles Einstein	.50	1.25	2.00	
87	The Loner - Bliss Lomax (H. S. Drago)	.50	1.25	2.00	W
88	Intent to Kill - Michael Bryan	.50	1.25	2.00	M
89	Battle Royal - Frank O'Rourke	.75	1.75	3.00	A
D90	The Last Enemy - Berton Roueche	.50	1.25	2.00	
91	Mad River - Donald Hamilton	.50	1.25	2.00	
92	Night Boat to Paris - Richard Jessup	.50	1.25	2.00	
93	Forever Funny - Bill Yates	.50	1.25	2.00	H
94	Atlantic Avenue - Albert Halper	.50	1.25	2.00	
95	The Devil's Spawn - Robert Carse	.50	1.25	2.00	
96	The Great Locomotive Chase - MacLennan Roberts movie tie-in	1.50	3.50	5.00	A
97	Juvenile Delinquency - Charles Preston	1.50	3.50	5.00	NF
FE98	Modern French Painting, 1855-1956 - Samuel Hunter	.50	1.25	2.00	NF
D99	Thirteen Great Stories - Daniel Talbot	.50	1.25	2.00	
FE100	Six Great Modern Plays - ed. Edward Parone 1956	.50	1.25	2.00	
101					
102					
103	The Angry Man - T. T. Flynn	.50	1.25	2.00	W
104	The Last Chance - Frank O'Rourke	.50	1.25	2.00	
105	The Pace That Kills - William Fuller	.50	1.25	2.00	
106	By My Victim - Robert Dietrich	.50	1.25	2.00	M
107	Singapore Passage - Donald Barr Chidsey	.75	1.75	3.00	A
108	Segundo - Frank O'Rourke	.50	1.25	2.00	
109	Cry Passion - Richard Jessup	.50	1.25	2.00	
A110	Riders West - anthology	.75	1.75	3.00	W
A111	The Big Success - Ian Gordon	.50	1.25	2.00	
A112	The Girl in 304 - Harold R. Daniels	.50	1.25	2.00	
A113	Murder in the Wind - John D. MacDonald	.75	1.75	3.00	
A114	The Big Bite - Charles Williams	.50	1.25	2.00	
A115	Maverick - Verne Athanas	2.00	4.00	7.50	W
A116	Kundu - Morris L. West	.50	1.25	2.00	
A117	Johnny Liddell's Morgue - Frank Kane	.50	1.25	2.00	M
A118	The Race of Giants - Matt Kinkaid	.50	1.25	2.00	
A119	Cimarron Trace - James Norman	.50	1.25	2.00	
A120	Wetback - William O'Farrell	.50	1.25	2.00	

A121	The Last Laugh - Charles Einstein	.50	1.25	2.00	
A122	The Branded Man - Luke Short	.50	1.25	2.00	W
A123	Assignment: Murder - Donald Hamilton	.50	1.25	2.00	M
A124	Rebel Gun - Arthur Stever	.50	1.25	2.00	W
A125	This is Little Lulu - Marge	3.00	6.00	12.00	H
A126	Key Witness - Frank Kane	.50	1.25	2.00	M
A127	Lone Hand - L. L. Foreman	.50	1.25	2.00	W
A128	The King and Four Queens - Theodore Sturgeon	3.00	6.00	12.00	W
A129	Bottoms Up! - Charles Preston	.50	1.25	2.00	H
A130	Death Trap - John D. MacDonald	.75	1.75	3.00	M
A131	The Bravados - Frank O'Rourke	.50	1.25	2.00	
A132	Under the Badge - C. Hall Thompson	.50	1.25	2.00	W
A133	The Girl in the Frame - William Fuller	.50	1.25	2.00	
A134	Bold Rider - Luke Short	.50	1.25	2.00	W
A135	Desert Guns - Steve Frazee	.50	1.25	2.00	W
A136	A Taste of Brass - Robert Donald Locke	.50	1.25	2.00	
A137	A Shady Place to Die - John Savage	.50	1.25	2.00	
A138	Showdown at Stony Crest - Joseph Wayne	.50	1.25	2.00	W
A139	The House of Numbers - Jack Finney	.50	1.25	2.00	
A140	Tall Wyoming - Dan Cushman	.50	1.25	2.00	W
A141	Murder on the Rocks - Robert Dietrich	.50	1.25	2.00	M
A142	The Living End - Frank Kane	.50	1.25	2.00	M
A143	The Outcast - Richard Ferber	.50	1.25	2.00	
A144	Death for Sale - Henry Kane	.50	1.25	2.00	M
A145	Murder in Majorca - Michael Bryan	.50	1.25	2.00	M
A146	The Dice Spelled Murder - Al Fray	.50	1.25	2.00	M
A147	Year of the Gun - Giff Cheshive	.50	1.25	2.00	W
A148	Treachery at Rock Point - Peter Dawson	.50	1.25	2.00	W
A149	Death at Flood Tide - Louis A. Brennan	.50	1.25	2.00	
A150	Tough Country - Frank Bonham 1958	.50	1.25	2.00	W
A151	The Man on the Blue - Luke Short	.50	1.25	2.00	W
A152	The Price of Murder - John D. MacDonald	.75	1.75	3.00	M
A153	Brad Dolan's Blonde Cargo - William Fuller	.50	1.25	2.00	
A154	Bought With a Gun - Luke Short 1958	.50	1.25	2.00	W
A155	Blackmail, Inc. - Robert Kyle	.50	1.25	2.00	
A156	The Body Looks Familiar - Richard Wormser	.50	1.25	2.00	M
A157	The Bravados - Frank O'Rourke	.50	1.25	2.00	
A158	Brad Dolan's Miami Manhung - William Fuller	.50	1.25	2.00	
A159	The Perfect Victim - James McKimmey	.50	1.25	2.00	
A160	A Bullet for a Blonde - Paul Kruger	.50	1.25	2.00	M
A161	Come Back for More - Al Fray	.50	1.25	2.00	M
A162	The Hostiles - Richard Ferber	.50	1.25	2.00	
A163	Under Cover of Night - Manning Lee Stokes	.50	1.25	2.00	M
A164	Talk of the Town - Charles Williams	.50	1.25	2.00	
A165	All the Way - Charles Williams	.50	1.25	2.00	
A166	Man from Nowhere - T. T. Flynn	.50	1.25	2.00	W
A167	Built for Trouble - Al Fray	.50	1.25	2.00	M
A168	Revenge - Jack Ehrlich	.50	1.25	2.00	
A169	The Concubine - Michael East	.50	1.25	2.00	
A170	The Snatch - Harold R. Daniels	.50	1.25	2.00	
A171	Buckskin Man - Thomas W. Blackburn	.50	1.25	2.00	W
A172	The Long Rope - Hal G. Evarts	.50	1.25	2.00	W
A173	Nellie the Nurse - Kaz	.75	1.75	3.00	H
A174	The Raiders - Richard Ferber 1959	.50	1.25	2.00	
A175	The House on Q Street - Robert Dietrich	.50	1.25	2.00	M
A176	77 Sunset Strip - Roy Huggins TV tie-in	2.00	4.00	7.50	M
A177	Sound of Gunfire - Frank Bonham	.50	1.25	2.00	W
A178	The Other Woman - Bill Yates	.50	1.25	2.00	H
A179	On Becoming a Woman - Irene Kane & Mary McGee Williams	.50	1.25	2.00	NF
A180	The Naked City - Sterling Silliphant	.75	1.75	3.00	
A181	Darby O'Gill and the Little People - Lawrence Edward Watkin movie tie - in	1.50	3.50	5.00	
A182	Sweet Cheat - Peter Duncan	.50	1.25	2.00	
A183	Laredo Road - Will C. Brown	.50	1.25	2.00	W
A184	Last Stand at Saber River - Elmore Leonard	.50	1.25	2.00	
A185	Winner Take All - James McKimmey	.50	1.25	2.00	
A186	Last Stage West - Frank Bonham	.50	1.25	2.00	W

A187	Kay Manion, M.D. - Adeline McElfresh	.50	1.25	2.00	R
A188	Corruption City - Horace McCoy	2.00	4.00	7.50	JD
A189	Tight Squeeze - William Fuller	.50	1.25	2.00	
A190	McCracken in Command - James Keene	.50	1.25	2.00	
A191	Texas Heller - E. M. Parsons	.50	1.25	2.00	W
A192	Model for Murder - Robert Kyle	.50	1.25	2.00	M
A193	Epitaph for a Tramp - David Markson	.50	1.25	2.00	
A194	The Deadly Duo - Richard Jessup	.50	1.25	2.00	
	1959				
B101	The Official American Medical Association Book of Health - W. W. Bauer	.50	1.25	2.00	NF
	1957				
B102	New Worlds of Modern Science - Leonard Engel	.50	1.25	2.00	NF
B103	SF: The Year's Greatest Science-Fiction and Fantasy - ed. Judith Merril	.75	1.75	3.00	SF
B104	The Walt Disney Story of Our Friend the Atom - Heinz Haber	.75	1.75	3.00	NF
B105	Moses and the Ten Commandments - Paul Ilton & MacLennan Roberts	.75	1.75	3.00	
B106	A Treasury of Faith - Leon McCauley	.50	1.25	2.00	
B107	Stories for the Dead of Night - ed. Don Congdon	.50	1.25	2.00	
B108	More Than Flesh - Louis A. Brennan	.50	1.25	2.00	
B109	The Fabulous Buccaneer - Robert Carse	.50	1.25	2.00	A
B110	SF: The Year's Greatest Science-Fiction and Fantasy, 2nd Annual Volume - ed. Judith Merril	.50	1.25	2.00	SF
B111	By Appointment Only - Russell Boltar	.50	1.25	2.00	
B112	A Man of Affairs - John D. MacDonald	.75	1.75	3.00	M
	1958				
B113	Sea Avenger - Jack Beater & MacLennan Roberts	.75	1.75	3.00	A
B114	Girl Out Back - Charles Williams	.50	1.25	2.00	
B115	The Big Country - Donald Hamilton	.75	1.75	3.00	W
B116	The Accused - Harold R. Daniels	.50	1.25	2.00	
B117	The Deceivers - John D. MacDonald	.75	1.75	3.00	M
B118	Lowdown - Richard Jessup	.50	1.25	2.00	
B119	SF: The Year's Greatest Science-Fiction and Fantasy, 3rd Annual Volume - ed. Judith Merril	.75	1.75	3.00	SF
B120	The Cosmic Rape - Theodore Sturgeon	1.50	3.50	5.00	SF
B121	Soft Touch - John D. MacDonald	.75	1.75	3.00	M
B122	Untamed - Warner Hall	.50	1.25	2.00	
B123	Syndicate Girl - Frank Kane	.50	1.25	2.00	M
	1959				
B124	The Two Lives of Dr. Stratton - Russell Boltar	.50	1.25	2.00	
B125	The Lineup - Frank Kane	.50	1.25	2.00	M
B126	The Strain - Kenneth E. Shiflet	.50	1.25	2.00	
B127	Deadly Welcome - John D. MacDonald	.75	1.75	3.00	M
B128	The Five Pennies - Grady Johnson	.50	1.25	2.00	
B129	SF: The Year's Greatest Science-Fiction and Fantasy, 4th Annual Volume - ed. Judith Merril	.75	1.75	3.00	SF
B130	Marauders' Moon - Luke Short	.50	1.25	2.00	W
B131	Girl on the Beach - George Sumner Albee	.50	1.25	2.00	
B132	Paula - Don Kingery	.50	1.25	2.00	
B133	The Flesh Merchants - Bob Thomas	.50	1.25	2.00	
B134					
B135	The Witch Finder - Thomas L. O'Brien	.50	1.25	2.00	
B136	The Joy Boys - Walt Grove	.75	1.75	3.00	
B137	Juke Box King - Frank Kane	.75	1.75	3.00	
B138	The Sirens of Titan - Kurt Vonnegut, Jr.	7.50	15.00	30.00	SF
	Orig., 1959				
B139	Sin Street - Bob Bristow	.50	1.25	2.00	
B140	Montana! - C. Hall Thompson	.50	1.25	2.00	
B141	The Lethal Sex - John D. MacDonald	.75	1.75	3.00	M
B142	Poker According to Maverick	.75	1.75	3.00	NF
	TV tie-in				
B143	Marital Blitz - Janice & Stanley Berenstain	.50	1.25	2.00	H
B148	Career - Victor Chapin	.50	1.25	2.00	
B152	Scent of Mystery - Kelley Roos	.50	1.25	2.00	M
C101	The American Heritage Reader	.50	1.25	2.00	
C102	A Popular History of Music - Carter Harman	.50	1.25	2.00	NF

C103	From Medicine Man to Freud - Jan Ehrenwald 1956	.50	1.25	2.00	NF
C104	The Second Ribald Reader - ed. A.M. Krich	.75	1.75	3.00	
C105	Great Scenes from Great Novels - ed. Robert Terrall	.50	1.25	2.00	
C106	The Handbook of Beauty - Constance Hart	.50	1.25	2.00	NF
C107	Combat: European Theater - World War II - Don Congdon	.75	1.75	3.00	NF
C108	Combat: Pacific Theater - World War II - Don Congdon	.75	1.75	3.00	NF

DELL LAUREL EDITIONS

(Dell Publishing Co.)

LB110	New Ways to Greater Word Power - Roger B. Goodman & David Lewin	.50	1.25	2.00	NF
LB111	The World in Space - Alexander Marshack	.50	1.25	2.00	NF
LB112	Hamlet - William Shakespeare	.50	1.25	2.00	
LB113	The Taming of the Shrew - William Shakespeare	.50	1.25	2.00	
LB114	Romeo and Juliet - William Shakespeare	.50	1.25	2.00	
LB115	Richard III - William Shakespeare	.50	1.25	2.00	
LB116	Great Flying Stories - Frank W. Anderson, Jr.	.50	1.25	2.00	
LB117	The Walt Disney Story of Our Friend the Atom - Heinz Haber	.75	1.75	3.00	NF
LB118	The Merchant of Venice - William Shakespeare	.50	1.25	2.00	
LB119	Julius Caesar - William Shakespeare	.50	1.25	2.00	
LB120	Poe - Edgar Allen Poe	.50	1.25	2.00	
LB121	Whitman - Walt Whitman	.50	1.25	2.00	
LB122	Coleridge - Samuel Taylor Coleridge	.50	1.25	2.00	
LB123	Wordsworth - William Wordsworth	.50	1.25	2.00	
LB124	Macbeth - William Shakespeare	.50	1.25	2.00	
LB125	Twelfth Night - William Shakespeare	.50	1.25	2.00	
LB126	Great Tales of Action and Adventure - George Bennett	.50	1.25	2.00	
LB127	Great Sea Stories - Alan Villiers	.50	1.25	2.00	
LB128	Kim - Rudyard Kipling	.50	1.25	2.00	A
LB129	Othello - William Shakespeare	.50	1.25	2.00	
LB130	As You Like It - William Shakespeare	.50	1.25	2.00	
LB131	Keats - John Keats	.50	1.25	2.00	
LB132	Longfellow - Henry Wadsworth Longfellow	.50	1.25	2.00	
LB133	The Winter's Tale - William Shakespeare	.50	1.25	2.00	
LB134	Henry IV, Part 1 - William Shakespeare 1959	.50	1.25	2.00	
LC101	Four Plays - George Bernard Shaw	.50	1.25	2.00	
LC102	Great English Short Stories - ed. Christopher Isherwood	.50	1.25	2.00	
LC103	Great American Short Stories - ed. Mary & Wallace Stegner	.50	1.25	2.00	
LC104	The New Dell Modern American Dictionary - Jess Stein	.50	1.25	2.00	NF
LC105	Common Wild Animals and Their Young - Rita and William Vandivert	.50	1.25	2.00	NF
LC106	The Modern Meat Cookbook - Jeannette Frank	.50	1.25	2.00	NF
LC107	Panorama: The Laurel Reader No. 1 - ed. R. F. Tannenbaum	.50	1.25	2.00	
LC108	Lincoln and the Civil War - Courtlandt Canby	.75	1.75	3.00	NF
LC109	Six Centuries of Great Poetry - Albert Erskine & Robert Penn Warren	.50	1.25	2.00	
LC110	Great Russian Short Stories - ed. Norris Houghton	.50	1.25	2.00	
LC111	Mark Twain - Mark Twain	.50	1.25	2.00	
LC112	A Catholic Prayer Book - Dale Francis	.50	1.25	2.00	
LC113	Jean-Christope - Romain Rolland	.50	1.25	2.00	
LC114	Martin Eden - Jack London	.50	1.25	2.00	
LC115	How to Draw the Human Figure - John R. Grabach	.50	1.25	2.00	NF

LC116	Emerson - Ralph Waldo Emerson	.50	1.25	2.00	
LC117	The Wings of the Dove - Henry James	.50	1.25	2.00	
LC118	Madame Bovary - Gustave Flaubert	.50	1.25	2.00	
LC119	Elmer Gantry - Sinclair Lewis	.50	1.25	2.00	
LC120	Child Behavior: Gesell Institute - Louise Bates Ames & Frances L. Ilg	.50	1.25	2.00	NF
LC121	The Aspern Papers and the Spoils of Poynton - Henry James	.50	1.25	2.00	
LC122	Pride and Prejudice - Jane Austen	.50	1.25	2.00	
LC123	Three Plays by Ibsen - Henrik Ibsen	.50	1.25	2.00	
LC124	Everybody's Book of Modern Diet and Nutrition - Henrietta Fleck & Elizabeth Munves	.50	1.25	2.00	NF
LC125	How to Draw and Paint - Henry Gasser 1959	.50	1.25	2.00	NF
LC126	Great Stories by Chekhov - Anton Chekhov	.50	1.25	2.00	
LC127	Great Italian Short Stories - ed. Pier Pasinetti	.50	1.25	2.00	
LC128	Sense and Sensibility - Jane Austen	.50	1.25	2.00	
LC129					
LC130	Poetry: A Modern Guide to its Understanding and Enjoyment - Elizabeth Drew	.50	1.25	2.00	
LC131	The House of the Dead - Fyodor Dostoyevsky	.50	1.25	2.00	
LC132	Six Great Modern Short Novels	.50	1.25	2.00	
LC133	Four Great Russian Short Novels	.50	1.25	2.00	
LC134	Voltaire - Voltaire	.50	1.25	2.00	
LC135	Maupassant - Guy de Maupassant	.50	1.25	2.00	
LC136	Washington Square and the Europeans - Henry James	.50	1.25	2.00	
LC137	Freud: His Life and His Mind - Helen W. Puner	.50	1.25	2.00	B
LC138	Lives of the Nobel Greeks - Plutarchus	.50	1.25	2.00	B
LC139	Lives of the Noble Romans - Plutarchus	.50	1.25	2.00	B
LC140	Stevenson - Robert Louis Stevenson	.50	1.25	2.00	
LX101	A History of the United States - William Miller	.50	1.25	2.00	NF
LX102	Short Story Masterpieces - ed. Albert Erskine & Robert Penn Warren	.50	1.25	2.00	
LX103	Six Great Modern Plays - ed. Edward Parone	.50	1.25	2.00	
LX104	Brideshead Revisited - Evelyn Waugh	.50	1.25	2.00	
LX105	Moby Dick - Herman Melville	.50	1.25	2.00	A
LX106	Crime and Punishment - Fyoder Dostoyersky	.50	1.25	2.00	
LX107					
LX108	Jude the Obscure - Thomas Hardy	.50	1.25	2.00	
LX109	The Titan - Theodore Dreiser	.50	1.25	2.00	
LX110	Six Centuries of Great Poetry - ed. Albert Erskine & Robert Penn Warren	.50	1.25	2.00	
LX111	Bulfinch's Mythology - Thomas Bulfinch	.50	1.25	2.00	
LX112	Ballet: A New Guide to the Liveliest Art - Walter Terry	.50	1.25	2.00	NF
LX113	Abraham Lincoln: The Prairie Years - Carl Sandburg	.75	1.75	3.00	B
LX114	Abraham Lincoln: The War Years, 1861-1864 - Carl Sandburg	.75	1.75	3.00	B
LX115	Abraham Lincoln: The War Years, 1864-1865 - Carl Sandburg	.75	1.75	3.00	B
LX116	Famous American Plays of the 20's - ed. Kenneth MacGowan	.75	1.75	3.00	
LX117					
LX120	How to Draw the Human Figure - John R. Grabach	.50	1.25	2.00	NF
LY101	An American Tragedy - Theodore Dreiser	.50	1.25	2.00	
LY102	Modern American Painting and Sculpture - Samuel Hunter	.50	1.25	2.00	NF

DELL 10 - CENT BOOKS

(Dell Publishing Company, Inc.)

Dell 10-Cent 1, c. Dell   Dell 10-Cent 3, c. Dell   Dell 10-Cent 4, c. Dell

(DELL 10 - CENT BOOKS, continued)
1	Trumpets West - Luke Short, 1951	4.00	8.00	12.50	W
2	Rain - W. S. Maugham	3.00	6.50	10.00	
3	Night Bus - Samuel H. Adams	3.00	6.50	10.00	
4	Locked Doors - Mary Roberts Rinehart	3.00	6.50	10.00	M
5	Bride From Broadway - Faith Baldwin	3.00	6.50	10.00	R
6	The Wedding Journey - Walter D. Edmonds	2.50	5.50	9.00	
7	Deadly is the Diamond - Mignon G. Eberhart	3.00	6.50	10.00	M
8	Journey for Life - Pearl S. Buck	3.00	6.50	10.00	
9	Strangers in Love - Vina Delmar	3.00	6.50	10.00	R
10	Trees Die at the Top - Edna Ferber	2.50	5.50	9.00	
11	Marihuana - William Irish	22.50	60.00	100.00	M
12	The Longhorn Legion - Norman A. Fox First ed., 1951	3.00	6.50	10.00	W
13	Sun, Sea and Sand - John P. Marquand	2.50	5.50	9.00	
14	The Name is Mary - Fannie Hurst	3.00	6.50	10.00	R
15	A Taste for Cognac - Brett Halliday	4.00	8.00	12.50	M
16	The Beachcomber - W. S. Maugham	2.50	5.50	9.00	
17	Remembering Laughter - Wallace Stegner	2.50	5.50	9.00	
18	Free Woman - Katharine Brush	3.00	6.50	10.00	
19	Death Walks Marble Halls - Lawrence Blochman First ed., 1951	4.00	8.00	12.50	M
20	Broken Arrow Range - Thomas W. Blackburn First ed., 1951	3.50	7.50	11.50	W
21	Door to Death - Rex Stout	5.00	11.00	20.00	M
22	Alibi for Israel - Mary Roberts Rinehart	3.00	6.50	10.00	M
23	The Lamp of God - Ellery Queen	5.00	11.00	20.00	M
24	Pal Joey - John O'Hara	2.50	5.50	9.00	
25	South of Cancer - John Hersey	2.50	5.50	9.00	
26	You'll Never See Me Again - William Irish First ed., 1951	15.00	35.00	50.00	M
27	Thief is an Ugly Word - Paul Gallico	4.00	8.00	12.50	
28	Beauty Marks the Spot - Kelley Roos	4.00	8.00	12.50	M
29	Delilah of the Back Stairs - Geoffrey Household	4.00	8.00	12.50	
30	Wife vs. Secretary - Faith Baldwin	4.00	8.00	12.50	R
31	Chinese Nightmare - Hugh Pentecost First ed., 1951	5.00	11.00	20.00	M
32	The Murderer Who Wanted More - Baynard Kendrick	4.00	8.00	12.50	M
33	The Case of the Dancing Sandwiches - Frederic Brown, First ed., 1951	15.00	35.00	50.00	M

Dell 10-Cent 9, c. Dell   Dell 10-Cent 11, c. Dell   Dell 10-Cent 15, c. Dell

Dell 10-Cent 35, c. Dell   Dell 10-Cent 36, c. Dell   Dell Told in Pict. 2, c. Dell

(DELL 10 - CENT BOOKS, continued)

34 Better Off Dead - Helen McCloy First ed., 1951	4.00	8.00	12.50	M
35 Superstition Farm - Perry Stowe	5.00	11.00	20.00	
36 Universe - Robert Heinlein, First ed., 1951	10.00	17.50	25.00	SF

DELL TOLD IN PICTURES

(Dell Publishing Company)

Digest size, all comic book style

1 Twice Loved 1950	12.50	27.50	45.00	R
2 Four Frightened Women - George Harmon Coxe 1950	15.00	35.00	60.00	M
3 Rich Girl, Poor Girl	12.50	27.50	45.00	R
4 I Met a Handsome Cowboy	12.50	27.50	45.00	R

DELL UNNUMBERED

(Dell Publishing Company)

Some digest size

nn Blondie and Dagwood in Footlight Folly - Chic Young 1947	12.50	30.00	50.00	H
nn Dick Tracy and the Woo-Woo Sisters - Chester Gould 1947	15.00	35.00	60.00	M
nn Hopalong Cassidy - Clarence E. Mulford nd, Movie tie-in, digest size	7.50	15.00	30.00	W

Dell Unnumbered nn, c. Dell   Dell Unnumbered nn, c. Dell   Dell Unnumbered nn, c. Dell

nn Jungle Belles -   5.00   10.00   20.00

DELL X-SERIES

(Dell Publishing Company)

X1 The James Beard Cookbook - James A. Beard &
    Isabel E. Calivert   .75   1.75   3.00   NF

DETECTIVE NOVEL CLASSIC

(Novel Selections, Inc.)

Digest size

3	Death by Remote Control - Emmett Hogarth	2.00	4.00	6.00	M
4	The Case is Closed - Patricia Wentworth	1.50	3.50	5.00	M
6	The Scarecrow Murders - Frederic Arnold Kummer	1.50	3.50	5.00	M
7	The Case of the Rusted Room - John Donavan	1.50	3.50	5.00	M
8	Murder Will Out - Jeanette Covert Nolan	1.50	3.50	5.00	M
9	Hong-Kong Airbase Murders - Van Wyck Mason	1.50	3.50	5.00	M
10	The Clue of the Twisted Face - Frederic Arnold Kummer	1.50	3.50	5.00	M
11	The Bathtub Murder Case - E. R. Punshon	1.50	3.50	5.00	M
13	Gone North - Charles Alden Seltzer	1.50	3.50	5.00	W
15	The Strange Death of Manny Square - A. B. Cunningham	1.50	3.50	5.00	M
18	The Penguin Pool - Stuart Palmer	1.50	3.50	5.00	M
23	Murder in the Mews - Helen Reilly	1.50	3.50	5.00	M
24	Little Hercules - F. Wallace	1.50	3.50	5.00	M
25	The Bancock Murder Case - A. B. Cunningham	1.50	3.50	5.00	M
27	Steps to Murder - Robert Portner Coehler	1.50	3.50	5.00	M
28	Dead Men Leave No Fingerprints - Whitman Chambers	1.50	3.50	5.00	M
31	Bodies are Where You Find Them - Brett Halliday	1.50	3.50	5.00	M
33	Murder by Latitude - Rufus King	1.50	3.50	5.00	M
34	Exit Screaming - Christopher Hale	1.50	3.50	5.00	M
35	Death is Like That - John Spain	1.50	3.50	5.00	M
36	Death and Bitters - Kit Christian	1.50	3.50	5.00	M
37	The Great Yant Mystery - A. B. Cunningham	1.50	3.50	5.00	M
38	A Murderer in this House - Rufus King	1.50	3.50	5.00	M
39	Death of Winter - Christoper Hale	1.50	3.50	5.00	M
41	The Gull Cove Murders - Eli Colter	1.50	3.50	5.00	M
42	The Cane-Patch Mystery - A. B. Cunningham	1.50	3.50	5.00	M
46	Death Visits the Apple Hole - A. B. Cunningham	1.50	3.50	5.00	M
48	Murder Makes a Racket - M. V. Heberden	1.50	3.50	5.00	M
49	I Can't Die Here - Jeannette Covert Nolan	1.50	3.50	5.00	M
51	Rumor Hath It - Christopher Hale	1.50	3.50	5.00	M
52	Murder Before Nidnight - A. B. Cunningham	1.50	3.50	5.00	M
54	Neck in a Noose - E. X. Ferrars	1.50	3.50	5.00	M

DIVERSEY POPULAR NOVELS

(Diversey Periodicals, Inc.)

Digest size

1	Broadway Virgin - Lois Bull 1949	7.50	15.00	30.00	E
2	Naked on Roller Skates - Maxwell Bodenheim	7.50	15.00	30.00	E

Note: Same cover as Novel Library no. 46.

DIVERSEY PRIZE NOVELS

Avon Fant. Reader 3,
1947 ©Avon

Avon 38, 1944 ©Avon

Berkley G-120, 1958 ©Berk

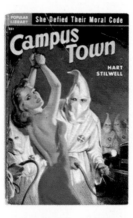

Dell 53, 1958 ©Dell

Popular Library 331,
1951 ©PopLib

Avon 256, 1950 ©Avon

Popular Library 59,
1945 ©Simon

Avon 344, 1951 ©Avon

Ace D-36, 1953 ©Ace

Pocket Book B44, 1951 © PkB

Ace D-52, 1954 © Ace

Yogi Mysteries nn, 1940
© Frank Munsey

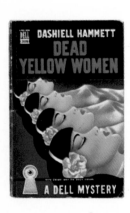

Dell 308, 1949 © Dell

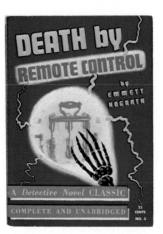

A Det. Novel Classic 3, 1940 © Hill

Banner Mysteries 2,
1945 © Banner

Dell 1, 1943 © Dell

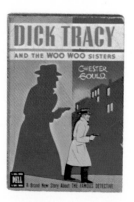

Dick Tracy, 1947
© Chicago Tribune

Popular Library 211,
1949 © PopLib

Hillman 41, 1950 ©Hill

Avon 285, 1950 ©Avon

Dell 264, 1948 ©Dell

Handi-Book 16, 1943 ©Quinn

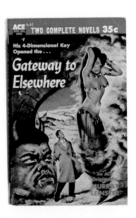

Ace D-53, 1954 ©Ace

Popular Library 221,
1950 ©PopLib

Bonded Mystery 1, 1946 ©Anson

Fantasy Novel 2,
1950 ©Avon

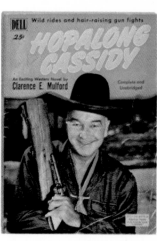

nn, nd ©Dell

Double Action Detective 2,
1943 ©Close

Eton E119, 1952 ©Eton

Ballantine 165, 1956 ©BB

Ace D-26, 1953 ©Ace

Dell 269, 1948 ©Dell

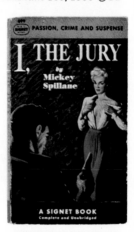

Signet 699, 1948 ©SigB

Ace D-15, 1953 ©Ace

Ace D-18, 1953 ©Ace

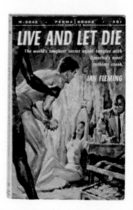

Perma M-3048, 1956 ©Perma

Avon 136, 1947 © Avon

Dell 10 Cents 11, 1951 © Dell

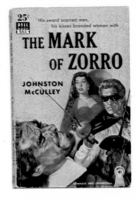

Dell 553, 1951 © Dell

Dell 265, 1948 © Dell

Diversey 2, 1949 © Div

Avon 222, 1950 © Avon

Ballantine 99, 1955 © BB

Popular Library 292,
1950 © PopLib

Giant Edition 2, 1952 © Univ

Popular Library 147,
1948 © PopLib

Diversey 1, 1948 © Div

Dell 600, 1952 © Dell

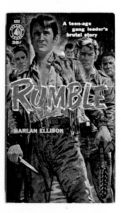

Pyramid G352, 1958 © PyB

Dell 172, 1947 © Dell

Eerie 4, 1945 © Eerie

Gold Medal 241, 1952 © Faw

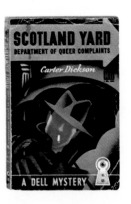

Dell 65, 1944 © Dell

Century Mystery 32, nd © Cen

Avon 324, 1951 ©Avon

Pyramid 21, 1950 © PyB

Popular Library 258,
1950 © PopLib

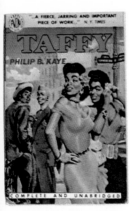

Avon 377, 1951 © Avon

Popular Library 217,
1950 © PopLib

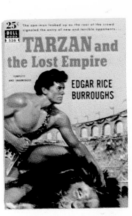

Dell 536, 1951 ©ERB

Avon 339, 1951 ©Avon

Dell 185, 1947 ©Dell

Ace D-1, 1952 © Ace

Thrilling Novels 21, nd ©PopLib

Amazing SF Novel nn,
1957 ©Z-D

Archer 35, 1952 ©Archer

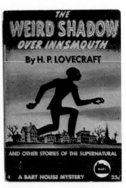

Bart House 4, 1944 ©Bart

Western Novel Classic 99,
nd ©Hill

Permabook P275,
1954 ©Perma

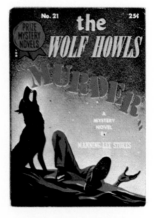

Prize Mystery Novel 21,
1946 ©Crest

Beacon 291, 1960 ©Glxy

Ace D-274, 1958 ©Ace

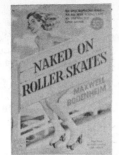

Detective Novel Classic 3,
c. NS

Diversey Popular Novels 1,
c. Div

Diversey Popular Novels 2,
c. Div

(DIVERSEY PRIZE NOVELS, continued)

(Diversey Periodicals, Inc.)

Digest size

3	The Passions of Linda Lane - Frances Marion 1949, aka Minnie Flynn	7.50	15.00	25.00	E
4	Fast Woman - Marty Holland	7.50	15.00	25.00	E
5	Love for Sale - John Wilstach 1949, aka The Fate of Fay Delroy	7.50	15.00	25.00	E
6	The Amorous Interne - Edward Reltid	7.50	15.00	25.00	E

DIVERSEY ROMANCE NOVELS

(Diversey Publishing Corporation)

Digest Size

1	Reform School Girl - Felice Swados
	   1948, aka House of Fury
	   Note: same cover as Reform School Girl
	   comic book
		75.00	165.00	275.00	E

DOCKET SERIES

(Oceana Publications)

1	The Holmes Reader - ed. Julius J. Marke 1955	1.50	3.50	5.00
2	The Freedom Reader - ed. Edwin S. Newman	1.50	3.50	5.00
3	The Marshall Reader - ed. Erwin C. Surrency	1.50	3.50	5.00
4	The Wilson Reader - ed. Frances Farmer 1956	1.50	3.50	5.00

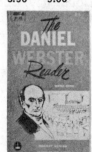

Diversey Romance 1, c. Div

Docket Series 3, c. Oceana

Docket Series 5, c. Oceana

DOMINO MYSTERIES

(Duchess Printing and Publishing Co., Ltd.)

Digest size

1 The "Q" Squad - Gerald Verner 1944	3.00	6.00	12.00	M

DOUBLE ACTION DETECTIVE

(Close-Up, Inc.)

Digest size

2 Hot Bullets for Love - Gentry Nyland 1943, aka Mr. South Burned His Mouth	2.00	4.00	7.50	M
3 Jealousy Pulls the Trigger - M. E. Corne 1943, aka A Magnet for Murder	2.00	4.00	7.50	M

DOUBLE-ACTION POCKETBOOK

(Columbia Publications, Inc.)

Digest size

nn City of Glass - Noel Loomis 1955	2.00	5.00	8.50	SF

DOUBLEDAY

(Doubleday and Company, Inc.)

nn The Farmer Takes a Hand - Marquis Childs Orig., 1952	.75	1.50	2.50	NF

DOUBLEDAY DORAN

(Doubleday, Doran and Company, Inc.)

Domino Mysteries 1, c. Duch

Double Action Det. 2, c. Close

Double Action Det. 3, c. Close

Double Action Pbk. nn, c. Col   Doubleday nn, c. DD   Doubleday Doran nn, c. DD

(DOUBLEDAY DORAN, continued)

Digest size

nn Come Wind, Come Weather - Daphne Du Maurier 1941	2.00	4.00	6.00	

DOUGLAS

(Douglas Publishing, Inc.)

nn Today's Business Market - John Garris 1954	1.50	3.50	5.00	NF

DUCHESS

(Duchess Printing and Publishing Co., Ltd.)

Canadian

nn Brigands of the Moon - John Campbell nd Note: Miscredited, actually written by Ray Cummings	2.00	4.00	7.50	SF
nn Bait for a Tiger - Bayard Veiller	1.50	3.50	5.00	M
nn Murder at the Mike - Charles Saxby	1.50	3.50	5.00	M
nn Run, Corpse, Run - Guy Pember-Hiller	1.50	3.50	5.00	M

EAGLE BOOKS

(Eagle Books, Inc./New American Library)

Duchess nn, c. Duch   Eagle Books E3, c. NA   Edell nn, c. Edell

(EAGLE BOOKS, continued)

nn(1)	Dear Sir - Juliet Lowell 1943	2.00	4.00	7.50	H
nn(2)	Kitty - Rosamond Marshall 1945	2.00	4.00	6.00	E
E3	Duchess Hotspur - Rosamond Marshall 1947	2.00	4.00	6.00	E

ECSTASY NOVEL

(Falcon Books, Inc.)

Digest size

nn	Intimate Confessions of an Artist's Model - Norman Bligh 1950	1.50	3.00	5.00	E

EDELL

(The Edell Company)

Digest size

nn	The Case of the Deadly Drops - Gerald Benedict	1.50	3.50	5.00	M

EERIE SERIES

(Eerie Publishing Co.)

Digest size

1	The Case of the Curious Heel - Ken Crossen nd	4.00	8.00	15.00	M
2	Murder in Mocking Valley - Will Crowell 1944	3.00	6.00	12.00	M
3	The Corpse Wore No Shoes - Donald Thompson	3.00	6.00	12.00	M
4	Satan Comes Across - Bennett Barlay 1945	3.00	6.00	12.00	M
5	Murder in the Radio Department - Alfred Eichler	3.00	6.00	12.00	M
6	The Pleasure Primer	3.00	6.00	12.00	
7	A Spy in the Room - Denison Clift	3.00	6.00	12.00	M
8	Homicide Johnny - Stephen Gould	3.00	6.00	12.00	M
9	Haunted Harbor - Dayle Douglas 1945	3.00	6.00	12.00	M

ETON BOOKS

Eerie Series 1, c. Eerie

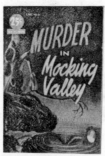

Eerie Series 2, c. Eerie

Eerie Series 4, c. Eerie

Eton Books ET106, c. Eton   Eton Books ET108, c. Eton   Eton Books E112, c. Eton

(ETON BOOKS, continued)
(Eton Books, Inc.)

ET 51	Sex Habits of American Women - Fritz Wittels, M. D.	3.00	6.00	12.00	NF
101	United States Book of Baby & Child Care 1951	2.50	6.00	10.00	NF
102	Sex Habits of American Women - Fritz Witties, M.D.	2.50	6.00	10.00	NF
103	The Hygiene of Marriage - Millard Spencer Everett	2.50	6.00	10.00	NF
ET104	Control Blood Pressure - Herman Pomeranz, M. D.	2.50	6.00	10.00	NF
ET105	How to Understand Your Dreams - Wilhelm Stekel	2.50	6.00	10.00	NF
ET106	The Show of Violence - Fredric Wertham	7.50	15.00	30.00	NF
ET107	Authentic Librettos of the Grand Opera	2.50	6.00	10.00	NF
ET108	This is Russia Un-Censored! - Edmund Stevens	2.50	6.00	10.00	NF
E109	Self-Mastery Through Psycho-Analysis - William J. Fielding 1952	2.50	6.00	10.00	NF
E110	I Killed Stalin - Sterling Noel	2.50	6.00	10.00	SF
E111	Sin in Their Blood - Ed Lacy Orig., 1952	2.50	6.00	10.00	M
E112	Kiss my Fist! - James Hadley Chase	3.00	6.00	12.00	M
E113	The Renegade Hills - Allan K. Echols Orig., 1952	2.50	6.00	10.00	W
E114	Give Me Your Love - Jerime Weldman Orig., 1952	2.50	6.00	10.00	E
E115	I'll Bring Her Back - Peter Cheyney aka Dark Bahama	2.50	6.00	10.00	
E116	The Marijuana Mob - James Hadley Chase	4.00	8.00	15.00	M
E117	Invitation to Dishonor - Eric Arthur	2.50	6.00	10.00	E
E118	Gun-Play in Killer canyon - Tevis Miller	2.50	6.00	10.00	W
E119	I Killed Stalin - Sterling Noel Illo in Parade of Pleasure	2.50	6.00	10.00	SF
E120	Mark it with a Stone - George Victor Martin	2.50	6.00	10.00	E
E121	Queer Patterns - Lilyan Brock	2.50	6.00	10.00	E
E122	Paris Escort - Daniel Harper Orig., 1953	2.00	4.00	7.50	E
E123	Strip for Violence - Ed Lacy Orig., 1953	2.50	6.00	10.00	M
E124	Tuck's Girl - Marcel Wallenstein Orig., 1953	2.00	4.00	7.50	
E125	Gunfighter - Paul Craig	2.00	4.00	7.50	W
E126					
E127	Stir up the Dust - William Colt MacDonald Orig., 1953	2.50	6.00	10.00	W
E128	Stagecoach to Hellfire Pass - Paul Evan Lehman	2.00	4.00	7.50	W
E129	Wit from Overseas - Roy Hoopes, Jr.	2.00	4.00	6.00	
E130	The Black Riders - Sam Meriwether	2.00	4.00	7.50	W
E131	Vengeance Valley - Allan K. Echols	2.00	4.00	7.50	W
E132	Hide-out - Larry Holden	2.00	4.00	7.50	M

EXOTIC NOVELS

(Falcon Books, Inc.)

Digest size

5	Buy My Love! - Perry Lindsay 1949, c-Rodewald	1.50	3.50	5.00	E
17	Ten Toes Up- Anthony Scott 1951	2.00	4.00	7.50	E
nn	Three Men and a Mistress - Florence Stonebraker 1950	1.50	3.50	5.00	E

FALCON BOOKS

(Falcon Books, Inc.)

Digest size

22	The Scarlet Bride - M. Reed	2.00	4.00	6.00	E
27	Lida Lynn - Daughter of Passion - Norma Dann	2.00	4.00	6.00	E
29	Mistress on a Deathbed! - Norman A. Daniels Orig., 1952	2.00	4.00	7.50	M
31	Slave Girl - Tom Roan	2.00	4.00	6.00	E
33	Yellow-Head! - Hodge Evens Orig., 1952	2.00	4.00	6.00	E
36	Junkie - Johnathan Craig Orig., 1952	4.00	8.00	15.00	E
38	Sweet Savage - Norman Daniels	2.00	4.00	6.00	E
40	Whip - Hand! - Hodge Evens Orig., 1952	2.00	4.00	7.50	E
41	The Evil Sleep! - Evan Hunter Orig., 1952	2.00	4.00	7.50	M
42	The Long Night - Bryce Walton	2.00	4.00	6.00	E
43	House of 1000 Desires - Mark Reed Orig., 1953	2.00	4.00	7.50	E

FAMOUS MYSTERY SERIES

(Howard Publications)

Digest size

Canadian

1	Murder Takes a Honeymoon - Edith Fleming 1940	2.00	4.00	7.50	M

FEDERAL

Exotic Novels 17, c. Falcon

Falcon Books 33, c. Falcon

Famous Myst. Series 1, c. How

Federal 2, c. Fed   Feiner nn, c. Feiner   Femack Publ. nn, c. Fem

(FEDERAL, continued)
(Federal Publishing Co.)

(Canadian)

2 Room Girl - Beth Brown 1951	1.50	3.00	5.00	E

FEINER

(J. P. Feiner)

Digest size

nn The Greatest Adventure Stories Ever Told -
     Arnold Shaw
     1945
	1.50	3.50	5.00	A

FEMACK PUBLICATIONS

(The Femack Company)

Digest size

nn He Died Laughing - Lawrence Lariar	1.50	3.50	5.00	M

FIESTA BOOKS

(Rio Publishing Corporation)

Digest size

1 The Lady was a Tramp - Nick Baroni	1.50	3.50	5.00	E
2 Ask for Therese - Evans Wall	1.50	3.50	5.00	E
Orig., 1952	1.50	3.50	5.00	E
3 Love Fetish - Evans Wall				

FIGHTING FORCES SERIES

(The Infantry Journal)

Some are digest size

Note: Some Fighting Forces Series titles are also Penguin Specials and are listed under that imprint.

F14 Report on the Army, 1939-1943 - George C. Marshall	1.50	3.50	5.00	NF
nn World War II - Roger W. Shugg and H. A. DeWeerd	1.50	3.50	5.00	NF
nn Selected Speeches and Statements - George C. Marshall	1.50	3.50	5.00	NF
nn Fishes and Shells of the Pacific World	1.50	3.50	5.00	NF
nn Plant Life of the Pacific World - Merrill	1.50	3.50	5.00	NF
nn Native Peoples of the Pacific World - Keesing	1.50	3.50	5.00	NF
nn Japan and the Japanese	1.50	3.50	5.00	NF
nn Japan's Military Masters - Hillis Lory	2.00	4.00	7.50	NF
nn Survival	2.00	4.00	7.00	
nn We Cannot Escape History - John Whitaker	1.50	3.50	5.00	NF
nn America's Navy in World War II - Gilbert Cant	1.50	3.50	5.00	NF
nn Abraham Lincoln and the Fifth Column - George Fort Milton 1943	1.50	3.50	5.00	NF
nn America in Arms - John McA. Palmer	1.50	3.50	5.00	
nn Animals of the Pacific World - Hill, Carter, & Tate	1.50	3.50	5.00	NF
nn The Battle is the Pay-off - Major Ingersoll	1.50	3.50	5.00	
nn Blitzkrieg: Armies on Wheels - S. L. A. Marshall	1.50	3.50	5.00	NF
nn Burma Surgeon - Gordon Seagrave	1.50	3.50	5.00	NF
nn The Capture of Attu	1.50	3.50	5.00	NF
nn Combat First Aid: How to Save Lives in Battle	1.50	3.50	5.00	NF
nn Conflict: The American Civil War - George Fort Milton	1.50	3.50	5.00	NF
nn Defense Against Chemical War	3.00	6.00	12.00	NF
nn Fear in Battle - John Dollard	1.50	3.50	5.00	
nn Freedom of Speech: Democratic Poetry and Prose	1.50	3.50	5.00	
nn Fundamentals of Electricity - Mott-Smith	1.50	3.50	5.00	NF
nn Fundamentals of Mathematics - Mott-Smith & Van de Water	1.50	3.50	5.00	NF
nn Gas Warfare - Alden H. Waitt	2.00	4.00	7.50	NF
nn The German Soldier: How He is Trained	2.00	4.00	7.50	NF
nn Great Soldiers of the First World War - H. A. DeWeerd	1.50	3.50	5.00	NF
nn The Gun - C. S. Forester	1.50	3.50	5.00	A
nn Hitler's Second Army - Alfred Vagts	1.50	3.50	5.00	NF
nn How to Abandon Ship - Richards & Banigan	2.00	4.00	7.50	NF
nn How to Shoot the U. S. Army Rifle	1.50	3.50	5.00	NF
nn Island Victory: How Kwajalein Was Won	1.50	3.50	5.00	NF
nn The Jap Soldier: How He is Trained	2.00	4.00	7.50	NF
nn Leadership for American Army Leaders - E. L. Munson	1.50	3.50	5.00	NF
nn The Living Thoughts of Clausewitz	1.50	3.50	5.00	
nn The Lost Battalion - Thomas M. Johnson & Fletcher Pratt 1943	1.50	3.50	5.00	NF
nn Machine Warfare - J. F. C. Fuller	1.50	3.50	5.00	NF
nn The Making of Modern China - Owen & Eleanor Lattimore	1.50	3.50	5.00	NF
nn The Nazi State - William Ebenstein	2.00	4.00	7.50	NF
nn Our Enemy Japan - Wilfrid Fleisher	2.00	4.00	7.50	NF
nn Reptiles of the Pacific World - A. Loveridge	1.50	3.50	5.00	NF

Fiesta Books 2, c. Rio

Fighting Forces F14, c. Infan

Fighting Forces nn, c. Infan

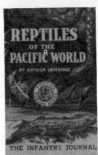

Fighting Forces nn, c. Infan   Fighting Western Novel 22, c. NS   Fighting Western 33, c. NS

(FIGHTING FORCES SERIES, continued)

nn	Patriot Battles, 1775-1782 - A. C. M. Azoy	1.50	3.50	5.00	NF
nn	Report on India - T. A. Raman	1.50	3.50	5.00	NF
nn	Rifleman Dodd - C. S. Forester	1.50	3.50	5.00	A
nn	Rifles and Machine Guns of the World's Armies - Johnson	1.50	3.50	5.00	NF
nn	The Russian Army - Walter Kerr	1.50	3.50	5.00	NF
nn	Scouting and Patrolling	1.50	3.50	5.00	NF
nn	Sergeant Terry Bull: His Ideas on War and Fighting - Terry Bull	1.50	3.50	5.00	
nn	Short History of the Army and Navy - Fletcher Pratt	1.50	3.50	5.00	NF
nn	So You're Going Overseas - R. S. Barker	1.50	3.50	5.00	NF
nn	The Story of West Point, 1802-1943 - R. E. Dupuy	1.50	3.50	5.00	NF
nn	Studies on War	1.50	3.50	5.00	NF
nn	Tank-Fighter Team - R. M. Gerard	1.50	3.50	5.00	NF
nn	Thesaurus of Humor	1.50	3.50	5.00	H
nn	Weapons for the Future - Johnson and Haven	1.50	3.50	5.00	NF
nn	What to do Aboard the Transport	1.50	3.50	5.00	NF
	Note: Co-publication with Science Service. Henius				
nn	Modern Battle: Campaigns of 1939 - 1941 - P. W. Thompson	1.50	3.50	5.00	NF
nn	New Ways of War - Tom Wintringham	1.50	3.50	5.00	NF
nn	Warships at Work - T. A. Hardy	1.50	3.50	5.00	NF
nn	Pipeline to Battle: Campaigns in Africa - Major Rainier	1.50	3.50	5.00	NF
nn	Engineer Training Notebook	1.50	3.50	5.00	NF
nn	Company Duties: A Checklist	1.50	3.50	5.00	NF
nn	Machine Gunner's Handbook - C. H. Coates	1.50	3.50	5.00	NF
nn	Driver Training: Handbook for Instructors	1.50	3.50	5.00	NF
nn	Keep 'em Rolling: Handbook for Drivers	1.50	3.50	5.00	NF
nn	You Must Be Fit	1.50	3.50	5.00	
nn	Platoon Record Book	1.50	3.50	5.00	NF
nn	Squad Record Book	1.50	3.50	5.00	NF
nn	Our Armed Forces: A Complete Description	1.50	3.50	5.00	NF
nn	Spanish Dictionary for the Soldier - Frank Henius	1.50	3.50	5.00	NF
nn	French Dictionary for the Soldier - Frank Henius	1.50	3.50	5.00	NF
nn	German Dictionary for the Soldier - Frank Henius	1.50	3.50	5.00	NF
nn	Italian Dictionary for the Soldier - Frank Henius	1.50	3.50	5.00	NF
nn	Italian Sentence Book for the Soldier - Frank Henius	1.50	3.50	5.00	NF

FIGHTING WESTERN NOVEL

(Novel Selections, Inc./Hillman)

Digest size

2	Under the Mesa Rim - C. Whipple	1.50	3.50	5.00	W
7	Stranger at Storm Ranch - Dan James	1.50	3.50	5.00	W

8 South of the Pass - Johnston McCulley	1.50	3.50	5.00	W
14 Law of the Trail - J. E. Grinstead	1.50	3.50	5.00	W
16 Trigger Trail - Roy Manning	1.50	3.50	5.00	W
20 Spectre Spread - Tom West	1.50	3.50	5.00	W
22 The Cougar of Canyon Caballo - Paul Evan Lehman	1.50	3.50	5.00	W
23 The Bar D Boss - Ranger Lee	1.50	3.50	5.00	W
25 The Drifting Kid - Will Ermine	1.50	3.50	5.00	W
26 Prairie Pinto - Lynn Westland	1.50	3.50	5.00	W
28 Prentiss of the Box 8 - Lynn Westland	1.50	3.50	5.00	W
30 Tall in the Saddle - Gordon Young	1.50	3.50	5.00	W
33 Black Creek Buckaroo - Anson Piper	1.50	3.50	5.00	W
34 Rustlers of TAble Butte - Ernie Phillips	1.50	3.50	5.00	W
38 Wild Horse Shorty - Nelson Nye	1.50	3.50	5.00	W
39 Brand of the Open Hand - Frank C. Robertson	1.50	3.50	5.00	W
40 Return to the Range - Lynn Westland	1.50	3.50	5.00	W
41 Blood of Kings - Nelson C. Nye	1.50	3.50	5.00	W

FINGERPRINT MYSTERY

(Readers Detective Book Service)

Digest size

nn Murder Rings Twice - Helen Joan Hultman aka Murder on Route 40	1.50	3.50	5.00	M
nn The Man Without a Head - Joseph Bowen	1.50	3.50	5.00	M

FIVE STAR MYSTERY

(Green Publishing Company)

Digest size

1 The Dress Circle Murders - Peter Yates Orig., 1945	3.00	6.00	12.00	M
3 You'll Die Laughing - Bruce Elliott Orig., 1945	2.00	4.00	7.00	M
13 The Laughing Buddha Murders - Richard Foster (K. F. Crossen)	2.00	4.00	7.00	M
15 The Case of the Phantom Fingerprints - Ken Crossen	2.00	4.00	7.00	M
16 Curtain Call for Murder - Peter Yates Orig., 1945	2.00	4.00	7.00	M
21 The Dress Circle Murders - Peter Yates	2.00	4.00	7.00	M
22 Murder out of Mind - Ken Crossen Orig., 1945	2.00	4.00	7.00	M
26 You'll Die Laughing - Bruce Elliott	2.00	4.00	7.00	M
28 Death Comes to Dinner - Peter Yates Orig., 1945	2.00	4.00	7.00	M
36 Invisible Man Murders - Richard Foster	2.00	4.00	7.00	M

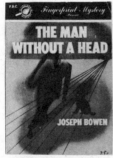

Fingerprint Mystery nn,   Five Star Mystery 1, c. Green   Five Star Mystery 3, c. Green
   c. Readers Det.

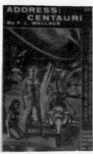

Galaxy SF Novels 11, c. Glxy Galaxy SF Novels 32, c. Glxy Galaxy SF Novels 34, c. Glxy

(FIVE STAR MYSTERY, continued)
    (Kendell Foster Crossen)
    Orig., 1945

37	Death in The Hands of Talent - Peter Yates	2.00	4.00	7.00	M
	Orig., 1945				
38	Murder Seeks an Agent - Wenzell Brown	2.00	4.00	7.00	M
	Orig., 1945				
41	Death's Long Shadow - Katharine Wolffe	2.00	4.00	7.00	M
	Orig., 1946				
42	Death Wears a Green Hat - Will Creed	2.00	4.00	7.00	M
	Orig., 1946				
43	Crime is of The Essence - Joe Csida	2.00	4.00	7.00	M
	Orig., 1946				
44	The Corpse is Indignant - Douglas Stapleton	2.00	4.00	7.00	M
	and Helen A. Carey				
	Orig., 1946				
45	Murder in The Rough - Leslie Allen (Horace	2.00	4.00	7.00	M
	Brown)				
	Orig., 1946				
46	Kill to Fit - Bruno Fischer	1.50	3.50	5.00	M

GALAXY SCIENCE FICTION NOVELS

(Galaxy Publishing Corp.)

1 - 31 are digest size

1	Sinister Barrier - Eric Frank Russell	1.50	3.50	5.00	SF
2	Legion of Space - Jack Williamson	1.50	3.50	5.00	SF
3	Prelude to Space - Arthur C. Clarke	1.50	3.50	5.00	SF
4	The Amphibians - S. Fowler Wright	1.50	3.50	5.00	SF
5	The World Below - S. Fowler Wright	1.50	3.50	5.00	SF
6	The Alien - Raymond F. Jones	1.50	3.50	5.00	SF
7	Empire - Clifford D. Simak	2.00	4.00	6.00	SF
8	Odd John - Olaf Stapledon	2.00	4.00	6.00	SF
9	Four Sided Triangle - William F. Temple	2.00	4.00	6.00	SF
10	Rat Race - Jay Franklin	2.00	4.00	6.00	SF
11	City in the Sea - Wilson Tucker	2.00	4.00	6.00	SF
12	The House of Many Worlds - Sam Merwin, Jr.	2.00	4.00	6.00	SF
13	Seeds of Life - John Taine	2.00	4.00	6.00	SF
14	Pebble in the Sky - Isaac Asimov	2.00	4.00	6.00	SF
15	Three Go Back - J. Leslie Mitchell	2.00	4.00	6.00	SF
16	The Warriors of Day - James Blish	2.00	4.00	6.00	SF
17	Well of the Worlds - Lewis Padgett	2.00	4.00	6.00	SF
18	City at World's End - Edmond Hamilton	2.00	4.00	6.00	SF
19	Jack of Eagles - James Blish	2.00	4.00	7.00	SF
20	The Black Galaxy - Murray Leinster	2.50	6.00	10.00	SF
21	The Humanoids - Jack Williamson	2.00	4.00	7.50	SF
22	Killer to Come - Sam Merwin, Jr.	2.00	4.00	7.50	SF
23	Murder in Space - David V. Reed	2.00	4.00	7.50	SF
24	Lest Darkness Fall - L. Sprague de Camp	2.50	6.00	10.00	SF
25	The Last Spaceship - Murray Leinster	2.50	6.00	10.00	SF
	1955				
26	Chessboard Planet - Lewis Padgett	2.00	4.00	7.50	SF
	aka The Fairy Chessman				

(GALAXY SCIENCE FICTION NOVELS, continued)

27	Tarnished Utopia - Malcolm Jameson	2.00	4.00	7.50	SF
28	Destiny Times Three - Fritz Leiber	4.00	8.00	15.00	SF
29	Fear - L. Ron Hubbard	4.00	8.00	15.00	SF
30	Double Jeopardy - Fletcher Pratt	4.00	8.00	15.00	SF
31	Shambleau - C. L. Moore	5.00	10.00	20.00	SF
32	Address: Centauri - F. L. Wallace c-Wood	2.50	6.00	10.00	SF
33	Mission of Gravity - Hal Clement c-Wood	2.50	6.00	10.00	SF
34	Twice in Time - Manly Wade Wellman c-Wood	2.50	6.00	10.00	SF
35	The Forever Machine - Mark Clifton & Frank Riley c-Wood	2.50	6.00	10.00	SF

GEM BOOKS

(Gem Books, Inc.)

Digest size

101	She Lived in Sin - Ralph Carter 1952	1.50	3.00	5.00	E
102	Shameful Love - Thomas Stone	1.50	3.00	5.00	E

GOLDEN WILLOW

(Golden Willow Press, Inc.)

Digest size

51	Rampage in the Rockies - Shoshone Green 1945	1.50	3.50	5.00	W
55	Murder by Schedule - Julian Hinckley 1946, aka The Letter in His Throat	1.50	3.50	5.00	M

GOLD MEDAL

(Fawcett Publications, Inc.)

nn(99)	The Best from True 1949	7.50	15.00	30.00	
nn(100)	What Today's Woman Should Know About Marriage and Sex	7.50	15.00	30.00	NF
101	We are the Public Enemies - Alan Hynd Orig., 1950	5.00	10.00	20.00	NF
102	Man Story - anthology First ed., 1950	4.00	8.00	15.00	A
103	Persian Cat - John Flagg	2.50	6.00	10.00	M

Golden Willow 55, c. GW

Gold Medal 99, c. Faw

Gold Medal 101, c. Faw

Gold Medal 105, c. Faw   Gold Medal 113, c. Faw   Gold Medal 124, c. Faw

(GOLD MEDAL, continued)

104 I'll Find You - Richard Himmel	2.50	6.00	10.00	M
105 Nude in Mink - Sax Rohmer	5.00	10.00	20.00	M
Orig., 1950				
106 Stretch Dawson - W. R. Burnett	2.50	6.00	10.00	W
107 The Flying Saucers are Real - Donald Keyhoe	2.50	6.00	10.00	UFO
108 Devil May Care - Wade Miller	2.50	6.00	10.00	M
109 The Awakening of Jenny - Lillian Colter	2.50	6.00	10.00	E
110 Million Dollar Murder - Edward Ronns	2.50	6.00	10.00	M
111 The Wild Horse - Les Savage, Jr.	2.50	6.00	10.00	W
112 Your Child and You - Sidonie Gruenberg	3.00	6.00	12.00	NF
113 The Violent Ones - Howard Hunt	3.00	6.00	12.00	M
114 No Business for a Lady - James Rubel	2.50	6.00	10.00	M
115 Help Wanted--For Murder - William L. Rohde	2.50	6.00	10.00	M
116 The Slaughtered Lovelies - Don Stanford	2.50	6.00	10.00	M
117 State Department Murders - Edward Ronns	2.50	6.00	10.00	M
118 The Goldfish Murders - Will Mitchell	2.50	6.00	10.00	M
119 The Tormented - Theodore Pratt	2.50	6.00	10.00	E
120 The Man Who Said No - Walt Grove	2.50	6.00		
121 The Desperado - Clifton Adams	2.50	6.00	10.00	W
122 One Wild Oat - MacKinlay Kantor	2.50	6.00	10.00	E
123 House of Flesh - Bruno Fischer	3.00	6.00	12.00	M
Orig., 1950				
124 The Brass Cupcake - John D. MacDonald	6.00	12.50	25.00	M
Orig., 1950				
125 The Obsessed - Gertrude Schweitzer	2.50	6.00	10.00	
1950				
126 Dallas - Will F. Jenkins (Murray Leinster)	3.00	6.00	12.00	W
Movie tie-in				
127 Case of the Vanishing Beauty - Richard S. Prather	2.50	6.00	10.00	M
128 Three Secrets - Margaret Lee Runbeck	2.50	6.00	10.00	
129 Mansion of Evil - Joseph Millard	10.00	25.00	40.00	M
Orig., 1950				
Note: Comic book format				
130 A Man of Parts - Vivian Connell	2.50	6.00	10.00	
131 Guns at Broken Bow - William Heuman	2.50	6.00	10.00	W
132 Women's Barracks - Tereska Torres	2.50	6.00	10.00	E
133 Catspaw Ordeal - Edward Ronns	2.50	6.00	10.00	
134 Hell-bent for Danger - Walt Grove	2.50	6.00	10.00	

Gold Medal 126, c. Faw   Gold Medal 129, c. Faw   Gold Medal 132, c. Faw

(GOLD MEDAL. continued)

135 Bar Guide - Virgil Partch & Ted Shane	3.00	6.00	12.00	H
136 Savage Bride - Cornell Woolrich	4.00	8.00	15.00	M
Orig., 1951				
137 War Bonnet Pass - Logan Stewart	2.50	6.00	10.00	W
138 The Corpse that Walked - Octavus Roy Cohen	2.50	6.00	10.00	M
139 Stolen Woman - Wade Miller	2.50	6.00	10.00	E
140 Gunfighter's Return - Leslie Ernenwein	2.50	6.00	10.00	W
141 Hill Girl - Charles Williams	2.50	6.00	10.00	E
Orig., 1951				
142 Jewel of the Java Sea - Dan Cushman	2.50	6.00	10.00	A
143 The Chinese Keyhole - Richard Himmel	2.50	6.00	10.00	M
144 Winchester Cut - Mark Sabin	2.50	6.00	10.00	W
145 High Red for Dead - William L. Rohde	2.50	6.00	10.00	M
Orig., 1951				
146 Roll the Wagons - William Heuman	2.50	6.00	10.00	W
147 Bodies in Bedlam - Richard S. Prather	2.50	6.00	10.00	M
148 The Lady Kills - Bruno Fischer	2.50	6.00	10.00	E
Orig., 1951				
149 Gunsmoke Reckoning - Joseph Chadwick	2.50	6.00	10.00	W
150 Come Murder Me - James Kieran	2.50	6.00	10.00	M
1951				
151 Death and the Naked Lady - John Flagg	2.50	6.00	10.00	
152 The Killer - Wade Miller	2.50	6.00	10.00	M
Orig., 1951				
153 Cocotte - Theodore Pratt	2.50	6.00	10.00	E
154 A Gun in His Hand - Victor Rosen	2.50	6.00	10.00	
155 The Apache - James Warner Bellah	2.50	6.00	10.00	W
156 The Texas Gun - Leslie Ernenwein	2.50	6.00	10.00	W
157 Westport Landing - Homer Hatton	2.50	6.00	10.00	
158 Naked Ebony - Dan Cushman	2.50	6.00	10.00	
159 Barren Land Murders - Luke Short	2.50	6.00	10.00	W
160 Catnips at Love and Marriage - Walter Chandoh & Rhar Dee	5.00	10.00	20.00	H
161 Son of the Flying Y - Will F. Jenkins (Murray Leinster)	3.00	6.00	12.00	
162 Bargain in Blood - Don Stanford	2.50	6.00	10.00	M
Orig., 1951				
163 Big City Girl - Charles Williams	2.50	6.00	10.00	E
Orig., 1951				
164 Murder for the Bride - John D. MacDonald	4.00	8.00	15.00	M
165 Everybody Had a Gun - Richard S. Prather	2.50	6.00	10.00	M
166 I Can't Stop Running - Edward Ronns	2.50	6.00	10.00	
Orig., 1951				
167 The Judas Hour - Howard Hunt	3.00	6.00	12.00	M
168 A Noose for the Desperado - Clifton Adams	2.50	6.00	10.00	W
169 Satan is a Woman - Gil Brewer	2.50	6.00	10.00	E
170 Death on a Ferris Wheel - Aylwin Lee Martin	2.50	6.00	10.00	M
171 I, Mobster - anonymous	3.00	6.00	12.00	
172 Lost Lady - Octavus Roy Cohen	2.50	6.00	10.00	M
173 The Tiger's Wife - Wade Miller	2.50	6.00	10.00	
174 Rider from Nowhere - Joseph Chadwick	2.50	6.00	10.00	W
175 Gay Ghastly Holiday - Sebastian Blayne	2.50	6.00	10.00	
1951				
176 Crockett's Woman - Eric Hatch	2.50	6.00	10.00	
177 This is Costello - Norton Mockridge & Robert Prall	4.00	8.00	15.00	NF
178 Cabin Road - John Faulkner	2.50	6.00	10.00	E

Gold Medal 138, c. Faw   Gold Medal 175, c. Faw   Gold Medal 177, c. Faw

Gold Medal 191, c. Faw   Gold Medal 208, c. Faw   Gold Medal 227, c. Faw

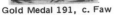

(GOLD MEDAL, continued)

179	I Have Gloria Kirby - Richard Himmel	2.50	6.00	10.00	M
	Orig., 1951				
180	The Girl in the Stateroom - Charles Boswell				
	& Lewis Thompson	3.00	6.00	12.00	NF
181	Shanghai Flame - A. S. Fleischman	2.50	6.00	10.00	E
	Orig., 1951				
182	They Died Healthy - Logan Stewart	2.50	6.00	10.00	
183	...And Be My Love - Ledru Baker, Jr.	2.50	6.00	10.00	E
	Orig., 1951				
184	Thunderclap - Jack Sheridan	2.50	6.00	10.00	E
	Orig., 1951				
185	We Never Called Him Henry - Harry Bennett				
	& Paul Marcus	2.00	4.00	7.50	B
186	Judge Me Not - John D. MacDonald	3.00	6.00	12.00	M
	Orig., 1951				
187	Hunt the Man Down - William Herman	2.50	6.00	10.00	W
188	Get Out of Town - Paul Connolly	2.50	6.00	10.00	
189	Cassidy's Girl - David Goodis	2.50	6.00	10.00	E
190	Fires that Destroy - Harry Whittington	2.50	6.00	10.00	
191	It's Your Money—Come and Get It -				
	Sidney Margolius	4.00	8.00	15.00	NF
192	The Devil's Mistress - Kenneth Thomas	2.50	6.00	10.00	
193	The Trail - Logan Stewart	2.50	6.00	10.00	W
194	The Decoy - Edward Ronns	2.50	6.00	10.00	M
195	Saratoga Mantrap - Dexter St. Clare	2.50	6.00	10.00	
196	So Rich, So Dead - Gil Brewer	2.50	6.00	10.00	
197	The Lady and the Cheetah - John Flagg	3.00	6.00	12.00	
198	To Hell Together - H. Vernor Dixon	2.50	6.00	10.00	E
199	Sumuru - Sax Rohmer	5.00	10.00	20.00	A
	Orig., 1951				
200	Weep for Me - John D. MacDonald	4.00	8.00	15.00	M
	Orig., 1951				
201	Stampede - Yukon Miles	2.50	6.00	10.00	W
202	The Unpossessed - William H. Fielding	2.50	6.00	10.00	
203	Find this Woman - Richard S. Prather	2.50	6.00	10.00	M
204	Death for Mr. Big - John Gonzales	2.50	6.00	10.00	
G205	Handsome - Theodore Pratt	2.50	6.00	10.00	
206	To Kiss or Kill - Day Keene	2.50	6.00	10.00	E
	Orig., 1951				
G207	River Girl - Charles Williams	2.50	6.00	10.00	E
	Orig., 1951				
208	Wild Blood - A. C. Abbott	2.50	6.00	10.00	W
209	Fools Walk In - Bruno Fischer	2.50	6.00	10.00	M
210	Don't Get Caught - Carter Cullen	2.50	6.00	10.00	
211	13 French Street - Gil Brewer	2.50	6.00	10.00	E
	Orig., 1951				
s212	Deep is the Pit - H. Vernor Dixon	2.50	6.00	10.00	E
	Orig., 1952				
213	The Golden Woman - Eric Hatch	2.50	6.00	10.00	
214	Fear Comes Calling - Aylwin Lee Martin	2.50	6.00	10.00	M
215	Conquest - Homer Hatton	2.50	6.00	10.00	
216	Red Runs the River - William Heuman	2.50	6.00	10.00	W
217	Passage to Terror - Edward Ronns	2.50	6.00	10.00	E
	Orig., 1952				
218	Here is My Body - Booth Mooney	2.50	6.00	10.00	
219	The Sheltering Night - Steve Fisher	2.50	6.00	10.00	
220	Give a Man a Gun - Leslie Ernenwein	2.50	6.00	10.00	W

221	The Forbidden Room - Jaclen Steele	2.50	6.00	10.00	
222	Spring Fire - Vin Packer	2.50	6.00	10.00	E
	Orig., 1952				
223	Look Behind You, Lady - A. S. Fleischman	2.50	6.00	10.00	
224	Tears are for Angels - Paul Connolly	2.50	6.00	10.00	
	Orig., 1952				
225	Home is the Sailor - Day Keene	2.00	4.00	7.50	
226	Of Tender Sin - David Goodis	2.00	4.00	7.50	
227	The Creeping Shadow - Sam Merwin, Jr.	3.00	6.00	12.00	
228	Appointment in Paris - Fay Adams	2.00	4.00	7.50	
229	Little Sister - Lee Roberts	2.50	6.00	10.00	E
	Orig., 1952				
230	The Colonel's Lady - Clifton Adams	2.50	6.00	10.00	W
231	The Road's End - Albert Conroy	2.00	4.00	7.50	E
	Orig., 1952				
232	Woman Soldier - Arnold Rodin	3.00	6.00	12.00	C
	Orig., 1952				
233	Way of a Wanton - Richard S. Prather	2.50	6.00	10.00	M
234	The Sharp Edge - Richard Himmel	2.50	6.00	10.00	
235	The Avenger - Matthew Blood	2.50	6.00	10.00	M
236	Lone Star - Borden Chase	2.50	6.00	10.00	W
237	Terror in the Sun - Richard Glendinning	2.50	6.00	10.00	E
	Orig., 1952				
238	Uncle Good's Girls - John Faulkner	2.50	6.00	10.00	E
239	Don't Cry, Beloved - Edward Ronns	2.50	6.00	10.00	M
240	The Damned - John D. MacDonald	3.00	6.00	12.00	M
241	Savage Interlude - Dan Cushman	3.00	6.00	12.00	A
242	Trapped - Richard Hayward	2.50	6.00	10.00	M
	Orig., 1952				
243	The Secret Rider - Logan Stewart	2.00	4.00	7.50	W
244	The Cheaters - Ledru Baker, Jr.	2.50	6.00	10.00	
245	Double Cross - Joseph Chadwick	2.50	6.00	10.00	W
	Orig., 1952				
246	The Scarlet Venus - Chalmers Green	2.50	6.00	10.00	E
	Orig., 1952				
247	Cry at Dusk - Lester Dent	3.00	6.00	12.00	M
	Orig., 1952				
248	Blackmailer - George Axelrod	2.50	6.00	10.00	
249	Cartoon Laffs from True - Clyde Carley	3.00	6.00	12.00	H
250	Dark Intruder - Vin Packer	2.00	4.00	7.50	
	1952				
251	The Caged - Fan Nichols	2.00	4.00	7.50	
252	Satan Takes the Helm - Calvin Clements	2.50	6.00	10.00	
253	The Crimson Frame - Aylwin Lee Martin	2.00	4.00	7.50	M
254	About Doctor Ferrel - Day Keene	2.00	4.00	7.50	E
	Orig., 1952				
255	The White Squaw - Larabie Sutter	2.50	6.00	10.00	W
256	Street of the Lost - David Goodis	2.00	4.00	7.50	E
	Orig., 1952				
257	Branded Woman - Wade Miller	2.50	6.00	10.00	
258	Escape to Love - Edward S. Aarons	2.00	4.00	7.50	
259	Walk in Fear - W. T. Ballard	2.00	4.00	7.50	
260	Men into Beasts - George Sylvester Viereck	2.50	6.00	10.00	M
261	Devil's Legacy - Joseph Chadwick	2.50	6.00	10.00	W
262	Who Evil Thinks - Richard Glendinning	2.50	6.00	10.00	
263	Love Me Now - John McPartland	2.50	6.00	10.00	E
	Orig., 1952				

Gold Medal 240, c. Faw   Gold Medal 241, c. Faw   Gold Medal 273, c. Faw

264	Brenda - Lehi Zane	2.00	4.00	7.50	E
	Orig., 1952				
265	Darling, It's Death - Richard S. Prather	2.00	4.00	7.50	M
266	Plunder - Benjamin Appel	2.00	4.00	7.50	C
267	Secret of Death Valley - William Heuman	2.00	4.00	7.50	W
268	Whisper Her Name - Howard Hunt	2.50	6.00	10.00	
269	The Devil Drives - Robert Ames	2.00	4.00	7.50	
270	The Fast Buck - Bruno Fischer	2.50	6.00	10.00	
	Orig., 1952				
271	Blood on the Sun - Chad Merriman	2.00	4.00	7.50	
272	Take Me as I Am - William H. Fielding	2.00	4.00	7.50	
273	Unholy Flame - Olga Rosmanith	3.00	6.00	12.00	E
	Orig., 1952				
274	Beyond Desire - Richard Himmel	2.00	4.00	7.50	
275	Move Along, Stranger - Frank Castle	2.00	4.00	7.50	
	1953				
276	Mountain Girl - Cord Wainer	2.00	4.00	7.50	E
	Orig., 1952				
277	Flight to Darkness - Gil Brewer	2.00	4.00	7.50	
278	That French Girl - Joseph Hilton	2.00	4.00	7.50	
279	The Big Guy - Wade Miller	2.00	4.00	7.50	
280	The Sinners - Edward S. Aarons	2.00	4.00	7.50	M
281	Swamp Brat - Allen O'Quinn	2.00	4.00	7.50	E
282	Woman of Cairo - John Flagg	2.00	4.00	7.50	
283	The Fire Goddess - Sax Rohmer	5.00	10.00	20.00	A
284	Whip Hand - Joseph Chadwick	2.00	4.00	7.50	W
285	Too Rich to Die - H. Vernor Dixon	2.00	4.00	7.50	
286	Hell Hath No Fury - Charles Williams	2.00	4.00	7.50	E
	Orig., 1953				
287	On to Santa Fe - William Heuman	2.00	4.00	7.50	W
288	Maggie - Her Marriage - Taylor Caldwell	2.00	4.00	7.50	E
	Orig., 1953				
289	The Chislers - Albert Conroy	2.50	6.00	10.00	E
	Orig., 1953				
290	Jungle She - Dan Cushman	2.50	6.00	10.00	
	Orig., 1953				
291	Whom Gods Destroy - Clifton Adams	2.00	4.00	7.50	
292	Run, Chico, Run - Wenzell Brown	2.50	6.00	10.00	JD
	Orig., 1953				
293	Mystery Raider - Leslie Ernenwein	2.00	4.00	7.50	W
294	The Girl in the Red Velvet Swing - Charles				
	Samuels	2.50	6.00	10.00	
295	Danger in Paradise - A. S. Fleischman	2.00	4.00	7.50	
296	Black Wings has my Angel - Elliott Chaze	2.00	4.00	7.50	
297	Lovers are Losers - Howard Hunt	2.00	4.00	7.50	
298	Dead Low Tide - John D. MacDonald	3.00	6.00	12.00	M
	Orig., 1953				
299	Six-gun Code - Perry Westwood	2.00	4.00	7.50	W
300	The Borgia Blade - Gardner F. Fox	2.50	6.00	10.00	A
	1953				
301	Leave Her to God - O. O. Osborne	2.00	4.00	7.50	
302	Masquerade into Madness - Russ Merservey	2.00	4.00	7.50	
303	Barge Girl - Calvin Clements	2.00	4.00	7.50	E
304	The Snatchers - Lionel White	2.00	4.00	7.50	
305	Ridge Runner - Chad Merriman	2.00	4.00	7.50	W
306	The Girl in the Death Cell - Fred J. Cook	2.00	4.00	7.50	NF
307	Witch of Salem - Benjamin Siegel	2.50	6.00	10.00	E
	Orig., 1953				
308	Hideaway - Nikki Content	2.00	4.00	7.50	
309	Sword in His Hand - John Vail	2.00	4.00	7.50	A
310	Keelboats North - William Heuman	2.00	4.00	7.50	W
311	Thieves Fall Out - Cameron Kay	2.00	4.00	7.50	
s312	Gold Medal Treasury of American Verse -				
	John Gilland Brunini	3.00	6.00	12.00	
313	War Bonnet Pass - Logan Stewart	2.00	4.00	6.00	W
314	Gunsmoke Reckoning - Joseph Chadwick	2.00	4.00	6.00	W
315	Saturday's Harvest - Paul Shelley	2.00	4.00	7.50	
316	Up a Winding Stair - H. Vernor Dixon	2.00	4.00	7.50	
317	Come Feed On Me - Morton Cooper	2.00	4.00	7.50	
318	Ambush at Rincon - Dudley Dean	2.00	4.00	7.50	W
319	The Crooked Mile - Norbert Fagan	2.00	4.00	7.50	
320	Escape from Morales - Virginia Myers	2.00	4.00	7.50	
321	Nude in Mink - Sax Rohmer	2.50	6.00	10.00	M
322	Guns at Broken Bow - William Heuman	2.00	4.00	6.00	
323	The Neon Jungle - John D. MacDonald	3.00	6.00	12.00	M

(GOLD MEDAL, continued)

324 Look Back to Love - Vin Packer	2.00	4.00	7.50	
325 Terror in the Night - Sebastian Blayne 1953	2.00	4.00	7.50	
326 Moment of Truth - Arnold Rodin	2.00	4.00	7.50	
327 Savage Stronghold - Logan Stewart	2.00	4.00	7.50	W
328 Madame Buccaneer - Gordon F. Fox Orig., 1953	2.50	6.00	10.00	A
329 Gunfighter's Return - Leslie Ernenwein	2.00	4.00	6.00	W
330 Roll the Wagons - William Heuman	2.00	4.00	6.00	W
331 South of the Sun - Wade Miller	2.00	4.00	7.50	
332 Timberjack - Dan Cushman	2.00	4.00	7.50	
333 To Love to Hate - Fay Adams	2.00	4.00	7.50	
334 The Girl in Lover's Lane - Charles Boswell & Lewis Thompson	2.00	4.00	7.50	NF
335 Valley of Angry Men - Matthew Gant	2.00	4.00	7.50	
336 Tokyo Doll - John McPartland	2.00	4.00	7.50	
337 Bar Guide - Virgil Partch & Ted Shane	2.50	6.00	10.00	H
338 Rider from Nowhere - Joseph Chadwick	2.00	4.00	6.00	W
s339 Escape to Eden - Theodore Pratt	2.00	4.00	7.50	
340 Nothing in Her Way - Charles Williams	2.00	4.00	7.50	
341 Ride a High Horse - Richard S. Prather	2.00	4.00	7.50	
342 Belle Bradley, Her Story	2.00	4.00	7.50	
343 Run for Your Life - Bruno Fischer	2.00	4.00	7.50	M
344 Wagon Train Woman - Alan Henry	2.00	4.00	7.50	W
345 Hell's Our Destination - Gil Brewer	2.00	4.00	7.50	
346 Son of the Flying Y - Will F. Jenkins (Murray Leinster)	2.50	6.00	10.00	W
347 Hondo - Louis L'Amour Orig., 1953	2.50	6.00	10.00	W
348 The Moon in the Gutter - David Goodis	2.00	4.00	7.50	
349 I Came to Kill - Gordon Davis	2.00	4.00	7.50	M
350 Rage in Texas - Howard Rigsby 1953	2.00	4.00	7.50	W
351 The Girl in Poison Cottage - Jim Bishop & H. Hoffmann	2.00	4.00	7.50	NF
352 Eagle on His Wrist - Homer Hatton	2.00	4.00	7.50	
353 The Fall of Suzanne Swift - V. A. McMillen	2.00	4.00	7.50	E
354 Big Red's Daughter - John McPartland	2.00	4.00	7.50	E
355 Big Stan - John Monahan 1954	2.00	4.00	7.50	
356 Paradise Motel - Jack Sheridan	2.00	4.00	7.50	
357 Guns Along the Wickiup - D. B. Newton	2.00	4.00	7.50	W
358 Pappy and the Promised Land - Jack Gotshall	2.00	4.00	7.50	
359 The Girl in the House of Hate - Charles Samuels & Louise Samuels	2.00	4.00	7.50	NF
360 One Sword for Love - Gardner F. Fox	2.50	6.00	10.00	A
361 Rampage - Leslie Ernenwein	2.00	4.00	7.50	W
362 Come Back, My Love - Edward S. Aarons Orig., 1954	2.00	4.00	7.50	M
363 Come Destroy Me - Vin Packer	2.00	4.00	7.50	
364 Gold Brick Cassie - David Loth	2.50	6.00	10.00	NF
365 Monte Carlo Mission - Vivian Connell	2.00	4.00	7.50	
366 This Woman is Mine - Harry Whittington	2.00	4.00	7.50	
367 Rails West - Logan Stewart	2.00	4.00	7.50	W
368 Malay Woman - A. S. Fleischman	2.00	4.00	7.50	A
369 Seminole - Theodore Pratt	3.00	6.00	12.00	A
370 A Lover for Cindy - H. Vernon Dixon	2.00	4.00	7.50	

Gold Medal 307, c. Faw

Gold Medal 347, c. Faw

Gold Medal 369, c. Faw

(GOLD MEDAL, continued)

371	Go Home, Stranger - Charles Williams	2.00	4.00	7.50	
372	Notorious - Day Keene	2.00	4.00	7.50	
373	Two Deaths Must Die - Richard Himmel	2.00	4.00	7.50	
374	Come Out Shooting - Joseph Chadwick	2.00	4.00	7.50	W
375	As a Man Falls - Howard Rigsby	2.00	4.00	7.50	
	1954				
376	Take Your Last Look - Matt Brady	2.00	4.00	7.50	
377	The Range Grabbers - Sidney Stewart	2.00	4.00	7.50	
378	Let Them Eat Bullets - Howard Schoenfeld	2.00	4.00	7.50	M
379	Women's Barracks - Tereska Torres	2.00	4.00	7.50	E
380	A Killer is Loose - Gil Brewer	2.00	4.00	7.50	
381	Fury on the Plains - Chad Merriman	2.00	4.00	7.50	W
382	One Against the Odds - Norbert Fagan	2.00	4.00	7.50	
383	Cartoon Fun from True	3.00	6.00	12.00	H
384	The Girl with the Scarlet Brand - Charles				
	Boswell & Lewis Thompson	2.00	4.00	7.50	NF
385	Sweet Money Girl - Benjamin Appel	2.00	4.00	7.50	
386	The Beautiful and Dead - Ross MacRoss	2.00	4.00	7.50	
d387	Driven - Richard Gehman	2.00	4.00	7.50	
388	I'll Take What's Mine - Nard Jones	2.00	4.00	7.50	
389	Retreat into Night - Richard Glendinning	2.00	4.00	7.50	
390	Renegade Gun - Joseph Chadwick	2.00	4.00	7.50	
391	Dear, Deadly Beloved - John Flagg	2.00	4.00	7.50	M
392	The Fabulous Finn - Don Cushman	2.00	4.00	7.50	
393	The Face of Evil - John McPartland	2.00	4.00	7.50	
394	The Gentleman Rogue - Gardner F. Fox	2.50	6.00	10.00	A
395	And Two Shall Meet - Raymond Mason	2.00	4.00	7.50	
396	The Dark Throne - John Vail	2.00	4.00	7.50	A
397	The Girl on the Gallows - Q. Patrick	2.50	6.00	10.00	M
398	Spring Fire - Vin Packer	2.00	4.00	6.00	E
399	A Woman for Henry - Allen O'Quinn	2.00	4.00	7.50	
400	Lucinda - Howard Rigsby	2.00	4.00	7.50	
	1954				
401	Saddle the Storm - Harry Whittington	2.00	4.00	7.50	
402	French for Murder - Bernard Mara	2.00	4.00	7.50	M
s403	Portrait of Lisa - William Brothers	2.00	4.00	7.50	
404	The Wickedest Man - Joseph Millard	2.00	4.00	7.50	
405	There Was a Crooked Man - Day Keene	2.00	4.00	7.50	
406	Affair in Tokyo - John McPartland	2.00	4.00	7.50	
407	Man Divided - Dean Douglas	2.00	4.00	7.50	
408	Return of Sumuru - Sax Rohmer	5.00	10.00	20.00	A
	Orig., 1954				
409	Some Must Die - Gil Brewer	2.00	4.00	7.50	
410	Uncle Good's Girls - John Faulkner	2.00	4.00	6.00	E
411	Black Horse Canyon - Les Savage, Jr.	2.50	6.00	10.00	W
412	Hell Ship to Kuma - Calvin Clements	2.00	4.00	7.50	
413	Always Leave 'em Dying - Richard S.				
	Prather	2.00	4.00	7.50	M
414	Ride for Texas - William Heuman	2.00	4.00	7.50	W
415	Runaway Black - Richard Marsten	2.00	4.00	7.50	
416	Jezebel in Crinoline - Homer Hatton	2.00	4.00	7.50	E
417	I am Legend - Richard Matheson	2.50	6.00	10.00	SF
	Orig., 1954				
418	13 French Street - Gil Brewer	2.00	4.00	7.50	
419	Come Murder Me - James Kieran	2.00	4.00	7.50	M
420	All These Condemned - John D. MacDonald	3.00	6.00	12.00	M
421	Smash-up - Theodore Pratt	2.00	4.00	7.50	
422	Two-Gun Law - Clifton Adams	2.00	4.00	7.50	W
423	Death is a Lovely Dame - Matthew Blood	2.00	4.00	7.50	M
424	Girl on the Run - Edward S. Aarons	2.00	4.00	7.50	M
425	Case of the Vanishing Beauty - Richard S.				
	Prather	2.00	4.00	6.00	M
	1954				
426	Whisper His Sin - Vin Packer	2.00	4.00	7.50	
427	Cry Down the Lonely Night - Milton White	2.00	4.00	7.50	
428	Street of No Return - David Goodis	2.00	4.00	7.50	
429	The Range Buster - William Heuman	2.00	4.00	7.50	W
430	Beautiful Humbug - William H. Fielding	2.00	4.00	7.50	
431	The Girl on the Lonely Beach - Fred J. Cook	2.00	4.00	7.50	NF
s432	Handsome - Theodore Pratt	2.00	4.00	7.50	
433	Somebody Loves Me - Nancy Morgan	2.00	4.00	7.50	
434	A Touch of Death - Charles Williams	2.00	4.00	7.50	
435	The Dangerous One - Robert Ames	2.00	4.00	7.50	
436	The Man from Riondo - Dudley Dean	2.00	4.00	7.50	W
437	So Wicked My Love - Bruno Fischer	2.00	4.00	7.50	M
438	Women of Kali - Gardner F. Fox	2.50	6.00	10.00	A

439	Cabin Road - John Faulkner	2.00	4.00	6.00	E
s440	The Cunning and the Haunted - Richard Jessup	2.00	4.00	7.50	
s441	Sow the Wild Wind - John Vail	2.00	4.00	7.50	A
442	Rebel Raider - Joseph Chadwick	2.00	4.00	7.50	W
443	Wild Breed - Ted Stratton	2.00	4.00	7.50	
444	Mission to Murder - Richard Glendinning	2.00	4.00	7.50	M
445	Funny Cartoons by VIP - Virgil Partch	3.00	6.00	12.00	H
	1955				
446	Hill Girl - Charles Williams	2.00	4.00	6.00	
447	Make My Coffin Strong - William R. Cox	2.00	4.00	7.50	
448	77 Rue Paradis - Gil Brewer	2.00	4.00	7.50	
449	The Mating Cry - Frank Daniels	2.00	4.00	7.50	
450	Strange but True	2.00	4.00	7.50	NF
	1955				
451	Bad Day at Black Rock - Howard Breslin	2.00	4.00	7.50	W
452	Outcast of Murder Mesa - Kenneth Fowler	2.00	4.00	7.50	W
s453	City of Women - Nancy Morgan	2.00	4.00	7.50	E
s454	The Hunger and the Hate - H. Vernor Dixon	2.00	4.00	7.50	
455	The Sin Shouter of Cabin Road - John Faulkner	2.00	4.00	7.50	E
456	Shanghai Incident - Steve Dodge	2.00	4.00	7.50	
457	Many Rivers to Cross - Steve Frazee	2.00	4.00	7.50	W
458	The Girl in Murder Flat - Mel Heimer	2.00	4.00	7.50	NF
459	Lady in Dread - Ryerson Johnson	2.00	4.00	7.50	
460	I'll Find You - Richard Himmel	2.00	4.00	6.00	
461	The Glitter and the Greed - Robert W. Taylor	2.00	4.00	7.50	
462	Funny Business - Charlest Preston	2.50	6.00	10.00	H
463	Strangers in My Bed - Allen O'Quinn	2.00	4.00	7.50	
464	Bullet Barricade - Leslie Ernenwein	2.00	4.00	7.50	W
465	A New Way to Eat and Get Slim - Donald G. Cooley	2.50	6.00	10.00	NF
466	Death was the Bridegroom - Charles Samuels	2.00	4.00	7.50	
s467	River Girl - Charles Williams	2.00	4.00	6.00	E
468	Forever is Today - Raymond Mason	2.00	4.00	6.00	
469	Mad Baxter - Wade Miller	2.00	4.00	7.50	M
470	The Big Caper - Lionel White	2.00	4.00	7.50	M
471	Song of the Gun - Dudley Dean	2.00	4.00	7.50	W
472	A Bullet for My Lady - Bernard Mara	2.00	4.00	7.50	M
473	Violence in the Night - Alan Hynd	2.00	4.00	7.50	
s474	The Tormented - Theodore Pratt	2.00	4.00	6.00	
475	Angels in the Gutter - Joseph Hilton	3.00	6.00	12.00	JD
	1955				
476	Blonde Savage - John Vail	2.00	4.00	7.50	A
477	Prey by Night - Malcolm Douglas	2.00	4.00	7.50	
478	Heller with a Gun - Louis L'Amour	2.50	6.00	10.00	W
479	The Soft Arms of Death - Richard Hayward	2.00	4.00	7.50	
480	The Girls in Nightmare House - Charles Boswell & Lewis Thompson	2.00	4.00	7.50	NF
481	The Damned - John D. MacDonald	2.00	4.00	6.00	
482	The Brass Cupcake - John D. MacDonald	2.00	4.00	6.00	M
483	Death's Sweet Song - Clifton Adams	2.00	4.00	7.50	
484	Rebel Wench - Gardner F. Fox	2.00	4.00	7.50	A
485	West to the Sun - Noel M. Loomis	2.00	4.00	7.50	W
486	Dark Heritage - John Foster	2.00	4.00	7.50	
487	The Truth about Belle Gunness - Lillian de la Torre	2.00	4.00	7.50	

Gold Medal 411, c. Faw

Gold Medal 417, c. Faw

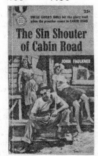

Gold Medal 455, c. Faw

Gold Medal 498, c. Faw   Gold Medal 509, c. Faw   Gold Medal 549, c. Faw

(GOLD MEDAL, continued)

488	Cry of the Flesh - Richard Himmel	2.00	4.00	7.50	
489	Find this Woman - Richard S. Prather	2.00	4.00	6.00	M
490	Mine to Avenge - Thomas Wills	2.00	4.00	7.50	
491	Assignment to Disaster - Edward S. Aarons	2.00	4.00	7.50	M
492	Plunder Range - Homer Hatton	2.00	4.00	7.50	
493	The Golden Frame - Joseph Chadwick	2.00	4.00	7.50	
494	Who Has Wilma Lathrop? - Day Keene	2.00	4.00	7.50	M
495	Hell Strip - Lee Richards	2.00	4.00	7.50	
496	Bodies in Bedlam - Richard S. Prather	2.00	4.00	6.00	M
497	Way of a Wanton - Richard S. Prather	2.00	4.00	6.00	M
498	One of Our H-Bombs is Missing - Frederick Hazlitt Brennan	3.00	6.00	12.00	M
499	Blood Alley - A. S. Fleischman Movie tie-in	2.00	4.00	7.50	A
500	So Fair, So Evil - Paul Connolly 1955	2.00	4.00	7.50	
501	Trouble Rides Tall - William Hopson	2.00	4.00	7.50	W
502	Homicide Hussy - Atha McGuire	2.00	4.00	7.50	M
503	Death Lies Deep - William Guinn	2.00	4.00	7.50	M
504	Everybody Had a Gun - Richard S. Prather	2.00	4.00	6.00	M
505	Darling, It's Death - Richard S. Prather	2.00	4.00	6.00	M
506	Stop this Man - Peter Rabe	2.00	4.00	7.50	
507	Murder in the Navy - Richard Marsten	2.00	4.00	7.50	M
508	Strip for Murder - Richard S. Prather	2.00	4.00	7.50	M
509	We Walk Alone - Ann Aldrich Orig., 1955	2.50	6.00	10.00	E
510	The Thrill Kids - Vin Packer	2.00	4.00	7.50	
511	The Broken Spur - Dudley Dean	2.00	4.00	7.50	W
512	Ride the Dark Storm - Nard Jones	2.00	4.00	7.50	
513	Stolen Woman - Wade Miller	2.00	4.00	6.00	
514	Shanghai Flame - A. S. Fleischman	2.00	4.00	6.00	
s515	A Rage to Die - Richard Jessup	2.00	4.00	7.50	
516	To Tame a Land - Louis L'amour	2.50	6.00	10.00	W
517	Journey into Death - Jack Johnson	2.00	4.00	7.50	
518	Awake and Die - Robert Ames	2.00	4.00	7.50	M
519	Lie Down with Lions - Marvin H. Albert	2.00	4.00	7.50	
520	Benny Muscles In - Peter Rabe	2.00	4.00	7.50	
521	The Killer - Wade Miller	2.00	4.00	6.00	
s522	Run, Chico, Run - Wenzell Brown	2.00	4.00	7.50	JD
523	The Second Longest Night - Stephen Marlowe	2.00	4.00	7.50	M
524	My Deadly Angel - John Chelton	2.00	4.00	7.50	
525	Your Sins and Mine - Taylor Caldwell	2.00	4.00	7.50	
526	Gunsmoke Empire - Lewis B. Patten	2.00	4.00	7.50	W
527	Renegade Brand - Richard Brister	2.00	4.00	7.50	W
528	A Shroud for Jesso - Peter Rabe	2.00	4.00	7.50	
529	The Decoy - Edward Ronns	2.00	4.00	6.00	
530	The Wounded and the Slain - David Goodis	2.00	4.00	7.50	
531	The Dead Darling - Jonathan Craig	2.00	4.00	7.50	M
532	The Neighbor's Kids - George Clark	2.00	4.00	7.50	
533	Gambling Man - Clifton Adams	2.00	4.00	7.50	
534	The Outlaw Breed - D. B. Newton	2.00	4.00	7.50	W
535	Port Orient - Dan Cushman	2.00	4.00	7.50	
536	Cocotte - Theodore Pratt	2.00	4.00	6.00	
537	House of Flesh - Bruno Fischer	2.00	4.00	6.00	M
538	The Flesh and Mr. Rawlie - Morton Cooper	2.00	4.00	7.50	
539	Rain of Terror - Malcolm Douglas 1955	2.00	4.00	7.50	

225

540 Zowie! Girl Meets Boy - Charles Preston	3.00	6.00	12.00	H
541 Horsemen from Hell - Homer Hatter	2.00	4.00	7.50	
542 The Lone Gun - Howard Rigsby	2.00	4.00	7.50	
543 The Chinese Keyhole - Richard Himmel	2.00	4.00	6.00	
544 Cassidy's Girl - David Goodis	2.00	4.00	6.00	E
545 Hell-bent for Danger - Walt Grove	2.00	4.00	6.00	
546 Killer in White - Tedd Thomey	2.00	4.00	7.50	
547 A House in Naples - Peter Rabe	2.00	4.00	7.50	
548 To Hell—And Texas - Giles A. Lutz	2.00	4.00	7.50	W
s549 Queen of Sheba - Gardner F. Fox	3.00	6.00	12.00	A
Orig., 1956				
s550 Down to Eternity - Richard O'Connor	2.00	4.00	7.50	
551 Too Many Crooks - Richard S. Prather	2.00	4.00	7.50	M
552 Men into Beasts - George Sylvester Viereck	2.00	4.00	6.00	
553 The Law and Jake Wade - Marvin Albert	2.00	4.00	7.50	W
554 The Violent Hours - Frank Castle	2.00	4.00	7.50	
555 Sinister Madonna - Sax Rohmer	5.00	10.00	20.00	A
Orig., 1956				
556 Hold Back the Sun - John Vail	2.00	4.00	7.50	A
557 Hot, Sweet and Blue - Jack Baird	2.00	4.00	7.50	
558 Trapped - Richard Hayward	2.00	4.00	6.00	
559 Woman Soldier - Arnold Rodin	2.00	4.00	7.50	C
560 The Guns of Fort Petticoat - C. William Harrison	2.00	4.00	7.50	W
561 Death Must Wait - Don Kingery	2.00	4.00	7.50	
562 This Gun for Gloria - Bernard Mara	2.00	4.00	7.50	M
563 Build My Gallows High - Roy B. Sparkia	2.00	4.00	7.50	
s564 Cry Blood - H. Vernor Dixon	2.00	4.00	7.50	
565 Little Sister - Lee Roberts	2.00	4.00	6.00	E
566 I Have Gloria Kirby - Richard Himmel	2.00	4.00	6.00	
567 The Golden Bawd - Giles A. Lutz	2.00	4.00	7.50	
568 Assignment—Treason - Edward S. Aarons	2.00	4.00	7.50	M
569 Gunfire at Salt Fork - William Hopson	2.00	4.00	7.50	W
570 My Mistress, Death - Robert Spafford	2.00	4.00	7.50	
571 I'll See You in Hell - John McPartland	2.00	4.00	7.50	
572 Look Behind You, Lady - A. S. Fleischman	2.00	4.00	6.00	
573 Rope Law - Lewis B. Patten	2.00	4.00	7.50	W
574 Danger for Breakfast - John McPartland	2.00	4.00	7.50	
575 Mecca for Murder - Stephen Marlowe	2.00	4.00	7.50	M
1956				
576 Catch a Falling Star - Reed Marr	2.00	4.00	7.50	
s577 The Shrinking Man - Richard Matheson	2.50	6.00	10.00	SF
578 Dark Intruder - Vin Packer	2.00	4.00	7.50	
579 The Road's End - Albert Conroy	2.00	4.00	7.50	
580 Rio Bravo - Gordon D. Shirreffs	2.00	4.00	7.50	W
581 The Young and Violent - Vin Packer	2.00	4.00	7.50	
582 Morgue for Venus - Jonathan Craig	2.00	4.00	7.50	M
s583 Hypnosis and You - Ben Benson & Howard D. Tawney	2.50	6.00	10.00	NF
584 The Diehards - Dudley Dean	2.00	4.00	7.50	W
585 Swamp Brat - Allen O'Quinn	2.00	4.00	6.00	
586 Let Them Eat Bullets - Howard Schoenfeld	2.00	4.00	6.00	
s587 Johnny Concho - Noel M. Loomis	2.00	4.00	7.50	W
Movie tie-in				
s588 The Innocent and Willing - Morton Cooper	2.00	4.00	7.50	
589 Love After Five - Raymond Mason	2.00	4.00	7.50	
s590 Edgar Cayce - Mystery Man of Miracles - Joseph Millard	2.00	4.00	7.50	NF
591 Knee-deep in Death - Bruno Fischer	2.00	4.00	7.50	M
592 The Wailing Frail - Richard S. Prather	2.00	4.00	7.50	M
593 Law of the Trigger - Clifton Adams	2.00	4.00	7.50	W
594 Kill the Boss Good-bye - Peter Rabe	2.00	4.00	7.50	
595 Brute in Brass - Harry Whittington	2.00	4.00	7.50	
596 The Wild Party - John McPartland	2.00	4.00	7.50	
s597 The Women with Claws - Williams Forrest	2.00	4.00	7.50	
598 Always Leave 'em Dying - Richard S. Prather	2.00	4.00	6.00	M
599 Mountain Girl - Cord Wainer	2.00	4.00	6.00	E
600 Fools Walk In - Bruno Fischer	2.00	4.00	6.00	M
1956				
601 Tough Hombre - Dudley Dean	2.00	4.00	7.50	W
602 White Warrior - Lewis B. Patten	2.00	4.00	7.50	W
603 Bring Him Back Dead - Day Keene	2.00	4.00	7.50	
604 The Name's Buchanan - Jonas Ward	2.00	4.00	7.50	W
605 Dead and Kicking - Frank Castle	2.00	4.00	7.50	

606	Operation—Murder - Lionel White	2.00	4.00	7.50	
s607	The Diamond Bikini - Charles Williams	2.00	4.00	7.50	
608	The Chiselers - Albert Conroy	2.00	4.00	6.00	E
609	The Borgia Blade - Gardner F. Fox	2.50	6.00	10.00	A
610	Don't Get Caught - Carter Cullen	2.00	4.00	6.00	
611	Desire in the Dust - Hany Whittington	2.00	4.00	7.50	
612	Dig My Grave Deep - Peter Rabe	2.00	4.00	7.50	
613	He Rode Alone - Steve Frazee	2.00	4.00	7.50	W
614	The Deadly Dames - Malcolm Douglas	2.00	4.00	7.50	
615	Three Violent People - Leonard Praskins & Barney Slater	2.00	4.00	7.50	
s616	Killer in Silk - H. Vernor Dixon	2.00	4.00	7.50	
617	About Doctor Ferrel - Day Keene	2.00	4.00	6.00	
s618	Handsome - Theodore Pratt	2.00	4.00	6.00	
619	Prairie Reckoning - Paul Durst	2.00	4.00	7.50	W
620	High Gun - Leslie Ernenwein	2.00	4.00	7.50	W
621	Assignment—Suicide - Edward S. Aarons	2.00	4.00	7.50	M
622	Murder on the Side - Day Keene	2.00	4.00	7.50	M
623	Down There - David Goodis	2.00	4.00	7.50	
s624	Dark Don't Catch Me - Vin Packer	2.00	4.00	7.50	
625	Go Home Stranger - Charles Williams	2.00	4.00	6.00	
	1956				
626	Of Tender Sin - David Goodis	2.00	4.00	6.00	E
627	Trouble is My Name - Stephen Marlowe	2.00	4.00	7.50	M
628	Murder in Monaco - John Flagg	2.00	4.00	7.50	M
629	The Deadly Chase - Carter Cullen	2.00	4.00	7.50	
630	The White Squaw - Larabie Sutter	2.00	4.00	6.00	
631	Violence Valley - William Heuman	2.00	4.00	7.50	W
s632	Search for Surrender - Borden Deal	2.00	4.00	7.50	
633	The Sin Shouter of Cabin Road - John Faulkner	2.00	4.00	6.00	E
634	State Department Murders - Edward Ronns	2.00	4.00	6.00	M
635	Seminole - Theodore Pratt	2.50	6.00	10.00	A
	1957				
636	Vengeance Under Law - Frank Castle	2.00	4.00	7.50	
637	Running Target - Steve Frazee	2.00	4.00	7.50	
638	Women Without Men - Reed Marr	2.00	4.00	7.50	
639	Bugles on the Prairie - Gordon D. Shirreffs	2.00	4.00	7.50	W
640	The Wicked Streets - Wenzell Brown	2.50	6.00	10.00	JD
s641	The Golden Sorrow - Theodore Pratt	2.00	4.00	7.50	
s642	Sweet Money Girl - Benjamin Appel	2.00	4.00	7.50	
643	I Am Legend - Richard Matheson	3.00	6.00	12.00	SF
644	Ride the Gold Mare - Ovid Demaris	2.00	4.00	6.00	
645	Case of the Cold Coquette - Jonathan Craig	2.00	4.00	7.50	M
646	The Reluctant Gun - Howard Rigsby	1.50	3.50	5.00	
647	Cheyenne Saturday - Richard Jessup	2.00	4.00	7.50	W
648	Terror Over London - Gardner F. Fox	2.50	6.00	10.00	M
s649	The Wings of Eagles - Walt Grove Movie tie-in	2.00	4.00	7.50	
650	The Corpse that Walked - Octavus Roy Cohen	1.50	3.50	5.00	M
	1957				
651	Big City Girl - Charles Williams	1.50	3.50	5.00	E
652	Street of the Lost - David Goodis	1.50	3.50	5.00	
s653	Odd Girl Out - Ann Bannon	2.00	4.00	6.00	
654	Pure Sweet Hell - Malcolm Douglas	2.00	4.00	6.00	
655	Gun in the Valley - Dudley Dean	2.00	4.00	6.00	W
656	Westward the Drums - L. A. Hearne	2.00	4.00	7.50	
657	The Cut is Death - Peter Rabe	2.00	4.00	6.00	
658	Murder is My Dish - Stephen Marlowe	2.00	4.00	6.00	M
659	Hell Strip - Lee Richards	1.50	3.50	5.00	
s660	The Young Don't Cry - Richard Jessup	2.00	4.00	6.00	
s661	The Maricopa Trail - Noel M. Loomis	2.00	4.00	7.50	W
662	Buchanan Says No - Jonas Ward	2.00	4.00	6.00	W
663	Death Takes the Bus - Lionel White	2.00	4.00	6.00	M
664	So I'm A Heel - Mike Heller	2.00	4.00	6.00	
665	Three's a Shroud - Richard S. Prather	2.00	4.00	6.00	M
666	Assignment--Stella Marni - Edward S. Aarons	2.00	4.00	6.00	M
667	Saddle Justice - Steven C. Lawrence	2.00	4.00	6.00	W
668	Don't Let Her Die - Tarn Scott	2.00	4.00	6.00	
669	So Young, So Wicked - Jonathan Craig	2.00	4.00	6.00	M
670	Agreement to Kill - Peter Rabe	2.00	4.00	6.00	
671	Lusty Conquest - Lee Richards	2.00	4.00	6.00	E
672	Long Ride West - Richard Jessup	2.00	4.00	6.00	W
s673	Women's Barracks - Tereska Torres	2.00	4.00	6.00	
674	Outlaw's Son - Clifton Adams	2.00	4.00	6.00	W

675	One Wild Oat - MacKinlay Kantor 1957	1.50	3.50	5.00	
676	Nice Guys Finish Dead - Albert Conroy	2.00	4.00	6.00	
677	Have Cat--Will Travel - Richard S. Prather	2.00	4.00	6.00	M
678	It's My Funeral - Peter Rabe	2.00	4.00	6.00	M
679	Gun Talk at Yuma - Frank Castle	2.00	4.00	6.00	W
680	The Hoods Take Over - Ovid Demaris	2.00	4.00	7.50	JD
681	Heller from Texas - William Heuman	2.00	4.00	6.00	W
682	The Tiger's Wife - Wade Miller	1.50	3.50	5.00	
683	A Noose for the Desperado - Clifton Adams	1.50	3.50	5.00	W
s684	Re-enter Fu Manchu - Sax Rohmer Orig., 1957	4.00	8.00	15.00	A
685	Sundown at Crazy Horse - Vechel Howard	2.00	4.00	6.00	W
686	Last Stand at Papago Wells - Louis L'Amour Orig., 1957	2.00	4.00	7.50	W
687	Hostage for a Hood - Lionel White	2.00	4.00	6.00	
s688	The Girl in the Belfry - Joseph Henry Jackson & Lenore Glen Offord	2.00	4.00	6.00	NF
689	Three-Day Terror - Vin Packer	2.00	4.00	6.00	
690	Crockett's Woman - Eric Hatch	1.50	3.50	5.00	
691	Fire in the Flesh - Richard Goodis	2.00	4.00	6.00	
692	Harry the Men High - Noel M. Loomis & Paul Leslie Peil	2.00	4.00	6.00	
693	Killers are My Meat - Stephen Marlowe	2.00	4.00	6.00	M
694	Murder in the Raw - Bruno Fischer	2.00	4.00	6.00	M
695	Lovely--And Lethal - Frank Castle	2.00	4.00	6.00	
696	Apache Rising - Marvin Albert	2.00	4.00	6.00	W
697	Hill Girl - Charles Williams	1.50	3.50	5.00	
698	The Baby Doll Murders - James O. Causey	2.00	4.00	6.00	M
699	Comanche Vengeance - Richard Jessup	2.00	4.00	6.00	W
700	The Tall Stranger - Louis L'Amour Orig., 1957	2.00	4.00	7.50	W
701	Run from the Hunter - Keith Grantland	2.00	4.00	6.00	
702	The Case of the Beautiful Body - Jonathan Craig	2.00	4.00	6.00	M
703	The Voodoo Murders - Michael Avallone	2.00	4.00	6.00	M
s704	This is Costello - Norton Mockridge & Robert Prall	2.00	4.00	7.50	NF
705	Stagecoach West - William Heuman	2.00	4.00	6.00	W
706	The Massacre at San Pablo - Lewis B. Pattern	2.00	4.00	6.00	W
707	Assignment--Budapest - Edward S. Aarons	2.00	4.00	6.00	M
708	The Brat - Gil Brewer	2.00	4.00	6.00	E
709	Murder in Red - Frank Castle	2.00	4.00	6.00	
710	Journey into Terror - Peter Rabe	2.00	4.00	6.00	
711	A Man of Parts - Vivian Connell	1.50	3.50	5.00	
712	The Wailing Frail - Richard S. Prather	1.50	3.50	5.00	M
713	Summons to Silverhorn - Kenneth Fowler	2.00	4.00	6.00	
714	Ambush on the Mesa - Gordon D. Shirreffs	2.00	4.00	6.00	W
715	Case of the Deadly Kiss - Milton K. Ozaki	2.00	4.00	6.00	M
716	Come Night, Come Evil - Jonathan Craig	2.00	4.00	6.00	M
717	For Love of Imabelle - Chester Himes	1.50	3.50	5.00	
718	The Crazy Mixed-Up Corpse - Michael Avallone Orig., 1957	2.00	4.00	6.00	M
719	Savage Bride - Cornell Woolrich	2.00	4.00	6.00	M
720	Barren Land Showdown - Luke Short aka Barren Land Murders	2.00	4.00	6.00	W

Gold Medal 700, c. Faw   Gold Medal 728, c. Faw   Gold Medal 736, c. Faw

721	Murder on the Line - William L. Rohde	2.00	4.00	6.00	M
722	A Town to Tame - Joseph Chadwick	1.50	3.50	5.00	W
723	Five Rode West - Lewis B. Patten	1.50	3.50	5.00	W
724	The Damned - John D. MacDonald	1.50	3.50	5.00	M
s725	The Great Debauch - Williams Forrest 1958	1.50	3.50	5.00	E
s726	Three Times Infinity - Leo Margulies	.75	1.75	3.00	SF
s727	We Too Must Love - Ann Aldrich Orig., 1958	2.00	4.00	7.50	E
728	Heller with A Gun - Louis L'Amour	.75	1.75	3.00	W
729	Uncle Good's Girls - John Faulkner	.75	1.75	3.00	E
730	Cabin Road - John Faulkner	.75	1.75	3.00	E
s731	5:45 to Suburbia - Vin Packer	.75	1.75	3.00	
732	Ripe Fruit - John McPartland	.75	1.75	3.00	
733	Guns of Rio Conches - Clair Huffaker	1.50	3.50	5.00	W
s734	Teen-age Terror - Wenzell Brown	2.00	4.00	7.50	JD
s735	The Rich and the Damned - Richard Himmel	.75	1.75	3.00	
736	Cowboy - Clair Huffaker Movie tie-in	2.00	4.00	7.50	W
737	Dead Low Tide - John D. MacDonald	.75	1.75	3.00	M
738	The Violent Ones - Howard Hunt	.75	1.75	3.00	
739	I, Mobster	.75	1.75	3.00	
740	Web of Murder - Harry Whittington	1.50	3.50	5.00	
741	Outcast Gun - Giles A. Lutz	1.50	3.50	5.00	W
742	One-man Massacre - Jonas Ward	1.50	3.50	5.00	W
743	I Like 'em Tough - Curt Cannon	1.50	3.50	5.00	
744	The Secret of Sylvia - Lee Borden	1.50	3.50	5.00	
745	Take a Murder, Darling - Richard S. Prather	1.50	3.50	5.00	M
s746	River Girl - Charles Williams	.75	1.75	3.00	E
747	The Hoods Come Calling - Nick Quany	2.00	4.00	6.00	JD
748	Badman's Holiday - Will Cook	1.50	3.50	5.00	W
749	Assignment-Angelina - Edward S. Aarons	1.50	3.50	5.00	M
750	The Lusting Drive - Ovid Demaris 1958	1.50	3.50	5.00	
s751	War with the Gizmos - Murray Leinster	1.50	3.50	5.00	SF
752	Dakota Boomtown - Frank Castle	1.50	3.50	5.00	W
753	So Wicked My Love - Bruno Fischer	.75	1.75	3.00	M
754	The Obsessed - Gertrude Schweitzer	.75	1.75	3.00	
755	The Lady Kills - Bruno Fischer	.75	1.75	3.00	M
756	The Law and Jake Wade - Marvin H. Albert	.75	1.75	3.00	W
s757	Sumuru - Sax Rohmer	1.50	3.50	5.00	A
758	Devil May Come - Wade Miller	.75	1.75	3.00	
759	Wyoming Jones - Richard Telfair	1.50	3.50	5.00	
760	The Bounty Killer - Marvin Albert	1.50	3.50	5.00	W
761	Park Avenue Tramp - Fletcher Flora	1.50	3.50	5.00	E
s762	The Tycoon and the Tigress - William R. Cox	1.50	3.50	5.00	
763	Stop this Man - Peter Rabe	.75	1.75	3.00	
s764	The Rise and Fall of Dr. Carey - O. O. Osborne	1.50	3.50	5.00	
765	No Business for A Lady - James Rubel	.75	1.75	3.00	
766	Catspaw Ordeal - Edward Ronns	.75	1.75	3.00	
767	Murder for the Bride - John D. MacDonald	.75	1.75	3.00	M
d768	The Lost Years of Jesus Revealed - Charles Francis Potter	2.00	4.00	6.00	NF
769	Violence is My Business - Stephen Marlowe	1.50	3.50	5.00	M
770	The Scrambled Yeggs - Richard S. Prather	1.50	3.50	5.00	M
771	Texas Outlaw - Richard Jessup	1.50	3.50	5.00	W
772	Feud at Forked River - Philip Ketcham	1.50	3.50	5.00	W
s773	Mission for Vengeance - Peter Rabe	1.50	3.50	5.00	
s774	We Walk Alone - Ann Aldrich	1.50	3.50	5.00	
775	Coffin for a Hood - Lionel White 1958	1.50	3.50	5.00	
776	Murder Comes Calling - Malcolm Douglas	1.50	3.50	5.00	
s777	Clemmie - John D. MacDonald	2.00	4.00	6.00	
778	Home is the Outlaw - Lewis B. Patten	1.50	3.50	5.00	W
779	Tucson - Paul Leslie Peil	1.50	3.50	5.00	
780	The Mob Says Murder - Albert Conroy	1.50	3.50	5.00	
781	Here is My Body - Booth Mooney	.75	1.75	3.00	
782	Judge Me Not - John D. MacDonald	.75	1.75	3.00	M
s783	The Fast Buck - Bruno Fischer	.75	1.75	3.00	M
784	Case of the Petticoat Murder - Jonathan Craig	1.50	3.50	5.00	M
785	The Forbidden Land - Dan Cushman	1.50	3.50	5.00	
786	Too Young to Die - Lionel White	1.50	3.50	5.00	
787	Death's Lovely Mask - John Flagg	1.50	3.50	5.00	M
788	Brand of a Texan - Steven C. Lawrence	1.50	3.50	5.00	W
789	Tall in the West - Vechel Howard	1.50	3.50	5.00	W

s790	The Neon Jungle - John D. MacDonald	.75	1.75	3.00	M
s791	Branded Woman - Wade Miller	.75	1.75	3.00	
792	The Brass Cupcake - John D. MacDonald	.75	1.75	3.00	M
s793	Spring Fire - Vin Packer	.75	1.75	3.00	
794	Trouble at Borrasca Rim - Mark Owen	1.50	3.50	5.00	
795	Case of the Cop's Wife - Milton K. Ozaki	.75	1.75	3.00	M
s796	Self-made Widow - Philip Race	.75	1.75	3.00	M
s797	The Evil Friendship - Vin Packer	.75	1.75	3.00	
798	Guns of North Texas - Will Cook	1.50	3.50	5.00	W
799	Assignment—Madeline - Edward S. Aarons	.75	1.75	3.00	M
800	Two Deaths Must Die - Richard Himmel	.75	1.75	3.00	M
s801	The Man Who Said No - Walt Grove 1958	.75	1.75	3.00	
s802	The Devil's Mistress - Kenneth Thomas	.50	1.25	2.00	
803	Buchanan Gets Mad - Jonas Ward	.75	1.75	3.00	W
804	Relentless Gun - Giles A. Lutz	.75	1.75	3.00	W
805	The Deadly Pay-off - William H. Duhart	.75	1.75	3.00	
806	Murder in Room 13 - Albert Conroy	.75	1.75	3.00	
807	Death Takes an Option - Neil MacNeil	.75	1.75	3.00	
808	Party Girl - Marvin H. Albert	.75	1.75	3.00	
s809	Plunder - Benjamin Appel	.50	1.25	2.00	C
810	The Killer - Wade Miller	.50	1.25	2.00	
811	Take Your Last Look - Matt Brady	.50	1.25	2.00	
s812	The Ungilded Lily - Morton Cooper	.75	1.75	3.00	
813	Terror is My Trade - Stephen Marlowe	.75	1.75	3.00	M
814	I'm Cannon--for Hire - Curt Cannon	.75	1.75	3.00	
815	Showdown at War Cloud - Lewis B. Patten	.75	1.75	3.00	W
816	Fort Desperation - Frank Castle	.75	1.75	3.00	W
s817	Slab Happy - Richard S. Prather	.75	1.75	3.00	M
818	Everybody Had a Gun - Richard S. Prather	.50	1.25	2.00	M
819	Bodies in Bedlam - Richard S. Prather	.50	1.25	2.00	M
820	Case of the Vanishing Beauty - Richard S. Prather	.50	1.25	2.00	M
821	Find this Woman - Richard S. Prather	.50	1.25	2.00	M
822	Man on the Run - Charles Williams	.75	1.75	3.00	
823	Passage to Samoa - Day Keene	.75	1.75	3.00	
824	Trail of a Tramp - Nick Quarry	.75	1.75	3.00	
s825	Blood on the Desert - Peter Rabe 1958	.75	1.75	3.00	
826	Renegade Posse - Marvin H. Albert	.75	1.75	3.00	W
827	Day of the Gun - Richard Telfair	.75	1.75	3.00	
s828	Naked Ebony - Dan Cushman	.50	1.25	2.00	A
s829	The Awakening of Jenny - Lillian Colter	.50	1.25	2.00	E
830	Way of a Wanton - Richard S. Prather	.50	1.25	2.00	M
831	Fires that Destroy - Harry Whittington	.50	1.25	2.00	
s832	The Monster from World's End - Murray Leinster	2.00	4.00	6.00	SF
d833	I Am a Woman - Ann Bannon	.75	1.75	3.00	
834	Assignment--Carlotta Cortez - Edward S. Aarons	.75	1.75	3.00	M
835	The Captain Must Die - Robert Colby	.75	1.75	3.00	
s836	Smoke in the Valley - Steve Frazee	.75	1.75	3.00	W
837	Outcast of Cripple Creek - Will Cook	.75	1.75	3.00	W
838	Darling, It's Death - Richard S. Prather	.50	1.25	2.00	M
d839	City of Women - Nancy Morgan	.50	1.25	2.00	
s840	Jewel of the Java Sea - Dan Cushman	.50	1.25	2.00	
841	...And Be My Love - Ledru Baker, Jr.	.50	1.25	2.00	
842	Wagon Train West - William Heuman	.75	1.75	3.00	W
843	Outlaw Marshal - Ray Hogan	.75	1.75	3.00	W
s844	Third on a Seesaw - Neil MacNeil	.75	1.75	3.00	
s845	Kitten with a Whip - Wade Miller	1.50	3.50	5.00	
846	That Jane from Maine - Marvin H. Albert 1959, Movie tie-in	1.50	3.50	5.00	
847	The Bloody Medallion - Richard Telfair	.75	1.75	3.00	
848	Strip for Murder - Richard S. Prather	.50	1.25	2.00	M
849	Always Leave 'em Dying - Richard S. Prather	.50	1.25	2.00	M
850	Too Many Crooks - Richard S. Prather 1959	.50	1.25	2.00	M
851	The Wailing Frail - Richard S. Prather	.50	1.25	2.00	M
d852	Tempest - R. V. Cassill Movie tie-in	1.50	3.50	5.00	A
s853	The Rest Must Die - Richard Foster	2.50	6.00	10.00	SF
854	Murder with Love - Vechel Howard	.75	1.75	3.00	
855	Secret of the Second Door - Robert Colby	.75	1.75	3.00	

856	The Reformed Gun - Marvin H. Albert	.75	1.75	3.00	
857	Savage Breed - Joseph Chadwick	.75	1.75	3.00	W
858	13 French Street - Gil Brewer	.50	1.25	2.00	E
s859	Beyond Desire - Richard Himmel	.50	1.25	2.00	E
860	Have Gat—Will Travel - Richard S. Prather	.50	1.25	2.00	M
s861	The Twisted Ones - Vin Packer	.75	1.75	3.00	
862	A Ticket to Hell - Harry Whittington	.75	1.75	3.00	
863	Assignment—Helene - Edward S. Aarons	.75	1.75	3.00	M
864	Bring Me Another Corpse - Peter Rabe	.75	1.75	3.00	M
865	Above the Palo Duro - Noel M. Loomis	.75	1.75	3.00	W
866	The Ruthless Men - Lewis B. Patten	.75	1.75	3.00	W
867	Smash-up - Theodore Pratt	.50	1.25	2.00	
868	Return of Sumuru - Sax Rohmer	2.00	4.00	6.00	A
s869	The Judas Hour - Howard Hunt	.75	1.75	3.00	
870	Let Them Eat Bullets - Howard Schoenfeld	.50	1.25	2.00	
871	Strangers in My Bed - Allen O'Quinn	.50	1.25	2.00	
872	Case of the Nervous Nude - Jonathan Craig	.75	1.75	3.00	M
873	Prowler in the Night - Jack Matcha	.75	1.75	3.00	
874	Take a Step to Murder - Day Keene	.75	1.75	3.00	M
875	Armande - Daniel May	.75	1.75	3.00	
	1959				
876	The Brave Rifles - Gordon D. Shirreffs	.75	1.75	3.00	W
877	The Homing Bullet - Giles A. Lutz	.75	1.75	3.00	W
878	Murder on Her Mind - Vechel Howard	.75	1.75	3.00	
879	Wake Up and Scream - Milton K. Ozaki	.75	1.75	3.00	M
880	Homicide Is My Game - Stephen Marlowe	.75	1.75	3.00	M
881	The Kingdom of Johnny Cool - John McPartland	.75	1.75	3.00	M
882	Lawless Guns - Dudley Dean	.75	1.75	3.00	W
883	Wyoming Jones for Hire - Richard Telfair	.75	1.75	3.00	
884	Weep for Me - John D. MacDonald	.50	1.25	2.00	M
885	The Mating Cry - Frank Daniels	.50	1.25	2.00	M
886	House of Flesh - Bruno Fischer	.50	1.25	2.00	M
s887	Over Her Dead Body - Richard S. Prather	.50	1.25	2.00	M
888	Killer Take All - Philip Race	.50	1.25	2.00	M
889	Backwoods Tramp - Harry Whittington	.75	1.75	3.00	E
890	The Corpse that Talked - Richard Telfair	.75	1.75	3.00	M
891	A Hole in the Head - Arnold Schulman	.75	1.75	3.00	
892	Marshal Without a Badge - Ray Hogan	.75	1.75	3.00	W
893	To Tame a Land - Louis L'Amour	.75	1.75	3.00	W
894	All These Condemned - John D. MacDonald	.75	1.75	3.00	M
895	Assignment to Disaster - Edward S. Aarons	.50	1.25	2.00	M
896	Three's a Shroud - Richard S. Prather	.50	1.25	2.00	M
s897	Cry Kill - Wenzell Brown	.75	1.75	3.00	
898	Two Guns for Hire - Neil MacNeil	.75	1.75	3.00	
899	Bier for a Chaser - Richard Foster	.75	1.75	3.00	
900	Return to Vikki - John Tomerlin	.75	1.75	3.00	
	1959				
901	The Lustful Ape - Bruno Fischer	.75	1.75	3.00	
902	Rider from Wind River - Marvin H. Albert	.75	1.75	3.00	W
s903	The Thrill Kids - Vin Packer	.75	1.75	3.00	
904	Cartoon Fun from True	2.00	4.00	6.00	H
905	Hondo - Louis L'Amour	.75	1.75	3.00	W
906	Assignment—Stella Marni - Edward S. Aarons	.50	1.25	2.00	M
s907	The Beach Girls - John D. MacDonald	1.50	3.50	5.00	M
s908	Uncle Sagamore and His Girls - Charles Williams	.75	1.75	3.00	E
909	The Last Night - John McPartland	.75	1.75	3.00	
s910	The Slasher - Ovid Demaris	.75	1.75	3.00	
s911	Assignment—Lili Lamaris - Edward S. Aarons	.75	1.75	3.00	M
912	Gun Shy - Dudley Dean & Les Savage, Jr.	.75	1.75	3.00	W
s913	Angels in the Gutter - Joseph Hilton	2.00	4.00	7.50	JD
914	Trouble Is My Name - Stephen Marlowe	.50	1.25	2.00	M
915	It's My Funeral - Peter Rabe	.50	1.25	2.00	
916	Bullet Barricade - Leslie Ernenwein	.50	1.25	2.00	W
s917	Teen-age Mafia - Wenzell Brown	2.00	4.00	7.50	JD
918	Pillow Talk - Marvin H. Albert Movie tie-in	1.50	3.50	5.00	
s919	Women in the Shadows - Ann Bannon	.75	1.75	3.00	
920	Top Man With a Gun - Lewis B. Patten	.75	1.75	3.00	W
921	The Wife Next·Door - R. V. Cassill	.75	1.75	3.00	
s922	To Hell Together - H. Vernor Dixon	.50	1.25	2.00	
923	Assignment—Suicide - Edward S. Aarons	.50	1.25	2.00	
924	The Avenger - Matthew Blood	.50	1.25	2.00	M
925	Song of the Gun - Dudley Dean	.50	1.25	2.00	W
	1959				

(GOLD MEDAL, continued)

d926	Double in Trouble - Stephen Marlowe & Richard S. Prather	.75	1.75	3.00	M
927	Ain't Gonna Rain No More - John Faulkner	.75	1.75	3.00	E
928	Second-hand Nude - Bruno Fischer	.75	1.75	3.00	M
s929	Emperor Fu Manchu - Sax Rohmer Orig., 1959	2.50	6.00	10.00	A
930	Case of the Village Tramp - Jonathan Craig	.75	1.75	3.00	M
931	Too Hot to Hold - Day Keene	.75	1.75	3.00	
932	The Secret of Apache Canyon - Richard Telfair	.75	1.75	3.00	W
s933	The Tormented - Theodore Pratt	.50	1.25	2.00	
934	Little Sister - Lee Roberts	.50	1.25	2.00	E
935	Many Rivers to Cross - Steve Frazee	.50	1.25	2.00	W
s936	The Big Guy - Wade Miller	.50	1.25	2.00	
s937	Four from Planet 5 - Murray Leinster Orig., 1959	2.00	4.00	6.00	SF
938	The Girl With No Place to Hide - Nick Quarry	.75	1.75	3.00	
939	Time Enough to Die - Peter Rabe	.75	1.75	3.00	
940	The Deadly Desire - Robert Colby	.75	1.75	3.00	
s941	The Young and Violent - Vin Packer	.50	1.25	2.00	
942	Witness this Woman - Gardner F. Fox	1.50	3.50	5.00	
943	Stage to Painted Creek - Vechel Howard	.75	1.75	3.00	W
944	The Range Buster - William Heuman	.50	1.25	2.00	W
945	The Tiger's Wife - Wade Miller	.50	1.25	2.00	
s946	Thunderclap - Jack Sheridan	.50	1.25	2.00	

GOLD STAR BOOKS

(New International Library, Inc.)

IL7-42	Tarzan & The Silver Globe - Barton Werper Orig., 1964	3.00	6.00	12.00	SF
IL7-49	Tarzan & The Cave City - Barton Werper Orig., 1964	3.00	6.00	12.00	A
IL7-54	Tarzan & The Snake People - Barton Werper Orig., 1964	3.00	6.00	12.00	SF
IL7-60	Tarzan & The Abominable Snowman - Barton Werper Orig., 1965	4.00	8.00	15.00	SF
IL7-65	Tarzan & The Winged Invaders - Barton Werper Orig., 1965	5.00	10.00	20.00	SF

Note: Barton Werper was the pseudonym of Peter and Peggy O'Neill Scott and this series, known as The New Tarzan Series, was unauthorized and stopped by legal action shortly after no. 5 was printed, with unsold copies being destroyed.

GRAPHIC

Gold Medal 929, c. Faw

Gold Star IL7-42, c. New

Gold Star IL7-54, c. New

Graphic 19, c. Graphic Graphic 81, c. Graphic Graphic 104, c. Graphic

(GRAPHIC, continued)

(Graphic Publishing Company, Inc.)

11	Murder--Queen High - Bill Miller & Bob Wade	2.00	4.00	6.00	M
	1949				
12	If I Live to Dine - Hillary Waugh	2.00	4.00	6.00	M
13	Flash--Hold for Murder - Paul Whelton	2.00	4.00	6.00	M
14	Death Commits Bigamy - James M. Fox	2.00	4.00	6.00	M
15	Tex - Clarence E. Mulford	2.00	4.00	6.00	W
16	Deadline at Dawn - William Irish	2.00	4.00	6.00	M
17	Call the Lady Indiscreet - Paul Whelton	1.50	3.50	5.00	
18	Dealing Out Death - W. T. Ballard	1.50	3.50	5.00	M
19	Lures of Death - Paul Whelton	1.50	3.50	5.00	
	1950				
20	Dilemma of the Dead Lady - William Irish	2.00	4.00	6.00	M
21	The Widow Gay - A. A. Marcus	1.50	3.50	5.00	M
22	Tough Cop - John Roeburt	1.50	3.50	5.00	M
23	The Man from Bar 20 - Clarence E. Mulford	2.00	4.00	6.00	W
24	Uninvited Corpse - Paul Whelton	1.50	3.50	5.00	M
25	The Singing Scorpion - William Colt				
	MacDonald	1.50	3.50	5.00	W
26	Murder Can't Stop - W. T. Ballard	1.50	3.50	5.00	M
27	Corpse on the Town - John Roeburt	1.50	3.50	5.00	M
28	Tex - Clarence E. Mulford	2.00	4.00	6.00	W
	1951				
29	Memo for Murder - Dal Wilmer	2.00	4.00	6.00	M
	Orig., 1951				
30	Runyon First and Last - Damon Runyon	2.00	4.00	6.00	
31	Deadly Night Call - William Irish	2.00	4.00	6.00	M
32	Hangover House - Sax Rohmer	2.00	4.00	7.50	M
33	The Dummy Murder Case - Milton K. Ozaki	2.00	4.00	6.00	M
	Orig., 1951				
34	Texas Men - Paul Evan Lehman	1.50	3.50	5.00	W
35	Walk the Bloody Boulevard - A. A. Marcus	1.50	3.50	5.00	M
36	Call Me Killer - Harry Whittington	1.50	3.50	5.00	M
37	Pardon My Blood - Paul Whetton	1.50	3.50	5.00	M
38	Tough Cop - John Roeburt	1.50	3.50	5.00	M
39	Vultures of Paradise Valley - Paul Evan				
	Lehman	1.50	3.50	5.00	W
40	The Crooked Circle - Manning Lee Stokes	1.50	3.50	5.00	M
41	Murder Is My Mistress - Harry Whittington	1.50	3.50	5.00	M
42	There Are Dead Men in Manhattan - John				
	Roeburt	1.50	3.50	5.00	M
43	If the Coffin Fits - Day Keene	1.50	3.50	5.00	M
	1952				
44	Gun Hawk - Leslie Ernewein	1.50	3.50	5.00	W
45	Death for a Hussy - Aylwin Lee Martin	1.50	3.50	5.00	M
46	Mourn the Hangman - Harry Whittington	1.50	3.50	5.00	M
47	Faces in the Dust - Paul Evan Lehman	1.50	3.50	5.00	W
48	Pattern for Murder - David Knight	1.50	3.50	5.00	M
49	In Comes Death - Paul Whelton	1.50	3.50	5.00	M
50	The Singing Scorpion - William Colt MacDonald	1.50	3.50	5.00	W
51	Framed in Guilt - Day Keene	1.50	3.50	5.00	M
52	There Oughta Be a Law! - Al Fagaly & Harry				
	Shorten	2.00	4.00	7.50	H
53	Tex - Clarence E. Mulford	1.50	3.50	5.00	W
54	Murder--Queen High - Bill Miller & Bob Wade	1.50	3.50	5.00	M

No.	Title - Author				
55	A Shot in the Dark - Richard Powell	1.50	3.50	5.00	M
56	Texas Men - Paul Evan Lehman	1.50	3.50	5.00	M
57	The Deadly Pick-up - Milton K. Ozaki 1953	1.50	3.50	5.00	M
58	Strange Witness - Day Keene	1.50	3.50	5.00	M
59	Dark Destiny - Edward Ronns	1.50	3.50	5.00	M
60	Dead Man's Tide - William Richards Orig., 1953	2.00	4.00	6.00	M
61	There Oughta Be a Law! - Al Fagaly & Harry Shorten	2.00	4.00	7.50	H
62	Gun Hawk - Leslie Ernenwein	1.50	3.50	5.00	W
63	Tough Cop - John Roeburt	1.50	3.50	5.00	M
64	Walk the Bloody Boulevard - A. A. Marcus	1.50	3.50	5.00	M
65	Murder Can't Stop - W. T. Ballard	1.50	3.50	5.00	M
66	Vultures of Paradise Valley - Paul Evan Lehman	1.50	3.50	5.00	W
67	Post-mark Homicide - A. A. Marcus aka The Widow Gay Note: Same cover as Harlequin 90.	1.50	3.50	5.00	M
68	The Net - Edward Ronns	1.50	3.50	5.00	M
69	Runyon First and Last - Damon Runyon	2.00	4.00	6.00	
70	Late Last Night - James Reach	1.50	3.50	5.00	M
71	Pardon My Blood - Paul Whelton 1954	1.50	3.50	5.00	M
72	Dealing Out Death - W. T. Ballard	1.50	3.50	5.00	M
73	Handle with Fear - Thomas B. Dewey	1.50	3.50	5.00	M
74	Two-gun Fury - Charles M. Martin	1.50	3.50	5.00	W
75	The Big Kiss-off - Day Keene	1.50	3.50	5.00	M
76	Say It with Murder - Edward Ronns	1.50	3.50	5.00	M
77	Gunman's Creed - L. P. Holmes	1.50	3.50	5.00	W
78	Hangover House - Sax Rohmer	2.00	4.00	6.00	M
79	Dressed to Kill - Milton Ozaki	1.50	3.50	5.00	M
80	Blood on the Range - Eli Colter	1.50	3.50	5.00	W
81	Deadly Night Call - William Irish	2.00	4.00	6.00	M
82	Stand Up and Die - Frances & Richard Lockridge	2.00	4.00	6.00	M
83	The Fatal Cast - Curtiss T. Gardner	1.50	3.50	5.00	M
84	Your Shot, Darling - Lillian Bergquist & Irving Moore	1.50	3.50	5.00	M
85	More there Oughta Be a Law! - Al Fagaly & Harry Shorten	2.00	4.00	7.50	H
86	Texas Pride - Charles M. Martin	1.50	3.50	5.00	W
87	Homicidal Lady - Day Keene Orig., 1954	2.00	4.00	6.00	M
88	Outlaw Justice - Ford Pendeton	1.50	3.50	5.00	M
89	The Scarab Murder Case - S. S. Van Dine	2.00	4.00	6.00	M
90	Too Young to Die - Robert O. Saber	1.50	3.50	5.00	M
91	Tex - Clarence E. Mulford	1.50	3.50	5.00	M
92	The Deadly Pick-up - Milton K. Ozaki	1.50	3.50	5.00	M
93	Say it With Bullets - Richard Powell	1.50	3.50	5.00	M
94	Model for Murder - Stephen Marlowe 1955	1.50	3.50	5.00	M
95	Call the Lady Indiscreet - Paul Whelton	1.50	3.50	5.00	M
96	Gun Lightning! - Steve Thurman	1.50	3.50	5.00	W
97	One Touch of Blood - Samm Sinclair Baker	1.50	3.50	5.00	M
98	Too Many Murderers - Manning Lee Stokes	1.50	3.50	5.00	M
99	Sucker Bait - Robert O. Saber	1.50	3.50	5.00	M
100	Faces in the Dust - Paul Evan Lehman	1.50	3.50	5.00	W
101	Cry Torment - Victor H. Johnson	1.50	3.50	5.00	M
102	Die by Night - M. S. Marble	1.50	3.50	5.00	M
103	Girl in the Red Dress - Richard Cargoe	1.50	3.50	5.00	
104	Mugs, Molls and Dr. Harvey - George Malcolm-Smith	2.00	4.00	6.00	H
105	Murder Has Many Faces - William Grew	1.50	3.50	5.00	M
106	Trap - George E. Jones	1.50	3.50	5.00	M
107	The Adventures of Ferd'nand - Mik	1.50	3.50	5.00	
108	Phantom Lady - William Irish	2.00	4.00	6.00	M
109	More There Oughta Be a Law! - Al Fagaly & Harry Shorten	2.00	4.00	7.50	H
110	The Hollow Man - John Roeburt	1.50	3.50	5.00	M
111	A Dame Called Murder - Robert O. Saber	1.50	3.50	5.00	M
112	Gun Hawk - Leslie Ernenwein	1.50	3.50	5.00	W
113	Unfinished Crime - Helen McCloy	1.50	3.50	5.00	M
114	They All Ran Away - Edward Ronns	1.50	3.50	5.00	M
115	Make Way for Murder - A. A. Marcus	1.50	3.50	5.00	M
116	Hell Rider - Ford Pendleton	1.50	3.50	5.00	W

Graphic 151, c. Graphic   Graphic G206, c. Graphic   Graphic G216, c. Graphic

(GRAPHIC, continued)

117 Murder Can't Wait - Manning Lee Stokes	1.50	3.50	5.00	M
118 And Kill Once More - Al Fray	1.50	3.50	5.00	M
119 Mood for Murder - Frank Gruber	1.50	3.50	5.00	M
1956				
120 Texas Guns - Leslie Ernenwein	1.50	3.50	5.00	W
121 Tough Cop - John Roeburt	1.50	3.50	5.00	M
122 Homicide Lost - William E. Vance	1.50	3.50	5.00	M
123 A Time for Murder - Robert O. Saber	1.50	3.50	5.00	M
124 Gunpoint! - John L. Shelley	1.50	3.50	5.00	
125 The Intruder - Octavus Roy Cohen	1.50	3.50	5.00	M
126 Murder's End - Robert Kelston	2.00	4.00	7.50	M
c-Maguire				
127 So Lovely to Kill - Harrison Wade	1.50	3.50	5.00	M
128 Two-gun Fury - Charles M. Martin	1.50	3.50	5.00	W
129 Six-gun Heritage - Brad Ward	1.50	3.50	5.00	W
130 Late Last Night - James Reach	1.50	3.50	5.00	M
131 This Kill Is Mine - Dean Evans	1.50	3.50	5.00	M
132 I Prefer Murder - Charles A. Landolf &				
Browning Norton	1.50	3.50	5.00	M
133 Gunmaster - Ford Pendleton	1.50	3.50	5.00	W
134 Who Dies There? - James Duff	2.00	4.00	6.00	M
Orig., 1956				
135 Murder--Very Dry - Samm Sinclair Baker	1.50	3.50	5.00	M
136 Killer's Choice - Stuart Brock	1.50	3.50	5.00	M
137 Blood on the Range - Eli Colter	1.50	3.50	5.00	W
138 The Corpse Next Door - John Farris	2.00	4.00	6.00	M
Orig., 1956				
139 Some Die Young - James Duff	1.50	3.50	5.00	M
140 Gun Trail - Mack Saunders	1.50	3.50	5.00	W
141 Dressed to Kill - Milton Ozaki	1.50	3.50	5.00	M
142 Fair Prey - Will Duke	1.50	3.50	5.00	M
143 Three Must Die! - Dan Gregory	1.50	3.50	5.00	M
144 Gunman's Creed - L. P. Holmes	1.50	3.50	5.00	W
1957				
145 While Murder Waits - Bruce Cassiday	1.50	3.50	5.00	M
146 Six-guns Wild - Gene Thompson	1.50	3.50	5.00	W
147 Killer, Take All! - James O. Causey	1.50	3.50	5.00	M
148 Say it With Bullets - Richard Powell	1.50	3.50	5.00	M
149 Murder Without Tears - Leonard Lupton	1.50	3.50	5.00	M
150 Too Young to Die - Robert O. Saber	1.50	3.50	5.00	M
151 Gun Proud - Lewis B. Patten	1.50	3.50	5.00	M
152 Call Me Deadly - Hal Braham	1.50	3.50	5.00	M
153 Gun Lightning! - Steve Thurman	1.50	3.50	5.00	W
154 Outlaw Justice - Ford Pendleton	1.50	3.50	5.00	W
155 Gun Chance - Ford Pendleton	1.50	3.50	5.00	W
156 Sucker Bait - Robert O. Saber	1.50	3.50	5.00	M
157 Hell Rider - Ford Pendleton	1.50	3.50	5.00	W

GRAPHIC G-SERIES

(Graphic Publishing Company, Inc.)

G101 Captain for Elizabeth - Jan Westcoff	2.00	4.00	6.00	A
1952				
G201 Captain for Elizabeth - Jan Westcoff	2.00	4.00	6.00	A
1953				

G202	River Queen - Charles N. Heckelmann	2.00	4.00	6.00	A
G203	45 Murderers - Craig Rice	2.00	4.00	6.00	M
G204	How to Live with Your Heart - Peter J. Stein Crohn 1954	2.00	4.00	6.00	NF
G205	King's Rogue - Max Peacock	2.00	4.00	6.00	A
G206	The Gladiators - Arthur Koestler	2.00	4.00	7.50	A
G207	Great Sea Stories of Modern Times - William McFee	2.00	4.00	6.00	A
G208	Swords for Charlemagne - Mario Pei 1955	2.00	4.00	6.00	A
G209	The Golden Blade - John Clou	2.00	4.00	6.00	A
G210	Gunman's Spawn - Ben Thompson	1.50	3.50	5.00	W
G211	Captain for Elizabeth - Jan Westcott	1.50	3.50	5.00	A
G212	Rogue Royal - Donn O'hara 1956, c-Maguire	2.00	4.00	7.50	A
G213	The Gladiators - Arthur Koestler	2.00	4.00	6.00	A
G214	Captain Bashful - Donald Barr Chidsey	2.00	4.00	6.00	A
G215	Call Me Duke - Harry Grey	1.50	3.50	5.00	M
G216	The Private Life of Helen of Troy - John Erskine	2.00	4.00	7.50	A
G217	Eve's Daughters - Laurette Pizer 1957	2.00	4.00	6.00	E
G218	Guns of Hell Valley - John Prescott	1.50	3.50	5.00	W
G219	Swords for Charlemagne - Mario Pei	2.00	4.00	6.00	A
G220	The Golden Blade - John Clou c-Maguire	2.00	4.00	7.50	A
G221	River Queen - Charles N. Heckelmann	2.00	4.00	6.00	A
G222	The Fair and the Bold - Donn O'Hara	2.00	4.00	6.00	A
G223	Gunman's Spawn - Ben Thompson	1.50	3.50	5.00	W

GREAT AMERICAN PUBLICATIONS, INC.

(Great American Publications, Inc.)

nn	Economy Driving - ed. Peter Bowman Orig., 1956	1.50	3.50	5.00	NF

GREEN

(Green Publishing Company)

Digest size

6	Some Like it Hot - Sidney Marshall	1.50	3.50	5.00	M
7	11 True Crimes - Joseph Gollomb	1.50	3.50	5.00	NF
8	The Laughing Loon - Josiah E. Greene	1.50	3.50	5.00	M
9	The Owl's Warning - Herman Landon	1.50	3.50	5.00	M
10	Death in the Sun - Charles Saxby Note: Incorrectly says 'first edition'	1.50	3.50	5.00	M
11	A Dagger in the Dark - Walter E. Eberhardt	1.50	3.50	5.00	M
12	Kill or Cure - William Francis	1.50	3.50	5.00	M

Graphic G217, c. Graphic   Great American Publ. nn, c. Great   Green 11, c. Green

Green 14, c. Green

Green Dragon 28, c. Ideal

Green Dragon 31, c. Ideal

(GREEN, continued)

13 Murder Stalks the Mayor - R. T. M. Scott	1.50	3.50	5.00	M
14 The Backstage Mystery - Octavus Roy Cohen	1.50	3.50	5.00	M

GREEN

(Larkin, Roosevelt, and Larkin, Ltd.)

Digest size

1 Rough on Rats - William Francis	2.00	4.00	6.00	M

GREEN

(R. W. Voigt)

Digest size

2 The Back Seat Murder - Herman Landon	2.00	4.00	6.00	M

GREEN DRAGON

(Ideal Distributing Company)

Some digest size

1 Murder Makes By-Lines - Kelliher Secrist Digest size	2.00	4.00	6.00	M
2 The Mausoleum Key - Norman A. Daniels Digest size	1.50	3.50	5.00	M
3 Johnny on the Spot - Amen Dell Digest size	2.00	4.00	6.00	M
4 A Murder a Day - Robert Avery Digest size	1.50	3.50	5.00	M
5 The Moscow Mystery - Iry Litrinoff Digest size	1.50	3.50	5.00	M
6 The Snatch - R. L. Goldman Digest size	1.50	3.50	5.00	M
7 Murder of the Night Club Lady - Anthony Abbot aka About the Murder of the Night Club Lady Digest size	2.00	4.00	6.00	M
8 A Most Immoral Murder - H. Ashbrook Digest size	1.50	3.50	5.00	M
9 Murder Moves On - Jack Dall Digest size	1.50	3.50	5.00	M
10 Death Plays Solitaire - R. L. Goldman Digest size	1.50	3.50	5.00	M
13 Ten Words of Poison - Barry Perowne Digest size	1.50	3.50	5.00	M

(GREEN DRAGON, continued)

16	Murder without Clues - Joseph L. Bonney Digest size	1.50	3.50	5.00	M
17	... And Death Drove On - Robert Fleming Digest size	1.50	3.50	5.00	M
18	Murder Comes Back - H. Ashbrook Digest size	1.50	3.50	5.00	M
19	Death Defies the Doctor - Denis Muir Digest size	1.50	3.50	5.00	M
21	The Man Who Was Murdered Twice - Robert H. Leitfred Digest size	1.50	3.50	5.00	M
23	I Thought I'd Die - David V. Reed First ed., nd, aka the Metal Monster Murders Digest size	2.00	4.00	6.00	M
25	She Screamed Blue Murder - Kelliher Secrist	2.00	4.00	6.00	M
26	Stone Dead - Patrick Laing	2.00	4.00	6.00	M
28	Headsman's Holiday - Dean Hawkins	2.00	4.00	6.00	M
29	The Late Lamented Lady - Marie Blizard	2.00	4.00	6.00	M
30	A Matter of Policy - Sam Merwin, Jr.	2.00	4.00	6.00	M
31	Murder by Magic - Amelia Reynolds Long	2.00	4.00	6.00	M
33	Death is Thy Neighbor - Laurence Dwight Smith	2.00	4.00	6.00	M

GRIFFIN BOOKS

(Griffin Books)

Digest size

nn	Love on Call - John Saxon	1.50	3.00	5.00	E
nn	Stolen Trade - Thomas Stone	1.50	3.00	5.00	E
nn	Confessions of a Hat Check Girl - C. Sturdy	1.50	3.00	5.00	E
nn	Hotel Love - W. McClellan	1.50	3.00	5.00	E

GUNFIRE WESTERN NOVEL

(Novel Selections, Inc./Hillman)

Digest size

6	The Morgan Trail - W. C. Tuttle	1.50	3.50	5.00	W
7	The Deputy Sheriff - Clarence E. Mulford	1.50	3.50	5.00	W
10	Prairie Fire - D. Bardwell	1.50	3.50	5.00	W
11	Rebel Ranger - William Colt MacDonald	1.50	3.50	5.00	W
12	Cowman's Jack-Pot - Frank C. Robertson	1.50	3.50	5.00	W
14	Six-Gun Melody - William Colt MacDonald	1.50	3.50	5.00	W
15	Getley's Gold - Frank C. Robertson c-Saunders	1.50	3.50	5.00	W
17	Thunderbird Trail - William Colt MacDonald	1.50	3.50	5.00	W
18	Dangerous Dust - Kim Knight	1.50	3.50	5.00	W
19	The Vanishing Gunslinger - William Colt MacDonald	1.50	3.50	5.00	W

Green Dragon 33, c. Ideal

Gunfire Western 25, c. NS

Gunfire Western 45, c. NS

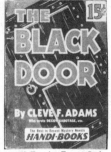

Gunfire Western 46, c. NS   Handi Books 1, c. Quinn   Handi Books 7, c. Quinn

(GUNFIRE WESTERN NOVEL, continued)

20	Grizzly Meadows - Frank C. Robertson	1.50	3.50	5.00	W
21	The Phantom Corral - Bliss Lomax (H. S. Drago)	1.50	3.50	5.00	W
22	The Three Mesquiteers - William Colt MacDonald	1.50	3.50	5.00	W
23	Dunn of the Double D - N. M. Newland	1.50	3.50	5.00	W
25	Boss of the OK - Brett Rider	1.50	3.50	5.00	W
28	Outlaw Guns - E. E. Halleran	1.50	3.50	5.00	W
34	Outlaw of Hidden Valley - John Sims	1.50	3.50	5.00	W
36	Fend at Silver Bend - J. E. Grinstead	1.50	3.50	5.00	W
41	Milk River Range - Lee Floren	1.50	3.50	5.00	W
42	Guns Along the Border - Charles H. Snow	1.50	3.50	5.00	W
43	The Long S - Lee Floren	1.50	3.50	5.00	W
45	Rebel on the Range - Ranger Lee	1.50	3.50	5.00	W
46	The Pride of Pine Creek - Frank C. Robertson	1.50	3.50	5.00	W
51	Smuggler's Range - Lee Floren	1.50	3.50	5.00	W

HANDI BOOKS

(Quinn Publishing Co., Inc.)

nn(1)	Odds on the Hot Seat - Judson Phillips 1941	5.00	10.00	20.00	M
nn(2)	Decoy - Cleve F. Adams	4.00	8.00	15.00	M
nn(3)	12 Chinks and a Woman - James Hadley Chase 1942	4.00	8.00	15.00	M
nn(4)	Seven Men - Theodore Roscoe	3.00	6.00	12.00	M
nn(5)	Curtains for the Copper - Thomas Polsky	3.00	6.00	12.00	M
nn(6)	A Bullet in his Cap - Robert Fleming	3.00	6.00	12.00	M
nn(7)	The Black Door - Cleve Adams	3.00	6.00	12.00	M
8	She Got What She Asked For - James Ronald	3.00	6.00	12.00	M
9	Vicious Circle - Manning Long	3.00	6.00	12.00	M
10	The Case of the Vanishing Women - Robert Archer	3.00	6.00	12.00	M
11	The Nine Dark Hours - Lenore Glen Offord	3.00	6.00	12.00	M
12	The Big Frame - Sam Merwin, Jr. 1943	3.00	6.00	12.00	M
13	Lazarus No. 7 - Richard Sale	5.00	10.00	20.00	SF
14	Black Alibi - Cornell Woolrich	3.00	6.00	12.00	M
15	The Case of the Walking Corpse - Brett Halliday	3.00	6.00	12.00	M
16	The 14th Trump - Judson Phillips	2.50	6.00	10.00	M
17	Footsteps Behind Her - Mitchell Wilson	2.50	6.00	10.00	M
18	The Unscrupulous Mr. Callaghan - Peter Cheyney	2.50	6.00	10.00	M
19	Passing Strange - Richard Sale	2.50	6.00	10.00	M
20	To a Blindfold Lady - Joseph Purtell	2.50	6.00	10.00	M
21	The Case of the Shivering Chorus Girls - James Atlee Phillips	2.50	6.00	10.00	M
22	The Blonde Died First - Dana Chambers 1944	2.50	6.00	10.00	M
23	Five Alarm Funeral - Stewart Sterling	2.50	6.00	10.00	M
24	Murder in Marble - Judson Phillips	2.50	6.00	10.00	M
25	Court of Shadows - Giles Jackson	2.50	6.00	10.00	M
26	To Catch a Thief - Daphne Sanders	2.50	6.00	10.00	M

(HANDI BOOKS, continued)

27	I Wake Up Screaming - Steve Fisher	2.50	6.00	10.00	M
28	The Frightened Man - Dana Chambers	2.50	6.00	10.00	M
29	The Woman in Red - Anthony Gilbert	2.50	6.00	10.00	M
30	The X-Ray Murders - M. Scott Michel	2.50	6.00	10.00	M
31	The Case of the Curious Chair - Richard Power	2.50	6.00	10.00	M
32	No Good from a Corpse - Leigh Bracket	3.00	6.00	12.00	M
33	Up Jumped the Devil - Cleve Adams	2.50	6.00	10.00	M
34	The Last Secret - Dana Chambers	4.00	8.00	15.00	SF

1945

35	The Snake in the Grass - James Howard Wellard	2.25	5.00	8.00	M
36	The Walls Came Tumbling Down - Jo Eisinger	2.25	5.00	8.00	M
37	The Dark Voyage - Hugh Addis	2.25	5.00	8.00	M
38	The Man with the Lumpy Nose - Lawrence Laviar	2.25	5.00	8.00	M
39	Send Another Coffin - F. G. Presnell	2.25	5.00	8.00	M
40	Dead Little Rich Girl - Norbert Davis	2.25	5.00	8.00	M
41	If I Kill Him - John & Ward Hawkins	2.25	5.00	8.00	M
42	The Fall Guy - Joe Barry	2.25	5.00	8.00	M
43	The Body on the Pavement - Gordon Meyrick	2.25	5.00	8.00	M
44	Knife in my Back - Sam Merwin, Jr.	2.25	5.00	8.00	M
45	The Blonde is Dead - John Dow aka The Little Boy Laughed	2.25	5.00	8.00	M
46	The Case of the Tearless Widow - John Roebutt	2.25	5.00	8.00	M

1946

47	Sweet Murder - M. Scott Michel	2.25	5.00	8.00	M
48	The Body Next Door - Eaton K. Goldthwaite	2.25	5.00	8.00	M
49	The Corpse Who Wouldn't Die - Ed Doherty	2.25	5.00	8.00	M
50	The Dangerous Dead - William Brandon	2.25	5.00	8.00	M
51	Darling, this is Death - Dana Chambers	2.25	5.00	8.00	M
52	The Triple Cross - Joe Barry	2.25	5.00	8.00	M
53	Puzzle for Players - Patrick Quentin	2.25	5.00	8.00	M
54	O, Murder Mine - Norbert Davis	2.25	5.00	8.00	M
55	Blood on the Cat - Nancy Rutledge	2.25	5.00	8.00	M
56	Lady with the Dice - Joel Townsley Rogers	2.50	6.00	10.00	M
57	Death Against Venus - Dana Chambers	2.25	5.00	8.00	M
58	The Corpse Awaits - Owen Fox Jerome	2.25	5.00	8.00	M

1947

59	One of these Seven - Carolynne & Malcolm Logan	2.25	5.00	8.00	M
60	The Black Key - M. Scott Michel	2.25	5.00	8.00	M
61	The Gloved Hand - Leigh Bryson	2.25	5.00	8.00	M
62	The Murder of the U. S. A. - Will F. Jenkins (Murray Leinster)	4.00	8.00	15.00	SF
63	The Clean-Up - Joe Barry	2.00	4.00	7.50	M
64	The Fourth Star - Richard Burke	2.00	4.00	7.50	M
65	Guilty Bystander - Wade Miller	2.00	4.00	7.50	M
66					
67					
68	Killers Play Rough - Adam Ring	2.00	4.00	7.50	M
69	Bullet Breed - Leslie Ernewein	2.00	4.00	7.50	W
70	Run for Your Life - Michael Stark	2.00	4.00	7.50	M

1948

71	The Range Maverick - Oscar J. Friend	2.00	4.00	7.50	W
72	Death About Face - Frank Kane	2.00	4.00	7.50	M
73	Only the Brave - Paul Evan Lehman	2.00	4.00	7.50	W
74	If You Have Tears - John Evans	2.00	4.00	7.50	M
75	Boss of Panamint - Leslie Ernewein	2.00	4.00	7.50	W
76	Cargo of Fear - Jay L. Currier	2.00	4.00	7.50	M

Handi Books 16, c. Quinn

Handi Books 27, c. Quinn

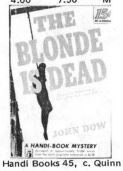

Handi Books 45, c. Quinn

Handi Books 62, c. Quinn   Handi Books 84, c. Quinn   Handi Books 129, c. Quinn

(HANDI BOOKS, continued)

77 Calamity Range - Paul Evan Lehman	2.00	4.00	7.50	W
78 This Deadly Dark - Lee Wilson	2.00	4.00	7.50	M
79 Gun Harvest - Oscar J. Friend	2.00	4.00	7.50	W
80 Not With my Neck - Tom Van Dycke & Ben Kerner	2.00	4.00	7.50	M
81 Empty Saddles - Al Cody	2.00	4.00	7.50	W
82 Witch's Moon - Giles Jackson 1949	2.00	4.00	7.50	M
83 The Faro Kid - Leslie Ernewein Note: Same Cover as Harlequin 89	2.00	4.00	7.50	W
84 Yaller Gal - Carolina Lee	2.00	4.00	7.50	E
85 The Great I Am - Lewis Graham	2.00	4.00	7.50	E
86 Dig Another Grave - Don Cameron	2.00	4.00	7.50	M
87 Idaho - Paul Evan Lehman	2.00	4.00	7.50	W
88 Hope to Die - Hillary Waugh	2.00	4.00	7.50	M
89 The King of Thunder Valley - Archie Joscelyn	2.00	4.00	7.50	W
90 Love to Burn - Peggy Gaddis	2.00	4.00	7.50	E
91 Lulie - Joan Sherman	2.00	4.00	7.50	E
92 The Girl with the Frightened Eyes - Lawrence Lariar	2.00	4.00	7.50	M
93 Rebel Yell - Leslie Ernewein	2.00	4.00	7.50	W
94 They All Died Young - Charles Boswell Orig., 1949	2.00	4.00	7.50	M
95 The Outcast of Lazy S - Eli Colter	2.00	4.00	7.50	W
96 The Black Dark Murders - Robert O. Saber	2.00	4.00	7.50	M
97 A Lover Would Be Nice - Hugh Herbert	2.00	4.00	7.50	E
98 Spider House - Van Wyck Mason	2.00	4.00	7.50	M
99 The Cold Trail - Paul Evan Lehman	2.00	4.00	7.50	W
100 Too Many Women - Milton K. Ozaki 1950	2.00	4.00	7.50	
101 The Range Doctor - Oscar J. Friend	2.00	4.00	7.50	W
102 Satan's Gal - Carolina Lee	2.00	4.00	7.50	E
103 Maverick Guns - J. E. Grinstead	2.00	4.00	7.50	W
104 The Restless Corpse - Alan Pruitt	2.00	4.00	7.50	M
105 The Rider from Yonder - Norman A. Fox	2.00	4.00	7.50	W
106 Three for the Money - Joe Barry	2.00	4.00	7.50	M
107 The Siren of Silver Valley - Paul Evan Lehman	2.00	4.00	7.50	W
108 The Affair of the Frigid Blonde - Robert O. Saber	2.00	4.00	7.50	M
109 Shannahan's Feud - Archie Joscelyn	2.00	4.00	7.50	W
110 The Glass Ladder - Paul W. Fairman	2.00	4.00	7.50	M
111 Renegade Ramrod - Leslie Ernewein	2.00	4.00	7.50	W
112 No Wings on a Cop - Cleve Adams	2.00	4.00	7.50	M
113 Barricade - Oscar J. Friend	2.00	4.00	7.50	W
114 False Face - Leslie Edgley	2.00	4.00	7.50	M
115 Range King - J. E. Grinstead	2.00	4.00	7.50	W
116 A Fiend in Need - Milton K. Ozaki	2.00	4.00	7.50	M
117 Thunder of Hoofs - Tex Holt	2.00	4.00	7.50	W
118 Window with the Sleeping Nude - Robert Leslie Bellem	2.00	4.00	7.50	M
119 Vengeance Valley - Paul Evan Lehman	2.00	4.00	7.50	W
120 Slay Ride for a Lady - Harry Whittington	2.00	4.00	7.50	W
121 Rawhide Summons - Brett Rider	2.00	4.00	7.50	W
122 Dark Memory - Edward Ronns	2.00	4.00	7.50	M
123 When Texans Rode - J. E. Grinstead	2.00	4.00	7.50	W
124 The Scented Flesh - Robert O. Saber 1951	2.00	4.00	7.50	M

(HANDI BOOKS, continued)

125 Valley of the Tyrant - Dick Pearce	2.00	4.00	7.50	W
126 Yaller Gal - Carolina Lee	2.00	4.00	7.50	E
127 The Faro Kid - Leslie Ernewein	2.00	4.00	7.50	W
128 Pursuit - Lawrence G. Blochman Orig., 1951	2.50	6.00	10.00	M
129 The Heiress of Copper Butte - Paul W. Fairman aka The Montana Vixen	2.00	4.00	7.50	W
130 The Dove - Robert O. Saber Orig., 1951	2.00	4.00	7.50	M
131 The Lady was a Tramp - Harry Whittington	2.00	4.00	7.50	M
132 Trail Rider - Lynn Westland	2.00	4.00	7.50	W
133 Boot Hill - Clay Weston	2.00	4.00	7.50	W
134 Murder is Dangerous - Saul Levinson c-Saunders	2.50	6.00	10.00	M
135 Typed for a Corpse - Alan Pruitt c-Saunders	2.50	6.00	10.00	M
136 Dark Canyon - Tex Holt c-Saunders	2.50	6.00	10.00	W
137 Yucca City Outlaw - William Hopson c-Saunders Note: Same cover as Harlequin no. 158.	2.50	6.00	10.00	W
138 The Brass Monkey - Harry Whittington	2.00	4.00	7.50	M
139 The Lady Killers - William T. Brannon 1951	2.00	4.00	7.50	M

HANDI-BOOKS WESTERN

(Quinn Publishing Co., Inc.)

1 The Cow Kingdom - Paul Evan Lehman 1947	2.00	4.00	7.50	W
2 Rio Renegade - Leslie Ernewein	1.50	3.50	5.00	W
3 The Long Noose - Oscar J. Friend	1.50	3.50	5.00	W
4 West of the Wolverine - Paul Evan Lehman	1.50	3.50	5.00	W

HANGMAN'S HOUSE

(Parsee Publications)

Some digest size

1 Murder on the Pike - Arville Nonweiler Digest size	2.00	4.00	6.00	M
2 Puzzle in Paint - Kootz (Samuel Melvin) Digest size	1.50	3.50	5.00	M
3 Murder in False Face - George Childerness Digest size	1.50	3.50	5.00	M
4 The Man Who Feared - Will F. Jenkins (Murray Leinster) Digest size	2.00	4.00	6.00	M
5 Death Gets a Head - A. R. McKenzie Digest size	2.00	4.00	6.00	M

Handi Books 137, c. Quinn

Handi Books 139, c. Quinn

Handi Books West. 1, c. Quinn

Hangman's House 13, c. Par   Hangman's House 15, c. Par   Hanro 2, c. Hanro

(HANGMAN'S HOUSE, continued)

6	Fit to Kill - Hans C. Owen Digest size	1.50	3.50	5.00	M
7	Murder on Beacon Hill - Gerald Brown Digest size	1.50	3.50	5.00	M
8	Death Like Thunder - Hugh Holman Digest size	1.50	3.50	5.00	M
9	The Corpse in the Cab - Aldin Vinton aka Mystery in Green, Digest size	1.50	3.50	5.00	M
10	Murder in Odd Sizes - Helen Joan Hultman Digest size	1.50	3.50	5.00	M
11	Murder Wore Green - Robert Portner Koehler Digest size	1.50	3.50	5.00	M
13	The Cowl of Doom - Edward Ronns aka Death in a Lighthouse	2.00	4.00	6.00	M
14	The Corpse that Spoke - Robert H. Leitfred	2.00	4.00	6.00	M
15	The Cipher of Death - F. L. Gregory	2.00	4.00	6.00	M
16	Thereby Hangs a Corpse - Clarence Mullen	2.00	4.00	5.00	M
17	The Road House Murders - Robert Portner Koehler	2.00	4.00	6.00	M
18	Memory of a Scream - David X. Manners	2.00	4.00	6.00	M
20	Murder Steals the Show - Lee Hirsch	2.00	4.00	6.00	M
21	Lady that's my Skull - Carl Shannon	2.00	4.00	6.00	M

HANRO

(Hanro Corporation)

Digest size

2	Shady Lady - Perry Lindsay	1.50	3.50	5.00	E
4	Confessions of a Part-Time Bride - Hall Bennett aka Make the Man Pay	1.50	3.50	5.00	E

HARLEQUIN

(Harlequin Books, Ltd.)

Canadian

1	The Manatee - Nancy Bruff 1949	3.00	7.50	15.00	A
2	Lost House - Frances Shelly Wees	3.00	7.50	15.00	
3	Maelstrom - Howard Hunt	3.00	7.50	15.00	
4	Double Image - Arthur Herbert Bryant	3.00	7.50	15.00	
5	Close to My Heart - Margaret Nichols	3.00	7.50	15.00	
6	Wolf of the Mesas - Charles H. Snow	3.00	7.50	15.00	W
7	The House on Craig Street - Ronald J. Cooke	3.00	7.50	15.00	
8	Honeymoon Mountain - Frances Shelley Wees	3.00	7.50	15.00	R
9	The Dark Page - Samuel Michael Fuller	3.00	7.50	15.00	
10	Here's Blood in Your Eye - Manning Long	3.00	7.50	15.00	M

(HARLEQUIN, continued)

11	The Wicked Lady Skelton - Magdalen King 'Hall	3.00	7.50	15.00	
12	A Killer is Loose Among Us - Robert Terrall	3.00	7.50	15.00	M
13	His Wife the Doctor - Joseph McCord	3.00	7.50	15.00	
14	Six-Guns of Sandoval - Charles H. Snow	3.00	7.50	15.00	W
15	Virgin with Butterflies - Tom Powers	3.00	7.50	15.00	E
16	No Nice Girl - Perry Lindsay	3.00	7.50	15.00	E
17	The D. A.'s Daughter - Herman Petersen	3.00	7.50	15.00	
18	Rebel of Ronde Valley - Charles H. Snow	3.00	7.50	15.00	W
19	Gina - George Albert Glay	3.00	7.50	15.00	E
20	Flame Vine - Helen Topping Miller	3.00	7.50	15.00	E
21	Renegade Ranger - Charles H. Snow	3.00	7.50	15.00	W
22	Crazy to Kill - Ann Cardwell	3.00	7.50	15.00	M
23	City for Conquest - Aben Kandel	3.00	7.50	15.00	
24	Painted Post Outlaws - Tom Gunn	3.00	7.50	15.00	W
25	Blondes Don't Cry - Merida Mace	3.00	7.50	15.00	
26	Gambling on Love - Gale Jordan	2.00	4.50	8.00	R
	1950				
27	Kiss Your Elbow - Alan Handley	3.00	7.50	15.00	
28	One Year with Grace - Martin Mooney	3.00	7.50	15.00	
29	Gunfighter Breed - Nelson C. Nye	3.00	7.50	15.00	W
30	Portrait of Love - Margaret Nichols	2.00	4.50	8.00	R
31	The Golden Feather - Theda Kenyon	3.00	7.50	15.00	
32	The Hollywood Mystery - Ben Hecht	3.00	7.50	15.00	M
33	Candle in the Morning - Helen Topping Miller	3.00	7.50	15.00	
34	Mobtown Clipper - S. S. Rabl	3.00	7.50	15.00	
35	Lush Valley - Patricia Campbell	3.00	7.50	15.00	
36	Murder Over Broadway - Fred Malina	3.00	7.50	15.00	M
37	Amaru - R. D. Frisbie	3.00	7.50	15.00	
38	Sheriff of Yavisa - Charles H. Snow	3.00	7.50	15.00	W
39	Be Still My Love - June Truesdell	2.00	4.50	8.00	R
40	Pass Key to Murder - Blair Reed	3.00	7.50	15.00	M
41	Panthers' Moon - Victor Canning	3.00	7.50	15.00	
42	House in Harlem - M. Scott Michel	3.00	7.50	15.00	E
43	The Clean-Up - Joe Barry	3.00	7.50	15.00	M
44	The So Blue Marble - Dorothy B. Hughes	2.00	4.50	8.00	M
45	Night and the City - Gerald Kersh	2.00	4.50	8.00	M
46	Fair Stranger - Cecile Gilmore	3.00	7.50	15.00	
47	Registered Nurse - Carl Sturdy	2.00	4.50	8.00	R
48	Poldrate Street - Garnett Weston	3.00	7.50	15.00	
49	Weep Not Fair Lady - John Evans	3.00	7.50	15.00	
50	One Way Street - Joseph McCord	3.00	7.50	15.00	
	1950				
51	The Pocket Purity Cook Book	2.00	4.50	8.00	NF
52	Livre De Cuisine Purity, Petit Format	2.00	4.50	8.00	NF
53	Pale Blonde of Sands St. - Wm. C. White	3.00	7.50	15.00	
54	Speak of the Devil - Elizabeth Sanxay Holding	3.00	7.50	15.00	M
55	Mr. Sandeman Loses His Life - Eugene Healy	3.00	7.50	15.00	
56	The Mayor of Cote St. Paul - Ronald J. Cooke	3.00	7.50	15.00	
57	Murder Man - William Bogart	3.00	7.50	15.00	M
58	Outposts of Vengeance - E. E. Halleran	3.00	7.50	15.00	W
59	Cardinal Rock - Richard Sale	3.00	7.50	15.00	
60	Lady Killer - Elizabeth Sanxay Holding	3.00	7.50	15.00	M
61	Shadow of the Badlands - E. E. Halleran	3.00	7.50	15.00	W
62	Message From A Corpse - Sam Merwin, Jr.	3.00	7.50	15.00	M
63	The Dangerous Dead - William Brandon	3.00	7.50	15.00	M
64	Sinister Warning - M. Scott Michel	3.00	7.50	15.00	
65	Bridewell Beauty - H. M. E. Clamp	2.00	4.50	8.00	R
66	Royce of the Royal Mounted - Ames Moore	3.00	7.50	15.00	A
67	Criss Cross - Don Tracy	3.00	7.50	15.00	M
68	The Queen City Murder Case - Wm. G. Bogart	3.00	7.50	15.00	M
69	Payoff in Black - Wm. G. Schofield	3.00	7.50	15.00	M
70	Knife in My Back - Sam Merwin, Jr.	3.00	7.50	15.00	M
71	Bouquet Knitter's Guide	2.00	4.50	8.00	NF
72	Night of Terror - Joy Brown	3.00	7.50	15.00	M
73	The King of Thunder Valley - Archie Joscelyn	3.00	7.50	15.00	W
74	Spider House - Van Wyck Mason	3.00	7.50	15.00	
75	Maverick Guns - J. E. Grinstead	3.00	7.50	15.00	W
	1950				
76	The Corpse Came Back - Amelia Reynolds Long	3.00	7.50	15.00	M

Harlequin 86, c. HB   Harlequin 89, c. HB   Harlequin 148, c. HB

(HARLEQUIN, continued)

77	A Night at Club Bagdad -				
	Owen Fox Jerome	3.00	7.50	15.00	
78	Rink Rat - Don MacMillan	3.00	7.50	15.00	
79	Lazarus No. 7 - Richard Sale	3.00	7.50	15.00	SF
80	The Case of the Six Bullets -				
	R. M. Laurenson	3.00	7.50	15.00	M
81	Idaho - Paul E. Lehman	3.00	7.50	15.00	W
82	The Cold Trail - Paul E. Lehman	3.00	7.50	15.00	W
83	The Fall Guy - Joe Barry	3.00	7.50	15.00	M
84	The Triple Cross - Joe Barry	3.00	7.50	15.00	M
85	She Died on the Stairway -				
	Knight Rhoades	3.00	7.50	15.00	M
86	Double Life - Owen Fox Jerome	3.00	7.50	15.00	
87	Murder in Miniatures - Sam Merwin, Jr.	3.00	7.50	15.00	M
88	Renegade Ramrod - Leslie Ernenwein	3.00	7.50	15.00	W
89	The Faro Kid - Leslie Ernenwein	3.00	7.50	15.00	W
	(Note: Same cover as Handi-Book 83)				
90	The Widow Gay - A. A. Marcus	2.00	4.50	8.00	M
	aka Post-mark Homicide				
	Note: Same cover as Graphic 67.				
91	Lady, That's My Skull - Carl Shannon	3.00	7.50	15.00	M
	1951				
92	Dig Another Grave - Don Cameron	3.00	7.50	15.00	M
93	Empty Saddles - Al Cody	3.00	7.50	15.00	W
94	The Range Doctor - Oscar J. Friend	2.00	4.50	8.00	
95	You're Lonely When You're Dead -				
	James Hadley Chase	3.00	7.50	15.00	M
96	The Rider From Yonder - Norman A. Fox	3.00	7.50	15.00	W
97	My Old Man's Badge - Ferguson Findley	3.00	7.50	15.00	
98	Jigger Moran - John Roeburt	3.00	7.50	15.00	M
99	Murder - Queen High - Bob Wade &				
	Bill Miller	3.00	7.50	15.00	M
100	Black Rider - Jackson Cole	3.00	7.50	15.00	W
	1951				
101	Three for the Money - Joe Barry	3.00	7.50	15.00	M
102	Wreath for a Redhead - Brian Moore	3.00	7.50	15.00	M
103	Wanton City - O. M. Hall	3.00	7.50	15.00	E
104	Tough Cop - John Roeburt	3.00	7.50	15.00	M
105	Vengeance Valley - Paul Evan Lehman	3.00	7.50	15.00	W
106	The Window with the Sleeping Nude -				
	Robert Leslie Bellem	3.00	7.50	15.00	M
107	The Man from Bar-20 -				
	Clarence E. Mulford	3.00	7.50	15.00	W
108	No Orchids for Miss Blandish -				
	James Hadley Chase	5.00	10.00	20.00	M
109	Corpse on the Town - John Roeburt	3.00	7.50	15.00	M
110	Tombstone Stage - William Hopson	3.00	7.50	15.00	W
111	The Flesh of the Orchid -				
	James Hadley Chase	3.00	7.50	15.00	M
112	Gina - George Albert Glay	3.00	7.50	15.00	E
113	Beyond the Blue Mountains - Jean Plaidy	2.00	4.50	8.00	
114	Johnny Saxon - William G. Bogart	3.00	7.50	15.00	N M
115	Manhatten Underworld - John Roeburt	3.00	7.50	15.00	M
116	Kill the Toff - John Creasey	3.00	7.50	15.00	M
117	The Executioners - Brian Moore	3.00	7.50	15.00	
118	Range Justice - Paul Evan Lehman	3.00	7.50	15.00	W
119	When Texans Ride - J. E. Grinstead	3.00	7.50	15.00	W

(HARLEQUIN, continued)

120	Slay Ride for a Lady - Harry Whittington	3.00	7.50	15.00	M
121	Run for Your Life - Michael Stark	3.00	7.50	15.00	M
122	A Matter of Policy - Sam Merwin, Jr.	3.00	7.50	15.00	M
123	Saddle Wolves - Allan K. Echols	3.00	7.50	15.00	W
124	The Dead Stay Dumb - James Hadley Chase	3.00	7.50	15.00	M
125	The Hidden Portal - Garnett Weston 1951	3.00	7.50	15.00	
126	Death About Face - Frank Kane	3.00	7.50	15.00	M
127	Dark Memory - Edward Ronns	3.00	7.50	15.00	M
128	Law of the '45 - Paul Evan Lehman	3.00	7.50	15.00	W
129	Hire This Killer - Ferguson Findley	3.00	7.50	15.00	M
130	Figure it Out for Yourself - James Hadley Chase	3.00	7.50	15.00	M
131	Tex - Clarence E. Mulford	3.00	7.50	15.00	W
132	False Face - Leslie Edgley	3.00	7.50	15.00	
133	Frontier Doctor - Bradford Scott	3.00	7.50	15.00	W
134	The Killers - George C. Henderson	3.00	7.50	15.00	
135	Lay Her Among the Lilies - James Hadley Chase	3.00	7.50	15.00	M
136	Boot Hill - Weston Clay	3.00	7.50	15.00	W
137	Berlin of Midnight - Robert Joseph	3.00	7.50	15.00	
138	Emma Hart - Lozania Prole	3.00	7.50	15.00	
139	The Glass Ladder - Paul W. Fairman	3.00	7.50	15.00	
140	The Lady Was a Tramp - Harry Whittington	3.00	7.50	15.00	M
141	Roger Sudden - Thomas H. Raddall	3.00	7.50	15.00	A
142	Doctor by Day - Thomas Stone	3.00	7.50	15.00	
143	Rebel Yell - Leslie Ernenwein	3.00	7.50	15.00	W
144	City for Conquest - Aben Kandel	3.00	7.50	15.00	
145	Rio Renegade - Leslie Ernenwein	3.00	7.50	15.00	W
146	Trail Rider - Lynn Westland	3.00	7.50	15.00	W
147	Pardon My Body - Dale Bogard	3.00	7.50	15.00	M
148	Wagon Train Westward - Lynn Westland 1952	3.00	7.50	15.00	W
149	Remembering Laughter - Wallace Stegner	3.00	7.50	15.00	
150	Paprika - Erich Von Stroheim 1952	3.00	7.50	15.00	E
151	The Great I Am - Lewis Graham	3.00	7.50	15.00	
152	Great Oaks - Ben Ames Williams	3.00	7.50	15.00	
153	Outlaw Valley - Al Cody	3.00	7.50	15.00	W
154	Rasputin and Crimes That Shook the World - Richard Hirsch	3.00	7.50	15.00	NF
155	Canyon of the Damned - Tex Holt	3.00	7.50	15.00	W
156	Blood of the North - James B. Hendryx	3.00	7.50	15.00	A
157	The Bizarre Sisters - Jay and Audrey Walz	3.00	7.50	15.00	E
158	Yucca City Outlaw - William Hopson c-Saunders Note: Same cover as Handi-Book 137.	3.00	7.50	15.00	W
159	The Smiling Tiger - Glen Offord	3.00	7.50	15.00	
160	Twelve Chinks and a Woman - James Hadley Chase	15.00	35.00	60.00	E
161	Health, Sex and Birth Control - Percy E. Ryberg, M.D.	2.00	4.50	8.00	NF
162	The River's End - James Oliver Curwood	3.00	7.50	15.00	
163	Guntown - Dan Carew	3.00	7.50	15.00	W
164	Captain for Elizabeth - Jan Westcott	3.00	7.50	15.00	A

Harlequin 160, c. HB

Harlequin 167, c. HB

Harlequin 186, c. HB

Harlequin 195, c. HB

Harlequin 203, c. HB

Harlequin 217, c. HB

(HARLEQUIN, continued)

165	Rats with Baby Faces - W. Stanley Moss	3.00	7.50	15.00	M
166	The Big Fist - Clyde B. Ragsdale	3.00	7.50	15.00	
167	Love Me - and Die! - Day Keene	3.00	7.50	15.00	M
168	Hunt the Killer - Day Keene	3.00	7.50	15.00	M
169	Lady of Cleves - Margaret Campbell Barnes	3.00	7.50	15.00	
170	The Sea is so Wide - Evelyn Eaton	3.00	7.50	15.00	A
171	Savage Justice - Leslie Ernenwein	3.00	7.50	15.00	W
172	Gun Law - Paul Evan Lehman	3.00	7.50	15.00	W
173	Anna - Anneke de Lange	2.00	4.50	8.00	
174	Murder is My Racket - Robert H. Leitfred	3.00	7.50	15.00	M
175	The Commandos - Elliot Arnold 1952	3.00	7.50	15.00	C
176	The Valley of Silent Men - James Oliver Curwood	3.00	7.50	15.00	A
177	The House that Stood Still - A. E. van Vogt	10.00	25.00	40.00	SF
178	The Goldsmith's Wife - Jean Plaidy	3.00	7.50	15.00	
179	Madame Serpent - Jean Plaidy	3.00	7.50	15.00	E
180	If the Coffin Fits - Day Keene	3.00	7.50	15.00	M
181	The Wicked Lady Skelton - Magdalen King-Hall	3.00	7.50	15.00	
182	Crime On My Hands - Carl G. Hodges	3.00	7.50	15.00	M
183	Evening Street - Katrina Johnson	3.00	7.50	15.00	
184	Black Jade - Angeline Taylor	3.00	7.50	15.00	
185	Naked Fury - Day Keene	3.00	7.50	15.00	
186	Why Be a Sucker - D.N. LeBourdais	3.00	7.50	15.00	NF
187	Shanghai Jezebel - Mark Corrigan	3.00	7.50	15.00	E
188	Beggars Might Ride - George Albert Glay	3.00	7.50	15.00	
189	The Nymph and the Lamp - Thomas H. Raddall	3.00	7.50	15.00	E
190	Slave Ship - H. B. Drake	3.00	7.50	15.00	A
191	Prison Doctor - Louis Berg, M.D.	3.00	7.50	15.00	
192	Swamp Willow - Edwina Elroy	3.00	7.50	15.00	E
193	The Firebrand - George Challis	3.00	7.50	15.00	A
194	Triggerman - Abel Shott	3.00	7.50	15.00	
195	Nine to Five - Harvey Smith	3.00	7.50	15.00	
196	His Majesty's Yankees - Thomas H. Raddall	3.00	7.50	15.00	A
197	Strictly for Cash - James Hadley Chase	3.00	7.50	15.00	M
198	The Rawhider - Charles N. Heckelmann	3.00	7.50	15.00	W
199	The Double Shuffle - James Hadley Chase	3.00	7.50	15.00	M
200	Doctor of Lonesome River - Edison Marshall 1952	3.00	7.50	15.00	A
201	The Unfulfilled - W. G. Hardy	3.00	7.50	15.00	
202	Copper Town - Paul W. Fairman	3.00	7.50	15.00	W
203	Daughter of Satan - Jean Plaidy	3.00	7.50	15.00	E
204	Gun Hawk - Leslie Ernenwein 1953	3.00	7.50	15.00	W
205	The Black Flame - Stanley G. Weinbaum	10.00	25.00	40.00	SF
206	You Never Know with Women - James Hadley Chase	3.00	7.50	15.00	E
207	Three Ships West - Harry Symons	3.00	7.50	15.00	
208	Pillar of Fire - George Borodin	3.00	7.50	15.00	
209	The Rock Cried Out - Edward Stanley	3.00	7.50	15.00	
210	McSorley's Wonderful Saloon - Joseph Mitchell	3.00	7.50	15.00	

211	The Cautious Amorist - Norman Lindsay	3.00	7.50	15.00	
212	Shooting Valley - Lynn Westland	3.00	7.50	15.00	W
213	The Royal Story - Richard J. Doyle	3.00	7.50	15.00	NF
214	Paprika - Erich von Stroheim	3.00	7.50	15.00	E
215	Turn Back the River - W. G. Hardy	3.00	7.50	15.00	
216	No Mean City - A. McArthur & H. Kingsley Long	3.00	7.50	15.00	
217	The Sea Hawk - Rafael Sabatini	3.00	7.50	15.00	A
218	The Golden Amazon - John Russell Fearn	15.00	30.00	50.00	SF
219	Girls in White - Rona Randall	3.00	7.50	15.00	
220	Masked Rider - Will Garth	3.00	7.50	15.00	W
221	The Great Impersonation - E. Phillips Oppenheim	3.00	7.50	15.00	A
222	Mad Mike - George Goodchild	3.00	7.50	15.00	
223	The Wages of Virtue - P. C. Wren	3.00	7.50	15.00	A
224	Lady Hobo - Beth Brown	3.00	7.50	15.00	E
225	Sir Rusty Sword - Phillip Lindsay	3.00	7.50	15.00	A
	1953				
226	The Owlhoot Trail - Buck Billings	3.00	7.50	15.00	W
227	We Too Can Die - Paul Le Butt	3.00	7.50	15.00	
228	Drums of Dambala - H. Bedford Jones	3.00	7.50	15.00	A
229	Framed in Guilt - Day Keene	3.00	7.50	15.00	M
230	Women Spies - Kurt Singer	5.00	10.00	20.00	E
231	Legionnaire - John Robb	3.00	7.50	15.00	A
232	Malay Gold - H. Bedford Jones	3.00	7.50	15.00	A
233	Die with Me Lady - Ronald Cocking	3.00	7.50	15.00	M
234	Rebound - Dick Diespecker	3.00	7.50	15.00	
235	General Duty Nurse - Lucy Agnes Hancock	2.00	4.50	8.00	R
236	Gun Thrower - William L. Hopson	3.00	7.50	15.00	W
237	Island of Escape - Alexander Key	3.00	7.50	15.00	
238	The Lost World - Sir Arthur Conan Doyle	5.00	10.00	20.00	SF
239	Mission of Revenge - Edison Marshall	3.00	7.50	15.00	
240	Violent Night - Whit Harrison	3.00	7.50	15.00	M
241	Son of the Gods - Rex Beach	3.00	7.50	15.00	A
242	The Murder on the Links - Agatha Christie	3.00	7.50	15.00	M
243	School for Love - Oliver Anderson	3.00	7.50	15.00	
244	Hostage - Archie Joscelyn	3.00	7.50	15.00	W
245	The Soft Touch - James Hadley Chase	3.00	7.50	15.00	M
246	The Law's Outlaw - Arnold Smith	3.00	7.50	15.00	
247	Dark Surgery - Ben Ames Williams	3.00	7.50	15.00	
248	Legion of the Lawless - Lynn Westland	3.00	7.50	15.00	
249	Come Blonde, Come Murder - Peter George	3.00	7.50	15.00	M
250	The Man in the Middle - Ferguson Findley	3.00	7.50	15.00	
	1953				
251	Doctor in Buckskin - T. D. Allen	3.00	7.50	15.00	
252	Legion of Dishonor - Ivan Lebedeff	3.00	7.50	15.00	A
253	Wake Up to Murder - Day Keene	3.00	7.50	15.00	M
254	Mesquite Johnny - Barry Cord	3.00	7.50	15.00	W
255	Lady, Here's Your Wreath - Raymond Marshall	3.00	7.50	15.00	M
256	No Wings on a Cop - Cleve F. Adams	3.00	7.50	15.00	M
257	One Man Front - George Murdoch Rennie	3.00	7.50	15.00	
258	World Behind Bars - Louis Berg, M.D.	3.00	7.50	15.00	NF
259	Silver City - Bradford Scott	3.00	7.50	15.00	W
260	The Outlaw Trail - Johnston McCulley	3.00	7.50	15.00	W
261	Light in the Wilderness - E. B. Osler	3.00	7.50	15.00	
262	The Body on Mount Royal - David Montrose	3.00	7.50	15.00	

Harlequin 225, c. HB

Harlequin 232, c. HB

Harlequin 240, c. HB

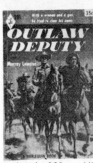

Harlequin 281, c. HB Harlequin 286, c. HB Harlequin 300, c. HB

(HARLEQUIN, continued)

263	Texas Showdown - Archie Joscelyn	3.00	7.50	15.00	W
264	Community Nurse - Lucy Agnes Hancock	2.00	4.50	8.00	R
265	The Paw in the Bottle - Raymond Marshall	3.00	7.50	15.00	
	1954				
266	Catalina - W. Somerset Maugham	3.00	7.50	15.00	
267	I'll Bury My Dead - James Hadley Chase	3.00	7.50	15.00	M
268	The Unholy Woman - Jean Plaidy	3.00	7.50	15.00	E
269	Queen Jezebel - Jean Plaidy	3.00	7.50	15.00	E
270	Fighting Buckaroo - Paul Evan Lehman	3.00	7.50	15.00	W
271	Mind Your Manners - Claire Wallace	3.00	7.50	15.00	
272	The Fabulous Nell Gwynne - Lozania Prole	3.00	7.50	15.00	
273	Holy Deadlock - A. P. Herbert	3.00	7.50	15.00	
274	Lost Valley - Al Cody	3.00	7.50	15.00	W
275	Hell's Horseman - William Hopson	3.00	7.50	15.00	W
	1954				
276	Conflict - E. V. Timms	3.00	7.50	15.00	A
277	Lady of China Street - Mark Corrigan	3.00	7.50	15.00	A
278	The Bait and the Trap - George Challis	3.00	7.50	15.00	A
279	Crime on my Hands - Carl G. Hodges	3.00	7.50	15.00	M
280	The Nut Brown Maid - Philip Lindsay	3.00	7.50	15.00	E
281	Outlaw Deputy - Murray Leinster	3.00	7.50	15.00	W
282	Frozen Frontier - Walter W. Liggett	3.00	7.50	15.00	
283	A Body for a Blonde - Ken McLeod	3.00	7.50	15.00	M
284	Calling Nurse Blair - Lucy Agnes Hancock	2.00	4.50	8.00	R
285	Texas Outlaw - Al Cody	3.00	7.50	15.00	W
286	Colonel Blood - Max Peacock	3.00	7.50	15.00	A
287	Gina - George Albert Glay	3.00	7.50	15.00	E
288	Bright Path to Adventure - Gordon Sinclair	3.00	7.50	15.00	A
289	The Black Donellys - Thomas P. Kelley	2.00	4.50	8.00	NF
290	The Violet Years - E. V. Timms	3.00	7.50	15.00	
291	Heart of Asia - Roy Chapman Andrews	3.00	7.50	15.00	NF
292	Nurse Barlow - Lucy Agnes Hancock	2.00	4.50	8.00	R
293	Mona - M. Coates Webster	3.00	7.50	15.00	
294	Girls in White - Rona Randall	3.00	7.50	15.00	
295	The Lost House - Frances Shelley Wees	3.00	7.50	15.00	
296	Half-Caste - Eric Baume	3.00	7.50	15.00	E
297	The Vice Merchants - Reed McCary	3.00	7.50	15.00	
298	Pride's Fancy - Thomas H. Raddall	3.00	7.50	15.00	A
299	Copper - Lieut. Tom McGrath	3.00	7.50	15.00	
300	Mallory - Raymond Marshall	3.00	7.50	15.00	
	1954				
301	Mary Read, Buccaneer - Philip Rush	3.00	7.50	15.00	A
302	The Nurse - Lucy Agnes Hancock	3.00	7.50	15.00	R
303	Captain Gentleman - Verne Fletcher	3.00	7.50	15.00	
304	High Saddle - William Hopson	3.00	7.50	15.00	W
305	Out of the Night - Robert O. Saber	3.00	7.50	15.00	M
306	Fabian of the Yard - Robert Fabian	3.00	7.50	15.00	NF
307	The Cage - Sydney Horler	3.00	7.50	15.00	E
308	Doctor Paul - Bette Allan	2.00	4.50	8.00	R
309	Notched Guns - William Hopson	3.00	7.50	15.00	W
310	Why Pick on Me - Raymond Marshall	3.00	7.50	15.00	
311	Convicted - David Goodis	3.00	7.50	15.00	
312	The Seeker - Thomas Burtis	3.00	7.50	15.00	
313	Hospital Nurse - Lucy Agnes Hancock	2.00	4.50	8.00	R
314	Forbidden - Lois Bull	3.00	7.50	15.00	
315	The Black Eagle - Thomas Burtis	3.00	7.50	15.00	
316	This Way for a Shroud - James Hadley Chase	3.00	7.50	15.00	M

317	Blonde's Requiem - Raymond Marshall	3.00	7.50	15.00	
318	The Half-Breed - M. Constantin-Weyer	3.00	7.50	15.00	
319	Woman Doctor - Dorothy Pierce Walker	3.00	7.50	15.00	
320	The Deathless Amazon - John Russell Fearn	10.00	25.00	40.00	SF
321	London After Dark - Fabian of the Yard	3.00	7.50	15.00	NF
322	The Web - Sydney Horler	3.00	7.50	15.00	M
323	Tiger by the Tail - James Hadley Chase 1955	3.00	7.50	15.00	M
324	West End Nurse - Lucy Agnes Hancock	2.00	4.50	8.00	R
325	Satan's Range - Al Cody 1955	3.00	7.50	15.00	W
326	Girl Intern - Elizabeth Seifert	2.00	4.50	8.00	R
327	The World's Worst Women - Bernard O'Donnell	5.00	10.00	20.00	E
328	The Wife Traders - Arthur Stringer	3.00	7.50	15.00	
329	People of the Night - Victor Russell	3.00	7.50	15.00	
330	Convict Town - E. V. Timms	5.00	10.00	20.00	E
331	Women in Chains - E. V. Timms	10.00	25.00	40.00	E
332	Staff Nurse - Lucy Agnes Hancock	2.00	4.50	8.00	R
333	Resident Nurse - Lucy Agnes Hancock	2.00	4.50	8.00	R
334	The Square Emerald - Edgar Wallace	3.00	7.50	15.00	M
335	Hoodlum Alley - Albert E. Ullman	3.00	7.50	15.00	M
336	The Good and the Bad - Joan Fleming	2.00	4.50	8.00	R
337	The Man in the Brown Suit - Agatha Christie	3.00	7.50	15.00	M
338	District Nurse - Lucy Agnes Hancock	2.00	4.50	8.00	R
339	Nurses Are People - Lucy Agnes Hancock	2.00	4.50	8.00	R
340	The Pick-Up - Raymond Marshall	3.00	7.50	15.00	
341	Ruthless - Raymond Marshall	3.00	7.50	15.00	
342	Nancy Craig, R.N. - Marcia Ford	2.00	4.50	8.00	R
343	Gun Thunder Valley - Al Cody	3.00	7.50	15.00	W
344	Village Doctor - Lucy Agnes Hancock	2.00	4.50	8.00	R
345	The Gunman - Al Cody	3.00	7.50	15.00	W
346	Doctor Bill - Lucy Agnes Hancock	2.00	4.50	8.00	R
347	Pat Whitney, R.N. - Lucy Agnes Hancock	2.00	4.50	8.00	R
348	The Doctor on Elm Street - Kay Hamilton 1956	2.00	4.50	8.00	R
349	The Four Just Men - Edgar Wallace	3.00	7.50	15.00	M
350	The Renegade - Walt Coburn 1956	3.00	7.50	15.00	W
351	Dr. Parrish, Resident - Sydney Thompson	2.00	4.50	8.00	R
352	The India-Rubber Men - Edgar Wallace	3.00	7.50	15.00	M
353	Gun Law - Paul Evan Lehman	3.00	7.50	15.00	W
354	Dark Bahama - Peter Cheyney	3.00	7.50	15.00	
355	Savage Justice - Leslie Ernenwein	3.00	7.50	15.00	W
356	Nurse's Aide - Lucy Agnes Hancock	2.00	4.50	8.00	R
357	Young Doctor Glenn - Kay Hamilton	2.00	4.50	8.00	R
358	Redrock Gold - Paul Evan Lehman	3.00	7.50	15.00	W
359	The Secret Adversary - Agatha Christie	3.00	7.50	15.00	M
360	Yucca City Outlaw - William Hopson	3.00	7.50	15.00	W
361	The Clue of the Silver Key - Edgar Wallace	3.00	7.50	15.00	M
362	Nora Was a Nurse - Peggy Dern	2.00	4.50	8.00	R
363	Doctor Alice's Daughter - Kay Hamilton	2.00	4.50	8.00	R
364	Surgeon in Charge - Elizabeth Seifert	2.00	4.50	8.00	R
365	Doctors Are Different - Dorothy Pierce Walker	2.00	4.50	8.00	R
366	The Brass Monkey - Harry Whittington	3.00	7.50	15.00	M
367	Hickory House - Kenneth Orvis	3.00	7.50	15.00	
368	Meredith Blake, M.D. - Peggy Gaddis	2.00	4.50	8.00	R
369	Three Doctors - Elizabeth Seifert	2.00	4.50	8.00	R
370	Appointment with Venus - Jerrard Tickell	3.00	7.50	15.00	
371	Renegade Ramrod - Leslie Ernenwein	3.00	7.50	15.00	W
372	Meet the Warrens - Lucy Agnes Hancock	2.00	4.50	8.00	R
373	Tonight, Josephine - Lozania Prole	3.00	7.50	15.00	
374	Valley of the Sun - Archie Joscelyn	3.00	7.50	15.00	W
375	Miss Doctor - Elizabeth Seifert	2.00	4.50	8.00	R
376	Blake Hospital - Dorothy Worley 1957	2.00	4.50	8.00	R
377	The Secret of Chimneys - Agatha Christie	3.00	7.50	15.00	M
378	The Ringer - Edgar Wallace	3.00	7.50	15.00	M
379	The Doctor Takes a Wife - Elizabeth Seifert	2.00	4.50	8.00	R
380	The River's End - James Oliver Curwood	3.00	7.50	15.00	A
381	Doctor Joel - Watkins E. Wright	2.00	4.50	8.00	R
382	Never Trust a Woman - Raymond Marshall	3.00	7.50	15.00	
383	Valley of Silent Men - James Oliver Curwood	3.00	7.50	15.00	A
384	Nurse Ellen - Peggy Dern	2.00	4.50	8.00	R
385	Eve - James Hadley Chase	3.00	7.50	15.00	
386	The Faro Kid - Leslie Ernenwein	3.00	7.50	15.00	W

387	White Face - Edgar Wallace	3.00	7.50	15.00	M
388	Doctor Scott - Peggy Dern	2.00	4.50	8.00	R
389	Circle F Cowboy - Chuck Martin	3.00	7.50	15.00	W
390	Adopted Derelicts - Bluebell S. Phillips	3.00	7.50	15.00	
391	How to Get More From Your Car - W. J. Young & E. R. McCrea	2.00	4.50	8.00	NF
392	Doctor of Mercy - Elizabeth Seifert	2.00	4.50	8.00	R
393	A Forest of Eyes - Victor Canning	3.00	7.50	15.00	
394	Lady Doctor - Peggy Gaddis	2.00	4.50	8.00	R
395	The Angel of Terror - Edgar Wallace	3.00	7.50	15.00	M
396	Double Cross Ranch - Will Watson	3.00	7.50	15.00	W
397	The Shorn Lamb - Lucy Agnes Hancock	2.00	4.50	8.00	R
398	Sagebrush - Wade Hamilton	3.00	7.50	15.00	W
399	Royce of the Royal Mounted - Amos Moore	3.00	7.50	15.00	W.
400	The Cage - Sydney Horter	3.00	7.50	15.00	M
	1957				
401	The Doctor Disagrees - Elizabeth Seifert	2.00	4.50	8.00	R
402	The Football Gravy Train - Frank O'Rourke	3.00	7.50	15.00	S
403	Next of Kin - George Goodchild	2.00	4.50	8.00	R
404	Law in the Saddle - Paul Evan Lehman	3.00	7.50	15.00	W
405	City Nurse - Peggy Gaddis	2.00	4.50	8.00	R
406	The Flaming Forest - James Oliver Curwood	3.00	7.50	15.00	A
407	The Hospital in Buwambo - Anne Vinton	2.00	4.50	8.00	R
408	Rink Rat - Don MacMillan	3.00	7.50	15.00	
409	Hospital Corridors - Mary Burchell	2.00	4.50	8.00	R
	1958				
410	Dark Journey - Sydney Horler	3.00	7.50	15.00	
411	Range King - J. E. Grinstead	3.00	7.50	15.00	W
412	Nurse Trenton - Caroline Trench	2.00	4.50	8.00	R
413	I'll Get You for This - James Hadley Chase	3.00	7.50	15.00	M
414	Devil's Portage - Charles Stoddard	3.00	7.50	15.00	
415	The Normal Child - Alan Brown, M.D.	2.00	4.50	8.00	NF
416	Doctor Lucy - Barbara Allen	2.00	4.50	8.00	R
417	Maverick Guns - J.E. Grinstead	3.00	7.50	15.00	W
418	The Feathered Serpent - Edgar Wallace	3.00	7.50	15.00	M
419	Nurse Warding Takes Charge - Caroline Trench	2.00	4.50	8.00	R
420	The Squeaker - Edgar Wallace	3.00	7.50	15.00	M
421	The Golden Amazon's Triumph - John Russell Fearn	10.00	25.00	40.00	SF
422	Then Come Kiss Me - Mary Burchell	2.00	4.50	8.00	R
423	Nurse Greve - Jane Arbor	2.00	4.50	8.00	R
424	Flashing Spikes - Frank O'Rourke	3.00	7.50	15.00	S
425	The Return of the Nighthawk - Sydney Horler	3.00	7.50	15.00	
	1958				
426	The World's Greatest Spy Stories - ed. Kurt Singer	3.00	7.50	15.00	
427	Nurse Brookes - Kate Norway	2.00	4.50	8.00	R
428	The Strange Countess - Edgar Wallace	3.00	7.50	15.00	M
429	Steele of the Royal Mounted - James Oliver Curwood	3.00	7.50	15.00	A
430	Ship's Nurse - Alex Stuart	2.00	4.50	8.00	R
431	The Silent Valley - Jean S. MacLeod	3.00	7.50	15.00	
432	The Lady Lost Her Head - Manning Lee Stokes	3.00	7.50	15.00	M
433	Because of Doctor Danville - Elizabeth Hoy	2.00	4.50	8.00	R
434	Dear Doctor Everett - Jean S. MacLeod	2.00	4.50	8.00	R
435	Canada's Greatest Crimes - Thomas P. Kelley	3.00	7.50	15.00	NF
436	Garrison Hospital - Alex Stuart	2.00	4.50	8.00	R
437	Saddlebag Surgeon - Robert Tyre	2.00	4.50	8.00	
438	Master of Surgery - Alex Stuart	2.00	4.50	8.00	
439	Hospital in Sudan - Anne Vinton	2.00	4.50	8.00	R
440	Pardon My Parka - Joan Walker	2.00	4.50	8.00	R
441	Murder on the Links - Agatha Christie	3.00	7.50	15.00	M
442	Curling with Ken Watson - Ken Watson	3.00	7.50	15.00	NF
443	Nurse on Call - Elizabeth Gilzean	2.00	4.50	8.00	R
444	Double Dan - Edgar Wallace	3.00	7.50	15.00	M
445	Nurse in the Tropics - Peggy Dern	2.00	4.50	8.00	R
446	To Please the Doctor - Marjorie Moore	2.00	4.50	8.00	R
447	The Crimson Circle - Edgar Wallace	3.00	7.50	15.00	M
	1959				
448	Bridal Array - Elizabeth Cadell	2.00	4.50	8.00	R
449	Nurse in Training - Elizabeth Hoy	2.00	4.50	8.00	R
450	Gay Canadian Rogues - Frank Rasky	3.00	7.50	15.00	NF
	1959				
451	Air Ambulance - Jean S. MacLeod	2.00	4.50	8.00	R

(HARLEQUIN, continued)

No.	Title				
452	Crescent Dream Book and Fortune Teller	3.00	7.50	15.00	NF
453	Corner Cupboard - Carlyle Allison	2.00	4.50	8.00	R
454	Nurse in Love - Jane Arbor	2.00	4.50	8.00	R
455	Smoke Over Sikanaska - J. S. Gowland	3.00	7.50	15.00	A
456	The Yellow Snake - Edgar Wallace	3.00	7.50	15.00	M
457	Physical Fitness for all the Family - Lloyd Percival	2.00	4.50	8.00	NF
458	Next Patient, Doctor Anne - Elizabeth Gilzean	2.00	4.50	8.00	R
459	Ring for the Nurse - Marjorie Moore	2.00	4.50	8.00	R
460	At the Villa Rose - A. E. W. Mason	2.00	4.50	8.00	R
461	For Ever and Ever - Mary Burchell	2.00	4.50	8.00	R
462	Love from a Surgeon - Elizabeth Gilzean	2.00	4.50	8.00	R
463	Nurse Brodie - Kate Norway	2.00	4.50	8.00	R
464	The Captain's Table - Alex Stuart	2.00	4.50	8.00	
465	My Greatest Crime Story - ed. Kurt Singer	3.00	7.50	15.00	
466	The Traitor's Gate - Edgar Wallace	3.00	7.50	15.00	M
467	Nurse to the Island - Caroline Trench	2.00	4.50	8.00	R
468	Surgeon of Distinction - Mary Burchell	2.00	4.50	8.00	R

HART BOOKS

(Horace Hart, Inc.)

Digest size

No.	Title				
K-1	The House of Creeping Horror - George F. Worts	1.50	3.50	5.00	M
K-2	The Diamonds of Death - Borden Chase aka Blue, White and Perfect	1.50	3.50	5.00	M

HERCULES

(Hercules Publishing Corporation)

Digest size

nn	D - as in Dead - Lawrence Treat 1943	1.50	3.50	5.00	M

HILLMAN BOOKS

(Hillman Periodicals, Inc.)

nn(1)	Let's Make Mary - Jack Hanley 1948	3.00	6.00	12.00	E
2	Tumbling River Range - W. C. Tuttle	3.00	6.00	12.00	W
3	Casanova's Memoirs - Giacomo Casanova	3.00	6.00	12.00	
4	Ironheart - William MacLeod Raine	3.00	6.00	12.00	W

Hart Books K-2, c. Hart

Hercules nn, c. Hercules

Hillman Books 2, c. Hill

Hillman Books 12, c. Hill

Hillman Books 15, c. Hill

Hillman Books 19, c. Hill

(HILLMAN BOOKS, continued)

5 Bluffer's Luck - W. C. Tutle	3.00	6.00	12.00	W
6 Riders of Buck River - William MacLeod Raine	3.00	6.00	12.00	W
7 Sex and Marriage Problems - E. B. Taylor	3.00	6.00	12.00	
8 I Chose Freedom - Victor Kravchenko	3.00	6.00	12.00	NF
9 Guns on the High Mesa - Arthur Henry Gooden	3.00	6.00	12.00	W
10 Murder Under Construction - Sue MacVeigh	3.00	6.00	12.00	M
11 Steve Yeager - William MacLeod Raine	3.00	6.00	12.00	W
12 Ten Droll Tales - Honore de Balzac	4.00	8.00	15.00	
Includes some science fiction/fantasy				
13 Hell in the Saddle - Ed Earl Repp	3.00	6.00	12.00	W
14 The Physiology of Love - Remy de Gourmont	3.00	6.00	12.00	NF
1949				
15 Hanging Judge - Bruce Hamilton	3.00	6.00	12.00	M
16 Gold - Clarence Budington Kelland	3.00	6.00	12.00	W
17 Gun Hawk - Ed Earl Repp	3.00	6.00	12.00	W
18 Collusion - Theodore D. Irwin	3.00	6.00	12.00	NF
19 The Red Rider of Smoky Range - Wm. Colt				
MacDonald	3.00	6.00	12.00	W
20 Dark Hazard - W. R. Burnett	3.00	6.00	12.00	M
21 Marriage, Sex, and Family Problems and How				
to Solve Them - John J. Anthony	3.00	6.00	12.00	NF
22 The Shadowed Trail - Arthur Henry Gooden	3.00	6.00	12.00	W
23 42 Days for Murder - Roger Torrey	3.00	6.00	12.00	M
24 The Trail of Danger - Wm. MacLeod Raine	3.00	6.00	12.00	W
25 The Deputy of Carabina - William Colt				
MacDonald	3.00	6.00	12.00	W
26 Straws in the Wind - W. C. Tuttle	3.00	6.00	12.00	W
27 Dead on Arrival	3.00	6.00	12.00	
28 The Redhead from Sun Dog - W. C. Tuttle	3.00	6.00	12.00	W
Note: Same cover as Western Novel Classic 89.				
29 Big-Town Round up - William MacLeod Raine	3.00	6.00	12.00	W
30 Buzzard Tracks - Tom J. Hopkins	3.00	6.00	12.00	W
31 Wheels in the Dust - William Colt MacDonald	3.00	6.00	12.00	W
32 Bear Paw - Dane Coolidge	3.00	6.00	12.00	W
33 Rusty Guns - Bliss Lomax	3.00	6.00	12.00	W
34 King of Crazy River - William Colt MacDonald	3.00	6.00	12.00	W
35 Smoky River - Tom Roan	3.00	6.00	12.00	W
36 King of the Bush - Wm. MacLeod Raine	3.00	6.00	12.00	W
37 Hashknife of Stormy River - W. C. Tuttle	3.00	6.00	12.00	W

Hillman Books 28, c. Hill

Hillman Books 33, c. Hill

Hillman Books 41, c. Hill

(HILLMAN BOOKS, continued)

38	Nothing More than Murder - Jim Thompson	3.00	6.00	12.00	M
39	Meet Mr. Mulliner - P. G. Wodehouse	3.00	6.00	12.00	H
40	Trouble at the JHC - W. C. Tuttle	3.00	6.00	12.00	W
41	The Dying Earth - Jack Vance	15.00	35.00	60.00	SF
	First ed., 1950				
42	Roaring River - William MacLeod Raine	3.00	6.00	12.00	W
43	Arizona Nights - Stewart Edward White	3.00	6.00	12.00	W
44	The Trusty Knaves - Eugene Manlove Rhodes	3.00	6.00	12.00	W
45	Story of a Russian Spy - Alexander Foote	2.50	6.00	10.00	B
	aka Handbook for Spies				
46	Copper Streak Trail - Eugene Manlove Rhodes	3.00	6.00	12.00	W
47	Scattergun Ranch - Tom J. Hopkins	3.00	6.00	12.00	W
48	Father of the Bride - Edward Streeter	2.50	6.00	10.00	
103	The Short Night - Russell Turner	2.00	4.00	6.00	
	1957				
104	Rimrock Town - William Heuman	2.00	4.00	6.00	W
105	The Matchmaker - Georges Simenon	2.00	4.00	7.50	M
106	Sex Without Guilt - Albert Ellis	2.00	4.00	6.00	NF
	1959				
107	The Tormentors - Robert Payne	2.00	4.00	6.00	
108	Roy Bean: Law West of the Pecos - C. L. Sonnichsen	2.00	4.00	7.50	NF
109	Horses, Women and Guns - Nelson Nye	2.00	4.00	7.50	W
110	The Greatest Lover in the World - Alex Austin	2.00	4.00	6.00	
111	Morocco Episode - William Brothers c-Maguire	2.00	4.00	6.00	M
112	The Sins of Skid Row - John White	2.00	4.00	6.00	
113	Soldier's Women - Stan Smith	2.00	4.00	6.00	
114	Temptation in a Southern Town - William L. Heath	2.00	4.00	6.00	E
115	Dead Warrior - John Myers Myers	2.00	4.00	7.50	
116	A Strange Innocence - Charles Mergendahl	2.00	4.00	6.00	
117	Cassandra - Frances Clippinger	2.00	4.00	6.00	E
118	The Jayhawkers - Saul Cooper	2.00	4.00	6.00	W
	Movie tie-in				
119	A Killer's Kiss - Hal Ellson	2.00	4.00	6.00	
120	Let's Make Mary - Jack Hanley	2.00	4.00	7.50	
121	The Sinful One - Edwina Mark	2.00	4.00	6.00	
122	Sixgun Helltown - Charles M. Martin	2.00	4.00	6.00	W
	aka Sixgun Town				
123	Savage Conqueror - Davenport Steward	2.00	4.00	6.00	
124	The Sinful Love - Calvin Turner	2.00	4.00	6.00	
125	Death is Confidential - Lawrence Lariar	2.00	4.00	6.00	
126	And Then Murder - Julius Fast	2.00	4.00	6.00	
127	Maverick Gun - Barry Cord	2.00	4.00	6.00	W
	aka Gun - Proddy Hombre				
128	Elisa - Edmond de Goncourt	2.00	4.00	6.00	
129	The Moments Between - Robert Ackworth	2.00	4.00	6.00	
130	The Elvis Presley Story - James Gregory	7.50	17.50	30.00	B
	First ed., 1960				

HILLMAN DETECTIVE NOVEL

(Hillman Periodicals, Inc.)

1	The Arabian Nights Murder - John Dickson Carr	5.00	10.00	20.00	M
	1943				

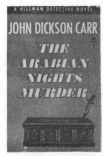

Hillman Books 114, c. Hill   Hillman Det. Novel 1, c. Hill   Howard nn, c. How

254

Infantry Journal J102, c. Infan   Intimate Novels 1, c. Design   Intimate Novels 32, c. Design

HIP BOOKS

(Hip Books, Inc.)

1 The Mystery of the Red Suitcase - Lula M. Day 1946	2.00	4.00	7.50	M

HOWARD

(F. E. Howard Publications)

Digest size

Canadian

nn I Hate You to Death - Keith Edgar 1944	1.50	3.50	5.00	M
nn True Mysteries and Murders - anthology	1.50	3.50	5.00	NF
nn Honduras Double Cross - Keith Edgar	1.50	3.50	5.00	M
nn The Incendiary Blonde - Keith Edgar	1.50	3.50	5.00	M

THE INFANTRY JOURNAL

(The Infantry Journal)

J101 Boomerang - William C. Shambliss 1945	1.50	3.50	5.00	A
J102 The U. S. Marines on Iwo Jima 1945	1.50	3.50	5.00	NF

INTIMATE NOVELS

(Design Publishing Company)

Digest size

1 Wayward Bride - Paul Gaillard 1950, aka One Unfaithful Year	2.00	4.00	7.50	E
3 Cheap Hotel - Gerald Foster aka Night Clerk	1.50	3.50	5.00	E
4 Plaything - Gordon Semple	1.50	3.50	5.00	E
6 Divorce Racket Girls - Jed Anthony	1.50	3.50	5.00	E
7 Greenwich Village Girl - Robert Norcross	2.00	4.00	6.00	E
8 Gin Wedding - Ann Lawrence	1.50	3.50	5.00	E
9 Temptress - Elliot Brewster	1.50	3.50	5.00	E

(INTIMATE NOVELS, continued)

10 Dangerous Trade - Charles Thornton	1.50	3.50	5.00	E
11 Swamp Girl - Perry Lindsay	2.00	4.00	6.00	E
12 Seventh Wife - Barry de Forest	1.50	3.50	5.00	E
13 Local Talent - Florence Stonebraker	1.50	3.50	5.00	E
14 Off Limits - Bruce Manning	1.50	3.50	5.00	E
15 Private Chauffeur - N. R. De Mexico	1.50	3.50	5.00	E
16 Lust for Love - Florence Stonebraker	1.50	3.50	5.00	E
17 The Sins of Janet Benson, Showgirl - Ben West	1.50	3.50	5.00	E
18 Hot Lips - Jack Hanley	1.50	3.50	5.00	E
19 Mail-Order Passion - Hall Bennett c-Gross Note: Same cover as Beacon no. B134.	1.50	3.50	5.00	E
20 Pleasure Alley - Ralph Carter Orig., 1952 Note: Same cover as Beacon B307.	1.50	3.50	5.00	E
21 Dr. Randolph's Women - Thomas Stone	1.50	3.50	5.00	E
22 Office Wife - Richard Grant aka Teaser	1.50	3.50	5.00	E
23 Ex-Mistress - Thomas Stone	1.50	3.50	5.00	E
24 The Whipping Room - Florenz Branch	1.50	3.50	5.00	E
25 Triangle of Sin - Bruce Manning	1.50	3.50	5.00	E
26 Very Private Secretary - Jack Hanley	1.50	3.50	5.00	E
27 Tramp Girl - Thomas Stone	1.50	3.50	5.00	E
28 Back Country Woman - Evans Wall aka A Time to Sow	1.50	3.50	5.00	E
29 Shameless Wife - Wayne Way	1.50	3.50	5.00	E
30 Tent-show Bride - Jack Hanley	1.50	3.50	5.00	E
31 Naked Desire - Henry Lewis Nixon Orig., 1953	1.50	3.50	5.00	E
32 Basement Gang - David Williams Orig., 1953 Note: Same cover as Stallion no. 213 and virtually identical to Beacon B260.	2.50	6.00	10.00	E
33 Scarlet City - Winchell Barry	1.50	3.50	5.00	E
34 Shack Woman - Kathie Keed	1.50	3.50	5.00	E
35 Private Practice - Thomas Stone	1.50	3.50	5.00	E
36 Waterfront Blonde - Gordon Semple	1.50	3.50	5.00	E
37 New York Model - Jack Hanley	1.50	3.50	5.00	E
38 Lily of New Orleans - Beth Brown	1.50	3.50	5.00	E
39 Dr. Breyton's Wife - Florenz Branch	1.50	3.50	5.00	E
40 Crusher's Girl - Gordon Semple	1.50	3.50	5.00	E
42 Village Girl - Reed	1.50	3.50	5.00	E
48 Cafe Society Sinner - Bruce Manning Orig., 1953	1.50	3.50	5.00	E
49 Strange Circle - Gale Sydney Orig., 1953	1.50	3.50	5.00	E
51 Ship's Doctor - Henry Lewis Nixon Orig., 1954	1.50	3.50	5.00	E
56 Odd Girl - Hal R. Moore	1.50	3.50	5.00	E

JACKET LIBRARY

(National Home Library Foundation)

1 Treasure Island - R. L. Stevenson 1932	4.00	8.00	15.00	A

Jacket Library 1, c. NH   Jacket Library nn, c. NH   James nn, c. James

2	The New Testament	4.00	8.00	15.00	
3	Green Mansions - W. H. Hudson	5.00	10.00	20.00	F
4	The Way of all Flesh - Samuel Butler	4.00	8.00	15.00	
5	The Merchant of Venice - William Shakespeare	4.00	8.00	15.00	
6	Emerson's Essays - Ralph Waldo Emerson	4.00	8.00	15.00	
7	Petre Goriot - Honore de Balzac	4.00	8.00	15.00	
8	Alice in Wonderland, Through the Looking Glass, Hunting of the Shark - Lewis Carroll	5.00	10.00	20.00	F
9	The Adventures of Tom Sawyer - Mark Twain	4.00	8.00	15.00	A
10	Tales of Sherlock Holmes - Arthur Conan Doyle	5.00	10.00	20.00	M
11	Under the Greenwood Tree - Thomas Hardy	4.00	8.00	15.00	
12	The Golden Treasury of Song and Verse	4.00	8.00	15.00	
13	Cyrano de Bergeros - Edmond Rostand 1933	4.00	8.00	15.00	A
14	Other People's Money - Louis D. Brandeis	4.00	8.00	15.00	NF
nn	The Art of Love - a Parisian Casanova	4.00	8.00	15.00	A
	Note: Ironically retitled reprint of Cyrano de Bergerac (no.13).				

JAMES

(C. L. R. James)

nn Mariners, Renegades and Castaways - C. L. R. James Orig., 1953	3.00	6.00	12.00	B

JONATHAN MYSTERY

(The Jonathan Press, Inc.)

Digest size

1	The Chinese Orange Mystery - Ellery Queen	1.50	3.50	5.00	M
2	Too Many Cooks - Rex Stout	.75	1.75	3.00	M
3	A Man Lay Dead - Ngaio Marsh	.75	1.75	3.00	M
4	The Bowstring Murders - Carter Dickson	.75	1.75	3.00	M
5	The French Powder Mystery - Ellery Queen	.75	1.75	3.00	M
6	Over My Dead Body - Rex Stout	.75	1.75	3.00	M
7	Murder for Christmas - Agatha Christie	.75	1.75	3.00	M
8	Maigret Sits it Out - Georges Simenon	.75	1.75	3.00	M
9	The Broken Vase - Rex Stout	.75	1.75	3.00	M
10	Death in the Air - Agatha Christie	.75	1.75	3.00	M
11	The Red Widow Murders - Carter Dickson	1.50	3.50	5.00	M
12	The Roman Hat Mystery - Ellery Queen	.75	1.75	3.00	M
13	N or M? - Agatha Christie	.50	1.25	2.00	M
14	The White Priory Murders - Carter Dickson	.75	1.75	3.00	M
15	Cordially Invited to Meet Death - Rex Stout	.75	1.75	3.00	M
16	Murder in Retrospect - Agatha Christie	.50	1.25	2.00	M
17	The Return of the Continental Op - Dashiell Hammett First ed., 1945	7.50	15.00	30.00	M
18	Maigret Returns - Georges Simenon	.75	1.75	3.00	M
19	The Plague Court Murders - Carter Dickson	.75	1.75	3.00	M
20	Passing Strange - Richard Sale	.50	1.25	2.00	M
21	Arrow Pointing Nowhere - Elizabeth Daly	.50	1.25	2.00	M
22	Design for Murder - Percival Wilde	.50	1.25	2.00	M
23	Black Alibi - Cornell Woolrich	.50	1.25	2.00	M
24	Lazarus No. 7 - Richard Sale	2.00	4.00	7.50	SF
25	It Walks by Night - John Dickson	.75	1.75	3.00	M
26	The Riddiges of Hildegarde Withers - Stuart Palmer	.50	1.25	2.00	M
27	Not Quite Dead Enough - Rex Stout	.75	1.75	3.00	M
28	Jethro Hammer - Michael Venning	.50	1.25	2.00	M
29	Dead Yellow Women - Dashiell Hammett First ed., 1947	7.50	15.00	30.00	M
30	The Glass Triangle - George Harmon Coxe	1.50	3.50	5.00	M
31	And so to Death - William Irish	.75	1.75	3.00	M
32	Dancers in Mourning - Margery Allingham	.75	1.75	3.00	M
33	The League of Frightened Men - Rex Stout	.75	1.75	3.00	M

(JONATHAN MYSTERY, continued)

34	Dear, Dead Women - Dana Chambers	.50	1.25	2.00	M
	aka The Case of Caroline Animus				
35	Build My Gallows High - Geoffrey Homes	.50	1.25	2.00	M
36	The Big Knockover - Dashiell Hammett	4.00	8.00	15.00	M
	1948, aka $106,000 Blood Money				
37	The Pinball Murders - Thomas B. Black	.40	1.25	2.00	M
38	The Frightened Man - Dana Chambers	.50	1.25	2.00	M
39	With Intent to Deceive - Manning Coles	.50	1.25	2.00	M
40	The Continental Op - Dashiell Hammett	2.00	4.00	7.50	M
41	The 3-13 Murders - Thomas B. Black	.50	1.25	2.00	M
42	The Billion Dollar Body - Joseph Shallit	.50	1.25	2.00	M
43	Darling, this is Death - Dana Chambers	.50	1.25	2.00	M
44	Dead Level - Russell Gordon	.50	1.25	2.00	M
45	The Spider Lily - Bruno Fischer	.50	1.25	2.00	M
46	The Last Secret - Dana Chambers	.50	1.25	2.00	M
47	Deadhead - Charles Marquis Warren	.50	1.25	2.00	M
48	The Creeping Siamese - Dashiell Hammett	7.50	15.00	30.00	M
	First ed., 1950				
49	Mr. Moto is so Sorry - John P. Marquand	.75	1.75	3.00	M
50	Death Against Venus - Dana Chambers	.50	1.25	2.00	M
51	The Black Angel - Cornell Woolrich	.50	1.25	2.00	M
52	No Hero - John P. Marquand	.50	1.25	2.00	M
53	Dangerous Blondes - Kelley Roos	.50	1.25	2.00	M
	aka If the Shroud Fits				
54	Ming Yellow - John P. Marquand	.50	1.25	2.00	M
55	Blood on the Blonde - Dana Chambers	.50	1.25	2.00	M
	aka Witch's Moon				
56	Dead Weight - Frank Kane	.50	1.25	2.00	M
57	Dangerous by Nature - Manning Coles	.50	1.25	2.00	M
58	The Blonde Died First - Dana Chambers	.50	1.25	2.00	M
59	Woman in the Dark - Dashiell Hammett	7.50	15.00	30.00	M
	First ed., 1951				
60	The Blue Ice - Hammond Innes	.50	1.25	2.00	M
61	The Black Path of Fear - Cornell Woolrich	.75	1.75	3.00	M
62	Now or Never - Manning Coles	.50	1.25	2.00	M
63	Rope for an Ape - Dana Chambers	.50	1.25	2.00	M
64	Bullet Proof - Frank Kane	.50	1.25	2.00	M
65	The Fifth Grave - Jonathan Latimer	.50	1.25	2.00	M
66	Die Like a Dog - Frank Gruber	.50	1.25	2.00	M
	aka The Hungry Dog				
67	Scared to Death - George Bagby	.50	1.25	2.00	M
68	Operation Manhunt - Manning Coles	.50	1.25	2.00	M
	aka Alias Uncle Hugo				
69	Murder in the Madhouse - Jonathan Latimer	.50	1.25	2.00	M
70	Kiss for a Killer - Dorothy B. Hughes	.50	1.25	2.00	M
	aka The Scarlet Imperial				
71	A Body for the Bride - George Bagby	.50	1.25	2.00	M
	aka The Original Carcase				
72	Too Tough to Die - Frank Gruber	.50	1.25	2.00	M
	aka The Lock and the Key				
73	Dead Drunk - George Bagby	.50	1.25	2.00	M
74	All that Glitters - Manning Coles	.50	1.25	2.00	M
75	Layout for a Corpse - Gene Goldsmith	.50	1.25	2.00	M
76	Fall Guy for a Killer - Frank Gruber	.50	1.25	2.00	M
	aka The Yellow Overcoat				
77	Some Dames are Deadly - Jonathan Latimer	.50	1.25	2.00	M
	aka Red Gardenias	.50	1.25	2.00	M
78	Payoff in Blood - Hal Calin	.50	1.25	2.00	M
	aka Rocks and Ruin				
79	Deadly Lure - Whitman Chambers	.50	1.25	2.00	M
80	Death Rides a Painted Horse - Robert Patrick Wilmot	.50	1.25	2.00	M
81	Lust to Kill - Edward Lee	.50	1.25	2.00	M
82	Naked Fear - John Farr	.50	1.25	2.00	M
	aka Don't Feed the Animals				
83	Give the Girl a Gun - Richard Deming	.50	1.25	2.00	M
	aka Whistle Past the Graveyard				
84	Headed for a Hearse - Jonathan Latimer	.50	1.25	2.00	M
85	The Long Arm of Murder - Frank Gruber	.50	1.25	2.00	M
86	Hell Street - Max Franklin	.50	1.25	2.00	M
87	Death Ain't Commercial - George Bagby	.50	1.25	2.00	M
88	The Smell of Fear - Spencer Dean	.50	1.25	2.00	M
	aka The Scent of Fear				
89	Once Over Deadly - Frank Gruber	.50	1.25	2.00	M
	aka The French Key Mystery	.50	1.25	2.00	M

Jonathan Mystery 17, c. Jon   Keep-Worthy Books 3, c. KW   Knickerbocker nn, c. Knic

(JONATHAN MYSTERY, continued)

90 The Man in the Green Hat - Manning Coles	.50	1.25	2.00	M
91 Hand-Picked to Die - Richard Deming	.50	1.25	2.00	M
aka Tweak the Devil's Nose				
92 A Shroud for Mr. Bundy - James M. Fox	.50	1.25	2.00	M
93 The Basle Express - Manning Coles	.50	1.25	2.00	M
94 Murder is Insane - Glenn Barns	.50	1.25	2.00	M
95 The Long Escape - David Dodge	.50	1.25	2.00	M
96 Rites for a Killer - James M. Fox	.50	1.25	2.00	M
aka The Bright Serpent				

KEEP-WORTHY BOOKS

(Keep-Worthy Books, Inc.)

1				
2				
3 Twelve of the World's Famous Adventure Books - ed. Julius Muller 1946	2.00	4.00	6.00	A
4 Twelve of the World's Famous Love Novels - ed. Julius Muller 1946	2.00	4.00	6.00	R

KNICKERBOCKER

(Knickerbocker Publishing Company)

Digest size

15 Palm Beach Apartment - Gail Jordan	1.50	3.50	5.00	E
nn Death Has a Will - Amelia Reynolds Long	2.00	4.00	6.00	M
nn Confessions of a Studio Model - Gladys Sloan	1.50	3.50	5.00	E
aka Studio Apartment				
nn Wayward Girl - Carlotta Baker	1.50	3.50	5.00	E
nn A Touch of Passion - John Saxon	1.50	3.50	5.00	E
nn Love for Sale - Charles S. Strong	1.50	3.50	5.00	E
nn The Sinful Sisters - Gladys Sloan	1.50	3.50	5.00	E
nn Pleasure After Hours - Florenz Branch	1.50	3.50	5.00	E
nn The Wife and the Wolf - Lee Jacquin	1.50	3.50	5.00	E
nn Excess Wife - Wright Williams	1.50	3.50	5.00	E
nn Professional Glamour Girl - Gail Jordan	1.50	3.50	5.00	E
nn Careless Caresses - Thomas Stone	1.50	3.50	5.00	E
nn Marriage Later - William Arthur	1.50	3.50	5.00	E
nn Made for Love - Gail Jordan	1.50	3.50	5.00	E
nn Tavern Girl - Glen Watkins	1.50	3.50	5.00	E
nn Small Town Virgin - Gail Jordan	1.50	3.50	5.00	E
nn A Talent for Love - Thomas Stone	1.50	3.50	5.00	E
nn Her Sacred Sin - H. A. Keller	1.50	3.50	5.00	E
nn Love at a Price - Robert Norcross	1.50	3.50	5.00	E
nn Torrid Love - Ralph Carter	1.50	3.50	5.00	E
aka Strictly a Wolf				

(KNICKERBOCKER, continued)

nn	Blonde Peril - Hall Bennett	1.50	3.50	5.00	E
nn	Studio Lovers - Lee Jacquin	1.50	3.50	5.00	E
nn	The Hard Boiled Blonde - Glen Watkins	1.50	3.50	5.00	E
nn	Immoral Woman - Charles S. Strong	1.50	3.50	5.00	E
nn	The Fallen Woman - Carlotta Baker	1.50	3.50	5.00	E
nn	Born to Sin - H. L. Gates	1.50	3.50	5.00	E
nn	The Wanton Blonde - Gail Jordan	1.50	3.50	5.00	E
	aka Blonde and Beautiful				
nn	Shameless Woman - Perry Lindsay	1.50	3.50	5.00	E
nn	Hotel Wife - Glen Watkins	1.50	3.50	5.00	E
nn	Her Day of Sin - H. A. Keller	1.50	3.50	5.00	E

LARCH

(Larch Publications)

1	Gag and Cartoon Book	1.50	3.50	5.00	
2	Joke and Cartoon Book	1.50	3.50	5.00	H
	1944				

LEISURE LIBRARY

(Leisure Library, Inc.)

Digest size

1	My Life is my Own - Jules-Jean Morac	3.00	6.00	12.00	E
2	Death for a Doll - Spike Morelli	3.00	6.00	12.00	E
3	Pick-Up Girl - Roland Vane	3.00	6.00	12.00	E
4	Make Mine a Shroud - Michael Storme	3.00	6.00	12.00	E
5	Hot Dames on Cold Slabs - Michael Storme	3.00	6.00	12.00	E
6	No Prude - Jules-Jean Morac	3.00	6.00	12.00	E
7	This Way for Hell - Spike Morelli	4.00	8.00	15.00	M
	1952, c-Heade				
8	White Slave Racket - Roland Vane	3.00	6.00	12.00	E
9	Two Smart Dames - Gene Ross	3.00	6.00	12.00	E
10	Midnight Sinner - Paul Renin	3.00	6.00	12.00	E
11	Curtains for Carla - Michael Storme	3.00	6.00	12.00	E
12	Bertrand and the Blondes - Jules Jean Morac	4.00	8.00	15.00	E
	1952, c-Heade				
13	Sorry for You, Beautiful - Gene Ross	4.00	8.00	15.00	E
	1952, c-Heade				
14	Wedding Night - Paul Renin	4.00	8.00	15.00	E
	1952, c-Heade				
15	Carmen was a Virgin - Michael Storme	3.00	6.00	12.00	E
16	Amorous Adventuress - Roland Vane	3.00	6.00	12.00	E
	1952, c-Heade				
17	Honey, Hold that Scream! - Tony Angelo	3.00	6.00	12.00	E
18	She Who Hesitates------------- - Paul Renin	3.00	6.00	12.00	E
19	A Corpse Spells Danger - Michael Storme	3.00	6.00	12.00	M
	1953				

Knickerbocker nn, c. Knic

Larch 2, c. Larch

Leisure Library 7, c. Leisure

Leisure Library 12, c. Leisure   Leisure Library 13, c. Leisure   Lion 10, c. Lion

(LEISURE LIBRARY, continued)

20 Pagan Interlude - Rosalind Brett	3.00	6.00	12.00	E
21 Curves Cause Trouble - Gene Ross 1953, c-Heade	3.00	6.00	12.00	E
22 Thou Shalt Not - Paul Renin	3.00	6.00	12.00	E
23 This Woman is Death - Michael Storme	3.00	6.00	12.00	E
24 White Man's Slave - Mary Clare	3.00	6.00	12.00	E

LEV GLEASON LIBRARY

(Lev Gleason Publications, Inc.)

Digest size

103 The Wench is Willing - Griffith James 1949	2.00	4.00	6.00	E

LION

(Lion Books, Inc.)

Also see Red Circle

8 Hungry Men - Edward Anderson 1949	5.00	10.00	20.00	
9 Anniversary - Ludwig Lewisohn	5.00	10.00	20.00	E
10 Canyon Hell - Peter Dawson aka High Country	5.00	10.00	20.00	W
11 The Blonde Body - Michael Morgan	5.00	10.00	20.00	M
14 The Lottery - Shirley Jackson	5.00	10.00	20.00	SF
15 Soft Shoulders - Peter Shelley	4.00	8.00	15.00	E
16 The Devil's Daughter - Peter Marsh	5.00	10.00	20.00	E
17 Dust of the Trail - Bennett Foster 1950	2.50	6.00	10.00	W
18 Christ in Concrete - Pietro di Donato	2.50	6.00	10.00	
19 He Ran all the Way - Sam Ross	3.00	6.00	12.00	M
20 Gambler's Gun Luck - Brett Austin	2.50	6.00	10.00	W
21 To Keep or Kill - Wilson Tucker	5.00	10.00	20.00	M
22 The French Touch - Jack Iams	2.50	6.00	10.00	
23 Baseball Stars of 1950 - Bruce Jacobs Orig., 1950	5.00	10.00	20.00	S
24 Twilight Men - Andre Tellier	2.50	6.00	10.00	
25 The Intimate Stranger - William Lynch 1950	2.50	6.00	10.00	E
26 The Outward Room - Millen Brand	2.50	6.00	10.00	
27 Dead Man's Gorge - E. B. Mann	2.50	6.00	10.00	W
28 Gun Devil! - W. Edmunds Claussen	2.50	6.00	10.00	W
29 Walk Hard - Talk Loud - Len Zinberg	2.50	6.00	10.00	
30 The Indiscreet Confessions of a Nice Girl - Anonymous	2.50	6.00	10.00	E
31 The Small Back Room - Nigel Balchin	2.50	6.00	10.00	E
32 Ceylon - Margaret Rebecca Lay	2.50	6.00	10.00	E

Lion 28, c. Lion

Lion 42, c. Lion

Lion 50, c. Lion

(LION, continued)

33 The Continental Touch - Josef Wechsberg	2.50	6.00	10.00	
34 Guns of Arizona - Charles N. Heckelmann	2.50	6.00	10.00	W
35 Man Tracks - Bennett Foster	2.50	6.00	10.00	W
36 The Road Through the Wall - Shirley Jackson	3.00	6.00	12.00	M
37 Guns on the Santa Fe - Peter Dawson	2.50	6.00	10.00	W
38 The Lustful Ape - Russell Graw	3.00	6.00	12.00	
39 Brain Guy - Benjamin Appel	2.50	6.00	10.00	M
40 All Thy Conquests - Alfred Hayes	2.50	6.00	10.00	
41 The Big Night - Stanley Ellin aka Dreadful Summit	2.50	6.00	10.00	E
42 Spring Riot - Jay Presson	2.50	6.00	10.00	E
43 Massacre - James Warner Bellah	2.50	6.00	10.00	W
44 His Dead Wife - Elizabeth Eastman	2.50	6.00	10.00	
45 Now Sleeps the Beast - Don Tracy	2.50	6.00	10.00	
46 A Slight Case of Scandal - Jack Iams aka Prematurely Gay	2.50	6.00	10.00	E
47 Trouble Follows Me - Kenneth Millar	2.50	6.00	10.00	M
48 The Dark Tunnel - Kenneth Millar	3.00	6.00	12.00	M
49 All Quiet on the Western Front - Erich Maria Remarque	3.00	6.00	12.00	C
50 Oregon Trunk - Dan J. Stevens	2.50	6.00	10.00	W
1951				
51 Tall, Dark and Dead - Kermit Jaediker	2.50	6.00	10.00	
52 No Letters for the Dead - Gale Wilhelm	3.00	6.00	12.00	E
53 Arena of Love - Helene Eliat	3.00	6.00	12.00	E
54 Joy Street - Clifton Cuthbert	2.50	6.00	10.00	
55 El Paso - W. Edmunds Claussen	2.50	6.00	10.00	W
56 The Glass Lady - Asa Bordages	2.50	6.00	10.00	E
57 Affair - Emily Hahn	2.50	6.00	10.00	
58 Art Colony - Clifton Cuthbert	2.50	6.00	10.00	E
59 Border Woman - Richard Carroll & Gregory Mason aka Mexican Gallop	2.50	6.00	10.00	W
60 Murders in Silk - Mike Teagle	2.50	6.00	10.00	M
61 Wolf Dog Range - Will Watson	2.50	6.00	10.00	W
62 Blondes are Skin Deep - Louis Trimble	2.50	6.00	10.00	M
63 Cage Me a Peacock - Noel Langley	2.50	6.00	10.00	E
64 The Savage - Mikhail Artzybasheff	2.50	6.00	10.00	E
65 Killers Five - William Hopson aka Sunset Ranch	2.50	6.00	10.00	W

Lion 53, c. Lion

Lion 70, c. Lion

Lion 71, c. Lion

Lion 82, c. Lion   Lion 116, c. Lion   Lion 125, c. Lion

(LION, continued)

66	The Ranch Cat - Wm Hopson aka Straight from Boot Hill	3.00	6.00	12.00	E
67	MacArthur - Man of Action - Frank Kelley & Cornelius Ryan	3.00	6.00	12.00	B
68	My Flesh is Sweet - Day Keene	2.50	6.00	10.00	E
69	The Cheat - Don Tracy aka Criss-Cross	2.50	6.00	10.00	E
70	We Too Are Drifting - Gale Wilhelm	3.00	6.00	12.00	E
71	America's Cities of Sin - Noah Sarlat	4.00	8.00	15.00	E
72	The Tigress - Jeff Bogar aka Payoff for Paula	2.50	6.00	10.00	E
73	Innocent Madame - Eleanore Browne 1952	2.50	6.00	10.00	E
74	Either is Love - Elisabeth Craigin	2.50	6.00	10.00	E
75	Die, Damn You! - Paul Durst	2.50	6.00	10.00	W
76	A Walk in the Sun - Harry Brown	2.50	6.00	10.00	C
77	The Lust of Private Cooper - James Gordon	2.50	6.00	10.00	E
78	Nevada Killing - Duke Montana aka Lynch Law in Perdition	2.50	6.00	10.00	W
79	My Gun, Her Body - Jeff Bogar Aka Dinah for Danger	2.50	6.00	10.00	E
80	Third Ward - Newark - Curtis Lucas	2.50	6.00	10.00	
81	The Lurking Man - Gerald Butler aka Mad with Much Heart	2.50	6.00	10.00	E
82	War in Korea - Marguerite Higgins	2.50	6.00	10.00	C
83	Bodies are Dust - P. J. Wolfson	2.50	6.00	10.00	
84	Earth Woman - Edwin J. Becker aka Coble Hill	2.50	6.00	10.00	E
85					
86					
87	You'll Get Yours - Thomas Wills	2.50	6.00	10.00	
88					
89	Route 28 - Ward Greene	2.50	6.00	10.00	E
90	Pistolman - Steve Frazee	2.50	6.00	10.00	W
91	So Low, So Lovely - Curtis Lucas	2.50	6.00	10.00	
92	South Sea Tales - Jack London	3.00	6.00	12.00	A
93	The Big Feeling - Daniel Karp Orig., 1952	2.50	6.00	10.00	E
94	Lona - John Evans aka If You Have Tears, c-Bergey	2.50	6.00	10.00	E
95	Hell's Kitchen - Benjamin Appel	2.50	6.00	10.00	M
96	Utah Hell Guns - Steve Frazee	2.50	6.00	10.00	W
97					
98	Prelude to a Certain Midnight - Gerald Kersh	3.00	6.00	12.00	
99	The Killer Inside Me - Jim Thompson Orig., 1952	2.50	6.00	10.00	
100	One is a Lonely Number - Bruce Elliot c-Bergey	2.50	6.00	10.00	E
101	Joy Street - Clifton Cuthbert	2.00	4.00	7.50	E
102	Bailey's Daughters - John DeMeyer	2.00	4.00	7.50	E
103	Eat Dog or Die! - C. William Harrison	2.50	6.00	10.00	W
104	Little Killer - Gene Paul Orig., 1952	2.50	6.00	10.00	
105	The Brotherhood of Velvet - David Karp	2.50	6.00	10.00	E
106	Sintown, U. S. A. - Noah Sarlat	4.00	8.00	15.00	E
107	Candidate - Voltaire	2.50	6.00	10.00	
108	Cropper's Cabin - Jim Thompson Orig., 1952	2.50	6.00	10.00	E

109	The Naked Storm - Simon Eisner (C. M. Kornbluth)	3.00	6.00	12.00	E
110	The Peddlers - Douglas Ring	2.50	6.00	10.00	
111	Company K - William March	2.50	6.00	10.00	C
112	The Man I Killed - Shel Walker	2.50	6.00	10.00	E
113	The Montana Vixen - Paul W. Fairman	2.50	6.00	10.00	W
	aka The Heiress of Copper Butte				
114	Luther - Roy Flannagan	3.00	6.00	12.00	E
115	Cora Potts - Ward Greene	2.50	6.00	10.00	E
116	Saskia - Claude Marais	3.00	6.00	12.00	E
117	Run the Wild River - D. L. Champion	2.50	6.00	10.00	
	1953				
118	The Haploids - Jerry Sohl	3.00	6.00	12.00	SF
119	Hardman - David Karp	2.50	6.00	10.00	
	Orig., 1953				
120	Recoil - Jim Thompson	2.50	6.00	10.00	
	Orig., 1953				
121	The Strange Path - Gale Wilhelm	3.00	6.00	12.00	E
122	Life and Death in Soviet Russia - El Campesino (Valentin Gonzalez & Julian Gorkin)	3.00	6.00	12.00	NF
123	Don't Dig Deeper - William Francis	2.50	6.00	10.00	E
124	The Burglar - David Goodis	2.50	6.00	10.00	M
	Orig., 1953				
125	Baseball Stars of 1953 - Bruce Jacobs	5.00	10.00	20.00	S
	Orig., 1953				
126	Mojave Guns - Roe Richmond	2.50	6.00	10.00	W
127	The Alcoholics - Jim Thompson	2.50	6.00	10.00	
128	His Great Journey - Manuel Komroff	2.00	4.00	7.50	
129	.44 - H. A. DeRosso	2.50	6.00	10.00	W
130	Sharp the Bugle Calls - Steve Frazee	2.50	6.00	10.00	W
	Orig., 1953				
131	Bourbon Street - G. H. Otis	2.50	6.00	10.00	M
	Orig., 1953				
132	Cry, Flesh - David Karp	2.50	6.00	10.00	
133	The Dark Chase - David Goodis	2.50	6.00	10.00	M
	aka Nightfall				
134	Colorado Creek - E. E. Hallerah	2.50	6.00	10.00	W
135	Half - Jordan Park (C. M. Kornbluth)	5.00	10.00	20.00	E
	Orig., 1953				
136	Fighting Man - Mark Morgan	2.50	6.00	10.00	
137	Someone Is Bleeding - Richard Matheson	4.00	8.00	15.00	M
	Orig., 1953				
138	Dark the Summer Dies - Walter Untermeyer, Jr.	2.50	6.00	10.00	E
	Orig., 1953				
139	Gunman's Grudge - George C. Appell	2.50	6.00	10.00	W
140	Cockpit - Warwick Scott	2.50	6.00	10.00	
141	Rooming House - Berton Roueche	2.50	6.00	10.00	E
	aka Black Weather				
142	"I Was There" - Ken Jones	2.50	6.00	10.00	NF
	Orig., 1953				
143	The Wild Bunch - Peter Dawson	2.50	6.00	10.00	W
144	A Tent on Corsica - Martin Quigley	2.50	6.00	10.00	
145	Malenkov - Robert Frazier	3.00	6.00	12.00	NF
	Orig., 1953				
146	Frankenstein - Mary Wollstonecraft Shelley	5.00	10.00	20.00	SF
147	The Wench and the Flame - Robert L. Trimnell	2.50	6.00	10.00	

Lion 128, c. Lion

Lion 135, c. Lion

Lion 145, c. Lion

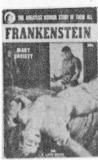

Lion 146, c. Lion   Lion 160, c. Lion   Lion 176, c. Lion

(LION, continued)

148	Doomsday - Warwick Scott	3.00	6.00	12.00	SF
	Orig., 1953			
149	Bad Boy - Jim Thompson	2.50	6.00	10.00	
150	Lawman's Feud - Steve Frazee	2.50	6.00	10.00	W
151	Slaughter Street - Louis Falstein	2.50	6.00	10.00	E
	Orig., 1953			
152	A Rage at Sea - Frederick Lorenz	2.50	6.00	10.00	E
	Orig., 1953			
153	Tough Guy - A. I. Bezzerides	2.50	6.00	10.00	
	aka Long Haul			
154	Naked in the Dark - Gene Paul	2.50	6.00	10.00	E
155	Savage Night - Jim Thompson	2.50	6.00	10.00	
156	Hero's Lust - Kermit Jaedicker	2.50	6.00	10.00	
157	The Lone Gunhawk - Frank Gruber	2.50	6.00	10.00	W
158	The Utah Kid - Roe Richmond	2.50	6.00	10.00	W
159	Sin People - George Milburn	2.50	6.00	10.00	E
	aka Oklahoma Town			
160	Sexual Practices of American Women - Christopher Gerould	5.00	10.00	20.00	NF
	Orig., 1953			
161	The Hoodlum - Eleazar Lipsky	2.50	6.00	10.00	
162	Angel - Curtis Lucas	2.50	6.00	10.00	
163	Gunsight - Frank Gruber	2.50	6.00	10.00	W
164	Platoon - Adam Singer	2.50	6.00	10.00	
165	The Big Lure - William Manners	2.50	6.00	10.00	
166	Dock Walloper - Benjamin Appel	2.50	6.00	10.00	M
167	Every Man's Bible - Manuel Komroff	5.00	10.00	20.00	
168	Killer's Crossing - Burt Arthur	2.50	6.00	10.00	W
169	The Gunslammer - Lee Floren	2.50	6.00	10.00	W
170	Sailor's Luck - Basil Heatter	2.50	6.00	10.00	
171	Hot Cargo - Gitt Otis	2.50	6.00	10.00	
172	Korea's Heroes - Bruce Jacobs	2.50	6.00	10.00	NF
173	The Dream and the Flesh - Vivian Connell	2.50	6.00	10.00	
	aka The Peacock is a Gentleman			
174	The Corrupters - William Francis	2.50	6.00	10.00	E
	Orig., 1953			
175	The Gun Trail - H. A. DeRosso	2.50	6.00	10.00	W
176	Valerie - Jordan Park (C. M. Kornbluth)	5.00	10.00	20.00	E
	c-Maguire			
177	Men and Women - William Kozlenko	2.50	6.00	10.00	
	Orig., 1953			
178	Bloody River - Paul Durst	2.50	6.00	10.00	W
179	Conjure Wife - Fritz Leiber	5.00	10.00	20.00	F
	c-Maguire			
180	Fury on Sunday - Richard Matheson	4.00	8.00	15.00	
181	The Oxbow Kill - C. William Harrison	2.50	6.00	10.00	
182	O'Mara - Laurence Greene	2.50	6.00	10.00	
183	Trouble on Crazyman - Sam Allison	2.50	6.00	10.00	W
184	The Criminal - Jim Thompson	2.50	6.00	10.00	M
	Orig., 1953			
185	The Kidnapper - Robert Bloch	3.00	6.00	12.00	
	1954			
186	The Blonde on the Street Corner - David Goodis	2.50	6.00	10.00	
187	The Dakota Deal - Riley Ryan	2.50	6.00	10.00	W
188	The Naked Year - Philip Atlee	2.50	6.00	10.00	E
	aka The Inheritors			

(LION, continued)

189	Two-Gun Texan - Burt Arthur	2.50	6.00	10.00	W
190	The Joy Wheel - Paul W. Fairman	2.50	6.00	10.00	
191	Strange Desires - J. Vernon Shea	2.50	6.00	10.00	
192	The Golden Gizmo - Jim Thompson	2.50	6.00	10.00	
193	Night Never Ends - Frederick Lorenz	2.50	6.00	10.00	
194	Baseball Stars of 1954 - Bruce Jacobs Orig., 1954	5.00	10.00	20.00	S
195	Apache Greed - William Hopson	2.50	6.00	10.00	W
196	A Dog's Head - Jean Dutourd	5.00	10.00	20.00	F
197	The Naked Night - Dan Brennan	2.50	6.00	10.00	
198	Sin Pit - Paul Meskil	2.50	6.00	10.00	
199	Ambush Hell - George C. Appell	2.50	6.00	10.00	W
200	The Long Thrill - Olga Rosmanith Orig., 1954	2.50	6.00	10.00	
201	Roughneck - Jim Thompson Orig., 1954	2.50	6.00	10.00	E
202	Hoboes and Harlots - George Milburn Orig., 1954	2.50	6.00	10.00	E
203	Whip Hand - Rod Patterson	2.50	6.00	10.00	W
204	Sleep with the Devil - Day Keene Orig., 1954	2.50	6.00	10.00	E
205	Human? - Judith Merril	4.00	8.00	15.00	SF
206	Alley Girl - Jonathan Craig Orig., 1954	2.50	6.00	10.00	M
207	Tiger Street - Elleston Treror	2.50	6.00	10.00	
208	Win - or else! - D. J. Michael Orig., 1954	2.50	6.00	10.00	S
209	A Way With Women - William Gwinn	2.50	6.00	10.00	
210	Joy, House - Day Keene	2.00	4.00	7.50	
211	Boss Man - Roy B. Sparkia	2.50	6.00	10.00	E
212	A Swell-Looking Babe - Jim Thompson	2.50	6.00	10.00	
213	Stag Gag - Sandy Nelkin & Pat Untermeyer	3.00	6.00	12.00	H
214	Fully Dressed and in His Right Mind - Michael Fessier	4.00	8.00	15.00	SF
215	Strange Sisters - Fletcher Flora	2.50	6.00	10.00	
216	Dormitory Women - R. V. Cassill	4.00	8.00	15.00	E
217	The Gunthrowers - Steve Frazee	2.50	6.00	10.00	W
218	A Hell of a Woman - Jim Thompson Orig., 1954	2.50	6.00	10.00	
219	Wharf Girl - William Manners	2.50	6.00	10.00	
220	Me 'an You - Jay Thomas Caldwell	2.50	6.00	10.00	
221	The Naked and the Lost - Franklin M. Davis, Jr.	2.50	6.00	10.00	
222	Evil Roots - Walter Untermeyer, Jr. Orig., 1954	2.50	6.00	10.00	E
223	The Savage Chase - Frederick Lorenz Orig., 1954	2.50	6.00	10.00	
224	Black Friday - David Goodis Orig., 1954	2.50	6.00	10.00	M
225	Jazz Bum - William Gwinn	2.50	6.00	10.00	
226	Tina - Robert Bruce	2.00	4.00	7.50	E
227	Sinner's Game - Linton Baldwin	2.00	4.00	7.50	E
228	Act of Violence - Basil Heatter	2.50	6.00	10.00	
229	Champs and Bums - Bucklin Moon	2.00	4.00	7.50	
230	False Night - Algis Budrys	4.00	8.00	15.00	SF
231	House of Evil - Clayre Lipman & Michel Lipman	2.50	6.00	10.00	E

Lion 192, c. Lion

Lion 196, c. Lion

Lion 216, c. Lion

266

Lion 233, c. Lion   Lion Library 1, c. Lion   Lion Library 6, c. Lion

(LION, continued)

232	Room for a Stranger - Constantine Fitzgibbon 1955	2.00	4.00	7.50
233	The Deluge - Leonardo da Vinci (ed. Robert Payne)	4.00	8.00	15.00	SF

LION LIBRARY/LION BOOK

(Lion Books, Inc.)

LL 1	Number One - John Dos Passos 1954	2.00	4.00	7.50	
LL 2	A Woman's Life - Guy de Maupassant	2.00	4.00	7.50	
LL 3	The Sky Block - Steve Frazee	2.50	6.00	10.00	SF
LL 4	The Flesh Baron - P. J. Wolfson aka Is My Flesh of Brass	2.50	6.00	10.00	
LL 5	The Sin and the Flesh - Lloyd S. Thompson	2.00	4.00	7.50	
LL 6	The Damned - Daniel Talbot	2.50	6.00	10.00	
LL 7	The Green Millenium - Fritz Leiber	2.50	6.00	10.00	SF
LL 8	Gods and Demons - Manuel Komroff	2.50	6.00	10.00	
LL 9	Passage to Violence - Stetson Kennedy Orig., 1954	2.00	4.00	7.50	
LL10	Escape to Nowhere - David Karp 1955	2.50	6.00	10.00	SF
LL11	Dark Plunder - Victor Rosen	2.00	4.00	7.50	E
LL12	Baseball Stars of 1955 - Bruce Jacobs Orig., 1955	4.00	8.00	15.00	S
LL13	Hell's Pavement - Damon Knight	2.50	6.00	10.00	SF
LL14	Lila - Curtis Lucas Orig., 1955	2.00	4.00	7.50	E
LL15	The Unleashed Will - Christopher Clark	2.00	4.00	7.50	E
LL16	The Passionate Season - Victor Wolfson	2.00	4.00	7.50	
LL17	The Best Cartoons from France - Edna Bennett	2.50	6.00	10.00	H
LL18	The Lost Men - Benedict Thielen	2.00	4.00	7.50	
LL19	The Hills Beyond - Thomas Wolfe	2.00	4.00	7.50	
LL20	Net of Outrage - William Derby	2.00	4.00	7.50	
LL21	How I Made a Million - Noah Sarlat	2.00	4.00	7.50	

Lion Library 8, c. Lion   Lion Library 12, c. Lion   Lion Library 153, c. Lion

LL22 The Wild Place - Bogart Carlaw	2.00	4.00	7.50	
LL23 How Like a God - Rex Stout	2.00	4.00	7.50	M
LL24 For Stags Only - Sandy Nelkin & Pat Untermeyer, Jr.	2.50	6.00	10.00	H
LL25 Galaxy of Ghouls - Judith Merril	3.00	6.00	12.00	SF
LL26 The Stork Didn't Bring You - Louis Pemberton	2.50	6.00	10.00	NF
LL27 A Mask of Guilt - Sigrid de Lima	2.00	4.00	7.50	
LL28 Don't You Weep, Don't You Moan - Richard Coleman	2.00	4.00	7.50	
LL29 Curve Ball Laughs - Herman L. Masin Orig., 1955	2.00	4.00	7.50	SH
LL30 Great Tales of the Deep South -	2.00	4.00	7.50	
LL31 Nineteen Stories - Graham Green	2.00	4.00	7.50	
LL32 Whipsaw - Wm MacLeod Raine	2.00	4.00	7.50	W
LL33 The Storm and the Silence - David Walker	2.00	4.00	7.50	
LL34 The Tunnel of Love - Peter DeVries	2.00	4.00	7.50	
LL35 The Fall of Valor - Charles Jackson	2.00	4.00	7.50	
LL36 Oregon Trunk - Dan J. Stevens	2.00	4.00	7.50	
LL37 Fruit of Desire - Willa Gibbs	2.00	4.00	7.50	
LL38 Cartoons the French Way - Rene Goscinny	2.50	6.00	10.00	H
LL39 Parent's Magazine Book of Baby Care - Eleanor S. Duncan	2.50	6.00	10.00	NF
LL40 Trouble Follows Me - Kenneth Millar	2.00	4.00	7.50	E
LL41 Collision - James Gordon	2.00	4.00	7.50	
LL42 Adventures of a Young Man - John Dos Passos	2.00	4.00	7.50	
LL43 The Kid from Dodge City - Bennett Foster	2.00	4.00	7.50	W
LL44 Desperate Asylum - Fletcher Flora	2.00	4.00	7.50	
LL45 The Night Before Dying - Robert M. Coates	2.00	4.00	7.50	
LL46 The Flesh Painter - Ad Gordon Orig., 1955, c-Gauguin	3.00	6.00	12.00	B
LL47 Strange Barriers - J. Vernon Shea	2.00	4.00	7.50	
LL48 The Naked and the Guilty - Ralph Ingersoll	2.00	4.00	7.50	
LL49 The Outward Room - Miller Brand	2.00	4.00	7.50	
LL50 Roberta Cowell's Story - Roberta Cowell	2.00	4.00	7.50	
LL51 Hungry Men - Edward Anderson	2.00	4.00	7.50	
LL52 I Die Slowly - Kenneth Millar	2.00	4.00	7.50	
LL53 Great Tales of City Dwellers - Alex Austin c-Maguire	2.00	4.00	7.50	
LL54 The Wild Breed - Frank Bonham	2.00	4.00	7.50	
LL55 Cora Potts - Ward Green	2.00	4.00	7.50	
LL56 Love - William Saroyan	2.00	4.00	7.50	
LL57 Ramrod - George C. Appell	2.00	4.00	7.50	W
LL58 The Saturday Evening Post Cartoons - John Bailey	2.50	6.00	10.00	H
LL59 He Ran All the Way - Sam Ross	2.00	4.00	7.50	
LL60 The Sins of Joy Monson - Ludwig Lewisohn	2.00	4.00	7.50	
LB61 Leashed Guns - Peter Dawson	2.00	4.00	7.50	W
LB62 Company K - William March	2.00	4.00	7.50	
LL63 A Party Everynight - Frederick Lorenz 1956	2.00	4.00	7.50	
LL64 Kill the Beloved - Lane Kauffmann	2.00	4.00	7.50	
LL65 Two Thieves - Manuel Komroff	2.00	4.00	7.50	
LL66 The Naked Year - Philip Atlee	2.00	4.00	7.50	
LL67 Pius XII: Eugenio Pacelli, Pope of Peace - Oscar Haleck & James F. Murray. Jr.	2.50	6.00	10.00	B
LL68 All Thy Conquests - Alfred Hayes	2.00	4.00	7.50	
LB69 Utah Hell Guns - Steve Frazee	2.00	4.00	7.50	W
LB70 Fighting Man - Mark Morgan	2.00	4.00	7.50	E
LL71 Cage Me a Peacock - Noel Langley	2.00	4.00	7.50	
LL72 Gunman's Land	2.00	4.00	7.50	W
LL73 A Handful of Hell - Noah Sarlat	2.00	4.00	7.50	
LL74 Baseball Stars of 1956 - Bruce Jacobs Orig., 1956	2.00	4.00	7.50	S
LL75 Joy Street - Clifton Cuthbert	2.00	4.00	6.00	E
LL76 The Heart in Exile - Rodney Garland	2.00	4.00	7.50	
LB77 Tough Kid - William Attaway aka Let Me Breathe Thunder	2.00	4.00	7.50	E
LB78 Pistolman - Steve Frazee	2.00	4.00	7.50	W
LL79 Slade - Ad Gordon	2.00	4.00	7.50	
LL80 Art Buchwald's Paris - Art Buchwald	2.00	4.00	7.50	
LL81 All Quiet on the Western Front - Erich Maria Remarque	2.00	4.00	7.50	C

LL82 Julie - George Milburn	2.00	4.00	7.50	
LL83 Rogues and Lovers - Noah Sarlat	2.00	4.00	7.50	E
LL84 To Keep or Kill - Wilson Tucker c-Maguire	2.50	6.00	10.00	M
LB85 Two-Gun Texan - Burt Arthur	2.00	4.00	7.50	W
LL86 The Girl on Crown Street - David Karp	2.00	4.00	7.50	
LB87 The Brass Bed - Fletcher Flora	2.00	4.00	7.50	
LL88 Great Tales of the Far West - Alex Austin	2.00	4.00	7.50	
LL89 The Gunslingers - Harry Widmer	2.00	4.00	7.50	W
LL90 Around the World in 80 Days - Jules Verne	2.00	4.00	7.50	A
LL91 A Knife is Silent - David Keaf	2.00	4.00	7.50	M
LB92 Lonely Boy Blues - Allan Kapelner	2.00	4.00	7.50	
LB93 Gunsight - Frank Grober	2.00	4.00	7.50	W
LB94 Luther - Roy Flannagan	2.00	4.00	7.50	
LL95 Stories for Stags - Eddie Davis	2.50	6.00	10.00	H
LL96 Kiss Her Goodbye - Wade Miller	2.00	4.00	7.50	M
LL97 Sorority House - Jordan Park (C. M. Kornbluth & Frederick Pohl)	2.50	6.00	10.00	E
LL98 Art Colony - Clifton Cuthbert	2.00	4.00	7.50	E
LB99 French and Frisky - Rene Goscinny	2.50	6.00	10.00	H
LB100 Gun Hell - Riley Ryan	2.00	4.00	7.50	W
LB101 The Utah Kid - Roe Richmond aka Gonestoga Cowboy	2.00	4.00	7.50	W
LL102 The Oracle - Edwin O'Connor	2.00	4.00	7.50	
LL103 Sports Laughs - Herman Le Masin Orig., 1956, c-Powers	2.00	4.00	7.50	SH
LL104 Ruby - Frederick Lorenz	2.00	4.00	7.50	
LL105 Bedtime Laughs - Paul Steiner	2.00	4.00	7.50	H
LL106 House of Dolls - Ka-tzetnik 135633	2.50	6.00	10.00	NF
LB107 Candide - Voltaire	2.00	4.00	7.50	
LB108 Lawman's Feud - Steve Frazee	2.00	4.00	7.50	W
LB109 Platoon - Adam Singer	2.00	4.00	7.50	
LL110 His Great Journey - Manuel Komroff	2.00	4.00	7.50	
LL111 Wives and Lovers - Alex Austin	2.00	4.00	7.50	
LL112 The Dream and the Flesh - Vivian Connell	2.00	4.00	7.50	
LL113 World so Wide - Sinclair Lewis	2.00	4.00	7.50	
LL114 Quintet - W. Somerset Maughm	2.00	4.00	7.50	
LB115 Paula - Gale Wilhelm aka No Letters for the Dead	2.00	4.00	7.50	
LB116 Alley Kids - Benjamin Appel aka Hells Kitchen	2.00	4.00	7.50	E
LB117 The Lone Gunhawk - Frank Gruber aka Smoky Road	2.00	4.00	7.50	W
LL118 The Cheat - Don Tracy	2.00	4.00	7.50	
LL119 College Humor - Sandy Nelkin	2.00	4.00	7.50	H
LL120 My Old Man - Richard B. Erno	2.00	4.00	7.50	
LL121 Desire and Damnation aka Come in at the Door	2.00	4.00	7.50	
LB122 Either is Love - Elisabeth Craigin	2.00	4.00	7.50	
LB123 The Oxbow Kill - C. William Harrison	2.00	4.00	7.50	
LB124 Recoil - Jim Thompson c-Maguire	2.00	4.00	7.50	
LL125 The Naked Storm - Simon Eisner (C. M. Kornbluth)	2.50	6.00	10.00	
LL126 Gil Paust's Gun Book - Gil Paust	2.50	6.00	10.00	NF
LL127 Combat! - Noah Sarlat	2.00	4.00	7.50	C
LL128 The Troubled Midnight - Rodney Garland	2.00	4.00	7.50	
LB129 You'll Get Yours - Thomas Wills	2.00	4.00	7.50	
LB130 The Hardboiled Lineup - Harry Widmer	2.50	6.00	10.00	
LB131 Nightfall - David Goodis aka The Dark Chase	2.00	4.00	7.50	M
LB132 Logan - Evan Hall aka Colorado Creek	2.00	4.00	7.50	
LL133 Rooming House - Berton Roueche	2.00	4.00	7.50	
LL134 Raft of Despair - Ensio Tiira	2.00	4.00	7.50	A
LL135 The Big Rape - James Wakefield Burke	2.00	4.00	7.50	
LL136 Leave Her to Heaven - Ben Ames Williams	2.00	4.00	7.50	
LB137 Killer's Game - Edward Hudiburg	2.00	4.00	7.50	
LB138 A Hell of a Woman - Jim Thompson	2.00	4.00	7.50	
LB139 Bloody River - Paul Durst	2.00	4.00	7.50	W
LL140 Bachelor's Anonymous - Vivian Connell	2.00	4.00	7.50	
LL141 Women without Men - Alex Austin	2.00	4.00	7.50	
LL142 The Kill-Off - Jim Thompson	2.00	4.00	7.50	
LL143 Thread of Evil - Charles Jackson	2.00	4.00	7.50	
LB144 Hot - Frederick Lorenz	2.00	4.00	7.50	
LB145 .44 - H. A. DeRosso	2.00	4.00	7.50	W

LL146					
LB147	The Naked Night - Dan Brenman 1957	2.00	4.00	7.50	
LL148	The Bedside Corpse - Stuart Friedman aka The Gray Eyes	2.00	4.00	7.50	M
LL149	A Killer Among Us - Ben Ames Williams	2.00	4.00	7.50	M
LL150	Baseball Stars of 1957 - Bruce Jacobs Orig., 1957	2.50	6.00	10.00	S
LL151	Brain Guy - Benjamin Appel	2.00	4.00	7.50	
LB152	Dolls are Murder - Harold Q. Masor	2.00	4.00	7.50	M
LB153	Valerie - Jordan Park (C. M. Kornbluth)	2.00	4.00	7.50	E
LB154	The Man from Texas - H. A. DeRosso aka The Gun Trail	2.00	4.00	7.50	W
LB155	The Gun-Hung Men - Leslie Ernenwein aka Rio Renegade	2.00	4.00	7.50	W
LB156	Hangtree Range - William Hopson	2.00	4.00	7.50	W
LB157	Wyoming War - Sam Allison aka Trouble on Crazyman	2.00	4.00	7.50	W
LL158	The Big Make - Gene Paul c-Maguire	2.00	4.00	7.50	
LL159					
LL160	Hoboes and Harlots - George Milburn	2.00	4.00	7.50	
LL161	Gunman's Grudge - George C. Appell	2.00	4.00	7.50	W
LL162					
LB163	LaSignora - Elio Bartolini	2.00	4.00	7.50	E
LB164	Whip Hard - Rod Patterson	2.00	4.00	7.50	W
LB165	A Rage at Sea - Frederick Lorenz c-Maguire	2.00	4.00	7.50	
LL166					
LL167	This is It! - Noah Sarlat c-Maguire	2.00	4.00	7.50	
LL168	The Bedside Bachelor - Paul Steiner	2.00	4.00	7.50	H
LL169					
LL170	The Red Lily - Anatole France	2.00	4.00	7.50	
LB171	The Sleeper - Holly Roth	2.00	4.00	7.50	
LB172	Slaughter Street - Louis Falstein c-Maguire	2.00	4.00	7.50	
LB173	The Gunthrowers - Steve Frazee	2.00	4.00	7.50	W
LL174	The Seventh Trumpet - Peter Julian	2.00	4.00	7.50	
LL175	Five Who Vanished - Robert Levin	2.00	4.00	7.50	

LOVE ROMANCE SERIES

(Palace Promotions)

Digest size

12	Love Above All - Eliot Brewster c-Cole Note: Although no. 12 is on the spine, no. 3 is on the cover.	2.00	4.00	7.50	R

LUCOM

(David Lucom, Publishers)

Digest size

nn	The Case of the Walking Corpse - Armstrong Livingston 1945	1.50	3.00	5.00	M

MAGABOOKS

(Galaxy Publishing Corp.)

Digest size

1	Radge of Infamy				SF
	The Sky is Falling - Lester del Rey	2.00	4.00	6.00	SF

Magazine Village 6, c. Mag   Manhattan nn, c. Manhattan   Mentor Books M39, c. NA

(MAGABOOKS, continued)

2 After Worlds End				SF
The Legion of Time - Jack Williamson	2.00	4.00	6.00	SF
3 Baby is Three				SF
...And My Fear is Great - Theodore Sturgeon	2.00	4.00	6.00	SF

MAGAZINE VILLAGE

(Magazine Village, Inc.)

Digest size

5 Confessions of a Park Avenue Playgirl - Carl Sturdy	1.50	3.50	5.00	E
aka Society Doctor				
6 Illicit Honeymoon - Lois Bull	2.00	4.00	6.00	E
1948, aka Seven Make a Honeymoon				
7 Hard Boiled Mistress - Lois Bull	1.50	3.50	5.00	E
1948, aka Mating Woman				
Note: Cover gives E. T. Keating as author.				

MANHATTAN

(Manhattan Fiction Publishing)

Digest size

nn Harem Nights - B. J. Vaswani	1.50	3.00	5.00	E
1947				

MENTOR BOOKS

(New American Library)

M26 American Essays - Charles B. Shaw	.75	1.75	3.00	
1948				
M27 Biography of the Earth - George Gamow	.75	1.75	3.00	NF
M28 Science and the Modern World - Alfred North Whitehead	.75	1.75	3.00	NF
M29 The Autobiography of an Ex-Coloured Man - James Weldon Johnson	1.50	3.50	5.00	
M30 America in Perspective - Henry Steele Commager	.75	1.75	3.00	
M31 Man in the Modern World - Julian Husley	.75	1.75	3.00	
M32 The Greek Way to Western Civilization - Edith Hamilton	.75	1.75	3.00	NF
M33 Indians of the Americas - John Collier	.75	1.75	3.00	NF
M34 The Law and You - Max Radin	.75	1.75	3.00	NF
M35 The Limitations of Science - J. W. N. Sullivan	.75	1.75	3.00	NF
1949				

M36	How to Know the Birds - Roger Tory Peterson	1.50	3.50	5.00	NF
M37	Russia - Bernard Pares	.75	1.75	3.00	NF
M38	The Age of Jackson - Arthur M. Schlesinger, Jr.	.75	1.75	3.00	NF
M39	Life on Other Worlds - H. Spencer Jones	1.50	3.50	5.00	
M40	Arts and the Man - Irwin Edman	.75	1.75	3.00	NF
M41	The Aims of Education - Alfred North Whitehead	.75	1.75	3.00	NF
M42	Ballet - George Amberg	.75	1.75	3.00	NF
M43	Science and the Moral Life - Max Otto	.75	1.75	3.00	NF
M44	The Coming of Age in Samoa - Margaret Mead	.75	1.75	3.00	NF
M45	Beethoven - J. W. N. Sullivan	.75	1.75	3.00	B
M46	The Iliad - Homerus 1950	.75	1.75	3.00	
M47	Music for the Millions - David Ewen	.75	1.75	3.00	NF
M48	How to Know the Wild Flowers - Alfred Stefferud	.75	1.75	3.00	NF
M49	The Revolt of the Masses - Jose Ortega y Gasset	.75	1.75	3.00	
M50	The Next Development in Man - Lancelot Law White 1950	.75	1.75	3.00	
M51	The Oregon Trail - Francis Parkman	.75	1.75	3.00	W
M52	New Handbook of the Heavens - Hubert J. Bernhard	.75	1.75	3.00	NF
M53	Reconstruction in Philosophy - John Dewey	.75	1.75	3.00	NF
M54	100 Modern Poems - Selden Rodman	.75	1.75	3.00	
M55	Life Stories of Men Who Shaped History - Plutarchus	.75	1.75	3.00	B
M56	Sex and Temperament in Three Primitive Societies - Margaret Mead	.75	1.75	3.00	NF
M57	Lenia - David Shub	.75	1.75	3.00	B
M58	Introduction to Economic Science - George Soule 1951	.75	1.75	3.00	NF
M59	The Democratic Way of Life - Eduard C. Lindeman & T. V. Smith	.75	1.75	3.00	NF
M60	The Summing Up - W. Somerset Maugham	.75	1.75	3.00	
M61	A Gallery of Americans - Frank Luther Mott	.75	1.75	3.00	B
M62	How to Know American Antiques - Alice Winchester	.75	1.75	3.00	NF
M63	How to Know the American Mammals - Ivan T. Sanderson	.75	1.75	3.00	NF
M64	Man Makes Himself - V. Gordon Childe	.75	1.75	3.00	
M65	The World of Copernicus - Angus Armitage	.75	1.75	3.00	NF
M66	The Meaning of Evolution - George Gaylord Simpson	.75	1.75	3.00	NF
M67	Psychopathology in Everyday Life - Sigmund Freud	.75	1.75	3.00	NF
M68	On Understanding Science - James B. Conant	.75	1.75	3.00	NF
M69	The Prince - Niccolo Machiavelli 1952	.75	1.75	3.00	
M70	Jefferson - Saul K. Padover	.75	1.75	3.00	B
M71	The Universe and Dr. Einstein - Lincoln Barnett	.75	1.75	3.00	NF
M72	Greek Historical Thought - Arnold J. Toynbee	.75	1.75	3.00	NF
Ms73	New World Writing No. 1	.75	1.75	3.00	
M74	Heredity, Race and Scoiety - Th. Dobzhansky & L. C. Dunn	.75	1.75	3.00	NF
M75	A World Apart - Gustaw Herling 1952	.75	1.75	3.00	
M76	Good Reading	.50	1.25	2.00	
M77	The Birth and Death of the Sun - George Gamow	.75	1.75	3.00	NF
M78	A Documentary History of the United States - Richard D. Heffner	.75	1.75	3.00	NF
Ms79	New World Writing No. 2	.75	1.75	3.00	
M80	American Diplomacy: 1900 - 1950 - George F. Kennan	.75	1.75	3.00	NF
M81	What to Listen for in Music - Aaron Copland 1953	.75	1.75	3.00	NF
M82	The Wonderful World of Books - Alfred Stefferud	.75	1.75	3.00	NF
M83	Out of My Life and Thought - Albert Schweitzer & Everett Skillings	.75	1.75	3.00	NF

M84	How to Know and Predict the Weather - Robert Moore Fisher	.75	1.75	3.00	NF
Ms85	New World Writing No. 3	.75	1.75	3.00	
Ms86	Mythology - Edith Hamilton	.75	1.75	3.00	
M87	Walden and Civil Disobedience - Henry David Thoreau	.75	1.75	3.00	
M88	A History of the World in 240 Pages - Rene Sedillot	.75	1.75	3.00	NF
M89	Patterns of Culture - Ruth Benedict	.75	1.75	3.00	NF
Ms90	The Golden Treasury - F. T. Palgrave & Oscar Williams	.75	1.75	3.00	
M91	Growing up in New Guinea - Margaret Mead	.75	1.75	3.00	NF
M92	The Odyssey - Homerus	.75	1.75	3.00	
M93	The Theory of the Leisure Class	.75	1.75	3.00	NF
Ms94	The Meaning of the Glorious Koran - Mohammed Marmaduke Pickthall	.75	1.75	3.00	
M95	The Living U. S. Constitution - Saul K. Padover	.75	1.75	3.00	NF
Ms96	New World Writing No. 4	.75	1.75	3.00	
Ms97	One Two Three...Infinity - George Gamow	.50	1.25	2.00	
M98	The Shaping of the Modern Mind - Crane Brinton	.50	1.25	2.00	NF
M99	Greek Civilization and Character - Arnold J. Toynbee	.75	1.75	3.00	NF
M100	The Sea Around Us - Rachel L. Carson	.75	1.75	3.00	NF
	1954				
MD101	Philosophy in a New Key - Susanne K. Langer	.75	1.75	3.00	NF
M102	Basic Selections from Emerson - Ralph Waldo Emerson	.75	1.75	3.00	
M103	The Song of God: Bhagavad-gita	.75	1.75	3.00	
M104	Highlights of Modern Literature - Francis Brown	.75	1.75	3.00	
M105	The Life of the Spider - John Crompton	.75	1.75	3.00	NF
Ms106	New World Writing No. 5	.50	1.25	2.00	
M107	Ethics in a Business Society - Douglass Cater & Marquis W. Childs	.50	1.25	2.00	
Ms108	An Analysis of the Kinsey Reports on Sexual Behavior in the Human Male and Female - Donald Porter Geddes	.75	1.75	3.00	NF
M109	The World of History - Courtlands Canby & Nancy E. Gross	.50	1.25	2.00	
Ms110	The Iliad - Homerus	.75	1.75	3.00	
M111	The Life of the Bee - Maurice Maeterlinck	.75	1.75	3.00	NF
Ms112	The Uses of the Past - Herbert J. Muller	.50	1.25	2.00	
Ms113	The Inferno - Dante Alighieri	.75	1.75	3.00	
Ms114	New Handbook of the Heavens - Hubert J. Bernhard & Others	.75	1.75	3.00	NF
M115	Men, Wages and Employment in the Modern U. S. Economy - George Soule	.50	1.25	2.00	
Ms116	The Holy Bible in Brief - James Reeves	.75	1.75	3.00	NF
Ms117	Leaves of Grass - Walt Whitman	.75	1.75	3.00	
Ms118	New World Writing No. 6	.50	1.25	2.00	
Ms119	Psychology of Sex - Havelock Ellis	.50	1.25	2.00	NF
Ms120	The Birth and Death of the Sun - George Gamow	.75	1.75	3.00	NF
Ms121	The Dynamics of Soviet Society - W. W. Rostow	.50	1.25	2.00	NF
MD122	Good Listening - R. D. Darrell	.50	1.25	2.00	NF
Ms123	Ballet in America - George Amberg	.75	1.75	3.00	NF
Ms124	Good Reading	.50	1.25	2.00	
M125	The Nature of the Universe - Fred Hoyle	.75	1.75	3.00	NF
	1955				
Ms126	The Age of Belief - Anne Fremantle	.75	1.75	3.00	NF
MD127	Here I Stand - Roland H. Bainton	.50	1.25	2.00	
M128	Under the Sea Wind - Rachel L. Carson	.75	1.75	3.00	NF
M129	The Way of Life - Lao-Tzu	.75	1.75	3.00	
MD130	New World Writing No. 7	.50	1.25	2.00	
MD131	The Teachings of the Compassionate Buddha - Edwin A. Burtt	.75	1.75	3.00	
MD132	The Creative Process - Brewster Ghiselin	.50	1.25	2.00	
MD133	Sex and Temperament in Three Primitive Societies - Margaret Mead	.50	1.25	2.00	NF
MD134	Cultural Patters and Technical Change - Margaret Mead	.75	1.75	3.00	NF
M135	The Law and You - Max Radin	.75	1.75	3.00	NF

M136	Mohammedanism - H. A. R. Gibb	.75	1.75	3.00	NF
MD137	American Essays - Charles B. Shaw	.75	1.75	3.00	
MD138	Biography of the Earth - George Gamow	.75	1.75	3.00	NF
MD139	Science and the Moral Life - Max Otto	.50	1.25	2.00	NF
MD140	Lenin - David Shub	.75	1.75	3.00	B
MD141	Adventures of Ideas - Alfred North Whitehead	.50	1.25	2.00	
MD142	The Age of Analysis - Morton White	.75	1.75	3.00	NF
M143	Ideas of the Great Economists - George Soule	.75	1.75	3.00	NF
MD144	Life on Other Worlds - H. Spencer Jones	.75	1.75	3.00	
MD145	The Age of Jackson - Arthur M. Schlesinger, Jr.	.75	1.75	3.00	NF
MD146	New World Writing No. 8	.50	1.25	2.00	
M147	A Primer of Freudian Psychology - Calvin S. Hall	.75	1.75	3.00	NF
MD148	Man in the Modern World - Julian Huxley	.50	1.25	2.00	
MD149	The Oregon Trail - Francis Parkman	.75	1.75	3.00	W
MD150	Male and Female - Margaret Mead 1955	.75	1.75	3.00	
M151	The Sayings of Confucius - Confucius	.75	1.75	3.00	
MD152	The Aims of Education - Alfred North Whitehead	.50	1.25	2.00	NF
MD153	The Coming of Age in Samoa - Margaret Mead	.75	1.75	3.00	NF
MD154	Man Makes Himself - V. Gordon Childe	.50	1.25	2.00	
M155	Scheherezade: Tales from the 1001 Nights	1.50	3.50	5.00	
M156	Company Manners - Louis Kronenberger	.50	1.25	2.00	
MD157	The Wonderful World of Books - Alfred Stefferud	.75	1.75	3.00	NF
MD158	The Age of Reason - Stuart Hampshire	.75	1.75	3.00	NF
M159	The Painter's Eye - Maurice Grosser	.75	1.75	3.00	NF
MD160	Jefferson - Saul K. Padover	.75	1.75	3.00	B
MD161	Democracy in America - Alexis de Tocqueville	.75	1.75	3.00	NF
MD162	Science and the Modern World - Alfred North Whitehead	.75	1.75	3.00	NF
MD163	Religion and the Rise of Capitalism - R. H. Tawney	.50	1.25	2.00	NF
MD164	Greek Historical Thought - Arnold J. Toynbee	.75	1.75	3.00	NF
MD165	Human Destiny - Pierre Lecomte du Nouy	.50	1.25	2.00	
MD166	Life Stories of Men Who Shaped History - Plutarchus	.75	1.75	3.00	B
MD167	Great Dialogues of Plato	.75	1.75	3.00	
M168	Books that Changed the World - Robert B. Downs	.50	1.25	2.00	
MD169	America in Perspective - Henry Steele Commager	.50	1.25	2.00	
MD170	New World Writing No. 9	.50	1.25	2.00	
MD171	Indians of the Americas - John Collier	.75	1.75	3.00	NF
MD172	The Age of Enlightenment - Isaiah Berlin	.75	1.75	3.00	NF
MD173	The Shaping of the Modern Mind - Crane Brinton	.50	1.25	2.00	
M174	The Public Philosophy - Walter Lippmann	.50	1.25	2.00	
MD175	American Skyline - Henry Hope Reed & Christopher Tunnard	.50	1.25	2.00	
MD176	Walden and Civil Disobedience - Henry David Thoreau	.75	1.75	3.00	
MD177	The Papal Encyclicals in Their Historical Context - Anne Fremantle	.75	1.75	3.00	NF
MD178	Good Reading	.50	1.25	2.00	
MD179	The Reader's Companion to World Literature - Lillian Herlands Hornstein	.50	1.25	2.00	
MD180	Dialogues of Alfred North Whitehead	.50	1.25	2.00	
M181	Christopher Columbus, Mariner - Samuel Eliot Morison	.75	1.75	3.00	B
MD182	Russia and America: Dangers and Prospects - Henry L. Roberts	.50	1.25	2.00	
MD183	New World Writing No. 10	.50	1.25	2.00	
MD184	The Age of Adventure - Giorgio deSantillana	.75	1.75	3.00	NF
MD185	The Age of Ideaology - Henry O. Aiken	.75	1.75	3.00	NF
MD186	100 American Poems - Selden Rodman	.75	1.75	3.00	
MD187	100 Modern Poems - Selden Rodman	.75	1.75	3.00	
MD188	The Cycle of American Literature -				

	Robert E. Spiller	.50	1.25	2.00	
	1957				
MD189	The Mentor Book of Religious Verse - Horace Gregory & Marya Zaturenska	.75	1.75	3.00	
MD190	The Nature of the Non-Western World - Vera Micheles Dean	.50	1.25	2.00	NF
MD191	On Life and Sex - Havelock Ellis	.50	1.25	2.00	NF
MD192	Realm of the Incas - Victor W. Von Hagen	.75	1.75	3.00	NF
MD193	Of the Imitation of Christ - Thomas a Kempis	.50	1.25	2.00	NF
M 194	The Upanishads	.75	1.75	3.00	
MD195	Eight Great Tragedies - Sylvan Barnet & Others	.50	1.25	2.00	
MD196	New World Writing No. 11	.50	1.25	2.00	
MD197	The Anvil of Civilization - Leonrad Cottrell	.75	1.75	3.00	NF
M 198	The Hedgehog and the Fox - Isaiah Berlin	.50	1.25	2.00	
MD199	The Living Talmud: the Wisdom of the Fathers	.75	1.75	3.00	
MD200	The Frontiers of Astronomy - Fred Hoyle	.75	1.75	3.00	NF
MD201	The Silver Treasury of Light Verse - Oscar Williams	.75	1.75	3.00	
MD202	On Love, Family and the Good Life - Plutarchus	.75	1.75	3.00	
MD203	The Summing Up - W. Somerset Maugham	.75	1.75	3.00	
MD204	Evolution in Action - Julian Huxley	.50	1.25	2.00	
MD205	Three Great Irishmen - Arland Ussher	.75	1.75	3.00	
MD206	The Negro in American Culture - Margaret Just Butcher	1.50	3.50	5.00	NF
MD207	Don Quixote - Miguel de Cervantes	.75	1.75	3.00	
MD208	Arms and Men - Walter Millis	.50	1.25	2.00	
MD209	Language - Joshua Whatmough	.50	1.25	2.00	NF
MD210	New World Writing No. 12	.50	1.25	2.00	
MD211	Enjoying Modern Art - Sarah Newmeyer	.50	1.25	2.00	NF
MD212	Modern Music - John Tasker Howard & James Lyons	.50	1.25	2.00	NF
MD213	The Roman Way to Western Civilization - Edith Hamilton	.75	1.75	3.00	NF
MD214	The Creation of the Universe - George Gamow	.75	1.75	3.00	NF
MD215	The Authentic New Testament	.50	1.25	2.00	
	1958				
MD216	Eight Great Comedies - Sylvan Barnet & Others	.50	1.25	2.00	
MD217	Medicine and Man - Ritchie Calder	.50	1.25	2.00	NF
MD218	The Theory of Business Enterprise - Thorstein Veblen	.50	1.25	2.00	NF
MD219	The Meaning of the Dead Sea Scrolls - A. Powell Davies	.75	1.75	3.00	NF
MD220	The United Nations and How it Works - David Cushman Coyle	.50	1.25	2.00	NF
MD221	The Varieties of Religious Experience - William James	.50	1.25	2.00	NF
MD222	The Origin of the Species - Charles Darwin	.75	1.75	3.00	NF
MT223	The Meaning of the Glorious Koran - Mohammed Marmaduke Pickthall	.75	1.75	3.00	
MD224	A Short History of India and Pakistan - T. Walter Wallbank	.50	1.25	2.00	NF
MD225	The Dark Ages - W. P. Ker	.75	1.75	3.00	NF
	1958				
MD226	The Greek Philosophers - Rex Warner	.75	1.75	3.00	NF
MD227	Human Types - Raymond Firth	.50	1.25	2.00	
MD228	The True Believer - Eric Hoffer	.50	1.25	2.00	
MD229	Books that Changed the World - Robert B. Downs	.75	1.75	3.00	NF
MD230	Russia - Bernard Pares	.50	1.25	2.00	
MD231	The Universe and Dr. Einstein - Lincoln Barnett	.75	1.75	3.00	NF
MT232	The Reader's Companion to World Literature - Lillian Herlands Horstein & Others	.50	1.25	2.00	
MT233	New World Writing No. 13	.50	1.25	2.00	
MD234	Relativity for the Layman - James A. Coleman	.50	1.25	2.00	
MT235	Great Writings of Goethe - Johann Wolfgang von Goethe	.75	1.75	3.00	

MD236	The Aztec: Man and Tribe - Victor W. Von Hagen	.75	1.75	3.00	NF
MD237	Bertrand Russell's Best - Bertrand Russell	.50	1.25	2.00	
MT238	The Oedipus Plays of Sophocles	.75	1.75	3.00	
MD239	Man: His First Million Years - Ashley Montagu	.75	1.75	3.00	NF
MD240	The Story of Jazz - Marshall Stearns	.75	1.75	3.00	NF
MT241	Three Great Plays of Euripides	.75	1.75	3.00	
MD242	The Edge of the Sea - Rachel L. Carson	.50	1.25	2.00	NF
MD243	A Treasury of Asian Literature - John D. Yohannan	.75	1.75	3.00	
MD244	Religion Without Revelation - Julian Huxley	.50	1.25	2.00	
MT245	The Golden Treasury - F. T. Palgrave & Oscar Williams	.50	1.25	2.00	
MT246	New World Writing No. 14	.50	1.25	2.00	
MD247	Stories from Shakespeare - Marchette Chute 1959	.50	1.25	2.00	
MT248	Mainsprings of Civilization - Ellsworth Huntington	.50	1.25	2.00	
MT249	Rebels and Redcoats - Hugh F. Rankin & George Scheer	.75	1.75	3.00	NF
MD250	The Statesman - Henry Taylor	.50	1.25	2.00	
MD251	The Origins of Oriental Civilization - Walter A. Fairservis, Jr.	.50	1.25	2.00	NF
MD252	The First Christian - A. Powell Davies	.50	1.25	2.00	
MD253	The Religions of Man - Huston Smith	.50	1.25	2.00	
MD254	The Young Caesar - Rex Warner	.75	1.75	3.00	B
MD255	Growing Up in New Guinea - Margaret Mead	.75	1.75	3.00	NF
MT256	The Papal Encyclicals in their Historical Context - Anne Fremantle	.75	1.75	3.00	
MT257	Stories from Shakespeare - Marchette Chute	.50	1.25	2.00	
MD258	The ABC of Relativity - Bertrand Russell	.50	1.25	2.00	
MD259	The Undiscovered Self - C. G. Jung	.75	1.75	3.00	NF
MT260	New World Writing No. 15	.50	1.25	2.00	
MD261	Music and Imagination - Aaron Copland	.75	1.75	3.00	NF
MT262	The History of Western Art - Erwin O. Christenson	.75	1.75	3.00	NF
MD263	The Liveliest Art - Arthur Knight	.50	1.25	2.00	
MD264	The Crust of the Earth - Samuel Rapport & Helen Wright	.75	1.75	3.00	NF
MD265	The Renaissance - Walter Pater	.75	1.75	3.00	NF
M 266					
MD267	The American Presidency - Clinton Rossiter	.50	1.25	2.00	
MD268					
M 269					
M 270					
MD271	A Primer of Freudian Psychology - Calvin S. Hall	.50	1.25	2.00	NF
MD272	The Sea Around Us - Rachel L. Carson	.50	1.25	2.00	NF
MD273	The Way of Zen - Alan W. Watts	.75	1.75	3.00	
MD274	A History of the Western World - L. J. Cheney	.50	1.25	2.00	
MD275	The Greek Experience - C. M. Bowra 1959	.75	1.75	3.00	
MD276	Understanding Chemistry - Lawrence P. Lessing	.50	1.25	2.00	NF
MD277	The Song of Songs	.75	1.75	3.00	
MD278	The March Up Country: Xenophon's Anabasis	.75	1.75	3.00	
MD279	Gestalt Psychology - Wolfgang Kohler	.75	1.75	3.00	NF
MT287	Eight Great Comedies - Sylvan Barnet & Others	.50	1.25	2.00	

MENTOR GUIDES

(New American Library of World Literature, Inc.)

G2	How to Know and Enjoy New York - Carl Maas 1949	2.00	4.00	7.50	NF

Mentor Guides G2, c. NA   Mercury Mystery 41, c. Merc   Mercury Mystery 82, c. Merc

MERCURY MYSTERY

(The American Mercury, Inc./Mercury Publications)

Digest size

1	The Postman Always Rings Twice - James M. Cain	1.50	3.50	5.00	M
2	Everything is Thunder - J. L. Hardy	.50	1.25	2.00	
3	Thirteen Steps - Whitman Chambers	.75	1.75	3.00	M
4	Company K - William March	.50	1.25	2.00	
5	Thieves Like Us - Edward Anderson	.75	1.75	3.00	M
6	Weeping is for Women - Donald Barr Chidsey	.50	1.25	2.00	
7	Diamond Jim Brady - Parker Morell	.50	1.25	2.00	
8	Hot Saturday - Harvey Fergusson	.50	1.25	2.00	
9	Criss-Cross - Don Tracy	.75	1.75	3.00	M
10	The General - C. S. Forester	.50	1.25	2.00	A
11	Mantrap - Sinclair Lewis	.50	1.25	2.00	
12	I Cover the Waterfront - Max Miller	.50	1.25	2.00	NF
13	To the Vanquished - I. A. R. Wylie	.50	1.25	2.00	
14	Death in the Deep South - Ward Greene	.75	1.75	3.00	M
15	Indelible - Elliot H. Paul	.50	1.25	2.00	
16	Once Too Often - Whitman Chambers	.50	1.25	2.00	M
17	The Prodigal Parents - Sinclair Lewis	.50	1.25	2.00	
18	The Loving Spirit - Daphne du Maurier	.50	1.25	2.00	
19	East Wind; West Wind - Pearl S. Buck	.50	1.25	2.00	
20	Cup of Gold - John Steinbeck	.75	1.75	3.00	A
21	The Missing Miniature - Erich Kastner	.50	1.25	2.00	
22	County Court - Roy Flannagan	.50	1.25	2.00	
23	The Devil in Satin - Dornford Yates	.50	1.25	2.00	
24	Divide by Two - Mildred Gilman	.50	1.25	2.00	
25	The Light that Failed - Rudyard Kipling	.75	1.75	3.00	A
26	Never in Vain - J. L. Hardy	.50	1.25	2.00	
27	The Dutch Shoe Mystery - Ellery Queen	.75	1.75	3.00	M
28	Jamaica Inn - Daphne du Maurier	.50	1.25	2.00	
29	Class Reunion - Franz Werfel	.50	1.25	2.00	
30	Dr. Norton's Wife - Mildred Walker	.50	1.25	2.00	
31	The Death of M. Gallet - Georges Simenon	.75	1.75	3.00	M
32	The Door Between - Ellery Queen	.75	1.75	3.00	M
33	Fifty Roads to Town - Frederick Nebel	.50	1.25	2.00	M
34	Strawstack - Dorothy Cameron Disney	.50	1.25	2.00	M
35	Death of Lord Haw Haw - Brett Rutledge	.50	1.25	2.00	M
36	The Siamese Twin Mystery - Ellery Queen	.75	1.75	3.00	M
37	Meet Nero Wolfe - Rex Stout	.75	1.75	3.00	M
38	Headed for a Hearse - Jonathan Latimer	.50	1.25	2.00	M
39	Halfway House - Ellery Queen	.75	1.75	3.00	M
40	The D. A. Calls it Murder - Erle Stanley Gardner	.50	1.25	2.00	M
41	Poirot Loses a Client - Agatha Christie	.50	1.25	2.00	M
42	The American Gun Mystery - Ellery Queen	.75	1.75	3.00	M
43	Murder at the Vicarage - Agatha Christie	.75	1.75	3.00	M
44	The Norths Meet Murder - Richard & Frances Lockridge	.75	1.75	3.00	M
45	The Listening House - Mabel Seeley	.50	1.25	2.00	M
46	The Incredible Theft - Agatha Christie	.75	1.75	3.00	M
47	The Four of Hearts - Ellery Queen	.75	1.75	3.00	M
48	The League of Frightened Men - Rex Stout	.75	1.75	3.00	M

#	Title				
49	Mystery Mile - Margery Allingham	.50	1.25	2.00	M
50	Murder in Mesopotamia - Agatha Christie	.75	1.75	3.00	M
51	Hasty Wedding - Mignon G. Eberhart	.50	1.25	2.00	M
52	The Unicorn Murders - Carter Dickson	1.50	3.50	5.00	M
53	Cards on the Table - Agatha Christie	.75	1.75	3.00	M
54	The Golden Swan Murder - Dorothy Cameron Disney	.50	1.25	2.00	M
55	Red Gardenias - Jonathan Latimer	.50	1.25	2.00	M
56	The D. A. Draws a Circle - Erle Stanley Gardner	.50	1.25	2.00	M
57	The Dragon's Teeth - Ellery Queen	.75	1.75	3.00	M
58	The Case of the Dangerous Dowager - Erle Stanley Gardner	.50	1.25	2.00	M
59	Thirteen at Dinner - Agatha Christie	.75	1.75	3.00	M
60	Good Night, Sheriff - Harrison R. Steeves	.50	1.25	2.00	M
61	The Singing Clock - Virginia Perdue	.50	1.25	2.00	M
62	The Clew of the Forgotten Murder - Erle Stanley Gardner	.50	1.25	2.00	M
63	A Toast to Tomorrow - Manning Coles	.50	1.25	2.00	M
64	The Black Curtain - Cornell Woolrich	.75	1.75	3.00	M
65	Verdict of Twelve - Raymond Postgate	.50	1.25	2.00	M
66	Death on the Nile - Agatha Christie	.75	1.75	3.00	M
67	Mystery in the Woodshet - Anthony Gilbert	.50	1.25	2.00	M
68	Challenge to the Reader - Ellery Queen	.75	1.75	3.00	M
69	The Secret of Chimneys - Agatha Christie	.75	1.75	3.00	M
70	A Taste of Honey - H. F. Heard	.50	1.25	2.00	M
71	Death in the Back Seat - Dorothy Cameron Disney	.50	1.25	2.00	M
72	Black Orchids - Rex Stout	.75	1.75	3.00	M
73	Keep It Quiet - Selwyn Jepson	.50	1.25	2.00	M
74	The Crying Sisters - Mabel Seeley	.50	1.25	2.00	M
75	The Case of the Haunted Brides - William DuBois	.50	1.25	2.00	M
76	Mystery Week-End - Percival Wilde	.50	1.25	2.00	M
77	Murder Out of Town - Frances & Richard Lockridge	.75	1.75	3.00	M
78	Folio on Florence White - Will Oursler	.50	1.25	2.00	M
79	The Nursing Home Murder - Ngaio Marsh & Dr. Henry Jellett	.75	1.75	3.00	M
80	He Fell Down Dead - Virginia Perdue	.50	1.25	2.00	M
81	Once Off Guard - J. H. Wallis	.50	1.25	2.00	M
82	I Wouldn't Be in Your Shoes - William Irish	.75	1.75	3.00	M
83	Tinsley's Bones - Percival Wilde	.50	1.25	2.00	M
84	The Moving Finger - Agatha Christie	.75	1.75	3.00	M
85	The Case of the Weird Sisters - Charlotte Armstrong	.50	1.25	2.00	M
86	The Trial of Vincent Doon - Will Oursler	.50	1.25	2.00	M
87	Donovan's Brain - Curt Siodmak	2.00	4.00	7.50	SF
88	The White Cockatoo - Mignon G. Eberhart	.50	1.25	2.00	M
89	Maigret to the Rescue - Georges Simenon	.75	1.75	3.00	M
90	The Bach Festival Murders - Blanche Bloch	.50	1.25	2.00	M
91	The Woman in Red - Anthony Gilbert	.50	1.25	2.00	M
92	The Case of the Foster Father - Virginia Perdue	.50	1.25	2.00	M
93	The Bride Dined Alone - Vera Kelsey	.50	1.25	2.00	M
94	The Black Paw - Constance & Gwenyth Little	.50	1.25	2.00	M
95	Look Your Last - John Stephen Strange	.50	1.25	2.00	M
96	The Smell of Money - Matthew Head	.50	1.25	2.00	M
97	The Rat Began to Gnaw the Rope - C. W. Grafton	.50	1.25	2.00	M
98	Keep it Quiet - Richard Hull	.50	1.25	2.00	M
99	The Spectral Bride - Joseph Shearing	.50	1.25	2.00	M
100	Murder on the Links - Agatha Christie	.50	1.25	2.00	M
101	Mr. Bowling Buys a Newspaper - Donald Henderson	.50	1.25	2.00	M
102	Beware the Hoot Owl - Nancy Rutledge	.50	1.25	2.00	M
103	Murder Through the Looking Glass - Michael Venning	.50	1.25	2.00	M
104	Footsteps Behind Her - Mitchell Wilson	.50	1.25	2.00	M
105	There was a Crooked Man - Kelley Roos	.50	1.25	2.00	M
106	The Undertaker Dies - Garnett Weston	.50	1.25	2.00	M
107	The Black Rustle - Constance & Gwenyth Little	.50	1.25	2.00	M
108	Thirty Days to Live - Anthony Gilbert	.50	1.25	2.00	M
109	Clues to Christabel - Mary Fitt	.50	1.25	2.00	M
110	Dr. Fell, Detective and Other Stories - John Dickson Carr First ed., 1947	5.00	10.00	20.00	M
111	Payment Deferred - C. S. Forester	.50	1.25	2.00	M

112	The Case Book of Mr. Campion - Margery Allingham	.50	1.25	2.00	M
113	Pattern for Murder - Ione Sandberg Shriber	.50	1.25	2.00	M
114	Dark Road - Doris Miles Disney	.50	1.25	2.00	M
115	Too Many Suspects - John Rhode	.50	1.25	2.00	M
116	The Outsiders - A. E. Martin	.50	1.25	2.00	M
117	Case of the Giant Killer - H. S. Branson	.50	1.25	2.00	M
118	The Hangover Murders - Adam Hobhouse	.50	1.25	2.00	M
119	When Last I Died - Gladys Mitchell	.50	1.25	2.00	M
120	Nightmare Town - Dashiell Hammett First ed., 1948	7.50	15.00	30.00	M
121	The Bandaged Nude - Robert Finnegan	.50	1.25	2.00	M
122	And Hope to Die - Richard Powell	.50	1.25	2.00	M
123	The Whitebird Murders - Thomas B. Black	.50	1.25	2.00	M
124	The Dying Room - Manning Lee Stokes	.50	1.25	2.00	M
125	Come and be Killed - Shelley Smith	.50	1.25	2.00	M
126	Let the Tiger Die - Manning Coles	.50	1.25	2.00	M
127	The Pikskin Bag - Bruno Fischer	.50	1.25	2.00	M
128	Fatal Bride - Van Siller aka The Curtain Between	.50	1.25	2.00	M
129	Death of a Tall Man - Frances & Richard Lockridge	.50	1.25	2.00	M
130	I am the Cat - Rosemary Kutak	.50	1.25	2.00	M
131	They Can Only Hang You Once - Dashiell Hammett aka The Adventures of Sam Spade	2.00	4.00	7.50	M
132	Legacy in Blood - Margery Allingham aka Flowers for the Judge	.50	1.25	2.00	M
133	Untidy Murder - Frances & Richard Lockridge	.75	1.75	3.00	M
134	Sweet and Deadly - David Duncan aka The Bramble Bush	.50	1.25	2.00	M
135	Dead Man Blues - William Irish	.50	1.25	2.00	M
136	Relative to Poison - E. C. R. Lorac	.50	1.25	2.00	M
137	I Want to go Home - Richard & Frances Lockridge	.50	1.25	2.00	M
138	The King and the Corpse - Max Murray	.50	1.25	2.00	M
139	Last Laugh, Mr. Moto - John P. Marquand	.75	1.75	3.00	M
140	Murder Makes Me Nervous - Margaret Scherf	.50	1.25	2.00	M
141	Call for the Saint - Leslie Charteris	.75	1.75	3.00	M
142	Too Good to be True - J. F. Hutton	.50	1.25	2.00	M
143	Nightmare - Edward S. Aarons	.50	1.25	2.00	M
144	Not Negotiable - Manning Coles	.50	1.25	2.00	M
145	Murder is Served - Frances & Richard Lockridge	.50	1.25	2.00	M
146	Rogue's Coat - Theodora DuBois	.50	1.25	2.00	M
147	The Beast Must Die - Nicholas Blake	.75	1.75	3.00	M
148	The Bulldog Has the Key - F. W. Bronson	.50	1.25	2.00	M
149	The Girl with the Hole in Her Head - Hampton Stone	.50	1.25	2.00	M
150	The Stalking Man - Wilson Tucker	2.00	4.00	6.00	M
151	And Dangerous to Know - Elizabeth Daly	.50	1.25	2.00	M
152	Terror in the Town - Edward Ronns	.50	1.25	2.00	M
153	The Leaden Bubble - H. C. Branson	.50	1.25	2.00	M
154	Spin Your Web, Lady! - Richard & Frances Lockridge	.75	1.75	3.00	M
155	Death From a Top Hat - Clayton Rawson	.50	1.25	2.00	M
156	Drop Dead - George Bagby	.50	1.25	2.00	M
157	Dig Me Later - Miriam-Ann Hagen	.50	1.25	2.00	M
158	House on Telegraph Hill - Dana Lyon aka The Frightened Child	.50	1.25	2.00	M
159	Sudden Vengeance - Edmind Crispin	.50	1.25	2.00	M
160	The Three Fears - Jonathan Stagge	.50	1.25	2.00	M
161	Dr. Bruderstein Vanishes - John Sherwood	.50	1.25	2.00	M
162	Death of a Nymph - Evelyn Piper aka The Motive	.50	1.25	2.00	M
163	Give Up the Ghost - Margaret Erskine	.50	1.25	2.00	M
164	Death at the Rodeo - Ellery Queen aka The American Gun Mystery	.50	1.25	2.00	M
165	Death and Letters - Elizabeth Daly	.50	1.25	2.00	M
166	Skeleton in the Closet - A. B. Cunningham	.50	1.25	2.00	M
167	Ill Wind - Ruth Fenisong	.50	1.25	2.00	M
168	Murder Comes Home - Anthony Gilbert	.50	1.25	2.00	M
169	The House in the Forest - Marten Cumberland	.50	1.25	2.00	M
170	Murder Goes to Press - Cicely Cairns	.50	1.25	2.00	M
171	Never Fight a Lady - Seldon Truss	.50	1.25	2.00	M

172 The Murder in Gay Ladies - James Ronald aka Murder in the Family	.50	1.25	2.00	M
173 The Sound of Murder - Kenneth Fearing aka The Loneliest Girl in the World	.50	1.25	2.00	M
174 A Noose for Her - Edmund Crispin aka The Long Divorce	.50	1.25	2.00	M
175 The Party was a Payoff - Elizabeth Sanxay Holding aka Too Many Bottles	.50	1.25	2.00	M
176 A Grave Case of Murder - Roger Bax	.50	1.25	2.00	M
177 Fish and Kill - Macdonald Hastings aka Cork on the Water	.50	1.25	2.00	M
178 D as in Dead - Lawrence Treat	.50	1.25	2.00	M
179 Blood on Baker Street - Anthony Boucher aka The Case of the Baker Street Irregulars	.75	1.75	3.00	M
180 The Body in the Bridal Bed - Richard Shattuck aka The Wedding Guest Sat on a Stone	.50	1.25	2.00	M
181 Murder Gone Mad - Philip MacDonald	.50	1.25	2.00	M
182 The Dead Don't Care - Jonathan Latimer	.50	1.25	2.00	M
183 Lady Marked for Murder - Peggy Bacon aka The Inward Eye	.50	1.25	2.00	M
184 Come Out Killing - Robert Reeves aka No Love Lost	.50	1.25	2.00	M
185 The Widow-Makers - Michael Blankfort	.50	1.25	2.00	M
186 Clues to Burn - Lenore Glen Offord	.50	1.25	2.00	M
187 The Pinball Murders - Thomas B. Black	.50	1.25	2.00	M
188 Death is a Lover - Nedra Tyre aka Mouse in Eternity	.50	1.25	2.00	M
189 The Missing Heiress - Bernice Carey	.50	1.25	2.00	M
190 The Christmas Murder - Cyril Hare aka An English Murder	.50	1.25	2.00	M
191 Kiss the Boss Goodbye - Frank Gruber aka The Last Doorbell	.50	1.25	2.00	M
192 Trial by Terror - Frances & Richard Lockridge aka Death by Association	.75	1.75	3.00	M
193 The Wrong Body - Anthony Gilbert	.50	1.25	2.00	M
194 With Blood and Kisses - Richard Shattuck aka The Snark was a Boojum	.50	1.25	2.00	M
195 The Screaming Bride - H. T. Teilhet aka A Private Undertaking	.50	1.25	2.00	M
196 Baltimore Madame - Helen Knowland aka Madame Baltimore	.50	1.25	2.00	M
197 Murder by the Day - Veronica Parker Johns	.50	1.25	2.00	M
198 Murder of a Mistress - John Sherwood aka Ambush for Anatol	.50	1.25	2.00	M
199 Blood Runs Cold - A. B. Cunningham aka The Hunter is the Hunted	.50	1.25	2.00	M
200 Killer in the Crowd - Josephine Tey aka The Man in the Queue	.50	1.25	2.00	M
201 The Deadly Chase - John M. Eshelman aka The Long Chase	.50	1.25	2.00	M
202 The Frightened Widow - Bernice Carey aka Their Nearest and Dearest	.50	1.25	2.00	M
203 The Bride of Death - Ngaio Marsh aka Spinsters in Jeopardy	.50	1.25	2.00	M
204 They Buried a Man - Mildred Davis	.50	1.25	2.00	M
205 You Die Today - Baynard Kendrick	.50	1.25	2.00	M
206 Death of a Cheat - John M. Eshelman	.50	1.25	2.00	M
207 Savage Breast - Manning Long	.50	1.25	2.00	M
208 Killer in the Straw - Richard & Frances Lockridge aka Death at the Gentle Bull	.75	1.75	3.00	M
209 The Blonde with the Deadly Past - Mabel Seeley aka The Whistling Shadow	.50	1.25	2.00	M

(Note: After no. 209, the series became Mercury
Mystery Book-Magazine.)

MERIT BOOKS

(Century Publications)

Digest size

Merit Books B-13, c. Cen

Metro nn. c. Metro

Midwood Publ. 4, c. Mid

(MERIT BOOKS, continued)

B-10	Operation Interstellar - George O. Smith 1950	2.25	5.00	8.00	SF
B-13	World of IF - Rog Phillips 1951	2.50	6.00	10.00	SF
B-14	Model for Love - Gerald Seton	1.50	3.50	5.00	E

METRO

(Metro Publications)

Digest size

nn	The Spy in the Room - Denison Clift	1.50	3.00	5.00	M
nn	Homicide Johnny - Stephen Gould	1.50	3.00	5.00	M

MIDWOOD PUBLICATIONS

(Midwood Enterprises, Inc.)

nn	There Oughta Be a Law! - Al Fagaly and Harry Shorten 1957	3.00	6.00	12.00	H
4	There Oughta Be a Law! - Al Fagaly and Harry Shorten 1958	3.00	6.00	12.00	H

MODERN SHORT STORY MONTHLY

(Avon Publishing Company, Inc.)

Digest Size

Modern Short Story 1, c. Avon

Modern Short Story 3 c. Avon

Modern Short Story 36 c. Avon

1	Cosmopolitans: 29 Short Stories - John O'Hara	2.50	6.00	10.00	
2	Files on Parade - John O'Hara	2.00	4.00	7.50	
3	To Step Aside - Noel Coward	2.00	4.00	7.50	
4	Inhale and Exhale - Wm Saroyan	2.00	4.00	7.50	
5	Ill Wind - James Hilton	2.00	4.00	7.50	
6	Selected Short Stories - Sinclair Lewis	2.00	4.00	7.50	
7	14 Great Stories - anthology	2.00	4.00	7.50	
8	First Person Singular - W. S. Maugham	2.00	4.00	7.50	
9	13 Great Stories - John Steinbeck 1943	2.00	4.00	7.50	
10	15 Selected Stories - James T. Farrell	2.00	4.00	7.50	
11	Selected Great Stories - Ben Hecht	2.00	4.00	7.50	
12	34 More Great Stories - Wm Saroyan	2.00	4.00	7.50	
13	Three Short Novels - Louis Bromfield	2.00	4.00	7.50	
14	22 Modern Stories - Erskine Caldwell	2.00	4.00	7.50	
15	13 Great Modern Stories - anthology	2.00	4.00	7.50	
16	Eight Long Short Stories - Fannie Hurst	2.00	4.00	7.50	
17	Selected Stories - Thomas Wolfe	2.00	4.00	7.50	
18	Ah King - W. S. Maugham	2.00	4.00	7.50	
19	They Brought Their Women - Edna Ferber	2.00	4.00	7.50	
20	Twelve Selected Modern Stories - anthology	2.00	4.00	7.50	
21	12 Great Modern Short Stories - James T. Farrell	2.00	4.00	7.50	
22	Career in C Major - J. M. Cain	2.00	4.00	7.50	
23	Great Stories of China - Pearl S. Buck	2.00	4.00	7.50	
24	Five Long Short Stories - Louis Bromfield	2.00	4.00	7.50	
25	The Bottle Collectors - Kenneth Roberts	2.00	4.00	7.50	
26	A Thousand and One Afternoons in New York - Ben Hecht	2.00	4.00	7.50	
27	Ten Hilarious Stories - Damon Runyon	2.00	4.00	7.50	
28	Too Bad - Dorothy Parker	2.00	4.00	7.50	
29	Hope of Heaven - John O'Hara	2.00	4.00	7.50	
30	Georgia Boy - Erskine Caldwell	2.00	4.00	7.50	
31	Everybody was Nice - Stephen Vincent Benet	2.00	4.00	7.50	
32	Welcome to the City - Irwin Shaw	2.00	4.00	7.50	
33	The Road to Recovery - Budd Shulberg	2.00	4.00	7.50	
34	Great Stories by Louis Bromfield	2.00	4.00	7.50	
35	Trembling of a Leaf - W. S. Maugham	2.00	4.00	7.50	
36	Stories of Love and Adventure - Rafael Sabatini	2.00	4.00	7.50	A
	Note: Same cover as Avon no. 84				
37	Another Selection of Ben Hecht's Sparkling Stories	2.00	4.00	7.50	
38	Stories of Intrigue - W. S. Maugham	2.00	4.00	7.50	
39	Stories of Venial Sin - John O'Hara	2.00	4.00	7.50	
40	Great Short Stories - Lion Feuchtwanger	2.00	4.00	7.50	
41	Ten Selected Stories - James T. Farrell	2.00	4.00	7.50	
42	Hollywood Love Clinic - anthology	2.50	6.00	10.00	
43	Intriguing Stories about East of Suez - W. S. Maugham	2.00	4.00	7.50	
44	Amok - and Other Stories of the Tropics - Stefan Zweig	2.00	4.00	7.50	
45	Hellbox - John O'Hara	2.00	4.00	7.50	
46	Love Among the Haystacks - D. H. Lawrence	2.00	4.00	7.50	
47	Delightful Stories about Love in Greenwich Village - Floyd Dell	2.50	6.00	10.00	
48	Diverting Tales of Cafe Society - Katharine Brush	2.50	6.00	10.00	

Modern Short Story 40
c. Avon

Modern Short Story 42
c. Avon

Modern Short Story 45
c. Avon

49	A Modern Lover - P. H. Lawrence	2.00	4.00	7.50	
50	All the Girls He Wanted - John O'Hara	2.00	4.00	7.50	

MONARCH BOOKS

(Monarch Books, Inc.)

101	Dark Hunger - Don James 1958	.75	1.75	3.00	
102	Winter Range - Alan LeMay	.50	1.25	2.00	W
103	Love Me Now - Fan Nichols	.50	1.25	2.00	
104	Rawhider from Texas - Dean Owen	.50	1.25	2.00	W
105	Shadow of the Mafia - Louis Malley	.50	1.25	2.00	
106	Rogue Lover - Leon Phillips 1959	.50	1.25	2.00	
107	Wild to Possess - Gil Brewer c-Maguire	.50	1.25	2.00	
108	Brand Fires on the Ridge - Ernest Haycox	.50	1.25	2.00	W
109	Marmaduke Rides Again - Brad Anderson	.50	1.25	2.00	H
110	Touch Me Not - Brian Harwin c-Maguire	.50	1.25	2.00	
111	Sword of Casanova - James Kendricks	.75	1.75	3.00	A
112	Spring of Desire - Louis Falstein	.50	1.25	2.00	
113	Thunderhead Range - Sam Bowie	.50	1.25	2.00	W
114	Killer Cop - Ferguson Findley	.50	1.25	2.00	
115	Madigan's Women - John Conway	.50	1.25	2.00	
116	Some Like It Tough - Jack Karney	.50	1.25	2.00	
117	Stronger than Passion - George Byram	.50	1.25	2.00	
118	Way of the Wicked - William Woolfolk	.50	1.25	2.00	E
119	Occasion of Sin - Robert William Taylor	.50	1.25	2.00	E
120	Take Me Home - Fletcher Flora	.50	1.25	2.00	E
121	Kiss Me Quick - Karl Kramer c-Maguire	.50	1.25	2.00	
122	Season for Love - Whitman Chambers	.50	1.25	2.00	
123	Beyond Our Pleasure - James Kendricks	.50	1.25	2.00	
124	All I Can Get - William Ard c-Maguire	.50	1.25	2.00	
125	Nikki - Stuart Friedman 1959 c-Maguire	.75	1.75	3.00	A
126	Law of the Gun - Max Brand	.50	1.25	2.00	W
127	Lust to Live - Peter W. Denzer	.50	1.25	2.00	
128	Hell is My Destination - John Conway	.50	1.25	2.00	E
129	End to Innocense - Robert Carse	.50	1.25	2.00	
130	We Burn Like Fire - Will Cook	.50	1.25	2.00	
131	The Darkness of Love - Harry Olive	.50	1.25	2.00	
132	Save Them for Violence - James M. Fox	.50	1.25	2.00	
133	The Flesh Peddlers - Frank Boyd c-Maguire	.75	1.75	3.00	E
134	Fury in the Heart - W. T. Ballard	.50	1.25	2.00	
135	Hangman's Mesa - Dan J. Sterens	.50	1.25	2.00	W
136	Not For a Curse - Karl Kramer	.50	1.25	2.00	
137	Jailbait Street - Hal Ellson	2.00	4.00	7.50	JD
138	Stephana - Joseph Foster	.50	1.25	2.00	
139	In Savage Surrender - Whitman Chambers	.50	1.25	2.00	
140	The Glory Jumpers - Delano Stagg	.50	1.25	2.00	
141	Falcons of France - James Norman Hall & Charles Nordhoff	.75	1.75	3.00	C
142	Night After Night - Steve Thurman	.50	1.25	2.00	
K50	Congo Song - Stuart Cloete 1958	.50	1.25	2.00	
K51	Polish Nights - Wldyslawa Chojnowska 1959	.50	1.25	2.00	
K52	This Naked Love - Helga Moray	.50	1.25	2.00	

MONARCH HUMAN BEHAVIOR SERIES

(Monarch Books, Inc.)

MB501	Women in Trouble - James Donner 1959 c-Maguire	.75	1.75	3.00	
MB502	The Sexual Side of Love - Don James	.75	1.75	3.00	NF
MB503	Tormented Women - Edward J. McGoldrick, Jr. c-Maguire	.75	1.75	3.00	

MURDER MYSTERY MONTHLY

(Avon Book Company/Avon Publising Company, Inc.)

Digest size

Continuation of Murder of the Month

2	Mysterious Mickey Finn - Elliot Paul 1942	4.00	8.00	15.00	M
3	Silinski - Master Criminal - Edgar Wallace	4.00	8.00	15.00	M
4	The French Key Mystery - Frank Gruber	4.00	8.00	15.00	M
5	Burn, Witch, Burn - A. A. Merritt	4.00	8.00	15.00	SF
6	The Postman Always Rings Twice - J. M. Cain	4.00	8.00	15.00	
7	The Big Sleep - Raymond Chandler	4.00	8.00	15.00	M
8	Maigret Aboard - Georges Simenon 1943	4.00	8.00	15.00	M
9	The Red Box - Rex Stout	4.00	8.00	15.00	M
10	Homicide for Hannah - Dwight V. Babcock	4.00	8.00	15.00	M
11	Creep Shadow Creep - A. A. Merritt	4.00	8.00	15.00	SF
12	Hungry Dog Murders - Frank Gruber	4.00	8.00	15.00	M
13	If the Shroud Fits - Kelley Roos	4.00	8.00	15.00	M
14	Whose Body? - Dorothy L. Sayers	4.00	8.00	15.00	M
15	Premeditated Murder - Peter Cheyney aka A Trap for Bellamy	4.00	8.00	15.00	M
16	Double Indemnity - James M. Cain First ed., 1943	5.00	10.00	20.00	M
17	Who Killed Chloe? - Margery Allingham aka Dancers in Mourning	4.00	8.00	15.00	M
18	The Moon Pool - A. A. Merritt 1944	4.00	8.00	15.00	SF
19	5 Murderers - Raymond Chandler First ed., 1944	7.50	15.00	30.00	M
20	The Embezzler - J. M. Cain	4.00	8.00	15.00	M
21	Counter Spy Murders - Peter Cheyney aka Dark Duet	4.00	8.00	15.00	M
22	Ace of Knaves - Leslie Charteris aka The Saint Goes into Action	4.00	8.00	15.00	M
23	Simon Lash, Private Detective - Frank Gruber	4.00	8.00	15.00	M
24	Dwellers in the Mirage - A. A. Merritt	4.00	8.00	15.00	SF
25	About the Murder of a Startled Lady - Anthony Abbot	4.00	8.00	15.00	M
26	The Mysterious Affair at Styles - Agatha Christie	4.00	8.00	15.00	M
27	The Black Angel - Cornell Woolrich	4.00	8.00	15.00	M
28	Five Criminals - Raymond Chandler First ed., 1945	7.50	15.00	30.00	M
29	The Face in the Abyss - A. A. Merritt	4.00	8.00	15.00	SF
30	Farewell to the Admiral - Peter Cheyney	4.00	8.00	15.00	M
31	If I Should Die Before I Wake - William Irish First ed., 1945	5.00	10.00	20.00	M
32	The Saint vs. Scotland Yard - Leslie Charteris	4.00	8.00	15.00	M
33	Nobody Lives Forever - W. R. Burnett	4.00	8.00	15.00	M
34	The Ship of Ishtar - A. A. Merritt	4.00	8.00	15.00	SF

Note: Uses retouched cover from the pulp magazine Argosy May 10, 1930

Murder Mystery 32, c. Avon   Murder Mystery 34, c. Avon   Murder Mystery 41, c. Avon

Murder Mystery 42, c. Avon   Murder Mystery 43, c. Avon   Murder Mystery 47, c. Avon

(MURDER MYSTERY MONTHLY, continued)

35	Flowers for the Judge - Margery Allingham 1946	4.00	8.00	15.00	M
36	They Never Say When - Peter Cheyney	4.00	8.00	15.00	M
37	Orchids to Murder - Hulbert Footner	4.00	8.00	15.00	M
38	Hannah Says Foul Play - Dwight V. Babcock First ed., 1946	4.00	8.00	15.00	M
39	Flash Casey - Detective - George Harmon Coxe First ed., 1946	4.00	8.00	15.00	M
40	High Sierra - W. R. Burnett	4.00	8.00	15.00	M
41	The Metal Monster - A. A. Merritt	4.00	8.00	15.00	SF
42	Borrowed Crime - William Irish First ed., 1946	5.00	10.00	20.00	M
43	Finger Man - Raymond Chandler First ed., 1946	7.50	15.00	30.00	M
44	Love's Lovely Counterfeit - J. M. Cain 1947	4.00	8.00	15.00	M
45	On the Spot - Edgar Wallace	4.00	8.00	15.00	M
46	Green Ice Murders - Raoul Whitfield 1947	4.00	8.00	15.00	M
47	The Blonde. the Gangster and the Private Eye - Dale Clark 1950, aka The Red Rods	5.00	10.00	20.00	M
48	Murder in Her Big Blue Eyes - Julius Long aka Keep the Coffins Coming	5.00	10.00	20.00	M
49	Lady, the Guy is Dead - Edward Ronns 1950, aka No Place to Live Note: Same cover as the comic The Saint no. 10.	5.00	10.00	20.00	M

MURDER OF THE MONTH

(Avon Book Company)

Digest size

Continued as Murder Mystery Monthly

1	Seven Footprints to Satan - A. A. Merritt 1942	5.00	10.00	20.00	SF

MYSTERY NOVEL CLASSIC

(Novel Selections, Inc.)

Digest size

48	Date for Murder - Louis Trimble	1.50	3.50	5.00	M
50	The Bride Brings Death - Darby St. John 1943	1.50	3.50	5.00	
53	The Ballot Box Murders - John Stephen Strange	1.50	3.50	5.00	M

(MYSTERY NOVEL CLASSIC, continued)

55	Murder Without Clues - Eleanor Pierson aka The Defense Rests	1.50	3.50	5.00	M
56	The Glass Slipper - Mignon G. Eberhart	1.50	3.50	5.00	M
57	Death Writes an Ad - Marion Holbrook aka Suitable for Framing	1.50	3.50	5.00	M
58	Hostess to Murder - Elizabeth Sanxay Holding	1.50	3.50	5.00	M
60	The Case of the Tainted Token - Kathleen Moore Knight aka Tainted Token	1.50	3.50	5.00	M
61	Bring Me Another Murder - Whitman Chambers	1.50	3.50	5.00	M
62	The Girl Died Laughing - Viola Paradise	1.50	3.50	5.00	M
63	Wanted: A Murderess - Marion Holbrook	1.50	3.50	5.00	M
65	Echo of a Bomb - Van Siller	1.50	3.50	5.00	M
66	Shadows on the Wall - Mary Reisner	1.50	3.50	5.00	M
67	A Girl Died Laughing - V. Paradise	1.50	3.00	5.00	M
70	Terror by Twilight - Kathleen Moore Knight	1.50	3.50	5.00	M
72	Escape While I Can - Melba Marlot	1.50	3.50	5.00	M
77	Death Checks In - Stephen Ransome	1.50	3.50	5.00	M
78	Let the Skeletons Rattle - Frederick C. Davis	1.50	3.00	5.00	M
83	The Cat's Cradle Murders - Jerome Barry aka Leopard Cat's Cradle	1.50	3.50	5.00	M

MYSTERY NOVEL OF THE MONTH

(Novel Selections, Inc.)

Digest size

nn	42 Days for Murder - Roger Torrey 1939	2.00	4.00	6.00	M
nn	The Merry-Go-Round of Murder - Joseph F. Dinneen 1939	2.00	4.00	6.00	M
nn	Murder on the S-23 - Steve Fisher	2.00	4.00	6.00	M
nn	Murders in Silk - Mike Teagle	2.00	4.00	6.00	M
nn	Murder by Proxy - Colver Harris	2.00	4.00	6.00	M
nn	Death is a Stowaway - Wesley Price	2.00	4.00	6.00	M
nn	The Case of the Severed Skull - H. Weiner 1940	2.00	4.00	6.00	M
nn	Liar Dice - J. S. Mosher 1941	2.00	4.00	6.00	M
19	Cradled in Murder! - Rudd Fleming 1941	2.00	4.00	6.00	M
23	Murder at Coney Island - James O'Hanlon	1.50	3.50	5.00	M
25	Murder by Invitation - Richard Hull	2.00	4.00	6.00	M
27	Grand Central Murder - Sue MacVeigh	1.50	3.50	5.00	M
28	Murder on Stage - Sutherland Scott 1941	2.00	4.00	6.00	M
35	Murder at Deer Lick - A. B. Cunningham	1.50	3.50	5.00	M
39	Murder on Every Floor - Ann Demarest 1942	1.50	3.50	5.00	M
40	The Clue of the Red Carnation - Burton Stevenson	1.50	3.50	5.00	M
41	The Case of the Blue Lacquer Box - George F. Worts	1.50	3.50	5.00	M

Murder of the Month 1
c. Avon

Myst. Novel Classic 56, c. NS

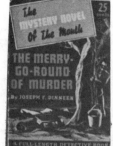

Mystery Novel/Month nn
c. NS

Mystery Novel/Month 25, c. NS

National Dairy nn
c. Nat. Dairy

News Stand Libr. 1A
c. Export

NATIONAL DAIRY
(National Dairy Products Corp.)

nn 641 Tested Recipes from the Sealtest Kitchens   .75   1.50   3.00   NF
    1954

NEWS STAND LIBRARY

(Export Publishing Enterprises Limited)

Canadian

1A	Negligee - Gladys Sloan	1.50	3.50	5.00	E
	1949				
5A	Sweet Serenader - George Willis	1.50	3.50	5.00	E
	1949, aka The Wild Faun				
7A	The Pagans - Jack Benedict	1.50	3.50	5.00	E
14A	Death Be My Destiny - Neil H. Perrin	1.50	3.50	5.00	E
	with dust jacket	3.00	6.00	12.00	
	1949				
15A	Jesse James - Thomas P. Kelley	2.00	4.00	7.50	NF
	1950				
16A	Daughters of Desire - Fletcher Knight	1.50	3.50	5.00	E
18A	Let Out the Beast - Leonard Fischer	2.50	6.00	10.00	SF
	1950				
20A	Sugar-Puss on Dorchester Street - Al Palmer	1.50	3.50	5.00	E
24A	Overnight Escapade - Stephen Mark	1.50	3.50	5.00	E
25	Call House Madam - Serge C. Wolsey	1.50	3.50	5.00	E
26A	He Learned About Women - Ted Greenshade	1.50	3.50	5.00	E
27A	Waste No Tears - Jarvis Warwick	1.50	3.50	5.00	E
	1950				
42	Gloria - Glen Watkins	1.50	3.50	5.00	E
	aka Fall Girl				
141	Destroy the U.S.A. - Will F. Jenkins (Murray	3.00	6.00	12.00	SF
	Leinster)				
	1950, aka Murder of the U.S.A.				

News Stand 14A w/dj
c. Export

News Stand 14A wo/dj
c. Export

News Stand 141, c. Export

No Imprint D1920, c. unknown No Imprint nn, c. unknown Novel Library 4, c. Div

NO IMPRINT

(Unknown Publisher)

D1920	How to Build and Operate a Model Railroad - Marshall McClintock 1955	1.50	3.50	5.00	NF

NO IMPRINT

(Unknown publisher)

Digest size

nn	War Birds-Diary of an Unknown Aviator 1951	3.00	6.00	9.00	C

NOVEL LIBRARY

(Diversey Publishing Corporation)

No.	Title				
1	3 Gorgeous Hussies - Jack Woodford 1948	7.50	15.00	30.00	E
2	Ecstasy Girl - Jack Woodford	5.00	12.50	15.00	E
3	Free Lovers - Jack Woodford aka Fiddler's Fee	4.00	10.00	20.00	E
4	The Passionate Princess - Jack Woodford aka Proxy Princess	5.00	12.50	25.00	E
5	Wanton Venus - Maurice LeBlanc	4.00	10.00	20.00	
6	Peeping Tom - Jack Woodford aka Come Into My Parlor	10.00	25.00	40.00	E
7	Grounds for Divorce - Jack Woodford aka Love at Last	4.00	10.00	20.00	E
8	The Regenerate Lover - P. H. Clarke	5.00	12.50	25.00	E

Novel Library 6, c. Div   Novel Library 8, c. Div   Novel Library 11, c. Div

Novel Library 26, c. Div   Novel Library 37, c. Div   Novel Library 46, c. Div

(NOVEL LIBRARY, continued)

    aka Young and Healthy

1949

9	The Street of Painted Lips - Maurice DeKobra	7.50	15.00	30.00	E
10	Woman Without Love? - Roswell Williams	7.50	15.00	30.00	E
11	The Villain and the Virgin - J. H. Chase	7.50	15.00	30.00	E
	aka No Orchids for Miss Blandish				
12	Uneasy Virtue - Dana Wilson	5.00	12.50	25.00	E
13	A Good Time Man - E. P. Keating	5.00	12.50	25.00	E
14	Gold Diggers - Lois Bull	5.00	12.50	25.00	E
15	Playthings of Desire - J. Wesley Putnam				E
16	Women to Love - Sinclair Drago	7.50	15.00	30.00	E
17	Frisco Gal - Clarkson Crane	7.50	15.00	30.00	E
	aka Naomi Martin				
18	Bedroom Eyes - Maurice DeKobra	7.50	15.00	35.00	E
19	Louis Beretti - D. H. Clarke	5.00	12.50	25.00	E
20	One Night with Nancy - Wilson Collison	7.50	15.00	30.00	E
21	Love Toy - Anonymous - H. S. Drago	7.50	15.00	30.00	E
22	Mirabelle: Woman of Passion - Ellen Caren	5.00	12.50	25.00	E
23	Broadway Virgin - Lois Bull	5.00	12.50	25.00	E
24	Infidelity - Arthur Weigall	7.50	15.00	30.00	E
25	Venus on Wheels - Maurice DeKobra	7.50	15.00	30.00	E
	1949				
26	The Immodest Maidens - Eleanore Browne	7.50	15.00	30.00	E
	aka Make Me Yours				
27	Ladies of Chance - Anthony Scott	7.50	15.00	30.00	E
28	The Love Clinic - Maurice DeKobra	7.50	15.00	30.00	E
29	All Dames are Dynamite - Timothy Trent	7.50	15.00	30.00	E
30	Diary of Death - Wilson Collison	5.00	12.50	25.00	E
31	Millions for Love - Colette Roberts	5.00	12.50	25.00	E
32	Dishonorable Darling - Wilson Gilison	5.00	12.50	25.00	E
	aka Farewell to Women				
	1950				
33	The Women in his Life - Eleanor Nash	7.50	12.50	25.00	E
	aka Bachelors are Made				
34	Crystal Girl - Stephen Longstreet	5.00	12.50	25.00	E
35	The Lady Said Yes - George Martin	5.00	12.50	25.00	E
36	Male and Female - Jack Woodford	5.00	12.50	25.00	E
37	Chinamen and a Woman - J. H. Chase	7.50	15.00	30.00	E
38	Sixty Seconds - Maxwell Bodenheim	7.50	15.00	30.00	E
39	No Bed of Her Own - Val Lewton	7.50	15.00	30.00	E
40	Wild Parties - Max Lief	7.50	15.00	30.00	E
41	Help Wanted - Male - Thomas Stone	5.00	12.50	25.00	E
	Note: Same cover as the Avon comic Romantic Love no. 9.				
42	Lady for Love - Alan Brener Schultz	7.50	15.00	30.00	E
43	How to Play Canasta - Richard L. Frey	2.50	5.00	10.00	NF
44	Teach Me to Love - Jack Woodford	5.00	12.50	25.00	E
45	Blonde Baggage - Marty Holland	10.00	25.00	40.00	E
46	Naked on Roller Skates - Maxwell Bodenheim	10.00	20.00	35.00	E
	Note: Same cover as Diversey Popular Novel no. 2.				

NOVEL SELECTIONS

(Novel Selections, Inc.)

Novel Selections 51, c. NS   Novels Inc. nn, c. Novels Inc.   Novels Inc. 10, c. Novels Inc.

(NOVEL SELECTIONS, continued)

51	The Bastard - Erskine Caldwell	1.50	3.50	5.00	E
52	Poor Fool - Erskine Caldwell	1.50	3.50	5.00	E

NOVELS INC.
(Novels Inc.)
Digest size

nn	Made for Loving - William Arthur c-Rodewald	1.00	3.50	5.00	E
nn	Sinner in Gingham - Gail Jordan	1.50	3.00	5.00	E
10	The Tigress - John Saxon	1.00	3.50	5.00	E

OMNIBUS
(Omnibus Publishing Company)
Digest size

nn	Night of Crime - Armstrong Livingston	1.50	3.50	5.00	M

ORIGINAL NOVELS
(Original Novels, Inc.)
Digest size

700	Women of the Night - Peggy Gaddis Orig., 1951, c-Gross	1.50	3.50	5.00	E

Original Novels 700, c. Orig   Original Novels 718, c. Orig   Original Novels 720, c. Orig

Original Novels 726, c. Orig   Original Novels 727, c. Orig   Original Novels 738, c. Orig

(ORIGINAL NOVELS, continued)

701	Backstage Affair - Amos Hatter	1.50	3.50	5.00	E
710	See No Evil - Kermit Welles	1.50	3.50	5.00	E
713	Sleep with the Devil - Reed McCary	1.50	3.50	5.00	E
714	Body and Passion - Whit Harrison	1.50	3.50	5.00	E
715	Wayward Nymph - Elisabeth Gill	1.50	3.50	5.00	E
716	Cellar Club - Albert L. Quandt	2.00	4.00	7.50	E
717	Sheila's Daughter - William Arnold	1.50	3.50	5.00	E
718	Savage Love - Whit Harrison	1.50	3.50	5.00	E
	Orig., 1952				
	c-Belarski				
719	Harlem Woman - William Arnold	2.00	4.00	7.50	E
720	Baby Sitter - Albert L. Quandt	1.50	3.50	5.00	E
	Orig., 1952				
721	Zip-Gun Angels - Albert L. Quandt	2.00	4.00	7.50	JD
	Note: Same cover as Star no. 750.				
722	City of Sin - Robert O. Saber	1.50	3.50	5.00	E
	Orig., 1952				
723	Backwoods Hussy - Hallam Whitney	1.50	3.50	5.00	E
724	Runaway Girl - William Arnold	.75	1.75	3.00	E
725	Ringside Jezebel - Kate Nickerson	.75	1.75	3.00	E
	Orig., 1953				
726	Dream Club - Albert L. Quandt	2.00	4.00	7.50	E
	aka Beyond Desire				
727	Visiting Nurse - Norman Bligh	.75	1.75	3.00	E
	Orig., 1953				
728	Baby Peddler - Albert L. Quandt	1.50	3.50	5.00	E
730	Waterfront Girl - Amos Hatter	1.50	3.50	5.00	E
733	Back Woods Hussy - Hallam Whitney	.75	1.75	3.00	E
738	Cellar Club - Albert L. Quandt	2.00	4.00	7.50	E
740	River Boat Girl - Norman Bligh	1.50	3.50	5.00	E
	c-Belarski				
741	Motel Mistress - Norman Bligh	.75	1.75	3.00	E
	aka Remembered Moment				
742	Shanty Road - Whit Harrison	1.50	3.50	5.00	E
743	Big City Nurse - Albert L. Quandt	.75	1.75	3.00	E
	aka Baby Peddler				
744	City Streets - Gene Harvey	1.50	3.50	5.00	E
746	French Alley - Matthew Clay	.75	1.75	3.00	E
	Orig., 1954				

PADELL

(Padell Book and Magazine Company)

Digest size

nn	From Dance Hall to White Slavery - John Dillon	5.00	10.00	20.00	E
nn	The Tragedies of the White Slaves - H. M. Lytle	5.00	10.00	20.00	E
	1945				

PARENTS INSTITUTE

(The Parents Institute, Inc.)

Digest size

nn Best Stories for Boys and Girls - anthology   4.00   8.00   15.00
    1938, includes Mickey Mouse and Pluto

PELICAN BOOKS

(New American Library)

Also see Mentor

P 1	Public Opinion - Walter Lippmann 1946	.50	1.25	2.00	NF
P 2	Patterns of Culture - Ruth Benedict	.50	1.25	2.00	NF
P 3	You and Music - Christian Darnton	.50	1.25	2.00	NF
P 4	The Birth and Death of the Sun - George Gamow	.75	1.75	3.00	NF
P 5	An Enemy of the People: Anti-Semitism - James Parkes	.50	1.25	2.00	NF
P 6	What Happened in History - V. Gordon Childe	.75	1.75	3.00	NF
P 7	The Physiology of Sex - Kenneth Walker	.50	1.25	2.00	NF
P 8	Mathematician's Delight - W. W. Sawyer	.50	1.25	2.00	NF
P 9	The Weather - Raymond Bush & George Kimble	.50	1.25	2.00	NF
P10	America's Role in the World Economy - Alvin H. Hansen	.50	1.25	2.00	NF
P11	Heredity, Race and Society - Th. Dobzhansky & L. C. Dunn	.75	1.75	3.00	NF
P12	The Story of Human Birth - Alan F. Guttmacher 1947	.50	1.25	2.00	NF
P13	Thomas Jefferson on Democracy	1.50	3.50	5.00	NF
P14	Introducing Shakespeare - G. B. Harrison	.50	1.25	2.00	NF
P15	Emerson: The Basic Writings of America's Sage - Ralph Waldo Emerson	.75	1.75	3.00	NF
P16	The Personality of Animals - H. Munro Fox	.75	1.75	3.00	NF
P17	Human Breeding and Survival - Guy I. Burch & Elmer Pendell	.75	1.75	3.00	NF
P18	Is Marriage Necessary? - George H. Bartlett	.50	1.25	2.00	NF
P19	Good Reading	.50	1.25	2.00	NF
P20	An Introduction to Modern Architecture - Elizabeth B. Mock & J. M. Richards	.75	1.75	3.00	NF
P21	The Odyssey - Homerus	.75	1.75	3.00	NF
P22	Religion and the Rise of Capitalism - R. H. Tawney	.75	1.75	3.00	NF
P23	Heredity, Race and Society - Th. Dobzhansky & L. C. Dunn	.50	1.25	2.00	NF
P24	Sweden: The Middle Way - Marquis W. Childs 1948	.50	1.25	2.00	NF
P25	Philosophy in a New Key - Susanne K. Langer	.50	1.25	2.00	NF

Padell nn, c. Padell

Parents Institute nn, c. PI

Pelican Books P13, c. NA

Penguin 528. c. Pen   Penguin 537, c. Pen   Penguin 587, c. Pen

PENGUIN

(Penguin Books, Inc.)

Also see Signet

60	The Dark Invader - Captain von Rintelen	2.00	4.00	6.00	
79	The Rasp - Philip MacDonald	2.00	4.00	7.50	M
239	Stealthy Terror - John Ferguson	2.00	4.00	6.00	M
276	The Case of the Late Pig - Margery Allingham	2.00	4.00	7.50	M
339	High Rising - Angela Thirkell	2.00	4.00	6.00	
501	Murder by an Aristocrat - Mignon G. Eberhart 1942	2.00	4.00	7.50	M
502	Pygmalion - George Bernard Shaw	2.00	4.00	6.00	
503	Death of a Ghost - Margery Allingham	2.00	4.00	7.50	M
	With dust jacket	5.00	10.00	20.00	
504	All Concerned Notified - Helen Reilly	2.00	4.00	7.50	M
505	The Mother - Pearl S. Buck	2.00	4.00	7.50	
506	Two Survived - Guy Pearce Jones	2.00	4.00	6.00	
507	The Physiology of Sex - Kenneth Walker	2.00	4.00	6.00	
508	Walden - Henry David Thoreau	2.00	4.00	6.00	
509	The Pastures of Heaven - John Steinbeck	2.00	4.00	6.00	
510	Trent's Own Case - Warner H. Allen & E. C. Bentley	2.00	4.00	6.00	M
511	Cause for Alarm - Eric Ambler	2.00	4.00	7.50	M
512	The Strange Case of Miss Annie Spragg - Louis Bromfield	2.00	4.00	7.50	
513	The Catalyst Club - George Dyer	2.00	4.00	6.00	
514	Tombstone - Walter Noble Burns	2.00	4.00	7.50	NF
515	The Confidential Agent - Graham Greene 1943	2.00	4.00	7.50	
516	Genghis Khan - Harold Lamb	2.00	4.00	7.50	B
517	Philosopher's Holiday - Irwin Edman	2.00	4.00	6.00	
518	The Middle Temple Murder - J. S. Fletcher	2.00	4.00	7.50	M
519	A Blunt Instrument - Georgette Heyer	2.00	4.00	7.50	M
520	The Saga of Billy the Kid - Walter Noble Burns	2.00	4.00	7.50	B
521	The Ox-bow Incident - Walter Van Tilburg Clark	2.00	4.00	7.50	W
522	Sabotage - Cleve F. Adams	2.00	4.00	7.50	
523	Leaves of Grass - Walt Whitman	2.00	4.00	7.50	
524	Pencil Points to Murder - W. A. Barber & R. F. Schabelitz	2.50	6.00	10.00	M
525	The Penguin Book of Sonnets - Carl Withers	2.00	4.00	7.50	
526	My Own Murderer - Richard Hull	2.00	4.00	7.50	M
527	The Telephone Booth Indian - A. J. Liebling	2.00	4.00	7.50	
528	The Blind Barber - John Dickson Carr	2.50	6.00	10.00	M
529	Kitty Foyle - Christopher Morley 1944	2.00	4.00	6.00	
530	The Ministry of Fear - Graham Greene	2.00	4.00	7.50	
531	Drawn Conclusion - W. A. Barber & R. F. Schabelitz	2.50	6.00	10.00	M
532	Hag's Nook - John Dickson Carr	2.50	6.00	10.00	M
533	The Purple Sickle Murder - Freeman Wills Crofts	2.00	4.00	7.50	

534	Black Plumes - Margery Allingham	2.00	4.00	7.50	
535	The Old Dark House - J. B. Priestley	2.00	4.00	7.50	
536	In Hazard - Richard Hughes	2.00	4.00	6.00	
537	Out of this World - Julius Fast	2.50	6.00	10.00	SF
538	The Laughing Fox - Frank Gruber	2.00	4.00	7.50	
	With dust jacket	5.00	10.00	20.00	
539	Laughing Boy - Oliver LaFarge	2.00	4.00	6.00	
540	My Name is Aram - William Saroyan	2.00	4.00	6.00	
541	Mr. Pinkerton Grows a Beard - David Frome	2.00	4.00	7.50	M
542	Murder Enters the Picture - W. A. Barber & R. F. Schabelitz	2.50	6.00	10.00	M
543	Shell of Death - Nicholas Blake	2.00	4.00	7.50	M
544	Ten Holy Horrors - Francis Beeding	2.00	4.00	7.50	M
545	The Talking Clock - Frank Gruber	2.00	4.00	7.50	
	With dust jacket	5.00	10.00	20.00	
546	O'Halloran's Luck - Stephen Vincent Benet	2.00	4.00	7.50	
547	Death of My Aunt - C. H. B. Kitchin	2.00	4.00	7.50	M
548	Black-Out in Gretley - J. B. Priestley	2.00	4.00	7.50	
549	Murders in Volume II - Elizabeth Daly	2.00	4.00	7.50	M
550	To Walk the Night - William Sloane	2.00	4.00	7.50	
551	Mr. Littlejohn - Martin Flavin	2.00	4.00	6.00	
552	Murder in Trinidad - John W. Vandercook	2.00	4.00	7.50	M
553	Nine times Nine - H. H. Holmes	2.00	4.00	7.50	M
	1945				
554	Tales of Piracy, Crime and Ghosts - Daniel Defoe	2.00	4.00	7.50	A
555	Dr. Toby finds Murder - Sturges Mason Schley	2.00	4.00	7.50	M
556	The Mycenaid - C. Everett Cooper	2.00	4.00	6.00	
557	McSorley's Wonderful Saloon - Joseph Mitchell	2.00	4.00	6.00	
558	Porgy - Du Bose Heyward	2.00	4.00	6.00	
559	Death of a Saboteur - Hulbert Footner	2.00	4.00	6.00	
560	Murder in Fiji - John W. Vandercook	2.00	4.00	7.50	M
561	Young Man with a Horn - Dorothy Baker	2.00	4.00	6.00	
562	Simon Lash, Private Detective - Frank Gruber	2.00	4.00	7.50	M
563	Appointment in Samarra - John O'Hara	2.00	4.00	6.00	
564	Maigret Travels South - Georges Simenon	2.50	6.00	10.00	M
565	Step in the Dark - Ethel Lina White	2.00	4.00	7.50	M
566	Say Yes to Murder - W. T. Ballard	2.00	4.00	7.50	M
567	Trouble in July - Erskine Caldwell	2.00	4.00	6.00	
568	Night Flight - Antoine de Saint Exupery	2.00	4.00	6.00	
569	Conceived in Liberty - Howard Fast	2.00	4.00	6.00	
570	And Berry Came Too - Dornford Yates	2.00	4.00	6.00	
571	Death Down East - Eleanor Blake	2.00	4.00	7.50	M
572	The Good Soldier Schweik - Jaroslav Hasek	2.00	4.00	6.00	
	1946				
573	The Turning Wheels - Stuart Cloete	2.00	4.00	6.00	
574	A Passage to India - E. M. Forster	2.00	4.00	7.50	
575	The Cask - Freeman Wills Crofts	2.00	4.00	7.50	M
576	The Lovely Lady - D. H. Lawrence	2.00	4.00	7.50	
577	Manhattan Transfer - John Dos Passos	2.00	4.00	6.00	
578	Bread and Wine - Ignazio Silone	2.00	4.00	6.00	
579	Patience of Maigret - Georges Simenon	2.50	6.00	10.00	M
580	Pal Joey - John O'Hara	2.00	4.00	6.00	
581	God's Little Acre - Erskine Caldwell	2.00	4.00	6.00	
582	Thunder on the Left - Christopher Morley	2.00	4.00	6.00	
583	Vein of Iron - Ellen Glasgow	2.00	4.00	6.00	
584	Dead Reckoning - Francis Bonnamy	2.00	4.00	6.00	M
585	Winesburg, Ohio - Sherwood Anderson	2.00	4.00	6.00	
586	The Rasp - Philip MacDonald	2.00	4.00	7.50	M
	With dust jacket	5.00	10.00	20.00	
587	Martin Eden - Jack London	2.00	4.00	7.50	
588	The Unvanquished - Howard Fast	2.00	4.00	6.00	
589	Back Street - Fannie Hurst	2.00	4.00	6.00	
590	Orlando - Virginia Woolf	2.00	4.00	7.50	
591	Mildred Pierce - James McCain	2.00	4.00	7.50	
592	Malice in Wonderland - Nicholas Blake	2.00	4.00	7.50	M
593	Handbook of Politics and Voters' Guide - Lowell Mellett	2.00	4.00	7.50	
594	Heavenly Discourse - Charles Erskine Scott Wood	2.00	4.00	6.00	
595	Cabbages and Kings - O. Henry	2.00	4.00	6.00	
596	The Heart is a Lonely Hunter - Carson McCullers	2.00	4.00	6.00	

(PENGUIN, continued)

597 The Summing Up - W. Somerset Maugham	2.00	4.00	6.00	
598 Put Out the Light - Ethel Lina White	2.00	4.00	6.00	M
599 Tortilla Flat - John Steinbeck	2.00	4.00	6.00	
600 Montana Rides! - Evan Evans	2.00	4.00	7.50	W
601 Jurgen - James Branch Cabell	2.00	4.00	7.50	F
602 The New Veteran - Charles G. Bolte	2.00	4.00	6.00	
603 Short Stories of James T. Farrell	2.00	4.00	6.00	
604 Trio - Dorothy Baker	2.00	4.00	6.00	
605 Cimarron - Edna Ferber	2.00	4.00	6.00	
606 A Rope of Sand - Francis Bonnamy	2.00	4.00	6.00	M
607 Pygmalion - George Bernard Shaw	2.00	4.00	6.00	
608 Major Barbara - George Bernard Shaw	2.00	4.00	6.00	
609 Saint Joan - George Bernard Shaw	2.00	4.00	6.00	
610 Lady Chatterley's Lover - D. H. Lawrence	2.00	4.00	7.50	
611 Messer Marco Polo - Donn Byrne	2.00	4.00	6.00	
612 Christianity Takes a Stand - William Scarlett	1.50	3.50	5.00	NF
613 The Odyssey - Homerus	2.00	4.00	6.00	A
614 The Penguin Hoyle - Albert H. Morehead & Geoffrey Mott-Smith	2.00	4.00	6.00	NF
615 Lady into Fox and A Man in the Zoo - David Garnett	2.00	4.00	7.50	F
616 Eleven of Diamonds - Baynard Kendrick	2.00	4.00	7.50	M
617 Saratoga Trunk - Edna Ferber	1.50	3.50	5.00	
1947				
618 The Perennial Boarder - Phoebe Atwood Taylor	2.00	4.00	6.00	
With dust jacket	5.00	10.00	20.00	
619 Almayer's Folly - Joseph Conrad	2.00	4.00	7.50	
620 Montana Rides Again - Evan Evans	1.50	3.50	5.00	W
621 Serenade - James M. Cain	2.00	4.00	7.50	
622 Looking for a Bluebird - Josef Wechsberg	1.50	3.50	5.00	
623 The Silver Jackass - Frank Gruber	2.00	4.00	6.00	
624 The Velvet Well - John Gearon	1.50	3.50	5.00	
625 Daisy Miller and an International Episode - Henry James	1.50	3.50	5.00	
626 The Purple Onion Mystery - Harriette Ashbrook	2.00	4.00	6.00	M
627 Tobacco Road - Erskine Caldwell	2.00	4.00	6.00	
628 The Innocent Voyage - Richard Hughes	1.50	3.50	5.00	
629 The King is Dead on Queen Street - Francis Bonnamy	2.00	4.00	6.00	M
630 Mother Wore Tights - Miriam Young	1.50	3.50	5.00	
631 A Funeral in Eden - Paul McGuire	1.50	3.50	5.00	
632 Sanctuary - William Faulkner	1.50	3.50	5.00	
633 Great Son - Edna Ferber	1.50	3.50	5.00	
634 The Unberable Bassington - Saki	2.00	4.00	6.00	
635 Blood on Lake Louisa - Baynard Kendrick	2.00	4.00	6.00	
636 The Voice of Bugle Ann and the Romance of Rosy Ridge - MacKinlay Kantor	1.50	3.50	5.00	
637 Hotel Splendide - Ludwig Bemelmans	1.50	3.50	5.00	
638 A Portrait of Jennie - Robert Nathan	1.50	3.50	5.00	
639 So Big - Edna Ferber	1.50	3.50	5.00	
640 Cartoons: All in Line - Saul Steinberg	2.00	4.00	7.50	H
641 Murder! Great True Crime Cases - Alan Hynd	2.00	4.00	6.00	NF
642 The Kiss of Death - Eleazar Lipsky	1.50	3.50	5.00	
643 Young Lonigan - James T. Farrell	1.50	3.50	5.00	
644 Short Stories of Thomas Wolfe	1.50	3.50	5.00	
645 Song of the Whip - Evan Evans	1.50	3.50	5.00	W
646 Journeyman - Erskine Caldwell	1.50	3.50	5.00	E
647 Uncle Tom's Children - Richard Wright	1.50	3.50	5.00	
648 Deadly Weapon - Wade Miller	2.00	4.00	6.00	M
649 The Tyranny of Sex - Ludwig Lewisohn	1.50	3.50	5.00	
650 American Beauty - Edna Ferber	1.50	3.50	5.00	
651 Market for Murder - Frank Gruber	2.00	4.00	6.00	M
652 The New Quiz Book - Albert H. Morehead & Geoffrey Mott-Smith	2.00	4.00	6.00	NF
653 Show Boat - Edna Ferber	2.00	4.00	6.00	
654 Great Western Stories - William Targ	2.00	4.00	6.00	W
655 Great Mystery Stories	2.00	4.00	7.50	M
656 Christ Stopped at Eboli - Carlo Levi	1.50	3.50	5.00	
657 Desire Me - Leonhard Frank	1.50	3.50	5.00	
658 Death of a Swagman - Arthur W. Upfield	2.50	6.00	10.00	
659 The Wild Palms - William Faulkner	1.50	3.50	5.00	

PENGUIN GUIDES

(Penguin Books, Inc.)

G1 The Penguin Guide to California - Carl Maas 1947	2.00	4.00	7.50	NF

PENGUIN SPECIALS

(Penguin Books, Inc./The Infantry Journal)

s 75 New Ways of War - Tom Wintringham	1.50	3.50	5.00	NF
With dust jacket 1940	3.00	6.00	10.00	
s 81 Russia - Bernard Pares 1943	1.50	3.50	5.00	NF
s 82 Aircraft Recognition - R. A. Saville-Sneath	1.50	3.50	5.00	NF
s201 What's that Plane - Walter Pitkin, Jr. 1942	1.50	3.50	5.00	NF
s202 New Soldier's Handbook	1.50	3.50	5.00	NF
s203 Guerrilla Warfare - "Yank" Levy	1.50	3.50	5.00	NF
s204 How the Jap Army Fights - Paul W. Thompson, others 1942	1.50	3.50	5.00	NF
s206 How Russia Prepared - Maurice Edelman	1.50	3.50	5.00	NF
s207 Christianity and Social Order - William Temple	.75	1.75	3.00	NF
s209 Americans vs. Germans 1942	1.50	3.50	5.00	NF
s210 Modern Battle - Paul W. Thompson	1.50	3.50	5.00	NF
s211 The Good Soldier Schweik - Jaroslav Hasek	.75	1.75	3.00	
s212 Psychology for the Fighting Man 1943	1.50	3.50	5.00	NF
s213 Empire in the Changing World - W. K. Hancock	.75	1.75	3.00	NF
s214 Hitler's Second Army - Alfred Hancock 1943	1.50	3.50	5.00	NF
s215 Handbook for Army Wives and Mothers - Catherine Redmond	1.50	3.50	5.00	NF
s216 A History of the War - Rudolf Modley	1.50	3.50	5.00	NF
s217 The Next Germany	1.50	3.50	5.00	NF
s218 Shipyard Diary of a Woman Welder - Augusta H. Clawson	1.50	3.50	5.00	NF
s219 The Moon is Down - John Steinbeck 1943	1.50	3.50	5.00	
s220 Guadacanal Diary - Richard Tregaskis 1943	1.50	3.50	5.00	C
s221 Thirty Seconds Over Tokyo - Ted W. Lawson 1944	1.50	3.50	5.00	C
s222 The British Navy's Air Arm - Owen Rutter	1.50	3.50	5.00	NF
s223 They Were Expendable - W. L. White	1.50	3.50	5.00	
s224 A Short History of the Army and Navy - Fletcher Pratt	1.50	3.50	5.00	NF
s225 G. I. Sketch Book - Aimee Crane	1.50	3.50	5.00	

Penguin Specials S75, c. Pen   Penguin Specials S218, c. Pen   Penguin Specials S229, c. Pen

s226	The Battle is the Pay-off - Ralph Ingersoll 1944	1.50	3.50	5.00	
s227	This is the Navy - Gilbert Cant	.75	1.75	3.00	NF
s229	Psychology for the Returning Serviceman - Marjorie van de Water 1945	1.50	3.50	5.00	NF
s230	I Knew Your Soldier - Eleanor Stevenson & Pete Martin	1.50	3.50	5.00	
s231	Cartoons for Fighters - Frank Brandt 1945	1.50	3.50	5.00	
s237	Pipeline to Battle - Peter W. Rainier	1.50	3.50	5.00	
s238	Storm - George R. Stewart	1.50	3.50	5.00	
s239	This is the Navy - Gilbert Cant	1.50	3.50	5.00	NF
s240	Island Victory - S. L. A. Marshall	1.50	3.50	5.00	

PENNANT

(Pennant Books/Bantam Books, Inc.)

P 1	Navajo Canyon - Thomas W. Blackburn 1953	2.00	4.00	7.50	W
P 2	The Last of the Plainsmen - Zane Grey	1.50	3.50	5.00	W
P 3	Epitaph for a Spy - Eric Ambler	1.50	3.50	5.00	M
P 4	Stamped for Murder - Ben Benson	1.50	3.50	5.00	M
P 5	In Those Days - Harvey Fergusson	1.50	3.50	5.00	W
P 6	Mojave - Edwin Corle	1.50	3.50	5.00	W
P 7	Vanity Row - W. R. Burnett	2.00	4.00	6.00	
P 8	Sunset Rider - Matt Stuart	1.50	3.50	5.00	W
P 9	Ruler of the Range - Peter Dawson	1.50	3.50	5.00	W
P10	Six-gun Boss - Clay Randall	1.50	3.50	5.00	W
P11	A Time to Kill - Geoffrey Household	1.50	3.50	5.00	M
P12	Warrant for a Wanton - Michael Gillian	1.50	3.50	5.00	
P13	Apache Desert - L. P. Holmes	1.50	3.50	5.00	W
P14	Action at War Bow Valley - Michael Carder	1.50	3.50	5.00	W
P15	Takeoff - C. M. Kornbluth	2.00	4.00	7.50	SF
P16	Lily in Her Coffin - Ben Benson	1.50	3.50	5.00	M
P17	Gunsmoke Over Big Muddy - Frank O'Rourke	1.50	3.50	5.00	W
P18	Wire in the Wind - Matt Stuart	1.50	3.50	5.00	W
P19	Reap the Wild Wind - Thelma Strabel	1.50	3.50	5.00	A
P20	Two and the Town - Henry Gregor Felsen	1.50	3.50	5.00	
P21	Border Graze - Dwight Bennett	1.50	3.50	5.00	W
P22	Long Ride - Peter Dawson	1.50	3.50	5.00	W
P23	Maneaters of Kumaon - Jim Corbett	1.50	3.50	5.00	NF
P24	Murder Won't Out - Russel Crouse	1.50	3.50	5.00	M
P25	High Starlight - L. P. Holmes	1.50	3.50	5.00	W
P26	Santa Fe Passage - Clay Fisher	1.50	3.50	5.00	W
P27	Burro Alley - Edwin Corle	1.50	3.50	5.00	
P28	Blackcock's Feather - Maurice Walsh	1.50	3.50	5.00	A
P29	The Naked Spur - Rolfe Bloom & Allan Ullman 1954	1.50	3.50	5.00	W
P30	Bold Raiders of the West - Frederick R. Bechdolt	2.00	4.00	6.00	W
P31	The Outlaw Years - Robert M. Coates	2.00	4.00	6.00	NF
P32	Walls Rise Up - George Sessions Perry	1.50	3.50	5.00	
P33	Shadow of the Butte - Thomas Thompson	1.50	3.50	5.00	W
P34	Dodge City: Queen of Cowtowns - Stanley Vestal	2.00	4.00	6.00	NF
P35	Walk the Dark Bridge - William O'Farrell	1.50	3.50	5.00	
P36	Elephant Bill - J. H. Williams	.75	1.75	3.00	NF
P37	Longhorn Empire - Will Ermine	1.50	3.50	5.00	W
P38	Outlaw Valley - Evan Evans (Max Brand)	1.50	3.50	5.00	W
P39	American Me - Beatrice Griffith	1.50	3.50	5.00	
P40	Doubloons - Charles B. Driscoll	1.50	3.50	5.00	A
P41	The Bronze Mermaid - Paul Ernst	1.50	3.50	5.00	
P42	Saddle-man - Matt Stuart	1.50	3.50	5.00	W
P43	Fort Starvation - Frank Gruber	1.50	3.50	5.00	W
P44	Adventures in Time and Space - Raymond J. Healy & J. Francis McComas	1.00	2.50	4.00	SF
P46	Guaracha Trail - George Parker	1.50	3.50	5.00	
P47	Tombstone - Clarence Budington Kelland	1.50	3.50	5.00	W
P48	When Oil Ran Red - Clay Randall	1.50	3.50	5.00	W
P49	The Sixpenny Dame - Eaton K. Goldthwaite	1.50	3.50	5.00	

(PENNANT, continued)

P50 One Way Ticket - Eugene O'Brien	1.50	3.50	5.00	
P51 A Vaquero of the Brush Country - J. Frank Dobie	2.00	4.00	6.00	NF
P52 The Border Queen - Nick Sumner	1.50	3.50	5.00	W
P53 Toll Mountain - Robert McCaig	1.50	3.50	5.00	
P54 To the Last Man - William E. Barrett	1.50	3.50	5.00	
P55 Repeat Performance - William O'Farrell	1.50	3.50	5.00	
P56 Beyond Human Ken - Judith Merril	2.00	4.00	6.00	SF
P57 Horse Thief Trail - Frederick R. Bechdolt	1.50	3.50	5.00	W
P59 Mostly Murder - Fredric Brown	2.00	4.00	7.50	M
P61 The Argosy Book of Sports Stories - Rogers Terrill	1.50	3.50	5.00	S
P62 Blind Entry - Merlyn Estin	1.50	3.50	5.00	
P64 The Stakes are High - Brent Ashabranner	1.50	3.50	5.00	
P65 In Winter Light - Edwin Corle	1.50	3.50	5.00	
P67 Dry Bones in the Valley - William MacLeod Raine	1.50	3.50	5.00	W
P69 The Nester - John S. Daniels	1.50	3.50	5.00	W
P70 Gentlemen Prefer Corpses - Max Arthur	1.50	3.50	5.00	M
P75 The Altered Ego - Jerry Sohl 1955	2.00	4.00	6.00	SF
P76 Whiplash - Brad Ward	1.50	3.50	5.00	W
P77 High Country - Peter Dawson	1.50	3.50	5.00	W
P78 The Hangman's Overture - J. Jerod Chouinard	1.50	3.50	5.00	M
P79 Code Three - James M. Fox	1.50	3.50	5.00	

PENNANT MYSTERY
(Maco Publishing)
Digest size

1 Death Out of Thin Air - Stuart Towne	1.50	3.50	5.00	M
2 The Six Iron Spiders - Phoebe Atwood Taylor	1.50	3.50	5.00	M
3 So Much Blood - Bruno Fischer	1.50	3.50	5.00	M
4 The Purple Parrot - C. B. Clason	1.50	3.50	5.00	M

PENNANT STUDENT EDITIONS
(Bantam Books, Inc.)

nn Life on the Mississippi - Mark Twain Note: Other titles exist in this series.	2.00	4.00	7.50

PERMA BOOKS
(Pocket Books, Inc.)

M1000 Peace of Soul - Fulton J. Sheen 1954	1.50	3.50	5.00	
M1600 The Greatest Book Ever Written - Fulton Oursler	1.50	3.50	5.00	
M2001 Texan-Killer - Gene Austin 1955	1.50	3.50	5.00	W
M3002 Too Dead to Run - Jason Manor	1.50	3.50	5.00	
M3003 Spur to the Smoke - Steve Frazee	1.50	3.50	5.00	W
M3004 Life Among the Savages - Shirley Jackson	.50	1.25	2.00	NF
M3005 Tender to Danger - Eliot Reed	1.50	3.50	5.00	M
M3006 Boy Gang - Mark Kennedy	3.00	6.00	12.00	JD
M3007 The Desperate Hours - Joseph Hayes	.75	1.75	3.00	E
M3008 Horse Thief Crossing - Tom J. Hopkins	1.50	3.50	5.00	W
M3009 Honky-tonk Woman - Bliss Lomax	1.50	3.50	5.00	W
M3010 The Crimson Clue - George Harmon Coxe	1.50	3.50	5.00	M

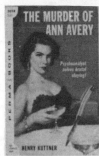

Perma Books M3048, c. PKB Perma Books M3058, c. PKB Perma Books M3074, c. PKB

(PERMA BOOKS, continued)

M3011	The Stainless Steel Kimono - Elliott Chaze	.75	1.75	3.00	H
M3012	Dead Game - Michael Avallone	1.50	3.50	5.00	
M3013	Massacre Trail - George C. Appell	1.50	3.50	5.00	W
M3014	End of the Gun - H. A. DeRosso	1.50	3.50	5.00	W
M3015	The Queen's Awards: Eighth Series - Ellery Queen	.75	1.75	3.00	M
M3016	The Secret Road - Bruce Lancaster	1.50	3.50	5.00	
M3017	The Big Water - Mark Derby	1.50	3.50	5.00	
M3018	Tejanos! - K. R. G. Granger	1.50	3.50	5.00	
M3019	Doubles in Death - William Grew	1.50	3.50	5.00	M
M3020	The Dreamers - J. Bigelow Clark	1.50	3.50	5.00	
M3021	The Settling of the Sage - Hal G. Evarts	1.50	3.50	5.00	W
M3022	The Big Boodle - Robert Sylvester	1.50	3.50	5.00	
M3023	Top Hand - Dwight Bennett	1.50	3.50	5.00	W
M3024	Frenchman's River - Will Ermine	1.50	3.50	5.00	W
M3025	The Maras Affair - Eliot Reed	1.50	3.50	5.00	M
M3026	Easy Money - Frank Peace	1.50	3.50	5.00	
	1956				
M3027	World Out of Mind - J. T. McIntosh c-Powers	2.00	4.00	7.50	SF
M3028	The Bad Step - Mark Derby	.75	1.75	3.00	
M3029	Do It Yourself - Morris Brickman	.75	1.75	3.00	NF
M3030	Border Fever - C. William Harrison	1.50	3.50	5.00	W
M3031	Fractured French - F. S. Pearson II & Richard Taylor	.75	1.75	3.00	H
M3032	The Mean Streets - Thomas B. Dewey	1.50	3.50	5.00	E
M3033	Blood Money - Dan J. Stevens	1.50	3.50	5.00	
M3034	Snow Fury - Richard Holden	3.00	6.00	12.00	SF
M3035	Bar 4 Roundup of Best Western Stories - Scott Meredith	1.50	3.50	5.00	W
M3036	Visa to Death - Ed Lacy c-Maguire	1.50	3.50	5.00	
M3037	Cop Hater - Ed McBain	1.50	3.50	5.00	M
M3038	Pay-off at Black Hawk - Harry Sinclair Drago	1.50	3.50	5.00	W
M3039	The Perma Quiz Book - Joseph Nathan Kane	1.50	3.50	5.00	NF
M3040	Sleep With Strangers - Dolores Hitchens	1.50	3.50	5.00	M
M3041	To Have and Have Not - Ernest Hemingway	.75	1.75	3.00	
M3042	From Here to Shimbashi - John Sack	.75	1.75	3.00	
M3043	Red Harvest - Dashiell Hammett	1.50	3.50	5.00	
M3044	Showdown Creek - Lucas Todd	1.50	3.50	5.00	W
M3045	The Avenger - Dwight Bennett	1.50	3.50	5.00	W
M3046	The Murder of Eleanor Pope - Henry Kuttner	2.00	4.00	7.50	M
M3047	Blessed Event - Bill O'Mally	.75	1.75	3.00	H
M3048	Live and Let Die - Ian Fleming	3.00	6.00	12.00	M
M3049	Tumbling Range Woman - Steve Frazee	1.50	3.50	5.00	W
M3050	Droodles - Roger Price	.75	1.75	3.00	H
	1956				
M3051	F. O. B. Murder - Bert & Dolores Hitchens	.75	1.75	3.00	M
M3052	The Brass Brigade - Frank Peace	.75	1.75	3.00	
M3053	Invasion of Privacy - Harry Kurnitz	.75	1.75	3.00	M
M3054	Play It Yourself - Jack Bassett,& Norman Monath	.75	1.75	3.00	
M3055	The Con Man - Ed McBain	.75	1.75	3.00	M
M3056	Green Hills of Africa - Ernest Hemingway	.75	1.75	3.00	

(PERMA BOOKS, continued)

M3057	The Perma X-Word Puzzle Book - Alexander Field	1.50	3.50	5.00	NF
M3058	The Murder of Ann Avery - Henry Kuttner	2.00	4.00	7.50	M
M3059	Hot Town - Frank Malachy	1.50	3.50	5.00	
M3060	Best Jokes for all Occasions - Jerry Lieberman & Powers Moulton	.75	1.75	3.00	H
M3061	The Mugger - Ed McBain	.75	1.75	3.00	M
M3062	The Pusher - Ed McBain	.75	1.75	3.00	M
M3063	Die in the Saddle - Lincoln Drew	.75	1.75	3.00	W
M3064	The Bloody Sevens - Jefferson Cooper 1957	1.50	3.50	5.00	
M3065	Wilbert - Gill Fox	.75	1.75	3.00	
M3066	Murder is Where You Find It - Robert P. Hansen	1.50	3.50	5.00	M
M3067	Pets--Including Women - Charles Preston	.75	1.75	3.00	H
M3068	Decision at Broken Butte - Harry Sinclair Drago	1.50	3.50	5.00	W
M3069	The Last Round - Frank O'Rourke	.75	1.75	3.00	W
M3070	Too Hot to Handle - Ian Fleming aka Moonraker	2.00	4.00	7.50	M
M3071	Chronide of the Calypso Clipper - John Jennings	1.50	3.50	5.00	A
M3072	Death in the Wind - Edwin Lanham	.75	1.75	3.00	
M3073	The Wild Life - Herbert Gold	.75	1.75	3.00	
M3074	The Maltese Falcon - Dashiell Hammett	1.50	3.50	5.00	M
M3075	Oh, What a Wonderful Wedding - Virginia Rowans 1957	.50	1.25	2.00	
M3076	Ellery Queen's Awards: Tenth Series - Ellery Queen	.75	1.75	3.00	M
M3077	Boomer - Clay Randall	.75	1.75	3.00	
M3078	Feeling No Pain - Bill O'Malley	.50	1.25	2.00	H
M3079	Unhappy Hooligan - Stuart Palmer	.75	1.75	3.00	M
M3080	The Splintered Man - M. E. Chaber	2.00	4.00	7.50	M
M3081	The Wild West Joke Book - Oren Arnold	.75	1.75	3.00	H
M3082	Bar 5 Roundup of Best Western Stories - Scott Meredith	1.50	3.50	5.00	W
M3083	Choice Cartoons from Sports Illustrated - Charles Preston	.75	1.75	3.00	H
M3084	Diamonds are Forever - Ian Fleming	2.00	4.00	7.50	M
M3085	Wild Grass - Harry Sinclair Drago	1.50	3.50	5.00	W
M3086	Montana Bad Man - Roe Richmond	.75	1.75	3.00	W
M3087	The Golden Widow - Floyd Mahannah	.75	1.75	3.00	
M3088	Pursuit - Lewis B. Patten	.75	1.75	3.00	W
M3089	The Brave, Bad Girls - Thomas B. Dewey	.75	1.75	3.00	
M3090	Don't Do it Yourself - Morris Brickman	.75	1.75	3.00	NF
M3091	The Men in Her Death - Stephen Ransome	.75	1.75	3.00	
M3092	Ride the Wind South - John Hunter	.75	1.75	3.00	
M3093	Unarmed Killer - William Harrison	1.50	3.50	5.00	W
M3094	This is My Funniest - Whit Burnett	.50	1.25	2.00	H
M3095	Shadow of the Rope - Ray Gaulden	.75	1.75	3.00	
M3096	Widow's Pique - Blair Treynor	.75	1.75	3.00	M
M3097	Vanishing Ladies - Richard Marsten	.75	1.75	3.00	
M3098	Red - Richard Vincent	.75	1.75	3.00	
M3099	Nurse Kathy - Adeline McElfresh 1958	.50	1.25	2.00	R
M3100	One-Way Ticket - Bert & Dolores Hitchens	.75	1.75	3.00	M
M3101	Cavalry Scout - Dee Brown	1.50	3.50	5.00	W
M3102	Marcia Blake, Publicity Girl - Nancy Webb	.50	1.25	2.00	R
M3103	The Saint Around the World - Leslie Charteris	.75	1.75	3.00	M
M3104	Lash of Idaho - Roe Richmond	.75	1.75	3.00	W
M3105	O'Malley's Nuns - Bill O'Malley	.75	1.75	3.00	H
M3106	Lead With Your Left - Ed Lacy	.75	1.75	3.00	
M3107	Yellow Rope - Lincoln Drew	.75	1.75	3.00	
M3108	Killer's Choice - Ed McBain	.75	1.75	3.00	M
M3109	The Lonely Law - Matt Stuart	.75	1.75	3.00	W
M3110	The Vengeful Men - Ray Gaulden	.75	1.75	3.00	
M3111	The Best from Manhunt - Scott Meredity & Sidney Meredith	1.50	3.50	5.00	
M3112	Three Trails - George C. Appell	.75	1.75	3.00	W
M3113	Killer's Payoff - Ed McBain	.75	1.75	3.00	M
M3114	Deadly Summer - Glenn M. Barns	.75	1.75	3.00	
M3115	Showdown at Sunset - Harry Sinclair Drago	1.50	3.50	5.00	W

Code	Title				
M3116	Bar 6 Roundup of Best Western Stories - Scott Meredith	1.50	3.50	5.00	W
M3117	Even the Wicked - Richard Marsten	.75	1.75	3.00	
M3118	Spearhead - Franklin M. Davis, Jr.	.75	1.75	3.00	
M3119	Lady Killer - Ed McBain	.75	1.75	3.00	M
M3120	Rifle Ranch - Lincoln Drew	.75	1.75	3.00	W
M3121					
M3122	The Velvet Ape - David C. Holmes	.75	1.75	3.00	
M3123	The Marshal from Deadwood - John Hunter	.75	1.75	3.00	
	1958				
M4001	Botany Bay - James Norman Hall & Charles Nordhoff	.75	1.75	3.00	
	1955				
M4002	The High and the Mighty - Ernest K. Gann	1.50	3.50	5.00	
M4003	Peace With God - Billy Graham	.50	1.25	2.00	
M4004	Anyone's My Name - Seymour Shubin	.50	1.25	2.00	
M4005	The Velbet Doublet - James Street	.75	1.75	3.00	
M4006	Corpus of Joe Bailey - Oakley Hall	.75	1.75	3.00	
M4007	The Time is Noon - Hiram Haydn	.75	1.75	3.00	
M4008	Storm Haven - Frank G. Slaughter	.75	1.75	3.00	
M4009	The Art of Living - Norman Vincent Peale	.50	1.25	2.00	
M4010	The Girl with the Glass Heart - Daniel Stern	.75	1.75	3.00	E
M4011	Stories of the Foreign Legion - Percival C. Wren	2.00	4.00	7.50	A
M4012	Sight Without Glasses - Harold M. Peppard	.50	1.25	2.00	NF
M4013	Be Glad You're Neurotic - Louis E. Bisch	.50	1.25	2.00	NF
M4014	Best Jokes - Powers Moulton	.50	1.25	2.00	H
M4015	Eat and Reduce - Victor H. Lindlahr	.50	1.25	2.00	NF
M4016	The Fundamentals of Contract Bridge - Charles H. Goren	.50	1.25	2.00	NF
M4017	Modern Parables - Fulton Oursler	.50	1.25	2.00	
M4018	New Standard Book of Model Letters for all Occasions - Leo J. Henkin	.50	1.25	2.00	
M4019	Sex and the Love-Life - William J. Fielding	.50	1.25	2.00	NF
M4020	Word Power Made Easy - Norman Lewis	.50	1.25	2.00	NF
M4021	The Perma Cross Word Puzzle Dictionary - Frank Eaton Newman	.50	1.25	2.00	NF
M4022	Operation Future - Groff Conklin	1.50	3.50	5.00	SF
M4023	Your Legal Advisor - Samuel G. Kling	.50	1.25	2.00	NF
M4024	The Well of Loneliness - Radclyffe Hall	.50	1.25	2.00	
M4025	Spencer Brade, M. D. - Frank G. Slaughter	.75	1.75	3.00	
	1955				
M4026	That None Should Die - Frank G. Slaughter	.75	1.75	3.00	
M4027	East Side General - Frank G. Slaughter	.75	1.75	3.00	
M4028	The Deap Six - Martin Dibner	.75	1.75	3.00	
M4029	To Hell and Back - Audie Murphy	.75	1.75	3.00	B
M4030	The Standard Bartender's Guide - Patrick Gavin Duffy & James A. Beard	.50	1.25	2.00	NF
M4031	The Song of Ruth - Frank G. Slaughter	.75	1.75	3.00	
M4032	Captain of the Medici - John J. Pugh	1.50	3.50	5.00	A
M4033	Lift Up Your Heart - Fulton J. Sheen	.50	1.25	2.00	
M4034	Soldier of Fortune - Ernest K. Gann	.75	1.75	3.00	
M4035	Your Child from 2 to 5 - Morton Edwards	.50	1.25	2.00	
M4036	The Greatest Faith Ever Known - Fulton Oursler	.75	1.75	3.00	
M4037	The Cotton Road - Frank Feville	.75	1.75	3.00	
M4038	A Touch of Glory - Frank G. Slaughter	.75	1.75	3.00	
	1956				
M4039	Prisoner in Paradise - Garet Rogers	.75	1.75	3.00	
M4040	But We Were Born Free - Elmer Davis	.50	1.25	2.00	
M4041	Lights Along the Shore - Fulton Oursler	.50	1.25	2.00	
M4042	Mardios Beach - Oakley Hall	.75	1.75	3.00	
M4043	The Silver Oar - Howard Breslin	.50	1.25	2.00	
M4044	Ceremony of Love - Thomas Williams	.50	1.25	2.00	
M4045	The Strongbox - Howard Swiggett	.75	1.75	3.00	
M4046	The Greatest Story Ever Told - Fulton Oursler	.75	1.75	3.00	
M4047	Divine Mistress - Frank G. Slaughter	.75	1.75	3.00	
M4048	Battle Surgeon - Frank G. Slaughter	.50	1.25	2.00	C
M4049	The Galileans - Frank G. Slaughter	.75	1.75	3.00	
M4050	Slattery's Hurricane - Herman Wouk	.75	1.75	3.00	
	1956				
M4051	The Healer - Frank G. Slaughter	.75	1.75	3.00	
M4052	The Hound of Earth - Vance Bourjaily	.50	1.25	2.00	
M4053	Air Surgeon - Frank G. Slaughter	.75	1.75	3.00	C
M4054	Fort Everglades - Frank G. Slaughter	2.00	4.00	7.50	A

(PERMA BOOKS, continued)

M4055	The Road to Bithyula - Frank G. Slaughter	.75	1.75	3.00	
M4056	South Sea Stories - W. Somerset Maugham	1.50	3.50	5.00	
M4057	Darien Venture - C. V. Terry	.75	1.75	3.00	
M4058	Shad Run - Howard Breslin	.75	1.75	3.00	
M4059	The Will to Live - Arnold A. Hutschnecker	.50	1.25	2.00	
M4060	Science and Surgery - Frank G. Slaughter	.50	1.25	2.00	
4061	Run Silent, Run Deep - Edward L. Beach	.75	1.75	3.00	C
M4062	Kon-Tiki - Thor Heyerdahl	.75	1.75	3.00	NF
M4063	Cell 2455, Death Row - Caryl Chessman	2.00	4.00	7.50	B
M4064	Flight from Natchez - Frank G. Slaughter	.75	1.75	3.00	
M4065	How to Eat Better for Less Money - Sam W. Aaron	.50	1.25	2.00	NF
M4066	The Complete Letter Writer - N. H. & S. K. Mayer	.50	1.25	2.00	NF
M4067	H. M. S. Ulysses - Alistair MacLean	.75	1.75	3.00	A
M4068	Winter Harvest - Norah Lofts	.50	1.25	2.00	
M4069	The Scarlet Cord - Frank G. Slaughter	.75	1.75	3.00	
M4070	The Highwayman - Noel B. Gerson	1.50	3.50	5.00	A
M4071	The Smiling Rebel - Harnett T. Kane	.75	1.75	3.00	
M4072	The Golden Isle - Frank G. Slaughter	.75	1.75	3.00	
M4073	The Dice of God - Hoffman Birney	.50	1.25	2.00	
M4074	How to Win and Hold a Mate - Samuel G. Kling	.50	1.25	2.00	NF
M4075	Christopher Humble - Charles B. Judah	.75	1.75	3.00	
	1957				
M4076	The Corsair - Madeleine Fabiola Kent	1.50	3.50	5.00	A
M4077	The Loving Couple - Virginia Rowans	.50	1.25	2.00	
M4078	Kentucky Pride - Gene Markey	.75	1.75	3.00	
M4079	The Wreck of the Mary Deare - Hammond Innes	.75	1.75	3.00	
M4080	Breakaway - Wally Depew	.50	1.25	2.00	
M4081	Position Unknown - Ian Mackersey	.75	1.75	3.00	
M4082	Murder of a Mistress - Henry Kuttner	3.00	6.00	12.00	M
M4083	Bellevve Is my Home - S. R. Cutolo	1.50	3.50	5.00	NF
M4084	Rate Yourself - Pauline Arnold	.50	1.25	2.00	NF
M4085	Underworld U. S. A. - Joseph F. Dinneen	1.50	3.50	5.00	NF
M4086	Diamond in the Sky - Mary Orr	.50	1.25	2.00	
M4087	The Warrior - Frank G. Slaughter	1.50	3.50	5.00	
M4088	Dracula - Bram Stoker	1.50	3.50	5.00	HO
M4089	The Guns of Navarone - Alistair MacLean	.75	1.75	3.00	C
M4090	The Calendar Epic - James Kubeck	.50	1.25	2.00	
M4091	Twilight for the Gods - Ernest K. Gann	.50	1.25	2.00	
M4092	Sword and Scalpel - Frank G. Slaughter	.75	1.75	3.00	
M4093	The Proving Flight - David Beaty	.75	1.75	3.00	
M4094	Star of Macedon - Karl V. Eiker	.75	1.75	3.00	
M4095	In the Wet - Nevil Shute	.50	1.25	2.00	
M4096	Murder of a Wife - Henry Kuttner	3.00	6.00	12.00	M
M4097	The Midwife of Pont Clery - Flora Sandstrom	.50	1.25	2.00	
M4098	Till the Rafters Ring - Roswell G. Ham, Jr.	.50	1.25	2.00	
M4099	The Tortured Path - Kendell Foster Crossen	.75	1.75	3.00	
M4100	The Golden Ones - C. V. Terry	.50	1.25	2.00	
	1958				
M4101	The Second Perma Quiz Book - Joseph Nathan Kane	1.50	3.50	5.00	
M4102	The Mask - Stuart Cloete	.50	1.25	2.00	
M4103	The Royai Vultures - Hillel Black & Sam Kolman	.75	1.75	3.00	
M4104	The Success - Helen Howe	.50	1.25	2.00	
M4105	The Country Club Set - Otis Carney	.50	1.25	2.00	
M4106	What to Tell Your Children About Sex - Adie Suehsdorf	.50	1.25	2.00	NF
M4107	Doctor Pygmalion - Maxwell Maltz	.50	1.25	2.00	
M4108	Give Me Possession - Paul Horgan	.50	1.25	2.00	
M4109	Flight Hostess - Emily Thorne	.50	1.25	2.00	
M4110	Astrology and You - Carroll Righter	.50	1.25	2.00	NF
M4111	The Mapmaker - Frank G. Slaughter	.75	1.75	3.00	
M4112	No Hiding Place - Beth Day	.50	1.25	2.00	
M4113	The Questing Sword - Jefferson Cooper	1.50	3.50	5.00	
M4114	The Bixby Girls - Rosamond Marshall	.50	1.25	2.00	
	1959				
M4115	Pork Chop Hill - S. L. A. Marshall Movie tie-in	1.50	3.50	5.00	
M4116	South by Jara Head - Alistair MacLean	.75	1.75	3.00	A
M4117	Veronica's Vell - Jefferson Cooper	.75	1.75	3.00	

M4118	The D. A.'s Man - Harold Danforth & James D. Horan	.50	1.25	2.00	
M4119	The Devil's Cross - Walter O'Meara	.75	1.75	3.00	
M4120	Wasp - Eric Frank Russell	.75	1.75	3.00	SF
M4121	The Forbidden Road - Victor Canning	.50	1.25	2.00	
M4122	The Counterfeit Traitor - Alexander Klein	.50	1.25	2.00	
M4123	Betty White's Teen-age Dance Book - Betty White	.50	1.25	2.00	NF
M4124	Imitation of Life - Fannie Hurst	.50	1.25	2.00	
M4125	10 Days to a Successful Memory - Joyce Brothers & Edward P. F. Eagan 1959	.50	1.25	2.00	NF
M4126	A Family Affair - Roger Eddy	.50	1.25	2.00	
M4127	Scent of Cloves - Norah Lofts	.50	1.25	2.00	
M4128	Home from the Hill - William Humphrey	.50	1.25	2.00	
M4129	His Majesty's Highwayman - Donald Barr Chidsey	1.50	3.50	5.00	A
M4130	Daybreak - Frank G. Slaughter	.50	1.25	2.00	
M4131	The Pocket Book of Household Hints - Holly Cantus	.50	1.25	2.00	NF
M4132	Warm Bodies - Donald R. Morris	.50	1.25	2.00	
M4133	A Man Against Fate - Frank Canizio & Robert Markel	.50	1.25	2.00	
M4134	Freud: His Dream and Sex Theories - Joseph Jastrow	.75	1.75	3.00	NF
M4135	The Southern Cross - Peter French	.50	1.25	2.00	
M4136	The Fundamentals of Fishing and Hunting - Byron Dalrymple	.75	1.75	3.00	
M4137					
M4138	Fun for the Family - Jerome S. Meyer	.50	1.25	2.00	NF
M4139	The Captives of Mora Island - Victor Canning	.75	1.75	3.00	
M4140	All About Men - Joseph H. Peck	.50	1.25	2.00	
M4141	The Cultured Man - Ashley Montagu	.75	1.75	3.00	NF
M4142	Top of the World - Hans Ruesch	.50	1.25	2.00	
M4145	The Widow's Tale - John Coates	.50	1.25	2.00	
M4146	Woman Obsessed - John Mantley	.50	1.25	2.00	
M4147	AMF Guide to Natural Bowling - Victor Kalman	.50	1.25	2.00	NF
M4148	A Guide to Better Living - N. H. & S. K. Mager	.50	1.25	2.00	NF
M4149	Sands of Mars - Arthur C. Clarke	.75	1.75	3.00	
M4150	Killer's Wedge - Ed McBain 1959	.75	1.75	3.00	M
M4151	Tales Out of (Night) School - Hy Gardner	.50	1.25	2.00	H
M4152	The Savage - Noel Clad	.75	1.75	3.00	
M4153	Settlement Nurse - Rosie M. Banks	.50	1.25	2.00	R
M4161	Journey to the Center of the Earth - Jules Verne Movie tie-in	1.50	3.50	5.00	SF
M4168	Hound-dog Man - Fred Gipson Movie tie-in	.75	1.75	3.00	
M4201	Red Harvest - Dashiell Hammett	.75	1.75	3.00	M
M5000	Son of a Hundred Kings - Thomas B. Costain 1955	1.50	3.50	5.00	A
M5001	A General Introduction to Psychoanalysis - Sigmund Freud	.75	1.75	3.00	NF
M5002	The Shorter Bartlett's Familiar Questions - John Bartlett	.75	1.75	3.00	NF
M5003	The Silver Chalice - Thomas B. Costain 1956	1.50	3.50	5.00	A
M5004	Stories of the Great Operas - Milton Cross	1.50	3.50	5.00	NF
M5005	The Story of the Bible - Hendrik Willem van Loon	1.50	3.50	5.00	NF
M5006	A Complete Guide to Gardening - Montague Free 1957	.75	1.75	3.00	NF
M5007	The Concise Treasury of Great Poems - Louis Untermeyer 1958	.50	1.25	2.00	
M5008	When Your Child is Ill - Samuel Karelitz	.50	1.25	2.00	NF
M5009	The Sexual Responsibility of Woman - Maxine Davis 1959	.50	1.25	2.00	

(PERMA BOOKS, continued)

M5010	The Well of Loneliness - Radclyffe Hall	.50	1.25	2.00	
M5011	Only in America - Harry Golden	.50	1.25	2.00	
M5012	The Legal Encyclopedia for Home and Business - Samuel G. Kling	.50	1.25	2.00	NF
M5013	Schifferes' Family Medical Encyclopedia - Justus J. Schifferes	.50	1.25	2.00	NF
M5014	The Greatest Book Ever Written - Fulton Oursler	.75	1.75	3.00	
M7500	Gone With the Wind - Margaret Mitchell 1958	.75	1.75	3.00	

PERMA BOOKS (Hardbound)

(Perma Books/Doubleday and Co., Inc.)

See Perma Books (Softbound)

P 1	Best Loved Poems - ed. MacKenzie	.75	1.75	3.00	
P 2	How to Write Letters for All Occasions - Alexander L. Sheff & Edna Ingalls	.75	1.75	3.00	NF
P 3	Best Quotations for All Occasions	.75	1.75	3.00	
P 4	Common Errors in English and How to Avoid Them - Alexander M. Witherspoon	.75	1.75	3.00	NF
P 5	The Standard Bartender's Guide - Patrick Duffy	.75	1.75	3.00	NF
P 6	Sex and the Love Life - William J. Fielding	.75	1.75	3.00	NF
P 7	Eat and Reduce! - Victor H. Lindlahr	.75	1.75	3.00	
P 8	Best Jokes for All Occasions - Moulton	.75	1.75	3.00	H
P 9	Ida Bailey Allen's Cook Book	.75	1.75	3.00	NF
P10	The Conquest of Fear - Basil King	.75	1.75	3.00	
P11	How Shall I Tell My Child? - Belle S. Mooney	.75	1.75	3.00	
P12	The Male Hormone - Paul de Kruif	.75	1.75	3.00	NF
P13	Something to Live By - Dorothea Kopplin	.75	1.75	3.00	
P14	Sight Without Glasses - Harold M. Peppard 1948	.75	1.75	3.00	NF
P15	Blackstone's Tricks Anyone Can Do	4.00	8.00	15.00	NF
P16	Fortune Telling for Fun and Popularity - Paul Showers	.75	1.75	3.00	NF
P17	Handy Encyclopedia of Useful Information	.75	1.75	3.00	NF
P18	Famous Sheriffs and Western Outlaws - William MacLeod Raine	2.00	4.00	7.50	NF
P19	Good English Made Easy - J. Milnor Dorey	.75	1.75	3.00	NF
P20	Mathematics for Home and Business - William	.75	1.75	3.00	NF
P21	Modern Sex Life - Edwin W. Hirsch	.75	1.75	3.00	NF
P22	Life with Mother - Clarence Day	.75	1.75	3.00	
P23	Strange Customs of Courtship and Marriage - William J. Fielding	.75	1.75	3.00	NF
P24	Brief Biographies of Famous Men and Woman - W. Stuart Sewell	.75	1.75	3.00	NF
P25	Handy Legal Adviser for Home and Business - Samuel G. Kling	.75	1.75	3.00	NF
P26	What Your Dreams Mean - Herbert Hespro	.75	1.75	3.00	
P27	Handbook for House Repairs - Louis Gelders & Eugene O'Hare	.75	1.75	3.00	NF
P28	A Short History of the World - J. Milnor Dorey	.75	1.75	3.00	NF

Perma Books P15, c. Perma

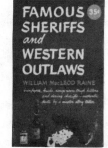

Perma Books P18, c. Perma

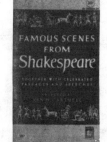

Perma Books P87, c. Perma

(PERMABOOKS, continued)

P29	In His Steps - Charles M. Sheldon	.75	1.75	3.00	
P30	Stories for Men - Charles Grayson	.75	1.75	3.00	
P31	The Art of Enjoying Music - Sigmund Spaeth	.75	1.75	3.00	NF
P32	Photography as a Hobby - Fred B. Barton	.75	1.75	3.00	NF
P33	Winning Poker - Oswald Jacoby	.75	1.75	3.00	NF
P34	The Handy Book of Hobbies - Geoffrey Mott-Smith	.75	1.75	3.00	NF
P35	Dale Carnegie's Five Minute Biographies	.75	1.75	3.00	NF
P36	Astrology for Everyone - Evangeline Adams	.75	1.75	3.00	
P37	Numerology - Morris C. Goodman	.75	1.75	3.00	NF
P38	Three Famous French Novels	.75	1.75	3.00	
P39	Character Reading Made Easy - Meier	.75	1.75	3.00	
P40	Stop Me If You've Heard This One - Lehr, Tinney, & Bower	.75	1.75	3.00	H
P41	Best Short Stories of Jack London	1.50	3.50	5.00	
P42	The Art of Living - Norman Vincent Peale	.50	1.25	2.00	
P43	The Human Body and How It Works - Tokay	.75	1.75	3.00	NF
P44	A Handy Illustrated Guide to Football	.75	1.75	3.00	NF
P45	The Golden Book of Prayer - D. B. Aldrich	.75	1.75	3.00	
P46	How to Control Worry - Matthew N. Chappell	.75	1.75	3.00	
P47	A Handy Illustrated Guide to Basketball	.75	1.75	3.00	NF
P48	Better Speech for You - Daniel P. Eginton	.75	1.75	3.00	NF
P49	The Man Nobody Knows - Bruce Barton	.75	1.75	3.00	
P50	Psychoanalysis and Love - Andre Tridon	.75	1.75	3.00	
P51	The Key to Your Personality - Charles B. Roth	.75	1.75	3.00	
P52	A Handy Illustrated Guide to Bowling	.75	1.75	3.00	NF
P53	A Handy Illustrated Guide to Boxing	.75	1.75	3.00	NF
P54	Magic Explained - Walter B. Gibson	10.00	25.00	40.00	NF
P55	The Handy Book of Indoor Games - Geoffrey Mott-Smith	.75	1.75	3.00	NF
P56					
P57	Understanding Human Nature - Alfred Adler	.75	1.75	3.00	
P58	Bridge Quiz Book - Charles H. Goren First ed., 1949	.75	1.75	3.00	NF
P59	Reading Handwriting for Fun and Popularity - Dorothy Sara	.75	1.75	3.00	NF
P60	Be Glad You're Neurotic - Louis E. Bisch	.75	1.75	3.00	
P61	Grammar Made Easy - Richard D. Mallery	.75	1.75	3.00	NF
P62	Permabook of Art Masterpieces - Ray Brock	.75	1.75	3.00	NF
P63	The Handy Book of Gardening - Wilkinson & Tiedjens	.75	1.75	3.00	NF
P64	The Meaning of Psychoanalysis - Martin W. Peck	.75	1.75	3.00	NF
P65	Know Your Real Abilities - C. V. & M. E. Broadley	.75	1.75	3.00	
P66	Stories of Famous Operas - Harold V. Milligan	.75	1.75	3.00	
P67	The Science Fiction Galaxy - Groff Conklin	3.00	6.00	12.00	SF
P68	How to Use Your Imagination to Make Money - C. B. Roth	.75	1.75	3.00	
P69	Favorite Verse of Edgar A. Guest 1950	.75	1.75	3.00	
P70	Perma Handy World Atlas	.75	1.75	3.00	NF
P71	Goren's Canasta Up-to-date - Charles H. Goren	.75	1.75	3.00	NF
P72	Meditations and My Daily Strength - Preston Bradley	.75	1.75	3.00	
P73	Personality Pointers - Jill Edwards	.75	1.75	3.00	
P74	South Sea Stories - W. Somerset Maugham	1.50	3.50	5.00	
P75	Manners for Millions - Sophie C. Hadida	.75	1.75	3.00	
P76	The Care and Handling of Dogs - Jack Baird	.75	1.75	3.00	NF
P77	A Handy Illustrated Guide to Baseball	.75	1.75	3.00	NF
P78	Buried Treasure - Ken Krippene	1.50	3.50	5.00	NF
P79	Everyday Speech - Bess Sondel	.75	1.75	3.00	NF
P80	The New Standard Ready Reckoner	.75	1.75	3.00	
P81	How to Read Palms - Litzka Raymond	.75	1.75	3.00	
P82	The Perma Week-End Companion - E. Mitchell	.75	1.75	3.00	
P83	How to Travel for Fun - Helen Eva Tates	.75	1.75	3.00	NF
P84					
P85	Dictionary of First Aid for Emergencies - H. Pomeranz	.75	1.75	3.00	NF
P86	The Perma Rhyming Dictionary - Langford Reed	.75	1.75	3.00	NF
P87	Famous Scenes from Shakespeare - Van H. Cartmell 1950	.75	1.75	3.00	
P88	Reading for Enjoyment - Donald MacCampbell	.75	1.75	3.00	NF

P89	The Perma Crossword Puzzle Dictionary - Frank Eaton Newman	.75	1.75	3.00	NF
P90	Essentials of Arithmetic - Henry Sticker	.75	1.75	3.00	NF
P91	The Perma Treasury of Love Poems - William Lord	.75	1.75	3.00	
P92	Favorite Stories from the Bible - S. E. Frost, Jr.	.75	1.75	3.00	
P93	Love and Idleness - Miguel Alcalde	.75	1.75	3.00	
P94	Perma Book of Ghost Stories - W. Bob Holland	4.00	8.00	15.00	
P95	Strange Tales of Famous Frauds - Henry & Dana Lee Thomas	1.50	3.50	5.00	NF
P96	Powdersmoke Justice - William Colt MacDonald	1.50	3.50	5.00	W
P97	You Can Win - Norman Vincent Peale	.50	1.25	2.00	
P99	Married Love - Marie Stopes	.75	1.75	3.00	NF
P100	Fundamentals of Contract Bridge - Charles H. Goren	.75	1.75	3.00	NF
P101	Careers That Change Your World - James Keller	.75	1.75	3.00	

PERMABOOKS (Softbound)

(Perma Books Doubleday and Company, Inc.)

Also see Permabooks (Hardbound)

P 5	The Standard Bartender's Guide - Patrick Gavin Duffy 1951	.75	1.75	3.00	NF
P 7	Eat and Reduce - Victor H. Lindlahr 1952	.75	1.75	3.00	NF
P 22	Life with Mother - Clarence Day	.75	1.75	3.00	
P 25	Handy Legal Advisor for Home and Business - Samuel G. Kling 1951	.75	1.75	3.00	NF
P 65	Know Your Real Abilities - Charles V. & Margaret E. Broadley 1953	.75	1.75	3.00	NF
P 89	The Perma Cross-Word Puzzle Dictionary - Frank Eaton Newman 1951	.75	1.75	3.00	NF
P 93	Love and Idleness - Miguel Alcalde 1951	.75	1.75	3.00	
P 98	New Standard Book of Model Letters for All Occasions - Leo J. Henkin 1951	1.50	3.50	5.00	NF
P102	Wind of the Western Sea - Giussepe Puzza	.75	1.75	3.00	
P103	Something for Nothing - P. D. Kappan	.75	1.75	3.00	
P104	One Plus One - Gunther Heiss	.75	1.75	3.00	
P105	Three Minutes a Day - James Keller	.75	1.75	3.00	NF
P106	How to Overcome Nervous Stomach Trouble - Joseph F. Montague	.75	1.75	3.00	NF
P107	In A Dark Garden - Frank G. Slaughter	.75	1.75	3.00	
P108	Unconquered - Neil H. Swanson	.75	1.75	3.00	
P109	One Tropical Night - Vicki Baum	1.50	3.50	5.00	
P110	Bell Timson - Marguerie Steen	.75	1.75	3.00	
P111	Castaway Island - William George Weekley	2.00	4.00	7.50	
P112	The Well of Loneliness - Radclyffe Hall	1.50	3.50	5.00	
P113	Poems for Men - Damon Runyon	2.00	4.00	7.50	
P114	The Mudlark - Theodore Bonnet	.75	1.75	3.00	
P115	The Chain - Paul I. Wellman	1.50	3.50	5.00	
P116	Fear is the Hunter - Hildegarde Tolman Tellhet	1.50	3.50	5.00	
P117	In the Grip of Terror - Groff Conklin	4.00	8.00	15.00	HO
P118	As Tough as They Come - Will Oursler	2.00	4.00	7.50	
P119	To Hell and Back - Audie Murphy	2.00	4.00	7.50	B
P120	The Case of the Little Doctor - Hilda Lewis	2.00	4.00	7.50	M
P121	The Golden Isle - Frank G. Slaughter	2.00	4.00	7.50	A
P122	New Stories for Men - Charles Grayson	.75	1.75	3.00	
P123	The Beautiful and the Damned - F. Scott Fitzgerald	1.50	3.50	5.00	

Permabooks P117, c. Perma   Permabooks P124, c. Perma   Permabooks P126, c. Perma

(PERMA BOOKS, continued)

P124 Arrest the Saint! - Leslie Charteris	4.00	8.00	15.00	M
P125 The Salem Frigate - John Jennings	2.00	4.00	7.50	A
1951				
P126 Spurs West! - Joseph T. Shaw	2.00	4.00	7.50	W
P127 Fair Wind to Java - Garland Roark	2.00	4.00	7.50	
P128 Night Without Stars - Winston Graham	1.50	3.50	5.00	
P129 The Walls of Jericho - Paul I. Wellman	1.50	3.50	5.00	
P130 The Thorndike - Barnhart Handy Pocket Distionary - Clarence Barnhart	.75	1.75	3.00	NF
P131 You Can Change the World - James Keller	.75	1.75	3.00	NF
P132 Chad Hanna - Walter D. Edmonds	1.50	3.50	5.00	
P133 The Sea Eagles - John Jennings	2.00	4.00	7.50	A
P134 The Raging Tide - Ernest K. Gann	1.50	3.50	5.00	
P135 The Greatest Story Ever Told - Fulton Oursler	.75	1.75	3.00	
P136 Quietly My Captain Waits - Evelyn Eaton	1.50	3.50	5.00	E
P137 Lusty Wind for Carolina - Inglis Fletcher	2.00	4.00	7.50	
P138 Black Judas - Burke Wilkinson aka Run Mongoose	2.00	4.00	7.50	E
P139 Rainbow in the Royals - Garland Roark	2.00	4.00	7.50	E
P140 Divine Mistress - Frank G. Slaughter	2.00	4.00	7.50	
P141 Land of Vengeance - John Jennings aka Call the New World	2.00	4.00	7.50	
P142 Angle with Spurs - Paul I. Wellman	1.50	3.50	5.00	
1952				
P143 Tidewater - Clifford Dowdey	.75	1.75	3.00	E
P144 Scarlet Cockerel - Garald Lagard	1.50	3.50	5.00	A
P145 Beyond the End of Time - Frederik Pohl	4.00	8.00	15.00	SF
P146 Tom Bone - Charles B. Judah	.75	1.75	3.00	E
P147 The Turning Wheels - Stuart Cloete	.75	1.75	3.00	E
P148 Guard of Honor - James Gould Cozzens	1.50	3.50	5.00	
P149 Phantom Fortress - Bruce Lancaster	1.50	3.50	5.00	
P150 The Man with One Talent - Josiah E. Greene	.75	1.75	3.00	
1952				
P151 Roanoke Hundred - Inglis Fletcher	2.00	4.00	7.50	
P152 The Color of Blood - E. Ralph Rundell	1.50	3.50	5.00	
P153 Before the Sun Goes Down - Elizabeth Metzger Howard	1.50	3.50	5.00	
P154 Gentleman's Agreement - Laura Z. Hobson	2.00	4.00	7.50	
P155 Fort Everglades - Frank G. Slaughter	2.00	4.00	7.50	
P156 If a man be mad - Harold Maine	2.00	4.00	7.50	
P157 River to the West - John Jennings	2.00	4.00	7.50	A
P158S Crusade in Europe - Dwight D. Eisenhower	1.50	3.50	5.00	
P159 Bugles Blow No More - Clifford Dowdey	1.50	3.50	5.00	
P160 The Mission of Jeffery Tomaly - Darwin L. Teilhet	.75	1.75	3.00	
P161 Woman in Love - Lucy Cores	1.50	3.50	5.00	
P162 The Ironmaster - Anne Powers	1.50	3.50	5.00	
P163 Morning Time - Charles O'Neill	1.50	3.50	5.00	
P164 My Lord America - Alex Rackowe	1.50	3.50	5.00	
P165S Lydia Bailey - Kenneth Roberts	1.50	3.50	5.00	
P166 The Plymouth Adventure - Ernest Gebler	1.50	3.50	5.00	
P167 Hear This Woman - Ana & Ben Pinchot	.75	1.75	3.00	
P168 Sir Pagan - Henry John Colyton	2.00	4.00	7.50	A
P169 Sing at My Wake - Jo Sinclair	.75	1.75	3.00	
P170 Be My Love - Harriet Hinsdale	1.50	3.50	5.00	E
P171 Bennett's Welcome - Inglis Fletcher	1.50	3.50	5.00	
P172 Government is Your Business - James Keller	.50	1.25	2.00	NF

P173 Rogue's Honor - Anne Powers	2.00	4.00	7.50	A
P174 Stronghold - Donald Barr Chidsey	2.00	4.00	7.50	A
P175 Victory in the Dust - Arthur Phillips 1952	1.50	3.50	5.00	
P176 Trumpet to Arms - Bruce Lancaster	1.50	3.50	5.00	
P177 Modern Parables - Fulton Oursler	.50	1.25	2.00	
P178S Green Dolphin Street - Elizabeth Goudge	.75	1.75	3.00	
P179 Big Old Sun - Robert Faherty	1.50	3.50	5.00	
P180 That None Should Die - Frank G. Slaughter	1.50	3.50	5.00	
P181 They Had a Glory - Davenport Steward	.75	1.75	3.00	
P182 King's Arrow - Joseph Patrick	2.00	4.00	7.50	A
P183 Some Thing To Live By - Dorothea S. Kopplin	.75	1.75	3.00	
P184 The Fundamentals of Contract Bridge - Charles H. Goren	.50	1.25	2.00	NF
P185 Journey to Nowhere - Martin Dibner aka The Bachelor Seals	1.50	3.50	5.00	
P186 Devil's Spawn - Wenzell Brown	4.00	8.00	15.00	A
P187S Murder, Inc. - Sid Feder & Burton B. Turkus	1.50	3.50	5.00	
P188 Restless Are the Sails - Evelyn Eaton	1.50	3.50	5.00	
P189 Men of Albemarle - Inglis Fletcher	3.00	6.00	12.00	A
P190 The Celebrity - Laura Z. Hobson	.75	1.75	3.00	
P191 Beau Geste - Percival C. Wren	2.00	4.00	7.50	A
P192 Detour - Norma Ciraci	1.50	3.50	5.00	E
P193 Silver Nutmeg - Norah Lofts 1953	2.00	4.00	7.50	E
P194 Dark Memory - Jonathan Latimer	1.50	3.50	5.00	
P195 Battle Surgeon - Frank G. Slaughter	1.50	3.50	5.00	C
P196 The Scarlet Patch - Bruce Lancaster	1.50	3.50	5.00	
P197 Port of Call - Maxwell Griffith	1.50	3.50	5.00	
P198 Slant of the Wild Wind - Garland Roark	1.50	3.50	5.00	E
P199S The Prodigal Women - Nancy Hale	1.50	3.50	5.00	
P200 Rogue Errant - Michael Leigh 1953	2.00	4.00	7.50	A
P201S The Story of the Bible - Hendrik Willem van Loon	2.00	4.00	7.50	NF
P202S A General Introduction to Psychoanalysis - Sigmund Freud	.75	1.75	3.00	NF
P203 Music Out of Dixie - Harold Sinclair	1.50	3.50	5.00	
P204 The Wire - David Walker	.75	1.75	3.00	
P205S The Shorter Bartlett's Familiar Quotations - John Bartlett	.75	1.75	3.00	NF
P206S The Concise Treasury of Great Poems - Louis Untermeyer	.75	1.75	3.00	
P207 Raleigh's Eden - Inglis Fletcher	3.00	6.00	12.00	A
P208 Grand Hotel - Vicki Baum	.75	1.75	3.00	
P209 Word Power Made Easy - Norman Lewis	.50	1.25	2.00	NF
P210 Schnozzola - Gene Fowler	3.00	6.00	12.00	B
P211 The Long Run - J. Bigelow Clark	.75	1.75	3.00	
P212S 7 Arts - Fernando Puma	.75	1.75	3.00	
P213S New Voices: American Writing Today - Don M. Wolfe	.50	1.25	2.00	
P214 To Hell and Back - Audie Murphy	.75	1.75	3.00	B
P215 The Gladiator - Thames Williamson	2.00	4.00	7.50	S
P216 Toil of the Brave - Inglis Fletcher	2.00	4.00	7.50	
P217S Show Biz - Abel Green & Joe Laurie, Jr.	1.50	3.50	5.00	NF
P218 East Side General - Frank G. Slaughter	.75	1.75	3.00	
P219 Venture in the East - Bruce Lancaster	1.50	3.50	5.00	
P220 In A Dark Garden - Frank G. Slaughter	.75	1.75	3.00	
p221 The Golden Isle - Frank G. Slaughter	1.50	3.50	5.00	
P222 Touched in Fire - John Tebbel	1.50	3.50	5.00	
P223 The Bengal Tiger - Hall Hunter	2.00	4.00	7.50	A
P224 Summer in Rome - Paul Hyde Bonner	.75	1.75	3.00	
P225 Beyond the Blue Mountains - Jean Plaidy 1953	1.50	3.50	5.00	
P226 Spencer Brade, M. D. - Frank G. Slaughter	.75	1.75	3.00	
P227 Swing the Big-Eyed Rabbit - John Pleasant McCoy	.75	1.75	3.00	E
P228 Immortal Wife - Irving Stone	.75	1.75	3.00	
P229 Front Office - Herbert Lyons	.75	1.75	3.00	
P230 Indian Summer - Robert Sylvester	1.50	3.50	5.00	
P231 The Golden Egg - James Pollak	.75	1.75	3.00	
P232 Beau Sabreur - Percival C. Wren	2.00	4.00	7.50	A
P233 Divine Mistress - Frank G. Slaughter	2.00	4.00	7.50	
P234 No Bugles Tonight - Bruce Lancaster	1.50	3.50	5.00	
P235 Yankee Woman - Eric Baume	2.00	4.00	7.50	A

Permabooks P207, c. Perma   Permabooks P236, c. Perma   Permabooks P275, c. Perma

(PERMABOOKS, continued)

P236	Shadow of Tomorrow - Frederik Pohl	3.00	6.00	12.00	SF
P237	Salome, the Princess of Galilee - Henry Denker	2.00	4.00	7.50	A
238	Trail End - Tom J. Hopkins	1.50	3.50	5.00	W
239	Women in Prison - Joan Henry	2.00	4.00	7.50	
P240	The Bowl of Brass - Paul I. Wellman	1.50	3.50	5.00	
P241	The Road to Bithynia - Frank G. Slaughter	.75	1.75	3.00	
P242	The Handy Home Medical Adviser - Morris Fishbein	.50	1.25	2.00	NF
P243	Kon Tiki - Thor Heyerdahl	1.50	3.50	5.00	NF
244	The Tall Delores - Michael Avallone	2.00	4.00	7.50	M
245	Memory of Love - Bessie Brever	1.50	3.50	5.00	
P246	Coins in the Fountain - John H. Secondari	1.50	3.50	5.00	
P247	My Love Must Wait - Ernestine Hill	.75	1.75	3.00	
P248	Panama Passage - Donald Barr Chidsey	1.50	3.50	5.00	
P249	Big Beverage - William T. Campbell	.75	1.75	3.00	
P250S	The Greatest Book Ever Written - Fulton Oursler	.75	1.75	3.00	
	1953				
251	The Old Man's Place - John B. Sanford	.75	1.75	3.00	
252	The Face in the Shadows - Peter Ordway	.75	1.75	3.00	M
253	To Have and Have Not - Ernest Hemingway	1.50	3.50	5.00	
P254	Crossroads in Time - Groff Conklin	2.00	4.00	7.50	SF
P255	By Valour and Arms - James Street	1.50	3.50	5.00	
P256	The Shadow and the Glory - John Jennings	2.00	4.00	7.50	A
257	The Secret Brand - Gene Austin	1.50	3.50	5.00	
258	The Assault - Allen R. Matthews	.75	1.75	3.00	
P259	Air Surgeon - Frank G. Slaughter	.75	1.75	3.00	C
P260	Thunder in the Wilderness - Harry Hamilton	.75	1.75	3.00	
P261	Baghdad-by-the-Bay - Herb Caen	.75	1.75	3.00	
P262S	7 Arts No. 2 - Fernando Puma	.50	1.25	2.00	
	1954				
263	The Comancheros - Paul I. Wellman	1.50	3.50	5.00	W
264	City - Clifford D. Simak	2.00	4.00	7.50	SF
265	Element of Risk - Mark Derby	.75	1.75	3.00	
P266	Bright to the Wanderer - Bruce Lancaster	1.50	3.50	5.00	
P267	Down and Out in Paris and London - George Orwell	.75	1.75	3.00	
P268	Queen's Gift - Inglis Fletcher	2.00	4.00	7.50	A
P269S	The Celluloid Jungle - Robert Carson	1.50	3.50	5.00	
270	Nine to Five - W. H. Prosser	.75	1.75	3.00	
271	Range War - Tom J. Hopkins	1.50	3.50	5.00	W
272	Why I Know There is a God - Fulton Oursler	.50	1.25	2.00	
P273	The Sinner of Saint Ambrose - Robert Raynolds	.75	1.75	3.00	E
P274	The Wreck of the Running Gale - Garland Roark	1.50	3.50	5.00	
P275	The White Rabbit - Bruce Marshall	5.00	10.00	20.00	C
	1954				
P276	The Will to Live - Arnold A. Hutschenecker	.75	1.75	3.00	
277	With Murder for Some - H. C. Huston	1.50	3.50	5.00	M
278	The Intruders - Robert Bright	.75	1.75	3.00	
279	The Lost World - Arthur Conan Doyle	2.00	4.00	7.50	SF
P280	Seed of Mischief - Willa Gibbs	.75	1.75	3.00	
P281	Killers in Africa - Alexander Lake	.75	1.75	3.00	
P282	The Proud Retreat - Clifford Dowdey	.75	1.75	3.00	A
P283	The Rifleman - John Brick	1.50	3.50	5.00	
P284S	The Silver Chalice - Thomas B. Costain	1.50	3.50	5.00	A

(PERMABOOKS, continued)

P285S	Gardening - Montague Free	.50	1.25	2.00	NF
286	The Condemned - Jo Pagano	.75	1.75	3.00	
287	The Crooked Man - Shelley Smith	.75	1.75	3.00	
288	Destination Revenge - Jim Conroy	.75	1.75	3.00	
289	The Spitting Image - Michael Avallone	1.50	3.50	5.00	
P290	The Galileans - Frank G. Slaughter	1.50	3.50	5.00	
P291	Outsiders: Children of Wonder - William Tenn	3.00	6.00	12.00	SF
P292	Day of the Harvest - Helen Upshaw	.75	1.75	3.00	
P293	Gentleman Ranker - John Jennings	2.00	4.00	7.50	A
P294	Gone with the Wind - Margaret Mitchell	1.50	3.50	5.00	
295	Escape the Thunder - Lonnie Coleman c-Maguire	.75	1.75	3.00	
P296	Green Hills of Africa - Ernest Hemingway	1.50	3.50	5.00	
297	Flying Saucers from Outer Space - Donald Keyhoe	1.50	3.50	5.00	
P298	The Golden Eagle - Noel B. Gerson	1.50	3.50	5.00	A
P299	The Southpaw - Mark Harris	.75	1.75	3.00	
P300	Father Divine: Holy Husband - Sara Harris 1954	.50	1.25	2.00	
P301	The High and the Mighty - Ernest K. Gann	2.00	4.00	7.50	
P305	The Babylonians - Nathaniel Norsen Weinreb	2.00	4.00	7.50	A
308	Tic-Polonga - Russ Anderton	.75	1.75	3.00	
310	Against the Fall of Night - Arthur C. Clarke	1.50	3.50	5.00	SF
P311	The Deep Six - Martin Dibner	.75	1.75	3.00	
P313	He Hanged Them High - Homer Croy	2.00	4.00	7.50	NF

PHANTOM BOOKS

(Hanro Corp.)

Digest size

500	Homicide Hotel - Joe Barry	2.00	4.00	7.50	M
501	Kisses Can Kill - Donnell Carey	2.00	4.00	7.50	M
502	The Deadly Lover - Robert O. Saber Orig., 1951	2.00	4.00	7.50	M
503	Married to Murder - Harry Whittington	2.00	4.00	7.50	M
504	Love Me and Die! - Day Keene	2.00	4.00	7.50	M
505	Satan's Widow	2.00	4.00	7.50	M
506	Crime on my Hands - Carl G. Hoges c-Gross	2.00	4.00	7.50	M
507	Hunt the Killer - Day Keene First ed., 1951	2.00	4.00	7.50	M
508	Swamp Kill - Whit Harrison Orig., 1952	2.00	4.00	7.50	M
509	Naked Fury - Day Keene Orig., 1952	2.00	4.00	7.50	M
510	Murder Doll - Robert O. Saber	2.00	4.00	7.50	M
511	Violent Night - Whit Harrison	2.00	4.00	7.50	M
512	No Way Out - Robert O. Saber Orig., 1952	2.00	4.00	7.50	M
513	Wake Up to Murder - Day Keene Orig., 1952	2.00	4.00	7.50	M

Phantom Books 502, c. Hanro   Phantom Books 508, c. Hanro   Phantom Books 513, c. Hanro

Phantom Mystery 1

Phoenix nn, c. Phoen

Pitman Ed. nn, c. Pitman

PHANTOM MYSTERY

(Unknown publisher)

1	Rocket to the Morgue - H. H. Holmes (Anthony Boucher) first ed., 1942	20.00	50.00	75.00	M

PHOENIX

(Phoenix Books)

nn	Tokyo Escapade - Shel Walker Orig., 1955	5.00	10.00	20.00	M

PITMAN EDITION

(Pitman Publishing Corporation)

nn	Franklin Delano Roosevelt: A Memorial - ed. Donald Porter Geddes	1.50	3.50	5.00	B

Note: Variant edition of Pocket Book No. 300

POCKET BOOK

(Pocket Books, Inc.)

nn	The Good Earth - Pearl S. Buck 1938 Introductory book of series	35.00	75.00	135.00
1	Lost Horizon - James Hilton 1939	25.00	60.00	100.00

Pocket Book 1, c. PKB

Pocket Book 10, c. PKB

Pocket Book 25, c. PKB

2	Wake Up and Live - Dorothea Brande	20.00	50.00	80.00	NF
3	Five Great Tragedies - William Shakespeare	20.00	50.00	80.00	
4	Topper - Thorne Smith	20.00	50.00	80.00	H
5	The Murder of Roger Ackroyd - Agatha Christie	20.00	50.00	80.00	M
6	Enough Rope - Dorothy Parker	20.00	50.00	80.00	
7	Wuthering Heights - Emily Bronte	20.00	50.00	80.00	
8	The Way of All Flesh - Samuel Butler	20.00	50.00	80.00	
9	The Bridge of San Luis Rey - Thornton Wilder	20.00	50.00	80.00	
10	Bambi - Felix Salten	20.00	50.00	80.00	
11	The Good Earth - Pearl S. Buck	5.00	10.00	20.00	
12	Great Short Stories - Guy de Maupassant	5.00	10.00	20.00	
13	Show Boat - Edna Ferber	3.00	6.00	12.00	
14	A Tale of Two Cities - Charles Dickens	3.00	6.00	12.00	
15	The Story of Mankind - Hendrik Willem Van Loon	3.00	6.00	12.00	NF
16	Green Mansions - W. H. Hudson	5.00	10.00	20.00	
17	The Chinese Orange Mystery - Ellery Queen	5.00	10.00	20.00	M
18	Pinocchio - Carlo Collodi	7.50	15.00	25.00	
19	Abraham Lincoln - Lord Charnwood	5.00	10.00	20.00	NF
20	The Return of the Native - Thomas Hardy	5.00	10.00	20.00	
21	Murder Must Advertise - Dorothy L. Sayers	4.00	8.00	15.00	M
22	The Swiss Family Robinson - Johann Wyss	4.00	8.00	15.00	A
23	The Autobiography of Benjamin Franklin - B. Franklin	3.00	6.00	12.00	NF
24	The Corpse with the Floating Foot - R. A. J. Walling	5.00	10.00	20.00	M
25	Treasure Island - Robert Louis Stevenson 1939	5.00	10.00	20.00	A
26	Elizabeth and Essex - Lytton Strachey	4.00	8.00	15.00	
27	Appointment in Samarra - John O'Hara	4.00	8.00	15.00	
28	Jeeves - P. G. Wodehouse	5.00	10.00	20.00	
29	A Christmas Carol - Charles Dickens	5.00	10.00	20.00	
30	The Little French Girl - Anne Douglas Sedgwick	4.00	8.00	15.00	
31	The Hunchback of Notre Dame - Volume I - Victor Hugo	5.00	10.00	20.00	A
32	The Hunchback of Notre Dame - Volume II - Victor Hugo	5.00	10.00	20.00	A
33	The Watchman's Clock - Leslie Ford	4.00	8.00	15.00	M
34	Gulliver's Travels - Jonathan Swift 1940 Movie tie-in	5.00	10.00	20.00	A
35	Beau Geste - Percival C. Wren	5.00	10.00	20.00	A
36	The Three Musketeers - Volume I - Alexandre Dumas	4.00	8.00	15.00	A
37	The Three Musketeers - Volume 2 - Alexandre Dumas	4.00	8.00	15.00	A
38	The Mystery of the Blue Train - Agatha Christie	5.00	10.00	20.00	M
39	Great Tales and Poems - Edgar Allen Poe	5.00	10.00	20.00	
40	The Man Nobody Knows - Bruce Barton	2.50	6.00	10.00	
41	The Constant Nymph - Margaret Kennedy	4.00	8.00	15.00	
42	Autobiography of Benvenuto Cellini - B. Cellini	4.00	8.00	15.00	NF
43	The Lodger - Marie Belloc Lowndes	4.00	8.00	15.00	
44	Mother - Kathleen Norris	4.00	8.00	15.00	
45	The Light that Failed - Rudyard Kipling	4.00	8.00	15.00	
46	The Bowstring Murders - Carter Dickson	5.00	10.00	20.00	M
47	Bring 'Em Back Alive - Edward Anthony & Frank Buck	4.00	8.00	15.00	A
48	Scarlet Sister Mary - Julia Peterkin	3.00	6.00	12.00	
49	Dr. Ehrlich's Magic Bullet - Paul deKruif (later editions retitled Microbe Hunters)	5.00	10.00	20.00	NF
50	The House Without a Key - Earl Derr Biggers 1940	5.00	10.00	20.00	M
51	Thunder on the Left - Christopher Morley	4.00	8.00	15.00	
52	The House of the Seven Gables - Nathaniel Hawthorne	4.00	8.00	15.00	
53	The Best of Damon Runyon - D. Runyon	4.00	8.00	15.00	
54	The Great Prince Shan - E. Phillips Oppenheim	4.00	8.00	15.00	
55	Our Town - Thornton Wilder	4.00	8.00	15.00	
56	The Green Bay Tree - Louis Bromfield	3.00	6.00	12.00	
57	After Such Pleasures - Dorothy Parker	3.00	6.00	12.00	

Pocket Book 34, c. PKB   Pocket Book 50, c. PKB   Pocket Book 95, c. PKB

(POCKET BOOK, continued)

58 Tom Brown's School Days - Thomas Hughes	4.00	8.00	15.00	
59 Think Fast, Mr. Moto - John P. Marquand	6.50	15.00	30.00	M
60 The Scandal of Father Brown - G. K. Chesterton	5.00	10.00	20.00	M
61 Bob, Son of Battle - Alfred Ollivant	4.00	8.00	15.00	A
62 The Pocket Book of Verse - M.E. Speare	3.00	6.00	12.00	
63 Pride and Prejudice - Jane Austin	3.00	6.00	12.00	
64 While the Patient Slept - Mignon G. Eberhart	3.00	6.00	12.00	M
65 The Four Million - O. Henry	3.00	6.00	12.00	
66 National Velvet - Enid Bagnold	4.00	8.00	15.00	
67 Heidi - Johanna Spyri	4.00	8.00	15.00	
68 How to Win Friends and Influence People - Dale Carnegie	3.00	6.00	12.00	NF
69 The Thirty-nine Steps - John Buchan	4.00	8.00	15.00	
70 The Mystery of the Dead Police - Philip MacDonald	4.00	8.00	15.00	M
71 The French Powder Mystery - Ellery Queen	4.00	8.00	15.00	M
72 Anne of Windy Poplars - L.M. Montgomery	5.00	10.00	20.00	
73 The Case of the Velvet Claws - Erle Stanley Gardner	3.00	6.00	12.00	M
74 The Unpleasantness at the Bellona Club - Dorothy L. Sayers	4.00	8.00	15.00	M
75 Little Men - Louisa May Alcott 1940	4.00	8.00	15.00	
76 Sunset Gun - Dorothy Parker	3.00	6.00	12.00	
77 The Roman Hat Mystery - Ellery Queen	3.00	6.00	12.00	M
78 Oh, You Tex! - William MacLeod Raine	4.00	8.00	15.00	W
79 Murder in the Calais Coach - Agatha Christie	4.00	8.00	15.00	M
80 Up from Slavery - Booker T. Washington	4.00	8.00	15.00	
81 The Red House Mystery - A. A. Milne	4.00	8.00	15.00	M
82 Captain Blood - Rafael Sabatini	4.00	8.00	15.00	A
83 A Puzzle for Fools - Patrick Quentin	4.00	8.00	15.00	M
84 The Riddle of the Sands - Erskine Childers	4.00	8.00	15.00	
85 Clouds of Witness - Dorothy L. Sayers	4.00	8.00	15.00	M
86 The Red Widow Murders - Carter Dickson	5.00	10.00	20.00	M
87 Mister Glencannon - Guy Gilpatric 1941	4.00	8.00	15.00	
88 The ABC Murders - Agatha Christie	4.00	8.00	15.00	M
89 And Now Good-bye - James Hilton	3.00	6.00	12.00	
90 The Case of the Sulky Girl - Erle Stanley Gardner	3.00	6.00	12.00	M
91 The Pocket Book of Short Stories - M. E. Speare	3.00	6.00	12.00	
92 The Pocket Bible	4.00	8.00	15.00	
93 Goodbye, Mr. Chips - James Hilton	4.00	8.00	15.00	
94 Greenmantle - John Buchan	3.00	6.00	12.00	
95 The Sherlock Holmes Pocket Book - Arthur Conan Doyle	7.50	15.00	30.00	M
96 Believe It or Not - Robert Ripley	5.00	10.00	20.00	NF
97 The Werewolf of Paris - Guy Endore	10.00	25.00	40.00	HO
98 The Circular Staircase - Mary Roberts Rinehart	3.00	6.00	12.00	M
99 The Adventures of Ellery Queen - E. Queen	4.00	8.00	15.00	M
100 The General Died at Dawn - Charles G. Booth 1941	10.00	20.00	35.00	
101 It Walks by Night - John Dickson Carr	5.00	10.00	20.00	M

Pocket Book 96, c. PKB   Pocket Book 100, c. PKB   Pocket Book 102, c. PKB

(POCKET BOOK, continued)

102	The Philadelphia Story - Philip Barry	4.00	8.00	15.00	
103	The Pocket Book of Great Detectives - Lee Wright	5.00	10.00	20.00	M
104	Nana - Emile Zola	4.00	8.00	10.00	M
105	Sir John Magill's Last Journey - Freeman Wills Crofts	4.00	8.00	10.00	M
106	The Case of the Lucky Legs - Erle Stanley Gardner	3.00	6.00	12.00	M
107	The Pocket Book of Etiquette - Margery Wilson	3.00	6.00	12.00	NF
108	The Pocket Reader - Philip Van Doren Stern	3.00	6.00	12.00	
109	The Siamese Twin Mystery - Ellery Queen	4.00	8.00	15.00	M
110	The Pocket Book of Boners Interior Illustrations - Dr. Suess	5.00	10.00	20.00	H
111	Mr. Pinkerton Finds a Body - David Frome	4.00	8.00	15.00	M
112	Fer-de-Lance - Rex Stout	4.00	8.00	15.00	M
113	Enter a Murderer - Ngaio Marsh	4.00	8.00	15.00	M
114	Five Great Comedies - William Shakespeare	3.00	6.00	12.00	
115	Dodsworth - Sinclair Lewis	3.00	6.00	12.00	
116	The Case of the Howling Dog - Erle Stanley Gardner	3.00	6.00	12.00	M
117	The Pocket Book of Mystery Stories - Lee Wright	4.00	8.00	15.00	M
118	We Are Not Alone - James Hilton	3.00	6.00	12.00	
119	The Pocket History of the World - H. G. Wells	4.00	8.00	15.00	NF
120	Life Begins at Forty - Walter B. Pitkin	3.00	6.00	12.00	
121	The Album - Mary Roberts Rinehart	3.00	6.00	12.00	M
122	The Simple Way of Poison - Leslie Ford	4.00	8.00	15.00	M
123	Dr. Jekyll and Mr. Hyde - Robert Louis Stevenson Movie tie-in	7.50	15.00	30.00	SF
124	Mr. Pinkerton Goes to Scotland Yard - David Frome	4.00	8.00	15.00	M
125	The Tragedy of X - Ellery Queen 1941	4.00	8.00	15.00	M
126	Pocket Self-Pronouncing Dictionary and Vocabulary Builder - William J. Pelo	3.00	6.00	12.00	NF
127	The Pocket Book of the War - Quincy Howe	3.00	6.00	12.00	NF
128	The Rubaiyat of Omar Khayyam - Omar Khayyam	3.00	6.00	12.00	

Pocket Book 123, c. PKB   Pocket Book 129, c. PKB   Pocket Book 139, c. PKB

Pocket Book 141, c. PKB   Pocket Book 151, c. PKB   Pocket Book 153, c. PKB

(POCKET BOOK, continued)

129	The Singapore Exile Murders - F. van Wyck Mason	3.00	6.00	12.00	M
130	Strong Poison - Dorothy L. Sayers	3.00	6.00	12.00	M
131	While Rome Burns - Alexander Woollcott	3.00	6.00	12.00	
132	The Pocket Quiz Book - Louise Crittenden & Rosejeanne Slifer	5.00	10.00	20.00	NF
133	The Black Camel - Earl Derr Biggers	5.00	10.00	20.00	M
134	The New Adventures of Ellery Queen - E. Queen	4.00	8.00	15.00	M
135	Long Remember - MacKinlay Kantor	3.00	6.00	12.00	
136	Without Armor - James Hilton 1942	3.00	6.00	12.00	
137	Death in a White Tie - Ngaio Marsh	2.50	6.00	10.00	M
138	The Case of the Caretaker's Cat - Erle Stanley Gardner	3.00	6.00	12.00	M
139	You Can't Do Business with Hitler - Douglas Miller	5.00	10.00	20.00	NF
140	The Door - Mary Roberts Rinehart	3.00	6.00	12.00	M
141	The Saint-Fiacre Affair - Georges Simenon	4.00	8.00	15.00	M
142	The Pocket Companion - Philip Van Doren Stern	3.00	6.00	12.00	
143	The Man Who Came to Dinner - Moss Hart & George S. Kaufman	3.00	6.00	12.00	
144	Singing Guns - Max Brand	3.00	6.00	12.00	W
145	The Pocket Book of Modern American Plays - Bennett Cerf	3.00	6.00	12.00	
146	The Spanish Cape Mystery - Ellery Queen	4.00	8.00	15.00	M
147	The Royal Road to Romance - Richard Halliburton	3.00	6.00	12.00	
148	The Pocket Book of Vegetable Gardening - Charles Nissley	4.00	8.00	15.00	NF
149	Escape - Ethel Vance	3.00	6.00	12.00	
150	The Office Wife - Faith Baldwin 1942	3.00	6.00	12.00	R
151	Hugger-Mugger in the Louvre - Elliot Paul	4.00	8.00	15.00	M
152	The Balcony - Dorothy Cameron Disney	4.00	8.00	15.00	M
153	The Man from Scotland Yard - David Frome	4.00	8.00	15.00	M
154	The Red Badge of Courage - Stephen Crane	3.00	6.00	12.00	
155	Hunger Fighters - Paul de Kruif	2.00	4.00	7.50	NF
156	The White Priory Murders - Carter Dickson	5.00	10.00	20.00	M
157	The Case of the Counterfeit Eye - Erle Stanley Gardner	3.00	6.00	12.00	M
158	Damon Runyon Favorites - D. Runyon	4.00	8.00	15.00	
159	Mrs. Miniver - Jan Struther	3.00	6.00	12.00	
160	The Art of Thinking - Ernest Dimnet	3.00	6.00	12.00	NF
161	The Spirit of the Border - Zane Grey	3.00	6.00	12.00	W
162	Arrowsmith - Sinclair Lewis	3.00	6.00	12.00	
163	Have his Carcase - Dorothy L. Sayers	4.00	8.00	15.00	M
164	A Puzzle for Players - Patrick Quentin	4.00	8.00	15.00	M
165	The Pocket Entertainer - Shirley Cunningham	3.00	6.00	12.00	NF
166	The Norths Meet Murder - Richard & Frances Lockridge	4.00	8.00	12.00	M
167	Peril at End House - Agatha Christie	4.00	8.00	12.00	M
168	The Chinese Parrot - Earl Derr Biggers	5.00	10.00	20.00	M
169	The Nutmeg Tree - Margery Sharp	3.00	6.00	12.00	
170	Defense Will Not Win the War - W.F. Kernan	3.00	6.00	12.00	NF
171	The Cape Cod Mystery - Phoebe Atwood Taylor	3.00	6.00	12.00	M

172	The Pocket Mystery Reader - Lee Wright	4.00	8.00	15.00	M
173	The Strategy of Terror - Edmond Taylor	4.00	8.00	15.00	NF
174	Beat to Quarters - C. S. Forester	3.00	6.00	12.00	
175	Green Light - Lloyd C. Douglas 1942	3.00	6.00	12.00	
176	The Pocket Book of Quotations - Henry Davidoff	3.00	6.00	12.00	NF
177	The Case of the Curious Bride - Erle Stanley Gardner	3.00	6.00	12.00	M
178	I Saw It Happen - Lewis Gannett	3.00	6.00	12.00	
179	The Greek Coffin Mystery - Ellery Queen	4.00	8.00	15.00	M
180	The Peacock Feather Murders - Carter Dickson	5.00	10.00	20.00	M
181	The Pocket Cook Book - Elizabeth Woody	4.00	8.00	15.00	NF
182	The Pocket Book of America - Philip Van Doren Stern	3.00	6.00	12.00	
183	The Return to Religion - Henry C. Link	3.00	6.00	12.00	
184	A Silent Witness - R. Austin Freeman	4.00	8.00	15.00	M
185	The Nine Tailors - Dorothy L. Sayers	4.00	8.00	15.00	M
186	Above Suspicion - Helen MacInnes	2.50	6.00	10.00	
187	The Pocket Book of Dog Stories - Harold Berman	3.00	6.00	12.00	
188	The Hurricane - James Norman Hall & Charles Nordhoff	2.50	6.00	10.00	A
189	My Sister Eileen - Ruth McKenney	3.00	6.00	12.00	
190	The Best of Mr. Fortune Stories - H.C. Bailey	5.00	10.00	20.00	M
191	Behind that Curtain - Earl Derr Biggers	5.00	10.00	20.00	M
192	Prelude to Victory - James B. Reston	3.00	6.00	12.00	
193	Journey into Fear - Eric Ambler	3.00	6.00	12.00	
194	The Coming Battle of Germany - William B. Ziff	3.00	6.00	12.00	NF
195	The Pocket History of the United States - Henry Steele Commager & Alan Nevius	3.00	6.00	12.00	NF
196	The Thin Man - Dashiell Hammett 1943	5.00	10.00	20.00	NF
197	The Pocket Book of War Humor - Bennett Cerf	3.00	6.00	12.00	H
198	The Human Body - Logan Clendening	3.00	6.00	12.00	NF
199	Arsenic and Old Lace - Joseph Kesselring	3.00	6.00	12.00	H
200	The Pocket Book of Flower Gardening 1943	3.00	6.00	12.00	NF
201	The Case of the Stuttering Bishop - Erle Stanley Gardner	2.00	4.00	7.50	M
202	The Dutch Shoe Mystery - Ellery Queen	4.00	8.00	15.00	M
203	Mission to Moscow - Joseph E. Davies	3.00	6.00	12.00	NF
204	Death Lights a Candle - Phoebe Atwood Taylor	3.00	6.00	12.00	M
205	Rebecca - Daphne du Maurier	3.00	6.00	12.00	
206	See Here, Private Hargrove - Marion Hargrove	2.00	4.00	7.50	H
207	Charlie Chan Carries On - Earl Derr Biggers	5.00	10.00	20.00	M
208	The Rubber Band - Rex Stout	5.00	10.00	20.00	M
209	Topper Takes a Trip - Thorne Smith	4.00	8.00	15.00	H
210	The Pocket Book of Crossword Puzzles - Margaret Petherbridge	5.00	10.00	20.00	NF
211	The Glass Key - Dashiell Hammett 1942	5.00	10.00	20.00	M
212	Farewell My Lovely - Raymond Chandler	5.00	10.00	20.00	M
213	The Pocket Book of True Crime Stories - Anthony Boucher 1943	4.00	8.00	15.00	NF
214	The Pocket Book of Science Fiction - Donald A. Wollheim	7.50	15.00	30.00	SF
215	Magnificent Obsession - Lloyd C. Douglas	3.00	6.00	12.00	
216	Mutiny on the Bounty - James Norman Hall & Charles Nordhoff	4.00	8.00	15.00	A
217	The Pocket Book of Home Canning - Elizabeth Beveridge	3.00	6.00	12.00	NF
218	Claudia - Rose Franken	2.00	4.00	7.50	
219	The Punch and Judy Murders - Carter Dickson	5.00	10.00	20.00	M
220	What to do till the Doctor Comes - Donald Armstrong & Grace T. Hallock	3.00	6.00	12.00	NF
221	Overture to Death - Ngaio Marsh	4.00	8.00	15.00	M
222	Fast Company - Marco Page	1.50	3.50	5.00	M
223	The Case of the Lame Canary - Erle Stanley Gardner	2.00	4.00	7.50	M

Pocket Book 253, c. PKB   Pocket Book 268 w/dj, c. PKB Pocket Book 268 wo/dj, c. PKB

(POCKET BOOK, continued)

224 The Great Impersonation - E. Phillips Oppenheim	1.50	3.50	5.00	
225 Into the Valley - John Hersey	3.00	6.00	12.00	
1943				
226 The House of Exile - Nora Wain	2.50	6.00	10.00	
227 The Egyptian Cross Myster - Ellery Queen	3.00	6.00	12.00	M
228 The Bigger They Come - A. A. Fair	2.50	6.00	10.00	M
229 One World - Wendell L. Willkie	2.50	6.00	10.00	
230 The Pocket Aviation Quiz Book - Milton Figen	4.00	8.00	15.00	NF
231 The Judas Window - Carter Dickson	5.00	10.00	20.00	M
232 A Coffin for Dimitrios - Eric Ambler	3.00	6.00	12.00	M
233 The Pocket Book of Cartoons - Bennett Cerf	4.00	8.00	15.00	H
234 Vogue's Pocket Book of Home Dressmaking	2.50	6.00	10.00	NF
235 Assignment in Brittany - Helen MacInnes	2.00	4.00	7.50	
236 The Pocket Book of Father Brown - G. K. Chesterton	4.00	8.00	15.00	M
237 Trial by Fury - Craig Rice	2.00	4.00	7.50	M
238 The Pocket Book of Modern American Short Stories - Philip Van Doren Stern	3.00	6.00	12.00	
239 How to Play Winning Checkers - Millard Hopper	3.00	6.00	12.00	NF
240 Madame Bovary - Gustave Flaubert	2.00	4.00	7.50	
1943				
241 Red Harvest - Dashiell Hammett	5.00	10.00	20.00	M
242 The Case of the Substitute Face - Erle Stanley Gardner	2.00	4.00	7.50	M
243 The Steinbeck Pocket Book - John Steinbeck	4.00	8.00	15.00	
244 U. S. Foreign Policy - Walter Lippmann	2.00	4.00	7.50	NF
1944				
245 The Four of Hearts - Ellery Queen	4.00	8.00	15.00	M
246 The Lady in the Morgue - Jonathan Latimer	4.00	8.00	15.00	M
247 No Surrender - Martha Albrand	3.00	6.00	12.00	
248 The Canary Murder Case - S. S. Van Dine	5.00	10.00	20.00	M
249 The Patriotic Murders - Agatha Christie	3.00	6.00	12.00	M
250 Destry Rides Again - Max Brand	2.50	6.00	10.00	W
1944				
251 The Ogden Nash Pocket Book - Ogden Nash	2.50	6.00	10.00	
252 The Case of the Dangerous Dowager - Erle Stanley Gardner	2.00	4.00	7.50	M
253 Phantom Lady - William Irish	4.00	8.00	15.00	M
254 The New Testament	4.00	8.00	15.00	
255 The New Pocket Quiz Book - Louise Crittenden & Rosejeanne Slifer	4.00	8.00	15.00	NF
256 The Greene Murder Case - S. S. Van Dine	5.00	10.00	20.00	M
257 Enter the Saint - Leslie Charteris	4.00	8.00	15.00	M
258 The Late George Apley - John P. Marquand	3.00	6.00	12.00	
259 Halfway House - Ellery Queen	4.00	8.00	15.00	M
260 The Pocket Book of Games - Albert H. Morehead	4.00	8.00	15.00	NF
261 And then there were None - Agatha Christie	3.00	6.00	12.00	M
262 The Somerset Maugham Pocket Book - W. S. Maugham	3.00	6.00	12.00	
263 The D. A. Calls it Murder - Erle Stanley Gardner	2.00	4.00	7.50	M
264 The Bellamy Trial - Frances Noyes Hart	2.50	6.00	10.00	
265 AAF: The Official Guide	2.50	6.00	10.00	NF

(POCKET BOOK, continued)

266	Lend-lease: Weapon for Victory - Edward R. Stettinius, Jr.	3.00	6.00	12.00	NF
267	Land Below the Wind - Agnes Newton Keith	3.00	6.00	12.00	
268	The Maltese Falcon - Dashiell Hammett	5.00	10.00	20.00	M
	with dust jacket	15.00	35.00	60.00	
269	Trent's Last Case - E. C. Benttey	3.00	6.00	12.00	M
270	The Devil to Pay - Ellery Queen	4.00	8.00	15.00	M
271	The Bride Wore Black - Cornell Woolrich	4.00	8.00	15.00	M
272	The Happy Highwayman - Leslie Charteris	4.00	8.00	15.00	M
273	Tarawa - Robert Sherrod	3.00	6.00	12.00	C
274	Here Is Your War - Ernie Pyle	2.00	4.00	7.50	NF
275	Random Harvest - James Hilton	3.00	6.00	12.00	
	1944				
276	The Story Pocket Book - Whit Burness	3.00	6.00	12.00	
277	The Case of the Sleepwalker's Niece - Erle Stanley Gardner	2.00	4.00	7.50	M
278	Experiment Perilous - Margaret Carpenter	3.00	6.00	12.00	
279	A Bell for Adano - John Hersey	2.00	4.00	7.50	
280	Life with Father - Clarence Day	3.00	6.00	12.00	H
281	Pastoral - Nevil Shute	2.00	4.00	7.50	
	1945				
282	The Human Comedy - William Saroyan	3.00	6.00	12.00	
283	Calamity Town - Ellery Queen	4.00	8.00	15.00	M
284	The Pocket Book of Adventure Stories - Philip Van Doren Stern	4.00	8.00	15.00	A
285	Evil Under the Sun - Agatha Christie	4.00	8.00	15.00	M
286	Background to Danger - Eric Ambler	4.00	8.00	15.00	M
287	The D. A. Holds a Candle - Erle Stanley Gardner	2.00	4.00	7.50	M
288	TVA: Democracy on the March - David E. Lilienthal	2.50	6.00	10.00	NF
289	Having a Wonderful Crime - Craig Rice	4.00	8.00	15.00	M
290	Jalna - Mazo de la Roche	2.00	4.00	7.50	
291	The Complete Sayings of Jesus - Arthur Hinds	4.00	8.00	15.00	
292	Take It Easy - Damon Runyon	4.00	8.00	15.00	
293	The Pocket Book of Western Stories - Harry E. Manle	3.00	6.00	12.00	W
294	The Pocket Book of Jokes - Bennett Cerf	2.50	6.00	10.00	H
295	The Dain Curse - Dashiell Hammett	5.00	10.00	20.00	M
296	Claudia and David - Rose Franken	2.00	4.00	7.50	
297	Death at the Bar - Ngaio Marsh	4.00	8.00	15.00	M
298	They'll Do It Every Time - Jimmy Hatlo	3.00	6.00	12.00	H
299	The Pocket Book of Basic English - I. A. Richards	3.00	6.00	12.00	NF
300	Franklin Delano Roosevelt: A Memorial - Donald Porter Geddes	1.50	3.50	5.00	B
	1945				
301	The Border Trumpet - Ernest Haycox	2.50	6.00	10.00	W
302	Young Doctor Galahad - Elizabeth Seifert	2.50	6.00	10.00	
303	The Reader Is Warned - Carter Dickson	5.00	10.00	20.00	M
304	Alexander Botts: Earthworm Tractors - William Hazlett Upson	3.00	6.00	12.00	
305	The Bishop Murder Case - S. S. Van Dine	5.00	10.00	20.00	M
306	Small Beer - Ludwig Bemelmans	3.00	6.00	12.00	
307	Trial and Error - Anthony Berkeley	3.00	6.00	12.00	M
	with dust jacket	10.00	20.00	35.00	
308	The Pocket Book of Modern Verse - Ted Malone	2.50	6.00	10.00	

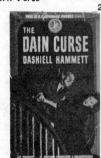

Pocket Book 272, c. PKB   Pocket Book 295, c. PKB   Pocket Book 298, c. PKB

Pocket Book 320, c. PKB Pocket Book 324 w/dj, c. PKB Pocket Book 324 wo/dj, c. PKB

POCKET BOOK, continued)

309	Rats, Lice and History - Hans Zinsser	3.00	6.00	12.00	NF
310	The Whoop-up Trail - B. M. Bower	3.00	6.00	12.00	W
311	White Collar Girl - Faith Baldwin	3.00	6.00	12.00	R
312	The Case of the Shoplifter's Shoe - Erle Stanley Gardner	2.00	4.00	7.50	M
313	The Tragedy of Y - Ellery Queen	2.00	4.00	7.50	M
314	The Bishop's Jaegers - Thorne Smith	2.00	4.00	7.50	H
315	Stalk the Hunter - Mitchell Wilson	3.00	6.00	12.00	
316	Fightin' Fool - Max Brand	2.50	6.00	10.00	W
317	On Borrowed Time - Lawrence Edward Watkin	2.50	6.00	10.00	
318	Farewell to Sport - Paul Gallico	2.50	6.00	10.00	S
319	Easy to Kill - Agatha Christie	2.50	6.00	10.00	M
320	The High Window - Raymond Chandler	5.00	10.00	20.00	M
321	Chicken Every Sunday - Rosemary Taylor	3.00	6.00	12.00	
	with dust jacket	10.00	20.00	35.00	
322	The Last Frontier - Howard Fast	2.50	6.00	10.00	W
323	Four Hundred Million Customers - Carl Crow	3.00	6.00	12.00	
324	Busman's Honeymoon - Dorothy L. Sayers	3.00	6.00	12.00	M
	with dust jacket	10.00	20.00	35.00	
325	The Sea-Wolf - Jack London	3.00	6.00	12.00	A
	1946				
326	There Was an Old Woman - Ellery Queen	2.50	6.00	10.00	M
327	Country Lawyer - Bellamy Partridge	2.50	6.00	10.00	
328	Warrant for X - Philip MacDonald	3.00	6.00	12.00	M
329	The Fashion in Shrouds - Margery Allingham	2.50	6.00	10.00	M
330	You Must Relax - Edmund Jacobson	3.00	6.00	12.00	
331	Verdict of Twelve - Raymond Postgate	3.00	6.00	12.00	
332	Junior Miss - Sally Benson	2.00	4.00	7.50	
333	The Benson Murder Case - S. S. Van Dine	5.00	10.00	20.00	M
334	The D. A. Draws a Circle - Erle Stanley Gardner	2.00	4.00	7.50	M
335	Nine--and Death Makes Ten - Carter Dickson	5.00	10.00	20.00	M
336	Blood Upon the Snow - Hilda Lawrence	2.50	6.00	10.00	M
337	Hopalong Cassidy Returns - Clarence E. Mulford	2.50	6.00	10.00	W
338	The Pocket History of the Second World War - Henry Steele Commager	2.50	6.00	10.00	NF
339	Young Widow - Clarissa Fairchild Cushman	2.00	4.00	7.50	
340	The Atomic Age Opens - Donald Porter Geddes	2.50	6.00	10.00	NF
341	The Body in the Library - Agatha Christie	2.50	6.00	10.00	M
342	The Pocket Book of Story Poems - Louis Untermeyer	2.00	4.00	7.50	
343	First Aid for the Ailing House - Rober B. Whitman	2.50	6.00	10.00	NF
344	Lust for Life - Irving Stone	2.50	6.00	10.00	
345	Spiderweb Trail - Eugene Cunningham	2.50	6.00	10.00	W
346	A Pinch of Poison - Richard & Frances Lockridge	2.50	6.00	10.00	M
347	The Phantom Filly - George Agnew Chamberlain	2.50	6.00	10.00	
348	Gringo Guns - Peter Field	2.00	4.00	7.50	W
349	Fielding's Folly - Frances Parkinson Keyes	2.00	4.00	7.50	
350	Death Turns the Tables - John Dickson Carr	4.00	8.00	15.00	M
	1946				

351	Color Scheme - Ngaio Marsh	2.50	6.00	10.00	M
352	Disputed Passage - Lloyd C. Douglas	1.50	3.50	5.00	
353	The Valley of Dry Bones - Arthur Henry Gooden	2.00	4.00	7.50	W
354	To Have and to Hold - Mary Johnston	2.00	4.00	7.50	
355	The Tragedy of Z - Ellery Queen	2.50	6.00	10.00	M
356	The Horse and Buggy Doctor - Arthur E. Hertzler	1.50	3.50	5.00	
357	Taps for Private Tussie - Jesse Stuart	2.00	4.00	7.50	
358	Men Against the Sea - James Norman Hall & Charles Nordhoff	2.00	4.00	7.50	A
359	Dragon Seed - Pearl S. Buck	2.00	4.00	7.50	
360	The Stephen Vincent Benet Pocketbook - Stephen Vincent Benet	2.00	4.00	7.50	
361	Home Sweet Homicide - Craig Rice	2.00	4.00	7.50	M
362	Steele of the Royal Mounted - James Oliver Curwood	2.00	4.00	7.50	A
363	Steamboat Round the Bend - Ben Lucien Burman	2.00	4.00	7.50	
364	The Journey Home - Zelda Popkin	2.00	4.00	7.50	
365	Dragonwyck - Anya Seton	2.00	4.00	7.50	
366	Barnaby - Crockett Johnson	2.00	4.00	7.50	
367	The Best-Loved Poems and Ballads of James Whitcomb Riley - J. W. Riley	2.00	4.00	7.50	
368	Murder Up My Sleeve - Erle Stanley Gardner	2.00	4.00	7.50	M
369	Silvertip - Max Brand	2.00	4.00	7.50	W
370	Action at Aquila - Hervey Allen	2.00	4.00	7.50	
371	The Last Trail - Zane Grey	2.00	4.00	7.50	W
372	The Emperor's Snuff Box - John Dickson Carr	3.00	6.00	12.00	M
373	Lad: A Dog - Albert Payson Terhune	2.00	4.00	7.50	
374	The Pocket Book of Robert Frost's Poems	2.00	4.00	7.50	
375	Whiteoaks of Jalna - Maxo de la Roche 1947	1.50	3.50	5.00	
376	Murder out of Town - Richard & Frances Lockridge	3.00	6.00	12.00	M
377	The Pocket Book of Baby & Child Care - Benjamin Spock	1.50	3.50	5.00	NF
378	The Case of the Perjured Parrot - Erle Stanley Gardner	2.00	4.00	7.50	M
379	Devils, Drugs and Doctors - Howard W. Haggard	2.50	6.00	10.00	
380	Medical Center - Faith Baldwin	1.50	3.50	5.00	R
381	The Murder of My Aunt - Richard Hull	2.00	4.00	7.50	M
382	Freedom Road - Howard Fast	2.00	4.00	7.50	
383	Roget's Pocket Thesaurus - Christopher Mawson & Katherine Whiting	2.00	4.00	7.50	NF
384	The Pocket Book of Ghost Stories - Philip Van Doren Stern	4.00	8.00	15.00	
385	The Red Right Hand - Joel Townsley Rogers	2.00	4.00	7.50	M
386	Seeing Is Believing - Carter Dickson	3.00	6.00	12.00	M
387	White Banners - Lloyd C. Douglas	2.00	4.00	7.50	
388	The Pocket Book of Humerous Verse - David McCord	2.00	4.00	7.50	H
389	The Lady in the Lake - Raymond Chandler	2.00	4.00	7.50	M
390	South of Rio Grande - Max Brand	2.00	4.00	7.50	W
391	The Lucky Stiff - Craig Rice	2.00	4.00	7.50	M
392	The Pocket Book of Erskine Caldwell Stories - E. Caldwell	2.00	4.00	7.50	
393	The Walsh Girls - Elizabeth Janeway	1.50	3.50	5.00	
394	The Bamboo Blonde - Dorothy B. Hughes	2.00	4.00	7.50	M
395	Cluny Brown - Margery Sharp	1.50	3.50	5.00	
396	Laugh with Leacock - Stephen Leacock	1.50	3.50	5.00	H
397	The Pocket Atlantic - Edward Weeks	1.50	3.50	5.00	
398	Towards Zero - Agatha Christie	2.00	4.00	7.50	M
399	The Fear Makers - Darwin L. Teilhet	2.00	4.00	7.50	
400	Madame Curie - Eve Curie 1946	2.00	4.00	7.50	B
401	The Passionate Witch - Thorne Smith	2.00	4.00	7.50	H
402	Darkness of Slumber - Rosemary Kutak	1.50	3.50	5.00	
403	Jamaica Inn - Daphne du Maurier	1.50	3.50	5.00	
404	Past Imperfect - Ilka Chase	1.50	3.50	5.00	
405	Forgive Us Our Trespasses - Lloyd C. Douglas	2.00	4.00	7.50	
406	Runyon a la Carte - Damon Runyon	2.00	4.00	7.50	
407	The D. A. Goes to Trial - Erle Stanley Gardner	2.00	4.00	7.50	M

Pocket Book 408, c. PKB   Pocket Book 426, c. PKB   Pocket Book 452, c. PKB

(POCKET BOOK, continued)

408	The Lost God and other Adventure Stories - John Russell	5.00	10.00	20.00	A
409	The Glorious Pool - Thorne Smith	2.00	4.00	7.50	H
410	The Covered Wagon - Emerson Hough	2.00	4.00	7.50	W
411	Death on the Aisle - Richard Lockridge & Frances Lockridge	2.50	6.00	10.00	M
412	Slim - William Wister Haines	2.00	4.00	7.50	
413	The Sea of Grass - Conrad Richter	2.00	4.00	7.50	
414	The Case of the Baited Hook - Erle Stanley Gardner	2.00	4.00	7.50	M
415	Frenchman's Creek - Daphne du Maurier	1.50	3.50	5.00	
416	Bill Stern's Favorite Boxing Stories - B. Stern	2.00	4.00	7.50	S
417	The Peter Arno Pocket Book - Peter Arno	2.00	4.00	7.50	H
418	The Razor's Edge - W. Somerset Maugham 1947	2.00	4.00	7.50	
419	Before the Fact - Francis Iles	2.00	4.00	7.50	M
420	A Puzzle for Puppets - Patrick Quentin	2.00	4.00	7.50	M
421	The Merriam-Webster Pocket Dictionary	2.00	4.00	7.50	NF
422	The Delicate Ape - Dorothy B. Hughes	2.00	4.00	7.50	M
423	The Fighting Four - Max Brand	2.00	4.00	7.50	W
424	The Pocket Treasury - Louis Untermeyer	1.50	3.50	5.00	
425	The G-string Murders - Gypsy Rose Lee 1947	1.50	3.50	5.00	M
426	The Second Believe It or Not - Robert Ripley	3.00	6.00	12.00	NF
427	The Innocent Flower - Charlotte Armstrong	2.00	4.00	7.50	M
428	The Night Life of the Gods - Thorne Smith	2.00	4.00	7.50	H
429	North of 36 - Emerson Hough	2.00	4.00	7.50	W
430	Good Night, Sweet Prince - Gene Fowler	1.50	3.50	5.00	
431	The Pocket Book of Famous French Short Stories - Eric Swenson	2.00	4.00	7.50	
432	Malice Aforethought - Francis Iles	3.00	6.00	12.00	M
433	The Song of Bernadette - Franz Werfel	1.50	3.50	5.00	
434	The Sunday Pigeon Murders - Craig Rice	2.00	4.00	7.50	M
435	Father Malachy's Miracle - Bruce Marshall	2.00	4.00	7.50	F
436	The Lost Gallows - John Dickson Carr	3.00	6.00	12.00	M
437	Death and the Dancing Footman - Ngaio Marsh	2.00	4.00	7.50	M
438	The Clue of the Forgotten Murder - Erle Stanley Gardner	1.50	3.50	5.00	M
439	A Time to Die - Hilda Lawrence	1.50	3.50	5.00	M
440	Wife for Sale - Kathleen Norris	1.50	3.50	5.00	
441	The Shepherd of the Hills - Harold Bell Wrigh	1.50	3.50	5.00	W
442	Daisy Kenyon - Elizabeth Joneway	1.50	3.50	5.00	
443	The Postman Always Rings Twice - James M. Cain	2.00	4.00	7.50	M
444	The Unsuspected - Charlotte Armstrong	1.50	3.50	5.00	M
445	Private Duty - Faith Baldwin	1.50	3.50	5.00	R
446	The Pocket Book of O. Henry Prize Stories - Herschel Brickell	1.50	3.50	5.00	
447	Turnabout - Thorne Smith	2.00	4.00	7.50	H
448	Castle Skull - John Dickson Carr	4.00	8.00	15.00	M
449	My Ten Years in a Quandary - Robert Benchley	2.00	4.00	7.50	H
450	The 2nd Pocket Book of Crossword Puzzles - Margaret Petherbridge 1947	4.00	8.00	15.00	NF
451	Rembered Death - Agatha Christie	2.00	4.00	7.50	M
452	Dracula - Bram Stoker	7.50	15.00	30.00	HO

No.	Title			
453	Mystery House - Kathleen Norris	1.50	3.50	5.00	
454	Dread Journey - Dorothy B. Hughes	2.00	4.00	7.50	M
455	The Treasure of the Sierra Madre - B. Traven	2.00	4.00	7.50	A
456	District Nurse - Faith Baldwin	1.50	3.50	5.00	R
457	Pitcairn's Island - James Norman Hall & Charles Nordhoff	2.00	4.00	7.50	A
458	Win, Place and Show - Robert Dowst	2.00	4.00	7.50	
459	Dragon's Teeth - Ellery Queen 1948	3.00	6.00	12.00	M
460	Slay the Loose Ladies - Patrick Quentin	2.00	4.00	7.50	M
461	The Thursday Turkey Murders - Craig Rice	2.00	4.00	7.50	M
462	How Green was my Valley - Richard Llewellyn	1.50	3.50	5.00	
463	Doctor's Wife - Maysie Greig	1.50	3.50	5.00	
464	The Case of the Rolling Bones - Erle Stanley Gardner	1.50	3.50	5.00	M
465	Death Comes as the End - Agatha Christie	2.00	4.00	7.50	M
466	Rim of the Desert - Ernest Haycox	2.00	4.00	7.50	W
467	Circle C Moves In - Brett Rider	2.00	4.00	7.50	W
468	The Case of the Silent Partner - Erle Stanley Gardner	1.50	3.50	5.00	M
469	Kitty - Rosamond Marshall	1.50	3.50	5.00	
470	A Lantern In Her Hand - Bess Streeter Aldrich	1.50	3.50	5.00	
471	The Door Between - Ellery Queen	2.50	6.00	10.00	M
472	Odd Man Out - F. L. Green	2.00	4.00	7.50	
473	Under Northern Stars - William MacLeod Raine	2.00	4.00	7.50	W
474	The Barbary Coast - Herbert Asbury	4.00	8.00	15.00	NF
475	Death of a Peer - Ngaio Marsh 1947	2.00	4.00	7.50	M
476	The Corpse Steps Out - Craig Rice	2.00	4.00	7.50	M
477	Tales from the Decameron - Giovanni Boccaccio	2.00	4.00	7.50	
478	Death--and the Gilded Man - Carter Dickson	3.00	6.00	12.00	M
479	Did She Fall? - Thorne Smith	2.00	4.00	7.50	H
480	Passion Flower - Kathleen Norris	1.50	3.50	5.00	
481	The Emperor's Physician - J. R. Perkins	2.00	4.00	7.50	
482	Deep Summer - Gwen Bristow 1948	2.00	4.00	7.50	
483	The King's General - Daphne du Maurier	2.00	4.00	7.50	
484	The Chair for Martin Rome - Henry Edward Helseth	2.00	4.00	7.50	
485	The Hollow - Agatha Christie	2.00	4.00	7.50	M
486	If Winter Comes - A. S. M. Hutchinson	2.00	4.00	7.50	
487	The Yukon Trail - William MacLeod Raine	2.00	4.00	7.50	W
488	Walls of Gold - Kathleen Norris	2.00	4.00	7.50	
489	I Am Gazing Into My 8-Ball - Earl Wilson	2.00	4.00	7.50	H
490	Skin and Bones - Thorne Smith	2.00	4.00	7.50	H
491	The Border Kid - Max Brand	1.50	3.50	5.00	W
492	The Deadly Pavilion - Hilda Lawrence	1.50	3.50	5.00	M
493	The Flying Yorkshireman - Eric Knight	2.50	6.00	10.00	F
494	My Favorite Sports Stories - Bill Stern	2.00	4.00	7.50	S
495	Carry on, Jeeves! - P. G. Wodehouse	2.50	6.00	10.00	H
496	Farmer Takes a Wife - John Gould	2.00	4.00	7.50	
497	A Connecticut Yankee In King Arthur's Court - Mark Twain	2.50	6.00	10.00	F
498	Mr. Adam - Pat Frank	2.50	6.00	10.00	SF
499	Another Claudia - Rose Franken	1.50	3.50	5.00	

Pocket Book 459, c. PKB   Pocket Book 465, c. PKB   Pocket Book 495, c. PKB

Pocket Book 524, c. PKB

Pocket Book 539, c. PKB

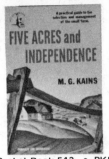

Pocket Book 543. c. PKB

(POCKET BOOK, continued)

500 The Sexual Side of Marriage - M. J. Exner 1948	2.50	6.00	10.00	NF
501 Payoff for the Banker - Richard & Frances Lockridge	2.50	6.00	10.00	M
502 High Tension - William Wister Haines	2.00	4.00	7.50	
503 Peabody's Mermaid - Guy Pearce & Constance Jones	2.50	6.00	10.00	F
504 Fun in Bed - Frank Scully	2.00	4.00	7.50	H
505 Mr. Blandings Builds his Dream House - Eric Hodgins Movie tie-in	2.50	6.00	10.00	
506 The Pursuit of Love - Nancy Mitford	1.50	3.50	5.00	
507 She Died a Lady - Carter Dickson	3.00	6.00	12.00	M
508 Deep Waters - Ruth Moore	2.00	4.00	7.50	
509 The Stolen Stallion - Max Brand	2.00	4.00	7.50	W
510 The Pocket Book of O. Henry Stories - O.Henry	2.00	4.00	7.50	
511 We Took to the Woods - Louise Dickinson Rich	2.00	4.00	7.50	
512 This is Murder - Erle Stanley Gardner	2.00	4.00	7.50	M
513 Rehersal for Love - Faith Baldwin	1.50	3.50	5.00	R
514 Flame of Sunset - L. P. Holmes	2.00	4.00	7.50	W
515 Anna Karenina - Leo Tolstoy	2.00	4.00	7.50	
516 Tales of the South Pacific - James A. Michener	2.50	6.00	10.00	
517 The Murderer is a Fox - Ellery Queen	2.00	4.00	7.50	M
518 The Stray Lamb - Thorne Smith	2.00	4.00	7.50	H
519 Oliver Twist - Charles Dickens	2.00	4.00	7.50	
520 Student Nurse - Lucy Agnes Hancock	2.00	4.00	7.50	
521 More Deaths Than One - Bruno Fischer	2.00	4.00	7.50	M
522 Freud: His Dream and Sex Theories - Joseph Jastrow	2.00	4.00	7.50	NF
523 The Longhorn Feud - Max Brand	2.00	4.00	7.50	M
524 The Double Take - Roy Huggins	2.50	6.00	10.00	M
525 The Foolish Virgin - Kathleen Norris 1948	1.50	3.50	5.00	
526 Desert Town - Ramona Stewart	2.00	4.00	7.50	
527 Final Curtain - Ngaio Marsh	2.00	4.00	7.50	M
528 The Big Midget Murders - Craig Rice	2.00	4.00	7.50	M
529 The Pocket Book of American Poems - Louis Untermeyer	2.00	4.00	7.50	
530 Guns on the Cimarron - Allan Vaughan Elston	2.00	4.00	7.50	W
531 Saddle and Ride - Ernest Haycox	2.00	4.00	7.50	W
532 Four Great Tragediew - William Shakespeare	2.00	4.00	7.50	
533 Four Great Comedies - William Shakespeare	2.00	4.00	7.50	
534 The Turquoise - Anya Seton	2.00	4.00	7.50	
535 Precious Bane - Mary Webb	1.50	3.50	5.00	
536 The Ballad and the Source - Rosamond Lehma Rosamond Lehmann	2.00	4.00	7.50	
537 The Shadowy Third - Marco Page	1.00	2.00	3.00	M
538 You Got to Stay Happy - Robert Carson	2.00	4.00	7.50	
539 Age of Consent - Norman Lindsay	2.00	4.00	7.50	E
540 Death of a Doll - Hilda Lawrence	2.00	4.00	7.50	M
541 Professional Lover - Maysie Greig	2.00	4.00	7.50	
542 Death Stalks the Range - Brett Rider	2.00	4.00	7.50	W
543 Five Acres and Independence - M. G. Kains	2.00	4.00	7.50	
544 The Case of the Turning Tide - Erle Stanley Gardner	2.00	4.00	7.50	M

323

(POCKET BOOK, continued)

545	The Pocket Book of True Stories - Ernest Heyn	2.50	6.00	10.00	
546	Rain in the Doorway - Thorne Smith	2.00	4.00	7.50	H
547	Silvertips Strike - Max Brand	2.00	4.00	7.50	W
548	Minute for Murder - Nicholas Blake	2.00	4.00	7.50	M
549	Younger Sister - Kathleen Norris	1.50	3.50	5.00	
550	Mister Roberts - Thomas Heggen	2.50	6.00	10.00	
	1948				
551	The Scarlet Letter - Nathaniel Hawthorne	2.00	4.00	7.50	
552	Silas Marner - George Eliot	2.00	4.00	7.50	
553	Economics in One Lesson - Henry Hazlitt	2.00	4.00	7.50	NF
554	Texas Triggers - Eugene Cunningham	2.00	4.00	7.50	
555	Bill Stern's Favorite Football Stories - B. Stern	3.00	6.00	12.00	S
556	Anything Can Happen - George & Helen Papashvily	2.00	4.00	7.50	
557	The Horizontal Man - Helen Eustis	2.00	4.00	7.50	
558	Bury Me Deep - Harold Q. Masur	2.00	4.00	7.50	M
559	Carmen and Other Stories - Prosper Merimee	2.00	4.00	7.50	
560	So Evil My Love - Joseph Shearing	2.00	4.00	7.50	
	1949				
561	The D. A. Cooks a Goose - Erle Stanley Gardner	2.00	4.00	7.50	M
562	The Babe Ruth Story - Bob Considine & Babe Ruth	3.00	6.00	12.00	B
563	Range Boss - D. B. Newton	2.00	4.00	7.50	W
564	A City of Bells - Elizabeth Goudge	2.00	4.00	7.50	
565	The French Quarter - Herbert Asbury	3.00	6.00	12.00	NF
566	The Egg and I - Betty MacDonald	2.00	4.00	7.50	H
567	Outlaws Three - Peter Field	2.00	4.00	7.50	W
568	The Curse of the Bronze Lamp - Carter Dickson	3.00	6.00	12.00	M
569	30 Days to a More Powerful Vocabulary - Wilfred Funk & Norman Lewis	1.00	2.00	3.00	NF
570	Rendezvous in Black - Cornell Woolrich	2.00	4.00	7.50	M
571	Command Decision - William Wister Haines	2.00	4.00	7.50	
572	Favorite Baseball Stories - Bill Stern	3.00	6.00	7.50	S
573	Sundown Jim - Ernest Haycox	2.00	4.00	7.50	W
574	Unmarried Couple - Maysie Greig	2.00	4.00	7.50	
575	The Chocolate Cobweb - Charlotte Armstrong	2.00	4.00	7.50	M
	1949				
576	Anna and the King of Siam - Margaret Landon	2.50	6.00	10.00	
577	The Foxes of Harrow - Frank Yerby	1.50	3.50	5.00	
578	The Pocket Book of Old Masters - Herman J. Wechsler	3.00	6.00	12.00	NF
579	Famous Artists and Their Models - Thomas Craven	3.00	6.00	12.00	NF
580	Fun for the Family - Jerome S. Meyer	2.00	4.00	7.50	NF
581	The Painted Veil - W. Somerset Maugham	2.00	4.00	7.50	
582	Wilders Walk Away - Herbert Brean	2.00	4.00	7.50	
583	Dr. Whitney's Secretary - Dorothy Pierce Walker	2.00	4.00	7.50	
584	King of the Range - Max Brand	2.00	4.00	7.50	W
585	Hit the Saddle - Allan Vaughan Elston	2.00	4.00	7.50	W
586	The Pocket Weekend Book - Philip Van Doren Stern	2.00	4.00	7.50	
587	In a Lonely Place - Dorothy B. Hughes c-Frank McCarthy	2.50	6.00	10.00	M

Pocket Book 545, c. PKB

Pocket Book 546, c. PKB

Pocket Book 579, c. PKB

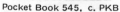

588	Conspirator - Humphrey Slater	2.00	4.00	7.50	
589	The Handsome Road - Gwen Bristow	2.00	4.00	7.50	
590	The Case of the Haunted Husband - Erle Stanley Gardner	2.00	4.00	7.50	M
591	Alexandra - Gladys Schmitt	2.00	4.00	7.50	
592	The Strange Case of Lucile Clery - Joseph Shearing	2.00	4.00	7.50	
593	The Call of the Wild - Jack London	2.00	4.00	7.50	A
594	Deep West - Ernest Haycox	2.00	4.00	7.50	W
595	The D. A. Calls a Turn - Erle Stanley Gardner	2.00	4.00	7.50	M
596	Try and Stop Me - Bennett Cerf	2.00	4.00	7.50	H
597	The Story of Mrs. Murphy - Natalie Anderson Scott	2.00	4.00	7.50	
598	Let's Explore Your Mind - Albert Edward Wiggam	2.00	4.00	7.50	
599	Secret Marriage - Kathleen Norris	2.00	4.00	7.50	
600	The Big Sky - A. B. Guthrie, Jr. 1949	2.00	4.00	7.50	W
601	Lani - Margaret Widdemer	2.00	4.00	7.50	
602	Too Late for Tears - Roy Huggins	2.50	6.00	10.00	M
603	Woman in Her Way - Faith Baldwin	2.00	4.00	7.50	R
604	Lost Stage Valley - Frank Bonham	2.00	4.00	7.50	W
605	Burned Fingers - Kathleen Norris	2.00	4.00	7.50	
606	Disposing of Henry - Roger Bax	2.00	4.00	7.50	M
607	Seven Short Novels from the Woman's Home Companion - Barthold Fles	2.00	4.00	7.50	
608	Action by Night - Ernest Haycox	2.00	4.00	7.50	W
609	Valley of Vanishing Men - Max Brand	2.00	4.00	7.50	W
610	West of the Law - Al Cody	2.00	4.00	7.50	W
611	Square Shooter - William MacLeod Raine	2.00	4.00	7.50	W
612	Moby Dick - Herman Melville	2.50	6.00	10.00	A
613	No Private Heaven - Faith Baldwin	2.00	4.00	7.50	R
614	Love is a Deadly Weapon - Patrick Quentin c-Frank McCarthy, aka Puzzle for Friends	2.50	6.00	10.00	M
615	Desert Island Decameron - H. Allen Smith	2.00	4.00	7.50	H
616	Kim - Rudyard Kipling	2.00	4.00	7.50	A
617	There is a Tide - Agatha Christie	2.00	4.00	7.50	M
618	The Big Con - David W. Maurer	2.00	4.00	7.50	
619	The Case of the Empty Tin - Erle Stanley Gardner	1.50	3.50	5.00	M
620	Circle C Carries On - Brett Rider c-Frank McCarthy	2.50	6.00	10.00	W
621	The Life and Times of the Shmoo - Al Capp	5.00	10.00	20.00	H
622	The Pocket Book of Great Operas - Henry Simon & Abraham Veinus	2.00	4.00	7.50	NF
623	Red Rust - Cornelia James Cannon	2.00	4.00	7.50	
624	Shoot the Works - Richard Ellington	2.00	4.00	7.50	M
625	Mink Coat - Kathleen Norris 1949	2.00	4.00	7.50	
626	Died in the Wool - Ngaio Marsh	2.00	4.00	7.50	M
627	The Renegade - L. L. Foreman	2.00	4.00	7.50	W
628	The Best of Wodehouse - P. G. Wodehouse First ed., 1949	5.00	10.00	20.00	H
629	Care and Training of Dogs - Arthur Frederick Jones	2.50	6.00	10.00	NF
630	So Well Remembered - James Hilton	2.00	4.00	7.50	
631	Jean-Christophe - Romain Rolland	2.00	4.00	7.50	
632	Black Ivory - Norman Collins	2.50	6.00	10.00	
633	My Late Wives - Carter Dickson	3.00	6.00	12.00	M
634	Silvertips Chase - Max Brand	2.00	4.00	7.50	W
635	Black Jade - Angeline Taylor	2.00	4.00	7.50	
636	What are the Odds? - Leo Guild	2.00	4.00	7.50	NF
637	Jed Blaine's Woman - Evelyn Wells	2.00	4.00	7.50	
638	The Room Upstairs - Mildred Davis	2.00	4.00	7.50	
639	The Man with My Face - Samuel W. Taylor	2.00	4.00	7.50	M
640	Canyon Passage - Ernest Haycox	2.00	4.00	7.50	W
641	Minute Mysteries - Austin Ripley	2.00	4.00	7.50	M
642	Pavilion of Women - Pearl S. Buck	2.00	4.00	7.50	
643	The Case of the Drowning Duck - Erle Stanley Gardner	1.50	3.50	5.00	M
644	Sister Carrie - Theodore Dreiser	2.00	4.00	7.50	
645	Stars In My Crown - Joe David Brown	2.00	4.00	7.50	
646	They Died with Their Boots On - Thomas Ripley	2.00	4.00	7.50	W

(POCKET BOOK, continued)

647	The Trial of Mary Dugan - Bayard Veiller & William Almon Wolff 1950	2.00	4.00	7.50	
648	Disaster Trail - Al Cody	2.00	4.00	7.50	W
649	The Saturday Evening Post Sports Stories - Red Smith	2.00	4.00	7.50	S
650	French Through Pictures - I. A. Richards 1950	2.00	4.00	7.50	NF
651	The Fourth Postman - Craig Rice	2.00	4.00	7.50	M
652	The Sea Chase - Andrew Geer	2.00	4.00	7.50	
653	Spotlight - Helen Topping Miller	2.00	4.00	7.50	
654	Consultation Room - Frederic Loomis	2.00	4.00	7.50	
655	The Vixens - Frank Yerby	2.00	4.00	7.50	
656	Man-size - William MacLeod Raine	2.00	4.00	7.50	W
657	The Bishop's Mantle - Agnes Sligh Turnbull	2.00	4.00	7.50	
658	Give Love the Air - Faith Baldwin	2.00	4.00	7.50	R
659	Voice Out of Darkness - Ursula Curtiss	2.00	4.00	7.50	M
660	Return of the Rio Kid - Don Davis	2.00	4.00	7.50	W
661	Gods and Goddesses in Art and Legend - Herman J. Wechsler	3.00	6.00	12.00	NF
662	The Blank Wall - Elisabeth Sanxay Holding	2.00	4.00	7.50	M
663	Renegade Ranch - Roy Manning	2.00	4.00	7.50	W
664	No Trumpet Before Him - Nelia Gardner White	2.00	4.00	7.50	
665	More Work for the Undertaker - Margery Allingham	2.00	4.00	7.50	M
666	The Girl on the Via Flaminia - Alfred Hayes	2.00	4.00	7.50	
667	The Case of the Smoking Chimney - Erle Stanley Gardner	1.50	3.50	5.00	M
668	Valley Thieves - Max Brand	2.00	4.00	7.50	W
669	Drury Lane's Last Case - Ellery Queen	2.00	4.00	7.50	M
670	The Casebook of Sherlock Holmes - Arthur Conan Doyle	2.50	6.00	10.00	M
671	The Franchise Affair - Josephine Tey	2.00	4.00	7.50	
672	Pilgrim's Inn - Elizabeth Goudge	2.00	4.00	7.50	
673	One Woman - Tiffany Thayer	2.00	4.00	7.50	
674	All You Need to Know About Fishing, Hunting and Camping - Byron Dalrymple	2.50	6.00	10.00	NF
675	Desert Rails - L. P. Holmes 1950	2.00	4.00	7.50	W
676	The Fate of the Immodest Blonde - Patrick Quentin	2.50	6.00	10.00	M
677	The Pocket Book of Greek Art - Thomas Craven	3.00	6.00	12.00	NF
678	The Case of the Buried Clock - Erle Stanley Gardner	1.50	3.50	5.00	M
679	Peony - Pearl S. Buck	2.00	4.00	7.50	
680	The Moving Target - John Ross MacDonald	2.00	4.00	7.50	M
681	Rampart Street - Everett & Olga Webber	2.00	4.00	7.50	
682	Small Talk - Syms	2.00	4.00	7.50	H
683	The Boss of the Lazy 9 - Peter Field	2.00	4.00	7.50	W
684	The Pocket Treasury of American Folklore - B. A. Botkin	2.00	4.00	7.50	
685	Wine, Women and Words - Billy Rose	2.00	4.00	7.50	B
686	Five O'Clock Surgeon - Dorothy Pierce Walker	2.00	4.00	7.50	
687	Flaming Irons - Max Brand	2.00	4.00	7.50	W
688	Three Men and Diana - Kathleen Norris	2.00	4.00	7.50	
689	The Case of the Drowsy Mosquito - Erle Stanley Gardner	1.50	3.50	5.00	M
690	Annie Jordan - Mary Brinker Post	2.00	4.00	7.50	
691	The Fighting Edge - William MacLeod Raine	2.00	4.00	7.50	W
692	Special Nurse - Lucy Agnes Hancock	1.50	3.50	5.00	
693	The Whispering Corpse - William P. McGivern	2.00	4.00	7.50	M
694	Killer's Range - E. B. Mann	2.00	4.00	7.50	W
695	Rhubarb - H. Allen Smith	3.00	6.00	12.00	H
696	The Big Sleep - Raymond Chandler	5.00	10.00	20.00	M
697	Without Magnolias - Bucklin Moon	2.00	4.00	7.50	
698	The Darker the Night - Herbert Brean	2.00	4.00	7.50	
699	No Benefit of Law - Brett Rider	2.00	4.00	7.50	W
700	Of Human Bondage - W. Somerset Maugham 1950	3.00	6.00	12.00	
701	Big Sol - Henry Von Rhau	2.00	4.00	7.50	
702	Desperado's Gold - L. L. Foreman	2.00	4.00	7.50	W
703	Rustlers' Canyon - E. E. Halleran	2.00	4.00	7.50	W
704	Suddenly a Corpse - Harold Q. Masur	2.00	4.00	7.50	M

(POCKET BOOK, continued)

No.	Title			
705	Hired Guns - Max Brand	2.00	4.00	7.50	W
706	Death Rides the Pecos - Davis Dresser	2.00	4.00	7.50	W
707	The Girl from Nowhere - Rae Foley	2.00	4.00	7.50	
708	The Pocket History of American Painting - James Thomas Flexner	3.00	6.00	12.00	NF
709	Halo in Brass - John Evans	2.00	4.00	7.50	
710	An Apple for Eye - Kathleen Norris	2.00	4.00	7.50	
711	Midnight Round-up - Peter Field	2.00	4.00	7.50	W
712	The Doctor at Coffin Gap - Les Savage, Jr.	2.00	4.00	7.50	W
713	Hound-dog Man - Fred Gipson	2.00	4.00	7.50	
714	The Asphalt Jungle - W. R. Burnett	2.50	6.00	10.00	JD
715	The University of Chicago Spanish-English, English-Spanish Dictionary - Carlos Castillo & others	3.00	6.00	12.00	NF
716	The Trouble with Murder - Roger Bax	2.00	4.00	7.50	M
717	The Bandit of the Black Hills - Max Brand	2.00	4.00	7.50	W
718	Great American Sports Humor - Mac Davis	2.00	4.00	7.50	SH
719	Singing Lariat - Will Ermine	2.00	4.00	7.50	W
720	Spanish through Pictures - I. A. Richards	2.00	4.00	7.50	NF
721	Border Breed - William MacLeod Raine	2.00	4.00	7.50	W
722	Opus 21 - Philip Wylie	1.50	3.50	5.00	
723	The Hearth and the Eagle - Anya Seton	2.00	4.00	7.50	
724	The Case of the Careless Kitten - Erle Stanley Gardner	2.00	4.00	7.50	M
725	Suitable for Framing - James Atlee Phillips 1950	2.00	4.00	7.50	M
726	Dusty Wagons - Matt Stuart	2.00	4.00	7.50	W
727	Perilous Passage - Arthur Mayse	2.00	4.00	7.50	
728	The Feather Merchants - Max Shulman	2.00	4.00	7.50	
729	Chesapeake Cavalier - Don Tracy	2.00	4.00	7.50	A
730	This is America - Max Herzberg	2.00	4.00	7.50	
731	The 3rd Pocket Book of Crossword Puzzles - Margaret Petherbridge	3.00	6.00	12.00	NF
732	Cowboy - Ross Sautee	2.00	4.00	7.50	W
733	Ghost Gold - Tom West	2.00	4.00	7.50	W
734	The Red Dress - John Watson	2.00	4.00	7.50	
735	The March Hare Murders - E. X. Ferrars	2.00	4.00	7.50	M
736	Coffin Corner - George Bagby	2.00	4.00	7.50	M
737	Murder One - Eleazar Lipsky	2.00	4.00	7.50	M
738	Dead Lion - Emery Bonett, John Bonett	2.00	4.00	7.50	
739	The Man Who Held Five Aces - Jean Leslie	2.00	4.00	7.50	
740	Ten Day's Wonder - Ellery Queen	2.00	4.00	7.50	M
741	The Case of the Jorneying Boy - Michael Innes	2.00	4.00	7.50	M
742	Head of a Traveller - Nicholas Blake	3.00	6.00	12.00	M
743	On the Dodge - William MacLeod Raine	2.00	4.00	7.50	W
744	Hunted Riders - Max Brand	2.00	4.00	7.50	W
745	Lord Johnnie - Leslie Turner White	2.00	4.00	7.50	
746	Wilderness Nurse - Marguerite Mooers Marshall	1.50	3.50	5.00	R
747	Combat - Van Van Praag	2.00	4.00	7.50	C
748	Call it Treason - George Howe 1951	2.00	4.00	7.50	
749	The Golden Hawk - Frank Yerby	2.00	4.00	7.50	A
750	The Little Sister - Raymond Chandler	5.00	10.00	20.00	M
751	The Perfect Hostess - Maureen Daly	2.00	4.00	7.50	
752	Beyond a Reasonable Doubt - C. W. Grafton	2.00	4.00	7.50	M
753	Crooked House - Agatha Christie	2.00	4.00	7.50	M
754	Riders by Night - Nelson Nye	2.00	4.00	7.50	W
755	The Human Side of Animals - Vance Packard	2.00	4.00	7.50	NF
756	It's a Crime - Richard Ellington	2.00	4.00	7.50	M
757	The Man With the Golden Arm - Nelson Algren	2.50	6.00	10.00	
758	The Case of the Crooked Candle - Erle Stanley Gardner	2.00	4.00	7.50	M
759	The Tenderfoot Kid - Peter Field	2.00	4.00	7.50	W
760	Outlaw Vengeance - Samuel A. Peeples	2.00	4.00	7.50	W
761	Rustlers' Moon - Will Ermine	2.00	4.00	7.50	W
762	Swing, Brother, Swing - Ngaio Marsh	2.00	4.00	7.50	M
763	All the Ship's at Sea - William J. Lederer	2.00	4.00	7.50	
764	Laughing Boy - Oliver LaFarge	2.00	4.00	7.50	
765	The Pocket Book of Great Drawings - Paul J. Sachs	3.00	6.00	12.00	NF
766	Law of the Gun - Brett Rider	2.00	4.00	7.50	W

(POCKET BOOK, continued)

767 The Big Wheel - John Brooks	2.00	4.00	7.50	
768 The Fight for the Sweetwater - Bliss Lomax	2.00	4.00	7.50	W
769 Bitter Creek - Al Cody	2.00	4.00	7.50	W
770 The Naked Eye - Gita Lewis & Henriette Martin	2.00	4.00	7.50	
771 The Brave Bulls - Tom Lea	3.00	6.00	12.00	
772 Ruggles of Red Gap - Harry Leon Wilson	1.50	3.50	5.00	H
773 My Dead Wife - William Worley	3.00	6.00	12.00	M
774 The House Without a Door - Thomas Sterling	2.00	4.00	7.50	
775 The 22 Brothers - Dana Sage 1951	2.00	4.00	7.50	
776 The End is Known - Geoffrey Holiday Hall	2.00	4.00	7.50	
777 So Young a Body - Frank Bunce	2.00	4.00	7.50	
778 Top of the World - Hans Rvesch	2.00	4.00	7.50	
779 And When She Was Bad She Was Murdered - Richard Starnes	2.00	4.00	7.50	M
780 The Way West - A. B. Guthrie, Jr.	2.00	4.00	7.50	W
781 Rustlers of Beacon Creek - Max Brand	2.00	4.00	7.50	W
782 Dialogues of Plato	2.00	4.00	7.50	
783 Outlaw Trail - E. E. Halleran	2.00	4.00	7.50	W
784 Come and Kill Me - Josephine Tey	2.00	4.00	7.50	
785 The Golden Fury - Marian Castle	2.00	4.00	7.50	
786 Very Cold for May - William P. McGivern	2.00	4.00	7.50	
787 Ranger's Luck - William MacLeod Raine	2.00	4.00	7.50	W
788 The Pocket Guide to the Wildflowers - Samuel Gottscho	3.00	6.00	12.00	NF
789 Ann Pillsbury's Baking Book - Ann Pillsbury	2.00	4.00	7.50	NF
790 Rough Justice - Ernest Haycox	2.00	4.00	7.50	W
791 Red Range - Eugene Cunningham	2.00	4.00	7.50	W
792 The Case of the Black-eyed Blonde - Erle Stanley Gardner	1.50	3.50	5.00	M
793 Diagnosis: Homicide - Lawrence G. Blochman	2.00	4.00	7.50	M
794 Broncho Apache - Paul I. Wellman	2.00	4.00	7.50	W
795 Hold Autumn in Your Hand - George Sessions Perry	2.00	4.00	7.50	
796 For Doctors Only - Francis Leo Golden	2.00	4.00	7.50	H
797 The Outlaw - Max Brand	2.00	4.00	7.50	W
798 Under the Skin - Phyllis Bottome	2.00	4.00	7.50	
799 Dardanelles Derelict - F. VanWyck Mason	2.00	4.00	7.50	
800 Conception, Pregnancy and Birth - J. D. Ratcliff 1951	2.00	4.00	7.50	NF
801 Reprisal - Arthur Gordon	2.00	4.00	7.50	
802 Big As Life - John Pleasant McCoy	2.00	4.00	7.50	
803 The Hide Rustlers - Les Savage, Jr.	2.00	4.00	7.50	W
804 The Deadly Miss Ashley - Frederick C. Davis	2.00	4.00	7.50	M
805 Mischief - Charlotte Armstrong	2.00	4.00	7.50	M
806 Murder's Web - Dorothy Dunn	2.00	4.00	7.50	M
807 Bullets for a Badman - Bennett Foster	2.00	4.00	7.50	W
808 The Sheriff of Painted Post - Tom Gunn	2.00	4.00	7.50	W
809 Colt Comrades - Bliss Lomax	2.00	4.00	7.50	W
810 The Freeholder - Joe David Brown	1.50	3.50	5.00	A
811 The Witch of Spring - William Shore	3.00	6.00	12.00	E
812 The Case of the Golddigger's Purse - Erle Stanley Gardner	1.50	3.50	5.00	M
813 Stone Cold Dead - Richard Ellington	2.00	4.00	7.50	M
814 The Poisoned Chocolates Case - Anthony Berkeley	2.00	4.00	7.50	M
815 The Sheriff's Son - William MacLeod Raine	2.00	4.00	7.50	W
816 Wall of Guns - Jim O'Mara	2.00	4.00	7.50	W
817 Something About Midnight - D. B. Olsen	2.00	4.00	7.50	M
818 High Valley - Charmian Clift & George Henry Johnston	2.00	4.00	7.50	
819 Mingo Dabney - James Street	2.00	4.00	7.50	A
820 A Murder is Announced - Agatha Christie	2.00	4.00	7.50	M
821 The Drowning Pool - John Ross MacDonald	2.00	4.00	7.50	M
822 Cat of Many Tails - Ellery Queen	2.00	4.00	7.50	M
823 Trouble is My Business - Raymond Chandler	5.00	10.00	20.00	M
824 The Road to San Jacinto - L. L. Foreman	2.00	4.00	7.50	W
825 Sexual Feeling in Married Men and Women - G. Lombard Kelly 1951	2.00	4.00	7.50	NF
826 Face of A Hero - Louis Falstein	2.00	4.00	7.50	
827 The Hepburn - Jan Westcott	2.00	4.00	7.50	

Pocket Book 823, c. PKB   Pocket Book 835, c. PKB   Pocket Book 866, c. PKB

(POCKET BOOK, continued)

828	Murder City - Oakley Hall	2.00	4.00	7.50	M
829	Murder of a Nymph - Margot Neville	2.00	4.00	7.50	M
830	Homeward Borne - Ruth Chatterton	2.00	4.00	7.50	
831	The San Quentin - Clinton T. Duffy & Dean Jennings	3.00	6.00	12.00	NF
832	The Case of the Half-Wakened Wife - Erle Stanley Gardner	1.50	3.50	5.00	M
833	Off Missing Persons - David Goodis	2.00	4.00	7.50	
834	Signal Guns at Sunup - John Jo Carpenter	2.00	4.00	7.50	
835	Alice in Wonderland and Other Favorites - Lewis Carroll	3.00	6.00	12.00	F
836	Attack - Perry Wolff	2.00	4.00	7.50	C
	1952				
837	The Golden Herd - Curt Carroll	2.00	4.00	7.50	
838	About Mrs. Leslie - Vina Delmar	2.00	4.00	7.50	E
839	Walk With the Devil - Elliott Arnold	2.00	4.00	7.50	
840	The Zebra Derby - Max Shulman	1.50	3.50	5.00	
841	Painted Post Law - Tom Gunn	2.00	4.00	7.50	W
842	Gun Showdown - William MacLeod Raine	2.00	4.00	7.50	W
843	The Great Snow - Henry Morton Robinson	2.00	4.00	7.50	
844	Each Bright River - Mildred Masterson McNeilly	2.00	4.00	7.50	
845	The Candy Kid - Dorothy B. Hughes	2.00	4.00	7.50	
846	Pick-up On Noon Street - Raymond Chandler	5.00	10.00	20.00	M
847	The Smoking Iron - Peter Field	2.00	4.00	7.50	W
848	Danger Trail - Max Brand	2.00	4.00	7.50	W
849	The Build-up Boys - Jeremy Kirk	2.00	4.00	7.50	
850	Foxfire - Anya Seton	2.00	4.00	7.50	
	1952				
851	White Witch Doctor - Louise A. Stinetorf	2.00	4.00	7.50	
852	Martha Logan's Meat Cook Book - Thora Campbell & Beth Bailey McLean	2.00	4.00	7.50	NF
853	Death on Treasure Trail - Don Davis	2.00	4.00	7.50	W
854	Why Slug A Postman? - Seldon Truss	2.00	4.00	7.50	
855	The Case of the Backward Mule - Erle Stanley Gardner	1.50	3.50	5.00	M
856	The Case of the Borrowed Brunette - Erle Stanley Gardner	1.50	3.50	5.00	M
857	Black Majesty - John W. Vandercook	2.00	4.00	7.50	A
858	Another Mug for the Bier - Ricard Starnes	2.00	4.00	7.50	M
859	Bold Passage - Frank Bonham	2.00	4.00	7.50	W
860	You Can't Live Forever - Harold Q. Masur	2.00	4.00	7.50	M
861	Grant of Kingdom - Harvey Fergusson	2.00	4.00	7.50	
862	The Beckoning Door - Mabel Seeley	2.00	4.00	7.50	M
863	The People Against O'Hara - Eleazar Lipsky	2.00	4.00	7.50	
864	By Rope and Lead - Ernest Haycox	2.00	4.00	7.50	W
865	Tonto Riley - Lee E. Wells	2.00	4.00	7.50	W
866	The Story of My Psychoanalysis - John Knight	4.00	8.00	15.00	NF
867	The Raid - John Brick	2.00	4.00	7.50	
868	The Strumpet Sea - Don Tracy	2.00	4.00	7.50	
869	The D. A. Breaks A Seal - Erle Stanley Gardner	2.00	4.00	7.50	M
870	Shield for Murder - William P. McGivern	2.00	4.00	7.50	M
871	The Hangman of Sleepy Valley - Davis Dresser c-Frank McCarthy	2.50	6.00	10.00	W
872	What the Doctor Ordered - Francis Leo Golden	2.00	4.00	7.50	H

(POCKET BOOK, continued)

873	Magnus the Magnificent - Leslie Turner White	1.50	3.50	5.00	A
874	Double, Double - Ellery Queen	2.00	4.00	7.50	M
875	The Hard-Boiled Omnibus - Joseph T. Shaw 1952	3.00	6.00	12.00	M
876	Double Cross Trail - E. E. Halleran	2.00	4.00	7.50	W
877	Gunman's Gold - Max Brand	2.00	4.00	7.50	W
878	Dark Laughter - Sherwood Anderson	2.00	4.00	7.50	
879	New York 22 - Ilka Chase	2.00	4.00	7.50	
880	The Black-Eyed Stranger - Charlotte Armstrong	2.00	4.00	7.50	
881	The Eleventh Hour - Robert B. Sinclair	2.00	4.00	7.50	
882	Death Rides the Night - Peter Field	2.00	4.00	7.50	W
883	The Captain - Russell Thacher	2.00	4.00	7.50	
884	The Sultan's Warrior - Bates Baldwin	2.50	6.00	10.00	A
885	Southern Territory - Robert Tallant	2.00	4.00	7.50	
886	The Case of the Fan-Dancer's Horse - Erle Stanley Gardner c-Bergey	1.50	3.50	5.00	M
887	Judgement on Deltchev - Eric Ambler	2.00	4.00	7.50	
888	Shadow Riders of the Yellowstone - Les Savage, Jr.	2.00	4.00	7.50	W
889	Beulah Land - H. L. Davis	2.00	4.00	7.50	
890	A Complete Guide to Home Sewing - Sylvia K. Mager	2.00	4.00	7.50	NF
891	The Unknown Lincoln - Dale Carnegie	2.50	6.00	10.00	NF
892	The Pocket Stamp Album - H. E. Harris	2.50	6.00	10.00	NF
893	Your Own Book of Campcraft - Catherine T. Hammett	2.00	4.00	7.50	NF
894	Horns for the Devil - Louis Malley	2.00	4.00	7.50	M
895	Mystery Ranch - Max Brand	2.00	4.00	7.50	W
896	Miami Murder-Go-Round - Marston LaFrance	2.00	4.00	7.50	M
897	They Come to Baghdad - Agatha Christie	2.00	4.00	7.50	M
898	Cop - Jack Karney	2.00	4.00	7.50	
899	Cobean's Naked Eye - Samuel E. Cobean	2.00	4.00	7.50	
900	Scirocco - Romualdo Romano 1952 c-Belarski	2.50	6.00	10.00	
901	Murder for the Holidays - Howard Rigsby	2.00	4.00	7.50	M
902	The End of the Trail - Peter Field	2.00	4.00	7.50	W
903	Miracle on 34th Street - Valentine Davies	5.00	10.00	20.00	F
904	Fear in the Night - Irving Schwartz	2.00	4.00	7.50	
905	The Women of Champion City - Doris Davis	2.50	6.00	10.00	E
906	Lynch-Rope Law - Davis Dresser	2.00	4.00	7.50	W
907	The Way Some People Die - John Ross MacDonald	2.00	4.00	7.50	M
908	New Tales of Space and Time - Raymond J. Healy	1.50	3.50	5.00	SF
909	The Case of the Lazy Lover - Erle Stanley Gardner 1953	1.50	3.50	5.00	M
910	The Streak - Max Brand	1.50	3.50	5.00	W
911	My Gun is My Law - Will Ermine	1.50	3.50	5.00	W
912	...And to My Beloved Husband - Philip Loraine	1.50	3.50	5.00	
913	Dark Dream - Robert Martin	1.50	3.50	5.00	
914	The Man from Thief River - Peter Field	1.50	3.50	5.00	W
915	Ruby - Vina Delmar 1952	1.50	3.50	5.00	
916	The Simple Art of Murder - Raymond Chandler	5.00	10.00	20.00	M

Pocket Book 882, c. PKB   Pocket Book 884, c. PKB   Pocket Book 903, c. PKB

917	The Other Body in Grant's Tomb - Richard Starnes	1.50	3.50	5.00	M
918	Shadows More Among Them - Edgar Mittelholzer	1.50	3.50	5.00	
919	The Lord God of the Flesh - Jules Romains	1.50	3.50	5.00	
920	Space Platform - Murray Leinster c-Bergey	2.50	6.00	10.00	SF
921	Rio Kid Justice - Don Davis	1.50	3.50	5.00	W
922	The Case of the Lonely Heiress - Erle Stanley Gardner	1.50	3.50	5.00	M
923	Hangman's Hat - Paul Ernst	1.50	3.50	5.00	
924	The Left Hand of God - William E. Barrett	1.50	3.50	5.00	
925	Favorite Hymns - Albert H. Morehead & James Morehead	2.00	4.00	7.50	NF
	1953				
926	The Origin of Evil - Ellery Queen	1.50	3.50	5.00	M
927	Red Blizzard - Clay Fisher	1.50	3.50	5.00	W
928	Power Golf - Ben Hogan	1.50	3.50	5.00	NF
929	Himalayan Assignment - F. VanWyck Mason	1.50	3.50	5.00	
930	The Hair-Trigger Kid - Max Brand	1.50	3.50	5.00	W
931	Reclining Figure - Marco Page	1.50	3.50	5.00	
932	Captain Barney - Jan Westcott	1.50	3.50	5.00	A
933	Basketball - Arnold "Red" Averbach	1.50	3.50	5.00	NF
934	Kill and Tell - Howard Rigsby	1.50	3.50	5.00	M
935	Out from Eden - Victoria Lincoln	1.50	3.50	5.00	
936	The Proud Ones - Verne Athanas	1.50	3.50	5.00	W
937	Sheriff on the Spot - Peter Field	1.50	3.50	5.00	W
938	Candlemas Bay - Ruth Moore	1.50	3.50	5.00	
939	The Sundowners - Jon Cleary	1.50	3.50	5.00	
940	Catch a Killer - Ursula Curtiss	1.50	3.50	5.00	M
941	Exit for a Dame - Richard Ellington	1.50	3.50	5.00	M
942	Painted Post Range - Tom Gunn	1.50	3.50	5.00	W
943	Planet of the Dreamers - John D. MacDonald	2.50	6.00	10.00	SF
944	Winds of Morning - H. L. Davis	1.50	3.50	5.00	
945	Floodtide - Frank Yerby	1.50	3.50	5.00	
946	River of Rogues - A. R. Beverley -Giddings	1.50	3.50	5.00	
947	The War of the Worlds - H. G. Wells	3.00	6.00	12.00	SF
948	Laughter Is Legal - Francis Lea Golden	1.50	3.50	5.00	H
949	Two Clues - Erle Stanley Gardner	1.50	3.50	5.00	M
950	Single Jack - Max Brand	1.50	3.50	5.00	W
	1953				
951	Portrait of A Marriage - Pearl S. Buck	1.50	3.50	5.00	
952	Stella - Jan de Hartog	1.50	3.50	5.00	
953	The Sea - Jan de Hartog	1.50	3.50	5.00	
954	Outlaw Thickets - Les Savage, Jr.	1.50	3.50	5.00	W
955	101 Best Loved Songs - Albert H. & James Morehead	2.00	4.00	7.50	NF
956	Mrs. McGinty's Dead - Agatha Christie	1.50	3.50	5.00	M
957	Woman's Medical Problems - Maxine Davis	1.50	3.50	5.00	NF
958	Outside the Law - Philip Loraine	1.50	3.50	5.00	
959	The Man from Nazareth - Harry Emerson Fosdick	1.50	3.50	5.00	
960	Calendar of Crime - Ellery Queen c-Richard Powers	2.50	6.00	10.00	M
961	The Crooked Frame - William P. McGivern	1.50	3.50	5.00	M
962	Canyon of Death - Peter Field	1.50	3.50	5.00	W
963	Excuse It, Please! - Cornelia Otis Skinner	1.50	3.50	5.00	
964	Trespass - Eugene Brown	1.50	3.50	5.00	
965	The Case of the Vagabond Virgin - Erle Stanley Gardner	1.50	3.50	5.00	M
966	The 4th Pocket book of Crossword Puzzles - Margaret Petherbridge Farrar	3.00	6.00	12.00	NF
967	Snaketrack - Frank Bonham	1.50	3.50	5.00	W
968	The Low Calorie Diet - Marvin Small	1.50	3.50	5.00	NF
969	The Tender Age - Russell Thacher	1.50	3.50	5.00	
970	The Diary of a Young Girl - Anne Frank	1.50	3.50	5.00	
971	Marked for Murder - John Ross MacDonald	1.50	3.50	5.00	M
972	Halfway to Timberline - Ward West	1.50	3.50	5.00	
973	Tough Company - Clem Colt	1.50	3.50	5.00	W
974	The Highland Hawk - Leslie Turner White	1.50	3.50	5.00	
975	Blood in Your Eye - Robert Patrick Wilmot	1.50	3.50	5.00	M
	1954				
976	The Case of the Dubious Bridegroom - Erle Stanley Gardner	1.50	3.50	5.00	M
977	Wild Drum Beat - F. VanWyck Mason	1.50	3.50	5.00	

(POCKET BOOK, continued)

978	Land of the Lawless - Les Savage, Jr.	1.50	3.50	5.00	W
979	Vengeance Trail - Max Brand	1.50	3.50	5.00	W
980	A Great Time to be Alive - Harry Emerson				
	Fosdick	1.50	3.50	5.00	
981	The Big Heat - William P. McGivern	1.50	3.50	5.00	M
982	Doctor Two-Guns - Peter Field	1.50	3.50	5.00	W
983	Pioneer Loves - Ernest Haycox	1.50	3.50	5.00	W
984	The Shining Tides - Win Brooks	1.50	3.50	5.00	
985	Worse than Murder - David Duncan	1.50	3.50	5.00	M
986	Watchdog of Thunder River - Will Ermine	1.50	3.50	5.00	W
987	The Whistler - E. B. Mann	1.50	3.50	5.00	W
988	Last Seen Wearing... - Hillary Waugh	1.50	3.50	5.00	M
989	Sands of Mars - Arthur C. Clarke	2.50	6.00	10.00	SF
990	Coyote Gulch - Peter Field	1.50	3.50	5.00	W
991	Border Guns - Max Brand	1.50	3.50	5.00	W
992	Ripley's New Believe it or Not! - Robert				
	Ripley	2.50	6.00	10.00	NF
993	The Hidden Flower - Pearl S. Buck	1.50	3.50	5.00	
994	April Snow - Lillian Budd	1.50	3.50	5.00	
995	The Medicine Whip - John & Margaret Harris	1.50	3.50	5.00	
996	Lyle Brown's Sports Quiz - Lyle Brown	1.50	3.50	5.00	S
997	Murder on Monday - Robert Patrick Wilmont	1.50	3.50	5.00	M
998	So Rich, So Lovely, and So Dead -				
	Harold Q. Masur	1.50	3.50	5.00	M
999	Rogue Valley - Verne Athanas	1.50	3.50	5.00	W
1000	The Little World of Don Camillo -				
	Giovanni Guareschi	1.50	3.50	5.00	
	1954				
1001	Homer Crist - John Brick	1.50	3.50	5.00	
1002	Painted Post Gunplay - Tom Gunn	1.50	3.50	5.00	W
1003	Funerals Are Fatal - Agatha Christie	1.50	3.50	5.00	M
1004	The Big Deal - Selig Seligman	1.50	3.50	5.00	
1005	The King Is Dead - Ellery Queen	1.50	3.50	5.00	M
1006	The Amber Fire - Don Tracy	1.50	3.50	5.00	
1007	My Best Science Fiction Story -				
	Leo Margulies & Oscar J. Friend	2.50	6.00	10.00	SF
1008	Windom's Way - James Ramsey Ullman	1.50	3.50	5.00	
1009	The Case of the Cautious Coquette -				
	Erle Stanley Gardner	1.50	3.50	5.00	M
1010	The D. A. Takes A Chance -				
	Erle Stanley Gardner	1.50	3.50	5.00	M
1011	Murder on the Frontier - Ernest Haycox	1.50	3.50	5.00	W
1012	Tale of Two Lovers - Henry Morton Robinson	1.50	3.50	5.00	
1013	Tales for Salesmen - Francis Leo Golden	1.50	3.50	5.00	H
1014	The Covered Wagon - Emerson Hope	1.50	3.50	5.00	W
1015	The Girls of Sanfrediano - Vasco Prutolini	1.50	3.50	5.00	
1016	Last Race - Jon Manchip White	1.50	3.50	5.00	
1017	Johnny Guitar - Roy Chanslor	1.50	3.50	5.00	
1018	The Gun Tamer - Max Brand	1.50	3.50	5.00	W
1019	In Love - Alfred Hayes	1.50	3.50	5.00	
1020	Meet Me at the Morgue - John Ross				
	MacDonald	1.50	3.50	5.00	M
1021	Murder with Mirrors - Agatha Christie	1.50	3.50	5.00	M
1022	Troubled Range - E. B. Mann	1.50	3.50	5.00	W
1023	Two-Gun Rio Kid - Don Davis	1.50	3.50	5.00	W
1024	The Barbarians - F. VanWyck Mason	1.50	3.50	5.00	A
1025	How to Stop Smoking - Herbert Brean	1.50	3.50	5.00	NF
	1954				
1026	The Intruder - Helen Fowler	1.50	3.50	5.00	
1027	Law Badge - Peter Field	1.50	3.50	5.00	W
1028	Outlaw - Ernest Haycox	1.50	3.50	5.00	W
1029	The Case of the Negligent Nymph -				
	Erle Stanley Gardner	1.50	3.50	5.00	M
1030	Rogue Cop - William P. McGivern	1.50	3.50	5.00	M
1031	Busted Range - Will Ermine	1.50	3.50	5.00	W
1032	The Colors of the Day - Romain Gary	1.50	3.50	5.00	
1033	The Night Horseman - Max Brand	1.50	3.50	5.00	W
1034	Walk Out on Death - Charlotte Armstrong	1.50	3.50	5.00	M
	1955				
1035	The Outlaw of Eagle's Nest - Peter Field	2.00	4.00	7.50	W
1036	A Pocket Full of Rye - Agatha Christie	2.00	4.00	7.50	M
1037	Space Tug - Murray Leinster	2.00	4.00	7.50	SF
1038	You Shall Know Them - Vercors	2.00	4.00	7.50	SF/M
1039	The Beautiful Frame - William Pearson	1.50	3.50	5.00	
1040	Boss of the Plains - Will Ermine	1.50	3.50	5.00	W

1041	The Case of the One-eyed Witness - Erle Stanley Gardner	1.50	3.50	5.00	M
1042	The Little Ark - Jan de Hartog	1.50	3.50	5.00	
1043	The Story of Esther Costello - Nicholas Monsarrat	1.50	3.50	5.00	
1044	The Long Goodbye - Raymond Chandler	4.00	8.00	15.00	
1045	Science Fiction Terror Tales - Groff Conklin	3.00	6.00	12.00	SF
1046	Time and Time Again - James Hilton	1.50	3.50	5.00	
1047	Rogue's Yarn - John Jennings	3.00	6.00	12.00	A
1048	Ride the Dark Hills - W. Edmunds Claussen	1.50	3.50	5.00	W
1049	The Scarlet Letters - Ellery Queen	1.50	3.50	5.00	M
1050	Three for the Money - James McConnaughey	1.50	3.50	5.00	
	1955				
1051	A Fair Wind Home - Ruth Moore	1.50	3.50	5.00	
1052	The D. A. Breaks an Egg - Erle Stanley Gardner	1.50	3.50	5.00	
1053	Crackers in Bed - Vic Fredericks	1.50	3.50	5.00	
1054	Gambler's Gold - Peter Field	1.50	3.50	5.00	W
1055	I Die Possessed - J. B. O'Sullivan	1.50	3.50	5.00	
1056	Seven Trails - Max Brand	1.50	3.50	5.00	
1057	How to Work with Tools and Wood - Fred Gross	1.50	3.50	5.00	NF
1058	Murder's Nest - Charlotte Armstrong	1.50	3.50	5.00	M
1059	Hero Driver - Alfred Coppel	1.50	3.50	5.00	
1060	Hired Hand - Nelson Nye	1.50	3.50	5.00	W
1061	Arrow in the Moon - John & Margaret Harris	1.50	3.50	5.00	
1062	Margin of Terror - William P. McGivern	1.50	3.50	5.00	
1063	The Case of the Musical Cow - Erle Stanley Gardner	1.50	3.50	5.00	M
1064	Stage Road to Denver - Allan Vaughan Elston	1.50	3.50	5.00	W
1065	The Tenderfoot - Max Brand	1.50	3.50	5.00	W
1066	The Conquest of Don Pedro - Harvey Fergusson	1.50	3.50	5.00	
1067	Don Camillo and His Flock - Giovanni Guareschi	1.50	3.50	5.00	
1068	Mustang Mesa - Peter Field	1.50	3.50	5.00	W
1069	Prairie Guns - Ernest Haycox	1.50	3.50	5.00	W
1070	The Victim was Important - Joe Rayter	1.50	3.50	5.00	M
1071	Arrow in the Hill - Jefferson Cooper	1.50	3.50	5.00	
1072	The 5th Pocket Book of Crossword Puzzles - Margaret Petherbridge Farrar	3.00	6.00	12.00	NF
1073	Cress Delahanty - Jessamyn West	1.50	3.50	5.00	
1074	Invaders of Earth - Groff Conklin	2.00	4.00	7.50	SF
1075	A Ray and a Bone - Hillary Waugh	1.50	3.50	5.00	
	1955				
1076	Captain Judas - F. VanWyck Mason	1.50	3.50	5.00	A
1077	The Deadly Climate - Ursula Curtiss	1.50	3.50	5.00	
1078	Five Against the House - Jack Finney	1.50	3.50	5.00	
1079	The Fool Killer - Helen Eustis	1.50	3.50	5.00	
1080	Baby Sitter's Guide, by Dennis the Menace - Hank Ketcham & Bob Harmon	2.00	4.00	7.50	H
1081	Ravaged Range - Peter Field	1.50	3.50	5.00	W
1082	The Glass Village - Ellery Queen	1.50	3.50	5.00	M
1083	And Sometimes Death - J. Valentine	1.50	3.50	5.00	
1084	The Untamed - Max Brand	1.50	3.50	5.00	W
1085	The Under Dog and Other Mysteries - Agatha Christie	1.50	3.50	5.00	M
1086	Wagon Wheel Gap - Allan Vaughan Elston	1.50	3.50	5.00	W
1087	The New Peter Arno Pocket Book - Peter Arno	1.50	3.50	5.00	
	1956				
1088	Guns in the Saddle - Peter Field	1.50	3.50	5.00	W
1089	The Case of the Fiery Fingers - Erle Stanley Gardner	1.50	3.50	5.00	M
1090	The Devil Threw Dice - Amber Dean	1.50	3.50	5.00	
1091	Rider of the Midnight Range - Will Ermine	1.50	3.50	5.00	W
1092	The Case of the Angry Mourner - Erle Stanley Gardner	1.50	3.50	5.00	M
1093	The Compleat Practical Joker - H. Allen Smith	1.50	3.50	5.00	H
1094	Death Rides the Dondrino - Roe Richmond	1.50	3.50	5.00	W
1095	Alibi for Murder - Charlotte Armstrong	1.50	3.50	5.00	M
1096	Doctor Hudson's Secret Journal - Lloyd C. Douglas	1.50	3.50	5.00	

(POCKET BOOK, continued)

No.	Title				
1097	Tragedy Trail - Max Brand	1.50	3.50	5.00	W
1098	Guys and Dolls - Damon Runyon	3.00	6.00	12.00	
1099	Good Morning, Miss Dove - Frances Gray Patton	1.50	3.50	5.00	
1100	Off the Cuff - Jerry Lieberman 1956	1.50	3.50	5.00	H
1101	Cry, Coyote - Steve Frazee	1.50	3.50	5.00	W
1102	A Most Contagious Game - Samuel Grafton	1.50	3.50	5.00	
1103	Showdown - Allan Vaughan Elston	1.50	3.50	5.00	W
1104	Once a Fighter... - Les Savage, Jr.	1.50	3.50	5.00	W
1105	Waterfront Cop - William P. McGivern	1.50	3.50	5.00	
1106	Fedding Your Baby and Child - Miriam E. Lowenberg & Benjamin Spock	1.50	3.50	5.00	NF
1107	The Case of the Moth-eaten Mink - Erle Stanley Gardner	1.50	3.50	5.00	M
1108	The Brass Command - Clay Fisher	1.50	3.50	5.00	W
1109	Don't Hang Me Too High - J.B. O'Sullivan	1.50	3.50	5.00	
1110	Governor's Choice - Martin Mayer	1.50	3.50	5.00	
1111	The Big Store - Oscar Schisgall	1.50	3.50	5.00	
1112	The Girl from Frisco - William Heuman	1.50	3.50	5.00	W
1113	Man of the West - Philip Yordan	1.50	3.50	5.00	
1114	So Many Steps to Death - Agatha Christie	1.50	3.50	5.00	M
1115	Two Tickets for Tangier - F. VanWyck Mason	1.50	3.50	5.00	
1116	Forbidden Valley - Allan Vaughan Elston	1.50	3.50	5.00	W
1117	The River Witch - Marjorie McIntyre	1.50	3.50	5.00	
1118	Q. B. I. - Ellery Queen	1.50	3.50	5.00	M
1119	Onions in the Stew - Betty MacDonald	1.50	3.50	5.00	
1120	Dragnet: Case No. 561 - David Knight TV tie-in	2.00	4.00	7.50	M
1121	The Case of the Grinning Gorilla - Erle Stanley Gardner	1.50	3.50	5.00	M
1122	The False Rider - Max Brand	1.50	3.50	5.00	W
1123	The Road to Laramie - Peter Field	1.50	3.50	5.00	W
1124	Cowboy, Say Your Prayers! - Will Ermine	1.50	3.50	5.00	W
1125	Dennis the Menace Rides Again - Hank Ketcham 1956	2.00	4.00	7.50	H
1126	The Jungle Kids - Evan Hunter	2.50	6.00	10.00	JD
1127	The Case of the Hesitant Hostess - Erle Stanley Gardner	1.50	3.50	5.00	M
1128	The Guns of Witchwater - Colby Wolford	1.50	3.50	5.00	
1129	The 6th Pocket Book of Crossword Puzzles - Margaret Petherbridge Farrar	1.50	3.50	5.00	NF
1130	Strictly for Laughs - Joey Adams	1.50	3.50	5.00	H
1131	The Treasure of Pleasant Valley - Frank Yerby	1.50	3.50	5.00	
1132	Asking for Trouble - Joe Rayter	1.50	3.50	5.00	
1133	Galloping Broncos - Max Brand	1.50	3.50	5.00	W
1134	The Iron Bronc - Will Ermine	1.50	3.50	5.00	W
1135	The Parson of Gunbarrel Basin - Nelson Nye	1.50	3.50	5.00	W
1136	Sinners and Shrouds - Jonathan Latimer	1.50	3.50	5.00	M
1137	The Big Pasture - Clay Fisher	1.50	3.50	5.00	W
1138	The Case of the Fugitive Nurse - Erle Stanley Gardner	1.50	3.50	5.00	M
1139	Castle Garac - Nicholas Monsarrat	1.50	3.50	5.00	
1140	The Invisible Man - H. G. Wells	4.00	8.00	15.00	SF
1141	Hunt the Man Down - William Pearson 1957	1.50	3.50	5.00	

Pocket Book 920, c. PKB

Pocket Book 1140, c. PKB

Pocket Book 1178, c. PKB

1142	The Lonely Grass - Nelson Nye	1.50	3.50	5.00	W
1143	Lysander - F. VanWyck Mason	1.50	3.50	5.00	
1144	The Laff Parade - Jerry Lieberman	1.50	3.50	5.00	H
1145	Stab in the Dark - Joe Rayter	1.50	3.50	5.00	
1146	The Dangerous Years - Douglass Wallop	1.50	3.50	5.00	
1147	Combat Nurse - Frieda K. Franklin	1.50	3.50	5.00	R
1148	The Last Rodeo - Ernest Haycox	1.50	3.50	5.00	W
1149	The Gambler - Max Brand	1.50	3.50	5.00	W
1150	The Man on the Couch - Mischa Richter 1957	1.50	3.50	5.00	
1151	Hickory Dickory Death - Agatha Christie	1.50	3.50	5.00	M
1152	The Men from the Boys - Ed Lacy	1.50	3.50	5.00	
1153	Wanted: Dennis the Menace - Hank Ketcham	2.00	4.00	7.50	H
1154	The 7th Pocket Book of Crossword Puzzles - Margaret Petherbridge Farrar	2.00	4.00	7.50	NF
1155	The Case of the Green-eyed Sister - Erle Stanley Gardner	1.50	3.50	5.00	M
1156	The 7 File - William P. McGivern	1.50	3.50	5.00	
1157	Widow's Web - Ursula Curtiss	1.50	3.50	5.00	M
1158	Cakes and Ale - W. Somerset Maugham	1.50	3.50	5.00	
1159	The Blue Mustang - Clay Fisher	1.50	3.50	5.00	W
1160	Double Entendre - Newton Wilson Hoke	1.50	3.50	5.00	
1161	Maverick's Return - Peter Field	1.50	3.50	5.00	W
1162	Combat Mission - Joe David Brown	1.50	3.50	5.00	
1163	The Wyoming Bubble - Allan Vaughan Elston	1.50	3.50	5.00	W
1164	The Bulls and the Bees - Roger Eddy	1.50	3.50	5.00	
1165	Ripley's Believe It or Not! 4th Series - Robert Ripley	2.50	6.00	10.00	NF
1166	Lone Wolf - Bennett Foster	1.50	3.50	5.00	W
1167	Inspector Queen's Own Case - Ellery Queen	1.50	3.50	5.00	M
1168	Smiling Desperado - Max Brand	1.50	3.50	5.00	W
1169	War on the Saddle Rock - Will Ermine	1.50	3.50	5.00	W
1170	The Case of the Restless Redhead - Erle Stanley Gardner	1.50	3.50	5.00	M
1171	When Strangers Meet - Robert Bloomfield	1.50	3.50	5.00	
1172	The Seven Islands - Jon Godden	1.50	3.50	5.00	
1173	Sheriff Wanted! - Peter Field	1.50	3.50	5.00	W
1174	Dead Man's Folly - Agatha Christie	1.50	3.50	5.00	M
1175	The 8th Pocket Book of Crossword Puzzles - Margaret Petherbridge Farrar 1957	2.00	4.00	7.50	NF
1176	Captain Nemesis - F. VanWyck Mason	1.50	3.50	5.00	A
1177	Old Yeller - Fred Gipson	1.50	3.50	5.00	A
1178	Rebecca's Pride - Donald McNutt Douglass	2.00	4.00	7.50	
1179	Dennis the Menace vs. Everybody - Hank Ketcham	2.00	4.00	7.50	H
1180	The Invisible Outlaw - Max Brand	1.50	3.50	5.00	W
1181	The Marked Men - Allan Vaughan Elston	1.50	3.50	5.00	W
1182	The 9th Pocket Book of Crossword Puzzles - Margaret Petherbridge Farrar	2.00	4.00	7.50	NF
1183	No Blade of Grass - John Christopher	2.00	4.00	7.50	SF
1184	The NBC Book of Stars - Earl Wilson	3.00	6.00	12.00	NF
1185	The Brave Cowboy - Edward Abbey	1.50	3.50	5.00	W
1186	Santa Fe Passage - Clay Fisher 1958	1.50	3.50	5.00	W
1187	Powder Valley Showdown - Peter Field	1.50	3.50	5.00	W
1188	The Abode of Love - AuGray Menen	1.50	3.50	5.00	
1189	My Kingdom for a Hearse - Craig Rice	1.50	3.50	5.00	M
1190	Outlaw Breed - Max Brand	1.50	3.50	5.00	W
1191	Last Stage to Aspen - Allan Vaughan Elston	1.50	3.50	5.00	W
1192	The Enemy Below - D. A. Rayner	1.50	3.50	5.00	
1193	Night Extra - William P. McGivern	1.50	3.50	5.00	
1194	Shottin' Melody - E. B. Mann	1.50	3.50	5.00	W
1195	Ripley's Believe It or Not! 5th Series - Robert Ripley	2.50	6.00	10.00	NF
1196	Wagonmaster - Robert Turner TV tie-in	2.00	4.00	7.50	
1197	Hard Man - Leo Katcher	1.50	3.50	5.00	
1198	Dragnet: The Case of the Courteous Killer - Richard Deming TV tie-in	2.00	4.00	7.50	M
1199	The Day the Money Stopped - Brendan Gill	1.50	3.50	5.00	
1200	Too Humerous to Mention - Charles Preston 1958	1.50	3.50	5.00	H
1201	The Sulu Sea Murders - F. VanWyck Mason	1.50	3.50	5.00	
1202	The Tank Destroyers - Lawrence H. Kahn	1.50	3.50	5.00	C

(POCKET BOOK, continued)

1203	Trail Partners - Max Brand	1.50	3.50	5.00	
1204	The O. S. S. and I - William J. Morgan	2.00	4.00	7.50	
1205	Return to Powder Valley - Peter Field	1.50	3.50	5.00	W
1206	The Murder of the Missing Link - Vercors	2.00	4.00	7.50	SF/M
1207	The Assault - Allen R. Matthews	1.50	3.50	5.00	C
1208	Ripley's Believe It or Not! 6th Series - Robert Ripley	2.50	6.00	10.00	NF
1209	Yellowstone Kelly - Clay Fisher Movie tie-in	2.00	4.00	7.50	W
1210	Betty Cornell's Glamour Guide for Teens - Betty Cornell	2.00	4.00	7.50	NF
1211	Grand Mesa - Allan Vaughan Elston	1.50	3.50	5.00	W
1212	Beyond the Call of Duty - Eugene Brown	1.50	3.50	5.00	
1213	Blacksnake Trail - Peter Field	1.50	3.50	5.00	W
1214	Dragnet: The Case of the Crime King - Richard Deming TV tie-in	2.00	4.00	7.50	M
1215	Knocked for a Loop - Craig Rice	1.50	3.50	5.00	M
1216	The Scout - Robert Turner TV tie-in	2.00	4.00	7.50	W
1217	Dennis the Menace: Household Hurricane - Hank Ketcham	2.00	4.00	7.50	H
1218	Ensign O'Toole and Me - William J. Lederer	1.50	3.50	5.00	
1219	The China Sea Murders - F. VanWyck Mason	2.00	4.00	7.50	M
1220	Murder on Delivery - Spencer Dean	1.50	3.50	5.00	M
1221	Speedy - Max Brand	1.50	3.50	5.00	W
1222	The Winds of Time - Chad Oliver c-Powers	2.00	4.00	7.50	SF
1223	The Gracious Lily Affair - F. VanWyck Mason 1959	1.50	3.50	5.00	
1224	Brother Sebastian - Chon Dory	1.50	3.50	5.00	H
1225	A Roman Affair - Ercole Patti	1.50	3.50	5.00	
1226	Wagons West! - Robert Turner	1.50	3.50	5.00	
1227	The 10th Pocket Book of Crossword Puzzles - Margaret Petherbridge Farrar	2.00	4.00	7.50	
1228	Blood on the Trail - Max Brand	1.50	3.50	5.00	W
1229	The Hit - Julian Mayfield	1.50	3.50	5.00	
1230	End of the Line - Bert Hitchens & Dolores Hitchens	1.50	3.50	5.00	M
1231	The Broken Angel - Floyd Mahannah	1.50	3.50	5.00	M
1232	The Man Who Shot Quantrill - George Appell	1.50	3.50	5.00	W
1233	Thanks to the Saint - Leslie Charteris	1.50	3.50	5.00	M
1234	Stranger in the Land - Colby Wolford	1.50	3.50	5.00	
1235	Big Man - Richard Marsten	1.50	3.50	5.00	
1236	Visiting Nurse - Margaret Howe	1.50	3.50	5.00	R
1237	Captain Seadog - Jefferson Cooper	2.00	4.00	7.50	A
1238	The Last Holdup - Sam Meriwether	2.50	3.50	5.00	W
1239	Fool's Gold - Delores Hitchens	1.50	3.50	5.00	
1240	The Lady Came to Kill - M. E. Chaber	1.50	3.50	5.00	M
1241	Outlaw Valley - Peter Field	1.50	3.50	5.00	W
1242	Brother Juniper - Justin McCarthy	1.50	3.50	5.00	H
1243	Surgical Nurse - Rosie M. Banks	1.50	3.50	5.00	R
1244	Fire Brain - Max Brand	1.50	3.50	5.00	W
1245	Substitute Doctor - Elizabeth Seifert	1.50	3.50	5.00	
1246	The Mission - Dean Brelis	1.50	3.50	5.00	
1247	The Angry Land - Frank Bass	1.50	3.50	5.00	
1248	Dishonor Among Thieves - Spencer Dean	1.50	3.50	5.00	M
1249	Badlands Buccaneer - John Hunter	1.50	3.50	5.00	W
1250	The Killer is Mine - Talmage Powell 1959	1.50	3.50	5.00	
1251	Beyond Wind River - Les Savage, Jr.	1.50	3.50	5.00	W
1252	Cairo Intrigue - William Manchester	1.50	3.50	5.00	
1253					
1254	Rio Grande Deadline - Allan Vaughan Elston	1.50	3.50	5.00	W
1255	Murder Takes a Wife - James Howard	1.50	3.50	5.00	M
1256	Never Kill a Cop - Lee Costigan	1.50	3.50	5.00	
1257	Rebel Basin - Harry Sinclair Drago	1.50	3.50	5.00	W
1258					
1259	A Hearse of Another Color - M. E. Chaber	1.50	3.50	5.00	M
1260	Trail from Needle Rock - Peter Field	1.50	3.50	5.00	W
1261	Mark Kilby Solves a Murder - Robert Caine Frazer	1.50	3.50	5.00	M

POCKET BOOKS (BRITISH)

Pocket Books B44, c. Jarrold Pocket Books Jr. J-48, c. PKB Pocket Books Jr. J-57, c. PKB

(POCKET BOOKS, continued)

(Jarrold and Sons Limited)

B44	The Concertgoer's Handbook - Hubert Foss	2.00	4.00	7.50	NF

POCKET BOOKS JR.

(Pocket Books, Inc.)

Continuation of Comet Books

J35	Ski Patrol - Montgomery Atwater	1.50	3.50	5.00	A
J36	Long Lash - Bertrand Shurtleff	1.50	3.50	5.00	
J37	Tom Sawyer - Mark Twain	1.50	3.50	5.00	A
J38	Baldy of Nome - Esther Birdsall Darling	1.50	3.50	5.00	A
J39	Sponger's Jinx - Bert Sackett	1.50	3.50	5.00	A
J40	Mountain Pony - Henry V. Larom	1.50	3.50	5.00	A
J41	Black Storm - Thomas C. Hinkle	1.50	3.50	5.00	W
J42	Huckleberry Finn - Mark Twain	1.50	3.50	5.00	A
J43	Black Beauty - Anna Sewell	1.50	3.50	5.00	
J44	Popularity Plus - Sally S. Simpson	1.50	3.50	5.00	
J45	Your Own Book of Funny Stories	1.50	3.50	5.00	H
J46	Your Own Book of Campcraft - Catherine T. Hammett	1.50	3.50	5.00	NF
J47	The Mystery of Batty Ridge - Allan Gregg	2.00	4.00	6.00	M
J48	Buffalo Bill - Shannon Garst	1.50	3.50	5.00	B
J49	Blue Treasure - Helen Girvan	1.50	3.50	5.00	
J50	Tiger Roan - Glenn Balch	1.50	3.50	5.00	
J51	Kingdom of Flying Men - Frederick Nelson Litten	1.50	3.50	5.00	
J52	Gridiron Challenge - Jackson Scholz	1.50	3.50	5.00	S
J53	Sue Barton, Senior Nurse - Helen Dore Boylston	1.50	3.50	5.00	R
J54	Logging Chance - M. H. Lasher	1.50	3.50	5.00	
J55	Touchdown Twins - Philip Harkins	1.50	3.50	5.00	S
J56	Cowdog - Ned Andrews	1.50	3.50	5.00	
J57	The Black Arrow - Robert Louis Stevenson	1.50	3.50	5.00	A
J58	Mustang - Thomas C. Hinkle	1.50	3.50	5.00	W
J59	Pirot Man - Dick Friendlich	1.50	3.50	5.00	S
J60	Buckskin Brigade - Jim Kjelgaard	1.50	3.50	5.00	A
	1951				
J61	Black Spaniel Mystery - Betty Cavanna	1.50	3.50	5.00	M
J62	Yellowstone Scout - William Marshall Rush	1.50	3.50	5.00	W
J63	The Great Houdini - Samuel Stein & Beryl Williams	1.50	3.50	5.00	B
J64	Secret Sea - Robb White	1.50	3.50	5.00	
J65	Mountain Pony and the Pinto Calf - Henry V. Larom	1.50	3.50	5.00	W
J66	High, Inside! - Guy Emery	1.50	3.50	5.00	
J67	The Kid Comes Back - John R. Tunis	1.50	3.50	5.00	S
J68	The Teen-age Manual - Edith Heal	1.50	3.50	5.00	NF
J69	Back to Treasure Island - H. A. Calahan	1.50	3.50	5.00	
J70	Shag - Thomas C. Hinkle	1.50	3.50	5.00	

J71	The Jinx Ship - Howard Pease	1.50	3.50	5.00	A
J72	Beyond Rope and Fence - David Grew	1.50	3.50	5.00	
J73	The Wind in the Rigging - Howard Pease	1.50	3.50	5.00	A
J74	Riders of the Gabilans - Graham Dean	1.50	3.50	5.00	
J75	Wolf Dogs of the North - Jack Hines	1.50	3.50	5.00	A
J76	The Ship Without a Crew - Howard Pease	1.50	3.50	5.00	A
J77	Partners of Powder Hole - Robert Davis	1.50	3.50	5.00	

POCKET LIBRARY

(Pocket Books, Inc.)

PL 1	Man and State: The Political Philosophers - Saxe Commins & Robert N. Linscott 1954	.75	1.75	3.00	NF
PL 2	Man and Man: The Social Philosophers - Saxe Commins & Robert N. Linscott	.50	1.25	2.00	NF
PL 3	Man and the Universe: The Philosophers of Science - Saxe Commins & Robert N. Linscott	.50	1.25	2.00	NF
PL 4	Man and Spirit: The Speculative Philosophers - Saxe Commins & Robert N. Linscott	.50	1.25	2.00	NF
PL 5	The Imitation of Christ - Thomas A. Kempis	.50	1.25	2.00	
PL 6	The Golden Ass of Apuleius - Apuleius Madaurensis	.75	1.75	3.00	
PL 7	Dialogues of Plato	.75	1.75	3.00	
PL 8	Famous Chinese Short Stories - Lin Yutang	1.50	3.50	5.00	
PL 9	Pride and Prejudice - Jane Austen	.50	1.25	2.00	
PL10	Wuthering Heights - Emily Bronte	.50	1.25	2.00	
PL11	The Story of Philosophy - Will Durant	.75	1.75	3.00	NF
PL12	The Story of Mankind - Hendrik Willem Van Loon	.75	1.75	3.00	NF
PL13	The Pocket Bible	.75	1.75	3.00	
PL14	The Great Short Stories of Robert Louis Stevenson	.75	1.75	3.00	
PL15	The House of the Seven Gables - Nathaniel Hawthorne	.75	1.75	3.00	
PL16	Tales from the Arabian Nights	.75	1.75	3.00	
PL17	The Way West - A. B. Guthrie, Jr.	.75	1.75	3.00	W
PL18	The Autobiography of Benjamin Franklin	.75	1.75	3.00	B
PL19	Ivanhoe - Walter Scott	.50	1.25	2.00	A
PL20	The Red Badge of Courage - Stephen Crane	.50	1.25	2.00	A
PL21	The Pocket Book of Great Operas - Henry Simon & Abraham Veinus	.75	1.75	3.00	
PL22	A Tale of Two Cities - Charles Dickens	.75	1.75	3.00	
PL23	The Return of the Native - Thomas Hardy	.50	1.25	2.00	
PL24	The Pocket Book of Modern American Short Stories - Philip van Doren Stern	.50	1.25	2.00	
PL25	Tess of the D'Urbervilles - Thomas Hardy	.50	1.25	2.00	
PL26	The Scarlet Letter - Nathaniel Hawthorne 1955	.75	1.75	3.00	
PL27	Silas Marner - George Eliot	.75	1.75	3.00	
PL28	Moby Dick - Herman Melville	.50	1.25	2.00	
PL29	Great Short Stories - Guy de Maupassant	.50	1.25	2.00	
PL30	Four Great Tragedies - William Shakespeare	.50	1.25	2.00	
PL31	Four Great Comedies - William Shakespeare	.50	1.25	2.00	
PL32	German Stories and Tales - Robert Pick	.75	1.75	3.00	
PL33	The Basic Ideas of Alexander Hamilton	.75	1.75	3.00	
PL34	Kidnapped - Robert Louis Stevenson	.75	1.75	3.00	
PL35	The New Pocket Anthology of American Verse - Oscar Williams 1955	.75	1.75	3.00	
PL36	The Bridge of San Luis Rey - Thornton Wilder	.50	1.25	2.00	
PL37	French Stories and Tales - Stanley Geist 1956	.75	1.75	3.00	
PL38	The Pocket Book of O. Henry Stories	.75	1.75	3.00	
PL39	The Adventures of Tom Sawyer - Mark Twain	.50	1.25	2.00	
PL40	Spanish Stories and Tales - Harriet de Onis	.75	1.75	3.00	
PL41	The Pocket Book of Verse - M. E. Speare	.75	1.75	3.00	
PL42	The Adventures of Huckleberry Finn - Mark Twain	.50	1.25	2.00	
PL43	Tales from the Decameron - Giovanni Boccaccio	.75	1.75	3.00	

PL44 Jane Eyre - Charlotte Bronte	.50	1.25	2.00
PL45 The Confessions of St. Augustine - Aurelius			
Augustinus	.75	1.75	3.00
PL46 Great Tales and Poems - Edgar Allan Poe	.75	1.75	3.00
PL47 The Pocket Book of Robert Frost's Poems	.75	1.75	3.00
PL48 Irish Stories and Tales - Devin A. Garrity	.75	1.75	3.00
PL49 Treasure Island - Robert Louis Stevenson	.75	1.75	3.00
PL50 Great Expectations - Charles Dickens	.75	1.75	3.00
PL51 Gulliver's Travels - Jonathan Swift	.75	1.75	3.00
1957			
PL52 The Mayor of Casterbridge - Thomas Hardy	.50	1.25	2.00
PL53 The Pilgrim's Progress - John Bunyan	.50	1.25	2.00
PL54 The Vicar of Wakefield - Oliver Goldsmith	.50	1.25	2.00
PL55 The Pocket Book of Short Stories -			
M. E. Speare	.50	1.25	2.00
PL56 The Confessions of Jean - Jacques Rousseau	.75	1.75	3.00
PL57 The Tragedy of King Lear - William			
Shakespeare	.50	1.25	2.00
PL58 Great Essays in Science - Martin Gardner	.50	1.25	2.00
PL59 The Marble Fawn - Nathaniel Hawthorne	.75	1.75	3.00
PL60 The Merchant of Venice - William Shakespeare	.50	1.25	2.00
PL61 The Tragedy of Othello, the Moor of Venice -			
William Shakespeare	.50	1.25	2.00
PL62 The Last of the Mohicans - James Fenimore			
Cooper	.75	1.75	3.00
PL63 Nana - Emile Zola	.50	1.25	2.00
1958			
PL64 The Tragedy of Hamlet, Prince of Denmark -			
William Shakespeare	.50	1.25	2.00
PL65 Mid-century - Orville Prescott	.50	1.25	2.00
PL66 The Tragedy of Julius Caesar - William			
Shakespeare	.50	1.25	2.00
PL67 A Midsummer's Night's Dream - William			
Shakespeare	.50	1.25	2.00
PL68 A Christmas Carol - Charles Dickens	.75	1.75	3.00
PL69 Madame Bovary - Gustave Flaubert	.50	1.25	2.00
PL70 The Tragedy of Macbeth - William			
Shakespeare	.50	1.25	2.00
1959			
PL71 Laughing Boy - Oliver La Farge	.50	1.25	2.00
PL500 The Story of Philosophy - Will Durant	.75	1.75	3.00
PL501 The Story of Mankind - Hendrik Willem			
Van Loon	.75	1.75	3.00
PL502 Ivanhoe - Walter Scott	.75	1.75	3.00
PL503 The New Pocket Anthology of American			
Verse - Oscar Williams	.75	1.75	3.00
PL504 Immortal Poems of the English Language -			
Oscar Williams	.75	1.75	3.00
PL505 The Pocket Book of Modern Verse - Oscar			
Williams	.50	1.25	2.00
PL506 Tales from the Arabian Nights	.75	1.75	3.00
PL507 Adam Bede - George Eliot	.50	1.25	2.00
1956			
PL508 Lorna Doone - R. D. Blackmore	.75	1.75	3.00
PL509 The Mill on the Floss - George Eliot	.75	1.75	3.00
PL510 Robinson Crusoe - Daniel Defoe	.50	1.25	2.00
PL511 The Life and Opinions of Tristram Shandy,			
Gentleman - Laurence Sterne	.50	1.25	2.00
PL512 The Pocket History of the United States -			
Henry Steele Commager & Allan Nevins	.50	1.25	2.00
PL513 The Way West - A. B. Guthrie, Jr.	.75	1.75	3.00
PL514 Oliver Twist - Charles Dickens	.75	1.75	3.00
1957			
PL515 The Pocket History of American Painting -			
James Thomas Flexner	1.50	3.50	5.00
PL516 Story Poems - Louis Untermeyer	.75	1.75	3.00
PL517 Don Quixote - Miguel de Cervantes	.75	1.75	3.00
PL518 Essays in Philosophy - James Bayley &			
Houston Peterson	.50	1.25	2.00
PL519 The Pocket Aristotle - Aristotle	.75	1.75	3.00
PL520 The Selected Essays of Montaigne -			
Michel de Montaigne	.50	1.25	2.00
PL521			
PL522 A Tale of Two Cities - Charles Dickens	.75	1.75	3.00
PL523			

(POCKET LIBRARY, continued)
PL524

PL525	Tess of the D'Urbervilles - Thomas Hardy	.50	1.25	2.00
PL544	Jane Eyre - Charlotte Bronte	.50	1.25	2.00
PL750	Vanity Fair - William Makepeace Thackeray	.50	1.25	2.00
PL751	David Copperfield - Charles Dickens	.75	1.75	3.00

POCKET LIBRARY OF GREAT ART

Pocket Books Inc./N. Abrams, Inc.)

A 1	Degas - Daniel Catton Rich 1953	.75	1.75	3.00	NF
A 2	El Greco - John F. Matthews	.75	1.75	3.00	NF
A 3	Toulouse-Lautrec - Samuel Hunter	.75	1.75	3.00	NF
A 4	Cezanne - Theodore Rousseau, Jr.	.75	1.75	3.00	NF
A 5	Dufy - Alfred Werner	.75	1.75	3.00	NF
A 6	Van Gogh - Robert Goldwater	.75	1.75	3.00	NF
A 7	The French Impressionists and Their Circle - Herman J. Wechsler	.75	1.75	3.00	NF
A 8	Rembrandt - Wilhelm Koehler	.75	1.75	3.00	NF
A 9	Botticelli - Frederick Hartt	.75	1.75	3.00	NF
A10	Matisse - Clement Greenberg	.75	1.75	3.00	NF
A11	Renoir - Milton S. Fox	.75	1.75	3.00	NF
A12	Utrillo - Alfred Werner	.75	1.75	3.00	NF
A13	Manet - S. Lane Faison, Jr. 1954	.75	1.75	3.00	NF
A14	Rouault - Jacques Maritain	.75	1.75	3.00	NF
A15	Gauguin - John Rewald	.75	1.75	3.00	NF
A16	Modigliani - Jacques Lipchitz	.75	1.75	3.00	NF
A17	Rubens - Julius S. Held	.75	1.75	3.00	NF
A18	Pissarro - John Rewald	.75	1.75	3.00	NF
A19	Velazquez - Margaretta Salinger	.75	1.75	3.00	NF
A20	Picasso (Blue and Rose Periods) - William S. Lieberman	.75	1.75	3.00	NF
A21	Bruegel - Wolfgang Stechow 1955	.75	1.75	3.00	NF
A22	Goya - Frederick S. Wight	.75	1.75	3.00	NF
A23	Michelangelo - Margaretta Salinger	.75	1.75	3.00	NF
A24	Flower Painting by the Great Masters - Margaret Fairbanks Marcus	.75	1.75	3.00	NF

PONY BOOKS

(Stamford House)

45	Your Life in the Atom World - John Houston Craige 1946	2.50	6.00	10.00	NF
46	The Singing Corpse - Bernard Dougall 1945	2.50	6.00	10.00	M
47	The Orange Divan - Valentine Williams	2.50	6.00	10.00	M
48	The Narrow Cell - Dale Clark	2.50	6.00	10.00	M

Pocket Library PL7. c. PKB   Pocket Library A15. c. PKB   Pocket Library A21. c. PKB

Pony Books 57, c. SH   Pony Books 59, c. SH   Pony Books 64, c. SH

(PONY BOOKS, continued)

49 The Corpse with the Red-Headed Friend - R. A. J. Walling	2.50	6.00	10.00	M
50 The Wager and the House at Fernwood - Fulton Oursler First ed., 1946	2.00	4.00	7.50	
51 The Heart Has Wings - Faith Baldwin	2.00	4.00	7.50	R
52 A Clue for Mr. Fortune - H. C. Bailey	2.50	6.00	10.00	M
53 Unhurrying Chase - Morris Markey First ed., 1946	2.50	6.00	10.00	
54 Cellini Smith: Detective - Robert Reeves	2.50	6.00	10.00	M
55 Second Hand Wife - Kathleen Norris	2.50	6.00	10.00	
56 Wanted: Someone Innocent - Margery Allingham First ed., 1946	2.50	6.00	10.00	M
57 The Stolen Squadron - Charles L. Leonard	2.00	4.00	7.50	C
58 Salt River Ranny - Nelson C. Nye	2.50	6.00	10.00	W
59 One Small Candle - Cecil Roberts	2.00	4.00	7.50	
60 The Bishop's Crime - H. C. Bailey	2.50	6.00	10.00	M
61 Fifty Famous Sports Stories - Caswell Adams First ed., 1946	2.00	4.00	7.50	S
62 The Inconvenient Corpse - E. P. Fenwick	2.50	6.00	10.00	M
63 Death and the Devil - Paul Whelton	2.50	6.00	10.00	M
64 Mr. Fortune Wonders - H. C. Bailey	2.50	6.00	10.00	M
65 The Quiz Crossword Puzzle Book Orig., 1946	4.00	7.00	12.00	NF
66 Blood of the North - James B. Hendryx	2.50	6.00	10.00	A

PONY BOOKS

(Weldun)

Canadian

123 The Waltz of Death - P. B. Maxon	2.00	4.00	7.50	M

POPULAR LIBRARY

(Popular Library, Inc.)

1 Saint Overboard - Leslie Charteris 1943	15.00	35.00	60.00	M
2 Danger in the Dark - Mignon G. Eberhart	5.00	10.00	20.00	M
3 Crime of Violence - Rufus King	5.00	10.00	20.00	M
4 Murder in the Madhouse - Jonathan Latimer	5.00	10.00	20.00	M
5 Miss Pinkerton - Mary Roberts Rinehart	5.00	10.00	20.00	M
6 Three Bright Pebbles - Leslie Ford	5.00	10.00	20.00	M
7 Death Demands an Audience - Helen Reilly	5.00	10.00	20.00	M
8 Death for Dear Clara-- Q. Patrick	5.00	10.00	20.00	M
9 The Eee Pie Murders - David Frome	4.00	8.00	15.00	M
10 To Wake the Dead - John Dickson Carr	5.00	10.00	20.00	M
11 The Stoneware Monkey - R. Austin Freeman	5.00	10.00	20.00	M
12 Death Sits on the Board - John Rhode	5.00	10.00	20.00	M

13 Valcour Meets Murder - Rufus King	2.50	6.00	10.00	M
14 The Criminal C. O. D. - Phoebe Atwood Taylor	5.00	10.00	20.00	M
15 The Third Eye - Ethel Lina White	2.50	6.00	10.00	M
16 The Dead Don't Care - Jonathan Latimer	4.00	8.00	15.00	M
17 The House on the Roof - Mignon G. Eberhart	4.00	8.00	15.00	M
18 Tragedy in the Hollow - Freeman Wills Crofts	3.00	6.00	12.00	M
19 The Crooked Hinge - John Dickson Carr	4.00	8.00	15.00	M
20 Murder in Shinbone Alley - Helen Reilly	3.00	6.00	12.00	M
21 The After House - Mary Roberts Rinehart	3.00	6.00	12.00	M
1944				
22 Murder Masks Miami - Rufus King	3.00	6.00	12.00	M
23 S. S. Murder - Q. Patrick	4.00	8.00	15.00	M
24 Reno Rendezvous - Leslie Ford	3.00	6.00	12.00	S
25 Out of Order - Phoebe Atwood Taylor	3.00	6.00	12.00	M
1944				
26 Mr. Pinkerton Has the Clue - David Frome	3.00	6.00	12.00	M
27 From this Dark Stairway - Mignon G. Eberhart	3.00	6.00	12.00	M
28 The Burning Court - John Dickson Carr	5.00	10.00	20.00	M
29 Weekend with Death - Patricia Wentworth	3.00	6.00	12.00	M
30 There's Trouble Brewing - Nicholas Blake	4.00	8.00	15.00	M
31 Murder by the Clock - Rufus King	3.00	6.00	12.00	M
32 The Wheel Spins - Ethel Lina White	4.00	8.00	15.00	M
Movie tie-in				
33 McKee of Centre Street - Helen Reilly	3.00	6.00	12.00	M
34 Mr. Pinkerton at the Old Angel - David Frome	3.00	6.00	12.00	M
35 The Mystery of Hunting's End - Mignon G. Eberhart	3.00	6.00	12.00	M
36 Death and the Maiden - Q. Patrick	4.00	8.00	15.00	M
37 Mother Finds a Body - Gypsy Rose Lee	3.00	6.00	12.00	M
38 The Dark Ships - Hulbert Footner	3.00	6.00	12.00	
39 In the Balance - Patricia Wentworth	3.00	6.00	12.00	M
40 The Stars Spell Death - Jonathan Stagge	3.00	6.00	12.00	M
41 The Smiler with the Knife - Nicholas Blake	4.00	8.00	15.00	M
42 Murdered: One by One - Francis Beeding	3.00	6.00	12.00	M
43 The Fatal Kiss Mystery - Rufus King	3.00	6.00	12.00	M
1945				
44 The Brass Chills - Hugh Pentecost	4.00	8.00	15.00	M
45 The Wrong Murder - Craig Rice	3.00	6.00	12.00	M
46 Sound of Revelry - Octavus Roy Cohen	4.00	8.00	15.00	M
47 Return to the Scene - Q. Patrick	4.00	8.00	15.00	M
aka The Green Diary				
48 Mr. Smith's Hat - Helen Reilly	3.00	6.00	12.00	M
49 Tiger Milk - David Garth	3.00	6.00	12.00	M
50 Green Shiver - Clyde B. Clason	3.00	6.00	12.00	
1945				
51 The Whispering Cup - Mabel Seeley	3.00	6.00	12.00	M
52 Murder by Prescription - Jonathan Stagge	3.00	6.00	12.00	M
53 Cancelled in Red - Hugh Pentecost	3.00	6.00	12.00	M
54 Her Heart in her Throat - Ethel Lina White	4.00	8.00	15.00	M
55 Murder in the Willett Family - Rufus King	3.00	6.00	12.00	M
56 Dead for a Ducat - Helen Reilly	3.00	6.00	12.00	M
57 The Twelve Disguises - Francis Beeding	3.00	6.00	12.00	M
58 The Turquoise Shop - Frances Crane	3.00	6.00	12.00	M
59 The Case of the Solid Key - Anthony Boucher	5.00	10.00	20.00	M
60 The Corpse in the Snowman - Nicholas Blake	4.00	8.00	15.00	M
61 The Mad Hatter Mystery - John Dickson Carr	4.00	8.00	15.00	M
62 The Yellow Taxi - Jonathan Stagge	3.00	6.00	12.00	M

Popular Library 1. c. Poplib   Popular Library 28, c. Poplib   Popular Library 59, c. Poplib

Popular Library 76, c. Poplib Popular Library 88, c. Poplib Popular Library 91, c. Poplib

(POPULAR LIBRARY, continued)

63 Sing a Song of Homicide - James R. Laugham	3.00	6.00	12.00	M
64 They Can't Hang Me - James Ronald	3.00	6.00	12.00	M
65 The Woman in the Picture - John August	3.00	6.00	12.00	
66 The Blind Side - Patricia Wentworth	3.00	6.00	12.00	M
67 Murder on the Yacht - Rufus King	3.00	6.00	12.00	M
68 The Cat Screams - Todd Downing	3.00	6.00	12.00	M
69 The Listening House - Mabel Seeley	3.00	6.00	12.00	M
1946				
70 Mr. Polton Explains - R. Austin Freeman	4.00	8.00	15.00	M
71 Hell Let Loose - Francis Beeding	3.00	6.00	12.00	M
72 Who Killed Aunt Maggie? - Medora Field	3.00	6.00	12.00	M
73 Hasty Wedding - Mignon G. Eberhart	3.00	6.00	12.00	M
74 Murder in Season - Octavus Roy Cohen	4.00	8.00	15.00	M
75 She Faded into Air - Ethel Lina White	3.00	6.00	12.00	M
1946				
76 Fog - Valentine Williams & Dorothy Rice Sims	3.00	6.00	12.00	M
77 Buckaroo - Eugene Cunningham	3.00	6.00	12.00	W
78 Timbal Gulch Trail - Max Brand	3.00	6.00	12.00	W
79 Rolling Stone - Patricia Wentworth	3.00	6.00	12.00	M
80 The Golden Box - Frances Crane	3.00	6.00	12.00	M
81 Three Thirds of a Ghost - Timothy Fuller	3.00	6.00	12.00	M
82 The 24th Horse - Hugh Pentecost	3.00	6.00	12.00	M
83 The Black-Headed Pins - Constance & Gwenyth				
Little	3.00	6.00	12.00	M
84 Challenge for Three - David Garth	3.00	6.00	12.00	M
85 Trouble Shooter - Ernest Haycox	3.00	6.00	12.00	W
86 Bucky Follows a Cold Trail - William MacLeod				
Raine	3.00	6.00	12.00	W
87 Fatal Descent - John Rhode & Carter Dickson	4.00	8.00	15.00	M
88 Romance in the First Degree - Octavus Roy				
Cohen	4.00	8.00	15.00	M
89 The Right Murder - Craig Rice	3.00	6.00	12.00	M
90 The Scarlet Circle - Jonathan Stagge	3.00	6.00	12.00	M
91 The Sea-Hawk - Rafael Sabatini	4.00	8.00	15.00	A
92 All Over but the Shooting - Richard Powell	2.00	4.00	7.50	M
93 The Blue Lacquer Box - George F. Worts	3.00	6.00	12.00	M
94 The Mortal Storm - Phyllis Bottome	2.00	4.00	7.50	M
95 The Red Law - Jackson Gregory	3.00	6.00	12.00	W
96 Singing River - W. C. Tuttle	3.00	6.00	12.00	W
97 A Variety of Weapons - Rufus King	3.00	6.00	12.00	M
98 Dividend on Death - Brett Halliday	3.00	6.00	12.00	M
99 Dead of the Night - John Rhode	4.00	8.00	15.00	M
100 The African Poison Murders - Elspeth Huxley	3.00	6.00	12.00	M
1947				
101 Lummox - Fanny Hurst	2.00	4.00	7.50	
102 Duel in the Sun - Niven Busch	2.50	6.00	10.00	W
Movie tie-in				
103 The Phantom Canoe - William Byron Mowrey	2.50	6.00	10.00	
1947				
104 Mesquite Jenkins, Tumbleweed - Clarence E.				
Mulford	3.00	6.00	12.00	W
105 The Case is Closed - Patricia Wentworth	3.00	6.00	12.00	M
106 The Corpse with the Eerie Eye - R. A. J.				
Walling	3.00	6.00	12.00	M
107 Crossword Puzzles	10.00	25.00	40.00	NF
108 The Yellow Violet - Frances Crane	3.00	6.00	12.00	M
109 I'll Sing at your Funeral - Hugh Pentecost	3.00	6.00	12.00	M
110 Congo Song - Stuart Cloete	4.00	8.00	15.00	E

343

Popular Libr. 107, c. Poplib   Popular Libr. 110, c. Poplib   Popular Libr. 119, c. Poplib

(POPULAR LIBRARY, continued)

111 Bedelia - Vera Caspary Movie tie-in	3.00	6.00	12.00	E
112 The Black Shrouds - Constance & Gwenyth Little	3.00	6.00	12.00	M
113 Crucible - Ben Ames Williams	3.00	6.00	12.00	
114 Ramrod - Luke Short	3.00	6.00	12.00	W
115 Popular Book of Cartoons - Ned L. Pines	5.00	10.00	20.00	H
116 The Red House - George Agnew Chamberlain Movie tie-in	4.00	8.00	15.00	M
117 This is Murder, Mr. Jones - Timothy Fuller	3.00	6.00	12.00	M
118 The Flying U's Last Stand - B. M. Bower	2.00	4.00	7.50	W
119 Firebrand - Tom Gill	3.00	6.00	12.00	W
120 The Spiral Staircase - Ethel Lina White	3.00	6.00	12.00	M
121 A Losing Game - Freeman Wills Crofts	3.00	6.00	12.00	M
122 The Adventures of Dr. Thorndyke - R. Austin Freeman	4.00	8.00	15.00	M
123 A Question of Proof - Nicholas Blake	4.00	8.00	15.00	M
124 Design in Evil - Rufus King	3.00	6.00	12.00	M
125 Said the Spider to the Fly - Richard Shattuck 1947	3.00	6.00	12.00	M
126 The Deadly Sunshade - Phoebe Atwood Taylor	3.00	6.00	12.00	M
127 Paradise Trail - William Byron Mowery	2.50	6.00	10.00	W
128 The Voice of the Pack - Edison Marshall	2.50	6.00	10.00	W
129 I Wake Up Screaming - Steve Fisher	3.00	6.00	12.00	M
130 The Mystery Companion - A. L. Furman	4.00	8.00	15.00	M
131 The Clock Strikes Twelve - Patricia Wentworth	3.00	6.00	12.00	M
132 Seven Keys to Baldpate - Earl Derr Biggers	4.00	8.00	15.00	M
133 Advance Agent - John August	3.00	6.00	12.00	
134 Fighting Blood - Gordon Young	2.50	6.00	10.00	W
135 Law Rides the Range - Walt Coburn	3.00	6.00	12.00	W
136 Appointment with Danger - David Garth aka Road to Glenfairlie	3.00	6.00	12.00	M
137 Six Times Death - William Irish	4.00	8.00	15.00	M

138 The Case Against Mrs. Ames - Arthur
   Somers Roche
   Note: Same cover as the pulp magazine Popular
   Detective, November 1945.
	3.00	6.00	12.00	M

139 The Corpse with the Grimy Glove - R. A. J.
   Walling
   1948
	2.50	6.00	10.00	M

Popular Libr. 129, c. Poplib   Popular Libr. 132, c. Poplib   Popular Libr. 136, c. Poplib

344

Popular Libr. 146, c. Poplib   Popular Libr. 147, c. Poplib   Popular Libr. 150, c. Poplib

(POPULAR LIBRARY, continued)

140	Secret Valley - Jackson Gregory	3.00	6.00	12.00	W
141	Winter Range - Alan LeMay	3.00	6.00	12.00	W
	Note: Same cover as the pulp magazine Range Riders Western, March 1947.				
142	Guardians of the Desert - Tom Gill	3.00	6.00	12.00	W
143	Free Grass - Ernest Haycox	3.00	6.00	12.00	W
144	Danger in Paradise - Octavus Roy Cohen	3.00	6.00	12.00	M
145	Gunsmoke Trail - William MacLeod Raine	3.00	6.00	12.00	W
146	Hopalong Cassidy Takes Cards - C. E. Mulford	4.00	8.00	15.00	W
147	The Private Life of Helen of Troy - John Erskine c-Bergey	7.50	15.00	30.00	E
148	The Ranger Way - Eugene Cunningham	2.50	6.00	10.00	W
149	Hidden Blood - W. C. Tuttle	3.00	6.00	12.00	W
	Note: Same cover as the pulp magazine Range Riders Western, Summer 1945.				
150	Crossword Puzzles, Book Two 1948	10.00	25.00	40.00	NF
151	Double Cross Ranch - Charles Alden Seltzer	3.00	6.00	12.00	W
152	Rancher's Revenge - Max Brand	2.50	6.00	10.00	W
153	The Secret of Father Brown - G. K. Chesterton	4.00	8.00	15.00	M
154	The Case of the Crumpled Knave - Anthony Boucher c-Belarski	7.50	15.00	30.00	M
155	The Dreadful Night - Ben Ames Williams c-Belarski	3.00	6.00	12.00	M
156	Popular Book of Western Stories - Leo Margulies	3.00	6.00	12.00	W
157	The Flying U Strikes - B. M. Bower	2.50	6.00	10.00	W
158	The Strangled Witness - Leslie Ford	5.00	10.00	20.00	M
159	About the Murder of the Circus Queen - Anthony Abbot	2.50	6.00	10.00	M
160	The Silver Star - Jackson Gregory	2.00	4.00	7.50	W
161	Thunder in the Dust - Alan Le May	3.00	6.00	12.00	W
162	Love Has no Alibi - Octavus Roy Cohen C-Belarski	3.00	6.00	12.00	M
163	Death at Sea - Richard Sale c-Belarski	5.00	10.00	20.00	M

Popular Libr. 154, c. Poplib   Popular Libr. 158, c. Poplib   Popular Libr. 161, c. Poplib

Popular Libr. 167, c. Poplib

Popular Libr. 169, c. Poplib

Popular Libr. 174, c. Poplib

(POPULAR LIBRARY, continued)

164	Lady in Peril - Ben Ames Williams c-Belarski	3.00	6.00	12.00	M
165	Valley of Vanishing Herds - W. C. Tuttle	2.50	6.00	10.00	W
166	Sky-pilot Cowboy - Walt Coburn	2.50	6.00	10.00	W
167	Pattern of Murder - Mignon G. Eberhart c-Belarski	3.00	6.00	12.00	M
168	Death and Taxes - David Dodge	3.00	6.00	12.00	M
169	The Bitter Tea of General Yen - Grace Zaring Stone 1949	5.00	10.00	20.00	E
170	Omnibus of American Humor - Robert N. Linscott	3.00	6.00	12.00	H
171	Chaffee of Roaring Horse - Ernest Haycox Note: Same cover as the pulp magazine Thrilling Western, November 1944.	2.00	4.00	6.00	W
172	Pistol Pardners - William MacLeod Raine	2.50	6.00	10.00	W
173	Death is a Lovely Lady - Ruth Fenisong aka Jenny Kissed Me	2.50	6.00	10.00	M
174	The Three Coffins - John Dickson Carr c-Belarski	2.50	6.00	10.00	M
175	Roaring Guns - Gordon Young 1949	2.50	6.00	10.00	W
176	Diamond River Range - Eugene Cunningham aka Diamond River Man Note: Same cover as the pulp magazine Range Riders Western, September 1947.	2.00	4.00	6.00	W
177	Some Day I'll Kill You - Dana Chambers	3.00	6.00	12.00	M
178	Death is Like That - John Spain	3.00	6.00	12.00	M
179	Outlaw Breed - William Byron Mowery	2.50	6.00	10.00	W
180	Wild West - Bertrand W. Sinclair	2.50	6.00	10.00	W
181	How I Pick Winners - Ken Kling	5.00	10.00	20.00	NF
182	Little Known Facts about Well Known People - Dale Carnegie	4.00	8.00	15.00	NF
183	Gentle Annie - MacKinlay Kantor c-Belarski	2.00	4.00	7.50	W
184	Marshal of Sundown - Jackson Gregory	2.00	4.00	6.00	W
185	Whispering Smith - Frank H. Sperman	2.00	4.00	7.50	
186	Cartoon Fun - Ned L. Pines	5.00	10.00	20.00	H
187	Selected Western Stories - Leo Maugulies	2.50	6.00	10.00	W

Popular Libr. 181, c. Poplib

Popular Libr. 190, c. Poplib

Popular Libr. 192, c. Poplib

Popular Libr. 211, c. Poplib   Popular Libr. 217, c. Poplib   Popular Libr. 221, c. Poplib

(POPULAR LIBRARY, continued)

188	The Yellow Overcoat - Frank Gruber	4.00	8.00	15.00	M
	Note: Same cover as the pulp magazine				
	Thrilling Detective, August, 1947				
	c-Belarski				
189	The Death Wish - Elisabeth Sanxay Holding	3.00	6.00	12.00	M
190	The Gay Bandit of the Border - Tom Gill	2.50	6.00	10.00	W
191	Barb Wire - Walt Coburn	2.00	4.00	6.00	W
192	Bodies are Where You Find Them - Brett Halliday	3.00	6.00	12.00	M
	c-Belarski				
193	The Case of the Constant God - Rufus King	3.00	6.00	12.00	M
	c-Belarski				
194	Death on Scurvy Street - Ben Ames Williams	2.50	6.00	10.00	M
	c-Belarski				
195	Ward 20 - James Warner Bellah	2.50	6.00	10.00	E
	c-Belarski				
196	There's Always Time to Die - Octavus Roy Cohen	3.00	6.00	12.00	M
	aka I Love You Again				
197	Pursuit of a Parcel - Patricia Wentworth	3.00	6.00	12.00	M
198	Hopalong Cassidy's Saddle Mate - Clarence E. Mulford	3.00	6.00	12.00	W
199	Whispering Range - Ernest Haycox	3.00	6.00	12.00	W
200	Bats in the Belfry - Norman Matson 1949	3.00	6.00	12.00	F
201	Blood on Her Shoe - Medora Field	2.00	4.00	7.50	M
	c-Belarski				
202	Shear the Black Sheep - David Dodge	2.00	4.00	7.50	M
203	Wild Horse Valley - W. C. Tuttle	2.00	4.00	7.50	W
204	Arizona Jim - Charles Alden Seltzer	2.00	4.00	7.50	W
205	Home is the Hangman - Richard Sale	3.00	6.00	12.00	M
	c-Belarski				
206	The Grindle Nightmare - Q. Patrick	4.00	8.00	15.00	M
	c-Belarski				
207	Reunion with Murder - Timothy Fuller	3.00	6.00	12.00	M
208	The Deputy at Snow Mountain - Edison Marshall	2.50	6.00	10.00	W
209	Gunsight Trail - Alan LeMay	2.50	6.00	10.00	W
210	That Winter - Merle Miller	2.50	6.00	10.00	E
211	The Doll's Trunk Murder - Helen Reilly	10.00	25.00	40.00	M
	c-Belarski				
212	Awake to Darkness - Richard McMullen	2.50	6.00	10.00	E
213	Rustlers' Gap - William MacLeod Raine	2.50	6.00	10.00	W
214	Guns in the Valley - William Byron Mowery	2.50	6.00	10.00	W
215	The Silver Forest - Ben Ames Williams	5.00	10.00	20.00	E
	c-Belarski				
216	Cup of Gold - John Steinbeck	3.00	6.00	12.00	A
217	Tales of Chinatown - Sax Rohmer	15.00	35.00	60.00	M
	c-Belarski				
218	The Pink Umbrella Murder - Frances Crane	4.00	8.00	15.00	M
	c-Belarski				
219	Duke - Hal Ellson	4.00	8.00	15.00	E
	c-Belarski				
220	The Damon Runyon Story - Ed Weiner	3.00	6.00	12.00	B
221	Gentlemen Prefer Blondes - Anita Loos	7.50	15.00	30.00	E
	c-Bergey				

Popular Libr. 223, c. Poplib   Popular Libr. 229, c. Poplib   Popular Libr. 236, c. Poplib

(POPULAR LIBRARY, continued)

222	Something's Got to Give - Marion Hargrove	2.50	6.00	10.00	H
223	Picture Quiz Book - John Paul Adams	10.00	25.00	40.00	NF
	1950, c-Schomburg				
224	Sun in Their Eyes - Monte Barrett	2.00	4.00	7.50	W
	c-Belarski				
225	Fast on the Draw - Gordon Young	2.00	4.00	6.00	W
	aka Red Clark Rides Alone				
226	Sudden Bill Dorn - Jackson Gregory	2.00	4.00	6.00	W
227	The Illustrious Corpse - Tiffany Thayer	3.00	6.00	12.00	M
	c-Belarski				
	Note: Same cover as the pulp magazine				
	Popular Detective, September 1948				
228	The Sex Machine - Shepherd Mead	4.00	8.00	15.00	SF
	aka The Magnificent MacInnes				
	c-Schomburg				
229	Homicide Johnny - Steve Fisher	5.00	10.00	20.00	M
	c-Belarski				
230	Focus - Arthur Miller	2.50	6.00	10.00	
	c-Belarski				
231	The Chuckling Fingers - Mabel Seeley	3.00	6.00	12.00	M
232	The Key - Patricia Wentworth	2.50	6.00	10.00	M
233	Macamba - Lilla Van Saher	3.00	6.00	12.00	E
234	Quick Triggers - Eugene Cunningham	2.50	6.00	10.00	W
	1950				
235	Starlight Rider - Ernest Haycox	2.00	4.00	7.50	W
236	Pikes Peek or Bust - Earl Wilson	4.00	8.00	15.00	H
	c-Schomburg				
237	Drums of Destiny - Peter Bourne	3.00	6.00	12.00	A
	c-Bergey				
238	She'll Be Dead by Morning - Dana Chambers	2.50	6.00	10.00	M
239	The Evil Star - John Spain	2.50	6.00	10.00	M
240	Acres and Pains - S. J. Perelman	2.50	6.00	10.00	H
241	Fortunes of Captain Blood - Rafael Sabatini	4.00	8.00	15.00	A
	Movie tie-in, c-Belarski				
242	Riders of the Smoky Land - Edison Marshall	2.50	6.00	10.00	W
243	Texas Breed - William MacLeod Raine	2.50	6.00	10.00	W
244	Find Me in Fire - Robert Lowry	7.50	15.00	30.00	E
245	Death is a Gold Coin - Ruth Fenisong	3.00	6.00	12.00	M
246	Murder by Latitude - Rufus King	3.00	6.00	12.00	M

Popular Libr. 237, c. Poplib   Popular Libr. 241, c. Poplib   Popular Libr. 244, c. Poplib

Popular Libr. 258, c. Poplib   Popular Libr. 273, c. Poplib   Popular Libr. 282, c. Poplib

(POPULAR LIBRARY, continued)

247	Not Too Narrow---Not Too Deep - Richard Sale	2.50	6.00	10.00	
248	The Great Ones - Ralph Ingersoll	2.50	6.00	10.00	E
249	Twisted Trails - W. C. Tuttle	2.50	6.00	10.00	W
250	Mavericks - Walt Coburn	2.50	6.00	10.00	W
	1950				
251	Eagle at My Eyes - Norman Katkov	2.50	6.00	10.00	E
252	Bullets for the Bridegroom - David Dodge	3.00	6.00	12.00	M
253	Yesterday's Murder - Craig Rice	3.00	6.00	12.00	M
254	The Pale Blonde of Sands Street - William Chapman White c-Bergey	3.00	6.00	12.00	E
255	The Lone Rider - Jackson Gregory	2.50	6.00	10.00	W
256	Drygulch Trail - William MacLeod Raine	2.50	6.00	10.00	W
257	Whistle Stop - Maritta M. Wolff	3.00	6.00	12.00	E
258	Six Nights of Mystery - William Irish First ed., 1950	7.50	15.00	30.00	M
259	Murder in the Mews - Helen Reilly	3.00	6.00	12.00	M
260	The Edge of Doom - Leo Brady Movie tie-in	2.00	4.00	7.50	M
261	Painted Ponies - Alan Le May	2.50	6.00	10.00	W
262	Guns of the Arrowhead - Gordon Young Note: Same cover as the pulp magazine Thrilling Western, November 1945.	2.50	6.00	10.00	
263	Murder at Cambridge - Q. Patrick	3.00	6.00	12.00	M
264	Dangerous Lady - Octavus Roy Cohen c-Belarski	2.50	6.00	10.00	M
265	The Girl in the Spike-Heeled Shoes - Martin Yoseloff	2.50	6.00	10.00	
266	The Captain's Lady - Basil Heatler c-Belarski	3.00	6.00	12.00	E
267	Turn of the Table - Jonathan Stagge	3.00	6.00	12.00	
268	The Nine Waxed Faces - Francis Beeding c-Belarski	3.00	6.00	12.00	M
269	Mirror, Mirror on the Wall - Mona Kent	2.00	4.00	6.00	E
270	Tempered Blade - Monte Barrett	2.50	6.00	10.00	A
271	Riders West - Ernest Haycox	2.50	6.00	10.00	W
272	Trail's End - Edison Marshall	2.50	6.00	10.00	W
273	The Big Eye - Max Ehrlich c-Bergey	4.00	8.00	15.00	SF
274	They Move with the Sun - Daniel Taylor	2.50	6.00	10.00	E
275	Murder at Midnight - Richard Sale 1950	2.50	6.00	10.00	M
276	Somewhere in this House - Rufus King c-Belarski	3.00	6.00	12.00	M
277	The Sure Thing - Merle Miller	2.50	6.00	10.00	E
278	The Hero - Millard Lampell c-Bergey	3.00	6.00	12.00	
279	Shortgrass - Hal G. Evarts	2.50	6.00	10.00	W
280	The River Bend Feud - William MacLeod Raine	2.50	6.00	10.00	W
281	That's My Baby - Josef A. Schneider	3.00	6.00	12.00	
282	The Four False Weapons - John Dickson Carr c-Belarski	4.00	8.00	15.00	M
283	Silence in Court - Patricia Wentworth Note: Same cover as the pulp magazine Detective Novel, August 1945.	2.00	4.00	7.50	M

Popular Libr. 292, c. Poplib   Popular Libr. 298, c. Poplib   Popular Libr. 299, c. Poplib

(POPULAR LIBRARY, continued)

284	Laura - Vera Caspary	2.00	4.00	7.50	
285	The Curtain Nevers Falls - Joey Adams c-Bergey	3.00	6.00	12.00	E
286	Murder of a Clergyman's Mistress - Anthony Abbot	3.00	6.00	12.00	
287	Don't Look Behind You - Samuel Rogers	2.50	6.00	10.00	
288	The Leather Pushers - H. C. Witwer c-Bergey	2.50	6.00	10.00	
289	Trail of the Macaw - Eugene Cunningham	2.00	4.00	6.00	W
290	The Ringtailed Rannyhans - Walt Coburn	2.00	4.00	7.50	W
291	The Wrath and the Wind - Alexander Key	3.00	6.00	12.00	A
292	Overboard - George F. Worts c-Belarski	7.50	15.00	30.00	E
293	The Hangman's Whip - Mignon G. Eberhart c-Belarski	5.00	10.00	20.00	M
	Note: Same cover as the pulp magazine Mystery Book, Summer 1949.				
294	The Two Worlds of Johnny Truro - George Sklar	2.00	4.00	6.00	E
295	The Wolf that Fed Us - Robert Lowry	2.00	4.00	7.50	E
296	The Dead Tree Gives No Shelter - Virgil Scott	2.00	4.00	6.00	E
297	Shotgun Gold - W. C. Tuttle	2.00	4.00	7.50	W
298	Guns of Mist River - Jackson Cole	2.00	4.00	7.50	W
299	A Woman of Samaria - James Wesley Ingles	7.50	15.00	30.00	E
300	The Winds of Fear - Hodding Carter c-Belarski	7.50	15.00	30.00	E
301	The Fifth Grave - Jonathan Latimer 1950 c-Belarski	2.50	6.00	10.00	M
302	The Old Battle Ax - Elisabeth Sanxay Holding c-Belarski	3.00	6.00	12.00	M
	Note: Same cover as the pulp magazine Detective Novel, Spring 1949.				
303	Bound Girl - Everett & Olga Webber	3.00	6.00	12.00	E
304	This Spring of Love - Charles Mergendahl 1951	2.00	4.00	6.00	
305	The Desert Hawk - Harry Sinclair Drago	2.00	4.00	7.50	W
306	The Haunted Hills - B. M. Bower	2.00	4.00	7.50	W
307	Her Life to Live - Oriana Atkinson aka Big Eyes, c-Bergey	7.50	15.00	30.00	E

Popular Libr. 300, c. Poplib   Popular Libr. 302, c. Poplib   Popular Libr. 307, c. Poplib

Popular Libr. 309, c. Poplib Popular Libr. 315, c. Poplib Popular Libr. 326, c. Poplib

(POPULAR LIBRARY, continued)

308 It's a Free Country - Ben Ames Williams	2.00	4.00	6.00	
309 The Dancing Detective - William Irish	5.00	10.00	20.00	M
310 Here Lies the Body - Richard Burke	3.00	6.00	12.00	M
311 Smoke Up the Valley - Monte Barrett	2.00	4.00	7.50	W
312 Mamie Brandon - Jack Sheridan	2.00	4.00	7.50	E
313 The Far Call - Jackson Gregory	2.00	4.00	7.50	W
314 Edge of Beyond - James B. Hendryx	2.00	4.00	7.50	
315 Check Your Wits - Jules Leopold	10.00	25.00	40.00	NF
316 Tuesday to Bed - Francis Sill Wickware	2.00	4.00	7.50	E
317 The Night Before Murder - Steve Fisher c-Belarski	2.50	6.00	10.00	M
318 The Deadly Dove - Rufus King	2.50	6.00	10.00	M
319 My Forbidden Past - Polan Banks	2.50	6.00	10.00	E
320 Excuse My Dust - Bellamy Partridge	2.50	6.00	10.00	H
321 Trouble on the Border - Gordon Young	2.00	4.00	7.50	W
322 Hell and High Water - William MacLeod Raine	2.00	4.00	7.50	W
323 Home Guide to Repair, Upkeep and Re-modeling - William H. Crouse	5.00	10.00	20.00	NF
324 My Old Man's Badge - Ferguson Findley	2.50	6.00	10.00	
325 Murder by the Dozen - Hugh Wiley 1951	2.50	6.00	10.00	M
326 Behind the Flying Saucers - Frank Scully c-Bergey	3.00	6.00	12.00	UFO
327 Stranger and Alone - J. Saunders Redding	2.50	6.00	10.00	
328 Soldiers' Daughters Never Cry - Audrey Erskine Lindop	2.50	6.00	10.00	E
329 Bullet Brand - Hal G. Evarts	2.00	4.00	7.50	W
330 The Trouble Trailer - W. C. Tuttle	2.00	4.00	7.50	W
331 Campus Town - Hart Stilwell	7.50	15.00	30.00	E
332 Don't Ever Love Me - Octavus Roy Cohen	3.00	6.00	12.00	M
333 Lonesome Road - Patricia Wentworth	2.50	6.00	10.00	M
334 The Magnificent Courtesan - Lozania Prole c-Belarski	5.00	10.00	20.00	E
335 Shadow of a Hero - Allan Chase	2.00	4.00	6.00	
336 The Parents' Manual - Anna W. M. Wolfe	5.00	10.00	20.00	NF
337 Ace in the Hole - Jackson Gregory	2.00	4.00	7.50	W
338 Starlight Pass - Tom Gill	2.00	4.00	7.50	W
339 The Lion and the Lamb - E. Phillips Oppenheim c-Belarski	2.50	6.00	10.00	

Popular Libr. 331, c. Poplib Popular Libr. 332, c. Poplib Popular Libr. 334, c. Poplib

(POPULAR LIBRARY, continued)

340	Smart Guy - William MacHaug aka The Affairs of O'Malley	2.50	6.00	10.00	M
341	Season for Passion - Lee Manning c-Belarski	2.50	6.00	10.00	C
342	End of Track - Ward Weaver	2.00	4.00	7.50	W
343	While Murder Waits - John Esteven c-Belarski	2.50	6.00	10.00	M
344	The Applegreen Cat - Frances Crane c-Belarski	7.50	15.00	30.00	M
345	Bullets at Clearwater - Edison Marshall	2.00	4.00	7.50	W
346	Ramrod - Luke Short	2.00	4.00	7.50	W
347	Hoodlum - Charley Robertson aka Shadow of a Cloud	2.00	4.00	6.00	E
348	Adios, O'Shaughnessy - Robert Tallman	2.50	6.00	10.00	E
349	Poison in Jest - John Dickson Carr	3.00	6.00	12.00	M
350	The Dogs Do Bark - Jonathan Stagge 1951	2.50	6.00	10.00	M
351	Tonight is Forever - Charles Mergendahl c-Bergey	2.50	6.00	10.00	
352	Cotton Moon - Catherine Tracy	2.00	4.00	7.50	E
353	The Big Corral - Al Cody	2.00	4.00	7.50	W
354	Gun Feud - W. C. Tuttle aka Wandering Dogies	2.00	4.00	7.50	E
355	I'll be Right Home, Ma - Henry Denker	2.50	6.00	10.00	E
356	This Woman is Mine - P. J. Wolfson aka All Women Die	2.00	4.00	6.00	E
357	How I Became a Girl Reporter - Hyman Goldberg	2.00	4.00	6.00	E
358	Mrs. Candy and Saturday Night - Robert Tallant c-Bergey	2.00	4.00	6.00	E
359	Beyond the Rio Grande - William MacLeod Raine	2.00	4.00	7.50	W
360	The Silver Desert - Ernest Haycox	2.00	4.00	7.50	W
361	Winter Kill - Steve Fisher c-Belarski	2.00	4.00	7.50	M
362	Never Walk Alone - Rufus King aka The Case of the Dowagers Etchings c-Belarski	2.00	4.00	7.50	M
363	The Traitor - William L. Shirer	2.00	4.00	6.00	M
364	The Ringing of the Glass - Preston Schoyer c-Belarski	2.00	4.00	7.50	
365	Copperbelt - Nigel Sligh	2.00	4.00	7.50	
366	Please Send Me Absolutely Free! - Arkady Leokum	2.00	4.00	6.00	E
367	Shotgun Guard - D. B. Newton	2.00	4.00	7.50	W
368	Apache Crossing - Will Ermine Note: Same cover as the pulp magazine Giant Western, August 1949.	2.00	4.00	7.50	W
369	My Love Wears Black - Octavus Roy Cohen	3.00	6.00	12.00	M
370	The Crying Sisters - Mabel Seeley	2.50	6.00	10.00	M
371	The Strumpet Sea - Ben Ames Williams	2.50	6.00	10.00	A
372	Wintertime - Jan Valtin	2.00	4.00	6.00	E
373	The Weeping and the Laughter - Vera Caspary	2.50	6.00	10.00	E
374	Dark Drums - Wenzell Brown	2.50	6.00	10.00	E
375	Texas Sheriff - Eugene Cunningham 1951	2.00	4.00	6.00	W
376	Trouble at Moon Dance - A. B. Guthrie, Jr.	2.00	4.00	6.00	W

 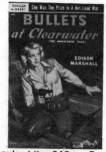 

Popular Libr. 344, c. Poplib   Popular Libr. 345, c. Poplib   Popular Libr. 368, c. Poplib

Popular Libr. 377, c. Poplib   Popular Libr. 379, c. Poplib   Popular Libr. 384, c. Poplib

(POPULAR LIBRARY, continued)

377	Shadow of Madness - Hugh Pentecost c-Bergey	3.00	6.00	12.00	M
378	You're Lonely When You're Dead - James Hadley Chase	2.50	6.00	10.00	M
379	No Narrow Path - Catharine Whitcomb aka The Hill of Glass, c-Belarski	3.00	6.00	12.00	E
380	Bear Guard - James Warner Bellah	2.00	4.00	6.00	W
381	Heads Off at Midnight - Francis Beeding	2.00	4.00	7.50	M
382	Dark Threat - Patricia Wentworth c-Belarski Note: Same cover as the pulp magazine Black Book Detective, Summer 1949.	2.00	4.00	7.50	M
383	The Man from Texas - Jackson Gregory	2.00	4.00	6.00	W
384	Range Boss - Gordon Young aka Red Clark, Range Boss Note: Same cover as the pulp magazine Hopalong Cassidy, Fall, 1950 (no. 1).	2.50	6.00	10.00	W
385	Once off Guard - J. H. Wallace	2.00	4.00	6.00	E
386	Cottage Sinister - Q. Patrick	2.00	4.00	6.00	M
387	Casualty - Robert Lowry	2.00	4.00	6.00	E
388	Hang My Wreath - Ward Weaver	2.00	4.00	6.00	
389	This Way Out - James Ronald	2.00	4.00	7.50	M
390	Trails by Night - Tom J. Hopkins	2.00	4.00	6.00	W
391	Mooney - William Brown Meloney	2.00	4.00	7.50	E
392	Jailbait - William Bernard Illo in Parade of Pleasure	3.00	6.00	12.00	JD
393	The Bed She Made - Leslie Waller 1952	2.00	4.00	6.00	E
394	Echo of Evil - Manuel Komroff	2.00	4.00	6.00	E
395	Day into Night - David Westheimer aka The Magic Fallacy	2.00	4.00	6.00	E
396	Love Me Sailor - Robert S. Close	2.00	4.00	6.00	
397	Border Feud - Tom Gill aka Red Earth	2.00	4.00	6.00	W
398	Trail Smoke - Ernest Haycox	2.00	4.00	6.00	W
399	Whirlpool - James Leal Henderson	2.00	4.00	6.00	E
400	Slay Ride - Frank Kane 1952	2.00	4.00	7.50	
401	Wine of Violence - Ralph Ingersoll	2.00	4.00	6.00	E

Popular Libr. 392, c. Poplib   Popular Libr. 410, c. Poplib   Popular Libr. 411, c. Poplib

402 Main Line - Livingston Biddle, Jr.	2.00	4.00	6.00	E
403 The Reef - Keith Wheeler	2.00	4.00	6.00	E
404 Divorce - James Warner Bellah	2.00	4.00	6.00	
405 Troubled Spring - John Brick	2.00	4.00	6.00	
406 Montana Road - Harry Sinclair Drago	2.00	4.00	6.00	W
407 Bonanza Gulch - Matt Stuart	2.00	4.00	6.00	W
408 Waterfront - Ferguson Findley	3.00	6.00	12.00	E
409 One by One - Fan Nichols	2.00	4.00	6.00	E
410 The Marx Brothers - Kyle Crichton	7.50	15.00	30.00	B
411 Revolt of the Triffids - John Wyndham	5.00	10.00	20.00	SF
aka Day of the Triffids, c-Bergey				
412 The Spell - Gustav Breuer	2.00	4.00	6.00	E
413 A Woman of Forty - Desmond Hall	2.00	4.00	6.00	
414 The Texas Kid - William MacLeod Raine	2.00	4.00	6.00	W
415 Pardners of the Dim Trails - Walt Coburn	2.00	4.00	6.00	W
416 The Perfect Frame - William Ard	2.00	4.00	6.00	E
417 A Yank on Piccadilly - C. L. McDermott	2.00	4.00	6.00	E
418 The Impudent Rifle - Dick Pearce	2.50	6.00	10.00	
419 Lower then Angels - Walter Karig	2.00	4.00	6.00	E
420 Trial by Gunsmoke - Jim O'Mara	2.00	4.00	6.00	W
421 A Matter of Morals - Joseph Gies	2.00	4.00	6.00	E
422 The Vanquished - Alan Marcus	2.00	4.00	6.00	C
aka Straw to Make Brick - c-Belarski				
423 Johnny Bogan - Leonora Baccante	2.00	4.00	6.00	E
424 Fright - George Hopley	3.00	6.00	12.00	M
425 Thunder Valley - Burt Arthur	2.00	4.00	6.00	W
1952				
426 The Black Door - Cleve F. Adams	2.00	4.00	6.00	M
427 More Beautiful than Murder - Octavus Roy				
Cohen c-Belarski	2.50	6.00	10.00	M
428 The Train from Pittsburgh - Julian Farsen	2.00	4.00	6.00	E
429 Two-gun Man - Gordon Young	2.00	4.00	6.00	W
430 Guardians of the Trail - Jackson Gregory	2.00	4.00	6.00	W
431 Strangler's Serenade - William Irish	3.00	6.00	12.00	M
c-Belarski				
432 The Great Mail Robbery - Clarence Budington				
Kelland c-Bergey	2.00	4.00	6.00	E
433 Bitter Fruit - Peter Packer	2.00	4.00	6.00	
434 So Deadly Fair - Gertrude Walker	2.00	4.00	7.50	E
435 The Lost Ones - Stevan Javellana	2.00	4.00	6.00	E
aka Without Seeing the Dawn				
436 Arizona Guns - William MacLeod Raine	2.00	4.00	6.00	W
437 Six-gun Gamble - D. B. Newton	2.00	4.00	6.00	W
438 At Sundown the Tiger - Ethel Mannin	2.00	4.00	6.00	
439 Rip Tide - Lee Wichelns	2.00	4.00	6.00	
440 The Cruel Dawn - Alfred Viazzi	2.50	6.00	10.00	E
441 Thief River - Nelson Nye	2.00	4.00	6.00	W
442 Head of the Mountain - Ernest Haycox	2.00	4.00	6.00	W
443 Sweet and Deadly - Verne Chute	2.00	4.00	6.00	
444 Isle of the Damned - George John Seaton	2.00	4.00	6.00	
445 Timbal Gulch Trail - Max Brand	2.00	4.00	6.00	W
446 The Night and the Naked - Gordon Merrick	2.00	4.00	6.00	E
aka The Strumpet Wind				
447 Dragon's Island - Jack Williamson	4.00	8.00	15.00	SF
c-Bergey				
448 You Can't Catch Me - Lawrence Lariar	2.00	4.00	7.50	E
449 Gunswift - Jack Byrne	2.00	4.00	6.00	W

Popular Libr. 431, c. Poplib   Popular Libr. 440, c. Poplib   Popular Libr. 447, c. Poplib

Popular Libr. 452, c. Poplib   Popular Libr. 495, c. Poplib   Popular Libr. 544, c. Poplib

(POPULAR LIBRARY, continued)

450	Trouble Shooter - Ernest Haycox	2.00	4.00	6.00	W
	1952				
451	Maharajah - Richard Cargoe	2.00	4.00	7.50	E
452	I'll Get Mine - Thurston Scott	2.00	4.00	7.50	E
453	Neither Five Nor Three - Helen MacInnes	2.00	4.00	6.00	E
454	Two-edged Vengeance - W. T. Ballard	2.00	4.00	6.00	W
455	Hellgate Canyon - Fred Delano	2.00	4.00	6.00	
456	What Price Murder - Cleve F. Adams	2.00	4.00	7.50	M
457	The Boy Came Back - Charles H.				
	Knickerbocker	2.00	4.00	6.00	E
458	Pray Love, Remember - Stephen Wendt	2.00	4.00	6.00	
459	Burmese Days - George Orwell	2.00	4.00	7.50	E
460	Rawhide Range - Ernest Haycox	2.00	4.00	6.00	W
461	Born to Trouble - Nelson Nye	2.00	4.00	6.00	W
462	A Bullet for My Love - Octavus Roy Cohen	2.00	4.00	7.50	M
463	The Big Bubble - Theodore Pratt	2.00	4.00	6.00	E
464	The Unfulfilled - W. G. Hardy	2.00	4.00	6.00	E
465	Guns of Vengeance - Jim O'Mara	2.00	4.00	6.00	W
466	The Outriders - Irving Raretch	2.00	4.00	6.00	
467	Shakedown - Ben Kerr	2.00	4.00	6.00	
468	Dark Surrender - Peter Packer	2.00	4.00	6.00	
469	Hard to Get - Edwin Gilbert	2.00	4.00	6.00	
470	Headline Crimes of the Year - Edward D.				
	Radin	2.50	6.00	10.00	
471	Range Beyond the Law - William MacLeod				
	Raine	2.00	4.00	6.00	W
472	Texan on the Prod - Philip Ketchum	2.00	4.00	6.00	W
473	Bluebeard's Seventh Wife - William Irish	7.50	15.00	30.00	M
	First ed., 1952				
474	The Night Thorn - Ian Gordon	2.00	4.00	7.50	E
	1953				
475	Rancher's Revenge - Max Brand	2.00	4.00	6.00	W
476	Showdown - W. T. Ballard & James C. Lynch	2.00	4.00	6.00	W
477	The Diary - William Ard	1.50	3.50	5.00	
478	Don't Crowd Me - Evan Hunter	2.00	4.00	6.00	
479	Torment - Scott Graham Williamson	2.00	4.00	6.00	E
480	Superstition Range - Parker Bonner	2.00	4.00	6.00	W
481	Desert of the Damned - Nelson Nye	2.00	4.00	6.00	W
482	Don't Get Caught - M. E. Chaber	2.00	4.00	6.00	M
	aka Hangman's Harvest				
483	Ask for Linda - Fan Nichols	2.00	4.00	6.00	E
484	The Girl Cage - Charles Mergendahl	2.00	4.00	6.00	E
485	Glitter - A. B. Shiffrin	1.50	3.50	5.00	E
486	Chaffee of Roaring Horse - Ernest Haycox	1.50	3.50	5.00	W
487	Quick Trigger Law - Jim O'Mara	2.00	4.00	6.00	W
488	Naked and Alone - Michael Lawrence	2.00	4.00	6.00	
489	Duel in the Sun - Niven Busch	1.50	3.50	5.00	W
490	Venables - Geoffrey Wagner	2.00	4.00	6.00	E
491	Blood on the Forge - William Attaway	1.50	3.50	5.00	
492	Incident at Sun Mountain - Todhunter				
	Ballard	2.00	4.00	6.00	W
493	High Mesa - Tex Grady	1.50	3.50	5.00	W
494	Double Cross - Mike Moran	2.00	4.00	6.00	
495	H is for Heroin - David Hulburd	2.50	6.00	10.00	E
496	Stranger in Our Midst - Robert Carson	2.00	4.00	6.00	E
497	You Can't See Around Corners - Jon Cleary	1.50	3.50	5.00	
498	Texas Rawhider - Jack Barton	1.50	3.50	5.00	W

#	Title - Author				
499	Guns of the Barricade Bunch - Philip Ketchum	2.00	4.00	6.00	W
500	Time to Kill - Terry Spain	2.00	4.00	6.00	E
501	The Closest Kin There Is - Clara Winston	2.00	4.00	6.00	E
502	A Girl for Danny - William Ard	1.50	3.50	5.00	
503	Rickey - Charles Calitri	1.50	3.50	5.00	
504	Joey Adams' Joke Book - Joey Adams	2.00	4.00	6.00	H
505	Ten Against Caesar - K. R. G. Granger	2.00	4.00	6.00	
506	Fighting Cowman - Louis Trimble	1.50	3.50	5.00	W
507	The Big Fear - Theo Durrant	1.50	3.50	5.00	
508	The Loving and the Daring - Francoise Mallet aka The Illusionist	1.50	3.50	5.00	E
509	Rage in the Wind - Boyd Cochrell	1.50	3.50	5.00	E
510	The Night Is Mine - David Davidson aka In Another Country	1.50	3.50	5.00	E
511	Renegade of Rainbow Basin - Hal G. Evarts	1.50	3.50	5.00	W
512	Ramrod from Hell - Ernie Wayne	1.50	3.50	5.00	
513	Beyond the Law - Edward D. Radin	2.00	4.00	6.00	NF
514	Darling, I Hate You - T. S. Matthews	1.50	3.50	5.00	
515	The Hard Way - Robert V. Williams	1.50	3.50	5.00	
516	Island in the Sky - Ernest K. Gann	2.00	4.00	6.00	A
517	Free Grass - Ernest Haycox	1.50	3.50	5.00	W
518	Rustler of the Owlhorns - Jim O'Mara	1.50	3.50	5.00	W
519	Blondes Die Young - Bill Peters	2.00	4.00	6.00	
520	The Tightrope - Stanley Kauffmann	1.50	3.50	5.00	E
521	Six Angels at My Back - John Bell Clayton	1.50	3.50	5.00	E
522	China Coaster - Don Smith	1.50	3.50	5.00	E
523	Facts of Life and Love for Teenagers - Evelyn Millis Duvall	2.00	4.00	7.50	NF
524	West of Quarantine - W. T. Ballard	1.50	3.50	5.00	W
525	Stranger from Texas - Ray Townsend	1.50	3.50	5.00	W
	1953				
526	You Can't Stop Me - William Ard	1.50	3.50	5.00	M
527	Bond of the Flesh - Rosamond Marshall	1.50	3.50	5.00	E
528	Hooked - Will Oursler & Laurence D. Smith	2.50	6.00	10.00	E
529	Liana - Martha Gellhorn	1.50	3.50	5.00	E
530	All the Way Down - M. E. Chaber	1.50	3.50	5.00	M
531	West of the Law - William MacLeod Raine	1.50	3.50	5.00	W
532	The Saddle Bum - Philip Ketchum	2.00	4.00	6.00	W
533	Smooth and Deadly - Quentin Renolyds aka I, Willie Sutton	2.50	6.00	10.00	NF
534	Strange Lovers - Armando Meoni	1.50	3.50	5.00	E
535	Thunder in the Dust - Alan LeMay	1.50	3.50	5.00	W
536	Count Me In - Fan Nichols	2.00	4.00	6.00	E
537	The Grim Canyon - Ernest Haycox	1.50	3.50	5.00	W
538	Point of a Gun - Dean Owen	1.50	3.50	5.00	W
539	Kiss Me Hard - Tom Brandt	1.50	3.50	5.00	
540	My Enemy, the World - Guido D'Agostino	1.50	3.50	5.00	E
541	This Heart, this Hunter - Hallie Burnett	1.50	3.50	5.00	
542	The Ranger Way - Eugene Cunningham	1.50	3.50	5.00	W
543	The Flesh and the Spirit - Charles Shaw aka Heaven Knows, Mr. Allison	2.00	4.00	6.00	E
544	The Mark of the Moon - Francis Gerard	4.00	8.00	15.00	E
545	The Silver Star - Jackson Gregory	1.50	3.50	5.00	W
546	Hard Rock Rancher - William E. Vance	1.50	3.50	5.00	W
547	Mother Finds a Body - Gypsy Rose Lee	1.50	3.50	5.00	M
548	Stay Away, Joe - Dan Cushman	1.50	3.50	5.00	
	1954				
549	Monkey on my Back - Wenzell Brown	2.00	4.00	6.00	E
550	Love for Lydia - H. E. Bates	1.50	3.50	5.00	E
551	I Dive for Treasure - Lt. Harry E. Rieseberg	2.00	4.00	6.00	A
552	High Iron - Todhunter Ballard	1.50	3.50	5.00	W
553	Texas Breed - William MacLeod Raine	1.50	3.50	5.00	W
554	Some Day I'll Kill You - Dana Chambers	1.50	3.50	5.00	M
555	Martha Crane - Charles Gorham	1.50	3.50	5.00	
556	Wilderness Rogue - Henry Schindall aka Let the Spring Come	1.50	3.50	5.00	A
557	Possessed - June Wetherell	1.50	3.50	5.00	
558	The Tiger in Summer - Michael Keon	2.00	4.00	6.00	E
559	Be Happier, Be Healthier - Gayelord Hauser	2.00	4.00	7.50	NF
560	Gunning for Trouble - L. L. Foreman	1.50	3.50	5.00	W
561	Gunsight Trail - Alan LeMay	1.50	3.50	5.00	W
562	I Take All - Robert Carson	1.50	3.50	5.00	
563	A Secret Story - William Saroyan	2.00	4.00	6.00	
564	The Sword of Satan - H. M. Mons	2.00	4.00	6.00	A
565	The Innocent at Large - Noel Langley	1.50	3.50	5.00	

Popular Libr. 566, c. Poplib   Popular Libr. 590, c. Poplib   Popular Libr. 660, c. Poplib

(POPULAR LIBRARY, continued)

566	Cradle of the Sun - John Clagget	2.00	4.00	6.00	A
567	Starlight Rider - Ernest Haycox	1.50	3.50	5.00	W
568	Shortgrass - Hal G. Evarts	1.50	3.50	5.00	W
569	A Private Party - William Ard	1.50	3.50	5.00	E
570	The Violent Wedding - Robert Lowry	1.50	3.50	5.00	
571	Isle of Demons - John Clarke Bowman	2.00	4.00	6.00	A
572	Country Girl - Richard McMullen	1.50	3.50	5.00	
573	The Girl in the Spike - Heeled Shoes - Martin Yoseloff	.75	1.75	3.00	
574	Fighting Blood - Gordon Young	1.50	3.50	5.00	W
575	The Texas Gun - Philip Ketchum	1.50	3.50	5.00	W
	1954				
576	The Dead Tree Gives No Shelter - Virgil Scott	.75	1.75	3.00	E
577	The Wire God - Jack Willard	1.50	3.50	5.00	
578	Rainbow Road - Davenport Steward	1.50	3.50	5.00	E
579	Are Your Troubles Psychosomatic? - J. A. Winter	2.00	4.00	7.50	NF
580	We Burn Like Candles - Bernice Kevinoky aka All the Young Summer Days	.75	1.75	3.00	
581	Dark Drums - Wenzell Brown	1.50	3.50	5.00	E
582	Highgrader - Hal G. Evarts	1.50	3.50	5.00	W
583	Rifle Pass - Dean Owen	1.50	3.50	5.00	W
584	Run, Brother, Run! - Tom Brandt	1.50	3.50	5.00	E
585	Rogue Wind - Ugo Moretti	1.50	3.50	5.00	
586	Devil Take Her - Fan Nichols	1.50	3.50	5.00	
587	Dark Streets of Paris - Jean-Louis Curtis	1.50	3.50	5.00	
588	The Mountain - Henri Troyat	1.50	3.50	5.00	
589	Guns Up - Ernest Haycox	1.50	3.50	5.00	W
590	Gold Town Gunman - Ray Townsend c-Saunders	2.00	4.00	6.00	W
591	No Angels for Me - William Ard	.75	1.75	3.00	
592	Teen-age Gangs - Madeline Darr & Dale Kramer	2.50	6.00	10.00	NF
593	The Gilded Hearse - Charles Gorham	.75	1.75	3.00	
594	The Brass God - Richard G. Hubler	.75	1.75	3.00	
595	Why We Behave as We Do - Frank S. Caprio	2.00	4.00	6.00	NF
596	Frontier Feud - Will Cook	1.50	3.50	5.00	W
597	Marshal of Sundown - Jackson Gregory	.75	1.75	3.00	W
598	The Innocent One - James Reach	.75	1.75	3.00	
599	The Night is my Undoing - Delmar Jackson	.75	1.75	3.00	
600	The Feared and the Fearless - Guthrie Wilson	1.50	3.50	5.00	C
601	The Naked Sword - Arthea Mitchell	2.00	4.00	6.00	A
602	The Dim View - Basil Heatter	1.50	3.50	5.00	E
603	Outlaw Brand - Parker Bonner	.75	1.75	3.00	W
604	Gun Law - Philip Ketchum	1.50	3.50	5.00	W
605	Crimes of Passion - Edward D. Radin	1.50	3.50	5.00	NF
606	The Departure - John Olden Sherry	.75	1.75	3.00	
607	Too Fast we Live - Richard Glendinning	.75	1.75	3.00	
608	The Wrath and the Wind - Alexander Key	1.50	3.50	5.00	A
609	The Survivors - Ronald McKie	.75	1.75	3.00	
610	Bad Men and Good	2.00	4.00	6.00	
611	Trail of the Damned - Jack Barton	1.50	3.50	5.00	W
612	Hot Freeze - Martin Brett	.75	1.75	3.00	
613	The Eternal Galilean - Fulton J. Sheen	1.50	3.50	5.00	NF
614	Mark of the Hunter - Gene Caesar	.75	1.75	3.00	
615	Give and Take - Thomas H. Raddall	.75	1.75	3.00	
616	Riders West - Ernest Haycox	.75	1.75	3.00	W

617	Rawhide Gunman - W. T. Ballard	1.50	3.50	5.00	W
618	Ten Roads to Hell - Robert Travers	1.50	3.50	5.00	
619	Naked to My Past - Frederic Wakeman	.75	1.75	3.00	
620	Everybody Slept Here - Elliott Arnold	.75	1.75	3.00	
621	Episode - Peter W. Denzer	1.50	3.50	5.00	
622	The Last Princess - Charles O. Locke	1.50	3.50	5.00	A
623	Renegade River - Ray Townsend	.75	1.75	3.00	W
624	Quick Triggers - Eugene Cunningham	.75	1.75	3.00	W
625	Flee the Night in Anger - Dan Keller	.75	1.75	3.00	
	1954				
626	All Passion Spent - Chandler Brossard	.75	1.75	3.00	
627	The Naked Hunter - William Woolfolk	.75	1.75	3.00	
628	Cry the Lonely Flesh - Jesse L. Lasky, Jr.	.75	1.75	3.00	E
629	Friend or Foe? - Oreste Pinto	.75	1.75	3.00	
630	Smoke up the Valley - Monte Barrett	.75	1.75	3.00	W
631	Prairie Guns - Will Cook	.75	1.75	3.00	W
632	Now It's My Turn - M. E. Chaber	1.50	3.50	5.00	M
633	Hotel Room - Natalie Anderson Scott	.75	1.75	3.00	
	1955				
634	Naked in the Night - Jon Cleary	.75	1.75	3.00	
635	The Wild Years - Donn O'Hara	.75	1.75	3.00	
636	Men and the Sea - Sterling Lord	1.50	3.50	5.00	
637	Six-gun Ambush - Max Brand	.75	1.75	3.00	W
638	Blizzard Range - W. T. Ballard	.75	1.75	3.00	W
639	Don't Come Crying to Me - William Ard	.75	1.75	3.00	
640	Kiss the Night Away - C. G. Lumbard	.75	1.75	3.00	
641	The Naked I - Roy Chanslor	.75	1.75	3.00	
642	I'll Never Let You Go - Fan Nichols	.75	1.75	3.00	E
643	Boldness Be My Friend - Richard Pape	.75	1.75	3.00	
644	Vengeance Trail - Ernest Haycox	.75	1.75	3.00	W
645	Desperation Valley - Philip Ketchum	1.50	3.50	5.00	
646	Up to Her Neck - John Newton Chance	.75	1.75	3.00	
647	Wide-Open Town - Robert F. Mirvish	.75	1.75	3.00	E
648	Naked Canvas - Warwick Scott	.75	1.75	3.00	E
649	Down the Dark Street - Siegel Fleisher	.75	1.75	3.00	
650	Fair Game - Karl Kramer	.75	1.75	3.00	
	1955				
651	Apache Agent - Hal G. Evarts	1.50	3.50	5.00	W
652	Fury at Painted Rock - Will Cook	.75	1.75	3.00	W
653	Down I Go - Ben Kerr	1.50	3.50	5.00	E
654	The Natur of Love - H. E. Bates	.75	1.75	3.00	
655	Dream of Innocence - Turnley Walker	.75	1.75	3.00	
656	Passion Road - Richard Glendinning	.75	1.75	3.00	
657	You Belong to Me - Sam Ross	.75	1.75	3.00	
658	Desire in the Streets - Renato Cannavale	.75	1.75	3.00	
659	Brand of Fury - Jack Barton	.75	1.75	3.00	W
660	You Asked For It - Ian Fleming	2.00	4.00	7.50	M
	aka Casino Royale				
661	Live and Let Live - Chesley Wilson	.75	1.75	3.00	
662	Deep is My Desire - Ian Gordon	.75	1.75	3.00	
663	Fast and Loose - Speed Lamkin	.75	1.75	3.00	
664	Night after Night - Leonard Nathan	.75	1.75	3.00	
665	Farewell, My Young Lover - Glenn Scott	.75	1.75	3.00	
666	Sundown Basin - Roy Townsend	.75	1.75	3.00	W
667	Blonde and Beautiful - Richard Foster	.75	1.75	3.00	
668	Strip the Heart - Jacquin Sanders	1.50	3.50	5.00	E
	aka Freakshow				
669	Sail the Dark Tide - Davenport Steward	.75	1.75	3.00	
670	The Bad One - Lowell Barrington	.75	1.75	3.00	
671	Drag Me Down - E. B. Stuart	.75	1.75	3.00	
672	A Time for Pleasure - Phyllis Hastings	.75	1.75	3.00	
673	Rider from Texas - Philip Ketchum	.75	1.75	3.00	W
674	Web of Passion - Edward D. Radin	.75	1.75	3.00	
675	Cry Hard, Cry Fast - John D. MacDonald	1.50	3.50	5.00	M
	1955				
676	This is My Night - Robert Lowry	.75	1.75	3.00	
677	Wicked We Love - Mordecai Richler	.75	1.75	3.00	
678	Bobby Sox - Marty Links	.75	1.75	3.00	H
679	Good-Time Girl - Conrad Maine	.75	1.75	3.00	
680	Trigger Trail - W.T. Ballard	.75	1.75	3.00	W
681	Don't Push Me Around - Elliott Gilbert	.75	1.75	3.00	
682	The Divine Romance - Fulton J. Sheen	.75	1.75	3.00	
683	The Valley of Love - H. E. Bates	.75	1.75	3.00	
684	Only the Brave - Allan R. Bosworth	.75	1.75	3.00	
685	The Big Rumble - Wenzell Brown	.75	1.75	3.00	
686	The Naked and the Damned - Robert Shafer	.75	1.75	3.00	

687	Bullet Range - Will Cook	.75	1.75	3.00	W
688	Surrender to Love - Charles Boswell & Lewis Thompson	.75	1.75	3.00	
689	The Lovers - Mitchell Wilson	.75	1.75	3.00	
690	The Long Watch - Robert F. Mirvish	.75	1.75	3.00	
691	All that Love Allows - Paul Darcy Boles	.75	1.75	3.00	
692	If You Are a Woman - Lee Graham	.75	1.75	3.00	
693	Desert Showdown - Max Brand aka Trouble Trail	.75	1.75	3.00	W
694	Forbidden Valley - Thomas Thompson	.75	1.75	3.00	W
695	Blondes are My Trouble - Martin Brett	.75	1.75	3.00	
696	I'll Cry Tomorrow - Lillian Roth	.75	1.75	3.00	
697	Contrary Pleasure - John D. MacDonald	1.50	3.50	5.00	
698	Oops! Wrong Party! - Syd Hoff	1.50	3.50	5.00	H
699	The Whole Town Knew - Francis Irby Gwaltney	.75	1.75	3.00	
700	Secret River and the Trail of the Barefoot Pony - Ernest Haycox	.75	1.75	3.00	
701	Trail Drive - Bill Gulick aka A Thousand for the Caribou	.75	1.75	3.00	
702	Sweet and Low-down - Jack Waer	.75	1.75	3.00	
703	Lovers in Torment - Gordon Merrick	.75	1.75	3.00	
704	The Judas Kiss - Jay J. Dratler	.75	1.75	3.00	
705	A New Desire - Stanley Kauffmann	.75	1.75	3.00	
706	Angel Face - Fan Nichols	.75	1.75	3.00	
707	Rawhide Guns - Frank Bonham	.75	1.75	3.00	W
708	Ambush Range - Jack Barton	.75	1.75	3.00	W
709	Show No Mercy - Lindsay Hardy	.75	1.75	3.00	
710	The World in the Evening - Christopher Isherwood	1.50	3.50	5.00	
711	Woman of Paris - Guy des Cars	.75	1.75	3.00	
712	Sigmund Freud for Everybody - Rachel Baker	1.50	3.50	5.00	NF
713	The Fall of Night - Giose Rimanelli	.75	1.75	3.00	
714	Saddlebow Rancher - Ray Townsend	.75	1.75	3.00	W
715	Guns Along the Chisholm - Will C. Brown	.75	1.75	3.00	W
716	After Dark, My Sweet - Jim Thompson	1.50	3.50	5.00	
717	Mistress of Rogues - Rosemond Marshall 1956, aka The Dollmaster	2.00	4.00	6.00	A
718	Carnival Girl - Richard Glendinning	1.50	3.50	5.00	
719	These Women - Gregory d'Alessio	.75	1.75	3.00	
720	Come and Get Me - Johnny Laredo	.75	1.75	3.00	
721	Brothers on the Trail - Max Brand	.75	1.75	3.00	W
722	The Fighting Texan - Will Cook	.75	1.75	3.00	W
723	Mr. Trouble - William Ard	.75	1.75	3.00	
724	The Widow - Georges Simenon	2.00	4.00	6.00	M
725	I'll Fix You - Hal Ellson 1956	.75	1.75	3.00	
726	The Fugitive Romans - William Murray	1.50	3.50	5.00	
727	Revolt of the Sinners - Ugo Zatterin	.75	1.75	3.00	
728	Gun Talk - Ernest Haycox	.75	1.75	3.00	W
729	The Vengeance Riders - Jack Barton	.75	1.75	3.00	W
730	My Love is Violent - Thomas B. Dewey	.75	1.75	3.00	
731	The Searchers - Alan LeMay	1.50	3.50	5.00	W
732	The Naked Hours - Wenzell Brown	.75	1.75	3.00	
733	The Double Life - Thomas Gallagher	.75	1.75	3.00	
734	The Violators - Israel Beckhardt & Wenzell Brown	.75	1.75	3.00	
735	Gunman from Texas - W. T. Ballard	.75	1.75	3.00	W
736	The Drifters - Allan R. Bosworth	.75	1.75	3.00	
737	You Live Once - John D. MacDonald	1.50	3.50	5.00	M
738	The Persistant Image - Gladys Schmitt	.75	1.75	3.00	
739	Wilderness Virgin - John Clagett	1.50	3.50	5.00	A
740	You've Got Me In Stitches - Lawrence Lariar	.75	1.75	3.00	
741	Ambush Rider - Hal G. Evarts	.75	1.75	3.00	W
742	Rawhide River - Cliff Farrell	.75	1.75	3.00	W
743	Jailbait - William Bernard	1.50	3.50	5.00	JD
744	I'm No Good - Peter W. Denzer	.75	1.75	3.00	
745	The Pitfall - Jay J. Dratler	.75	1.75	3.00	
746	The Savage Streets - Floyd Miller	1.50	3.50	5.00	
747	Wine of Desire - LaSelle Gilman	.75	1.75	3.00	
748	Trumpets to the West - Will Cook	.75	1.75	3.00	W
749	Death Cries in the Streets - Samuel A. Krasney	.75	1.75	3.00	
750	Border Town Girl - John D. MacDonald 1956	1.50	3.50	5.00	M

751	Hotel Fever - Arnold Gifford	.75	1.75	3.00	
752	Dark Night of Love - Calvin Clements	.75	1.75	3.00	
753	To Hate and to Love - Frieda K. Franklin	.75	1.75	3.00	
754	Let Me Alone - Donald Windham	.75	1.75	3.00	
755	The Mountain Men - Bill Gulick	.75	1.75	3.00	W
756	Hell is a City - William Ard	.75	1.75	3.00	
757	Duke - Hal Ellson	2.00	4.00	6.00	E
758	The Last Party - Robert Lowry	.75	1.75	3.00	
759	Fair in Love and War - Denton Whitson	.75	1.75	3.00	
760	I Get What I Want - Larry Heller	.75	1.75	3.00	
761	The Man from Missouri - Frank Gruber	.75	1.75	3.00	W
762	The Innocent and the Wicked - Phyllis Hastings	.75	1.75	3.00	
763	I Fear You Not - Ben Kerr	.75	1.75	3.00	
764	Why Johnny Can't Read - Rudolf Flesch	.75	1.75	3.00	
765	The Cruel Tower - William B. Hartley	.75	1.75	3.00	
766	Fraulein Lili Marlene - James Wakefield Burke	1.50	3.50	5.00	
767	A Rider of the High Mesa - Ernest Haycox	.75	1.75	3.00	W
768	Gun in His Hand - Jack Barton	.75	1.75	3.00	W
769	Run...Run...Run... - Frank Taubes	.75	1.75	3.00	
770	The Actor - Niven Busch	.75	1.75	3.00	
771	A Night Out - Basil Heatter	.75	1.75	3.00	
772	Guns of the Lawless - W. T. Ballard	.75	1.75	3.00	W
773	Apache Ambush - Will Cook	.75	1.75	3.00	W
774	Walk a Wicked Mile - Robert P. Hansen	.75	1.75	3.00	
775	Behold this Woman - David Goodis	.75	1.75	3.00	
	1956				
776	This Is It - Hal Ellson	.75	1.75	3.00	
777	Love from France - Edna Bennett & Brant House	.75	1.75	3.00	
778	The Night Raiders - Hal G. Evarts	.75	1.75	3.00	W
779	Born to Gunsmoke - Thomas Thompson	.75	1.75	3.00	W
780	Murder Makes Me Mad - Ferguson Findley	.75	1.75	3.00	
781	Take All You Can Get - Steve Fisher	.75	1.75	3.00	
782	The Hustlers - Sam Ross	.75	1.75	3.00	
783	The Man From Idaho - Dan Temple	.75	1.75	3.00	W
784	The Return of the Rancher - Frank Austin	.75	1.75	3.00	W
785	Damned if He Does - Ben Kerr	.75	1.75	3.00	
786	Moods and Truths - Fulton J. Sheen	.75	1.75	3.00	NF
787	The Dream Peddlers - Floyd Miller	.75	1.75	3.00	
788	The Gunpointer - Dean Owen	.75	1.75	3.00	W
789	Powder Smoke - Jackson Gregory	.75	1.75	3.00	W
790	Run While You Can - William Woolfolk	.75	1.75	3.00	
791	He Walks by Night - Fan Nichols	.75	1.75	3.00	
	1957				
792	Ramrod - Luke Short	.75	1.75	3.00	W
793	Day of the .44 - Jack Barton	.75	1.75	3.00	W
794	The Tramplers - Jason Manor	.75	1.75	3.00	
795	Marmaduke - Brad Anderson & Phil Leeming	1.50	3.50	5.00	H
796	The Silver Desert - Ernest Haycox	.75	1.75	3.00	W
797	Six-gun Maverick - Philip Ketchum	.75	1.75	3.00	W
798	Spin the Glass Web - Max Ehrlich	.75	1.75	3.00	
799	Sabrina Kane - Will Cook	.75	1.75	3.00	W
800	Island of the Pit - Vincent James	.75	1.75	3.00	
	1957				
801	The Jackson Trail - Max Brand	.75	1.75	3.00	W
802	Last-chance Range - Dean Owen	.75	1.75	3.00	W
803	Club 17 - Ben Kerr	.75	1.75	3.00	
804	On the Prod - Ernest Haycox	.75	1.75	3.00	W
805	Arizona Guns - William MacLeod Raine	.75	1.75	3.00	W
806	The Deadly Finger - Henry Kane	1.50	3.50	5.00	M
807	The Girls from Goldfield - Jacquin Sanders	.75	1.75	3.00	
808	Fort Vengeance - Gordon D. Shirreffs	.75	1.75	3.00	W
809	My Brother's Wife - Harry Davis	.75	1.75	3.00	
810	Maverick Empire - Lewis Ford	.75	1.75	3.00	W
811	Flee from Terror - Martin Brett	.75	1.75	3.00	
812	Laugh Yourself Well - Eddie Davis	1.50	3.50	5.00	H
813	Dead Man's Trail - Philip Ketchum	.75	1.75	3.00	
814	Silver Bullets - C. S. Park	.75	1.75	3.00	W
815	Swamp Fire - Don Kingery	.75	1.75	3.00	
816	And Where She Stops - Thomas B. Dewey	.75	1.75	3.00	
817	Calibre - Irving Shulman	.75	1.75	3.00	
818	Doctor Paradise - Jay J. Dratler	.75	1.75	3.00	
819	Let the Sky Fall - Roger Dee	.75	1.75	3.00	
820	Teen-age Gangs - Madeline Karr & Dale Kramer	2.00	4.00	6.00	NF

P. L. Eagle EB19, c. Poplib   P. L. Eagle EB37, c. Poplib   P. L. Eagle EB71, c. Poplib

(POPULAR LIBRARY, continued)

821	The Whipping Boy - S. E. Pfoutz	.75	1.75	3.00	
822	Valley Vultures - Max Brand	.75	1.75	3.00	W
823	One Thing On My Mind - Herbert D. Kastle	.75	1.75	3.00	
824	A Girl, a Man and a River - John Hawkins & Ward Hawkins	.75	1.75	3.00	
825	Scandal in Troy - Eva Hemmer Hansen 1957	.75	1.75	3.00	
826	The Mustangers - Jack Barton	.75	1.75	3.00	W
827	Lone Hand from Texas - Will Cook	.75	1.75	3.00	W
828	Sunset Strip - James Reach	.75	1.75	3.00	
829	Death in the Stacks - Max Arthur	.75	1.75	3.00	M
830	The Empty Trap - John D. MacDonald	1.50	3.50	5.00	M
831	Dead Man Range - Ernest Haycox	.75	1.75	3.00	W
832	Massacre Creek - Gordon D. Shirreffs 1958	.75	1.75	3.00	W
833	The Plundered Land - Coe Williams	.75	1.75	3.00	
834	Red Range - Eugene Cunningham	.75	1.75	3.00	W
835	The Avenging Gun - J. L. Bouma	.75	1.75	3.00	W

POPULAR LIBRARY EAGLE

(Popular Library, Inc.)

EB	1	The Captain's Lady - Basil Heatter 1953	2.00	4.00	7.50	E
EB	2	Rustlers' Gap - William MacLeod Raine	1.50	3.50	5.00	W
EB	3	Ward 20 - James Warner Bellah	.75	1.75	3.00	E
EB	4	Whispering Range - Ernest Haycox	1.50	3.50	5.00	W
EB	5	She'll Be Dead by Morning - Dana Chambers	1.50	3.50	5.00	M
EB	6	The Loves of Lucrezia - Francesca Wright 1954	1.50	3.50	5.00	E
EB	7	Yellowstone Passage - Coe Williams	1.50	3.50	5.00	W
EB	8	The Pale Blonde of Sands Street - William Chapman White	1.50	3.50	5.00	
EB	9	Julia - Margot Bland	.75	1.75	3.00	
EB	10	The Red Law - Jackson Gregory	1.50	3.50	5.00	W
EB	11	Macamba - Lilla van Saher	1.50	3.50	5.00	E
EB	12	Flight or Run - Giles A. Lutz	1.50	3.50	5.00	W
EB	13	Gentle Annie - MacKinlay Kantor	1.50	3.50	5.00	W
EB	14	Gunmen's Grass - Lewis Ford	1.50	3.50	5.00	W
EB	15	The G-String Murders - Gypsy Rose Lee	.75	1.75	3.00	M
EB	16	Satan Was a Man - Edward Hale Bierstadt	1.50	3.50	5.00	
EB	17	Secret Valley - Jackson Gregory	1.50	3.50	5.00	W
EB	18	This Spring of Love - Charles Mergendahl	.75	1.75	3.00	
EB	19	Desert Cache - Dave Barron	1.50	3.50	5.00	
EB	20	The Boat - Walter Gibson	.75	1.75	3.00	
EB	21	The River Bend Feud - William MacLead Raine	1.50	3.50	5.00	W
EB	22	Born of the Sun - Geoffrey Wagner	.75	1.75	3.00	
EB	23	Troopers West - Forbes Parkhill	1.50	3.50	5.00	W
EB	24	Passion is the Gale - Jane Winton	.75	1.75	3.00	
EB	25	Trouble Trail - Coe Williams 1954	1.50	3.50	5.00	W

EB 26	The Eagle and the Wind - Herbert E. Stover	1.50	3.50	5.00	
EB 27	Pistol Pardners - William MacLeod Raine	1.50	3.50	5.00	W
EB 28	The Tough Ones - Whit & Hallie Burnett	.75	1.75	3.00	
EB 29	Danger Trail - J. L. Bouma	1.50	3.50	5.00	W
EB 30	I'll Get You Yet - James Howard	.75	1.75	3.00	
EB 31	Six-gun Buckaroo - Clem Colt	1.50	3.50	5.00	W
EB 32	The Girl from Easy Street - Richard Foster 1955	1.50	3.50	5.00	
EB 33	Brush Rider - Dean Owen	1.50	3.50	5.00	W
EB 34	Too Hard to Handle - Derrick Nabarro	1.50	3.50	5.00	
EB 35	Drygulch Trail - William MacLeod Raine	1.50	3.50	5.00	W
EB 36	Tombolo - Nicholas Fersen	1.50	3.50	5.00	
EB 37	Outlaw River - Dan Temple	1.50	3.50	5.00	W
EB 38	That Girl on the River - Ted Fox	1.50	3.50	5.00	E
EB 39	Go For Your Gun - Coe Williams	1.50	3.50	5.00	W
EB 40	Tonight and Forever - Simon Kent	1.50	3.50	5.00	
EB 41	Texas Spurs - J. L. Bouma	1.50	3.50	5.00	W
EB 42	The Girl in the Red Jaguar - Jason Manor	1.50	3.50	5.00	E
EB 43	Reluctant Gunman - William MacLeod Raine	1.50	3.50	5.00	W
EB 44	Leave it to Me - George Joseph	.75	1.75	3.00	
EB 45	Apache War Cry - William E. Vance	1.50	3.50	5.00	W
EB 46	I Like it Tough - James Howard	1.50	3.50	5.00	
EB 47	Fugitive's Canyon - Hal G. Evarts	1.50	3.50	5.00	W
EB 48	River of Eyes - Lawrence Earl	.75	1.75	3.00	
EB 49	Gunfighter from Montana - Lewis Ford	1.50	3.50	5.00	W
EB 50	Don't Get in My Way - Frances Clippinger 1955	.75	1.75	3.00	
EB 51	Beyond the Rio Grande - William MacLeod Raine	1.50	3.50	5.00	W
EB 52	Time to Embrace - Joseph Foster	.75	1.75	3.00	
EB 53	Fighting Indians of the West - David C. Cooke	1.50	3.50	5.00	NF
EB 54	Barbary Slave - Kevin Matthews	2.00	4.00	7.50	A
EB 55	Mesquire Maverick - Eugene Cunningham	1.50	3.50	5.00	W
EB 56	No Halo for Me - Jason Manor 1956	1.50	3.50	5.00	
EB 57	Longhorn Stampede - Philip Ketchum	1.50	3.50	5.00	W
EB 58	Lament for a Lover - Patricia Highsmith	1.50	3.50	5.00	
EB 59	Six-gun Feud - William MacLeod Raine	1.50	3.50	5.00	W
EB 60	Storm Fear - Clinton Seeley	.75	1.75	3.00	
EB 61	Border Vengeance - J. L. Bouman	1.50	3.50	5.00	W
EB 62	Strange Customs of Courship and Marriage - William J. Fielding	.75	1.75	3.00	NF
EB 63	Apache Crossing - Will Ermine	1.50	3.50	5.00	W
EB 64	The Battle Done - S. Leonard Rubinstein	.75	1.75	3.00	
EB 65	The Elkhorn Feud - Philip Ketchum	1.50	3.50	5.00	W
EB 66	All or Nothing - Max Catto	.75	1.75	3.00	
EB 67	Desert Feud - William MacLeod Raine	1.50	3.50	5.00	W
EB 68	Don't Say No - Olga Rosmanith	1.50	3.50	5.00	
EB 69	Hard Rock Town - Joseph Gage	.75	1.75	3.00	
EB 70	Blow Out My Torch - James Howard	.75	1.75	3.00	
EB 71	Montana Road - Harry Sinclair Drago	1.50	3.50	5.00	W
EB 72	Hard and Fast - U. S. Anderson	.75	1.75	3.00	
EB 73	The Texas Kid - William MacLeod Raine	1.50	3.50	5.00	W
EB 74	Maracaibo - Sterling Silliphant	1.50	3.50	5.00	
EB 75	The Big Gun - Philip Ketchum 1956	1.50	3.50	5.00	
EB 76	The Bed She Made - Leslie Waller	.75	1.75	3.00	E
EB 77	Defiance Mountain - Frank Bonham	1.50	3.50	5.00	W
EB 78	Tory Mistress - Kevin Matthews	1.50	3.50	5.00	A
EB 79	Desert of the Damned - Nelson Nye	.75	1.75	3.00	W
EB 80	Judas Journey - Lee Roberts 1957	.75	1.75	3.00	
EB 81	High Grass Valley - Wayne D. Overholser & William MacLeod Raine	1.50	3.50	5.00	W
EB 82	Free Ride - James M. Fox	.75	1.75	3.00	
EB 83	Roundup - W. T. Ballard	1.50	3.50	5.00	W
EB 84	The Loving and the Daring - Francoise Mallet	1.50	3.50	5.00	E
EB 85	Man Without a Gun - Hal G. Evarts	.75	1.75	3.00	W
EB 86	The Spoiled Children - Philippe Heriat	.75	1.75	3.00	
EB 87	Burning Valley - J. L. Bouma	.75	1.75	3.00	W
EB 88	Heaven Knows, Mr. Allison - Charles Shaw	.75	1.75	3.00	

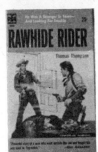

P. L. Eagle EB89, c. Poplib   Popular Libr. G102, c. Poplib   Popular Libr. G112, c. Poplib

(POPULAR LIBRARY EAGLE, continued)

EB 89	Rawhide Rider - Thomas Thompson	.75	1.75	3.00	W
EB 90	Die on Easy Street - James Howard	.75	1.75	3.00	
EB 91	Trouble on the Brazos - Will C. Brown	.75	1.75	3.00	W
EB 92	In Search of Love - William Fain	.75	1.75	3.00	
EB 93	Trail Town Marshal - W. T. Ballard	.75	1.75	3.00	W
EB 94	Duel in the Sun - Niven Busch	.75	1.75	3.00	W
EB 95	I am fifteen...and I Don't Want to Die -				
	Christine Arnothy	.75	1.75	3.00	
EB 96	Just So Far - Floyd Miller	.75	1.75	3.00	
EB 97	More Bobby Sox - Marty Links	.75	1.75	3.00	W
EB 98	California Passage - Cliff Farrell	.75	1.75	3.00	W
EB 99	Bullet Lease - Dan Temple	.75	1.75	3.00	W
EB100	Portrait of Rene - Harry Davis	.75	1.75	3.00	
	1957				
EB101	Border Breed - William MacLeod Raine	.75	1.75	3.00	W
	1958				
EB102	Stay Away, Joe - Dan Cushman	.75	1.75	3.00	
EB103	Hardcase Range - Jackson Gregory	.75	1.75	3.00	W
EB104	The Blonde and Johnny Malloy - Ben Kerr	.75	1.75	3.00	

POPULAR LIBRARY G - SERIES

(Popular Library, Inc.)

G100	Sangaree - Frank G. Slaughter	1.50	3.50	5.00	A
	1952				
G101	The Nymph and the Lamp - Thomas H. Raddall	1.50	3.50	5.00	
G102	From the Sea and the Jungle - Robert Carse	1.50	3.50	5.00	
G103	Mask of Glory - Dan Levin	1.50	3.50	5.00	
G104	Savage Cavalier - Noel B. Gerson	1.50	3.50	5.00	A
G105	The Big Cage - Robert Lowry	1.50	3.50	5.00	
G106	Courtroom - Quentin Reynolds	1.50	3.50	5.00	
G107	The Golden Road - Peter Bourne	2.50	6.00	10.00	A
G108	Red Lion Inn - Robert Payne	1.50	3.50	5.00	
G109	The Glorious Three - June Wetherell	1.50	3.50	5.00	
G110	Congo Song - Stuart Cloete	1.50	3.50	5.00	E
G111	The Forsaken - Ferenc Kormendi	1.50	3.50	5.00	
G112	Point Venus - Susanne McConnaughey	1.50	3.50	5.00	E
G113	Marianne - Rhys Davies	1.50	3.50	5.00	
G114	Find Me in Fire - Robert Lowry	1.50	3.50	5.00	E
G115	The Naked Rich - Vivian Connell	1.50	3.50	5.00	
G116	Sword of Fortune - Noel B. Gerson	2.50	6.00	10.00	A
	1953				
G117	Angle of Attack - Joseph Landon	1.50	3.50	5.00	
G118	The Forest Cavalier - Roy Flannagan	1.50	3.50	5.00	A
G119	Jasmine Street - Clifford Dowdey	1.50	3.50	5.00	
G120	The City Beyond - Lucille Emerick	1.50	3.50	5.00	
G121	Look Down in Mercy - Walter Baxter	1.50	3.50	5.00	
G122	After the Big House - Fred Berson	1.50	3.50	5.00	
G123	Charlie Dell - Anderson Wayne	1.50	3.50	5.00	
G124	Afraid of the Dark - Mark Derby	1.50	3.50	5.00	
G125	The Beach House - Stephen Longstreet	1.50	3.50	5.00	
G126	The Big Rape - James Wakefield Burke	1.50	3.50	5.00	
G127	The Scarlet Sword - H. E. Bates	1.50	3.50	5.00	
G128	One Winter in Boston - Robert M. Smith	1.50	3.50	5.00	

G129	Free and Easy - June Wetherell	1.50	3.50	5.00	
G130	Tisa - Helga Moray	2.50	6.00	10.00	E
G131	The Gathering Darkness - Thomas Gallagher	1.50	3.50	5.00	
G132	Watch for the Dawn - Stuart Cloete	1.50	3.50	5.00	
G133	Three Comrades - Erich Maria Remarque	1.50	3.50	5.00	
	Illo in Parade of Pleasure				
G134	Whistle Stop - Maritta Wolff	1.50	3.50	5.00	E
G135	When the Gods Are Silent - Mikhail Soloviev	1.50	3.50	5.00	
	B&W Illo in Parade of Pleasure				
G136	Prince Bart - Jay Richard Kennedy	1.50	3.50	5.00	
G137	Sun in Their Eyes - Monte Barrett	1.50	3.50	5.00	W
G138	Blood Royal - Robert Payne	2.50	6.00	10.00	A
G139	Marie of the Isles - Robert Gaillard	1.50	3.50	5.00	
G140	A House Is Not a Home - Polly Adler	1.50	3.50	5.00	
G141	These Items of Desire - Louis A. Brennan	1.50	3.50	5.00	
G142	The Hot and the Cool - Edwin Gilbert	1.50	3.50	5.00	
G143	Rage to Love - Frank Tilsley	1.50	3.50	5.00	
G144	The Strong Don't Cry - Estelle Slater	1.50	3.50	5.00	
	1955				
G145	The Flesh Is Real - Irving Shulman	1.50	3.50	5.00	
G146	Rumble on the Docks - Frank Paley	2.50	6.00	10.00	
G147	This Is Temptation - James Ronald	1.50	3.50	5.00	
G148	The Only Sin - Anne Powers	1.50	3.50	5.00	
G149	Never Say Love - Pierre Sichel	1.50	3.50	5.00	
G150	The Girl From Rome - Michel Durafour	1.50	3.50	5.00	
G151	The Image and the Search - Walter Baxter	1.50	3.50	5.00	
G152	The Golden Wildcat - Margaret Widdemer	1.50	3.50	5.00	
G153	A Time to Love and a Time to Die - Erich Maria Remarque	1.50	3.50	5.00	
G154	Many Loves Have I - William Brown Meloney	1.50	3.50	5.00	
G155	The Luciano Story - Sid Feder, Joachim Joesten	2.50	6.00	10.00	NF
	1956				
G156	Tomorrow! - Philip Wylie	3.00	6.00	12.00	SF
G157	The Iron Maiden - Edwin Lanham	1.50	3.50	5.00	
G158	Between Darkness and Day - Gordon Merrick	1.50	3.50	5.00	
G159	Louisiana Cavalier - Everett Webber	1.50	3.50	5.00	
G160	The Tormented - Audrey Erskine Lindop	1.50	3.50	5.00	
G161	Diversey - MacKinlay Kantor	1.50	3.50	5.00	
G162	The Reckless Years - Virginia Oakey	1.50	3.50	5.00	
G163	Sangaree - Frank G. Slaughter	1.50	3.50	5.00	
G164	Red Carpet for Mamie Eisenhower - Alden Hatch	1.50	3.50	5.00	
G165	Never Too Young - Joseph Weeks	1.50	3.50	5.00	
G166	Headquarters - Quentin Reynolds	1.50	3.50	5.00	
G167	A Room in Paris - Peggy Mann	1.50	3.50	5.00	
G168	The Four Winds - David Beaty	1.50	3.50	5.00	
G169	Captain Whitecap - John Clagett	1.50	3.50	5.00	A
G170	Folies - Bergere - Paul Derval	1.50	3.50	5.00	
G171	A Tale for Midnight - Frederic Prokosch	1.50	3.50	5.00	
G172	The Other Side of Paradise - Paul Hyde Bonner	1.50	3.50	5.00	
G173	The Night Is So Dark - Robert M. Coates	1.50	3.50	5.00	
G174	Red Sky at Midnight - Robert F. Mirvish	1.50	3.50	5.00	
G175	Children of the Dark - Irving Shulman	1.50	3.50	5.00	
	1957				
G176	Rogue Cavalier - Rosamond Marshall	1.50	3.50	5.00	A
G177	Her French Husband - Phyllis Hastings	1.50	3.50	5.00	
G178	Hot Winds of Summer - John H. Secondari	1.50	3.50	5.00	
G179	The Wild Country - Louis Bromfield	1.50	3.50	5.00	

Popular Libr. G125, c. Poplib   Popular Libr. G130, c. Poplib   Popular Libr. G138, c. Poplib

G180	Hang My Wreath - Ward Weaver	1.50	3.50	5.00	
G181	Erika - James McGovern	1.50	3.50	5.00	
G182	Girls on Parole - Katherine Sullivan	1.50	3.50	5.00	
G183	Man of the World - Stanley Kauffmann	1.50	3.50	5.00	
G184	The Last Voyage of the Lusitania - A. A. Hoehling, Mary Hoehling (cover supposedly by Kelly Freas)	1.50	3.50	5.00	NF
G185	Honey From a Dark Hive - Bernice Kavinoky	1.50	3.50	5.00	
G186	The Sultan's Warrior - Bates Baldwin	1.50	3.50	5.00	A
G187	The Quick and the Loving - Clifford Irving	1.50	3.50	5.00	
G188	Episode in the Sun - Curry Holden	1.50	3.50	5.00	
G189	All the Trumpets Sounded - W. G. Hardy	1.50	3.50	5.00	
G190	Happy Marriage - John A. O'Brien	1.50	3.50	5.00	
G191	Savage Cavalier - Noel B. Gerson	1.50	3.50	5.00	
G192	The Sleepless Moon - H. E. Bates	1.50	3.50	5.00	
G193	Keep the Aspidistra Flying - George Orwell	1.50	3.50	5.00	
G194	A Cry of Children - John Horne Burns	1.50	3.50	5.00	
G195	The Valley of God - Irene Patai	1.50	3.50	5.00	
G196	Sisters of the Night - Jess Stearn	1.50	3.50	5.00	
G197	On the Dodge - William MacLeod Raine	1.50	3.50	5.00	W
G198	A House in Peking - Robert Payne	1.50	3.50	5.00	
G199	The Miracle of Lourdes - Ruth Cranston	1.50	3.50	5.00	
G200	Way of a Buccaneer - Davenport Steward	1.50	3.50	5.00	A
G201	The Red Sands of Santa Maria - Bill Murphy	.75	1.75	3.00	
G202	Ten Days in August - Bernard Frizell	.75	1.75	3.00	
G203	Facts of Life and Love for Teenagers - Evelyn Millis Duvall	1.50	3.50	5.00	NF
G204	Dust in the Sun - Jon Cleary	.75	1.75	3.00	
G205	Mamba - Stuart Cloete	.75	1.75	3.00	
G206	The Beach House - Stephen Longstreet	.75	1.75	3.00	
G207	Tempered Blade - Monte Barrett	1.50	3.50	5.00	A
G208	Lady Sings the Blues - William Dufty and Billy Holiday	2.50	6.00	10.00	B
	1958				
G209	Life Is Worth Living - Fulton J. Sheen	.75	1.75	3.00	
G210	Jubilee - John Brick	.75	1.75	3.00	
G211	Pitchman - Robin Moore	.75	1.75	3.00	
G212	Work of Darkness - Jack Karney	.75	1.75	3.00	
G213	So Far From Spring - Peggy Simpson Curry	.75	1.75	3.00	
G214	Burmese Days - George Orwell	1.50	3.50	5.00	E
G215	The Red Room - Francoise Mallet	.75	1.75	3.00	
G216	Joey Adams' Joke Book - Joey Adams	1.50	3.50	5.00	H
G217	The Silver Lion - Noel B. Gerson	1.50	3.50	5.00	
G218	Trouble Shooter - Ernest Haycox	.75	1.75	3.00	W
G219	Bond of the Flesh - Rosamond Marshall	.75	1.75	3.00	
G220	What's Left of April - Robert Lowry	.75	1.75	3.00	
G221	A House on the Rhine - Frances Faviell	.75	1.75	3.00	
G222	Walk Through the Valley - Borden Deal	.75	1.75	3.00	
G223	The Sheriff's Son - William MacLeod Raine	.75	1.75	3.00	W
G224	Sex Attitudes in the Home - Ralph G. Eckert	1.50	3.50	5.00	NF
G225	The Hell Bent Kid - Charles O. Locke	.75	1.75	3.00	
G226	God Is Late - Christine Arnothy	.75	1.75	3.00	
G227	Pride of Innocence - David Buckley	.75	1.75	3.00	
G228	They Died in the Chair - Wenzell Brown	1.50	3.50	5.00	
G229	Awake to Darkness - Richard McMullen	.75	1.75	3.00	E
G230	The Happy Valley - Max Brand	.75	1.75	3.00	W
G231	I Know My Love - Fan Nichols	.75	1.75	3.00	
G232	The Man From Yuma - Hal G. Evarts	.75	1.75	3.00	W
G233	Give Us This Day - Sidney Stewart	.75	1.75	3.00	
G234	The Priest - Joseph Caruso	.75	1.75	3.00	
G235	Six Angels at My Back - John Bell Clayton	.75	1.75	3.00	E
G236	Cry Scandal - William Ard	.75	1.75	3.00	
G237	Chaffee of Roaring Horse - Ernest Haycox	.75	1.75	3.00	W
G238	Texas Triggers - Eugene Cunningham	.75	1.75	3.00	W
G239	I Take the Rap - Gordon Shelly	.75	1.75	3.00	
G240	Gun Hand - Cliff Farrell	.75	1.75	3.00	W
G241	Don't Touch Me - MacKinlay Kantor	.75	1.75	3.00	
G242	Dream of a Woman - Jay J. Dratler	.75	1.75	3.00	
G243	Queen of the East - Alexander Baron	1.50	3.50	5.00	
G244	From the Sea and the Jungle - Robert Carse	.75	1.75	3.00	
G245	Manhunt - Donald MacKenzie	.75	1.75	3.00	
G246	Man-Size - William MacLeod Raine	.75	1.75	3.00	W
G247	Showdown in the Sun - Bill Gulick	.75	1.75	3.00	W
G248	The Deadly Reasons - Edward D. Radin	.75	1.75	3.00	
G249	Saddle Tramp - W. T. Ballard	.75	1.75	3.00	W
G250	The Squirrel Cage - Edwin Gilbert	.75	1.75	3.00	

G251	Best Seller - William Murray	.75	1.75	3.00	
G252	The Kind of Guy I Am - Robert McAllister and Floyd Miller	.75	1.75	3.00	
G253	Liana - Martha Gellhorn	.75	1.75	3.00	E
G254	Trial by Fire - Charles Elliott	.75	1.75	3.00	
G255	Rawhide Gunman - W. T. Ballard	.75	1.75	3.00	W
G256	Caribbean Cavalier - Davenport Steward	1.50	3.50	5.00	A
G257	The Silver Star - Jackson Gregory	.75	1.75	3.00	W
G258	The Rib of the Hawk - Rosamond Marshall	.75	1.75	3.00	
G259	The Violent Wedding - Robert Lowry	.75	1.75	3.00	
G260	Calendar Model - Gloria Gale	.75	1.75	3.00	
G261	Free Grass - Ernest Haycox	.75	1.75	3.00	W
G262	Take a Number - Armando T. Perretta	.75	1.75	3.00	
G263	Apache Agent - Hal G. Evarts	.75	1.75	3.00	W
G264	Square Shooter - William MacLeod Raine	.75	1.75	3.00	W
G265	This Is for Keeps - George Joseph	.75	1.75	3.00	
G266	Life Without Father - Muriel Resnik	.75	1.75	3.00	
G267	Painted Ponies - Alan LeMay	.75	1.75	3.00	W
G268	The Big Bubble - Theodore Pratt c-Maguire	.75	1.75	3.00	E
G269	All for a Woman - Jay J. Dratler	.75	1.75	3.00	
G270	Dead or Alive - Max Brand	.75	1.75	3.00	W
G271	Cry Hard, Cry Fast - John D. MacDonald	.75	1.75	3.00	M
G272	Spiderweb Trail - Eugene Cunningham	.75	1.75	3.00	W
G273	The Life of All Living - Fulton J. Sheen	.75	1.75	3.00	
G274	Trouble at Moon Dance - A. B. Guthrie, Jr.	.75	1.75	3.00	W
G275	Tiger by the Tail - Charles Mergendahl	.75	1.75	3.00	
G276	Fury at Painted Rock - Will Cook	.75	1.75	3.00	W
G277	Don't Crowd Me - Evan Hunter	.75	1.75	3.00	
G278	Bullet Ambush - William MacLeod Raine	.75	1.75	3.00	W
G279	The Cut of the Ax - Delmar Jackson	.75	1.75	3.00	
G280	The Naked Rich - Vivian Connell	.75	1.75	3.00	
G281	A Strange Affair - Felix Jackson	.75	1.75	3.00	
G282	The Man Inside - M. E. Chaber	1.50	3.50	5.00	M
G283	Trail Smoke - Ernest Haycox	.75	1.75	3.00	W
G284	The Wicked Blade - Robert Carse	.75	1.75	3.00	
G285	Rage on the Bar - Geoffrey Wagner	.75	1.75	3.00	
G286	Showdown at Pistol Flat - C. S. Park	.75	1.75	3.00	W
G287	I'll Get Mine - Thurston Scott	.75	1.75	3.00	
G288	Shadow Valley - Gordon D. Shirreffs	.75	1.75	3.00	W
G289	Seize the Day - Saul Bellow	.75	1.75	3.00	
G290	Naked to My Pride - Howard Rigsby	.75	1.75	3.00	
G291	The Devil Must - Tom Wicker	.75	1.75	3.00	
G292	Ramrod From Hell - Leslie Ernenwein	.75	1.75	3.00	W
G293	Woman of Egypt - Kevin Matthews	1.50	3.50	5.00	A
G294	Buckaroo - Eugene Cunningham	.75	1.75	3.00	W
G295	The Tough Tenderfoot - William MacLeod Raine	.75	1.75	3.00	W
G296	The Closest Kin There Is - Clara Winston	.75	1.75	3.00	E
G297	We Burn Like Candles - Bernice Kavinoky 1959	.75	1.75	3.00	E
G298	Love Is a Four-letter Word - Anita Rowe Block	.75	1.75	3.00	
G299	Gold in the Sky - Max Catto	.75	1.75	3.00	
G300	Lone Rider - Ernest Haycox	.75	1.75	3.00	W
G301	Boy With a Gun - James Dean Sanderson	.75	1.75	3.00	
G302	Go to Sleep, Jeannie - Thomas B. Dewey	.75	1.75	3.00	
G303	End of Track - Ward Weaver (Van Wyck Mason)	.75	1.75	3.00	W
G304	Cry, Brother, Cry - Jack Karney	.75	1.75	3.00	
G305	The River Bend Feud - William MacLeod Raine	.75	1.75	3.00	W
G306	The Staked Plain - Frank X. Tolbert	.75	1.75	3.00	W E
G307	The Boy Came Back - Charles H. Knickerbocker	.75	1.75	3.00	E
G308	The Last Hero - Peter W. Denzer	.75	1.75	3.00	
G309	Trouble on the Massacre - W. T. Ballard	.75	1.75	3.00	W
G310	Time to Remember - Anderson Wayne	.75	1.75	3.00	
G311	The Losers - Clifford Irving	.75	1.75	3.00	
G312	The Last Princess - Charles O. Locke	.75	1.75	3.00	A
G313	Double Agent - Gene Stackelberg	.75	1.75	3.00	
G314	Guns of Abilene - James B. Chaffin	.75	1.75	3.00	W
G315	The Time of the Panther - Wesley Ford Davis	.75	1.75	3.00	
G316	Face of a Hero - Louis Falstein	.75	1.75	3.00	
G317	Dark Drums - Wenzell Brown	.75	1.75	3.00	E
G318	Riders West - Ernest Haycox	.75	1.75	3.00	W
G319	The Savage Affair - Virgil Scott	.75	1.75	3.00	
G320	Two-edged Vengeance - W. T. Ballard	.75	1.75	3.00	W
G321	Jailbait - William Bernard	1.75	3.50	5.00	JD
G322	The Untamed Breed - Jack Barton	.75	1.75	3.00	W
G323	Beyond My Worth - Lillian Roth	.75	1.75	3.00	

G324	Breaking Point - Jacob Presser	.75	1.75	3.00	
G325	Ask for Linda - Fan Nichols	.75	1.75	3.00	E
G326	Starlight Rider - Ernest Haycox	.75	1.75	3.00	W
G327	Timbal Gulch Trail - Max Brand	.75	1.75	3.00	W
G328	A Private Party - William Ard	.75	1.75	3.00	E
G329	New York Call Girl - Robert Lowry	.75	1.75	3.00	E
G330	After Long Silence - Robert Gutwillig	.75	1.75	3.00	
G331	Bitter Fruit - Peter Packer	.75	1.75	3.00	
G332	Texas Sheriff - Eugene Cunningham	.75	1.75	3.00	W
G333	That Randall Girl - Samuel Edwards	.75	1.75	3.00	E
G334	A Secret Story - William Saroyan	1.50	3.50	5.00	
G335	Showdown - W. T. Ballard, James C. Lynch	.75	1.75	3.00	W
G336	Johnny Bogan - Leonora Baccante	.75	1.75	3.00	E
G337	Decision at Piute Wells - Philip Ketchum	.75	1.75	3.00	W
G338	Blondes Die Young - Bill Peters	.75	1.75	3.00	
G339	The Young Life - Leo Townsend	.75	1.75	3.00	
G340	See How They Burn - Edwin Gilbert	.75	1.75	3.00	
G341	Cradle of the Sun - John Clagett	1.50	3.50	5.00	A
G342	Prodigal Shepherd - Al Hirshberg and Robert Pfau	.75	1.75	3.00	
G343	The Texas Kid - William MacLeod Raine	.75	1.75	3.00	W
G344	The Night and the Naked - Gordon Merrick	.75	1.75	3.00	E
G345	Thunder in the Dust - Alan LeMay	.75	1.75	3.00	W
G346	I'll Get You Yet - James Howard	.75	1.75	3.00	
G347	Guns of the Tom Dee and The Valley of the Rogue - Ernest Haycox	.75	1.75	3.00	W
G348	Free and Easy - June Wetherell	.75	1.75	3.00	
G349	The Eagle and the Wind - Herbert E. Stover	.75	1.75	3.00	
G350	Ward 20 - James Warner Bellah	.75	1.75	3.00	E
G351	Head of the Mountain - Ernest Haycox	.75	1.75	3.00	W
G352	The Tough Ones - Whit and Hallie Burnett	.75	1.75	3.00	
G353	Gold Town Gunman - Ray Townsend	.75	1.75	3.00	W
G354	Naked and Alone - Michael Lawrence	.75	1.75	3.00	
G355	Gun Law - Philip Ketchum	.75	1.75	3.00	W
G356	The Groves of Desire - Nathaniel Norsen Weinreb	.75	1.75	3.00	
G357	Drums of Empire - Robert Carse	.75	1.75	3.00	
G358	Duke - Hal Ellson	1.50	3.50	5.00	
G359	Violent Valley - Wade Ashburn	.75	1.75	3.00	
G360	Love Is a Man's Affair - Fred Kerner	.75	1.75	3.00	
G361	Texas Breed - William MacLeod Raine	.75	1.75	3.00	W
G362	The Girl in the Red Jaguar - Jason Manor	.75	1.75	3.00	E
G363	Gunsight Trail - Alan LeMay	.75	1.75	3.00	W
G364	Good Housekeeping's the Better Way	.75	1.75	3.00	NF
G365	Spring in Fialta - Vladimir Nabokov	.75	1.75	3.00	
G366	Danny and the Boys - Robert Traver	.75	1.75	3.00	
G367	Rawhide Range - Ernest Haycox	.75	1.75	3.00	W
G368	Julia - Margot Bland	.75	1.75	3.00	
G369	Rancher's Revenge - Max Brand	.75	1.75	3.00	W
G370	Rifle Pass - Dean Owen	.75	1.75	3.00	W
G371	Cindy and I - Joey Adams	.75	1.75	3.00	
G372	This Spring of Love - Charles Mergendahl	.75	1.75	3.00	
G373	The Sins of Maria - Bruce Cameron	.75	1.75	3.00	
G374	Pistol Pardners - William MacLeod Raine	.75	1.75	3.00	W
G375	So Strong a Flame - Bernice Kavinoky	.75	1.75	3.00	
G376	Lily and the Sergeant - Martin Yoseloff	.75	1.75	3.00	
G377	The Girls on the 10th Floor - Steve Allen	.75	1.75	3.00	
G378	Outlaw River - Dan Temple	.75	1.75	3.00	W
G379	Gentle Annie - MacKinlay Kantor	.75	1.75	3.00	W
G380	Marshal of Sundown - Jackson Gregory	.75	1.75	3.00	W
G381	Seek Out and Destroy - James D. Horan	.75	1.75	3.00	
G382	Aimee - M. L. Law	.75	1.75	3.00	E
G383	The Dr. Lewis Affair - Lane Johnstone	.75	1.75	3.00	
G384	Guadalcanal Diary - Richard Tregaskis	.75	1.75	3.00	C
G385	Country Girl - Richard McMullen	.75	1.75	3.00	E
G386	A Matter of Morals - Joseph Gies	.75	1.75	3.00	E
G387	Texas Spurs - J. L. Bouma	.75	1.75	3.00	W
G388	Brush Rider - Dean Owen	.75	1.75	3.00	W
G389	Gunfire Man - Philip Ketchum	.75	1.75	3.00	W
G390	Desert Feud - William MacLeod Raine	.75	1.75	3.00	W
G391	The Scarlet Guidon - Ray Toepfer	.75	1.75	3.00	
G392	The Living Wood - Louis de Wohl	.75	1.75	3.00	
G393	The Loves of Lucrezia - Francesca Wright	.75	1.75	3.00	
G394	Beyond the Rio Grande - William MacLeod Raine	.75	1.75	3.00	W
G395	Find Me in Fire - Robert Lowry	.75	1.75	3.00	E

G396	The Man From Texas - Jackson Gregory	.75	1.75	3.00	W
G397	Trouble Trail - Coe Williams	.75	1.75	3.00	W
G398	Six-gun Ambush - Max Brand	.75	1.75	3.00	W

POPULAR LIBRARY PC-SERIES

(Popular Library, Inc.)

PC300	Adventures of Captain David Grief - Jack London	2.00	4.00	6.00	A
PC400	Be My Guest - Conrad Hilton	2.00	4.00	6.00	NF

POPULAR LIBRARY SP-SERIES

(Popular Library, Inc.)

SP 2	The Adventures of Augie March - Saul Bellow 1955	1.50	3.50	5.00	
SP 3	Crossword Puzzles 1956	3.00	6.00	12.00	NF
SP 4	The Doctors - Andre Soubiran	1.50	3.50	5.00	
SP 5	Between Heaven and Hell - Francis Irby Gwaltney	1.50	3.50	5.00	
SP 6	Auntie Mame - Patrick Dennis	1.50	3.50	5.00	
SP 7	A Tree Grows in Brooklyn - Betty Smith	1.50	3.50	5.00	
SP 8	Courtroom - Quentin Reynolds 1957	1.50	3.50	5.00	
SP 9	Roll Back the Sky - Ward Taylor	1.50	3.50	5.00	
SP10	The Spear - Louis de Wohl	1.50	3.50	5.00	
SP11	The Butchers - Leonard Bishop	1.50	3.50	5.00	
SP12	Big Fella - Henry W. Clune 1958	1.50	3.50	5.00	
SP13	Onionhead - Weldon Hill	1.50	3.50	5.00	H
SP14	Three Comrades - Erich Maria Remarque	1.50	3.50	5.00	C
SP15	Webster's New World Dictionary of the American Language - David B. Guralnik	2.00	4.00	6.00	NF
SP16	Guestward ho! - Patrick Dennis & Barbara Hooton	1.50	3.50	5.00	
SP17	The Nymph and the Lamp - Thomas H. Raddall	1.50	3.50	5.00	E
SP18	Shadow of the Moon - M. M. Kaye	1.50	3.50	5.00	
SP19	The Wind in His Fists - John Jennings	2.00	4.00	6.00	A
SP20	The Forest Cavalier - Roy Flannagan	1.50	3.50	5.00	A
SP21	A Time to Love and a Time to Die - Erich Maria Remarque	1.50	3.50	5.00	C
SP22	If I Forget Thee - Robert S. de Ropp	1.50	3.50	5.00	
SP23	Dream of Innocence - Turnley Walker	1.50	3.50	5.00	
SP24	Lower the Angels - Walter Karig	1.50	3.50	5.00	E
SP25	Tisa - Helga Moray 1958	2.00	4.00	6.00	A
SP26	Woman Surgeon - Else K. La Roe	1.50	3.50	5.00	
SP27	A Moment of Warmth - Francis Irby Gwaltney	1.50	3.50	5.00	
SP28	Drums of Destiny - Peter Bourne	2.00	4.00	6.00	A
SP29	Good Deeds Must Be Punished - Irving Shulman	1.50	3.50	5.00	
SP30	The Philanderer - Stanley Kauffmann	1.50	3.50	5.00	
SP31	The City of Libertines - W. G. Hardy	2.00	4.00	5.00	
SP32	My Father--My Son - William Duffy & Edward G. Robinson, Jr.	3.00	6.00	12.00	
SP33	Marie of the Isles - Robert Gaillard	1.50	3.50	5.00	
SP34	Red Lion Inn - Robert Payne	1.50	3.50	5.00	A
SP35	The Late Liz - Elizabeth Burns	1.50	3.50	5.00	
SP36	A House is Not a Home - Polly Adler	1.50	3.50	5.00	
SP37	Love for Lydia - H. E. Bates	1.50	3.50	5.00	E
SP38	A Tale for Midnight - Frederic Prokosch	1.50	3.50	5.00	
SP39	Whistle Stop - Maritta Wolff	1.50	3.50	5.00	E
SP40	Blood Royal - Robert Payne	1.50	3.50	5.00	A
SP41	Look Down in Mercy - Walter Baxter	1.50	3.50	5.00	
SP42	The Good Housekeeping Book of Baby and Child Care - L. Emmett Holt, Jr.	1.50	3.50	5.00	NF

SP43 Rage to Love - Frank Tilsley	1.50	3.50	5.00	
SP44 Dark Fury - Helga Moray	1.50	3.50	5.00	
SP45 These Items of Desire - Louis A. Brennan	1.50	3.50	5.00	
SP46 The Big Cage - Robert Lowry	1.50	3.50	5.00	
SP47 The Strong Don't Cry - Estelle Slater	1.50	3.50	5.00	
SP48 The Insider - James Kelly	1.50	3.50	5.00	
SP49 Love Affair - Robert Carson	1.50	3.50	5.00	E
SP50 Kingsblood Royal - Sinclair Lewis 1959	1.50	3.50	5.00	
SP51 The Greater Glory - Lester Gorn	1.50	3.50	5.00	
SP52 The Golden Touch - Al Dewlen	1.50	3.50	5.00	
SP53 The Great Days - John Dos Passos	1.50	3.50	5.00	
SP100 Man Into Woman - Niels Hoyer	2.50	6.00	10.00	NF

POPULAR LIBRARY W-SERIES

(Popular Library, Inc.)

W400 I, James Dean - T. T. Thomas	3.00	6.00	12.00
W500 Fire Down Below - Simon Kent	1.50	3.50	5.00
W600 The Treasury of Ribaldry - Volume 1 - Louis Untermeyer	2.00	4.00	6.00

PREMIER BOOKS

(Fawcett Publications, Inc.)

S12 The Power of Positive Living - Douglas Lurton 1955	.50	1.25	2.00	NF
S13 How to Write and Speak Effective English - Edward Frank Allen	.50	1.25	2.00	NF
S14 The Enjoyment of Love in Marriage - LeMon Clark	.50	1.25	2.00	NF
S15 Best Quotations for all Occasions - Lewis C. Henry	.50	1.25	2.00	NF
S16 The Art of Thinking - Ernest Dimnet	.50	1.25	2.00	NF
S17 Mademoiselle de Maupin - Theophile Gautier	.50	1.25	2.00	
S18 Look Younger, Live Longer - Gaylord Hauser 1956	.50	1.25	2.00	NF
S19 The Way of Woman - Johnson E. Fairchild	.50	1.25	2.00	NF
S20 Philosophy for Pleasure - Hector Hawton	.50	1.25	2.00	NF
S21 The Fascinating Insect World of J. Henri Fabre - Edwin Way Teale	.50	1.25	2.00	NF
S22 Your Key to Happiness - Harold Sherman	.50	1.25	2.00	NF
d23 The Sex Life of Wild Animals - Eugene Burns	.75	1.75	3.00	NF
S24 The Strange Story of Our Earth - A. Hyatt Verrill	.50	1.25	2.00	NF
S25 My Life as an Indian - J. W. Schultz	.75	1.75	3.00	NF
S26 The Living Tide - N. S. Berrill	.50	1.25	2.00	NF
S27 A Key to the Heavens - Leo Mattersdorf	.50	1.25	2.00	NF
S28 The Wisdom and Ideas of Plato - David Appel, Eugene Freeman	.75	1.75	3.00	NF
S29 A Book About American History - George Stimpson	.75	1.75	3.00	NF
S30 The World's Ten Greatest Novels - W. Somerset Maugham	.75	1.75	3.00	
S31 The Benjamin Franklin Sampler	.75	1.75	3.00	
S32 American Ballads - David Jordan, Charles O'Brien Kennedy	1.50	3.50	5.00	
S33 The Origin of Things - Julius E. Lips	.50	1.25	2.00	NF
d34 Abraham Lincoln - Emil Ludwig	.75	1.75	3.00	B
S35 Understanding Other People - Stuart Palmer	.50	1.25	2.00	NF
S36 Party Fun and Games - Alexander Van Rensselaer 1956	.50	1.25	2.00	NF
S37 According to Hoyle - Richard Frey	.75	1.75	3.00	NF
S38 Unfaithful - Frank S. Caprio	.50	1.25	2.00	
S39 The Great Religions by Which Men Live - Tynette Hills, Floyd H. Ross	.50	1.25	2.00	NF

(PREMIER BOOKS, continued)

d40	George Washington - W. E. Woodward	.50	1.25	2.00	B
S41	The Home Book of Italian Cooking - Angela Catanzaro 1957	.50	1.25	2.00	NF
S42	How You Can Forecast the Weather - Eric Sloane	.50	1.25	2.00	NF
S43	Discover Your Self! - Stephen Lackner	.50	1.25	2.00	NF
S44	Animal Wonder World - Frank Lane	.50	1.25	2.00	NF
d45	Meet General Grant - W. E. Woodward	.50	1.25	2.00	B
S46	What Your Dreams Mean - Emil A. Gutheil	.50	1.25	2.00	NF
S47	Boswell's Johnson Sampler - James Boswell	.50	1.25	2.00	
S48	How to Make Psychology Work for You - Abraham P. Sperling	.50	1.25	2.00	NF
S49	Crucibles: the Story of Chemistry - Bernard Jaffe	.50	1.25	2.00	NF
d50	Man's Emerging Mind - N. J. Berrill	.50	1.25	2.00	NF
d51	The Miracle of Language - Charlton Laird	.50	1.25	2.00	NF
d52	Understanding Human Nature - Alfred Adler	.50	1.25	2.00	NF
d53	The Kipling Sampler - Rudyard Kipling	.75	1.75	3.00	
d54	Shakespeare Without Tears - Margaret Webster	.50	1.25	2.00	
d55	The Son of Man - Emil Ludwig	.50	1.25	2.00	NF
d56	Fun with Mathematics - Jerome S. Meyer	.50	1.25	2.00	NF
d57	Cure Your Nerves Yourself - Louis E. Bisch	.50	1.25	2.00	NF
d58	Mirror for Man - Clyde Kluckhohn	.50	1.25	2.00	NF
d59	The Practical Way to a Better Memory - Bruno Furst	.50	1.25	2.00	NF
d60	They Walked with God - Michael Williams	.50	1.25	2.00	NF
d61	The Living Thoughts of Thomas Jefferson	.75	1.75	3.00	
d62	Freedom from Money Worries - Martha & Price A. Patton 1958	.50	1.25	2.00	NF
d63	The Living Thoughts of Henry David Thoreau	.75	1.75	3.00	
d64	How to Understand Music - Oscar Thompson	.50	1.25	2.00	NF
d65	Riddles of Science - J. Arthur Thomson	.50	1.25	2.00	NF
d66	Becoming a Mother - Marvin H. Albert, T. R. Seidman	.50	1.25	2.00	NF
d67	The Living Thoughts of Ralph Waldo Emerson	.75	1.75	3.00	
d68	See Without Glasses - Ralph MacFadyen	.50	1.25	2.00	NF
d69	Magic, Myth and Medicine - D. T. Atkinson	.50	1.25	2.00	NF
d70	The Growth of Physical Science - James Jeans	.50	1.25	2.00	NF
d71	How to Live With Yourself and Like It - Henry Clay Lindgren	.50	1.25	2.00	NF
d72	The Living Thoughts of Machiavelli - Niccolo Machiavelli	.75	1.75	3.00	
d73	How to Use the Power of Prayer - Harold Sherman	.50	1.25	2.00	NF
d74	The Living Thoughts of Confucius - Confucius 1959	.75	1.75	3.00	
d75	Philosophy for Pleasure - Hector Hawton	.50	1.25	2.00	NF
d76	The Living Thoughts of Spinoza - Benedictus de Spinoza	.75	1.75	3.00	
d77	Your Key to Happiness - Harold Sherman	.50	1.25	2.00	NF
d78	Understanding Other People - Stuart Palmer (S35)	.50	1.25	2.00	NF
d79	The Story of America - Hendrik Willem Van Loon	.75	1.75	3.00	NF
d80	You and the Universe - N. J. Berrill	.50	1.25	2.00	NF
d81	Much Loved Books, Volume 1 - James O'Donnell Bennett	.50	1.25	2.00	
d82	The Living Thoughts of Darwin - Charles Darwin	.50	1.25	2.00	
d83	The Inhabited Universe - Derek D. Dempster, Kenneth W. Gatland	.50	1.25	2.00	NF
d84	The Wisdom and Ideas of Plato - David Appel, Eugene Freeman	.75	1.75	3.00	
d85	Readings from World Religions - Selwyn Gurney Champion, Dorothy Short	.50	1.25	2.00	NF
d86	Discover Yourself! - Stephen Lackner	.50	1.25	2.00	NF

PRIZE

(Century Publications)

Prize 64, c. Cen   Prize 88, c. Cen   Prize Mystery 13, c. Crest

(PRIZE, continued)

64	Too Loose - Carlotta Baker	2.00	4.00	7.50	E
88	Hell's Horseman - William Hopson	2.00	4.00	7.50	W

PRIZE LOVE NOVELS

(Crestwood Publishing Co., Inc.)

Digest size

22	Old Man's Darling - John Saxon	1.50	3.50	5.00	R

PRIZE MYSTERY NOVELS

(Crestwood Publishing Company)

Digest size

1	The Rose Petal Murders - Charles G. Givens 1943	2.00	4.00	6.00	M
4	Hot Ice - R. J. Casey	1.50	3.50	5.00	M
5	And Sudden Death - Cleve F. Adams	1.50	3.50	5.00	M
6	Fall Guy for Murder - Lawrence Goldman	1.50	3.50	5.00	M
7	The Great Insurance Murders - Milton Propper	1.50	3.50	5.00	M
8	The Station Wagon Murder - Milton Propper 1944	1.50	3.50	5.00	M
9	The Third Owl - Robert J. Casey	1.50	3.50	5.00	M
10	Murder on Safari - Elspeth Huxley	1.50	3.50	5.00	M
11	The Frightened Girl - Michael Crombie	1.50	3.50	5.00	M
12	The Third Degree - Joe Barry	1.50	3.50	5.00	M
13	Sinner's Castle - S. Andrew Wood	1.50	3.50	5.00	M
14	The Purple Pony Murders - Sidney E. Porcelain 1945	1.50	3.50	5.00	M
15	The Camp-Meeting Murders - Vance Randolph & Nancy Clemens	1.50	3.50	5.00	M

Prize Mystery 14, c. Crest   Prize Mystery 21, c. Crest   Prize Mystery 27, c. Crest

16	Murder Without Motive - R. L. Goldman	1.50	3.50	5.00	M
17	Invitation to Kill - Gardner Low	1.50	3.50	5.00	M
18	Out on Bail - R. L. Goldman	1.50	3.50	5.00	M
19	Murder for Breakfast - Peter Hunt	1.50	3.50	5.00	M
20	Murder is Forgetful - William G. Bogart	1.50	3.50	5.00	M
21	The Wolf Howls Murder - Manning Lee Stokes 1946	1.50	3.50	5.00	M
22	Message from a Corpse - Sam Merwin, Jr.	1.50	3.50	5.00	M
23	Never Say Die - M. Malmar	1.50	3.50	5.00	M
25	The Thorne Theater Mystery - J. Willard	1.50	3.50	5.00	M
27	It's My Own Funeral - Dana Lyon 1947	1.50	3.50	5.00	M
28	Two Names for Death - E. P. Fenwick	1.50	3.50	5.00	M
29	The Straw Donkey Case - A. S. Fleischman	1.50	3.50	5.00	M
30	Major Crime - Oliver Keystone	1.50	3.50	5.00	M

PRIZE SCIENCE FICTION NOVELS

(Crestwood Publishing Co., Inc.)

Digest size

10	Fight for Life - Murray Leinster	2.50	6.00	10.00	SF
11	Sojarr of Titan - Manly Wade Wellman First ed., nd	2.50	6.00	10.00	SF

PRIZE WESTERN NOVELS

(Crestwood Publishing Co., Inc.)

Digest size

27	Silver City Rangers - Herbert Shappiro 1948	1.50	3.50	5.00	W
29	Gunmaster of Saddleback - D. B. Newton	1.50	3.00	5.00	W
30	Smoke of the .45 - Harry S. Drago	1.50	3.50	5.00	
32	Powder Smoke Blood - Clav Star	1.50	3.50	5.00	
34	Ramrod Vengeance - John Sims	1.50	3.50	5.00	W
35	Wyoming Trail - Walter A. Tompkins	1.50	3.50	5.00	W
36	Bravo Trail - Leigh Carder	1.50	3.50	5.00	W
37	Valley of Death - Burt Arthur	1.50	3.50	5.00	W
38	Yellow Dust - V. J. Hanson	1.50	3.50	5.00	W
39	Trouble Buster - Earl Sumner	1.50	3.50	5.00	W
40	Guns of Powder River - Lee Floren	1.50	3.50	5.00	W

PUTNAM

(G. P. Putnams Sons)

Prize SF Novels 11, c. Crest

Prize Western 27, c. Crest

Prize Western 35, c. Crest

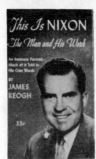

Putnam nn, c. Put   Pyramid Books 11, c. Pyb   Pyramid Books 21, c. Pyb

(PUTNAM, continued)
nn This is Nixon: The Man and his Work -
      James Keogh   1.50   3.50   5.00   NF
      1956

PYRAMID BOOKS

(Almat Publishing Corp./Pyramid Books)

Note: 1 - 10 do not exist
11	Passionate Virgin - Perry Lindsay	5.00	10.00	20.00	E
	1949, aka Brief Pleasure				
12	Reckless Passion - Gordon Sample	3.00	6.00	12.00	E
13	The Heart Beats Once - Lyon Colliers	3.00	6.00	12.00	
14	Blonde Mistress - Hall Bennett	3.00	6.00	12.00	E
15	Palm Beach Apartment - Gail Jordan	2.00	4.00	7.50	E
16	Set-up for Murder - Peter Cheyney	3.00	6.00	12.00	M
	1950				
17	Tavern Girl - Glen Watkins	3.00	6.00	12.00	E
18	Shameless Honeymoon - Thomas Stone	2.00	4.00	7.50	E
19	The Moonstone - Wilkie Collins	3.00	6.00	12.00	M
20	Terror in Times Square - Alan Handley	3.00	6.00	12.00	M
21	Sin Street - Dorine Manners	3.00	6.00	12.00	E
22	The Dead Men Grin - Bruno Fischer	3.00	6.00	12.00	M
23	Cry Shame! - Katherine Everard	3.00	6.00	12.00	E
24	The Manatee - Nancy Bruff	3.00	6.00	12.00	E
25	The Orphan Outlaw - Clarence E. Mulford	3.00	6.00	12.00	W
26	Arizona Ranger - A. Scott Leslie	3.00	6.00	12.00	W
27	Sinful Cities of the Western World -				
	Hendrik de Leeuw	3.00	6.00	12.00	E
28	The Shame of Mary Quinn - Clifton Cuthbert	3.00	6.00	12.00	E
29	Stairway to Death - Bruno Fischer	3.00	6.00	12.00	M
30	Madeleine - anonymous	2.00	4.00	7.50	E
31	Tough Town - Jack Karney	2.00	4.00	7.50	E
	1951, aka The Ragged Edge				
32	The Divided Path - Nial Kent	2.00	4.00	7.50	E
33	Roadside Night - Erwin N. Nistler &				
	Gerry P. Broderick	2.00	4.00	7.50	E

Pyramid Books 28, c. Pyb   Pyramid Books 31, c. Pyb   Pyramid Books 58, c. Pyb

34	Rustlers' Range - Bradford Scott	2.00	4.00	7.50	W
35	French Doctor - Louis-Charles Royer	2.00	4.00	7.50	E
36	Tombstone Trail - A. Scott Leslie	2.00	4.00	7.50	W
37	Farm Girl - William Brown Meloney	3.00	6.00	12.00	E
	aka Rusty to the Sun				
38	The Raft - Robert Trumbull	3.00	6.00	12.00	A
39	Swamp Girl - Evans Wall	3.00	6.00	12.00	E
40	Texas Fury - Jackson Cole	2.00	4.00	7.50	W
41	The House of Madame Tellier -				
	Guy de Maupassant	3.00	6.00	12.00	E
	1952				
G42	The King's Mistress - Jean Plaidy	3.00	6.00	12.00	E
	aka The Goldsmith's Wife				
G43	Teen-Age Vice! - Courtney Ryley Cooper	4.00	8.00	15.00	JD
44	The Stranger in Boots - A. Scott Leslie	2.00	4.00	7.50	W
45	I am a Fugitive from a Chain Gang -				
	Robert E. Burns	5.00	10.00	20.00	
	movie tie-in				
46	23 Women - anonymous	4.00	8.00	15.00	E
47	Thunder Range - Jackson Cole	2.00	4.00	7.50	W
G48	Cage of Lust - Allan Seager	2.00	4.00	7.50	E
	aka Equinox				
49	A Diary of Love - Maude Hutchins	2.00	4.00	7.50	E
G50	Yama, the Hell-hole - Alexandre Kuprin	3.00	6.00	12.00	E
	1952				
51	Border Hell - Jackson Cole	2.00	4.00	7.50	W
G52	Tillie - David Westheimer	3.00	6.00	12.00	E
	1952, aka Summer on the Water				
53	The Bruiser - Jim Tully	2.00	4.00	7.50	
G54	Yankee Trader - Stanley Morton	2.00	4.00	7.50	E
55	Downfall - Bentz Plagemann	2.00	4.00	7.50	E
56	The Death Riders - Jackson Cole	2.00	4.00	7.50	W
G57	The Wild Ones - Vardis Fisher	2.00	4.00	7.50	E
58	Female Convict - as told to Vincent E. Burns	3.00	6.00	12.00	NF
G59	Sweet Man - Gilmore Millen	3.00	6.00	12.00	E
G60	Bitter Love - Dyson Taylor	2.00	4.00	7.50	E
61	The Texan - A. Scott Leslie	2.00	4.00	7.50	W
62	Let's Go Naked - Don Wollheim	3.00	6.00	12.00	E
63	Apache Devil - Edwin Corle	3.00	6.00	12.00	W
G64	The Heavenly Sinner - Everett Harre	2.00	4.00	7.50	E
65	One Way Street - Nick Morino	2.00	4.00	7.50	
66	Trigger Law - Jackson Cole	2.00	4.00	7.50	W
G67	Hospital Doctor - Edward Young	2.00	4.00	7.50	E
68	Georgia Hotel - Scott Laurence	2.00	4.00	7.50	E
G69	The Brute - Buy des Cars	2.00	4.00	7.50	E
70	Massacre Canyon - Jackson Cole	2.00	4.00	7.50	W
	1953				
71	A Woman of Paris - Andre Tellier	2.00	4.00	7.50	E
G72	The Dark Urge - Robert W. Taylor	2.00	4.00	7.50	E
73	Killer Country - Jackson Cole	2.00	4.00	7.50	E
74	The Come-On - Whitman Chambers	2.00	4.00	7.50	E
G75	Pirate Wench - Frank Shay	3.00	6.00	12.00	A
	1953				
76	Two Years Before the Mast -				
	Richard Henry Dana	2.00	4.00	7.50	A
G77	Stella and Joe - Lester Cohen	2.00	4.00	7.50	E
	1953, aka Coming Home				
78	Blood Feud - Dave Ricks	2.00	4.00	7.50	W

Pyramid Books 63, c. Pyb   Pyramid Books 68, c. Pyb   Pyramid Books 76, c. Pyb

Pyramid Books 80, c. Pyb   Pyramid Books 84, c. Pyb   Pyramid Books 92, c. Pyb

(PYRAMID BOOKS, continued)

79	The Heel - William L. Rohde	2.00	4.00	7.50	E
80	Beware the Lady - Cornell Woolrich	3.00	6.00	12.00	E
	1953, aka The Bride Wore Black				
81	Texas Fists - Jackson Cole	2.00	4.00	7.50	W
82	Loves of Groya - Marion Chapman	2.00	4.00	7.50	E
83	The Bohemian - Jules Koslow	2.00	4.00	7.50	E
84	Love Camp - Louis-Charles Royer	4.00	8.00	15.00	E
85	Chinese Lover - Charles Pettit	3.00	6.00	12.00	E
G86	The Spitfires - Beril Becker	2.00	4.00	7.50	E
	1953, aka Whirlwind in Petticoats				
87	Gun-Runners - Jackson Cole	2.00	4.00	7.50	W
G88	The Moonstone - Wilkie Collins	2.00	4.00	7.50	M
89	She-Devil - Harry Hervey	2.00	4.00	7.50	E
90	Chicago Woman - Robert O. Saber	2.00	4.00	7.50	E
	aka The Dove				
91	Land Grab - Jackson Cole	2.00	4.00	7.50	W
92	Road Show - Jim Tully	3.00	6.00	12.00	E
93	Houseboy - Walton Fairbanks	3.00	6.00	12.00	E
94	Sailor's Leave - Brian Moore	2.00	4.00	7.50	E
95	Showdown Trail - William Colt MacDonald	2.00	4.00	7.50	W
96	Mimi - Robert W. Taylor	2.00	4.00	7.50	E
	1953				
97	The Big Fake - Murray Forbes	2.00	4.00	7.50	E
	1953, aka Hollow Triumph				
98	The Sea Tyrant - Peter Freuchen	2.00	4.00	7.50	E
99	There Goes Shorty Higgins - Jack Karney	2.00	4.00	7.50	A
100	Cellini - Beneveuutlo Cellini	2.00	4.00	7.50	A
	1953				
101	Cow Thief - William Colt MacDonald	2.00	4.00	7.50	W
102	African Mistress - Louis-Charles Royer	3.00	6.00	12.00	E
103	Backstairs - L. K. Scott	2.00	4.00	7.50	E
104	Big Mike - Charles Givens	2.00	4.00	7.50	M
	1953, aka Anchor Money				
105	Lesson in Love - Emile Zola	2.00	4.00	7.50	E
	aka Pot-Bouille				
106	The Ordeal of Pvt. Heath - Jeb Stuart	2.00	4.00	7.50	
107	Scandal - Robert W. Taylor	2.00	4.00	7.50	E
	Original, 1954				
108	Texas Tornado - Jackson Cole	2.00	4.00	7.50	W
109	After Dark - Max White	2.00	4.00	7.50	E
110	The Redhead from Chicago - Louis-Charles Royer	2.00	4.00	7.50	E
111	Gun Town - Jackson Cole	2.00	4.00	7.50	W
112	Hill Man - John Garth	2.00	4.00	7.50	E
113	Sporting Lady - Gene Gauntier	2.00	4.00	7.50	E
114	The Harem - Louis-Charles Royer	3.00	6.00	12.00	E
115	Two-Gun Deputy - William Colt MacDonald	2.00	4.00	7.50	W
116	His Kind of Woman - Michael Morgan	2.00	4.00	7.50	E
117	Outlawed - Jackson Cole	2.00	4.00	7.50	W
118	Woman on the Wall - Marshall McClintock	2.00	4.00	7.50	E
119	The Great Balsamo - Maurice Zolotow	2.00	4.00	7.50	E
G120	The Counsul at Sunset - Gerald Hanley	1.50	3.50	5.00	E
121	With Sirens Screaming - Ernest Booth	1.50	3.50	5.00	E
122	I Was a Drug Addict - Leroy Street & David Loth	3.00	6.00	12.00	
123	Blind Alley - Bant Singer	1.50	3.50	5.00	
124	Bullets High - Jackson Cole	2.00	4.00	7.50	W

(PYRAMID BOOKS, continued)

#	Title - Author				
125	Bold Moment - Victor H. Johnson	2.00	4.00	7.50	E
	1954, aka The Horncasters				
126	The Junk Pusher - Robert W. Taylor	3.00	6.00	12.00	E
G127	Teen-Age Vice! - Courtney Ryley Cooper	3.00	6.00	12.00	NF
128	One for the Road - Robert Dietrich	1.50	3.50	5.00	E
G129	Dark Brother - Gerald Gordon	3.00	6.00	12.00	E
130	A Diary of Love - Maude Hutchins	2.00	4.00	7.50	E
131	Ex-Con - Stuart Friedman	2.00	4.00	7.50	
132	Jungle Heat - Dale Wilmer	1.50	3.50	5.00	
	Orig., 1954				
133	Pierre's Woman - Jacques de Bout	1.50	3.50	5.00	E
134	Savage Triangle - Louis-Charles Royer	2.00	4.00	7.50	E
135	The Cheat - Robert Dietrich	1.50	3.50	5.00	E
136	Night in Manila - John Laugdon	1.50	3.50	5.00	E
G137	The King's Mistress - Jean Plaidy	2.00	4.00	7.50	E
138	His Father's Wife - Day Keene	1.50	3.50	5.00	E
	Orig., 1954				
139	I Was a House Detective - Dev Collans &				
	Stewart Sterling	2.00	4.00	7.50	E
	1955				
G140	Yankee Trader - Stanley Morton	3.00	6.00	12.00	E
G141	The Wild Ones - Vardis Fisher	3.00	6.00	12.00	E
G142	Sweet Man - Gilmore Millen	3.00	6.00	12.00	E
143	Lovers in the Sun - Robert Payne	1.50	3.50	5.00	E
	Orig., 1955				
144	Texas Manhunt - Jackson Cole	2.00	4.00	7.50	W
G145	Cage of Lust - Allan Seager	1.50	3.50	5.00	E
G146	The Heavenly Sinner - Everett Harre	1.50	3.50	5.00	E
147	For I Have Sinned	1.50	3.50	5.00	E
148	Roadside Night - Gerry P. Broderick &				
	Erwin N. Nistler	1.50	3.50	5.00	E
149	The Texan - A. Scott Leslie	1.50	3.50	5.00	W
G150	Devil's Cargo - Si Podolin	2.00	4.00	7.50	E
	1955				
151	The Proposition - Hunt Collins	1.50	3.50	5.00	E
152	Just Married	2.00	4.00	7.50	H
153	Gunsmoke Trail - Jackson Cole	1.50	3.50	5.00	W
G154	Farm Girl - William Brown Meloney	2.00	4.00	7.50	E
155	Trouble Shooter - Jackson Cole	1.50	3.50	5.00	W
156	Dangerous Game - anthology	1.50	3.50	5.00	A
G157	Shriek with Pleasure - Toni Howard	1.50	3.50	5.00	E
158	Diary of a Nun - Oscar de Mejo	1.50	3.50	5.00	
159	One Way Street - Nick Marino	2.00	4.00	7.50	
G160	Tell Me, Doctor - Dr. Henry B. Safford	1.50	3.50	5.00	NF
G161	Mademoiselle De Maupin - Theophile Gautier	2.00	4.00	7.50	E
162	Gun-Blaze - Jackson Cole	1.50	3.50	5.00	W
163	Bed of Hate - Si Podolin	1.50	3.50	5.00	E
164	Of a Strange Woman - James Wakefield Burke	1.50	3.50	5.00	E
165	Town Quarry - Martin Manners	1.50	3.50	5.00	E
166	French Doctor - Louis-Charles Royer	2.00	4.00	7.50	E
167	Texas Fury - Jackson Cole	2.00	4.00	7.50	W
168	Swamp Girl - Evans Wall	2.00	4.00	7.50	E
169	Shadow at Noon - Harry White	1.50	3.50	5.00	W
G170	Strange Friends - Agnete Holk	1.50	3.50	5.00	E
171	Two-Gun Devil - Jackson Cole	1.50	3.50	5.00	W
172	The Range Kid - William Cole MacDonald	1.50	3.50	5.00	W
173	Brand of Cain - Wade B. Cantrell	1.50	3.50	5.00	W
174	The Wanton Hour - Lewis Clay	1.50	3.50	5.00	E

Pyramid Books 125, c. Pyb   Pyramid Books 144, c. Pyb   Pyramid Books 156, c. Pyb

Pyramid Books 183, c. Pyb   Pyramid Books 209, c. Pyb   Pyramid Books 238, c. Pyb

(PYRAMID BOOKS, continued)

175	Madeleine - anonymous	1.50	3.50	5.00	E
176	Love Off-Limits - Arthur Curtin 1956	1.50	3.50	5.00	E
G177	Pere Goriot - Honore De Balzac	1.50	3.50	5.00	
178	The Texas Terror - Bradford Scott	1.50	3.50	5.00	W
179	The Shame of Mary Quinn - Clifton Cuthbert	1.50	3.50	5.00	E
G180	The Seed of McCoy - Jack London	3.00	6.00	12.00	A
G181	My Sister, My Bride - Merriam Modell	2.00	4.00	7.50	E
182	The Owlhoot Trail - Buck Billings	1.50	3.50	5.00	W
183	The World's Worst Women - Bernard O'Donnell	3.00	6.00	12.00	E
G184	A Way Home - Theodore Sturgeon (ed. by Groff Conklin)	2.00	4.00	7.50	SF
G185	The Sin Underneath - Beutz Plagemann aka Into the Labyrinth aka Downfall	1.50	3.50	5.00	E
186	Trigger Talk - Bradford Scott	1.50	3.50	5.00	
187	Gunman's Gold - Johnston McCulley	2.00	4.00	7.50	W
R188	It's Never Too Late to Leave - Anna K. Daniels	1.50	3.50	5.00	
G189	Shadows & Shame - John Taylor	1.50	3.50	5.00	E
190	Badland's Boss - Bradford Scott	1.50	3.50	5.00	W
191	Female Convict - as told to Vincent G. Burns	2.00	4.00	7.50	NF
192	Range Rebel - Gordon D. Shirreffs	1.50	3.50	5.00	W
193	Taking a Turn for the Nurse - Kaz	2.00	4.00	7.50	H
194	The Gunhand - Paul Evan Lehman	1.50	3.50	5.00	W
195	The Six-Gun Syndicate - Norman A. Fox	1.50	3.50	5.00	W
196	Let's Go Naked - ed. Donald A. Wollheim	2.00	4.00	7.50	H
G197	The Future Mr. Dolan - Charles Gorhom	1.50	3.50	5.00	E
198	Hell and High Water - ed. Michael Dewell	1.50	3.50	5.00	A
199	Canyon Killers - Bradford Scott	1.50	3.50	5.00	W
200	The Girl on the Couch - Georgiana Hunter 156	1.50	3.50	5.00	E
G201	Celeste - Rosamond Marshall	1.50	3.50	5.00	E
R202	The House of Madame Tellier - Guy de Maupassant	1.50	3.50	5.00	E
203	Lynch Law - Paul Evan	1.50	3.50	5.00	W
204	The Stranger in Boots - A. Scott Leslie	1.50	3.50	5.00	W
205	Playgirls, U. S. A. - Eddie Davis	1.50	3.50	5.00	
G206	Creep into Thy Narrow Bed - Leonard Bishop	1.50	3.50	5.00	E
R207	Yama, the Hell-Hole - Alexandre Kuprin	2.00	4.00	7.50	E
208	The Big Gun - James Cavanaugh	1.50	3.50	5.00	W
209	Gunsmoke Over Texas - Bradford Scott	1.50	3.50	5.00	W
R210	Women and Vodka - ed. Mark Merrill	2.00	4.00	7.50	E
R211	Drinkers of Darkness - Gerald Hanley	1.50	3.50	5.00	E
G212	The Other Side of the Street - Shirley Jackson	2.00	4.00		
G213	The Miracle of Growth - Arnold Sundgaard	1.50	3.50	5.00	NF
G214	Tomorrow and Tomorrow - Hunt Collins	2.00	4.00	7.50	SF
215	Houseboy - Walton Fairbanks	1.50	3.50	5.00	E
216	Outlaw Brand - Tom West	1.50	3.50	5.00	W
G217	The Man from Paris - Louis Charles Royer	1.50	3.50	5.00	E
G218	Wild Country - Noel M. Loomis	1.50	3.50	5.00	E
219	The Avenger - Bradford Scott	1.50	3.50	5.00	W
220	Border Blood - Bradford Scott	1.50	3.50	5.00	W
221	Pyramid Crossword Book - Jack Luzzatto	3.00	6.00	12.00	NF
G222	The Jealous Mistress - Paul Elbogen	1.50	3.50	5.00	E
R223	The Intimate Problems of Women - Henry B. Safford	2.00	4.00	7.50	NF

G224	The Damned One - Guy des Cars	1.50	3.50	5.00	E
225	A gunman Rode North - William Hopson 1956	1.50	3.50	5.00	W
G226	Give Me a Little Something - William L. Rohde	1.50	3.50	5.00	E
G227	The Love Makers - Mark Merrill	1.50	3.50	5.00	E
G228	Handwriting Analysis - Dorothy Sara	1.50	3.50	5.00	NF
229	Bold Moment - Victor H. Johnson aka The Horncasters	1.50	3.50	5.00	E
230	Reach for Your Guns - Curtis Bishop	1.50	3.50	5.00	W
231	Flaming Lead - William Colt MacDonald	1.50	3.50	5.00	W
R232	Woman Without Love - Andre Maurois	1.50	3.50	5.00	E
G233	Tillie - David Westheimer	2.00	4.00	7.50	E
G234	Men Against the Stars - Martin Greenberg 1957	1.50	3.50	5.00	SF
235	One for the Road - Robert Dietrich	1.50	3.50	5.00	E
R236	The Hearth and the Strangeness - N. Martin Kramer	1.50	3.50	5.00	E
R237	How to Help Your Husband Get Ahead - Mrs. Dale Carnegie	1.50	3.50	5.00	
238	Dead Man's Trail - Bradford Scott	1.50	3.50	5.00	W
G239	Feud at Five Rivers - Jack April	1.50	3.50	5.00	W
G240	Sex Is Better in College - ed. Henry Boltinoff	2.00	4.00	7.50	H
G241	The Night it Happened - Martin Manners	1.50	3.50	5.00	E
G242	Come See Them Die - Harold Hadley	1.50	3.50	5.00	
R243	Death Be Not Proud - John Gunther	1.50	3.50	5.00	
G244	Gone to Texas - ed. Leo Marguiles	1.50	3.50	5.00	W
245	Blood Brand - Larry Lawson	1.50	3.50	5.00	W
R246	Sex and Marriage - Havelock Ellis	1.50	3.50	5.00	NF
G247	The Synthetic Man - Theodore Sturgeon	2.00	4.00	7.50	SF
G248	Tonight It's Me - Robert Schlick	1.50	3.50	5.00	
G249	Sin Street - Dorine Manners	1.50	3.50	5.00	E
250	The Gun Crasher - William L. Rohde 1957	1.50	3.50	5.00	W
251	Rimrock Raiders - Leslie Scott	1.50	3.50	5.00	W
G252	Teenage Vice! - Courtney Ryley Cooper	2.00	4.00	7.50	JD
G253	Unrepentant Sinners - Lovis-Charles Royer	.75	1.75	3.00	
G254	The Lusty Men - William R. Cox	.75	1.75	3.00	
255	Double-cross Ranch - Stuart Brock	1.50	3.50	5.00	W
R256	Why Can't We Have a Baby? - James Henry Ferguson	1.50	3.50	5.00	
R257	Crescent City - William E. Wilson	.75	1.75	3.00	
258	Powder Burn - Bradford Scott	1.50	3.50	5.00	W
259	Gunhand's Play - Archie Joscelyn	1.50	3.50	5.00	W
G260	The First Time - Chandler Brossard	.75	1.75	3.00	
G261	I Was a House Detective - Dev Collans & Stewart Sterling	1.50	3.50	5.00	E
G262	Twilight Men - Andre Tellier	1.50	3.50	5.00	
G263	Taboo - James Wakefield Burke	1.50	3.50	5.00	E
264	Curse of Texas Gold - Bradford Scott	1.50	3.50	5.00	W
265	Bravo Trail - Eugene Cunningham	1.50	3.50	5.00	W
G266	His Father's Wife - Day Keene	.75	1.75	3.00	E
G267	The Fourth World - Daphne Athas	.75	1.75	3.00	
G268	Impossible Greeting Cards - Len Levinson	.75	1.75	3.00	
269	Gunsmoke Mesa - Dan James	1.50	3.50	5.00	W
G270	Stairway to Death - Bruno Fischer	1.50	3.50	5.00	M
G271	The Young Punks - ed. Leo Margulies	1.50	3.50	5.00	
G272	Georgia Hotel - Scott Lawrence	.75	1.75	3.00	E
R273	Take Off Your Mask - Ludwig Eidelberg	.75	1.75	3.00	
G274	This Girl for Hire - G. G. Fickling	.75	1.75	3.00	
G275	The Fuzzy Pink Nightgown - Sylvia Tate 1957	.75	1.75	3.00	
G276	Thunderbird Trail - William Colt MacDonald	1.50	3.50	5.00	W
G277	The Law Bringers - Bliss Lomax (H.S. Drago)	1.50	3.50	5.00	W
G278	Bitter Love - Dyson Taylor	.75	1.75	3.00	E
R279	Inherit the Night - Robert Christie	.75	1.75	3.00	
G280	Yellow Kid Weil - William T. Brannon	2.00	4.00	7.50	B
R281	Gestapo - Edward Crankshaw	1.50	3.50	5.00	
282	The Texas Hawk - Bradford Scott	.75	1.75	3.00	W
G283	V. I. P. - William L. Rohde	.75	1.75	3.00	
G284	The Name Is Chambers - Henry Kane	.75	1.75	3.00	M
G285	All His Women - Daniel Taylor	.75	1.75	3.00	
286	Two-gun Deputy - William Colt MacDonald	.75	1.75	3.00	W
287	The Sheriff - Forrest Covington	.75	1.75	3.00	W
G288	Smoke Among the Plains - Vingie Roe	.75	1.75	3.00	W
R289	I Am Adam - Maxine Kaufman	.75	1.75	3.00	

Pyramid Books R290, c. Pyb Pyramid Books G352, c. Pyb Pyramid Books G392, c. Pyb

(PYRAMID BOOKS, continued)

R290	Frankenstein - Mary Wollstonecraft Shelley	1.50	3.50	5.00	SF
G291	Isle of the Damned - George John Seaton	1.50	3.50	5.00	
G292	You're Wrong, Delaney - Charles Shaw	.75	1.75	3.00	
293	Death Canyon - Bradford Scott	.75	1.75	3.00	W
294	The Range Kid - William Colt MacDonald	.75	1.75	3.00	W
G295	The Daughter - Arthur Markowitz	.75	1.75	3.00	
G296	Here's the Answer - Albert Mitchell	.75	1.75	3.00	
G297	Hospital Doctor - Edward Young	.75	1.75	3.00	E
G298	Hellflower - George O. Smith	2.00	4.00	7.50	SF
G299	Perfect 36 - Ed Spingarn	.75	1.75	3.00	
R300	Michael Strogoff - Jules Verne	1.50	3.50	5.00	A
	1957				
G301	She-Devil - Harry Hervey	.75	1.75	3.00	E
302	Tombstone Showdown - Leslie Scott	.75	1.75	3.00	W
303	Blood-moon Range - Bob Obets	.75	1.75	3.00	W
G304	The Case of the Attic Lover - Alan Hynd	.75	1.75	3.00	
R305	Mrs. Parkington - Louis Bromfield	.75	1.75	3.00	
	c-Maguire				
G306	Dead Wrong - Larry Holden	.75	1.75	3.00	
307	The Hard Men - Roe Richmond	.75	1.75	3.00	W
	1958, aka Riders of Red Butte				
308	Shootin' Man - Bradford Scott	.75	1.75	3.00	W
G309	Yaller Gal - Carolina Lee	1.50	3.50	5.00	E
G310	The Wild Ones - Vardis Fisher	.75	1.75	3.00	E
G311	Fury With Legs - Gil Lawrence	.75	1.75	3.00	
G312	Bedlam - Andre Soubiran	.75	1.75	3.00	
	c-Maguire				
G313	Flame of the Osage - Fred Grove	.75	1.75	3.00	W
314	High Trail - R. D. Whitinger	.75	1.75	3.00	W
G315	City Limits - Nick Marino	.75	1.75	3.00	
R316	The Affairs of Casanova - Giacomo Casanova	.75	1.75	3.00	E
G317	French Doctor - Louis-Charles Royer	.75	1.75	3.00	E
R318	The Death of Hitler's Germany - Georges Blond	2.00	4.00	7.50	NF
319	The Blaze of Guns - Bradford Scott	.75	1.75	3.00	W
G320	Love Camp - Louis-Charles Royer	2.00	4.00	7.50	
G321	The Hills Beyond - Thomas Wolfe	.75	1.75	3.00	
G322	Twenty-one - Jack Barry	.75	1.75	3.00	
G323	Seven Days to Death - J. J. Marric	.75	1.75	3.00	M
G324	Baseball Stars of 1958 - Ray Robinson	1.50	3.50	5.00	S
325	Naked Spurs - Larry Lawson	.75	1.75	3.00	W
	1958				
G326	House of Dolls - Ka-Tzetnik	1.50	3.50	5.00	NF
G327	Take My Face - Peter Held (Jack Vance)	3.00	6.00	12.00	M
G328	The Mustard Seed - Vicki Baum	.75	1.75	3.00	
G329	Hangtree Country - Eric Allen	.75	1.75	3.00	W
R330	Hitler's Secret Service - Walter Schellenberg	1.50	3.50	5.00	NF
G331	Curve Ball Laughs - Herman L. Masin	.75	1.75	3.00	H
G332	The Skylark of Space - E. E. "Doc" Smith	1.50	3.50	5.00	SF
333	Railtown Sheriff - Stuart Brock	.75	1.75	3.00	W
G334	The Girl on the Couch - Georgiana Hunter	.75	1.75	3.00	E
G335	Gideon's Night - J. J. Marric	.75	1.75	3.00	M
G336	Cropper's Cabin - Jim Thompson	.75	1.75	3.00	
G337	Operation Cicero - L. C. Moyzisch	1.50	3.50	5.00	NF
G338	The Sleeper - Holly Roth	.75	1.75	3.00	
G339	Who? - Algis Budrys	1.50	3.50	5.00	SF
R340	Brainwashing - Edward Hunter	1.50	3.50	5.00	

G341	Strange Fulfillment - Denys Val Baker	.75	1.75	3.00	
G342	Never the Same Again - Gerald Tesch	.75	1.75	3.00	
G343	Bed and Broad - ed. Henry Boltinoff	.75	1.75	3.00	H
G344	A Gun for Honey - G. G. Fickling	.75	1.75	3.00	
G345	Prison Girl - Wenzell Brown c-Maguire	1.50	3.50	5.00	E
G346	Cartoons for Men Only - Sandy Nelkin	.75	1.75	3.00	H
347	The Young Texan - Paul Evan Lehman	.75	1.75	3.00	W
G348	House of Hate - W. Craig Thomas	.75	1.75	3.00	
G349	The Lost Combat - Ralph Leveridge	.75	1.75	3.00	
G350	The Name is Malone - Craig Rice	.75	1.75	3.00	M
	1958				
G351	70,000 to 1 - Quentin Reynolds	.75	1.75	3.00	
G352	Rumble - Harlan Ellison	10.00	25.00	40.00	JD
	orig., 1958				
G353	Room to Swing - Ed Lacy c-Maguire	.75	1.75	3.00	M
G354	Night Man - Lucille Fletcher & Allan Ullman	.75	1.75	3.00	
G355	The Case of the Nameless Corpse -				
	Clarence Budington Kelland	.75	1.75	3.00	
G356	Lincoln's Commando - Ralph J. Roske &				
	Charles Van Doren	1.50	3.50	5.00	NF
G357	Mr. Arkadin - Orson Welles	1.50	3.50	5.00	
G358	Killer Colt - James Woodruff Smith	.75	1.75	3.00	W
G359	Sidewalk Caesar - Donald Honig	.75	1.75	3.00	
G360	The Megstone Plot - Andrew Garve	.75	1.75	3.00	
G361	The Scarlet Treasury of Great Confessions -				
	Whit Burnett	1.50	3.50	5.00	
G362	Good Luck to the Corpse - Max Murray	.75	1.75	3.00	M
G363	The Mad Marshal - William Colt MacDonald	.75	1.75	3.00	W
G364	The Bad Girls - Bud Clifton	.75	1.75	3.00	
G365	All Thy Conquests - Alfred Hayes	.75	1.75	3.00	
G366	Girl on the Loose - G. G. Fickling	.75	1.75	3.00	
R367	My Brother's Bride - William March	.75	1.75	3.00	
G368	The Man of Cold Rages - Jordan Park				
	(C. M. Kornbluth)	3.00	6.00	12.00	
G369	Summer Boy - Walter Lowrey	.75	1.75	3.00	
370	Thunderbird Range - W. C. Tuttle	1.50	3.50	5.00	W
G371	I Cried in the Dark - Ann Scott	.75	1.75	3.00	
G372	The Crimson in the Purple - Holly Roth	.75	1.75	3.00	
	c-Maguire				
G373	The Fastest Man Alive - Frank K. Everest, Jr.				
	& John Guenther	.75	1.75	3.00	NF
G374	Death is My Cancing Partner -				
	Cornell Woolrich	1.50	3.50	5.00	M
G375	Platoon - Adam Singer	.75	1.75	3.00	
	1958				
G376	West of the Pecos - Paul Evan	.75	1.75	3.00	W
G377	Female Convict - as told to Vincent G. Burns	1.50	3.50	5.00	NF
G378	An Outcast of the Islands - Joseph Conrad	1.50	3.50	5.00	
	Orig., 1959				
G379	The Spy - Vincent Brome	.75	1.75	3.00	
G380	These Lonely, These Dead - Robert Colby	.75	1.75	3.00	
G381	The New Italian Cook Book - Rose L. Sorce	1.50	3.50	5.00	NF
G382	So Soon to Die - Jeremy York	.75	1.75	3.00	
G383	The Silver Dark - Herbert Clyde Lewis	.75	1.75	3.00	
G384	Whisper of Love - Fletcher Flora	.75	1.75	3.00	
G385	The Survivor - John Ehle	.75	1.75	3.00	
G386	The Young Punks - ed. Leo Margulies	1.50	3.50	5.00	
G387	The Dream and the Flesh - Vivian Connell	.75	1.75	3.00	
	c-Maguire				
G388	Never Smile at Children - E. T. French	.75	1.75	3.00	
389	Gallows Trail - Garth Davis	.75	1.75	3.00	W
G390	Vera - Robert Scott Taylor	.75	1.75	3.00	
G391	The Black Orchid - Edward Ronns	.75	1.75	3.00	
G392	Baseball Stars of 1959 - Ray Robinson	2.00	4.00	7.50	S
G393	The Lost One - Dana Lyon	.75	1.75	3.00	
394	How Sharp the Point - P. J. Wolfson	.75	1.75	3.00	W
	Orig., 1959				
G395	So Dead, My Lovely - Day Keene	.75	1.75	3.00	M
	c-Maguire				
396	The Longhorn Brand - Wade Hamilton	.75	1.75	3.00	W
G397	Off the Beaten Orbit - Judith Merril	2.00	4.00	7.50	SF
G398	Sins of Their Fathers - Marjorie Rittwagen	.75	1.75	3.00	
G399	The Beauty Makers - Nedda Lamont	.75	1.75	3.00	
G400	The Husband - Vera Caspary	.75	1.75	3.00	
	1959				

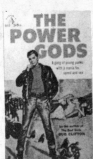  

Pyramid Books G410, c. Pyb Pyramid Books R419, c. Pyb Pyramid Books G462, c. Pyb

(PYRAMID BOOKS, continued)

G401	Five Who Vanished - Robert Levin	.75	1.75	3.00	
G402	City of Chains - William E. Pettit	.75	1.75	3.00	
403	Rimrock Renegade - Wade Hamilton	.75	1.75	3.00	W
G404	Take Off Your Mask - Ludwig Eidelberg	.75	1.75	3.00	
G405	Al Capone - John Roeburt	1.50	3.50	5.00	
G406	War Fish - George Grider & Lydel Sims	.75	1.75	3.00	C
G407	The Affair - Hans Koningsberger	.75	1.75	3.00	
G408	Hilda, Take Heed - Jeremy York	.75	1.75	3.00	
409	Dead in Texas - Bradford Scott	.75	1.75	3.00	W
G410	The Power Gods - Bud Clifton	2.00	4.00	7.50	JD
G411	Honey in the Flesh - G. G. Fickling	.75	1.75	3.00	
G412	The Oracle - Edwin O'Connor	.75	1.75	3.00	
	c-Maguire				
G413	The Shame of Mary Quinn - Clifton Cuthbert	.75	1.75	3.00	E
G414	Born Innocent - Creighton Brown-Burnham	.75	1.75		
G415	The Bride is Much Too Beautiful - Odette Joyeux	.75	1.75	3.00	
G416	The Falling Torch - Algis Budrys	2.00	4.00	7.50	SF
G417	The Red Lily - Anatole France	.75	1.75	3.00	
R418	Five Soldiers - Paul Vialar	.75	1.75	3.00	C
R419	The Divine Passion - Vardis Fisher	3.00	6.00	12.00	E
	c-Maguire				
420	Texas Badman - Bradford Scott	.75	1.75	3.00	W
G421	The Passionate Season - Victor Wolfson	.75	1.75	3.00	
G422	Mamma's Boarding House - John D. Fitzgerald	.75	1.75	3.00	
G423	Make Mine Love - Faber Birren	.75	1.75	3.00	
G424	The Banker's Daughter - Vladimir B. Grinioff	.75	1.75	3.00	
G425	Acts of Violence - William Kozlenko	.75	1.75	3.00	
	1959				
426	The Range Terror - Bradford Scott	.75	1.75	3.00	
	orig., Walt Sladewestern				
G427	A Really Sincere Guy - Robert Van Riper	.75	1.75	3.00	
G428	Celeste - Rosamond Marshall	.75	1.75	3.00	E
G429	Crime Cop - Larry Holden	.75	1.75	3.00	
G430	That Kind of Woman - Robert Lowry	.75	1.75	3.00	
G431	One to Grow On - Nathaniel Benchley	.75	1.75	3.00	
G432	Private Eyeful - Henry Kane	.75	1.75	3.00	M
	c-Maguire				
R433	10,000 Eyes - Richard Collier	.75	1.75	3.00	
G434	Four for the Future - ed. Groff Conklin	1.50	3.50	5.00	SF
435	Texas Vengeance - Bradford Scott	.75	1.75	3.00	W
G436	A Diary of Love - Maude Hutchins	.75	1.75	3.00	E
G437	Slaughter Street - Louis Falstein	.75	1.75	3.00	
G438	So Love Returns - Robert Nathan	.75	1.75	3.00	
G439	The Hoods Ride In - Wenzell Brown	2.00	4.00	7.50	JD
G440	No Nice Girl - Gale Wilhelm	.75	1.75	3.00	
G441	Seeds of Murder - Jeremy York	.75	1.75	3.00	
442	Gun Law - Bradford Scott	.75	1.75	3.00	W
G443	Dark Violence - Lee Bergman	.75	1.75	3.00	
G444	Cut Me In - Jack Karney	.75	1.75	3.00	
G445	But Not for Me - Edward Ronns	.75	1.75	3.00	
G446	The Magnificent Female - Cecil Saint-Laurent	.75	1.75	3.00	
R447	Leave Her to Heaven - Ben Ames Williams	.75	1.75	3.00	
G448	Dead in Bead - Day Keene	.75	1.75	3.00	M
G449	The Future Mr. Dolan - Charles Gorham	.75	1.75	3.00	
G450	Enemy in Sight - J. E. MacDonnell	.75	1.75	3.00	
	1959				

G451	Guns Between Suns - William Colt MacDonald	.75	1.75	3.00	W
G452	The Divided Path - Nial Kent	.75	1.75	3.00	E
G453	Girl on the Prowl - G. G. Fickling	.75	1.75	3.00	E
G454	Possessed - Anne Chamberlain	.75	1.75	3.00	
455	Holster Law - Bradford Scott orig., 1959	.75	1.75	3.00	W
G456	Hungry Men - Edward Anderson	.75	1.75	3.00	
G457	The Big Bedroom - Edward Ronns	.75	1.75	3.00	
G458	Man of Many Minds - E. Everett Evans	2.00	4.00	7.50	SF
R459	Cookbook of Fabulous Foods for People You Love - Carolyn Coggins	.75	1.75	3.00	NF
G460	Farm Girl - William Brown Meloney	.75	1.75	3.00	E
G461	The Long Night - Julian Mayfield	.75	1.75	3.00	
G462	Fire in My Blood - Lady Newborough c-Maguire	3.00	6.00	12.00	E
G463	Court Martial - Jack Ehrlich	.75	1.75	3.00	
G464	Tough Cop - John Roeburt	.75	1.75	3.00	
G465	The Loner - James Woodruff Smith	.75	1.75	3.00	
G466	Rooming House - Berton Roueche	.75	1.75	3.00	
G467	Gestapo - Edward Crankshaw	1.50	3.50	5.00	
G468	The Woman Racket - Gil Lawrence	1.50	3.50	5.00	
469	Maggy - Sara Seale	2.00	4.50	8.00	R
470	The Cat in the Convoy - William G. Schofield	3.00	7.50	15.00	
471	Nursey Hilary - Peggy Gaddis	2.00	4.50	8.00	R
472	Young Doctor Kirkdene - Elizabeth Hoy	2.00	4.50	8.00	R
473	The Cockoo in Spring - Elizabeth Cadell	2.00	4.50	8.00	R
474	Towards the Dawn - Jane Arbor	2.00	4.50	8.00	R
475	The Mind of Mr. J.G. Reeder - Edgar Wallace 1959	3.00	7.50	15.00	M
476	Nurse Jess - Joyce Dingwell	2.00	4.50	8.00	R
477	Hospital Blue - Anne Vinton	2.00	4.50	8.00	R
478	Dear Trustee - Mary Burchell	2.00	4.50	8.00	R
479	The Case of the Ebony Queen - Cleo Adkins	3.00	7.50	15.00	
480	Grey Cup Cavalcade - Tony Allan	3.00	7.50	15.00	
481	Bachelor of Medicine - Alex Stuart	2.00	4.50	8.00	R
482	Nurse Harlowe - Jane Arbor	2.00	4.50	8.00	R
483	My Heart has Wings - Elizabeth Hoy	2.00	4.50	8.00	R
484	The Northing Tramp - Edgar Wallace	3.00	7.50	15.00	M
485	Island Hospital - Elizabeth Houghton	2.00	4.50	8.00	R
486	Nurse Carll's New Post - Caroline Trench	2.00	4.50	8.00	R
487	The Happy Enterprise - Eleanor Farnes	2.00	4.50	8.00	
488	The Man Who Died Twice - Sydney Horler	3.00	7.50	15.00	
489	Consulting Surgeon - Jane Arbor	2.00	4.50	8.00	R
490	Nurse MacLean Goes West - Elizabeth Gilzean	2.00	4.50	8.00	R
491	Nurse Tennant - Elizabeth Hoy	2.00	4.50	8.00	R
492	Hospital Pro - Marjorie Moore	2.00	4.50	8.00	R
493	The Man at the Carlton - Edgar Wallace	3.00	7.50	15.00	M
494	Love is my Reason - Mary Burchell	2.00	4.50	8.00	R
495	Nurse with a Dream - Norrey Ford	2.00	4.50	8.00	R
496	Nurse in White - Lucy Agnes Hancock	2.00	4.50	8.00	R
497	Doctor Garth - Elizabeth Hoy	2.00	4.50	8.00	R
498	Nurse Atholl Returns - Jane Arbor	2.00	4.50	8.00	R
499	Junior Pro - Kate Norway	2.00	4.50	8.00	R
500	Honorary Surgeon - Marjorie Moore 1959	2.00	4.50	8.00	R
501	Do Something Dangerous - Elizabeth Hoy	2.00	4.50	8.00	R

PYRAMID ROYAL

Some Pyramid Royal editions are part of the regular Pyramid series.

(Pyramid Books)

PR10	The Compact Bible 1956	1.50	3.50	5.00	
PR11	The Moonstone - Wilkie Collins 1958	1.50	3.50	5.00	M
PR12	Two Years Before the Mast - Richard Henry Dana	.75	1.75	3.00	A
PG13	The Sky Block - Steve Frazee	1.50	3.50	5.00	SF
PR14	I married a Hunter - Marjorie Michael	.75	1.75	3.00	

Pyramid Royal PG17, c. Pyb Quarter Books 19, c. Mag   Quarter Books 25, c. Mag

(PYRAMID ROYAL, continued)

PR15	The Lost World - Arthur Conan Doyle	1.50	3.50	5.00	SF
PR16	The Scarlet Pimpernel - Baroness Orczy	1.50	3.50	5.00	A
PG17	Go, Man, Go - Edgar Williams & Dave Zinkoff	.75	1.75	3.00	
PG18	Sports Laughs - Herman L. Masin	.75	1.75	3.00	H
PR19	It's Never Too Late to Love - Anna K. Daniels 1959	.75	1.75	3.00	
PR20	The Dog Who Wouldn't Be - Farley Mowat	.75	1.75	3.00	
PR21	Pere Goriot - Honore de Balzac	.75	1.75	3.00	
PR22	The Miracle of Growth - Arnold Sundgaard	.75	1.75	3.00	NF
PR23	Handwriting Analysis - Dorothy Sara	.75	1.75	3.00	NF
PG24	Daughter of the Gold Rush - Corey Ford & Klondy Nelson	.75	1.75	3.00	
PR25	Lady Chatterley's Lover - D. H. Lawrence	.75	1.75	3.00	
PG26	At Home in India - Cynthia Bowles	.75	1.75	3.00	

QUARTER BOOKS

(Magazine Village, Inc./Astro Distributing Corp.)

Digest size

1	Part-time Virgin - James Clayford	2.00	4.00	6.00	E
2	Week-end Girl - James Clayford	1.50	3.50	5.00	E
4	Any Man's Girl	1.50	3.50	5.00	E
5	Divorce Bait	1.50	3.50	5.00	E
10	Confessions of a Goodtime Girl	1.50	3.50	5.00	E
11	Confessions of a Party Wife	1.50	3.50	5.00	E
12	Shakedown Dame - Dorothy Herzog	1.50	3.50	5.00	E
16	Wedding Night Confession - James Clayford	1.50	3.50	5.00	E
17	Careless Virgin - James Clayford	1.50	3.50	5.00	E
19	Bed Time Girl - James Clayford	1.50	3.50	5.00	E
20	Fighting Horse Valley - Murray Leinster	2.50	6.00	10.00	W
21	Shamed - Luther Gordon	1.50	3.50	5.00	E
22	Unfaithful	1.50	3.50	5.00	E
23	Passion's Mistress	1.50	3.50	5.00	E
25	Wanted Dead or Alive - Murray Leinster	2.50	6.00	10.00	W
26	Respectable Harlot	1.50	3.50	5.00	E
27	Sinful	1.50	3.50	5.00	E
28	Lure for Love	1.50	3.50	5.00	E
29	Immoral! - Luther Gordon aka The Naked Escape	1.50	3.50	5.00	E
30	Marriage Can Wait	1.50	3.50	5.00	E
31	Wicked	1.50	3.50	5.00	E
32	Careless - James Clayford	1.50	3.50	5.00	E
33	Naughty Virgin	1.50	3.50	5.00	E
34	Pleasure Girl	1.50	3.50	5.00	E
35	Ecstasy - Luther Gordon	1.50	3.50	5.00	E
36	Tempted	1.50	3.50	5.00	E
37	Love Cheat	1.50	3.50	5.00	E
38	Wolf Trap Blonde - Luther Gordon 1949, aka Marriage Agency	1.50	3.50	5.00	E
39	Frenchie	1.50	3.50	5.00	E

40	Night of Passion	1.50	3.50	5.00	E
41	Pick-Up - Harmon Bellamy	2.00	4.00	7.50	E
	aka Sacrifice, c-Gross				
42	Midnight Sinner	1.50	3.50	5.00	E
44	Bad Woman - Russell Higgins	1.50	3.50	5.00	E
	1949				
47	Sin Child - Norman Bligh	1.50	3.50	5.00	E
	1949				
48	As Good as Married - Perry Lindsay	1.50	3.50	5.00	E
49	The Intimate Affairs of a Burlesque Queen -	1.50	3.50	5.00	E
	R. Higgins				
50	Overnight Blonde - Charles E. Colohan	1.50	3.50	5.00	E
	aka Big Blonde				
51	Wild Passion - Watkins E. Wright	1.50	3.50	5.00	E
53	Virgin No More - Charles E. Colohan	1.50	3.50	5.00	E
54	Illicit Desires - H. M. Appel	2.00	4.00	6.00	E
	c-Gross				
67	Shamed! - L. Gordon	1.50	3.50	5.00	E
80	Frisco Dame - Florence Stonebraker	1.50	3.50	5.00	E
81	Fast, Loose, and Lovely - Norman Bligh	1.50	3.50	5.00	E
82	Illicit Pleasure - Peggy Gaddis	1.50	3.50	5.00	E
87	Ticket to Passion - Albert L. Quandt	1.50	3.50	5.00	E
88	Untamed Woman - Amos Hatter	1.50	3.50	5.00	E
89	The Lady is Taboo - Norman Bligh	2.00	4.00	6.00	E
	Orig., 1951, c-Gross				
91	Street Girl - Albert L. Quandt	1.50	3.50	5.00	E
92	Three Men and a Mistress - Florence				
	Stonebraker	2.00	4.00	6.00	E
	c-Gross				
94	Confessions of an Artist's Model - Norman Bligh	1.50	3.50	5.00	E
95	Diary of a Pleasure Cruise - Anthony Scott	1.50	3.50	5.00	E
	aka Stolen Sins				

QUICK READER

(Royce Publishers)

3" x 4 3/4" small size

101	Stories of Guy de Maupassant	4.00	8.50	15.00	
	1943				
102	The Killer - Stewart Edward White	4.00	8.50	15.00	
103	Nana - Emile Zola	4.00	8.50	15.00	E
104	The Chillers	4.00	8.50	15.00	
105	You'll Laugh Your Head Off	4.00	8.50	15.00	H
106	Great Short Stories - authology	4.00	8.50	15.00	
107	The Florentine Dagger - Ben Hecht	4.00	8.50	15.00	A
108	Webster's Dictionary	4.00	8.50	15.00	NF
109	Bushido - Alexandre Pernikoff	7.50	17.50	30.00	C
110	Jane Eyre - Charlotte Bronte	4.00	8.50	15.00	
111	Here's Reading You'll Enjoy	4.00	8.50	15.00	
112	More Fun than Looking Though a Keyhole	4.00	8.50	15.00	H
113	Murder on Shark Island - Jack DeWitt	4.00	8.50	15.00	M
114	Crime and Punishment - Fyodor Dostoyevsky	4.00	8.50	15.00	

Quick Reader 104, c. Royce Quick Reader 105, c. Royce Quick Reader 107, c. Royce

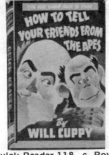

Quick Reader 109, c. Royce   Quick Reader 118, c. Royce   Quick Reader 128, c. Royce

(QUICK READER, continued)

115	How to Safeguard Your Income, Children	4.00	8.50	15.00	NF
116	Try this for Size - authology	4.00	8.50	15.00	
117	Count Bruga - Ben Hecht	4.00	8.50	15.00	
118	How to Tell Your Friends from the Apes - Will Cuppy	4.00	8.50	15.00	H
119	A Tale of Two Cities - Chas. Dickens	4.00	8.50	15.00	
120	Time Out for Murder - E. Queen & others	5.00	12.50	20.00	M
121	The Curve of the Catenary - M.R. Rinehart	4.00	8.50	15.00	M
122	Wuthering Heights - Emily Bronte	4.00	8.50	15.00	
	1944				
123	True Murders Not Quite Solved - Alvin F. Harlow	4.00	8.50	15.00	NF
124	15 Short Short Surprise Stories - anthology	4.00	8.50	15.00	
125	Strictly on the Funny Side	4.00	8.50	15.00	H
	1944				
126	Love is a Funny Business - anthology	4.00	8.50	15.00	H
127	Celebrated Stories Made into Movies	4.00	8.50	15.00	
128	Cat and Mouse - Hugh Pentecost	5.00	12.50	20.00	M
129	The Way of all Flesh - Samuel Butler	4.00	8.50	15.00	
130	Treasure Island - R. L. Stevenson	4.00	8.50	15.00	A
131	Seven Keys to Baldpate - Earl Derr Biggers	5.00	12.50	20.00	M
	1945				
132	I'll Be Glad When You're Dead - Dana Lyon	4.00	8.50	15.00	M
133	Gentlemen Prefer Blondes - Anita Loos	4.00	8.50	15.00	
134	Mr. Pinkerton - Passage for One - David Frome	4.00	8.50	15.00	M
135	Humorous Ghost Stories	4.00	8.50	15.00	H
136	Gulliver's Travels - Jonathan Swift	4.00	8.50	15.00	A
137	Bedside Bedlam - anthology	4.00	8.50	15.00	H
138	Mademoiselle de Maupin - Theophile Gautier	4.00	8.50	15.00	
139	One Side Please - authology	4.00	8.50	15.00	H
140	The Best of Edgar Allan Poe	4.00	8.50	15.00	
141	Quick Reader Bible	4.00	8.50	15.00	
142	Dr. Jekyll and Mr. Hyde - R.L. Stevenson	5.00	12.50	20.00	SF
143	Great Comedies Made into Movies	4.00	8.50	15.00	
144	Unforgettable French Love Stories	4.00	8.50	15.00	
145	The Dead Man's Tale - Hugh Pentecost	4.00	8.50	15.00	M
146					
147					
148	Blind Trail at Sunrise - W.C. Tuttle	4.00	8.50	15.00	W
149	Camille - Alexandre Dumas	4.00	8.50	15.00	

RAINBOW

(Magazine Productions, Inc.)

Digest size

101	Thrill Girl - Gene Harvey	1.50	3.50	5.00	E
	1950				
102	Reno Tramp - Florence Stonebraker	1.50	3.50	5.00	E
109	Her Candle Burns Hot! - Hodge Evens	1.50	3.50	5.00	E
	1951				
120	The Nude Stranger - Mark Reed	1.50	3.50	5.00	E
	Orig., 1952				

Rainbow 127, c. MP   Rainbow 128, c. MP   Rainbow 103, c. CP

(RAINBOW, continued)

124	Bedroom with a View - David Wade Orig., 1952, c-Gross	2.00	4.00	6.00	E
127	The Big Woman - Mel Colton Orig., 1953	2.00	4.00	6.00	E
128	The Twist! - Norma Dann Orig., 1953	1.50	3.50	5.00	E
129	Only Human - David Wade Orig., 1953	1.50	3.50	5.00	E

RAINBOW BOOKS

(The Colonial Press, Inc.)

Digest size

103	Ten Perfect Crimes - Hank Sterling 1954	1.50	3.50	5.00	NF

READERS CHOICE LIBRARY

(St. John Publishing Company)

Some digest size

2	Smoky Road - Frank Gruber Digest size	1.50	3.50	5.00	W
3	Gina - George Albert Glay	1.50	3.50	5.00	M
4	The Powder Burner - Frank C. Robertson Digest size	1.50	3.50	5.00	W
5	The Stranger from Texas - Allan K. Echols Digest size	1.50	3.50	5.00	W
7	Shoe the Wild Mare - Gene Fowler	1.50	3.50	5.00	W
8	Green Light for Death - Frank Kane	2.00	4.00	6.00	M
11	Stranger than Fruit - Vera Caspary	1.50	3.50	5.00	E

Readers Choice 4, c. Stj   Readers Choice 8, c. Stj   Readers Choice 13, c. Stj

Readers Choice 23, c. Stj   Reader's League nn, c. RL   Red Arrow 7, c. Red

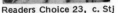

(READERS CHOICE LIBRARY, continued)

12	Nightmare - William Irish aka I Wouldn't Be in Your Shoes	2.00	4.00	6.00	M
13	Western Outlaw - Frank Gruber Digest size	1.50	3.50	5.00	W
14	Trouble Shootin' Man - Frank C. Robertson Digest size	1.50	3.50	5.00	W
15	The Lock and the Key - Frank Gruber Digest size	1.50	3.50	5.00	M
16	Murder '97 - Frank Gruber Digest size	1.50	3.50	5.00	M
17	Gun Crazy - Wayne D. Overholser Digest size	1.50	3.50	5.00	W
18	Bloody Saddlers - L. P. Holmes Digest size	1.50	3.50	5.00	W
19	Broken Lance - Frank Gruber Digest size	1.50	3.50	5.00	W
20	Trumpet in the Dust - Gene Fowler	1.50	3.50	5.00	E
24	Red Rustlers - Frank C. Robertson	1.50	3.50	5.00	W
25	Bonanza Queen - Zola Ross	1.50	3.50	5.00	E
33	Prairie Guns - E. E. Halleran Digest size	1.50	3.50	5.00	W
37	They Call It Sin - Alberta Stedman Eagan	1.50	3.50	5.00	E
38	Death Is My Lover - Stuart Brock	1.50	3.50	5.00	E
39	Lover Boy - Eric Rhodes Hayden	1.50	3.50	5.00	E

READER'S LEAGUE

(Readers League of America)

nn	Red Harvest - Dashiell Hammett	2.50	6.00	10.00	M
nn	The Case of the Dangerous Dowager - Erle Stanley Gardner	1.50	3.50	5.00	M
nn	The Four of Hearts - Ellery Queen	1.50	3.50	5.00	M
nn	Jeeves - P. G. Wodehouse	2.00	4.00	7.50	H
nn	Enter the Saint - Leslie Charteris	2.00	4.00	6.00	M
nn	The Case of the Substitute Face - Erle Stanley Gardner	1.50	3.50	5.00	M
nn	The Four of Hearts - Ellery Queen	1.50	3.50	5.00	M
nn	The Pocket Entertainer 1942	2.00	4.00	6.00	NF
nn	Phantom Lady - William Irish	2.00	4.00	7.50	M
nn	The Egyptian Cross Mystery - Ellery Queen	1.50	3.50	5.00	M
nn	The Case of the Stuttering Bishop - Erle Stanley Gardner	1.50	3.50	5.00	M
nn	Halfway House - Ellery Queen	1.50	3.50	5.00	M
nn	Jeeves - P. G. Wodehouse	2.00	4.00	7.50	H

RED ARROW BOOKS

(Red Arrow Books)

1	Thirteen at Dinner - Agatha Christie 1939	4.00	8.00	15.00	M

(RED ARROW BOOKS, continued)

2	Murder-on-Hudson - Jennifer Jones	4.00	8.00	15.00	M
3	Murders in Praed Street - John Rhode	4.00	8.00	15.00	M
4	Death in the Library - Philip Ketchum	4.00	8.00	15.00	M
5	Death Wears a White Gardenia - Zelda Popkin	4.00	8.00	15.00	M
6	My South Sea Island - Eric Musprat	4.00	8.00	15.00	
7	Yankee Komisar - Commander S. M. Riis	4.00	8.00	15.00	
8	Girl Hunt - Laurence D. Smith	4.00	8.00	15.00	
9	The Seven Sleepers - Francis Beeding	4.00	8.00	15.00	A
10	Captain Nemesis - F. Van Wyck Mason	4.00	8.00	15.00	A
11	Windswept - Olga Moore	4.00	8.00	15.00	
12	Pirate's Purchase - Ben Ames Williams	4.00	8.00	15.00	A

RED CIRCLE

(Select Publications, Inc.)

Also see Lion

1	Sex Life and You - Jules Archer & Maxine Sawyer 1949	7.50	15.00	30.00	NF
2	Passionate Fool - John Moroso aka Poor Passionate Fool	5.00	10.00	20.00	E
3	Leg Artist - Gene Harvey	5.00	10.00	20.00	E
4	Blonde Menace - Don Martin aka Shed No Tears	5.00	10.00	20.00	E
5	Body or Soul - Royal Peters	5.00	10.00	20.00	E
6	Passion in the Dust - Paul Evan Lehman	4.00	8.00	15.00	W
7	Hot Date - Elliot Storm aka Shame Girl	4.00	8.00	15.00	E
12	Why Get Married? - Token West	5.00	10.00	20.00	E
13	Carnival of Love - Anthony Scott 1949, aka Mardi Gras Madness	5.00	10.00	20.00	E

RED DAGGER MYSTERY

(Dagger House, Inc.)

Digest size

21	Death for a Hussy - Allison Holt 1946, aka Bier for a Hussy	1.50	3.50	5.00	M
25	Murder from the Mind - Patrick Laing 1947	1.50	3.50	5.00	M
27	There Are Dead Men in Manhattan - John Roeburt 1947	1.50	3.50	5.00	M
29	Blood on the Beach - H. Holley 1947	1.50	3.50	5.00	M

RED SEAL BOOKS

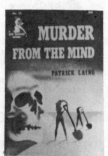

Red Circle 1, c. Select   Red Dagger 21, c. Dagger   Red Dagger 25, c. Dagger

Red Seal 7, c. Faw   Red Seal 22, c. Faw   Red Seal 24, c. Faw

(RED SEAL BOOKS, continued)

(Fawcett Publications, Inc.)

7	The Sky Tramps - Dennison O'Hara Orig., 1952	2.00	4.00	7.50	E
8	Each Life to Live - Richard Gehman Orig., 1952	2.00	4.00	6.00	E
9	This Woman - Albert Idell Orig., 1952	2.00	4.00	6.00	E
10	Naked in the Streets - Ryerson Johnson	2.00	4.00	6.00	E
11	Out of the Sea - Don Smith Orig., 1952	2.00	4.00	6.00	A
12	City of Women - Nancy Morgan Orig., 1952	2.00	4.00	7.50	E
13	The Sea Waifs - John Vail Orig., 1952	2.50	6.00	10.00	E
14	Halo for a Heel - Mike Skelly Orig., 1952	2.00	4.00	6.00	E
15	Bride of the Sword - Homer Hatten	2.00	4.00	6.00	A
16	The Golden Sorrow - Theodore Pratt	2.00	4.00	6.00	E
17	The Quest - O. O. Osborne Orig., 1952	2.00	4.00	6.00	E
18	The Marriage Bed - H. Vernor Dixon	2.00	4.00	6.00	E
19	Lili of Paris - Fay Adams Orig., 1952	2.00	4.00	6.00	E
20	Girl from Town - Jack Sheridan Orig., 1952	2.00	4.00	6.00	E
21	Be Still My Heart - Steve Fisher	2.00	4.00	6.00	
22	American Ballads Orig., 1952	2.00	4.00	6.00	NF
23	The Magnificent Moll - John Gonzales	2.00	4.00	6.00	E
24	One for Hell - Jada M. Davis	2.00	4.00	6.00	E
25	Thy Name is Woman - Hilda Van Siller Orig., 1952	3.00	6.00	12.00	E
26	This, too, is Love - Sam Ross	2.00	4.00	6.00	E
27	Love Isn't for Now - John Vail Orig., 1953	2.00	4.00	6.00	E
28	Mississippi Flame - Ryerson Johnson	2.00	4.00	6.00	E
29	Fare Thee Well - Robert Spafford Orig., 1953	2.00	4.00	6.00	E

RETAIL DISTRIBUTORS

(Retail Distributors, Inc.)

nn	World's Champs - Lester Bromberg 1958	1.50	3.50	6.00	S
101	Hoodlums Los Angeles - Ted Prager & Larry Craft 1959	1.50	3.50	6.00	NF
102	Hoodlums New York - Ted Prager & Leeds Moberley 1959	1.50	3.50	6.00	NF

REX STOUT MYSTERY

(Avon Book Company/Avon Detective - Mysteries, Inc.)

Digest size

1	Includes Stout, Hammett, Christie, Fischer, Others 1945	4.00	8.00	15.00	M
2	1945	3.00	6.00	12.00	M
3	1946	3.00	6.00	12.00	M
4	Includes Dickson, Freeman, Starrett, Blackwood, Others 1946	3.00	6.00	12.00	M
5		3.00	6.00	12.00	M
6		3.00	6.00	12.00	M
7		3.00	6.00	12.00	M
8	Includes Woolrich, Crofts, Collier, Starrett, Others 1947	3.00	6.00	12.00	M
9	1947	3.00	6.00	12.00	M

ROMANTIC NOVELS

(Romantic Reprints)

Digest size

nn	Dance Hall Girl - Ann Lawrence c-Rodewald	1.50	3.50	5.00	E
nn	Reckless Girl - John Saxon	1.50	3.50	5.00	E

ROYAL GIANT EDITION

(Royal Books/Universal Publishing and Distributing Corp.)

Digest size

Also see Universal Giant Edition

12	Jimgrim Sahib - Talbot Mundy aka Jimgrim	4.00	8.00	15.00	A
13	Note: May not exist.				
14	Matador - Marguerite Steen	3.00	6.00	12.00	A
15	Highlights from Yank	3.00	6.00	12.00	
16	Stalingrad - Theodor Plievier	3.00	6.00	12.00	C
17	The Other Stranger - Daoma Winston Orig., 1953				E
	Adam and Two Eves - anonymous	3.00	6.00	12.00	E

Rex Stout 1, c. Avon

Rex Stout 8, c. Avon

Romantic Novels nn, c. RN

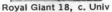

Royal Giant 18, c. Univ   Royal Giant 19, c. Univ   R. W. nn, c. R. W.

(ROYAL GIANT EDITION, continued)

18 Allan Quatermain - H. Rider Haggard				A
King Solomon's Mines - H. Rider Haggard	4.00	8.00	15.00	A
19 Trek East - Talbot Mundy	4.00	8.00	15.00	A
aka The Ivory Trail				
20 Full Moon - Talbot Mundy				A
High Priest of California - Charles Willeford	4.00	8.00	15.00	E
Orig., 1953				
21 Highway Episode - George Weller	3.00	6.00	12.00	E
aka Clutch and Differential				
22 Gonzaga's Woman - John Jakes				E
Orig., 1953				
Affair in Araby - Talbot Mundy	4.00	8.00	15.00	A
aka The King in Check				
23 The Case of Sergeant Grischa - Arnold Zweig	3.00	6.00	12.00	C
24 Roxana - Daniel Defoe	4.00	8.00	15.00	E
25 Mademoiselle De Maupin - Theophile Gantier				E
Candide - Voltaire	4.00	8.00	15.00	E
26 The Harem of Hsi Men - anthology	5.00	10.00	20.00	E
27 Confessions of a Psychiatrist - Henry Lewis Nixon				E
Orig., 1954				
The Woman He Wanted - Daoma Winston	4.00	8.00	15.00	E
Orig., 1954				
28 The Unnatural Son - Mark Twain				A
aka Puddnhead Wilson				
A Connecticut Yankee in King Arthur's Court - Mark Twain	3.00	6.00	12.00	F
29 The Way of all Flesh - Samuel Butler	3.00	6.00	12.00	E

RUTLEDGE BOOKS

(Scholastic Book Services)

Digest size

RP10 The Buccaneer - Iris Vinton	1.00	2.50	4.00	A
1959, Movie tie-in				

R. W.

(The R. W. Company)

Digest size

nn The Vice Czar Murders - Franklin Charles	1.50	3.50	5.00	M

SAINT MYSTERY LIBRARY

(Great American Publications, Inc.)

118 Stairway to Murder - Leslie Charteris 1959	1.00	2.50	4.00	M
119 Witness to Death - Leslie Charteris	1.00	2.50	4.00	M
120 Murder Set to Music - Leslie Charteris	2.00	4.00	6.00	M
Title story by Fredric Brown				
121 The Frightened Millionaire - Leslie Charteris	1.00	2.50	4.00	M
122 Murder Made in Moscow - Leslie Charteris	1.00	2.50	4.00	M
Title story by Baynard Kendrick				
123 Murder in the Family - Leslie Charteris	1.00	2.50	4.00	M
124 Death Stops at a Tourist Camp - Leslie Charteris	1.00	2.50	4.00	M
125 Red Snow in Darjeeling - Leslie Charteris	1.00	2.50	4.00	M
Title story by Lawrence G. Blochman				
126 Executioner's Signature - Leslie Charteris 1960	1.00	2.50	4.00	M
127 Murder Seeks an Agent - Leslie Charteris	1.00	2.50	4.00	M
Title story by Wenzell Brown				
128 Let Her Kill Herself - Leslie Charteris	1.00	2.50	4.00	M
129 Innocent Bystander - Craig Rice	1.00	2.50	4.00	M
130 Death Walks in Marble Halls - Leslie Charteris	1.00	2.60	4.00	M
Title story by Lawrence G. Blochman				
131 Rum and Cocoa Murders - Leslie Charteris	.75	1.75	3.00	M
Title story by Wenzell Brown				

SCIENCE SERVICE

(Science Service)

nn Science from Shipboard 1943	1.50	3.50	6.00	NF

SHOOTING SCRIPT

(Catholic Digest/Catechetical Guild)

nn Guilty of Treason - Emmet Lavery 1950, movie tie-in	2.00	4.00	7.50

SIGNET

(New American Library of World Literature, Inc.)

Also see Penguin

660 100 American Poems - Selden Rodman 1948	1.50	3.50	5.00
661 Tragic Ground - Erskine Caldwell	1.50	3.50	5.00
662 Invitation to the Waltz - Rosamond Lehman	1.50	3.50	5.00
663 As Good as Dead - Thomas B. Dewey	1.50	3.50	5.00
664 Portrait of the Artist as a Young Man - James Joyce	2.00	4.00	6.00

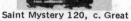

Saint Mystery 120, c. Great   Science Service nn, c. SS   Shooting Script nn, c. Cath

Signet 699, c. Sigb   Signet 705, c. Sigb   Signet 757, c. Sigb

(SIGNET, continued)

665 Strange Fruit - Lillian Smith	2.00	4.00	6.00	
666 The Valley of Hunted Men - Paul Evan Lehman	2.00	4.00	6.00	W
667 The Pinkerton Case Book - Alan Hynd	2.00	4.00	6.00	
668 The Dim View - Basil Heatter	2.00	4.00	6.00	
669 The Caballero - Johnston McCulley	2.00	4.00	6.00	W
670 They Shoot Horses, Don't They? - Horace McCoy	2.00	4.00	7.50	
671 Darkness at Noon - Arthur Koestler	1.50	3.50	5.00	
672 Cattle Kingdom - Alan LeMay	2.00	4.00	6.00	W
673 Sons of the Saddle - William MacLeod Raine	2.00	4.00	6.00	W
674 Mine Own Executioner - Nigel Balchin	1.50	3.50	5.00	
675 About the Kinsey Report - Enid Curie & Donald Porter Geddes	1.50	3.50	5.00	NF
676 Ariane - Claude Anet	2.00	4.00	6.00	E
677 Guilty Bystander - Wade Miller	2.00	4.00	6.00	
678 The Signet Crossword Puzzle Book - Albert Morehead & Geoffrey Mott-Smith	2.00	4.00	7.50	NF
679 Laramie Rides Again - Will Ermine	2.00	4.00	6.00	W
680 Past All Dishonor - James M. Cain	2.00	4.00	7.50	
681 Contract Bridge for Everyone - Ely Culbertson	1.50	3.50	5.00	NF
682 Blood of the West - Paul Evan Lehman	2.00	4.00	6.00	W
683 The Lost Weekend - Charles Jackson	2.00	4.00	6.00	
684 Slay the Murderer - Hugh Holman	2.00	4.00	6.00	M
685 Lobo Law - Will Ermine	2.00	4.00	6.00	W
686 A House in the Uplands - Erskine Caldwell	2.00	4.00	6.00	
687 Shore Leave - Frederic Wakeman	1.50	3.50	5.00	
688 High Pockets - Herbert Shappiro	1.50	3.50	5.00	
689 The Silver Tombstone - Frank Gruber	2.00	4.00	6.00	
690 No Pockets in a Shroud - Horace McCoy	2.00	4.00	7.50	
691 All the Girls we Loved - Prudencio De Pereda	1.50	3.50	5.00	
692 The Old Man - William Faulkner	2.00	4.00	6.00	
693 I Love You, I Love You, I Love You - Ludwig Bemelmans	2.00	4.00	6.00	
694 Lawless Range - Charles N. Heckelmann	2.00	4.00	6.00	W
695 Fatal Step - Wade Miller	2.00	4.00	6.00	
696 The Snake Pit - Mary Jane Ward	2.00	4.00	6.00	
697 Look Homeward, Angel, Part II - Thomas Wolfe	2.00	4.00	6.00	
698 Black Sombrero - William Colt MacDonald	2.00	4.00	6.00	W
699 I, the Jury - Mickey Spillane	4.00	8.00	15.00	M
Used in Parade of Pleasure, pg. 172				
700 Other Voices, Other Rooms - Truman Capote 1949	2.50	6.00	10.00	
701 Finnley Wren - Philip Wylie	2.00	4.00	6.00	
702 The Vehement Flame - Ludwig Lewisohn	2.00	4.00	6.00	
703 Find My Killer - Manly Wade Wellman	2.00	4.00	6.00	M
704 Gold of Smoky Mesa - Johnston McCulley	2.00	4.00	6.00	W
705 A Woman in the House - Erskine Caldwell	2.00	4.00	6.00	
706 Last of the Conquerors - William Gardner Smith	2.00	4.00	6.00	
707 The Honest Dealer - Frank Gruber	2.00	4.00	6.00	
708 The Texan - Herbert Shapiro	2.00	4.00	6.00	W
709 Deadlier than the Male - James E. Gunn	2.00	4.00	6.00	

710 The Street - Ann Petry	1.50	3.50	5.00	
711 Love in Dishevelment - David Greenhood	1.50	3.50	5.00	
712 The Fighting Tenderfoot - William MacLeod Raine	2.00	4.00	6.00	W
713 Murder as a Fine Art - Francis Bonnamy	2.00	4.00	6.00	M
714 The Gilded Hearse - Charles Gorham	2.00	4.00	6.00	
715 The Fall of Valor - Charles Jackson	1.50	3.50	5.00	
716 We Were Strange - Robert Sylvester	1.50	3.50	5.00	
717 A Son of Arizona - Charles Alden Seltzer	2.00	4.00	6.00	W
718 Another Man's Poison - Hugh Holman	1.50	3.50	5.00	
719 Baseball for Everyone - Joe Di Maggio	2.00	4.00	7.50	S
720 The Butterfly - James M. Cain	2.00	4.00	7.50	
721 Night of Flame - Warren Desmond	1.50	3.50	5.00	
722 Uneasy Street - Wade Miller	2.00	4.00	6.00	
723 The Crimson Quirt - William Colt MacDonald	2.00	4.00	6.00	W
724 The Golden Sleep - Vivian Connell	2.00	4.00	6.00	
725 At Heaven's Gate - Robert Penn Warren 1949	1.50	3.50	5.00	
726 The Whispering Master - Frank Gruber	2.00	4.00	6.00	
727 Trigger Justice - Leslie Ernenwein	2.00	4.00	6.00	W
728 Lona Hanson - Thomas Savage	1.50	3.50	5.00	
729 Stranger in Town - Howard Hunt	2.00	4.00	7.50	
730 The Body in the Bed - Bill S. Ballinger	2.00	4.00	7.50	M
731 Montana Man - Paul Evan Lehman	2.00	4.00	7.50	W
732 The Sure Hand of God - Erskine Caldwell	2.00	4.00	6.00	E
733 Crime and Punishment - Fyodor Dostoyevsky	2.00	4.00	6.00	
734 My Name is Aram - William Saroyan	2.00	4.00	6.00	
735 Everybody Sleph Here - Elliott Arnold	1.50	3.50	5.00	
736 Draw the Curtain Close - Thomas B. Dewey	2.00	4.00	6.00	M
737 Brave in the Saddle - Will Ermine	2.00	4.00	6.00	W
738 Nightmare Alley - William Lindsay Gresham	2.00	4.00	7.50	E
739 Beyond the Forest - Stuart Engstrand	2.00	4.00	6.00	E
740 Whistling Lead - Eugene Cunningham	2.00	4.00	6.00	W
741 Life in a Putty Knife Factory - H. Allen Smith	1.50	3.50	5.00	H
742 Kill or Cure - William Francis	2.00	4.00	6.00	
743 Intruder in the Dust - William Faulkner	2.00	4.00	6.00	
744 The Christian Demand for Social Justice - William Scarlett	2.00	4.00	6.00	NF
745 The Ox-Bow Incident - Walter Van Tilburg Clark	2.00	4.00	6.00	W
746 Human Destiny - Pierre Lecomte du Nouy	1.50	3.50	5.00	NF
747 Walden - Henry David Thoreau	2.00	4.00	6.00	
748 Mistress Glory - Susan Morley	2.00	4.00	6.00	E
749 For Ever Wilt Thou Love - Ludwig Lewisohn	2.00	4.00	6.00	E
750 Devil in the Flesh - Raymond Radiguet 1949	2.00	4.00	6.00	
751 Love Without Fear - Eustace Chesser	1.50	3.50	5.00	NF
752 The Future Mr. Dolan - Charles Gorham	2.00	4.00	7.50	JD
753 The Gamecock Murders - Frank Gruber	2.00	4.00	6.00	M
754 Kiss Tomorrow Good-bye - Horace McCoy	2.00	4.00	7.50	E
755 An American Tragedy - Theodore Dreiser	1.50	3.50	5.00	
756 If He Hollers Let Him Go - Chester Himes	2.00	4.00	7.50	
757 Brother of the Cheyennes - Max Brand	2.00	4.00	6.00	W
758 Clattering Hoofs - William MacLeod Raine	2.00	4.00	6.00	W
759 Everybody Does it and the Embezzler - James M. Cain	2.00	4.00	7.50	
760 Georgia Boy - Erskine Caldwell 1950	2.00	4.00	6.00	
761 Country Place - Ann Petry	2.00	4.00	6.00	
762 You Can Change the World - James Keller	1.50	3.50	5.00	NF
763 The Weeper and the Blackmailer - Richard H. Rovere	1.50	3.50	5.00	
764 Six-Shooter Showdown - William Colt MacDonald	2.00	4.00	6.00	W
765 Murder All Over - Cleve F. Adams aka Up Jumped the Devil	2.00	4.00	7.50	M
766 Appointment in Samarra - John O. Hara	1.50	3.50	5.00	
767 Alien Land - Willard Savoy	2.00	4.00	7.50	E
768 Dark Encounter - Howard Hunt aka Maelstrom	2.00	4.00	7.50	
769 Margaret - Caroline Slade	2.00	4.00	7.50	E
770 Two Loves - Elliott Arnold	1.50	3.50	5.00	
771 Killer's Choice - Wade Miller aka Devil on Two Sticks	2.00	4.00	6.00	M

772 Three Musketeers and a Lady - Tiffany Thayer	2.00	4.00	7.50	A
773 The City and the Pillar - Gore Vidal	2.00	4.00	7.50	
774 The Body Beautiful - Bill S. Balliner	2.00	4.00	6.00	M
775 Vengeance Trail - Charles N. Heckelmann 1950	2.00	4.00	6.00	W
776 Now I Lay Me Down to Sleep - Ludwig Bemelmans	1.50	3.50	5.00	
777 Laughter in the Dark - Vladimir Nabokov	2.00	4.00	6.00	
778 I Am Thinking of my Darling - Vincent McHugh	2.00	4.00	7.50	
779 Ellen Rogers - James T. Farrell	2.00	4.00	6.00	E
780 The Restless Hands - Bruno Fischer	2.00	4.00	6.00	M
781 The Outer Edges - Charles Jackson	1.50	3.50	5.00	E
782 The Buckaroo - Burt Arthur	2.00	4.00	6.00	E
783 The Saxon Charm - Frederic Wakeman	2.00	4.00	6.00	E
784 Double Indemnity - James M. Cain	2.00	4.00	7.50	M
785 Horseback Hellion - George Owen Baxter	2.00	4.00	6.00	W
786 The Sling and the Arrow - Stuart Engstrand	1.50	3.50	5.00	E
787 The Hanging Heiress - Richard Wirmser	2.00	4.00	6.00	M
788 Having a Baby - Alan F. Guttmacher	2.00	4.00	6.00	NF
789 The Love-making of Max-Robert - Robert Shaplen	1.50	3.50	5.00	
790 Lily Henry - Mae Cooper	1.50	3.50	5.00	
791 My Gun is Quick - Mickey Spillane	3.00	6.00	12.00	M
792 The Shadow Rider - William Colt MacDonald	2.00	4.00	6.00	W
793 Kitty Foyle - Christoper Morley	1.50	3.50	5.00	
S794 Native Son - Richard Wright	2.00	4.00	6.00	
795 Healthy Babies are Happy Babies - Josephine H. Kenyon & Ruth K. Russell	2.00	4.00	6.00	NF
S796 Arch of Triumph - Erich Maria Remarque	2.00	4.00	6.00	
797 A Tale of Poor Lovers - Vasco Pratolini	1.50	3.50	5.00	
798 1984 - George Orwell	3.00	6.00	12.00	SF
799 The Fourth Letter - Frank Gruber	2.00	4.00	6.00	
800 Fannie Farmer's Handy Cook Book 1950	2.00	4.00	6.00	NF
801 The Track of the Cat - Walter Van Tilburg Clark	2.00	4.00	6.00	W
802AB Knock on Any Door - Willard Motley	2.00	4.00	6.00	JD
803 World Full of Strangers - David Alman	1.50	3.50	5.00	E
804 Night Rider - Robert Penn Warren	2.00	4.00	6.00	E
805 The Runaways - Carl Bottume aka The Hills Around Havana	2.00	4.00	6.00	E
806 Powdersmoke Feud - William MacLeod Raine	2.00	4.00	6.00	W
807 The Bandaged Nude - Robert Finneyan	2.00	4.00	6.00	
808 The New American Webster Dictionary	2.00	4.00	6.00	NF
809AB Forever Amber - Kathleen Winsor	1.50	3.50	5.00	
810 The Young Manhood of Studs Lonigan - James T. Farrell	2.00	4.00	6.00	
811 The Moth - James M. Cain	2.00	4.00	6.00	
812 Beyond the Moon - Edmond Hamilton	2.00	4.00	7.50	SF
813 The World Next Door - Fritz Peters	1.50	3.50	5.00	
814 Room for Murder - Thomas B. Dewey	2.00	4.00	6.00	
815 Wanted--Dead or Alive - Gordon Young	2.00	4.00	6.00	W
816 Tortilla Flat - John Steinbeck	2.00	4.00	6.00	
817AB The Young Lions - Irwin Shaw	1.50	3.50	5.00	
818 A Swell-looking Girl - Erskine Caldwell aka American Earth	2.00	4.00	6.00	E
819 The Lonely - Paul Gallico	2.00	4.00	6.00	
820 Shriek with Pleasure - Toni Howard	2.00	4.00	6.00	E
821 Sleep No More - Sam S. Taylor	1.50	3.50	5.00	
822 Trigger Man - Burt Arthur	2.00	4.00	6.00	W
823 The Wastrel - Frederic Wakeman	1.50	3.50	5.00	
824 State Fair - Phil Ston	2.00	4.00	6.00	
825 Knight's Gambit - William Faulkner 1950	2.00	4.00	6.00	
826 Son of the Giant - Stuart Engstrand	1.50	3.50	5.00	
827 A Job of Murder - Frank Gruber	2.00	4.00	6.00	
828 Gunsmoke - Leslie Ernenwein	2.00	4.00	6.00	W
829 Lilly Crackell - Caroline Slade	2.00	4.00	6.00	
830 Night onto Night - Philip Wylie	2.00	4.00	6.00	E
831 Saturday Night - James T. Farrell	2.00	4.00	6.00	E
832 Love Knows No Barriers - Will Thomas aka God is for White Folks	2.00	4.00	7.50	E
833 The Flesh was Told - Bruno Fischer	2.00	4.00	7.50	M

834	Heart of Darkness and the Secret Sharer - Joseph Conrad	2.00	4.00	7.50	
835	Dead Man's Gold - William Colt MacDonald	2.00	4.00	6.00	W
836	Montana Riders! - Evan Evans	2.00	4.00	6.00	
	1951				
837AB	The Naked and the Dead - Norman Mailer	2.00	4.00	6.00	
838	This Very Earth - Erskine Caldwell	1.50	3.50	5.00	
839	Limbo Tower - William Lindsay Greshman	1.50	3.50	5.00	
840	The Sheltering Sky - Paul Bowles	1.50	3.50	5.00	E
841	Black Boy - Richard Wright	1.50	3.50	5.00	
842	Two-Bit Rancher - Charles N. Heckelmann	2.00	4.00	6.00	W
843	Calamity Fair - Wade Miller	1.50	3.50	5.00	E
S844	The Woman of Rome - Alberto Moravia	1.50	3.50	5.00	E
845	Tiger in the Garden - Speed Lamkin	1.50	3.50	5.00	E
846	The Short Cut - Ennio Flaiano	1.50	3.50	5.00	E
847	The Man Who Sold the Moon - Robert A. Heinlein	2.00	4.00	6.00	SF
848	The Conquest of Happiness - Bertrand Russell	1.50	3.50	5.00	
849	Brother of the Kid - Paul Evan Lehman	2.00	4.00	6.00	W
850	The Private Eye - Cleve F. Adams	2.00	4.00	6.00	M
	1951				
S851	The Strange Land - Ned Calmer	1.50	3.50	5.00	
852	Vengeance is Mine - Mickey Spillane	3.00	6.00	12.00	M
	Used in Parade of Pleasure, pg. 180-82				
853	Black Gold - Jewel Gibson	1.50	3.50	5.00	E
854	Memory and Desire - Leonora Hornblow	1.50	3.50	5.00	
855	The Snow was Black - Georges Simenon	2.00	4.00	7.50	M
856	Mean as Hell - Dee Harkey	1.50	3.50	5.00	
857	Meg - Theodora Keogh	1.50	3.50	5.00	
858	Dirty Eddie - Ludwig Bermelmans	1.50	3.50	5.00	
859	The Consumer's Guide to Better Buying - Sidney Margolius	1.50	3.50	5.00	NF
860	Follow Me Down - Shelby Foote	1.50	3.50	5.00	E
861	Prettiest Girl in Town - Thomas Fall	1.50	3.50	5.00	E
862	Courage and Confidence from the Bible - Walter L. Moore	1.50	3.50	5.00	NF
863	Pylon - William Faulkner	1.50	3.50	5.00	
864	Strangers and Lovers - Edwin Gran Gerry	1.50	3.50	5.00	E
865	I. O. U.--Murder - William Francis	2.00	4.00	6.00	M
	aka Rough on Rats				
866	Trouble Town - Burt Arthur	1.50	3.50	5.00	W
867	They Sought for Paradise - Stuart Engstrand	1.50	3.50	5.00	
868AB	Star Money - Kathleen Winsor	.50	1.25	2.00	
869	Kneel to the Rising Sun - Erskine Caldwell	1.50	3.50	5.00	
870	Time for Love - Margaret Lee Runbeck	1.50	3.50	5.00	E
871	The Dog Star - Donald Windham	1.50	3.50	5.00	E
872	There's No Home - Alexander Baron	.50	1.25	2.00	E
	aka The Wine of Etna				
873	Appointment with Fear - Donald Stokes	1.50	3.50	5.00	
874	Hell for Leather - Leslie Ernenwein	1.50	3.50	5.00	W
S875	Judgment Day - James T. Farrell	1.50	3.50	5.00	
	1951				
876	A Stretch on the River - Richard Bissell	1.50	3.50	5.00	
877	Cry of Violence - Joseph Kessel	1.50	3.50	5.00	
878	A Tree of Night - Truman Capote	2.00	4.00	6.00	
879	No Luck for A Lady - Floyd Mahannah	2.00	4.00	7.50	
	aka The Yellow Hearse				
880	Gunsight Range - William Colt MacDonald	1.50	3.50	5.00	W
881	Fertility in Marriage - Louis Portnoy & Jules Saltman	1.50	3.50	5.00	NF
882	The Day After Tomorrow - Robert A. Heinlein	1.50	3.50	5.00	SF
883	Stone Cold Blonde - Adam Knight	2.00	4.00	6.00	M
884	I Should Have Stayed Home - Horace McCoy	2.00	4.00	7.50	
885	Buckskin Marshal - Will Ermine	1.50	3.50	5.00	W
886	The Daughter - Arthur Markowitz	1.50	3.50	5.00	
887	Soldier's Pay - William Faulkner	1.50	3.50	5.00	
888	One Lonely Night - Mickey Spillane	2.00	4.00	7.50	M
	Used in Parade of Pleasure, pg. 175				
889	Your Way to Popularity & Personal Power - James Bender & Lee Graham	.50	1.25	2.00	NF
890	The Invaders - Stuart Engstrand	1.50	3.50	5.00	
891	Gunplay Valley - Joseph Wayne	1.50	3.50	5.00	W
892	The Silent Dust - Bruno Fischer	1.50	3.50	5.00	M
S893	Bernard Carr - James T. Farrell	1.50	3.50	5.00	E

Signet 894, c. Sigb	Signet 898, c. Sigb	Signet 923, c. Sigb

(SIGNET, continued)

894	Cornbread Aristocrat - Claud Garner	1.50	3.50	5.00	E
895	The Triumph of Willie Pond - Caroline Slade	1.50	3.50	5.00	E
896	Jubel's Children - Lenard Kaufman	1.50	3.50	5.00	E
897	Portrait in Smoke - Bill S. Ballinger	1.50	3.50	5.00	M
898	A Texas Cowboy - Charles A. Siringo	1.50	3.50	5.00	W
899	The Humorous Side of Erskine Caldwell	.75	1.75	3.00	
900	A Wind is Rising - William Russell	1.50	3.50	5.00	
	1951				
901	Good is for Angels - Christopher Clark	1.50	3.50	5.00	E
902	Contraband - Cleve Adams	2.00	4.00	6.00	M
	Illo in Parade of Pleasure				
903	High, Wide and Handsome - Curt Brandon	1.50	3.00	5.00	
904AB	The Rains Came - Louis Bromfield	.75	1.75	3.00	
905	Thunder Mountain - Theodore Pratt	1.50	3.50	5.00	
906	Love is the One with Wings - Philip van Doren Stern	1.50	3.50	5.00	
907	Anger at Innocence - William Gardner Smith	1.50	3.50	5.00	
908	Murder Change - Wade Miller	1.50	3.50	5.00	M
909	Butcher's Dozen - John Bartlow Martin	1.50	3.50	5.00	
910	Let the Guns Roar! - Charles N. Heckelmann	1.50	3.50	5.00	W
911	The Young Lovers - Meyor Levin	.75	1.75	3.00	
912	A Family Romance - Elizabeth Pollet	1.50	3.50	5.00	
913	They Don't Dance Much - James Ross	1.50	3.50	5.00	E
914	Mission: Interplanetary - A. E. Van Vogt	2.00	4.00	7.50	SF
915	The Big Kill - Mickey Spillane	2.00	4.00	7.50	M
	Used in Parade of Pleasure, pg. 178				
916	Bugles in the Night - Arthur Herbert	1.50	3.50	5.00	
	1952				
917	A Streetcar Named Desire - Tennessee Williams	2.00	4.00	7.50	
918	A Place Called Estherville - Erskine Caldwell	2.00	4.00	6.00	E
919	The Delicate Prey - Paul Bowles	2.00	4.00	6.00	
920	Murder for Madame - Adam Knight	2.00	4.00	6.00	M
921AB	Moulin Rouge - Pierre LaMure	1.50	3.50	5.00	
922	Conjugal Love - Alberto Moravia	1.50	3.50	5.00	
923	Laird's Choice - Rosamond Marshall	1.50	3.50	5.00	
S924	The Promising Young Men - George Sklar	.75	1.75	3.00	
925	The Killer Brand - William Colt MacDonald	1.50	3.50	5.00	W
	1952				
D926	A World I Never Made - James T. Farrell	1.50	3.50	5.00	E
927	Renee - H. R. Lenormand	1.50	3.50	5.00	
928	Deadly Weapon - Wade Miller	1.50	3.50	5.00	M
D929	The Seven Storey Mountain - Thomas Merton	.75	1.75	3.00	
930	Finistere - Fritz Peters	.75	1.75	3.00	E
S931	The Troubled Air - Irwin Shaw	1.50	3.50	5.00	
932	The Long Wait - Mickey Spillane	2.00	4.00	7.50	M
	Used in Parade of Pleasure, pg. 179				
933	Southways - Erskine Caldwell	1.50	3.50	5.00	
T934	The Fountainhead - Ayn Rand	1.50	3.50	5.00	
935	Montana Rides Again - Evan Evans	.75	1.75	3.00	W
936	Sabotage - Cleve F. Adams	1.50	3.50	5.00	
937	Goodbye to Berlin - Christopher Isherwood	1.50	3.50	5.00	
938	Where Town Begins - Richard R. Werry	.75	1.75	3.00	
939	China Station - Donald R. Morris	.75	1.75	3.00	
940	Walk on the Water - Ralph Leveridge	.75	1.75	3.00	
941	There's One in Every Town - James Aswell	.75	1.75	3.00	

(SIGNET, continued)

942	Pressure - Charles Francis Coe	.75	1.75	3.00	
943	The Green Hills of Earth - Robert A. Heinlein	2.00	4.00	6.00	SF
944	The Loved and the Lost - Morley Callaghan	.75	1.75	3.00	
945	Rock Wagram - William Saroyan	.75	1.75	3.00	
D946	No Star is Lost - James T. Farrell	1.50	3.50	5.00	
947	See How they Run - Don M. Mankiewicz	.75	1.75	3.00	
948	The Girl in His Past - Georges Simenon	2.00	4.00	7.50	M
949	The Kiss-off - Douglas Heyes	1.50	3.50	5.00	
950	Only the Dead Know Brooklyn - Thomas Wolfe	1.50	3.50	5.00	
	1952				
951	Elinda - Frances Clippinger	.75	1.75	3.00	
952	Stirrups in the Dust - Burt Arthur	1.50	3.50	5.00	W
953	A Grove of Fever Trees - Daphne Rooke	.75	1.75	3.00	
S954	Mister Smith - Louis Bromfield	.75	1.75	2.00	
955	The Roman Spring of Mrs. Stone - Tennessee Williams	1.50	3.50	5.00	
S956	The Stubborn Heart - Frank G. Slaughter	.75	1.75	3.00	
957	The Broken Body - Floyd Mahannah	1.50	3.50	5.00	E
958	The Double Door - Theodora Keogh	.75	1.75	3.00	
959	The Revolt of Mamie Stover - William Bradford Huie	1.50	3.50	5.00	E
960	Two Adolescents - Alberto Moravia	.75	1.75	3.00	
S961	Back Street - Fannie Hurst	.50	1.25	2.00	
962	The Face of Innocence - William Sansom	.75	1.75	3.00	
963	The Caravan Passes - George Tabori	.75	1.75	3.00	E
964	The Heart of a Man - Georges Simenon	2.00	4.00	6.00	
965	Fighting Ramrod - Charles N. Heckelmann	1.50	3.50	5.00	W
966	Death is a Round Black Ball - Mike Roscoe	1.50	3.50	5.00	M
D967	Lie Down in Darkness - William Styron	.50	1.25	2.00	
968	The Long November - James Benson Nablo	.50	1.25	2.00	
969	A Hero of Our Time - Vasco Pratolini	.50	1.25	2.00	
970	Love in a Dry Season - Shelby Foote	.50	1.25	2.00	
S971	The Sky is Red - Guiseppe Berto	.50	1.25	2.00	
972	Those Devils in Baggy Pants - Ross Carter	.50	1.25	2.00	C
973	The Six-Gun Kid - William MacLeod Raine	1.50	3.50	5.00	W
974	Who Walk in Darkness - Chandler Brossard	.75	1.75	3.00	
D975	World Enough and Time - Robert Penn Warren	.75	1.75	3.00	
	1952				
976	The Temptress - Rosamond Marshall	.75	1.75	3.00	
977	The Unvanquished - William Faulkner	.75	1.75	3.00	
978	Tobacco Road - Jack Kirkland	1.50	3.50	5.00	
S979	Possession - Louis Bromfield	.75	1.75	3.00	
980	The Puppet Masters - Robert A. Heinlein	2.00	4.00	6.00	SF
981	The Lonely Hearts Murders - Wenzell Brown	1.50	3.50	5.00	M
982	Gunhawk Harvest - Leslie Ernenwein	.75	1.75	3.00	W
983	Episode in Palmetto - Erskine Caldwell	.75	1.75	3.00	E
	1953				
984	The Unwanted - Dante Arfelli	.75	1.75	3.00	
S985	The Age of Longing - Arthur Koestler	.75	1.75	3.00	
986	Your Body and Your Mind - Frank G. Slaughter	.75	1.75	3.00	
987	Reach to the Stars - Calder Willingham	.75	1.75	3.00	
988	Stripped for Murder - Bruno Fischer	1.50	3.50	5.00	M
	Illo in Parade of Pleasure				
989	Trouble in Tombstone - Tom J. Hopkins	.75	1.75	3.00	W
990	Sailor's Choice - Carl Bottume	.75	1.75	3.00	

Signet 953, c. Sigb

Signet 959, c. Sigb

Signet 1034, c. Sigb

991	Moulded in Earth - Richard Vaughan	.75	1.75	3.00	
D992	We Fished All Night - Willard Motley	.75	1.75	3.00	
993	Act of Passion - Georges Simenon	2.00	4.00	6.00	
994	When Boyhood Dreams Came True - James T. Farrell	1.50	3.50	5.00	
995	Night at the Vulcan - Ngaio Marsh	1.50	3.50	5.00	M
996	Doubtful Valley - George Garland	.75	1.75	3.00	
997	Leopard in the Grass - Desmond Stewart	.75	1.75	3.00	
998	Moira - Julian Green	.75	1.75	3.00	
S999	The Hoods - Harry Gray	1.50	3.50	5.00	
1000	Kiss Me, Deadly - Mickey Spillane	2.00	4.00	7.50	M
	Illo in Parade of Pleasure				
1001	The Catcher in the Rye - J. D. Salinger	1.50	3.50	5.00	
1002	Let It Come Down - Paul Bowles	.75	1.75	3.00	
1003	Dangerous Voyage - Gore Vidal	1.50	3.50	5.00	
1004	Sybil - Louis Auchincloss	.75	1.75	3.00	
1005	Blind Cartridges - William Colt MacDonald	1.50	3.50	5.00	W
1006	Captive in the Night - Donald Stokes	.75	1.75	3.00	
1007	Destination: Universe! - A. E. Van Vogt	2.00	4.00	6.00	SF
1008	You and Your Heart - H. M. Marvin	.50	1.25	2.00	NF
D1009	Down All Your Streets - Leonard Bishop	.75	1.75	3.00	
S1010	Back of Town - Maritta Wolff	.75	1.75	3.00	
1011	Dream of Eden - Winston Brebner aka The Second Circle	.75	1.75	3.00	
1012	The Blessing - Nancy Mitford	.75	1.75	3.00	
1013	Shoot to Kill - Wade Miller	.75	1.75	3.00	M
1014	They Lived by their Guns	1.50	3.50	5.00	
1015	Song of the Whip - Evan Evans	.75	1.75	3.00	W
1016	The Courting of Susie Brown - Erskine Caldwell	.75	1.75	3.00	
S1017	Scalpel - Horace McCoy	2.00	4.00	6.00	
S1018	Dream of Innocence - Turnley Walker	.75	1.75	3.00	
1019	Barbary Shore - Norman Mailer	1.50	3.50	5.00	E
1020	The Glass Harp - Truman Capote	1.50	3.50	5.00	
1021	Mittee - Daphne Rooke	.75	1.75	3.00	
1022	Knife at my Back - Adam Knight	1.50	3.50	5.00	M
S1023	Spark of Life - Erich Maria Remarque	1.50	3.50	5.00	E
1024	A Husband in the House - Stuart Engstrand	.75	1.75	3.00	
S1025	The Green Bay Tree - Louis Bromfield	.75	1.75	3.00	
	1953				
1026	Frail Barrier - Philip Gillon	.75	1.75	3.00	
1027	The Devil's Passkey - Jimmy Shannon	.75	1.75	3.00	
1028	The Snake Stomper - Joseph Wayne	.75	1.75	3.00	W
1029	Wise Blood - Flannery O'Connor	.75	1.75	3.00	
D1030	Invisible Man - Ralph Ellison	.75	1.75	3.00	
1031	An American Dream Girl - James T. Farrell	.75	1.75	3.00	
S1032	Sartoris - William Faulkner	1.50	3.50	5.00	
1033	My Life in Crime - John Bartlow Martin	1.50	3.50	5.00	NF
1034	I Take this Woman - George Simenon	2.00	4.00	7.50	M
1035	To End the Night - Alex Gaby	.75	1.75	3.00	
1036	Death in the Fifth Position - Edgar Box	1.50	3.50	5.00	M
1037	Bugle's Wake - Curt Brandon	.75	1.75	3.00	W
S1038	Rage of the Soul - Vincent Sheean	.75	1.75	3.00	
S1039	Sons and Lovers - D. H. Lawrence	1.50	3.50	5.00	
1040	The Darkening Door - Bill S. Ballinger	1.50	3.50	5.00	M
S1041	This Dear Encounter - Catherine Hutter	.75	1.75	3.00	
1042	The Red Carnation - Elio Vittorini	.75	1.75	3.00	
S1043	Submarine! - Edward L. Beach	.75	1.75	3.00	C
1044	Tomorrow, the Stars - Robert A. Heinlein	2.00	4.00	6.00	SF
1045	Trigger Vengeance - B. M. Bower	.75	1.75	3.00	W
1046	Brother of the Cheyennes - Max Brand	.75	1.75	3.00	W
1047	Wives and Husbands - David Duncan c-Maguire	2.00	4.00	7.50	E
1048	By Anyother Name - Roy Michaels	.75	1.75	3.00	
1049	Street Music - Theodora Keogh	.75	1.75	3.00	
1050	Pistol Pete - Frank Eaton	.75	1.75	3.00	W
	1953				
S1051	Scollay Square - Pearl Schiff	.75	1.75	3.00	
S1052	Heaven Pays No Dividends - Richard Kaufmann c-Maguire	.75	1.75	3.00	
1053	The Brigand - Giuseppe Berto	.75	1.75	3.00	
1054	Naked to Mine Enemies - Susan Yorke	.75	1.75	3.00	
S1055	The Consumer's Guide to Better Buying - Sidney Margolius	.75	1.75	3.00	NF
1056	The Mistress - H. C. Branner	.75	1.75	3.00	
1057	No Head for Her Pillow - Sam S. Taylor	.75	1.75	3.00	

1058 Ashes - Charles Francis Coe	.75	1.75	3.00	
1059 Ranger Man - William Colt MacDonald	.75	1.75	3.00	W
1060 Riddle Me This - Mike Roscoe	.75	1.75	3.00	
1061 The Naked Streets - Vasco Pratolini	.75	1.75	3.00	
S1062 Natural Child - Calder Willingham	.75	1.75	3.00	
1063 Home Is Upriver - Brian Horwin	.75	1.75	3.00	
1064 The Descent - Fritz Peters	.75	1.75	3.00	
1065 A Funeral for Sabella - Robert Travers	.75	1.75	3.00	
D1066 Father and Son - James T. Farrell	.75	1.75	3.00	
1067 Crime Without Punishment - Guenther Reinhardt	.75	1.75	3.00	
D1068 Confessors of the Name - Gladys Schmitt c-Maguire	.75	1.75	3.00	
1069 Justice Comes to Tomahawk - William MacLeod Raine	.75	1.75	3.00	W
S1070 The Best Thing that Ever Happened - Warren Leslie	.75	1.75	3.00	
S1071 The Conformist - Alberto Moravia	.75	1.75	3.00	
1072 A Cow is Too Much Trouble in Los Angeles - Joseph Foster	.75	1.75	3.00	
1073 Four Days in a Lifetime - Georges Simenon	2.00	4.00	7.50	M
S1074 Strange Fruit - Lillian Smith	.75	1.75	3.00	
T1075 From Here to Eternity - James Jones	1.50	3.50	5.00	C
1953				
1076 The Big Sin - Jack Webb	1.50	3.50	5.00	
1077 By Gun and Spur - Joseph Wayne	.75	1.75	3.00	W
S1078 The Curve and the Tusk - Stuart Cloete	.75	1.75	3.00	
S1079 Sanctuary and Requiem for a Nun - William Faulkner	1.50	3.50	5.00	
S1080 Caesar's Angel - Mary Anne Amsbary	.75	1.75	3.00	
1081 The Disguises of Love - Robie Macauley	.75	1.75	3.00	
1082 The Currents of Space - Isaac Asimov	2.00	4.00	6.00	SF
1083 The Day I Died - Lawrence Lariar	.75	1.75	3.00	
1084 Deadlier than the Male - James E. Gunn	1.50	3.50	5.00	
1085 The Saga of Billy the Kid - Walter Noble Burns	1.50	3.50	5.00	B
S1086 Lady Chatterley's Lover - D. H. Lawrence	1.50	3.50	5.00	
1087 Appointment in Samarra - John O'Hara	1.50	3.50	5.00	
1088 Young Man with a Horn - Dorothy Baker	.75	1.75	3.00	
1089 Guilty Bystander - Wade Miller	.75	1.75	3.00	M
1954				
S1090 The Mountain and the Valley - Ernest Buckler	.75	1.75	3.00	
1091 A Lamp for Nightfall - Erskine Caldwell	.75	1.75	3.00	
1092 Depends What You Mean By Love - Nicholas Monsarrat	.75	1.75	3.00	
1093 Death Before Bedtime - Edgar Box	1.50	3.50	5.00	M
S1094 Amazon Head-Hunters - Lewis Cotlow	1.50	3.50	5.00	
1095 Uncle Tom's Children - Richard Wright	.75	1.75	3.00	
1096 Gigi and Julie de Carneilhan - Sidonie Colette	.75	1.75	3.00	
1097 The Waitress - William Fisher	.75	1.75	3.00	
S1098 The Skin - Curzio Malaparte	.75	1.75	3.00	
1099 The Center of the Stage - Gerald Sykes	.75	1.75	3.00	
1100 The Tattooed Heart - Theodora Keogh	.75	1.75	3.00	
1954				
1101 The Big Dry - George Garland	.75	1.75	3.00	
D1102 Night Shift - Maritta Wolff	.75	1.75	3.00	
1103 The Sunburned Corpse - Adam Knight	.75	1.75	3.00	M
1104 Shiloh - Shelby Foote	.75	1.75	3.00	
1105 The Demolished Man - Alfred Bester	2.00	4.00	7.50	SF
1106 A Breed Apart - Fleming MacLiesh	.75	1.75	3.00	
D1107 Days of My Love - Leonard Bishop	.75	1.75	3.00	
1108 Hell in his Holsters - Charles N. Heckelmann	.75	1.75	3.00	W
1109 The Brothers Rico - Georges Simenon	2.00	4.00	7.50	M
1110 Portrait of the Damned - Richard McKaye c-Maguire	.75	1.75	3.00	
1111 Nine Stories - J. D. Salinger	.75	1.75	3.00	
1112 The Double Shuffle - James Hadley Chase	1.50	3.50	5.00	M
1113 The Execution of Private Slovik - William Bradford Huie	1.50	3.50	5.00	C
S1114 The Outsider - Richard Wright	.75	1.75	3.00	
1115 The Lost Year - Robert Hazel	.75	1.75	3.00	
1116 Morning, Winter and Night - John Nairne Michaelson	.75	1.75	3.00	
1117 The Moon and the Bonfires - Cesare Pavese	.75	1.75	3.00	

Signet 1134, c. Sigb   Signet 1144, c. Sigb   Signet 1149, c. Sigb

(SIGNET, continued)

S1118	My Days of Anger - James T. Farrell	1.50	3.50	5.00	
1119	Murder, Madness and the Law - Louis H. Cohen c-Maguire	2.00	4.00	7.50	M
1120	Smoke Bellew - Jack London	1.50	3.50	5.00	
1121	The Birds and the Bees - James Aswell	.75	1.75	3.00	
1122	The Fancy Dress Party - Alberto Moravia	.75	1.75	3.00	
S1123	The Street - Ann Petry	2.00	4.00	6.00	E
1124	Belle - Georges Simenon	2.00	4.00	7.50	M
1125					
1126	The Naked Heart - John Lee Weldon	.75	1.75	3.00	
	1954				
1127	The Time Masters - Wilson Tucker	2.00	4.00	6.00	SF
1128	The Long Wind - Joseph Wayne	.75	1.75	3.00	W
1129	Pajama - Richard Bissell	.75	1.75	3.00	
D1130	Trial by Darkness - Charles Gorham	.75	1.75	3.00	
S1131	Cancel All Our Vows - John D. MacDonald	1.50	3.50	5.00	M
1132	The Face of the Deep - Jacob Twersky	.75	1.75	3.00	
S1133	The Time of Man - Elizabeth Madox Roberts	.75	1.75	3.00	
1134	The Beautiful Trap - Bill S. Ballinger	.75	1.75	3.00	M
1135	The Texan - Burt Arthur	.75	1.75	3.00	W
1136	We Are the Living - Erskine Caldwell	.75	1.75	3.00	
S1137	A House of Her Own - Robert F. Mirvish	.75	1.75	3.00	
1138	Go Tell It on the Mountain - James Baldwin	.75	1.75	3.00	
1139	Kiss and Kill - Adam Knight	1.50	3.50	5.00	M
1140	Guns of the Frontier - William MacLeod Raine	1.50	3.50	5.00	W
S1141	Blue Earth - John H. Burgess	.75	1.75	3.00	
1142	Branded - A. C. Abbott	.75	1.75	3.00	
S1143	A Law for the Lion - Louis Auchincloss	.75	1.75	3.00	
1144	The Bottom of the Bottle - Georges Simenon	2.00	4.00	7.50	M
1145	The Money Song - Arnold Shaw	.75	1.75	3.00	
1146	The Wayward Ones - Sara Harris	.75	1.75	3.00	
1147	A Kiss Before Dying - Ira Levin	.75	1.75	3.00	
S1148	The Wild Palms and the Old Man - William Faulkner	1.50	3.50	5.00	
1149	The Naked Angel - Jack Webb c-Maguire	2.00	4.00	7.50	M
S1150	Portrait of the Artist as a Young Man - James Joyce	1.50	3.50	5.00	
	1955				
1151	Mafia - Ed Reid	1.50	3.50	5.00	
1152	Galatea - James M. Cain	1.50	3.50	5.00	
1153	Serenade - James M. Cain	1.50	3.50	5.00	
1154	Requiem for a Redhead - Lindsay Hardy	.75	1.75	3.00	
1155	Awakening - Jean-Baptiste Rossi	.75	1.75	3.00	
D1156	The Chain in the Heart - Hubert Creekmore	.75	1.75	3.00	
S1157	The Hive - Camilo Jose Cela	.75	1.75	3.00	
1158	This Man and this Woman - James T. Farrell	1.50	3.50	5.00	
1159	The Scattered Seed - Stuart Engstrand	.75	1.75	3.00	
1160	The Ox-Bow Incident - Walter Van Tilburg Clark	.75	1.75	3.00	W
1161	Assignment in Eternity - Robert A. Heinlein	2.00	4.00	6.00	SF
S1162	Mud on the Stars - William Bradford Huie	.75	1.75	3.00	
1163	The General's Wench - Rosamond Marshall	.75	1.75	3.00	
1164	The Black City - M. F. Caulfield	.75	1.75	3.00	
1165	The Color of His Blood - Marris Murray	.75	1.75	3.00	

(SIGNET, continued)

1166	The Young and Hungry-hearted - James Aswell	.75	1.75	3.00	
1167	Let the Night Cry - Charles Wells	.75	1.75	3.00	
1168	Law and Order, Unlimited - William Colt MacDonald	1.50	3.50	5.00	W
D1169	Forever Amber - Kathleen Winsor	.50	1.25	2.00	
1170	Time for Love - Margaret Lee Runbeck	.75	1.75	3.00	
S1171	Search for the Sun - Charles Furcolowe	.75	1.75	3.00	
1172	A Private Stair - David Loughlin	.75	1.75	3.00	

1955

1173	The Spider in the Cup - Norman Hales	.75	1.75	3.00	
1174	Texas Hellion - J. H. Plenn	.75	1.75	3.00	W
1175	Devil in the Flesh - Raymond Radiguet	.75	1.75	3.00	
1176	The Sling and the Arrow - Stuart Engstrand	.75	1.75	3.00	
1177	Proud Youth - Alexander Eliot	.75	1.75	3.00	
S1178	The Housewarming - George Sklar	.75	1.75	3.00	
1179	The Lie - Peggy Goodin	.75	1.75	3.00	
1180	Fatal Step - Wade Miller	.75	1.75	3.00	M
1181	Six-Shooter Showdown - William Colt MacDonald	.75	1.75	3.00	W
1182	The Snake Pit - Mary Jane Ward	.75	1.75	3.00	
D1183	A Many-Splendored Thing - Suyin Han	.75	1.75	3.00	
1184	Thunder in the Heart - John Lee Weldon	.75	1.75	3.00	
1185	Room Clerk - Herbert Gold	.75	1.75	3.00	
1186	All the Way Home - Walter Freeman	.75	1.75	3.00	
1187	I'll Bury My Dead - James Hadley Chase	1.50	3.50	5.00	M
1188	Inspector Maigret and the Strangled Stripper - Georges Simenon c-Maguire	2.00	4.00	7.50	M
S1189	Cheri and the Last of Cheri - Sidonie Colette	.75	1.75	3.00	
1190	Kitty - Rosamond Marshall	.75	1.75	3.00	
1191	The Final Hours - Jose Suarez Carreno	.75	1.75	3.00	
1192	A Texas Cowboy - Charles A. Siringo	1.50	3.50	5.00	W
1193	River in My Blood - Richard Bissell	.75	1.75	3.00	
1194	Revolt in 2100 - Robert A. Heinlein	2.00	4.00	6.00	SF
1195	The Butterfly - James M. Cain	1.50	3.50	5.00	
1196	Mean as Hell - Dee Harkey	.75	1.75	3.00	
S1197	Street of the Barefoot Lovers - Joseph Foster	.75	1.75	3.00	
D1198	Love is a Bridge - Charles Bracelen Flood	.75	1.75	3.00	
D1199	The Complete Stories of Erskine Caldwell	.75	1.75	3.00	
S1200	The Jungle Seas - Arthur A. Ageton	.75	1.75	3.00	

1955

1201	Bamboo - Robert O. Bowen	.75	1.75	3.00	
1202	Out of the Red Brush - Kermit Daugherty	.75	1.75	3.00	
1203	Win, Place and Die! - Lawrence Lariar	.75	1.75	3.00	M
1204	Love Trap - Lionel White	.75	1.75	3.00	
S1205	Tombstone - Walter Noble Burns	1.50	3.50	5.00	NF
D1206	The Cry and the Covenant - Morton Thompson	.75	1.75	3.00	
1207	Three Sinners in Paris - Toni Howard	.75	1.75	3.00	
1208	Live for Today - Vincent Sheean c-Maguire	.75	1.75	3.00	
1209	The Fascinator - Theodora Keogh	.75	1.75	3.00	
1210	My Husband Keeps Telling Me to go to Hell - Ella Bentley Arthur	.75	1.75	3.00	
D1211	The Hoods - Harry Grey	1.50	3.50	5.00	

Signet 1173, c. Sigb

Signet 1182, c. Sigb

Signet 1188, c. Sigb

402

Signet 1221, c. Sigb   Signet 1233, c. Sigb   Signet 1234, c. Sigb

(SIGNET, continued)

T1212 A Child of the Century - Ben Hecht	.75	1.75	3.00	
S1213 The Time of Indifference - Alberto Moravia	.75	1.75	3.00	
S1214 Life of Davy Crockett - Davy Crockett	1.50	3.50	5.00	B
S1215 Lost Island - Graham McInnes	.75	1.75	3.00	
1216 Slice of Hell - Mike Roscoe	.75	1.75	3.00	
c-Maguire				
1217 Death Likes it Hot - Edgar Box	1.50	3.50	5.00	M
1218 The City and the Pillar - Gore Vidal	1.50	3.50	5.00	
1219 Cattle Kingdom - Alan LeMay	1.50	3.50	5.00	W
S1220 Darkness at Noon - Arthur Koestler	.75	1.75	3.00	
1221 The Black Donnellys - Thomas P. Kelley	.75	1.75	3.00	NF
S1222 The Eternal Voyagers - Robert F. Mirvish	.75	1.75	3.00	
1223 First Affair - Raffaele LaCapria	.75	1.75	3.00	
1224 The Space Frontiers - Roger Lee Vernon	2.00	4.00	6.00	SF
1225 The Last Kill - Charles Wells	.75	1.75	3.00	
1955 c-Maguire				
1226 Violent Streets - Dale Kramer	1.50	3.50	5.00	
D1227 The Lovers - Kathleen Winsor	.50	1.25	2.00	
1228 Sons of the Saddle - William MacLeod				
Raine	.75	1.75	3.00	W
D1229 Moby Dick - Herman Melville	1.50	3.50	5.00	A
1230 High Water - Richard Bissell	.75	1.75	3.00	
1231 The Farmer's Bride - Robert Hazel	.75	1.75	3.00	
1232 Hard Man with a Gun - Charles N.				
Heckelmann	.75	1.75	3.00	W
1233 The Damned Lovely - Jack Webb	2.00	4.00	7.50	M
c-Maguire				
1234 This Thing Called Love - Harve Breit &				
Marc Slonim	.75	1.75	3.00	
1235 Killer's Choice - Wade Miller	.75	1.75	3.00	M
1236 The Rose Tattoo - Tennessee Williams	.75	1.75	3.00	
D1237 The Lying Days - Nadine Gordimer	.75	1.75	3.00	
S1238 Everything Happens at Night - Bernard Wolfe	.75	1.75	3.00	
1239 Warrior's Return - Ted Pittenger	.75	1.75	3.00	
S1240 The Caves of Steel - Isaac Asimov	2.00	4.00	6.00	SF
1241 To Find a Killer - Lionel White	2.00	4.00	7.50	M
c-Maguire				
1242 Web of Gunsmoke - Will Hickok	.75	1.75	3.00	W
1243 The Body in the Bed - Bill S. Ballinger	.75	1.75	3.00	M
D1244 The Gold of their Bodies - Charles Gorham	.75	1.75	3.00	
S1245 Satchmo - Louis Armstrong	1.50	3.50	5.00	B
1246 Nights of Love and Laughter - Henry Miller	2.50	6.00	10.00	
1247 So Cold, My Bed - Sam S. Taylor	2.00	4.00	7.50	
c-Maguire				
1248 Inspector Maigret and the Killers - Georges				
Simenon	2.00	4.00	7.50	M
S1249 The Sheltering Sky - Paul Bowles	.75	1.75	3.00	
1250 The Golden Sleep - Vivian Connell	.75	1.75	3.00	
1955				
1251 Laramie Rides Alone - Will Ermine	.75	1.75	3.00	W
S1252 Goodbye to Berlin - Christopher Isherwood	.75	1.75	3.00	
S1253 Intruder in the Dust - William Faulkner	.75	1.75	3.00	
S1254 Heart of Darkness and the Secret Sharer -				
Joseph Conrad	1.50	3.50	5.00	
1255 The Unholy Three and Other Stories - Louis				
Auchincloss	.75	1.75	3.00	
1256 The Bleeding Scissors - Bruno Fischer	.75	1.75	3.00	M
c-Maguire				

1257	Uneasy Street - Wade Miller	.75	1.75	3.00	
1258	Montana Man - Paul Evan Lehman	.75	1.75	3.00	W
T1259	The Narrows - Ann Petry	.50	1.25	2.00	
D1260	The Farm - Louis Bromfield	.50	1.25	2.00	E
1261	How Green Was My Sex Life - Lawrence Lariar	.75	1.75	3.00	
S1262	A Streetcar Named Desire - Tennessee Williams	2.00	4.00	7.50	
D1263	The Rains Came - Louis Bromfield	.50	1.25	2.00	
	1956				
1264	The Primitive - Chester Himes	.75	1.75	3.00	
T1265	Not as a Stranger - Morton Thompson	.50	1.25	2.00	
S1266	The Soft Voice of the Serpent - Nadine Gordimer	.50	1.25	2.00	
1267	Margaret - Caroline Slade	.50	1.25	2.00	
1268	Stopover for Murder - Floyd Mahannah c-Maguire	.75	1.75	3.00	M
1269	Whistling Lead - Eugene Cunningham	.75	1.75	3.00	
1270	Calamity Fair - Wade Miller c-Maguire	2.00	4.00	7.50	M
S1271	Fifty Roads to Town - Earl Hammer, Jr.	1.50	3.50	5.00	
1272	Love and Money - Erskine Caldwell	.75	1.75	3.00	
S1273	The Blue Hussar - Roger Nimier	.75	1.75	3.00	
1274	The Body Beautiful - Bill S. Ballinger	.75	1.75	3.00	M
1275	The Face of Time - James T. Farrell 1956 c-Maguire	.75	1.75	3.00	
1276	I'll Kill You Next! - Adam Knight c-Maguire	2.00	4.00	7.50	M
1277	Bunch Grass - Joseph Wayne	.75	1.75	3.00	W
1278	Dirty Eddie - Ludwig Bemelmans	.75	1.75	3.00	
S1279	Making of a Mistress - Susan Morley	.75	1.75	3.00	
S1280	General Billy Mitchell - Roger Burlingame	1.50	3.50	5.00	B
S1281	Adventures in the Skin Trade - Dylan Thomas	1.50	3.50	5.00	
S1282	I, Robot - Isaac Asimov	2.50	6.00	10.00	SF
1283	The Nightshade Ring - Lindsay Hardy	.75	1.75	3.00	
1284	Meg - Theodora Keogh	.75	1.75	3.00	
S1285	No Time for Sergeants - Mac Hyman	.75	1.75	3.00	
1286	The Big Steal - Earle Basinsky	.75	1.75	3.00	M
1287	Lobo Law - Will Ermine	.75	1.75	3.00	W
1288	Conjugal Love - Alberto Moravia	.75	1.75	3.00	
1289	Animal Farm - George Orwell	2.50	6.00	10.00	
S1290	Too Late the Phalarope - Alan Paton	.75	1.75	3.00	
D1291	The Royal Box - Frances Parkinson Keyes	.75	1.75	3.00	
S1292	The Enemy - Wirt Williams	.75	1.75	3.00	
1293	I Stole $16,000,000 - Thomas P. Kelley & Herbert Emerson Wilson	1.50	3.50	5.00	NF
1294	Violence in Velvet - Michael Avallone c-Maguire	1.50	3.50	5.00	M
1295	The Lonely - Paul Gallico	.75	1.75	3.00	
1296	The Delicate Prey - Paul Bowles	.75	1.75	3.00	
1297	The Valley of Hunted Men - Paul Evan Lehman	.75	1.75	3.00	W
1298	Contraband - Cleve F. Adams	.75	1.75	3.00	
D1299	The Third Generation - Chester Himes	.75	1.75	3.00	
1300	Washington Lowdown - Larston Farrar	.75	1.75	3.00	
	1956				
1301	The Secret of Mary Magdalene - Paul Ilton	.75	1.75	3.00	
1302	Gunplay Valley - Joseph Wayne	.75	1.75	3.00	W
1303	The Six-Gun Kid - William MacLeod Raine	.75	1.75	3.00	W
1304	Winesburg, Ohio - Sherwood Anderson	.50	1.25	2.00	
D1305	Boswell's London Journal - James Boswell	.75	1.75	3.00	
S1306	A Ghost at Noon - Alberto Moravia	.75	1.75	3.00	
S1307	Murder in Paradise - Richard Gehman	.75	1.75	3.00	M
S1308	The Girl in the Dogwood Cabin - Calder Willingham	.75	1.75	3.00	
S1309	The Whispers of Love - Marguerite Duras	.75	1.75	3.00	
1310	The Killing - Lionel White c-Maguire	.75	1.75	3.00	
1311	The Broken Doll - Jack Webb c-Maguire	1.50	3.50	5.00	
1312	The Fastest Gun in Texas - C. J. LaRoche & J. H. Plenn	1.50	3.50	5.00	
1313	The Tent of the Wicked - Robert Switzer	.75	1.75	3.00	
1314	There's One in Every Town - James Aswell	.75	1.75	3.00	
1315	Knight's Gambit - William Faulkner	.75	1.75	3.00	

1316	The Glass Playpen - Edwin Fadiman, Jr. c-Maguire	.75	1.75	3.00	
1317	A Devil in Paradise - Henry Miller	1.50	3.50	5.00	
S1318	The Black Prince and Other Stories - Shirley Ann Grau	.75	1.75	3.00	
1319	The Tooth and the Nail - Bill S. Ballinger c-Maguire	.75	1.75	3.00	M
1320	Shore Leave - Frederic Wakeman	.75	1.75	3.00	
1321	Portrait in Smoke - Bill S. Ballinger	.75	1.75	3.00	M
1322	Stone Cold Blonde - Adam Knight c-Maguire	2.00	4.00	7.50	M
1323	Buckskin Marshal - Will Ermine	.75	1.75	3.00	W
1324	Delay En Route - Jerry Weil c-Maguire	.75	1.75	3.00	
1325	The Navigator - Jules Roy	.75	1.75	3.00	
	1956				
1326	Nightmare Alley - William Lindsay Gresham	.75	1.75	3.00	
1327	The Snow Was Black - Georges Simenon	2.00	4.00	6.00	M
D1328	The New American Handy College Dictionary - Albert H. Morehead & Loy Morehead	.75	1.75	3.00	NF
1329	The Kiss-off - Douglas Heyes	.75	1.75	3.00	
D1330	Band of Angels - Robert Penn Warren	.75	1.75	3.00	
1331	Black Sombrero - William Colt MacDonald	.75	1.75	3.00	W
1332	Julie - Andrew L. Stone c-Maguire	.75	1.75	3.00	
S1333	The Glass Harp and A Tree of Night - Truman Capote	1.50	3.50	5.00	
1334	Baby Doll - Tennessee Williams	1.50	3.50	5.00	
1335	The Living Idol - Robert Switzer c-Maguire	3.00	6.00	12.00	E
S1336	Nectar in a Sieve - Kamala Markandaya	.75	1.75	3.00	
S1337	The Alien Heart - Catherine Hutter	.75	1.75	3.00	
1338	Inspector Maigret in New York's Underworld - Georges Simenon c-Maguire	2.00	4.00	6.00	M
1339	Return of the Texan - Burt Arthur	.75	1.75	3.00	W
1340	Trigger Justice - Leslie Ernenwein	.75	1.75	3.00	W
1341	The Wayward Ones - Sara Harris	.75	1.75	3.00	
1342	Gretta - Erskine Caldwell	.75	1.75	3.00	
1343	Tea and Sympathy - Robert Anderson	.75	1.75	3.00	
1344	Good Night, Sailor - J. Inchardi	.75	1.75	3.00	
S1345	A Good Man is Hard to Find - Flannery O'Connor	.75	1.75	3.00	
S1346	Operation: Outer Space - Murray Leinster	2.00	4.00	6.00	SF
1347	Girl Running - Adam Knight	.75	1.75	3.00	M
S1348	The Teahouse of the August Moon - Vern Sneider	.75	1.75	3.00	
1349	French Girls are Vi cious - James T. Farrell	.75	1.75	3.00	
1350	Office Wife - Jerry Weil	.75	1.75	3.00	
	1957				
1351	Death is a Cold, Keen Edge - Earle Basinsky c-Maguire	.75	1.75	3.00	M
1352	Blood of the West - Paul Evan Lehman	.75	1.75	3.00	W
1353	The Slander of Witches - Richard Gehman	.75	1.75	3.00	
1354	Night Flight - Antoine de Saint Exupery	.75	1.75	3.00	
D1355	The Strangeland - Ned Calmer	.75	1.75	3.00	
S1356	Anastasia - Marcelle Maurette	.75	1.75	3.00	
1357	A Stranger in Eden - Desmond Stewart	.75	1.75	3.00	
1358	One Tear for My Grave - Mike Roscoe c-Maguire	.75	1.75	3.00	M
1359	Desire Me - Leonhard Frank	.75	1.75	3.00	
1360	Brave in the Saddle - Will Ermine	.75	1.75	3.00	W
1361	Ever Since Adam and Eve - Alfred Andriola & Mel Casson	.75	1.75	3.00	
S1362	Quicksand - William Brinkley	.75	1.75	3.00	
S1363	The Tyranny of Sex - Ludwig Lewisohn	.75	1.75	3.00	
S1364	The Girl He Left Behind - Marion Hargrove	.50	1.25	2.00	
S1365	The Angry Hills - Leon Uris	.75	1.75	3.00	C
1366	Death Rider - J. O. Barnwell	.75	1.75	3.00	
	1957				
S1367	Gift from the Sea - Anne Morrow Lindbergh	.75	1.75	3.00	
D1368	1,000,000 Delinquents - Benjamin Fine	1.50	3.50	5.00	
1369	Shoot to Kill - Wade Miller	.75	1.75	3.00	M
S1370	The Short Cut - Ennio Flaiano	.75	1.75	3.00	

S1371	I Leap Over the Wall - Monica Baldwin	.75	1.75	3.00	
1372	Two Adolescents - Alberto Moravia	.75	1.75	3.00	
1373	Bullet Law - Charles N. Heckelmann	.75	1.75	3.00	W
1374	An Act of Violence - Edwin Fadiman, Jr.	.75	1.75	3.00	
D1375	The Deer Park - Norman Mailer	.75	1.75	3.00	
	1957				
1376	Strangers in the House - Georges Simenon	2.00	4.00	6.00	M
1377	The Life, the Loves, the Adventurs of Omar Khayyam - Manuel Komroff	.75	1.75	3.00	
1378	Flight into Terror - Lionel White	.75	1.75	3.00	
	c-Maguire				
1379	The Bandaged Nude - Robert Finnegan	.75	1.75	3.00	
1380	Tortilla Flat - John Steinbeck	.75	1.75	3.00	
1381	The Story of Sandy - Susan Stanhope Wexler	.75	1.75	3.00	
1382	What am I Doing Here? - Abner Dean	.75	1.75	3.00	
1383	Killer in the House - Borden Deal	.75	1.75	3.00	
1384	The Return of the Kid - Joseph Wayne	.75	1.75	3.00	W
S1385	The Bachelor Party - Paddy Chayefsky	.75	1.75	3.00	
	Movie tie-in				
D1386	End as a Man - Calder Willingham	.75	1.75	3.00	
S1387	Look Not Upon Me - Denys Jones	.75	1.75	3.00	
T1388	Andersonville - MacKinlay Kantor	1.00	2.00	3.50	NF
S1389	The Stars, My Destination - Alfred Bester	2.00	4.00	6.00	SF
1390	The Wastrel - Frederic Wakeman	.75	1.75	3.00	
D1391	The Long Ships - Frans G. Bengtsson	.75	1.75	3.00	W
S1392	Cat Man - Edward Hoagland	.75	1.75	3.00	E
1393	Paint on Their Faces - Jerry Weil	.75	1.75	3.00	
	c-Maguire				
1394					
1395	Murder for Madame - Adam Knight	.75	1.75	3.00	M
1396	Clattering Hoofs - William MacLeod Raine	.75	1.75	3.00	W
1397	In A Summer Season - Ludwig Lewisohn	.75	1.75	3.00	
1398	Montana Rides! - Evan Evans	.75	1.75	3.00	W
1399	The Last Days of Sodom and Gomorrah - Paul Ilton c-Maguire	3.00	6.00	12.00	E
S1400	Lizzie - Shirley Jackson	.75	1.75	3.00	
	1957				
1401	Trigger Man - Burt Arthur	.75	1.75	3.00	W
1402	Ripening Seed - Sidonie Colette	.75	1.75	3.00	
1403	Quick-Trigger Country - Clem Colt	.75	1.75	3.00	W
1404	Love in the Afternoon - Claude Anet	.75	1.75	3.00	
1405	The Private Eye - Cleve F. Adams	.75	1.75	3.00	M
	c-Maguire				
1406					
D1407	Beyond Desire - Pierre LaMure	.75	1.75	3.00	
S1408	More Deaths than One - Stuart Engstrand	.75	1.75	3.00	
S1409	The Prince and the Showgirl - Terence Rattigan	2.00	4.00	6.00	
	Movie tie-in				
D1410	Heart of Darkness and the Secret Sharer - Joseph Conrad	.75	1.75	3.00	
D1411	Confessions of Felix Krull, Confidence Man - Thomas Mann	.75	1.75	3.00	NF
S1412	A Hatful of Rain - Michael Vincente Gazzo	.75	1.75	3.00	
S1413	Sweet Smell of Success - Ernest Lehman	.75	1.75	3.00	
1414	Flint - Gil Dodge	.75	1.75	3.00	
S1415	The Night Before Chancellorsville - Shelby Foote	.75	1.75	3.00	

Signet 1301, c. Sigb

Signet S1334, c. Sigb

Signet 1399, c. Sigb

1416 The Killer Brand - William Colt MacDonald	.75	1.75	3.00	W
1417 This Very Earth - Erskine Caldwell	.75	1.75	3.00	
1418 Doubtful Valley - George Garland	.50	1.25	2.00	
1419 Sabotage - Cleve F. Adams	.75	1.75	3.00	
S1420 The Deliverance of Sister Cecilia - William Brinkley & Sister Cecilia	.50	1.25	2.00	
1421 The Hitchhiker - Georges Simenon	2.00	4.00	6.00	M
1422 The Bad Blonde - Jack Webb	1.50	3.50	5.00	
c-Maguire				
1423 The Manhunter - Matthew Gant	.75	1.75	3.00	
S1424 This is the West - Robert West Howard	.75	1.75	3.00	NF
S1425 Pajama - Richard Bissell	.50	1.25	2.00	
1957				
S1426 Country Place - Ann Petry	.50	1.25	2.00	
1427 Double Indemnity - James M. Cain	.75	1.75	3.00	
c-Maguire				
D1428 Lady Chatterley's Lover - D. H. Lawrence	.75	1.75	3.00	
1429 The Unfaithful Wife - Jules Roy	.50	1.25	2.00	
S1430 Gulf Coast Stories - Erskine Caldwell	.75	1.75	3.00	
D1431 New American Roget's College Thesaurus in Dictionary Form	.50	1.25	2.00	NF
1432 The Hard Guys - John B. Sanford	.50	1.25	2.00	
S1433 The Martian Way and Other Stories - Isaac Asimov	1.50	3.50	5.00	SF
1434 The Tight Corner - Sam Ross	.50	1.25	2.00	
1435 The Man from Yesterday - John S. Daniels	.75	1.75	3.00	
1436 Montana Rides Again - Evan Evans	.75	1.75	3.00	W
S1437 Appointment in Samarra - John O'Hara	.50	1.25	2.00	
D1438 Lucy Crown - Irwin Shaw	.50	1.25	2.00	
S1439 Ruby McCollum - William Bradford Huie	.50	1.25	2.00	
1440 Coral Comes High - George P. Hunt	.50	1.25	2.00	
1441 The Mountain Boys - Paul Webb	.50	1.25	2.00	
1442 The House Next Door - Lionel White	.50	1.25	2.00	
1443 Gunsmoke in Nevada - Burt Arthur	.75	1.75	3.00	W
S1444 Double Star - Robert A. Heinlein	1.50	3.50	5.00	SF
1445 Love's Lovely Counterfeit - James M. Cain	.75	1.75	3.00	
1446 The Comedian and Other Stories - Ernest Lehman	.50	1.25	2.00	
1447 Secret of Hidden Valley - Loring Hutchinson	.50	1.25	2.00	
1448 Find My Killer - Manly Wade Wellman	.75	1.75	3.00	
c-Maguire				
1449 Nobody Dies in Paris - Jerry Weil	.50	1.25	2.00	
1450 Shore Leave - Frederic Wakeman	.50	1.25	2.00	
1957				
S1451 Comfort Me With Apples - Peter De Vries	.50	1.25	2.00	
S1452 I'm Owen Harrison Harding - James Whitfield Ellison	.50	1.25	2.00	
S1453 Tip on a Dead Jockey - Irwin Shaw	.50	1.25	2.00	
T1454 Marjorie Morningstar - Herman Wouk	.50	1.25	2.00	
D1455 The Field of Vision - Wright Morris	.50	1.25	2.00	
1456 A House in the Uplands - Erskine Caldwell	.50	1.25	2.00	
S1457 A Dangerous Woman - James T. Farrell	.75	1.75	3.00	
D1458 Don't Go Near the Water - William Brinkley	.50	1.25	2.00	
S1459 Submarine! - Edward L. Beach	.75	1.75	3.00	C
S1460 This is Goggle - Bentz Plagemann	.50	1.25	2.00	
1461 Wild Town - Jim Thompson	2.00	4.00	6.00	
c-Maguire				
S1462 Bitter Victory - Rene Hardy	.50	1.25	2.00	
S1463 Modern Sex Life - Edwin Hirsch	.50	1.25	2.00	
S1464 The City and the Stars - Arthur C. Clarke	2.00	4.00	6.00	SF
1465 The Fugitive - Georges Simenon	2.00	4.00	6.00	M
S1466 Those Devils in Baggy Pants - Ross Carter	.50	1.25	2.00	C
S1467 A Walk in the Sun - Harry Brown	.50	1.25	2.00	
T1468 The Fountainhead - Ayn Rand	.75	1.75	3.00	
D1469 The Amazing Crime and Trial of Leopold and Loeb - Maureen McKernan	.75	1.75	3.00	NF
S1470 The Ox-Bow Incident - Walter Van Tilburg Clark	.50	1.25	2.00	W
1471 Old Soldiers Never Die - Wolf Mankowitz	.50	1.25	2.00	
1472 Kill Once, Kill Twice - Kyle Hunt	.50	1.25	2.00	
c-Maguire				
1473 Bandido - Nelson Nye	.75	1.75	3.00	W
1474 The Flesh was Cold - Bruno Fischer	.75	1.75	3.00	M
c-Maguire				

(SIGNET, continued)

No.	Title				
1475	Death in the Fifth Position - Edgar Box 1957	.75	1.75	3.00	M
S1476	The FBI in Action - Ken Jones	.50	1.25	2.00	
D1477	Raquel - Lion Feuchtwanger	.50	1.25	2.00	
S1478	War! - Alex Austin	.50	1.25	2.00	C
1479	A Place Called Estherville - Erskine Caldwell	.50	1.25	2.00	
1480	The Sins of Sandra Shaw - Larston Farrar 1958	.50	1.25	2.00	
1481	Thirty Notches - Brad Ward	.75	1.75	3.00	W
1482	Guilty Bystander - Wade Miller	.75	1.75	3.00	
1483	Powdersmoke Feud - William MacLeod Raine	.75	1.75	3.00	W
1484	Death Likes it Hot - Edgar Box	.75	1.75	3.00	M
S1485	Pylon - William Faulkner	.50	1.25	2.00	
D1486	Sanctuary and Requiem for a Nun	.50	1.25	2.00	
D1487	The Last Parallel - Martin Russ	.50	1.25	2.00	
T1488	The Brothers Karamazov - Fyodor Dostoyevsky	.50	1.25	2.00	
1489	Sing, Boy, Sing - Richard Vincent	.50	1.25	2.00	
D1490	Too Much, Too Soon - Diana Barrymore & Gerold Frank	.50	1.25	2.00	
S1491	Kitty Foyle - Christopher Morley	.50	1.25	2.00	
1492	Violent Hours - Robert Walsh	.50	1.25	2.00	
S1493	The End of Eternity - Isaac Asimov	2.00	4.00	6.00	SF
1494	The Wife of the Red-haired Man - Bill S. Ballinger	.75	1.75	3.00	M
S1495	Last of the Great Outlaws - Homer Croy	1.50	3.50	5.00	NF
T1496	The Young Lions - Irwin Shaw	.50	1.25	2.00	
S1497	The Sacrilege of Alan Kent - Erskine Caldwell	.50	1.25	2.00	
D1498	Nine Stories - J. D. Salinger	.50	1.25	2.00	
S1499	Cat Man - Edward Hoagland	.75	1.75	3.00	E
S1500	Mafia - Ed Reid 1958	.50	1.25	2.00	
S1501	The Long Hot Summer - William Faulkner Movie tie-in	1.50	3.50	5.00	
S1502	Desire Under the Elms - Eugene O'Neill	.50	1.25	2.00	
D1503	Grandfather Stories - Samuel Hopkins Adams	.50	1.25	2.00	
1504	West Side Jungle - Jason Ridgway	.50	1.25	2.00	
1505	Smoke of the Gun - John S. Daniels	.50	1.25	2.00	W
D1506	Able Company - D. J. Hollands	.50	1.25	2.00	
S1507	The Tunnel of Love - Peter DeVries	.50	1.25	2.00	
1508	Cry Terror - Andrew L. Stone c-Maguire	2.00	4.00	6.00	
D1509	Sons and Lovers - D. H. Lawrence	.75	1.75	3.00	
D1510	The Conformist - Alberto Moravia	.50	1.25	2.00	
S1511	Intruder in the Dust - William Faulkner	.50	1.25	2.00	
S1512	The Invisible Flag - Peter Bamm	.50	1.25	2.00	
S1513	The Barbarian and the Geisha - Robert Payne Movie tie-in	2.00	4.00	6.00	
S1514	The Assistant - Bernard Malamud	.50	1.25	2.00	
1515	Hang By Your Neck - Henry Kane	.75	1.75	3.00	M
1516	Maverick Marshal - Nelson Nye	.75	1.75	3.00	W
S1517	Duchess Hotspur - Rosamond Marshall	.50	1.25	2.00	
T1518	Studs Lonigan - James T. Farrell	.75	1.75	3.00	
D1519	Gallery of Women - Bernard Glemser	.75	1.75	3.00	
S1520	Bitter Honeymoon - Alberto Moravia	.50	1.25	2.00	
S1521	Soldier's Three - Humphrey Slater	.50	1.25	2.00	
S1522	Company K - William March	.50	1.25	2.00	
1523	Edge of Panic - Henry Kane	.75	1.75	3.00	M
S1524	Starburst - Alfred Bester	1.50	3.50	5.00	SF
S1525	Gigi and Julie de Carneilhan - Sidonie Colette 1958	.50	1.25	2.00	
1526	Death Before Bedtime - Edgar Box c-Maguire	.75	1.75	3.00	M
1527	The Body - Carter Brown	.75	1.75	3.00	M
1528	The Nightwalkers - Beverley Cross	.50	1.25	2.00	
D1529	A Streetcar Named Desire - Tennessee Williams	.75	1.75	3.00	
D1530	No Time for Sergeants - Mac Hyman	.50	1.25	2.00	
S1531	Love Among the Cannibals - Wright Morris	.50	1.25	2.00	
S1532	Some Inner Fury - Kamala Markandaya	.50	1.25	2.00	
S1533	Branded West - Don Ward	.50	1.25	2.00	W
S1534	43,000 Years Later - Horace Coon	2.00	4.00	6.00	SF
S1535	A Thirsty Evil - Gore Vidal	.75	1.75	3.00	

| | Signet 1500, c. Sigb | Signet 1555, c. Sigb | Signet 1563, c. Sigb |

(SIGNET, continued)

1536	A Texan Came Riding - Frank O'Rourke	.50	1.25	2.00	W
S1537	The Green Hills of Earth - Robert A. Heinlein	1.50	3.50	5.00	SF
1538	Dame in Danger - Thomas B. Dewey c-Maguire	.75	1.75	3.00	
1539	The Case of the Dead Divorcee - William Holder	.50	1.25	2.00	M
1540	No Luck for a Lady - Floyd Mahannah c-Maguire	.50	1.25	2.00	
1541	The Restless Gun - Will Hickok	.50	1.25	2.00	W
D1542	Whispers of the Flesh - Fletcher Flora	.50	1.25	2.00	
D1543	Silent Grow the Guns - MacKinlay Kantor	.50	1.25	2.00	
S1544	The Puppet Masters - Robert A. Heinlein	1.50	3.50	5.00	SF
D1545	Bread and Wine - Ignazio Silone	.50	1.25	2.00	
D1546	Bon Voyage! - Joseph & Marrijane Hayes	.50	1.25	2.00	
T1547	A Dictionary of American-English Usage - Margaret Nicholson	.50	1.25	2.00	NF
D1548	The Love-seekers - Leonora Hornblow	.50	1.25	2.00	
T1549	The Naked and the Dead - Norman Mailer	.50	1.25	2.00	
D1550	Birdman of Alcatraz - Thomas E. Gaddis	.50	1.25	2.00	
	1958				
S15551	My Fair Lady - Alan Jay Lerner	.50	1.25	2.00	
D1552	The World of Suzie Wong - Raymond Mason Movie tie-in	.75	1.75	3.00	
S1553	Selected Stories - Liam O'Flaherty	.50	1.25	2.00	
1554	Escapade - Jerry Weil	.50	1.25	2.00	
1555	Hell to Pay - William R. Cox	1.50	3.50	5.00	JD
1556	The Brass Halo - Jack Webb c-Maguire	.75	1.75	3.00	
S1557	The Wild Bunch - James D. Horan	1.50	3.50	5.00	NF
S1558	Destination: Universe - A. E. Van Vogt	1.50	3.50	5.00	SF
S1559	Giovanni's Room - James Baldwin	.50	1.25	2.00	
S1560	My Name Is Rose - Theodora Keogh	.50	1.25	2.00	
D1561	The Girl with the Swansdown Seat - Cyril Pearl	.50	1.25	2.00	
D1562	On the Beach - Nevil Shute	.75	1.75	3.00	
S1563	From Russia, with Love - Ian Fleming	1.50	3.50	5.00	
S1564	This Very Earth - Erskine Caldwell	.50	1.25	2.00	
1565	The Blonde - Carter Brown	.75	1.75	3.00	M
1566	Damaron's Gun - Wesley Ray	.50	1.25	2.00	
T1567	Forever Amber - Kathleen Winsor	.50	1.25	2.00	
S1568	Certain Women - Erskine Caldwell	.50	1.25	2.00	
S1569	Room at the Top - John Braine	.50	1.25	2.00	
S1570	Nine Miles to Reno - Jill Stern	.50	1.25	2.00	
S1571	Henry the Last - Giuseppe Puzza	.50	1.25	2.00	
S1572	Portrait of a Mobster - Harry Grey	.75	1.75	3.00	
1573	Kill a Wicked Man - Kyle Hunt	.50	1.25	2.00	
D1574	Moulin Rouge - Pierre LaMure	.50	1.25	2.00	
D1575	The Hoods - Harry Grey	.75	1.75	3.00	
	1959				
D1576	Knock on Any Door - Willard Motley	.50	1.25	2.00	
S1577	The Day After Tomorrow - Robert A. Heinlein	1.50	3.50	5.00	SF
T1578	Remember Me to God - Myron S. Kaufmann	.50	1.25	2.00	
S1579	Not Yet--- - Tereska Torres	.50	1.25	2.00	
S1580	Subways are for Sleeping - Edmund Love	.50	1.25	2.00	

1581 The Heart of a Stranger - Lionel Olay	.50	1.25	2.00	
1582 The Doll's Smile - Eva Boros	.50	1.25	2.00	
S1583 The Deep Range - Arthur C. Clarke	2.00	4.00	6.00	SF
1584 The Getaway - Jim Thompson	1.50	3.50	5.00	
1585 Formula for Murder - Bill S. Ballinger	.50	1.25	2.00	M
1586 The Case of the Strangled Starlet - James Hadley Chase	.75	1.75	3.00	M
S1587 I Want to Live! - Tabor Rawson Movie tie-in	.75	1.75	3.00	
1588 The Crimson Quirt - William Colt MacDonald	.50	1.25	2.00	W
S1589 The Sure Hand of God - Erskine Caldwell	.50	1.25	2.00	
S1590 Cat on a Hot Tin Roof - Tennessee Williams Movie tie-in	1.50	3.50	5.00	
D1591 The American Woman - Eric J. Dingwall	.50	1.25	2.00	
S1592 Journeyman - Erskine Caldwell	.50	1.25	2.00	
S1593 The Demolished Man - Alfred Bester	1.50	3.50	5.00	SF
1594 The Mistress - Carter Brown	.50	1.25	2.00	M
1595 The Decks Ran Red - Andrew L. Stone	.50	1.25	2.00	
D1596 The Woman of Rome - Alberto Moravia	.50	1.25	2.00	
S1597 Sigrid and the Sergeant - Robert Buckner	.50	1.25	2.00	
S1598 Episode in Palmetto - Erskine Caldwell	.50	1.25	2.00	
S1599 The Knife - Theon Wright	.50	1.25	2.00	
D1600 America, with Love - Kathleen Winsor	.50	1.25	2.00	
1958				
D1601 The Called and the Chosen - Monica Baldwin	.50	1.25	2.00	
S1602 Summer in Salandar - H. E. Bates	.50	1.25	2.00	
S1603 A Restless Breed - J. William Terry	.50	1.25	2.00	
S1604 Fortune is a Woman - Hermes Nye	.50	1.25	2.00	
1605 Ute Country - John S. Daniels	.50	1.25	2.00	W
1606 The Corpse - Carter Brown	.50	1.25	2.00	M
1607 Gunsmoke Men - L. L. Foreman	.50	1.25	2.00	W
S1608 Trouble in July - Erskine Caldwell	.50	1.25	2.00	
S1609 Separate Tables - Terence Rattigan	.50	1.25	2.00	
1959				
S1610 Expense Account - Joe Morgan	.50	1.25	2.00	
S1611 Tragic Ground - Erskine Caldwell	.50	1.25	2.00	
S1612 Roman Tales - Alberto Moravia	.75	1.75	3.00	
S1613 Nobody Cares for Me - Sara Harris	.50	1.25	2.00	
D1614 Sartoris - William Faulkner	.50	1.25	2.00	
S1615 Animal Farm - George Orwell	.75	1.75	3.00	
S1616 The Unvanquished - William Faulkner	.50	1.25	2.00	
D1617 Man of Montmartre - Ethel & Stephen Longstreet	.50	1.25	2.00	
1618 Texas Hellion - J. H. Plenn	.50	1.25	2.00	W
D1619 On the Road - Jack Kerouac	1.50	3.50	5.00	
1620 The Lover - Carter Brown	.50	1.25	2.00	M
S1621 The Courting of Susie Brown - Erskine Caldwell	.50	1.25	2.00	
S1622 The Seedling Star - James Blish	.75	1.75	3.00	SF
S1623 A Place Called Estherville - Erskine Caldwell	.50	1.25	2.00	
S1624 Saturday Night - James T. Farrell	.50	1.25	2.00	
S1625 The Blessing - Nancy Mitford	.50	1.25	2.00	
1959				
S1626 Last Train from Gun Hill - Gordon D. Shirreffs Movie tie-in	.75	1.75	3.00	W
D1627 Grandfather Stories - Samuel Hopkins Adams	.50	1.25	2.00	
D1628 The Sound and the Fury - William Faulkner	.50	1.25	2.00	
D1629 Soldier's Pay - William Faulkner	.50	1.25	2.00	
D1630 Arch of Triumph - Erich Maria Remarque	.50	1.25	2.00	
1631 The Overlanders - Nelson Nye	.50	1.25	2.00	W
1632 The Caballero - Johnston McCulley	.75	1.75	3.00	W
1633 The Victim - Carter Brown	.50	1.25	2.00	M
1634 The Last Blitzkrieg - Walter Freeman	.50	1.25	2.00	
1635 The Fastest Gun in Texas - C. J. LaRoche & J. H. Plenn	.75	1.75	3.00	
1636 The Whispering Master - Frank Gruber	.50	1.25	2.00	
T1637 Some Came Running - James Jones	.50	1.25	2.00	
D1638 Darkness at Noon - Arthur Koestler	.50	1.25	2.00	
S1639 The Door into Summer - Robert A. Heinlein	1.50	3.50	5.00	SF
D1640 1984 - George Orwell	.75	1.75	3.00	SF
D1641 The Shadow and the Peak - Raymond Mason	.50	1.25	2.00	
1642 An Eye for an Eye - John B. West	.50	1.25	2.00	
D1643 The Wild Palms and the Old Man - William Faulkner	.50	1.25	2.00	

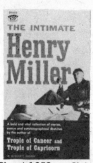

Signet 1653, c. Sigb

Signet 1670, c. Sigb

Signet 1723, c. Sigb

(SIGNET, continued)

S1644	The Man Who Sold the Moon - Robert A. Heinlein	.75	1.75	3.00	SF
T1645	Never so Few - Tom T. Chamales	.50	1.25	2.00	
1646	Dormitory Women - R. V. Cassill c-Maguire	1.50	3.50	5.00	
S1647	The Bedside Man - William M. Gaines	1.50	3.50	5.00	H
S1648	The Mackerel Plaza - Peter De Vries	.50	1.25	2.00	
S1649	The Darling Buds of May - H. E. Bates	.50	1.25	2.00	
S1650	Miri - Peter Sourian	.50	1.25	2.00	
	1959				
S1651	Wolf Whistle and Other Stories - William Bradford Huie	.50	1.25	2.00	
S1652	Beat, Beat, Beat - William F. Brown	.50	1.25	2.00	
D1653	The Intimate Henry Miller - Henry Miller	1.50	3.50	5.00	
1654	The Loving and the Dead - Carter Brown	.50	1.25	2.00	M
1655	Slattery's Range - Richard Wormser	.50	1.25	2.00	
S1656	Some Like It Hot - I. A. L. Diamond & Billy Wilder	2.00	4.00	7.50	
	Movie tie-in				
D1657	Two Women - Alberto Moravia	.50	1.25	2.00	
S1658	The Silent Service - William C. Chambliss	.50	1.25	2.00	
S1659	Something About a Soldier - Mark Harris	.50	1.25	2.00	
1660	Night Ward - Noah Gordon	.50	1.25	2.00	
T1661	And Quiet Flows the Don - Mikhail Sholokhov	.75	1.75	3.00	
1662	Kiss Her Goodbye - Wade Miller	.50	1.25	2.00	
1663	Walk Softly, Witch - Carter Brown	.50	1.25	2.00	M
S1664	The Roman Spring of Mrs. Stone - Tennessee Williams	.50	1.25	2.00	
S1665	Cancel All Our Vows - John D. MacDonald	.50	1.25	2.00	M
S1666	Georgia Boy - Erskine Caldwell	.50	1.25	2.00	
D1667	The Catcher in the Rye - J. D. Salinger	.50	1.25	2.00	
T1668	The Time of the Dragons - Alice Ekert-Rotholz	.50	1.25	2.00	
D1669	Safe Conduct - Boris Pasternak	.50	1.25	2.00	
S1670	Doctor No - Ian Fleming	1.50	3.50	5.00	
S1671	The Dangerous American - A. E. Hotchner	.50	1.25	2.00	
S1672	A Lamp for Nightfall - Erskine Caldwell	.50	1.25	2.00	
S1673	The Black Cloud - Fred Hoyle	1.50	3.50	5.00	SF
1674	The Passionate - Carter Brown	.50	1.25	2.00	M
1675	Trail of the Restless Gun - Will Hickok	.50	1.25	2.00	W
	1959				
D1676	Sir Fool - Thomas Skinner Willings	.50	1.25	2.00	
1677	The Silver Tombstone Mystery - Frank Gruber	.50	1.25	2.00	M
D1678	Lola - Dario Fernandez-Florez	.50	1.25	2.00	
D1679	They Came to Cordura - Glendon Swarthout	.75	1.75	3.00	
D1680	Chiara - Gene d'Olive	.50	1.25	2.00	
D1681	Ben-Hur - Lew Wallace	.75	1.75	3.00	
S1682	The Slot - John Clagett	.50	1.25	2.00	
S1683	No Time Like Tomorrow - Brian W. Aldiss	.50	1.25	2.00	SF
S1684	The Wounds of Hunger - Luis Spota	.50	1.25	2.00	
S1685	Follow Me Down - Shelby Foote	.50	1.25	2.00	
1686	Gun Code - Philip Ketchum	.75	1.75	3.00	W
1687	Violent Streets - Dale Kramer	.75	1.75	3.00	
1688	Wake Up With a Stranger - Fletcher Flora	.50	1.25	2.00	
S1689	The Loved and the Lost - Morley Callaghan	.50	1.25	2.00	
S1690	The Roman and the Slave Girl - John Medford Morgan	.75	1.75	3.00	

S1691	Crow Killer - Robert Bunker & Raymond Thorp	.75	1.75	3.00	W
D1692	Nautilus 90 North - William R. Anderson & Clay Blair, Jr.	.50	1.25	2.00	
D1693	Let No Man Write My Epitaph - Willard Motley	.50	1.25	2.00	
1694	None But the Lethal Heart - Carter Brown	.50	1.25	2.00	M
1695	Brand of a Man - Thomas Thompson	.50	1.25	2.00	W
1696	Shock Treatment - James Hadley Chase	.50	1.25	2.00	
1697	Stirrups in the Dust - Burt Arthur	.50	1.25	2.00	W
S1698	No But I Saw the Movie - Peter DeVries	.50	1.25	2.00	
S1699	Revolt in 2100 - Robert A. Heinlein	.75	1.75	3.00	SF
S1700	The Big Kill - Mickey Spillane	.75	1.75	3.00	M

1959

S1701	Son of Mad - William M. Gaines	1.50	3.50	5.00	H
Q1702	Atlas Shrugged - Ayn Rand	.75	1.75	3.00	
S1703	Frontier - MacKinlay Kantor	.75	1.75	3.00	
1704	Manuela - William Woods	.50	1.25	2.00	
S1705	The Long Wait - Mickey Spillane	.75	1.75	3.00	M
S1706	The Eighth Day of the Week - Marek Hasko	.50	1.25	2.00	
1707	Invitation to Violence - Lionel White	.50	1.25	2.00	
S1708	You Tell My Son - Rex Pratt	.50	1.25	2.00	
D1709	Around the World with Auntie Mame - Patrick Dennis	.50	1.25	2.00	
S1710	Vengeance is Mine - Mickey Spillane	.75	1.75	3.00	M
S1711	Summer of the Seventeenth Doll - Ray Lawler	.50	1.25	2.00	
S1712	Entry E - Richard Frede	.50	1.25	2.00	
1713	The Wanton - Carter Brown	.50	1.25	2.00	M
1714	Apache Warpath - George Garland	.50	1.25	2.00	W
1715	Ambuscade - Frank O'Rourke	.50	1.25	2.00	
1716					
T1717	The Mountain Is Young - Suyin Han	.50	1.25	2.00	
D1718	The Dharma Bums - Jack Kerouac	1.50	3.50	5.00	
S1719	Galactic Cluster - James Blish	1.50	3.50	5.00	SF
S1720	The Blue Angel - Heinrich Mann	.50	1.25	2.00	
S1721	Devil in the Flesh - Raymond Radiguet	.50	1.25	2.00	
1722	Suddenly by Violence - Carter Brown	.50	1.25	2.00	M
S1723	Live and Let Die - Ian Fleming	1.50	3.50	5.00	
1724	Triple Slay - Adam Knight	.50	1.25	2.00	M
D1725	Star Money - Kathleen Winsor	.50	1.25	2.00	

1959

T1726	The Hard Blue Sky - Shirley Ann Grau	.50	1.25	2.00	
D1727	Breakfast at Tiffany's - Truman Capote	.75	1.75	3.00	
S1728	One Lonely Night - Mickey Spillane	.75	1.75	3.00	M
S1729	The Other Side of the Sky - Arthur C. Clarke	1.50	3.50	5.00	SF
1730	The Longest Second - Bill S. Ballinger	.50	1.25	2.00	M
S1731	A Stretch on the River - Richard Bissell	.50	1.25	2.00	
S1732	The Incident - Marc Rivette	.50	1.25	2.00	
S1733	Kneel to the Rising Sun - Erskine Caldwell	.50	1.25	2.00	
S1734	Southways - Erskine Caldwell	.50	1.25	2.00	
S1735	We Are the Living - Erskine Caldwell	.50	1.25	2.00	
D1736	Lady Chatterley's Lover - D. H. Lawrence	.50	1.25	2.00	
S1737	Tortilla Flat - John Steinbeck	.50	1.25	2.00	
1738	The Dame - Carter Brown	.50	1.25	2.00	M
S1739	A Swell-Looking Girl - Erskine Caldwell	.50	1.25	2.00	
D1740	The Rainbow and the Rose - Nevil Shute	.50	1.25	2.00	
1741					
Q1742	A Child of the Century - Ben Hecht	.50	1.25	2.00	
S1743	The Girl in the Freudian Slip - William F. Brown	.50	1.25	2.00	
1744	The Dead-Shot Kit - Philip Ketchum	.50	1.25	2.00	W
S1745					
D1746	Strike Heaven on the Face - Charles Calitri	.50	1.25	2.00	
S1747	The Lovely Lady - D. H. Lawrence	.50	1.25	2.00	
1748	Desperate Rider - Frank O'Rourke	.50	1.25	2.00	W
1749	The Guilty are Afraid - James Hadley Chase	.75	1.75	3.00	M
1750	Terror Comes Creeping - Carter Brown	.50	1.25	2.00	M

SIGNET CLASSICS

(New American Library of World Literature, Inc.)

Code	Title / Author				
CD 1	Adolphe and the Red Notebook - Benjamin Constant 1959	.75	1.75	3.00	
CD 2	The Adventures of Tom Sawyer - Mark Twain	.75	1.75	3.00	
CD 3	Animal Farm - George Orwell	.75	1.75	3.00	
CD 4	Heart of Darkness and the Secret Sharer - Joseph Conrad	.75	1.75	3.00	
CD 5	The Adventures of Huckleberry Finn - Mark Twain	.75	1.75	3.00	
CD 6	Kidnapped - Robert Louis Stevenson	.75	1.75	3.00	A
CD 7	The Return of the Native - Thomas Hardy	.75	1.75	3.00	
CD 8	The Scarlet Letter - Nathaniel Hawthorne	.75	1.75	3.00	
CD 9	The Unvanquished - William Faulkner	.75	1.75	3.00	
CD10	Wuthering Heights - Emily Bronte	.75	1.75	3.00	

SIGNET KEY

(New American Library of World Literature, Inc.)

Code	Title / Author				
K300	Gandhi: His Life and Message for the World - Louis Fischer 1954	.75	1.75	3.00	B
K301	How to Make a Success of Your Marriage - Dr. Eustace Chesser	.50	1.25	2.00	NF
K302	Speak Better—Write Better—English - Horace Coon	.50	1.25	2.00	NF
K303	The United States Political System and How It Works - David Cushman Coyle	.50	1.25	2.00	NF
K304	A Brief History of the United States - Franklin Escher, Jr.	.75	1.75	3.00	NF
K305	Flower Arrangements Anyone Can Do Anywhere - Matilda Rogers	.75	1.75	3.00	NF
K306	Lives of Destiny as Told for the Reader's Digest - Donald Culross Peattie	.75	1.75	3.00	B
Ks307	Hoyle's Rules of Games - Albert H. Morehead & Geoffrey Mott-Smith	1.00	2.00	3.00	NF
K308	How the Great Religions Began - Joseph Gaer	1.00	2.00	3.00	NF
K309	Diet to Suit Yourself - Walter Ross	.50	1.25	2.00	NF
Ks310	A Treasury of Wisdom and Inspiration - David St. Leger	.50	1.25	2.00	
Ks311	Andy's Everyday Encyclopedia - Ellen Wales	.50	1.25	2.00	NF
K312	The Householder's Manual - Richard Kent	.50	1.25	2.00	NF
K313	Your Way to Popularity and Personal Power - James Bender & Lee Graham	.50	1.25	2.00	
Ks314	How to Help Your Child in School - Lawrence K. & Mary Frank	.50	1.25	2.00	NF
KD315	God's Wonderful World - Agnes Lockie Mason & Phyllis Brown Ohanian	.75	1.75	3.00	
Ks316	How to Land the Job You Want - Jules Z. Willing	.50	1.25	2.00	NF
Ks317	Flight into Space - Jonathan N. Leonard	.75	1.75	3.00	NF
Ks318	Hobbies for Pleasure and Profit - Horace Coon 1955	.75	1.75	3.00	NF
KD319	The Life of Abraham Lincoln - Stefan Lorant Lorant	1.50	3.50	5.00	B
Ks320	Science in Our Lives - Ritchie Calder	.50	1.25	2.00	NF
K321	Benjamin Franklin - Roger Burlingame	1.50	3.50	5.00	B
Ks322	The Conquest of Happiness - Bertrand Russell	.50	1.25	2.00	
Ks323	The Handy Book of Gardening - Victor A. Tiedjens & Albert E. Wilkinson	.50	1.25	2.00	NF
Ks324	The United Nations and How it Works - David Cushman Coyle	.50	1.25	2.00	NF
Ks325	Your Guide to Financial Security - Sidney Margolius	.50	1.25	2.00	NF
Ks326	The Nature of Living Things - C. Brooke Worth & Robert K. Enders	.75	1.75	3.00	NF
Ks327	Machines that Built America - Roger Burlingame	.75	1.75	3.00	NF
KD328	How to Know American Antiques - Alice Winchester	.75	1.75	3.00	NF

Ks329	Fifty Years a Surgeon - Robert T. Morris	.50	1.25	2.00	NF
Ks330	The Crust of the Earth - Samuel Rapport & Helen Wright	.75	1.75	3.00	NF
KD331	Stories of Famous Operas - Harold Vincent Milligan	.75	1.75	3.00	NF
Ks332	Having a Baby - Alan F. Guttmacher	.50	1.25	2.00	NF
Ks333	The Web of Life - John H. Storer	.50	1.25	2.00	
	1956				
Ks334	The American Presidency - Clinton Rossiter	.50	1.25	2.00	NF
K335	How to Live Without Liquor - Ralph A. Habas	.50	1.25	2.00	
K336	The Unknown—Is it Nearer? - Eric J. Dingwall & John Langdon-Davies	.50	1.25	2.00	
K337	Henry Ford - Roger Burlingame	.75	1.75	3.00	B
Ks338	Live Without Fear - T. V. Smith	.50	1.25	2.00	
Ks339	The Meaning of the Dead Sea Scrolls - A. Powell Davies	.75	1.75	3.00	NF
KD340	American Folk Tales and Songs - Richard Chase	1.50	3.50	5.00	NF
Ks341	How to be a Better Member - Horace Coon	.50	1.25	2.00	NF
Ks342	Sight without Glasses - Harold M. Peppard	.50	1.25	2.00	NF
Ks343	The Ten Commandments - A. Powell Davies	.75	1.75	3.00	NF
Ks344	Call it Experience - Erskine Caldwell	.50	1.25	2.00	
Ks345	Seeds of Life - John Langdon-Davies	.50	1.25	2.00	NF
	1957				
KD346	How to Know the Minerals and Rocks - Richard M. Pearl	.75	1.75	3.00	NF
KD347	How to Know the Birds - Roger Tory Peterson	.75	1.75	3.00	NF
Ks348	The Eloquence of Winston Churchill - Winston Churchill	.75	1.75	3.00	NF
KD349	How to Know the American Mammals - Ivan T. Sanderson	.75	1.75	3.00	NF
Ks350	Here's How! A Round-the-World Bar Guide - Lawrence G. Blochman	.75	1.75	3.00	NF
KD351	Electronics for Everyone - Monroe Upton	.50	1.25	2.00	NF
Ks352	The Shape of Tomorrow - George Soule	.50	1.25	2.00	NF
KD353	How to Know and Predict the Weather - Robert Moore Fisher	.50	1.25	2.00	NF
K354	Speak Better-Write Better—English - Horace Coon	.50	1.25	2.00	NF
KD355	The Human Body and How it Works - Elbert Tokay	.50	1.25	2.00	NF
KD356	You and Your Heart - H. M. Marvin	.50	1.25	2.00	NF
KD357	Gods, Heroes and Men of Ancient Greece - W. H. D. Rouse	.75	1.75	3.00	
KD358	Pregnancy and Birth - Alan F. Guttmacher	.50	1.25	2.00	NF
	1958				
KD359	How the Great Religions Began - Joseph Gaer	.75	1.75	3.00	NF
Ks360	Satellites, Rockets and Outer Space - Willy Ley	.75	1.75	3.00	NF
K361	Magic House of Numbers - Irving Adler	.50	1.25	2.00	NF
KD362	Buffalo Bill and the Wild West - Henry Blackman Sell & Victor Weybright	.75	1.75	3.00	B
KD363	Hoyle's Rules of Games - Albert H. Morehead & Geoffrey Mott-Smith	1.00	2.00	3.00	NF
K364	The Stars - Irving Adler	.50	1.25	2.00	NF
KD365	Your Body and Your Mind - Frank G. Slaughter	.50	1.25	2.00	NF
K366					
Ks367	A Brief History of the United States - Franklin Escher, Jr.	.50	1.25	2.00	NF
	1959				
KD368	The Complete Italian System of Winning Bridge - Edgar Kaplan	.50	1.25	2.00	NF
K369	How Life Began - Irving Adler	.50	1.25	2.00	NF
Ks370	How to Spell and Increase Your Word Power - Horace Coon	.50	1.25	2.00	NF
KD371	The Bible was Right - Hugh J. Schonfield	.50	1.25	2.00	
KD372	Your Adolescent at Home and in School - Lawrence K. & Mary Frank	.50	1.25	2.00	NF
KD373	The New American Guide to Colleges - Gene R. Hawes	.50	1.25	2.00	NF

Stallion 206, c. Univ

Star Books 29, c. SG

Star Books 30, c. SG

STALLION BOOKS

(Stallion Books/Universal Publishing and Distributing Corporation)

Digest size

206	The Queer Sisters - Steve Harragan	2.00	4.00	7.50	M
213	Reefer Club - Luke Roberts	2.50	6.00	10.00	E
	Note: Same cover as Intimate No. 32 and virtually identical to Beacon No. B260				

STAR BOOKS

(Star Guidance, Inc./Publication House, Inc.)

Digest size

1	Texas Gun Slinger - Murray Leinster	2.50	6.00	10.00	W
3	Outlaw Guns - Murray Leinster	2.50	6.00	10.00	W
6	The Flaming Guns - Burt Arthur	1.50	3.50	5.00	W
7	Bad Hombre - Archie Joscelyn Orig., 1950, c-Gross	1.50	3.50	5.00	W
8	Range Justice - Paul Evan Lehman Orig., 1950, c-Gross	1.50	3.50	5.00	W
9	Border Wolves - Archie Joscelyn c-Gross	1.50	3.50	5.00	W
10	Law of the .45 - Paul Evan Lehman	1.50	3.50	5.00	W
11	Killer's Moon - Burt Arthur Orig., 1950, c-Gross	1.50	3.50	5.00	W
12	The Black Rider - Burt Arthur Orig., 1950, c-Gross	1.50	3.50	5.00	W
13	Gun-Thunder Valley - Archie Joscelyn	1.50	3.50	5.00	W
14	The Vengeance Trail - Archie Joscelyn	1.50	3.50	5.00	W
15	The Long Trail North - Lee Floren Orig., 1951	1.50	3.50	5.00	W
16	The Sheep Killers - Paul Evan Lehman Orig., 1951	1.50	3.50	5.00	W
17	Two-Gun Trail - Lee Floren Orig., 1951	1.50	3.50	5.00	W
18	Wyoming Outlaw - Archie Joselyn	1.50	3.50	5.00	W
19	Duel on the Range - Burt Arthur	1.50	3.50	5.00	W
20	Rustler's Trail - Lee Floren Orig., 1951	1.50	3.50	5.00	W
21	Black Gunsmoke - Lee Floren Orig., 1951, c-Gross	1.50	3.50	5.00	W
22	Texas Vengeance - Paul Evan Lehman c-Gross	1.50	3.50	5.00	W
24	Gun-Thunder Valley - Archie Joscelyn	1.50	3.50	5.00	W
27	Deputy's Revenge - Lee Floren 1952, aka The Long Trail North	1.50	3.50	5.00	W
42	Two-Gun Vengeance - Archie Joscelyn	1.50	3.50	5.00	W

STORK ORIGINAL NOVEL

(Star Guidance, Inc.)

Digest size

nn	Life of Passion - Gordon Semple Orig., 1949, c-Rodewald	2.00	4.00	7.50	E
6	The Sins of Donna Kenyon - Ralph Carter	2.00	4.00	7.50	E
7	Raging Passion's - Thomas Stone Orig., 1950, c-Cole	2.50	6.00	10.00	E
8	Two Sinners - Lee Jackquin c-Cole	2.50	6.00	10.00	E
28	Texas Guns - Paul Evan Lehman aka Range Justice, c-Gross	1.50	3.50	5.00	W
29	Duel at Killman Creek - Archie Joscelyn aka Border Wolves, c-Gross	1.50	3.50	5.00	W
30	Texas Outlaw - Archie Joscelyn 1952, aka Bad Hombre, c-Gross	1.50	3.50	5.00	W
750	Boy-Crazy - Albert L. Quandt 1955 Note: Same cover as Original no. 721.	2.00	4.00	6.00	JD
754	Cellar Club - Albert L. Quandt	2.00	4.00	6.00	JD
758	Sinners Club - Harry Whittington 1956	1.50	3.50	5.00	E
760	Waterfront Girl - Amos Hatter	1.50	3.50	5.00	E
768	Ward Nurse - M. Coleman	1.50	3.50	5.00	E

STOVEL-ADVOCATE

(Stovel-Advocate Press Ltd.)
Canadian

nn	Grey Cup or Bust - Tony Allan 1954	2.00	4.00	7.50	S

STUART

(Stuart Art Gallery, Inc.)

nn	Precious Rubbish - Theodore L. Shaw Orig., 1956	1.50	3.50	5.00	NF
nn	Critical Quackery - Theodore L. Shaw	1.50	3.50	5.00	NF

SUPERIOR REPRINTS

(The Military Service Publishing Company)

M637	White Magic - Faith Baldwin 1944	1.00	2.00	3.50	R

Stork Orig. nn, c. SG

Superior M642, c. Mil

Superior M650, c. Mil

M638	Ol' Man Adam an' His Chillun - Roark Bradford	1.00	2.00	3.50	
M639	Unexpected Night - Elizabeth Daly	1.00	2.00	3.50	M
M640	An April Afternoon - Philip Wylie	1.00	2.00	3.50	
M641	Family Affair - Ione Sundberg Shriber	1.00	2.00	3.50	
M642	The Rynox Murder Mystery - Philip MacDonald	1.50	3.50	5.00	M
M643	Cartoons by George Price - George Price 1945	1.50	3.50	5.00	H
M644	Emberrassment of Riches - Marjorie Fischer	1.00	2.00	3.50	
M645	Murder in Mink - Robert George Dean	1.00	2.00	3.50	M
M646	The Love Nest, and other Stories - Ring Lardner	1.50	3.50	5.00	H
M647	Inquest - Percival Wilde	1.00	2.00	3.50	
M648	One Foot in Heaven - Hartzell Spence	1.00	2.00	3.50	
M649	The Navy Colt - Frank Gruber	1.00	2.00	3.50	
M650	The Informer - Liam O'Flaherty	1.00	2.00	3.50	
M651	Mr. Angel Comes Aboard - Charles G. Booth	1.00	2.00	3.50	
M652	This Gun for Hire - Graham Greene	1.50	3.50	5.00	
M653	The House Without the Door - Elizabeth Daly	1.00	2.00	3.50	M
M654	On Ice - Robert George Dean	1.00	2.00	3.50	M
M655	The Mighty Blockhead - Frank Gruber	1.00	2.00	3.50	
M656	Saki Sampler - H. H. Munro	1.50	3.50	5.00	F
M657	Good Night, Sheriff - Harrison R. Steeves	1.00	2.00	3.50	

SUSPENSE NOVELS

(Farrell Publishing Corporation)

Digest size

1	Strange Pursuit - N. R. De Mexico	1.50	3.50	5.00	M
2	The Case of the Lonely Lovers - Will Daemer 1951	1.50	3.50	5.00	M
3	Naked Villainy - Carl G. Hodges	1.50	3.50	5.00	M

TECH

(Tech Books, Inc.)

Digest size

1	The Black Rider - Herbert Shapiro	2.00	4.00	7.50	W
2	Murder is my Racket - Rbt. H. Leitfred aka Death Cancels the Evidence	2.00	4.00	7.50	M
nn	Murder Man - William Bogart	2.00	4.00	7.50	M

TECH MYSTERY

(Tech Mysteries, Inc.)

Digest size

1	The Candle - Linton C. Hopkins	1.50	3.50	5.00	M
2	Murder is my Racket - Robert H. Leitfred aka	1.00	2.00	3.00	M
nn	Murder Man - William Bogart	1.00	2.00	3.00	M

TECH WESTERN

(Tech Books, Inc.)

Digest size

Tech Mystery 1, c. Tech

Tech Western 1, c. Tech

Thriller Book nn, c. Lev

(TECH WESTERN, continued)

1	The Black Rider - Herbert Shapiro	1.50	3.50	5.00	W

THRILLER BOOK, A
(Lev Gleason Publications, Inc.)
3½" x 5¾" size

nn	Big Shot Gangsters, Their Crimes, Careers and Deaths - Stanford Quayle, 1947 c-Cole	4.00	8.00	15.00	NF
nn	The Greatest Prison Breaks of All Time - Michael Finn, c-Cole	4.00	8.00	15.00	NF
nn	How Detectives Catch Crooks - Stanford Quayle, c-Cole	4.00	8.00	15.00	NF
nn	10 Most Terrible Crimes of All Time - Stanford Quayle, c-Cole	4.00	8.00	15.00	NF
nn	Mysteries of Magic, Mind Reading and Hypnotism Explained - Hamilton Holt c-Cole	4.00	8.00	15.00	NF

THRILLER NOVEL CLASSIC
(Novel Selections, Inc.)
Digest size

1	Secret Agent No. 1 - Frederick Frost	2.00	4.00	7.50	M
3	The Yellow Strangler - Colin Robertson	2.00	4.00	7.50	M
4	The Insidious Dr. Fu-Manchu - Sax Rohmer	2.00	4.00	7.50	M
5	Lord of Terror - Sidney Horler	2.00	4.00	7.50	M
9	The Golden Scorpion - Sax Rohmer	2.00	4.00	7.50	M
10	The White Wolf - Franklin Gregory	2.00	4.00	7.50	SF

Thriller Book nn, c. Lev

Thriller Novel 1, c. NS

Thriller Novel 3, c. NS

Thriller Novel 16, c. NS   Thrilling Nov. 12, c. Poplib   Thrilling Nov. 15, c. Poplib

(THRILLER NOVEL CLASSIC, continued)

12	The Bamboo Whistle - Frederick Frost	1.50	3.50	5.00	
13	Invasion - Whitman Chambers	2.00	4.00	7.50	SF
14	Bulldog Drummond Meets a Murderess - H. C. McNeile	2.00	4.00	6.00	M
16	The Saint in Miami - Leslie Charteris	2.00	4.00	6.00	M
19	Eleven Were Brave - Francis Beeding	1.50	3.50	5.00	
20	Night Attack - Lee Crosby	1.50	3.50	5.00	
21	Design in Evil - Rufus King	1.50	3.50	5.00	M
22	Cradled in Fear - Anita Boutell	1.50	3.50	5.00	
23	Poison in Jest - John Dickson Carr	2.00	4.00	6.00	M
26	Deep Lay the Dead - Frederick C. Davis	1.50	3.50	5.00	
27	Assignment to Death - Charles L. Leonard	1.50	3.50	5.00	
29	The Black Path of Fear - Cornell Woolrich	1.50	3.50	5.00	M
33	Murder for Empire - Kim Knight	1.50	3.50	5.00	S
34	Action at World's End - Whitman Chambers	1.50	3.50	5.00	
35	Death at Abu Mina - Peter William aka The Affair at Abu Mina	1.50	3.50	5.00	
37	Murder in Silence - George Selmark	1.50	3.50	5.00	M

THRILLING BOOKS/NOVELS

(Popular Library, Inc.)

Digest size

11	Trail Dust - Clarence E. Mulford	2.00	4.00	6.00	W
12	Texas Man - William MacLeod Raine	2.00	4.00	6.00	W
13	Holster Law - Gordon Young	2.00	4.00	6.00	W
14	Square Deal Sanderson - Charles Alden Seltzer	2.00	4.00	6.00	W
15	The Quirt - B. M. Bower	2.00	4.00	6.00	W
16	Cow Country Law - Frank C. Robertson	2.00	4.00	6.00	W
17	Man to Man - Jackson Gregory	2.00	4.00	6.00	W
18	Guns of Paradise Bend - William White	2.00	4.00	6.00	W
19	Two Rangers from Texas - Caddo Cameron	2.00	4.00	6.00	W
20	Rustler's Valley - Clarence E. Mulford	2.00	4.00	6.00	W
21	Trigger Gospel - Harry Sinclair Drago	2.00	4.00	6.00	W

Thrilling Nov. 16, c. Poplib   Thrilling Nov. 20, c. Poplib   Thrilling Nov. 21, c. Poplib

(THRILLING BOOKS/NOVELS, continued)

22	Hot Lead Trail - Charles Alden Seltzer aka The Red Brand	2.00	4.00	7.50	W
23	Gunman from Abilene - Gordon Young aka Red Clark to the Rescue	2.00	4.00	6.00	W
24	Heart of a Ranger - William Patterson White	2.00	4.00	6.00	W
25	Longhorns of Hate - Frank C. Robinson	2.00	4.00	6.00	W
27	It's Hell to be a Ranger - Caddo Cameron	2.00	4.00	6.00	W
28	Riders of the Rocker K - S. Payne	2.00	4.00	6.00	W
29	Bring Me His Ears - Clarence E. Mulford	2.00	4.00	6.00	W
30	Thorson of Thunder Gulch - Norman A. Fox	2.00	4.00	6.00	W

TOBY

(Toby Press, Inc.)

Digest size

nn	Dangerous People Orig., 1952	1.50	3.00	6.00	NF
nn	Space Pirate - Jack Vance Orig., 1953	3.50	7.50	15.00	SF
nn	Escape Orig., 1953	1.50	3.00	6.00	A
nn	Sunset Showdown - Steve Frazee Orig., 1953	1.50	3.00	6.00	W
nn	Private Lives - E. Whitfield	2.00	4.00	7.50	NF
nn	The Lil Abner Square Dance Book - F. Leifer	2.00	4.00	7.50	NF

TRAVELLERS POCKET LIBRARY BEST-SELLER

(Ward-Hill Books)

100	Passion Is a Gentle Whip - Milton H. Gropper 1949	2.00	4.00	7.50	E
103	Venus in Furs - Leopold Sacher-Masoch 1949	4.00	8.00	15.00	E

TRIPLE NICKEL LIBRARY

(Solomon & Gelman, Inc.)

Digest size

1	The Adventures of Davy Crockett	2.00	4.00	7.50	A
2	Davy Crockett and Danger from the Mountain - Nat Wilson	2.00	4.00	7.50	A
3	The Life of Wild Bill Hickok -	2.00	4.00	7.50	W
4	1955				

Toby nn, c. Toby

Toby nn, c. Toby

Travellers PL 103, c. Ward

Triple Nickel 5, c. Sol   Triple Nickel 7, c. Sol   Trophy 402, c. Royce

(TRIPLE NICKEL LIBRARY, continued)

5 Barbie Lane and Mystery of the Egyptian Museum - Lucy Carlton, 1955	2.00	4.00	7.50	M
6 The Power Boys and the Riddle of the Sunken Ship - Arthur Benwood 1956	2.00	4.00	7.50	M
7 The Power Boys in the Castle of Curious Creatures - Arthur Benwood , 1956	2.00	4.00	7.50	M
8 The Power Boys and the Mystery of the Marble Face - Arthur Benwood	2.00	4.00	7.50	M

TROPHY BOOKS

(Royce Publishers)

402 The Pilditch Puzzle - W. B. M. Ferguson 1946	15.00	35.00	50.00	M

UNI - BOOKS

(Universal Publishing and Distributing Corp.)

Digest size

4 Wicked - Eleanor Gates	1.50	3.50	5.00	E
9 Warped Women - Janet Pritchard	1.50	3.50	5.00	E
10 Without Consent - M. Pili Grilli	1.50	3.50	5.00	E
13 Tormented - R. Meeker	1.50	3.50	5.00	E
14 Stripper - Wright Williams	1.50	3.50	5.00	E
15 The Thing that Made Love - David V. Reed	3.00	6.00	12.00	SF
16 Raw Passion - Charles Martin	1.50	3.50	5.00	W
18 Love Cheat - William Arthur	1.50	3.50	5.00	E
21 Hideaway - Peggy Gaddis	1.50	3.50	5.00	E
23 Sin Ship - Janet Pritchard	1.50	3.50	5.00	E
24 Badge of Shame - A. Abram	1.50	3.50	5.00	E

Uni-Books 30, c. Univ   Uni-Books 32, c. Univ   Uni-Books 42, c. Univ

26	The Fiend - Gerlad Foster	1.50	3.50	5.00	E
	aka Lust				
29	Brutal Kisses - H. M. Appel	1.50	3.50	5.00	E
	aka The Farmer's Daughter				
30	Eurasian Girl - Richard Grant	1.50	3.50	5.00	E
32	Loves of a Girl Wrestler - Ben West	2.50	6.00	10.00	E
	Note: Cover is almost identical to Beacon B112				
33	White Trash - Beulan Poynter	1.50	3.50	5.00	E
	Orig., 1952				
35	Slave Ship - H. B. Drake	1.50	3.50	5.00	E
36	Hoyden of the Hills - Ann Lawrence	1.50	3.50	5.00	E
37	Student Nurse - Gail Jordan	1.50	3.50	5.00	E
38	Secrets of a Co-Ed - Ben West	1.50	3.50	5.00	E
39	Pleasure Resort Women - Gordon Semple	1.50	3.50	5.00	E
41	She Devil - John Saxon	1.50	3.50	5.00	E
42	Side-Show Girl - Steve Harragan	2.00	4.00	7.50	M
44	Sin is a Redhead - Steve Harragan	2.00	4.00	7.50	M
45	Bad Sister - Evans Wall	1.50	3.50	5.00	E
46	Smuggled Sin - Steve Harragan	2.00	4.00	7.50	M
47	Kiss of the Damned - Steve Harragan	2.00	4.00	7.50	M
48	Women of Paris - L. H. Brenning	1.50	3.50	5.00	E
49	Reefer Club - Luke Roberts	2.50	6.00	10.00	E
50	River Woman - Evans Wall	1.50	3.50	5.00	E
51	Dirt Farm - Mitchell	1.50	3.50	5.00	E
52	The Shayne Dame - Steve Harragan	2.00	4.00	7.50	M
53	Wild Body - Manning Clay	1.50	3.50	5.00	E
54	Carney's Burlesque - Steve Harragan	2.00	4.00	7.50	M
56	Her Last Lover - Kelsey Freeman	1.50	3.50	5.00	E
	aka Last Lover				
57	Three Bad Girls - Bart Frane	2.00	4.00	7.50	M
60	Savage Eve - Jack Woodford	1.50	3.50	5.00	E
62	Hungry for Love - Gerge Willis	1.50	3.50	5.00	E
	aka Wild Faun				
63	Passion in the Pines - Jack Woodford	1.50	3.50	5.00	E
64	Cuban Heel - Steve Harragan	2.00	4.00	7.50	M
	Orig., nd				
65	Hillbilly in High Heels - Jeff Bogar	1.50	3.50	5.00	E
66	Witch on Wheels - Bill Bolton	1.50	3.50	5.00	E
67	Male Virgin - Jack Woodford	1.50	3.50	5.00	E
70	Wild Oats - Harry Whittington	1.50	3.50	5.00	E
71	Swamp Hoyden - Jack Woodford & John B. Thompson	1.50	3.50	5.00	E
73	Cabin Fever - Orrie Hitt	1.50	3.50	5.00	E
	Orig., 1954				
76	Below the Belt - R. Lucas	2.00	4.00	7.50	E
78	Out of Bounds - Ernest L. Matthews, Jr.	2.00	4.00	6.00	E

UNITED STATES PLAYING CARD COMPANY

(United States Playing Card Co./Whitman Publishing Company)

3768	50 Card Games for Children - Vernon Quinn	.75	1.50	2.50	NF
	1946				

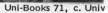

Uni-Books 71, c. Univ

U.S. Playing Card 3768, c. Whit   Universal Giant 1, c. Univ

Universal Giant 2, c. Univ   Universal Giant 4, c. Univ   Universal Giant 5, c. Univ

UNIVERSAL GIANT EDITION

(Universal Publishing and Distributing Corp.)

Digest size, see Royal Giant Edition

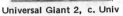

1	Prime Sucker - Harry Whittington Orig., 1952				E
	The Hussy - Idabel Williams	5.00	10.00	20.00	E
2	Paprika - Erich von Stoheim	7.50	15.00	30.00	E
3	His Majesty O'Keefe - Klingman and Green	4.00	8.00	15.00	A
4	Dope Doll - Steve Harragan				E
	The Bigamy Kiss - Steve Harragan	7.50	15.00	30.00	E
5	Bulls, Blood and Passion - David Williams, Orig.				E
	The Sinful Ones - Fritz Leiber First ed., 1953	5.00	10.00	20.00	SF
6	The Private Life of Julius Caesar - William Marston	5.00	10.00	20.00	E E
7	Savage Mistress - Jon Hartt				
	Concubine - Elsie Dean	5.00	10.00	20.00	E
8	The Lusty Land - Valerie Taylor				E
	Forbidden Fruit -	5.00	10.00	20.00	E
9	Aphrodide's Lover - Arthur MacArthur	5.00	10.00	20.00	E
10	The Memoirs of Casanova - Jacques Casanova	4.00	8.00	15.00	E
11	The Queen's Warrant - Talbot Mundy, First ed., 1953				A
	Paths of Glory - Humphrey Cobb	5.00	10.00	20.00	C

UNIVERSAL ROMANCE

(Unknown Publisher)

Digest size

nn	Any Man's Woman - Cecil Barr	.75	1.75	3.00	E

VALUE BOOKS

(Value Books, Inc.)

102	Strive and Succeed - Horatio Alger	2.00	4.00	6.00	A
104	Brave and Bold - Horatio Alger	2.00	4.00	6.00	A
105	Making His Way - Horatio Alger	2.00	4.00	6.00	A

VANITAS

(The Harvard Lampoon, Inc.)

(VANITAS, continued)

V4402 Alligator - I*n Fl*m*ng Orig., 1962	4.50	9.00	15.00	H

VENUS BOOKS

(Star Guidance, Inc.)

Digest size

104 Beach Party - Peggy Gaddis aka Lovers No More	1.50	3.50	5.00	E
106 Overnight - Norman Bligh	1.50	3.50	5.00	E
108 Cutie - Gene Harvey aka Passion's Slave	1.50	3.50	5.00	E
109 Lover Boy - H. Bellamy	1.50	3.50	5.00	E
110 Hard-Boiled - Harmon Bellamy 1950, aka Struggle	1.50	3.50	5.00	E
111 Pick-Up Alley - Albert L. Quandt	1.50	3.50	5.00	E
112 Temptation - Peggy Gaddis	1.50	3.50	5.00	E
113 Reckless - James Clayford	1.50	3.50	5.00	E
114 Confessions of a Carnival Dancer - Gene Harvey	1.50	3.50	5.00	E
115 Journey into Ecstasy - Albert L. Quandt	1.50	3.50	5.00	E
116 One Wild Night - Peggy Gaddis	1.50	3.50	5.00	E
119 No Time for Marriage - David Charlson	1.50	3.50	5.00	E
120 The Naked Night - Norman Bligh Orig., 1951	1.50	3.50	5.00	E
121 Girl of the Slum - Albert L. Quandt	1.50	3.50	5.00	E
122 Pleasure at Midnight - Peggy Gaddis	1.50	3.50	5.00	E
123 Emotions of Fire - Peggy Gaddis	1.50	3.50	5.00	E
124 She Couldn't Be Good - Gene Harvey	1.50	3.50	5.00	E
130 The Men She Knew - Norman Bligh	1.50	3.50	5.00	E
133 She Tried to be Good - Florence Stonebraker Orig., 1951	1.50	3.50	5.00	E
134 The Doctor's Wife - Arthur Marin	1.50	3.50	5.00	E
135 Night Nurse - David Charlson Orig., 1951	1.50	3.50	5.00	E
136 Torch Singer - William Arnold	1.50	3.50	5.00	E
137 Lost to Desire - Peggy Gaddis Orig., 1952	1.50	3.50	5.00	E
138 Reckless - Joan Sherman Orig., 1952	1.50	3.50	5.00	E
139 The Naked Canvas - William Arnold Orig., 1952, c-Gross	1.50	3.50	5.00	E
140 Oriental Nights - Florence Stonebraker Orig., 1952	1.50	3.50	5.00	E
141 Strip Street - Gene Harvey Orig., 1952	1.50	3.50	5.00	E
143 Lovers in the Sun - Joan Sherman Orig., 1952	1.50	3.50	5.00	E
144 The Innocent Wanton - Kermit Welles Orig., 1952	1.50	3.50	5.00	E
145 Frenchie - David Charlson Orig., 1952	1.50	3.50	5.00	E

Value Books 104, c. Value

Vanitas nn, c. Harvard

Venus 133, c. SG

Venus 154, c. SG

Venus 162, c. SG

Vital Book 1, c. Vital

(VENUS BOOKS, continued)

146	Call It Marriage - Gail Jordan Orig., 1952	1.50	3.50	5.00	E
147	Weekend of Madness - Joan Tucker	1.50	3.50	5.00	E
148	Remembered Moment - Norman Bligh Orig., 1952	1.50	3.50	5.00	E
149	Runaway Lovers - Peggy Gaddis Orig., 1952	1.50	3.50	5.00	E
150	The Affairs of a Leading Lady - Jane Manning Orig., 1952	1.50	3.50	5.00	E
151	Young Wife - Norman Bligh	1.50	3.50	5.00	E
152	Passion Is a Woman - Kale Nickerson	1.50	3.50	5.00	E
153	Sailor's Weekend - Whit Harrison	1.50	3.50	5.00	E
154	Hired Girl - Amos Hatter Orig., 1953	1.50	3.50	5.00	E
156	The Doctor's Wife - A. Marin	1.50	3.50	5.00	E
162	Wayward Nurse - Norman Bligh c-Belarski	2.00	4.00	6.00	E
165	Passion is a Woman - Kate Nickerson c-Belarski	2.00	4.00	6.00	E
167	Young Secretary - Joan Tucker Orig., 1954	1.50	3.50	5.00	E
169	Strip Street - Gene Harvey	1.50	3.50	5.00	E
170	Male Ward - M. Coleman c-Belarski	1.50	3.50	5.00	E
171	Beach Girl - Joan Sherman aka Lovers in the Sun	1.50	3.50	5.00	E
172	Farmer's Woman - Peggy Gaddis	1.50	3.50	5.00	E
173	Young Doctor - Frank Haskell Orig., 1954, c-Belarski	2.00	4.00	6.00	E
178	Wild Sister - K. Welles	1.50	3.50	5.00	E
190	Farmer's Woman - Peggy Gaddis	1.50	3.50	5.00	E
193	Waterfront Club - Joan Tucker	1.50	3.50	5.00	E

VITAL BOOK

(Vital Publications, Inc.)

Digest size

1	Empire of Crime - Nicholas Carter	5.00	10.00	20.00	M
2	Murder Unlimited - Nicholas Carter	4.00	8.00	15.00	M
3	Death Has Green Eyes - Nicholas Carter	4.00	8.00	15.00	M
4	Park Avenue Murder - Nicholas Carter	4.00	8.00	15.00	M

VULCAN MYSTERY

(Vulcan Publishing, Inc.)

Digest size

3	The Laughing Buddha Murder - Richard Foster 1944	1.50	3.50	5.00	M

(VULCAN MYSTERY, continued)

5	The Case of the Phantom Fingerprints - Ken Crossen Orig., 1945	1.50	3.50	5.00	M
6	Curtain Call for Murder - Peter Yates Orig., 1945	1.50	3.50	5.00	M

WASHINGTON SQUARE PRESS

(Washington Square Press, Inc./Pocket Books, Inc.)

W 1	English Through Pictures - Book 1 - Christine Gibson & I. A. Richards 1959	.75	1.75	3.00	NF
W 2	First Steps in Reading English - Christine Gibson & I. A. Richards	.50	1.25	2.00	NF
W 4	English Through Pictures - Book 2 Christine Gibson & I. A. Richards	.50	1.25	2.00	NF
W 8	French Through Pictures - Book 1 - I. A. Richards & Others	.50	1.25	2.00	NF
W 18	A First Workbook of French - Christine Gibson & I. A. Richards	.50	1.25	2.00	NF
W 15	German Through Pictures - Book 1 - I. A. Richards & Others	.50	1.25	2.00	NF
W 22	Italian Through Pictures - Book 1 - I. A. Richards & Others	.50	1.25	2.00	NF
W 30	Spanish Through Pictures - Book 1 - I. A. Richards & Others	.50	1.25	2.00	NF
W 38	Hebrew Through Pictures - Book 1 - I. A. Richards & Others	.75	1.75	3.00	NF
W 39	Hebrew Reader - I. A. Richards & Others	.75	1.75	3.00	NF
W 99	Oedipus the King - Sophocles	.75	1.75	3.00	
W100	Doctor Faustus - Christopher Marlowe	.75	1.75	3.00	
W101	The Duchess of Malfi - John Webster	.75	1.75	3.00	
W115	Macbeth - William Shakespeare	.50	1.25	2.00	
W121	Romeo and Juliet - William Shakespeare	.50	1.25	2.00	
W550	Collected Lyrics - Edna St. Vincent Millay	.50	1.25	2.00	
W551	Collected Sonnets - Edna St. Vincent Millay	.50	1.25	2.00	
W561	The Way of All Flesh - Samuel Butler	.50	1.25	2.00	

WESTERN ACTION NOVEL

(Hillman Periodicals, Inc./Novel Selections)

Digest size

1	Round-up in the River - Frank C. Robertson	2.00	4.00	6.00	W
2	The Riddle of Ramrod Ridge - William Colt MacDonald	1.50	3.50	5.00	W
3	Powder Smoke Fence - Bennett Foster	1.50	3.50	5.00	W
4	Donovan Rides - Arthur Henry Gooden	1.50	3.50	5.00	W

WESTERN NOVEL CLASSIC

(Hillman Periodicals, Inc./Novel Selections)

Digest size

22	The Sheriff's Son - William MacLeod Raine	1.50	3.50	5.00	W
24	Thunder on the Range - Frank C. Robertson	1.50	3.50	5.00	W
32	Thunder Ranch - Clarence E. Mulford aka Me an' Shorty	1.50	3.50	5.00	W
33	Tumbling River Range - W. C. Tuttle	1.50	3.50	5.00	W
36	Hopalong Cassidy and the Eagles Brood - Clarence E. Mulford	2.00	4.00	6.00	W
37	Black Sombrero - William Colt MacDonald	1.50	3.50	5.00	W
38	Red Range - Eugene Cunningham	1.50	3.50	5.00	W

West. Nov. Classic 37, c. Hill   West. Nov. Classic 45, c. Hill   West. Nov. Classic 50, c. Hill

(WESTERN NOVEL CLASSIC, continued)

39	Trail's End - William MacLeod Raine	1.50	3.50	5.00	W
40	War on the Cimarron - Luke Short	1.50	3.50	5.00	W
43	Whistling Lead - Eugene Cunningham	1.50	3.50	5.00	W
44	Roaring River Range - Arthur Henry Gooden	1.50	3.50	5.00	W
45	The Feud at Single Shot - Luke Short	1.50	3.50	5.00	W
46	The Tin God of Twisted River - W. C. Tuttle	1.50	3.50	5.00	W
50	The Dead-Line - W. C. Tuttle	1.50	3.50	5.00	W
55	Hash Knife of the Double Bar 8 - W. C. Tuttle	1.50	3.50	5.00	W
67	Sudden Takes Charge - O. Strange	1.50	3.50	5.00	W
68	Rough Mesa - J. Trace	1.50	3.50	5.00	W
69	South to Sonora - Ryerson Johnson	1.50	3.50	5.00	W
72	Gunsmoke in the Hills - Ray Palmer Tracy	1.50	3.50	5.00	W
74	Renegade Range - Tom West	1.50	3.50	5.00	W
81	Black Gold Stampede - Ed Moore	1.50	3.50	5.00	W
83	The Firebrand from Burnt Creek - Frank C. Robertson	1.50	3.50	5.00	W
84	Blood on the Sage - L. Legner	1.50	3.50	5.00	W
85	Black River Ranch - Lynn Westland	1.50	3.50	5.00	W
89	Marked Man - Harold Channing Wire	1.50	3.50	5.00	W
	Note: Same cover as Hillman 28				
90	Gunsmoke Galoot - Leslie Ernewein	1.50	3.50	5.00	W
91	Meddling Maverick - Tom West	1.50	3.50	5.00	W
96	Closed Range - Bliss Lomax (H. S. Drago)	1.50	3.50	5.00	W
99	Horsethief Pass - Charles H. Snow	1.50	3.50	5.00	W
100	Barbed Wire Empire - Will Ermine	1.50	3.50	5.00	W
105	Dakota Marshall - Lynn Westland	1.50	3.50	5.00	W
106	Lawless Legion - Will Ermine	1.50	3.50	5.00	W
107	Poison Springs - Eli Colter	1.50	3.50	5.00	W
109	Blow, Desert Winds - William Corcoran	1.50	3.50	5.00	W

WESTERN NOVEL OF THE MONTH

(Hillman Periodicals, Inc./Novel Selections)

Digest size

4	Hell on the Pecos - Ed Earl Repp	1.50	3.50	5.00	W
5	The Gun Tamer - Max Brand	1.50	3.50	5.00	W
19	Suicide Ranch - Ed Earl Repp	1.50	3.50	5.00	W
21	Pistol Passport - Eugene Cunningham	1.50	3.50	5.00	W

WESTERN THRILLER

(Vital Publications, Inc.)

Digest size

4	Open Land Renegades - Tom J. Hopkins 1948	1.50	3.50	5.00	W

THE WEST IN ACTION

(Astro Distributing Corporation)

Digest size

1 Outlaw Sheriff - Murray Leinster 1948	4.00	8.00	15.00	W
2 Guns Along the Western Trail - Murray Leinster	4.00	8.00	15.00	W
3 Kid Deputy - Murray Leinster 1948	4.00	8.00	15.00	W
4 Two-Gun Showdown - Murray Leinster	4.00	8.00	15.00	W

WHITMAN

(Whitman Publishing Company)

556 Pinocchio 1939, movie tie-in (Disney)	10.00	25.00	40.00

WIDE WORLD

(Peters Publishing Company)

1 A World in Crisis? - Allan Forester 1952	1.50	3.50	5.00	NF
2 Republicans Today - Philip Arthur 1952	1.50	3.50	5.00	NF
3 Democrats Today - Philip Arthur 1952	1.50	3.50	5.00	NF
4				
5 Cold War Politics - John Breamer 1953	1.50	3.50	5.00	NF

YOGI MYSTERIES

(Wiegers Publishing Company)

Digest size

nn Death from Nowhere - Stuart Towne (Clayton Rawson)	3.00	6.00	12.00	M

ZENITH

(Zenith Books, Inc.)

West in Action 1, c. Astro

Whitman 556, c. Whit

Yogi Mysteries nn, c. WP

Zenith ZB3, c. Zenith   Zenith ZB39, c. Zenith   Zenith ZB40, c. Zenith

(ZENITH, continued)

ZB 1	The Sisters - Charles Jackson 1958	.75	1.75	3.00	E
ZB 2	All Over Town - George Milburn	.75	1.75	3.00	
ZB 3	Johnny Purple - John Wyllie	.75	1.75	3.00	M
ZB 4	Die Screaming - Jo Pagano	.75	1.75	3.00	M
ZB 5	The Best Cartoons from Argosy	.75	1.75	3.00	H
ZB 6	The Oral Roberts Reader - Oral Roberts	.50	1.25	2.00	
ZB 7	The Girl from Hateville - Gil Brewer	.75	1.75	3.00	E
ZB 8	Adventure in Paradise - Emile C. Schurmacher	.75	1.75	3.00	A
ZB 9	The Man Without a Face - John Eugene Hasry	.75	1.75	3.00	
ZB10	Rawhiders - Tom Roan	.75	1.75	3.00	W
ZB11	The Long Desire - Max Weatherly 1959	.75	1.75	3.00	E
ZB12	The Rascal's Guide - Bruce Jay Friedman	.75	1.75	3.00	
ZB13					
ZB14	The People Maker - Damon Knight	1.50	3.50	5.00	SF
ZB15	Etched in Murder - Ken Jones	.75	1.75	3.00	M
ZB16					
ZB17					
ZB18	Blonde Bait - Ed Lacy	.75	1.75	3.00	M
ZB19	The Deadly Doll - Henry Kane	.75	1.75	3.00	M
ZB20	Fall Girl - Richard Deming	.75	1.75	3.00	M
ZB21	Young Sinner - Elisabeth Gill	.75	1.75	3.00	E
ZB22	Georgia Girl - Bart Frame	.75	1.75	3.00	E
ZB23	A Fine and Private Place - Ann Hebson	.75	1.75	3.00	E
ZB24	Moran's Woman - Day Keene	.75	1.75	3.00	E
ZB25	The Sweet Blonde Trap - William Campbell Gault 1959	.75	1.75	3.00	M
ZB26					
ZB27					
ZB28	Your Body and Its Care - Richard E. Winter	.50	1.25	2.00	NF
ZB29	Sweet and Deadly - A. Boyd Correll & Philip MacDonald	.75	1.75	3.00	M
ZB30	Strangers on Friday - Harry Whittington	.75	1.75	3.00	M
ZB31					
ZB32					
ZB33	The Gray Flannel Shroud - Henry Slesar	.75	1.75	3.00	M
ZB34	Frenchie - David Charlson	.75	1.75	3.00	E
ZB35					
ZB36					
ZB37					
ZB38					
ZB39	The Blonde on Borrowed Time - B. X. Sanborn aka The Doom-maker 1960	.75	1.75	3.00	M
ZB40	Corpus Earthling - Louis Charbonneau Orig., 1960	2.00	4.00	7.50	SF
ZB41					
ZB42					
ZB43	The Hot Sand of Hell - Christopher Landon aka Ice Cold in Alex 1960, Movie tie-in	.75	1.75	3.00	C
ZB44					
ZB45					
ZB46					

LATE ADDITIONS

AVON DETECTIVE MYSTERIES
(Avon Detective - Mysteries, Inc.)
Digest size

1 1947	3.00	6.00	12.00	M
2 Includes Carter Dickson, Eberhart, others, 1947 Note: Same cover as Avon no. 104 and Murder Mystery Monthly no. 13.	3.00	6.00	12.00	M
3 Includes Gruber, Rohmer, Brown, others, 1947 Note: Partially the same cover as Avon no. 122 and the pulp Private Detective Stories, October 1944	3.00	6.00	12.00	M

AVON ROMANCE NOVEL MONTHLY
(Avon Publishing Co., Inc.)
Digest size

2 Love Should be Laughter - Frances S. Moore	4.00	8.00	15.00	E

Avon Det. Mysteries 2, c. Avon

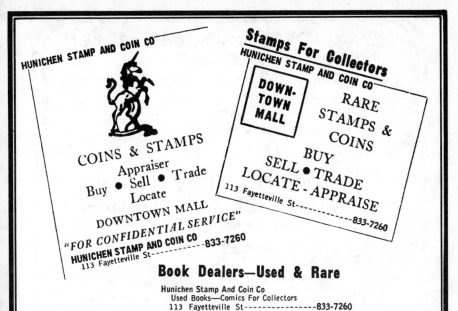

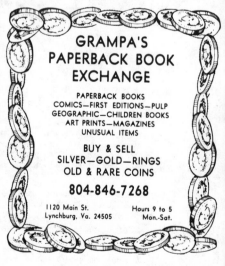